## Video Cases

## Part Ending Strategic Cases

# MARKETING

# MARKETING

## FOURTEENTH EDITION

**William M. Pride**
*Texas A & M University*

**O. C. Ferrell**
*University of New Mexico*

**Houghton Mifflin Company**    Boston   New York

*To Nancy, Michael, and Allen Pride*
*To Linda Ferrell*

*Publisher:* George Hoffman
*Marketing Manager:* Mike Schenk
*Marketing Assistant:* Erin Lane
*Sponsoring Editor:* Katie Rose
*Development Editor:* Amy Whitaker and Suzanna Smith
*Editorial Assistant:* John Powers
*Senior Project Editor:* Rachel D'Angelo Wimberly
*Editorial Assistant:* Anthony D'Aries
*Art/Design Coordinator:* Jill Haber
*Cover Design Manager:* Anne Katzeff
*Photo Editor:* Jennifer Meyer Dare
*Composition Buyer:* Chuck Dutton
*New Title Project Manager:* Priscilla Manchester

Cover image credit: © Luis Castenada, Inc., The Image Bank, Getty Images.

Printed in the U.S.A.

Library of Congress Control Number: 2006938349

Library Edition:
ISBN 10: 0-618-79970-2
ISBN 13: 978-0-618-79970-1

For orders, use loose-leaf text ISBNs:
ISBN 10: 0-618-79963-X
ISBN 13: 978-0-618-79963-3

1 2 3 4 5 6 7 8 9 — CRK — 12 11 10 09 08

# Brief Contents

v

# Contents

**Note:** Each chapter concludes with a Summary, Important Terms, Discussion & Review Questions, Application Questions, globalEDGE, and Internet Exercises.

# 6 Business Markets and Buying Behavior 149

# 7 Reaching Global Markets 173

## PART 4
# Using Technology, Information, and Target Market Analysis 211

# 8 E-Marketing and Customer Relationship Management 212

# 16   Wholesaling and Physical Distribution                                       431

# 17   Retailing and Direct Marketing                                              461

**PART 7**
# Promotion Decisions                                                              491

# 18   Integrated Marketing Communications                                         492

## 19 Advertising and Public Relations                                                    519

## 20 Personal Selling and Sales Promotion                                               545

# The Challenges of Teaching and Learning Marketing

**M**arketing continues to be one of the most dynamic dimensions of business. *Marketing: Concepts and Strategies* leads the market by adapting and responding to the changing marketing environment. Our approach is to balance new knowledge with insights from best practices to present students the most up-to-date principles of marketing text possible. The past ten years have provided new information technology that requires adaptation in teaching, learning, and practice of marketing. The global competitive environment has created new pressures to develop marketing strategies that reach beyond national boundaries.

To address these challenges, this new edition has undergone the most extensive revision ever, reaching far beyond new examples, boxes, cases and videos to carefully analyzing and rebuilding content in each chapter. These revision decisions were based on research, reviews, and assistance from content experts. The global marketing chapter, for example, has been completely revised with the assistance of Tomas Hult, Michigan State University. The current balance of trade deficit and global market opportunity require international integration throughout the text. The e-marketing and customer-relationship management chapter has likewise been updated and enhanced to reflect recent developments in this area. The text's definition of marketing has been modified to be consistent with the new American Marketing Association definition of marketing.

Details of this extensive revision are available in the transition guide in the Instructor's Resource Manual. We have also made efforts to improve all teaching ancillaries and student learning tools. PowerPoints continue to be a very popular teaching device and a special effort has been made to upgrade the PowerPoint program to enhance classroom teaching. The authors and publisher have worked together to provide a competent teaching package and ancillaries that are unsurpassed in the marketplace.

The authors maintain a hands-on approach to teaching the course and revising the text and its ancillaries. This results in an integrated teaching package and approach that is accurate, sound, and successful in reaching students. The outcome of this involvement fosters trust and confidence in the teaching package and in student learning outcomes.

# Keeping Pace with the Challenges and the Changing World

Many changes in the marketing environment have occurred since the last edition. Advancing technologies, particularly in the area of customer relationship management, help in understanding customers. The Internet and e-marketing strategies continue to create new opportunities for marketing success. Direct marketing, supply chain management, and growth of large retailers such as Wal-Mart, Best Buy, and IKEA—just some of the companies we feature in this edition—are changing the competitive forces. Starbucks' success reveals that consumers are trading up to services and experiences that provide enjoyment in a busy world. At the same time many of the companies we examine such as Life is good.®, Whole Foods, and Nestlé are contributing more to society by providing environmentally responsible products and promoting fair trade activities to enhance the welfare of all marketing channel

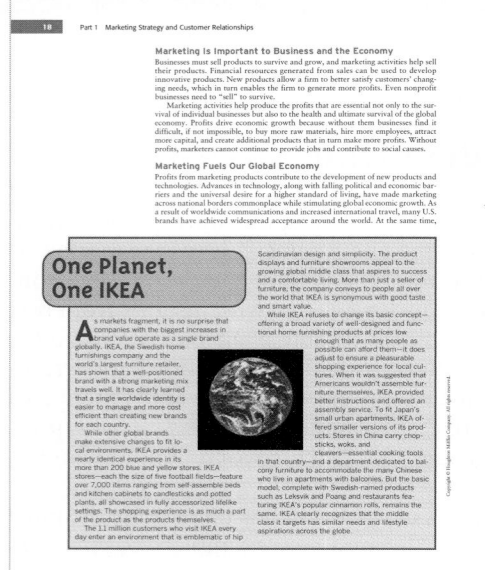

members. Ethics and social responsibility in marketing continue to be requirements-not options-in relating to customers and other stakeholders. All of these changes are emphasized in the content, examples, and boxes of this edition.

As mentioned before, we also examine the challenges that marketers face in developing global marketing strategies. Many of our products come from foreign markets, and foreign markets represent a sizable opportunity for U.S. products. Consider that China, which has developed the second largest world economy in output behind the U.S., has become the largest broadband DSL market, and companies such as Motorola and Intel have invested billions of dollars in China. Likewise, India's growing middle class, with more than 300 million consumers, is buying consumer products from companies such as Procter & Gamble and Coca-Cola. Conversely, Wal-Mart is now purchasing 20 percent of its merchandise from Chinese producers. These shifts in international markets mean that students need to understand how global marketing strategies are developed and implemented in a dynamic and complex world. We provide a revised chapter on this issue as well as exercises, boxed features, cases, examples, and content throughout the text.

An introductory marketing text must be revised on a timely basis to remain up to date and reflect current changes in marketing and the marketing environment. Significant content changes were made to reflect the adaptation of traditional marketing principles to existing cultural, social, legal, and technology trends. The practice of marketing is dynamic and new approaches continue to evolve. Throughout the text we have updated content with the most recent research that supports the frameworks and best practices for marketing.

# Features of the Book

As with previous editions, this edition of the text provides a comprehensive and practical introduction to marketing that is both easy to teach and to learn. *Marketing: Concepts and Strategies* continues to be one of the most widely adopted introductory textbooks in the world. We appreciate the confidence that adopters have placed in our textbook and continue to work hard to make sure that, as in previous editions, this edition keeps pace with changes. The entire text is structured to excite students about the subject and to help them learn completely and efficiently.

■ An *organizational model* at the beginning of each part provides a "roadmap" of the text and a visual tool for understanding the connection among various components.

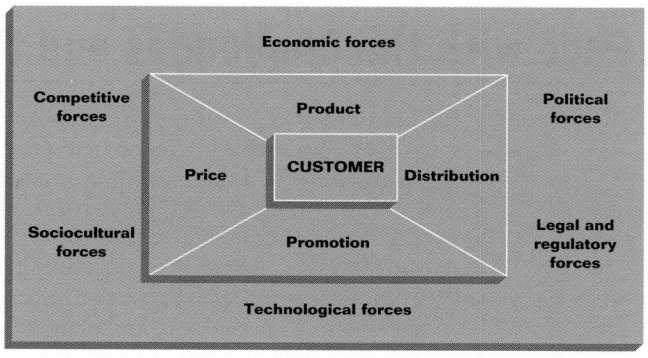

■ *Learning objectives* at the start of each chapter present concrete expectations about what students are to learn as they read the chapter.

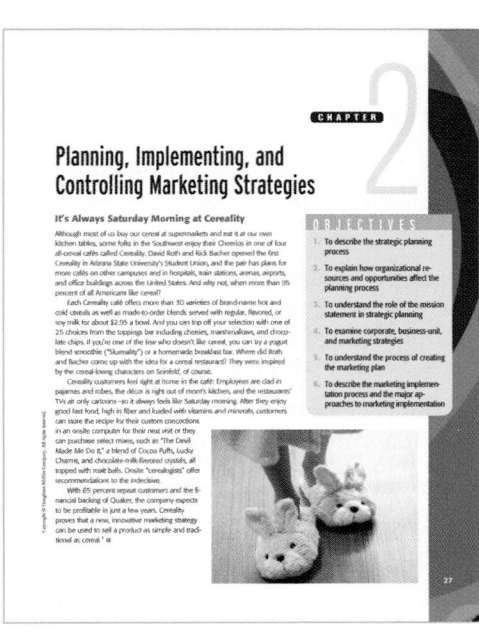

■ An *opening vignette* about a particular organization or current market trend introduces the topic for each chapter. The issues in these vignettes surround a variety of goods and services from diverse organizations such as Red Bull, Timberland, the Container Store, Levi Strauss, and the Broadway show *Wicked*. Through these vignettes, students are exposed to contemporary marketing realities and are better prepared to understand and apply the concepts they will explore in the text.

■ *Key term definitions* appear in the margins to help students build their marketing vocabulary.

■ Figures, tables, photographs, advertisements, and snapshot features increase comprehension and stimulate interest.

■ *Boxed features* reinforce students' awareness of the particular issues affecting marketing and the types of choices and decisions marketers must make. Topics range from ethics and global marketing to building customer relationships and ways to target ever-changing markets. Featured are trends such as yoga moms, aging baby boomers, and buzz marketing at teens, and companies such as Nickelodeon, Netflicks, and Iams.

## Iams Aims at Pet Lovers

To many people today, pets are part of their families, and they want their pets to have the best. Iams, which markets the Iams and Eukanuba pet food brands, recognized this trend and shifted its focus. Today, it markets high-quality pet food, fancy pet treats, sauces, and other items that allow pet lovers to spoil their pets. For example, the company created Multi-Cat cat food for customers concerned about feeding cats in multi-cat households in which one cat might be overweight while another was not.

Now owned by Procter & Gamble, Iams has begun marketing pet products that mirror those intended for humans. For example, the company now applies a technology borrowed from P&G's Crest toothpaste to put a tarter-control coating on all adult pet food. The coating was added to pet treats in 2006. Iams also plans to produce a line of pet shampoo.

Iams faces stiff competition from Nestlé's Purina and Wal-Mart's Ol'Roy, but it is currently the number 1 national pet food brand based on dollar sales. And it continues to research new possibilities in pet supplies. For example, it is currently looking into creating pet products connected to P&G's Swiffer and Febreze brands. The company is also branching out through its Iams Pet Imaging Centers and by offering pet health insurance.

■ A complete *chapter summary* reviews the major topics discussed, and the list of *important terms* provides another end-of-chapter study aid to expand students' marketing vocabulary.

■ *Discussion and review questions* at the end of each chapter encourage further study and exploration of chapter content, and *application questions* enhance students' comprehension of important topics.

■ Two **globalEDGE™** exercises invite students to look at the global economy and ways to market to it and from within it. These exercises are  provided by the Center for International Business Education and Research at Michigan State University (CIBER@MSU), the founders of the **globalEDGE** website. A knowledge web-portal that connects international business professionals worldwide to a wealth of information, insights, and learning resources on global business activities, the site is the most comprehensive international business resource on the Internet and the world's leading online source in international business as ranked by Google, Yahoo, MSN, and AOL.

■ An *Internet exercise* at the end of each chapter asks students to examine a website and assess one or more strategic issues associated

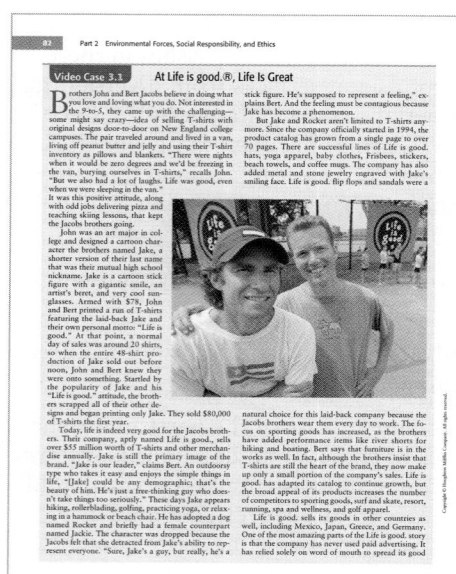

with the site. This section also points students to the various learning tools that are available on the text's website.

■ Two in-depth *cases* at the end of each chapter help students understand the application of chapter concepts. One of the end-of-chapter cases is related to a video segment. Some examples of companies highlighted in the cases are Travelocity, Life is good.®, Newbury Comics, and REI.

■ A *strategic case* at the end of each part helps students integrate the diverse concepts that have been discussed within the related chapters. Some of the organizations highlighted in these cases include Reebok, XM Satellite Radio and Texas Instruments.

■ *Appendixes* discuss marketing career opportunities, explore financial analysis in marketing, and present a sample marketing plan.

■ A comprehensive *glossary* defines more than 625 important marketing terms.

# Text Organization

We have organized the eight parts of *Marketing: Concepts and Strategies* to give students a theoretical and practical understanding of marketing decision making.

**Part 1**    **Marketing Strategy and Customer Relationships**
Provides an overview of marketing, strategic marketing planning, and implementation

**Part 2**    **Environmental Forces, Social Responsibility, and Ethics**
Provides an overview of the marketing environment, social responsibility, and ethics

**Part 3**    **Markets and Customer Behavior**
Focuses on consumer and business buying behavior, and global and international marketing

**Part 4**    **Using Technology and Information to Build Customer Relationships**
Covers e-marketing, customer relationship management, marketing research, information systems, target market segmentation, and positioning

**Part 5**    **Product Decisions**
Discusses product concepts, developing and managing products, branding, packaging, and services marketing

**Part 6**    **Distribution Decisions**
Provides coverage of marketing channels, supply chain management, wholesaling, physical distribution, retailing, and direct marketing

**Part 7**    **Promotion Decisions**
Focuses on integrated communications, advertising, public relations, personal selling, and sales promotion

**Part 8**    **Pricing Decisions**
Covers pricing concepts and the setting of prices in a dynamic marketing environment

# What's New to This Edition?

This edition is revised and updated to address the dynamic issues emerging in the current technology-driven environment, while continuing to stress the importance of traditional marketing issues. These revisions assist students in gaining a full understanding of marketing practices pertinent today and helping them anticipate increasing future changes.

## Organizational Changes

■ *Extensive reorganization.* Six chapters have been reordered and revised to accommodate their new position within the text to address reviewer feedback. To satisfy the teaching requirements of adopters, the new organization places a greater emphasis on buyer behavior and satisfies feedback indicating a preference to cover target markets and positioning prior to discussing the various major elements of the marketing mix. We believe this new structure will facilitate student learning from a more holistic perspective.

■ *Changes in the coverage of global marketing.* The global marketing chapter has been extensively revised and strengthened to facilitate teaching and student learning. The chapter now includes coverage of the influence of government, various competitive forces, social responsibility issues such as cultural relativism, outsourcing, and types of global organizational structures. This revision should help prepare students for the increasingly global nature of marketing in the twenty-first century.

■ *Changes in the treatment of e-marketing and customer relationship management.* In response to the rapidly changing nature of customer relationship management, we have updated and revised this section of this chapter. This chapter has also been updated to reflect new trends in the constantly changing environment of the Internet. This allows for greater integration of technology into the discussion of marketing mix elements throughout the remainder of the text.

## Changes In Every Chapter

■ *Opening vignettes.* All of the chapter opening vignettes are new. They are written to introduce the theme of each chapter by focusing on actual companies and how they deal with real-world situations.

■ *Boxed features.* Each chapter includes two boxed features that highlight important themes such as ethics, social responsibility, customer relationships, global marketing and technology. Most of the boxed features are new in this edition; a few have been significantly updated and revised since the last edition.

■ *New Snapshot features.* All twenty-two Snapshot features are new and engage students by highlighting interesting, up-to-date statistics that link marketing theory to the real world.

■ *New research.* Throughout the text we have updated content with the most recent research that supports the frameworks and best practices for marketing.

■ *New illustrations and examples.* New advertisements from well-known firms are employed to illustrate chapter topics. Experiences of real-world companies are used to exemplify marketing concepts and strategies throughout the text. Most of these examples are new. Others have been updated or expanded.

■ *End-of-chapter cases.* Each chapter contains two cases, including a video case, profiling firms to illustrate concrete application of marketing strategies and concepts. Many of the cases are new to this edition.

- *End-of-part Strategic Cases.* These eight cases incorporate issues found throughout all the chapters in each part and require students to integrate the content of these multiple chapters to answer the questions at the end of each case. Three of these cases are new and the others have been updated.

- *Marketing Entrepreneurs.* This new feature highlights everyday individuals who have used innovative marketing to launch a new business.

**marketing ENTREPRENEURS**

**Frank Hickingbotham**
THE BUSINESS: TCBY Enterprises, Inc.
FOUNDED: 1981

During an outing at Neiman-Marcus, Georgia Hickingbotham encouraged her husband Frank to try the peach-flavored frozen yogurt she bought while taking a break from shopping. Frank, not a yogurt fan, reluctantly did. "This can't be yogurt," he said, and, thus, the TCBY brand was born out of the initials of that outburst (although later the initials came to stand for "The Country's Best Yogurt"). The unique taste that melted "Mr. H.'s" dislike of yogurt was developed by Daniel Brackeen, a dairy genius from Dallas. The Hickingbothams arranged to purchase and distribute his product. And with that, Frank—founder, chairman of the board, and CEO of TCBY Enterprises, Inc.—started the company with a first-day sale on September 23, 1981, of $153.69. There are now about 3,000 TCBY locations in operation worldwide, and the TCBY brand is franchised in over 60 countries. In 2000, TCBY was acquired by Capricorn Investors for about $140 million (the startup cost in 1981 was about $150,000). Capricorn is principal shareholder of Mrs. Fields Famous Brands, LLC.

# A Comprehensive Instructional Resource Package

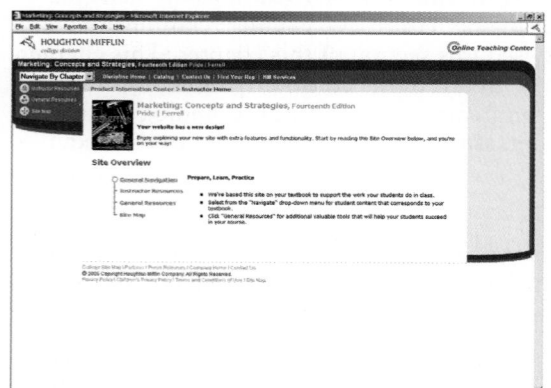

For instructors, this edition of *Marketing* includes an exceptionally comprehensive package of teaching materials.

- ***Online Teaching Center instructor's website.*** This continually updated, password-protected site includes valuable tools to help design and teach the course. The website has been redesigned to enhance its ease of use, so that you can spend your time preparing for class rather than clicking links. Website content includes sample syllabi, downloadable text files from the *Instructor's Resource Manual,* role-play exercises, both basic and premium PowerPoint® slides, *CRS (Classroom Response System) Clicker Content,* the new Integrated Lecture Outline, and more. Also, we provide a downloadable educational game written by John Drea of Western Illinois University. This easy-to-use game makes in-class review challenging and fun, and has been proven to increase students' test scores.

  In addition, you can preview our unique custom content modules featuring extended content on the latest Marketing topics. From here, you can determine which modules would enhance your instruction and your students' learning. To customize your text with modules, contact your Houghton Mifflin sales representative.

**The NFL's Super Bowl:**
**The Pinnacle of Event Marketing**

▶ *Prepared and written by Dr. Chuck Tomkovick, University of Wisconsin–Eau Claire, and Dr. Rama Yelkur, University of Wisconsin–Eau Claire*

When the National Football League (NFL) first sanctioned competition between its own champion and the top team from the rival American Football League, CBS and NBC (the two major television networks that broadcast the January 15, 1967, game) held the event in such low esteem that they didn't even keep a copy of their live telecasts. Back then, the game tickets sold for $12, the average cost for a 30-second ad during the telecasts was $42,000, approximately 40 million viewers watched the game on television, and so few people attended the game in Los Angeles that NFL officials asked the spectators to sit in the middle of the stadium so the TV cameras that panned the action could make it seem like the stands were full. Halftime entertainment was provided by the University of Michigan and the University of Arizona marching bands. The game was played in the afternoon, so as not to conflict with such evening prime-time viewing heavyweights as The Ed Sullivan Show, which featured The Rolling Stones that night. Fast-forwarding to today, a lot has changed. Super Bowl XL was watched by over 140 million viewers in America and by nearly 1 billion worldwide in more than 225 countries and territories. Since its inception, the cost of airing TV ads has risen by over 5,000%, to a staggering $2.5 million for every 30 seconds of commercial airtime for Super Bowl XL. Detroit was the lucky host for the 2006 game, the event was played and aired in the evening, and the halftime entertainment was provided by, well, yes, the Rolling Stones.

EM-1

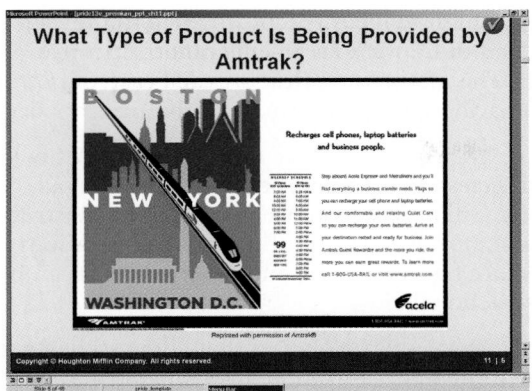

- **PowerPoint® slide presentations.** You can now enhance your lecture with a variety of PowerPoint options. For each chapter, traditional PowerPoint slides related to the learning objectives have been specially developed for this book. The slides contain outlines suitable for use in class lectures and discussions as well as selected figures and tables from the text. Premium PowerPoint slides have also been created to provide instructors with up-to-date unique content to increase student application and interest. The Premium PowerPoint slides offer such multimedia content as advertisements, video clips, weblinks, surveys and graphs, and important terms.

- **Classroom Management Systems.** With *Eduspace* powered by Blackboard and *Blackboard/WebCT* course management tools, instructors can create and customize online course materials to use in distance learning, distributed learning, or as a supplement to traditional classes. Each system includes a variety of study aids for instructors, including a gradebook, the Instructor's Resource Manual, Integrated Lecture Outlines, test pools, traditional and premium PowerPoint slides, Classroom Response System (CRS) clicker content, ACE practice tests and auto-graded quizzes, links to web content, all end-of-chapter questions from the textbook with suggested answers, Video Activities, and more.

- **Test Bank. HMTesting**, the computerized test bank, provides more than 4,000 test items including true/false, multiple-choice, and essay questions. Each objective test item is accompanied by the correct answer, a main text page reference, and a key that shows whether the question tests knowledge, comprehension, or application. *HMTesting* also provides difficulty and discrimination ratings derived from actual class testing for many of the multiple-choice questions. When preparing a test, instructors are able to select, edit, and add questions, or generate randomly selected questions to produce a test master for easy duplication. An Online Testing System and gradebook function allows instructors to administer tests via a network system, modem, or personal computer, and sets up a new class, records grades from tests or assignments, analyzes grades, and produces class and individual statistics. This program can be used on both PCs and Macintosh computers.

- **Instructor's Resource Manual.** Written by the text's authors, the *Instructor's Resource Manual* includes a complete set of teaching tools. For each text chapter, there is (1) a teaching resources quick reference guide, (2) a purpose and perspective statement, (3) special class exercises, (4) a debate issue, (5) a chapter quiz, (6) answers to discussion and review questions, (7) comments on the end-of-chapter cases, and (8) video information.

- **Integrated Lecture Outlines.** All multimedia instructor support is now integrated into a chapter outline prepared by the authors. This useful tool will provide cues for incorporating the video, PowerPoint slides—including appropriate video clips and ads—overhead transparencies, and additional text features. Encapsulate your students on everything the Pride and Ferrell program has to offer!

- **CRS (Classroom Response System) Clicker Content.** Using state-of-the-art wireless technology and text-specific Pride/Ferrell content, a Classroom Response System (CRS) provides a convenient and inexpensive way to gauge student comprehension, deliver quizzes or exams, and provide "on-the-spot" assessment. Ideal for any classroom, a CRS is a customizable handheld response system that will complement any teaching style. Various answering modes, question types, and display options mean that a CRS is as functional as you want it to be. As a testing platform, as an assessment tool, or simply as a way to increase interactivity in the classroom, a CRS provides the technology you need to transform a lecture into a dynamic learning environment. Content is available on the Instructor Website.

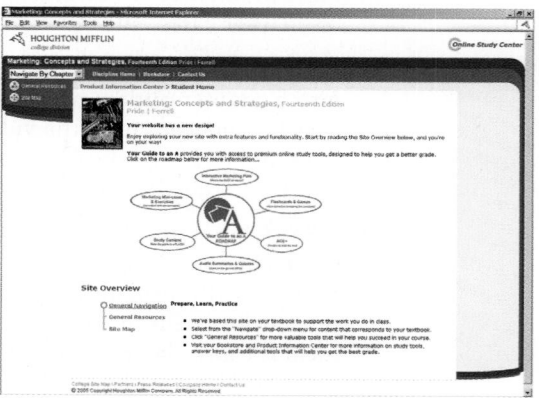

■ *Marketing Video Series.* This series contains videos specifically tied to the end-of-chapter video cases. More than half of the video segments in the series are new to the 14th Edition. The *Instructor's Resource Manual* and *Integrated Lecture Outline* provide specific information about each video segment.

■ *Online color transparencies.* A set of color transparencies, available on the text-specific Online Teaching Center, offers the instructor visual teaching assistance. About half of these are illustrations from the text. The rest are figures, tables, and diagrams that can be used as additional instructional aids.

■ *Role-play exercises.* Three role-play exercises that allow students to assume various roles within an organization are available in the *Instructor's Resource Manual* and on the instructor's web site. The exercises are designed to help students understand the real-world challenges of decision making in marketing. Decisions require a strategic response from groups or teams. These exercises simulate a real-world experience, and give students an opportunity to apply the marketing concepts covered in the text. Accompanying the exercises is in-depth information concerning their implementation and evaluation.

■ *Call-in test service.* This service lets instructors select items from the *Test Bank* and call our toll-free number to order printed tests.

# A Format and Supplements to Meet Student Needs

### Text Format

We have heard students' complaints about price. In response, we continue to offer all the benefits of a comprehensive textbook, but in the convenient, low-cost loose-leaf format. Students have told us they like this format—they can carry only those chapters they need, and it is available for about two-thirds the cost of a hardcover textbook. For professors or students who want a bound book, we do offer the traditional hardcover, Library Edition version. We also offer a low-cost ebook version of the text. For more information about an ebook, contact your Houghton Mifflin sales representative.

### Supporting Supplements

The complete package available with *Marketing: Concepts and Strategies* includes support materials that facilitate student learning.

*Pride/Ferrell Marketing Online Study Center.* Our student website at **www.prideferrell.com** contains the following:

■ *Your Guide to an 'A'* provides students with access to premium online study tools, designed to help students get a better grade. These assets include:
- ACE+
- MP3
- Study Content in Flash
- Interactive Marketing Plan
- Flashcards and Crosswords
- Marketing mini-cases and exercises

■ Please use the code in the *Your Guide to an A* passkey that came with new copies of your textbook. If you purchased a used textbook, the passkey is available for purchase through your bookstore or through Houghton Mifflin's eCommerce (go to **college.hmco.com/pic/prideferrellmarketing14e** and click on the **"Purchase Product"** link for *Your Guide to an A*).

■ *Interactive Marketing Plan.* In this edition, the *Marketing Plan Worksheets* have been revamped and reproduced within an interactive and multimedia environment. A video program has been developed around the worksheets, allowing students to follow a company through the trials and tribulations of launching a new product. This video will help place the conceptual marketing plan into an applicable light and will be supported by a summary of the specific stages of the marketing plan as well as a sample plan based on the events of the video. These elements act as the 1-2-3 punch supporting the student while completing his or her own plan, the last step of the *Interactive Marketing Plan. The Plan* is broken up into 3 functional sections that can either be completed in one simple project or carried over throughout the semester. *Available with the "Guide to an 'A'" passkey in the* **Online Study Center.**

■ *Audio Chapter Review MP3* downloadable files. The MP3 files provide unique audio chapter summaries and test-preppers for the on-the-go student. *Available with the "Guide to an 'A'" passkey in the* **Online Study Center.**

■ *ACE & ACE+ online self-tests.* Written by the text authors, these questions allow students to practice taking tests and get immediate scoring results. ACE + questions *available with the "Guide to an 'A'" passkey in the* **Online Study Center.**

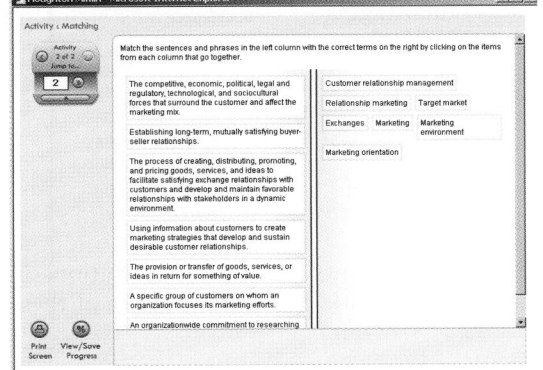

■ *Online Study Content in Flash.* Written by the text's authors, this supplement helps students review and integrate key marketing concepts. The *Study Content* questions are different from those in the online study aids and include chapter outlines as well as matching, true/false, multiple choice, and mini-case sample tests with answers. *Available with the "Guide to an 'A'" passkey in the* **Online Study Center.**

■ *Flashcards.* These study tools will help students review concepts and prepare for tests. *Available with the "Guide to an 'A'" Media Passkey.*

■ *Company links.* Hot links to companies featured in the text are provided so that students can further their research and understanding of the marketing practices of these companies.

■ *Online glossary & chapter summary.* These sections help students review key concepts and definitions.

■ *Career Center.* Downloadable "Personal Career Plan Worksheets" and links to various marketing careers websites will help students explore their options and plan their job search.

# Your Comments and Suggestions are Valued

Bill Pride and O.C. Ferrell have been co-authors of *Marketing: Concepts and Strategies* for three decades. Their major focus has been on teaching and preparing learning material for introductory marketing students. They have both traveled extensively to work with students and understand the needs of professors of introductory marketing courses. Both authors teach this marketing course on a regular basis and test the materials included in the book, *Test Bank*, and other ancillary materials to make sure they are effective in the classroom.

Through the years, professors and students have sent us many helpful suggestions for improving the text and ancillary components. We invite your comments, questions, and criticisms. We want to do our best to provide materials that enhance the teaching and learning of marketing concepts and strategies. Your suggestions will be sincerely appreciated. Please write us, or e-mail us at w-pride@tamu.edu or OCFerrell@mgt.unm.edu, or call 979-845-5857 (Pride) or 505-277-3468 (Ferrell). You can also send a feedback message through the website at **http://www.prideferrell.com**.

# Acknowledgments

Like most textbooks, this one reflects the ideas of many academicians and practitioners who have contributed to the development of the marketing discipline. We appreciate the opportunity to present their ideas in this book.

A special faculty advisory board assisted us in making decisions during the development of the text and the instructional package. For being "on-call" and available to answer questions and make valuable suggestions, we are grateful to those who participated:

Sana Akili
*Iowa State University*

Katrece Albert
*Southern University*

Frank Barber
*Cuyahoga Community College*

Nancy Bloom
*Nassau Community College*

Sandra Coyne
*Springfield College*

Kent Drummond
*University of Wyoming*

Robert Garrity
*University of Hawaii*

John Hafer
*University of Nebraska at Omaha*

David Hansen
*Texas Southern University*

Kathleen Krentler
*San Diego State University*

Marilyn L. Liebrenz-Himes
*George Washington University*

Edna Ragins
*North Carolina A&T State University*

Janice Williams
*University of Central Oklahoma*

John Withey
*Indiana University—South Bend*

A number of individuals have made helpful comments and recommendations in their reviews of this and earlier editions. We appreciate the generous help of these reviewers:

Zafar U. Ahmed
*Minot State University*

Thomas Ainscough
*University of Massachusetts—Dartmouth*

Joe F. Alexander
*University of Northern Colorado*

Mark I. Alpert
*University of Texas at Austin*

David M. Ambrose
*University of Nebraska*

David Andrus
*Kansas State University*

Linda K. Anglin
*Minnesota State University*

George Avellano
*Central State University*

Emin Babakus
*University of Memphis*

Julie Baker
*Texas Christian University*

Siva Balasubramanian
*Southern Illinois University*

Joseph Ballenger
*Stephen F. Austin State University*

Guy Banville
*Creighton University*

Joseph Barr
*Framingham State College*

Thomas E. Barry
*Southern Methodist University*

Charles A. Bearchell
*California State University—
Northridge*

Richard C. Becherer
*University of Tennessee—
Chattanooga*

Walter H. Beck, Sr.
*Reinhardt College*

Russell Belk
*University of Utah*

W.R. Berdine
*California State Polytechnic Institute*

Karen Berger
*Pace University*

Bob Berl
*University of Memphis*

Stewart W. Bither
*Pennsylvania State University*

Roger Blackwell
*Ohio State University*

Peter Bloch
*University of Missouri—Columbia*

Wanda Blockhus
*San Jose State University*

Paul N. Bloom
*University of North Carolina*

James P. Boespflug
*Arapahoe Community College*

Joseph G. Bonnice
*Manhattan College*

John Boos
*Ohio Wesleyan University*

Jenell Bramlage
*University of Northwestern Ohio*

James Brock
*Susquehanna College*

John R. Brooks, Jr.
*Houston Baptist University*

William G. Browne
*Oregon State University*

John Buckley
*Orange County Community College*

Gul T. Butaney
*Bentley College*

James Cagley
*University of Tulsa*

Pat J. Calabros
*University of Texas—Arlington*

Linda Calderone
*State University of New York
College of Technology at
Farmingdale*

Joseph Cangelosi
*University of Central Arkansas*

William J. Carner
*University of Texas—Austin*

James C. Carroll
*University of Central Arkansas*

Terry M. Chambers
*Westminster College*

Lawrence Chase
*Tompkins Cortland Community
College*

Larry Chonko
*Baylor University*

Barbara Coe
*University of North Texas*

Ernest F. Cooke
*Loyola College—Baltimore*

Robert Copley
*University of Louisville*

John I. Coppett
*University of Houston—Clear Lake*

Robert Corey
*West Virginia University*

Deborah L. Cowles
*Virginia Commonwealth University*

Melvin R. Crask
*University of Georgia*

William L. Cron
*Texas Christian University*

Gary Cutler
*Dyersburg State Community College*

Bernice N. Dandridge
*Diablo Valley College*

Lloyd M. DeBoer
*George Mason University*

Sally Dibb
*University of Warwick*

Ralph DiPietro
*Montclair State University*

Paul Dishman
*Idaho State University*

Suresh Divakar
*State University of New York—
Buffalo*

Casey L. Donoho
*Northern Arizona University*

Peter T. Doukas
*Westchester Community College*

Lee R. Duffus
*Florida Gulf Coast University*

Robert F. Dwyer
*University of Cincinnati*

Roland Eyears
*Central Ohio Technical College*

Thomas Falcone
*Indiana University of Pennsylvania*

James Finch
*University of Wisconsin—La Crosse*

Letty C. Fisher
*SUNY/Westchester Community
College*

Renée Florsheim
*Loyola Marymount University*

Charles W. Ford
*Arkansas State University*

John Fraedrich
*Southern Illinois University,
Carbondale*

David J. Fritzsche
*University of Washington*

Donald A. Fuller
*University of Central Florida*

Terry Gable
*Truman State University*

Ralph Gaedeke
*California State University,
Sacramento*

Cathy Goodwin
*University of Manitoba*

Geoffrey L. Gordon
*Northern Illinois University*

Robert Grafton-Small
*University of Strathclyde*

Harrison Grathwohl
*California State University—Chico*

Alan A. Greco
*North Carolina A&T State University*

Blaine S. Greenfield
*Bucks County Community College*

Thomas V. Greer
*University of Maryland*

Sharon F. Gregg
*Middle Tennessee University*

Jim L. Grimm
*Illinois State University*

Charles Gross
*University of New Hampshire*

Joseph Guiltinan
*University of Notre Dame*

Richard C. Hansen
*Ferris State University*

Nancy Hanson-Rasmussen
*University of Wisconsin—Eau Claire*

Robert R. Harmon
*Portland State University*

Mary C. Harrison
*Amber University*

Lorraine Hartley
*Franklin University*

Michael Hartline
*Florida State University*

Timothy Hartman
*Ohio University*

Salah S. Hassan
*George Washington University*

Manoj Hastak
*American University*

Del I. Hawkins
*University of Oregon*

Dean Headley
*Wichita State University*

Esther Headley
*Wichita State University*

Debbora Heflin-Bullock
*California State Polytechnic University—Pomona*

Merlin Henry
*Rancho Santiago College*

Lois Herr
*Elizabethtown College*

Charles L. Hilton
*Eastern Kentucky University*

Elizabeth C. Hirschman
*Rutgers, State University of New Jersey*

George C. Hozier
*University of New Mexico*

John R. Huser
*Illinois Central College*

Joan M. Inzinga
*Bay Path College*

Ron Johnson
*Colorado Mountain College*

Theodore F. Jula
*Stonehill College*

Peter F. Kaminski
*Northern Illinois University*

Yvonne Karsten
*Minnesota State University*

Jerome Katrichis
*Temple University*

James Kellaris
*University of Cincinnati*

Alvin Kelly
*Florida A&M University*

Philip Kemp
*DePaul University*

Sylvia Keyes
*Bridgewater State College*

William M. Kincaid, Jr.
*Oklahoma State University*

Roy Klages
*State University of New York at Albany*

Douglas Kornemann
*Milwaukee Area Technical College*

Patricia Laidler
*Massasoit Community College*

Bernard LaLond
*Ohio State University*

Richard A. Lancioni
*Temple University*

Irene Lange
*California State University—Fullerton*

Geoffrey P. Lantos
*Stonehill College*

Charles L. Lapp
*University of Texas—Dallas*

Virginia Larson
*San Jose State University*

John Lavin
*Waukesha County Technical Institute*

Marilyn Lavin
*University of Wisconsin—Whitewater*

Hugh E. Law
*East Tennessee University*

Monle Lee
*Indiana University—South Bend*

Ron Lennon
*Barry University*

Richard C. Leventhal
*Metropolitan State College*

Marilyn Liebrenz-Himes
*George Washington University*

Jay D. Lindquist
*Western Michigan University*

Terry Loe
*Kennesaw State University*

Mary Logan
*Southwestern Assemblies of God College*

Paul Londrigan
*Mott Community College*

Anthony Lucas
*Community College of Allegheny County*

George Lucas
*U.S. Learning, Inc.*

William Lundstrom
*Cleveland State University*

Rhonda Mack
*College of Charleston*

Stan Madden
*Baylor University*

Patricia M. Manninen
*North Shore Community College*

Gerald L. Manning
*Des Moines Area Community College*

Lalita A. Manrai
*University of Delaware*

Franklyn Manu
*Morgan State University*

Allen S. Marber
*University of Bridgeport*

Gayle J. Marco
*Robert Morris College*

James McAlexander
*Oregon State University*

Donald McCartney
*University of Wisconsin—Green Bay*

Anthony McGann
*University of Wyoming*

Jack McNiff
*State University of New York College of Technology at Farmington*

Lee Meadow
*Eastern Illinois University*

Carla Meeske
*University of Oregon*

Jeffrey A. Meier
*Fox Valley Technical College*

James Meszaros
*County College of Morris*

Brain Meyer
*Minnesota State University*

Martin Meyers
*University of Wisconsin—Stevens Point*

Stephen J. Miller
*Oklahoma State University*

William Moller
*University of Michigan*

Kent B. Monroe
*University of Illinois*

Carlos W. Moore
*Baylor University*

Carol Morris-Calder
*Loyola Marymount University*

David Murphy
*Madisonville Community College*

Keith Murray
*Bryant College*

Sue Ellen Neeley
*University of Houston—Clear Lake*

Carolyn Y. Nicholson
*Stetson University*

Francis L. Notturno, Sr.
*Owens Community College*

Terrence V. O'Brien
*Northern Illinois University*

James R. Ogden
*Kutztown University of Pennsylvania*

Mike O'Neill
*California State University—Chico*

Robert S. Owen
*State University of New York—Oswego*

Allan Palmer
*University of North Carolina at Charlotte*

David P. Paul, III
*Monmouth University*

Teresa Pavia
*University of Utah*

John Perrachione
*Truman State University*

Michael Peters
*Boston College*

Linda Pettijohn
*Missouri State University*

Lana Podolak
*Community College of Beaver County*

Raymond E. Polchow
*Muskingum Area Technical College*

Thomas Ponzurick
*West Virginia University*

William Presutti
*Duquesne University*

Kathy Pullins
*Columbus State Community College*

Edna J. Ragins
*North Carolina A&T State University*

Daniel Rajaratnam
*Baylor University*

Mohammed Rawwas
*University of Northern Iowa*

James D. Reed
*Louisiana State University—Shreveport*

William Rhey
*University of Tampa*

Glen Riecken
*East Tennessee State University*

Winston Ring
*University of Wisconsin—Milwaukee*

Ed Riordan
*Wayne State University*

Robert A. Robicheaux
*University of Alabama—Birmingham*

Robert H. Ross
*Wichita State University*

Vicki Rostedt
*The University of Akron*

Michael L. Rothschild
*University of Wisconsin—Madison*

Bert Rosenbloom
*Drexel University*

Kenneth L. Rowe
*Arizona State University*

Elise Sautter
*New Mexico State University*

Ronald Schill
*Brigham Young University*

Bodo Schlegelmilch
*Vienna University of Economics and Business Administration*

Edward Schmitt
*Villanova University*

Thomas Schori
*Illinois State University*

Donald Sciglimpaglia
*San Diego State University*

Stanley Scott
*University of Alaska—Anchorage*

Harold S. Sekiguchi
*University of Nevada—Reno*

Gilbert Seligman
*Dutchess Community College*

Richard J. Semenik
*University of Utah*

Beheruz N. Sethna
*Lamar University*

Morris A. Shapero
*Schiller International University*

Terence A. Shimp
*University of South Carolina*

Mark Siders
*Southern Oregon University*

Carolyn F. Siegel
*Eastern Kentucky University*

Dean C. Siewers
*Rochester Institute of Technology*

Lyndon Simkin
*University of Warwick*

Roberta Slater
*Cedar Crest College*

Paul J. Solomon
*University of South Florida*

Sheldon Somerstein
*City University of New York*

Eric R. Spangenberg
*University of Mississippi*

Rosann L. Spiro
*Indiana University*

William Staples
*University of Houston—Clear Lake*

Bruce Stern
*Portland State University*

Claire F. Sullivan
*Metropolitan State University*

Carmen Sunda
*University of New Orleans*

Robert Swerdlow
*Lamar University*

Steven A. Taylor
*Illinois State University*

Hal Teer
*James Madison University*

Ira Teich
*Long Island University—C.W. Post*

Debbie Thorne
*Texas State University*

Dillard Tinsley
*Stephen F. Austin State University*

Sharynn Tomlin
*Angelo State University*

Hale Tongren
*George Mason University*

James Underwood
*University of Southwest Louisiana—Lafayette*

Barbara Unger
*Western Washington University*

Tinus Van Drunen
*University Twente (Netherlands)*

Dale Varble
*Indiana State University*

R. Vish Viswanathan
*University of Northern Colorado*

Charles Vitaska
*Metropolitan State College*

Kirk Wakefield
*Baylor University*

Harlan Wallingford
*Pace University*

Jacquelyn Warwick
*Andrews University*

James F. Wenthe
*Georgia College*

Sumner M. White
*Massachusetts Bay Community College*

Alan R. Wiman
*Rider College*

Ken Wright
*West Australia College of Advanced Education—Churchland Campus*

We deeply appreciate the assistance of Gwyneth V. Walters, Carmen Powers, and Jack Powers for providing editorial suggestions, technical assistance, and support. For assistance in completing numerous tasks associated with the text and supplements, we express appreciation to Melanie Drever, Alexi Sherrill, Clarissa Means, Tammy Lemke, Dana Egg, Somia Qaiyum, and Kari Kelley.

Tomas Hult, Michigan State University, completely revised the Global Marketing chapter. In addition, he assisted in providing the **globalEdge** exercises at the end of each chapter in the book. He provided advice in helping to integrate the global dimension through the text. Michael Hartline, Florida State University, helped in the development of the marketing plan outline and the sample marketing plan in Appendix C, as well as the career worksheets on the website. We also wish to thank John Drea, Western Illinois University, for developing the *Who Wants to Be an 'A' Student* game.

We express appreciation for the support and encouragement given to us by our colleagues at Texas A&M University and University of New Mexico. We are also grateful for the comments and suggestions we receive from our own students, student focus groups, and student correspondents who provide ongoing feedback through the website.

A number of talented professionals at Houghton Mifflin have contributed to the development of this book. We are especially grateful to George Hoffman, Rachel D'Angelo Wimberly, Mike Schenk, Marcy Kagan, Katie Rose, Suzanna Smith, Sharon Donahue, Naomi Kornhauser, and Amy Whitaker. Their inspiration, patience, support, and friendship are invaluable.

*William M. Pride*
*O. C. Ferrell*

## About the Authors

**William M. Pride** is Professor of Marketing, Mays Business School at Texas A&M University. He received his Ph.D. from Louisiana State University. He is the author of Houghton Mifflin Company's *Business* text, a market leader.

Dr. Pride's research interests are in advertising, promotion, and distribution channels. Dr. Pride's research articles have appeared in major journals in the fields of advertising and marketing such as *Journal of Marketing*, *Journal of Marketing Research*, *Journal of the Academy of Marketing Science*, and the *Journal of Advertising*.

Dr. Pride is a member of the American Marketing Association, Academy of Marketing Science, Association of Collegiate Marketing Educators, Society for Marketing Advances and the Marketing Management Association.

Dr. Pride has taught principles of marketing and other marketing courses for more than 30 years at both the undergraduate and graduate levels.

**O. C. Ferrell** is Professor of Marketing and Creative Enterprise Scholar, Anderson Schools of Management, University of New Mexico. He recently served as the Bill Daniels Distinguished Professor of Business Ethics at the University of Wyoming and previously as Chair of the Colorado State University Marketing Department. He has also been on the faculties of University of Memphis, Texas A&M University, and Illinois State University. He received his Ph.D. in Marketing from Louisiana State University.

He is past president of the Academic Council of the American Marketing Association and chaired the American Marketing Association Ethics Committee. Under his leadership, the committee developed the AMA Code of Ethics and the AMA Code of Ethics for Marketing on the Internet. He is currently a member of the advisory committee for the AMA marketing certification program. In addition, he is a former member of the Academy of Marketing Science Board of Governors and is a Society of Marketing Advances and Southwestern Marketing Association Fellow. He currently serves as Marketing Ethics and Social Issues Section Editor of the *Journal of Macromarketing*.

Ferrell is the co-author of 18 books and approximately 75 articles. His articles have been published in the *Journal of Marketing Research*, *Journal of Marketing*, *Journal of Business Ethics*, *Journal of Business Research*, *Journal of the Academy of Marketing Science*, *Journal of Public Policy Marketing*, as well as other journals.

**part**

# Marketing Strategy and Customer Relationships

**P**art 1 introduces the field of marketing and offers a broad perspective from which to explore and analyze various components of the marketing discipline. **Chapter 1** defines *marketing* and explores several key concepts, including customers and target markets, the marketing mix, the marketing concept, customer relationships, value-driven marketing, and the importance of marketing in the global economy. **Chapter 2** provides an overview of strategic marketing issues, such as the role of the mission statement; corporate, business-unit, and marketing strategies; and the creation of the marketing plan.

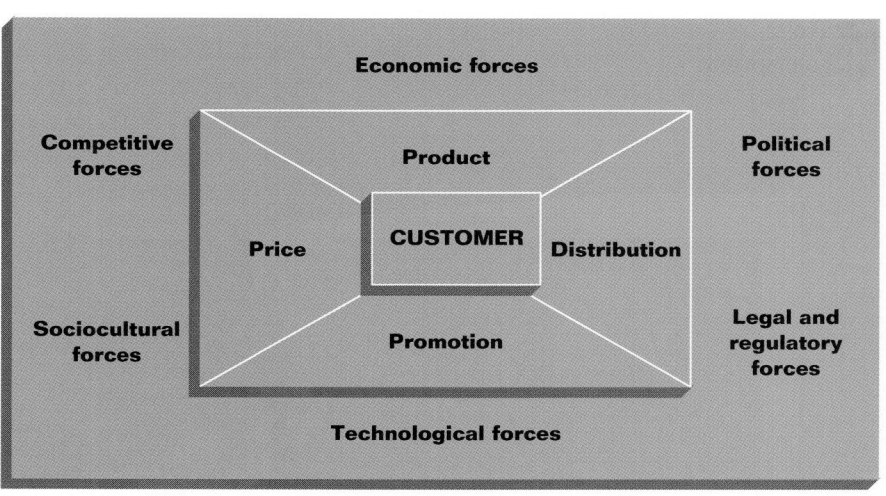

# An Overview of Strategic Marketing

## Red Bull Has Wings

Sleek in its blue and silver can, Red Bull is a huge marketing success. While established cola giants struggle with flat sales, upstart Red Bull has brought new energy to the marketplace.

Red Bull, which originated in Austria, commands 60 percent of its market share against competitors like Hype, Rockstar, Monster, Pimp Juice, and Bong Water. In fact, without this berry flavored beverage featuring mysterious additives taurine and glucuronolactone, there would not even be a market for all the other energy drinks currently crowding the shelves. While still a relatively small market, the energy drink category grew 75 percent in 2005 to $3.3 billion in sales. Even giants Pepsi and Coke have introduced their own versions. Pepsi has Mountain Dew AMP and Mountain Dew MDX, while Coke offers Full Throttle and Tab Energy—a twist on the 1970s soft drink Tab, which is targeted at women.

Energy drinks have about three times the caffeine of a regular soft drink and are loaded with sugar—it's clear why they provide an instant rush. And people are willing to pay for that buzz: from $2 for an 8-ounce can of Red Bull (double the price of a 12-ounce can of Coke) to $2.50 for a 16-ounce can of Rockstar or Monster.

Red Bull's marketing group is broken into decentralized units throughout the United States. Each marketing and salesperson is expected to take responsibility for the brand and act like an entrepreneur, working with distributors to find retail accounts at popular venues frequented by the local in crowd. They select only five accounts in an area to give the product an aura of exclusivity and encourage retailers to aggressively merchandise the brand to keep the product franchise.

Red Bull's marketing teams use a variety of techniques to create brand awareness. Beyond traditional commercials, they have used dance clubs, deejays, and even New York City cab drivers to spread the word. While others spend millions for superstars like Christina Aguilera, Red Bull relies on buzz from hip youngsters as well as the sponsorship of approximately 500 extreme athletes who surf in Nova Scotia in January or jump out of planes to swim the English Channel.

One of the brand's favorite targets is alternative sports venues. It's involved in national and regional events, including the Red Bull Huckfest ski and snowboard competition in Utah. Its fleet of show planes, the Flying Bulls, appears at air shows around the world. These events are naturals for reaching potential customers.

Red Bull also uses consumer education teams, hiring hip locals in target areas to drive Red Bull cars (small sporty blue and silver vehicles with a large Red Bull can mounted on the back) and hand out samples. However, what consumers see in one city may be entirely different from what they see in another city. Red Bull's marketing philosophy is to adapt its approach to the local market. It's all part of the mystique![1] ■

Like all organizations, the maker of Red Bull attempts to develop products that customers want, communicate useful information about them to excite interest, price them appropriately, and make them available when and where customers want to buy them. Even if an organization does all these things well, however, competition from marketers of similar products, economic conditions, and other factors may affect the company's success. Such factors influence the decisions that all organizations must make in strategic marketing.

This chapter introduces the strategic marketing concepts and decisions covered throughout the text. First, we develop a definition of *marketing* and explore each element of the definition in detail. Next, we introduce the marketing concept and consider several issues associated with implementing it. We also take a brief look at the management of customer relationships and then at the concept of value, which customers are demanding today more than ever before. We next explore the process of marketing management, which includes planning, organizing, implementing, and controlling marketing activities to encourage marketing exchanges. Finally, we examine the importance of marketing in our global society.

# Defining *Marketing*

**marketing** The process of creating, distributing, promoting, and pricing goods, services, and ideas to facilitate satisfying exchange relationships with customers and develop and maintain favorable relationships with stakeholders in a dynamic environment

**customers** The purchasers of organizations' products; the focal point of all marketing activities

If you ask several people what *marketing* is, you are likely to hear a variety of descriptions. Although many people think marketing is advertising or selling, marketing actually encompasses many more activities than most people realize. In this book, we define **marketing** as the process of creating, distributing, promoting, and pricing goods, services, and ideas to facilitate satisfying exchange relationships with customers and develop and maintain favorable relationships with stakeholders in a dynamic environment. Our definition is consistent with the American Marketing Association (AMA), which defines marketing as "an organizational function and a set of processes for creating, communicating, and delivering value to customers and for managing customer relationships in ways that benefit the organization and its stakeholders."[2] Let's take a closer look at selected parts of our definition.

## Marketing Focuses on Customers

As the purchasers of the products that organizations develop, promote, distribute, and price, **customers** are the focal point of all marketing activities (see Figure 1.1 on p. 4). Organizations must define their products not as what they produce but as what they do to satisfy customers. The Walt Disney Company, for example, is not in the business of establishing theme parks; it is in the business of making people happy. At Disney World, customers are guests, the crowd is an audience, and employees are cast members. Customer satisfaction and enjoyment can come from anything received when buying and using a product.

The essence of marketing is to develop satisfying exchange relationships from which both customers and marketers benefit. The customer expects to gain a reward or benefit in excess of the costs incurred in a marketing transaction. The marketer expects to gain something of value in return, generally the price charged for the

**figure 1.1**

## COMPONENTS OF STRATEGIC MARKETING

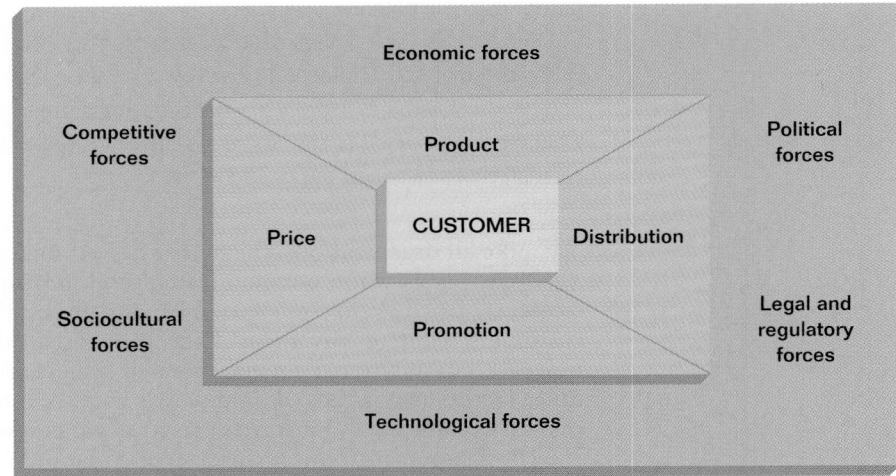

product. Through buyer-seller interactions, a customer develops expectations about the seller's future behavior. To fulfill these expectations, the marketer must deliver on promises made. Over time, this interaction results in interdependencies between the two parties. Fast-food restaurants such as Wendy's and Burger King depend on repeat purchases from satisfied customers—many often live or work a few miles from these restaurants—while customer expectations revolve around quality food, good value, and dependable service.

Organizations generally focus their marketing efforts on a specific group of customers, called a **target market.** Marketing managers may define a target market as a vast number of people or a relatively small group. Rolls-Royce, for example, targets its automobiles at a small, very exclusive market: wealthy people who want the ultimate in prestige in an automobile. Other companies target multiple markets, with different products, promotion, prices, and distribution systems for each one. Nike uses this strategy, marketing different types of shoes and apparel to meet specific needs of cross-trainers, rock climbers, basketball players, aerobics enthusiasts, and other athletic-shoe buyers. We explore the concept of target markets in more detail in Chapter 10.

**target market** A specific group of customers on whom an organization focuses its marketing efforts

### Marketing Deals with Products, Distribution, Promotion, and Price

Marketing is more than simply advertising or selling a product; it involves developing and managing a product that will satisfy customer needs. It focuses on making the product available in the right place and at a price acceptable to buyers. It also requires communicating information that helps customers determine if the product will satisfy their needs. These activities are planned, organized, implemented, and controlled to meet the needs of customers within the target market. Marketers refer to these activities—product, distribution, promotion, and pricing—as the **marketing mix** because they decide what type of each element to use and in what amounts. A primary goal of a marketing manager is to create and maintain the right mix of these elements to satisfy customers' needs for a general product type. Note in Figure 1.1 that the marketing mix is built around the customer.

Marketing managers strive to develop a marketing mix that matches the needs of customers in the target market. The marketing mix for DeWalt power tools, for example, combines rugged, high-quality products with coordinated distribution, promotion, and price appropriate for the target market of primarily professional contractors. The marketing mix for Black & Decker power tools differs from that of

**marketing mix** Four marketing activities—product, distribution, promotion, and pricing—that a firm can control to meet the needs of customers within its target markets

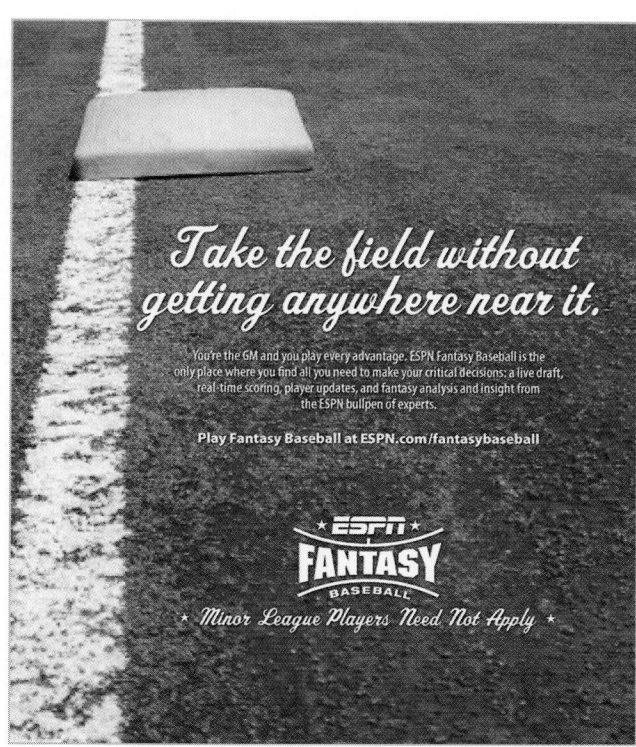

**Appealing to Target Markets**

This Neutrogena skin care advertisement targets young women. ESPN promotes its Fantasy Baseball primarily to men.

**product** A good, a service, or an idea

DeWalt—even though the two brands are owned by the same firm—with lower prices and broader distribution.[3]

Before marketers can develop a marketing mix, they must collect in-depth, up-to-date information about customer needs. Such information might include data about the age, income, ethnicity, gender, and educational level of people in the target market, their preferences for product features, their attitudes toward competitors' products, and the frequency with which they use the product. Research by Dunkin' Donuts, for example, revealed that its customers would welcome new menu items such as iced beverages, espresso drinks, and bagel breakfast sandwiches. This information helped the company refine its strategy of targeting workday on-the-go customers rather than compete directly against Starbucks.[4] In Chapter 9, we explore how organizations gather marketing research data. Armed with such data, marketing managers are better able to develop a marketing mix that satisfies a specific target market.

Let's look more closely at the decisions and activities related to each marketing mix variable.

**The Product Variable.** Successful marketing efforts result in **products** that become a part of everyday life. Consider the satisfaction customers have had over the years from Coca-Cola, Levi's jeans, Visa credit cards, Tylenol pain relievers, and 3M Post-it Notes. The product variable of the marketing mix deals with researching customers' needs and wants and designing a product that satisfies them. A product can be a good, a service, or an idea. A good is a physical entity you can touch. A Toyota Scion, an iPod, a Duracell battery, and a puppy available for adoption at an animal shelter are examples of goods. A service is the application of human and mechanical efforts to people or objects to provide intangible benefits to customers. Air travel, dry cleaning, hair cutting, banking, insurance, medical care, and day care are examples of services. Ideas include concepts, philosophies, images, and issues. For instance, a marriage counselor, for a fee, gives spouses ideas to help improve their relationship. Other marketers of ideas include political parties, churches, and schools. Note, however, that the actual production of tangible goods is not a marketing activity.

The product variable also involves creating or modifying brand names and packaging, and may include decisions regarding warranty and repair services. Even one of the world's best basketball players is a global brand. Yao Ming, the Houston Rockets center, has endorsed products from McDonald's, PepsiCo, and Reebok, many of which are marketed in his Chinese homeland.[5]

Product variable decisions and related activities are important because they are directly involved in creating products that address customers' needs and wants. To maintain an assortment of products that helps an organization achieve its goals, marketers must develop new products, modify existing ones, and eliminate those that no longer satisfy enough buyers or that yield unacceptable profits. In the funeral home industry, for example, some companies have developed new products such as DVD memoirs, grave markers that display photos along with a soundtrack, and caskets with drawers to hold mementos from the bereaved. To appeal to the growing number of people who prefer to be cremated, other firms are offering more cremation and memorial services.[6] We consider such product issues and many more in Chapters 11 through 14.

**The Distribution Variable.** To satisfy customers, products must be available at the right time and in convenient locations. For example, discount chain rivals Wal-Mart and Target are both opening in-store health clinics to make routine medical services such as sports physicals, flu shots, and strep-throat tests available to their customers without an appointment during pharmacy hours, including evenings and weekends. To keep the costs down to $25 to $60 per visit, the convenient clinics are staffed by nurse practitioners who can consult with physicians by telephone if needed.[7] In dealing with the distribution variable, a marketing manager makes products available in the quantities desired to as many target market customers as possible, keeping total inventory, transportation, and storage costs as low as possible. A marketing manager may also select and motivate intermediaries (wholesalers and retailers), establish and maintain inventory control procedures, and develop and manage transportation and storage systems. The Internet and other technologies have also dramatically influenced the distribution variable. Companies can now make their products available throughout the world without maintaining facilities in each country. We examine distribution issues in Chapters 15 through 17.

**The Promotion Variable.** The promotion variable relates to activities used to inform individuals or groups about the organization and its products. Promotion can aim to increase public awareness of the organization and of new or existing products. Procter & Gamble, for example, is using NASCAR driver Tony Stewart to convey the masculinity and endurance of its Old Spice Red Zone antiperspirant.[8] Promotional activities can also educate customers about product features or urge people to take a particular stance on a political or social issue, such as smoking or drug abuse. For example, rising natural gas and gasoline prices prompted the U.S. Energy Department to launch an advertising campaign featuring an Energy Hog mascot to urge the public to conserve energy, especially with regard to home heating. The campaign also used booklets, temporary tattoos for children, and two websites—one for children with games and one for adults with information about energy-saving tips and appliances.[9] Promotion can also help sustain interest in established products that have been available for decades, such as Arm & Hammer baking soda or Ivory soap. Many companies are using the Internet and the Web to communicate information about themselves and their products. Ragu's website, for example, offers Italian phrases, recipes, and a sweepstakes, while Southwest Airlines' website enables customers to make flight reservations. In Chapters 18 through 20, we take a detailed look at promotion activities.

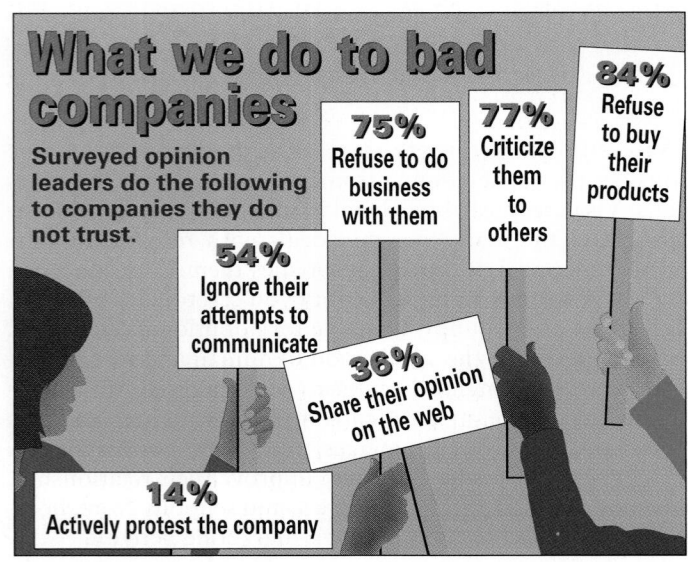

*Source:* 2006 Edelman Trust Barometer.

**The Price Variable.** The price variable relates to decisions and actions associated with establishing pricing objectives and policies and determining product prices. Price is a critical component of the marketing mix because customers are concerned about the value obtained in an exchange. Price is often used as a competitive tool, and intense price competition sometimes leads to price wars. Airlines, for example, develop complex systems for determining the right price for each seat on a specific flight. High prices can be used competitively to establish a product's image. Waterman and Mont Blanc pens, for example, have an image of high quality and high price that has given them significant status. On the other hand, some luxury goods marketers are now offering lower priced versions of their products to appeal to middle-class consumers who want to "trade up" to prestigious brand names. Handbag maker Coach, for example, markets fabric wristlets for $78 as well as vintage leather wristlets that sell for much more.[10] We explore pricing decisions in Chapters 21 and 22.

The marketing mix variables are often viewed as controllable because they can be modified. However, there are limits to how much marketing managers can alter them. Economic conditions, competitive structure, or government regulations may prevent a manager from adjusting prices frequently or significantly. Making changes in the size, shape, and design of most tangible goods is expensive; therefore, such product features cannot be altered very often. In addition, promotional campaigns and methods used to distribute products ordinarily cannot be rewritten or revamped overnight.

## Marketing Builds Relationships with Customers and Other Stakeholders

**exchange** The provision or transfer of goods, services, or ideas in return for something of value

Individuals and organizations engage in marketing to facilitate **exchanges**, the provision or transfer of goods, services, or ideas in return for something of value. Any product (good, service, or even idea) may be involved in a marketing exchange. We assume only that individuals and organizations expect to gain a reward in excess of the costs incurred.

For an exchange to take place, four conditions must exist. First, two or more individuals, groups, or organizations must participate, and each must possess something of value that the other party desires. Second, the exchange should provide a benefit or satisfaction to both parties in the transaction. Third, each party must have confidence in the promise of the "something of value" held by the other. If you go to a Cold Play concert, for example, you go with the expectation of a great performance. Finally, to build trust, the parties to the exchange must meet expectations.

Figure 1.2 (on p. 8) depicts the exchange process. The arrows indicate that the parties communicate that each has something of value available to exchange. An exchange will not necessarily take place just because these conditions exist; marketing activities can occur even without an actual transaction or sale. You may see an ad for a plasma TV, for instance, but you may never buy the product. When an exchange occurs, products are traded for other products or for financial resources.

Marketing activities should attempt to create and maintain satisfying exchange relationships. To maintain an exchange relationship, buyers must be satisfied with the obtained good, service, or idea, and sellers must be satisfied with the financial reward or something else of value received. A dissatisfied customer who lacks trust in the relationship often searches for alternative organizations or products.

**stakeholders** Constituents who have a "stake" or claim in some aspect of a company's products, operations, markets, industry, and outcomes

Marketers are concerned with building relationships not only with customers but also with relevant stakeholders. **Stakeholders** include those constituents who have a "stake," or claim, in some aspect of a company's products, operations, markets, industry, and outcomes; stakeholders include customers, employees, investors and shareholders, suppliers, governments, communities, and many others. Stakeholders have the power to provide or withdraw needed resources or influence customer opinion about a firm's marketing strategy and products. Developing and maintaining favorable relations with stakeholders is crucial to the long-term growth of an organization and its products.

**figure 1.2**

### EXCHANGE BETWEEN BUYER AND SELLER

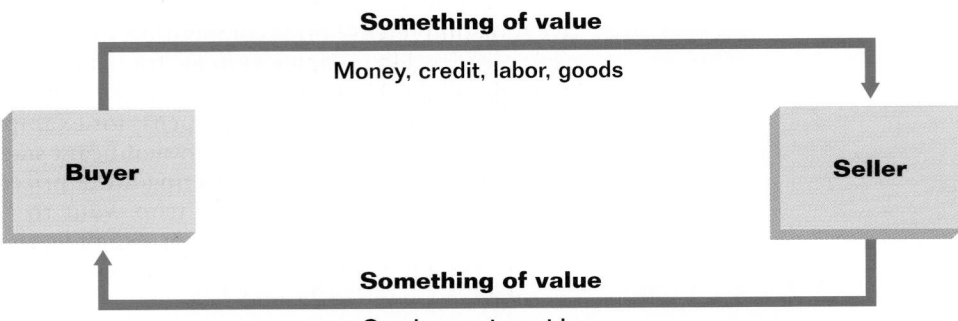

**Something of value**

Money, credit, labor, goods

**Buyer** → **Seller**

**Something of value**

Goods, services, ideas

## Marketing Occurs in a Dynamic Environment

**marketing environment** The competitive, economic, political, legal and regulatory, technological, and sociocultural forces that surround the customer and affect the marketing mix

Marketing activities do not take place in a vacuum. The **marketing environment,** which includes competitive, economic, political, legal and regulatory, technological, and sociocultural forces, surrounds the customer and affects the marketing mix (see Figure 1.1). The effects of these forces on buyers and sellers can be dramatic and difficult to predict. They can create threats to marketers, but they can also generate opportunities for new products and new methods of reaching customers.

The forces of the marketing environment affect a marketer's ability to facilitate exchanges in three general ways. First, they influence customers by affecting their lifestyles, standards of living, and preferences and needs for products. Because a marketing manager tries to develop and adjust the marketing mix to satisfy customers, effects of environmental forces on customers also have an indirect impact on marketing mix components. The merging of telecommunications and computer technologies, for example, allows FedEx Corporation to interact with customers via the Web. FedEx customers can track packages from their home or office computers and send e-mail feedback to FedEx about its services. This technology thus enables FedEx to gather marketing research information directly from customers. Second, marketing environment forces help determine whether and how a marketing manager can perform certain marketing activities. Third, environmental forces may affect a marketing manager's decisions and actions by influencing buyers' reactions to the firm's marketing mix.

Marketing environment forces can fluctuate quickly and dramatically, which is one reason that marketing is so interesting and challenging. Because these forces are closely interrelated, changes in one may cause changes in others. For example, evidence linking children's consumption of soft drinks and fast foods to health issues such as obesity, diabetes, and osteoporosis has exposed marketers of such products to negative publicity and generated calls for legislation regulating the sale of soft drinks in public schools. Some companies have responded to these concerns by reformulating products to make them healthier or even introducing new products. PepsiCo, for example, introduced Tropicana FruitWise bars and Life cereal with yogurt and began a marketing campaign to help consumers identify healthier eating choices. The company placed a green "Smart Spot" on more than 200 products that meet nutrition criteria on limits on fat, cholesterol, sodium, and added sugar, such as Baked Lay's potato chips and Tropicana orange juice.[11]

Changes in the marketing environment produce uncertainty for marketers and at times hurt marketing efforts, but they also create opportunities. Marketers who are alert to changes in environmental forces can adjust to and influence these changes and can capitalize on the opportunities such changes provide. Sharper Image, for example, was once a high-tech gadget boutique, always looking for the next calculator, robot, or other hot product from Sony, Panasonic, and other manufacturers. Today the national retail chain stays on top of social and technological trends by stocking new inventions and designing and marketing its own ideas. With an average purchase of $128 per customer, 80 percent of Sharper Image's revenues now come from its own products, such as the Turbo-Groomer, the Automatic Eyeglass Cleaner, and the Saxxy, a software-powered kazoo.[12]

Marketing mix elements—product, distribution, promotion, and price—are factors over which an organization has control; the forces of the environment, however, are far less controllable. But even though marketers know they cannot predict changes in the marketing environment with certainty, they must nevertheless plan for them. Because these environmental forces have such a profound effect on marketing activities, we explore each of them in considerable depth in Chapter 3.

# Understanding the Marketing Concept

Some firms have sought success by buying land, building a factory, equipping it with people and machines, and then making a product they believe buyers need. However, these firms frequently fail to attract customers with what they have to offer because they defined their business as "making a product" rather than as "helping potential customers satisfy their needs and wants." For example, when compact discs became more popular than vinyl records, turntable manufacturers had an opportunity to develop new products to satisfy customers' needs for home entertainment. Companies that did not pursue this opportunity, such as Dual and Empire, are no longer in business. Such organizations failed to implement the marketing concept. Likewise, the growing popularity of MP3 technology has enabled firms such as Apple Computer to develop products like the iPod to satisfy consumers' desire to store customized music libraries. Instead of buying CDs, a consumer can download a song for 99 cents from Apple's iTunes.

**marketing concept** A philosophy that an organization should try to provide products that satisfy customers' needs through a coordinated set of activities that also allows the organization to achieve its goals

According to the **marketing concept**, an organization should try to provide products that satisfy customers' needs through a coordinated set of activities that also allows the organization to achieve its goals. Customer satisfaction is the major focus of the marketing concept. To implement the marketing concept, an organization strives to determine what buyers want and uses this information to develop satisfying products. It focuses on customer analysis, competitor analysis, and integration of the firm's resources to provide customer value and satisfaction as well as generate long-term profits.[13] The firm must also continue to alter, adapt, and develop products to keep pace with customers' changing desires and preferences. Ben & Jerry's, for example, continuously assesses customer demand for ice cream and sorbet. On its website, it maintains a "flavor graveyard" that lists combinations that were tried and ultimately failed. It also notes its top ten flavors each month. Pharmaceutical companies such as Merck and Pfizer continually strive to develop new products to fight infectious diseases, viruses, cancer, and other medical problems. Drugs that lower cholesterol, control diabetes, alleviate depression, or improve the quality of life in other ways also provide huge profits for the drug companies. When a new product is approved—such as a grape-flavored chewable form of the allergy medication Zyrtec for young allergy sufferers—the company must undertake marketing activities to reach customers and communicate the product's benefits and any potential side effects. Thus, the marketing concept emphasizes that marketing begins and ends with customers. Research has found a positive association between customer satisfaction and shareholder value.[14]

The marketing concept is not a second definition of *marketing*. It is a management philosophy guiding an organization's overall activities. This philosophy affects all organizational activities, not just marketing. Production, finance, accounting, human resources, and marketing departments must work together.

The marketing concept is also not a philanthropic philosophy aimed at helping customers at the expense of the organization. A firm that adopts the marketing concept must satisfy not only its customers' objectives but also its own, or it

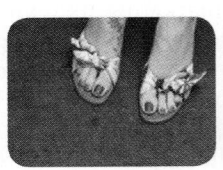

You are not silver, gold, or platinum. You are you.

Your "you-ness" [if that's a word] is worth protecting.

That's why we offer free Citi® Identity Theft Solutions just for being a customer.

Because if there's one thing we all have in common, it's that each of us is unique.

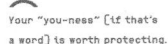

citi.com                Live richly.

**The Marketing Concept**

These companies communicate that they are customer-oriented, which is a part of the marketing concept. State Farm's slogan, "Like a good neighbor, State Farm is there," indicates that this company is attempting to satisfy customers' needs.

will not stay in business long. The overall objectives of a business might relate to increasing profits, market share, sales, or a combination of the three. The marketing concept stresses that an organization can best achieve these objectives by being customer oriented. Thus, implementing the marketing concept should benefit the organization as well as its customers.

It is important for marketers to consider not only their current buyers' needs but also the long-term needs of society. Striving to satisfy customers' desires by sacrificing society's long-term welfare is unacceptable. For example, while many parents want disposable diapers that are comfortable, absorbent, and safe for their babies, society in general does not want nonbiodegradable disposable diapers that create tremendous landfill problems now and for the future. Marketers are expected to act in a socially responsible manner, an idea we discuss in more detail in Chapter 4.

## Evolution of the Marketing Concept

The marketing concept may seem to be an obvious approach to running a business. However, businesspeople have not always believed that the best way to make sales and profits is to satisfy customers (see Figure 1.3).

## marketing
# ENTREPRENEURS

**Lambert Family Throwed Rolls**

THE BUSINESS: Lambert's Café: The only home of "Throwed Rolls"

FOUNDED: 1942

SUCCESS: Bakes more than 2,246,400 rolls a year

**W**ith just 14 cents in their pockets, Earl and Agnes Lambert borrowed $1,500 and opened a small café in Sikeston, Missouri, on March 13, 1942. Before long, Lambert's Café, which seated just 41 people, was a quaint eatery known for its hearty servings. When his father died in 1976, Norman Ray, Earl and Agnes's son, took over the café. In May of that year, while handing out oven-fresh rolls during a busy lunch hour, a hungry patron out of arms' reach told Norman to just throw him the @$%# thing. Thus was born the slogan, "If it doesn't say Lambert's, it's not. . .Throwed Rolls." Since then, Lambert's has been throwing rolls to thousands of diners who come from all over just to catch them—and to fill up on home-style food such as rib eye steak, white beans, and fried okra. Lambert's now operates out of three locations in two states and seats nearly 1,300 people.

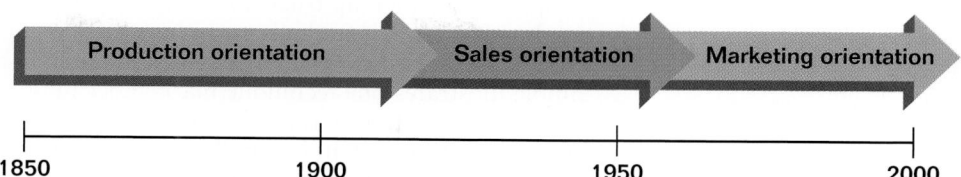

**figure 1.3**

## THE EVOLUTION OF THE MARKETING CONCEPT

Production orientation → Sales orientation → Marketing orientation

1850          1900          1950          2000

**The Production Orientation.** During the second half of the nineteenth century, the Industrial Revolution was in full swing in the United States. Electricity, rail transportation, division of labor, assembly lines, and mass production made it possible to produce goods more efficiently. With new technology and new ways of using labor, products poured into the marketplace, where demand for manufactured goods was strong.

**The Sales Orientation.** In the 1920s, strong demand for products subsided, and businesses realized they would have to "sell" products to buyers. From the mid-1920s to the early 1950s, businesses viewed sales as the major means of increasing profits and came to adopt a sales orientation. Businesspeople believed the most important marketing activities were personal selling, advertising, and distribution. Today some people incorrectly equate marketing with a sales orientation.

**The Marketing Orientation.** By the early 1950s, some businesspeople began to recognize that efficient production and extensive promotion did not guarantee that customers would buy products. These businesses, and many others since, found they must first determine what customers want and then produce these products rather than making the products first and then trying to persuade customers that they need them. As more organizations realized the importance of satisfying customers' needs, U.S. businesses entered the marketing era, one of marketing orientation.

**marketing orientation** An organizationwide commitment to researching and responding to customer needs

A **marketing orientation** requires the "organizationwide generation of market intelligence pertaining to current and future customer needs, dissemination of the intelligence across departments, and organizationwide responsiveness to it."[15] Marketing orientation is linked to new product innovation by developing a strategic focus to explore and develop new products to serve target markets.[16] Top management, marketing managers, nonmarketing managers (those in production, finance, human resources, and so on), and customers are all important in developing and carrying out a marketing orientation. Unless marketing managers provide continuous customer-focused leadership with minimal interdepartmental conflict, achieving a marketing orientation will be difficult. Nonmarketing managers must communicate with marketing managers to share information important to understanding the customer. Finally, a marketing orientation involves being responsive to ever-changing customer needs and wants. For example, to accomplish this, Amazon.com follows buyers' online purchases and recommends related purchases. Trying to assess what customers want, a difficult task to begin with, is further complicated by the speed with which fashions and tastes can change. Today businesses want to satisfy customers and build meaningful, long-term buyer-seller relationships. Doing so helps a firm boost its own financial value.[17]

## Implementing the Marketing Concept

A philosophy may sound reasonable and look good on paper, but that does not mean it can be put into practice easily. To implement the marketing concept, a marketing-oriented organization must accept some general conditions and recognize and deal with several problems. Consequently, the marketing concept has yet to be fully accepted by all U.S. businesses. Management must first establish an information system to discover customers' real needs and then use the information to create satisfying products. Nissan, for example, conducted intensive marketing research before launching its first full-size pickup truck, the Titan. The company interviewed truck buyers about their specific needs and wants for a vehicle. Surveys were conducted at a variety of locations including hunting expos, gun shows, and other events frequented by pick up truck owners.

In addition, Nissan had researchers drive competing trucks for a month to learn first hand about how the large vehicles handle in a variety of situations.[18] This example illustrates one technique marketers can use to obtain information about customers' desires and to respond in a way that forges a positive marketing relationship. An information system is usually expensive; management must commit money and time for its development and maintenance. But without an adequate information system, an organization cannot be marketing oriented.

To satisfy customers' objectives as well as its own, a company must also coordinate all its activities. This may require restructuring the internal operations and overall objectives of one or more departments. Nanotechnology, for example, represents opportunities for advances in pumps, gears, and switches to perform physical tasks. However, application and commercialization of this technology requires marketing knowledge related to customers' needs and product uses. If the head of the marketing unit is not a member of the organization's top-level management, a new technology may fail to sufficiently address actual customer needs and desires. Implementing the marketing concept demands the support not only of top management but also of managers and staff across all functions and levels of the organization.

# Managing Customer Relationships

Achieving the full profit potential of each customer relationship should be the fundamental goal of every marketing strategy. Marketing relationships with customers are the lifeblood of all businesses. At the most basic level, profits can be obtained through relationships by (1) acquiring new customers, (2) enhancing the profitability of existing customers, and (3) extending the duration of customer relationships. Implementing the marketing concept means optimizing the exchange relationship—the relationship between a company's investment in customer relationships and the return generated by customers' loyalty and retention.[19]

Maintaining positive relationships with customers is an important goal for marketers. The term **relationship marketing** refers to "long-term, mutually beneficial arrangements in which both the buyer and seller focus on value enhancement through the creation of more satisfying exchanges."[20] Relationship marketing continually deepens the buyer's trust in the company, which, as the customer's confidence grows, in turn increases the firm's understanding of the customer's needs. Successful marketers respond to customer needs and strive to increase value to buyers over time. Eventually this interaction becomes a solid relationship that allows for cooperation and mutual dependency.

To build long-term customer relationships, marketers are increasingly turning to marketing research and information technology. **Customer relationship management (CRM)** focuses on using information about customers to create marketing strategies that develop and sustain desirable customer relationships. By increasing customer value over time, organizations try to retain and increase long-term profitability through customer loyalty.[21] For example, AmSouth Bank, a financial institution with branches throughout the southeastern United States, promotes itself as "The Relationship Bank" and offers every financial service a business or consumer could conceivably need. Instead of focusing on acquiring new customers, AmSouth strives to serve all the financial needs of each individual customer, thereby acquiring a greater share of each customer's financial business.[22]

Managing customer relationships requires identifying patterns of buying behavior and using that information to focus on the most promising and profitable customers. Companies must be sensitive to customers' requirements and desires, and es-

**relationship marketing** Establishing long-term, mutually satisfying buyer-seller relationships

**customer relationship management (CRM)** Using information about customers to create marketing strategies that develop and sustain desirable customer relationships

tablish communication to build customers' trust and loyalty. Consider that the lifetime value of a Lexus customer is about 50 times that of a Taco Bell customer, but remember, there are many more Taco Bell customers. For either organization, a customer is important. A customer's lifetime value results from his or her frequency of purchases, average value of purchases, and brand-switching patterns.[23] In general, when marketers focus on customers chosen for their lifetime value, they earn higher profits in future periods than when they focus on customers selected for other reasons.[24] Because the loss of a loyal potential lifetime customer can result in lower profits, managing customer relationships has become a major focus of strategic marketing today.

Through the use of Internet-based marketing strategies (e-marketing), companies can personalize customer relationships on a nearly one-on-one basis. A wide range of products, such as computers, jeans, golf clubs, cosmetics, and greeting cards, can be tailored for specific customers. CRM provides a strategic bridge between information technology and marketing strategies aimed at long-term relationships with high-revenue customers.[25] Thus, information technology helps Amazon.com manage customer relationships to build value and increase sales and satisfaction. We take a closer look at some of these e-marketing strategies in Chapter 8.

# Value-Driven Marketing

**value** A customer's subjective assessment of benefits relative to costs in determining the worth of a product

Value is an important element of managing long-term customer relationships and implementing the marketing concept. We view **value** as a customer's subjective assessment of benefits relative to costs in determining the worth of a product (customer value = customer benefits − customer costs). From a company's perspective, there is a tradeoff between increasing the value offered to a customer and maximizing the profits from a transaction.[26]

Customer benefits include anything a buyer receives in an exchange. Hotels and motels, for example, basically provide a room with a bed and bathroom, but each firm provides a different level of service, amenities, and atmosphere to satisfy its guests. Hampton Inns offers the minimum services necessary to maintain a quality, efficient, low-price overnight accommodation. In contrast, the Ritz Carlton provides every imaginable service a guest might desire and strives to ensure that all service is of the highest quality. Customers judge which type of accommodation offers the best value according to the benefits they desire and their willingness and ability to pay for the costs associated with those benefits.

Customer costs include anything a buyer must give up to obtain the benefits the product provides. The most obvious cost is the monetary price of the product, but nonmonetary costs can be equally important in a customer's determination of value. Two nonmonetary costs are the time and effort customers expend to find and purchase desired products. To reduce time and effort, a company can increase product availability, thereby making it more convenient for buyers to purchase the firm's products. Another nonmonetary cost is risk, which can be reduced by offering good basic warranties or extended warranties for an additional charge.[27] Another risk reduction strategy is the offer of a 100 percent satisfaction guarantee. This strategy is increasingly popular in today's catalog/telephone/Internet shopping environment. L.L. Bean, for example, uses such a guarantee to reduce the risk involved in ordering merchandise from its catalogs and online store.

The process people use to determine the value of a product is not highly scientific. We all tend to get a feel for the worth of products based on our own expectations and previous experiences. We can, for example, compare the value of tires, batteries, and computers directly with the value of competing products. We evaluate movies, sporting events, and performances by entertainers on the more subjective basis of personal preferences and emotions. For most purchases, we do not consciously try to calculate the associated benefits and costs. It becomes an instinctive feeling that Kellogg's Corn Flakes are a good value or that McDonald's is a good place to take

**Value-Driven Marketing**

Rapala uses value to promote its products. Tide promotes the value of its stain-fighting ability to those with family heirlooms.

children for a quick lunch. The purchase of an automobile or a mountain bike may have emotional components, but more conscious decision making may also figure in the process of determining value.

In developing marketing activities, it is important to recognize that customers receive benefits based on their experiences. For example, many computer buyers consider services such as fast delivery, ease of installation, technical advice, and training assistance to be important elements of the product. Customers also derive benefits from the act of shopping and selecting products. These benefits can be affected by the atmosphere or environment of a store, such as Red Lobster's nautical theme. Even the ease of navigating a website can have a tremendous impact on perceived value. For this reason, General Motors has developed a user-friendly way to navigate its website for researching and pricing vehicles. Using the Internet to compare a Saturn with a Mercedes could result in different customers viewing each automobile as an excellent value. Owners have highly rated the Saturn as providing low-cost, reliable transportation and having dealers who provide outstanding service. A Mercedes may cost twice as much but has been rated as a better-engineered automobile that also has a higher social status than the Saturn. Different customers may view each car as being an exceptional value for their own personal satisfaction.

The marketing mix can be used to enhance perceptions of value. A product that demonstrates value usually has a feature or an enhancement that provides benefits. Promotional activities can also help create an image and prestige characteristics that customers consider in their assessment of a product's value. In some cases, value may simply be perceived as the lowest price. Many customers may not care about the quality of the paper towels they buy; they simply want the cheapest ones for use in cleaning up spills because they plan to throw them in the trash anyway. On the other hand, more people are looking for the fastest, most convenient way to achieve a certain goal and therefore become insensitive to pricing. For example, many busy customers are buying more prepared meals in supermarkets to take home and serve quickly, even though these meals cost considerably more than meals prepared from scratch. In such cases, the products with the greatest convenience may be perceived as having the greatest value. The availability or distribution of products can also enhance their value. Taco Bell, for example, wants to have its Mexican fast-food products available at any time and any place people are thinking about consuming food. It has therefore introduced Taco Bell products into supermarkets, vending machines, college campuses, and other convenient locations. Thus, the development of an effective marketing strategy requires understanding the needs and desires of customers and designing a marketing mix to satisfy them and provide the value they want.

# Will Your Relationship Last? Your Bear Will!

**M**arketing, like our personal lives, is all about building and maintaining relationships. People have wants, needs, and expectations, and there are companies who are looking to meet or exceed them. Sometimes it takes a company some time to figure out which customer wants and needs they are best suited to satisfy. The Vermont Teddy Bear Company is a case in point.

The Vermont Teddy Bear Company was founded in 1981 to manufacture and sell cuddly teddy bears. Sales were in hibernation for years in its three retail stores until the company started promoting its Bear-Gram—a delivery service via a toll-free phone number—and sales roared to life. Radio ads were developed that positioned the Bear-Gram as the convenient, creative alternative to flowers. Today the company offers over 100 varieties of bears with names like Stud Muffin, Love Bandit, Sweetheart, and Red Hot Redneck. The bears are also themed for popular gift-giving occasions such as Valentine's Day, birthdays, and anniversaries, as well as to extend such sentiments as get well and congratulations. They also offer teddy bears to honor people in their line of work; bears outfitted as police officers and firefighters are two popular choices. All Vermont Teddy Bears are hand made and guaranteed for life.

A major factor in the company's success has been their ability to personalize the recipient's "bear experience." Each bear is packaged in a box with an air hole (so the bear can breathe) and a warning not to turn the box upside down lest you give your bear a headache. Other soft touches include Bear Coun-

selors, who assist customers with the selection and personalization of their bears; an invitation to visit the factory; and free bear repairs at the Vermont Teddy Bear Hospital. Today, there are over 500,000 people enrolled in the company's PreFur'd customer loyalty program.

As sales grew, the company was repositioned as a gift delivery company. Its product offerings now include PajamaGrams, TastyGrams, and Calyx & Corolla, a floral catalog business. At the root of the company's successful transition into a gift delivery business was its ability to generate new marketing and product ideas that appeal to gift givers, as well as to come up with innovative processes to ensure customer satisfaction. Clearly The Vermont Teddy Bear Company is meeting its customers' expectations.

# Marketing Management

**marketing management** The process of planning, organizing, implementing, and controlling marketing activities to facilitate exchanges effectively and efficiently

**Marketing management** is the process of planning, organizing, implementing, and controlling marketing activities to facilitate exchanges effectively and efficiently. Effectiveness and efficiency are important dimensions of this definition. *Effectiveness* is the degree to which an exchange helps achieve an organization's objectives. *Efficiency* refers to minimizing the resources an organization must spend to achieve a specific level of desired exchanges. Thus, the overall goal of marketing management is to facilitate highly desirable exchanges and to minimize the costs of doing so.

Planning is a systematic process of assessing opportunities and resources, determining marketing objectives, and developing a marketing strategy and plans for implementation and control. Planning determines when and how marketing activities are performed and who performs them. It forces marketing managers to think ahead, establish objectives, and consider future marketing activities and their impact on society. Effective planning also reduces or eliminates daily crises.

Organizing marketing activities involves developing the internal structure of the marketing unit. The structure is the key to directing marketing activities. The marketing unit can be organized by functions, products, regions, types of customers, or a combination of all four.

Proper implementation of marketing plans hinges on coordination of marketing activities, motivation of marketing personnel, and effective communication within the unit. Marketing managers must motivate marketing personnel, coordinate their activities, and integrate their activities both with those in other areas of the company and with the marketing efforts of personnel in external organizations, such as advertising agencies and research firms. If McDonald's runs a promotion advertising Big Macs for 99 cents, proper implementation of this plan requires that each of the company's restaurants has enough staff and product on hand to handle the increased demand. An organization's communication system must allow the marketing manager to stay in contact with high-level management, with managers of other functional areas within the firm, and with personnel involved in marketing activities both inside and outside the organization.

The marketing control process consists of establishing performance standards, comparing actual performance with established standards, and reducing the difference between desired and actual performance. An effective control process has four requirements. First, it should ensure a rate of information flow that allows the marketing manager to detect quickly any differences between actual and planned levels of performance. Second, it must accurately monitor various activities and be flexible enough to accommodate changes. Third, the costs of the control process must be low relative to costs that would arise without controls. Finally, the control process should be designed so that both managers and subordinates can understand it. We examine the development, organization, implementation, and controlling of marketing strategies in greater detail in the next chapter.

# The Importance of Marketing in Our Global Economy

Our definition of *marketing* and discussion of marketing activities reveal some of the obvious reasons the study of marketing is relevant in today's world. In this section, we look at how marketing affects us as individuals and at its role in our increasingly global society.

### Marketing Costs Consume a Sizable Portion of Buyers' Dollars

Studying marketing will make you aware that many marketing activities are necessary to provide satisfying goods and services. Obviously these activities cost money. About one-half of a buyer's dollar goes for marketing costs. If you spend $12 on a new CD, 50 to 60 percent goes toward marketing expenses, including promotion and distribution, as well as profit margin. The production (pressing) of the CD represents about $1, or 6.25 percent of its price. A family with a monthly income of $3,000 that allocates $600 to taxes and savings spends about $2,400 for goods and services. Of this amount, $1,200 goes for marketing activities. If marketing expenses consume that much of your dollar, you should know how this money is used.

## Marketing Is Used in Nonprofit Organizations

Although the term *marketing* may bring to mind advertising for Estée Lauder, Toyota, and Microsoft, marketing is also important in organizations working to achieve goals other than ordinary business objectives such as profit. Government agencies at the federal, state, and local levels engage in marketing activities to fulfill their mission and goals. The U.S. Army, for example, uses promotion, including television advertisements and event sponsorships, to communicate the benefits of enlisting to potential recruits. The U.S. Agriculture Department launched a promotional website with games to help teach kids about eating right according to its revised "Food Pyramid."[28] Universities and colleges also engage in marketing activities to recruit new students as well as donations from alumni and businesses.

In the private sector, nonprofit organizations employ marketing activities to create, distribute, promote, and even price programs that benefit particular segments of society. Habitat for Humanity, for example, must promote its philosophy of low-income housing to the public to raise funds and donations of supplies to build or renovate housing for low-income families who contribute "sweat equity" to the construction of their own homes. In a recent year, such activities helped nonprofit organizations raise nearly $249 billion in philanthropic contributions to assist them in fulfilling their missions.[29]

**Nonprofit Organizations Use Marketing**

Nonprofit organizations such as these use advertisements to promote their causes.

## Marketing Is Important to Business and the Economy

Businesses must sell products to survive and grow, and marketing activities help sell their products. Financial resources generated from sales can be used to develop innovative products. New products allow a firm to better satisfy customers'

changing needs, which in turn enables the firm to generate more profits. Even non-profit businesses need to "sell" to survive.

Marketing activities help produce the profits that are essential not only to the survival of individual businesses but also to the health and ultimate survival of the global economy. Profits drive economic growth because without them businesses find it difficult, if not impossible, to buy more raw materials, hire more employees, attract more capital, and create additional products that in turn make more profits. Without profits, marketers cannot continue to provide jobs and contribute to social causes.

### Marketing Fuels Our Global Economy

Profits from marketing products contribute to the development of new products and technologies. Advances in technology, along with falling political and economic barriers and the universal desire for a higher standard of living, have made marketing across national borders commonplace while stimulating global economic growth. As a result of worldwide communications and increased international travel, many U.S. brands have achieved widespread acceptance around the world. At the same time, customers in the United States have greater choices among the products they buy as foreign brands such as Toyota (Japan), Bayer (Germany), and BP (Great Britain) now sell alongside U.S. brands such as Ford, Tylenol, and Chevron. People around the world watch CNN and MTV on Toshiba and Sony televisions they purchased at

# One Planet, One IKEA

As markets fragment, it is no surprise that companies with the biggest increases in brand value operate as a single brand globally. IKEA, the Swedish home furnishings company and the world's largest furniture retailer, has shown that a well-positioned brand with a strong marketing mix travels well. It has clearly learned that a single worldwide identity is easier to manage and more cost efficient than creating new brands for each country.

While other global brands make extensive changes to fit local environments, IKEA provides a nearly identical experience in its more than 200 blue and yellow stores. IKEA stores—each the size of five football fields—feature over 7,000 items ranging from self-assemble beds and kitchen cabinets to candlesticks and potted plants, all showcased in fully accessorized lifelike settings. The shopping experience is as much a part of the product as the products themselves.

The 1.1 million customers who visit IKEA every day enter an environment that is emblematic of hip

Scandinavian design and simplicity. The product displays and furniture showrooms appeal to the growing global middle class that aspires to success and a comfortable living. More than just a seller of furniture, the company conveys to people all over the world that IKEA is synonymous with good taste and smart value.

While IKEA refuses to change its basic concept—offering a broad variety of well-designed and functional home furnishing products at prices low enough that as many people as possible can afford them—it does adjust to ensure a pleasurable shopping experience for local cultures. When it was suggested that Americans wouldn't assemble furniture themselves, IKEA provided better instructions and offered an assembly service. To fit Japan's small urban apartments, IKEA offered smaller versions of its products. Stores in China carry chopsticks, woks, and cleavers—essential cooking tools in that country—and a department dedicated to balcony furniture to accommodate the many Chinese who live in apartments with balconies. But the basic model, complete with Swedish-named products such as Leksvik and Poang and restaurants featuring IKEA's popular cinnamon rolls, remains the same. IKEA clearly recognizes that the middle class it targets has similar needs and lifestyle aspirations across the globe.

Wal-Mart. Some well-known brands have been sold to foreign companies: Lenovo, a Chinese firm, purchased IBM's personal computer unit.[30] Electronic commerce via the Internet now enables businesses of all sizes to reach buyers worldwide. We explore the international markets and opportunities for global marketing in Chapter 7.

## Marketing Knowledge Enhances Consumer Awareness

Besides contributing to the well-being of our economy, marketing activities help improve the quality of our lives. Studying marketing allows us to assess a product's value and flaws more effectively. We can determine which marketing efforts need improvement and how to attain that goal. For example, an unsatisfactory experience with a warranty may make you wish for stricter law enforcement so that sellers would fulfill their promises. You may also wish you had more accurate information about a product before you purchased it. Understanding marketing enables us to evaluate corrective measures (such as laws, regulations, and industry guidelines) that could stop unfair, damaging, or unethical marketing practices. Thus, understanding how marketing activities work can help you be a better consumer.

## Marketing Connects People Through Technology

Technology, especially computers and telecommunications, helps marketers understand and satisfy more customers than ever before. Over the phone and online, customers can provide feedback about their experiences with a company's products. Even products such as Dasani bottled water provide a customer service number and a website for questions or comments. This feedback helps marketers refine and improve their products to better satisfy customer needs. In addition to feedback, the Internet also allows companies to provide tremendous amounts of information about their products to consumers and to interact with them through e-mail. A consumer shopping for a personal digital assistant, for example, can visit the Blackberry website to compare its features to those of a smartphone such as the Palm Treo or visit a price comparison website to find the best price.

The Internet has also become a vital tool for marketing to other businesses. In fact, online sales now exceed $100 billion, accounting for more than 2 percent of all retail sales.[31] Successful companies are using technology in their marketing strategies to develop profitable relationships with these customers. We look more closely at marketing on the Internet in Chapter 8.

## Socially Responsible Marketing: Promoting the Welfare of Customers and Society

The success of our economic system depends on marketers whose values promote trust and cooperative relationships in which customers are treated with respect. The public is increasingly insisting that social responsibility and ethical concerns be considered in planning and implementing marketing activities. Although some marketers' irresponsible or unethical activities end up on the front pages of *USA Today* or the *Wall Street Journal*, more firms are working to develop a responsible approach to developing long-term relationships with customers and society. For example, Staples, the office-supply superstore chain, has provided financial support and donated more than $400,000 worth of school supplies to the School, Home & Office Products Association (SHOPA) Kids in Need Foundation, which provides school supplies to needy children and teachers in low-income schools, through its

**Marketing and the Growth of Technology**

eBay uses technology to facilitate the marketing of a multitude of products.

search.ebay.com/hula skirts
/portable video games
/mystery novels
/baseball tickets
/all-terrain tires
/dome tents
/stain removers

/ranch land
/hedge trimmers
/golf shoes
/video cellphones
/flip-flops
/digital sports watches
/horseshoe sets

/laptops
/swimming trunks
/digital cameras
/sprinklers
/lawnmowers
/sun hats
/artificial turf

you can get it on ebY.

Staples Foundation for Learning.[32] By addressing concerns about the impact of marketing on society, a firm can protect the interests of the general public and the natural environment. We examine these issues and many others as we develop a framework for understanding more about marketing in the remainder of this book.

### Marketing Offers Many Exciting Career Prospects

From 25 to 33 percent of all civilian workers in the United States perform marketing activities. The marketing field offers a variety of interesting and challenging career opportunities throughout the world, such as personal selling, advertising, packaging, transportation, storage, marketing research, product development, wholesaling, and retailing. In addition, many individuals working for nonbusiness organizations engage in marketing activities to promote political, educational, cultural, church, civic, and charitable activities. Whether a person earns a living through marketing activities or performs them voluntarily for a nonprofit group, marketing knowledge and skills are valuable personal and professional assets.

## SUMMARY

Marketing is the process of creating, distributing, promoting, and pricing goods, services, and ideas to facilitate satisfying exchange relationships with customers and develop and maintain favorable relationships with stakeholders in a dynamic environment. As the purchasers of the products that organizations develop, promote, distribute, and price, customers are the focal point of all marketing activities. The essence of marketing is to develop satisfying exchanges from which both customers and marketers benefit. Organizations generally focus their marketing efforts on a specific group of customers called a target market.

Marketing involves developing and managing a product that will satisfy customer needs, making the product available in the right place and at a price acceptable to customers, and communicating information that helps customers determine if the product will satisfy their needs. These activities—product, distribution, promotion, and pricing—are known as the marketing mix because marketing managers decide what type of each element to use and in what amounts. Marketing managers strive to develop a marketing mix that matches the needs of customers in the target market. Before marketers can develop a marketing mix, they must collect in-depth, up-to-date information about customer needs. The product variable of the marketing mix deals with researching customers' needs and wants and designing a product that satisfies them. A product can be a good, a service, or an idea. In dealing with the distribution variable, a marketing manager tries to make products available in the quantities desired to as many customers as possible. The promotion variable relates to activities used to inform individuals or groups about the organization and its products. The price variable involves decisions and actions associated with establishing pricing policies and determining product prices. These

marketing mix variables are often viewed as controllable because they can be changed, but there are limits to how much they can be altered.

Individuals and organizations engage in marketing to facilitate exchanges—the provision or transfer of goods, services, and ideas in return for something of value. Four conditions must exist for an exchange to occur. First, two or more individuals, groups, or organizations must participate, and each must possess something of value that the other party desires. Second, the exchange should provide a benefit or satisfaction to both parties involved in the transaction. Third, each party must have confidence in the promise of the "something of value" held by the other. Finally, to build trust, the parties to the exchange must meet expectations. Marketing activities should attempt to create and maintain satisfying exchange relationships.

The marketing environment, which includes competitive, economic, political, legal and regulatory, technological, and sociocultural forces, surrounds the customer and the marketing mix. These forces can create threats to marketers, but they also generate opportunities for new products and new methods of reaching customers. These forces can fluctuate quickly and dramatically.

According to the marketing concept, an organization should try to provide products that satisfy customers' needs through a coordinated set of activities that also allows the organization to achieve its goals. Customer satisfaction is the marketing concept's major objective. The philosophy of the marketing concept emerged in the United States during the 1950s after the production and sales eras. Organizations that develop activities consistent with the marketing concept become marketing-oriented organizations. To implement the marketing concept, a marketing-oriented organization must establish an information system to discover customers' needs and use the information to create satisfying products. It must also coordinate all its activities and develop marketing mixes that create value for customers in order to satisfy their needs.

Relationship marketing involves establishing long-term, mutually satisfying buyer-seller relationships. Customer relationship management (CRM) focuses on using information about customers to create marketing strategies that develop and sustain desirable customer relationships. Managing customer relationships requires identifying patterns of buying behavior and using that information to focus on the most promising and profitable customers.

Value is a customer's subjective assessment of benefits relative to costs in determining the worth of a product. Benefits include anything a buyer receives in an exchange; costs include anything a buyer must give up to obtain the benefits the product provides. The marketing mix can be used to enhance perceptions of value.

Marketing management is the process of planning, organizing, implementing, and controlling marketing activities to facilitate effective and efficient exchanges. Planning is a systematic process of assessing opportunities and resources, determining marketing objectives, developing a marketing strategy, and preparing for implementation

and control. Organizing marketing activities involves developing the marketing unit's internal structure. Proper implementation of marketing plans depends on coordinating marketing activities, motivating marketing personnel, and communicating effectively within the unit. The marketing control process consists of establishing performance standards, comparing actual performance with established standards, and reducing the difference between desired and actual performance.

Marketing is important in our society in many ways. Marketing costs absorb about half of each buyer's dollar. Marketing activities are performed in both business and nonprofit organizations. Marketing activities help business organizations generate profits and help fuel the increasingly global economy. Knowledge of marketing enhances consumer awareness. New technology improves marketers' ability to connect with customers. Socially responsible marketing can promote the welfare of customers and society. Finally, marketing offers many exciting career opportunities.

**ACE self-test**

Please visit the student website at **www.prideferrell.com** for ACE Self-Test questions that will help you prepare for exams.

## IMPORTANT TERMS

| | | | |
|---|---|---|---|
| Marketing | Product | Marketing concept | Customer relationship |
| Customers | Exchange | Marketing orientation | management (CRM) |
| Target market | Stakeholders | Relationship marketing | Value |
| Marketing mix | Marketing environment | | Marketing management |

## DISCUSSION & REVIEW QUESTIONS

1. What is marketing? How did you define the term before you read this chapter?

2. What is the focus of all marketing activities? Why?

3. What are the four variables of the marketing mix? Why are these elements known as variables?

4. What conditions must exist before a marketing exchange can occur? Describe a recent exchange in which you participated.

5. What are the forces in the marketing environment? How much control does a marketing manager have over these forces?

6. Discuss the basic elements of the marketing concept. Which businesses in your area use this philosophy? Explain why.

7. How can an organization implement the marketing concept?

8. What is customer relationship management? Why is it so important to "manage" this relationship?

9. What is value? How can marketers use the marketing mix to enhance customers' perception of value?

10. What types of activities are involved in the marketing management process?

11. Why is marketing important in our society? Why should you study marketing?

## APPLICATION QUESTIONS

1. Identify several businesses in your area that have not adopted the marketing concept. What characteristics of these organizations indicate nonacceptance of the marketing concept?

2. Identify possible target markets for the following products:
   a. Kellogg's Corn Flakes
   b. Wilson tennis rackets
   c. Disney World
   d. Diet Pepsi

3. Discuss the variables of the marketing mix (product, price, promotion, and distribution) as they might relate to each of the following:
   a. a trucking company
   b. a men's clothing store
   c. a skating rink
   d. a campus bookstore

1. *Forbes* magazine publishes a composite ranking as a part of its Forbes Global 2000 based on four common business measures: sales, profit, assets, and market value. This information can be particularly useful if your firm intends to enter a new global market sector. Use the search term "composite ranking" at **http://globaledge.msu.edu/ibrd** to find the most recent Forbes 2000 ranking and then sort based on category. What are the top three semiconductor firms based on sales? In which country is each firm based?

2. Your firm is planning to develop a customer relationship management (CRM) initiative after it internationalizes. One way to understand the similarity or dissimilarity of markets and cultures is to use Hofstede's cultural dimensions, based on scores for 56 countries. Hofstede's cultural dimensions can be found using the search term "56 countries" at **http://globaledge.msu.edu/ibrd** to access the Geert Hofstede Resource Center and then the link called Hofstede Scores. The Power Distance Index (PDI) can be valuable in developing a CRM strategy. What are the five countries scoring lowest on Hofstede's PDI? Are these countries on the same continent? Are they geographically close?

## INTERNET Exercise

Visit **www.prideferrell.com** for resources to help you master the material in this chapter, plus materials that will help you expand your marketing knowledge, including Internet exercise updates, ACE Self-Tests, hotlinks to companies featured in this chapter, and much more.

### The American Marketing Association

The American Marketing Association (AMA) is the marketing discipline's primary professional organization. In addition to sponsoring academic research, publishing marketing literature, and organizing meetings of local businesspeople with student members, it helps individual members find employment in member firms. To see what the AMA has to offer you, visit the AMA website at **www.marketingpower.com**.

1. What type of information is available on the AMA website to assist students in planning their careers and finding jobs?
2. If you joined a student chapter of the AMA, what benefits would you receive?
3. What marketing mix variable does the AMA's Internet marketing efforts exemplify?

## Video Case 1.1 — Want Your Bagel Finagled?

Finagle A Bagel, a fast-growing Boston-based small business co-owned by Alan Litchman and Laura Trust, is at the forefront of one of the freshest concepts in the food service business: fresh food. The 20 stores bake a new batch of bagels every hour and receive deliveries of cheeses, vegetables, and other sandwich, soup, and salad ingredients every day. Store employees make everything to order to satisfy each "guest" —Finagle A Bagel's term for a customer. Patrons like this arrangement because they get fresh food prepared to their exact preferences—whether it's extra cheese on a bagel pizza or no onions in a salad—along with prompt, friendly service.

"Every sandwich, every salad is built to order, so there's a lot of communication between the customers and the cashiers, the customers and the sandwich makers, the customers and the managers," explains Trust. As a result, Finagle A Bagel's employees have ample opportunity to build customer relationships and encourage repeat business. Mirna Hernandez of the Tremont Street store in downtown Boston, for example, is so familiar with what many of the "regulars" order that she springs into action as soon as they enter the store. "We know what they want, and we just ring it in and take care of them," she says. Some employees even know their customers by name and make conversation as they create a sandwich or fill a coffee container.

Over time, the owners have introduced a wide range of bagels, sandwiches, soups, and salads linked to the core bagel product. Some of the most popular offerings include a breakfast bagel pizza, salads with bagel-chip croutons, and BLT (bacon-lettuce-tomato) bagel sandwiches. In any case, bagels—round, flat, seeded, plain, crowned with cheese, or cut into croutons—form the basis of every menu item at Finagle A Bagel. "So many other shops will just grab onto whatever is hot, whatever is trendy, in a 'me-too' strategy," observes Heather Robertson, director of marketing, human resources, and research and development. In contrast, she says, "We do bagels—that's what we do

best. And any menu item in our stores really needs to reaffirm that as our core concept." That's the first of Finagle A Bagel's marketing rules.

To identify a new product idea, Robertson and her colleagues conduct informal research by talking with both customers and employees. They also browse food magazines and cookbooks for ideas about out-of-the-ordinary flavors, taste combinations, and preparation methods. When developing a new bagel variety, Robertson looks for ideas that are innovative yet appealing: "If someone else has a sun-dried tomato bagel, that's all the more reason for me not to do it. People look at Finagle A Bagel as kind of the trendsetter." Once the marketing staff comes up with a promising idea, the next step is to write up a formula or recipe, walk downstairs to the dough factory, and mix up a test batch. Through trial and error, they refine the idea until they like the way the bagel or sandwich looks and tastes. One such idea is the scooped-out bagel, which has three-fourths of the calories and carbohydrates as a regular bagel, for those customers following a low-carb diet. To further reinforce the brand and reward customer loyalty, Finagle A Bagel introduced the Frequent Finagler card. Cardholders receive one point for every dollar spent in a Finagle A Bagel store and can redeem accumulated points for coffee, juice, sandwiches, or a dozen bagels (actually a *baker's dozen*, meaning 13 instead of 12). To join, customers register at the company's website **(www.finagleabagel.com).** From then on, says Litchman, "It's a web-based program where customers can log on, check their points, and receive free gifts by mail. The Frequent Finagler is our big push right now to use technology as a means of generating store traffic."

Pricing is an important consideration in the competitive world of quick-serve food. This is where another of Finagle A Bagel's marketing rules comes in. Regardless of cost, the company will not compromise quality. Therefore, the first step in pricing a new product is to find the best possible ingredients and then examine the costs and calculate an approximate retail price. After thinking about what a customer might expect to pay for such a menu item, shopping the competition, and talking with some customers, the company settles on a price that represents "a great product for a fair value," says Robertson. Although Finagle A Bagel's rental costs vary, the owners price menu items the same in both higher-rent and lower-rent stores. "We have considered adjusting prices based upon the location of the store, but we haven't done it because it can backfire in a very significant way," Trust explains. "People expect to be treated fairly, regardless of where they live."

Although Finagle A Bagel competes with other bagel chains in and around Boston, its competition goes well beyond restaurants in that category. "You compete with a person selling a cup of coffee, you compete with a grocery store selling a salad," Litchman notes. "People only have so many 'dining dollars' and you need to convince them to spend those dining dollars in your store." Finagle A Bagel's competitive advantages are high-quality, fresh products; courteous and competent employees; and clean, attractive, and inviting restaurants.

Social responsibility is an integral part of Finagle A Bagel's operations. Rather than simply throwing away unsold bagels at the end of the day, the owners donate the bagels to schools, shelters, and other nonprofit organizations. When local nonprofit groups hold fundraising events, the owners contribute bagels to feed the volunteers. Over the years, Finagle A Bagel has pro-

vided bagels to bicyclists raising money for St. Jude Children's Research Hospital, to swimmers raising money for breast cancer research, and to people building community playgrounds. Also, the owners are strongly committed to being fair to their customers by offering good value and a good experience. "Something that we need to remember and instill in our people all the time," Trust emphasizes, "is that customers are coming in and your responsibility is to give them the best that you can give them."

Even with 400-plus employees, the owners find that owning a business is a nonstop proposition. "Our typical day never ends," says Trust. They are continually visiting stores, dealing with suppliers, reviewing financial results, and planning for the future. Despite all these responsibilities, this husband-and-wife entrepreneurial team enjoys applying their educational background and business experience to build a business that satisfies thousands of customers every day.[33]

## Questions for Discussion

1. Describe Finagle A Bagel's marketing mix.
2. What forces from the marketing environment provide opportunities for Finagle A Bagel?
3. What forces might threaten the firm's marketing strategy?
4. Does Finagle A Bagel appear to be implementing the marketing concept? Explain your answer.

---

**Case 1.2**                 # Indy: The Great Race

Championship Auto Racing Teams (CART) was created in 1978 when 18 out of 21 automobile racing team owners left the United States Auto Club (USAC) to form a new league for open-wheel racing in the United States. Originally sanctioned in the mid-1950s by the USAC, open-wheel racing refers to cars that have an open cockpit with the engine housed at the rear of the vehicle, typical of cars used in the Indianapolis 500 race each year. However, dissatisfaction with USAC's administration and promotion of open-wheel racing prompted Roger Penske, Dan Gurney, Pat Patrick, and 15 other highly respected figures in U.S. motor sports to found CART (whose name was changed to Champ Car in 2003).

During its first 17 years, Champ Car dominated auto racing in the United States, and open-wheel racing enjoyed greater attention than other forms of racing, including stock-car racing associated with NASCAR. In the 1980s, Champ Car attracted legendary driver Mario Andretti and gained further foreign media cov-

erage when Formula 1 champion Nigel Mansell teamed up with Andretti and with Brazil's Emerson Fittipaldi for great finishes at Champ Car races.

Although Champ Car enjoyed increasing popularity in the early 1990s, Anton H. "Tony" George, whose family founded the Indianapolis 500 and developed it into the world-renowned auto race, was concerned that Champ Car was beginning to lose sight of the interests of U.S. open-wheel racing. Despite Champ Car's attempt to reorganize its board of directors to include Tony George, in 1994 he announced he was creating a new open-wheel league to compete with Champ Car beginning in 1996. His proposed Indy Racing League (IRL) was divisive to open-wheel racing in the United States as team owners were forced to choose whether to remain with Champ Car or move to the new league. George further deepened the rift when he proposed a "25/8" rule for the 1996 Indianapolis 500: the first 25 positions in the 33-car field would go to IRL members.

Despite the apparent duplication of open-wheel racing by Champ Car and IRL, there are significant differences between the two organizations. First, the leagues differ with respect to the types of racecourses employed. IRL races are held exclusively on oval tracks, whereas the majority of Champ Car races are run on road courses—either permanent racetrack facilities or temporary courses that run through the streets of an urban area. Because it is more difficult for racers to pass on road courses, they place a premium on drivers' skills to successfully navigate a track. On the other hand, oval track racing is influenced more by the horsepower and aerodynamics of the race cars, placing an emphasis on engineering and technical expertise to gain an edge over competitors.

Second, Champ Car and IRL differ in terms of the geographic scope of their leagues and drivers. The IRL is strictly a U.S. circuit. In contrast, Champ Car's drivers represent North America, South America, and Europe, and its 2006 schedule included races in the United States, Canada, Mexico, Australia, and South Korea. Champ Car also places greater emphasis on geographic allegiances with the Nations Cup, an award that recognizes the country whose drivers scored the best overall finish during the Champ Car season. As a result of Champ Car's international focus, it enjoys greater television exposure outside the United States as annually televised Champ Car races reach more than 980 million fans in 195 countries.

Champ Car has continued to be a dominant force in U.S. open-wheel racing after the initial split with the IRL. In fact, in 1998, Champ Car was incorporated and became a publicly traded company on the New York Stock Exchange. In 2000, two Champ Car teams resumed racing in the Indianapolis 500, and one won. Then Champ Car slowly began to lose ground against the IRL. Champ Car races in Brazil and Texas were cancelled during the 2001 season, resulting in public relations embarrassments for the organization. Top management turmoil was evident, too, as Champ Car went through four chief executive officers during 2000 and 2001.

When Champ Car and IRL split before the 1996 season, the breakup did more than split the racing teams. Fans tended to follow the league in which their favorite drivers raced rather than following both leagues. More important, sponsorship support was split between the two open-wheel leagues. Television broadcasts of Champ Car races could be instrumental in expanding the league's following, but Champ Car has been mired in an unfavorable television rights deal. Champ Car must pay to have its races broadcast, whereas IRL is paid by ABC for the rights to broadcast its races on ABC and ESPN. The limited reach of Champ Car's television broadcasts may have contributed to additional problems with sponsor relationships. Three major partners left Champ Car in recent seasons. Honda and Toyota, which provided engines

and technical support to Champ Car and its teams, left for deals with IRL. FedEx, which shipped a great deal of cargo to Champ Car racing sites in foreign markets, discontinued its title-sponsor relationship with Champ Car after the 2002 season. Champ Car ART successfully enlisted two new major series sponsors for the 2003 season and renamed the Champ Car series "Bridgestone Presents Champ Car World Series Powered by Ford."

Champ Car's viability as a major racing league was also harmed by the defection of key racing teams to IRL, including Roger Penske, Michael Andretti, and Chip Ganassi. Their absence meant that Champ Car might not be able to field the 18 cars needed to hold races. Champ Car responded by offering financial incentives to team owners to ensure enough cars would participate in its races. Also, Champ Car was forced to become the promoter of its own races after losing promoters in some markets. The combined result of an unfavorable television deal, sponsor and team owner defections, and increased costs of holding races forced Champ Car into a perilous financial position.

Champ Car's financial position continued to deteriorate during 2003, and company reports of increased operating costs and sluggish advertising and sponsorship revenue ultimately sent the organization into bankruptcy proceedings. Shortly after that, a group of investors, including some Champ Car team owners, purchased the embattled company for 56 cents per share. The group formed Open Wheel Racing Series LLC and planned to continue operating under the name Bridgestone Presents The Champ Car World Series Powered by Ford.

The new owners have many decisions to consider, including ways to define their product, how to promote races, where to race, and how to price their product for their race fans (customers). They moved quickly to secure new sponsorships and race-car teams. By 2005, the organization had gained several new sponsors, including Bridgestone, Ford, and Sherwin-Williams, and new teams, like the Newman/Wachs team run by famed driver Eddie Wachs and actor Paul Newman, himself a race-car driver. Moreover, race attendance reached record levels in 2005. The organization is also exploring the possibility of new races in China and Japan.

Nonetheless, U.S. auto racing fans seem to prefer oval track racing, as evidenced by NASCAR's strong race attendance and television ratings. However, IRL races on many of the same oval tracks as NASCAR but draws a fraction of the fans, with the Indianapolis 500 being a notable exception. Moreover, proponents of street and road course racing point to the fact that such venues lend themselves to creating a festival atmosphere around a race, including concerts, volleyball games, and beer gardens. Some racing fans insist that IRL and Champ Car must reunite for the betterment of auto racing, but the notion remains controversial. In any case, to compete against the growing popularity of NASCAR and to continue to grow, Champ Car must carefully analyze its target market and create a marketing mix to develop a successful long-term marketing strategy.[34]

## Questions for Discussion

1. Identify the product that the Champ Car World Series offers its race-car fans (customers).

2. What can the Champ Car World Series do to better promote its products? How should gaining sponsorships fit into its promotional plans?

3. How can the Champ Car World Series use the strengths of its international driver and race events to its advantage? Relate its selection of race courses and events to the concept of distribution presented in the chapter.

# Planning, Implementing, and Controlling Marketing Strategies

## It's Always Saturday Morning at Cereality

Although most of us buy our cereal at supermarkets and eat it at our own kitchen tables, some folks in the Southwest enjoy their Cheerios in one of four all-cereal cafés called Cereality. David Roth and Rick Bacher opened the first Cereality in Arizona State University's Student Union, and the pair has plans for more cafés on other campuses and in hospitals, train stations, arenas, airports, and office buildings across the United States. And why not, when more than 95 percent of all Americans like cereal?

Each Cereality café offers more than 30 varieties of brand-name hot and cold cereals as well as made-to-order blends served with regular, flavored, or soy milk for about $2.95 a bowl. And you can top off your selection with one of 25 choices from the toppings bar including cherries, marshmallows, and chocolate chips. If you're one of the few who doesn't like cereal, you can try a yogurt blend smoothie ("Slurreality") or a homemade breakfast bar. Where did Roth and Bacher come up with the idea for a cereal restaurant? They were inspired by the cereal-loving characters on *Seinfeld*, of course.

Cereality customers feel right at home in the café: Employees are clad in pajamas and robes, the décor is right out of mom's kitchen, and the restaurants' TVs air only cartoons—so it always feels like Saturday morning. After they enjoy good fast food, high in fiber and loaded with vitamins and minerals, customers can store the recipe for their custom concoctions in an onsite computer for their next visit or they can purchase select mixes, such as "The Devil Made Me Do It," a blend of Cocoa Puffs, Lucky Charms, and chocolate-milk-flavored crystals, all topped with malt balls. Onsite "cerealogists" offer recommendations to the indecisive.

With 65 percent repeat customers and the financial backing of Quaker, the company expects to be profitable in just a few years. Cereality proves that a new, innovative marketing strategy can be used to sell a product as simple and traditional as cereal.[1] ■

## OBJECTIVES

1. To describe the strategic planning process

2. To explain how organizational resources and opportunities affect the planning process

3. To understand the role of the mission statement in strategic planning

4. To examine corporate, business-unit, and marketing strategies

5. To understand the process of creating the marketing plan

6. To describe the marketing implementation process and the major approaches to marketing implementation

**W**ith competition increasing, Cereality and many other companies are spending more time and resources on strategic planning, that is, on determining how to use their resources and abilities to achieve their objectives and satisfy their customers. Although most of this book deals with specific marketing decisions and strategies, this chapter focuses on "the big picture": all the functional areas and activities—finance, production, human resources, and research and development, as well as marketing—that must be coordinated to reach organizational goals. To effectively implement the marketing concept of satisfying customers and achieving organizational goals, all organizations must engage in strategic planning.

We begin this chapter with an overview of the strategic planning process. Next, we examine how organizational resources and opportunities affect strategic planning and the role played by the organization's mission statement. After discussing the development of both corporate and business-unit strategy, we explore the nature of marketing strategy and the creation of the marketing plan. These elements provide a framework for the development and implementation of marketing strategies, as we will see throughout the remainder of this book.

# Understanding the Strategic Planning Process

**strategic planning** The process of establishing an organizational mission and formulating goals, corporate strategy, marketing objectives, marketing strategy, and a marketing plan

Through the process of **strategic planning**, a firm establishes an organizational mission and formulates goals, corporate strategy, marketing objectives, marketing strategy, and, finally, a marketing plan.[2] A marketing orientation should guide the process of strategic planning to ensure that a concern for customer satisfaction is an integral part of the process. A marketing orientation is also important for the successful implementation of marketing strategies.[3] Figure 2.1 shows the components of strategic planning.

**figure 2.1**

## COMPONENTS OF STRATEGIC PLANNING

**Source:** From *Marketing Strategy,* 2nd Edition by FERRELL. 2002. Reprinted with permission of South-Western, a division of Thomson Learning: **www** .thomsonrights.com. Fax 800-730-2215.

MMMMMMMMMMMMMMMMORE PLEASE.
TEA CAN DO THAT.

New Lipton' Green Iced Tea is something that tastes good and is rich in naturally protective antioxidants. How's that for balance? Learn more at Lipton.com

**The Marketing Concept**
Lipton targets health-concious consumers with its green tea.

The process begins with a detailed analysis of the organization's strengths and weaknesses and with identification of opportunities and threats within the marketing environment. Based on this analysis, the firm can establish or revise its mission and goals, and then develop corporate strategies to achieve those goals. Next, each functional area of the organization (marketing, production, finance, human resources, etc.) establishes its own objectives and develops strategies to achieve them.[4] The objectives and strategies of each functional area must support the organization's overall goals and mission. The strategies of each functional area should also be coordinated with a focus on marketing orientation.

Because our focus is marketing, we are, of course, most interested in the development of marketing objectives and strategies. Marketing objectives should be designed so that their achievement will contribute to the corporate strategy and so they can be accomplished through efficient use of the firm's resources. To achieve its marketing objectives, an organization must develop a **marketing strategy**, which includes identifying and analyzing a target market and developing a marketing mix to meet the needs of individuals in that market. Thus, a marketing strategy includes a plan of action for developing, distributing, promoting, and pricing products that meet the needs of the target market. Marketing strategy is best formulated when it reflects the overall direction of the organization and is coordinated with all the firm's functional areas. When properly implemented and controlled, a marketing strategy will contribute to the achievement not only of marketing objectives but also of the organization's overall goals. Consider that Apple's successful marketing strategy for its iPod line of music players helped revitalize the computer firm's reputation for excellent design, which may transfer to other Apple products. The firm even designed its iMac G5 computer to mimic the look of an iPod with rounded corners and a translucent shell.[5]

The strategic planning process ultimately yields a marketing strategy that is the framework for a **marketing plan**, a written document that specifies the activities to be performed to implement and control the organization's marketing activities. In the remainder of this chapter, we discuss the major components of the strategic

**marketing strategy** A plan of action for identifying and analyzing a target market and developing a marketing mix to meet the needs of that market

**marketing plan** A written document that specifies the activities to be performed to implement and control the organization's marketing activities

planning process: organizational opportunities and resources, organizational mission and goals, corporate and business-unit strategy, marketing strategy, and the role of the marketing plan.

# Assessing Organizational Resources and Opportunities

**core competencies** Things a firm does extremely well, which sometimes give it an advantage over its competition

**market opportunity** A combination of circumstances and timing that permits an organization to take action to reach a particular target market

**strategic windows** Temporary periods of optimal fit between the key requirements of a market and the particular capabilities of a firm competing in that market

The strategic planning process begins with an analysis of the marketing environment. As we will see in Chapter 3, economic, competitive, political, legal and regulatory, sociocultural, and technological forces can threaten an organization and influence its overall goals; they also affect the amount and type of resources the firm can acquire. However, these environmental forces can create favorable opportunities as well—opportunities that can be translated into overall organizational goals and marketing objectives. Organizational culture and information use affect the extent to which managers perceive such opportunities as situations on which they can successfully capitalize.[6]

Any strategic planning effort must assess the organization's available financial and human resources and capabilities, as well as how the level of these factors is likely to change in the future, as additional resources may be needed to achieve the organization's goals and mission.[7] Resources indirectly affect marketing and financial performance by helping to create customer satisfaction and loyalty.[8] Resources can also include goodwill, reputation, and brand names. The reputation and well-known brand names of Rolex watches and IBM computers, for example, are resources that give these firms an advantage over their competitors. Such strengths also include **core competencies**, things a firm does extremely well—sometimes so well that they give the company an advantage over its competition. For example, the Chipotle fast-casual restaurant chain has built an advantage over competitors such as Baja Fresh Mexican Grill and Moe's Southwest Grill through competitive prices and a simple menu of good food prepared in plain view of customers.[9]

Analysis of the marketing environment involves not only an assessment of resources but also identification of opportunities in the marketplace. When the right combination of circumstances and timing permits an organization to take action to reach a particular target market, a **market opportunity** exists. For example, advances in computer technology and the growth of the Internet have enabled real estate firms to provide prospective homebuyers with databases of homes for sale all over the country. At **www.realtor.com**, the website of the National Association of Realtors, buyers have access to a wealth of information about homes for sale, including photos, floor plans, and virtual tours, as well as details about neighborhoods, schools, and shopping. The Internet represents a powerful market opportunity for real estate firms because its visual nature is perfectly suited to the task of shopping for a home. Such opportunities are often called **strategic windows**, temporary periods of optimal fit between the key requirements of a market and the particular capabilities of a firm competing in that market.[10]

When a company matches a core competency to opportunities it has discovered in the marketplace, it is said to have a

**Assessing Organizational Resources and Opportunities**
Although La-Z-Boy's core competency is recliners, it is now expanding to other products.

**Market Opportunity**

Because so many people are pet owners, companies such as VPI Pet Insurance and Gel Pedic have many market opportunities.

**competitive advantage** The result of a company's matching a core competency to opportunities it has discovered in the marketplace

**competitive advantage**. In some cases, a company may possess manufacturing, technical, or marketing skills that it can match to market opportunities to create a competitive advantage. For example, eBay pioneered the online auction and built the premier site where 75 million users around the world buy and sell products. By analyzing its customer base, eBay found an opportunity to improve growth by targeting the nearly 23 million small businesses in the United States, many of which already use the auction site to buy and sell construction, restaurant, and other business equipment. To appeal to this important market, eBay sought ways to improve customers' online shopping experience.[11]

## marketing ENTREPRENEURS

**Ryan Garman**

THE BUSINESS: AllDorm.com

FOUNDED: 2000

SUCCESS: $25 million in sales

Two years after an arduous half-day journey in a U-Haul van from his Las Vegas home to his dorm room at Santa Clara University in California, Ryan Garman had an epiphany. Instead of hauling all of the things he needed for his dorm room with him, it would have been nice to have them delivered before he even arrived. So in 2000, Garman and a couple of dorm buddies founded AllDorm.com, an e-commerce site that caters to college students across the nation by allowing them to make online purchases of items such as beanbag chairs, microwaves, mini-fridges, and bed sheets, which are then delivered to their dorms before they arrive on campus. By eliminating inventory, having minimal office space, and using few employees, AllDorm maintains its edge. Today, AllDorm is partnered with more than 250 universities and offers more than 6,000 items to choose from on its website.

It's difficult to do a
side-by-side comparison when
your binoculars stand alone.

**Competitive Advantage**
Leupold has produced binoculars for nearly a century.

## SWOT Analysis

**SWOT analysis** Assessment of an organization's strengths, weaknesses, opportunities, and threats

One tool marketers use to assess an organization's strengths, weaknesses, opportunities, and threats is the **SWOT analysis**. Strengths and weaknesses are internal factors that can influence an organization's ability to satisfy its target markets. Strengths refer to competitive advantages or core competencies that give the firm an advantage in meeting the needs of its target markets. John Deere, for example, promotes its service, experience, and reputation in the farm equipment business to emphasize the craftsmanship used in its lawn tractors and mowers for city dwellers. Weaknesses refer to any limitations a company faces in developing or implementing a marketing strategy. Consider that America Online, the leading Internet service provider, brings in half the online advertising revenue of other online services such as Google, MSN, and Yahoo! at a time when online advertising has accelerated dramatically.[12] Both strengths and weaknesses should be examined from a customer perspective because they are meaningful only when they help or hinder the firm in meeting customer needs. Only those strengths that relate to satisfying customers should be considered true competitive advantages. Likewise, weaknesses that directly affect customer satisfaction should be considered competitive disadvantages. To boost online ad revenue, AOL has redesigned its website and added more content, such as a news ticker and more sports and music, to boost usage by members and thereby make it more attractive to online advertisers.[13]

Opportunities and threats exist independently of the firm and therefore represent issues to be considered by all organizations, even those that do not compete

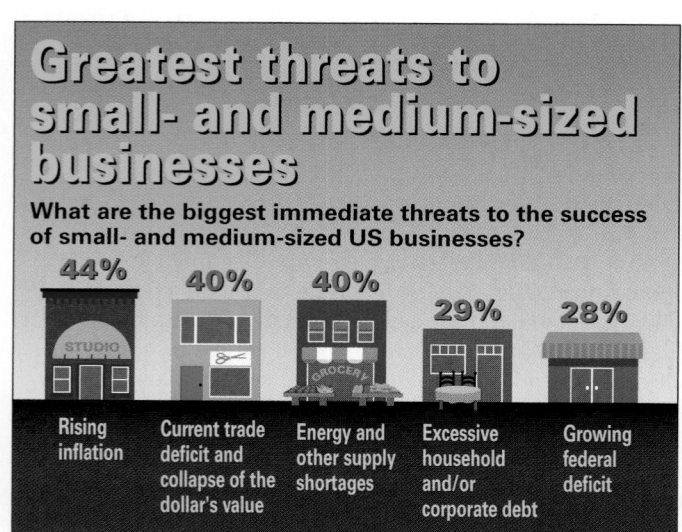

**Greatest threats to small- and medium-sized businesses**

**What are the biggest immediate threats to the success of small- and medium-sized US businesses?**

44% Rising inflation
40% Current trade deficit and collapse of the dollar's value
40% Energy and other supply shortages
29% Excessive household and/or corporate debt
28% Growing federal deficit

*Source:* Data from Interland Business Barometer (www.interland.com). Margin of error: ±3 percentage points.

## figure 2.2

### THE FOUR-CELL SWOT MATRIX

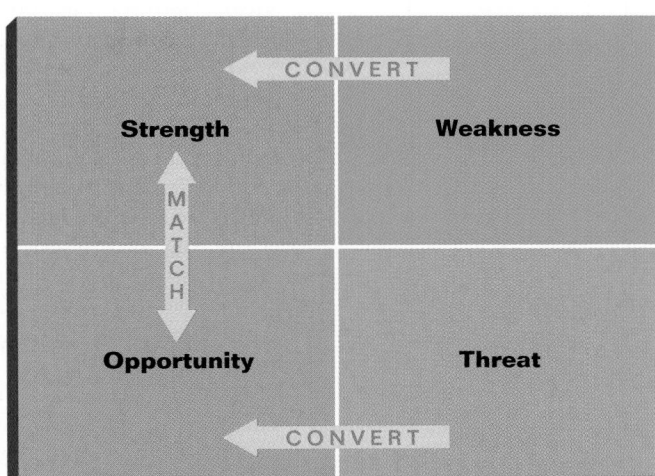

**Source:** Adapted from Nigel F. Piercy, *Market-Led Strategic Change.* Copyright © 1992 Butterworth-Heinemann Ltd., p. 371. Reprinted with permission.

with the firm. *Opportunities* refer to favorable conditions in the environment that could produce rewards for the organization if acted on properly. That is, opportunities are situations that exist but must be exploited for the firm to benefit from them. *Threats*, on the other hand, refer to conditions or barriers that may prevent the firm from reaching its objectives. For example, consumers today are buying fewer music CDs, in part because many believe CD prices are too high. CD sales declined by 31 percent over a three-year period as consumers downloaded more music from online sharing networks such as Kazaa or shifted their entertainment dollars to video games and DVDs.[14] An organization must act on threats to prevent them from limiting its capabilities. For example, to counter the threat of declining music sales, Universal Music Group slashed the wholesale price of CDs by artists such as Jay-Z and Shania Twain by as much as 31 percent.[15] Opportunities and threats can stem from many sources within the environment. When a competitor's introduction of a new product threatens a firm, a defensive strategy may be required. If the firm can develop and launch a new product that meets or exceeds the competition's offering, it can transform the threat into an opportunity.[16]

Figure 2.2 depicts a four-cell SWOT matrix that can help managers in the planning process. When an organization matches internal strengths to external opportunities, it creates competitive advantages in meeting the needs of its customers. In addition, an organization should act to convert internal weaknesses into strengths and external threats into opportunities. Ford Motor Company, for instance, converted the threats posed by rising gasoline prices and the growing acceptance of hybrid gas-electric cars from Japanese automakers into opportunities when it introduced a hybrid version of its Escape sport-utility vehicle, making the 36-mile-per-gallon Escape the first hybrid SUV available.[17] A firm that lacks adequate marketing skills can hire outside consultants to help convert a weakness into a strength.

# Establishing an Organizational Mission and Goals

**mission statement** A long-term view, or vision, of what the organization wants to become

Once an organization has assessed its resources and opportunities, it can begin to establish goals and strategies to take advantage of those opportunities. The goals of any organization should derive from its **mission statement**, a long-term view, or vision, of what the organization wants to become. Herbal tea marketer Celestial Seasonings, for example, says that its mission is "To create and sell healthful, naturally oriented products that nurture people's bodies and uplift their souls."[18]

When an organization decides on its mission, it really answers two questions: Who are our customers? What is our core competency? Although these questions appear very simple, they are two of the most important questions any firm must answer. Defining customers' needs and wants gives direction to what the company must do to satisfy them.

Companies try to develop and manage their *corporate identity*—their unique symbols, personalities, and philosophies—to support all corporate activities including marketing. Managing identity requires broadcasting mission goals and values, sending a consistent image, and implementing visual identity with stakeholders. Mission statements, goals, and objectives must be properly implemented to achieve the desired corporate identity.[19] New Leaf Paper Company, for example, has developed a mission and identity based on principles of sustainability and ecology that are unique in the paper industry. Half the fiber New Leaf uses in its paper comes from postconsumer waste instead of virgin tree pulp. The small firm's sales have increased more than four times in the last six years, spurring larger paper companies to introduce their own "green" paper products.[20]

An organization's goals and objectives, derived from its mission statement, guide the remainder of its planning efforts. Goals focus on the end results the organization seeks. Starbucks' mission statement, for example, incorporates the company's goals of striving for a high-quality product, a sound financial position, and community responsibility.

**marketing objective** A statement of what is to be accomplished through marketing activities

A **marketing objective** states what is to be accomplished through marketing activities. A marketing objective of Ritz-Carlton hotels, for example, is to have more than 90 percent of its customers indicate they had a memorable experience at the hotel. Marketing objectives should be based on a careful study of the SWOT analysis and should relate to matching strengths to opportunities and/or converting weaknesses or threats. These objectives can be stated in terms of product introduction, product improvement or innovation, sales volume, profitability, market share, pricing, distribution, advertising, or employee training activities.

Marketing objectives should possess certain characteristics. First, a marketing objective should be expressed in clear, simple terms so that all marketing personnel understand exactly what they are trying to achieve. Second, an objective should be written so that it can be measured accurately. This allows the organization to determine if and when the objective has been achieved. If an objective is to increase market share by 10 percent, the firm should be able to measure market share changes accurately. Third, a marketing objective should specify a time frame for its accomplishment. A firm that sets an objective of introducing a new product should state the time period in which to do this. Finally, a marketing objective should be consistent with both business-unit and corporate strategy. This ensures that the firm's mission is carried out at all levels of the organization.

# Developing Corporate, Business-Unit, and Marketing Strategies

In any organization, strategic planning begins at the corporate level and proceeds downward to the business-unit and marketing levels. Corporate strategy is the broadest of these three levels and should be developed with the organization's overall mission in mind. Business-unit strategy should be consistent with the corporate strategy, and marketing strategy should be consistent with both the business-unit and corporate strategies. Figure 2.3 shows the relationships among these planning levels.

## Corporate Strategy

**corporate strategy** A strategy that determines the means for utilizing resources in the various functional areas to reach the organization's goals

**Corporate strategy** determines the means for utilizing resources in the functional areas of marketing, production, finance, research and development, and human resources to reach the organization's goals. A corporate strategy determines not only the scope of the business but also its resource deployment, competitive advantages,

**figure 2.3**

**LEVELS OF STRATEGIC PLANNING**

Mission statement

Corporate strategy

Business-unit strategy

Marketing strategy

Marketing mix elements
▶ Product
▶ Distribution
▶ Promotion
▶ Pricing

**Corporate Strategy**

Citibank ties its Advantage card to travel and adventure.

and overall coordination of functional areas. In particular, top management's marketing expertise and deployment of resources for addressing markets contribute to sales growth and profitability.[21] Corporate strategy addresses the two questions posed in the organization's mission statement: Who are our customers? What is our core competency? The term *corporate* in this context does not apply solely to corporations; corporate strategy is used by all organizations, from the smallest sole proprietorship to the largest multinational corporation.

Corporate strategy planners are concerned with broad issues such as corporate culture, competition, differentiation, diversification, interrelationships among business units, and environmental and social issues. They attempt to match the resources of the organization with the opportunities and threats in the environment. Sara Lee, for example, sold its retail coffee unit including its well-known brand Chock full o'Nuts for $82.5 million in order to make greater investments in its core businesses of food, beverages, and household and body care, as well as to increase its shareholder value through dividends.[22] Corporate strategy planners are also concerned with defining the scope and role of the firm's business units so that the units are coordinated to reach the ends desired. A firm's corporate strategy may affect its technological competence and ability to innovate.[23]

## Business-Unit Strategy

After analyzing corporate operations and performance, the next step in strategic planning is to determine future business directions and develop strategies for individual business units. A **strategic business unit (SBU)** is a division, product line, or other profit center within the parent company. Borden's strategic business units, for example, consist of dairy products, snacks, pasta, niche grocery products like RealLemon juice and Cremora coffee creamer, and other units such as glue and paints. Each of these units sells a distinct set of products to an identifiable group of customers, and each competes with a well-defined set of competitors. The revenues, costs, investments, and strategic plans of each SBU can be separated from those of the parent company and evaluated. SBUs operate in a variety of markets, all with differing growth rates, opportunities, degrees of competition, and profit-making potential.

Strategic planners should recognize the strategic performance capabilities of each SBU and carefully allocate scarce resources among those divisions. This requires market-focused flexibility in considering changes in the environment.[24] Several tools allow a firm's portfolio of strategic business units, or even individual products, to be classified and visually displayed according to the attractiveness of various markets and the business's relative market share within those markets. A **market** is a group of individuals and/or organizations that have needs for products in a product class and have the ability, willingness, and authority to purchase those products. The percentage of a market that actually buys a specific product from a particular company is referred to as that product's (or business unit's) **market share**. Hershey Foods, for example, controls 43 percent of the market for chocolate candy in the United States, while its rivals Masterfoods and Nestlé command 23 percent and 8 percent, respec-

**strategic business unit (SBU)** A division, product line, or other profit center within the parent company

**market** A group of individuals and/or organizations that have needs for products in a product class and have the ability, willingness, and authority to purchase those products

**market share** The percentage of a market that actually buys a specific product from a particular company

# Sears Holdings: Merging to Success

Just 18 months after emerging from bankruptcy, Kmart announced that it would pay $11 billion to purchase Sears & Roebuck. The merged firm, Sears Holdings, has 3,500 stores, making it the number 3 retailer after Wal-Mart and Home Depot. Many believe that the new company will be able to achieve tremendous cost savings that will result in lower prices for consumers—and give retail giant Wal-Mart more competition.

Although most individual Sears and Kmart stores retained their current names, some Kmart stores turned into Sears stores, and both stores began to promote each other's brands. The challenge will be to blend the two organizations into one customer-focused culture. One way to accomplish this is through the leveraging of current brands and reputations. Sears is well known for its Kenmore appliances, Craftsman tools, Diehard batteries, and Lands' End apparel, while Kmart is known for Martha Stewart Everyday, Sesame Street, and Thalia Sodi.

Allowing Sears and Kmart to sell each other's exclusive products is only one part of the strategy. Sears' long-time business model had relied on mall locations, but in recent years the retailing landscape has shifted to stand-alone "big box" retail stores. Many Kmart stores are located in prime locations outside malls and can now be converted to Sears stores.

For Sears Holdings to be successful, it will need to engage in the strategic planning process, establishing an organizational mission, goals, corporate strategy, marketing objectives, and a marketing strategy. Only by successfully assessing opportunities and appropriately implementing strategies can the new company be successful.

**figure 2.4**   GROWTH SHARE MATRIX DEVELOPED BY THE BOSTON CONSULTING GROUP

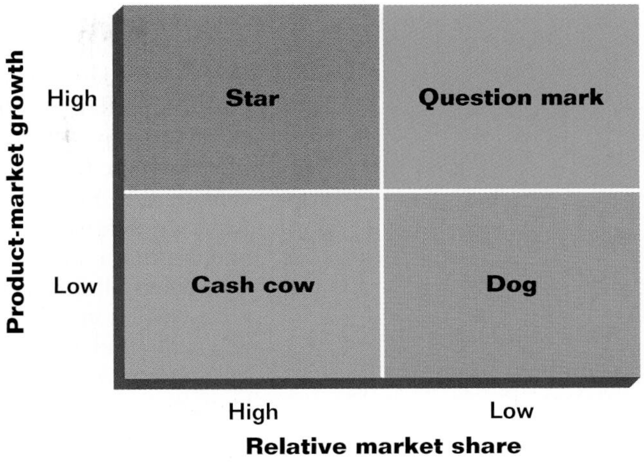

**Source:** *Perspectives,* No. 66, "The Product Portfolio." Reprinted by permission from The Boston Consulting Group, Inc., Boston, MA. Copyright © 1970.

**market growth/market share matrix** A strategic planning tool based on the philosophy that a product's market growth rate and market share are important considerations in its determining marketing strategy

tively.[25] Product quality, order of entry into the market, and market share have been associated with SBU success.[26]

One of the most helpful tools is the **market growth/market share matrix**, the Boston Consulting Group (BCG) approach, which is based on the philosophy that a product's market growth rate and its market share are important considerations in determining its marketing strategy. All the firm's SBUs and products should be integrated into a single, overall matrix and evaluated to determine appropriate strategies for individual products and overall portfolio strategies. Managers can use this model to determine and classify each product's expected future cash contributions and future cash requirements. The BCG analytical approach is more of a diagnostic tool than a guide for making strategy prescriptions.

Figure 2.4, which is based on work by the BCG, enables the strategic planner to classify a firm's products into four basic types: stars, cash cows, dogs, and question marks.[27] *Stars* are products with a dominant share of the market and good prospects for growth. However, they use more cash than they generate to finance growth, add capacity, and increase market share. An example of a star might be Apple's iPod MP3 player. *Cash cows* have a dominant share of the market but low prospects for growth; typically they generate more cash than is required to maintain market share. Bounty, the best-selling paper towels in the United States, represents a cash cow for Procter & Gamble. *Dogs* have a subordinate share of the market and low prospects for growth; these products are often found in established markets. The Oldsmobile brand may have been considered a dog at General Motors; its declining profits and market share contributed to GM's decision to eliminate the brand. *Question marks,* sometimes called "problem children," have a small share of a growing market and generally require a large amount of cash to build market share. Mercedes mountain bikes, for example, are a question mark relative to Mercedes's automobile products.

The long-term health of an organization depends on having some products that generate cash (and provide acceptable profits) and others that use cash to support growth. Among the indicators of overall health are the size and vulnerability of the cash cows; the prospects for the stars, if any; and the number of question marks and dogs. Particular attention should be paid to those products with large cash appetites. Unless the company has an abundant cash flow, it cannot afford to sponsor many such products at one time. If resources, including debt capacity, are spread too thin, the company will end up with too many marginal products and will be unable to finance promising new-product entries or acquisitions in the future.

## Marketing Strategy

The next phase in strategic planning is the development of sound strategies for each functional area of the organization, including marketing. Corporate strategy and marketing strategy must balance and synchronize the organization's mission and goals with stakeholder relationships. This means that marketing must deliver value and be responsible in facilitating effective relationships with all relevant stakeholders.[28] Consider that customers depend on the Coca-Cola Company to provide a standardized, reliable, satisfying soft drink or beverage anyplace in the world. Due to its efforts to expand distribution to every possible location, Coca-Cola sells 33 percent of its volume in Europe and the Middle East, 31 percent in North America, 22 percent in the Asian/Pacific region, 10 percent in Latin America, and 5 percent in Africa.[29] The company continues to introduce new products, expand distribution, and maintain a high-quality product. Coca-Cola is also a good "corporate citizen," donating millions of dollars to education, health and human services, and disaster-plagued regions each year. An effective marketing strategy must gain the support of key stakeholders including employees, investors, and communities, as well as channel members such as franchisees. Consider what happened when Burger King launched a $340 million advertising campaign featuring a heavy metal band named Coq Roq. Franchisees, vital to the distribution of Burger King products, felt the marketing strategy targeted too narrow of a market—teenage males—and worried that

# Procter & Gamble Cleans Up Around the World

Consumers around the world trust Procter & Gamble (P&G). They count on Crest, Charmin, and Gillette, among many other brand names and hundreds of other products, to improve the quality of their lives. P&G markets nearly 300 brands in 140 countries, and employs nearly 98,000 people in nearly 80 countries. P&G's core product categories—baby care, fabric care, feminine care, and hair care—are number 1 in terms of both global sales and global market share and generate more than half of the company's total profits. One percentage point increase in market share across these four core businesses is worth about $1 billion in annual sales and more then $150 million in annual earnings.

P&G's foundation is household products, but it is moving toward balancing this group of products with those geared toward health and beauty, since health-care and baby-care business now represent nearly half of the company's sales and profits. Personal health-care sales have more than doubled in the past three years, significantly outpacing market growth. In China, P&G's laundry and oral-care mar-

ket shares have more than doubled in the past three years. And in Russia, laundry, hair care, and oral care are all category leaders that have grown rapidly over the last three years.

P&G's ability to market superior products that improve the lives of its worldwide customers ensures that the company's future is indeed bright.

it might alienate other desirable markets. Their dissatisfaction with the campaign and overall marketing strategy resulted in a complete communication breakdown in the Burger King national franchise organization.[30] The complexity of marketing strategy decisions requires the identification of key stakeholders and their support or reaction to marketing activities.[31] There is a need in marketing to develop more of a stakeholder orientation to go beyond markets, competitors, and channel members to understand and address all stakeholder concerns.[32]

Within the marketing area, a strategy is typically designed around two components: (1) the selection of a target market and (2) the creation of a marketing mix that will satisfy the needs of the chosen target market. A marketing strategy articulates the best use of the firm's resources and tactics to achieve its marketing objectives. It should also match customers' desire for value with the organization's distinctive capabilities. Internal capabilities should be used to maximize external opportunities. The planning process should be guided by a marketing-oriented organizational culture and processes.[33] A comprehensive strategy involves a thorough search for information, the analysis of many potential courses of action, and the use of specific criteria for making decisions regarding strategy development and implementation.[34] When properly implemented, a sound marketing strategy enables a company to achieve its business-unit and corporate objectives. Although corporate, business-unit, and marketing strategies all overlap to some extent, the marketing strategy is the most detailed and specific of the three.

**Target Market Selection.**  Selecting an appropriate target market may be the most important decision a company has to make in the planning process because the target market must be chosen before the organization can adapt its marketing mix to meet this market's needs and preferences. Defining the target market and developing an appropriate marketing mix are the keys to strategic success. Consider that there are 80 million consumers in "Generation Y"—those born between 1977 and 1994—in the United States, and they command about $170 billion a year in spending power. These "Ys" are skeptical and resourceful, and more comfortable with cellphones, instant messaging, and Internet shopping than any other market. This represents a significant opportunity for marketers willing to adapt their marketing mixes to satisfy the needs of this important target market.[35] If a company selects the wrong target market, all other marketing decisions will be made in vain. Ford Motor, for example, experienced poor sales of its reintroduced Thunderbird, in part because its $35,000 to $40,000 price tag was too steep for the retro-styled convertible's target market of younger baby boomers and older Generation Xers. However, the Thunderbird could not compete with similarly priced luxury, high-performance vehicles like the BMW Z4 and the Audi TT, which offer greater horsepower and more features.[36]

Accurate target market selection is crucial to productive marketing efforts. Products and even companies sometimes fail because marketers do not identify appropriate customer groups at whom to aim their efforts. Organizations that try to be all things to all people rarely satisfy the needs of any customer group very well. An organization's management therefore should designate which customer groups the firm is trying to serve and gather adequate information about those customers. Identification and analysis of a target market provide a foundation on which the firm can develop a marketing mix.

Engineered to easily navigate
the most complex obstacle course ever created.

Your living room.

the ball dyson

The new Dyson Ball turns and maneuvers unlike any other vacuum. And, of course, it doesn't lose suction.
Test-drive one today. 1-866-693-9766 or dyson.com

**Target Market Selection**

Dyson targets homeowners with its high-tech vacuum cleaners.

When exploring possible target markets, marketing managers try to evaluate how entering them would affect the company's sales, costs, and profits. Marketing information should be organized to facilitate a focus on the chosen target customers. Accounting and information systems, for example, can be used to track revenues and costs by customer (or group of customers). In addition, managers and employees need to be rewarded for focusing on profitable customers. Teamwork skills can be developed with organizational structures that promote a customer orientation that allows quick responses to changes in the marketing environment.[37]

Marketers should also assess whether the company has the resources to develop the right mix of product, price, promotion, and distribution to meet the needs of a particular target market. In addition, they should determine if satisfying those needs is consistent with the firm's overall objectives and mission. When Amazon.com, the number 1 Internet bookseller, began selling electronics on its website, it made the decision with the belief that efforts to target this market would increase profits and be consistent with its objective to be the largest online retailer. The size and number of competitors already marketing products in potential target markets are concerns as well.

**Creating the Marketing Mix.** The selection of a target market serves as the basis for creating a marketing mix to satisfy the needs of that market. The decisions made in creating a marketing mix are only as good as the organization's understanding of its target market. This understanding typically comes from careful, in-depth research into the characteristics of the target market. Thus, while demographic information is important, the organization should also analyze customer needs, preferences, and behavior with respect to product design, pricing, distribution, and promotion. For example, Toyota's marketing research about Generation Y drivers found that they practically live in their cars, and many even keep a change of clothes handy in their vehicles. As a result of this research, Toyota designed its Scion as a "home on wheels," with a 15-volt outlet for plugging in a computer, reclining front seats for napping, and a powerful audio system for listening to MP3 music files, all for a $12,500 price tag.[38]

Marketing mix decisions should have two additional characteristics: consistency and flexibility. All marketing mix decisions should be consistent with the business-unit and corporate strategies. Such consistency allows the organization to achieve its objectives on all three levels of planning. Flexibility, on the other hand, permits the organization to alter the marketing mix in response to changes in market conditions, competition, and customer needs. Marketing strategy flexibility has a positive influence on organizational performance. Marketing orientation and strategic flexibility complement each other to help the organization manage varying environmental conditions.[39]

The concept of the four marketing mix variables has stood the test of time, providing marketers with a rich set of questions for the four most important decisions in strategic marketing. Consider the efforts of Harley-Davidson to improve its competitive position. The company worked to improve its product by eliminating oil leaks and other problems, and set prices that customers consider fair. The firm used promotional tools to build a community of Harley riders renowned for their camaraderie. Harley-Davidson also fostered strong relationships with the dealers that distribute the company's motorcycles and related products and that reinforce the firm's promotional messages. Even the Internet has not diminished the importance of finding the right marketing mix, although it has affected specific marketing mix elements. Amazon.com, for example, has exploited information technology to facilitate sales promotion by offering product feedback from other customers to help shoppers make purchase decisions.[40]

At the marketing mix level, a firm can detail how it will achieve a competitive advantage. To gain an advantage, the firm must do something better than its competition. In other words, its products must be of higher quality, its prices must be consistent with the level of quality (value), its distribution methods must be efficient and cost as little as possible, and its promotion must be more effective than the competition's. It is also important that the firm attempt to make these advantages sustainable. A **sustainable competitive advantage** is one that the competition cannot copy. Wal-Mart, for example, maintains a sustainable competitive advantage over Kmart because of its highly efficient and low-cost distribution system. This advantage allows Wal-Mart to offer lower prices. Maintaining a sustainable competitive advantage requires flexibility in the marketing mix when facing uncertain competitive environments.[41]

**sustainable competitive advantage**  An advantage that the competition cannot copy

# Creating the Marketing Plan

**marketing planning**  The process of assessing marketing opportunities and resources, determining marketing objectives, defining marketing strategies, and establishing guidelines for implementation and control of the marketing program

A major concern in the strategic planning process is **marketing planning**, the systematic process of assessing marketing opportunities and resources, determining marketing objectives, defining marketing strategies, and establishing guidelines for implementation and control of the marketing program. The outcome of marketing planning is the development of a marketing plan. As noted earlier, a marketing plan is a written document that outlines and explains all the activities necessary to implement marketing strategies. It describes the firm's current position or situation, establishes marketing objectives for the product or product group, and specifies how the organization will attempt to achieve those objectives.

Developing a clear, well-written marketing plan, though time consuming, is important. The plan is the basis for internal communication among employees. It covers the assignment of responsibilities and tasks, as well as schedules for implementation. It presents objectives and specifies how resources are to be allocated to achieve those objectives. Finally, it helps marketing managers monitor and evaluate the performance of a marketing strategy.

Marketing planning and implementation are inextricably linked in successful companies. The marketing plan provides a framework to stimulate thinking and provide strategic direction, while implementation occurs as an adaptive response to day-to-day issues, opportunities, and unanticipated situations—for example, increasing interest rates or an economic slowdown—that cannot be incorporated into marketing plans. Implementation-related adaptations directly affect an organization's marketing orientation, rate of growth, and strategic effectiveness.[42]

Organizations use many different formats when devising marketing plans. Plans may be written for strategic business units, product lines, individual products or brands, or specific markets. Most plans share some common ground, however, by including many of the same components. Table 2.1 (on p. 42) describes the major parts of a typical marketing plan.

# Implementing Marketing Strategies

**marketing implementation**  The process of putting marketing strategies into action

**intended strategy**  The strategy the company decided on during the planning phase and wants to use

**realized strategy**  The strategy that actually takes place

**Marketing implementation** is the process of putting marketing strategies into action. Although implementation is often neglected in favor of strategic planning, the implementation process itself can determine whether a marketing strategy succeeds. It is also important to recognize that marketing strategies almost always turn out differently than expected. In essence, all organizations have two types of strategy: intended strategy and realized strategy.[43] The **intended strategy** is the strategy the organization decided on during the planning phase and wants to use, whereas the **realized strategy** is the strategy that actually takes place. The difference between the two is often the result of how the intended strategy is implemented. For example, Chrysler's PT Cruiser was originally marketed to young drivers, but the retro-styled vehicle ultimately proved more popular with their nostalgic baby boomer parents. Just 4 percent of the PT Cruiser's buyers were from the car's intended target market of drivers under 25.[44] The realized strategy, though not necessarily any better or worse than the intended strategy, often does not live up to planners' expectations.

| table 2.1 | COMPONENTS OF THE MARKETING PLAN | |
|---|---|---|
| **Plan Component** | **Component Summary** | **Highlights** |
| Executive Summary | One- to two-page synopsis of the entire marketing plan | |
| Environmental Analysis | Information about the company's current situation with respect to the marketing environment | 1. Assessment of marketing environment factors<br>2. Assessment of target market(s)<br>3. Assessment of current marketing objectives and performance |
| SWOT Analysis | Assessment of the organization's strengths, weaknesses, opportunities, and threats | 1. Strengths<br>2. Weaknesses<br>3. Opportunities<br>4. Threats |
| Marketing Objectives | Specification of the firm's marketing objectives | Qualitative measures of what is to be accomplished |
| Marketing Strategies | Outline of how the firm will achieve its objectives | 1. Target market(s)<br>2. Marketing mix |
| Marketing Implementation | Outline of how the firm will implement its marketing strategies | 1. Marketing organization<br>2. Activities and responsibilities<br>3. Implementation timetable |
| Evaluation and Control | Explanation of how the firm will measure and evaluate the results of the implemented plan | 1. Performance standards<br>2. Financial controls<br>3. Monitoring procedures (audits) |

## Approaches to Marketing Implementation

Just as organizations can achieve their goals by using different marketing strategies, they can implement their marketing strategies by using different approaches. In this section, we discuss two general approaches to marketing implementation: internal marketing and total quality management. Both approaches represent mindsets that marketing managers may adopt when organizing and planning marketing activities. These approaches are not mutually exclusive; indeed, many companies adopt both when designing marketing activities.

**Internal Marketing.** **External customers** are the individuals who patronize a business—the familiar definition of customers—whereas **internal customers** are the company's employees. For implementation to succeed, the needs of both groups of customers must be met. If internal customers are not satisfied, it is likely external customers will not be satisfied either. Thus, in addition to targeting marketing activities at external customers, a firm uses internal marketing to attract, motivate, and retain qualified internal customers by designing internal products (jobs) that satisfy their wants and needs. **Internal marketing** is a management philosophy that coordinates internal exchanges between the organization and its employees to achieve successful external exchanges between the organization and its customers.[45]

Generally speaking, internal marketing refers to the managerial actions necessary to make all members of the marketing organization understand and accept their respective roles in implementing the marketing strategy. Thus, marketing managers need to focus internally on employees as well as externally on customers.[46] This means that all internal customers, from the president of the company down to the hourly workers on the shop floor, must understand the roles they play in carrying out their jobs and implementing the marketing strategy. In short, anyone invested in

**external customers** Individuals who patronize a business

**internal customers** A company's employees

**internal marketing** A management philosophy that coordinates internal exchanges between the organization and its employees to achieve successful external exchanges between the organization and its customers

the firm, both marketers and those who perform other functions, must recognize the tenet of customer orientation and service that underlies the marketing concept.

Like external marketing activities, internal marketing may involve market segmentation, product development, research, distribution, and even public relations and sales promotion.[47] For example, an organization may sponsor sales contests to inspire sales personnel to boost their selling efforts. This helps employees (and ultimately the company) to understand customers' needs and problems, teaches them valuable new skills, and heightens their enthusiasm for their regular jobs. In addition, many companies use planning sessions, websites, workshops, letters, formal reports, and personal conversations to ensure that employees comprehend the corporate mission, the organization's goals, and the marketing strategy. The ultimate results are more satisfied employees and improved customer relations.

**Total Quality Management.** Quality has become a major concern in many organizations, particularly in light of intense foreign competition, more demanding customers, and poorer profit performance owing to reduced market share and higher costs. To regain a competitive edge, a number of firms have adopted a total quality management approach. **Total quality management (TQM)** is a philosophy that uniform commitment to quality in all areas of the organization will promote a culture that meets customers' perceptions of quality. Indeed, research has shown that quality orientation and marketing orientation are complementary and together are sources of superior performance.[48] TQM involves coordinating efforts to improve customer satisfaction, increasing employee participation and empowerment, forming and strengthening supplier partnerships, and facilitating an organizational culture of continuous quality improvement. It requires continuous quality improvement and employee empowerment.

Continuous improvement of an organization's goods and services is built around the notion that quality is free; in contrast, *not* having high-quality goods and services can be very expensive, especially in terms of dissatisfied customers.[49] A primary tool of the continuous improvement process is **benchmarking**, comparing the quality of the organization's goods, services, or processes with that of the best-performing companies in the industry.[50] Benchmarking fosters organizational "learning" by helping firms identify and enhance valuable marketing capabilities.[51] Benchmarking lets the organization assess where it stands competitively in its industry, thus giving it a goal to aim for over time.

Ultimately TQM succeeds or fails because of the efforts of the organization's employees. Thus, employee recruitment, selection, and training are critical to the success of marketing implementation. **Empowerment** gives customer-contact employees the authority and responsibility to make marketing decisions without seeking the approval of their supervisors.[52] Although employees at any level in an organization can be empowered to make decisions, empowerment is used most often at the frontline, where employees interact daily with customers.

One characteristic of empowerment is that employees can perform their jobs the way they see fit, as long as their methods and outcomes are consistent with the organization's mission. However, empowering employees is successful only if the organization is guided by an overall corporate vision, shared goals, and a culture that supports the TQM effort.[53] For example, Ritz-Carlton hotels give each customer-contact employee permission to take care of customer needs as he or she observes issues. A great deal of time, effort, and patience is needed to develop and sustain a quality-oriented culture in an organization.

## Organizing Marketing Activities

The structure and relationships of a marketing unit, including lines of authority and responsibility that connect and coordinate individuals, strongly affect marketing activities. Firms that truly adopt the marketing concept develop a distinct organizational culture: a culture based on a shared set of beliefs that makes the customer's needs the pivotal point of the firm's decisions about strategy and operations.[54] Instead of developing products in a vacuum and then trying to persuade customers to purchase

**total quality management (TQM)** A philosophy that uniform commitment to quality in all areas of the organization will promote a culture that meets customers' perceptions of quality

**benchmarking** Comparing the quality of the firm's goods, services, or processes with that of its best-performing competitors

**empowerment** Giving customer-contact employees authority and responsibility to make marketing decisions without seeking approval of their supervisors

them, companies using the marketing concept begin with an orientation toward their customers' needs and desires. Recreational Equipment, Inc. (REI), for example, gives customers a chance to try out sporting goods in conditions that approximate how the products will actually be used. Customers can try out hiking boots on a simulated hiking path with a variety of trail surfaces and inclines or test climbing gear on an indoor climbing wall. In addition, REI offers clinics to customers, such as "Rock Climbing Basics," "Basic Backpacking," and "REI's Outdoor School."

If the marketing concept serves as a guiding philosophy, the marketing unit will be closely coordinated with other functional areas such as production, finance, and human resources. Marketing must interact with other departments in a number of key areas. It needs to work with manufacturing in determining the volume and variety of the company's products. Those in charge of production rely on marketers for accurate sales forecasts. Research and development departments depend heavily on information gathered by marketers about product features and benefits consumers desire. Decisions made by the physical distribution department hinge on information about the urgency of delivery schedules and cost/service tradeoffs. Information technology is often a crucial ingredient in effectively managing customer relationships, but successful customer relationship management programs must include every department involved in customer relations.[55]

How effectively a firm's marketing management can plan and implement marketing strategies also depends on how the marketing unit is organized. Organizing marketing activities in ways that mesh with a firm's strategic marketing approach enhances performance.[56] Effective organizational planning can give the firm a competitive advantage. The organizational structure of a marketing department establishes the authority relationships among marketing personnel and specifies who is responsible for making certain decisions and performing particular activities. This internal structure helps direct marketing activities.

**centralized organization** A structure in which top-level managers delegate little authority to lower levels

**decentralized organization** A structure in which decisionmaking authority is delegated as far down the chain of command as possible

One crucial decision regarding structural authority is centralization versus decentralization. In a **centralized organization**, top-level managers delegate little authority to lower levels. In a **decentralized organization**, decisionmaking authority is delegated as far down the chain of command as possible. The decision to centralize or decentralize the organization directly affects marketing. Most traditional organizations are highly centralized. In these organizations, most, if not all, marketing decisions are made at the top levels. However, as organizations become more marketing oriented, centralized decisionmaking proves somewhat ineffective. In these organizations, decentralized authority allows the company to respond to customer needs more quickly.

No single approach to organizing a marketing unit works equally well in all businesses. The best approach or approaches depend on the number and diversity of the firm's products, the characteristics and needs of the people in the target market, and many other factors. A marketing unit can be organized according to (1) functions, (2) products, (3) regions, or (4) types of customers. Firms often use some combination of these organizational approaches. Product features may dictate that the marketing unit be structured by products, whereas customer characteristics may require that it be organized by geographic region or by types of customers. By using more than one type of structure, a flexible marketing unit can develop and implement marketing plans to match customers' needs precisely.

**Organizing by Functions.** Some marketing departments are organized by general marketing functions, such as marketing research, product development, distribution, sales, advertising, and customer relations. The personnel who direct these functions report directly to the top-level marketing executive. This structure is fairly common because it works well for some businesses with centralized marketing operations, such as Ford and General Motors. In more decentralized firms, such as grocery store chains, functional organization can cause serious coordination problems. However, the functional approach may suit a large, centralized company whose products and customers are neither numerous nor diverse.

**Organizing by Products.** An organization that produces and markets diverse products may find the functional approach inadequate. The decisions and problems related to a single marketing function for one product may be quite different from those related to the same marketing function for another product. As a result, businesses that produce diverse products sometimes organize their marketing units according to product groups. Organizing by product groups gives a firm the flexibility to develop special marketing mixes for different products. Procter & Gamble, like many firms in the consumer packaged goods industry, is organized by product group. Although organizing by products allows a company to remain flexible, this approach can be rather expensive unless efficient categories of products are grouped together to reduce duplication and improve coordination of product management.

**Organizing by Regions.** A large company that markets products nationally (or internationally) may organize its marketing activities by geographic regions. Managers of marketing functions for each region report to their regional marketing manager; all the regional marketing managers report directly to the executive marketing manager. Frito-Lay, for example, is organized into four regional divisions, allowing the company to get closer to its customers and respond more quickly and efficiently to regional competitors. This form of organization is especially effective for a firm whose customers' characteristics and needs vary greatly from one region to another. Firms that try to penetrate the national market intensively may divide regions into subregions.

**Organizing by Types of Customers.** Sometimes a company's marketing unit is organized according to types of customers. This form of internal organization works well for a firm that has several groups of customers whose needs and problems differ significantly. For example, Bic may sell pens to large retail stores, wholesalers, and institutions. Retailers may want more rapid delivery of small shipments and more personal selling by the producer than do either wholesalers or institutional buyers. Because the marketing decisions and activities required for these two groups of customers differ considerably, the company may find it efficient to organize its marketing unit by types of customers.

## Controlling Marketing Activities

To achieve both marketing and general organizational objectives, marketing managers must effectively control marketing efforts. The **marketing control process** consists of establishing performance standards, evaluating actual performance by comparing it with established standards, and reducing the differences between desired and actual performance.

Although the control function is a fundamental management activity, it has received little attention in marketing. Organizations have both formal and informal control systems. The formal marketing control process, as mentioned earlier, involves performance standards, evaluation of actual performance, and corrective action to remedy shortfalls (see Figure 2.5 on p. 46). The informal control process involves self-control, social or group control, and cultural control through acceptance of the firm's value system. Which type of control system dominates depends on the environmental context of the firm.[57] We now discuss these steps in the formal control process and consider the major problems they involve.

**Establishing Performance Standards.** Planning and controlling are closely linked because plans include statements about what is to be accomplished. For purposes of control, these statements function as performance standards. A **performance standard** is an expected level of performance against which actual performance can be compared. A performance standard might be a 20 percent reduction in customer complaints, a monthly sales quota of $150,000, or a 10 percent increase per month in new-customer accounts. General Motors, for example, had a goal of selling 31,000 Corvette C6s in the United States in 2005.[58] As stated earlier, performance standards should be tied to organizational goals.

**Evaluating Actual Performance.** To compare actual performance with performance standards, marketing managers must know what employees within the com-

**marketing control process**
Establishing performance standards, evaluating actual performance by comparing it with established standards, and reducing the differences between desired and actual performance

**performance standard** An expected level of performance against which actual performance can be compared

figure 2.5

### THE MARKETING CONTROL PROCESS

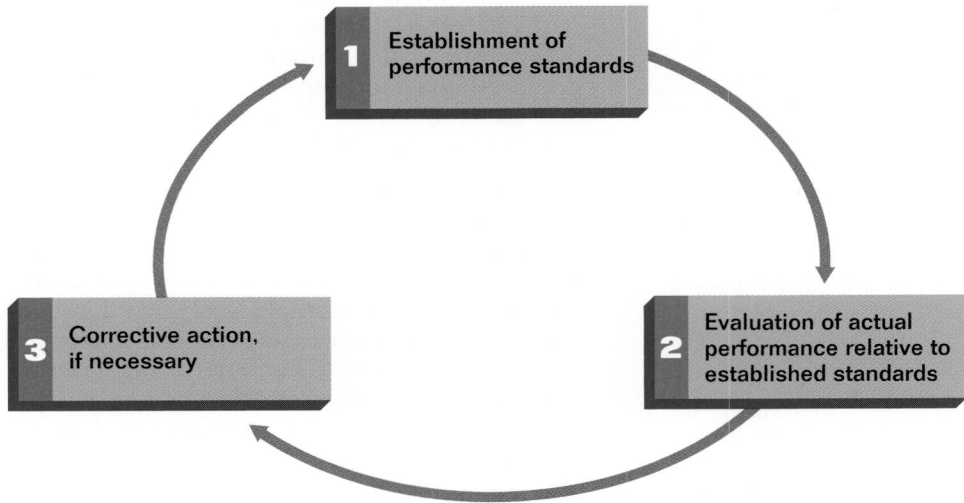

pany are doing and have information about the activities of external organizations that provide the firm with marketing assistance. For example, Saturn, like many automakers, uses many measures to evaluate its product and service levels, including how well it ranks on the J. D. Power & Associates Customer Service Index. In 2005, Saturn ranked number 3 among all automakers, up from number 6 in 2004, behind only Lincoln and Cadillac.[59] Records of actual performance are compared with performance standards to determine whether and how much of a discrepancy exists. For example, if General Motors had determined that only 25,000 Corvettes were sold in 2005, a discrepancy would have existed because its goal was 31,000 vehicles.

**Taking Corrective Action.** Marketing managers have several options for reducing a discrepancy between established performance standards and actual performance. They can take steps to improve actual performance, reduce or totally change the performance standard, or do both. At Wal-Mart, for example, managers implemented a strategy not to employ its usual steep discounts during the holiday shopping season, but when that strategy resulted in sluggish sales, they quickly slashed prices on key products and ran full-page newspaper ads to promote the lower prices.[60] To improve actual performance, the marketing manager may have to use better methods of motivating marketing personnel or find more effective techniques for coordinating marketing efforts.

**Problems in Controlling Marketing Activities.** In their efforts to control marketing activities, marketing managers frequently run into several problems. Often the information required to control marketing activities is unavailable or is available only at a high cost. Although marketing controls should be flexible enough to allow for environmental changes, the frequency, intensity, and unpredictability of such changes may hamper control. In addition, the time lag between marketing activities and their results limits a marketing manager's ability to measure the effectiveness of specific marketing activities. This is especially true for all advertising activities.

Because marketing and other business activities overlap, marketing managers cannot determine the precise costs of marketing activities. Without an accurate measure of marketing costs, it is difficult to know if the outcome of marketing activities is worth the expense. Finally, marketing control may be difficult because it is very hard to develop exact performance standards for marketing personnel.

## SUMMARY

Through the process of strategic planning, a firm identifies or establishes an organizational mission and goals, corporate strategy, marketing goals and objectives, marketing strategy, and a marketing plan. To achieve its marketing objectives, an organization must develop a marketing strategy, which includes identifying a target market and developing a plan of action for developing, distributing, promoting, and pricing products that meet the needs of customers in that target market. The strategic planning process ultimately yields the framework for a marketing plan, a written document that specifies the activities to be performed for implementing and controlling an organization's marketing activities.

The marketing environment, including economic, competitive, political, legal and regulatory, sociocultural, and technological forces, can affect the resources a firm can acquire and create favorable opportunities. Resources may include core competencies, which are things that a firm does extremely well, sometimes so well that it gives the company an advantage over its competition. When the right combination of circumstances and timing permit an organization to take action toward reaching a particular target market, a market opportunity exists. Strategic windows are temporary periods of optimal fit between the key requirements of a market and the particular capabilities of a firm competing in that market. When a company matches a core competency to opportunities it has discovered in the marketplace, it is said to have a competitive advantage.

An organization's goals should be derived from its mission statement, a long-term view, or vision, of what the organization wants to become. A well-formulated mission statement helps give an organization a clear purpose and direction, distinguish it from competitors, provide direction for strategic planning, and foster a focus on customers. An organization's goals and objectives, which focus on the end results sought, guide the remainder of its planning efforts.

Corporate strategy determines the means for utilizing resources in the areas of production, finance, research and development, human resources, and marketing to reach the organization's goals. Business-unit strategy focuses on strategic business units (SBUs)—divisions, product lines, or other profit centers within the parent company used to define areas for consideration in a specific strategic market plan. The Boston Consulting Group's market growth/market share matrix integrates a firm's products or SBUs into a single, overall matrix for evaluation to determine appropriate strategies for individual products and business units. Marketing strategies, the most detailed and specific of the three levels of strategy, are composed of two elements: the selection of a target market and the creation of a marketing mix that will satisfy the needs of the chosen target market. The selection of a target market serves as the basis for the creation of the marketing mix to satisfy the needs of that market. Marketing mix decisions should also be consistent with business-unit and corporate strategies and be flexible enough to respond to changes in market conditions, competition, and customer needs. Different elements of the marketing mix can be changed to accommodate different marketing strategies.

The outcome of marketing planning is the development of a marketing plan, which outlines all the activities necessary to implement marketing strategies. The plan fosters communication among employees, assigns responsibilities and schedules, specifies how resources are to be allocated to achieve objectives, and helps marketing managers monitor and evaluate the performance of a marketing strategy.

Marketing implementation is the process of executing marketing strategies. Marketing strategies do not always turn out as expected. Realized marketing strategies often differ from the intended strategies because of issues related to implementation. Proper implementation requires efficient organizational structures and effective control and evaluation.

One major approach to marketing implementation is internal marketing, a management philosophy that coordinates internal exchanges between the organization and its employees to achieve successful external exchanges between the organization and its customers. For strategy implementation to be successful, the needs of both internal and external customers must be met. Another approach is total quality management (TQM), which relies heavily on the talents of employees to continually improve the quality of the organization's goods and services.

**ACE self-test**

Please visit the student website at **www.prideferrell.com** for ACE Self-Test questions that will help you prepare for exams.

## IMPORTANT TERMS

Strategic planning
Marketing strategy
Marketing plan
Core competencies
Market opportunity
Strategic window
Competitive advantage
SWOT analysis
Mission statement

Marketing objective
Corporate strategy
Strategic business unit (SBU)
Market
Market share
Market growth/market share matrix
Sustainable competitive advantage

Marketing planning
Marketing implementation
Intended strategy
Realized strategy
External customers
Internal customers
Internal marketing
Total quality management (TQM)
Benchmarking

Empowerment
Centralized organization
Decentralized organization
Marketing control process
Performance standard

## DISCUSSION & REVIEW QUESTIONS

1. Identify the major components of strategic planning, and explain how they are interrelated.
2. What are the two major parts of a marketing strategy?
3. What are some issues to consider in analyzing a firm's resources and opportunities? How do these issues affect marketing objectives and marketing strategy?
4. How important is the SWOT analysis to the marketing planning process?
5. How should organizations set marketing objectives?
6. Explain how an organization can create a competitive advantage at the corporate, business-unit, and marketing strategy levels.

7. Refer to question 6. How can an organization make its competitive advantages sustainable over time? How difficult is it to create sustainable competitive advantages?
8. What benefits do marketing managers gain from planning? Is planning necessary for long-run survival? Why or why not?
9. Why does an organization's intended strategy often differ from its realized strategy?
10. Why might an organization use multiple bases for organizing its marketing unit?
11. What are the major steps of the marketing control process?

## APPLICATION QUESTIONS

1. Contact three organizations that appear to be successful. Ask one of the company's managers or executives if he or she would share with you the company's mission statement or organizational goals. Obtain as much information as possible about the statement and organizational goals. Discuss how the statement matches the criteria outlined in the text.
2. Assume you own a new, family-style restaurant that will open for business in the coming year. Formulate a long-term goal for the company, and then develop short-term goals to help you achieve the long-term goal.
3. Amazon.com identified an opportunity to capitalize on a desire of many consumers to shop at home. This strategic window gave Amazon.com a very competitive position in a new market. Consider the

opportunities that may be present in your city, your region, or the United States as a whole. Identify a strategic window, and discuss how a company could take advantage of this opportunity. What kind of core competencies are necessary?

4. Marketing units may be organized according to functions, products, regions, or types of customers. Describe how you would organize the marketing units for the following:
   a. A toothpaste with whitener; a toothpaste with extra-strong nicotine cleaners; a toothpaste with bubble-gum flavor
   b. A national line offering all types of winter and summer sports clothing for men and women
   c. A life insurance company that provides life, health, and disability insurance

**globalEDGE™**

1. Rankings of the world's largest manufacturing companies provide a variety of data. Rankings by industry can be found using the search term "largest manufacturing companies" at **http://globaledge.msu.edu/ibrd** to access *IndustryWeek*'s IW 1000 ranking. Perform a SWOT (i.e., strengths, weaknesses, opportunities, and threats) analysis of the top five firms in the apparel industry. From the information included, which firm has the strongest market position? Analyze all firms in the apparel industry. Which five firms have the weakest positions?

2. Your firm is currently developing a marketing strategy based on the expected age of both the Canadian and U.S. populations for the foreseeable future. By analyzing the population pyramids provided in the International Data Base (IDB) by the U.S. Census Bureau, you can better understand the estimated demographic shifts from 2000 to 2025 and 2050 for both countries. The population pyramids can be found using the search term "international data base" at **http://globaledge.msu.edu/ibrd** to reach the U.S. Census Bureau's International Data Base (IDB), and then choosing the Population Pyramid link. Provide a summary of your findings.

**INTERNET Exercise**

Visit **www.prideferrell.com** for resources to help you master the material in this chapter, plus materials that will help you expand your marketing knowledge, including Internet exercise updates, ACE Self-Tests, hotlinks to companies featured in this chapter, and much more.

## Sony

Internet analysts have praised Sony's website as one of the best organized and most informative on the Internet. See why by accessing **www.sony.com**.

1. Based on the information provided on the website, describe Sony's SBUs.
2. Based on your existing knowledge of Sony as an innovative leader in the consumer electronics industry, describe the company's primary competitive advantage. How does Sony's website support this competitive advantage?
3. Assess the quality and effectiveness of Sony's website. Specifically, perform a preliminary SWOT analysis comparing Sony's website with other high-quality websites you have visited.

**Video Case 2.1**

## Green Mountain Coffee Roasters Brews Up the Best Market Strategy

Green Mountain Coffee Roasters, Inc. is a leader in the specialty coffee industry. Founded in 1981 as a small café in Waitsfield, Vermont, Green Mountain quickly gained a reputation for its high quality, and demand for its freshly roasted coffee grew among local restaurants and inns. Incorporated in 1993, the firm today markets $161 million worth of coffee and related products through a coordinated multichannel distribution network with both wholesale and direct-to-consumer operations. This distribution network is designed to maximize brand recognition and product availability.

Green Mountain derives the majority of its revenue from more than 7,000 wholesale customer accounts located primarily in the eastern United States. The wholesale operation serves customers such as supermarkets, specialty food stores, convenience stores, food service companies, hotels, restaurants, universities, and office coffee services. Many of these wholesale customers then resell the coffee in whole bean or ground form for home consumption or brew and sell coffee beverages at their places of business.

Green Mountain Coffee roasts 40 varieties of high-quality Arabica coffee beans and offers more than 100 selections of coffee such as single-origin, estate, and certified organic coffee, as well as proprietary blends and flavored coffees sold under the Green Mountain Coffee Roasters and Newman's Own Organics brand names. It has made a point of marketing certified Fair Trade™ coffees that help struggling coffee farmers earn fair market value for their efforts. It carefully selects its coffee beans and then roasts them to maximize their taste and flavor differences. Green Mountain coffee is delivered in a variety of packages including whole bean, fractional packages, and premium one-cup coffee pods.

Green Mountain's objective is to be the leading specialty coffee company. It aims to achieve the highest market share in its target markets while maximizing company values. To meet these objectives, Green Mountain differentiates and reinforces the Green Mountain Coffee brand by distributing only the highest quality products, providing superior customer service and distribution, stressing corporate governance and employee development, and implementing socially responsible business practices. Through these strategies, Green Mountain believes it engenders a high degree of customer loyalty.

The company employs 670 people but has a flat organizational structure, which makes all employees responsible for implementation. Although it has functional departments that vary across the company, there are typically about four layers of hierarchy in each department. There is openness in all aspects of communication that allows employees to have regular access to all levels of the organization, including CEO Bob Stiller. The company urges each employee to voice his or her opinions and ideas. This encourages passion and commitment so that employees get to the heart of issues and challenges instead of playing office politics. In this way, Green Mountain has fostered a culture that involves its workers in decision making and challenges them to find solutions to problems. Empowering employees to this degree means that the company may sometimes appear chaotic, but the communication across channels in what is sometimes termed a "constellation of communication" ensures the collaborative nature of getting things done.

In addition to growing sales and a reputation for quality, Green Mountain Coffee Roasters has been ranked among *Forbes* magazine's list of 200 Best Small Companies in America for six consecutive years. The company's commitment to social responsibility—not only to secure fair trade prices for coffee growers but also its support of social and environmental programs in coffee-growing regions—earned it a second place on *Business Ethics* magazine's annual list of 100 Best Corporate Citizens in 2005, up from its 2004 position of fifth.[61]

## Questions for Discussion

1. Describe Green Mountain's marketing strategy.
2. How does Green Mountain use implementation to achieve success in a very competitive market?
3. How does empowerment work at Green Mountain?

---

| Case **2.2** | ## A Turnaround King Helps Burger King Recover |

Burger King, founded in Miami in 1954 by James McLamore and David Edgerton, serves almost 12 million customers a day at more than 11,000 restaurants in 60 countries. However, since the early 1990s the profits and success of Burger King restaurants have steadily declined, while rivals McDonald's and Wendy's grabbed its market share. While 10 CEOs passed through Burger King in 14 years, CEO number 11, Greg Brenneman, is finally turning things around. This charismatic, driven CEO has implemented new strategies that have boosted sales 6.8 percent in restaurants open more than a year—the largest increase in more than ten years. The company's market share is also expected to show improvement this year after falling since 1999.

Brenneman certainly has experience with corporate turnarounds. Before taking the lead at Burger King, he helped turn around PwC Consulting and helped facilitate that company's merger with IBM Global Services. This merger earned the title of "deal of the year" from *Institutional Investor* magazine. Prior to that, Brenneman spent six years at the helm of Continental Airlines, helping to return the company to profitability after 16 years of losses. Although Brenneman has an MBA from Harvard Business School, he attributes much of his success to growing up on a Kansas farm, where days began at 6 a.m. and ended late in the evening, and where he developed a strong work ethic. His early jobs included manicuring golf courses and working at a furniture warehouse. Those who work with him view him as intelligent, aggressive, and quick. Even Edgerton feels Brenneman is the first CEO in a long time who listens to everyone.

To approach the issues facing Burger King, Brenneman took a simple path and initiated the "Go Forward Plan," which required a single sheet of paper to articulate. He set straightforward goals for the company: to earn money, bring in more customers/build enthusiasm in existing customers, and motivate BK employees. To reach those goals, he first slashed the costs of building new Burger King restaurants from $1.3 million to $970,000 by recommending making new stores smaller. His idea was supported by research that suggested that most customers currently order food to go, so the new Burger King prototype (one of which is already open in Miami) has about half the previous number of seats. The kitchens of these new stores are also smaller to make preparation more efficient. In addition, Brenneman wants the new stores built with materials readily available at Home Depot. Doing all of this may save up to 50 percent on the price of land, which should enable franchisees to achieve profits more quickly. In addition to reducing the size of the new restaurants, the company has introduced a new "industrial chic" decoration scheme, which executives believe will be a major draw for customers. About 12 of the new stores were open by the fall of 2005. When Brenneman took the reins at Burger King, the company had just one project idea on the table. To take the company forward, he is determined that now there will always be at least 30 project ideas in the works. His first project was the Enormous Omelet Sandwich, which raised breakfast profits 20 percent.

One of Brenneman's biggest challenges is soothing franchisees, who are vital to the firm's continuing success. In particular, one group of franchisees is unhappy that a recent $340 million ad campaign targets teenage males at the expense of other market segments, especially women. While some franchisees worry that the advertising focus is too narrow, a spokeswoman for Burger King says that sales—the only way to measure success—have been up since the campaign began. Other issues of concern to franchisees relate to new menu items, pricing, and hours of operations. Given that 90 percent of Burger King restaurants are franchised, Brenneman clearly has work to do to settle these issues.

Despite these issues, Brenneman is optimistic about Burger King's future. There are signs to support his optimism. For example, customer satisfaction is at an all-time high according to the University of Michigan's American Customer Satisfaction Index, at a time when McDonald's has seen customer satisfaction decline. In 2005 Burger King opened more restaurants than it closed—a first since the 1990s. The company is also opening new restaurants overseas, with new locations in Brazil and China. All told, the company opened 300 to 350 international locations in 2005.

Even given the challenges to be faced, employees and franchisees alike are rooting for Brenneman and the success of Burger King. The company still has a way to go to return to the successful levels of the early 1990s, but Brenneman is certainly laying solid groundwork for success.

While it is simply a matter of watching to see how Burger King's future sales fare, Brenneman—who now rises at 4 a.m. and is at work by 4:30 and has successful company turnarounds under his belt—may be just the man to keep sales on the rise.[62]

## Questions for Discussion

1. Briefly describe the target market and marketing mix used by Burger King.
2. Do you believe that targeting teenage males at the expense of other markets, especially women, is an appropriate strategy?
3. Have Burger King's strategic marketing planning efforts been successful? Why or why not?

## Strategic Case 1   FedEx Packages Marketing for Overnight Success

In 1973, Frederick W. Smith founded Federal Express Corporation with part of an $8 million inheritance. At the time, the U.S. Postal Service and United Parcel Service (UPS) provided the only means of delivering packages, and they often took several days or more to get packages to their destinations. While a student at Yale in 1965, Smith studied topology, a mathematical discipline dedicated to geometric configurations. He applied these principles to a business plan and envisioned a hub system from which packages could be delivered across the globe. Smith wrote a paper proposing an independent overnight delivery service. Although he received a C on the paper, Smith never lost sight of his vision. He believed many businesses would be willing to pay more to get letters, documents, and packages delivered overnight. He was right.

Federal Express began shipping packages overnight from Memphis, Tennessee, on April 17, 1973. On that first night of operations, the company handled six packages, one of which was a birthday present sent by Smith himself. Today FedEx Corporation handles more than 3 million overnight packages and documents a day and more than 6 million shipments a day around the world, including the hot markets of India, China, and Brazil. FedEx controls more than 50 percent of the overnight delivery market, with an astounding $31 billion in total revenue. FedEx does not view itself as being in the package and document transport business; rather, it describes its business as delivering "certainty." FedEx delivers this certainty by connecting the global economy with a wide range of transportation, information, and supply chain services.

FedEx Express and FedEx Ground provide the bulk of the company's business, offering valuable services to anyone who needs to deliver letters, documents, and packages. Whether it is dropped off at one of nearly 42,000 drop boxes or 715 world service centers or picked up by a FedEx courier, each package is taken to a local FedEx office, where it is trucked to the nearest airport. The package is flown to one of the company's distribution "hubs" for sorting and then flown to the airport nearest its destination. The package is then trucked to another FedEx office, where a courier picks it up and hand delivers it to the correct recipient. All of this takes place overnight, with many packages delivered before 8:00 a.m. the following day. FedEx confirms that roughly 99 percent of its deliveries are made on time.

To achieve this highly successful delivery rate,

FedEx maintains an impressive infrastructure of equipment and processes. The company owns more than 70,000 vehicles, and its 677 aircraft fly more than 500,000 miles every day. FedEx operates its own weather forecasting service, ensuring that most of its flights arrive within 15 minutes of schedule. The hub envisioned by Smith in college is located in Memphis, Tennessee. FedEx takes over control of Memphis International Airport at roughly 11:00 each night. For an hour every night, FedEx planes begin to arrive in Memphis and land side by side on parallel runways every minute. After the packages are sorted, all FedEx planes take off in time to reach their destinations. Beginning at 2:48 a.m. every Monday through Friday, FedEx dispatches eight to twelve aircraft every six minutes. By 4:12 a.m., FedEx has launched about 150 aircraft to over 136 domestic and international destinations. Not all packages are shipped via air; whenever possible, FedEx uses ground transportation to save on expenses. For international deliveries, FedEx uses a combination of direct services and independent contractors. To handle the logistics of its large number of planes, FedEx relies on high-tech software originally developed by NASA. The program displays real-time maps of the airport layout, runways, aircraft, taxiways, and gates. With a single click of the mouse, the operator can receive detailed information about an individual airplane's arrival and departure times.

### Growth and Expansion

FedEx has been expanding its reach by merging with Kinko's, partnering with its former competitor. FedEx purchased Kinko's in 2004 to provide new business services and expand FedEx shipping options at Kinko's nationwide stores. The purchase followed rival UPS's acquisition of 3,000 Mail Boxes Etc. stores. Renamed as the UPS Stores, that acquisition put UPS closer to small- and medium-size customers and high-profit, infrequent shippers. FedEx's purchase of Kinko's, which operates in 11 countries, is expected to help the company reach new customers and expand in Asia and Europe.

In 2001, FedEx Express expanded its reach further with the announcement of two seven-year service agreements with the U.S. Postal Service. In the first agreement, FedEx Express provides air transportation for certain postal services, including Priority Mail. The second agreement gives FedEx Express the option to place a drop box in every U.S. post office. FedEx did not get the exclusive rights to drop boxes, which left open the potential for UPS to negotiate its own agreement with the postal service. Both FedEx and the postal service operate competitively and maintain separate services in all other categories.

One of the most important keys to success for FedEx is its flexibility. FedEx always has to be ready to deal with the unexpected or the uncontrollable. "That's the nature of the business," says Dave Bronczek, the head of FedEx's Express division. Natural disasters are a natural obstacle in the shipping business. In 2004 and 2005, FedEx had to rely on contingency plans to successfully navigate the 57 tropical storms that threatened to interrupt its business. "We're used to dealing with crisis," says Bronczek. When television reporters covered the inability of FEMA workers and Army personnel to communicate during post–Hurricane Katrina rescue operations, FedEx came to the rescue. The company contacted FEMA and offered use of its intact radio network to aid rescue workers. Every day, some part of the globe visited by FedEx is experiencing some type of political or natural unrest. This is the reason FedEx has implemented disaster drills covering everything from bioterrorism to typhoons. Each night eight planes sit in Memphis with fuel, supplies, and communications gear ready to deploy to a FedEx facility in need. Also, five cargoless planes roam the skies, ready to help out in cases of unexpected volume, air emergencies, or broken down planes.

## FedEx Relies Heavily on Information Technology

Despite its tremendous successes, FedEx has faced some difficult times in its efforts to grow and compete against strong rivals. The overnight delivery market matured very rapidly as intense competition from the U.S. Postal Service, UPS, Emery, DHL, RPS, and electronic document delivery (i.e., fax machines and e-mail) forced FedEx to search for viable means of expansion. In 1984, facing a growing threat from electronic document delivery, FedEx introduced its ZapMail service for customers who could not afford expensive fax machines. For $35, FedEx would fax up to 10 pages of text to any FedEx site around the world. The document was then hand-delivered to its recipient. Soon after the service was introduced, the price of fax machines plummeted, ultimately forcing FedEx to drop ZapMail after losing close to $200 million.

Many analysts still argue that the overnight delivery market could eventually lose as much as 30 percent of its letter business to electronic document delivery, especially e-mail. This trend may be balanced by the enormous growth of online businesses that rely on shipping services to deliver merchandise. This boom of clicking, buying, and shipping led to a record-breaking holiday season for FedEx recently. The company experienced all-time highs in business and broke its own records with 9 million packages handled in a single day.

FedEx constantly strives to improve its services by enhancing its distribution networks, transportation infrastructure, information technology, and employee performance. FedEx also continues to invest heavily in information technology by installing computer terminals at customers' offices and giving away its proprietary tracking software. Today the vast majority of FedEx customers—more than 70 percent—electronically generate their own pickup and delivery requests. FedEx has also moved more aggressively into e-commerce with respect to order fulfillment for business-to-business and business-to-consumer merchants. For example, FedEx's Home Delivery network has grown rapidly and now reaches virtually every U.S. residential address.

FedEx offers several electronic tools, applications, and online interfaces for customers to integrate into their processes to shorten response time, reduce inventory costs, generate better returns, and simplify their shipping. FedEx InSight was the first online application to offer proactive, real-time status information on inbound, outbound, and third-party shipments. It enables customers to identify issues instantly and address them before they become problems. In addition, FedEx InSight allows customers to see the progress of their shipments without requiring a tracking number, giving them convenient and unprecedented data visibility critical to effective management of their supply chain systems. FedEx technology enables customers, couriers, and contract delivery personnel to access the company's information systems networks by wireless technology anytime, anywhere. In fact, FedEx was the first transportation company to embrace wireless technology—more than two decades ago—and continues to be a leader in the use of innovative wireless solutions.

## Why Is FedEx Successful?

As FedEx moves ahead, the company has a lot going for it. No other carrier can match FedEx's global capabilities or one-stop shopping—at least not yet. To increase its competitiveness, FedEx is focusing on increasing revenue and reducing costs through tighter integration and consolidation, improved productivity, and reduced capital expenditures.

FedEx has been successful for many reasons. First, FedEx tries to stay focused on its mission statement, which is:

FedEx will produce superior financial returns for shareowners by providing high value-added supply chain, transportation, business and related information services through focused operating companies. Customer requirements will be met in the highest quality manner appropriate to each market segment served. FedEx will strive to develop mutually rewarding relationships with its employees, partners and suppliers. Safety will be the first consideration in all operations. Corporate activities will be conducted to the highest ethical and professional standards.

A second reason is the company's enviable corporate culture and workforce. Because employees are critical to the company's success, FedEx strives to hire the best people and offers them the best training and compensation in the industry. FedEx employees are loyal, highly efficient, and extremely effective in delivering good service. In fact, FedEx employees claim to have "purple blood" to match the company's official color. It is not surprising that FedEx has been named one of the "100 Best Companies to Work For" for eight consecutive years.

A third reason for FedEx's success is its technology and customer relationship management. The company's focus on "delivering certainty" has allowed it to home in on opportunities that give FedEx additional capabilities in innovative information technology solutions.

A final reason for FedEx's success is its highly effective marketing. FedEx is a master at recognizing untapped customer needs and building relationships. FedEx is also never content to sit on its laurels as it constantly strives to improve service and offer more options to its customers. After 30 years of success, there is little doubt that Fred Smith's C paper has become an indispensable part of the business world.[63]

**Questions for Discussion**

1. Which three environmental forces are likely to have the greatest effects on FedEx? Explain your answer.
2. What are the major strengths, weaknesses, opportunities, and threats (SWOT) associated with FedEx?
3. Is there evidence that FedEx has attempted to adopt and use the marketing concept? Explain.
4. Evaluate FedEx's mission statement. Explain the major strengths and weaknesses of this mission statement.

# Environmental Forces, Social Responsibility, and Ethics

**P**art 2 deals with the marketing environment and examines concepts, influences, and trends both in the United States and abroad. **Chapter 3** examines competitive, economic, political, legal, regulatory, technological, and sociocultural forces in the marketing environment, which can have profound effects on marketing strategies. **Chapter 4** explores the role of ethical and social responsibility issues in marketing decisions.

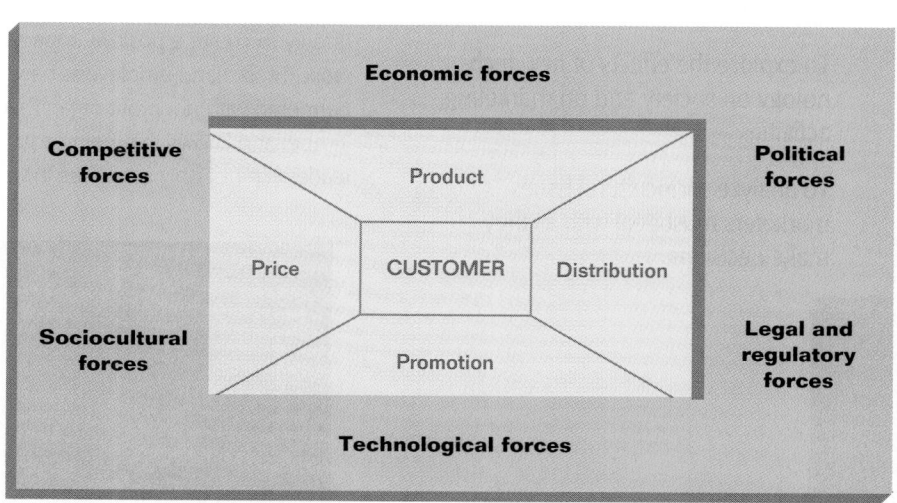

# CHAPTER 3

# The Marketing Environment

## OBJECTIVES

1. To recognize the importance of environmental scanning and analysis

2. To understand how competitive and economic factors affect organizations' ability to compete and customers' ability and willingness to buy products

3. To identify the types of political forces in the marketing environment

4. To understand how laws, government regulations, and self-regulatory agencies affect marketing activities

5. To explore the effects of new technology on society and on marketing activities

6. To analyze sociocultural issues marketers must deal with as they make decisions

### Timberland: Walking in Nature's Shoes

The Timberland Company is a global leader in the design, manufacturing, and marketing of premium-quality footwear, apparel, and accessories for consumers who love the outdoors. Its iconic yellow boot with the embossed tree logo is found in department and specialty stores as well as in Timberland retail stores worldwide. Timberland is not only known for its quality products, but also is recognized as one of the most socially responsible corporations in the world. Recently, Timberland received the Ron Brown Award for Corporate Leadership, the only presidential award that recognizes companies for outstanding achievement in community relations.

Among the company's goals are the fostering of engaged citizenship, environmental stewardship, and global human rights. To cultivate citizenship, the company created the Path of Service program, which provides 40 hours of pay to those employees who engage in community service activities. Through a myriad of service events and programs, employees invest their time, skills, and energy to create a positive impact on the communities in which they live and work. Timberland employees have invested more than 278,000 hours and partnered with nonprofit organizations in 27 countries around the world. Timberland knows that being a good citizen is good for business. This civic leadership not only advances the community in which Timberland does

business, but also provides benefits to the company in the form of a more energetic, dedicated, and loyal workforce.

Timberland also pursues a number of practices to preserve Earth's resources, such as designing its "Earthwatch" boots with natural and recycled compounds, using water-based adhesives, searching for new ways to manufacture products without having to use hazardous chemicals, and conserving energy to help combat climate change.

Through its Code of Conduct program, Timberland works to ensure that its products are made in workplaces that are fair, safe, and nondiscriminatory. The company is equally committed to improving the quality of life for its global business partners' employees. Beyond training factory management, educating factory workers, and auditing for compliance with its Code of Conduct, Timberland also partners with nongovernmental organizations and international agencies such as Verité, CARE, and Social Accountability International to ensure that its programs address current needs.

Timberland's reputation for social responsibility is well deserved. By creating programs that further its goals, the company shows that it values both people and the environment. And Timberland clearly understands that people like to do business with companies whose values they share.[1] ■

Companies like Timberland are modifying marketing strategies in response to changes in the marketing environment. Because recognizing and addressing such changes in the marketing environment are crucial to marketing success, we will focus in detail on the forces that contribute to these changes.

This chapter explores the competitive, economic, political, legal and regulatory, technological, and sociocultural forces that constitute the marketing environment. First, we define the marketing environment and consider why it is critical to scan and analyze it. Next, we discuss the effects of competitive forces and explore the influence of general economic conditions: prosperity, recession, depression, and recovery. We also examine buying power and look at the forces that influence consumers' willingness to spend. We then discuss the political forces that generate government actions affecting marketing activities and examine the effects of laws and regulatory agencies on these activities. After analyzing the major dimensions of the technological forces in the environment, we consider the impact of sociocultural forces on marketing efforts.

# Examining and Responding to the Marketing Environment

The marketing environment consists of external forces that directly or indirectly influence an organization's acquisition of inputs (human, financial, natural resources and raw materials, and information) and creation of outputs (goods, services, or ideas). As we saw in Chapter 1, the marketing environment includes six such forces: competitive, economic, political, legal and regulatory, technological, and sociocultural.

Whether fluctuating rapidly or slowly, environmental forces are always dynamic. Changes in the marketing environment create uncertainty, threats, and opportunities for marketers. Consider that after uncertainty in the Middle East and the effects of hurricanes Katrina and Rita led to escalating fuel costs, many automakers saw sales of their gas-guzzling sport-utility vehicles plummet. For some firms, though, the situation proved fortuitous, as Honda, Nissan, and Toyota gained sales when many consumers switched to more fuel-efficient vehicles, like the Toyota Prius.[2] Although the future is not very predictable, marketers try to forecast what may happen. We can say with certainty that marketers continue to modify their marketing strategies and plans in response to dynamic environmental forces. Consider how technological changes have affected the products offered by computer companies and how the public's growing concern with health and fitness has influenced the products of clothing,

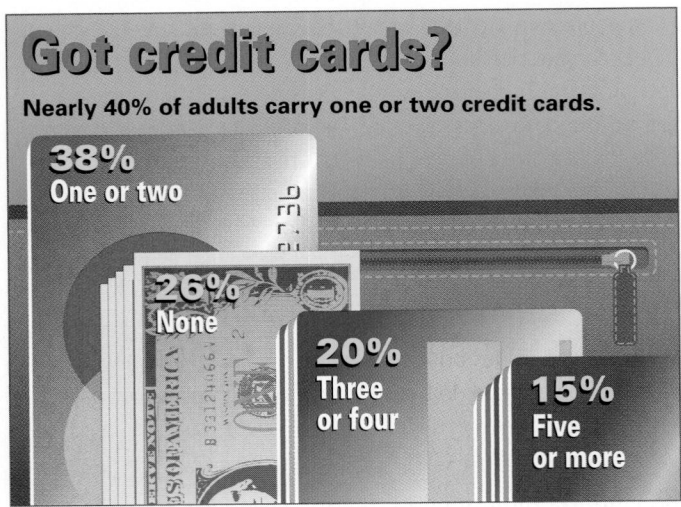

# Got credit cards?

**Nearly 40% of adults carry one or two credit cards.**

**38%**
One or two

**26%**
None

**20%**
Three
or four

**15%**
Five
or more

*Source:* Ipsos News Center.

**environmental scanning** The process of collecting information about forces in the marketing environment

**environmental analysis** The process of assessing and interpreting the information gathered through environmental scanning

food, exercise equipment, and health-care companies. Marketing managers who fail to recognize changes in environmental forces leave their firms unprepared to capitalize on marketing opportunities or to cope with threats created by those changes. Monitoring the environment is crucial to an organization's survival and to the long-term achievement of its goals.

## Environmental Scanning and Analysis

To monitor changes in the marketing environment effectively, marketers engage in environmental scanning and analysis. **Environmental scanning** is the process of collecting information about forces in the marketing environment. Scanning involves observation; secondary sources such as business, trade, government, and general-interest publications; and marketing research. The Internet has become a popular scanning tool since it makes data more accessible and allows companies to gather needed information quickly. Environmental scanning gives companies an edge over competitors in allowing them to take advantage of current trends. However, simply gathering information about competitors and customers is not enough; companies must know *how* to use that information in the strategic planning process. Managers must be careful not to gather so much information that sheer volume makes analysis impossible.

**Environmental analysis** is the process of assessing and interpreting the information gathered through environmental scanning. A manager evaluates the information for accuracy, tries to resolve inconsistencies in the data, and, if warranted, assigns significance to the findings. Evaluating this information should enable the manager to identify potential threats and opportunities linked to environmental changes. Understanding the current state of the marketing environment and recognizing threats and opportunities arising from changes within it help companies in their strategic planning. In particular, it can help marketing managers assess the performance of current marketing efforts and develop future marketing strategies.

## Responding to Environmental Forces

Marketing managers take two general approaches to environmental forces: accepting them as uncontrollable or attempting to influence and shape them. An organization that views environmental forces as uncontrollable remains passive and reactive toward the environment. Instead of trying to influence forces in the environment, its marketing managers adjust current marketing strategies to environmental changes. They approach with caution market opportunities discovered through environmental scanning and analysis. On the other hand, marketing managers who believe environmental forces can be shaped adopt a more proactive approach. For example, if a market is blocked by traditional environmental constraints, proactive marketing managers may apply economic, psychological, political, and promotional skills to gain access to and operate within it. Once they identify what is constraining a market opportunity, they assess the power of the various parties involved and develop strategies to overcome the obstructing environmental forces. Microsoft and Intel, for example, have responded to political, legal, and regulatory concerns about their power in the computer industry by communicating the value of their competitive approaches to various publics. The computer giants contend that their competitive success results in superior products for their customers.

A proactive approach can be constructive and bring desired results. To influence environmental forces, marketing managers seek to identify market opportunities or to extract greater benefits relative to costs from existing market opportunities. For example, a firm losing sales to competitors with lower-priced products develops a

First One To Save The Planet Wins.

We're all working for a better world. Cleaner air, a better environment and more natural resources. A worthy goal. At Toyota, we've been working on Hybrid Synergy Drive® for the past 40 years. The result? A technology that not only dramatically increases fuel economy but also creates far fewer smog-forming emissions. You'll find Hybrid Synergy Drive® on the Prius, Highlander Hybrid and, soon, the Camry Hybrid. In fact, we're working toward the day when you'll find it on all Toyota vehicles. Because we think you'll agree, better mileage and less pollution is a winning combination.

To learn more, visit toyota.com

HYBRID SYNERGY DRIVE

**Responding to Environmental Forces**
Toyota produces hybrid cars in response to both customer demand and its own desires to exceed regulatory agency emissions standards.

technology that makes its production processes more efficient, thus allowing it to lower prices of its own products. Political action is another way to affect environmental forces. The pharmaceutical industry, for example, has lobbied very effectively for fewer restrictions on prescription drug marketing. However, managers must recognize that there are limits to the degree that environmental forces can be shaped. Although an organization may be able to influence legislation through lobbying, it is unlikely that a single organization can significantly increase the national birthrate or move the economy from recession to prosperity.

We cannot say whether a reactive or a proactive approach to environmental forces is better. For some organizations the passive, reactive approach is more appropriate, but for others the aggressive approach leads to better performance. Selection of a particular approach depends on an organization's managerial philosophies, objectives, financial resources, customers, and human skills, as well as on the environment within which the organization operates. Both organizational factors and managers' personal characteristics affect the variety of responses to changing environmental conditions. Microsoft, for example, can take a proactive approach because of its financial resources and the highly visible image of its founder, Bill Gates.

In the remainder of this chapter, we explore in greater detail the six environmental forces—competitive, economic, political, legal and regulatory, technological, and sociocultural—that interact to create opportunities and threats that must be considered in strategic planning.

# Competitive Forces

Few firms, if any, operate free of competition. In fact, for most goods and services, customers have many alternatives from which to choose. For example, the five best-selling soft drinks are Coke Classic, Pepsi-Cola, Diet Coke, Mountain Dew, and Sprite.[3] Thus, when marketing managers define the target market(s) their firm will serve, they simultaneously establish a set of competitors.[4] In addition, marketing managers must consider the type of competitive structure in which the firm operates. In this section, we examine types of competition and competitive structures, as well as the importance of monitoring competitors' actions.

## Types of Competitors

Broadly speaking, all firms compete with one another for customers' dollars. More practically, however, a marketer generally defines **competition** as other firms that market products that are similar to or can be substituted for its products in the same geographic area. These competitors can be classified into one of four types. **Brand competitors** market products with similar features and benefits to the same customers at similar prices. For example, a thirsty, calorie-conscious customer may

**competition** Other organizations that market products that are similar to or can be substituted for a marketer's products in the same geographic area

**brand competitors** Firms that market products with similar features and benefits to the same customers at similar prices

Drawn from nature.
From deep beneath the surface, filtered through ancient rock in the lush volcanic region of Auvergne. Volvic, natural spring water.

*Volvic*
Created by volcanoes
www.volvic-na.com

**Brand Competition**
Volvic bottled water has many competitors, including Fiji, Evian, and Deer Park.

**product competitors** Firms that compete in the same product class but market products with different features, benefits, and prices

**generic competitors** Firms that provide very different products that solve the same problem or satisfy the same basic customer need

**total budget competitors** Firms that compete for the limited financial resources of the same customers

**monopoly** A competitive structure in which an organization offers a product that has no close substitutes, making that organization the sole source of supply

choose a diet soda such as Diet Coke or Diet Pepsi from the soda machine. However, these sodas face competition from other types of beverages. **Product competitors** compete in the same product class but market products with different features, benefits, and prices. The thirsty dieter, for instance, might purchase iced tea, juice, mineral water, or bottled water instead of a soda. **Generic competitors** provide very different products that solve the same problem or satisfy the same basic customer need. Our dieter, for example, might simply have a glass of water from the kitchen tap to satisfy her thirst. **Total budget competitors** compete for the limited financial resources of the same customers.[5] Total budget competitors for Diet Coke, for example, might include gum, a newspaper, and bananas. Although all four types of competition can affect a firm's marketing performance, brand competitors are the most significant because buyers typically see the different products of these firms as direct substitutes for one another. Consequently marketers tend to concentrate environmental analyses on brand competitors.

## Types of Competitive Structures

The number of firms that supply a product may affect the strength of competitors. When just one or a few firms control supply, competitive factors exert a different form of influence on marketing activities than when many competitors exist. Table 3.1 presents four general types of competitive structures: monopoly, oligopoly, monopolistic competition, and pure competition.

A **monopoly** exists when an organization offers a product that has no close substitutes, making that organization the sole source of supply. Because the organization has no competitors, it controls supply of the product completely and, as a single seller, can erect barriers to potential competitors. In reality, most monopolies surviving today are local utilities, which are heavily regulated by local, state, or federal agencies. These monopolies are tolerated because of the tremendous financial resources needed to develop and operate them. For example, few organizations can obtain the financial or political resources to mount any competition against a local

| table 3.1 | SELECTED CHARACTERISTICS OF COMPETITIVE STRUCTURES | | | |
|---|---|---|---|---|
| Type of Structure | Number of Competitors | Ease of Entry into Market | Product | Example |
| Monopoly | One | Many barriers | Almost no substitutes | Fort Collins (Colorado) Water Utilities |
| Oligopoly | Few | Some barriers | Homogeneous or differentiated (with real or perceived differences) | General Motors (autos) |
| Monopolistic competition | Many | Few barriers | Product differentiation, with many substitutes | Levi Strauss (jeans) |
| Pure competition | Unlimited | No barriers | Homogeneous products | Vegetable farm (sweet corn) |

**oligopoly** A competitive structure in which a few sellers control the supply of a large proportion of a product

**monopolistic competition** A competitive structure in which a firm has many potential competitors and tries to develop a marketing strategy to differentiate its product

**pure competition** A market structure characterized by an extremely large number of sellers, none strong enough to significantly influence price or supply

water supplier. On the other hand, competition is increasing in the electric and cable television industries.

An **oligopoly** exists when a few sellers control the supply of a large proportion of a product. In this case, each seller considers the reactions of other sellers to changes in marketing activities. Products facing oligopolistic competition may be homogeneous, such as aluminum, or differentiated, such as automobiles. Usually barriers of some sort make it difficult to enter the market and compete with oligopolies. For example, because of the enormous financial outlay required, few companies or individuals could afford to enter the oil-refining or steel-producing industry. Moreover, some industries demand special technical or marketing skills, a qualification that deters entry of many potential competitors.

**Monopolistic competition** exists when a firm with many potential competitors attempts to develop a marketing strategy to differentiate its product. For example, Levi Strauss has established an advantage for its blue jeans through a well-known trademark, design, advertising, and a reputation for quality. Although many competing brands of blue jeans are available, this firm has carved out a market niche by emphasizing differences in its products.

**Pure competition**, if it existed at all, would entail a large number of sellers, none of which could significantly influence price or supply. Products would be homogeneous, and entry into the market would be easy. The closest thing to an example of pure competition is an unregulated farmers' market, where local growers gather to sell their produce.

Pure competition is an ideal at one end of the continuum; monopoly is at the other end. Most marketers function in a competitive environment somewhere between these two extremes.

## Monitoring Competition

Marketers need to monitor the actions of major competitors to determine what specific strategies competitors are using and how those strategies affect their own. Price is one marketing strategy variable that most competitors monitor. When AirTran or Southwest Airlines lowers its fare on a route, most major airlines attempt to match the price. Monitoring guides marketers in developing competitive advantages and in adjusting current marketing strategies and planning new ones.

In monitoring competition, it is not enough to analyze available information; the firm must develop a system for gathering ongoing information about competitors. Understanding the market and what customers want, as well as what the competition is providing, will help the firm maintain a marketing orientation.[6] Information about competitors allows marketing managers to assess the performance of their own marketing efforts and to recognize the strengths and weaknesses in their own marketing strategies. In addition, organizations are rewarded for taking risks and dealing with the uncertainty created by inadequate information.[7] Data about market shares, product movement, sales volume, and expenditure levels can be useful. However, accurate information on these matters is often difficult to obtain.

# Economic Forces

Economic forces in the marketing environment influence both marketers' and customers' decisions and activities. In this section, we examine the effects of general economic conditions as well as buying power and the factors that affect people's willingness to spend.

## Economic Conditions

The overall state of the economy fluctuates in all countries. Changes in general economic conditions affect (and are affected by) supply and demand, buying power, willingness to spend, consumer expenditure levels, and intensity of competitive behavior. Therefore, current economic conditions and changes in the economy have a broad impact on the success of organizations' marketing strategies.

**business cycle** A pattern of economic fluctuations that has four stages: prosperity, recession, depression, and recovery

Fluctuations in the economy follow a general pattern, often referred to as the **business cycle**. In the traditional view, the business cycle consists of four stages: prosperity, recession, depression, and recovery. From a global perspective, different regions of the world may be in different stages of the business cycle during the same period. Throughout much of the last decade, for example, the United States experienced booming growth (prosperity). The U.S. economy began to slow in 2000, with a brief recession, especially in high-technology industries, in 2001. Japan, however, endured a recession during most of the last decade and into the early 2000s. Economic variation in the global marketplace creates a planning challenge for firms that sell products in multiple markets around the world.

**prosperity** A stage of the business cycle characterized by low unemployment and relatively high total income, which together ensure high buying power (provided the inflation rate stays low)

During **prosperity**, unemployment is low and total income is relatively high. Assuming a low inflation rate, this combination ensures high buying power. If the economic outlook remains prosperous, consumers generally are willing to buy. In the prosperity stage, marketers often expand their product offerings to take advantage of increased buying power. They can sometimes capture a larger market share by intensifying distribution and promotion efforts.

**recession** A stage of the business cycle during which unemployment rises and total buying power declines, stifling both consumer and business spending

Because unemployment rises during a **recession**, total buying power declines. These factors, usually accompanied by consumer pessimism, often stifle both consumer and business spending. As buying power decreases, many customers may become more price and value conscious, and look for basic, functional products. During a recession, some firms make the mistake of drastically reducing their marketing efforts, thus damaging their ability to survive. Obviously, however, marketers should consider some revision of their marketing activities during a recessionary period. Because consumers are more concerned about the functional value of products, a company should focus its marketing research on determining precisely what functions buyers want and make sure those functions become part of its products. Promotional efforts should emphasize value and utility. For example, KeepMedia, an online periodical content archive, discovered consumers wanted to pay for quality periodical content on the Internet but were unwilling to pay a separate fee for each title across the Web as they do for magazines offline. The company CEO put together recent editorial materials from recognizable publications at one flat fee.[8]

**depression** A stage of the business cycle when unemployment is extremely high, wages are very low, total disposable income is at a minimum, and consumers lack confidence in the economy

A prolonged recession may become a **depression**, a period in which unemployment is extremely high, wages are very low, total disposable income is at a minimum, and consumers lack confidence in the economy. A depression usually lasts for an extended period, often years, and has been experienced by Russia, Mexico, and Brazil in the last decade. Although evidence supports maintaining or even increasing spending during economic slowdowns, marketing budgets are more likely to be cut in the face of an economic downturn.

During **recovery**, the economy moves from recession or depression toward prosperity. During this period, high unemployment begins to decline, total disposable income increases, and the economic gloom that reduced consumers' willingness to buy subsides. Both the ability and the willingness to buy rise. Marketers face some problems during recovery; for example, it is difficult to ascertain how quickly and to what level prosperity will return. In this stage, marketers should maintain as much flexibility in their marketing strategies as possible so they can make the needed adjustments.

## Buying Power

The strength of a person's **buying power** depends on economic conditions and the size of the resources—money, goods, and services that can be traded in an exchange—that enable the individual to make purchases. The major financial sources of buying power are income, credit, and wealth. For an individual, **income** is the amount of money received through wages, rents, investments, pensions, and subsidy payments for a given period, such as a month or a year. Normally this money is allocated among taxes, spending for goods and services, and savings. The median annual household income in the United States is approximately $44,389.[9] However, because of differences in people's educational levels, abilities, occupations, and wealth, income is not equally distributed in this country.

Marketers are most interested in the amount of money left after payment of taxes because this **disposable income** is used for spending or saving. Because disposable income is a ready source of buying power, the total amount available in a nation is important to marketers. Several factors determine the size of total disposable income. One is the total amount of income, which is affected by wage levels, the rate of unemployment, interest rates, and dividend rates. Because disposable income is income left after taxes are paid, the number and amount of taxes directly affect the size of total disposable income. When taxes rise, disposable income declines; when taxes fall, disposable income increases.

Disposable income that is available for spending and saving after an individual has purchased the basic necessities of food, clothing, and shelter is called **discretionary income**. People use discretionary income to purchase entertainment, vacations, automobiles, education, pets, furniture, appliances, and so on. Changes in total discretionary income affect sales of these products, especially automobiles, furniture, large appliances, and other costly durable goods.

Credit enables people to spend future income now or in the near future. However, credit increases current buying power at the expense of future buying power. Several factors determine whether people use or forgo credit. First, credit must be available. Interest rates too affect buyers' decisions to use credit, especially for expensive purchases such as homes, appliances, and automobiles. When interest rates are low, the total cost of automobiles and houses becomes more affordable. In the United States, low interest rates over the past ten years induced many buyers to take on the high level of debt necessary to own a home, fueling a tremendous boom in the construction of new homes and the sale of older homes. In contrast, when interest rates are high, consumers are more likely to delay buying such expensive items. Use of credit is also affected by credit terms, such as size of the down payment and amount and number of monthly payments.

**Wealth** is the accumulation of past income, natural resources, and financial resources. It exists in many forms, including cash, securities, savings accounts, jewelry, and real estate. Like income, wealth is unevenly distributed. A person can have a high income and very little wealth. It is also possible, but not likely, for a person to have great wealth but little income. The significance of wealth to marketers is that as people become wealthier, they gain buying power in three ways: they can use their wealth to make current purchases, to generate income, and to acquire large amounts of credit.

**recovery** A stage of the business cycle in which the economy moves from recession or depression toward prosperity

**buying power** Resources, such as money, goods, and services, that can be traded in an exchange

**income** For an individual, the amount of money received through wages, rents, investments, pensions, and subsidy payments for a given period

**disposable income** After-tax income

**discretionary income** Disposable income available for spending and saving after an individual has purchased the basic necessities of food, clothing, and shelter

**wealth** The accumulation of past income, natural resources, and financial resources

Income, credit, and wealth equip consumers with buying power to purchase goods and services. Marketing managers need to be aware of current levels and expected changes in buying power in their own markets because buying power directly affects the types and quantities of goods and services customers purchase. Information about buying power is available from government sources, trade associations, and research agencies. One of the most current and comprehensive sources of buying power data is the *Sales & Marketing Management Survey of Buying Power,* published annually by *Sales & Marketing Management* magazine. Having buying power, however, does not mean consumers will buy. They must also be willing to use their buying power.

## Willingness to Spend

**willingness to spend** An inclination to buy because of expected satisfaction from a product, influenced by the ability to buy and numerous psychological and social forces

People's **willingness to spend**—their inclination to buy because of expected satisfaction from a product—is, to some degree, related to their ability to buy. That is, people are sometimes more willing to buy if they have the buying power. However, a number of other elements also influence willingness to spend. Some elements affect specific products; others influence spending in general. A product's price and value influence almost all of us. Cross pens, for example, appeal to customers who are willing to spend more for fine writing instruments even when lower-priced pens are readily available. Increasingly, middle-class consumers seem more willing to spend on high-price luxury products, such as Coach purses, BMW automobiles, and spa vacations, although they may shop for discounted groceries and other basic products at Wal-Mart and Target in order to afford the upscale products.[10] The amount of satisfaction received from a product already owned may also influence customers' desire to buy other products. Satisfaction depends not only on the quality of the currently owned product but also on numerous psychological and social forces. The American Customer Satisfaction Index, computed by the National Quality Research Center at the University of Michigan (see Figure 3.1), offers an indicator of customer satisfaction with a wide variety of businesses.

Factors that affect consumers' general willingness to spend are expectations about future employment, income levels, prices, family size, and general economic conditions. Willingness to spend ordinarily declines if people are unsure whether or how long they will be employed, and usually increases if people are reasonably certain of higher incomes in the future. Expectations of rising prices in the near future may also increase willingness to spend in the present. For a given level of buying power, the larger the family, the greater the willingness to spend. One reason for this relationship is that as the size of a family increases, more dollars must be spent to provide the basic necessities to sustain family members.

**figure 3.1**

## AMERICAN CUSTOMER SATISFACTION INDEX

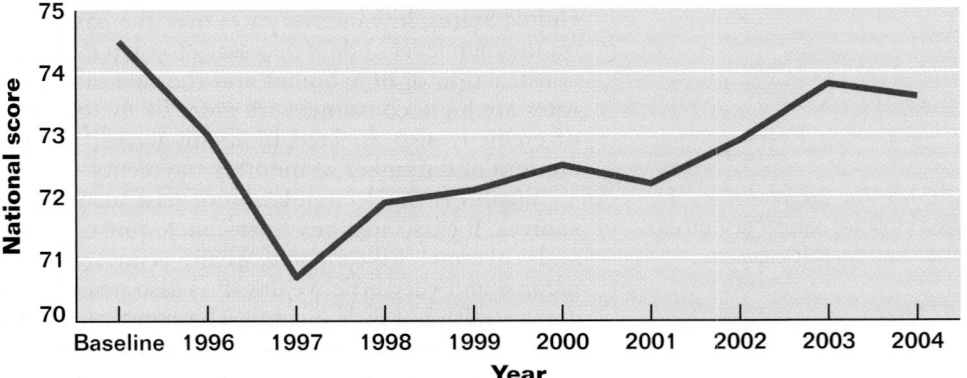

**Source:** "American Customer Satisfaction Index," University of Michigan Business School, Sept. 2005, **www.theacsi.com.**

# Political Forces

Political, legal, and regulatory forces of the marketing environment are closely inter-related. Legislation is enacted, legal decisions are interpreted by courts, and regulatory agencies are created and operated, for the most part, by elected or appointed officials. Legislation and regulations (or their lack) reflect the current political outlook. Consequently the political forces of the marketing environment have the potential to influence marketing decisions and strategies.

Marketing organizations strive to maintain good relations with elected and appointed political officials for several reasons. Political officials well disposed toward particular firms or industries are less likely to create or enforce laws and regulations unfavorable to those companies. For example, political officials who believe oil companies are making honest efforts to control pollution are unlikely to create and enforce highly restrictive pollution control laws. In addition, governments are big buyers, and political officials can influence how much a government agency purchases and from whom. Finally, political officials can play key roles in helping organizations secure foreign markets.

Many marketers view political forces as beyond their control and simply adjust to conditions arising from those forces. Some firms, however, seek to influence the political process. In some cases, organizations publicly protest the actions of legislative bodies. More often, organizations help elect to political offices individuals who regard them positively. Much of this help is in the form of campaign contributions. Although laws restrict direct corporate contributions to campaign funds, corporate influence may be channeled into campaigns through executives' or stockholders' personal contributions. Such actions violate the spirit of corporate campaign contribution laws. A sizable donation to a campaign fund may carry an implicit understanding that the elected official will perform political favors for the executive's firm.

Although laws limit corporate contributions to campaign funds for specific candidates, it is legal for businesses and other organizations to contribute to political parties. Some companies even choose to donate to more than one party. These donations are made in the form of "soft money," which refers to money that is donated to a political party with no specification on how the money will be spent. Some corporations give large sums to candidates, particularly in presidential elections, as shown in Table 3.2. Marketers can also influence the political process through

| table 3.2 | TOP CORPORATE DONORS BY POLITICAL PARTY | | | |
|---|---|---|---|---|
| | Democrat | Amount | Republican | Amount |
| 1 | United Parcel Service | $226,173 | 1  United Parcel Service | $550,125 |
| 2 | AT&T | $199,000 | 2  AT&T | $435,300 |
| 3 | Northrop Grumman | $198,500 | 3  Pfizer, Inc. | $377,750 |
| 4 | AFLAC Incorporated | $193,500 | 4  General Electric | $346,650 |
| 5 | General Electric | $193,350 | 5  Union Pacific | $332,275 |
| 6 | General Dynamics | $168,500 | 6  Bank of America | $303,250 |
| 7 | BellSouth | $166,100 | 7  Northrup Grumman | $293,000 |
| 8 | Boeing | $166,000 | 8  R. J. Reynolds | $284,500 |
| 9 | Raytheon | $161,250 | 9  General Dynamics | $279,000 |
| 10 | Comcast | $153,950 | 10  Federal Express | $270,900 |

political action committees (PACs) that solicit donations from individuals and then contribute those funds to candidates running for political office. Companies are barred by federal law from donating directly to candidates for federal offices or to PACs, but they can organize PACs to which their executives, employees, and stockholders can make significant donations as individuals. Companies can also participate in the political process through lobbying to persuade public and/or government officials to favor a particular position in decisionmaking. Many organizations concerned about the threat of legislation or regulation that may negatively affect their operations employ lobbyists to communicate their concerns to elected officials. For example, a World Health Organization (WHO) study suggested a relationship between food advertising and childhood obesity. These findings prompted the U.S. advertising industry to mount lobbying and public relations efforts to influence the regulation of food advertising.[11]

# Legal and Regulatory Forces

A number of federal laws influence marketing decisions and activities. Table 3.3 lists some of the most important laws. In addition to discussing these laws, which deal with competition and consumer protection, this section examines the effects of regulatory agencies and self-regulatory forces on marketing efforts.

## Procompetitive Legislation

Procompetitive laws are designed to preserve competition. Most of these laws were enacted to end various antitrade practices deemed unacceptable by society. The Sherman Antitrust Act, for example, was passed in 1890 to prevent businesses from restraining trade and monopolizing markets. Examples of illegal anticompetitive practices include stealing trade secrets or obtaining other confidential information from a competitor's employees, trademark and copyright infringement, price fixing, false advertising, and deceptive selling methods such as "bait and switch" and false representation of products. For example, the Lanham Act (1946) and the Federal Trademark Dilution Act (1995) help companies protect their trademarks (brand names, logos, and other registered symbols) against infringement. The latter also requires users of names that match or parallel existing trademarks to relinquish them to prevent confusion among consumers. Antitrust laws also authorize the government to punish companies that engage in such anticompetitive practices. For example, Korean-based Samsung Electronics and its U.S. subsidiary Samsung Semiconductor paid a $300 million criminal fine for participating in an international conspiracy to fix prices in the market for dynamic random access memory (DRAM).[12]

## Consumer Protection Legislation

Consumer protection legislation is not a recent development. During the mid-1800s, lawmakers in many states passed laws to prohibit adulteration of food and drugs. However, consumer protection laws at the federal level mushroomed in the mid-1960s and early 1970s. A number of them deal with consumer safety, such as the food and drug acts, designed to protect people from actual and potential physical harm caused by adulteration or mislabeling. Other laws prohibit the sale of various hazardous products, such as flammable fabrics and toys that may injure children. Others concern automobile safety. Congress has also passed several laws concerning information disclosure. Some require that information about specific products, such as textiles, furs, cigarettes, and automobiles, be provided on labels. Other laws focus on particular marketing activities: product development and testing, packaging, labeling, advertising, and consumer financing. For example, concerns about companies' online collection and use of personal information, especially about children, resulted in the passage of the Children's Online Privacy Protection Act, which prohibits websites and Internet providers from seeking personal information from children under age 13 without parental consent.

**table 3.3   MAJOR FEDERAL LAWS AFFECTING MARKETING DECISIONS**

| Name and Date Enacted | Purpose |
| --- | --- |
| Sherman Antitrust Act (1890) | Prohibits contracts, combinations, or conspiracies to restrain trade; establishes as a misdemeanor monopolizing or attempting to monopolize |
| Clayton Act (1914) | Prohibits specific practices such as price discrimination, exclusive-dealer arrangements, and stock acquisitions whose effect may noticeably lessen competition or tend to create a monopoly |
| Federal Trade Commission Act (1914) | Created the Federal Trade Commission; also gives the FTC investigatory powers to be used in preventing unfair methods of competition |
| Robinson-Patman Act (1936) | Prohibits price discrimination that lessens competition among wholesalers or retailers; prohibits producers from giving disproportionate services or facilities to large buyers |
| Wheeler-Lea Act (1938) | Prohibits unfair and deceptive acts and practices regardless of whether competition is injured; places advertising of foods and drugs under the jurisdiction of the FTC |
| Lanham Act (1946) | Provides protections for and regulation of brand names, brand marks, trade names, and trademarks |
| Celler-Kefauver Act (1950) | Prohibits any corporation engaged in commerce from acquiring the whole or any part of the stock or other share of the capital assets of another corporation when the effect would substantially lessen competition or tend to create a monopoly |
| Fair Packaging and Labeling Act (1966) | Prohibits unfair or deceptive packaging or labeling of consumer products |
| Magnuson-Moss Warranty (FTC) Act (1975) | Provides for minimum disclosure standards for written consumer product warranties; defines minimum consent standards for written warranties; allows the FTC to prescribe interpretive rules in policy statements regarding unfair or deceptive practices |
| Consumer Goods Pricing Act (1975) | Prohibits the use of price maintenance agreements among manufacturers and resellers in interstate commerce |
| Trademark Counterfeiting Act (1980) | Imposes civil and criminal penalties against those who deal in counterfeit consumer goods or any counterfeit goods that can threaten health or safety |
| Trademark Law Revision Act (1988) | Amends the Lanham Act to allow brands not yet introduced to be protected through registration with the Patent and Trademark Office |
| Nutrition Labeling and Education Act (1990) | Prohibits exaggerated health claims; requires all processed foods to contain labels with nutritional information |
| Telephone Consumer Protection Act (1991) | Establishes procedures to avoid unwanted telephone solicitations; prohibits marketers from using an automated telephone dialing system or an artificial or prerecorded voice to certain telephone lines |
| Federal Trademark Dilution Act (1995) | Grants trademark owners the right to protect trademarks and requires relinquishment of names that match or parallel existing trademarks |
| Digital Millennium Copyright Act (1996) | Refined copyright laws to protect digital versions of copyrighted materials, including music and movies |
| Children's Online Privacy Protection Act (2000) | Regulates the collection of personally identifiable information (name, address, e-mail address, hobbies, interests, or information collected through cookies) online from children under age 13 |
| Do Not Call Implementation Act (2003) | Directs the FCC and FTC to coordinate so that their rules are consistent regarding telemarketing call practices including the Do Not Call Registry and other lists, as well as call abandonment |

## Encouraging Compliance with Laws and Regulations

Marketing activities are sometimes at the forefront of organizational misconduct, with fraud and antitrust violations the most frequently sentenced organizational crimes. Legal violations usually begin when marketers develop programs that unwittingly overstep legal bounds. Many marketers lack experience in dealing with complex legal actions and decisions. Some test the limits of certain laws by operating in a legally questionable way to see how far they can get with certain practices before being prosecuted. Other marketers interpret regulations and statutes very strictly to avoid violating a vague law. When marketers interpret laws in relation to specific marketing practices, they often analyze recent court decisions both to better understand what the law is intended to do and to predict future court interpretations.

To ensure that marketers comply with the law, the federal government is moving toward greater organizational accountability for misconduct. The U.S. Sentencing Commission (USSC) introduced a detailed set of guidelines to regulate the sentencing of companies convicted of breaking the law. The basic philosophy of the Federal Sentencing Guidelines for Organizations is that companies are responsible for crimes committed by their employees. These guidelines were designed not only to hold companies as well as employees accountable for illegal actions but also to streamline sentencing and fine structures for offenses. (Previously laws punished only those employees directly responsible for an offense, not the company.) The underlying assumption is that "good citizen corporations" maintain compliance systems and internal controls to prevent misconduct and educate employees about questionable activities. Thus, the new guidelines focus on crime prevention and detection by mitigating penalties for firms that have chosen to develop such compliance programs should one of their employees engage in misconduct. The Sarbanes-Oxley Act, passed in 2002 in response to numerous corporate accounting scandals, further stiffened penalties for corporate fraud and required greater transparency in financial reporting.

The bottom line is that unless a marketer works in a company with an effective compliance program that meets the minimum requirements of the U.S. Sentencing Commission's recommendations, both the individual and the company face severe penalties if the marketer violates the law. For example, Daiwa Bank was hit with a $340 million fine for misrepresenting financial information, and Archer Daniels Midland received a $100 million fine for price fixing. Further, the Federal Sentencing Guidelines for individuals often mandate substantial prison sentences even for first-time offenders convicted of a felony such as antitrust, fraud, import/export violations, or environmental crimes.

## Regulatory Agencies

Federal regulatory agencies influence many marketing activities, including product development, pricing, packaging, advertising, personal selling, and distribution. Usually these bodies have the power to enforce specific laws, as well as some discretion in establishing operating rules and regulations to guide certain types of industry practices. Because of this discretion and overlapping areas of responsibility, confusion or conflict regarding which agencies have jurisdiction over which marketing activities is common.

**Federal Trade Commission (FTC)** An agency that regulates a variety of business practices and curbs false advertising, misleading pricing, and deceptive packaging and labeling

Of all the federal regulatory units, the **Federal Trade Commission (FTC)** most heavily influences marketing activities. Although the FTC regulates a variety of business practices, it allocates a large portion of resources to curbing false advertising, misleading pricing, and deceptive packaging and labeling. When it has reason to believe a firm is violating a law, the commission typically issues a complaint stating that the business is in violation and takes appropriate action. For example, the FTC filed a complaint against Emerson Direct, Inc. (doing business as Council on Natural Health) for making unsubstantiated claims that its "Smoke Away" smoking-cessation product would help smokers quit easily, quickly, permanently, and without side effects. The FTC's complaint further charged that two doctors who endorsed the product did not properly use their expertise or have the claimed expertise. The company settled

figure 3.2

## FEDERAL TRADE COMMISSION ENFORCEMENT TOOLS

| Cease-and-desist order | Consent decree | Redress | Corrective advertising | Civil penalties |
|---|---|---|---|---|
| A court order to a business to stop engaging in an illegal practice | An order for a business to stop engaging in questionable activities to avoid prosecution (In 2005, 10,021 were issued) | Money paid to customer to settle or resolve a complaint | A requirement that a business make new advertisement to correct misinformation | Court-ordered civil fines for up to $10,000 per day for violating a cease-and-desist order |

Source: www.ftc.gov.

the charges for $1.3 million and agreed to make no more unsubstantiated claims about its product.[13] If after a company is issued a complaint it continues the questionable practice, the FTC can issue a cease-and-desist order demanding that the business stop doing whatever caused the complaint. The firm can appeal to the federal courts to have the order rescinded. However, the FTC can seek civil penalties in court, up to a maximum penalty of $10,000 a day for each infraction if a cease-and-desist order is violated.

The commission can also require companies to run corrective advertising in response to previous ads deemed misleading (see Figure 3.2). This mandated corrective advertising is proving to be costly to some companies. The FTC has emerged as one of the leading enforcement agencies for consumer protection issues on the Internet. For example, the FTC is taking action against D Squared Solutions LLC, alleging the firm sells software that exploits a security hole in Microsoft's Messenger Service utility to send full-screen ads to consumers, and then advertises software that would block the pop-up ads. "It's an unfair practice to [send] advertisements that create a problem and then charge consumers for the solution," said Howard Beales, director of the FTC's Bureau of Consumer Protection.[14]

The FTC also assists businesses in complying with laws and evaluates new marketing methods every year. For example, the agency has held hearings to help firms establish guidelines for avoiding charges of price fixing, deceptive advertising, and questionable telemarketing practices. It has also held conferences and hearings on electronic (Internet) commerce. When general sets of guidelines are needed to improve business practices in a particular industry, the FTC sometimes encourages firms within that industry to establish a set of trade practices voluntarily. The FTC may even sponsor a conference bringing together industry leaders and consumers for this purpose.

Unlike the FTC, other regulatory units are limited to dealing with specific products, services, or business activities. For example, the Food and Drug Administration (FDA) enforces regulations prohibiting the sale and distribution of adulterated, misbranded, or hazardous food and drug products. Table 3.4 (on p. 70) outlines the areas of responsibility of six federal regulatory agencies.

In addition, all states, as well as many cities and towns, have regulatory agencies that enforce laws and regulations regarding marketing practices within their states or municipalities. State and local regulatory agencies try not to establish regulations that conflict with those of federal regulatory agencies. They generally enforce laws dealing with the production and sale of particular goods and services. The utility, insurance, financial, and liquor industries are commonly regulated by state agencies. Among these agencies' targets are misleading advertising and pricing. Recent legal actions suggest that states are taking a firmer stance against perceived deceptive pricing practices and are using basic consumer research to define deceptive pricing.

## table 3.4   MAJOR FEDERAL REGULATORY AGENCIES

| Agency | Major Areas of Responsibility |
|---|---|
| Federal Trade Commission (FTC) | Enforces laws and guidelines regarding business practices; takes action to stop false and deceptive advertising, pricing, packaging, and labeling |
| Food and Drug Administration (FDA) | Enforces laws and regulations to prevent distribution of adulterated or misbranded foods, drugs, medical devices, cosmetics, veterinary products, and potentially hazardous consumer products |
| Consumer Product Safety Commission (CPSC) | Ensures compliance with the Consumer Product Safety Act; protects the public from unreasonable risk of injury from any consumer product not covered by other regulatory agencies |
| Federal Communications Commission (FCC) | Regulates communication by wire, radio, and television in interstate and foreign commerce |
| Environmental Protection Agency (EPA) | Develops and enforces environmental protection standards and conducts research into the adverse effects of pollution |
| Federal Power Commission (FPC) | Regulates rates and sales of natural gas producers, thereby affecting the supply and price of gas available to consumers; also regulates wholesale rates for electricity and gas, pipeline construction, and U.S. imports and exports of natural gas and electricity |

## Self-Regulatory Forces

In an attempt to be good corporate citizens and prevent government intervention, some businesses try to regulate themselves. Kraft Foods, for example, stopped advertising sugary snacks and cereals to children under 12 in response to growing concerns about childhood obesity and its effects on children's long-term health. While some competitors were astonished by the decision, Kraft executives recognized that if food product marketers did not begin to police themselves, the government could impose restrictions on advertising to children and the industry could face potential lawsuits.[15] Similarly, a number of trade associations have developed self-regulatory programs. Though these programs are not a direct outgrowth of laws, many were established to stop or stall the development of laws and governmental regulatory groups that would regulate the associations' marketing practices. Sometimes trade associations establish ethics codes by which their members must abide or risk censure or exclusion from the association. For example, the Pharmaceutical Research and Manufacturers of America released its "Guiding Principles" to function as a set of voluntary industry rules for drug companies to follow when advertising directly to consumers. Some of the key guidelines are explained in detail in Table 3.5.[16]

**Better Business Bureau (BBB)**
A system of nongovernmental, independent, local regulatory agencies supported by local businesses that helps settle problems between customers and specific business firms

Perhaps the best-known self-regulatory group is the **Better Business Bureau (BBB)**, which is a system of nongovernmental, independent, local regulatory agencies that are supported by local businesses. More than 150 bureaus help settle problems between consumers and specific business firms. Each bureau also acts to preserve good business practices in a locality, although it usually lacks strong enforcement tools for dealing with firms that employ questionable practices. When a firm continues to violate what the Better Business Bureau believes to be good business practices, the bureau warns consumers through local newspapers or broadcast media. If the offending organization is a BBB member, it may be expelled from the local bureau. For

| table 3.5 | SELECTED DIRECT-TO-CONSUMER PHARMACEUTICAL AD GUIDELINES |
|---|---|
| Doctor information | Doctors must be informed about a product before it is marketed to consumers. |
| Schedule of advertisements | Advertisements must be aired at times for age-appropriate viewers. (Ads for Viagra and similar medications, for example, must appear at later hours.) |
| Identification of health condition | Advertisements must include the health condition the drug treats and include more than only the product name. |
| Advertisement review by FDA | All new television advertising must be submitted to the FDA before being broadcast. |
| Suggestions of other positive health-related actions | Advertisements must include other positive health-related behaviors. |

example, Cingular Wireless had its membership revoked by the Better Business Bureau of Upstate New York for having too many unresolved complaints on file.[17]

The Council of Better Business Bureaus is a national organization composed of all local Better Business Bureaus. The National Advertising Division (NAD) of the Council operates a self-regulatory program that investigates claims regarding alleged deceptive advertising. For example, after NAD received a complaint from Pfizer, a pharmaceutical firm, it asked the FTC and the FDA to further investigate whether Aventis's advertising for its Allegra prescription allergy medicine misleads consumers about the effectiveness of Pfizer's Benadryl, an over-the-counter allergy medicine.[18]

**National Advertising Review Board (NARB)** A self-regulatory unit that considers challenges to issues raised by the National Advertising Division (an arm of the Council of Better Business Bureaus) about an advertisement

Another self-regulatory entity, the **National Advertising Review Board (NARB)**, considers cases in which an advertiser challenges issues raised by the NAD about an advertisement. Cases are reviewed by panels drawn from NARB members representing advertisers, agencies, and the public. The NARB, sponsored by the Council of Better Business Bureaus and three advertising trade organizations, has no official enforcement powers. However, if a firm refuses to comply with its decision, the NARB may publicize the questionable practice and file a complaint with the FTC. For example, Sidney Frank Importing Company appealed to the NARB about an NAD order to abandon its claim that the company's Grey Goose Vodka is "rated the No. 1 Tasting Vodka in the World." The NARB concurred with the NAD on the issue. Frank refused to comply with the NARB, and the NARB referred the case to the FTC and the Alcohol and Tobacco Tax and Trade Bureau.[19]

Self-regulatory programs have several advantages over governmental laws and regulatory agencies. Establishment and implementation are usually less expensive, and guidelines are generally more realistic and operational. In addition, effective self-regulatory programs reduce the need to expand government bureaucracy. However, these programs have several limitations. When a trade association creates a set of industry guidelines for its members, nonmember firms do not have to abide by them. Furthermore, many self-regulatory programs lack the tools or authority to enforce guidelines. Finally, guidelines in self-regulatory programs are often less strict than those established by government agencies.

# Technological Forces

The word *technology* brings to mind scientific advances such as information technology and biotechnology, which have resulted in the Internet, cellphones, cloning, stem-cell research, pharmaceutical products, lasers, and more. Technology has revolutionized the products created and offered by marketers and the channels by which they communicate about those products. However, even though these innovations

**technology** The application of knowledge and tools to solve problems and perform tasks more efficiently

are outgrowths of technology, none of them *are* technology. **Technology** is the application of knowledge and tools to solve problems and perform tasks more efficiently. Technology grows out of research performed by businesses, universities, government agencies, and nonprofit organizations. More than half of this research is paid for by the federal government, which supports research in such diverse areas as health, defense, agriculture, energy, and pollution.

The rapid technological growth of the last several decades is expected to accelerate. It has transformed the U.S. economy into the most productive in the world and provided Americans with an ever-higher standard of living and tremendous opportunities for sustained business expansion. Technology and technological advancements clearly influence buyers' and marketers' decisions, so let's take a closer look at the impact of technology and its use in the marketplace.

## Impact of Technology

Technology determines how we, as members of society, satisfy our physiological needs. In various ways and to varying degrees, eating and drinking habits, sleeping patterns, sexual activities, health care, and work performance are all influenced by both existing technology and changes in technology. Because of the technological revolution in communications, for example, marketers can now reach vast numbers of people more efficiently through a variety of media. E-mail, voice mail, cellphones, pagers, and PDAs help marketers stay in touch with clients, make appointments, and handle last-minute orders or cancellations. Some companies, including Ford Motor, are even abandoning the use of traditional wired telephones in favor of exclusive use of cellphones in the workplace.[20] A growing number of U.S. households have given up their "land lines" in favor of using cellphones as their primary phones, and growth in wireless subscriptions is expected to continue at a compounded 2.9 percent through 2010.[21]

Personal computers are now in about 65 percent of U.S. consumers' homes, and millions of PCs include broadband or modems for accessing the Internet.[22] Telecom-

**The Impact of Technology**
Monster.com has changed the way people search for jobs, by allowing them to post résumés online. Honda's new Element sports an MP3 jack.

muting—using telecommunications technology to work from home or other nontraditional areas—is an increasingly popular use of computer technology. About 44.4 million employees telecommute for at least part of their workweeks, and marketing has become a significant telecommuting job.[23] Although we enjoy the benefits of communicating through the Internet, we are increasingly concerned about protecting our privacy and intellectual property. Likewise, although health and medical research have created new drugs that save lives, cloning and genetically modified foods have become controversial issues in many segments of society. In various ways and to varying degrees, home environments, health care, leisure, and work performance are all influenced by both current technology and advances in technology.[24]

The effects of technology relate to such characteristics as dynamics, reach, and the self-sustaining nature of technological progress. The *dynamics* of technology involve the constant change that often challenges the structures of social institutions, including social relationships, the legal system, religion, education, business, and leisure. *Reach* refers to the broad nature of technology as it moves through society. Consider the impact of cellphones. The ability to call from almost any location has many benefits but also negative side effects, including increases in traffic accidents, increased noise pollution, and fears about potential health risks.[25]

The *self-sustaining* nature of technology relates to the fact that technology acts as a catalyst to spur even faster development. As new innovations are introduced, they stimulate the need for more advancements to facilitate further development. For example, the Internet has created the need for ever-faster transmission of signals through broadband connections such as high-speed phone lines (DSL), satellites, and cable.

# Technology Goes to the Dogs

Americans love their pets. A recent survey by the American Animal Hospital Association reveals that four out of five pet owners consider their pets to be their children, and market trends confirm this. The pet industry has more than doubled in size in the past 10 years from $17 billion to $36 billion, making it the seventh largest retail segment in the nation. Fueling this trend are empty nesters and young adults who are having children later and spending their time and energy with their animals. As well, the pet industry has grown increasingly sophisticated at consumer marketing and has introduced a steady stream of new, high-tech pet products, all of which are vying for pet owners' dollars.

For example, the ThirstAlert! from JoBananas Club flashes red lights when the water level in your pet's bowl gets low. A deluxe version is scheduled for release next year that will send an e-mail or text message to let you know when your pet's bowl is empty. The Careful Clipper by Dogmatic marks the first renovation to the pet nail clipper in 20 years. It features an ergonomic handle and flexible snake light that allows you to see through almost any nail to avoid cutting the quick. The K&H Cool Bed absorbs heat from your pet and radiates the heat back into the air. And the Petmate Electronic Portion Control LeBistro is a programmable, electronic dispenser that holds more than 5 pounds of food and dispenses portions of up to 3 cups at selected times in the day.

With Americans falling more in love with their pets, this industry is quickly growing and is proving to be as responsive to technology as any other market.

**marketing**
## ENTREPRENEURS

**Jo Waldron**

THE BUSINESS: Able Planet Inc.

FOUNDED: 2003

SUCCESS: Allows the over 34 million Americans and 500 million worldwide with mild to profound hearing loss to communicate through telecommunications

After a lifetime of silence and 18 months of research and development, Jo Waldron, together with veteran audiologist Dr. Joan Burleigh, invented a revolutionary microtechnology called Able Planet. Smaller than a grain of rice, the microtech device is easily integrated into any phone, wireless, cell, or handheld set and interacts directly with the T-coil component of hearing aids. Instead of using a magnetic field to amplify the sound, Able Planet creates audio within the hearing aid itself, allowing users to hear up to 80 percent better. Soon we could be seeing Able Planet technology in devices such as stereos, computers, TVs, and more. Jo Waldron saw a need, helped create a new product, and has established effective distribution.

Technology initiates a change process that creates new opportunities for new technologies in every industry segment or personal life experience that it touches. At some point, there is a multiplier effect that causes still greater demand for more change to improve performance.[26]

The expanding opportunities for e-commerce, the sharing of business information, and the ability to maintain business relationships and conduct business transactions via telecommunications networks are already changing the relationship between businesses and consumers.[27] More and more people are turning to the Internet to purchase computers and related peripherals, software, books, music, and even furniture. Consumers are increasingly using the Internet to book travel reservations, transact banking business, and trade securities. The forces unleashed by the Internet are particularly important in business-to-business relationships, where uncertainties are being reduced by improving the quantity, reliability, and timeliness of information. Numerous companies are moving toward making most of their purchases online. Business-to-business Internet sales are more than $5 trillion.[28]

### Adoption and Use of Technology

Many companies lose their status as market leaders because they fail to keep up with technological changes. It is important for firms to determine when a technology is changing the industry and to define the strategic influence of the new technology. For example, wireless devices in use today include radios, cellphones, laptop computers, TVs, pagers, and car keys. To remain competitive, companies today must keep up with and adapt to technological advances.

The extent to which a firm can protect inventions stemming from research also influences its use of technology. How secure a product is from imitation depends on how easily others can copy it without violating its patent. If groundbreaking products and processes cannot be protected through patents, a company is less likely to market them and make the benefits of its research available to competitors.

Through a procedure known as *technology assessment*, managers try to foresee the effects of new products and processes on their firm's operations, on other business organizations, and on society in general. With information obtained through a technology assessment, management tries to estimate whether benefits of adopting a specific technology outweigh costs to the firm and to society at large. The degree to which a business is technologically based also influences its managers' response to technology.

# Sociocultural Forces

**sociocultural forces** The influences in a society and its culture(s) that change people's attitudes, beliefs, norms, customs, and lifestyles

**Sociocultural forces** are the influences in a society and its culture(s) that bring about changes in people's attitudes, beliefs, norms, customs, and lifestyles. Profoundly affecting how people live, these forces help determine what, where, how, and when people buy products. Like the other environmental forces, sociocultural forces present marketers with both challenges and opportunities. For a closer look at sociocultural forces, we examine three major issues: demographic and diversity characteristics, cultural values, and consumerism.

## Demographic and Diversity Characteristics

Changes in a population's demographic characteristics—age, gender, race, ethnicity, marital and parental status, income, and education—have a significant bearing on relationships and individual behavior. These shifts lead to changes in how people live and ultimately in their consumption of such products as food, clothing, housing, transportation, communication, recreation, education, and health services. We look at a few of the changes in demographics and diversity that are affecting marketing activities.

One demographic change affecting the marketplace is the increasing proportion of older consumers. According to the U.S. Bureau of the Census, the number of people age 65 and older is expected to more than double by the year 2050, reaching 96 million.[29] Consequently, marketers can expect significant increases in the demand for health-care services, recreation, tourism, retirement housing, and selected skin-care products. Del Webb Development Company is one firm taking advantage of this opportunity by creating several Sun City retirement communities for mature adults. In addition to providing housing, facilities, and activities designed for older residents, Del Webb's developments are typically situated to take advantage of a location's moderate climate, outdoor opportunities, and proximity to nearby cultural events. To reach older customers effectively, of course, marketers must understand the diversity within the mature market with respect to geographic location, income, marital status, and limitations in mobility and self-care.

The number of singles is also on the rise. Nearly 41 percent of U.S. adults are single, and many plan to remain that way. Moreover, single men living alone comprise 11 percent of all households (up from 3.5 percent in 1970), and single women living alone make up nearly 15 percent (up from 7.3 percent in 1970).[30] Single people have quite different spending patterns than couples and families with children. They are less likely to own homes and thus buy less furniture and fewer appliances. They spend more heavily on convenience foods, restaurants, travel, entertainment, and recreation. In addition, they tend to prefer smaller packages, whereas families often buy bulk goods and products packaged in multiple servings.

**Demographic Changes**
Today in the U.S., the rate of growth is higher in older age categories than in younger age categories. Some marketers are changing their product offerings to provide a greater number of products that meet the needs of older people.

The United States is entering another baby boom, with nearly 81 million Americans age 19 or younger. The new baby boom represents 28 percent of the total population; the original baby boomers, born between 1946 and 1964, account for nearly 27 percent.[31] The children of the original baby boomers differ from one another radically in terms of race, living arrangements, and socioeconomic status. Thus, the newest baby boom is much more diverse than previous generations.

Another noteworthy population trend is the increasingly multicultural nature of U.S. society. The number of immigrants into the United States has steadily risen during the last 40 years. In the 1960s, 3.3 million people immigrated to the United States; in the 1970s, 4.5 million came here; in the 1980s, 7.3 million arrived; and in the 1990s, the United States received 9.1 million immigrants.[32] In contrast to earlier immigrants, very few recent ones are of European origin. Another reason for the increasing cultural diversification of the United States is that most recent immigrants are relatively young, whereas U.S. citizens of European origin are growing older. These younger immigrants tend to have more children than their older counterparts, further shifting the population balance. By the turn of the twentieth century, the U.S. population had shifted from one dominated by whites to one consisting largely of three racial and ethnic groups: whites, blacks, and Hispanics. The U.S. government projects that by the year 2050, more than 102 million Hispanics, 61 million blacks, and 33 million Asians will call the United States home.[33] Figure 3.3 depicts how experts believe the U.S. population will change over the next 50 years.

# Boomers: Not Babies Anymore

Few factors have influenced the U.S. marketing environment more than the emergence of the baby boom generation. In one year alone, 1946, 3.4 million Americans were born, a jump from 2.8 million the year before. This birthrate explosion lasted 19 years and added 78 million people to the United States, which represented 26 percent of the population.

The baby boomers redefined every stage of the life cycle as they passed through it. They created the youth culture that brought us jeans, rock music, sexual permissiveness, and political alienation. Now this aging but still active generation controls 70 percent of the total net worth in the United States. Over the next 15 years, a boomer will turn 60 every 7 seconds. These older boomers will exert strong influence on the media as well as on industries such as fitness, food, and pharma-

ceuticals as they place more emphasis on their own well-being.

As the boomers get older, their needs and tastes will change, and successful marketers will change with them. Palo Alto–based IDEO, a product design firm, uses empathy tools to simulate the struggles that face the world's aging population. By using weighted gloves and boots, restrictive clothing, and glasses to impair vision, IDEO explores challenges faced by the elderly or disabled. Other companies, such as Ford Motor, have used similar technologies. Ford has begun using a specially designed suit to simulate the challenges faced by elderly drivers. Whirlpool has unveiled elevated washers and dryers that make it easier to load and unload laundry. Home Depot has expanded the company's services to help older customers make home improvements.

As the bulk of the U.S. population continues to age, companies must be mindful of the changes and challenges facing older customers. Those companies that adapt their products and services to this wealthy demographic will reap the benefits of the roughly $1.7 trillion spent annually by older Americans.

**figure 3.3**

## U.S. POPULATION PROJECTIONS BY RACE

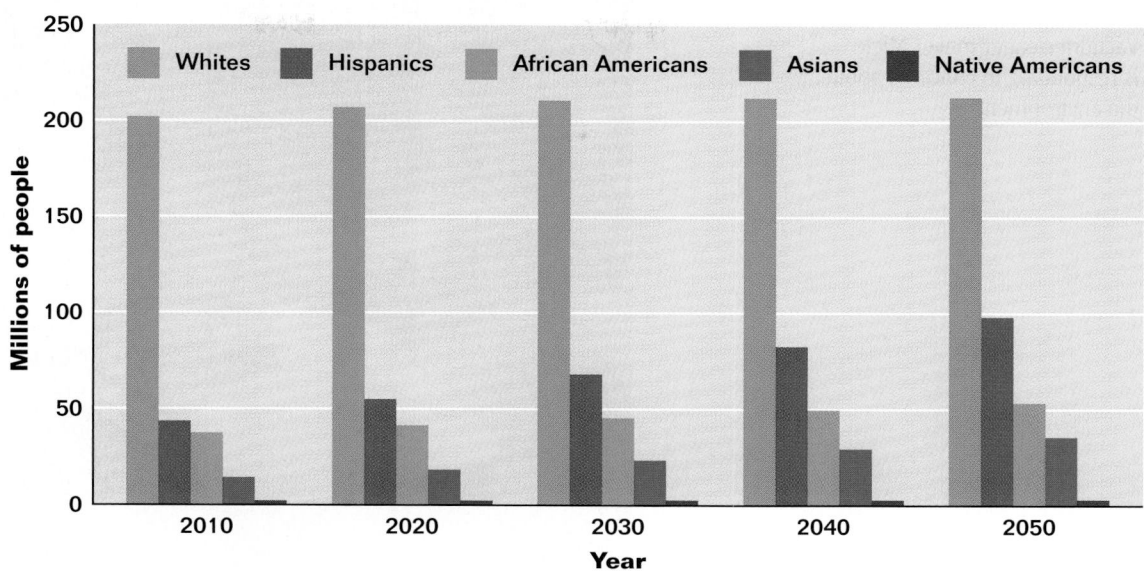

**Source:** U.S. Bureau of the Census, *Statistical Abstract of the United States,* 2000; Reed Business Info, July 11, 2005.

Marketers recognize that these profound changes in the U.S. population bring unique problems and opportunities. Hispanics, for example, wield about $736 billion in annual buying power, and experts project that figure will grow to $1,087 billion by 2010.[34] But a diverse population means a more diverse customer base, and marketing practices must be modified—and diversified—to meet its changing needs. Home and personal-care product company Unilever researched what messages appeal to Hispanic women and launched "*Secretos de belleza,*" a beauty secrets campaign honoring Latin women who serve their communities. Burger King sponsored the Latin Grammy Awards and an "Empowering Latinas" tour by *Catlina* magazine during Hispanic Heritage Month.[35] General Motors increased its minority marketing budget from $70 million to $140 million in 2002 and boosted it more than 50 percent for 2003, recognizing the growing buying power of ethnically diverse customers.[36]

### Cultural Values

Changes in cultural values have dramatically influenced people's needs and desires for products. Although cultural values do not shift overnight, they do change at varying speeds. Marketers try to monitor these changes, knowing this information can equip them to predict changes in consumers' needs for products at least in the near future.

Starting in the late 1980s, issues of health, nutrition, and exercise grew in importance. People today are more concerned about the foods they eat and thus are choosing healthier products. Compared to those in the previous two decades, Americans today are more likely to favor smoke-free environments and to consume less alcohol. They have also altered their sexual behavior to reduce the risk of contracting sexually transmitted diseases. Marketers have responded with a proliferation of foods, beverages, and exercise products that fit this new lifestyle, as well as with programs to help people quit smoking and contraceptives that are safer and more effective. Americans are also becoming increasingly open to alternative medicines and nutritionally improved foods. As a result, sales of organic foods, herbs and herbal remedies, vitamins, and dietary supplements have escalated. More marketers are investing in research into traditional herbal medicines and fortified foods to take advantage of this market opportunity. Celestial Seasonings, for example, has

**Cultural Values**
Changes in cultural values have resulted in a greater emphasis on preserving the environment. Vacuum cleaner maker Miele is responding to concerns about the environment.

developed herbal teas like Mama Bear's Cold Care, with Echinacea and mint, and Sleepytime, with chamomile.

The major source of cultural values is the family. For years, when asked about the most important aspects of their lives, adults specified family issues and a happy marriage. Today, however, only one out of three marriages is predicted to last. Values regarding the permanence of marriage are changing. Because a happy marriage is prized so highly, more people are willing to give up an unhappy one and seek a different marriage partner or opt to stay single. Children remain important, however. Marketers have responded with safer, upscale baby gear and supplies, children's electronics, and family entertainment products. Marketers are also aiming more marketing efforts directly at children because children often play pivotal roles in purchasing decisions.

Children and family values are also factors in the trend toward more eat-out and take-out meals. Busy families in which both parents work are usually eager to spend less time in the kitchen and more time together enjoying themselves. Beneficiaries of this trend have primarily been fast-food and casual restaurants like McDonald's, Taco Bell, and Applebee's, but 75 percent of grocery stores have added more ready-to-cook or ready-to-serve meal components to meet the needs of busy customers. Some also offer dine-in cafés.

Today's consumers are more and more concerned about the natural environment. One of society's environmental hurdles is proper disposal of waste, especially of nondegradable materials such as disposable diapers and polystyrene packaging. Companies have responded by developing more environmentally sensitive products and packaging. Procter & Gamble, for example, uses recycled materials in some of its packaging and sells environment-friendly refills. Raytheon has developed a new Amana refrigerator that does not use chlorofluorocarbons (CFCs), which harm the earth's ozone layer. A number of marketers sponsor recycling programs and encourage their customers to take part in them. Many organizations, including America's Electric Utility Companies and Phillips Petroleum, take pride in their efforts to protect the environment.

## Consumerism

**Consumerism** involves organized efforts by individuals, groups, and organizations to protect consumers' rights. The movement's major forces are individual consumer advocates, consumer organizations and other interest groups, consumer education, and consumer laws.

To achieve their objectives, consumers and their advocates write letters or send e-mails to companies, lobby government agencies, broadcast public service announcements, and boycott companies whose activities they deem irresponsible. Consider that most consumers would like to eliminate telemarketing and e-mail spam, and many have joined organizations and groups attempting to stop these activities. Companies that consistently and willfully ignore society's wishes on these issues fuel public desire for a regulatory response.[37] For example, several organizations evaluate children's products for safety, often announcing dangerous products before Christmas so parents can avoid them. Other actions by the consumer movement have resulted in seat belts and air bags in automobiles, dolphin-free tuna, the banning of unsafe three-wheel motorized vehicles, and numerous laws regulating product safety and information. We take a closer look at consumerism in the next chapter.

## SUMMARY

The marketing environment consists of external forces that directly or indirectly influence an organization's acquisition of inputs (personnel, financial resources, raw materials, and information) and generation of outputs (goods, services, and ideas). The marketing environment includes competitive, economic, political, legal and regulatory, technological, and sociocultural forces.

Environmental scanning is the process of collecting information about forces in the marketing environment; environmental analysis is the process of assessing and interpreting information obtained in scanning. This information helps marketing managers predict opportunities and threats associated with environmental fluctuation. Marketing managers may assume either a passive, reactive approach or a proactive, aggressive approach in responding to these environmental fluctuations. The choice depends on the organization's structures and needs and on the composition of environmental forces that affect it.

All businesses compete for customers' dollars. A marketer, however, generally defines *competition* as other firms that market products that are similar to or can be substituted for its products in the same geographic area. These competitors can be classified into one of four types: brand competitors, product competitors, generic competitors, and total budget competitors. The number of firms controlling the supply of a product may affect the strength of competitors. The four general types of competitive structures are monopoly, oligopoly, monopolistic competition, and pure competition. Marketers monitor what competitors are currently doing and assess changes occurring in the competitive environment.

General economic conditions, buying power, and willingness to spend can strongly influence marketing decisions and activities. The overall state of the economy fluctuates in a general pattern known as the business cycle, which consists of four stages: prosperity, recession, depression, and recovery. Consumers' goods, services, and financial holdings make up their buying power, or ability to purchase. Financial sources of buying power are income, credit, and wealth. After-tax income used for spending or saving is disposable income. Disposable income left after an individual has purchased the basic necessities of food, clothes, and shelter is discretionary income. Factors affecting buyers' willingness to spend include product price; level of satisfaction obtained from currently used products; family size; and expectations about future employment, income, prices, and general economic conditions.

The political, legal, and regulatory forces of the marketing environment are closely interrelated. The political environment may determine what laws and regulations affecting specific marketers are enacted and how much the government purchases and from which suppliers. It can also be important in helping organizations secure foreign markets.

Federal legislation affecting marketing activities can be divided into procompetitive legislation—laws designed to preserve and encourage competition—and consumer protection laws, which generally relate to product safety and information disclosure. Actual effects of legislation are determined by how marketers and courts interpret the laws. Federal guidelines for sentencing violations of these laws represent an attempt to force marketers to comply with the laws.

Federal, state, and local regulatory agencies usually have power to enforce specific laws and some discretion in establishing operating rules and drawing up regulations to guide certain types of industry practices. Industry self-regulation represents another regulatory force; marketers view this type of regulation more favorably than government action because they have more opportunity to take part in creating guidelines. Self-regulation may be less expensive than government regulation, and its guidelines are generally more realistic. However, such regulation generally cannot ensure compliance as effectively as government agencies.

Technology is the application of knowledge and tools to solve problems and perform tasks more efficiently. Consumer demand, product development, packaging, promotion, prices, and distribution systems are all influenced directly by technology.

Sociocultural forces are the influences in a society and its culture that result in changes in attitudes, beliefs, norms, customs, and lifestyles. Major sociocultural issues directly affecting marketers include demographic and diversity characteristics, cultural values, and consumerism.

Changes in a population's demographic characteristics, such as age, income, race, and ethnicity, can lead to changes in that population's consumption of products. Changes in cultural values, such as those relating to health, nutrition, family, and the natural environment, have had striking effects on people's needs for products and therefore are closely monitored by marketers. Consumerism involves the efforts of individuals, groups, and organizations to protect consumers' rights. Consumer rights organizations inform and organize other consumers, raise issues, help businesses develop consumer-oriented programs, and pressure lawmakers to enact consumer protection laws.

**ACE self-test**

Please visit the student website at **www.prideferrell.com** for ACE Self-Test questions that will help you prepare for exams.

## IMPORTANT TERMS

| | | | |
|---|---|---|---|
| Environmental scanning | Oligopoly | Buying power | Better Business Bureau |
| Environmental analysis | Monopolistic competition | Income | (BBB) |
| Competition | Pure competition | Disposable income | National Advertising |
| Brand competitors | Business cycle | Discretionary income | Review Board (NARB) |
| Product competitors | Prosperity | Wealth | Technology |
| Generic competitors | Recession | Willingness to spend | Sociocultural forces |
| Total budget competitors | Depression | Federal Trade Commission | Consumerism |
| Monopoly | Recovery | (FTC) | |

## DISCUSSION & REVIEW QUESTIONS

1. Why are environmental scanning and analysis important to marketers?

2. What are the four types of competition? Which is most important to marketers?

3. In what ways can each of the business cycle stages affect consumers' reactions to marketing strategies?

4. What business cycle stage are we experiencing currently? How is this stage affecting business firms in your area?

5. Define *income, disposable income,* and *discretionary income.* How does each type of income affect consumer buying power?

6. How do wealth and consumer credit affect consumer buying power?

7. What factors influence a buyer's willingness to spend?

8. Describe marketers' attempts to influence political forces.

9. What types of problems do marketers experience as they interpret legislation?

10. What are the goals of the Federal Trade Commission? List the ways in which the FTC affects marketing activities. Do you think a single regulatory agency should have such broad jurisdiction over so many marketing practices? Why or why not?

11. Name several nongovernmental regulatory forces. Do you believe self-regulation is more or less effective than governmental regulatory agencies? Why?

12. What does the term *technology* mean to you? Do the benefits of technology outweigh its costs and potential dangers? Defend your answer.

13. Discuss the impact of technology on marketing activities.

14. What factors determine whether a business organization adopts and uses technology?

15. What evidence exists that cultural diversity is increasing in the United States?

16. In what ways are cultural values changing? How are marketers responding to these changes?

17. Describe consumerism. Analyze some active consumer forces in your area.

## APPLICATION QUESTIONS

1. Assume you are opening one of the following retail stores. Identify publications at the library or online that provide information about the environmental forces likely to affect the store. Briefly summarize the information each source provides.
   a. Convenience store
   b. Women's clothing store
   c. Grocery store
   d. Fast-food restaurant
   e. Furniture store

2. For each of the following products, identify brand competitors, product competitors, generic competitors, and total budget competitors.
   a. Dodge Caravan minivan
   b. Levi's jeans
   c. America Online

3. Technological advances and sociocultural forces have a great impact on marketers. Identify at least one technological advance and one sociocultural change that has affected you as a consumer. Explain the impact of each change on your needs as a customer.

**globalEDGE™**

1. Free trade influences the global marketing environment in many ways. Though contingent on the bylaws of a specific free trade agreement, such contracts between countries typically increase the number of competitors from abroad contending with current players in the market. The Free Trade Area of the Americas (FTAA) is one such example. More information about this trade agreement can be found using the search term "FTAA" at **http://global edge.msu.edu/ibrd** to access the FTAA. How many FTAA members are there? Besides the United States, which are the most prominent members? Are there any countries that are conspicuously absent?

2. Globalization is a phenomenon that is affecting many countries. As a result, your firm is attempting to define its own role in a globalizing environment with a particular focus on western Europe. Public opinion regarding the globalization trend is likely to influence many competitive and market forces worldwide for a prolonged period of time. To gain valuable information about attitudes toward globalization in western European countries, use the search term "public opinion analysis" at **http://globaledge.msu. edu/ibrd** to access the Eurobarometer website and follow the Globalization link. To help your firm develop its European marketing strategy, identify the top two markets that support globalization and the top four markets that oppose globalization. From these results, what conclusions do you draw in your effort to enter these markets?

**INTERNET Exercise**

Visit **www.prideferrell.com** for resources to help you master the material in this chapter, plus materials that will help you expand your marketing knowledge, including Internet exercise updates, ACE Self-Tests, hotlinks to companies featured in this chapter, and much more.

### The Federal Trade Commission

To learn more about the Federal Trade Commission and its functions, look at the FTC's website at **www.ftc.gov**.

1. Based on information on the website, describe the FTC's impact on marketing.
2. Examine the sections entitled Newsroom and Formal Actions. Describe three recent incidents of illegal or inappropriate marketing activities and the FTC's response to those actions.
3. How could the FTC's website assist a company in avoiding misconduct?

## Video Case 3.1   At Life is good.®, Life Is Great

Brothers John and Bert Jacobs believe in doing what you love and loving what you do. Not interested in the 9-to-5, they came up with the challenging—some might say crazy—idea of selling T-shirts with original designs door-to-door on New England college campuses. The pair traveled around and lived in a van, living off peanut butter and jelly and using their T-shirt inventory as pillows and blankets. "There were nights when it would be zero degrees and we'd be freezing in the van, burying ourselves in T-shirts," recalls John. "But we also had a lot of laughs. Life was good, even when we were sleeping in the van." It was this positive attitude, along with odd jobs delivering pizza and teaching skiing lessons, that kept the Jacobs brothers going.

John was an art major in college and designed a cartoon character the brothers named Jake, a shorter version of their last name that was their mutual high school nickname. Jake is a cartoon stick figure with a gigantic smile, an artist's beret, and very cool sunglasses. Armed with $78, John and Bert printed a run of T-shirts featuring the laid-back Jake and their own personal motto: "Life is good." At that point, a normal day of sales was around 20 shirts, so when the entire 48-shirt production of Jake sold out before noon, John and Bert knew they were onto something. Startled by the popularity of Jake and his "Life is good." attitude, the brothers scrapped all of their other designs and began printing only Jake. They sold $80,000 of T-shirts the first year.

Today, life is indeed very good for the Jacobs brothers. Their company, aptly named Life is good., sells over $55 million worth of T-shirts and other merchandise annually. Jake is still the primary image of the brand. "Jake is our leader," claims Bert. An outdoorsy type who takes it easy and enjoys the simple things in life, "[Jake] could be any demographic; that's the beauty of him. He's just a free-thinking guy who doesn't take things too seriously." These days Jake appears hiking, rollerblading, golfing, practicing yoga, or relaxing in a hammock or beach chair. He has adopted a dog named Rocket and briefly had a female counterpart named Jackie. The character was dropped because the Jacobs felt that she detracted from Jake's ability to represent everyone. "Sure, Jake's a guy, but really, he's a stick figure. He's supposed to represent a feeling," explains Bert. And the feeling must be contagious because Jake has become a phenomenon.

But Jake and Rocket aren't limited to T-shirts anymore. Since the company officially started in 1994, the product catalog has grown from a single page to over 70 pages. There are successful lines of Life is good. hats, yoga apparel, baby clothes, Frisbees, stickers, beach towels, and coffee mugs. The company has also added metal and stone jewelry engraved with Jake's smiling face. Life is good. flip flops and sandals were a natural choice for this laid-back company because the Jacobs brothers wear them every day to work. The focus on sporting goods has increased, as the brothers have added performance items like river shorts for hiking and boating. Bert says that furniture is in the works as well. In fact, although the brothers insist that T-shirts are still the heart of the brand, they now make up only a small portion of the company's sales. Life is good. has adapted its catalog to continue growth, but the broad appeal of its products increases the number of competitors to sporting goods, surf and skate, resort, running, spa and wellness, and golf apparel.

Life is good. sells its goods in other countries as well, including Mexico, Japan, Greece, and Germany. One of the most amazing parts of the Life is good. story is that the company has never used paid advertising. It has relied solely on word of mouth to spread its good cheer. The company briefly considered developing radio spots, but decided to donate the money to charity instead. Bert and John aren't content to merely spread a positive vibe; they also want to create positive change, especially for children. The brothers work with several New England–based charitable organizations to help underprivileged and sick children. Life is good. spends its entire promotional budget on holding several outdoor festivals every year. All of the proceeds from these events are donated to Project Joy and Camp Sunshine. The brothers consider the festivals the most important part of their business. "Being able to impact the lives of children is much more fulfilling than a pile of money and a Mercedes Benz," says Bert.

Because of their focus on creating positive change, this unconventional duo has rejected several multimillion-dollar buyout offers. Instead, they are focusing on keeping Life is good. on the right track financially and

socially. Although Life is good. is constantly adapting to change, the Jacobs brothers haven't changed a bit. They believe that the same positive outlook that got them through those cold nights in the back of their van is the key to their continued success. "The foundation of our brand is optimism, and optimism is timeless," explains Bert. "It always has a place in every demographic and in every economy, and it's always something that's in need."[38]

### Questions for Discussion

1. Which marketing environment forces are likely to have the greatest impact on Life is good.?
2. What types of organizations are most likely to exert the greatest competitive forces on Life is good.?
3. Are there environmental forces that have contributed to the success of Life is good.? Explain.

## Case 3.2     Chipping Away the Fat at Frito-Lay

Frito-Lay knows that yesterday's recipe for success is not necessarily today's. Owned by PepsiCo, Frito-Lay sells 15 billion bags of salty snacks every year under such well-known brands as Lay's, Doritos, Cheetos, Tostitos, and Ruffles. However, sales of potato chips and other similar snacks have flattened in recent years in part due to growing public concerns about widespread obesity and the health consequences of certain fats. The resulting changes in customer attitudes and regulatory guidelines have prompted Frito-Lay to reformulate both its recipes and its marketing efforts.

Food manufacturers turned to partially hydrogenated oils to enhance snack taste, texture, and stability after health experts linked the saturated fats in butter and palm oil to higher cholesterol levels and coronary heart disease. Years later, however, experts determined that these partially hydrogenated vegetable oils, also known as trans fats, were themselves linked to the risk of heart disease and diabetes. In Europe, Unilever took the early initiative in responding to these concerns by voluntarily reducing or eliminating trans fats. In fact, the success of Unilever's trans-fat-free margarine encouraged competing food manufacturers to introduce margarines made without trans fats.

In the United States, the Food and Drug Administration (FDA) deliberated for ten years before requiring manufacturers to specify the amount of trans fats on food labels. As long as they did not have to change their labels, most major food manufacturers had resisted reducing or eliminating trans fats because of the expense of developing new products and changing processing

systems. Meanwhile, however, customers were learning more about the dangers of trans fats, and some were switching to healthier snack alternatives. This benefited companies marketing organic and "all-natural" snacks without trans fats, but put more pressure on companies marketing snacks containing trans fats.

Frito-Lay was already offering some low-fat, reduced-fat, and no-fat snacks. For example, it made Lay's potato chips with corn oil rather than trans fats. Parent PepsiCo's senior management also recognized that customers' attitudes toward health and diet were changing. PepsiCo had invited prominent doctors to a health and wellness conference attended by representatives of Frito-Lay and other divisions. Frito-Lay's CEO vividly remembers that after the doctors told the group, "The single biggest thing you could do is to eliminate trans fats," he decided to do just that. Although this required investing in new production technologies and locating substitute ingredients, the CEO was convinced that the reformulated snacks would be more appealing to customers. Moreover, he believed the decision would demonstrate Frito-Lay's leadership within the industry, an important competitive consideration.

Based on this decision, Frito-Lay product developers came up with trans-fat-free recipes, and the company announced the changeover with a $2 million ad campaign. The headline was clear and to the point: "Great News! America's Favorite Snacks Have 0 Grams of Trans Fats." In addition, the company worked with a doctor to create a special Smart Snack label for products that meet certain nutritional guidelines for calorie, fat, trans fat, and sodium content. The company later changed that label to a green Smart Spot label in 2005 to help customers find healthier snacks quickly. Frito-Lay's parent company also boosted promotional efforts of Smart Spot–labeled products targeted at minority communities.

Eyeing the growing demand for natural products, Frito-Lay also created a line of natural, reduced-fat potato chips and introduced salty-snack alternatives such as snack bars and breakfast bars. "Today's consumers are more aware of what they eat, and we know they want better snack choices," explained Frito-Lay's vice president of North American marketing.

The company was the first in the industry to list trans-fat information on snack food labels, two years ahead of the January 2006 deadline for the new labeling set by the FDA. Kraft and other Frito-Lay competitors also prepared for the change by revamping their products to reduce or replace trans fats and adding label information to comply with the new regulations. Nutrition experts agree that eliminating trans fats is a step in the right direction, but some express reservations about promoting chips and similar snacks on the basis of diet and health. "A no-trans-fat potato chip has just as many calories as a trans-fat chip," stresses a spokesperson at the Center for Science in the Public Interest.

Because Frito-Lay had addressed the trans-fat challenge in advance of new food labeling rules, it could seize the opportunity to introduce new flavors and new snacks based on feedback from marketing research. The vice president of potato chip marketing com-

mented, "We're going back to basics with an emphasis on flavor. Consumers told us that flavor is the number one driver for eating chips." Other studies indicated that customers were choosing Procter & Gamble's Pringles crisps over Lay's chips because they wanted a "clean-eating snack." Therefore, after five years of research, development, and testing, the company introduced Lay's Stax—uniform, scoop-shaped potato crisps in a resealable plastic container—to compete head-on with Pringles.

Thanks to the new labeling requirement and increased public awareness of the health risks of trans fats, the $90 billion snack category will never be the same. Some customers will go out of their way to find snacks without trans fats, and some will use label information to compare the amount of trans fats when choosing among competing brands. Either way, Frito-Lay is in a position to benefit. Sales of Smart Spot–labeled products have already climbed 13 percent and now account for 41 percent of PepsiCo's North American sales.[39]

## Questions for Discussion

1. How did competition affect Frito-Lay's responses to the changes in the marketing environment? How did cultural values affect the decisions made by food manufacturers in the snack food industry?
2. Why would Frito-Lay make a point of being the first food manufacturer to eliminate trans fats from its best-selling snack products years before the new labeling requirement took effect?

# Social Responsibility and Ethics in Marketing

## Cartoon Characters Lighten Up

Companies have been using cartoon characters in advertising since Mickey Mouse appeared on the Post Toasties cereal box in 1935. But today children's advocates are growing increasingly concerned about the amount of advertising targeted at children, and particularly about the use of popular cartoon characters to promote unhealthy foods to children. Studies by the Kaiser Family Foundation found that the average child sees about 40,000 advertisements a year on television, most of which endorse candy, cereal, fast food, and soft drinks. A report by the Institute of Medicine provided "strong evidence" that advertising is linked with obesity in young children.

The Kaiser studies suggest that food ads may not only influence the food choices children make but may confuse them regarding what is good for them and what is not. They also found that companies can have a positive impact on children by using their favorite characters to advertise healthier foods. The Institute of Medicine has also recommended that food companies use licensed characters to promote only healthful food choices.

Although some companies have been silent on the issue thus far, others are making positive changes. Kraft Foods, for example, decided to curtail advertising sugary snacks and cereals to children and has begun limiting its use of cartoon characters in an effort to support better nutrition for children younger than 12. PepsiCo has begun labeling some of its products to help children identify more healthful choices. Although Kellogg is using Chicken Little to advertise its cereal Fruit Loops, the cereal boxes show Chicken Little teaching children how to choose healthy breakfast foods, and Viacom recently agreed to place SpongeBob SquarePants on spinach packages. Although some companies are making efforts to encourage healthier food choices for children, the food industry as a whole needs to agree on the definition of a healthy food—no easy task and something many would rather not do.[1] ■

OBJECTIVES

1. To understand the concept and dimensions of social responsibility

2. To define and describe the importance of marketing ethics

3. To become familiar with ways to improve ethical decisions in marketing

4. To understand the role of social responsibility and ethics in improving marketing performance

Most marketers operate responsibly and within the limits of the law. However, some companies engage in activities that customers, other marketers, and society in general deem unacceptable. Such activities include questionable selling practices, bribery, price discrimination, deceptive advertising, misleading packaging, and marketing defective products. Practices of this kind raise questions about marketers' obligations to society. Inherent in these questions are the issues of social responsibility and marketing ethics.

Because social responsibility and ethics often have profound impacts on the success of marketing strategies, we devote this chapter to their role in marketing decision making. We begin by defining social responsibility and exploring its dimensions. We then discuss social responsibility issues, such as the natural environment and the marketer's role as a member of the community. Next, we define and examine the role of ethics in marketing decisions. We consider ethical issues in marketing, the ethical decision making process, and ways to improve ethical conduct in marketing. Finally, we incorporate social responsibility and ethics into strategic market planning.

# The Nature of Social Responsibility

**social responsibility** An organization's obligation to maximize its positive impact and minimize its negative impact on society

In marketing, **social responsibility** refers to an organization's obligation to maximize its positive impact and minimize its negative impact on society. Social responsibility thus deals with the total effect of all marketing decisions on society. In marketing, social responsibility includes the managerial processes needed to monitor, satisfy, and even exceed stakeholder expectations and needs.[2] Remember from Chapter 1 that stakeholders are groups that have a "stake," or claim, in some aspect of a company's products, operations, markets, industry, and outcomes.

Ample evidence demonstrates that ignoring stakeholders' demands for responsible marketing can destroy customers' trust and even prompt government regulations. Irresponsible actions that anger customers, employees, or competitors may not only jeopardize a marketer's financial standing but have legal repercussions as well. For instance, after news reports that pharmaceutical giant Merck was aware that its arthritis-fighting drug Vioxx may cause heart problems, the firm's stock plummeted and hundreds of lawsuits were filed against the company. The company had already pulled the drug from the market.[3] In contrast, socially responsible activities can generate positive publicity and boost sales. The Breast Cancer Awareness Crusade sponsored by Avon Products, for example, has helped raise nearly $400 million to fund community-based breast cancer education and early detection services. Within the first few years of the Awareness Crusade, hundreds of stories about Avon's efforts appeared in major media, which contributed to an increase in company sales. Avon, a marketer of women's cosmetics, is also known for employing a large number of women and promoting them to top management; the firm has more female top managers (86 percent) than any other Fortune 500 company.[4]

Recycling that's easy to wrap around.

Wrapping yourself around a plan that recycles your used rechargeable batteries is easy. Check the batteries in your cordless and cellular phones, camcorders, cordless power tools, laptop computers, digital cameras, and two-way radios. If they no longer hold a charge, recycle them by visiting one of many collection sites nationwide, including those retailers listed below. For a complete list of rechargeable battery drop-off locations, visit **www.call2recycle.org** or call toll free **877-2-RECYCLE**.

Recycle your rechargeable batteries.

call②recycle
A Rechargeable Battery Recycling Corporation program

Recycle at one of these national retailers:   BatteriesPlus.+   BestBuy   Office DEPOT   RadioShack.   Sears   STAPLES   ⊙ TARGET

©2006 Rechargeable Battery Recycling Corporation. Founded in 1994, RBRC is a non-profit organization dedicated to recycling rechargeable batteries and cellular phones. For more information: www.rbrc.org or 1-800-8-BATTERY. To learn more about the animal featured in this ad, visit our web site.

**The Nature of Social Responsibility**

Recognizing their environmental responsibility, companies such as Target, Staples, and Sears encourage recycling of batteries.

Socially responsible efforts like Avon's have a positive impact on local communities; at the same time, they indirectly help the sponsoring organization by attracting goodwill, publicity, and potential customers and employees. Thus, while social responsibility is certainly a positive concept in itself, most organizations embrace it in the expectation of indirect long-term benefits. Our own research suggests that an organizational culture that is conducive to social responsibility engenders greater employee commitment and improved business performance.[5] Table 4.1 provides a sampling of companies that have chosen to make social responsibility a strategic long-term objective.

## The Dimensions of Social Responsibility

Socially responsible organizations strive for **marketing citizenship** by adopting a strategic focus for fulfilling the economic, legal, ethical, and philanthropic social responsibilities that their stakeholders expect of them. Companies that consider the diverse perspectives of stakeholders in their daily operations and strategic planning

| table 4.1 | BUSINESS ETHICS BEST CORPORATE CITIZENS 2006 |
|---|---|
| 1 | Green Mountain Coffee Roasters, Inc. |
| 2 | Hewlett-Packard Company |
| 3 | Advanced Micro Devices, Inc. |
| 4 | Motorola, Inc. |
| 5 | Agilent Technologies, Inc. |
| 6 | Timberland Company (The) |
| 7 | Salesforce.com, Inc. |
| 8 | Cisco Systems, Inc. |
| 9 | Dell Inc. |
| 10 | Texas Instruments Incorporated |
| 11 | Intel Corporation |
| 12 | Johnson and Johnson |
| 13 | NIKE, Inc. |
| 14 | General Mills Incorporated |
| 15 | Pitney Bowes, Inc. |
| 16 | Wells Fargo & Company |
| 17 | Starbucks Corporation |
| 18 | Wainright Bank & Trust Company |
| 19 | St. Paul Travelers Companies, Inc. (The) |
| 20 | Ecolab Inc. |

**Source:** From "100 Corporations: Best Corporate Citizens 2005," *Business Ethics,* Spring 2005, p. 22. Reprinted with permission from *Business Ethics,* PO Box 8439, Minneapolis, MN 55408. **www.business-ethics.com**.

**The Dimensions of Social Responsibility**

Chevron addresses the very issue that consumers have with its products.

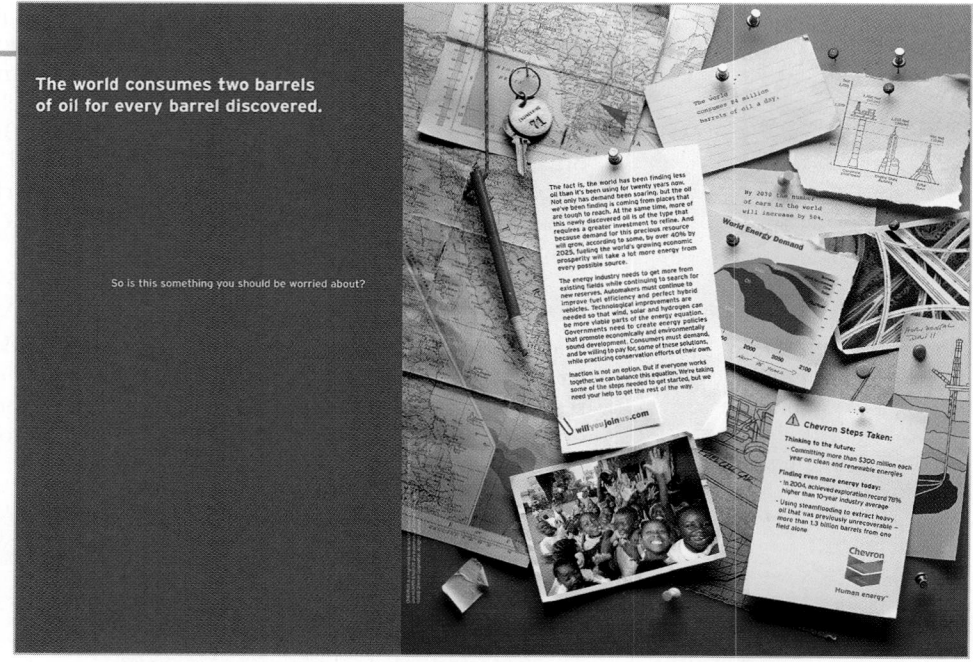

The world consumes two barrels of oil for every barrel discovered.

So is this something you should be worried about?

are said to have a *stakeholder orientation,* an important element of social responsibility.[6] A stakeholder orientation in marketing goes beyond customers, competitors, and regulators to include understanding and addressing the needs of all stakeholders, including communities and special interest groups. As a result, organizations are now under pressure to undertake initiatives that demonstrate a balanced perspective on stakeholder interests.[7] Ford Motor, for example, has secured stakeholder input on a number of issues including human rights and climate change.[8] As Figure 4.1 shows, the economic, legal, ethical, and philanthropic dimensions of social responsibility can be viewed as a pyramid.[9] The economic and legal aspects have long been

**figure 4.1**

## THE PYRAMID OF CORPORATE SOCIAL RESPONSIBILITY

**Source:** From Archie B. Carroll, "The Pyramid of Corporate Social Responsibility: Toward the Moral Management of Organizational Stakeholders," adaptation of Figure 3, p. 42. Reprinted from *Business Horizons,* July/Aug. 1991. Copyright © 1991 by the Foundation for the School of Business at Indiana University. Reprinted with permission.

**RESPONSIBILITIES**

**Philanthropic**
*Be a good
corporate citizen*
▶ Contribute resources to the
community; improve quality of life

**Ethical**
*Be ethical*
▶ Obligation to do what is right, just, and fair
▶ Avoid harm

**Legal**
*Obey the law*
▶ Law is society's codification of right and wrong
▶ Play by the rules of the game

**Economic**
*Be profitable*
▶ The foundation upon which all others rest

acknowledged, whereas ethical and philanthropic issues have gained recognition more recently.

At the most basic level, all companies have an economic responsibility to be profitable so they can provide a return on investment to their owners and investors, create jobs for the community, and contribute goods and services to the economy. How organizations relate to stockholders, employees, competitors, customers, the community, and the natural environment affects the economy. When economic downturns or poor decisions lead companies to lay off employees, communities often suffer as they attempt to absorb the displaced employees. Customers may experience diminished levels of service as a result of fewer experienced employees. Stock prices often decline when layoffs are announced, affecting the value of shareholders' investment portfolios. Moreover, stressed-out employees facing demands to reduce expenses may make poor decisions that affect the natural environment, product quality, employee rights, and customer service. An organization's sense of economic responsibility is especially significant for employees, raising such issues as equal job opportunities, workplace diversity, job safety, health, and employee privacy. Economic responsibilities require finding a balance between society's demand for social responsibility and investors' desire for profits.

Marketers also have an economic responsibility to compete fairly. Size frequently gives companies an advantage over rivals. Large firms can often generate economies of scale that allow them to put smaller firms out of business. Consequently small companies and even whole communities may resist the efforts of firms like Wal-Mart, Home Depot, and Best Buy to open stores in their vicinity. These firms are able to operate at such low costs that small, local firms cannot compete. Though consumers appreciate lower prices, the failure of small businesses creates unemployment for some members of the community. Such issues create concerns about social responsibility for organizations, communities, and consumers.

# Nestlé in Africa: Doing the Right Thing

Since Nestlé opened the first of 27 African factories in South Africa in 1927, African consumers have come to view Nestlé products as a familiar part of their lives. The company employs about 11,500 people in Africa, and only 120 of them are non-Africans. And Nestlé's suppliers provide about 50,000 additional jobs there. In 2004, the dean of the University of Ibadan's Faculty of Social Sciences reported that in Nigeria "Nestlé employees earn more than the average in manufacturing. . . . More than 75% said that if given the choice to change jobs, they would decline."

Nestlé is the largest direct buyer of coffee in the world. Although it does not own farmland in Africa, it does work to help local farmers improve the quality of their crops and often their incomes. Improving the quality helps the farmers become more competitive in the global market.

The company is committed to improving farming labor standards, promoting local African products, preserving water, creating less waste, offering nutrition education, and fostering free trade. Nestlé also contributes to the United Nation's Millennium Development Goals in Africa, which are to eliminate extreme poverty and hunger, achieve universal primary education, promote gender equality and empower women, lessen child mortality, improve maternal health, combat HIV/AIDS and other diseases, foster environmental sustainability, and develop a global partnership for development. Peter Brabeck-Letmathe, Nestlé's chief executive, says, "We can really do good—not only for the communities and countries we're working with, but also for us."

Marketers are also expected, of course, to obey laws and regulations. The efforts of elected representatives and special-interest groups to promote responsible corporate behavior have resulted in laws and regulations designed to keep U.S. companies' actions within the range of acceptable conduct. When marketers engage in deceptive practices to advance their own interests over those of others, charges of fraud may result. In general, fraud is any purposeful communication that deceives, manipulates, or conceals facts in order to create a false impression. It is considered a crime, and convictions may result in fines, imprisonment, or both. Fraud costs U.S. companies more than $600 billion a year; the average company loses about 6 percent of total revenues to fraud and abuses committed by its own employees.[10]

When customers, interest groups, or businesses become outraged over what they perceive as irresponsibility on the part of a marketing organization, they may urge their legislators to draft new legislation to regulate the behavior or engage in litigation to force the organization to "play by the rules." Office Depot, for example, filed a lawsuit against Staples, accusing its rival of trademark infringement, unfair competition, false advertising, and deceptive trade practices for allegedly improperly buying online advertisements at search engines that redirected potential customers to Staples' website.[11]

# Wal-Mart Struggles to Satisfy Stakeholders

Wal-Mart is the world's largest company, with 5,000 stores and 1.7 million employees around the globe; its revenues are in excess of $300 billion. It is often called a "retail giant," but some argue that this is an understatement given the enormous influence the company wields. This power has enormous ethical and social implications.

Suppliers report that Wal-Mart can dictate almost every aspect of their operations—from product design to prices—in an effort to deliver maximum savings to the consumer. To meet Wal-Mart's demands for lower prices, some suppliers have been forced to lay off employees or to move operations to countries where production costs are lower. Companies that balk risk finding their products replaced by a competitor's on Wal-Mart's lucrative shelves.

Wal-Mart stores can also

wreak havoc on businesses and workers in communities. The demise of local businesses means the loss of jobs, and although Wal-Mart may rehire some workers, Wal-Mart employees generally receive lower pay and fewer benefits than workers at other retail stores. Because of the vast Wal-Mart workforce, these policies have been blamed for driving down retail wages across the United States. Other ethical and legal issues relate to allegations that Wal-Mart workers have been forced to work "off the clock" and that the company has discriminated against women and minorities in promotions to management positions.

Unquestionably there are benefits to Wal-Mart's philosophy: it has compelled suppliers to concentrate on efficiency and to innovate with new products, revived more than one floundering company, and directly and indirectly saved consumers an estimated $100 billion a year. But the real costs of Wal-Mart's philosophy have yet to be tallied. As the world's largest retailer, it must accept the public scrutiny and social responsibilities that come with the territory.

**marketing ethics** Principles and standards that define acceptable marketing conduct as determined by various stakeholders

Economic and legal responsibilities are the most basic levels of social responsibility for a good reason: failure to consider them may mean that a marketer is not around long enough to engage in ethical or philanthropic activities. Beyond these dimensions is **marketing ethics**, principles and standards that define acceptable conduct in marketing as determined by various stakeholders, including the public, government regulators, private-interest groups, consumers, industry, and the organization itself. The most basic of these principles have been codified as laws and regulations to encourage marketers to conform to society's expectations for conduct. However, marketing ethics goes beyond legal issues. Ethical marketing decisions foster trust, which helps build long-term marketing relationships. We take a more detailed look at the ethical dimension of social responsibility later in this chapter.

At the top of the pyramid of corporate responsibility (see Figure 4.1) are philanthropic responsibilities. These responsibilities, which go beyond marketing ethics, are not required of a company, but they promote human welfare or goodwill, as do the economic, legal, and ethical dimensions of social responsibility. That many companies have demonstrated philanthropic responsibility is evidenced by the more than $12 billion in annual corporate donations and contributions to environmental and social causes.[12] After Hurricane Katrina killed more than 1,000 people and devastated New Orleans and parts of the Gulf Coast, many corporations—including Anheuser-Busch, BP, Capitol One, Cingular, DuPont, General Motors, Lowe's, Office Depot, Toyota, Wal-Mart, and many more—donated millions of dollars in cash, supplies, equipment, food, and medicine to help victims. Other firms matched employee donations or provided mechanisms through which customers could donate funds and supplies to help with relief efforts.[13] Even small companies participate in philanthropy through donations and volunteer support of local causes and national charities, such as the Red Cross and the United Way.

**cause-related marketing** The practice of linking products to a particular social cause on an ongoing or short-term basis

More companies than ever are adopting a strategic approach to corporate philanthropy. Many firms link their products to a particular social cause on an ongoing or short-term basis, a practice known as **cause-related marketing**. American Express, for example, donated $1 to the St. Jude's Research Hospital for every American Express Gift Card purchased.[14] Such cause-related programs tend to appeal to consumers because they provide an additional reason to "feel good" about a particular purchase. Marketers like the programs because well-designed ones increase sales and create feelings of respect and admiration for the companies involved. Indeed, research suggests that attitudes toward both the cause and the product may be enhanced when consumers view the association as plausible and favorable.[15] Research further indicates that such corporate support of causes generates trust in a company for 80 percent of those surveyed.[16]

**strategic philanthropy** The synergistic use of organizational core competencies and resources to address key stakeholders' interests and achieve both organizational and social benefits

Some companies are beginning to extend the concept of corporate philanthropy beyond financial contributions by adopting a **strategic philanthropy** approach, the synergistic use of organizational core competencies and resources to address key stakeholders' interests and achieve both organizational and social benefits. Strategic philanthropy involves employees, organizational resources and expertise, and the ability to link those assets to the concerns of key stakeholders, including employees, customers, suppliers, and social needs. Strategic philanthropy involves both financial and nonfinancial contributions to stakeholders (employee time, goods and services, and company technology and equipment, as well as facilities), but it also benefits the company.[17] Home Depot, for example,

## marketing ENTREPRENEURS

**Amy Simmons**

THE BUSINESS: Amy's Ice Cream

FOUNDED: 1984

SUCCESS: $5 million in sales through 13 stores and a wholesale business

Back in 1984, Amy Simmons knew that traditional corporate life was just not for her. Having worked in an ice cream store while in college, Amy was familiar with the business, so she and a partner wrote a hot check for the first month's rent and opened Amy's Ice Cream in Austin, Texas. The store's high-quality ingredients and creative flavors, coupled with the zany antics of its behind-the-counter "scoopers," quickly gained it a loyal following and made Amy an Austin icon. Now with 160 employees and many locations, Amy's Ice Cream eschews advertising in favor of spending money supporting local charities such as Austin public television, Candlelighter's Childhood Cancer Foundation, and Austin Partners in Education. The company's brand new, state-of-the-art 6,000 square foot factory, which includes numerous energy-saving devices, was recycled from an old post office.

has been progressive in aligning its expertise and resources to address community needs. Its relationship with Habitat for Humanity gives employees a chance to improve their skills and bring direct knowledge back into the workplace to benefit customers. It also enhances Home Depot's image of expertise as the "do-it-yourself" center. Home Depot also responds to customers' needs during disasters such as hurricanes. During natural disasters, some home building supply and hardware stores have taken advantage of customers by inflating prices on emergency materials, but Home Depot opens its stores 24 hours a day and makes materials available at reduced costs to help customers survive the disaster.[18]

## Social Responsibility Issues

Although social responsibility may seem to be an abstract ideal, managers make decisions related to social responsibility every day. To be successful, a business must determine what customers, government regulators, and competitors, as well as society in general, want or expect in terms of social responsibility. Table 4.2 summarizes three major categories of social responsibility issues: the natural environment, consumerism, and community relations.

**The Natural Environment.**  One of the more common ways marketers demonstrate social responsibility is through programs designed to protect and preserve the natural environment. Many companies are making contributions to environmental protection organizations, sponsoring and participating in clean-up events, promoting recycling, retooling manufacturing processes to minimize waste and pollution, and generally reevaluating the effects of their products on the natural environment. Procter & Gamble, for example, uses recycled materials in some of its packaging and sells refills for some products, which reduces packaging waste. Wal-Mart provides on-site recycling for customers and encourages its suppliers to reduce wasteful packaging. It also opened a "green" store in McKinney, Texas, that uses a 120-foot-tall wind turbine to generate electricity, a rain-water harvesting pond that provides 95 percent of the water needed for irrigation, and many other environmentally friendly and energy-saving features. Although the store is a prototype, the store manager says many of its features may one day be standard in all new Wal-Mart stores.[19] Such efforts generate positive publicity and often increase sales for the companies involved.

**green marketing** The specific development, pricing, promotion, and distribution of products that do not harm the natural environment

**Green marketing** refers to the specific development, pricing, promotion, and distribution of products that do not harm the natural environment. Toyota and Honda, for example, have succeeded in marketing "hybrid" cars that use electric motors to augment their internal-combustion engines, improving the vehicles' fuel economy without reducing their power. Ford Motor introduced the first hybrid SUV, the Escape, in 2005.[20] New Leaf Paper has taken a leadership role in the pa-

| table 4.2 | SOCIAL RESPONSIBILITY ISSUES | |
|---|---|---|
| **Issue** | **Description** | **Major Social Concerns** |
| Natural environment | Consumers insisting not only on a good quality of life but on a healthful environment so they can maintain a high standard of living during their lifetimes | Conservation<br>Water pollution<br>Air pollution<br>Land pollution |
| Consumerism | Activities undertaken by independent individuals, groups, and organizations to protect their rights as consumers | The right to safety<br>The right to be informed<br>The right to choose<br>The right to be heard |
| Community relations | Society eager to have marketers contribute to its well-being, wishing to know what marketers do to help solve social problems | Equality issues<br>Disadvantaged members of society<br>Safety and health<br>Education and general welfare |

**Environmental Responsibility**

Earth Share, a consortium of the world's leading conservation groups, works to protect the environment.

**figure 4.2**

### THE EUROPEAN ECO-LABEL

per-production industry, producing paper made from 50–100 percent postconsumer waste instead of virgin tree pulp. The small firm's success has forced many larger competitors to introduce their own sustainable paper products. The growing trend of recycled papers is saving trees and reducing the amount of solid waste going into landfills.[21] On the other hand, some stakeholders, including customers, try to dictate companies' use of responsible suppliers and sources of products.[22] Aveda, for example, maker of earth-friendly personal-care products, only places magazine ads in those magazines printed on recycled paper. The requirement has already prompted *Natural Health* to switch to recycled paper.[23]

Many products have been certified as "green" by environmental organizations such as Green Seal and carry a special logo identifying their organization as green marketers. Lumber products at Home Depot, for example, may carry a seal from the Forest Stewardship Council to indicate they were harvested from sustainable forests using environmentally friendly methods.[24] Likewise, most Chiquita bananas are certified through the Rainforest Alliance's Better Banana Project as having been grown with more environmentally and labor-friendly practices.[25] In Europe, companies can voluntarily apply for the European Eco-label to indicate that their products are less harmful to the environment than competing products, based on scientifically determined criteria (see Figure 4.2).

Although demand for economic, legal, and ethical solutions to environmental problems is widespread, the environmental movement in marketing includes many different groups whose values and goals often conflict. Some environmentalists and marketers believe companies should work to protect and preserve the natural environment by implementing the following goals:

**1.** *Eliminate the concept of waste.* Recognizing that pollution and waste usually stem from inefficiency, the question is not what to do with waste but how to make things without waste.

**2.** *Reinvent the concept of a product.* Products should be reduced to only three types and eventually just two. The first type is consumables, which are eaten or, when placed in the ground, turn into soil with few harmful side effects. The second type is durable goods—such as cars, televisions, computers, and refrigerators— which should be made, used, and returned to the manufacturer within a closed-loop system. Such products should be designed for disassembly and recycling. The third category is unsalables and includes such products as radioactive materials,

**Green Marketing**

Ford recognizes the importance of producing hybrid vehicles to help protect the natural environment.

heavy metals, and toxins. These products should always belong to the original makers, who should be responsible for the products and their full life cycle effects. Reclassifying products in this way encourages manufacturers to design products more efficiently.

**3.** *Make prices reflect the cost.* Every product should reflect or at least approximate its actual cost—not only the direct cost of production but also the cost of air, water, and soil. For example, the cost of a gallon of gasoline, according to the World Resources Institute in Washington, D.C., is approximately $4.50 when pollution, waste disposal, health effects, and defense expenditures like those of the Persian Gulf and Iraq Wars are factored in.

**4.** *Make environmentalism profitable.* Consumers are beginning to recognize that competition in the marketplace should not occur between companies harming the environment and those trying to save it.[26]

**Consumerism.** Another significant issue in socially responsible marketing is consumerism, which we defined in Chapter 3 as the efforts of independent individuals, groups, and organizations to protect the rights of consumers. A number of interest groups and individuals have taken action against companies they consider irresponsible by lobbying government officials and agencies, engaging in letter-writing campaigns and boycotts, and making public service announcements. Some consumers choose to boycott firms and products out of a desire to support a cause and make a difference.[27] How a firm handles customer complaints affects consumer evaluations and in turn customer satisfaction and loyalty.[28] Indeed, research suggests that angry consumers not only fail to make repeat purchases but may retaliate against the source of their dissatisfaction.[29] The consumer movement has been helped by news-format television programs, such as *Dateline, 60 Minutes,* and *Prime Time Live,* as well as by 24-hour news coverage from CNN and MSNBC. The Internet too has changed the way consumers obtain information about companies' goods, services, and activities.

Ralph Nader, one of the best-known consumer activists, continues to crusade for consumer rights. Consumer activism by Nader and others has resulted in legislation requiring many features that make cars safer: seat belts, air bags, padded dashboards, stronger door latches, head restraints, shatterproof windshields, and collapsible steering columns. Activists' efforts have also facilitated the passage of several

*Source:* Data from TIAA-CREF Trust. Margin of error ±3 percentage points.

consumer protection laws, including the Wholesome Meat Act of 1967, the Radiation Control for Health and Safety Act of 1968, the Clean Water Act of 1972, and the Toxic Substance Act of 1976.

Also of great importance to the consumer movement are four basic rights spelled out in a consumer "bill of rights" drafted by President John F. Kennedy. These rights include the right to safety, the right to be informed, the right to choose, and the right to be heard.

Ensuring consumers' *right to safety* means marketers are obligated not to market a product that they know could harm consumers. This right can be extended to imply that all products must be safe for their intended use, include thorough and explicit instructions for proper and safe use, and have been tested to ensure reliability and quality.

Consumers' *right to be informed* means consumers should have access to and the opportunity to review all relevant information about a product before buying it. Many laws require specific labeling on product packaging to satisfy this right. In addition, labels on alcoholic and tobacco products must inform consumers that these products may cause illness and other problems.

The *right to choose* means consumers should have access to a variety of products and services at competitive prices. They should also be assured of satisfactory quality and service at a fair price. Activities that reduce competition among businesses in an industry might jeopardize this right.

The *right to be heard* ensures that consumers' interests will receive full and sympathetic consideration in the formulation of government policy. The right to be heard also promises consumers fair treatment when they complain to marketers about products. This right benefits marketers too because when consumers complain about a product, the manufacturer can use this information to modify the product and make it more satisfying.

**Community Relations.** Social responsibility also extends to marketers' roles as community members. Individual communities expect marketers to make philanthropic contributions to civic projects and institutions and to be "good corporate citizens." The Weaver Street Market Cooperative in Carrboro, North Carolina, for example, serves as a community hub and live music venue, as well as a farmer's market and food store emphasizing sustainable and local food products. It has also used its resources to support a community radio station, affordable housing, and a satellite market to serve consumers nearby.[30]

While most charitable donations come from individuals, corporate philanthropy is on the rise. Target, for example, contributes significant resources to education, including fundraising and scholarship programs that assist teachers and students as well as direct donations of more than $154 million to schools. Through the retailer's Take Charge of Education program, customers using a Target Guest Card can designate a specific school to which Target donates 1 percent of their total purchase. This program is designed to make customers feel their purchases are benefiting their community while increasing the use of Target Guest Cards.[31]

Smaller firms can also make positive contributions to their communities. For example, Colorado-based New Belgium Brewing Company donates $1 for every barrel of beer brewed to charities within the markets it serves. The brewery divides the funds among states in proportion to interests and needs, considering environmental, human services, drug and alcohol awareness, and cultural issues.[32] From a positive perspective, a marketer can significantly improve its community's quality of life through employment opportunities, economic development, and financial contributions to educational, health, cultural, and recreational causes.[33]

# Marketing Ethics

As noted earlier, marketing ethics is a dimension of social responsibility involving principles and standards that define acceptable conduct in marketing. Acceptable standards of conduct in making individual and group decisions in marketing are determined by various stakeholders and by an organization's ethical climate.

Marketers should be aware of ethical standards for acceptable conduct from several viewpoints: company, industry, government, customers, special-interest groups, and society at large. When marketing activities deviate from accepted standards, the exchange process can break down, resulting in customer dissatisfaction, lack of trust, and lawsuits. In recent years, a number of ethical scandals have resulted in a massive loss of confidence in the integrity of U.S. businesses.[34] In fact, 73 percent of consumers say they would boycott the products of a socially irresponsible company, and 90 percent would consider switching to a competitor's products.[35] Sony BMG Music Entertainment, for example, was sharply criticized for including copy-protection software on millions of CDs. Although most marketers of music have sought innovative ways to stifle rampant CD piracy, many consumers felt that Sony's copy-protection software went too far because it could potentially disable computers or enable a hacker to unleash a virus if the CD was played on a Windows-based computer. At least one state attorney general launched an investigation into charges that the company used the software to secretly collect information on consumers' computers and send it back to the company. Sony ultimately recalled an estimated 4.7 million CDs, at a projected cost of $2 to $4 million, but not before generating considerable consumer anger and confusion over the technology as well as at least one class-action lawsuit.[36] When marketers engage in activities that deviate from accepted principles, continued marketing exchanges become difficult, if not impossible. The best time to deal with such problems is during the strategic planning process, not after major problems materialize.

As we already noted, marketing ethics goes beyond legal issues. Marketing decisions based on ethical considerations foster mutual trust in marketing relationships. Although we often try to draw a boundary between legal and ethical issues, the distinction between the two is frequently blurred in decision making. Marketers operate in an environment in which overlapping legal and ethical issues color many decisions. To separate legal and ethical decisions, one must assume that marketing managers can instinctively differentiate legal and ethical issues. However, while the legal ramifications of some issues and problems may be obvious, others are not. Questionable decisions and actions often result in disputes that must be resolved through litigation. The legal system therefore provides a formal venue for marketers to resolve ethical disputes as well as legal ones. Hasbro, for example, filed suit against a Pennsylvania man who marketed a board game called Ghettopoly. Hasbro's suit accused David Chang's game of unlawfully copying the packaging and logo of Hasbro's long-selling Monopoly board game and causing "irreparable injury" to Hasbro's reputation and goodwill. After minority-rights activists complained that Ghettopoly promoted negative stereotypes of African Americans, some retailers stopped selling the game.[37] Indeed, most ethical disputes reported in the media involve the legal system at some level. In many cases, however, settlements are reached without requiring the decision of a judge or jury.

Before we proceed with our discussion of ethics in marketing, it is important to state that it is not our purpose to question anyone's ethical beliefs or personal convictions. Nor is it our purpose to examine the conduct of consumers, although some do behave unethically (engaging, for instance, in coupon fraud, shoplifting, returning clothing after wearing it, and other abuses). Instead, our goal here is to underscore the importance of resolving ethical issues in marketing and to help you learn about marketing ethics.

## Ethical Issues in Marketing

**ethical issue** An identifiable problem, situation, or opportunity requiring a choice among several actions that must be evaluated as right or wrong, ethical or unethical

An **ethical issue** is an identifiable problem, situation, or opportunity requiring an individual or organization to choose from among several actions that must be evaluated as right or wrong, ethical or unethical. Any time an activity causes marketing managers or customers in their target market to feel manipulated or cheated, a marketing ethical issue exists, regardless of the legality of that activity. For example, organizational objectives that call for increased profits or market share may pressure marketers to knowingly bring an unsafe product to market. Such pressures represent ethical issues. Regardless of the reasons behind specific ethical issues, marketers must be able to identify those issues and decide how to resolve them. To do so requires familiarity with the many kinds of ethical issues that may arise in marketing. Research suggests that the greater the consequences associated with an issue, the more likely it will be recognized as an ethics issue and the more important it will be to making an ethical decision.[38] Some examples of ethical issues related to product, promotion, price, and distribution (the marketing mix) appear in Table 4.3.

Product-related ethical issues generally arise when marketers fail to disclose risks associated with a product or information regarding the function, value, or use of a product. Most automobile companies have experienced negative publicity associated with design or safety issues that resulted in a government-required recall of specific models. Pressures can build to substitute inferior materials or product components to reduce costs. Ethical issues also arise when marketers fail to inform customers about existing conditions or changes in product quality; such failure is a form of dishonesty about the nature of the product. Consider the introduction of a new size of candy bar, labeled with a banner touting its "new larger size." However, when placed in vending machines alongside older candy bars of the same brand, it was apparent that the product was actually slightly *smaller* than the candy bar it replaced. Although this could have been a mistake, the firm still has to defend and deal with the consequences of its actions.

Promotion can create ethical issues in a variety of ways, among them false or misleading advertising and manipulative or deceptive sales promotions, tactics, and publicity. One controversial issue in the area of promotion is the promotion of pharmaceuticals that require a doctor's prescription directly to consumers. Proponents of the practice argue that it arms consumers with more information about products that may be beneficial for their conditions. Critics worry about the potential for overtreatment and have called for tighter guidelines on the promotion of drugs. With new studies suggesting that pharmaceutical ads are strongly influencing both doctors and consumers and consumers growing wary of the ads, the Pharmaceutical Researchers and Manufacturers of America announced plans to release voluntary guidelines to better self-regulate the industry.[39] Another major ethical issue in promotion pertains to the marketing of video games that allegedly promote violence and weapons to children. Many other ethical issues are linked to promotion, including the use of bribery in personal selling situations. Even a bribe that is offered to bene-

| table 4.3 | SAMPLE ETHICAL ISSUES RELATED TO THE MARKETING MIX |
|---|---|
| Product Issue<br>*Product information* | Covering up defects that could cause harm to a consumer; withholding critical performance information that could affect a purchase decision. |
| Distribution Issue<br>*Counterfeiting* | Counterfeit products are widespread, especially in the areas of computer software, clothing, and audio and video products. The Internet has facilitated the distribution of counterfeit products. |
| Promotion Issue<br>*Advertising* | Deceptive advertising or withholding important product information in a personal-selling situation. |
| Pricing Issue<br>*Pricing* | Indicating that an advertised sale price is a reduction below the regular price when in fact that is not the case. |

fit the organization is usually considered unethical. Because it jeopardizes trust and fairness, it hurts the organization in the long run.

In pricing, common ethical issues are price fixing, predatory pricing, and failure to disclose the full price of a purchase. The emotional and subjective nature of price creates many situations in which misunderstandings between the seller and buyer cause ethical problems. Marketers have the right to price their products to earn a reasonable profit, but ethical issues may crop up when a company seeks to earn high profits at the expense of its customers. Some pharmaceutical companies, for example, have been accused of pricing products at exorbitant levels and taking advantage of customers who must purchase the medicine to survive or to maintain their quality of life. Another issue relates to quantity surcharges that occur when consumers are effectively overcharged for buying a larger package size of the same grocery product.[40]

Ethical issues in distribution involve relationships among producers and marketing middlemen. Marketing middlemen, or intermediaries (wholesalers and retailers), facilitate the flow of products from the producer to the ultimate customer. Each intermediary performs a different role and agrees to certain rights, responsibilities, and rewards associated with that role. For example, producers expect wholesalers and retailers to honor agreements and keep them informed of inventory needs. Other serious ethical issues with regard to distribution include manipulating a product's availability for purposes of exploitation and using coercion to force intermediaries to behave in a specific manner. Several companies have been accused of channel stuffing, which involves shipping surplus inventory to wholesalers and retailers at an excessive rate, typically before the end of a quarter. The practice may conceal declining demand for a product or inflate financial statement earnings, misleading investors.[41]

### The Nature of Marketing Ethics

To grasp the significance of ethics in marketing decision making, it is helpful to examine the factors that influence the ethical decision making process. As Figure 4.3 shows, individual factors, opportunity, and organizational relationships interact to determine ethical decisions in marketing.

**Individual Factors.** When people need to resolve ethical conflicts in their daily lives, they often base their decisions on their own values and principles of right or wrong. For example, a study by the Josephson Institute of Ethics reported that 62 percent of students admitted to cheating on a test at least once in the past year, and 82 percent admitted to lying to their parents in the past year. One out of three students confessed to plagiarizing documents from the Internet in the same period.[42] People learn values and principles through socialization by family members, social groups, religion, and formal education. In the workplace, however, research has es-

**figure 4.3**

**FACTORS THAT INFLUENCE THE ETHICAL DECISION MAKING PROCESS IN MARKETING**

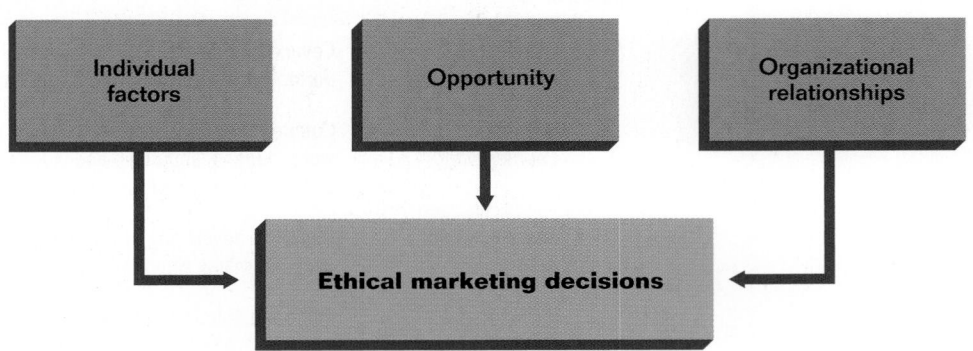

Communication with your teens can be a form of prevention. In fact, teens whose parents lay out rules and expectations for them are far less likely to try pot and other drugs. **Be clear. Be firm. Be a parent.** For information, call 1-800-788-2800 or visit www.theantidrug.com.

if you're not telling them NO you're telling them YES

**PARENTS.**
THE ANTI-DRUG.

**Individual Factors**

Organizations such as "Parents—The Anti-Drug" focus on character development among teenagers.

tablished that an organization's values often have more influence on marketing decisions than do a person's own values.[43]

**Organizational Relationships.** Although people can and do make ethical choices pertaining to marketing decisions, no one operates in a vacuum.[44] Ethical choices in marketing are most often made jointly, in work groups and committees or in conversations and discussions with coworkers. Marketing employees resolve ethical issues based not only on what they learned from their own backgrounds but also on what they learn from others in the organization. The outcome of this learning process depends on the strength of each individual's personal values, opportunity for unethical behavior, and exposure to others who behave ethically or unethically. Superiors, peers, and subordinates in the organization influence the ethical decision making process. Although people outside the organization, such as family members and friends, also influence decision makers, organizational culture and structure operate through organizational relationships to influence ethical decisions.

**Organizational, or corporate, culture** is a set of values, beliefs, goals, norms, and rituals that members of an organization share. These values also help shape employees' satisfaction with their employer, which may affect the quality of the service they provide to customers. A firm's culture may be expressed formally through codes of conduct, memos, manuals, dress codes, and ceremonies, but it is also conveyed informally through work habits, extracurricular activities, and anecdotes. An organization's culture gives its members meaning and suggests rules for how to behave and deal with problems within the organization.

With regard to organizational structure, most experts agree that the chief executive officer or vice president of marketing sets the ethical tone for the entire marketing organization. Lower-level managers obtain their cues from top managers, but they too impose some of their personal values on the company. This interaction between corporate culture and executive leadership helps determine the firm's ethical value system.

Coworkers' influence on an individual's ethical choices depends on the person's exposure to unethical behavior. Especially in gray areas, the more a person is exposed to unethical activity by others in the organizational environment, the more likely he or she is to behave unethically. Most marketing employees take their cues from coworkers in learning how to solve problems, including ethical problems.[45] For example, the 2005 National Business Ethics Survey (NBES) found that 52 percent of employees had observed at least one type of misconduct in the past year; just over one-half of them (55 percent) had reported the misconduct to management.[46] Table 4.4 (on p. 100) lists some commonly observed types of observed misconduct. Moreover, research suggests that marketing employees who perceive their work environment as ethical experience less role conflict and ambiguity, are more satisfied with their jobs, and are more committed to their employer.[47]

**organizational (corporate) culture** A set of values, beliefs, goals, norms, and rituals that members of an organization share

**table 4.4   TYPES AND INCIDENCES OF OBSERVED MISCONDUCT**

| Type of Conduct Observed | Employees Observing It (%) |
| --- | --- |
| Abusive or intimidating behavior toward employees | 21 |
| Lying to employees, customers, vendors, or the public | 19 |
| A situation that places employee interests over organizational interests | 18 |
| Safety regulation violations | 16 |
| Misreporting of actual time worked | 16 |
| Discrimination on the basis of race, color, gender, age, or similar categories | 12 |
| Stealing or theft | 11 |
| Sexual harassment | 9 |

**Source:** From "Survey Documents State of Ethics in the Workplace," Ethics Resource Center, press release, Oct. 12, 2005, **www.ethics.org/nbes/nbes2005/release.html.** Reprinted by permission of Ethics Resource Center.

Organizational pressure plays a key role in creating ethical issues. For example, because of pressure to meet a schedule, a superior may ask a salesperson to lie to a customer over the phone about a late product shipment. Similarly, pressure to meet a sales quota may result in overly aggressive sales tactics. Research in this area indicates that superiors and coworkers can generate organizational pressure, which plays a key role in creating ethical issues. Nearly all marketers face difficult issues whose solutions are not obvious or that present conflicts between organizational objectives and personal ethics.

**Opportunity.** Another factor that may shape ethical decisions in marketing is opportunity, that is, conditions that limit barriers or provide rewards. A marketing employee who takes advantage of an opportunity to act unethically and is rewarded or suffers no penalty may repeat such acts as other opportunities arise. For example, a salesperson who receives a raise after using a deceptive sales presentation to increase sales is being rewarded and thus will probably continue the behavior. Indeed, opportunity to engage in unethical conduct is often a better predictor of unethical activities than are personal values.[48] Beyond rewards and the absence of punishment, other elements in the business environment may create opportunities. Professional codes of conduct and ethics-related corporate policy also influence opportunity by prescribing what behaviors are acceptable, as we will see later. The larger the rewards and the milder the punishment for unethical conduct, the greater is the likelihood that unethical behavior will occur.

However, just as the majority of people who go into retail stores do not try to shoplift at each opportunity, most marketing managers do not try to take advantage of every opportunity for unethical behavior in their organizations. Although marketing managers often perceive many opportunities to engage in unethical conduct in their companies and industries, research suggests that most refrain from taking advantage of such opportunities. Moreover, most marketing managers do not believe unethical conduct in general results in success.[49] Individual factors as well as organizational culture may influence whether an individual becomes opportunistic and tries to take advantage of situations unethically.

## Improving Ethical Conduct in Marketing

It is possible to improve ethical conduct in an organization by hiring ethical employees and eliminating unethical ones, and by improving the organization's ethical

SHE NEEDS HER FUR MORE THAN YOU DO

Please choose compassion as *your* fashion.

THE HUMANE SOCIETY
OF THE UNITED STATES
2100 L Street, NW, Washington, DC 20037
202-452-1100

www.hsus.org/fur

©2005 The HSUS. All rights reserved.

**Improving Ethical Conduct in Marketing**
Both for-profit and nonprofit organizations such as the Humane Society are guided by ethics and compliance programs.

standards. One way to approach improvement of an organization's ethical standards is to use a "bad apple–bad barrel" analogy. Some people always do things in their own self-interest, regardless of organizational goals or accepted moral standards; they are sometimes called "bad apples." To eliminate unethical conduct, an organization must rid itself of bad apples through screening techniques and enforcement of the firm's ethical standards. However, organizations sometimes become "bad barrels" themselves, not because the individuals within them are unethical but because the pressures to survive and succeed create conditions (opportunities) that reward unethical behavior. One way to resolve the problem of the bad barrel is to redesign the organization's image and culture so that it conforms to industry and societal norms of ethical conduct.[50]

If top management develops and enforces ethical and legal compliance programs to encourage ethical decision making, it becomes a force to help individuals make better decisions. The 2005 National Business Ethics Survey found that formal ethics programs are an essential element of strong corporate cultures.[51] Ethics programs that include written standards of conduct, ethics training, ethics advice lines or offices, and systems for anonymous reporting increase the likelihood that employees will report misconduct observed in the workplace. When top managers talk about the importance of ethics, inform employees, keep promises, and model ethical behavior, employees observe significantly fewer instances of unethical conduct. According to the 2005 NBES, employees who reported observations of misconduct to management did so because they thought it was the right thing to do. They also indicated that they felt they had the support of top management and that corrective action would result from their report. Figure 4.4 (on p. 102) lists some of the reasons employees cited for not reporting observed misconduct.[52] When marketers understand the policies and requirements for ethical conduct, they can more easily resolve ethical conflicts. However, marketers can never fully abdicate their personal ethical responsibility in making decisions. Claiming to be an agent of the business ("the company told me to do it") is unacceptable as a legal excuse and is even less defensible from an ethical perspective.[53]

**Codes of Conduct.** Without compliance programs and uniform standards and policies regarding conduct, it is hard for employees to determine what conduct is acceptable within the company. In the absence of such programs and standards, employees will generally make decisions based on their observations of how coworkers and superiors behave. To improve ethics, many organizations have developed **codes of conduct** (also called *codes of ethics*) consisting of formalized rules and standards that describe what the company expects of its employees. Most large corporations have formal codes of conduct. Tyco, for example, established a Guide to Ethical Conduct as part of a major corporate overhaul that involved forcing out nearly 300 managers, dramatic changes in reporting relationships, and many more initiatives to ensure that Tyco developed an ethical corporate culture.[54] Codes of

**codes of conduct** Formalized rules and standards that describe what the company expects of its employees

**figure 4.4**

## REASONS EMPLOYEES DO NOT REPORT ETHICAL MISCONDUCT

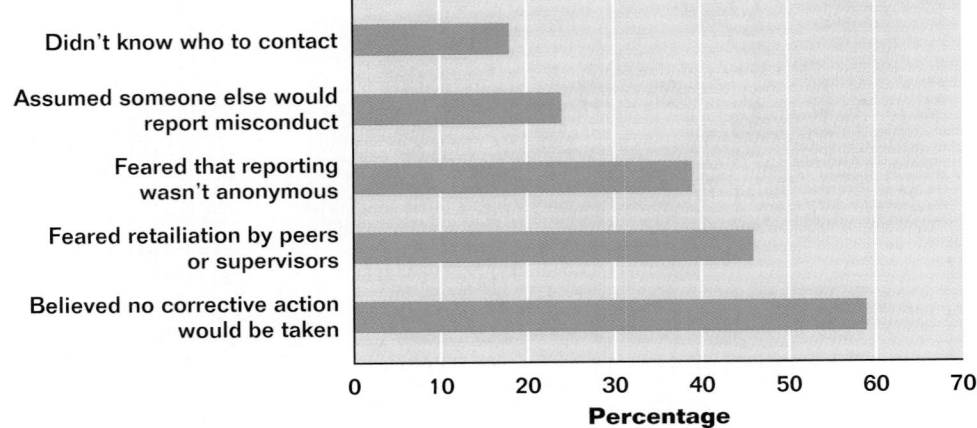

**Source:** From National Business Ethics Survey, "How Employees View Ethics in Their Organizations 1994-2005," Ethics Resource Center 2005, p. 29. © Ethics Resource Center, Washington, DC. Reprinted with permission.

conduct promote ethical behavior by reducing opportunities for unethical behavior; employees know both what is expected of them and what kind of punishment they face if they violate the rules. Codes help marketers deal with ethical issues or dilemmas that develop in daily operations by prescribing or limiting specific activities. At Hospital Corporation of America (HCA), for example, the code of conduct specifies that any violation of the code may trigger an oral warning, written warning, written reprimand, suspension, termination, and/or restitution, depending on the nature, severity, and frequency of the violation.[55] Codes of conduct have also made companies that subcontract manufacturing operations abroad more aware of the ethical issues associated with supporting facilities that underpay and even abuse their workforce. The American Apparel & Footwear Association, for example, has endorsed the principles and certification program of Worldwide Responsible Apparel Production (WRAP), a nonprofit organization dedicated to promoting and certifying "lawful, humane, and ethical manufacturing throughout the world." Companies that endorse the principles are expected to allow independent monitoring to ensure their contractors are complying with the principles.[56]

Codes of conduct do not have to be so detailed that they take every situation into account, but they should provide guidelines that enable employees to achieve organizational objectives in an ethical, acceptable manner. The American Marketing Association Code of Ethics, reprinted in Table 4.5, does not cover every possible ethical issue, but it provides a useful overview of what marketers believe are sound principles for guiding marketing activities. This code serves as a helpful model for structuring an organization's code of conduct.

**Ethics Officers.** Organizational compliance programs must also have oversight by high-ranking persons in the organization known to respect legal and ethical standards. Ethics officers are typically responsible for creating and distributing a code of conduct, enforcing the code, and meeting with organizational members to discuss or provide advice about ethical issues. Many firms have created ethics officer positions, including the New York Stock Exchange, Marsh & McLennan, Nortel Networks, and Computer Associates International.[57] At Tyco, for example, senior vice president of corporate governance Eric Pillmore is in the process of revamping the firm's ethics program. In addition to revising the company's code of conduct, Pillmore, who reports directly to Tyco's board of directors, is responsible for providing ethics training.[58]

Many ethics officers also employ toll-free telephone "hotlines" to provide advice, anonymously when desired, to employees who believe they face an ethical issue. Since the passage of the 2002 Sarbanes-Oxley Act, more companies have imple-

## table 4.5   CODE OF ETHICS OF THE AMERICAN MARKETING ASSOCIATION

### ETHICAL NORMS AND VALUES FOR MARKETERS

**Preamble**

The American Marketing Association commits itself to promoting the highest standard of professional ethical norms and values for its members. Norms are established standards of conduct expected and maintained by society and/or professional organizations. Values represent the collective conception of what people find desirable, important and morally proper. Values serve as the criteria for evaluating the actions of others. Marketing practitioners must recognize that they serve not only their enterprises but also act as stewards of society in creating, facilitating and executing the efficient and effective transactions that are part of the greater economy. In this role, marketers should embrace the highest ethical norms of practicing professionals as well as the ethical values implied by their responsibility toward stakeholders (e.g., customers, employees, investors, channel members, regulators and the host community).

**General Norms**

1.  Marketers must first do no harm. This means doing work for which they are appropriately trained or experienced so that they can actively add value to their organizations and customers. It also means adhering to all applicable laws and regulations as well as embodying high ethical standards in the choices they make.

2.  Marketers must foster trust in the marketing system. This means that products are appropriate for their intended and promoted uses. It requires that marketing communications about goods and services are not intentionally deceptive or misleading. It suggests building relationships that provide for the equitable adjustment and/or redress of customer grievances. It implies striving for good faith and fair dealing so as to contribute toward the efficacy of the exchange process.

3.  Marketers should embrace, communicate and practice the fundamental ethical values that will improve consumer confidence in the integrity of the marketing exchange system. These basic values are intentionally aspirational and include: Honesty, Responsibility, Fairness, Respect, Openness and Citizenship.

**Ethical Values**

Honesty—this means being truthful and forthright in our dealings with customers and stakeholders.

We will tell the truth in all situations and at all times.

We will offer products of value that do what we claim in our communications.

We will stand behind our products if they fail to deliver their claimed benefits.

We will honor our explicit and implicit commitments and promises.

Responsibility—this involves accepting the consequences of our marketing decisions and strategies.

We will make strenuous efforts to serve the needs of our customers.

We will avoid using coercion with all stakeholders.

We will acknowledge the social obligations to stakeholders that come with increased marketing and economic power.

We will recognize our special commitments to economically vulnerable segments of the market such as children, the elderly and others who may be substantially disadvantaged.

Fairness—this has to do with justly trying to balance the needs of the buyer with the interests of the seller.

We will clearly represent our products in selling, advertising and other forms of communication; this includes the avoidance of false, misleading and deceptive promotion.

We will reject manipulations and sales tactics that harm customer trust.

We will not engage in price fixing, predatory pricing, price gouging or "bait and switch" tactics.

We will not knowingly participate in material conflicts of interest.

Respect—this addresses the basic human dignity of all stakeholders.

We will value individual differences even as we avoid customer stereotyping or depicting demographic groups (e.g., gender, race, sexual) in a negative or dehumanizing way in our promotions.

We will listen to the needs of our customers and make all reasonable efforts to monitor and improve their satisfaction on an on-going basis.

We will make a special effort to understand suppliers, intermediaries and distributors from other cultures.

We will appropriately acknowledge the contributions of others, such as consultants, employees and co-workers, to our marketing endeavors.

*continued*

| table 4.5 | CODE OF ETHICS OF THE AMERICAN MARKETING ASSOCIATION (continued) |
|---|---|

Openness—this focuses on creating transparency in our marketing operations.

We will strive to communicate clearly with all our constituencies.

We will accept constructive criticism from our customers and other stakeholders.

We will explain significant product or service risks, component substitutions or other foreseeable eventualities affecting the customer or their perception of the purchase decision.

We will fully disclose list prices and terms of financing as well as available price deals and adjustments.

Citizenship—this involves a strategic focus on fulfilling the economic, legal, philanthropic and societal responsibilities that serve stakeholders.

We will strive to protect the natural environment in the execution of marketing campaigns.

We will give back to the community through volunteerism and charitable donations.

We will work to contribute to the overall betterment of marketing and its reputation.

We will encourage supply chain members to ensure that trade is fair for all participants, including producers in developing countries.

**Implementation**

Finally, we recognize that every industry sector and marketing sub-discipline (e.g., marketing research, e-commerce, direct selling, direct marketing, advertising, etc.) has its own specific ethical issues that require policies and commentary. An array of such codes can be accessed via links on the AMA website. We encourage all such groups to develop and/or refine their industry and discipline-specific codes of ethics in order to supplement these general norms and values.

**Source:** Copyright © 2004 by the American Marketing Association.

mented anonymous hotlines for employees to report misconduct; many companies, including Halliburton and Coca-Cola, have contracted the operation of these hotlines to third parties, such as EthicsPoint, Global Compliance Services, National Hotline Services, and Pinkerton Consulting & Investigations. Although the majority of incidents reported to these hotlines have been minor infractions, one caller identified kickbacks from suppliers, and another reported on a multimillion-dollar falsified contract.[59]

**Implementing Ethical and Legal Compliance Programs.**  To nurture ethical conduct in marketing, open communication and coaching on ethical issues are essential. This requires providing employees with ethics training, clear channels of communication, and follow-up support throughout the organization.

It is important that companies consistently enforce standards and impose penalties or punishment on those who violate codes of conduct and ethics policies. Clear Channel Communications, for example, fired two executives and disciplined other employees for violating the firm's policies on "payola," the illegal practice of accepting payment for playing songs on the air without divulging such deals. The firm, which owns approximately 1,200 radio stations, also required station managers and programming personnel to undergo additional training on its policies.[60] In addition, companies must take reasonable steps in response to violations of standards and, as appropriate, revise their compliance programs to diminish the likelihood of future misconduct. To succeed, a compliance program must be viewed as a part of the overall marketing strategy implementation. If ethics officers and other executives are not committed to the principles and initiatives of marketing ethics and social responsibility, the program's effectiveness will be in question.

Although the virtues of honesty, fairness, and openness are often assumed to be self-evident and universally accepted, marketing strategy decisions involve complex and detailed matters in which correctness may not be so clear-cut. A high level of personal morality may not be sufficient to prevent an individual from violating the law in an organizational context in which even experienced lawyers debate the exact meaning of the law. Because it is impossible to train all members of an organization as lawyers, the identification of ethical issues and implementation of compliance programs and codes of conduct that incorporate both legal and ethical concerns constitute the best approach to preventing violations and avoiding litigation. Codifying ethical standards into meaningful policies that spell out what is and is not acceptable gives marketers an opportunity to reduce the probability of behavior that could create legal problems. Without proper ethical training and guidance, it is impossible for the average marketing manager to understand the exact boundaries of illegality in the areas of price fixing, copyright violations, fraud, export/import violations, and so on. A corporate focus on ethics helps create a buffer zone around issues that could trigger serious legal complications for the company.

# Incorporating Social Responsibility and Ethics into Strategic Planning

Although the concepts of marketing ethics and social responsibility are often used interchangeably, it is important to distinguish between them. *Ethics* relates to individual and group decisions—judgments about what is right or wrong in a particular decision making situation—whereas *social responsibility* deals with the total effect of marketing decisions on society. The two concepts are interrelated because a company that supports socially responsible decisions and adheres to a code of conduct is likely to have a positive effect on society. Because ethics and social responsibility programs can be profitable as well, an increasing number of companies are incorporating them into their overall strategic market planning.

**Incorporating Social Responsibility and Ethics**

Siemens prides itself on global innovation, providing equipment that processes 70 percent of the growing U.S. ethanol production.

## table 4.6   ORGANIZATIONAL AUDIT OF SOCIAL RESPONSIBILITY AND ETHICS CONTROL MECHANISMS

Answer True or False for each statement.

T    F    1. No mechanism exists for top management to detect social responsibility and ethical issues relating to employees, customers, the community, and society.

T    F    2. There is no formal or informal communication within the organization about procedures and activities that are considered acceptable behavior.

T    F    3. The organization fails to communicate its ethical standards to suppliers, customers, and groups that have a relationship with the organization.

T    F    4. There is an environment of deception, repression, and cover-ups concerning events that could be embarrassing to the company.

T    F    5. Compensation systems are totally dependent on economic performance.

T    F    6. The only concerns about environmental impact are those that are legally required.

T    F    7. Concern for the ethical value systems of the community with regard to the firm's activities is absent.

T    F    8. Products are described in a misleading manner, with no information on negative impact or limitations communicated to customers.

*True answers indicate a lack of control mechanisms, which, if implemented, could improve ethics and social responsibility.*

As we have emphasized throughout this chapter, ethics is one dimension of social responsibility. Being socially responsible relates to doing what is economically sound, legal, ethical, and socially conscious. One way to evaluate whether a specific activity is ethical and socially responsible is to ask other members of the organization if they approve of it. Contact with concerned consumer groups and industry or government regulatory groups may be helpful. A check to see whether there is a specific company policy about an activity may help resolve ethical questions. If other organization members approve of the activity and it is legal and customary within the industry, chances are the activity is acceptable from both an ethical and a social responsibility perspective. Table 4.6 provides an audit of mechanisms to help control ethics and social responsibility in marketing.

A rule of thumb for resolving ethical and social responsibility issues is that if an issue can withstand open discussion that results in agreement or limited debate, an acceptable solution may exist. Nevertheless, even after a final decision is reached, different viewpoints on the issue may remain. Openness is not the end-all solution to the ethics problem. However, it creates trust and facilitates learning relationships.[61]

## The Challenge of Ethical and Socially Responsible Behavior

To promote socially responsible and ethical behavior while achieving organizational goals, marketers must monitor changes and trends in society's values. Consider that as aging baby boomers see increased rates of obesity, diabetes, heart conditions, and other chronic illnesses, many companies in the food industry are responding by introducing or adapting products to address their needs. Their approaches range from special brands and labels to introducing low-fat, low-sugar, whole-grain, and other specialty-food requirements to maintaining separate shelf space for products that target these conditions. Developing a more user-friendly grocery store for these consumers is both socially responsible and lucrative.[62] Likewise, when consumers began to demand greater transparency, or openness, from companies in the wake of a number of ethics scandals, transparency became a factor in most marketing and management decisions.[63] An organization's top management must assume some responsibility for employees' conduct by establishing and enforcing policies that address society's desires.

After determining what society wants, marketers must attempt to predict the long-term effects of decisions pertaining to those wants. Specialists outside the company, such as doctors, lawyers, and scientists, are often consulted, but sometimes there is a lack of agreement within a discipline as to what is an acceptable marketing decision. Forty years ago, for example, tobacco marketers promoted cigarettes as being good for one's health. Today, years after the discovery that cigarette smoking is linked to cancer and other medical problems, society's attitude toward smoking has changed, and marketers face new social responsibilities, such as providing a smoke-free atmosphere for customers. Most major hotel chains allocate at least some of their rooms to nonsmokers, many rental car companies provide smoke-free cars, and most other businesses within the food, travel, and entertainment industries provide smoke-free environments or sections.

Many of society's demands impose costs. For example, society wants a cleaner environment and the preservation of wildlife and their habitats, but it also wants low-priced products. Consider the plight of the gas station owner who asked his customers if they would be willing to spend an additional 1 cent per gallon if he instituted an air filtration system to eliminate harmful fumes. The majority indicated they supported his plan. However, when the system was installed and the price increased, many customers switched to a lower-cost competitor across the street. Thus, companies must carefully balance the costs of providing low-priced products against the costs of manufacturing, packaging, and distributing their products in an environmentally responsible manner.

In trying to satisfy the desires of one group, marketers may dissatisfy others. Regarding the smoking debate, for example, marketers must balance nonsmokers' desire for a smoke-free environment against smokers' desire, or need, to continue to smoke. Some anti-tobacco crusaders call for the complete elimination of tobacco products to ensure a smoke-free world. However, this attitude fails to consider the difficulty smokers have in quitting (now that tobacco marketers have admitted their product is addictive) and the impact on U.S. communities and states that depend on tobacco crops for their economic survival. Thus, this issue, like most ethical and social responsibility issues, cannot be viewed in black and white.

Balancing society's demands to satisfy all members of society is difficult, if not impossible. Marketers must evaluate the extent to which members of society are willing to pay for what they want. For instance, customers may want more information about a product but be unwilling to pay the costs the firm incurs in providing the data. Marketers who want to make socially responsible decisions may find the task a challenge because, ultimately, they must ensure their economic survival.

## Social Responsibility and Ethics Improve Marketing Performance

Do not think, however, that the challenge is not worth the effort. On the contrary, increasing evidence indicates that being socially responsible and ethical pays off. Research suggests that a relationship exists between a marketing orientation and an organizational climate that supports marketing ethics and social responsibility. This relationship implies that being ethically and socially concerned is consistent with meeting the demands of customers and other stakeholders. By encouraging employees to understand their markets, companies can help them respond to stakeholders' demands.[64]

There is a direct association between corporate social responsibility and profits.[65] In a survey of consumers, nearly 86 percent indicated that when quality and price are similar among competitors, they would be more likely to buy from the company associated with a particular cause. In addition, young adults aged 18–25 are especially likely to take a company's citizenship efforts into account when making not only purchasing but also employment and investment decisions.[66]

Thus, recognition is growing that the long-term value of conducting business in a

**Social Responsibility Improves Marketing Performance**

Merck believes its social responsibility program, providing medicines free to those who can't afford them, links to their financial performance

socially responsible manner far outweighs short-term costs.[67] Companies that fail to develop strategies and programs to incorporate ethics and social responsibility into their organizational culture may pay the price with poor marketing performance and the potential costs of legal violations, civil litigation, and damaging publicity when questionable activities are made public. Because marketing ethics and social responsibility are not always viewed as organizational performance issues, many managers do not believe they need to consider them in the strategic planning process. Individuals also have different ideas as to what is ethical or unethical, leading them to confuse the need for workplace ethics and the right to maintain their own personal values and ethics. While the concepts are undoubtedly controversial, it is possible—and desirable—to incorporate ethics and social responsibility into the planning process.

## SUMMARY

Social responsibility refers to an organization's obligation to maximize its positive impact and minimize its negative impact on society. It deals with the total effect of all marketing decisions on society. Although social responsibility is a positive concept, most organizations embrace it in the expectation of indirect long-term benefits.

Marketing citizenship involves adopting a strategic focus for fulfilling the economic, legal, ethical, and philanthropic social responsibilities expected of organizations by their stakeholders, those constituents who have a stake, or claim, in some aspect of the company's products, oper-

ations, markets, industry, and outcomes. At the most basic level, companies have an economic responsibility to be profitable so they can provide a return on investment to their stockholders, create jobs for the community, and contribute goods and services to the economy. Marketers are also expected to obey laws and regulations. Marketing ethics refers to principles and standards that define acceptable conduct in marketing as determined by various stakeholders, including the public, government regulators, private-interest groups, industry, and the organization itself. Philanthropic responsibilities go beyond marketing ethics; they are not required of a company, but they promote human welfare or goodwill. Many firms use cause-related marketing, the practice of linking products to a social cause on an ongoing or short-term basis. Strategic philanthropy is the synergistic use of organizational core competencies and resources to address key stakeholders' interests and achieve both organizational and social benefits.

Three major categories of social responsibility issues are the natural environment, consumerism, and community relations. One of the more common ways marketers demonstrate social responsibility is through programs designed to protect and preserve the natural environment. Green marketing refers to the specific development, pricing, promotion, and distribution of products that do not harm the environment. Consumerism consists of the efforts of independent individuals, groups, and organizations to protect the rights of consumers. Consumers expect to have the right to safety, the right to be informed, the right to choose, and the right to be heard. Many marketers view social responsibility as including contributions of resources (money, products, and time) to community causes such as the natural environment, arts and recreation, disadvantaged members of the community, and education.

Whereas social responsibility is achieved by balancing the interests of all stakeholders in the organization, ethics relates to acceptable standards of conduct in making individual and group decisions. Marketing ethics goes beyond legal issues. Ethical marketing decisions foster mutual trust in marketing relationships.

An ethical issue is an identifiable problem, situation, or opportunity requiring an individual or organization to choose from among several actions that must be evaluated as right or wrong, ethical or unethical. A number of ethical issues relate to the marketing mix (product, promotion, price, and distribution).

Individual factors, organizational relationships, and opportunity interact to determine ethical decisions in marketing. Individuals often base their decisions on their own values and principles of right or wrong. However, ethical choices in marketing are most often made jointly, in work groups and committees or in conversations and discussions with coworkers. Organizational culture and structure operate through organizational relationships (with superiors, peers, and subordinates) to influence eth-

ical decisions. Organizational, or corporate, culture is a set of values, beliefs, goals, norms, and rituals that members of an organization share. The more a person is exposed to unethical activity by others in the organizational environment, the more likely he or she is to behave unethically. Organizational pressure plays a key role in creating ethical issues, as does opportunity, conditions that limit barriers or provide rewards.

It is possible to improve ethical behavior in an organization by hiring ethical employees and eliminating unethical ones, and by improving the organization's ethical standards. If top management develops and enforces ethics and legal compliance programs to encourage ethical decision making, it becomes a force to help individuals make better decisions. To improve company ethics, many organizations have developed codes of conduct, formalized rules and standards that describe what the company expects of its employees. A marketing compliance program must have oversight by a high-ranking organization member known to abide by legal and common ethical standards; this person is usually called an ethics officer. To nurture ethical conduct in marketing, open communication and coaching on ethical issues are essential. This requires providing employees with ethics training, clear channels of communication, and follow-up support throughout the organization. Companies must consistently enforce standards and impose penalties or punishment on those who violate codes of conduct.

An increasing number of companies are incorporating ethics and social responsibility programs into their overall strategic market planning. To promote socially responsible and ethical behavior while achieving organizational goals, marketers must monitor changes and trends in society's values. They must determine what society wants and attempt to predict the long-term effects of their decisions. Costs are associated with many of society's demands, and balancing those demands to satisfy all of society is difficult. However, increasing evidence indicates that being socially responsible and ethical results in valuable benefits: an enhanced public reputation (which can increase market share), costs savings, and profits.

**ACE self-test**

Please visit the student website at **www.prideferrell.com** for ACE Self-Test questions that will help you prepare for exams.

## IMPORTANT TERMS

| | | | |
|---|---|---|---|
| Social responsibility | Cause-related marketing | Ethical issue | Codes of conduct |
| Marketing citizenship | Strategic philanthropy | Organizational culture | |
| Marketing ethics | Green marketing | (corporate) | |

## DISCUSSION & REVIEW QUESTIONS

1. What is social responsibility? Why is it important?

2. What are stakeholders? What role do they play in strategic marketing decisions?

3. What are four dimensions of social responsibility? What impact do they have on marketing decisions?

4. What is strategic philanthropy? How does it differ from more traditional philanthropic efforts?

5. What are some major social responsibility issues? Give an example of each.

6. What is the difference between ethics and social responsibility?

7. Why is ethics an important consideration in marketing decisions?

8. How do the factors that influence ethical or unethical decisions interact?

9. What ethical conflicts may exist if business employees fly on certain airlines just to receive benefits for their personal "frequent flier" programs?

10. Give an example of how ethical issues can affect each component of the marketing mix.

11. How can the ethical decisions involved in marketing be improved?

12. How can people with different personal values work together to make ethical decisions in organizations?

13. What tradeoffs might a company have to make to be socially responsible and responsive to society's demands?

14. What evidence exists that being socially responsible and ethical is worthwhile?

## APPLICATION QUESTIONS

1. Some organizations promote their social responsibility. These companies often claim that being ethical is good business and that it pays to be a "good corporate citizen." Identify an organization in your community that has a reputation for being ethical and socially responsible. What activities account for this image? Is the company successful? Why or why not?

2. If you had to conduct a social audit of your organization's ethics and social responsibility, what information would most interest you? What key stakeholders would you want to communicate with? How could such an audit assist the company in improving its ethics and social responsibility?

3. Suppose that in your job you face situations that require you to make decisions about what is right or wrong and then act on these decisions. Describe such a situation. Without disclosing your actual decision, explain what you based it on. What and whom did you think of when you were considering what to do? Why did you consider them?

4. Consumers interact with many businesses daily and weekly. Not only do companies in an industry acquire a reputation for being ethical or unethical; entire industries also become known as ethical or unethical. Identify two types of businesses with which you or others you know have had the most conflict involving ethical issues. Describe those ethical issues.

1. Corporate social responsibility is an emerging area of interest for firms. As such, many companies have conducted research and developed reports on corporate social responsibility. One such report is the KPMG International Survey of Corporate Responsibility Reporting. This report can be accessed using the search term "international survey" at **http://globaledge.msu.edu/ibrd**. In the most recent report, which category of corporate social responsibility was most widely reported, and what does it say?

2. The use of bribery in the business setting is an important ethical dilemma many companies face both domesti-cally and globally. While bribery is illegal for U.S. companies to use as a business strategy, there are still industries and countries in which it is perceived as acceptable. Transparency International's Bribe Payers Index, which assesses the perceived level of bribery in each country, can be found using the search term "bribe payers" at **http://globaledge.msu.edu/ibrd**. Using the most recent index, find the three industries in which bribery is perceived to be least prevalent. How does this compare with the three industries thought to have the largest problems with bribery?

## INTERNET Exercise

Visit **www.prideferrell.com** for resources to help you master the material in this chapter, plus materials that will help you expand your marketing knowledge, including Internet exercise updates, ACE Self-Tests, hotlinks to companies featured in this chapter, and much more.

## Business for Social Responsibility

Business for Social Responsibility (BSR) is a nonprofit organization for companies desiring to operate responsibly and demonstrate respect for ethical values, people, communities, and the natural environment. Founded in 1992, BSR offers members practical information, research, educational programs, and technical assistance as well as the opportunity to network with peers on current social responsibility issues. To learn more about this organization and access its many resources, visit **www.bsr.org**.

1. What types of businesses join BSR, and why?
2. Describe the services available to member companies. How can these services help companies improve their performances?
3. Peruse the "CRS Issue Areas and Information Links" and find the reports on ethics codes and training. Using these reports, list some examples of corporate codes of ethics and training.

## Video Case 4.1

# PETCO: Putting Pets First Earns Loyal Customers

PETCO Animal Supplies is the nation's number 2 specialty pet supply retailer, with more than 750 stores in 48 states and the District of Columbia. Its pet-related products include pet food, pet supplies, grooming products, toys, novelty items, vitamins, veterinary supplies, and small pets such as fish, birds, and hamsters. It does not sell cats or dogs, however. PETCO strives to offer customers a complete assortment of pet-related products and services at competitive prices at convenient locations and through its website, www.petco.com, with a high level of customer service.

Most PETCO stores are 12,000 to 15,000 square feet and conveniently located near local neighborhood shopping destinations, such as supermarkets, bookstores, coffee shops, dry cleaners, and video stores, where its target customers make regular weekly shopping trips. PETCO executives believe the company is well positioned, in terms of both product offerings and location, to benefit from favorable long-term demographic trends: a growing pet population and an increasing willingness of "pet parents" to spend on their pets. Indeed, the U.S. pet population has now reached 378 million companion animals, including 143 million cats and dogs. An estimated 62 percent of all U.S. households own at least one pet, and three-quarters of those households have two or more pets. The trend to have more pets and the number of pet-owning households will continue to grow, driven by an increasing number of children under 18 as well as a growing population of empty nesters whose pets become their new children. U.S. retail sales of pet food, supplies, small animals (ex-

cluding cats and dogs), and services grew to approximately $34 billion in 2004.

PETCO was founded on the principle of "connecting with the community." One of its most important missions is to promote the health, well-being, and humane treatment of animals. It strives to carry out this mission through vendor-selection programs, pet-adoption programs, and partnerships with animal-welfare organizations. The company is involved every year in a number of programs to raise money for local communities and local animal initiatives.

Recognizing that between 5 and 10 million pets are euthanized in the United States every year, PETCO launched an annual "Spay Today" initiative in 2000 to address the growing problem of pet overpopulation in the United States. The "Spay Today" funds come from customer donations at PETCO stores, where customers are encouraged to round up their purchases to the nearest dollar or more. In 2005, PETCO launched the "Think Adoption First" program, which supports and promotes the human-animal bond. It is a program that sets the standard for responsibility and community involvement for the industry. The "Spring a Pet" fundraiser encourages pet lovers to donate $1, $5, $10, or $20 to animal welfare causes. Donors received a personalized cutout bunny as a reminder of their generosity. In 2005, $1.51 million was raised and each PETCO store selected an animal welfare organization to be the recipient of the money raised at its location. The Tree of Hope program encourages customers to think of animals during the

Christmas season. Customers visiting PETCO during the Christmas season can purchase card ornaments, the proceeds of which go to animal welfare charities. The PETCO Foundation also sponsors "Kind News," a Humane Education Program that educates children about humane treatment of companion animals and fellow human beings. It features stories about responsible pet environmental concerns and issues as well as information on all types of animals.

Like all companies, PETCO operates in an environment in which a single negative incident can influence customers' perceptions of a firm's image and reputation instantly and potentially for years afterwards. Because pets engender such strong emotional attachments, it is especially important for companies that sell pets and pet products to be able to provide a rapid response to justify or to correct activities that may arouse potentially negative perceptions. The focus should be on a commitment to make correct decisions and to continually assess and address the risks of operating the business.

All retailers are subject to criticisms and must remain vigilant to maintain internal controls that provide assurance that employees and other partners follow ethical codes. PETCO accomplishes this through an ethics office and by developing an ethical corporate culture. PETCO has also developed and implemented a comprehensive Code of Ethics, which addresses all areas of organizational risk associated with human resources, conflicts of interests, and appropriate behavior in the workplace. The code's primary emphasis is that animals always come first—PETCO insists that the well-being of animals in its care is of paramount importance. In the case of PETCO, a desire to do the right thing and to train all organizational members to make ethical decisions assures not only success in the marketplace but a significant contribution to society.[68]

### Questions for Discussion

1. How does PETCO's ethics program help manage the risks associated with the pet industry?
2. How can PETCO's social responsibility programs advance its marketing strategy?
3. Why is it important for PETCO to train all of its employees to understand and implement its ethical policies?

---

## Case 4.2        On Doing Good at Ford Motor

Ford Motor Company was founded in 1903 and grew into one of the world's largest corporations, selling nearly 7 million vehicles worldwide. When founder Henry Ford ran the company in the early twentieth century, he often recycled materials—turning wooden crates into running boards, for example—to keep costs down. In more recent decades, however, Ford has not been known for its environmental record, as evidenced most recently by environmentalists' ridicule of the gas-guzzling Ford Expedition SUV and the firm's failure to achieve a much-publicized goal of improving fuel efficiency on SUVs by 25 percent. Now Henry Ford's grandson, chairman and CEO William Clay Ford, Jr., wants to change that record.

When Bill Ford stepped into the CEO's office in 2001, he brought his own values to the company and established far-reaching environmental, quality, and competitive goals for the company. Under his tenure, the company has improved quality, innovation, and cost efficiency. Ford also became the first carmaker to achieve ISO 14001 certification, a series of international environmental standards. Ford Motor also makes significant donations and grants to causes associated with education, the environment, public policy, health and social programs, civic affairs and community development, and arts and humanities, typically through its Ford Motor Company Fund foundation.

One example of Bill Ford's environmental focus is a new assembly plant in the Ford Rouge Center that features efficient and flexible manufacturing processes as well as "breakthrough" environmental methods for storm-water management, energy use, air quality, and soil restoration. The roof of the Dearborn, Michigan, factory is a four-layer, mat-like system topped with drought-resistant plants, which acts like a giant sponge, absorbing rainfall and reducing polluted storm-water run-off, as well as an insulating blanket that helps sharply reduce energy consumption in all weather. Although the environmentally friendly roof added $3.6 million to the factory's cost, the firm will reap millions in savings by reducing energy expenses and eliminating the need for expensive storm sewers and storm-water treatment systems. The company has likewise invested in green facilities using solar, wind, and other technologies designed to reduce energy consumption and emissions. At the Lima Engine Plant, for example, cold water from quarries on the plant site is used to help cool the facility, saving $300,000 a year in operating costs. These initiatives have helped Food reap significant water and energy savings. Its facilities now use 18 percent less energy overall and 5 billion fewer gallons of water than they did in 2000.

Another example of the company's environmental focus is its new focus on technologies that promise to improve the fuel efficiency of and reduce emissions from vehicles wearing Ford-owned marques. The company is aggressively pursuing fuel-cell technology, which may allow cars of the future to have great fuel efficiency and zero emissions, and working to develop cleaner burning conventional and diesel engines. Ford's E-450 hydrogen engine shuttle buses are the first commercially available hydrogen vehicles in North America. In particular, Ford has taken a leadership position in the area of hybrid vehicles, which employ an electric engine to augment the traditional gasoline engine to improve fuel efficiency. The first of these hybrid vehicles is the Escape SUV, which gets 36 miles to the gallon, about 50 percent more than a conventional Escape. With demand for hybrids escalating along with gasoline prices, the company ultimately intends to offer hybrid engines on half its models.

Although Bill Ford has been criticized by some analysts and investors for applying his personal values to Ford operations, he strongly believes his approach is the right strategy for taking the firm into its second century of operations. He points out that reducing Ford's use of nonrenewable materials will help it cut costs, and he believes that a stronger focus on social and environmental priorities will help better position Ford to respond to increasingly stringent government regulations around the world. He also recognizes that society's growing interest in environmental issues will foster a strong market for "green" products and technologies that can generate new revenue streams for the company. And perhaps most important, he acknowledges that consumers seem to assign greater value to brands that are associated with a strong commitment to social and environmental responsibility, and that more socially responsible companies can better attract and retain employees.

Will Ford's performance changes get environmentalists and other critics off his back? He says, "Tackling environmental and social issues is not something a company does *after* it is profitable; it must be something we do to *be* more profitable." He believes that being more environmentally responsible will ultimately result in a better reputation with stakeholders, particularly customers and employees; a stronger bottom line; and a safer environment.[69]

## Questions for Discussion

1. Describe the social responsibility issues that Ford Motor seems to be targeting. How do these issues relate to the firm's target markets? To other stakeholders?
2. What level of corporate social responsibility does Bill Ford have to his company and its stakeholders?
3. Debate Bill Ford's justifications for making Ford more environmentally and socially responsible.

## Strategic Case 2    Texas Instruments

### Introduction

Texas Instruments (TI) strives to develop the most effective organizational ethics and compliance program possible. The company knows it is vital to identify potential risks and uncover the existence of activities or events that relate to misconduct. It also understands that it must have the infrastructure and a plan in place to deal with unethical issues or events, which must include a rapid response system. Through explicit codes of conduct and statements of values and ethics documented in organizational communication, TI must maintain the values, the culture, and the expectations for conduct that employees hold about daily life within the firm. This same goal is also accomplished implicitly through stories about ethical decisions, by treatment of customer and employee complaints, and by the way that meetings are conducted. Another way employees learn a company's code of conduct is by noticing which behaviors and accomplishments get rewarded and recognized and which behaviors are criticized, ignored, or punished.

Texas Instruments Incorporated (NYSE: TXN) is headquartered in Dallas, Texas and has manufacturing, design, or sales operations in more than 25 countries. It has three separate business segments: (1) Semiconductor, which accounts for about 85 percent of its revenue; (2) Sensors & Controls, which accounts for about 10 percent of its revenue; and (3) Educational & Productivity Solutions, which accounts for about 5 percent of its revenue. Its largest geographic sources of revenue, in order, are Asia (excluding Japan), Europe, the United States, and Japan. The company's vision is world leadership in digital solutions for the networked society. It wants to accomplish this with excellence in everything it does; by producing products and technologies that make them and its customers substantially different from the competition, by competing in high-growth markets, and by providing consistently good financial performance.

### Background and History

The company was founded in 1930 as Geophysical Service Inc. (GSI), a pioneering provider of seismic exploration services. In December 1941, four GSI managers purchased the company, as the U.S. entered World War II. During the war the company began manufacturing submarine detection equipment for the U.S. Navy, and following the war, became a supplier of defense systems and launched a strategy that would completely change the company. In 1951, the company changed its name to Texas Instruments (TI) to reflect the change in its business strategy and entered the semiconductor business in 1952.

TI designed the first transistor radio in 1954, the handheld calculator in 1967, and the single-chip microcomputer in 1971. It was assigned the first patent on a single-chip microprocessor in 1973. TI is usually given credit with Intel for the almost simultaneous invention of the microprocessor.

TI also created the first commercial silicon transistor and invented the integrated circuit. It continued to manufacture equipment for use in the seismic industry, as well as providing seismic services. TI sold its GSI subsidiary to Halliburton in 1988 and in the early 1990s began a strategic process of focusing on its semiconductor business, primarily digital signal processors and analog semiconductors. Few companies can match the 75-year record of innovations from TI. Today TI continues to work in processing and interpreting signals, and its products are used in many things that are an integral part of our daily lives—from the single-chip mobile phone solution to cable modems, home theaters, wireless Internet, digital cameras, and advanced automotive systems. TI is also working on new signal processing innovations that will help create cars that drive themselves and allow the blind to see, as well as much more.

### The Business of TI

Semiconductors are the electronic building blocks used to create modern electronic systems and equipment. Semiconductors come in two basic forms: individual transistors, and integrated circuits (generally known as "chips") that combine different transistors on a single piece of material to form a complete electronic circuit. TI's Semiconductor segment designs, manufactures, and sells integrated circuits.

The global semiconductor market is characterized by constant, though generally incremental, advances in product designs and manufacturing methods. Typically, new chips are produced in limited quantities at first and then ramp to high-volume production over time. Chip prices and manufacturing costs tend to decline over time as manufacturing methods and product life cycles mature.

The "semiconductor cycle" is an important concept that refers to the ebb and flow of supply and demand. The semiconductor market is characterized by periods of tight supply caused by strong demand and/or insufficient manufacturing capacity, followed by periods of surplus products caused by declining demand and/or excess manufacturing capacity. This cycle is affected by the significant time and capital required to build and maintain semiconductor manufacturing facilities.

TI was the world's third-largest semiconductor company in 2004 in terms of revenue. Historically, its Semiconductor segment averages a significantly higher growth rate than its other two business segments. About 75 percent of Semiconductor revenue comes from its core products, which are analog semiconductors and digital signal processors, or DSPs. These products enhance, and often make possible, a variety of applications that serve the communications, computer, consumer, automotive, and industrial markets. The company believes that virtually all of today's digital electronic equipment requires some form of analog or digital signal processing.

TI also designs and manufactures other types of semiconductors, such as Digital Light Processing™ devices that enable exceptionally clear video, and microprocessors that serve as the brains of high-end computer servers. Knowledge about the systems its products go into is becoming increasingly important because it enables TI to differentiate its product offerings for its customers. Where a customer may have previously required multiple chips for a system to operate, TI now uses its system-level knowledge to integrate the functionality of those multiple chips onto fewer chips. A recent example is its single-chip cellphone, which combines the functionality of many separate chips onto a single chip. The digitization of electronics also requires more high-performance analog functionality. With expertise in both digital signal processing and analog at the system level, TI believes it is one of a very few semiconductor companies capable of integrating both technologies onto a single chip.

In addition, TI enables its customers, particularly original design manufacturers (ODMs), to take advantage of its system-level knowledge. This speeds its customers' time to market by making available to them standard chipsets and reference designs. Reference designs are technical blueprints that contain all the essential elements in a system. Customers using its reference designs, such as cellphone ODMs, may enhance or modify the design as required. TI's ability to deliver integrated solutions and system-level knowledge allows its customers to create more advanced systems and products.

In each of its product categories, TI faces significant competition. TI believes that competitive performance in the semiconductor market depends upon several factors, including the breadth of a company's product line as well as technological innovation, quality, reliability, price, customer service, technical support, and scale.

### Employee Stakeholders

TI employs approximately 35,200 people worldwide, with about 16,100 in the United States. During the last year TI's job growth was a -6 percent, or a reduction of 1,076 people, while its voluntary turnover was 5 percent. TI's workforce is made up of 34 percent minorities and 25 percent women. The company supports diversity through 30 employee-networking groups. Among them are the "lesbian and gay employee network," "Christian Values Initiative," and "Muslim Initiative." TI has also been mentioned as one of nine companies that have a "Best 401k Match" — it offers a 100 percent match up to 4 percent of total compensation. In addition to financial incentives, Texas Instruments offers employees ancillary benefits such as flexible work options, an employee trip reduction program, an onsite concierge, a day-spa, elder care, a summer camp for kids, and even special interest clubs such as a flying club.

TI's flexible work arrangements include flex-time, part-time, compressed work-week schedules, and telecommuting. It has New Mothers Rooms for nursing mothers in all major facilities and an online parent's network for employees to share information on issues related to children and parenting. Onsite seminars on topics such as parenting, childcare, elder care, and other work-life balance issues are yet another benefit. TI also has corporate wellness programs, services, and recreation associations, which include a childcare room at the onsite Dallas fitness center. Its wellness programs include tobacco cessation programs, travel well programs for worldwide employees, and immunizations and preventive screenings for TI employees. TI also provides onsite walking and weight management programs as well as nutrition resources to ensure that its employees are as healthy as possible. Its benefits include discount programs at daycare centers, education assistance, adoption benefits, life insurance options, pretax reimbursement accounts for dependent care and health care, and an employee assistance program— which offers confidential counseling for TIers and their family members. TI also offers a time bank program that allows accrued time off to be used for any reason.

Not only has TI been on the 2005 list of Best Employers for Healthy Lifestyles, from the National Business Group on Health's Institute on the Costs and Health Effects of Obesity, it was also listed on the 2005 Healthcare Heroes Award in the *Dallas Business Journal*. In 1998 it also received the C. Everett Koop National Health Award for excellence in health risk reduction and cost reduction programs, which is part of The Health Project at the University of Stanford.

TI is ranked 83rd on the Fortune list of 100 Best Companies to work for in 2006, up three positions from 86th in 2005. It is the sixth year that TI has been on the list. This list is based on two criteria: an evaluation of the policies and culture of each company and the opinions of the company's employees. The opinions of employees are given a weight of two-thirds of the total score, and are based on responses to a 57-question survey of 350 randomly selected employees. The remaining one-third of the score is based on an evaluation of each company's demographic makeup, pay, and benefits programs and culture. Companies are scored in four areas: credibility (communication to employees), respect (opportunities and benefits), fairness (compensation, diversity), and pride/camaraderie (philanthropy, celebrations).

TI also ranked 50th on the Business Ethics Magazine's 100 Best Corporate Citizens in 2005. The aim of the list is to identify firms that excel at serving a variety of stakeholders with excellence and integrity. For each company the list rates eight categories—shareholders, community, minorities and women, employees, environment, human rights, customers, and governance. For each area, strengths and concerns are matched against each other to arrive at the final score. TI is also a member of the Domini 400 Social Index and has won numerous awards for corporate citizenship and ethics as well as for being a good employer and for its diversity.

TI is also concerned with the environment, safety, and health. It is a "Sony Green Partner" for supplying components, devices, and materials to ensure the production of environmentally friendly products. TI is also building a "green" chip factory in Richardson, near Dallas. Although China, Taiwan, and Singapore were all tempting alternatives, TI proposed a challenge to the design team: if the TI design team and community leaders could find a way to build the new factory for $180 million less than the last Dallas factory built in the late 1990s, then TI would locate in Dallas. The design team did it. Instead of three floors, the new design has just two and it is expected to cut utility costs by 20 percent and water usage by 35 percent. Creative design and engineering will eliminate waste and reduce energy usage. Almost all of the waste from the building construction is being recycled and all the urinals are waterless.

## TI Ethics Program

TI has always been concerned about ethics in its company. The company believes that maintaining the highest ethical standards requires a partnership between employees and employers. It proactively supports employees by communicating values and giving individual guidance, while empowered employees participate actively in problem-solving. In 1987, TI decided to

actively support employees by establishing a TI ethics office and appointing a TI ethics director. The TI Ethics Office has three primary functions:

To ensure that business policies and practices continue to be aligned with ethical principles.
To clearly communicate ethical expectations.
To provide multiple channels for feedback through which people can ask questions, voice concerns, and seek resolution to ethical issues.

TI has strong documented requirements for ethical business practices. These include the TI Standard Policies and Procedures, The TI Commitment, and "The Values and Ethics of TI" booklet. The TI Values and Principles are:

Integrity—respect and value people, be honest
Innovation—learn and create, act boldly
Commitment—take responsibility, commit to win.

The Ethics quick test is also an integral part of everything TI does. It is included in the Code of Ethics booklet as a punchout card to put in a wallet or purse, and it is printed on the TI mouse pads given to employees.

The TI Ethics Quick Test:

Is the action legal?
Does it comply with our values?
If you do it, will you feel bad?
How will it look in the newspaper?
If you know its wrong, don't do it!
If you're not sure, ask.
Keep asking until you get an answer.

There are many resources and alternative communication channels available to help ensure compliance—whether as an individual or as a company. The compliance procedures are:

*Take Direct Action.* The best and most effective approach is to fix problems on the spot. If employees are considering an action or see a proposed action that raises ethical concerns, they should raise the ethical concerns right away. Frequently—perhaps usually—merely highlighting and discussing the issue will result in actions that achieve the desired goal in full compliance with TI's Values and Ethics Statement and the Code of Business Conduct. Employees should use available resources, including the Code of Ethics, the Values and Ethics Statement, the Code of Business Conduct, the Ethics Quick Test, Policies, Business Rules, Chart of Accounts, and other guidance.

*Consult Your Supervisor.* TI supervisors know employees assignments and circumstances better than anyone else. TI supervisors can often help employees find answers and solutions if the one that is being tried just doesn't seem to fit.

***Talk with Human Resources.*** If for any reason employees cannot communicate with a supervisor or local managers, they should contact the site Human Resources. The TI HR staff is there to help employees resolve many issues. Employees may counsel with them at any time.

***Call the TI Law Department.*** For questions regarding contracts, pricing practices, or anything with a legal orientation, the TI Law Department can help employees find the answers. There are attorneys assigned to assist each business group, as well as attorneys who specialize in the areas of law that TI most frequently encounters.

***Get On-Line.*** TI is an information-rich company. There are many sites on its intranet, where TI-specific information can be found.

***Contact the TI Ethics Office.*** At any time, for any reason, employees can contact the TI Ethics Office for answers to questions, including any concerns about accounting, internal accounting controls, or auditing matters. They may even remain anonymous.[70]

## Questions for Discussion

1. How effectively has TI managed the ethical and legal environment?
2. What are the ethical and legal risks associated with competing in TI's industries?
3. How would you describe TI's organizational culture?
4. Is there room for improvement in TI's ethics program?

# part 3

# Markets and Customer Behavior

**P**art **3** focuses on consumer, business, and global markets and on buyer behavior. The development of a marketing strategy begins with customers. Understanding elements that affect buying decisions enables marketers to better analyze customers' needs and evaluate how specific marketing strategies can satisfy those needs. **Chapter 5** examines consumer buying decision processes and factors that influence buying decisions. **Chapter 6** explores business markets, business customers, the buying center, and the business buying decision process. **Chapter 7** focuses on the nature, involvement, and strategy of marketing in a global economy.

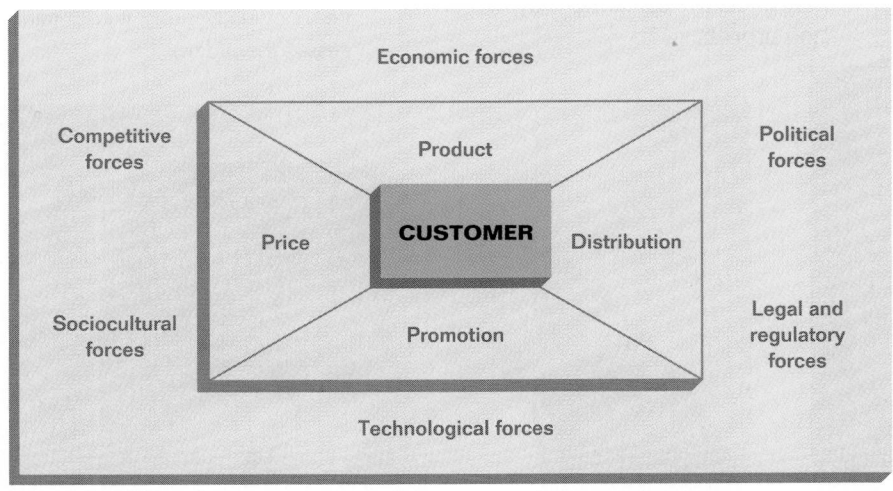

# 5

# Consumer Buying Behavior

1. To understand consumers' level of involvement with a product and describe the types of consumer problem-solving processes

2. To recognize the stages of the consumer buying decision process

3. To explore how situational influences may affect the consumer buying decision process

4. To understand the psychological influences that may affect the consumer buying decision process

5. To examine the social influences that may affect the consumer buying decision process

## Why Leave the House? Use the Mouse!

Online shopping is big—BIG—business! Last year Americans bought goods and services worth $81 billion from online retailers, a figure expected to jump to $95 billion this year, and to $144 billion by 2010. This means that U.S. residents will increase their online spending for retail products and services at an average of 12 percent annually for the next four years.

What accounts for such impressive growth? Well, since the dawn of e-commerce, there has been a steady stream of new online shoppers. Each year more and more people have become Internet-savvy and have felt more and more confident about shopping securely online—for everything from iTunes at Apple to collectibles at eBay. People far and wide are learning about the benefits of shopping online, benefits such as the ease of comparing products and prices and the ability to shop anytime of day or night. Plus, a recent study by MIT found that it is the ability to *find* products easily that prompts many consumers to shop the Internet. For example, while a brick and mortar bookstore may not be able to afford or have the space to keep titles on its shelves that sell only one or two copies a year, Amazon.com can fill an order without keeping millions of books in inventory. (When the company gets an order for an item not in inventory, it goes right to the publisher, gets the book, and processes the order.)

So what does all of this growth mean to marketers? Plenty. As online shopping matures, more people become online shoppers and eventually new customers are harder to come by. In response, online retailers and marketers will have to focus on growing their sales by attracting their competitor's customers and by keeping their current customers loyal. Coupons, free delivery, and "rewards" for frequent shoppers or users of the online store's credit card represent opportunities to attract new customers and keep existing customers devoted. Other routes for growth include improved processes:

one study suggests that online shoppers are likely to shop at sites that offer delivery services that are both reliable and flexible and that offer guaranteed online security.

Clearly, online shopping is big business—that's getting even bigger. What an opportunity![1] ■

**B**oth online and traditional marketers go to great lengths to understand their customers' needs and gain a better grasp of customers' buying behavior. Marketers attempt to understand buying behavior for several reasons. First, customers' reactions to a firm's marketing strategy have a great impact on the firm's success. Second, as we saw in Chapter 1, the marketing concept stresses that a firm should create a marketing mix that satisfies customers. To find out what satisfies buyers, marketers must examine the main influences on what, where, when, and how consumers buy. Third, by gaining a deeper understanding of the factors that affect buying behavior, marketers are in a better position to predict how consumers will respond to marketing strategies.

We begin this chapter by examining how a customer's level of involvement with a product affects the type of problem solving employed and by discussing the types of consumer problem-solving processes. Then we analyze the major stages of the consumer buying decision process, beginning with problem recognition, information search, and evaluation of alternatives and proceeding through purchase and postpurchase evaluation. Next, we examine situational influences—surroundings, time, purchase reason, and buyer's mood and condition—that affect purchasing decisions. We go on to consider psychological influences on purchasing decisions: perception, motives, learning, attitudes, personality and self-concept, and lifestyles. We conclude with a discussion of social influences that affect buying behavior, including roles, family, reference groups and opinion leaders, social classes, and culture and subcultures.

# Consumer Markets and Consumer Buying Behavior

**consumer market** Purchasers and household members who intend to consume or benefit from the purchased products and do not buy products to make profits

**buying behavior** The decision processes and acts of people involved in buying and using products

**consumer buying behavior** The decision processes and purchasing activities of people who purchase products for personal or household use and not for business purposes

In Chapter 2, we defined a market as a group of individuals and/or organizations that have needs for products in a product class and have the ability, willingness, and authority to purchase those products. Markets can be divided into two categories: consumer markets and business markets. (Business markets are discussed in Chapter 6.) The division is based on the characteristics of the individuals and groups that comprise specific markets and the purposes for which they buy products. A **consumer market** consists of purchasers and household members who intend to consume or benefit from the purchased products and do not buy products for the primary purpose of making a profit. Each of us belongs to numerous consumer markets for products such as housing, food, clothing, vehicles, personal services, appliances, furniture, and recreational equipment. A firm's ability to develop and sustain satisfying customer relationships requires an understanding of **buying behavior**, the decision processes and acts of people involved in buying and using products. **Consumer buying behavior** refers to the buying behavior of ultimate consumers, those who purchase products for personal or household use and not for business purposes.

# Level of Involvement and Consumer Problem-Solving Processes

**level of involvement** An individual's intensity of interest in a product and the importance of the product for that person

In order to acquire and maintain products that satisfy their current and future needs, consumers engage in problem solving. People engage in different types of problem-solving processes depending on the nature of the products involved. The amount of effort, both mental and physical, that buyers expend in solving problems also varies considerably. A major determinant of the type of problem-solving process employed depends on the customer's **level of involvement**, the degree of interest in a product and the importance the individual places on that product. High-involvement products tend to be those that are visible to others (such as clothing, furniture, or automobiles) and are expensive. High-importance issues, such as health care, are also associated with high levels of involvement. Low-involvement products tend to be less expensive and have less associated social risk, such as many grocery items. A person's interest in a product or product category that is ongoing and long term is referred to as *enduring involvement*. For example, a consumer interested in technology might always have the most advanced electronic devices, read electronics magazines, and work in a related field. However, most consumers have an enduring involvement with only a very few activities or items. In contrast, *situational involvement* is temporary and dynamic, and results from a particular set of circumstances, such as the need to buy a new car after being involved in an accident. For a short time period, the consumer will visit car dealerships, visit a car company's website, or even purchase automotive-related magazines or books. However, once the car purchase is made, the consumer's interest and involvement tapers off. Consumer involvement may be attached to product categories (such as sports), loyalty to a specific brand, interest in a specific advertisement (e.g., a funny commercial) or a medium (such as a particular television show), or to certain decisions and behaviors (e.g., a love of shopping). On the other hand, a consumer may find a particular advertisement entertaining, yet have little involvement with the brand advertised because of loyalty to another brand.[2] Involvement level, as well as other factors, affects a person's selection of one of three types of consumer problem solving: routinized response behavior, limited problem solving, or extended problem solving (Table 5.1).

**routinized response behavior**
A consumer problem-solving process used when buying frequently purchased, low-cost items that require very little search-and-decision effort

A consumer uses **routinized response behavior** when buying frequently purchased, low-cost items needing very little search-and-decision effort. When buying such items, a consumer may prefer a particular brand but is familiar with several brands in the product class and views more than one as acceptable. Typically, low-involvement products are bought through routinized response behavior, that is, almost automatically. For example, most buyers spend little time or effort selecting soft drinks or cereals.

**limited problem solving** A consumer problem-solving process used when purchasing products occasionally or needing information about an unfamiliar brand in a familiar product category

Buyers engage in **limited problem solving** when buying products occasionally or when they need to obtain information about an unfamiliar brand in a familiar product category. This type of problem solving requires a moderate amount of time for information gathering and deliberation. For example, if Procter & Gamble introduces an improved Tide laundry detergent, buyers will seek additional information about the new product, perhaps by asking a friend who has used it or watching a commercial about it, before making a trial purchase.

**extended problem solving** A consumer problem-solving process employed when purchasing unfamiliar, expensive, or infrequently bought products

The most complex type of problem solving, **extended problem solving**, occurs when purchasing unfamiliar, expensive, or infrequently bought products—for instance, a car, home, or college education. The buyer uses many criteria to evaluate alternative brands or choices and spends much time seeking information and deciding on the purchase. Extended problem solving is frequently used for purchasing high-involvement products.

Purchase of a particular product does not always elicit the same type of problem-solving process. In some instances, we engage in extended problem solving the first

| table 5.1 | CONSUMER PROBLEM SOLVING | | |
|---|---|---|---|
| | **Routinized Response** | **Limited** | **Extended** |
| Product cost | Low | Low to moderate | High |
| Search effort | Little | Little to moderate | Extensive |
| Time spent | Short | Short to medium | Lengthy |
| Brand preference | More than one is acceptable, although one may be preferred | Several | Varies; usually many |

time we buy a certain product but find that limited problem solving suffices when we buy it again. If a routinely purchased, formerly satisfying brand no longer satisfies us, we may use limited or extended problem solving to switch to a new brand. Thus, if we notice that the brand of pain reliever we normally buy is no longer working, we may seek out a different brand through limited problem solving. Most consumers occasionally make purchases solely on impulse and not on the basis of any of these three problem-solving processes. **Impulse buying** involves no conscious planning but results from a powerful urge to buy something immediately.

**impulse buying** An unplanned buying behavior resulting from a powerful urge to buy something immediately

# Consumer Buying Decision Process

**consumer buying decision process** A five-stage purchase decision process that includes problem recognition, information search, evaluation of alternatives, purchase, and postpurchase evaluation

The **consumer buying decision process**, shown in Figure 5.1, includes five stages: problem recognition, information search, evaluation of alternatives, purchase, and postpurchase evaluation. Before we examine each stage, consider these important points. First, the actual act of purchasing is just one stage in the process, and usually not the first stage. Second, even though we indicate that a purchase occurs, not all decision processes lead to a purchase; individuals may end the process at any stage. Finally, not all consumer decisions include all five stages. People engaged in extended problem solving usually go through all stages of this decision process, whereas those engaged in limited problem solving and routinized response behavior may omit some stages.

## Problem Recognition

Problem recognition occurs when a buyer becomes aware of a difference between a desired state and an actual condition. Consider a student who owns a nonprogrammable calculator and learns she needs a programmable one for her math course. She recognizes that a difference exists between the desired state—having a programmable calculator—and her actual condition. She therefore decides to buy a new calculator.

The speed of consumer problem recognition can be quite rapid or rather slow. Sometimes a person has a problem or need but is unaware of it. Marketers use sales personnel, advertising, and packaging to help trigger recognition of such needs or problems. For example, a university bookstore may advertise programmable

**figure 5.1**

**CONSUMER BUYING DECISION PROCESS AND POSSIBLE INFLUENCES ON THE PROCESS**

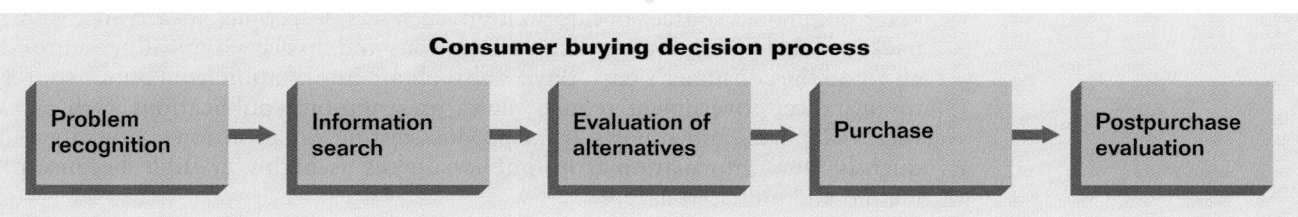

**Possible influences on the decision process**

| **Situational influences** | **Psychological influences** | **Social influences** |
|---|---|---|
| ▸ Physical surroundings | ▸ Perception | ▸ Roles |
| ▸ Social surroundings | ▸ Motives | ▸ Family |
| ▸ Time | ▸ Learning | ▸ Reference groups |
| ▸ Purchase reason | ▸ Attitudes | ▸ Opinion leaders |
| ▸ Buyer's mood and condition | ▸ Personality and self-concept | ▸ Social classes |
| | ▸ Lifestyles | ▸ Culture and subcultures |

**Consumer buying decision process**

Problem recognition → Information search → Evaluation of alternatives → Purchase → Postpurchase evaluation

Protect his habitat. And yours.

When you recycle your rechargeable batteries, you preserve his environment – and ours. Check the batteries in your cordless power tools, cordless and cellular phones, camcorders, laptop computers, digital cameras, and two-way radios. If they no longer hold a charge, recycle them by visiting one of many collection sites nationwide, including those retailers listed below. For a complete list of rechargeable battery drop-off locations, visit www.call2recycle.org or call toll free 877-2-RECYCLE.

Recycle your rechargeable batteries.

call②recycle
A Rechargeable Battery Recycling Corporation program

Recycle at one of these national retailers:   BLACK&DECKER   Home Depot   LOWE'S   RadioShack.   Sears   TARGET

**Problem Recognition**

In this advertisement, Call2Recycle stimulates problem recognition–in this case, what to do with used batteries. Problem recognition is the first stage in the consumer buying process.

calculators in the school newspaper at the beginning of the term. Students who see the advertisement may recognize that they need these calculators for their course work.

## Information Search

After recognizing the problem or need, a buyer (if continuing the decision process) searches for product information that will help resolve the problem or satisfy the need. For example, after recognizing her need for a programmable calculator, the above-mentioned student may search for information about different types and brands of calculators. She acquires information over time from her surroundings. However, the information's impact depends on how she interprets it.

An information search has two aspects. In an **internal search**, buyers search their memories for information about products that might solve their problem. If they cannot retrieve enough information from memory to make a decision, they seek additional information from outside sources in an **external search**. The external search may focus on communication with friends or relatives, comparison of available brands and prices, marketer-dominated sources, and/or public sources. For example, one survey found that the Internet is the preferred information source among car shoppers in online households, especially for pricing information.[3] An individual's personal contacts—friends, relatives, and associates—often are influential sources of information because the person trusts and respects them. Utilizing marketer-dominated sources of information, such as salespeople, advertising, websites, package labeling, and in-store demonstrations and displays, typically requires little effort on the consumer's part. Buyers also obtain information from public sources—for instance, government reports, news presentations, publications such as *Consumer Reports,* and reports from product-testing organizations. Consumers frequently view information from public sources as highly credible because of its factual and unbiased nature.

**internal search** An information search in which buyers search their memories for information about products that might solve their problem

**external search** An information search in which buyers seek information from sources other than memory

**Framing Product Attributes**
Gillette frames product attributes of its Fusion razor by advertising features such as "5-blade shaving surface technology," "precision trimmer blade," "comfortable," and "stylish."

Repetition, a technique well known to advertisers, increases consumers' learning of information. When seeing or hearing an advertising message for the first time, recipients may not grasp all its important details, but they learn more details as the message is repeated. Nevertheless, even when commercials are initially effective, repetition eventually may cause wear-out, meaning consumers pay less attention to the commercial and respond to it less favorably than they did at first. Information can be presented verbally, numerically, or visually. Marketers pay great attention to the visual components of their advertising materials.

## Evaluation of Alternatives

A successful information search within a product category yields a group of brands that a buyer views as possible alternatives. This group of brands is sometimes called a **consideration set** (also called an *evoked set*). For example, a consideration set of programmable calculators might include those made by Texas Instruments, Hewlett-Packard, Sharp, and Canon.

To assess the products in a consideration set, the buyer uses **evaluative criteria**, objective characteristics (such as the size of a calculator) and subjective characteristics (such as style) that are important to the buyer. For example, one calculator buyer may want a rechargeable unit with a large display and large buttons, whereas another may have no size preferences but dislikes rechargeable calculators. The buyer also assigns a certain level of importance to each criterion: some features and characteristics carry more weight than others. Using the criteria, the buyer rates and eventually ranks brands in the consideration set. The evaluation stage may yield no brand the buyer is willing to purchase. In that case, a further information search may be necessary.

Marketers may influence consumers' evaluations by *framing* the alternatives, that is, describing the alternatives and their attributes in a certain manner. Framing can make a characteristic seem more important to a consumer and facilitate its recall from memory. For example, by stressing a car's superior comfort and safety features over those of a competitor's, a carmaker can direct consumers' attention toward these points of superiority. Framing probably influences the decision processes of inexperienced buyers more than those of experienced ones. If the evaluation of alternatives yields one or more brands the consumer is willing to buy, he or she is ready to move on to the next stage of the decision process: the purchase.

## Purchase

In the purchase stage, the consumer chooses the product or brand to be bought. Selection is based on the outcome of the evaluation stage and on other dimensions. Product availability may influence which brand is purchased. For example, if the brand ranked highest in evaluation is unavailable, the buyer may purchase the brand ranked second. If a consumer wants a pair of black Nikes and cannot find them in his size, he may buy a pair of black Reeboks.

During this stage, buyers also pick the seller from which they will buy the product. The choice of seller may affect final product selection and therefore the terms of

**consideration set** A group of brands within a product category that a buyer views as alternatives for possible purchase

**evaluative criteria** Objective and subjective characteristics that are important to a buyer

sale, which, if negotiable, are determined at this stage. Other issues, such as price, delivery, warranties, maintenance agreements, installation, and credit arrangements, are also settled. Finally, the actual purchase takes place during this stage, unless the consumer decides to terminate the buying decision process.

## Postpurchase Evaluation

After the purchase, the buyer begins evaluating the product to ascertain if its actual performance meets expected levels. Many criteria used in evaluating alternatives are applied again during postpurchase evaluation. The outcome of this stage is either satisfaction or dissatisfaction, which influences whether the consumer complains, communicates with other possible buyers, and repurchases the brand or product.

**cognitive dissonance** A buyer's doubts shortly after a purchase about whether the decision was the right one

Shortly after purchase of an expensive product, evaluation may result in **cognitive dissonance**, doubts in the buyer's mind about whether purchasing the product was the right decision. For example, after buying a $199 iPod, the consumer may feel guilty about the purchase or wonder whether she purchased the right brand and quality. Cognitive dissonance is most likely to arise when a person has recently bought an expensive, high-involvement product that lacks some of the desirable features of competing brands. A buyer experiencing cognitive dissonance may attempt to return the product or seek positive information about it to justify choosing it. Marketers sometimes attempt to reduce cognitive dissonance by having salespeople telephone recent purchasers to make sure they are satisfied with their new purchases. At times, recent buyers are sent results of studies showing that other consumers are very satisfied with the brand.

As Figure 5.1 shows, three major categories of influences are believed to affect the consumer buying decision process: situational, psychological, and social. In the remainder of this chapter, we focus on these influences. Although we discuss each major influence separately, their effects on the consumer decision process are interrelated.

Marketers employ a number of marketing research techniques, some of which will be discussed in Chapter 9, to better understand their customers' buying decision processes and factors that influence those buying decision processes. Both conventional and unconventional marketing research methods are used.

# Situational Influences on the Buying Decision Process

**situational influences** Influences resulting from circumstances, time, and location that affect the consumer buying decision process

**Situational influences** result from circumstances, time, and location that affect the consumer buying decision process. For example, buying an automobile tire after noticing, while washing your car, that the tire is badly worn is a different experience from buying a tire right after a blowout on the highway derails your vacation. Situational factors can influence the buyer during any stage of the consumer buying decision process and may cause the individual to shorten, lengthen, or terminate the process.

Situational factors can be classified into five categories: physical surroundings, social surroundings, time perspective, reason for purchase, and the buyer's momentary mood and condition.[4] Physical surroundings include location, store atmosphere, aromas, sounds, lighting, weather, and other factors in the physical environment in which the decision process occurs. Marketers at some banks, department stores, and specialty stores go to considerable effort and expense to create physical settings conducive to making purchase decisions. Numerous restaurant chains, such as Olive Garden and Chili's, invest heavily in facilities, often building from the ground up, to provide special surroundings that enhance customers' dining experiences.

In some settings, dimensions such as weather, traffic sounds, and odors are clearly beyond marketers' control; instead marketers must try to make customers more comfortable. General climatic conditions, for example, may influence a customer's decision to buy a specific type of vehicle (such as an SUV) and certain acces-

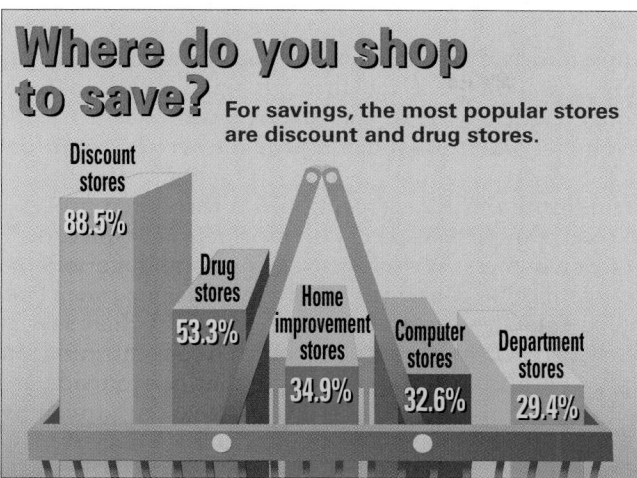

*Source:* Data from American Research Group, April 2005.

sories (such as four-wheel drive). Current weather conditions, depending on whether they are favorable or unfavorable, may either encourage or discourage consumers to go shopping to seek out specific products. Social surroundings include characteristics and interactions of others who are present during a purchase decision, such as friends, relatives, salespeople, and other customers. Buyers may feel pressured to behave in a certain way because they are in a public place such as a restaurant, store, or sports arena. Thoughts about who will be around when the product is used or consumed is also a dimension of the social setting. An overcrowded store or an argument between a customer and a salesperson may cause consumers to leave the store.

The time dimension, too, influences the buying decision process in several ways, such as the amount of time required to become knowledgeable about a product, to search for it, and to buy and use it. For instance, more men are buying diamond engagement rings online partly to make an informed decision at their own convenience. A high-end Internet jeweler like Blue Nile features interactive tools on its website to help men educate themselves about diamonds and then select a unique combination from its large inventory of diamonds and settings.[5] Time plays a major role in that the buyer considers the possible frequency of product use, the length of time required to use the product, and the length of the overall product life. Other time dimensions that influence purchases include time of day, day of the week or month, seasons, and holidays. The amount of time pressure a consumer is under affects how much time is devoted to purchase decisions. A customer under severe time constraints is likely either to make a quick purchase decision or to delay a decision.

The purchase reason raises the questions of what exactly the product purchase should accomplish and for whom. Generally, consumers purchase an item for their own use, for household use, or as a gift. For example, people who are buying a gift may buy a different product from one they would buy for themselves. If you own a Cross pen, for example, it is unlikely that you bought it for yourself.

The buyer's momentary moods (such as anger, anxiety, contentment) or momentary conditions (fatigue, illness, being flush with cash) may have a bearing on the consumer buying decision process. These moods or conditions immediately precede the current situation and are not chronic. Any of these moods or conditions can affect a person's ability and desire to search for information, receive information, or seek and evaluate alternatives. They can also significantly influence a consumer's postpurchase evaluation.

# Psychological Influences on the Buying Decision Process

**psychological influences**
Factors that in part determine people's general behavior, thus influencing their behavior as consumers

**Psychological influences** partly determine people's general behavior and thus influence their behavior as consumers. Primary psychological influences on consumer behavior are perception, motives, learning, attitudes, personality and self-concept, and lifestyles. Even though these psychological factors operate internally, they are very much affected by social forces outside the individual.

## Perception

**perception** The process of selecting, organizing, and interpreting information inputs to produce meaning

Different people perceive the same thing at the same time in different ways. When you first look at the illustration below, do you see the fish changing into birds or the birds changing into fish? Similarly, an individual may perceive the same item in a number of ways at different times. **Perception** is the process of selecting, organizing,

**Fish or Fowl?**

Do you see fish changing into birds or birds changing into fish?

and interpreting information inputs to produce meaning. **Information inputs** are sensations received through sight, taste, hearing, smell, and touch. When we hear an advertisement, see a friend, smell polluted air or water, or touch a product, we receive information inputs.

As the definition indicates, perception is a three-step process. Although we receive numerous pieces of information at once, only a few reach our awareness. We select some inputs and ignore others because we cannot be conscious of all inputs at one time. This process is called **selective exposure** because an individual selects which inputs will reach awareness. If you are concentrating on this paragraph, you probably are not aware that cars outside are making noise, that the room light is on, or that you are touching this page. Even though you receive these inputs, they do not reach your awareness until they are pointed out.

An individual's current set of needs affects selective exposure. Information inputs that relate to one's strongest needs at a given time are more likely to be selected to reach awareness. It is not by random chance that many fast-food commercials are aired near mealtimes. Customers are more likely to tune in to these advertisements at these times.

The selective nature of perception may result not only in selective exposure but also in two other conditions: selective distortion and selective retention. **Selective distortion** is changing or twisting currently received information; it occurs when a person receives information inconsistent with personal feelings or beliefs. For example, on seeing an advertisement promoting a disliked brand, a viewer may distort the information to make it more consistent with prior views. This distortion substantially lessens the effect of the advertisement on the individual. In **selective retention**, a person remembers information inputs that support personal feelings and beliefs and forgets inputs that do not. After hearing a sales presentation and leaving a store, for example, a customer may forget many selling points if they contradict personal beliefs.

The second step in the process of perception is perceptual organization. Information inputs that reach awareness are not received in an organized form. To produce meaning, an individual must mentally organize and integrate new information with what is already stored in memory. People use several methods to organize. One method, called *closure*, occurs when a person mentally fills in missing elements in a pattern or statement. In an attempt to draw attention to its brand, an advertiser will capitalize on closure by using incomplete images, sounds, or statements in its advertisements.

Interpretation, the third step in the perceptual process, is the assignment of meaning to what has been organized. A person bases interpretation on what he or she expects or what is familiar. For this reason, a manufacturer that changes a product or its package faces a major problem: when people are looking for the old, familiar product or package, they may not recognize the new one. For instance, when Smucker's redesigned its packaging, marketers told designers that, although they wanted a more contemporary package design, they also wanted a classic look so that customers would perceive the products to be the familiar ones they had been buying for years. Unless a product or package change is accompanied by a promotional program that makes people aware of the change, an organization may suffer a sales decline.

Although marketers cannot control buyers' perceptions, they often try to influence them through information. Several problems may arise from such attempts,

**information inputs** Sensations received through sight, taste, hearing, smell, and touch

**selective exposure** The process by which some inputs are selected to reach awareness and others are not

**selective distortion** An individual's changing or twisting of information that is inconsistent with personal feelings or beliefs

**selective retention** Remembering information inputs that support personal feelings and beliefs and forgetting inputs that do not

however. First, a consumer's perceptual process may operate such that a seller's information never reaches that person. For example, a buyer may block out a salesperson's presentation. Second, a buyer may receive a seller's information but perceive it differently than was intended. For example, when a toothpaste producer advertises that "35 percent of the people who use this toothpaste have fewer cavities," a customer might infer that 65 percent of users have more cavities. Third, a buyer who perceives information inputs to be inconsistent with prior beliefs is likely to forget the information quickly.

## Motives

**motive** An internal energizing force that directs a person's behavior toward satisfying needs or achieving goals

A **motive** is an internal energizing force that directs a person's activities toward satisfying needs or achieving goals. Buyers' actions are affected by a set of motives rather than by just one motive. At a single point in time, some of a person's motives are stronger than others. For example, a person's motives for having a cup of coffee are much stronger right after waking up than just before going to bed. Motives also affect the direction and intensity of behavior. Some motives may help an individual achieve his or her goals, whereas others create barriers to goal achievement.

Abraham Maslow, an American psychologist, conceived a theory of motivation based on a hierarchy of needs. According to Maslow, humans seek to satisfy five levels of needs, from most important to least important, as shown in Figure 5.2. This sequence is known as **Maslow's hierarchy of needs**. Once needs at one level are met, humans seek to fulfill needs at the next level up in the hierarchy.

**Maslow's hierarchy of needs** The five levels of needs that humans seek to satisfy, from most to least important

At the most basic level are *physiological needs*, requirements for survival such as food, water, sex, clothing, and shelter, which people try to satisfy first. Food and beverage marketers often appeal to physiological needs. Marketers of whitening toothpastes such as Ultrabrite sometimes promote their brands based on sex appeal.

At the next level are *safety needs*, which include security and freedom from physical and emotional pain and suffering. Life insurance, automobile air bags, carbon monoxide detectors, vitamins, and decay-fighting toothpastes are products that consumers purchase to meet safety needs.

Next are *social needs*, the human requirements for love and affection and a sense of belonging. Advertisements frequently appeal to social needs. Ads for cosmetics and other beauty products, jewelry, and even cars often suggest that purchasing these products will bring love. Certain types of trendy clothing, such as Abercrombie jeans, Nike athletic shoes, or T-shirts imprinted with logos or slogans, appeal to the customer's need to belong.

**patronage motives** Motives that influence where a person purchases products on a regular basis

At the level of *esteem needs*, people require respect and recognition from others as well as self-esteem, a sense of one's own worth. Owning a Lexus automobile, having a beauty makeover, or flying first class can satisfy esteem needs. At the top of the hierarchy are *self-actualization needs*. These refer to people's need to grow and develop and to become all they are capable of becoming. Some products that satisfy these needs include fitness center memberships, education, self-improvement workshops, and skiing lessons. In its recruiting advertisements, the U.S. Army told potential enlistees to "be all that you can be in the Army," a message that implies that people can reach their full potential by enlisting in the U.S. Army.

Motives that influence where a person purchases products on a regular basis are called **patronage motives**. A buyer may shop at a specific store because of such patronage motives as price, service, location, product variety, or friendliness of salespeople. To capitalize on patronage motives, marketers try to determine why regular customers patronize a particular store and to emphasize these characteristics in the store's marketing mix.

**figure 5.2**

### MASLOW'S HIERARCHY OF NEEDS

Self-actualization needs
Esteem needs
Social needs
Safety needs
Physiological needs

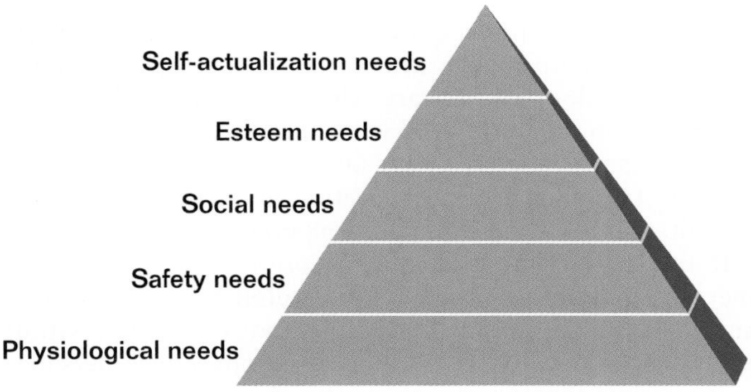

Maslow believed that people seek to fulfill five categories of needs.

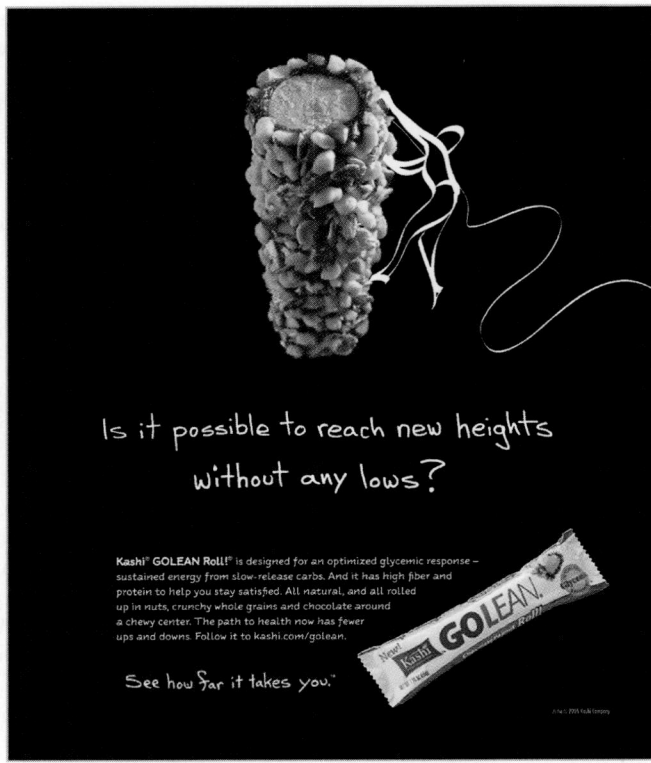

## Learning

The American Society for the Prevention of Cruelty to Animals and the maker of Kashi GoLean Bars attempt to change thought processes and behaviors with their advertisements.

**learning** Changes in an individual's thought processes and behavior caused by information and experience

## Learning

**Learning** refers to changes in a person's thought processes and behavior caused by information and experience. Consequences of behavior strongly influence the learning process. Behaviors that result in satisfying consequences tend to be repeated. For example, a consumer who buys a Snickers candy bar and enjoys the taste is more likely to buy a Snickers again. In fact, the individual will probably continue to purchase that brand until it no longer provides satisfaction. When effects of the behavior are no longer satisfying, the person may switch brands or stop eating candy bars altogether.

When making purchasing decisions, buyers process information. Individuals' abilities in this regard differ. The type of information inexperienced buyers use may differ from the type used by experienced shoppers familiar with the product and purchase situation. Thus, two potential purchasers of an antique desk may use different types of information in making their purchase decisions. The inexperienced buyer may judge the desk's value by price, whereas the more experienced buyer may seek information about the manufacturer, period, and place of origin to judge the desk's quality and value. Consumers lacking experience may seek information from others when making a purchase and even take along an informed "purchase pal." More experienced buyers have greater self-confidence and more knowledge about the product and can recognize which product features are reliable cues to product quality. For example, Safeway decided to launch its Safeway.com online grocery shopping service in Portland, Oregon, and Vancouver, Washington, because consumers in those two cities were already familiar with the operation and offerings of web-based grocery stores. As a result, these consumers had the experience and knowledge, and thus were more likely to understand and use Safeway.com.[6]

Marketers help customers learn about their products by helping them gain experience with them. Free samples, sometimes coupled with coupons, can successfully encourage trial and reduce purchase risk. For example, because some consumers may be wary of exotic menu items, restaurants sometimes offer free samples. In-store demonstrations foster knowledge of product uses. A software producer may use point-of-sale product demonstrations to introduce a new product. Test drives give potential new-car purchasers some experience with the automobile's features.

Consumers also learn by experiencing products indirectly through information from salespeople, advertisements, websites, friends, and relatives. Through sales personnel and advertisements, marketers offer information before (and sometimes after) purchases to influence what consumers learn and to create more favorable attitudes toward the product. However, their efforts are seldom fully successful. Marketers encounter problems in attracting and holding consumers' attention, providing consumers with important information for making purchase decisions, and convincing them to try the product.

## Attitudes

**attitude** An individual's enduring evaluation of feelings about and behavioral tendencies toward an object or idea

An **attitude** is an individual's enduring evaluation of feelings about and behavioral tendencies toward an object or idea. The objects toward which we have attitudes may be tangible or intangible, living or nonliving. For example, we have attitudes toward sex, religion, politics, and music, just as we do toward cars, football, and breakfast cereals. Although attitudes can change, they tend to generally remain stable and do not vary from moment to moment. However, all of a person's attitudes do not have equal impact at any one time; some are stronger than others. Individuals acquire attitudes through experience and interaction with other people.

An attitude consists of three major components: cognitive, affective, and behavioral. The cognitive component is the person's knowledge and information about the object or idea. The affective component comprises the individual's feelings and

**Attempting to Change Attitudes**

Mothers Against Drunk Driving works to educate people about the dangers of drunk driving.

emotions toward the object or idea. The behavioral component manifests itself in the person's actions regarding the object or idea. Changes in one of these components may or may not alter the other components. Thus, a consumer may become more knowledgeable about a specific brand without changing the affective or behavioral components of his or her attitude toward that brand.

Consumer attitudes toward a company and its products greatly influence success or failure of the firm's marketing strategy. When consumers have strong negative attitudes toward one or more aspects of a firm's marketing practices, they may not only stop using its products but also urge relatives and friends to do likewise.

Because attitudes play such an important part in determining consumer behavior, marketers should measure consumer attitudes toward prices, package designs, brand names, advertisements, salespeople, repair services, store locations, features of existing or proposed products, and social responsibility efforts. Several methods help marketers gauge these attitudes. One of the simplest ways is to question people directly. Marion General Hospital in Marion, Indiana, for example, asked Press Ganey Associates to ask patients about their hospital experiences, including the food. The research firm found that satisfaction with Marion General's food service ranked in the 40th percentile. To help boost customer satisfaction with the hospital's food, the hospital consulted with a Fort Wayne hospital whose food service ranked in the 90th percentile. After implementing several ideas from the consultation, Marion General's food satisfaction score rose into the 70th percentile and ultimately reached a rating in the '90s.[7] Marketers also evaluate attitudes through attitude scales. An **attitude scale** usually consists of a series of adjectives, phrases, or sentences about an object. Respondents indicate the intensity of their feelings toward the object by reacting to the adjectives, phrases, or sentences in a certain way. For example, a marketer measuring people's attitudes toward shopping might ask respondents to indicate the extent to which they agree or disagree with a number of statements, such as "Shopping is more fun than watching television." By using an attitude scale, a marketing research company was able to identify and classify six major types of clothing purchasers. The scale was based on such attributes as demographics, media use, and purchase behavior.

When marketers determine that a significant number of consumers have negative attitudes toward an aspect of a marketing mix, they may try to change those attitudes to make them more favorable. This task is generally lengthy, expensive, and difficult, and may require extensive promotional efforts. For example, the California Prune Growers, an organization of prune producers, has tried to use advertising to change consumers' attitudes toward prunes by presenting them as a nutritious snack high in potassium and fiber. To alter consumers' responses so that more of them buy a given brand, a firm might launch an information-focused campaign to change the cognitive component of a consumer's attitude or a persuasive (emotional) campaign to influence the affective component. Distributing free samples might help change the behavioral component. Both business and nonbusiness organizations try to change people's attitudes about many things, from health and safety to prices and product features.

**attitude scale** A means of measuring consumer attitudes by gauging the intensity of individuals' reactions to adjectives, phrases, or sentences about an object

**personality** A set of internal traits and distinct behavioral tendencies that result in consistent patterns of behavior in certain situations

## Personality and Self-Concept

**Personality** is a set of internal traits and distinct behavioral tendencies that result in consistent patterns of behavior in certain situations. An individual's personality arises from hereditary characteristics

## marketing ENTREPRENEURS

**M**elissa and Mallory Gollick of Denver, Colorado, share more in common than your average siblings. They both became entrepreneurs at the tender age of 9. Melissa, now 20, is the founder and operator of MelMaps, a computer graphics firm specializing in location, vicinity, site, and floor maps. Over the past 9 years, she has established a loyal clientele of local real estate agents and bankers. Her younger sister Mallory, who is now 18, owns and operates Jungle Beans, a company that sells gourmet Costa Rican coffee beans to the tune of 40 kilos (88 pounds) a week.

**Melissa and Mallory Gollick**

**THEIR BUSINESSES:** MelMaps and Jungle Beans

**FOUNDED AT AGE:** 9

**SUCCESS:** Loyal customers

and personal experiences that make the person unique. Personalities typically are described as having one or more characteristics, such as compulsiveness, ambition, gregariousness, dogmatism, authoritarianism, introversion, extroversion, and competitiveness. Marketing researchers look for relationships between such characteristics and buying behavior. Even though a few links between several personality traits and buyer behavior have been determined, results of many studies have been inconclusive. The weak association between personality and buying behavior may be the result of unreliable measures rather than a lack of a relationship. A number of marketers are convinced that consumers' personalities do influence types and brands of products purchased. For example, the type of clothing, jewelry, or automobile a person buys may reflect one or more personality characteristics.

At times marketers aim advertising at certain types of personalities. For example, ads for certain cigarette brands are directed toward specific personality types. Marketers focus on positively valued personality characteristics, such as security consciousness, sociability, independence, or competitiveness, rather than on negatively valued ones, such as insensitivity or timidity.

**self-concept** A perception or view of oneself

A person's self-concept is closely linked to personality. **Self-concept** (sometimes called *self-image*) is a perception or view of oneself. Individuals develop and alter their self-concepts based on an interaction between psychological and social dimensions. Research shows that buyers purchase products that reflect and enhance their self-concepts and that purchase decisions are important to the development and maintenance of a stable self-concept. Consumers' self-concepts may influence whether they buy a product in a specific product category and may affect brand selection as well as where they buy. For example, home improvement retailer Lowe's is targeting women—who make 90 percent of household decisions about home decor and home improvement—using self-concept as the basis of its advertising message. "Only Lowe's has everything and everyone to help your house tell the story about who you really are," says the company's advertising tag line.[8]

**lifestyle** An individual's pattern of living expressed through activities, interests, and opinions

## Lifestyles

A **lifestyle** is an individual's pattern of living expressed through activities, interests, and opinions. Lifestyle patterns include the ways people spend time, the extent of their interaction with others, and their general outlook on life and living. People partially determine their own lifestyles, but the pattern is also affected by personality and by demographic factors such as age, education, income, and social class. Lifestyles are measured through a lengthy series of questions.

Lifestyles have a strong impact on many aspects of the consumer buying decision process, from problem recognition to postpurchase evaluation. Lifestyles influence consumers' product needs, brand preferences, types of media used, and how and where they shop.

**Lifestyles**

A variety of purchasing decisions are partially influenced by lifestyles.

# Social Influences on the Buying Decision Process

**social influences** The forces other people exert on one's buying behavior

Forces that other people exert on buying behavior are called **social influences**. As Figure 5.1 shows, they are grouped into five major areas: roles, family, reference groups and opinion leaders, social classes, and culture and subcultures.

## Roles

**role** Actions and activities that a person in a particular position is supposed to perform based on expectations of the individual and surrounding persons

All of us occupy positions within groups, organizations, and institutions. Associated with each position is a **role**, a set of actions and activities a person in a particular position is supposed to perform based on expectations of both the individual and surrounding persons. Because people occupy numerous positions, they have many roles. For example, a man may perform the roles of son, husband, father, employee or employer, church member, civic organization member, and student in an evening college class. Thus, multiple sets of expectations are placed on each person's behavior.

An individual's roles influence both general behavior and buying behavior. The demands of a person's many roles may be diverse and even inconsistent. Consider the various types of clothes that you buy and wear depending on whether you are going to class, to work, to a party, or to the gym. You and others involved in these settings have expectations about what is acceptable clothing for these events. Thus, the expectations of those around us affect our purchases of clothing and many other products.

# Yoga Mamas: Today's Choosy Mothers

Soccer moms move over—there's a hot new spender in town. She buys $150 designer diaper bags, pricey organic baby foods and lotions, and Italian leather toddler shoes at Nordstrom's. She is an emerging class of woman that marketers call Yoga Mamas. The name is not meant to imply that all of these women practice yoga (though most do), but rather that they share similar lifestyles.

These middle- and upper-income mothers, age 25 to 40, are more interested in getting in touch with their inner selves and pampering their children than being on-the-go housewives. To them motherhood is a personal statement. No matter what their income, they spend lavishly on their babies and toddlers. They're more apt than soccer moms to want that $700 Bugaboo stroller and more inclined to buy products like organic food and clothing for their young ones. They tend to be more educated and have more disposable income to spend on fewer children than past generations.

Yoga Mamas are revolutionizing the baby products market as evidenced by the brisk sales of premium-priced products. Sales of specialty baby toiletries have tripled in the past five years, and it is estimated that sales of furnishings and accessories for infants, such as strollers and car seats, will jump from $7 billion in 1998 to $11 billion in 2007: a 57 percent increase. Further, sales of infant and toddler clothing increased by approximately 33 percent in the last five years—a time period when overall apparel sales declined.

Beyond their own purchasing power, these women tend to be trendsetters and opinion leaders. They have active lifestyles, share common interests with other moms, and are prolific Internet users. If they are satisfied with their product, they might inform 50 other mothers, who then become potential prospects. Yoga Mamas are clearly a group that marketers should pay attention to.

## Family Influences and Consumer Buying Decisions

**consumer socialization** The process through which a person acquires the knowledge and skills to function as a consumer

Family influences have a very direct impact on the consumer buying decision process. Parents teach children how to cope with a variety of problems, including those dealing with purchase decisions. **Consumer socialization** is the process through which a person acquires the knowledge and skills to function as a consumer. Often children gain this knowledge and set of skills by observing parents and older siblings in purchase situations, as well as through their own purchase experiences. Children observe brand preferences and buying practices in their families and, as adults, retain some of these brand preferences and buying practices as they establish and raise their own families. Buying decisions made by a family are a combination of group and individual decision making.

Although female roles continue to change, women still make buying decisions related to many household items, including health-care products, laundry supplies, paper products, and foods. Spouses participate jointly in the purchase of a variety of products, especially durable goods. Due to changes in men's roles, a significant proportion of men are major grocery shoppers. Children make many purchase decisions and influence numerous household purchase decisions. Knowing that children wield considerable influence over food brand preferences, H. J. Heinz is targeting them with EZ Squirt green, blue, or purple ketchup in a squeeze bottle. Kids like squeezing squiggly colored patterns on their hamburgers, and parents like the ketchup's extra vitamin C.[9]

The family life cycle stage affects individual and joint needs of family members. (Family life cycle stages are discussed in Chapter 10.) For example, consider how the car needs of recently married "twenty-somethings" differ from those of the same couple when they are "forty-somethings" with a 13-year-old daughter and a 17-year-old son. Family life cycle changes can affect which family members are involved in purchase decisions and the types of products purchased.

The extent to which either one or both of the two adult family members take part in family decision making varies among families and product categories. As shown in Table 5.2, there are four types of family decisions: autonomic, husband-dominant, wife-dominant, and syncratic. In autonomic decision making, each adult household member makes an equal number of decisions. In husband-dominant or wife-dominant decision making, the husband or the wife makes most of the family decisions. Syncratic decision making means both partners jointly make most decisions concerning purchases. The type of family decision making employed depends on the values and attitudes of family members. However, research indicates that women are the primary decision makers for 80 to 85 percent of all consumer buying decisions.[10]

When two or more family members participate in a purchase, their roles may dictate that each is responsible for performing certain purchase-related tasks, such as

**table 5.2   TYPES OF FAMILY DECISION MAKING**

| Decision Making Type | Decision Maker | Types of Products |
|---|---|---|
| Husband-dominant | Male head-of-household | Lawn mowers, hardware and tools, stereos, refrigerators, washer and dryer |
| Wife-dominant | Female head-of-household | Children's clothing, women's clothing, groceries, pots and pans, toiletries, home decoration |
| Autonomic | Equally likely to be made by the husband or wife, but not by both | Men's clothing, luggage, toys and games, sporting equipment, cameras |
| Syncratic | Made jointly by husband and wife | Vacations, TVs, living room furniture, carpets, financial planning services, family cars |

initiating the idea, gathering information, determining if the product is affordable, deciding whether to buy the product, or selecting the specific brand. The specific purchase tasks performed depend on the types of products being considered, the kind of family purchase decision process typically employed, and the amount of influence children have in the decision process. Thus, different family members may play different roles in the family buying process.

Within a household, an individual may perform one or more roles related to making buying decisions. The gatekeeper is the household member who collects and controls information. This may include price and quality comparisons, locations of sellers, and assessment of which brand best suits the family's needs. For example, if a family is planning a summer vacation, the gatekeeper might compare prices for hotels and airfare. The influencer is a family member who expresses his or her opinions and tries to influence buying decisions. In the vacation example, an influencer might be a child who wants to go to Disney World or a teenager who wants only to go snowboarding. The decider is a member who makes the buying choice. This role switches based on the type and expense of the product being purchased. In the case of a vacation, the decider will more likely be the adults, who use a combination of information, influences, and their own preferences. The buyer is a member who actually makes the purchase. After the family has decided to go to Disney World, the buyer will make all of the actual travel purchases. The user is a household member who consumes or uses the product. In this Disney World example, all members of the family would be users.

## Reference Groups

**reference group** A group that a person identifies with so strongly that he or she adopts the values, attitudes, and behavior of group members

A **reference group** is a group that a person identifies with so strongly that he or she adopts the values, attitudes, and behavior of group members. Reference groups can be large or small. Most people have several reference groups, such as families, work-related groups, fraternities or sororities, civic clubs, professional organizations, or church-related groups.

# Big Spending on the Teen Scene

Thirty-two million teens represent a strong force in the marketplace. Teens are active consumers in terms of both the money they spend and the influence they wield among their peers and families.

It is estimated that U.S. teen spending will reach $190 billion this year. Favorite products of this age group include CDs, fast food, clothes, makeup, movie tickets, accessories, school supplies, books, magazines, shoes, and hair-care products. Teenage girls as well as boys like electronic gear, notably cellphones, which they use to stay in touch with each other almost constantly. Teenagers are also important sales drivers of video games and portable entertainment devices such as iPods and DVD players.

Teenagers shape their parents' consumer habits to such an extent that one industry source estimates that 37 percent of car purchases are influenced by them. Those in this age group are also strong influencers of family computer and consumer electronics purchases. Most parents wouldn't dare buy a computer or digital video recorder without consulting their techno-savvy teen. Teenagers also influence what other teens buy. According to one economist, "Consumption is a thoroughly social activity, and what one person buys, wears, drives or eats affects the desires and behaviors of those around them." This is especially true for teenagers, who are greatly influenced by the desires and behaviors of their peer groups.

Teenagers are a diverse, growing, and crucial market group in the United States today. Their beliefs, attitudes, and behaviors do and will affect buying trends for several years.

In general, there are three major types of reference groups: membership, aspirational, and disassociative. A membership reference group is one to which an individual actually belongs; the individual identifies with group members strongly enough to take on the values, attitudes, and behaviors of people in that group. An aspirational reference group is a group to which a person aspires to belong; the individual desires to be like those group members. A group that a person does not wish to be associated with is a disassociative or negative reference group; the individual does not want to take on the values, attitudes, and behavior of group members.

A reference group may serve as an individual's point of comparison and source of information. A customer's behavior may change to be more in line with actions and beliefs of group members. For example, a person may stop buying one brand of shirts and switch to another based on reference group members' advice. An individual may also seek information from the reference group about other factors regarding a prospective purchase, such as where to buy a certain product.

The extent to which a reference group affects a purchase decision depends on the product's conspicuousness and on the individual's susceptibility to reference group influence. Generally, the more conspicuous a product, the more likely that the purchase decision will be influenced by reference groups. A product's conspicuousness is determined by whether others can see it and whether it can attract attention. Reference groups can affect whether a person does or does not buy a product at all, buys a type of product within a product category, or buys a specific brand.

A marketer sometimes tries to use reference group influence in advertisements by suggesting that people in a specific group buy a product and are highly satisfied with it. In this type of appeal, the advertiser hopes that many people will accept the suggested group as a reference group and buy (or react more favorably to) the product. Whether this kind of advertising succeeds depends on three factors: how effectively the advertisement communicates the message, the type of product, and the individual's susceptibility to reference group influence.

## Opinion Leaders

**opinion leader** A member of an informal group who provides information about a specific topic to other group members

An **opinion leader** is a member of an informal group who provides information about a specific topic, like software, to other group members who seek that information. He or she is in a position or has knowledge or expertise that makes him or her a credible source of information about a few topics. Opinion leaders are easily accessible and they are viewed by other group members as being well informed about a particular topic. Opinion leaders are not the foremost authority on all topics, but because such individuals know they are opinion leaders, they feel a responsibility to remain informed about a topic and thus seek out advertisements, manufacturers' brochures, salespeople, and other sources of information.

An opinion leader is likely to be most influential when consumers have high product involvement but low product knowledge, when they share the opinion leader's values and attitudes, and when the product details are numerous or complicated. Possible opinion leaders and topics are shown in Table 5.3.

**table 5.3**    **EXAMPLES OF OPINION LEADERS AND TOPICS**

| Opinion Leader | Possible Topics |
| --- | --- |
| Local religious leader | Charities to support, political ideas, lifestyle choices |
| Sorority president | Clothing and shoe purchases, hair styles, nail and hair salons |
| "Movie buff" friend | Movies to see in theater or rent, DVDs to buy, television programs to watch |
| Family doctor | Prescription drugs, vitamins, health products |
| "Techie" acquaintance | Computer and other electronics purchases, software purchases, Internet service choices, video game purchases |

## Social Classes

**social class** An open group of individuals with similar social rank

In all societies, people rank others into higher or lower positions of respect. This ranking process, called social stratification, results in social classes. A **social class** is an open aggregate of people with similar social rank. A class is referred to as *open* because people can move into and out of it. Criteria for grouping people into classes vary from one society to another. In the United States, we take into account many factors, including occupation, education, income, wealth, race, ethnic group, and possessions. A person who is ranking someone does not necessarily apply all of a society's criteria. Sometimes, too, the role of income tends to be overemphasized in social class determination. Although income does help determine social class, the other factors also play a role. Within social classes, both incomes and spending habits differ significantly among members.

Analyses of social class in the United States commonly divide people into three to seven categories. Social scientist Richard P. Coleman suggests that for purposes of consumer analysis the population is divided into the four major status groups shown in Table 5.4. However, he cautions marketers that considerable diversity exists in people's life situations within each status group.

To some degree, individuals within social classes develop and assume common behavioral patterns. They may have similar attitudes, values, language patterns, and possessions. Social class influences many aspects of people's lives. Because people have the most frequent interaction with people from within their own social class, most people are more likely to be influenced by others within their own class than by those in other classes. For example, it affects their chances of having children and their children's chances of surviving infancy. It influences their childhood training, choice of religion, financial planning decisions, access to higher education, selection of occupation, and leisure time activities. Because social class has a bearing on so many aspects of a person's life, it also affects buying decisions.

Social class influences people's spending, saving, and credit practices. It determines to some extent the type, quality, and quantity of products a person buys and uses. For example, it affects purchases of clothing, foods, financial and health-care services, travel, recreation, entertainment, and home furnishings. The behaviors of people in one class can influence consumers in others. Most common is the "trickle-down" effect in which members of lower classes attempt to emulate members of higher social classes, such as purchasing expensive automobiles, homes, appliances, and other status symbols. For example, couture fashions designed for the upper class influence the clothing sold in department stores frequented by the middle class, which eventually influences the working class who shop at discount clothing stores. Less often, status float will occur, when a product that is traditionally associated with a lower class gains status and usage among upper classes. Blue jeans, for example, were originally worn exclusively by the working class. Youth of the 1950s began wearing them as symbol of rebellion against their parents. By the 1970s and 1980s, jeans had also been adopted by upper-class youth when they began to acquire designer labels. Today, blue jeans are acceptable attire for all social classes and cost anywhere from $9.99 to the $2 million fetched by Jennifer Lopez's Sweetface diamond-covered denims that feature a 17-carat diamond on the top buckle.[11]

Social class also affects an individual's shopping patterns and types of stores patronized. In some instances, marketers attempt to focus on certain social classes through store location and interior design, product design and features, pricing strategies, personal sales efforts, and advertising. Many companies focus on the middle and working classes because they account for such a large portion of the population. Outside the U.S., the middle class is growing in India, China, and other countries, making these consumers increasingly desirable to marketers as well. Some firms target different classes with different products. BMW, for example, introduced several models priced in the mid $20,000 range to target middle-class consumers, although it usually targets upper-class customers with more expensive vehicles.

## Culture and Subcultures

**culture** The accumulation of values, knowledge, beliefs, customs, objects, and concepts of a society

**Culture** is the accumulation of values, knowledge, beliefs, customs, objects, and concepts that a society uses to cope with its environment and passes on to future generations. Examples of objects are foods, furniture, buildings, clothing, and tools. Concepts include education, welfare, and laws. Culture also includes core values and the

| table 5.4 | SOCIAL CLASS BEHAVIORAL TRAITS AND PURCHASING CHARACTERISTICS | |
|---|---|---|
| **Class (% of Population)** | **Behavioral Traits** | **Buying Characteristics** |
| Upper (14%); includes upper-upper, lower-upper, upper-middle | Income varies among the groups, but goals are the same; Various lifestyles: preppy, conventional, intellectual, etc.; Neighborhood and prestigious schooling important | Prize quality merchandise; Favor prestigious brands; Products purchased must reflect good taste; Invest in art; Spend money on travel, theater, books, tennis, golf, and swimming clubs |
| Middle (32%) | Often in management; Considered white collar; Prize good schools in a well-maintained neighborhood; Often emulate the upper class; Enjoy travel and physical activity; Often very involved in children's school and sports activities | Like fashionable items; Consult experts via books, articles, etc., before purchasing; Spend for experiences they consider worthwhile for their children (e.g., ski trips, college education); Tour packages, weekend trips; Attractive home furnishings |
| Working (38%) | Emphasis on family, and especially for economic and emotional supports (e.g., job opportunity tips, help in times of trouble); Blue collar; Earn good incomes; Enjoy mechanical items and recreational activities; Enjoy leisure time after working hard | Buy vehicles and equipment related to recreation, camping, and selected sports; Strong sense of value; Shop for best bargains at off-price and discount stores; Purchase automotive equipment for making repairs; Enjoy local travel, recreational parks |
| Lower (16%) | Often unemployed due to situations beyond their control (e.g., layoffs, company takeovers); Can include individuals on welfare and homeless individuals; Often have strong religious beliefs; May be forced to live in less desirable neighborhoods; In spite of their problems, often good-hearted toward others; Enjoy everyday activities when possible | Most products purchased are for survival; Ability to convert discarded goods into usable items |

**Source:** Adapted with permission from Richard P. Coleman, "The Continuing Significance of Social Class to Marketing," *Journal of Consumer Research,* Dec. 1983, pp. 265–280. Data from Wayne D. Hoyer and Deborah J. MacInnis, *Consumer Behavior*, 3rd ed. (Boston: Houghton Mifflin, 2004), p. 333.

VICTORIA JEALOUSE
PROFESSIONAL SNOWBOARDER
(P):MARK SELIGER

burton.com

**Subculture Based on Age**

Marketers sometimes aim marketing mixes at age-based subcultures.

degree of acceptability of a wide range of behaviors in a specific society. For example, in U.S. culture, customers as well as businesspeople are expected to behave ethically.

Culture influences buying behavior because it permeates our daily lives. Our culture determines what we wear and eat and where we reside and travel. Society's interest in the healthfulness of food affects food companies' approaches to developing and promoting their products. Culture also influences how we buy and use products and our satisfaction from them. In the U.S. culture, makers of furniture, cars, and clothing strive to understand how people's color preferences are changing.

Because culture determines product purchases and uses to some degree, cultural changes affect product development, promotion, distribution, and pricing. Food marketers, for example, have made a multitude of changes in their marketing efforts. Thirty years ago, most U.S. families ate at least two meals a day together, and the mother spent four to six hours a day preparing those meals. Today more than 75 percent of women between ages 25 and 54 work outside the home, and average family incomes have risen considerably. These shifts, along with scarcity of time, have resulted in dramatic changes in the national per capita consumption of certain food products, such as take-out foods, frozen dinners, and shelf-stable foods.

When U.S. marketers sell products in other countries, they realize the tremendous impact those cultures have on product purchases and use. Global marketers find that people in other regions of the world have different attitudes, values, and needs, which call for different methods of doing business as well as different types of marketing mixes. Some international marketers fail because they do not or cannot adjust to cultural differences.

**subcultures** A group of individuals whose characteristic values and behavior patterns are similar and different from those of the surrounding culture

A culture consists of various subcultures. **Subcultures** are groups of individuals whose characteristic values and behavior patterns are similar and different from those of the surrounding culture. Subcultural boundaries are usually based on geographic designations and demographic characteristics, such as age, religion, race, and ethnicity. U.S. culture is marked by a number of different subcultures. Among them are West Coast, teenage, Asian American, and college students. Within subcultures, greater similarities exist in people's attitudes, values, and actions than within the broader culture. Relative to other subcultures, individuals in one subculture may have stronger preferences for specific types of clothing, furniture, or foods. It is important to understand that a person can be a member of more than one subculture and that the behavioral patterns and values attributed to specific subcultures do not necessarily apply to all group members.

The percentage of the U.S. population comprising ethnic and racial subcultures is expected to grow. By 2050, about one-half of the U.S. population will be members of racial and ethnic minorities. The U.S. Census Bureau reports that the three largest and fastest-growing ethnic U.S. subcultures are African Americans, Hispanics, and Asians. The population growth of these subcultures interests marketers. Businesses recognize that to succeed, their marketing strategies will have to take into account the values, needs, interests, shopping patterns, and buying habits of various subcultures.

**African American Subculture.** In the United States, the African American subculture represents 12 percent of the population.[12] Like all subcultures, African American consumers possess distinct buying patterns. For example, African American consumers spend more money on utilities, footwear, children's apparel, groceries, and housing than do white consumers. Conversely, African Americans tend to spend less on vehicles, health care, entertainment, pensions, and eating out.[13]

Recently, Procter & Gamble Company began an initiative to increase marketing aimed at the African American community. By including African American actors in its ads, the company believes it can encourage a positive response to its products, increasing sales among African American consumers, while still maintaining ties with white consumers. For example, if an African American family is featured in an ad, the white consumers will see a heartwarming bond between family members. The African American viewers will note the inclusion of their race and feel a stronger connection to the product.[14]

Other corporations are reaching out to the African American community by celebrating Black History Month. Chrysler Group, partnering with DaimlerChrysler African American Network, organized an assortment of festivities to commemorate Black History Month by holding exhibits, concerts, and guest speakers to help increase awareness about the African American community and their vital contributions to present-day society.[15] Hawaiian Punch also supports Black History Month with a national contest inviting schoolchildren to learn about historical African American figures.[16] McDonald's launched 365Black™, a program that celebrates Black History all year round. The following year, it introduced 365Black™ Awards, which honor African Americans for their outstanding achievements.

**Hispanic Subculture.** Hispanics represent 14 percent of the U.S. population.[17] When considering the buying behavior of Hispanics, marketers must keep in mind that this subculture is really composed of nearly two dozen nationalities, including Cuban, Mexican, Puerto Rican, Caribbean, Spanish, and Dominican. Each has its own history and unique culture that affect consumer preferences and buying behavior. They should also recognize that the terms *Hispanic* and *Latino* refer to an ethnic category rather than a racial distinction. Because of the group's growth and purchasing power, understanding the Hispanic subculture is critical to marketers. In general, Hispanics have strong family values, concern for product quality, and strong brand loyalty. Studies reveal that the majority of Hispanic consumers not only are brand loyal but also will pay more for a well-known brand.[18] Like African American consumers, Hispanics spend more on housing, groceries, telephone services, and children's apparel and shoes. But they also spend more on furniture, appliances, and eating out, while they spend less than average on health care, entertainment, and education.[19]

To attract this powerful subculture, marketers are taking Hispanic values and preferences into account when developing products and creating advertising and promotions. Reebok, for example, markets to young Hispanics through a website, **www.barriorbk.com**, using music and Latino celebrities. The company has also established a relationship with the Mexican soccer team, Chivas, to help market its athletic products in Mexico and the United States.[20] The company launched a monthly Spanish magazine and a Sunday advertising circular.

White consumers, especially between the ages of 12 and 34, continue to be influenced by minority cultures, especially in areas such as fashion, entertainment, dining, sports, and music.[21] Thanks to this increasing appeal, advertisers have made a beneficial discovery. They can target both white and Hispanic consumers by hiring famous Hispanic people to appear in their ad campaigns. PepsiCo, for example, put Latina pop star Shakira in its ads, while Bell South hired actress Daisy Fuentes to appear in a commercial emphasizing the importance of friends and family. The ad aired both in English and Spanish.[22]

**Asian American Subculture.** The term *Asian American* includes people from more than 15 ethnic groups, including Filipinos, Chinese, Japanese, Asian Indians, Koreans, and Vietnamese, and this group represents 4.2 percent of the U.S. population. The individual language, religion, and value system of each group influences its members' purchasing decisions. Some traits of this subculture, however, carry across ethnic divisions, including an emphasis on hard work, strong family ties, and a high value placed on education.[23] Asian Americans are the fastest-growing U.S. subculture. They also have the most money, the best education, and the largest percentage of professionals and managers of all U.S. minorities. Asian Americans tend to spend more than the average U.S. household on housing, telecom services, groceries and dining out, education, public transportation, children's clothing, and personal insurance and pensions. They typically spend less than average on utilities, vehicles, entertainment, and health care.[24]

Retailers with a large population of Chinese shoppers have begun to capitalize on this group's celebration of the Lunar New Year. For example, during this period in the Los Angeles area, supermarkets stock traditional Chinese holiday foods and items used in the celebration, such as candles, greeting cards, and party goods. The McDonald's website features a link about the Chinese New Year and describes traditional ways of celebrating the important holiday. The website also features an extensive assortment of facts about different Asian cultures and the holidays they celebrate. Several eateries headquartered abroad are now catering to the tastes of Asians living in the United States. Maria's Bakery based in Hong Kong, Ten Ren based in Taiwan, and Woo Lae Oak based in South Korea have all opened restaurants in Washington, D.C., and other areas. With a few menu changes, these companies are successfully introducing their foods to other U.S. customers.[25]

## SUMMARY

A consumer market is comprised of purchasers and household members who intend to consume or benefit from the purchased products and do not buy products to make profits. Buying behavior consists of the decision processes and acts of people involved in buying and using products. Consumer buying behavior is the buying behavior of ultimate consumers.

An individual's level of involvement—the importance and intensity of interest in a product in a particular situation—affects the type of problem-solving process used. Enduring involvement is an ongoing interest in a product class because of personal relevance, whereas situational involvement is a temporary interest stemming from the particular circumstance or environment in which buyers find themselves. There are three kinds of consumer problem solving: routinized response behavior, limited problem solving, and extended problem solving. Consumers rely on routinized response behavior when buying frequently purchased, low-cost items requiring little search-and-decision effort. Limited problem solving is used for products purchased occasionally or when buyers need to acquire information about an unfamiliar brand in a familiar product category. Consumers engage in extended problem solving when purchasing an unfamiliar, expensive, or infrequently bought product. Purchase of a

certain product does not always elicit the same type of decision making. Impulse buying is not a consciously planned buying behavior but involves a powerful urge to buy something immediately.

The consumer buying decision process includes five stages: problem recognition, information search, evaluation of alternatives, purchase, and postpurchase evaluation. Not all decision processes culminate in a purchase, nor do all consumer decisions include all five stages. Problem recognition occurs when buyers become aware of a difference between a desired state and an actual condition. After recognizing the problem or need, buyers search for information about products to help resolve the problem or satisfy the need. In the internal search, buyers search their memories for information about products that might solve the problem. If they cannot retrieve from memory enough information for a decision, they seek additional information through an external search. A successful search yields a group of brands, called a consideration set, that a buyer views as possible alternatives. To evaluate the products in the consideration set, the buyer establishes certain criteria by which to compare, rate, and rank different products. Marketers can influence consumers' evaluations by framing alternatives.

In the purchase stage, consumers select products or brands on the basis of results from the evaluation stage and on other dimensions. Buyers also choose the seller from whom they will buy the product. After the purchase, buyers evaluate the product to determine if its actual performance meets expected levels. Shortly after the purchase of an expensive product, for example, the postpurchase evaluation may result in cognitive dissonance, dissatisfaction brought on by the consumer's doubts as to whether he or she should have bought the product in the first place or would have been better off buying another desirable brand.

Three major categories of influences affect the consumer buying decision process: situational, psychological, and social. Situational influences are external circumstances or conditions existing when a consumer makes a purchase decision. Situational influences include surroundings, time, reason for purchase, and the buyer's mood and condition.

Psychological influences partly determine people's general behavior, thus influencing their behavior as consumers. The primary psychological influences on consumer behavior are perception, motives, learning, attitudes, personality and self-concept, and lifestyles. Perception is the process of selecting, organizing, and interpreting information inputs (sensations received through sight, taste, hearing, smell, and touch) to produce meaning. The three steps in the perceptual process are selection, organization, and interpretation. Individuals have numerous perceptions of packages, products, brands, and organizations that affect their buying decision processes. A motive is an internal energizing force that orients a person's activities toward satisfying needs or achieving goals. Learning refers to changes in a person's thought processes and behavior caused by information and experience. Marketers try to shape what consumers learn to influence what they buy. An attitude is an individual's enduring evaluation, feelings, and behavioral tendencies toward an object or idea and consists of three major components: cognitive, affective, and behavioral. Personality is the set of traits and behaviors that make a person

unique. Self-concept, closely linked to personality, is one's perception or view of oneself. Research indicates that buyers purchase products that reflect and enhance their self-concepts. Lifestyle is an individual's pattern of living expressed through activities, interests, and opinions. Lifestyles influence consumers' needs, brand preferences, and how and where they shop.

Social influences are forces that other people exert on buying behavior. They include roles, family, reference groups and opinion leaders, social class, and culture and subcultures. Everyone occupies positions within groups, organizations, and institutions, and each position has a role, a set of actions and activities that a person in a particular position is supposed to perform based on expectations of both the individual and surrounding persons. In a family, children learn from parents and older siblings how to make decisions, such as purchase decisions. Consumer socialization is the process through which a person acquires the knowledge and skills to function as a consumer. The consumer socialization process is partially accomplished through family influences. A reference group is a group that a person identifies with so strongly that he or she adopts the values, attitudes, and behavior of group members. The three major types of reference groups are membership, aspirational, and disassociative. An opinion leader is a member of an informal group who provides information about a specific topic to other group members. A social class is an open group of individuals with similar social rank. Social class influences people's spending, saving, and credit practices. Culture is the accumulation of values, knowledge, beliefs, customs, objects, and concepts that a society uses to cope with its environment and passes on to future generations. A culture is made up of subcultures, groups of individuals whose characteristic values and behavior patterns are similar and different from those of the surrounding culture. U.S. marketers focus on three major ethnic subcultures: African American, Hispanic, and Asian American.

**ACE self-test**

Please visit the student website at **www.prideferrell.com** for ACE Self-Test questions that will help you prepare for exams.

---

## IMPORTANT TERMS

Consumer market
Buying behavior
Consumer buying behavior
Level of involvement
Routinized response behavior
Limited problem solving
Extended problem solving
Impulse buying

Consumer buying decision process
Internal search
External search
Consideration set
Evaluative criteria
Cognitive dissonance
Situational influences
Psychological influences
Perception
Information inputs

Selective exposure
Selective distortion
Selective retention
Motive
Maslow's hierarchy of needs
Patronage motives
Learning
Attitude
Attitude scale
Personality

Self-concept
Lifestyle
Social influences
Role
Consumer socialization
Reference group
Opinion leader
Social class
Culture
Subculture

## DISCUSSION & REVIEW QUESTIONS

1. How does a consumer's level of involvement affect his or her choice of problem-solving process?

2. Name the types of consumer problem-solving processes. List some products you have bought using each type. Have you ever bought a product on impulse? If so, describe the circumstances.

3. What are the major stages in the consumer buying decision process? Are all these stages used in all consumer purchase decisions? Why or why not?

4. What are the categories of situational factors that influence consumer buying behavior? Explain how each of these factors influences buyers' decisions.

5. What is selective exposure? Why do people engage in it?

6. How do marketers attempt to shape consumers' learning?

7. Why are marketers concerned about consumer attitudes?

8. In what ways do lifestyles affect the consumer buying decision process?

9. How do roles affect a person's buying behavior? Provide examples.

10. What are family influences, and how do they affect buying behavior?

11. What are reference groups? How do they influence buying behavior? Name some of your own reference groups.

12. How does an opinion leader influence the buying decision process of reference group members?

13. In what ways does social class affect a person's purchase decisions?

14. What is culture? How does it affect a person's buying behavior?

15. Describe the subcultures to which you belong. Identify buying behavior that is unique to one of your subcultures.

## APPLICATION QUESTIONS

1. Consumers use one of three problem-solving processes when purchasing goods or services: routinized response behavior, limited problem solving, or extended problem solving. Describe three buying experiences you have had (one for each type of problem solving), and identify which problem-solving type you used. Discuss why that particular process was appropriate.

2. The consumer buying process consists of five stages: problem recognition, information search, evaluation of alternatives, purchase, and postpurchase evaluation. Not every buying decision goes through all five stages, and the process does not necessarily conclude in a purchase. Interview a classmate about the last purchase he or she made. Report the stages used and those skipped, if any.

3. Attitudes toward products or companies often affect consumer behavior. The three components of an attitude are cognitive, affective, and behavioral. Briefly describe how a beer company might alter the cognitive and affective components of consumer attitudes toward beer products and toward the company.

4. An individual's roles influence that person's buying behavior. Identify two of your roles and give an example of how they have influenced your buying decisions.

5. Select five brands of toothpaste and explain how the appeals used in advertising these brands relate to Maslow's hierarchy of needs.

**globalEDGE™**

1. Marketers may define subcultures by a variety of demographic characteristics including ethnicity, income, or social class. Another attribute that can define a subculture is religion. To find information about religion in the United States and other countries, use the search term "global statistics" at **http://globaledge.msu.edu/ibrd**. Follow the link to Global Data and then to Religion by Country. Using this information, how might you segment the U.S. population according to religion? Are there any defining characteristics that marketers may use for the U.S. religions listed? Choose four other countries and report any commonalities or differences. Are there any differences in your sample of five countries that might be important to marketers?

2. Your firm is currently designing the next generation of mountain climbing accessories and footwear. To understand the needs and behaviors of this distinctive global market segment, you must perform market research in a variety of countries. From your own knowledge on the subject, you know that the number of Mt. Everest ascents per capita, developed by NationMaster.com, is an excellent measure of mountain climbing's popularity. To access this information, use the search term "compare various statistics" at **http://globaledge.msu.edu/ibrd** Determine the top five countries in mountain climbing popularity. In which three countries would you conduct focus groups to develop your new product line?

**INTERNET Exercise**

Visit **www.prideferrell.com** for resources to help you master the material in this chapter, plus materials that will help you expand your marketing knowledge, including Internet exercise updates, ACE Self-Tests, hotlinks to companies featured in this chapter, and much more.

**Amazon.com**

Some mass market e-commerce sites, such as Amazon.com, have extended the concept of customization to their customer base. Amazon.com has created an affinity group by drawing on certain users' likes and dislikes to make product recommendations to other users. Check out this pioneering online retailer at **www.amazon.com**.
1. What might motivate some consumers to read a "Top Selling" list?
2. Is the consumer's level of involvement with an online book purchase likely to be high or low?
3. Discuss the consumer buying decision process as it relates to a decision to purchase from Amazon.com.

**Video Case 5.1**   **Want the Low Down? Consumer Reports Has It**

For more than 70 years, Consumer Reports has been helping people to buy right. A subsidiary of Consumer Union, Consumer Reports first began operations in 1936. The company is an independent, nonprofit organization whose stated mission is to strive for a fair, just, and safe marketplace for all consumers. Also, Consumer Reports attempts to empower consumers to protect themselves by teaching them about products to make better buying decisions.

The company's National Testing and Research Center in Yonkers, New York, is the largest nonprofit educational and consumer product testing center in the world. Credibility has been its key to success, and Consumer Reports works hard at maintaining its independence and impartiality by accepting no outside advertising or free samples and maintaining no other agenda than the interests of consumers. The company supports itself through the sale of information about products and services, individual contributions, and a few noncommercial grants. *Consumer Reports* magazine has about 4 million subscribers. ConsumerReports.org is the largest publication-based subscription website in the world with more than 2 million online subscribers.

Before a product enters one of Consumer Reports' dozens of labs, it has been carefully researched as to manufacturers' claims and consumer demand in the marketplace. Products are tested not only against government and industry standards but also on how consumers use them in everyday situations. Consumer Reports employs more than 150 anonymous shoppers in 60 U.S. cities to buy the products for testing. Laboratory testing is supplemented through an annual questionnaire that is sent to subscribers that generates over 900,000 returns.

The stakes are high for Consumer Reports to be accurate in its product evaluations. In some cases, the health and the lives of consumers are at stake. Consumer Reports recently investigated the multibillion-dollar nutritional supplements business and found that highly dangerous supplements were being legally sold in mainstream U.S. stores and on the Internet. Consumer Reports pointed out that a nutritional supplement's safety claims do not have to be scientifically supported and that the government does not require warning labels of potential dangers. An article profiled a consumer who suffered severe kidney damage after taking Chinese herbs. The woman had to undergo a kidney transplant and sued the therapist that recommended the products and several companies that manufactured them.

Consumer Reports also faces the risk of lawsuits. Obviously, companies are not happy when Consumer Reports disputes their claims or publishes test results that disparage their products. The company has been sued 15 times in its 70-year existence and has prevailed in every case. Clearly, the nature of Consumer Reports' type of business makes Consumer Union vulnerable to lawsuits. However, its track record speaks volumes about its accuracy and integrity.

Consumer Reports has continued to keep abreast of technology and consumer buying habits. Just prior to the Christmas buying season, Consumer Reports announced ShopSmart, a new service designed specifically for the way people shop. ShopSmart delivers independent expert ratings, reviews, and prices on thousands of popular consumer products to subscribers over their cellphones, wherever and whenever they shop. The service is available on major cellphone carriers for a monthly fee billed to the subscriber's cellphone account.

ShopSmart will change the way people shop by supplying them with detailed product and pricing information at the point of purchase. For example, a mom

out shopping for a plasma screen TV for her family sees a sale on one of the latest models, and a salesperson assures her that it is flat-out the best TV at an unbeatable price. With a price tag of $2,000, she wants to make sure she buys the best product at the best value. By dialing ShopSmart on her cellphone, she can get a product rating, see the suggested price for the TV, and even determine if the same model is available in another store at a lower price.

"Consumer Reports ShopSmart was created with all types of shoppers in mind including the impulse buyer at the counter facing an aggressive salesperson and the researcher in the parking lot contemplating an important purchase," said the senior director and general manager of information products for Consumer Reports. "The service works for every lifestyle—from the teenager out shopping for a new MP3 player to expecting parents buying a new space heater."

Seventy years later, Consumer Reports is still helping customers to buy right.[26]

## Questions for Discussion

1. What elements of the consumer buying decision process does Consumer Reports' information most impact? In what ways?
2. In what ways could information in Consumer Reports contribute to or help reduce cognitive dissonance? Explain.
3. How can Consumer Reports help a buyer to make a better purchase decision?

## Case 5.2   AutoTrader.com Fuels Online Auto Buying

AutoTrader.com operates the largest virtual used-car lot in the United States. Founded in 1997, this fast-growing company has accelerated beyond competitors eBay and cars.com to capture a dominant share of the online used-car market. At any one time, the AutoTrader website (**www.autotrader.com**) features classified ads for more than 2 million cars, both new and used. Buyers and sellers make contact through the site to negotiate the final terms for purchases. Today AutoTrader's customers can choose from vehicles offered by 40,000 dealers and 250,000 individuals across the United States.

When AutoTrader first opened its online business, few people had ever bought or sold a vehicle on the Internet. Therefore, the company's initial challenge was to change the habits of consumers and dealers who were accustomed to using newspaper classified advertising for used-car transactions. Instead of charging dealers for every listing, as newspapers did, AutoTrader decided to set a flat monthly fee for posting any number of descriptions and photos. Because dealers did not have to pay separately for every car listed, they could afford to post information about every vehicle in their inventories.

As more dealers signed up and listed cars for sale, the website became more attractive to consumers who wanted to choose from a large selection of vehicles. However, the company still had to educate its primary target market, 25- to 49-year-old men, about an unfamiliar buying process. AutoTrader's solution was to run informative television commercials showing step by step how to use its site. Its policy of charging buyers no fee to browse or buy was a plus. Soon the site was drawing more than 5.5 million visitors every month.

Next, AutoTrader targeted a slightly younger segment of 18- to 24-year-olds because research showed that these first-time buyers account for a significant percentage of used-car purchasers. The company hired a video game specialist to adapt the look of its fast-paced television commercials to an online promotion titled "Slide into Your Ride." Players earned prizes for correctly lining up three cars by matching their colors and were entered in a sweepstakes to win a $25,000 AutoTrader shopping spree and other prizes.

Knowing that students typically search for used cars before heading off for college in the fall, AutoTrader scheduled this promotional game for August and September. The company placed banner ads on popular websites and sent e-mail announcements to its online newsletter subscribers, as well as to people on a *Sports Illustrated* list. Although this promotion cost $1 million, it was a good investment because it raised brand awareness and drew an additional 500,000 visitors to the site during the first month alone.

More than half the visitors who played the game were women, and about one-third of the players were in the 18- to 24-year-old age group. More than 60 percent of the players signed up to receive AutoTrader's monthly online newsletter, enabling the company to continue building relationships with these potential buyers. Equally important, several hundred thousand players searched for used cars on the AutoTrader site during the promotional period.

Meanwhile, AutoTrader noticed that online auctions were becoming more popular. At one time it cooperated with eBay, the world's best-known auction site, to link the two sites so consumers could search for cars on either one. After monitoring buyer behavior for two years, AutoTrader ended the agreement and created its own vehicle auction operation, going into direct competition with eBay. "We did a lot of research and studied very closely the behavior of auction style users on our site," says Chip Perry, AutoTrader's CEO. He acknowledges that eBay is the "current major player in an extremely small niche segment of the car business." At the same time, he sees plenty of room for AutoTrader to profitably serve customers in this $2 billion market segment.

As its annual vehicle sales accelerate past $100 million, AutoTrader is not putting on the brakes. The company continues to reinforce brand recognition through television advertising, especially during the weeks leading up to the busy fall buying season. And it constantly introduces new features to draw new visitors and serve the nearly 10 million qualified buyers who use the site every month to check the listings, compare prices, and buy or bid on vehicles. The firm's success can be measured in part by its number 1 rank in J. D. Powers & Associates satisfaction survey of used-vehicle dealers.[27]

### Questions for Discussion

1. In what ways has AutoTrader helped potential car buyers learn how to buy cars online?
2. In which stage of the consumer buying decision process would AutoTrader's television commercials be most likely to influence potential car buyers to use AutoTrader's website? Why?
3. Why is it important for AutoTrader to influence first-time buyers' perceptions of its site through online promotions such as "Slide into Your Ride"?

## CHAPTER 6

# Business Markets and Buying Behavior

## Naturally Potatoes? Naturally.

Naturally Potatoes was founded in the mid-1990s by a group of savvy potato farmers in Mars Hill, Aroostook County, Maine. The county's economy had long relied on potato farming, but in the 1990s, the potato market was in decline. Inspired by packaged, prewashed lettuce mixes, Rodney McCrum, Francis Fitzpatrick, and other local farmers decided to create fresh-cut potato products to fit into the preprepared produce market. McCrum put together 14 investors and set to work building a $15 million plant to process the potatoes. This move increased the company's growth by 30 percent and its sales by $20 million annually.

Naturally Potatoes sells to two markets—food service/restaurants and retailers who resell the products to ultimate consumers. Today the company is focused on the food service/restaurant end, but it plans to increase its concentration on the retail end in the future. With more consumers looking for nearly ready-to-eat food to fit their busy lifestyles, the company predicts that its packaged potatoes will be a hit in supermarkets.

With its highly automated plant, Naturally Potatoes needs just 70 employees to process 50 million potatoes annually. The machines wash, peel, and chop the potatoes. The company's mashed potatoes are cooked through, but the diced potatoes are 80 percent cooked so that chefs in restaurants or people at home can easily and quickly finish cooking them. Once processed, the potatoes

are put in plastic bags and shipped in refrigerated trucks. Depending on the product, the potatoes are good for 30 to 60 days.

Naturally Potatoes faces competition from Reser's Fine Foods, which sells Potato Express, and Michael Foods, which markets Simply Potatoes. Both companies, like Naturally Potatoes, serve both the food service/restaurant and retail industries. Right now, despite a supposed decline in potato consumption, all three companies are thriving and believe that further success is ahead.[1] ■

S erving business markets effectively requires understanding those markets. Marketers at Naturally Potatoes go to considerable lengths to understand their customers so they can provide better services and develop and maintain long-term customer relationships. Like consumer marketers, business marketers are concerned about satisfying their customers.

In this chapter, we look at business markets and business buying decision processes. We first discuss various kinds of business markets and the types of buyers making up those markets. Next, we explore several dimensions of business buying, such as characteristics of transactions, attributes and concerns of buyers, methods of buying, and distinctive features of demand for products sold to business purchasers. We then examine how business buying decisions are made and who makes the purchases. Finally, we consider how business markets are analyzed.

# Business Markets

**business market** Individuals or groups that purchase a specific kind of product for resale, direct use in producing other products, or use in general daily operations

A **business market** (also called a *business-to-business market* or *B2B market*) consists of individuals or groups that purchase a specific kind of product for one of three purposes: resale, direct use in producing other products, or use in general daily operations. Marketing to businesses employs the same concepts as marketing to ultimate consumers, such as defining target markets, understanding buying behavior, and developing effective marketing mixes, but we devote a complete chapter to business marketing because there are structural and behavioral differences in business markets. A company marketing to another company must understand how its product will affect other firms in the marketing channel, such as resellers and other manufacturers. Business products can also be technically complex and the market often consists of sophisticated buyers.

Because the business market consists of relatively smaller customer populations, a segment of the market could be as small as a few customers.[2] The market for railway equipment in the United States, for example, is limited to a few major carriers. On the other hand, a business product can be a commodity, such as corn or a bolt or screw, but the quantity purchased and the buying methods differ significantly from the consumer market. Business marketing is often based on long-term mutually profitable relationships across members of the marketing channel. Networks of suppliers and customers recognize the importance of building strong alliances based on cooperation, trust, and collaboration.[3] Manufacturers may even co-develop new products with business customers sharing marketing research, production, scheduling, inventory management, and information systems. For example, when the largest distributor for independent book publishers, Consortium Book & Sales Distribution Inc., discovered its information technology system was obsolete, the firm partnered with Integrated Knowledge Systems, Inc., to develop a new database to track book sales in real time to let publishers know which titles sell well and which should be eliminated. In this case, the marketer custom designed IT solutions with the customer to resolve its operational services and efficiency concerns.[4] Although business marketing can be based on collaborative long-term buyer-seller relationships, there are also transactions based on timely exchanges of basic products at highly competitive market prices. For most business marketers, the goal is understanding customer needs and providing a value-added exchange that shifts from attracting customers to keeping customers and developing relationships.[5]

| table 6.1   NUMBER OF ESTABLISHMENTS IN INDUSTRY GROUPS | |
| --- | --- |
| **Industry** | **Number of Establishments** |
| Agriculture, forestry, fishing and hunting | 26,600 |
| Mining | 23,900 |
| Construction | 710,300 |
| Manufacturing | 344,300 |
| Transportation, warehousing, utilities | 213,500 |
| Finance, insurance, real estate | 773,400 |
| Services | 2,536,300 |

**Source:** U.S. Bureau of the Census, *Statistical Abstract of the United States*, 2006 (Washington, DC: Government Printing Office, 2006), p. 513.

The four categories of business markets are producer, reseller, government, and institutional. In the remainder of this section, we discuss each of these types of markets.

## Producer Markets

**producer markets** Individuals and business organizations that purchase products to make profits by using them to produce other products or using them in their operations

Individuals and business organizations that purchase products for the purpose of making a profit by using them to produce other products or using them in their operations are classified as **producer markets.** Producer markets include buyers of raw materials, as well as purchasers of semifinished and finished items, used to produce other products. For example, manufacturers buy raw materials and component parts for direct use in product production. Grocery stores and supermarkets are part of producer markets for numerous support products such as paper and plastic bags, counters, and scanners. Farmers are part of producer markets for farm machinery, fertilizer, seed, and livestock. Producer markets include a broad array of industries ranging from agriculture, forestry, fisheries, and mining to construction, transportation, communications, and utilities. As Table 6.1 indicates, the number of business establishments in national producer markets is enormous.

Manufacturers are geographically concentrated. More than half are located in only seven states: New York, California, Pennsylvania, Illinois, Ohio, New Jersey, and Michigan. This concentration sometimes enables businesses that sell to producer markets to serve them more efficiently. Within certain states, production in a specific industry may account for a sizable proportion of that industry's total production.

## Reseller Markets

**reseller markets** Intermediaries that buy finished goods and resell them for profit

**Reseller markets** consist of intermediaries, such as wholesalers and retailers, which buy finished goods and resell them for profit. Aside from making minor alterations, resellers do not change the physical characteristics of the products they handle. Except for items producers sell directly to consumers, all products sold to consumer markets are first sold to reseller markets.

Wholesalers purchase products for resale to retailers, to other wholesalers, and to producers, governments, and institutions. Arrow Electronics, for example, buys computer chips and other electronics components and resells them to producers of subsystems for cellphones, computers, and automobiles. Of the 438,000 wholesalers in the United States, a large number are located in New York, California, Illinois, Texas, Ohio, Pennsylvania, and Florida.[6] Although some products are sold directly to end users, many manufacturers sell their products to wholesalers, which in turn sell the products to other firms in the distribution system. Thus, wholesalers are very

**Reseller Markets**

The Garlic Company and Carolina Turkey are food service resellers that provide ingredients to restaurants.

important in helping producers get products to customers. Professional buyers and buying committees make wholesalers' initial purchase decisions. Reordering is often automated.

Retailers purchase products and resell them to final consumers. There are approximately 1.1 million retailers in the United States, employing more than 15 million people and generating more than $3.1 trillion in annual sales.[7] Some retailers—Home Depot, PetSmart, and Staples, for example—carry a large number of items. Supermarkets may handle as many as 30,000 different products. In small, individually owned retail stores, owners or managers make purchasing decisions. In chain stores, a central office buyer or buying committee frequently decides whether a product will be made available for selection by store managers. For most products, however, local managers make the actual buying decisions for a particular store.

When making purchase decisions, resellers consider several factors. They evaluate the level of demand for a product to determine in what quantity and at what prices the product can be resold. Retailers assess the amount of space required to handle a product relative to its potential profit, sometimes on the basis of sales per square foot of selling area. Because customers often depend on resellers to have products available when needed, resellers typically appraise a supplier's ability to provide adequate quantities when and where wanted. Resellers also take into account the ease of placing orders and the availability of technical assistance and training programs from producers. When resellers consider buying a product not previously carried, they try to determine whether the product competes with or complements products they currently handle. These types of concerns distinguish reseller markets from other markets.

## Government Markets

**government markets** Federal, state, county, or local governments that buy goods and services to support their internal operations and provide products to their constituencies

Federal, state, county, and local governments make up **government markets**. These markets spend billions of dollars annually for a variety of goods and services to support their internal operations and provide citizens with such products as highways, education, water, energy, and national defense. The federal government spends about $466 billion annually on national defense alone. Government expenditures annually account for about 20 percent of the U.S. gross domestic product.[8] Besides the federal government, there are 50 state governments, 3,034 county governments, and 84,491 local governments.[9] The amount spent by federal, state, and local units during the last 30 years has increased rapidly because the total number of government units and the services they provide have both increased. Costs of providing these services have also risen.

The types and quantities of products bought by government markets reflect social demands on various government agencies. As citizens' needs for government services change, so does demand for products by government markets. For example, the U.S. Department of State granted Identix a contract to supply large-scale facial recognition systems for visa processing, a capability that has become increasingly important in today's world.[10] Although it is common to hear of large corporations being awarded government contracts, in fact businesses of all sizes market to government agencies. For example, VM Manufacturing, a small New York firm specializing in aircraft and commercial parts, used ePublicBids to help it win contracts of up to $100,000 with defense supply centers in Philadelphia and Richmond.[11]

Because government agencies spend public funds to buy the products needed to provide services, they are accountable to the public. This accountability explains

# Brighton's Bright Idea

**B**righton is a California-based company that markets accessories such as fragrances, sunglasses, jewelry, and gifts for the home. Having owned a small store in the past, CEO Jerry Kohl knew what it meant to be an independent retailer. He treats his business customers—6,000 independent retailers—like the valued customers they are. Kohl knows that Brighton will prosper if it focuses on building special relationships with smaller stores. He and his managers continually research what their resellers need to satisfy customers and to increase their own profits. Studying shoppers' buying behavior leads to many new ideas for increasing store traffic, encouraging brand loyalty, and boosting sales.

Equally important, Brighton gives resellers the tools they need to serve their customers more effectively. For example, Brighton sales representatives travel the country visiting retailers and educating their sales staffs about Brighton products—how a handbag or belt is made, why it lasts longer, and how customers benefit. They update store owners on the latest promotions and gather retailers' sales tips and success stories to share with Brighton's entire reseller network.

In addition, retailers receive useful reference books such as *M.I.S.S. (Marketing Is Simply Smart)* and a subscription to the colorful *Brighton View* newsletter. Each newsletter offers insights into customer behavior; describes new products; explains promotions such as the "Think Pink Too" bracelet, which raises money for breast cancer research; and helps owners analyze Brighton products' sales and inventory levels. Finally, owners of stores that sell at least $150,000 worth of Brighton products in a year receive a free trip to the company's annual convention in Hawaii. By marketing through smaller specialty stores and pampering his retail customers, Kohl has built Brighton into a major accessories company that benefits his retail customers. Pretty bright idea.

their relatively complex set of buying procedures. Some firms do not even try to sell to government buyers because they want to avoid the tangle of red tape. However, many marketers have learned to deal efficiently with government procedures and do not find them a stumbling block. For certain products, such as defense-related items, the government may be the only customer. The U.S. Government Printing Office publishes and distributes several documents explaining buying procedures and describing the types of products various federal agencies purchase.

Governments make purchases through bids or negotiated contracts. Although companies may be reluctant to approach government markets because of the complicated bidding process, once they understand the rules of this process, some firms routinely penetrate government markets. To make a sale under the bid system, firms must apply and be approved for placement on a list of qualified bidders. When a government unit wants to buy, it sends out a detailed description of the products to qualified bidders. Businesses wishing to sell such products submit bids. The government unit is usually required to accept the lowest bid.

When buying nonstandard or highly complex products, a government unit often uses a negotiated contract. Under this procedure, the government unit selects only a few firms and then negotiates specifications and terms; it eventually awards the contract to one of the negotiating firms. Most large defense-related contracts, once held by such companies as McDonnell Douglas and General Dynamics, traditionally were negotiated in this fashion. However, as the number and size of such contracts have declined, these companies have had to strengthen their marketing efforts and look to other markets. Although government markets can impose intimidating requirements, they can also be very lucrative.

### Institutional Markets

**institutional markets** Organizations with charitable, educational, community, or other nonbusiness goals

Organizations with charitable, educational, community, or other nonbusiness goals constitute **institutional markets**. Members of institutional markets include churches, some hospitals, fraternities and sororities, charitable organizations, and private colleges. Institutions purchase millions of dollars' worth of products annually to provide goods, services, and ideas to congregations, students, patients, and others. Because institutions often have different goals and fewer resources than other types of organizations, marketers may use special marketing efforts to serve them. For example, Hussey Seating in Maine sells stadium seating to schools, colleges, churches, and other institutions, as well as to sports arenas around the world. The family-owned business shows its support for institutional customers through assistance with school funding and reduced-cost construction of local economic development projects.[12]

# Dimensions of Marketing to Business Customers

Now that we have considered different types of business customers, we look at several dimensions of marketing to business customers. We examine characteristics of transactions with business customers and then discuss attributes of business customers and some of their primary concerns when making purchase decisions. Next, we consider buying methods and major types of purchases. Finally, we discuss the characteristics of demand for business products.

## Characteristics of Transactions with Business Customers

Transactions between businesses differ from consumer sales in several ways. Orders by business customers tend to be much larger than individual consumer sales. An airline, for example, may order multiple jet airplanes costing several million dollars each. Suppliers often must sell products in large quantities to make profits; consequently they prefer not to sell to customers who place small orders. For example, Airborne Express competes successfully against FedEx and UPS by providing low-cost overnight delivery services primarily to businesses that buy such services in high volume.

Some business purchases involve expensive items, such as computer systems. Other products, such as raw materials and component items, are used continuously in production, and their supply may need frequent replenishing. The contract regarding terms of sale of these items is likely to be a long-term agreement.

Discussions and negotiations associated with business purchases can require considerable marketing time and selling effort. Purchasing decisions are often made by committee, orders are frequently large and expensive, and products may be custom built. Several people or departments in the purchasing organization are often involved. For example, one department expresses a need for a product, a second department develops the specifications, a third stipulates maximum expenditures, and a fourth places the order.

**reciprocity** An arrangement unique to business marketing in which two organizations agree to buy from each other

One practice unique to business markets is **reciprocity,** an arrangement in which two organizations agree to buy from each other. Reciprocal agreements that threaten competition are illegal. The Federal Trade Commission and the Justice Department take actions to stop anticompetitive reciprocal practices. Nonetheless, a certain amount of reciprocal activity occurs among small businesses and, to a lesser extent, among larger companies. Because reciprocity influences purchasing agents to deal only with certain suppliers, it can lower morale among agents and lead to less than optimal purchases.

## Attributes of Business Customers

Business customers typically demand detailed information about a product's functional features and technical specifications to ensure that it meets their needs. Personal goals, however, may also influence business buying behavior. Most purchasing agents seek the psychological satisfaction that comes with organizational advancement and financial rewards. Agents who consistently exhibit rational business buying behavior are likely to attain these personal goals because they help their firms achieve organizational objectives. Today many suppliers and their customers build and maintain mutually beneficial relationships, sometimes called *partnerships*. Researchers find that even in a partnership between a small vendor and a large corporate buyer, a strong partnership exists because high levels of interpersonal trust can lead to higher levels of commitment to the partnership by both organizations.[13]

## Primary Concerns of Business Customers

When making purchasing decisions, business customers take into account a variety of factors. Among their chief considerations are price, product quality, service, and supplier relationships. Price matters greatly to business customers because it influences operating costs and costs of goods sold, which in turn affect selling price, profit margin, and ultimately the ability to compete. When purchasing major equipment, a business customer views price as the amount of investment necessary to obtain a certain level of return or savings. A business customer is likely to compare the price of a product with the benefits the product will yield to the organization.

Most business customers try to achieve and maintain a specific level of quality in the products they buy. To achieve this goal, most firms establish standards (usually stated as a percentage of defects allowed) for these products and buy them on the basis of a set of expressed characteristics, commonly called *specifications*. A customer evaluates the quality of the products being considered to determine whether they meet specifications. If a product fails to meet specifications or malfunctions for the ultimate consumer, the customer may drop that product's supplier and switch to a different one. On the other hand, customers are ordinarily cautious about buying products that exceed specifications because such products often cost more, thus increasing the organization's overall costs. Specifications are designed to meet a customer's wants, and anything that does not contribute to meeting those wants may be considered wasteful.

Business buyers value service. Services offered by suppliers directly and indirectly influence customers' costs, sales, and profits. In some instances, the mix of customer services is the major means by which marketers gain a competitive advantage. Typical

WE CREATED A
SUPPLY CHAIN
THAT GOES
WHERE TRUCKS
ONLY DREAM OF.

On thousands of narrow streets in cities and villages all over Central America, you'll find tiendas ... tiny stores selling groceries and essentials. Food companies face a unique challenge delivering refrigerated foods to these out-of-the-way places. So Cargill's supply chain specialists fit a solution to the need. Sales representatives travel on maneuverable motorcycles equipped with iceboxes and handheld computers ... delivering the products tiendas need, when they need them. Proving that a delivery system doesn't have to be big to be efficient. This is how Cargill works with customers.

*collaborate  >  create  >  succeed*

**Cargill**
Nourishing Ideas. Nourishing People.™

www.cargillcreates.com

**Primary Concerns of Business Customers**

Cargill focuses on supplier relationships, a primary concern of small grocery stores.

services customers desire are market information, inventory maintenance, on-time delivery, and repair services. Business buyers are likely to need technical product information, data regarding demand, information about general economic conditions, or supply and delivery information. Maintaining adequate inventory is critical because it helps make products accessible when a customer needs them and reduces the customer's inventory requirements and costs. Because business customers are usually responsible for ensuring that products are on hand and ready for use when needed, on-time delivery is crucial. Furthermore, reliable, on-time delivery saves business customers money because it enables them to carry less inventory. For example, Dell opened an enterprise command center similar to those it operates in the United States and in Limerick, Ireland, to provide around-the-clock support for its business customers in Europe, the Middle East, and Africa.[14] Purchasers of machinery are especially concerned about obtaining repair services and replacement parts quickly because inoperable equipment is costly. Caterpillar Inc., manufacturer of earth-moving, construction, and materials-handling machinery, has built an international reputation, as well as a competitive advantage, by providing prompt service and replacement parts for its products around the world. Business customers are likely to resist a supplier's effort to implement a new technology if there are questions about the technology's compatibility, reliability, or other factors that could cause the supplier to fail to deliver on promises.[15]

Quality of service is a critical issue because customer expectations about service have broadened. Using traditional service quality standards based only on traditional manufacturing and accounting systems is not enough. Communication channels that allow customers to ask questions, voice complaints, submit orders, and trace shipments are indispensable components of service. Marketers should strive for uniformity of service, simplicity, truthfulness, and accuracy. They should also develop customer service objectives and monitor customer service programs. Firms can monitor service by formally surveying customers or informally calling on customers and asking questions about the service they receive. Expending the time and effort to ensure that customers are happy can greatly benefit marketers by increasing customer retention. One study found that boosting customer retention by 5 percent could double a small firm's profitability.[16]

Finally, business customers are concerned about the costs of developing and maintaining relationships with their suppliers. By developing relationships and building trust with a particular supplier, buyers can reduce their search efforts and uncertainty about monetary prices.[17] Business customers have to keep in mind the overall fit of a purchase including its potential to reduce inventory and carrying costs as well as to increase inventory turnover and ability to move the right products to the right place at the right time. The entire business can be damaged by a single supplier's failure to be a good partner.[18]

## Methods of Business Buying

Although no two business buyers do their jobs the same way, most use one or more of the following purchase methods: *description, inspection, sampling,* and *negotiation.* When products are standardized according to certain characteristics (such as size, shape, weight, and color) and graded using such standards, a business buyer may be able to purchase simply by describing or specifying quantity, grade, and other attributes. Agricultural products often fall into this category. Sometimes buyers specify a particular brand or its equivalent when describing the desired product. Purchases on the basis of description are especially common between a buyer and seller with an ongoing relationship built on trust.

Certain products, such as industrial equipment, used vehicles, and buildings, have unique characteristics and may vary with regard to condition. For example, a particular used truck may have a bad transmission. Consequently, business buyers of such products must base purchase decisions on inspection.

Sampling entails taking a specimen of the product from the lot and evaluating it on the assumption that its characteristics represent the entire lot. This method is appropriate when the product is homogeneous—for instance, grain—and examining the entire lot is not physically or economically feasible.

Some purchases by businesses are based on negotiated contracts. In certain instances, buyers describe exactly what they need and ask sellers to submit bids. They

**Methods of Buying**

Titleist makes a standardized product that can be customized.

then negotiate with the suppliers that submit the most attractive bids. This approach may be used when acquiring commercial vehicles, for example. In other cases, the buyer may be unable to identify specifically what is to be purchased and can provide only a general description, as might be the case for a piece of custom-made equipment. A buyer and seller might negotiate a contract that specifies a base price and provides for the payment of additional costs and fees. These contracts are most commonly used for one-time projects such as buildings, capital equipment, and special projects.

### Types of Business Purchases

Most business purchases are one of three types: new-task, straight rebuy, or modified rebuy purchase. Each type is subject to different influences and thus requires business marketers to modify their selling approaches appropriately.[19] In a **new-task purchase**, an organization makes an initial purchase of an item to be used to perform a new job or solve a new problem. A new-task purchase may require development of product specifications, vendor specifications, and procedures for future purchases of that product. To make the initial purchase, the business buyer usually needs much information. New-task purchases are important to suppliers because if business buyers are satisfied with the products, suppliers may be able to sell buyers large quantities of them for many years.

A **straight rebuy purchase** occurs when buyers purchase the same products routinely under approximately the same terms of sale. Buyers require little information for these routine purchase decisions and tend to use familiar suppliers that have pro-

**new-task purchase** An initial purchase by an organization of an item to be used to perform a new job or solve a new problem

**straight rebuy purchase** A routine purchase of the same products by a business buyer

# The Focus Is on Service at IBM

IBM provides technology and support services to help companies operate. Based on earnings, IBM is number 1 in information technology (IT) services, hardware, and financing; it is number 2 in software. Over the years, IBM has transferred its focus from computer hardware to computer services.

In 2003, IBM made some big changes and refined its business model. The company sold its personal computer division to Lenovo, a Chinese firm, and phased out its presence in creating and selling hard disk drives, memory chips, and networking hardware. Instead, the company decided to focus on forming and maintaining collaborative relationships and providing services to solve the information management needs of its business customers. Some of the major shifts IBM has made are the restructuring of its business skills, assets, and delivery capabilities to meet the needs of customers wanting to blend IT with business operations. IBM is always moving forward and reinventing its focus through effective customer relationship strategies.

Today, IBM continues to make its business more tangible, flexible, and innovative. The company vows to create a global reach and utilize the talent available worldwide by giving authority and resources to those working in close contact with its clients. IBM's target customers include companies such as General Motors, which is outsourcing $15 billion worth of IT contracts. To satisfy the auto giant, IBM will have to adjust to GM's demands for smaller contracts and standardized ways of doing things. In addition, it will need to develop a close partnership and craft the right value proposition to a company that is attempting to restructure in the highly competitive automotive market. IBM must also compete with EDS, Hewlett-Packard, and CapGemini, as well as other IT firms, to get its share of GM's business. With IBM's new focus, every new customer represents a challenge to craft precisely the right service.

**Types of Business Purchases**

Audiovisual solutions from companies such as AVW-TELAV are often purchased for new-task applications linked to desired specifications. Magma identifies chip buyers' needs in computer technology.

**modified rebuy purchase** A new-task purchase that is changed on subsequent orders or when the requirements of a straight rebuy purchase are modified

**derived demand** Demand for industrial products that stems from demand for consumer products

vided satisfactory service and products in the past. These marketers try to set up automatic reordering systems to make reordering easy and convenient for business buyers. A supplier may even monitor the business buyer's inventories and indicate to the buyer what should be ordered and when. For example, Degussa Construction Chemicals Operations, Inc., a chemical manufacturer, contracts with freight carrier Dist-Tech to manage and deliver its products with real-time shipment tracking.[20] Such a contract represents a straight rebuy purchase because the contract implies an understanding of a continued service.

In a **modified rebuy purchase**, a new-task purchase is changed the second or third time it is ordered or requirements associated with a straight rebuy purchase are modified. A business buyer might seek faster delivery, lower prices, or a different quality level of product specifications. A modified rebuy situation may cause regular suppliers to become more competitive to keep the account since other suppliers could obtain the business. When a firm changes the terms of a service contract, such as for telecommunication services, it has made a modified purchase. Gateway Computer Systems is expanding its commercial business by focusing on small businesses by offering on-site help and online educational resources. This effort may give Gateway a competitive advantage in serving small firms making modified rebuy purchases.[21]

## Demand for Business Products

Unlike consumer demand, demand for business products (also called *industrial demand*) can be characterized as (1) derived, (2) inelastic, (3) joint, or (4) fluctuating.

**Derived Demand.** Because business customers, especially producers, buy products for direct or indirect use in the production of goods and services to satisfy consumers' needs, the demand for business products derives from the demand for consumer products; it is therefore called **derived demand.** In the long run, no demand for business products is totally unrelated to the demand for consumer products.

We dispose of waste properly. Before it becomes a problem.

We don't simply remove waste, we manage it responsibly. Trust our network of more than 80 distribution centers, including numerous EPA-permitted storage facilities, and our 24 years of waste management experience, to assist with your compliance. Because we don't own waste processing facilities, you can depend on us for unbiased service. As a leading distributor of chemicals, plastics and composites for many of the world's premier suppliers, the added dimension of our Environmental Services group lets us provide full-circle solutions. Get more than peace of mind. Get a strategic partner who brings more to the table than materials. Every day.

**ASHLAND**
ASHLAND DISTRIBUTION

DISTRIBUTION DONE RIGHT™. FROM DELIVERY TO DISPOSAL. VISIT US AT WWW.ASHDIST.COM OR CALL 800-531-7106

#@%&!

**Derived Demand**

Ashland helps identify and resolve waste management issues.

**inelastic demand** Demand that is not significantly altered by a price increase or decrease

The derived nature of demand is usually multilevel. Business marketers at different levels are affected by a change in consumer demand for a particular product. For instance, consumers have become concerned with health and good nutrition and, as a result, are purchasing more products with less fat, cholesterol, and sodium. When consumers reduced their purchases of high-fat foods, a change occurred in the demand for products marketed by food processors, equipment manufacturers, and suppliers of raw materials associated with these products. Change in consumer demand for a product affects demand for all firms involved in the production of that product.

**Inelastic Demand.** With **inelastic demand**, a price increase or decrease will not significantly alter demand for a business product. Because some business products contain a number of parts, price increases affecting only one or two parts may yield only a slightly higher per-unit production cost. When a sizable price increase for a component represents a large proportion of the product's cost, demand may become more elastic because the price increase in the component causes the price at the consumer level to rise sharply. For example, if aircraft engine manufacturers substantially increase the price of engines, forcing Boeing to raise the prices of the aircraft it manufactures, the demand for airliners may become more elastic as airlines reconsider whether they can afford to buy new aircraft. An increase in the price of windshields, however, is unlikely to greatly affect either the price of or the demand for airliners.

Inelasticity applies only to industry demand for business products, not to the demand an individual firm faces. Suppose a spark plug producer increases the price of spark plugs sold to small-engine manufacturers, but its competitors continue to maintain lower prices. The spark plug company will probably experience reduced unit sales because most small-engine producers will switch to lower-priced brands. A specific firm is vulnerable to elastic demand, even if industry demand for a spe-

## marketing ENTREPRENEURS

**Shazad Mohamed**

HIS BUSINESS: GlobalTek Solutions

FOUNDED AT AGE: 12

SUCCESS: Revenues of over $1 million a year

**W**hen someone hears that Shazad Mohamed was able to carry his company through the dot-com bust and technology downturn of the early 2000s, they might assume that he is a seasoned CEO with years of experience. While Mohamed is by all measures an entrepreneurial wunderkind, he is still in his teens. His company, GlobalTek Solutions, develops software for use by governments and in the health-care industry. He plans to initiate international projects in countries such as India and Pakistan in upcoming years.

**joint demand** Demand involving the use of two or more items in combination to produce a product

cific business product is inelastic. We will take another look at price elasticity in Chapter 21.

**Joint Demand.** Demand for certain business products, especially raw materials and components, is subject to joint demand. **Joint demand** occurs when two or more items are used in combination to produce a product. For example, a firm that manufactures axes needs the same number of ax handles as it does ax blades. These two products thus are demanded jointly. If a shortage of ax handles exists, the producer buys fewer ax blades. Understanding the effects of joint demand is particularly important for a marketer selling multiple jointly demanded items. Such a marketer realizes that when a customer begins purchasing one of the jointly demanded items, a good opportunity exists to sell related products.

**Fluctuating Demand.** Because the demand for business products is derived from consumer demand, it may fluctuate enormously. In general, when particular consumer products are in high demand, their producers buy large quantities of raw materials and components to ensure meeting long-run production requirements. In addition, these producers may expand production capacity, which entails acquiring new equipment and machinery, more workers, and more raw materials and component parts. Conversely, a decline in demand for certain consumer goods significantly reduces demand for business products used to produce those goods.

Marketers of business products may notice changes in demand when customers alter inventory policies, perhaps because of expectations about future demand. For example, if several dishwasher manufacturers that buy timers from one producer increase their inventory of timers from a two-week to a one-month supply, the timer producer will have a significant, immediate increase in demand.

Sometimes price changes lead to surprising temporary changes in demand. A price increase for a business product may initially cause business customers to buy more of the item because they expect the price to rise further. Similarly, demand for a business product may decrease significantly following a price cut because buyers are waiting for further price reductions. Fluctuations in demand can be substantial in industries in which prices change frequently.

# Business Buying Decisions

**business (organizational) buying behavior** The purchase behavior of producers, government units, institutions, and resellers

**buying center** The people within an organization who make business purchase decisions

**Business (organizational) buying behavior** refers to the purchase behavior of producers, government units, institutions, and resellers. Although several factors affecting consumer buying behavior (discussed in the previous chapter) also influence business buying behavior, a number of factors are unique to the latter. In this section, we first analyze the buying center to learn who participates in business purchase decisions. Then we focus on the stages of the buying decision process and the factors that affect it.

## The Buying Center

Relatively few business purchase decisions are made by just one person; often they are made through a buying center. The **buying center** is the group of people within the organization who make business purchase decisions. They include users, influencers, buyers, deciders, and gatekeepers.[22] One person may perform several roles. These participants share some goals and risks associated with their decisions.

Users are the organization members who actually use the product being acquired. They frequently initiate the purchase process and/or generate purchase specifications. After the purchase, they evaluate product performance relative to the specifications.

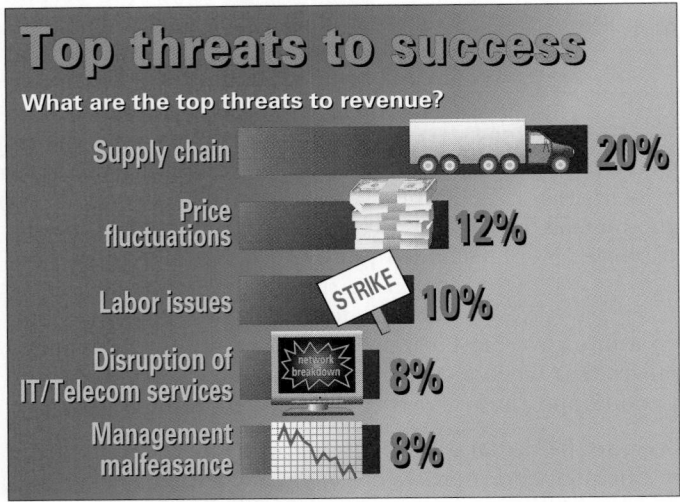

**Top threats to success**

What are the top threats to revenue?

| | |
|---|---|
| Supply chain | 20% |
| Price fluctuations | 12% |
| Labor issues | 10% |
| Disruption of IT/Telecom services | 8% |
| Management malfeasance | 8% |

*Source:* Data From Managing Business Risk in 2006 and Beyond, FM Global and Harris/Interactive. Margin of error ±4 percentage points.

Influencers are often technical personnel, such as engineers, who help develop the specifications and evaluate alternative products. Technical personnel are especially important influencers when products being considered involve new, advanced technology.

Buyers select suppliers and negotiate terms of purchase. They may also become involved in developing specifications. Buyers are sometimes called purchasing agents or purchasing managers. Their choices of vendors and products, especially for new-task purchases, are heavily influenced by people occupying other roles in the buying center. For straight rebuy purchases, the buyer plays a major role in vendor selection and negotiations.

Deciders actually choose the products. Although buyers may be deciders, it is not unusual for different people to occupy these roles. For routinely purchased items, buyers are commonly deciders. However, a buyer may not be authorized to make purchases exceeding a certain dollar limit, in which case higher-level management personnel are deciders.

Finally, gatekeepers, such as secretaries and technical personnel, control the flow of information to and among people occupying other roles in the buying center. Buyers who deal directly with vendors also may be gatekeepers because they can control information flows. The flow of information from a supplier's sales representatives to users and influencers is often controlled by personnel in the purchasing department.

The number and structure of an organization's buying centers are affected by the organization's size and market position, the volume and types of products being purchased, and the firm's overall managerial philosophy regarding exactly who should be involved in purchase decisions. The size of a buying center is influenced by the stage of the buying decision process and by the type of purchase. The size of the buying center likely would be larger for a new-task purchase than for a straight rebuy. Varying goals among members of a buying center can have both positive and negative effects on the purchasing process.

A marketer attempting to sell to a business customer should determine who is in the buying center, the types of decisions each individual makes, and which individuals are most influential in the decision process. Because in some instances many people make up the buying center, marketers cannot feasibly contact all participants. Instead, they must be certain to contact a few of the most influential.

### Stages of the Business Buying Decision Process

Like consumers, businesses follow a buying decision process. This process is summarized in the lower portion of Figure 6.1. In the first stage, one or more individuals recognize that a problem or need exists. Problem recognition may arise under a variety of circumstances, for instance, when machines malfunction or a firm modifies an existing product or introduces a new one. Individuals in the buying center, such as users, influencers, or buyers, may be involved in problem recognition, but it may be stimulated by external sources, such as sales representatives or advertisements.

The second stage of the process, development of product specifications, requires that buying center participants assess the problem or need and determine what is necessary to resolve or satisfy it. During this stage, users and influencers, such as engineers, often provide information and advice for developing product specifications. By assessing and describing needs, the organization should be able to establish product specifications.

| figure 6.1 | BUSINESS (ORGANIZATIONAL) BUYING DECISION PROCESS AND FACTORS THAT MAY INFLUENCE IT |

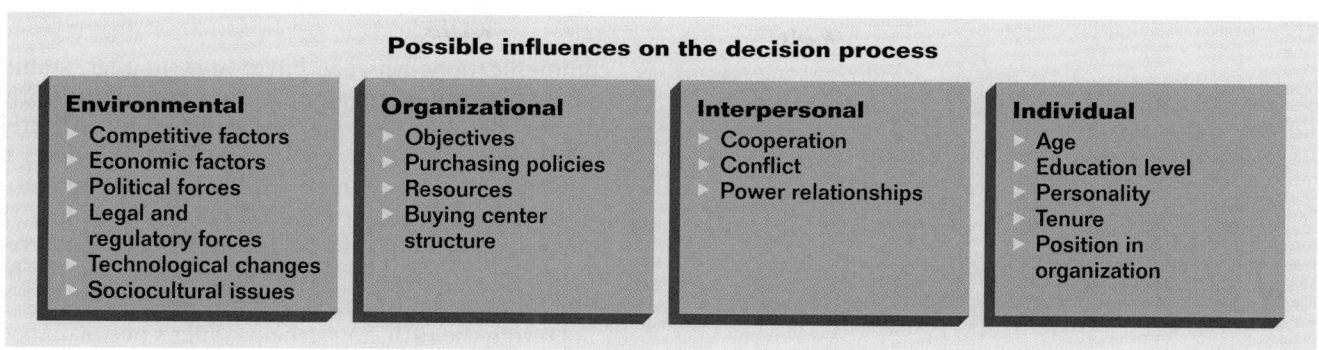

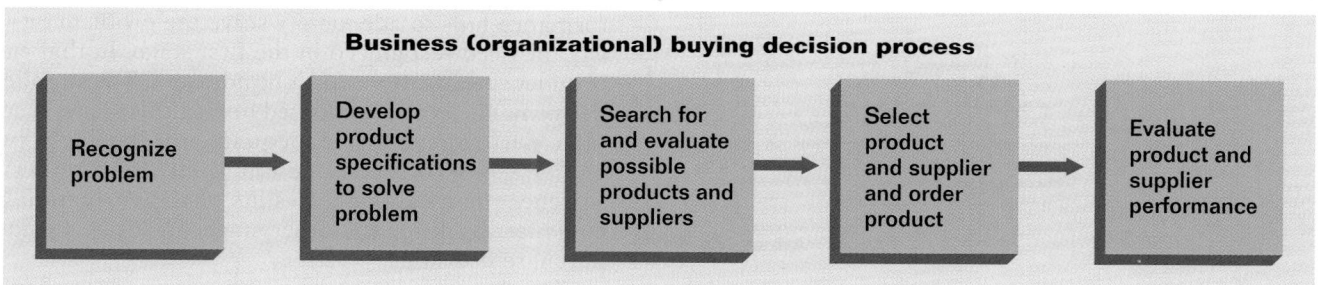

**value analysis** An evaluation of each component of a potential purchase

**vendor analysis** A formal, systematic evaluation of current and potential vendors

**multiple sourcing** An organization's decision to use several suppliers

**sole sourcing** An organization's decision to use only one supplier

Searching for and evaluating potential products and suppliers is the third stage in the decision process. Search activities may involve looking in company files and trade directories; contacting suppliers for information; soliciting proposals from known vendors; and examining websites, catalogs, and trade publications. To facilitate a vendor search, some organizations, such as Wal-Mart, advertise their desire to build partnerships with specific types of vendors, such as those owned by women or by minorities. During this stage, some organizations engage in **value analysis**, an evaluation of each component of a potential purchase. Value analysis examines quality, design, materials, and possibly item reduction or deletion to acquire the product in the most cost-effective way. Some vendors may be deemed unacceptable because they are not large enough to supply needed quantities; others may be excluded because of poor delivery and service records. Sometimes the product is not available from any existing vendor and the buyer must find a company known for its innovation, such as 3M, to design and make it. Products are evaluated to make sure they meet or exceed product specifications developed in the second stage. Usually suppliers are judged according to multiple criteria. A number of firms employ **vendor analysis**, a formal, systematic evaluation of current and potential vendors, focusing on such characteristics as price, product quality, delivery service, product availability, and overall reliability.

Results of deliberations and assessments in the third stage are used during the fourth stage to select the product to be purchased and the supplier from which to buy it. In some cases, the buyer selects and uses several suppliers, a process known as **multiple sourcing**. In others, only one supplier is selected, a situation called **sole sourcing**. For example, Best Buy and UPS recently agreed to an exclusive shipping relationship that resulted in greater savings, efficiencies, and customer loyalty for both companies.[23] Firms with federal government contracts are required to have several sources for an item. Sole sourcing has traditionally been discouraged except when a product is available from only one company. Sole sourcing is much more common today, however, partly because such an arrangement means better

**Supplier Diversity**
American Airlines focuses on supplier diversity.

communications between buyer and supplier, stability and higher profits for suppliers, and often lower prices for buyers. However, many organizations still prefer multiple sourcing because this approach lessens the possibility of disruption caused by strikes, shortages, or bankruptcies. The actual product is ordered in this fourth stage, and specific details regarding terms, credit arrangements, delivery dates and methods, and technical assistance are finalized.

During the fifth stage, the product's performance is evaluated by comparing it with specifications. Sometimes the product meets the specifications, but its performance fails to adequately solve the problem or satisfy the need recognized in the first stage. In that case, product specifications must be adjusted. The supplier's performance is also evaluated during this stage. If supplier performance is inadequate, the business purchaser seeks corrective action from the supplier or searches for a new one. Results of the evaluation become feedback for the other stages in future business purchase decisions.

This business buying decision process is used in its entirety primarily for new-task purchases. Several stages, but not necessarily all, are used for modified rebuy and straight rebuy situations.

## Influences on the Business Buying Decision Process

Figure 6.1 also lists four major categories of factors that influence business buying decisions: environmental, organizational, interpersonal, and individual.

Environmental factors include competitive and economic factors, political forces, legal and regulatory forces, technological changes, and sociocultural issues. These factors generate considerable uncertainty for an organization, which can make individuals in the buying center apprehensive about certain types of purchases. Changes in one or more environmental forces can create new purchasing opportunities and threats. For example, changes in competition and technology can make buying decisions difficult for products such as software, computers, and telecommunications equipment. On the other hand, many business marketers believe the Internet can reduce their customer service costs and allow firms to improve relationships with business customers.[24]

Organizational factors influencing the buying decision process include the company's objectives, purchasing policies, and resources, as well as the size and composition of its buying center. An organization may have certain buying policies to which buying center participants must conform. For instance, a firm's policies may mandate unusually long- or short-term contracts, perhaps longer or shorter than most sellers desire. General Motors, for example, limits technology contracts to five years, even though the industry standard is seven- or ten-year contracts. The company has also imposed strict standardized sets of operating rules governing its awarding of contracts. These rules give GM greater flexibility and control but create additional challenges for firms marketing to the auto giant.[25] An organization's financial resources may require special credit arrangements. Any of these conditions could affect purchase decisions.

Interpersonal factors are the relationships among people in the buying center. Trust among all members of collaborative partnerships is crucial, particularly in purchases involving customized products.[26] Use of power and level of conflict among buying center participants influence business buying decisions. Certain individuals in the buying center may be better communicators and more persuasive than others. Often these interpersonal dynamics are hidden, making them difficult for marketers to assess.

Individual factors are personal characteristics of participants in the buying center, such as age, education level, personality, and tenure and position in the organization. For example, a 55-year-old manager who has been in the organization for 25 years may affect decisions made by the buying center differently than a 30-year-old person employed only two years. How influential these factors are depends on the buying situation; the type of product being purchased; and whether the purchase is new-task, modified rebuy, or straight rebuy. Negotiating styles of people vary within an organization and from one organization to another. To be effective, marketers must know customers well enough to be aware of these individual factors and their potential effects on purchase decisions.

# Using Industrial Classification Systems

Marketers have access to a considerable amount of information about potential business customers since much of this information is available through government and industry publications and websites. Marketers use this information to identify potential business customers and to estimate their purchase potential.

## Identifying Potential Business Customers

Much information about business customers is based on industrial classification systems. In the United States, marketers traditionally have relied on the *Standard Industrial Classification (SIC) system*, which the federal government developed to classify selected economic characteristics of industrial, commercial, financial, and service organizations. However, the SIC system has been replaced by a new industry classification system called the **North American Industry Classification System (NAICS)**. NAICS is a single industry classification system used by the United States, Canada, and Mexico to generate comparable statistics among the three partners of the North American Free Trade Agreement (NAFTA). The NAICS classification is based on the types of production activities performed. NAICS is similar to the International Standard Industrial Classification (ISIC) system used in Europe and many other parts of the world. Whereas the SIC system divided industrial activity into ten divisions, NAICS divides it into 20 sectors. NAICS contains 1,172 industry classifications, compared with 1,004 in the SIC system. NAICS is more comprehensive and up to date, and it provides considerably more information about service industries and high-tech products.[27] A sample comparison of the SIC system and NAICS appears in Table 6.2 (on p. 166). Over the next few years, all three NAFTA countries will convert from previously used industrial classification systems to NAICS.

Industrial classification systems are ready-made tools that enable marketers to categorize organizations into groups based mainly on the types of goods and services provided. Although an industrial classification system is a vehicle for segmentation, it is most appropriately used in conjunction with other types of data to determine exactly how many and which customers a marketer can reach.

Input-output analysis works well in conjunction with an industrial classification system. This type of analysis is based on the assumption that the output, or sales, of one industry are the input, or purchases, of other industries. **Input-output data** identify what types of industries purchase the products of a particular industry. A major source of national input-output data is the *Survey of Current Business*, published by the Office of Business Economics, U.S. Department of Commerce. After learning which industries purchase the major portion of an industry's output, the next step is to find the industrial classification numbers for those industries. Because firms are grouped differently in input-output tables and industrial classification systems, ascertaining industrial classification numbers can be difficult. However, the Office of

**North American Industry Classification System (NAICS)** An industry classification system that generates comparable statistics among the United States, Canada, and Mexico

**input-output data** Information that identifies what types of industries purchase the products of a particular industry

**table 6.2** COMPARISON OF THE SIC SYSTEM AND NAICS FOR MANUFACTURERS OF MAGNETIC AND OPTICAL MEDIA

| SIC Hierarchy | | NAICS Hierarchy | |
| --- | --- | --- | --- |
| Division D | Manufacturing | Sector 31–33 | Manufacturing |
| Major Group 36 | Manufacturers of electronic and other electrical equipment, except computer equipment | Subsector 334 | Computer and electronic manufacturing |
| Industry Subgroup 369 | Manufacturers of miscellaneous electrical machinery, equipment, and supplies | Industry Group 3346 | Manufacturing and reproduction of optical media |
| Detailed Industry 3695 | Manufacturers of magnetic and optical recording media | Industry 33461 | Manufacturing and reproduction of magnetic and optical media |
| | | U.S. Industry 334611 | U.S.-specific reproduction of software |

**Source:** Copyright © 1998, Manufacturers' Agents National Association, 23016 Mill Creek Road, P.O. Box 3467, Laguna Hills, CA 92654-3467. Phone (949) 859-4040; fax (949) 855-2973. All rights reserved. Reproduction without permission is strictly prohibited.

Business Economics provides some limited conversion tables with input-output data. These tables can help marketers assign classification numbers to industry categories used in input-output analysis.

After determining the classification numbers of industries that buy the firm's output, a marketer is in a position to ascertain the number of organizations that are potential buyers. Government sources, such as the *Census of Business,* the *Census of Manufacturers,* and *County Business Patterns,* report the number of establishments, the value of industry shipments, the number of employees, the percentage of imports and exports, and industry growth rates within classifications. Commercial sources also provide information about organizations categorized by industrial classifications.

A marketer can take several approaches to determine the identities and locations of organizations in specific groups. One approach is to use state directories or commercial industrial directories, such as *Standard & Poor's Register* and Dun & Bradstreet's *Million Dollar Directory.* These sources contain such information about a firm as its name, industrial classification, address, phone number, and annual sales. By referring to one or more of these sources, marketers isolate business customers with industrial classification numbers, determine their locations, and develop lists of potential customers by desired geographic area. A more expedient, although more expensive, approach is to use a commercial data service. Dun & Bradstreet, for example, can provide a list of organizations that fall into a particular industrial classification group. For each company on the list, Dun & Bradstreet gives the name, location, sales volume, number of employees, type of products handled, names of chief executives, and other pertinent information. Either method can effectively identify and locate a group of potential customers. However, a marketer probably cannot pursue all organizations on the list. Because some companies have greater purchasing potential than others, marketers must determine which customer or customer group to pursue.

## Estimating Purchase Potential

To estimate the purchase potential of business customers or groups of customers, a marketer must find a relationship between the size of potential customers' purchases and a variable available in industrial classification data, such as the number of employees. For example, a paint manufacturer might attempt to determine the average number of gallons purchased by a specific type of potential customer relative to the number of employees. A marketer with no previous experience in this market segment will probably have to survey a random sample of potential customers to establish a relationship between purchase sizes and numbers of employees. Once this relationship is established, it can be applied to customer groups to estimate their potential purchases. After deriving these estimates, the marketer is in a position to select the customer groups with the most sales and profit potential.

Despite their usefulness, industrial classification data pose several problems. First, a few industries do not have specific designations. Second, because a transfer of products from one establishment to another is counted as a part of total shipments, double counting may occur when products are shipped between two establishments within the same firm. Third, because the Census Bureau is prohibited from providing data that identify specific business organizations, some data, such as value of total shipments, may be understated. Finally, because government agencies provide industrial classification data, a significant lag usually exists between data collection time and the time the information is released.

## SUMMARY

Business (B2B) markets consist of individuals and groups that purchase a specific kind of product for resale, direct use in producing other products, or use in day-to-day operations. Producer markets include those individuals and business organizations that purchase products for the purpose of making a profit by using them to produce other products or as part of their operations. Intermediaries that buy finished products and resell them to make a profit are classified as reseller markets. Government markets consist of federal, state, county, and local governments, which spend billions of dollars annually for goods and services to support internal operations and to provide citizens with needed services. Organizations with charitable, educational, community, or other nonprofit goals constitute institutional markets.

Transactions involving business customers differ from consumer transactions in several ways. Such transactions tend to be larger, and negotiations occur less frequently, though they are often lengthy. They frequently involve more than one person or department in the purchasing organization. They may also involve reciprocity, an arrangement in which two organizations agree to buy from each other. Business customers are usually better informed than ultimate consumers and more likely to seek information about a product's features and technical specifications.

When purchasing products, business customers are particularly concerned about quality, service, price, and supplier relationships. Quality is important because it directly affects the quality of products the buyer's firm produces. To achieve an exact level of quality, organizations often buy products on the basis of a set of expressed characteristics, called specifications. Because services have such a direct influence on a firm's costs, sales, and profits, factors such as market information, on-time delivery, and availability of parts are crucial to a business buyer. Although business customers do not depend solely on price to decide which products to buy, price is of primary concern because it directly influences profitability.

Business buyers use several purchasing methods, including description, inspection, sampling, and negotiation. Most organizational purchases are new-task, straight rebuy, or modified rebuy. In a new-task purchase, an organization makes an initial purchase of items to be used to perform new jobs or solve new problems. In a modified rebuy purchase, a new-task purchase is changed the second or third time it is ordered or requirements associated with a straight rebuy purchase are modified. A straight rebuy purchase occurs when a buyer purchases the same products routinely under approximately the same terms of sale.

Industrial demand differs from consumer demand along several dimensions. Industrial demand derives from demand for consumer products. At the industry level, industrial demand is inelastic. If an industrial item's price changes, product demand will not change as much proportionally. Some industrial products are subject to joint demand, which occurs when two or more items are used in combination to make a product. Finally, because organizational demand derives from consumer demand, the demand for business products can fluctuate widely.

Business (or organizational) buying behavior refers to the purchase behavior of producers, resellers, government units, and institutions. Business purchase decisions are made through a buying center, the group of people involved in making such purchase decisions. Users are those in the organization who actually use the product. Influencers help develop specifications and evaluate alternative products for possible use. Buyers select suppliers and negotiate purchase terms. Deciders choose the products. Gatekeepers control the flow of information to and among individuals occupying other roles in the buying center.

The stages of the business buying decision process are problem recognition, development of product specifications to solve problems, search for and evaluation of products and suppliers, selection and ordering of the most appropriate product, and evaluation of the product's and supplier's performance.

Four categories of factors influence business buying decisions: environmental, organizational, interpersonal, and individual. Environmental factors include competitive forces, economic conditions, political forces, laws and regulations, technological changes, and sociocultural factors. Business factors include the company's objectives, purchasing policies, and resources, as well as the size and composition of its buying center. Interpersonal factors are the relationships among people in the buying center. Individual factors are personal characteristics of members of

the buying center, such as age, education level, personality, and tenure and position in the organization.

Business marketers have a considerable amount of information available for use in planning marketing strategies. Much of this information is based on an industrial classification system, which categorizes businesses into major industry groups, industry subgroups, and detailed industry categories. An industrial classification system—like the North American Industry Classification System (NAICS) used by the United States, Canada, and Mexico—provides marketers with information needed to identify business customer groups. It can best be used for this purpose in conjunction with other information, such as input-output data. After identifying target industries, a marketer can obtain the names and locations of potential customers by using government and commercial data sources. Marketers then must estimate potential purchases of business customers by finding a relationship between a potential customer's purchases and a variable available in industrial classification data.

**ACE self-test**

Please visit the student website at **www.prideferrell.com** for ACE Self-Test questions that will help you prepare for exams.

---

## IMPORTANT TERMS

| | | | |
|---|---|---|---|
| Business market | New-task purchase | Business (organizational) buying behavior | Sole sourcing |
| Producer markets | Straight rebuy purchase | | North American Industry Classification System (NAICS) |
| Reseller market | Modified rebuy purchase | Buying center | |
| Government market | Derived demand | Value analysis | Input-output data |
| Institutional market | Inelastic demand | Vendor analysis | |
| Reciprocity | Joint demand | Multiple sourcing | |

---

## DISCUSSION & REVIEW QUESTIONS

1. Identify, describe, and give examples of the four major types of business markets.

2. Why might business customers generally be considered more rational in their purchasing behavior than ultimate consumers?

3. What are the primary concerns of business customers?

4. List several characteristics that differentiate transactions involving business customers from consumer transactions.

5. What are the commonly used methods of business buying?

6. Why do buyers involved in straight rebuy purchases require less information than those making new-task purchases?

7. How does demand for business products differ from consumer demand?

8. What are the major components of a firm's buying center?

9. Identify the stages of the business buying decision process. How is this decision process used when making straight rebuys?

10. How do environmental, business, interpersonal, and individual factors affect business purchases?

11. What function does an industrial classification system help marketers perform?

12. List some sources that a business marketer can use to determine the names and addresses of potential customers.

## APPLICATION QUESTIONS

1. Identify organizations in your area that fit each business market category: producer, reseller, government, and institutional. Explain your classifications.

2. Indicate the method of buying (description, inspection, sampling, or negotiation) an organization would be most likely to use when purchasing each of the following items. Defend your selections.

   a. A building for the home office of a light bulb manufacturer

   b. Wool for a clothing manufacturer

   c. An Alaskan cruise for a company retreat, assuming a regular travel agency is used

   d. One-inch nails for a building contractor

3. Purchases by businesses may be described as new-task, modified rebuy, or straight rebuy. Categorize the following purchase decisions and explain your choices.

   a. Bob has purchased toothpicks from Smith Restaurant Supply for 25 years and recently placed an order for yellow toothpicks rather than the usual white ones.

   b. Jill's investment company has been purchasing envelopes from AAA Office Supply for a year and now needs to purchase boxes to mail year-end portfolio summaries to clients. Jill calls AAA to purchase these boxes.

   c. Reliance Insurance has been supplying its salespeople with small personal computers to assist in their sales efforts. The company recently agreed to begin supplying them with faster, more sophisticated computers.

4. Identifying qualified customers is important to the survival of any organization. NAICS provides helpful information about many different businesses. Find the NAICS manual at the library and identify the NAICS code for the following items.

   a. Chocolate candy bars

   b. Automobile tires

   c. Men's running shoes

globalEDGE™

1. The world market for steel plays a vital role on projects involving the construction of bridges, buildings, automobiles, and aircraft. After attending a conference sponsored by the International Iron and Steel Institute (IISI), you learn that the "World Steel in Figures" report can help your firm reassess its strategy for sourcing steel on the global market to be a better arbiter for clients. To access this report, use the search term "IISI" at **http://globaledge.msu.edu/ibrd**. Currently, your sourcing strategy is similar to typical North American companies. As such, from which regions does your company source steel? In which countries might your firm aim to find new sources for steel?

2. Part of your firm's evaluation of a supplier's performance is based on the degree to which it seamlessly delivers goods and materials. A recent complication for global suppliers is an initiative to enhance shipping container security for international trade and transport. A report concerning container security for international trade and transportation can be found using the search term "international trade and transport" at **http://globaledge.msu.edu/ibrd**. At the United Nations Conference on Trade and Development (UNCTAD) website, click on the Transport & Trade Logistics link, go to the Documents section, and look for a report on Container Security. What are the four parts of this program? Based on this, do you think your firm should change its evaluation of supplier performance?

## General Electric Company

General Electric Company is a highly diversified, global corporation with many divisions. GEPolymerland.com is the online site for GE's resins business. Visit the site at **www.GEPolymerland.com**.

1. At what types of business markets are GE's resin products targeted?
2. How does GEPolymerland address some of the concerns of business customers?
3. What environmental factors do you think affect demand for GE resin products?

---

## Video Case 6.1    Lextant Corporation: Design Research at Its Best

These days, competition is fierce. It's no longer possible just to make a product and hope that it sells; products must be designed with end users in mind. Lextant Corporation provides design research for its business customers, including PepsiCo, Procter & Gamble, Motorola, Goodyear, Whirlpool, Microsoft, and Hard Rock Café. Its name comes from the word *lexicon,* meaning "a vocabulary or language"—in this case, a language of consumers. The privately held Columbus, Ohio–based company strives to translate this language into actionable insights, equipping its clients to design for the motivations, behaviors, and desires of their own customers.

Lextant was founded with one fundamental goal—to help companies achieve a sustainable competitive advantage by understanding their end users and designing products to satisfy them. To achieve this goal, Lextant examines what motivates and drives people and presents this information to its clients so that they can make informed decisions about the products they are designing. Lextant brings together teams of experts in psychology, sociology, anthropology, human factors, industrial design, and interaction design, and it combines ethnographic, participatory, marketing, behavioral, and usability research techniques to provide tools to make products better. Then researchers learn from consumers by following them in everything they do in their environment. Finally, researchers design systems that will yield the desired results for the firm's clients.

Lextant researchers discover what end users want by getting a broad view of people and trying to know and understand them, often by observing them in their own environment. They understand the importance of observing people actually using the products being studied in their place of usage. It is important in this process to really listen to end users when they explain what matters to them. Lextant has two approaches for collecting data. The first is qualitative—through the context and environment of the user. The second is quantitative—based on what the client wants. The quantitative approach involves presenting prototypes of a product to a sample of end users. These clients then use the sample product and give feedback on what they like and don't like about the product, as well as suggestions on how the product could be improved.

In some cases, Lextant uses focus groups to discover information for its clients. Researchers bring people together at a central facility to use and test the product and provide feedback about its design, color, and ease of use. This method is especially useful when budget or time is limited because it permits researchers to gather information at a central location in a short time and results in instant feedback.

Once researchers have collected the data from various sources, they are often confronted with an overwhelming amount of data. They must analyze the data to find the patterns and recognize anomalies that occur in only a few cases. Researchers use affinity diagrams and Post-it Notes stuck to the wall to help the process flow. By having Post-it Notes labeled with each important characteristic, it is easy to move the parts around until the relevant story becomes clear. By having many pictures of the users and the environments in which a product is used, it is possible for any person in the organization to come into the room and understand the consumers: their personas, attitudes, and motivations.

Employees at Lextant immerse themselves in the information that they gather to evaluate which information is relevant while at the same time discarding useless information. It is then possible to see where people say similar things and to focus on those and find out what is wrong with certain products.

Clients of Lextant are often surprised by the findings of the Lextant team, especially when it comes to identifying ways that they can modify their existing products to better satisfy end users. For example, Lextant helped Hard Rock Café to answer the question, "Is our website experience helping or hurting our brand?" Indeed, its website was challenging to navigate and was sapping online sales. Lextant helped the restaurant chain develop an easy-to-use, compelling website to help rejuvenate the legendary brand. Lextant researchers examined the Hard Rock website from the customers' perspective, documented the user goals and ideal experiences, and then developed an architecture that facilitated desired activity flows. The research firm created a complete prototype featuring an intuitive Café locator, personalization features, and a streamlined shopping process. This enabled Hard Rock to corroborate and refine site concepts before making significant investments in implementation.

Lextant provides a business product that has a derived demand from producing products that delight consumers. Design research is not about the what, but rather the why. If you understand why people do not like an existing design, then it is possible to design a new solution.[28]

### Questions for Discussion

1. Why is the Lextant product a derived demand business product?
2. What types of business markets does Lextant serve?
3. When purchasing Lextant services, what type of buying method would be used: description, sampling, inspection, or negotiation?

---

| Case 6.2 | WebMD Delivers Online Services to Health-Care Providers |
|---|---|

How do doctors, hospitals, pharmaceutical firms, laboratories, health insurers, pharmacies, and medical suppliers stay connected to deliver quality health-care services to consumers? The divisions of WebMD (**www.webmd.com**) aim to provide the common connection. For physicians and clinics, WebMD Practice Services offers office management systems to manage appointments, handle billing, maintain patient files, and track insurance claims. These services help medical practitioners streamline their office procedures for higher productivity. Doctors can also use WebMD Practice Services to access patients' medical records, insurance coverage, and treatment options via their PDAs. This convenience not only saves time but also allows doctors to check patient information while patients wait and replaces reams of paperwork.

Each medical visit sets in motion a tide of transactions among doctors, insurers, pharmacies, hospitals, laboratories, and others—a tide that WebMD Envoy can help stem. As the market leader in electronic health-care transaction processing, WebMD Envoy reduces paperwork by putting claims and payments in digital form, arranging online prescriptions, and transmitting laboratory test orders and reports. This service is especially important as the U.S. medical industry works to comply with federally mandated standards for electronic exchange of information.

WebMD Envoy was already processing 2.5 billion digital transactions annually before WebMD acquired Medifax-EDI, a company that checks a patient's health insurance coverage and determines eligibility for medical services. The combination makes WebMD Envoy a more powerful competitor, in part because Medifax-EDI's customer base, mainly hospitals and Medicaid providers, complements WebMD Envoy's customer base of doctors, dentists, and insurers. In addition, the combined company offers a much wider array of services and can therefore expedite processing of nearly any medical visit's administrative and financial details, from start to finish. Its business customers save a lot of money when they convert from manual to electronic claims processing. A doctor's office might spend up to $6 to process a claim by hand, but the cost drops below

$1 when the office processes a claim electronically. WebMD's CEO estimates that customers pay an average of 21 cents for each digital transaction processed.

Every participant in the health-care network needs timely medical information, especially patients and doctors. On the business side, health-care professionals can use WebMD's Medscape website to obtain articles from medical journals, follow presentations at recent medical conferences, look up the latest medical developments, and take continuing medical education courses. More than 2 million medical professionals use this site to stay current in their areas of expertise. On the consumer side, WebMD Health is one of the best-known online sources of information about the latest medical breakthroughs, health news, specific diseases and conditions, support communities, and medical education. This popular website draws 20 million consumers every month and provides medical news to millions more through deals with America Online and other Internet portals.

Despite its promise, WebMD's high-tech strategy faces several challenges. First, the competition is becoming more intense. Rivals such as Per-sé Technologies and MedAvant Healthcare Solutions are active in some of the same business markets WebMD serves. Second, WebMD may wind up with lower transaction volumes or be forced to cut prices if health insurers choose to strengthen their ties with doctors by providing electronic transaction processing for free. The company will face similar threats if many hospitals and clinics create their own electronic processing systems rather than paying WebMD or other firms to handle digital transac-tions. Some hospitals have made the transition to software that connects their systems for processing purposes, sharply reducing the need for outside processing services. For example, Sharp HealthCare, based in California, now processes the majority of its claims through an internal system, although it still pays WebMD to handle a small number of transactions.

Third, health-care providers are particularly interested in goods and services tailored to their specialties. However, they are reluctant to sign up for fee-based services, such as a monthly subscription for accessing medical information through a handheld device, unless they believe they will get a solid payback. They value short-term benefits such as improving productivity, but also want to know they will enjoy long-term benefits that make the cost worthwhile. Therefore, as medical knowledge expands and government regulations evolve, WebMD will have to stay tuned to its customers' needs and priorities and add innovations to remain ahead of competitors.[29]

## Questions for Discussion

1. Which of the environmental influences that can affect the business buying process are creating opportunities for WebMD?
2. Which of the organizational influences that can affect the business buying process could pose threats for WebMD?
3. Would a customer who prefers multiple sourcing welcome WebMD's acquisition of Medifax-EDI if the customer previously contracted for services from both companies? Explain.

## CHAPTER 7

# Reaching Global Markets

## iPod: Surely One of Apple's Greatest Hits

Today, just about everyone has an iPod. Well, perhaps not everyone. But the Queen of England has one. So does the President of the United States. And the Pope. Fashion designer Karl Lagerfeldt has more than 70 of them storing his collection of more than 60,000 CDs.

From its start in 1976 with the introduction of Apple I to the more recent phenomenon of the iPod, Apple Computer Inc. has achieved legendary status worldwide with its innovations. Whether it's the latest incarnation of the original iPod that was first introduced in October 2001 or the later additions such as the iPod shuffle or iPod nano, one of the most remarkable things about the iPod family is its almost universal appeal. It's been embraced not just by U.S. teenagers, but by people worldwide, young and old. Sit in a Starbucks in New York or San Francisco or venture out to a sidewalk cafe in Beijing, Melbourne, Rio de Janeiro, Stockholm, or Tokyo and the parade of iPods works like a universal ad for Apple. The company currently dominates the MP3 player market with its Microsoft-like 75 percent share worldwide.

The iPod is simply an entirely new way to listen to music, and the global marketplace is taking notice. Numerous companies are hopping on the bandwagon by developing products that go along with iPods. For example, San Francisco–based Levi Strauss is launching its Levi's RedWire DLX jeans that have a docking station in the pocket and a control panel sewn into the coin pocket. At $200 a pair, "This brings blue jeans into the 21st century. . . . The idea is to merge fashion and technology," says Levi spokeswoman Amy Jasmer.

The automobile industry is also paying close attention to the iPod. "Customers have been asking for iPod connectivity," said Randy Ewers, director, Mopar Accessories Portfolio Team. Most carmakers now offer iPod integration. In cars made by the Chrysler Group—such as Chrysler, Jeep, and Dodge—seamless iPod integration means that drivers can listen to their iPods through their cars' audio systems. They have the traditional features of their iPods at their fingertips

## OBJECTIVES

1. To understand the nature of global marketing strategy

2. To analyze the environmental forces affecting international marketing efforts

3. To understand several important international trade agreements

4. To identify methods of international market entry

5. To examine various forms of global organizational structures

6. To examine the use of the marketing mix internationally

via the radio or steering wheel controls, and they can view selections on the radio display.

Accessories made specifically for iPod range from fashionable cases to Bose speaker systems. No doubt the iPod will continue to inspire new products and new marketing strategies the world over. It's time to Listen Up![1] ■

Before picking up an Egg McMuffin at McDonald's this morning, a young woman in Hong Kong may have brightened her smile with Colgate toothpaste and highlighted her eyes with Avon eye shadow. Her brother, on business that same day in Frankfurt, may cash a check in a local Citicorp branch bank. Elsewhere that day, a Polish office worker may lunch on a pizza from Pizza Hut, fried chicken from KFC, or a taco from Taco Bell. An Australian mother shopping for a birthday present in Melbourne may drop in at Daimaru, a Japanese department store, while a New Yorker in Syracuse may shop for a train set for his two-year-old at the Lost Forest, an Australian toy boutique. The earth is now populated by about 6.5 billion people whose lives are intertwined in one tremendous global marketplace. In fact, global trade in goods and services reached $11 trillion in 2004, an increase of 18 percent compared with 2003.[2]

In deference to the increasingly global nature of marketing, we devote this chapter to the unique features of global markets and international marketing. We begin by exploring the environmental forces that create opportunities and threats for international marketers. Next, we consider several regional trade alliances, markets, and agreements. Finally, we examine the levels of commitment by firms to international marketing and their degree of involvement in it. These factors must be considered in any marketing plan that includes an international component.

# The Nature of Global Marketing Strategy

**international marketing** Developing and performing marketing activities across national boundaries

Technological advances and rapidly changing political and economic conditions are making it easier than ever for companies to market their products internationally as well as at home. **International marketing** involves developing and performing marketing activities across national boundaries. For example, Wal-Mart has more than 1.5 million employees and operates more than 5,300 stores in ten countries, including the United States, Brazil, and China, while Starbucks serves 20 million customers a week at more than 10,000 shops in 30 countries.[3]

Firms are finding that international markets provide tremendous opportunities for growth. At the same time, governments and industry leaders often argue that too few firms take full advantage of international opportunities. The result is a wide variance in trade balances for countries. For example, the trade balance of the United States has been significantly negative—more imports than exports—for decades, while a strong-growth economy such as China has a positive trade balance.[4] To assist firms in their internationalization efforts, many countries offer significant practical assistance and valuable benchmarking research that will help their domestic firms become more competitive globally.

Consider the Commercial Service, the global business solutions unit of the U.S. Department of Commerce. It offers U.S. firms wide and deep practical knowledge of international markets and industries, a unique global network, inventive use of information technology, and a focus on small and medium-sized businesses.[5] Another example is the benchmarking of best international practices that is conducted by the network of CIBERs—Centers for International Business Education and Research—at leading business schools in the United States.[6] These 30 CIBERs are funded by the U.S. government to help U.S. firms become more competitive globally. A major element of the assistance that these governmental organizations can provide firms (especially small and medium-sized firms) is knowledge of the internationalization process of firms.

BE AN
EXPERT IN
OVERSEAS
MARKETS.

*Do you live an InterContinental life?*

INTERCONTINENTAL.
HOTELS & RESORTS

**Global Strategy Thinking**

Intercontinental touts its global strategy capabilities.

Before the so-called born global firm became a widespread viable organizational form around the early 1990s, most firms entered the international marketplace incrementally as they gained knowledge about various markets and opportunities. Becoming more internationally oriented was typically a slow and deliberate process. However, some firms had the knowledge and resources to speed up their commitment and investment in the international marketplace. Born globals—typically small technology-based firms operating in international markets within two years of their establishment and realizing as much as 70 percent of their sales outside the domestic home market—challenged the traditional internationalization process and especially its incremental nature and slow developmental speed.[7]

These born global firms export their products almost immediately after being established in market niches in which they compete with larger, more established firms. Whether the traditional approach, the born global approach, or an approach that merges attributes of both approaches is adopted to market the firm's products and services, international marketing strategy is a critical element of a firm's global operations. Today, global competition in most industries is intense and becoming increasingly fierce with the addition of newly emerging markets and firms.

For example, to combat new competition, online retailer Amazon.com has nine distribution centers from Nevada to Germany that fill their current flow of about 30 orders per second and ship them to customers in more than 200 countries.[8] In fact, most of the world's population and two-thirds of its total purchasing power are outside the United States. Accessing these markets can promote innovation, while intensifying global competition spurs companies to market better, less expensive products. Most automobile marketers, for instance, are now attempting to develop products for use by customers worldwide. In the future, only a few automobile brands may be recognized globally. Some of these are likely to be from General Motors, whose many globally recognized brands include Saab, Opel, Chevrolet, and Cadillac. Others may come from Japan's Toyota Motors, which aggressively markets automobiles and trucks around the world and looks to overtake GM as the top automaker in the next few years.[9]

# Environmental Forces in Global Markets

Firms that enter international markets often find they must make significant adjustments in their marketing strategies. The environmental forces that affect foreign markets may differ dramatically from those affecting domestic markets. Thus, a successful international marketing strategy requires a careful environmental analysis. Conducting research to understand the needs and desires of international customers is crucial to global marketing success. Many firms have demonstrated that such efforts can generate tremendous financial rewards, increase market share, and heighten customer awareness of their products around the world. In this section, we explore how differences in the competitive, economic, political, legal and regulatory,

**Staying Ahead of the Competition**

Datapipe focuses on delivering competitive worldwide services.

technological, and sociocultural environmental forces in other countries can profoundly affect marketing activities.

## Competitive Forces

Competition is often viewed as a staple of the global marketplace. Customers thrive on the choices offered by competition, and firms constantly seek opportunities to outmaneuver their competition to gain customers' loyalty. Firms typically identify their competition when they establish target markets worldwide. Customers seek alternative solutions to their product needs by identifying firms that can compete to solve their needs. However, the increasingly interconnected international marketplace and advances in technology have resulted in competitive forces that are unique to the international marketplace.

As in domestic markets, the products offered by the competition and the ways they are marketed are key competitive forces internationally. However, beyond the types of competition (i.e., brand, product, generic, and total budget competition) and types of competitive structures (i.e., monopoly, oligopoly, monopolistic competition, and pure competition) that are discussed in Chapter 3, firms operating internationally also need to

■ attend to the competitive forces in the countries they target

■ identify the interdependence of countries and the global competitors in those markets

■ be mindful of a new breed of customers—the global customer

Each country has unique competitive aspects—often founded in the other environmental forces (i.e., sociocultural, technological, political, legal, regulatory, and economic forces)—that are often independent of the competitors in that country

## table 7.1  A RANKING OF THE MOST COMPETITIVE COUNTRIES IN THE WORLD

| | |
|---|---|
| 1. Finland | 11. Netherlands |
| 2. United States | 12. Japan |
| 3. Sweden | 13. United Kingdom |
| 4. Denmark | 14. Canada |
| 5. Taiwan | 15. Germany |
| 6. Singapore | 16. New Zealand |
| 7. Iceland | 17. South Korea |
| 8. Switzerland | 18. United Arab Emirates |
| 9. Norway | 19. Qatar |
| 10. Australia | 20. Estonia |

**Source:** From Lopezcarlos/Porter/Shwab, *The Global Competitiveness Report 2005–2006*, World Economic Forum. Reproduced with permission of Palgrave Macmillan.

market. The most globally competitive countries are listed in Table 7.1. While competitors drive competition, country markets establish the infrastructure for the type of competition that can take place. For example, Microsoft's almost monopolistic dominance in the U.S. marketplace (and most other countries' markets) has led the U.S. government and U.S. firms to a long-standing legal battle over the firm's business practices vis-à-vis its competition.[10] Other countries allow monopoly structures to exist. For example, most alcohol sales in Sweden are made through the governmental store Systembolaget, which is legally supported by the Swedish Alcohol Retail Monopoly.[11] According to Systembolaget, the Swedish Alcohol Retail Monopoly exists for one reason: "To minimize alcohol-related problems by selling alcohol in a responsible way, without profit motive."

The interdependence between countries and their strategic relevance for multinational firms has long been a critical component of international competition.[12] These interdependencies are a function of governmental activity, trade agreements like the European Union (EU) and the North American Free Trade Agreement (NAFTA), and cultural differences. The result has been the formation of the "triad blocks" of North America, the EU, and Japan. Firms can clearly operate in more than the triad blocks, but the successful international firms typically need to have a solid position in each of the triad blocks to be successful in the long term. Success internationally is a function of the strategic interdependence firms can create across the triad blocks as well as across the other country and region markets targeted. In fact, in only a few industries—such as consumer electronics—should a firm strive to develop a global strategy. For most manufacturing firms and for almost all service firms, adopting a regional approach makes more sense (and in many cases, a country-specific approach is still needed).

The new breed of customer—the global customer—has changed the landscape of international competition drastically.[13] Firms used to simply produce products or services and provide local markets with information about the features and uses of their products or services. Customers seldom had opportunities to compare products from competitors, know details about the competing products' features, and compare other options beyond the local (country or region) markets. However, not only do customers who travel the globe expect to be able to buy the same product in most of the world's more than 200 countries, they also expect that the product they buy in their local store in Miami will have the same features as similar products sold in London or even in Beijing. If the quality of the product or its features are more advanced in an international market, customers will soon demand that their local markets offer the same product at the same or lower prices.

## Economic Forces

Global marketers need to understand the international trade system, particularly the economic stability of individual nations, as well as trade barriers that may stifle marketing efforts. Economic differences among nations—differences in standards of living, credit, buying power, income distribution, national resources, exchange rates, and the like—dictate many of the adjustments firms must make in marketing internationally.

The United States and western Europe are more stable economically than many other regions of the world. However, even these economies have downturns in regular cycles. In recent years, a number of countries, including Korea, Russia, Singapore, and Thailand, have experienced economic problems such as depressions, high unemployment, corporate bankruptcies, instability in currency markets, trade imbalances, and financial systems that need major reforms. Even more stable developing countries, such as Mexico and Brazil, tend to have greater fluctuations in their business cycles than the United States does. Economic instability can disrupt the markets for U.S. products in places that otherwise might be excellent marketing opportunities.

Beyond assessing the stability of a nation's economy, marketers should consider whether that nation imposes trade restrictions, such as tariffs. An **import tariff** is any duty levied by a nation on goods bought outside its borders and brought in. Because they raise the prices of foreign goods, tariffs impede free trade between nations. Tariffs are usually designed either to raise revenue for a country or to protect domestic products.

Nontariff trade barriers include quotas and embargoes. A **quota** is a limit on the amount of goods an importing country will accept for certain product categories in a specific period of time. An **embargo** is a government's suspension of trade in a particular product or with a given country. Embargoes are generally directed at specific goods or countries and are established for political, health, or religious reasons. For example, the United States forbids the importation of cigars from Cuba for political reasons. However, demand for Cuban cigars is so strong that many enter the U.S. market illegally. Laws regarding pricing policies may also serve as trade barriers. Great Britain, for example, has weaker antitrust laws than the United States and is generally more accepting of price collusion. Consequently many products cost more in Britain than in the United States. Because customers may be unable to afford the higher prices of imported products, such policies effectively create barriers to foreign trade.

**Exchange controls,** government restrictions on the amount of a particular currency that can be bought or sold, may also limit international trade. They can force businesspeople to buy and sell foreign products through a central agency, such as a central bank. On the other hand, to promote international trade, some countries have joined to form free trade zones, multinational economic communities that eliminate tariffs and other trade barriers. Such regional trade alliances are discussed later in the chapter. Foreign currency exchange rates also affect the prices marketers can charge in foreign markets. Fluctuations in the international monetary market can change the prices charged across national boundaries on a daily basis. Thus these fluctuations must be considered in any international marketing strategy.

Countries may limit imports to maintain a favorable balance of trade. The **balance of trade** is the difference in value between a nation's exports and its imports. When a nation exports more products than it imports, a favorable balance of trade exists because money is flowing into the country. The United States had a negative balance of trade for goods and services of $725 billion in 2005, the largest deficit ever.[14] A negative balance of trade is considered harmful because it means U.S. dollars are supporting foreign economies at the expense of U.S. companies and workers. At the same time, individuals living in the United States benefit from the assortment of imported products and their typically lower prices.

In terms of the value of all products produced by a nation, the United States has the largest gross domestic product in the world, nearly $12.5 trillion in 2005.[15] **Gross domestic product (GDP)** is an overall measure of a nation's economic standing; it is the market value of a nation's total output of goods and services for a given period. However, it does not take into account the concept of GDP in relation to population (GDP per capita). The United States has a GDP per capita of $35,700. Switzerland is roughly 230 times smaller than the United States—a little larger than the state of Maryland—but its population density is six times greater than that of the United States.

Although Switzerland's GDP is about one-fortieth the size of the United States' GDP, its GDP per capita is about the same. Even Canada, which is comparable in size to the United States, has a lower GDP and GDP per capita.[16] Table 7.2 provides a comparative economic analysis of Switzerland, Canada, and the United States.

**import tariff** A duty levied by a nation on goods bought outside its borders and brought in

**quota** A limit on the amount of goods an importing country will accept for certain product categories in a specific period of time

**embargo** A government's suspension of trade in a particular product or with a given country

**exchange controls** Government restrictions on the amount of a particular currency that can be bought or sold

**balance of trade** The difference in value between a nation's exports and its imports

**gross domestic product (GDP)** The market value of a nation's total output of goods and services for a given period; an overall measure of economic standing

| table 7.2 | A COMPARATIVE ECONOMIC ANALYSIS OF CANADA, SWITZERLAND, AND THE UNITED STATES | | |
|---|---|---|---|
| | **Canada** | **Switzerland** | **United States** |
| **Land area (sq. mi.)** | 3,560,219 | 15,355 | 3,539,227 |
| **Population (millions)** | 32.21 | 7.41 | 290.34 |
| **Population density (persons per sq. mi.)** | 9 | 482 | 82 |
| **GDP, 2002 ($ billions)** | $725 | $268 | $10,383 |
| **GDP per capita** | $23,074 | $36,722 | $36,121 |

**Source:** U.S. Bureau of the Census, *Statistical Abstract of the United States*, 2004 (Washington DC: Government Printing Office, 2005), pp. 841–843, 853.

Knowledge about per capita income, credit, and the distribution of income provides general insights into market potential.

Opportunities for international trade are not limited to countries with the highest incomes. Some nations are progressing at a much faster rate than they were a few years ago, and these countries—especially in Latin America, Africa, eastern Europe, and the Middle East—have great market potential. An annual study by the Center for International Business Education and Research at Michigan State University provides updated rankings on emerging markets on the globalEDGE website (**http://globaledge.msu.edu/ibrd/marketpot.asp**). The 2006 update of the EMPI features Hong Kong and Singapore at the top of the most attractive emerging markets. China has been steadily climbing up in the index and now ranks third. Ranking as the fourth most attractive export market is South Korea. At the other extreme are South Africa, Venezuela, and Columbia, all suffering from extended economic recessions. However, marketers must understand the political and legal environments before they can convert buying power of customers in these countries into actual demand for specific products.

## Political Forces

The political, legal, and regulatory forces of the environment are closely intertwined in the United States. To a large degree, the same is true in many countries internationally. Typically, legislation is enacted, legal decisions are interpreted, and regulatory agencies are operated by elected or appointed officials. A country's legal and regulatory infrastructure is a direct reflection of the political climate in the country. In some countries, this political climate is determined by the people via elections, while in other countries leaders are appointed or have assumed leadership based on certain powers. While laws and regulations have direct effects on a firm's operations in a country, political forces are indirect and often not clearly known in all country markets. For example, the need to work with the government of China to enter and establish operations in the country has been a highly political process since the Communist rule started.

To offset the potential political negatives that may exist in a country or region, firms (and often their home-country governments) strive to maintain good relations with political officials in the targeted countries. Some countries also establish specific mechanisms to better understand the political and business climates around the world, for the benefit of the country's firms. For example, in the United States, the Centers for International Business Education and Research (CIBERs) were created under the Omnibus Trade and Competitiveness Act of 1988 to increase and promote the capacity of the United States for international understanding and economic enterprise.[17] Much of what these CIBERs focus on deals with the political business climate of world markets.

The political climate in a country or region, political officials in a country, and political officials in charge of trade agreements directly affect the legislation and regulations (or lack thereof). Within industries, elected or appointed officials of influential industry associations also set the tone for the regulatory environment guiding operations in a particular industry. For example, the American Marketing Association (**www.marketingpower.com**)—one of the largest professional associations for marketers with 38,000 members worldwide in every area of marketing—has established Ethical Norms and Values for Marketers that guide the marketing profession in the United States.[18]

### Legal and Regulatory Forces

A nation's political system, laws, regulatory bodies, special-interest groups, and courts all have great impact on international marketing. A government's policies toward public and private enterprise, consumers, and foreign firms influence marketing across national boundaries. Some countries have established import barriers. Many nontariff barriers, such as quotas and minimum price levels set on imports, port-of-entry taxes, and stringent health and safety requirements, still make it difficult for U.S. companies to export their products. For example, the collectivistic nature of Japanese culture and the high-context nature of Japanese communication make some types of direct marketing messages less effective and may predispose many Japanese to support greater regulation of direct marketing practices.[19] A government's attitude toward importers has a direct impact on the economic feasibility of exporting to that country.

# globalEDGE: The Net's International Business Resource

From its beginning as a single webpage in 1994, globalEDGE has expanded to be the most comprehensive international business resource on the Internet. With over 5,000 online resources and up-to-date statistics and business news for nearly 200 countries, globalEDGE is the world's leading online source in international business as ranked by Google, Yahoo!, MSN, and America Online.

Created by the Center for International Business Education and Research at Michigan State University (MSU-CIBER), globalEDGE is a knowledge web portal that connects international business professionals worldwide to a wealth of information, insights, and learning resources on global business activities.

The MSU-CIBER team of entrepreneurs does the work for you, uncovering and organizing the best international business and trade sites available. Each resource is categorized by topic, which are relevant for today's international business environment. The knowledge is free, providing you unlimited access to the information and tools needed to improve a firm's global competitiveness. The site offers the following:

- **Global Resources,** with more than 5,000 online resources
- **Country Insights,** with a wealth of information on all countries
- **News & Views:** latest issues in international business and marketing
- **Academy:** extensive research and teaching resources
- **Diagnostic Tools:** decision-support tools for managers

The global answers are at globalEDGE.

On the globalEDGE?
All the information you need on 200 global markets is just one click away... and you've already paid for it.*

The world's leading online source for international business information.** Several thousand online resources are mined daily for news and information. Get all the data you need - when you need it.

Visit us today. Membership is free.
http://globalEDGE.msu.edu

*globalEDGE.msu.edu was created by the Center for International Business Education and Research at Michigan State University (MSU-CIBER) and is funded by U.S. government grants and other sponsorships.
**globalEDGE is the #1 web resource for 'international business' information in the world, based on rankings by Google as of March 8, 2006.

Differences in national standards of ethics are illustrated by what the Mexicans call *la mordida,* "the bite." The use of payoffs and bribes is deeply entrenched in many governments. Because U.S. trade and corporate policy, as well as U.S. law, prohibits direct involvement in payoffs and bribes, U.S. companies may have a hard time competing with foreign firms that engage in these practices. Some U.S. businesses that refuse to make payoffs are forced to hire local consultants, public relations firms, or advertising agencies, which results in indirect payoffs. The ultimate decision about whether to give small tips or gifts where they are customary must be based on a company's code of ethics. However, under the Foreign Corrupt Practices Act of 1977, it is illegal for U.S. firms to attempt to make large payments or bribes to influence policy decisions of foreign governments. Nevertheless, facilitating payments, or small payments to support the performance of standard tasks, are often acceptable. The Foreign Corrupt Practices Act also subjects all publicly held U.S. corporations to rigorous internal controls and recordkeeping requirements for their overseas operations.

## Sociocultural Forces

Cultural, social, and ethical differences among countries (and their subcultures) can have significant effects on marketing activities. Because marketing activities are primarily social in purpose, they are influenced by beliefs and values regarding family, religion, education, health, and recreation. For example, in Greece, where sunbathing is a common form of recreation, U.S. products such as Johnson & Johnson Baby Sunblock have a large target market. By identifying major sociocultural variations among countries, marketers lay the groundwork for an effective adaptation of marketing strategy. For instance, when Little Caesars opened new franchise pizza outlets abroad, it made some menu changes to accommodate local tastes and social norms. In Japan, Little Caesars' pizzas are garnished with asparagus, potatoes, squid, or seaweed. Turkish menus include a local pastry for dessert, while Middle Eastern menus exclude pork.[20] Although football is a popular sport in the United States and a major opportunity for many television advertisers, soccer is the most popular televised sport in Europe (and the largest sport in the world). Most important, marketing communications often must be translated into other languages. For example, New Horizons Computer Learning Centers, the world's largest independent IT training firm, has translated course materials into 14 languages and adapted marketing campaigns to serve customers in 45 countries.[21]

It can be difficult to transfer marketing symbols, trademarks, logos, and even products to international markets, especially if they are associated with objects that have profound religious or cultural significance in a particular culture. For example, when Big Boy opened a new restaurant in Bangkok, it quickly became popular with European and U.S. tourists, but the local Thais refused to eat there. Instead they placed gifts of rice and incense at the feet of the Big Boy statue—a chubby boy holding a hamburger—which reminded them of Buddha. In Japan, customers were forced to tiptoe around a logo painted on the floor at the entrance to an Athlete's Foot store because in Japan it is taboo to step on a crest. On the other hand, A&W's Great Root Beer is a U.S. icon that has been successfully translated around the world: it appeals to customers everywhere.[22]

Cultural differences may also affect marketing negotiations and decision making behavior. For example, consumers in Russia found the U.S.-style energetic happiness of McDonald's employees insincere and offensive when the company opened its first stores in the country.[23] Although U.S. and Taiwanese sales agents are

**Cultural Differences**

American Indian College Fund realizes that students are highly influenced by cultural and family values.

equally sensitive to customer interests, research suggest that the Taiwanese are more sensitive to the interests of their companies and competitors and less attuned to the interests of colleagues. Identifying such differences in work-related values of employees across different nationalities helps companies design more effective sales management practices.[24] However, the use of U.S. sales management techniques among Polish retail salespeople has been successful despite many cultural, economic, and political differences in the environments.[25] Table 7.3 offers a sampling of behaviors that may be viewed as rude, insensitive, or offensive in global business negotiations. Cultural differences in the emphasis placed on personal relationships, status, and decision making styles have been known to complicate dealings between Americans and businesspeople from other countries. In the Far East, a gift may be considered a necessary introduction before negotiation, whereas in the United States or Canada, a gift may be misconstrued as an illegal bribe.

Buyers' perceptions of other countries can influence product adoption and use. For example, research indicates that Japanese consumers evaluate products from Japan more favorably than those from other countries regardless of product superiority. Americans, however, evaluate domestic products more favorably than foreign ones only when the U.S. products are superior to products from other countries.[26] When people are unfamiliar with products from another country, their perceptions of the country itself may affect their attitude toward the product and help determine whether they will buy it. If a country has a reputation for producing quality products and therefore has a positive image in consumers' minds, marketers of products from that country will want to make the country of origin well known. For example, a generally favorable image of Western computer technology has fueled sales of U.S. personal computers and Microsoft software in Japan. On the other hand, marketers may want to dissociate themselves from a particular country in some cases. For ex-

| table 7.3 | A SAMPLING OF CROSS-CULTURAL BEHAVIORAL DIFFERENCES |
|---|---|
| **Country** | **Behaviors Viewed as Rude or Otherwise Unacceptable** |
| Belgium | Talking with your hands in your pockets |
| Egypt | Showing the sole of your shoe (as when legs are crossed) |
| England | Pushing your way in front of others standing in a line |
| Finland | Standing with your arms folded across your chest |
| France | Chewing gum, yawning, or conversing loudly in public |
| Hong Kong | Blinking conspicuously during conversation |
| India | Expressing anger |
| Japan | Talking about price during negotiations |
| New Zealand | Using toothpicks or chewing gum in public |
| Sri Lanka | Touching, leaning on, or sitting on an image of Buddha |
| Thailand | Stepping on a doorsill when entering a building |
| Zambia | Pointing directly at someone or something |

**Source:** "Gestures Around the World," Web of Culture, **www.webofculture.com/worldsmart/gestures.html** (accessed July 5, 2001).

ample, because the world has not always viewed Mexico as producing quality products, Volkswagen may not want to advertise that some of the models it sells in the United States, including the Beetle, are made in Mexico.

When products are introduced from one nation into another, acceptance is far more likely if similarities exist between the two cultures. It used to be that firms identified cultural differences and tried to modify their products and services to fit the customers' needs. Nowadays, firms identify similarities and stress those in their product offerings. For example, due to the global sensitivity regarding food, middle-class U.S. families are eating more like their counterparts in Japan, France, and Canada. Europeans are eating more like Americans. For international marketers, cultural differences have implications for product development, advertising, packaging, and pricing. Schlotzsky's, for example, experienced slower-than-expected sales when it opened a new restaurant in Beijing. Although the Texas-based sandwich chain has enjoyed great success in the United States, Chinese consumers are less accustomed to eating foods with their hands, and they often like to share their meals with companions, which is difficult to do with a sandwich. The company hopes that training staff and placing pictures on restaurant tables to demonstrate how to hold and eat its large sandwiches will help sales in China.[27]

Differences in ethical standards can also affect marketing efforts. For example, there are significant differences between the expectations of U.S. versus French and German consumers regarding the social responsibilities of business.[28] In China and Vietnam, standards regarding intellectual property differ dramatically from those in the United States, creating potential conflicts for marketers of computer software, music, and books. Because of differences in cultural and ethical standards, many companies are working both individually and collectively to establish ethics programs and standards for international business conduct.[29] Levi Strauss's code of ethics, for example, bars the firm from manufacturing in countries where workers are known to be abused. Starbucks's global code of ethics strives to protect agricultural workers who harvest coffee beans.

## Technological Forces

Advances in technology have made international marketing much easier. Interactive web systems, instant messaging, and iPod downloads (along with the traditional vehicles of voice mail, e-mail, fax, and cellular phones) make international marketing activities more affordable and convenient. Internet use has accelerated dramatically within the United States and abroad. In Europe, more than 50 percent of households have Internet access at home or work, pushing e-commerce revenues to $16.4 billion.[30] In Japan, 56 million are logging on to the Internet, and 18 million Russians have Internet access.[31] The majority of young adults (age 16 to 24) in Europe prefer advertisements on the Web over any other media vehicle; these ads are more directly targeting their needs.[32]

In many developing countries that lack the level of technological infrastructure found in the United States and Japan, marketers are beginning to capitalize on opportunities to leapfrog existing technology. For example, cellular and wireless phone technology is reaching many countries at a more affordable rate than traditional hard-wired telephone systems. Consequently opportunities for growth in the cellphone market remain strong in Southeast Asia, Africa, and the Middle East. In war-torn Iraq, many firms are fiercely competing for opportunities to rebuild the nation's telecommunications infrastructure, and MCI and Motorola have already won contracts to develop cellphone networks there.[33] Hewlett-Packard also hopes to bring new technologies to less developed countries. The company has launched World e-Inclusion, an economic development initiative that seeks to apply technology-based solutions to empower people in developing countries. Pilot programs for the initiative have already yielded high-speed Internet connections for remote villages in Central America and specialized software for coffee growers in Sumatra.[34]

# Global Ethical and Social Responsibility Issues

When businesspeople travel, they sometimes perceive that other business cultures have different modes of operation. This uneasiness is especially pronounced for businesspeople who have not traveled extensively or interacted much with foreigners in business or social settings. For example, a perception exists among many in the United States that U.S. firms are often different from those in other countries. This implied perspective of "us" versus "them" is also common in other countries. Table 7.4 indicates the countries that businesspeople, risk analysts, and the general public perceived as the most and least corrupt. In business, the idea that "we" differ from "them" is called the self-reference criterion (SRC).

The SRC is the unconscious reference to one's own cultural values, experiences, and knowledge. When confronted with a situation, we react on the basis of knowledge we have accumulated over a lifetime, which is usually grounded in our culture of origin (and often rooted in our religious beliefs). Our reactions are based on meanings, values, and symbols that relate to our culture but may not have the same relevance to people of other cultures. In the United States, for example, **dumping**—the practice of

**dumping** The practice of charging high prices for products sold in domestic markets while selling the same products in foreign markets at low prices, often below the costs of exporting them

| table 7.4 | PERCEPTIONS OF THE LEAST AND MOST CORRUPT COUNTRIES |
|---|---|

| Least Corrupt | Most Corrupt |
|---|---|
| 1. Iceland (9.7) | 1. Bangladesh (1.7), Chad |
| 2. Finland (9.6), New Zealand | 2. Haiti (1.8), Myanmar, Turkmenistan |
| 3. Denmark (9.5) | 3. Cote d'Ivoire (1.9), Equatorial Guinea, Nigeria |
| 4. Singapore (9.4) | 4. Angola (2.0) |
| 5. Sweden (9.2) | 5. Congo, Democratic Republic (2.1), Kenya, Pakistan, Paraguay, Somalia, Sudan, Tajikistan |
| 6. Switzerland (9.1) | 6. Azerbaijan (2.2), Cameroon, Ethiopia, Indonesia, Iraq, Liberia, Uzbekistan |
| 7. Norway (8.9) | 7. Burundi (2.3), Cambodia, Republic of Congo, Georgia, Kyrgyzstan, Papua New Guinea, Venezuela |
| 8. Australia (8.8) | 8. Albania (2.4), Niger, Russia, Sierra Leon |
| 9. Austria (8.7) | 9. Afghanistan (2.5), Bolivia, Ecuador, Guatemala, Guyana, Libya, Nepal, Philippines, Uganda |
| 10. United Kingdom (8.6), Netherlands | 10. Belarus (2.6), Eritrea, Honduras, Kazakhstan, Nicaragua, Palestine, Ukraine, Vietnam, Zambia, Zimbabwe |
| 11. Luxembourg (8.5) | 11. Gambia (2.7), Macedonia, Swaziland, Yemen |
| 12. Canada (8.4) | 12. Algeria (2.8), Argentina, Madagascar, Malawi, Mozambique, Serbia and Montenegro |
| 13. Hong Kong (8.3) | 13. Armenia (2.9) Benin, Bosnia and Herzegovina, Gabon, India, Mali, Moldova, Tanzania |
| 14. Germany (8.2) | 14. Dominican Republic (3.0), Mongolia, Romania |
| 15. United States (7.6) | 15. Lebanon (3.1), Rwanda |
| Corruption Scale: 10 = Least Corrupt, 1 = Most Corrupt. | |

**Source:** The results presented in this paper rely on data from the "Transparency International Corruption Perceptions Index 2005," provided by Transparency International, **http://ww1.transparency.org/cpi/2005/dnld/media_pack_en.pdf** Reprinted by permission of Transparency International.

**Global Diversity**

Diversity is a value that can lead to increased competitiveness around the world.

**cultural relativism** The concept that morality varies from one culture to another and that business practices are therefore differentially defined as right or wrong by particular cultures

charging high prices for products sold in domestic markets while selling the same products in foreign markets at low prices, often below the costs of exporting them—is viewed negatively, and the United States has a number of antidumping laws.

However, many businesspeople adopt the principle of "When in Rome, do as the Romans do." These businesspeople adapt to the cultural practices of the country they are in and use the host country's cultural practices as the rationalization for sometimes straying from their own ethical values when doing business internationally. For example, by defending the payment of bribes or "greasing the wheels of business" and other questionable practices in this fashion, some businesspeople are resorting to **cultural relativism**—the concept that morality varies from one culture to another and that business practices are therefore differentially defined as right or wrong by particular cultures.

For example, ExxonMobil Corporation and Royal Dutch/Shell Group have invested heavily in developing the oil reserves of Sakhalin Island, a Russian territory north of Japan. The companies have invested $22 billion in oil and gas drilling equipment not only because there may be as much as 13 billion barrels of oil in its waters but also because Russia's environmental rules are almost nonexistent and seldom enforced. However, the seismic blasting and toxic mud associated with developing the area's oil fields are hazardous to the endangered Western Pacific grey whale. If a spill or other accident were to occur, the nearest cleanup equipment is 50 miles away, making it impractical to save salmon and other animal species from harm.[35] Although the Russian government and people who live in the area are happy about the jobs created, in this case the multinational investment group seems to be applying Russian cultural values toward the natural environment rather than the more stringent ones of their own countries.

This example illustrates why multinational corporations have been the subject of much ethical criticism, and their impact on the countries in which they do business has been hotly debated. Their size and financial clout enable MNCs to control money supplies, employment, and even the economic well-being of less-developed countries. In some instances, MNCs have controlled entire cultures and countries. For example, a Los Angeles judge recently ruled that Unocal may be liable for the conduct of the government of Myanmar (formerly known as Burma), as documents presented in court contended that forced labor was commonly used in Myanmar to build Unocal projects and that workers' refusal to work resulted in their imprisonment and/or execution at the hands of the Myanmar army.

At the same time, a large number of MNCs also strive to be good global citizens with strong ethical values. Texas Instruments (TI), for example, has adopted a three-level global approach to ethical integrity that asks: (1) "Are we complying with all legal requirements on a local level?" (2) "Are there business practices or requirements at the local level which impact how we interact with co-workers in other parts of the world?" and (3) "Do some of our practices need to be adapted based on the local laws and customers of a specific locale? On what basis do we define our universal standards that apply to TI employees everywhere?" TI generally follows conservative rules regarding the giving and receiving of gifts. However, what may be considered an excessive gift in the United States may be viewed differently according to the local customs of other parts of the world. TI used to define gift limits in terms of U.S. dollars, but now it specifies that gift-giving should not be used in a way that exerts undue pressure to win business or implies a quid pro quo.[36]

TI and many other firms, including Coca-Cola, Du Pont, Hewlett-Packard, Levi Strauss & Company, Texaco, and Wal-Mart, endorse following responsible business practices internationally. These companies support a globally based resource system called Business for Social Responsibility (BSR). BSR tracks emerging issues and trends, provides information on corporate leadership and best practices, conducts educational workshops and training, and assists organizations in developing practical business ethics tools. It addresses such issues as community investment, corporate social responsibility, the environment, governance, and accountability. BSR has also established formal partnerships with other organizations that focus on corporate responsibility in Brazil, Israel, the United Kingdom, Chile, and Panama.[37]

# Regional Trade Alliances, Markets, and Agreements

Although many more firms are beginning to view the world as one huge marketplace, various regional trade alliances and specific markets affect companies engaging in international marketing; some create opportunities, and others impose constraints. In fact, while trade agreements in various forms have been around for centuries, the last century can be classified as the trade agreement period in the world's international development. Today, there are about 180 trade agreements around the world compared with only a select handful in the early 1960s. In this section, we examine several of the more critical regional trade alliances, markets, and changing conditions affecting markets. These include the North American Free Trade Agreement, the European Union, the Common Market of the Southern Cone, Asia-Pacific Economic Cooperation, and the World Trade Organization.

### The North American Free Trade Agreement (NAFTA)

**North American Free Trade Agreement (NAFTA)** An alliance that merges Canada, Mexico, and the United States into a single market

The **North American Free Trade Agreement (NAFTA)**, implemented in 1994, effectively merged Canada, Mexico, and the United States into one market of more than 430 million consumers.[38] NAFTA will eliminate virtually all tariffs on goods produced and traded among Canada, Mexico, and the United States to create a free trade area by 2009. The estimated annual output for this trade alliance is more than $11 trillion.[39]

NAFTA makes it easier for U.S. businesses to invest in Mexico and Canada; provides protection for intellectual property (of special interest to high-technology and entertainment industries); expands trade by requiring equal treatment of U.S. firms

**World Alliances**

The Skyteam Alliance, with its ten member airlines, provides flexibility and a broad array of choices for international travelers.

in both countries; and simplifies country-of-origin rules, hindering Japan's use of Mexico as a staging ground for further penetration into U.S. markets. Although most tariffs on products coming to the United States will be lifted, duties on more sensitive products, such as household glassware, footware, and some fruits and vegetables, will be phased out over a 15-year period.

Canada's 32.5 million consumers are relatively affluent, with a per capita GDP of $29,800.[40] Trade between the United States and Canada totals approximately $411 billion.[41] Currently exports to Canada support approximately 1.5 million U.S. jobs. Canadian investments in U.S. companies are also increasing, and various markets, including air travel, are opening as regulatory barriers dissolve.[42]

With a per capita GDP of $9,000, Mexico's 105 million consumers are less affluent than Canadian consumers. However, they bought $107 billion worth of U.S. products last year. In fact, Mexico has become the United States' second-largest trading market, after Canada.[43] Many U.S. companies, including Hewlett-Packard, IBM, and General Motors, have taken advantage of Mexico's low labor costs and close proximity to the United States to set up production facilities, sometimes called *maquiladoras*. Production at the *maquiladoras*, especially in the automotive, electronics, and apparel industries, has increased significantly as companies as diverse as Ford, John Deere, Motorola, Sara Lee, Kimberly-Clark, and VF Corporation set up facilities in north-central Mexican states. With the *maquiladoras* accounting for roughly half of Mexico's exports, Mexico has risen to become the world's twelfth-largest economy.[44] Although Mexico experienced financial instability throughout the 1990s, privatization of some government-owned firms and other measures instituted by the Mexican government and businesses, along with a booming U.S. economy, have helped Mexico's economy. Moreover, increasing trade between the United States and Canada constitutes a strong base of support for the ultimate success of NAFTA.

Mexico's membership in NAFTA links the United States and Canada with other Latin American countries, providing additional opportunities to integrate trade among all the nations in the Western Hemisphere. Indeed, efforts to create a free trade agreement among the 34 nations of North and South America are in process among the countries in the region (**www.ftaa-alca.org**). Like NAFTA, the Free Trade Area of the Americas (FTAA) will progressively eliminate trade barriers and create the world's largest free trade zone, with 800 million people.[45] A related trade agreement—the Central American Dominican Republic Free Trade Agreement (CAFTA-DR)—among Costa Rica, the Dominican Republic, El Salvador, Guatemala, Honduras, Nicaragua, and the United States has also been approved in all those countries except Costa Rica. The CAFTA-DR agreement is not yet in effect but will have great influence on trade in the region when (and if) implemented (see **www.ita.doc.gov/cafta** for more information).

Despite its benefits, NAFTA has been controversial, and disputes continue to arise over its implementation. Archer Daniels Midland, for example, filed a claim against the Mexican government for losses resulting from a tax on soft drinks containing high-fructose corn syrup, which the company believes violates the provisions of NAFTA.[46] While many Americans feared the agreement would erase jobs in the United States, Mexicans have been disappointed that it failed to create more jobs.

Moreover, Mexico's rising standard of living has increased the cost of doing business there; some 850 *maquiladoras* have closed their doors and transferred work to China and other nations where labor costs are lower. Indeed, China has become the United States' second-largest source of imported goods.[47]

Although NAFTA has been controversial, it has become a positive factor for U.S. firms wishing to engage in international marketing. Because licensing requirements have been relaxed under the pact, smaller businesses that previously could not afford to invest in Mexico and Canada will be able to do business in those markets without having to locate there. NAFTA's long phase-in period provides ample time for adjustment for those firms affected by reduced tariffs on imports. Furthermore, increased competition should lead to a more efficient market, and the long-term prospects of including most Western Hemisphere countries in the alliance promise additional opportunities for U.S. marketers.

## The European Union (EU)

**European Union (EU)** An alliance that promotes trade among its member countries in Europe

The **European Union (EU)**, sometimes also referred to as the *European Community* or *Common Market*, was established in 1958 to promote trade among its members, which initially included Belgium, France, Italy, West Germany, Luxembourg, and the Netherlands. In 1991 East and West Germany united, and by 1995 the United Kingdom, Spain, Denmark, Greece, Portugal, Ireland, Austria, Finland, and Sweden had joined as well. (Cyprus, Poland, Hungary, the Czech Republic, Slovenia, Estonia, Latvia, Lithuania, Slovakia, and Malta joined in 2004; Romania, Bulgaria, and Turkey have requested membership as well.[48])

Until 1993 each nation functioned as a separate market, but in that year the members officially unified into one of the largest single world markets, which today includes more than 450 million consumers in 25 countries. The EU is a relatively diverse set of democratic European countries. It is not a state that is intended to replace existing country states, nor is it an organization for international cooperation. Instead, its member states have common institutions to which they delegate some of their sovereignty to allow specific matters of joint interest to be decided at the European level. The primary goals of the EU are to establish European citizenship; ensure freedom, security, and justice; promote economic and social progress; and assert Europe's role in world trade.[49]

To facilitate free trade among members, the EU is working toward standardizing business regulations and requirements, import duties, and value-added taxes; eliminating customs checks; and creating a standardized currency for use by all members. Many European nations (Austria, Belgium, Finland, France, Germany, Ireland, Italy, Luxembourg, the Netherlands, Portugal, and Spain) are linked to a common currency, the *euro*; however, several EU members have rejected use of the euro in their countries (e.g., Denmark, Sweden, and the United Kingdom). Although the common currency requires many marketers to modify their pricing strategies and subjects them to increased competition, the use of a single currency frees companies that sell goods among European countries from the nuisance of dealing with complex exchange rates.[50] The long-term goals are to eliminate all trade barriers within the EU, improve the economic efficiency of the EU nations, and stimulate economic growth, thus making the union's economy more competitive in global markets, particularly against Japan and other Pacific Rim nations, and North America.

As the EU nations attempt to function as one large market, consumers in the EU may become more homogeneous in their needs and wants. Marketers should be aware, however, that cultural differences among the nations may require modifications in the marketing mix for customers in each nation. Differences in tastes and preferences in these diverse markets are significant for international marketers. But there is evidence that such differences may be diminishing, especially within the younger population that includes teenagers and young professionals. Gathering information about these distinct tastes and preferences is likely to remain a very important factor in developing marketing mixes that satisfy the needs of European customers.

## The Common Market of the Southern Cone (MERCOSUR)

**Common Market of the Southern Cone (MERCOSUR)** An alliance that promotes the free circulation of goods, services, and production factors, and has a common external tariff and commercial policy among member nations in South America

**Asia-Pacific Economic Cooperation (APEC)** An alliance that promotes open trade and economic and technical cooperation among member nations throughout the world

The **Common Market of the Southern Cone (MERCOSUR)** was established in 1991 under the Treaty of Asunción to unite Argentina, Brazil, Paraguay, and Uruguay as a free trade alliance. Venezuela became a new member in December 2005, and Bolivia is in the process of being invited to become a full member. Currently, Bolivia, Chile, Colombia, Ecuador, and Peru have associate member status. The alliance represents two-thirds of South America's population and has a combined GDP of more than $800 billion, making it the third-largest trading bloc behind NAFTA and the EU. Like NAFTA, MERCOSUR promotes "the free circulation of goods, services and production factors among the countries" and establishes a common external tariff and commercial policy.[51]

## Asia-Pacific Economic Cooperation (APEC)

The **Asia-Pacific Economic Cooperation (APEC)**, established in 1989, promotes open trade and economic and technical cooperation among member nations, which initially included Australia, Brunei Darussalam, Canada, Indonesia, Japan, Korea, Malaysia, New Zealand, the Philippines, Singapore, Thailand, and the United States. Since then the alliance has grown to include China, Hong Kong, Chinese Taipei, Mexico, Papua New Guinea, Chile, Peru, Russia, and Vietnam. The 21-member alliance represents 2.5 billion consumers, has a combined GDP of $19 trillion, and accounts for nearly 47 percent of global trade. APEC differs from other international trade alliances in its commitment to facilitating business and its practice of allowing the business/private sector to participate in a wide range of APEC activities.[52]

Despite economic turmoil and a recession in Asia in recent years, companies of the APEC have become increasingly competitive and sophisticated in global business in the last two decades. Moreover, the markets of the APEC offer tremendous opportunities to marketers who understand them. In fact, the APEC region has consistently been the most economically dynamic part of the world. In its first decade, the APEC countries generated almost 70 percent of worldwide economic growth and the APEC region consistently outperformed the rest of the world.[53]

Japanese firms in particular have made tremendous inroads on world markets for automobiles, motorcycles, watches, cameras, and audio and video equipment. Products from Sony, Sanyo, Toyota, Mitsubishi, Canon, Suzuki, and Toshiba are sold all over the world and have set standards of quality by which other products are often judged. Sony is often viewed as the benchmark of the global company. Despite the high volume of trade between the United States and Japan, the two economies are less integrated than the U.S. economy is with Canada and western Europe. If Japan imported goods at the same rate as other major nations, the United States would sell billions of dollars more each year to Japan.

The People's Republic of China, a country of 1.3 billion people, has launched a program of economic reform to stimulate its economy by privatizing many industries, restructuring its banking system, and increasing public spending on infrastructure (including railways and telecommunications).[54] As a result, China has become a manufacturing powerhouse, with an economy growing at a rate of 7 percent a year.[55] Many foreign companies, including General Motors, Volkswagen, and Toyota, are opening factories in China to take advantage of its low labor costs.[56] Nike and Adidas have shifted most of their shoe production to China, and recently China has become a major producer of compact disc players, cellular phones, portable stereos, and personal computers. The potential of China's consumer market is so vast that it is almost impossible to measure, but doing business in China also entails many risks. Political and economic instability, especially inflation, corruption, and erratic policy shifts, have undercut marketers' efforts to stake a claim in what could become the world's largest market. Moreover, piracy is a major issue, and protecting a brand name in China is difficult. Because copying is a tradition in China and laws protecting copyrights and intellectual property are weak and minimally enforced, the country is flooded with counterfeit videos, movies, compact discs, computer software, furniture, and clothing.

**General Agreement on Tariffs and Trade (GATT)** An agreement among nations to reduce worldwide tariffs and increase international trade

**World Trade Organization (WTO)** An entity that promotes free trade among member nations by eliminating trade barriers and educating individuals, companies, and governments about trade rules around the world

## World Trade Organization (WTO)

Like NAFTA and the EU, the **General Agreement on Tariffs and Trade (GATT)** was based on negotiations among member countries to reduce worldwide tariffs and increase international trade in the wake of World War II. Originally signed by 23 nations in 1947, GATT was the precursor to the **World Trade Organization (WTO)** trading system that provides a forum for tariff negotiations, reduces trade restrictions, promotes discussion and resolution of international trade problems, and provides rules to prevent dumping (i.e., the selling of products at unfairly low prices). As one of the youngest international organizations, the WTO came into being in 1995 as a result of the Uruguay Round (1988–1994) of negotiations. Broadly, WTO is the main worldwide organization that deals with the rules of trade between nations; its main function is to ensure that trade flows as smoothly, predictably, and freely as possible between nations. In 2006, 149 nations were members of the WTO.[57]

Fulfilling the purpose of the WTO requires eliminating trade barriers; educating individuals, companies, and governments about trade rules around the world; and assuring global markets that no sudden changes of policy will occur. At the heart of the WTO are agreements that provide legal ground rules for international commerce and trade policy. Based in Geneva, Switzerland, the WTO also serves as a forum for dispute resolution.[58] For example, after the EU and seven countries protested a U.S. tariff on imported steel, WTO investigated and ultimately ruled the U.S. duties illegal under international trade rules. The United States had imposed the tariffs to protect domestic steel producers from less expensive imported steel, but the WTO found that the United States had failed to prove that its steel industry had been harmed by dumping.[59] Facing the prospect of retaliatory sanctions against U.S. goods, the United States dropped the tariffs 16 months early after the ruling.[60]

# International Entry Modes

Marketers enter international markets and continue to engage in marketing activities at several levels of international involvement. Traditionally, firms have adopted one of four different modes of entering an international market; each successive "stage" represents different degrees of international involvement (i.e., the "Uppsala Model"):[61]

Stage 1: No regular export activities.
Stage 2: Export via independent representatives (agents)
Stage 3: Establishment of one or more sales subsidiaries internationally
Stage 4: Establishment of international production/manufacturing facilities

As Figure 7.1 shows, today a firm's international involvement covers a wide spectrum, from purely domestic marketing to global marketing. Domestic marketing involves marketing strategies aimed at markets within the home country; at the other extreme, global marketing entails developing marketing strategies for the entire world (or at least more than one major region of the world). Many firms with an international presence start out as small companies serving local and regional domestic markets and expand to national markets before considering opportunities in foreign markets (the born global firm, described earlier, is one exception to this internationalization process). Limited exporting may occur even if a firm makes little or no effort to obtain foreign sales. Foreign buyers may seek out the company and/or its products, or a distributor may discover the firm's products and export them. The level of commitment to international marketing is a major variable in global marketing strategies. In this section, we examine importing and exporting, trading companies, licensing and franchising, contract manufacturing, joint ventures, direct ownership, and some of the other approaches to international involvement.

**figure 7.1**

### LEVELS OF INVOLVEMENT IN GLOBAL MARKETING

**Globalized marketing**
Marketing strategies are developed for the entire world
(or more than one major region), with the focus on the
similarities across regions and country markets.

**Regional marketing**
Marketing strategies are developed for each major region, with
the countries in the region being marketed to in the same way
based on similarities across the region's country markets.

**Multinational marketing**
International markets are a consideration in the marketing
strategy, with customization for the country markets based on
critical differences across regions and country markets.

**Limited exporting**
The firm develops no international marketing strategies, but
international distributors, foreign firms, or selected
customers purchase some of its products.

**Domestic marketing**
All marketing strategies focus on the market
in the country of origin.

## Importing and Exporting

Importing and exporting require the least amount of effort and commitment of resources. **Importing** is the purchase of products from a foreign source. **Exporting**, the sale of products to foreign markets, enables firms of all sizes to participate in global business. A firm may find an exporting intermediary to take over most marketing functions associated with marketing to other countries. This approach entails minimal effort and cost. Modifications in packaging, labeling, style, or color may be the major expenses in adapting a product for the foreign market.

Export agents bring together buyers and sellers from different countries and collect a commission for arranging sales. Export houses and export merchants purchase products from different companies and then sell them abroad. They are specialists at understanding customers' needs in global markets. Using exporting intermediaries involves limited risk because no foreign direct investment (FDI) is required.

Buyers from foreign companies and governments provide a direct method of exporting and eliminate the need for an intermediary. These buyers encourage international exchange by contacting overseas firms about their needs and the opportunities available in exporting to them. Indeed, research suggests that many small firms tend to rely heavily on such native contacts, especially in developed markets, and remain production oriented rather than marketing oriented in their approach to international marketing.[62] Domestic firms that want to export with minimal effort and investment should seek out export intermediaries. Once a company becomes involved in exporting, it usually develops more knowledge of the country and becomes more confident in its competitiveness.[63] The U.S. government offers a wealth of trade and exporting services at **www.export.gov**, the official gateway to international trade support

**importing** The purchase of products from a foreign source

**exporting** The sale of products to foreign markets

**Business Across Borders**

The Orchard Network guides firms in their cross-border activities to reduce risk and increase each firm's potential.

provided by a collaboration of agencies such as the Department of Commerce, Department of State, U.S. Commercial Service, and the Small Business Administration.

## Trading Companies

**trading company** A company that links buyers and sellers in different countries

Marketers sometimes employ a **trading company**, which links buyers and sellers in different countries but is not involved in manufacturing and does not own assets related to manufacturing. Trading companies buy products in one country at the lowest price consistent with quality and sell them to buyers in another country. For instance, SCiNet (**www.scinet-corp.com**) offers a 24-hour-per-day online world trade system that connects 17 million companies in 245 countries, offering more than 50 million products and services. The SCiNet system offers online payments and handles customs, tariffs, and inspections of goods for their clients. A trading company acts like a wholesaler, taking on much of the responsibility of finding markets while facilitating all marketing aspects of a transaction. An important function of trading companies is taking title to products and performing all the activities necessary to move the products to the targeted foreign country. For example, large grain-trading companies operating out of home offices in both the United States and overseas control a major portion of the world's trade in basic food commodities. These trading companies sell homogeneous agricultural commodities that can be stored and moved rapidly in response to market conditions.

Trading companies reduce risk for firms seeking to get involved in international marketing. A trading company provides producers with information about products that meet quality and price expectations in domestic and international markets. Additional services a trading company may provide include consulting, marketing research, advertising, insurance, product research and design, legal assistance, warehousing, and foreign exchange.

## Licensing and Franchising

**licensing** An alternative to direct investment requiring a licensee to pay commissions or royalties on sales or supplies used in manufacturing

When potential markets are found across national boundaries, and when production, technical assistance, or marketing know-how is required, **licensing** is an alternative to direct investment. The licensee (the owner of the foreign operation) pays commissions or royalties on sales or supplies used in manufacturing. The licensee may also pay an initial down payment or fee when the licensing agreement is signed. Exchanges of management techniques or technical assistance are primary reasons for licensing agreements. Yoplait, for example, is a French yogurt that is licensed for

## marketing ENTREPRENEURS

**Frank Hickingbotham**

THE BUSINESS: TCBY Enterprises, Inc.

FOUNDED: 1981

During an outing at Neiman-Marcus, Georgia Hickingbotham encouraged her husband Frank to try the peach-flavored frozen yogurt she bought while taking a break from shopping. Frank, not a yogurt fan, reluctantly did. "This can't be yogurt," he said, and, thus, the TCBY brand was born out of the initials of that outburst (although later the initials came to stand for "The Country's Best Yogurt"). The unique taste that melted "Mr. H.'s" dislike of yogurt was developed by Daniel Brackeen, a dairy genius from Dallas. The Hickingbothams arranged to purchase and distribute his product. And with that, Frank—founder, chairman of the board, and CEO of TCBY Enterprises, Inc.—started the company with a first-day sale on September 23, 1981, of $153.69. There are now about 3,000 TCBY locations in operation worldwide, and the TCBY brand is franchised in over 60 countries. In 2000, TCBY was acquired by Capricorn Investors for about $140 million (the startup cost in 1981 was about $150,000). Capricorn is principal shareholder of Mrs. Fields Famous Brands, LLC.

production in the United States; the Yoplait brand tries to maintain a French image. Similarly, sports organizations such as the International Olympic Committee (IOC), which is responsible for the Olympic Games, typically concentrate on organizing their sporting events while licensing the merchandise and other products that are sold.

Licensing is an attractive alternative when resources are unavailable for direct investment or when the core competencies of the firm or organization are not related to the product being sold (such as in the case of Olympics merchandise). Licensing can also be a viable alternative when the political stability of a foreign country is in doubt. In addition, licensing is especially advantageous for small manufacturers wanting to launch a well-known brand internationally. For example, Questor Corporation owns the Spalding name but produces not a single golf club or tennis ball itself; all Spalding sporting products are licensed worldwide.

**Franchising** is a form of licensing in which a company (the franchiser) grants a franchisee the right to market its product, using its name, logo, methods of operation, advertising, products, and other elements associated with the franchiser's business, in return for a financial commitment and an agreement to conduct business in accordance with the franchiser's standard of operations. This arrangement allows franchisers to minimize the risks of international marketing in four ways: (1) the franchiser does not have to put up a large capital investment; (2) the franchiser's revenue stream is fairly consistent because franchisees pay a fixed fee and royalties; (3) the franchiser retains control of its name and increases global penetration of its product; and (4) franchise agreements ensure a certain standard of behavior from franchisees, which protects the franchise name.[64] Subway, Pizza Hut, and KFC are "top ten" franchisers in the world; other well-known franchisers with international visibility include Holiday Inn, Marriott, McDonald's, and Wendy's.

### Contract Manufacturing

**Contract manufacturing** occurs when a company hires a foreign firm to produce a designated volume of the firm's product (or a component of a product) to specification and the final product carries the domestic firm's name. The Gap, for example, relies on contract manufacturing for some of its apparel; Reebok uses Korean contract manufacturers to produce many of its athletic shoes. Marketing may be handled by the contract manufacturer or by the contracting company.

Three specific forms of contract manufacturing have become popular in the last decade: outsourcing, offshoring, and offshore outsourcing. **Outsourcing** is defined as the contracting of noncore operations or jobs from internal production within a business to an external entity that specializes in that operation. For example, outsourcing certain elements of a firm's operations to China and Mexico has become popular. The majority of all footwear is now produced in China, regardless of the brand on the shoe you wear. **Offshoring** is defined as moving a business process that was done domestically at the local factory to a foreign country, regardless of whether the production accomplished in the foreign country is performed by the local company (e.g., in a wholly owned subsidiary) or a third party (e.g., subcontractor). Typically, the production is moved to reap the advantages of lower cost of operations in

**franchising** A form of licensing in which a franchiser, in exchange for a financial commitment, grants a franchisee the right to market its product in accordance with the franchiser's standards

**contract manufacturing** The practice of hiring a foreign firm to produce a designated volume of the domestic firm's product or a component of it to specification; the final product carries the domestic firm's name

**outsourcing** The practice of contracting noncore operations with an organization that specializes in that operation

**offshoring** The practice of moving a business process that was done domestically at the local factory to a foreign country, regardless of whether the production accomplished in the foreign country is performed by the local company (e.g., in a wholly owned subsidiary) or a third party (e.g., subcontractor)

**offshore outsourcing** The practice of contracting with an organization to perform some or all business functions in a country other than the country in which the product or service will be sold

**joint venture** A partnership between a domestic firm and a foreign firm or government

**strategic alliance** A partnership formed to create a competitive advantage on a worldwide basis

the foreign location. **Offshore outsourcing** is the practice of contracting with an organization to perform some or all business functions in a country other than the country in which the product or service will be sold.

## Joint Ventures

In international marketing, a **joint venture** is a partnership between a domestic firm and a foreign firm or government. Joint ventures are especially popular in industries that require large investments, such as natural resources extraction or automobile manufacturing. Control of the joint venture may be split equally, or one party may control decision making. Joint ventures are often a political necessity because of nationalism and government restrictions on foreign ownership. They may occur when acquisition or internal development is not feasible or when the risks and constraints leave no other alternative. They also provide legitimacy in the eyes of the host country's citizens. Local partners have firsthand knowledge of the economic and sociopolitical environment and the workings of available distribution networks, and they may have privileged access to local resources (raw materials, labor management, and so on). However, joint venture relationships require trust throughout the relationship to provide a foreign partner with a ready means of implementing its own marketing strategy.[65] Joint ventures are assuming greater global importance because of cost advantages and the number of inexperienced firms entering foreign markets. They may be the result of a tradeoff between a firm's desire for completely unambiguous control of an enterprise and its quest for additional resources.

**Strategic alliances** are partnerships formed to create competitive advantage on a worldwide basis. They are very similar to joint ventures, but while joint ventures are defined in scope, strategic alliances are typically represented by an agreement to work together (which can ultimately mean more involvement than a joint venture). In an international strategic alliance, the firms in the alliance may have been traditional rivals competing for the same market. They may also be competing in certain markets while working together in other markets where it is beneficial for both parties. An example of such an alliance is New United Motor Manufacturing, Inc. (NUMMI), formed by Toyota and General Motors to make automobiles for both firms. This alliance united the quality engineering of Japanese cars with the marketing expertise and market access of General Motors. Today NUMMI manufactures the popular Toyota Tacoma compact pickup truck, as well as the Toyota Corolla, Pontiac Vibe, and a right-hand-drive Toyota Voltz for sale in Japan.[66] While joint ventures are formed to create a new identity, partners in international strategic alliances often retain their distinct identities, with each partner bringing a core competency to the union.

The success rate of international alliances could be higher if a better fit between the companies existed. A strategic alliance should focus on a joint market opportunity from which all partners can benefit.[67] In the automobile, computer, and airline industries, strategic alliances are becoming the predominant means of competing internationally. Competition in these industries is so fierce and the costs of competing on a global basis are so high that few firms have all the resources needed to do it alone. Firms that lack the internal resources essential for international success may seek to collaborate with other companies. A shared mode of leadership among partner corporations combines joint abilities and allows collaboration from a distance. Focusing on customer value and implementing innovative ways to compete create a winning strategy.[68] One such collaboration is the Sky Team Alliance—involving Northwest Airlines, KLM, Aero Mexico, Air France,

**snapshot**

# Top 10 global franchisers

1. Subway
2. Quiznos Sub
3. Curves
4. The UPS Store
5. Pizza Hut, Inc.
6. WSI Internet
7. KFC Corp.
8. Century 21 Real Estate LLC
9. RE/MAX Int'l. Inc.
10. Jani-King

*Source:* "Top 10 Global Franchises for 2006," *Entrepreneur,* www.entrepreneur.com/franzone/rank/0,6584,12-12-IN-2006-0,00.html (accessed Apr. 13, 2006).

Alitalia, Continental Airlines, TSA Czech Airlines, Delta, and Korean Air—which is designed to improve customer service among the nine firms.

## Direct Ownership

**direct ownership** A situation in which a company owns subsidiaries or other facilities overseas

Once a company makes a long-term commitment to marketing in a foreign country that has a promising market as well as a suitable political and economic environment, **direct ownership** of a foreign subsidiary or division is a possibility. Mexico's Gigante grocery chain, for example, has opened stores in Los Angeles and southern California, where it hopes its name will appeal to the large Hispanic population there.[69] Most foreign investment covers only manufacturing equipment or personnel because the expenses of developing a separate foreign distribution system can be tremendous. The opening of retail stores in Europe, Canada, or Mexico can require a staggering financial investment in facilities, research, and management.

**multinational enterprise** A firm that has operations or subsidiaries in many countries

The term **multinational enterprise**, sometimes called multinational corporation, refers to a firm that has operations or subsidiaries in many countries. Often the parent company is based in one country and carries on production, management, and marketing activities in other countries. The firm's subsidiaries may be autonomous so they can respond to the needs of individual international markets or they may be part of a global network that is led by the headquarters' operations.

At the same time, a wholly owned foreign subsidiary may be allowed to operate independently of the parent company to give its management more freedom to adjust to the local environment. Cooperative arrangements are developed to assist in marketing efforts, production, and management. A wholly owned foreign subsidiary may export products to the home country, its market may serve as a test market for the firm's global products, or it may be a component of the firm's globalization efforts. Some U.S. automobile manufacturers, for example, import cars built by their foreign subsidiaries. A foreign subsidiary offers important tax, tariff, and other operating advantages. Table 7.5 lists the ten largest global corporations.

One of the greatest advantages is the cross-cultural approach. A subsidiary usually operates under foreign management so that it can develop a local identity. In particular, the firm (i.e., seller) is often expected to adapt, if needed, to the buyer's culture. Interestingly, the cultural values of customers in the younger age group (30 years and younger) is becoming increasingly similar around the world. Today, a 20-year-old in Russia is increasingly similar in mindset to a 20-year-old in China and a 20-year-old in the United States. This makes marketing products and services to the

### table 7.5 — THE TEN LARGEST GLOBAL CORPORATIONS

| Rank | Company | Country | Industry | Revenues (in millions) |
|------|---------|---------|----------|------------------------|
| 1 | Wal-Mart Stores | U.S. | General merchandiser | $287,989.0 |
| 2 | BP | Britain | Petroleum refining | $285,059.0 |
| 3 | Exxon Mobil | U.S. | Petroleum refining | $270,772.0 |
| 4 | Royal Dutch/Shell Group | Netherlands/Britain | Petroleum refining | $268,690.0 |
| 5 | General Motors | U.S. | Motor vehicles | $193,517.0 |
| 6 | DaimlerChrysler | Germany | Motor vehicles | $176,687.5 |
| 7 | Toyota Motor | Japan | Motor vehicles | $172,616.3 |
| 8 | Ford Motor | U.S. | Motor vehicles | $172,233.0 |
| 9 | General Electric | U.S. | Diversified financials | $152,866.0 |
| 10 | Total | France | Petroleum refining | $152,609.5 |

**Source:** "Global 500: The World's Largest Corporations," *Fortune,* July 25, 2005. © 2005 Time Inc. All rights reserved.

younger population easier today than it was only ten years ago. Nevertheless, there is still great danger involved in having a wholly owned subsidiary in some parts of the world due to political uncertainty, terrorism threats, and economic instability.

# Global Organizational Structures

**organizational structure** The way in which a firm divides its operations into separate functions and/or value-adding units and coordinates its activities

Firms develop their international marketing strategies and manage their marketing mix (i.e., product, distribution, promotion, and price) by developing and maintaining an organizational form that best leverages their resources and core competencies. This **organizational structure** is defined as the way in which a firm divides its operations into separate functions and/or value-adding units and coordinates its activities. The modes of entry, described in the previous section, can be adopted by any firm doing business internationally. However, most firms undergo a step-by-step development in their internationalization efforts of the firm's people, processes, functions, culture, and structure.[70]

The pyramid in Figure 7.2 symbolizes how deeply rooted the international operations and values are in the firm, with the base of the pyramid—structure—being the most difficult to change (especially in the short term). Three basic structures of international organizations exist: export departments, international divisions, and internationally integrated structures (e.g., product division structures, geographic area structures, and matrix structures). The existing structure of the firm, or the structure that the firm chooses to adopt, has implications for international marketing strategy.

## Export Departments

For most firms, the early stages of international development are often ad hoc and not fully planned. During this early internationalization effort, sales opportunities in the global marketplace motivate the firm to engage internationally. For example, born global firms make exporting a primary objective from their inceptions. At the same time, for most firms engaging internationally for the first time, very minimal, if any, organizational adjustments take place to accommodate the international sales

<table>
<tr><td>figure 7.2</td></tr>
</table>

**ORGANIZATIONAL ARCHITECTURE**

**People**

**Processes**
How global decisions are made and how work gets done

**Functions**
Business functions such as finance, HR, production, marketing, and accounting

**Culture**
The norms, values, beliefs, and artifacts that are shared among the people throughout the global organization

**Structure**
Export departments, international divisions, and internationally integrated organizations

of the firm. Foreign sales—defined as sales outside the firm's home country—are typically so small that many firms cannot justify allocating structural or other resources to the internationalization effort in the infancy of internationalization.

Exporting, licensing, and using trading companies are preferred modes of international market entry for firms with an export department structure. Some firms develop the export department as a subunit of the marketing department, while others organize it as a department that structurally coexists at an equal level with the other functional units. Clipsal, the Australian maker of more than 20,000 different lines of eletrical accessories, has taken its number 1 position in Australia and achieved international success led by its high-quality products and operations of its export department. Clipsal's "Export Department offers global support in many areas and this has resulted in a level of teamwork that has significantly strengthened the Clipsal brand throughout the world."[71]

Another unique case of developing a successful export operation early after its inception is the born global firm of Logitech International. Logitech, founded in 1981, is a publicly traded Swiss company (traded in the United States on the Nasdaq with a symbol of LOGI). Logitech designs personal peripherals that enable people to effectively work, play, and communicate in the digital world. Their products include webcams, mice, trackballs, keyboards, speakers, headsets, interactive gaming devices, digital pens, and advanced universal remote controls.

As demand for its products and services grows or commitments of the firm increase due to internationalization efforts, the firm's structure develops. Many firms evolve from using their export department structure to forming an international division.

## International Divisions

The international division of a firm centralizes all of the responsibility for international operations (and in many cases, all international activities also become centralized in the international division). The typical international division concentrates human resources (i.e., international expertise) into one unit and serves as the central point for all information flow related to international operations (e.g., international market opportunities, international research and development). At the same time, firms with an international division structure take advantage of economies of scale by keeping manufacturing and related functions within the domestic divisions. Firms with international divisions can be at a relatively early as well as a rather mature stage of their international development. As such, these firms use exporting, licensing and franchising, trading companies, contract manufacturing, and joint ventures as possible modes of international market entry.

This international division structure illustrates the critical importance of coordination and cooperation between domestic and international operations. Frequent interaction and strategic planning meetings are needed to make this structure work effectively. In particular, firms that use an international division structure are often organized domestically on the basis of functions or product divisions, while the international division operates based on geography. This means that coordination and strategic alignment across domestic divisions and the international division is critical to success. At the same time, lack of coordination between domestic and international operations is commonly the most significant flaw in the international division structure.

An example of a firm that has used the international division structure to achieve worldwide success is Abbott Laboratories, a $22 billion diversified health-care company that develops products and services that span prevention and diagnosis to treatment and cure. As international sales grew in the late 1960s, the firm added an international division to its structure. This international division structure has benefits and drawbacks for Abbott, as it does for other firms using it.

Some argue that to offset the natural "isolation" that may result between domestic and international operations in this structure, the international division structure should be used only when the firm (1) intends to market only a small assortment of products or services internationally and (2) when foreign sales account for only a small portion of total sales. When the product assortment increases or the percentage of foreign sales becomes significant, an internationally integrated structure should be adopted.

### Internationally Integrated Structures

A number of different internationally integrated structures have been developed and implemented by firms in their quest to achieve success globally. The three most common structures are the product division structure, the geographic area structure, and the global matrix structure. Firms with these varied structures have multiple choices for international market entry similar to international divisions (e.g., exporting, licensing and franchising, trading companies, contract manufacturing, and joint ventures). However, firms with internationally integrated structures are the most likely to engage in direct ownership activities internationally.

The product division structure is the form used by the majority of multinational firms. This structure lends itself well to firms that are diversified, often driven by their current domestic operations. Each division is a self-contained entity with responsibility for its own operations, whether it is based on a country or regional structure. However, the worldwide headquarters maintains the overall responsibility for the strategic direction of the firm, while the product division is in charge of implementation. Procter & Gamble has a long-standing tradition of operating as a product division structure, with leading brands such as Pampers, Tide, Ariel, Always, Pantene, Bounty, Folgers, Pringles, Charmin, Downy, Crest, and Olay.

The geographic area structure lends itself well to firms with a low degree of diversification. Under this domestically influenced functional structure, the world is divided into logical geographical areas based on the firms' operations and the customers' characteristics. Accenture, a global management consulting firm, operates worldwide largely based on a geographic area structure. Each area tends to be relatively self-contained, and integration across areas is typically via the worldwide or the regional headquarters. This structure facilitates local responsiveness, but it is not ideal for reducing global costs and transferring core knowledge across the firm's geographic units. A key issue in geographic area structures, as in almost all multinational corporations, is the need to become more regionally and globally integrated.

The global matrix structure was designed to achieve both global integration and local responsiveness. Asea Brown Boveri (ABB), a Swedish-Swiss engineering multinational, is the best-known firm to implement a global matrix structure. ABB is an international leader in power and automation technologies that enable customers to improve their performance while lowering environmental impact. Global matrix structures theoretically facilitate a simultaneous focus on realizing local responsiveness, cost efficiencies, and knowledge transfers. However, few firms can operate a global matrix well since the structure is based on, for example, product and geographic divisions simultaneously (or a combination of any two traditional structures). This means that employees belong to two divisions and often report to two managers throughout the hierarchies of the firm. An effectively implemented global matrix structure has the benefit of being global in scope while also being nimble and responsive locally. However, a poorly implemented global matrix structure results in added bureaucracy and indecisiveness in leadership and implementation.

# The International Marketing Mix: Customization Versus Globalization

Like domestic marketers, international marketers develop marketing strategies to serve specific target markets. Traditionally international marketing strategies have customized marketing mixes according to cultural, regional, and national differences. Table 7.6 provides a sample of international issues related to product, distribution, promotion, and price. For example, many soap and detergent manufacturers

## table 7.6 MARKETING MIX ISSUES INTERNATIONALLY

**Sample International Issues**

**Product Element**

| | |
|---|---|
| Core Product | Is there a commonality of the customer's needs across countries? What will the product be used for and in what context? |
| Product Adoption | How is awareness created for the product in the various country markets? How and where is the product typically bought? |
| Managing Products | How are truly new products managed in the country markets vis-à-vis existing products or products that have been modified slightly? |
| Branding | Is the brand accepted widely around the world? Does the home country help or hurt the brand perception of the consumer? |

**Distribution Element**

| | |
|---|---|
| Marketing Channels | What is the role of the channel intermediaries internationally? Where is value created beyond the domestic borders of the firm? |
| Physical Distribution | Is the movement of products the most efficient from the home country to the foreign market or to a regional warehouse? |
| Retail Stores | What is the availability of different types of retail stores in the various country markets? |
| Retailing Strategy | Where do customers typically shop in the targeted countries—downtown, in suburbs, or in malls? |

**Promotion Element**

| | |
|---|---|
| Advertising | Some countries' customers prefer firm-specific advertising instead of product-specific advertising. How does this affect advertising? |
| Public Relations | How is public relations used to manage the stakeholders' interests internationally? Are the stakeholders' interests different worldwide? |
| Personal Selling | What product types require personal selling internationally? Does it differ from how those products are sold domestically? |
| Sales Promotion | Is coupon usage a widespread activity in the targeted international markets? What other forms of sales promotion should be used? |

**Pricing Element**

| | |
|---|---|
| Core Price | Is price a critical component of the value equation of the product in the targeted country markets? |
| Analysis of Demand | Is the demand curve similar internationally as it is domestically? Will a change in price drastically change demand? |
| Demand, Cost, and Profit Relationships | What are the fixed and variable costs when marketing the product internationally? Are they similar to the domestic setting? |
| Determination of Price | How does the pricing strategy, environmental forces, business practices, and cultural values affect price? |

adapt their products to local water conditions, equipment, and washing habits. Colgate-Palmolive even devised an inexpensive, plastic, hand-powered washing machine for use in households that have no electricity in less developed countries. Coca-Cola markets distinct versions of its soft drinks for the tastes of different regions of the world; it also contributes to local causes and customizes promotion to feature local people, humor, and sports teams in its advertising.[72] Realizing that both similarities and differences exist across countries is a critical first step to developing the appropriate marketing strategy effort targeted to particular international markets. Today, many firms strive to build their marketing strategies around similarities that exist instead of customizing around differences.

**globalization** The development of marketing strategies that treat the entire world (or its major regions) as a single entity

For many firms, **globalization** of marketing is the goal; it involves developing marketing strategies as though the entire world (or its major regions) were a single entity: a globalized firm markets standardized products in the same way everywhere.[73] Nike and Adidas shoes, for example, are standardized worldwide. Other examples of globalized products include electronic communications equipment, Western U.S. clothing, movies, soft drinks, rock and alternative music CDs, cosmetics, and toothpaste. Sony televisions, Levi jeans, and U.S. cigarette brands post year-to-year gains in the world market.

For many years, organizations have attempted to globalize their marketing mixes as much as possible by employing standardized products, promotion campaigns, prices, and distribution channels for all markets. The economic and competitive payoffs for globalized marketing strategies are certainly great. Brand name, product characteristics, packaging, and labeling are among the easiest marketing mix vari-

# Indonesia: The New Economic Powerhouse?

With 25 percent of the world's total population, China's 1.3 billion people confer considerable market power, and its economy is growing at an astounding 9.5 percent a year. Likewise, India, with its 1.1 billion people, information technology focus, and good gross domestic product (GDP) growth rate is getting the world's attention. Most firms today spend considerable resources on either sourcing from China and India or marketing their products in those countries. Is Indonesia the next country where substantial outsourcing and market gains can be found?

Indonesia, with its large population (more than 240 million people), a good GDP growth rate (4.9 percent in 2005), and a workforce that is more untapped by Western firms than those in China and India, presents itself as a strong possibility as the next country of note. Indonesia has a market-based economy, but the government plays a significant role. The Indonesian government owns close to 160 enterprises and is setting prices on several basic products such as fuel, rice, and electricity.

Inaugurated in 2004, Yudhoyono is Indonesia's first directly elected leader. Yudhoyono led a highly skilled response to the devastating tsunami in December 2004, and he then exhibited a leader's touch in signing an important peace pact to end the long-running rebellion in the province of Aceh. The ethnically and politically fractured Malay archipelago is increasingly becoming a stable market. In fact, Douglas Ramage, the Asia Foundation's Indonesia representative, calls Indonesia "the sleeper democratization success story" in Asia.

Indonesia has vast natural resources outside Java, including crude oil, natural gas, tin, copper, and gold. It is the world's second-largest exporter of natural gas (after Russia). Major agricultural products include rice, tea, coffee, spices, and rubber. The country's major trading partners are Japan, the United States, and the surrounding nations of Singapore, Malaysia, and Australia.

ables to standardize; media allocation, retail outlets, and price may be more difficult. In the end, the degree of similarity among the various environmental and market conditions determines the feasibility and degree of globalization. A successful globalization strategy often depends on the extent to which a firm is able to implement the idea of "think globally, act locally."[74] Even take-out food lends itself to globalization: McDonald's, KFC, and Taco Bell restaurants satisfy hungry customers in both hemispheres, although menus may be altered slightly to satisfy local tastes.

International marketing demands some strategic planning if a firm is to incorporate foreign sales into its overall marketing strategy. International marketing activities often require customized marketing mixes to achieve the firm's goals. Globalization requires a total commitment to the world, regions, or multinational areas as an integral part of the firm's markets; world or regional markets become as important as domestic ones. Regardless of the extent to which a firm chooses to globalize its marketing strategy, extensive environmental analysis and marketing research are necessary to understand the needs and desires of the target market(s) and successfully implement the chosen marketing strategy. A global presence does not automatically result in a global competitive advantage. However, a global presence generates five opportunities for creating value: (1) to adapt to local market differences, (2) to exploit economies of global scale, (3) to exploit economies of global scope, (4) to mine optimal locations for activities and resources, and (5) to maximize the transfer of knowledge across locations.[75] To exploit these opportunities, marketers need to conduct marketing research and work within the constraints of the international environment and regional trade alliances, markets, and agreements.

Pacific Rim regions such as South Korea, Thailand, Singapore, Taiwan, and Hong Kong have become major manufacturing and financial centers. Even before Korean brand names such as Samsung, Daewoo, and Hyundai became household words, these products prospered under U.S. company labels, including GE, GTE, RCA, and JCPenney. Singapore boasts huge global markets for rubber goods and pharmaceuticals. Hong Kong is still a strong commercial center after being transferred to Chinese control. Vietnam is becoming one of Asia's fastest-growing markets for U.S. businesses, but Taiwan may have the most promising future of all the Pacific Rim nations as a strong local economy and low import barriers draw increasing imports. Firms from Thailand and Malaysia are also thriving, carving out niches in the world markets for a variety of products from toys to automobile parts.

## SUMMARY

International marketing involves developing and performing marketing activities across national boundaries. International markets can provide tremendous opportunities for growth and renewed opportunity for the firm.

A detailed analysis of the environment is essential before a company enters an international market. Environmental aspects of special importance include cultural, social, ethical, economic, political, legal, and technological forces. Because marketing activities are primarily social in purpose, they are influenced by beliefs and values regarding family, religion, education, health, and recreation. Cultural differences may affect marketing negotiations, decision making behavior, and product adoption and use. A nation's economic stability and trade barriers can affect marketing efforts. Significant trade barriers include import tariffs, quotas, embargoes, and exchange controls. Gross domestic product (GDP) and GDP per capita are common measures of a nation's economic

standing. Political and legal forces include a nation's political system, laws, regulatory bodies, special-interest groups, and courts. Advances in technology have greatly facilitated international marketing.

Various regional trade alliances and specific markets create both opportunities and constraints for companies engaged in international marketing. These include the North American Free Trade Agreement, the European Union, the Common Market of the Southern Cone, Asia-Pacific Economic Cooperation, and the World Trade Organization.

There are several ways to get involved in international marketing. Importing (the purchase of products from a foreign source) and exporting (the sale of products to foreign markets) are the easiest and most flexible methods. Marketers may employ a trading company, which links buyers and sellers in different countries but is not involved in manufacturing and does not own assets related to manufacturing. Licensing and franchising are arrangements whereby one firm pays fees to another for the use of its name, expertise, and supplies. Contract manufacturing occurs when a company hires a foreign firm to produce a designated volume of the domestic firm's product to specification, and the final product carries the domestic firm's name. Joint ventures are partnerships between a domestic firm and a foreign firm or government. Strategic alliances are partnerships formed to create competitive advantage on a worldwide basis. Finally, a firm can build its own marketing or production facilities overseas. When companies have direct ownership of facilities in many countries, they may be considered multinational enterprises.

Although most firms adjust their marketing mixes for differences in target markets, some firms standardize their marketing efforts worldwide. Traditional full-scale international marketing involvement is based on products customized according to cultural, regional, and national differences. Globalization, however, involves developing marketing strategies as if the entire world (or regions of it) were a single entity; a globalized firm markets standardized products in the same way everywhere. International marketing demands some strategic planning if a firm is to incorporate foreign sales into its overall marketing strategy.

**ACE self-test**

Please visit the student website at **www.prideferrell.com** for ACE Self-Test questions that will help you prepare for exams.

## IMPORTANT TERMS

International marketing
Import tariff
Quota
Embargo
Exchange controls
Balance of trade
Gross domestic product (GDP)
North American Free Trade Agreement (NAFTA)

European Union (EU)
Common Market of the Southern Cone (MERCOSUR)
Asia-Pacific Economic Cooperation (APEC)
General Agreement on Tariffs and Trade (GATT)

Dumping
World Trade Organization (WTO)
Importing
Exporting
Trading company
Licensing
Franchising

Contract manufacturing
Outsourcing
Offshoring
Offshore outsourcing
Joint venture
Strategic alliance
Direct ownership
Multinational enterprise
Globalization

## DISCUSSION & REVIEW QUESTIONS

1. How does international marketing differ from domestic marketing?

2. What factors must marketers consider as they decide whether to engage in international marketing?

3. Why are the largest industrial corporations in the United States so committed to international marketing?

4. Why do you think this chapter focuses on an analysis of the international marketing environment?

5. If you were asked to provide a small tip (or bribe) to have a document approved in a foreign nation where this practice is customary, what would you do?

6. How will NAFTA affect marketing opportunities for U.S. products in North America (the United States, Mexico, and Canada)?

7. What should marketers consider as they decide whether to license or enter into a joint venture in a foreign nation?

8. Discuss the impact of strategic alliances on international marketing strategies.

9. Contrast globalization with customization of marketing strategies. Is one practice better than the other?

10. What are some of the product issues that you need to consider when marketing luxury automobiles in Australia, Brazil, Singapore, South Africa, and Sweden?

## APPLICATION QUESTIONS

1. To successfully implement marketing strategies in the international marketplace, a marketer must understand the complexities of the global marketing environment. Which environmental forces (sociocultural, economic, political/legal, or technological) might a marketer need to consider when marketing the following products in the international marketplace, and why?

   a. Barbie dolls

   b. Beer

   c. Financial services

   d. Television sets

2. Many firms, including Procter & Gamble, FedEx, and Occidental Petroleum, wish to do business in Eastern Europe and in the countries that were once part of the former Soviet Union. What events could occur that would make marketing in these countries more difficult? What events might make it easier?

3. This chapter discusses various organizational approaches to international marketing. Which would be the best arrangements for international marketing of the following products, and why?

   a. Construction equipment

   b. Cosmetics

   c. Automobiles

4. Procter & Gamble has made a substantial commitment to foreign markets, especially in Latin America. Its actions may be described as a "globalization of marketing." Describe how a shoe manufacturer (e.g., Wolverine World Wide) would go from domestic marketing to limited exporting, to international marketing, and finally to a globalization of marketing. Give examples of some activities that might be involved in this process.

globalEDGE™

1. Tariffs play a significant role in global markets. Sometimes designed to protect industries from excessive foreign competition, tariffs may be imposed by countries for political, economic, or legal reasons. Find data pertaining to the Free Trade Area of America (FTAA) in the Trade and Tariff Database by using the search term "FTAA" at **http://globaledge.msu.edu/ibrd**. From the Trade and Tariff Database in the FTAA website, open the HTML version and then click on the Tariffs link, then the Tariffs button, and then choose Tariffs to Imports. Next, click on the Ranking button. Determine the top five industries in the United States benefiting from tariffs. Compare this list to the top five industries with tariffs in Mexico. Are there any differences or similarities that you notice?

2. An important element in designing your firm's internationalization strategy is to identify markets that are most similar and different culturally. Because your firm is based in the United States, one approach to determine this is to calculate the average difference in scores from the United States for each country based on Hofstede's five cultural dimensions for 56 countries. Hofstede's cultural dimensions can be found using the search term "56 countries" at **http://globaledge.msu.edu/ibrd**. At the Geert Hofstede Resource Center, there will be a link called Hofstede Scores. Which five countries are most similar to the United States? Which five countries are least similar?

**INTERNET Exercise**

## FTD

Founded in 1910 as "Florists' Telegraph Delivery," FTD was the first company to offer a "flowers-by-wire" service. FTD does not itself deliver flowers but depends on local florists to provide this service. In 1994, FTD expanded its toll-free telephone-ordering service by establishing a website. Visit the site at **www.ftd.com**.

1. Click on International. Select a country to which you would like to send flowers. Summarize the delivery and pricing information that would apply to that country.
2. Determine the cost of sending fresh-cut seasonal flowers to Germany.
3. What are the benefits of this global distribution system for sending flowers worldwide? What other consumer products could be distributed globally through the Internet?

## Video Case 7.1    IDG: Communicating Across Cultures Is Key

International Data Group (IDG) was founded in 1964 by Patrick McGovern. A true visionary in the information technology field, McGovern is now chairman of the board of IDG. However, it is clear that his vision is still driving the firm:

The information technology market looks dramatically different today [in 2006] than it did when we started IDG in 1964. At that time, the United States accounted for nearly 80% of all IT spending. Today with globalization accelerating, it accounts for 35%.

For more than 40 years, IDG has maintained and reinforced our commitment to identify and expand into new growth markets. The result is the most dynamic, most trusted worldwide family of publications, web sites, research services, and events in the industry. Technology buyers throughout the world depend on IDG's timely and trusted information resources. We've taken the lead in the largest and fastest growing markets to create globally branded product lines that reach more than 120 million buyers in 85 countries representing 95% of worldwide IT spending.

IDG has been ranked by *Fortune* magazine as one of the "100 Best Companies to Work For" for the last sev-

eral years. It was the only media firm in the 2004 ranking based on *Fortune*'s survey. The magazine noted IDG's decentralized management style as a particularly impressive feature that made it a favored company for employees. "We have focused on building an organization that is a rewarding place to work and that meets customer requirements. . . . IDG operates via the corporate values of respect and dignity for each individual. . . . [W]e invest in our people, foster an action-oriented 'let's try it attitude,' and keep responsive to the marketplace," said Patrick McGovern.

This responsiveness to the global marketplace is impressive as well. For example, IDG has more than 300 newspapers and magazines internationally, including *Computerworld, InfoWorld, Network World, PC World, Macworld,* and the CIO global publishing product lines. Currently, more than 100 million people in 85 countries read IDG's publications. Second, IDG also produces more than 170 events in about 40 countries. It has a comprehensive portfolio of technology-focused tradeshows, conferences, and events. Third, IDG prides itself on being the premier global provider of market intelligence, advisory services, and events for the IT industries; over 775 IDG analysts in 50 countries provide global, regional, and local expertise on IT. Fourth, IDG's online presence includes 400 websites in over 80 countries; these are supported by a network of more than 2,000 journalists.

IDG values proper communication around the world and thrives on communicating effectively with all its target markets in 85 countries. Managers stress the importance of proper communication, including proper translation from the home language to the preferred foreign language. At the same time, they know the value of English as the preferred business language around the world.

Patrick McGovern's founding vision for IDG is to "improve the lives of people worldwide by providing information on information technology that could make them more productive in their jobs and happier in their lives." Given the focus on information, clear communication is perhaps the most crucial aspect of IDG regardless of which product line is the focus. IDG is responsive locally while taking advantage of global operations. Specifically, IDG employs local nationals on its editorial staff to report on stories of particular interest to its local readers. And IDG has more than 100 individual business units, each operating with a high degree of decentralized authority and autonomy (which

was also noted by *Fortune* as the key aspect of why IDG is such an admired firm). At the same time, the IDG News Service, an internal newswire, links more than a thousand IDG editors and journalists. They distribute news, features, commentary, and other editorial resources, which enables IDG publications to supplement local coverage with articles of a global nature.

IDG is a part of the lives of a large number of people, many who do not know their involvement with the firm's products. As long as IDG provides proper communication that carries internationally, we will continue to buy their products and receive great value in return.[76]

## Questions for Discussion

1. How has IDG developed such a successful international marketing strategy?
2. What can other firms learn from their attention to communication style internationally?
3. How would you compare IDG's worldwide marketing strategy with that of Microsoft in the information technology sector and that of *USAToday* in the newspaper (publication) sector?
4. Do you think IDG's global marketing strategy meets the requirements of the concept of globalization as described in this chapter?

---

## Case 7.2      Gillette: One of P&G's Best Brands

For those of you who have ever used a wet razor, whether it was for shaving your face, legs, head, or other body parts, chances are you used a Gillette brand razor. After all, the Gillette Company, which also makes the popular Duracell battery, owns over 70 percent of the $1.7 billion men's razor market in the United States, and the company has a dominant share of the worldwide razor market as well. And the international marketplace is changing, at least for Gillette's competitors.

On October 1, 2005, the merger of the Gillette Company and the Procter & Gamble Company was completed. This merger stands to profoundly affect the international marketplace. It represents a powerful merger of two giants spanning several global industries and centuries of experience and success (P&G was

founded in 1837 and Gillette was founded in 1901).

Founded by King C. Gillette, the Gillette Company was one of the first great multinational organizations and, some would say, a marvel of marketing effectiveness—a trait that has also been synonymous with P&G. Just four years after founding Gillette in Boston, King Gillette opened a branch office in London, and the company quickly gained sales and profits throughout western Europe. About 20 years later, Gillette said of his safety razor, "There is no other article for individual use so universally known or widely distributed. In my travels, I have found it in the most northern town in Norway and in the heart of the Sahara Desert." From the beginning, Gillette set out to offer consumers high-quality shaving products that would satisfy their basic grooming needs at a fair price. Having gained more than half of the entire razor and blades market, Gillette's manufacturing efficiency allowed it to implement marketing programs on a large scale, which helped the company gain both profits and market leadership.

Today the Gillette Company is the world leader in male grooming products, a category that includes blades, razors, and shaving preparations, and in selected female grooming products, such as wet-shaving products and hair removal devices. In addition, the company holds the number 1 position worldwide in alkaline batteries and in manual and power toothbrushes. Gillette's manufacturing operations are conducted at 32 facilities in 15 countries, and products are distributed through wholesalers, retailers, and agents in more than 200 countries and territories.

Gillette's Mach3 and Mach3 Turbo shaving systems, which reap $2 billion in sales annually, remain the best-selling men's shavers, and its line of Venus razors leads the women's shaver market. "Gillette's blade and razor business is the single most valuable franchise in the household products and cosmetics industries," said William H. Steele, an analyst at Bank of America Securities. The blade and razor segment accounts for roughly 40 percent of Gillette's sales and more than 70 percent of the company's profits. Sales in this segment have more than doubled in the last decade, and the outlook for this segment is promising as the shaving population increases, particularly in such locations as Asia, eastern Europe, and Latin America. The company's progress in its principal line of business reflects the success of its technologically advanced products, including the Mach3 system.

The worldwide success of the Mach3 was not a simple task, however. It took ten years, 35 patents, $200 million in research and development, $550 million in capital investments, and $300 million in marketing efforts to make Mach3 successful. And all of these resources were spent on an item that costs roughly $6.50 to consumers. The marketing campaign for Mach3 is a fascinating one. Specifically, Gillette's goal for Mach3 was a worldwide product launch, not just a domestic one. As such, the company needed to ensure that it had enough Mach3 products in the global supply chain to satisfy the likely strong global demand. Any stockouts would be very costly to Gillette's market position and image and endanger its aggressive product launch. Mostly successful in its launch, the Mach3 razor set the tone for the marketplace and for how to launch such a product globally. Much of the launch success of the Venus razor for women is owed to the carefully delineated process of the Mach3 razor. Gillette used largely the same strategy for the Venus as it did for Mach3.

Gillette's current strategy in the personal-care market is to focus resources on core grooming products such as deodorants/antiperspirants and shaving prepa-rations while providing supporting products in key markets. The premier brand in this product mix is the Gillette Series, which includes shaving gels and foams, as well as Gillette Series antiperspirants and deodorants. The personal-care segment also includes many of Gillette's best-known and most respected brands, including Foamy shaving cream and Right Guard, Soft & Dri, and Dry Idea deodorants/antiperspirants.

The Gillette Company also owns Braun, which turned in a record performance in 1997 but has since struggled to contribute profits. As a result, Braun is no longer considered one of the company's primary business segments. However, Gillette still values Braun's shaving products, oral-care products, and hair removal (epilation) devices, which fit well with the company's emphasis on product innovation and with its other business segments. Other Braun products—namely, kitchen appliances, personal-care products, and health-care instruments—do not fit as well with Gillette's focus. As a result, the company has contemplated selling most of the Braun line but keeping the key products in shaving, oral care, and hair removal.

Another brand in Gillette's stable is Oral-B, which develops and markets a broad range of superior oral-care products worldwide in a strong and well-established partnership with dental professionals. Led by toothbrushes, the Oral-B line also includes interdental products, specialty toothpastes, mouth rinses, and professional dental products. Sales and profits continue to increase in this segment as a function of technological developments and product innovations. For example, the Oral-B Triumph toothbrush features innovative technology with a FlossAction brushhead for superior cleaning.

With the acquisition of Duracell International, Gillette instantly achieved worldwide leadership in the alkaline battery market. Duracell leads this market with approximately a 40 percent share. This segment is key to Gillette's portfolio and complements P&G's portfolio well. Duracell products generate sizable sales and profits. Also, Duracell and Gillette share many characteristics, including global brand franchises, common distribution channels, and geographic expansion potential. With the company's backing, Duracell enjoys significant economies of scale and greater market penetration through P&G's worldwide distribution network.

Each day around the world, more than 1 billion people interact with Gillette products, while 2 billion times a day customers interact with P&G brands. Both Gillette and P&G have gained leadership positions through their strategies of managing their businesses with long-term, global perspectives. This ability to generate long-term, profitable growth in a changing global marketplace rests on several fundamental strengths, including a constantly increasing accumulation of scientific knowledge; innovative products that embody meaningful technological advances; and an immense manufacturing capability to produce billions of products every year reliably, efficiently, and cost effectively. Gillette's and P&G's strengths have created strong and enduring consumer brand loyalty around the world. Now, what can these firms do together? One prediction is that the merger between Gillette and Procter & Gamble will make consumers' brand loyalty even stronger—could this be the case?[77]

## Questions for Discussion

1. What environmental factors have contributed to Gillette's success in global markets? What forces may have created challenges for the company?
2. What strategy does Gillette appear to have adopted for international marketing?
3. How can Gillette continue to compete effectively in the battery and grooming markets after the merger with Procter & Gamble?

Mattel Takes on Global Challenges

Mattel, Inc., with about $5 billion in annual revenues, is the world leader in the design, manufacture, and marketing of children's toys. The company's major toy brands include Barbie (with more than 120 different Barbie dolls), Fisher-Price, Disney entertainment lines, Hot Wheels and Matchbox cars, Tyco Toys, American Girl, and games such as UNO. In addition, Mattel promotes international sales by tailoring toys for specific global markets instead of simply modifying favorites from the United States. Headquartered in El Segundo, California, Mattel also has offices in more than 40 countries and markets its products in more than 155 nations.

Mattel's marketing prowess and reach have paid off. In a poll conducted by the annual Power Brands study, Mattel had strong popularity among consumers. As many as four out of ten people said that if they were shopping for toys, Mattel would be the brand they most prefer. Retailers also singled out Mattel as the number 1 performer, with more than six out of ten mentions. This survey showed that both children and adults are enthused about Mattel and its line of products. Mattel and Fisher-Price names continually top surveys of consumers who are asked about their brand preferences when buying toys in discount stores or superstores. The same consumers mention Barbie and Hot Wheels repeatedly.

**Customer Orientation at Mattel**

Mattel's management philosophy focuses on satisfying customers' needs and wants. For example, Mattel redesigned Barbie to more naturally reflect a "normal" athletic woman in an attempt to meet the demand for a more realistic doll. Barbie has also taken on many different professions to reach a wider audience. These product modifications and extensions are designed to meet consumer and social demands while still accomplishing company objectives. Some Hot Wheels cars now sport NASCAR logos to meet consumer demand for more merchandise related to this popular televised sport.

Mattel's pursuit of interactive multimedia is an attempt to adapt to the shorter span of time young girls spend playing with Barbie and other dolls and more traditional toys. Increasingly children are turning to more interactive toys, and Mattel acquired the Learning Company to meet and capitalize on this demand. This acquisition, however, did not prove profitable for Mattel, and the company eventually sold the division.

As another indicator of its commitment to customers, Mattel regularly employs market research to ensure that its strategy and tactics match customer desires. This is combined with research and development in an effort to release new products yearly based on

these consumer needs and wants. A recent addition to the Mattel product lines includes the construction and activity set called Ello. The product is meant to compete with Lego AG and draw girls to building toys, which traditionally have been geared almost exclusively to boys. Mattel research teams watched girls play with pipe cleaners, scissors, glue, paper, and cardboard and concluded that girls wanted to make panels and tell stories about the space. The idea behind Ello is to build a house or figures using interconnecting plastic shapes, allowing girls to build and create while engaging in social play. Mattel hopes Ello will be a globally recognized brand with a unique name that does not require translation.

**Mattel's Core Products—Barbie**

The first Barbie doll sported open-toed shoes, a ponytail, sunglasses, earrings, and a zebra-striped bathing suit. Fashions and accessories were also available for the doll. Whereas buyers at the annual Toy Fair in New York City took no interest in Barbie, little girls of the time certainly did. The intense demand seen at the retail stores was insufficiently met for several years; Mattel just could not produce the Barbie dolls fast enough. Barbie is one of Mattel's major product lines, accounting for more than 50 percent of its total sales.

March 2005 marked the forty-fifth anniversary of Barbie. It also heralded a new Barbie campaign called "More than a Doll," which encourages girls to be anything from athletes to computer experts to dreamers. The campaign is an attempt to retain the interest of girls for a longer time, beyond the usual post-Barbie age of seven, by making Barbie more "real" to older girls. "From fashion selection to vintage collection, she's everything." And in 2004 Barbie even split from Ken. After 43 years together, Barbie and Ken decided to break up—leaving Barbie as a more independent can-do (doll) woman.

Perhaps Barbie's slipping in popularity in the early part of the century had something to do with the breakup. Mattel reacted by introducing a line of My Scene dolls, which includes a multicultural Barbie, aimed at older girls referred to as "tweens." The tween market consists of girls ages eight to 12 who would rather watch MTV than play with dolls. The website **www.myscene.com** engages girls in the lives of four friends living in the Big City through short "shows" and music videos. Other efforts targeted at tweens include the Mystery Squad (a crime-solving crew) and the Barbie doll as Elle Woods, which is a tribute to the blonde character in the film *Legally Blonde 2: Red, White and Blonde.*

### Hot Wheels

With more than 15 million boys ages five to 15 collecting Hot Wheels cars, this line of small die-cast vehicles is now involved with almost every racing circuit in the world, including NASCAR (National Association for Stock Car Auto Racing), Formula One, NHRA (National Hot Rod Association), CART (Championship Auto Racing Teams), AMA (American Motorcycle Association), and many others. This immense popularity has created a group of young collectors: the average boy collector owns more than 41 Hot Wheels.

Hot Wheels celebrated its thirty-fifth anniversary in 2003 with a massive marketing campaign called the Hot Wheels Highway 35 World Race. Mattel created a story- and character-based package that included collectible cars, racetracks, comic books, home videos, a video game, a television network special, and an online race. The idea was to appeal to the many age groups of collectors Mattel has acquired in recent years.

### Fisher-Price

Acquired in 1993 as a wholly owned subsidiary, Fisher-Price is the umbrella brand for all of Mattel's infant and preschool lines. The brand is trusted by parents all over the world and appears on everything from children's software to eyewear, books, and bicycles. Some of the classic products include the Rock-a-Stack and Little People play sets. New favorites include Power Wheels vehicles and Rescue Heroes, a line of firefighter action figures that has been in great demand since the tragedy of September 11, 2001. Through licensing agreements, the brand also develops character-based toys such as *Sesame Street's* Elmo and Big Bird and Disney's Winnie the Pooh and Mickey Mouse.

Fisher-Price has built trust with parents by creating products that are educational, safe, and useful. For example, during recent years, the brand has earned high regard for innovative car seats and nursery monitors. One project includes collaboration with Microsoft to develop an activity table that teaches infants through preschoolers with "smart technology." Fisher-Price keeps pace with the interests of today's families

through innovative learning toys and award-winning baby gear.

### International Sales

Under current CEO Robert A. Eckert's leadership, Mattel has maintained its strategy of strong expansion overseas with a goal of raising international sales to 50 percent. International sales increased 13 percent from 2000 to 2001 and another 11 percent from 2001 to 2002. Of the 34 percent of sales in 2002, two-thirds are in Europe, one-third in Latin America, and a small percentage in the Asia-Pacific region. And in the past year (2005), international sales increased (by about 3 percent) while domestic sales declined (by about 3 percent). The international segment has benefited from Mattel's strategic focus on globalization of brands, including improved product availability, better alignment of worldwide marketing and sales plans, and strong product launches.

Worldwide, Mattel's most recognized product continues to be Barbie. In a study conducted by Interbrand and published in *Business Week*, Barbie was the only Mattel brand that made the list of the 2002 "100 Best Global Brands" (although the brand has since dropped out of the top 100). However, the traditional Barbie doll is receiving a cool welcome in some international markets. The Malaysian Consumers' Association of Penanghas tried to ban Barbie because of her non-Asian appearance and the lack of creativity needed to play with her. The public and media soon protested against the ban. But government agencies in other countries, such as Iran, are carrying out similar campaigns against Barbie.

### Ethics and Responsibility at Mattel

Like most organizations, Mattel has recognized the different responsibilities it has to various stakeholders, including customers, employees, investors, suppliers, and the community, in its products, markets, and business outcomes. Mattel demonstrates a commitment to economic, legal, ethical, and philanthropic responsibilities.

Mattel's core products and business environment can present ethical issues. For example, because its products are designed primarily for children, the company must be sensitive to societal concerns about children's rights. In addition, the international environment often complicates business transactions, especially in the areas of employee rights and safety in manufacturing facilities. Different legal systems and cultural expectations about business can create ethical conflict. Finally, the use of technology may present ethical dilemmas, especially with regard to consumer privacy. Mattel has recognized these potential issues and has taken steps to strengthen its commitment to business ethics and social responsibility.

Advances in technology have created special issues

for Mattel's marketing efforts. Mattel recognizes that because it markets to children, it has the responsibility to communicate with parents about corporate marketing strategy. The company has taken special steps to inform both children and adults about its philosophy regarding Internet-based marketing tools, such as the Hot Wheels website.

At the Barbie.com website, parents are encouraged to read and follow Mattel's suggestions on Internet safety. This parents' page provides tips for creating rules and regulations for their children's use of the Internet. There is also a sample Internet Safety Promise for children and parents to complete, forming a "contract" to engage in smart, safe, and responsible behavior when surfing the Web.

Today Mattel faces many market opportunities and threats, including the rate at which children are maturing and abandoning toys, the role of technology in consumer products, and purchasing power and consumer needs in global markets. Mattel's sales growth potential, especially in the international markets, continues to grow. For a company that began with two friends making picture frames, Mattel has demonstrated marketing dexterity. But the next few years will test the firm's resolve and strategy within the highly competitive but lucrative toy market.[78]

## Questions for Discussion

1. Describe Mattel's target market for Barbie and Hot Wheels. How did the firm's marketing strategy appeal to this market internationally?
2. How has Mattel tried to be a socially responsible firm in its numerous world markets?
3. What environmental forces have created challenges for Mattel as it continues expansion into global markets? Which markets have created opportunities?

# part 4

# Using Technology, Information, and Target Market Analysis

**P**art 4 examines how marketers use technology and information about customers in greater detail. **Chapter 8** explores how marketers use information technology to build long-term relationships with customers by targeting them more precisely than ever before. Both e-marketing and customer relationship management are presented in the context of building an effective marketing strategy. **Chapter 9** provides a foundation for analyzing buyers through a discussion of marketing information systems and the basic steps in the marketing research process. **Chapter 10** focuses on one of the major steps in marketing strategy development: selecting and analyzing target markets.

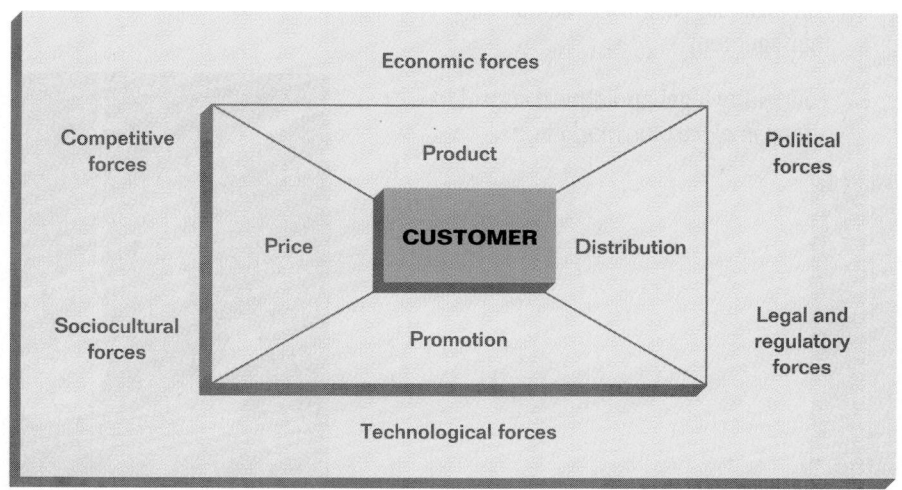

## CHAPTER 8

# E-Marketing and Customer Relationship Management

## OBJECTIVES

1. To define *electronic marketing* and *electronic commerce* and recognize their increasing importance in strategic planning

2. To understand the characteristics of electronic marketing—addressability, interactivity, memory, control, accessibility, and digitalization—and how they differentiate electronic marketing from traditional marketing activities

3. To examine how the characteristics of electronic marketing affect marketing strategy

4. To understand how electronic marketing and information technology can facilitate customer relationship management

5. To identify legal and ethical considerations in electronic marketing

## "Hey, Hey . . . We're the Arctic Monkeys": E-Marketing Rocks

Thanks in great part to e-marketing, the Arctic Monkeys, a four-piece indie rock band that was established in 2002 in Sheffield, England, skyrocketed to fame in three short years. About a year after the band's formation, demo CDs—handed out at small concert gigs—were downloaded to the Internet. Loyal fans shared the music via cyberspace, people began to take notice, and the band's fan base increased tremendously. In 2004 the band began to receive attention from BBC Radio 1 and the British press based on the offerings floating around the Net. In fact, some of their music is available only via download.

The Arctic Monkeys resisted the idea of signing with a record label for quite some time, even going as far as forbidding record company scouts from attending their concerts. Since the group had a large number of sold-out shows across the U.K., thanks primarily to electronic word of mouth, they weren't sure they needed representation. However, in 2005 they signed with Domino Records' owner Laurence Bell, a representative who signs only artists whose music he personally likes. The Arctic Monkeys' debut album, *Whatever People Say I Am, That's What I'm Not*, which includes the single "I Bet You Look Good on the Dance Floor," was released in 2006. The album has become the fastest- selling

debut album in U.K. chart history. In fact, the album is outselling all top 20 albums put together.

The band won "Best New Act" at the 2006 Brit Awards and made history yet again by being named both "Best New Band" and "Best British Band" in the same year at the 2006 NME Awards. The Arctic Monkeys' quick rise to fame has astounded those in the music business, some of whom say they haven't seen anything like it since the Beatles.[1] ■

T he phenomenal growth of the Internet presents exciting opportunities for companies, including rock bands, to forge interactive relationships with consumers and business customers. The interactive nature of the Internet has made it possible to target markets more precisely and even reach markets that previously were inaccessible. It also facilitates customer relationship management, allowing companies to network with manufacturers, wholesalers, retailers, suppliers, and outsource firms to serve customers more efficiently. Because of its ability to enhance the exchange of information between customer and marketer, the Internet has become an important component of most firms' marketing strategies.

We devote this chapter to exploring this exciting frontier. We begin by defining *electronic marketing* and exploring its context within marketing strategies. Next, we examine the characteristics that differentiate electronic marketing activities from traditional ones and explore how marketers are using the Internet strategically to build competitive advantage. Then we take a closer look at the role of the Internet and electronic marketing in managing customer relationships. Finally, we consider some of the ethical and legal implications that affect Internet marketing.

# Electronic Marketing

**electronic commerce (e-commerce)** Sharing business information, maintaining business relationships, and conducting business transactions by means of telecommunications networks

**electronic marketing (e-marketing)** The strategic process of creating, distributing, promoting, and pricing products for targeted customers in the virtual environment of the Internet

A number of terms have been coined to describe marketing activities and commercial transactions on the Internet. One of the most popular terms is **electronic commerce**, or **e-commerce**, defined as "the sharing of business information, maintaining business relationships, and conducting business transactions by means of telecommunications networks."[2] In this chapter, we focus on how the Internet, especially the World Wide Web, relates to all aspects of marketing, including strategic planning. Thus, we use the term **electronic marketing**, or **e-marketing**, to refer to the strategic process of creating, distributing, promoting, and pricing products for targeted customers in the virtual environment of the Internet.

One of the most important benefits of e-marketing is the ability of marketers and customers to share information. Through company websites, consumers can learn about a firm's products, including features, specifications, and even prices. Many websites also provide feedback mechanisms through which customers can ask questions, voice complaints, indicate preferences, and otherwise communicate about their needs and desires. The Internet has changed the way marketers communicate and develop relationships not only with their customers but also with their employees and suppliers. Lockheed Martin, for example, created a global network linking 80 suppliers to help build a new stealth fighter jet. The company expects the project to save about $25 million a year during product development.[3] Many companies use e-mail, groupware (software that allows people in different locations to access and work on the same file or document over the Internet), instant messaging, blogs, videoconferencing, and other technologies to coordinate activities and communicate with employees. Because such technology facilitates and lowers the cost of communications, the Internet can contribute significantly to any industry or activity that depends on the flow of information, such as software, entertainment, health care, education, travel services, and government services.[4] The Homeland Security Department, for example, created a secure Web-based network that lets emergency services share information and coordinate responses to disasters. The Disaster Management Interoperability Services system facilitates vital communications during disasters and may benefit the country in the event of a terrorist attack.[5] Indeed,

**Electronic Marketing**

Through the Internet, companies can offer customers unique services. RealSimpleRewards.com offers rewards and samples to subscribers of *Real Simple* magazine.

research has found that using the Internet for communication and administration activities has a greater effect on business performance than higher-profile activities such as order taking and procurement.[6]

Telecommunications technology offers additional benefits to marketers, including rapid response, expanded customer service capability (e.g., 24 hours a day, 7 days a week, or 24/7), decreased operating costs, and reduced geographic barriers. Data networks have decreased cycle and decision times and permitted companies to treat customers more efficiently.[7] In today's fast-paced world, the ability to shop for books, clothes, and other merchandise at midnight, when traditional stores are usually closed, is a benefit for both buyers and sellers. Indeed, research by comScore Networks found that 20 percent of online shopping occurs between 9 p.m. and 9 a.m.[8] The Internet allows even small firms to reduce the impact of geography on their operations. For example, Coastal Tool & Supply, a small power tool and supply store in Connecticut, has generated sales from around the world through its website.

Despite these benefits, many companies that chose to make the Internet the core of their marketing strategies—often called "dot-coms"—failed to earn profits or acquire sufficient resources to remain in business. Many dot-coms went bankrupt because they thought the only thing that mattered was brand awareness. In reality, however, Internet markets are more similar to traditional markets than they are different.[9] Thus, successful e-marketing strategies, like traditional marketing strategies, depend on creating, distributing, promoting, and pricing products that customers need or want, not merely developing a brand name or reducing the costs associated with online transactions. In fact, traditional retailers continue to do quite well in some areas that many people thought the Internet would dominate just a few years ago. For example, although many marketers believed there would be a shift to buying cars online, experts estimate that just 5.4 percent of all new cars will be sold via the Internet in 2008. Research suggests that online shoppers are very concerned about price, and a firm's profits can vanish quickly as competition drives prices down. Few consumers are willing to spend \$30,000 online to purchase a new automobile. However, consumers are increasingly making car-buying decisions on the basis of information found online.[10]

Indeed, e-marketing has not changed all industries, although it has had more of an impact in some industries in which the costs of business and customer transactions are very high. For example, trading stock has become significantly easier and less expensive for customers who can go online and execute their own orders. Firms such as E*Trade and Charles Schwab have been innovators in this area, and traditional brokerage firms such as Merrill Lynch have had to introduce online trading for their customers to remain competitive. In many other industries, however, the impact of e-marketing may be incremental.

## Consumer-Generated Electronic Marketing

While Internet-based marketing has generated exciting opportunities to interact with consumers, it is important to recognize that electronic marketing and related technologies are more consumer-driven than traditional markets. Two major factors have caused consumer-generated information to gain importance:

1. Consumers' desire to learn about other consumers' opinions and experiences

2. Consumers' increased ability to find information from other consumers' postings and to forward information about their own experiences[11]

Indeed, consumers often rely on the recommendations and suggestions from friends and family when making purchasing decisions. These informal exchanges of communication are often referred to as word of mouth, but online or electronic word-of-mouth practices are advancing rapidly.[12]

Today marketers must recognize the impact of not only websites but also instant messaging, blogs, online forums, mailing lists, and wikis, as well as text messaging via cellphones and podcasts via MP3 players (see Table 8.1). **Blogs** (short for "weblogs") are web-based journals in which writers can editorialize and interact with other Internet users, while **wikis** are software that create an interface that enables users to add or edit the content of some types of websites (also called wikis or wikipages). One of the best-known wikis is Wikipedia.com, an online encyclopedia. Marketers must also monitor websites with less than flattering names, such as

**blogs** Web-based journals in which people can editorialize and interact with other Internet users

**wikis** Software that create an interface that enables users to add or edit the content of some types of websites (also called wikis or wikipages)

| table 8.1 | TECHNOLOGIES THAT PROVIDE CONSUMERS WITH MARKETING INFORMATION |
|---|---|
| Blogs | Online journals in which people can post entries about their personal experiences, interests, and hobbies |
| MP3 Player | Allows users to listen to music or voice recordings in MP3 format |
| Handheld and wireless devices | Web-enabled devices including cellphones, personal digital assistants, and integrated devices such as Blackberries that permit users to access the Internet |
| Podcasts | Audio or video files, such as radio programs or videos, that can be downloaded from the Internet using either RSS or Atom syndication for listening on mobile devices and personal computers. The subscription feed of automatically delivered new content distinguishes a podcast from a simple download or real-time audio streaming. |

walmart-blows.com, ihatedell.net, or targetsucks.com in order to gain insight into public opinion about their firms. Social networks, such as MySpace.com, CarSpace.com, livejournal.com, or Slashdot.com, allow subscribers to blog and share anecdotes and experiences, often with pictures, audio, or even videos. For example, after Jeff Jarvis had an unhappy experience with Dell's ineffective attempts to resolve problems with his new laptop, he wrote about it on his blog. Within days his blog became one of the most visited websites, and it triggered a surge of Dell horror stories across the Web. Soon after when people typed "Dell" into search engines, Jarvis's blog and websites with unflattering names would appear on the first listings page.[13]

Although one estimate indicates that Google handles an estimated two-thirds of the world's Internet search queries, people may use several different search engines, and new search engines are evolving for almost every subject. Each search engine may be tailored to a different specific task, such as searching blog postings, video clips, or Internet shopping sites like Become.com. They permit users to look for specific targeted information that traditional search engines cannot supply. Startups such as Jeteye and Kaboodle use the experiences of prior searchers to refine searches and offer more useful results. These "social searches" instill human preferences into computer search algorithms to unearth more relevant and useful information. Yahoo! recently acquired five startups focused on building online community content in the hopes that this will improve searching through people.[14]

## Basic Characteristics of Electronic Marketing

Although e-marketing is similar to traditional marketing, it is helpful to understand the basic characteristics that distinguish this environment from the traditional marketing environment. These characteristics include addressability, interactivity, memory, control, accessibility, and digitalization.

**Addressability.** The technology of the Internet makes it possible for visitors to a website to identify themselves and provide information about their product needs and wants before making a purchase. The ability of a marketer to identify customers before they make a purchase is called **addressability**. Many websites encourage visitors to register to maximize their use of the site or to gain access to premium areas; some even require it. Registration forms typically ask for basic information, such as name, e-mail address, age, and occupation, from which marketers can build user profiles to enhance their marketing efforts. CDNow (a partner of Amazon.com), for example, asks music lovers to supply information about their listening tastes so the company can recommend new releases. Some websites even offer contests and prizes to encourage users to register. Marketers can also conduct surveys to learn more about the people who access their websites, offering prizes as motivation to participate.

> **addressability** A marketer's ability to identify customers before they make a purchase

Addressability represents the ultimate expression of the marketing concept. With the knowledge about individual customers garnered through the Web, marketers can tailor marketing mixes more precisely to target customers with narrow interests, such as recorded blues music or golf. Addressability also facilitates tracking website visits and online buying activity, which makes it easier for marketers to accumulate data about individual customers to enhance future marketing efforts. Amazon.com, for example, stores data about customers' purchases and uses that information to make recommendations the next time they visit the site.

> **cookie** An identifying string of text stored on a website visitor's computer

Some website software can store a **cookie**, an identifying string of text, on a visitor's computer. Marketers use cookies to track how often a particular user visits the website, what he or she may look at while there, and in what sequence. Cookies also permit website visitors to customize services, such as virtual shopping carts, as well as the particular content they see when they log onto a webpage. CNN, for example, allows visitors to its website to create a custom news page tailored to their particular interests. The use of cookies to store customer information can be an ethical issue, however, depending on how the data are used. If a website owner can use cookies to link a visitor's interests to a name and address, that information could be sold to advertisers and other parties without the visitor's consent or even knowledge. The

**Addressability**

Addressability is a company's ability to identify customers before they make a purchase.

potential for misuse of cookies has made many consumers wary of this technology. Because technology allows access to large quantities of data about customers' use of websites, companies must carefully consider how the use of such information affects individuals' privacy, as we discuss in more detail later in this chapter.

**interactivity** The ability to allow customers to express their needs and wants directly to the firm in response to the firm's marketing communications

**Interactivity.** Another distinguishing characteristic of e-marketing is **interactivity**, which allows customers to express their needs and wants directly to the firm in response to its marketing communications. This means marketers can interact with prospective customers in real time (or at least a close approximation of it). Of course, salespeople have always been able to do this, but at a much greater cost. The Web provides the advantages of a virtual sales representative, with broader market coverage and at lower cost.

Interactivity helps marketers maintain high-quality relationships with existing customers by shaping customer expectations and perceptions. Customers with a higher expectation of continuing a relationship with a marketer are more likely to maintain that relationship even after a less than satisfactory experience with that firm.[15] To help build such relationships, companies are using the Internet to share increasing levels of information with customers. Amazon.com, for example, launched Search Inside the Book, which enables customers to search for a word or phrase in 120,000 books. After the new feature was introduced, sales for searchable books rose by 9 percent over books not included in the service.[16]

One implication of interactivity is that a firm's customers can also communicate with other customers (and noncustomers) through mailing lists, blogs, and word of mouth. For this reason, differences in the amount and type of information possessed by marketers and their customers are less pronounced than in the past. One result is that the new- and used-car businesses have become considerably more competitive because buyers are coming into dealerships armed with more complete product and cost information obtained through comparison shopping on the Net. By providing information, ideas, and a context for interacting with other customers, e-marketers can enhance customers' interest in and involvement with their products.

Interactivity also enables marketers to capitalize on the concept of community to help customers derive value from the firm's products and website. **Community** refers to a sense of group membership or feeling of belonging by individual members of a group.[17] One such community is Tripod, a website where Generation Xers can create their own webpages and chat or exchange messages on bulletin boards about topics ranging from cars and computers to health and careers. Another example is iVillage, a website targeted at women. Because such communities have well-defined demographics and share common interests, they represent a valuable audience for marketers, which typically fund the sites through advertising.

Another way to interact with customers is through blogs. There are an estimated 5 million blogs on a variety of topics, including companies, brands, and products, and they can be positive—raves about Manolo shoes, for example—or negative—such as rages against Wal-Mart, Kmart, and Best Buy. When Shayne McQuade invented a backpack with solar panels that let backpackers keep their gadgets charged, a friend mentioned the product on his blog, which soon led to references and discussions on other blogs, and ultimately, created a positive "buzz" and orders for the new product. Companies are increasingly establishing blogs to interact with customers. General Motors, for example, hosts the GM Smallblock Engine blog, where employees and customers marvel over Corvettes and other GM vehicles.[18]

**Memory.**  **Memory** refers to a firm's ability to access databases or data warehouses containing individual customer profiles and purchase histories and use these data in real time to customize its marketing offer to a specific customer. A **database** is a collection of information arranged for easy access and retrieval. Although companies have had database systems for many years, the information these systems contain did not become available on a real-time basis until fairly recently. Current software technology allows a marketer to identify a specific visitor to its website instantaneously, locate that customer's profile in its database, and then display the customer's past purchases or suggest new products based on past purchases while he or she is still at the site. For example, Bluefly, an online clothing retailer, asks visitors to provide their e-mail addresses, clothing preferences, brand preferences, and sizes so it can create a customized online catalog of clothing that matches the customer's specified preferences. The firm uses customer purchase profiles to manage its merchandise buying. Whenever it adds new clothing items to its inventory, it checks them against its database of customer preferences and, if it finds a match, alerts the individual in an e-mail message. Applying memory to large numbers of customers represents a significant advantage when a firm uses it to learn more about individual customers each time they visit the firm's website.

**Control.**  In the context of e-marketing, **control** refers to customers' ability to regulate the information they view and the rate and sequence of their exposure to that information. The Web is sometimes referred to as a *pull* medium because users determine what they view at websites; website operators' ability to control the content users look at and in what sequence is limited. In contrast, television can be characterized as a *push* medium because the broadcaster determines what the viewer sees once she or he has selected a particular channel. Both television and radio provide "limited exposure control" (you see or hear whatever is broadcast until you change the station).

For e-marketers, the primary implication of control is that attracting—and retaining—customers' attention is more difficult. Marketers have to work harder and more creatively to communicate the value of their websites clearly and quickly, or the viewer may lose interest and move on to another site. With literally hundreds of millions of unique pages of content available to any web surfer, simply putting a

**community** A sense of group membership or feeling of belonging by individual members

**memory** The ability to access databases or data warehouses containing individual customer profiles and purchase histories and use these data in real time to customize a marketing offer

**database** A collection of information arranged for easy access and retrieval

**control** Customers' ability to regulate the information they view and the rate and sequence of their exposure to that information

## marketing ENTREPRENEURS

**Matt Drudge**

**THE BUSINESS:** Drudge, Inc.

**FOUNDED:** 1995

**SUCCESS:** $800,000 annual revenues

In 1995, with only an e-mail address, a website, and a knack for uncovering and "telling" stories, Matt Drudge started one of the most successful and controversial online newspapers of our time, the *Drudge Report*. With a staff of two (including himself), Drudge compiles his "news" and "gossip" from a variety of daily newspapers, wire services, and most important, thousands of daily e-mail tips. The site then directs its readers via web links to online news sources that are already reporting on the stories. With the majority of the *Drudge Report*'s revenue coming from advertising, which accounts for around $100,000 monthly, and with his newspaper's minimal overhead, Drudge can clear around $3,500 a day and still have time for leisure.

website on the Internet does not guarantee anyone will visit it or make a purchase. Publicizing the website may require innovative promotional activities. For this reason, many firms pay millions of dollars to advertise their products or websites on high-traffic sites such as America Online (AOL). Because of AOL's growing status as a **portal** (a multiservice website that serves as a gateway to other websites), firms are eager to link to it and other such sites to help draw attention to their own sites. Indeed, consumers spend most of their time online on portal sites such as MSN and Yahoo!, checking e-mail, tracking stocks, and perusing news, sports, and weather.

**Accessibility.** An extraordinary amount of information is available on the Internet. The ability to obtain information is referred to as **accessibility**. Because customers can access in-depth information about competing products, prices, reviews, and so forth, they are much better informed about a firm's products and their relative value than ever before. Someone looking to buy a new truck, for example, can go to the websites of Ford, Toyota, and Dodge to compare the features of the Ford F-150, the Toyota Tundra, and the Dodge Ram. The truck buyer can also access online magazines and pricing guides to get more specific information about product features, performance, and prices. Many new- and used-car buyers turn to independent websites such as Kelley Blue Book, Edmunds, and Autobytel for pricing information before they go to a dealership to negotiate for a new vehicle.

Accessibility dramatically increases competition for Internet users' attention. Without substantial promotion, such as advertising on portals like AOL, MSN, Yahoo!, and other high-traffic sites, it is becoming increasingly difficult to attract a visitor's attention to a particular website. Consequently e-marketers have to be increasingly creative and innovative to attract visitors to their sites.

Accessibility also relates to making information available for employees to service customers. Krispy Kreme, for example, has a network that provides store managers with a wealth of information, ranging from instructional videos and ordering recommendations based on each store's order history to weather forecasts, because consumers are more likely to buy donuts when the temperature falls. Having so much information readily accessible allows employees to focus on customers instead of paperwork.[19]

**Digitalization. Digitalization** is the ability to represent a product, or at least some of its benefits, as digital bits of information. Digitalization allows marketers to use the Internet to distribute, promote, and sell those features apart from the physical item itself. FedEx, for example, has developed web-based software that allows consumers and business customers to track their own packages from starting point to destination. Distributed over the Web at very low cost, the online tracking system adds value to FedEx's delivery services. Digitalization can be enhanced for users who have broadband access to the Internet because broadband's faster connections allow streaming audio and video and other new technologies.

In addition to providing distribution efficiencies, digitizing part of a product's features allows new combinations of features and services to be created quickly and inexpensively. For example, a service station that keeps a customer's history of automotive oil changes in a database can e-mail that customer when the next oil change is due and at the same time suggest other types of preventive maintenance, such as tire rotation or a tune-up. Digital features are easy to mix and match to meet the demands of individual customers.

**portal** A multiservice website that serves as a gateway to other websites

**accessibility** The ability to obtain information available on the Internet

**digitalization** The ability to represent a product, or at least some of its benefits, as digital bits of information

**Digitalization**

Napster offers music downloads of over 1 million songs.

## E-Marketing Strategies

Now that we have examined some distinguishing characteristics of doing business on the Internet, let's consider how these characteristics affect marketing strategy. Marketing strategy involves creating a marketing mix to satisfy individuals in a target market, regardless of whether those individuals are accessible online or through more traditional avenues. However, there are significant differences in how the marketing mix components are developed and combined into a marketing strategy in the electronic environment of the Web. As we continue this discussion, keep in mind that the Internet is a very dynamic environment, and therefore e-marketing strategies may need to be modified frequently to keep pace.

**Product Considerations.** The growth of the Internet and the World Wide Web presents exciting opportunities for marketing products to both consumers and organizations. Computers and computer peripherals, industrial supplies, and packaged software are the leading business purchases online. Experts project that e-commerce sales will grow eightfold, to $6 trillion by 2011.[20] Consumer products account for a small but growing percentage of Internet transactions, with food and beverage, sporting goods, and home goods among the fastest-growing online consumer purchases. Through e-marketing, companies can provide products, including goods, services, and ideas, that offer unique benefits and improve customer satisfaction.

The online marketing of goods such as computer hardware and software, books, videos, DVDs, CDs, toys, automobiles, and even groceries is accelerating rapidly. For example, Internet grocers such as FreshDirect and Peapod expect to see online sales of food and beverages grow from $2.4 billion to $6.5 billion by 2008.[21] Based in New York City, FreshDirect uses technology to provide made-to-order meat, produce, bakery items, and other grocery products at prices up to 25 percent less than competitors.[22] Autobytel has established an effective model for online auto sales by helping consumers find the best prices on their preferred models and then arranging for local delivery. However, low profit margins due to customized deliveries have challenged the ability of firms to deliver tangible goods.

Services may have the greatest potential for online marketing success. Many websites offer or enhance services ranging from home- and car-buying assistance to travel reservations and stock trading. At Century 21's website, consumers can search for the home of their dreams anywhere in the United States, get information about mortgages and credit, read tips on buying real estate, and learn about the company's relocation services. Airlines are increasingly booking flights via their websites. Southwest Airlines, for example, booked 59 percent of the airplane tickets it sold in 2005 online.[23]

The proliferation of information on the World Wide Web has itself spawned new services. Web search engines and directories such as Google, Yahoo!, Lycos, and Excite are among the most heavily accessed sites on the Internet. Without these services, which track and index the vast quantity of information available on the Web, the task of finding something of interest would be tantamount to searching for the proverbial needle in a haystack. Many of these services, most notably Yahoo!, have evolved into portals by offering additional services, including news, weather, chat rooms, free e-mail accounts, and shopping.

Even ideas have potential for success on the Internet. Web-based distance learning and educational programs are becoming increasingly popular. Corporate employee training is a $55 billion a year industry, and online training modules are growing rapidly. Kinko's, for example, replaced 51 employee-training centers with a web-based training network that lets workers take online courses on the company's products and policies.[24] Additional ideas being marketed online include marriage and personal counseling; medical, tax, and legal advice; and even psychic services.

**Distribution Considerations.**   The role of distribution is to make products available at the right time at the right place in the right quantities. The Internet can be viewed as a new distribution channel. Physical distribution is especially compatible

### E-Marketing Strategies

The growth of the Internet has spawned immeasurable opportunity for online service companies like Careerbuilder.com and Monster.com. They refine their marketing messages to consider both job hunters and head hunters.

with e-marketing. The ability to process orders electronically and increase the speed of communications via the Internet reduces inefficiencies, costs, and redundancies throughout the marketing channel. Most trucking firms now accept orders through the Internet, for example, but Yellow Transportation feeds order data from the Internet and the firm's call centers into a custom program to determine how many drivers it needs to schedule at each of its 335 facilities across the nation. By helping Yellow schedule 19,300 Teamsters and 8,250 trucks, the system saves the company approximately $100 million a year.[25]

More firms are exploiting advances in information technology to synchronize the relationships between their manufacturing or product assembly and their customer contact operations. This increase in information sharing among the firm's various

# ING DIRECT: Internet Banking—and Innovation—at Its Best

In the United States alone, more than 4 million people save their money at the online bank ING DIRECT, a subsidiary of the Amsterdam-based ING Group. For a bank that has only four brick and mortar locations in the whole country, that's saying something. And it isn't just Americans who have been lured to the Dutch company. Sixteen million customers are served by ING DIRECT in Australia, Austria, Canada, France, Germany, Italy, Spain, and the United Kingdom.

What is the company's success secret? In a word, innovation. ING DIRECT has built a reputation as an easy-to-use, reliable bank, while it has rejected traditional banking conventions. Instead of providing high-service contact on every corner, it exploits a range of technological innovations that make it possible to move money around the world electronically. Instead of showering customers with free toasters, it offers them low-cost, simple banking products. Instead of interacting directly with its customers (such one-on-one service would be expensive and time-consuming), ING DIRECT relies on paperless transactions, which reduce costs and improve speed, efficiency, and service to its clients.

The company's marketing strategy is seamless. Its tagline states its aim succinctly: *Save your Money.* Its logo is no stately flag or imposing rock, but a simple bright orange, hard-to-miss circle. And you know those brick and mortar locations? They're *cafés,* where customers can attend seminars; surf the Net; ask questions of on-site sales associates; and, yes, have a cup of coffee.

ING studied the lifestyles and habits of its most profitable customers and applied what it learned to attract prospects with similar characteristics. Its target customers are Internet-savvy, savings-minded parents aged 30 to 50. The bank's typical customer is comfortable but not wealthy, with average deposits of around $14,000.

ING DIRECT meets its goal of low-cost, simple transactions by letting savers open accounts with no fees and no minimums, and by consistently offering one of the best interest rates in the United States. Its mortgages have no application fee; a simple no-hassle application; and great rates that, compared to the 30-year fixed mortgages offered by traditional banks, can save customers thousands of dollars on their mortgages.

When ING DIRECT says it, they mean it: *Save your Money.*

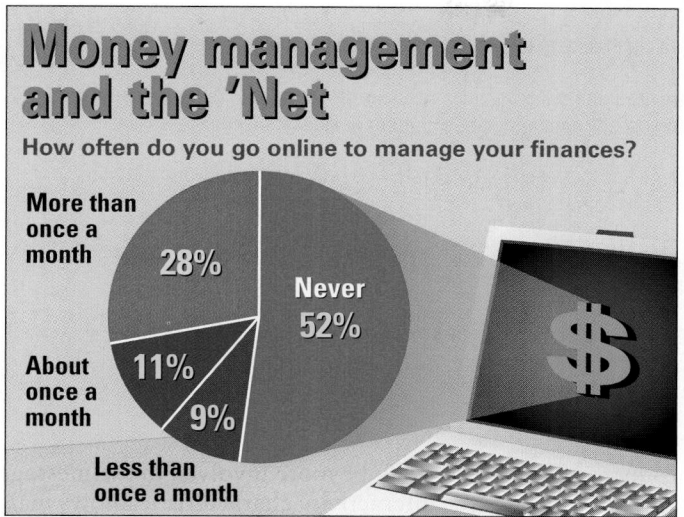

*Source:* Data from Ipsos Internet Survey. Margin of error: ±3 percentage points.

operations makes product customization easier to accomplish. Marketers can use their websites to query customers about their needs and then manufacture products that exactly fit those needs. Gateway and Dell, for example, help customers build their own computers by asking them to specify what components to include; the firms then assemble and ship the customized products directly to the customers in a few days. Imperial Sugar lets customers place orders, check stock, and track shipments via its website, which now accounts for 10 percent of the firm's sales.[26]

One of the most visible members of any marketing channel is the retailer, and the Internet is increasingly becoming a retail venue. Jupiter Media Metrix projects that by 2010 the percentage of the population shopping online will grow to 71 percent and online retail sales in the United States will climb to $144 billion.[27] The Internet provides an opportunity for marketers of everything from computers to travel reservations to encourage exchanges. Amazon.com, for example, sold more than $8 billion of books, CDs, DVDs, videos, toys, games, and electronics directly from its website in 2005.[28] Indeed, Amazon.com's success at marketing books online has been so phenomenal that many imitators have adopted its retailing model for everything from CDs to toys. Another retailing venture is online auctioneers, such as eBay, which auction everything from fine wines and golf clubs to computer goods and electronics.

**Promotion Considerations.** The Internet is an interactive medium that can be used to inform, entertain, and persuade target markets to accept an organization's products. In fact, gathering information about goods and services is one of the main reasons people use the Internet. College students in particular say they are influenced by Internet ads when buying online or just researching product purchases.[29] The accessibility and interactivity of the Internet allow marketers to complement their traditional media usage for promotional efforts. The control characteristic of e-marketing means that customers who visit a firm's website are there because they choose to be, indicating they are interested in the firm's products and therefore can be at least somewhat involved in its website's message and dialogue. For these reasons, the Internet represents a highly cost-effective communication tool for small businesses.

Many companies augment their TV and print advertising campaigns with web-based promotions. Kraft, Ragu, and Splenda, for example, have created websites with recipes and entertaining tips to help consumers get the most out of their products. Many movie studios have set up websites at which visitors can view clips of their latest releases, and television commercials for new movies often encourage viewers to visit these sites. In addition, many companies choose to advertise their goods, services, and ideas on portals, search engines, and even other firms' websites. Table 8.2 (on p. 224) describes the most common types of advertisements found on websites. More than 80 percent of companies now include the Internet as an advertising medium.[30]

Many marketers are also offering buying incentives and adding value to their products online through the use of sales promotions, especially coupons. Several websites, including coolsavings.com, valupage.com, and valpak.com, offer online coupons for their members.

The characteristics of e-marketing make promotional efforts on the Internet significantly different from those using more traditional media. First, because Internet users can control what they see, customers who visit a firm's website are there because they choose to be, which implies, as pointed out previously, that they are

| table 8.2 | TYPES OF ADVERTISING ON WEBSITES |
|---|---|
| Banner ads | Small rectangular, static, or animated ads that typically appear at the top of a webpage |
| Keyword ads | Ads that relate to text or subject matter specified in a web search |
| Button ads | Small square or rectangular ads bearing a corporate or brand name or logo and usually appearing at the bottom or side of a webpage |
| Pop-up ads | Large ads that open in a separate web browser window on top of the website being viewed |
| Pop-under ads | Large ads that open in a new browser window underneath the website being viewed |
| Sponsorship ads | Ads that integrate companies' brands and products with the editorial content of certain websites |

interested in the firm's products and therefore may be more involved in the message and dialogue provided at the site. Second, the interactivity characteristic allows marketers to enter into dialogues with customers to learn more about their interests and needs. This information can then be used to tailor promotional messages to individual customers. In fact, customized communications can help reduce information overload and improve buying decisions, which can enhance customer relationships.[31] Finally, addressability can make marketing efforts directed at specific customers more effective. Indeed, direct marketing combined with effective analysis of customer databases may become one of e-marketing's most valuable promotional tools.

**Pricing Considerations.** Pricing relates to perceptions of value and is the most flexible element of the marketing mix. Electronic marketing facilitates both price and nonprice competition because the accessibility characteristic of e-marketing gives consumers access to more information about the costs and prices of products than has ever been available to them before. As mentioned earlier, car shoppers can access automakers' webpages, configure an ideal vehicle, and get instant feedback on its cost. They can also visit Autobytel, Edmund's, and other websites to obtain comparative pricing information on both new and used cars to help them find the best value.

# Customer Relationship Management

One characteristic of companies engaged in e-marketing is a renewed focus on relationship marketing by building customer loyalty and retaining desired customers—in other words, on customer relationship management (CRM). As we noted in Chapter 1, CRM focuses on using information about customers to create marketing strategies that develop and sustain desirable long-term customer relationships. Procter & Gamble, for example, encourages Oil of Olay customers to join Club Olay, an online community with some 4 million members. In exchange for beauty tips, coupons, and special offers, the website collects some information about customers and their use of the skin-care product.[32] CRM focuses on analyzing and using databases and leveraging technologies to identify strategies and methods that will maximize the lifetime value of each desirable customer to the firm.[33] Four dimensions of CRM include top management involvement and commitment; organizational alignment (people, systems, and processes); customer differentiation and management; and technology to develop analytical, collaborative, and operational management.[34]

A focus on customer relationship management is possible in e-marketing because of marketers' ability to target individual customers. This effort is enhanced over time as customers invest time and effort into "teaching" the firm what they want. This investment in the firm also increases the costs a customer would incur by switching to another company. Once a customer has learned to trade stocks online through Charles Schwab, for example, there is a cost associated with leaving to find a new brokerage firm: another firm may offer less service, and it may take time to find a new firm and learn a new system. Any time a marketer can learn more about its customers to strengthen the match between its marketing mix and target customers' desires and preferences, it increases the perceived costs of switching to another firm. Strong customer identification with a company can also help build meaningful relationships and even turn customers into "champions" of those companies and their products.[35]

E-marketing permits companies to target customers more precisely and accurately than ever before. The addressability, interactivity, and memory characteristics of e-marketing allow marketers to identify specific customers, establish interactive dialogues with them to learn about their needs, and combine this information with their purchase histories to customize products to meet those needs. Like many online retailers, Amazon.com stores and analyzes purchase data to understand each customer's interests. This information helps the retailer improve its ability to satisfy individual customers and thereby increase sales of books, music, movies, and other products to each customer. The ability to identify individual customers allows marketers to shift their focus from targeting groups of similar customers to increasing their share of an individual customer's purchases. Thus, the emphasis shifts from *share of market* to *share of customer*. However, improving share of customer by maximizing customer loyalty can be difficult.[36]

**Database Marketing**

Database marketing uses an electronic information database.

## Database Marketing

CRM employs database marketing techniques to identify different types of customers and develop specific strategies for interacting with each customer. It incorporates three elements:

1. Identifying and building a database of current and potential consumers, including a wide range of demographic, lifestyle, and purchase information

2. Delivering differential messages according to each consumer's preferences and characteristics through established and new media channels

3. Tracking customer relationships to monitor the costs of retaining individual customers and the lifetime value of their purchases[37]

It is important for marketers to distinguish *active* customers—those likely to continue buying from the firm—from *inactive* customers—those who are likely to defect and those who have already defected. This information should help to (a) identify profitable inactive customers who can be reactivated, (b) remove inactive unprofitable customers from the customer database, and (c) identify active customers who should be targeted with regular marketing activities.[38] Table 8.3 (on p. 226) examines types of databases and how marketers can use them for customer relationship management.

Another aspect of CRM is supplier relationship marketing (SRM), which also uses databases to manage relationships and communications with vendors and other individuals and companies that supply goods, services, and ideas to a firm. SRM uses information technology to develop databases and measures for

How rough is *too rough?*

CAUTION EXTREME ROUGH ROAD

**Lansmont Field Instruments**
- Hands-Free Data Collection
- 90-Day Battery Life; set-it and forget-it
- Small Size, Light Weight

**Lansmont**
Field-to-Lab

800-LANSMONT
www.lansmont.com

| table 8.3 | TYPES OF DATABASES | |
|---|---|---|
| | **What Are They?** | **What Do They Do?** |
| Customer databases | Contain information about a company's current customers and thereby form the core of any marketing database | Store basic data—name, address, zip code, and telephone number; demographic data—age, gender, marital status, education, income, and so on; psychographic data—values, activities, interests, preferences, and so on; transaction histories; inquiries and referrals |
| Prospect databases | Contain information about prospects—noncustomers with profiles similar to those of existing customers; should include as much information about prospects as the customer database does about current customers | Supply information to be used to design marketing campaigns to target prospects and turn them into lifetime customers |
| Cluster databases | Contain information about relatively small clusters of people who can be defined based on geographic reference, affinity (e.g., clubs and associations), and lifestyle reference groups; people in the same cluster tend to have similar interests, attitudes, purchasing habits, and preferences | Help marketers identify clusters to which prospective customers belong and to customize marketing communications according to membership of prospective customers in specific clusters |
| Enhancement databases | Collect additional information about customers and prospects—demographic and psychographic data, transaction histories, address changes, income changes, privacy status, and new product categories recently purchased | Help marketers better target advertising and marketing campaigns, expand brand reach, improve acquisition and retention rates and thereby profitability |

**Source:** Adapted from V. Kumar, "Customer Relationship Management," custom module for William M. Pride and O. C. Ferrell, *Marketing,* 14th ed. (Boston: Houghton Mifflin, 2006), www.prideferrell.com.

assessing and managing these relationships. It is necessary to monitor supplier relationships and track performance in order to assess quality and determine vendors' value to the overall operation. These systems and processes are important in creating value and effective relationships with a firm's own customers.[39] Consider that Trader Joe's Company, a specialty food retailer, had to drop award-winning Bingham Hill Cheese products from its product mix due to frequent inventory stockouts and lost sales from lack of product availability. Bingham Hill was too small a supplier to serve a large company like Trader Joe's.[40]

## Customer Lifetime Value

Focusing on share of customer requires recognizing that all customers have different needs and that all customers do not have equal value to a firm. Thus, a firm should ensure that individual target customers have sufficient potential to justify such specialized efforts. Indeed, one benefit arising from the addressability characteristic of e-marketing is that firms can track and analyze individual customers' purchases and identify the most profitable and loyal customers. The most basic application of this idea is the 80/20 rule: 80 percent of business profits come from 20 percent of customers. Although this idea is not new, advances in technology and data collection techniques now permit firms to profile customers in real time. The goal is to assess the worth of individual customers and thus estimate their lifetime value to the firm. The concept of customer lifetime value (CLV) may include not only an individual's propensity to engage in purchases but also his or her strong word-of-mouth communication about the firm's products.[41] Some customers—those who require considerable hand-holding or who return products frequently—may simply be too expensive to retain given the low level of profits they generate. Companies can discourage these unprofitable customers by requiring them to pay higher fees for additional services. For example, many banks and brokerages charge hefty maintenance fees on small accounts. Such practices allow firms to focus their resources on developing and managing long-term relationships with more profitable customers.[42] Developing systematic CRM procedures is thus one of the most important steps in managing relationships.[43]

Thus, managing customer relationships requires allocating resources selectively to different customers based on the economic value of their relationship to the firm. CLV is a key measurement that forecasts a customer's lifetime economic contribution based on continued relationship marketing efforts. It can be calculated by taking the sum of the customer's present value contributions to profit margins over a specific timeframe. For example, the lifetime value of a Lexus customer could be predicted by how many new automobiles Lexus could sell the customer over a period of years and developing a summation of the contribution to margins across the time period. The sales value has been estimated at $600,000. Data from past customer behavior and other information of the effectiveness of relationship efforts could assist in this projection. While this is not an exact science, knowing a customer's potential lifetime value can help marketers determine how best to allocate resources to marketing strategies to sustain that customer over a lifetime.

CLV is the only gauge that incorporates revenue, expense, and customer behavior and adopts a customer-centric approach.[44] As such, the concept can help companies confront marketing issues with greater confidence by exploring these questions:

- Which customers should be provided with preferential and sometimes personal treatment?

- With which customers should the firm interact through inexpensive channels like the Internet or the telephone and which should be let go altogether?

- How do firms decide the timing of an offering to a customer?

- Which prospects will make good customers in the future, and therefore are worthwhile to attract now?

- How many and what resources should the firm allocate to secure future business with a current customer?

- How should firms monitor customer activity to determine whether adjustments to their marketing initiatives are required?[45]

If a company truly understands each customer's lifetime value, it can maximize its own value by boosting the number, scope, and duration of value-enhancing customer relationships. To do that, managers would have to determine how much revenue each customer would generate in the future and subtract the expected costs of acquiring, serving, and keeping that customer.[46] Thus the concept of CLV helps marketers adopt appropriate marketing activities today to increase future profitability.

## Technology Drives CRM

CRM focuses on building satisfying exchange relationships between buyers and sellers by gathering useful data at all customer-contact points—telephone, fax, online, and personal—and analyzing those data to better understand customers' needs and desires. Companies are increasingly automating and managing customer relationships through technology. Indeed, one fast-growing area of CRM is customer support and call-center software, which helps companies capture information about all interactions with customers and provides a profile of the most important aspects of the customer experience on the Web and on the phone. Using technology, marketers can analyze interactions with customers to identify performance issues and even build a library of "best practices" for customer interaction.[47] Customer support and call-center software can focus on those aspects of customer interaction that are most relevant to performance, such as how long customers have to wait on the phone to ask a question of a service representative or how long they must wait to receive a response from an online request. This technology can also help marketers determine whether call-center personnel are missing opportunities to promote additional products or provide better service. For example, after buying a new Saab automobile, the customer is supposed to meet a service mechanic who can answer any technical questions about the car during the first service visit. Saab follows up this visit with a telephone survey to determine whether the new-car buyer met the Saab mechanic and to learn about the buyer's experience with the first service call.

Sales automation software can link a firm's sales force to e-marketing applications that facilitate selling and providing service to customers. Often these applications enable customers to assist themselves instead of using traditional sales and service organizations. At Cisco, for example, 80 percent of all customer support questions can be answered online through the firm's website, eliminating 75,000 phone calls a

# Mining Customer Opinions with Technology

Successful marketers take the time to study and understand consumer buying behavior because it can influence the strategies a company uses to reach a particular target market. Increasingly, many companies such as Citigroup, Johnson & Johnson, Pfizer, and Procter & Gamble are turning to online software to create large-scale focus groups to help them understand their customers and their needs and wants. Companies that sell such software aim to help marketers listen to what their customers want rather than designing marketing campaigns based on generic strategies.

For years, companies have brought together small groups of people for traditional face-to-face focus groups to discuss products while marketers listen (often from another room) to their interactions. Edmund Sarraille, CEO of Informative, which markets the new focus-group software, says that the advantage of large-scale online focus groups is that they can reach a much larger audience and therefore capture a much wider range of ideas and opinions. This may yield more accurate information about what customers want.

Consider that for years, Lego has been producing the same Lego sets based on feedback from traditional focus groups. When Informative conducted an online focus group for the company involving 10,000 people—all Lego customers who were invited via e-mail to participate in an online contest regarding new products—the result was essentially brainstorming in cyberspace, which resulted in customers suggesting departures from Lego's traditional toys.

Although there are many challenges regarding this new software and its uses—for example, some suggest online research may be skewed toward Internet users—online focus groups are much less expensive than traditional ones. Informative and Communispace, another company marketing similar software, are doing a healthy business with high-profile clients, and it appears, at least for now, that this new research method may be a good way to go.

month.[48] In addition, CRM systems can provide sales managers with information that helps them develop the best product solutions for customers and thus maximize service. Dell Computer, for example, employs CRM data to identify those customers with the greatest need for computer hardware and then provides these select customers with additional value in the form of free, secure, customized websites. These "premier pages" allow customers—typically large companies—to check their order status, arrange deliveries, and troubleshoot problems. Although Dell collects considerable data about its customers from its online sales transactions, the company avoids selling customer lists to outside vendors.[49] CRM applications such as that used by Dell include software for marketing automation, sales automation, and customer support and call centers.

It is important to distinguish between CRM systems and CRM processes. CRM systems, including computers and software, integrate relevant customer and product information. CRM processes involve the measures required to retain customers and provide effective marketing initiatives through continuous interaction with customers.[50] CRM systems provide the infrastructure needed to secure the data that generate information for marketing strategies.

## Customer Satisfaction Is the End Result of CRM

Although technology drives CRM and can help companies build relationships with desirable customers, it is too often used as a cost reduction tactic or a tool for selling, with little thought toward developing and sustaining long-term relationships. Some companies spend millions to develop CRM systems, yet fail to achieve the associated benefits. These companies often see themselves as sophisticated users of technology to manage customers, but they do not view customers as assets. CRM is effective only when it is developed as a relationship-building tool. CRM is a process of reaching out to customers and building trust, not a technology solution for customer sales.[51] In addition, service quality and satisfaction depend on customer contact employees' commitment to their company and its customers as well as technology.[52]

Perhaps because of the software and information technology associated with collecting information from consumers and responding to their desires, some critics view CRM as a form of manipulation. It is possible to use information about customers at their expense to obtain quick results—for example, charging higher prices whenever possible and using available data to maximize profits. However, using CRM to foster customer loyalty does not require collecting every conceivable piece of data from consumers or trying to sell customers products they don't want. Marketers should not try to control customers; they should try to develop relationships that derive from the trust gained over many transactions and are sustained by customers' belief that the company genuinely desires their continued patronage.[53] Trust reduces the costs associated with worrying about whether expectations will be honored and simplifies customers' buying efforts in the future.

What marketers can do with CRM technology is identify their most valuable customers so they can make an investment in building long-term relationships with those customers.[54] To be successful, marketers must measure the effectiveness of their CRM systems in terms of their progress toward developing satisfactory customer relationships. Fewer than 20 percent of companies track customer retention, but developing and assessing customer loyalty is important in managing long-term customer relationships. At **www.loyaltyeffect.com**, a survey asks customers whether a company is worthy of their loyalty. Companies that rank high in customer loyalty on the survey include Enterprise Rent-a-Car, Harley-Davidson, L. L. Bean, and Northwestern Mutual.[55]

The most important component of CRM is remembering that it is not about technology but about relationships with customers. It has proven useful for business-to-business, business-to-customer, and nonprofit marketing. In all cases, high-contact relationships may require greater effort in developing organizational identity.[56] CRM systems should ensure that marketers listen to customers and then respond to their needs and concerns to build long-term relationships. The Internet can provide a valuable listening post and serve as a medium to manage customer relationships.[57]

# Legal and Ethical Issues in E-Marketing

How marketers use technology to gather information—both online and offline—to foster long-term relationships with customers has raised numerous legal and ethical issues. The popularity and widespread use of the Internet grew so quickly that global legal systems have been unable to keep pace with advances in technology. Among the issues of concern are personal privacy, unsolicited e-mail, and misappropriation of copyrighted intellectual property.

One of the most significant privacy issues involves the personal information companies collect from website visitors. A survey by the Progress and Freedom Foundation found that 96 percent of popular commercial websites collect personally identifying information from visitors.[58] Several companies, including Qwest Communications International Inc. and Comcast Corporation, have been criticized for improperly using personal data, both online and offline.[59] Cookies are the most common means of obtaining such information. Some people fear the collection of personal information from website users may violate users' privacy, especially if done without their knowledge.

In response to privacy concerns, some companies are cutting back on the amount of information they collect. The 96 percent of websites identified by the Progress and Freedom Foundation survey as collectors of personal information was down from 99 percent two years before, and 84 percent of the surveyed sites indicated they are collecting fewer data than previously.[60] Public concerns about online privacy remain, however, and many professionals in the industry are urging self-policing on this issue to head off potential regulation. One effort toward self-policing is the online privacy program developed by the BBBOnLine subsidiary of the Council of Better Business Bureaus (see Figure 8.1). The program awards a privacy seal to companies that clearly disclose to their website visitors what information they are collecting and how they are using it.[61]

Few laws specifically address personal privacy in the context of e-marketing, but the standards for acceptable marketing conduct implicit in other laws and regulations can generally be applied to e-marketing. Personal privacy is protected by the U.S. Constitution; various Supreme Court rulings; and laws such as the 1971 Fair

---

**figure 8.1**

### THE BBBONLINE PRIVACY SEAL AND PROGRAM EXPLANATION

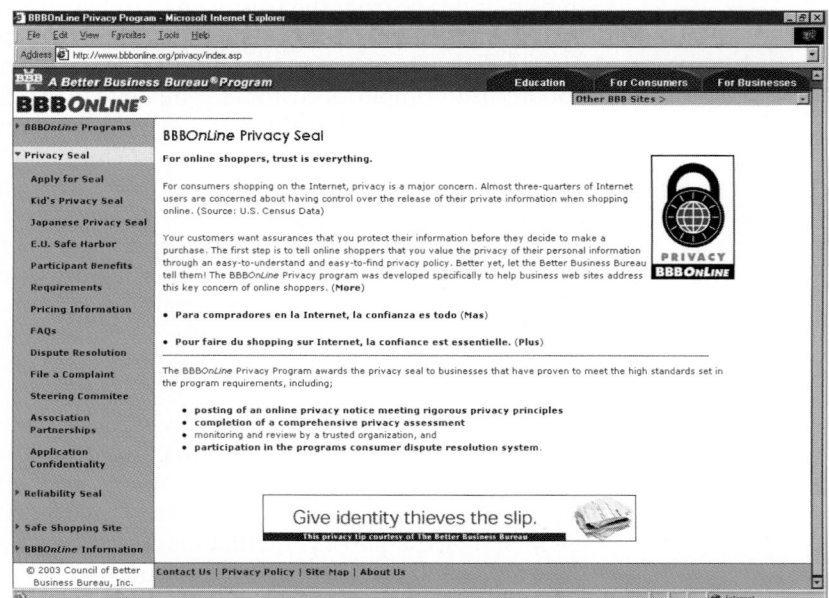

**Source:** Reprinted by permission of the Council of Better Business, Inc.

stop spam now

Shut it off with SurfControl E-mail Filter.

Only SurfControl E-mail Filter stops unwanted content using advanced Adaptive Reasoning Technology, artificial intelligence, and an Anti-Spam Agent that blocks virtually 100% of spam at the server. This simple-to-use enterprise solution also blocks inappropriate content, secures confidential data, optimizes network bandwidth and adds a layer of protection against viruses. And, it's easy to install on any SMTP or Exchange platform.

So get that spam out of your hair once and for all. Download SurfControl E-mail Filter now for a free 30-day evaluation.

Visit www.surfcontrol.com or call 1 800.368.3366

SurfControl®
The World's #1 Web & E-mail Filtering Company

**Legal and Ethical Issues in E-Marketing**
SurfControl stops unwanted e-mails, blocks inappropriate content, and secures confidential data.

Credit Reporting Act, the 1978 Right to Financial Privacy Act, and the 1974 Privacy Act, which deals with the release of government records. However, with few regulations on how businesses use information, companies can legally buy and sell information about customers to gain competitive advantage. Some have suggested that if personal data were treated as property, customers would have greater control over their use.

The most serious strides toward regulating privacy issues associated with e-marketing are emerging in Europe. The 1998 European Union Directive on Data Protection specifically requires companies to explain how the personal information they collect will be used and to obtain the individual's permission. Companies must make customer data files available on request, just as U.S. credit reporting firms must grant customers access to their personal credit histories. The law also bars website operators from selling e-mail addresses and using cookies to track visitors' movements and preferences without first obtaining permission. Because of this legislation, no company may deliver personal information about EU citizens to countries whose privacy laws do not meet EU standards.[62] The directive may ultimately establish a precedent for Internet privacy that other nations emulate.

**spam** Unsolicited commercial e-mail

**Spam**, or unsolicited commercial e-mail (UCE), has become a major source of frustration with the Internet. Many Internet users believe spam violates their privacy and steals their resources. Many companies despise spam because it costs them nearly $22 billion a year in lost productivity, new equipment, antispam filters, and labor. By some estimates, spam accounts for more than 75 percent of all e-mail.[63] Spam has been likened to receiving a direct-mail promotional piece with postage due. Some angry recipients of spam have organized boycotts against companies that advertise in this manner. Other recipients, however, appreciate the opportunity to learn about new products, as indicated in Figure 8.2 (on p. 232).

Most commercial online services (e.g., America Online) and Internet service providers offer their subscribers the option to filter out e-mail from certain Internet addresses that generate a large volume of spam. Businesses are installing software to filter out spam from outside their networks. Some firms have filed lawsuits against spammers under the Controlling the Assault of Non-Solicited Pornography and Marketing (CAN-SPAM) Law, which went into effect in 2004 and bans fraudulent or deceptive unsolicited commercial e-mail and requires senders to provide information on how recipients can opt out of receiving additional messages. However, spammers appear to be ignoring the law and finding creative ways to get around spam filters.[64] Increasingly, spam originates from outside the United States.

The Internet has also created issues associated with intellectual property, the copyrighted or trademarked ideas and creative materials developed to solve problems, carry out applications, and educate and entertain others. Intellectual property losses in the United States total more than $11 billion a year in lost revenue from the illegal copying of computer programs, movies, compact discs, and books. This issue has become a global concern because of disparities in enforcement of laws through-

**figure 8.2**

## TYPES OF GOODS AND SERVICES MARKETED THROUGH SPAM

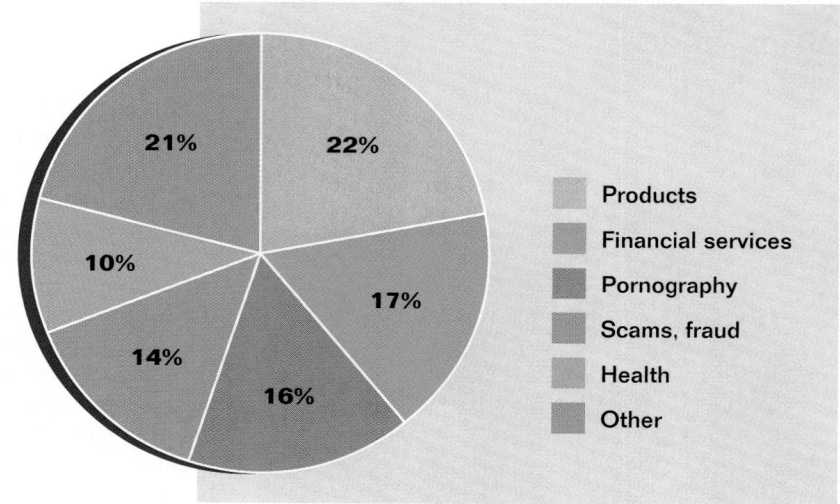

- Products
- Financial services
- Pornography
- Scams, fraud
- Health
- Other

**Source:** Ferris Research, in "Spam for Everyone," *The New York Times*, Jan. 31, 2005, www.nytimes.com.

out the world. The software industry estimates that worldwide piracy costs its companies roughly $12 billion every year.[65] The Digital Millennium Copyright Act (DMCA) was passed to protect copyrighted materials on the Internet. Intellectual property rights issues have file-sharing services such as Napster, Kaaza, Grockster, and eDonkey scrambling to reinvent their business models to address a Supreme Court ruling supporting the Recording Industry Association of America's efforts to protect its members' copyrighted music. File-sharing via eDonkey, the most popular file-sharing service, accounts for more than one-third of the volume of data sent over the Web. Whether eDonkey can become a legal way to market and share music will determine whether the industry persists as a black market for illegal, pirated tunes or evolves to comprise legitimate businesses.[66] Even Google has run into problems related to copyrights in providing searches. In one case, Google was required to remove images that failed three of four tests of fair use. Because Google sells ads that run alongside search results, the image search service does not fall under the noncommercial freedom to transmit others' copyrighted images.[67]

Protecting trademarks can also be problematic. For example, some companies have discovered that another firm has registered a URL that duplicates or is very similar to their own trademarks. The "cyber-squatter" then attempts to sell the right to use the URL to the legal trademark owner. Companies such as Taco Bell, MTC, and KFC have paid thousands of dollars to gain control of domain names that match or parallel their company trademarks.[68] To help companies address this conflict, Congress passed the Federal Trademark Dilution Act of 1995, which gives trademark owners the right to protect their trademarks, prevents the use of trademark-protected entities, and requires the relinquishment of names that duplicate or closely parallel registered trademarks.

As the Internet continues to evolve, more legal and ethical issues will certainly arise. Recognizing this, the American Marketing Association has developed a Code of Ethics for Marketing on the Internet (see Table 8.4). Such self-regulatory policies may help head off government regulation of electronic marketing and commerce. Marketers and all other users of the Internet should make an effort to learn and abide by basic "netiquette" (Internet etiquette) to ensure they get the most out of the resources available on this growing medium. Fortunately, most marketers recognize the need for mutual respect and trust when communicating in any public medium. They know that doing so will allow them to maximize the tremendous opportunities the Internet offers to foster long-term relationships with customers.

| table 8.4 | AMERICAN MARKETING ASSOCIATION CODE OF ETHICS FOR MARKETING ON THE INTERNET |
|---|---|

### Preamble

The Internet, including online computer communications, has become increasingly important to marketers' activities, as they provide exchanges and access to markets worldwide. The ability to interact with stakeholders has created new marketing opportunities and risks that are not currently specifically addressed in the American Marketing Association Code of Ethics. The American Marketing Association Code of Ethics for Internet marketing provides additional guidance and direction for ethical responsibility in this dynamic area of marketing. The American Marketing Association is committed to ethical professional conduct and has adopted these principles for using the Internet, including online marketing activities utilizing network computers.

### General Responsibilities

Internet marketers must assess the risks and take responsibility for the consequences of their activities. Internet marketers' professional conduct must be guided by:

1. Support of professional ethics to avoid harm by protecting the rights of privacy, ownership and access.

2. Adherence to all applicable laws and regulations with no use of Internet marketing that would be illegal, if conducted by mail, telephone, fax or other media.

3. Awareness of changes in regulations related to Internet marketing.

4. Effective communication to organizational members on risks and policies related to Internet marketing, when appropriate.

5. Organizational commitment to ethical Internet practices communicated to employees, customers and relevant stakeholders.

### Privacy

Information collected from customers should be confidential and used only for expressed purposes. All data, especially confidential customer data, should be safeguarded against unauthorized access. The expressed wishes of others should be respected with regard to the receipt of unsolicited e-mail messages.

### Ownership

Information obtained from the Internet sources should be properly authorized and documented. Information ownership should be safeguarded and respected. Marketers should respect the integrity and ownership of computer and network systems.

### Access

Marketers should treat access to accounts, passwords, and other information as confidential, and only examine or disclose content when authorized by a responsible party. The integrity of others' information systems should be respected with regard to placement of information, advertising or messages.

**Source:** From the American Marketing Association, **www.ama.org/about/ama/ethcode.asp**. Reprinted with permission.

## SUMMARY

Electronic commerce (e-commerce) refers to sharing business information, maintaining business relationships, and conducting business transactions by means of telecommunications networks. Electronic marketing (e-marketing) is the strategic process of creating, distributing, promoting, and pricing products for targeted customers in the virtual environment of the Internet. The Internet has changed the way marketers communicate and develop relationships with their customers, employees, and suppliers. Telecommunications technology offers marketers potential advantages, including rapid response, expanded customer service capability, reduced costs of operation, and diminished geographic barriers. Despite these benefits, many Internet companies failed because they did not realize Internet markets are more similar to traditional markets than they are different and thus require the same marketing principles. Consumer-generated marketing information through instant messaging, blogs, online forums, mailing lists, and wikis, as well as text messaging and podcasts, has become more important.

Addressability is a marketer's ability to identify customers before they make a purchase. One way websites achieve addressability is through the use of cookies, strings of text placed on a visitor's computer. Interactivity allows customers to express their needs and wants directly to a firm in response to its marketing communications. It also enables marketers to capitalize on the concept of community and customers to derive value from the use of the firm's products and websites. Memory refers to a firm's ability to access collections of information in databases or data warehouses containing individual customer profiles and purchase histories. Firms can then use these data in real time to customize their marketing offers to specific customers. Control refers to customers' ability to regulate the information they view, as well as the rate and sequence of their exposure to that information. Accessibility refers to customers' ability to obtain the vast amount of information available on the Internet. Digitalization is the representation of a product, or at least the representation of some of its benefits, as digital bits of information.

The addressability, interactivity, and memory characteristics of e-marketing enable marketers to identify specific customers, establish interactive dialogues with them to learn their needs, and combine this information with their purchase histories to customize products to meet their needs. Thus, e-marketers can focus on building customer loyalty and retaining customers.

The growth of the Internet and the World Wide Web presents opportunities for marketing products (goods, services, and ideas) to both consumers and organizations. The Internet can also be viewed as a new distribution channel. The ability to process orders electronically and to increase the speed of communications via the Internet reduces inefficiencies, costs, and redundancies throughout the marketing channel. The Internet is an interactive medium that can be used to inform, entertain, and persuade target markets to accept an organization's products. The accessibility of the Internet presents marketers with an opportunity to expand and complement their traditional media promotional efforts. The Internet gives consumers access to more information about the costs and prices of products than has ever been available to them before.

One characteristic of companies engaged in e-marketing is a focus on customer relationship management (CRM), which employs information about customers to create marketing strategies that develop and sustain desirable long-term customer relationships. The addressability, interactivity, and memory characteristics of e-marketing allow marketers to identify specific customers, establish interactive dialogues with them to learn about their needs, and combine this information with customers' purchase histories to tailor products that meet those needs. It also permits marketers to shift their focus from share of market to share of customer. CRM employs database marketing techniques to identify different types of customers and develop specific strategies for interacting with each customer. The goal is to assess the worth of individual customers and thus estimate their customer lifetime value (CLV). Although technology drives CRM and can help companies build relationships with desirable customers, customer relationship management cannot be effective unless it is developed as a relationship-building tool.

One of the most controversial issues in e-marketing is personal privacy, especially the personal information companies collect from website visitors, often through the use of cookies. Additional issues relate to spam, or unsolicited commercial e-mail (UCE), and misappropriation of copyrighted or trademarked intellectual property. More issues are likely to emerge as the Internet and e-marketing continue to evolve.

**ACE self-test**

Please visit the student website at **www.prideferrell.com** for ACE Self-Test questions that will help you prepare for exams.

## IMPORTANT TERMS

Electronic commerce
  (e-commerce)
Electronic marketing
  (e-marketing)
Blogs

Wikis
Addressability
Cookie
Interactivity
Community

Memory
Database
Control
Portal

Accessibility
Digitalization
Spam

## DISCUSSION & REVIEW QUESTIONS

1. How does addressability differentiate e-marketing from the traditional marketing environment? How do marketers use cookies to achieve addressability?

2. Define *interactivity* and explain its significance. How can marketers exploit this characteristic to improve relations with customers?

3. Memory gives marketers quick access to customers' purchase histories. How can a firm use this capability to customize its product offerings?

4. Explain the distinction between *push* and *pull* media. What is the significance of control in terms of using websites to market products?

5. What is the significance of digitalization?

6. How can marketers exploit the characteristics of the Internet to improve the product element of their marketing mixes?

7. How do the characteristics of e-marketing affect the promotion element of the marketing mix?

8. How does e-marketing facilitate customer relationship management?

9. How can technology help marketers improve their relationships with customers?

10. Electronic marketing has raised several ethical questions related to consumer privacy. How can cookies be misused? Should the government regulate the use of cookies by marketers?

## APPLICATION QUESTIONS

1. Amazon.com is one of the Web's most recognizable marketers. Visit the company's website at **www.amazon.com**, and describe how the company adds value to its customers' buying experience.

2. Some products are better suited than others to electronic marketing activity. For example, Art.com specializes in selling art prints via its online store. The ability to display a variety of prints in many different categories gives customers a convenient and efficient way to search for art. On the other hand, General Electric has a website displaying its appliances, but customers must visit a retailer to purchase them.

Visit **www.art.com** and **www.geappliances.com**, and compare how each firm uses the electronic environment of the Internet to enhance its marketing efforts.

3. Visit the website **www.covisint.com** and evaluate the nature of the business customers attracted. Who is the target audience for this business marketing site? Describe the types of firms currently doing business through this exchange. What other types of organizations might be attracted? Is it appropriate to sell any banner advertising on a site such as this? What other industries might benefit from developing similar e-marketing exchange hubs?

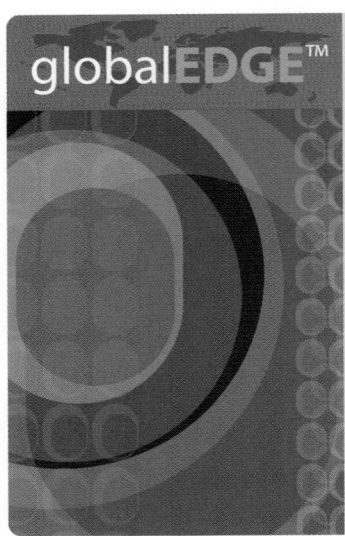

1. If your firm wanted to market goods or services to potential customers via the Internet, your marketing efforts may be affected by the number of Internet service providers (ISPs) existing in a particular market. NationMaster.com's Internet Service Providers listing, which offers valuable assistance in comparing various statistics worldwide on the topic, can be found using the search term "compare various statistics" at **http://globaledge.msu.edu/ibrd**. Once you have reached the NationMaster.com site, select the Internet category and the subcategory of Internet Service Providers. What are the top ten countries by number of ISPs? From this, divide these ten countries into two groups: highly decentralized and highly centralized per capita. What conclusions can be made from this?

2. Your firm wants to know which ten countries are most prepared for e-commerce. A ranking of the level of "e-readiness" of various markets worldwide can be accessed by using the search term "e-readiness" at **http://globaledge.msu.edu/ibrd** . If your firm was aiming to develop its international e-commerce competence, how can this information influence your firm's marketing strategy?

---

## INTERNET Exercise

Visit **www.prideferrell.com** for resources to help you master the material in this chapter, plus materials that will help you expand your marketing knowledge, including Internet exercise updates, ACE Self-Tests, hotlinks to companies featured in this chapter, and much more.

### iVillage.com

One example of an online community is iVillage. Explore the content of this website at **www.ivillage.com**.

1. What target market can marketers access through iVillage?
2. How can marketers target this community to market their goods and services?
3. Based on your understanding of the characteristics of e-marketing, analyze the advertisements you observe on this website.

---

## Video Case 8.1    The Gnome Helps Fuel a Turnaround at Travelocity

Travelocity was launched on March 12, 1996, by Sabre Interactive, a division of AMR Corporation, which at the time owned the Sabre Reservations System and American Airlines. Today Travelocity is the most popular travel service on the Web and the sixth-largest travel agency in the United States, with sales of more than $500 million. Teams of employees working in seven U.S. offices work together to bring consumers the best in airline reservations, hotel rooms, cruises, vacation packages, car rentals, and last-minute deals. Travelocity operates or powers websites in five languages across four continents. It was named the "World's Leading Travel Internet Site" for the eighth consecutive year at the World Travel Awards in 2005, and it has led all travel sites—including airline and hotel sites—in customer respect, based on a study released by the Customer Respect Group. It holds the highest possible ranking from *Consumer Reports*.

When Travelocity began in 1996, it was one of the first Internet travel websites. By 2000 and 2001, however, it had stopped growing and was fading as the pioneer brand. Travelocity executives recognized that they needed to refocus the company on more profitable products. The reality is that selling airline tickets does not make money, but selling hotels and travel packages does. Consequently, Travelocity implemented a strategy of cross-selling and up-selling to help customers get a more complete travel experience. It focused on serving as a more complete advocate for travelers by providing a more affordable and more rewarding travel experience. The result: Travelocity's package segment

grew by more than 100 percent a year between 2003 and 2005.

Despite the improving outlook, executives felt that the company needed to stand behind travelers in a way that no other online travel company did. They decided to spend a year developing a Customer Bill of Rights to guarantee that everything that customers book will be right and if it isn't, then the company will work with its partners to fix the problem. For example, if a customer books a hotel with a swimming pool, but finds the swimming pool closed upon arrival, Travelocity will, at its own expense, find a comparable or better quality hotel and move the customer there. Travelocity maintains a 24-hour hotline open seven days a week to ensure that customers get what they want. The Travelocity Guarantee allays the concerns of Travelocity customers who may be worried about booking online. The company stood by the guarantee even when it made a mistake and sold $0 tickets to Fiji for a short time.

The company paired the new guarantee with the "Roaming Gnome Enforcer of the Travelocity Guarantee" in television and other advertising. The Roaming Gnome advertising campaign represented an effort to humanize the Travelocity brand. The character embodied the joy of travel and symbolized getting out of the garden and seeing the world with new eyes. The advertising campaign created a tremendous buzz about Travelocity and boosted revenues by 37 percent. The gnome also won the American Marketing Association Gold EFIE award for Best Retail advertising campaign.

Travelocity partners with American Express Travel, AOL Travel, Yahoo! Travel, many other firms. In this way, Travelocity has a much larger market share, and because it represents so many firms, it has more power both with consumers and suppliers. The network partnering is especially important when it comes to marketing to customers. Travelocity can piggyback off its partners to use their tried-and-tested marketing techniques with its own customers. In this way, Travelocity and its partners gain from the synergies of their partnerships.

Travelocity is also experimenting with creative ways of marketing to its customers. It was a sponsor of the CBS series *Amazing Race*, and the competitors even had to find a gnome and carry him across the finish line. Although it was a huge investment for Travelocity, it paid off with increases in sales in only eight weeks. Executives believe that by going beyond 30-second commercials and banner ads, Travelocity is part of the complete entertainment mix of customers. Travelocity also uses search-engine marketing, spending much of its online advertising budget on paid keyword search ads. Although click-through advertising is vital, Travelocity has estimated that as many as a quarter of the people who came to Travelocity through search marketing would have come to the website anyway because Travelocity is such a well-known brand.

Travelocity also regularly tests its website for ease of use. It has seven testers in a room to find out where people are confused and where things can be improved. It has used this method to radically change its website. One of the things it realized was that people forget passwords. To counteract this problem Travelocity changed the system so that customers re-entered their credit card information, address and e-mail address and used these things to pull up their profile, rather than relying on passwords. This change resulted in overnight increases in revenues of 10 percent. Executives realized that if you make using the website hard, then people will go elsewhere.[69]

## Questions for Discussion

1. What is the role of consumer-generated information in helping Travelocity succeed?
2. Describe the marketing decisions that have helped Travelocity be so successful.
3. How did Travelocity use the Roaming Gnome as a symbol to communicate with its target market?

## Case 8.2  eBay Auctions It All

One of the best-known Internet companies is eBay, whose stated mission is "to provide a global trading platform where practically anyone can trade practically anything." The leading online auction site has grown into a community of more than 100 million registered users around the world who can buy or sell literally anything from automobiles, boats, and furniture to jewelry, musical instruments, electronics, and collectibles. The auction site, described by CEO Meg Whitman as a "dynamic self-regulating economy," transacts nearly $15 billion in merchandise a year, more than the gross domestic product of many countries, giving it 80 percent of the online auction market. The firm sells more used vehicles than the nation's number 1 dealer, AutoNation. Unlike many high-tech dot-com companies, eBay has been profitable almost from the beginning. The company's revenues topped $4.5 billion in 2005, and its double-digit annual growth rate is expected to continue for the foreseeable future.

Why has eBay been so successful when so many other Internet startups have failed? Many people believe the company's success is due largely to the leadership of Whitman, who ranked first on a recent *Fortune* list of the most powerful women in business. Whitman, who gained experience at Hasbro, FTD, Stride Rite, Disney, and Procter & Gamble before taking the reins at eBay, keeps the company focused on the "big-picture" objectives and key priorities, such as keeping company expenses down and building a world-class executive team to keep the company on its fast-growing profitable pace. She expects to meet company objectives by making smart acquisition decisions; reaching new customers, including more corporate ones; and opening a fixed-price bazaar. Whitman believes her most valuable contribution to eBay's success is the development of a work ethic and an organizational culture that focuses on a fun, open, and trusting environment.

Another reason for the company's success is its responsiveness to its users. For example, eBay's Voice of the Customer program brings in a dozen buyers and sellers every month to question about how they work and what else eBay could do to improve. In addition, the firm holds hour-long teleconferences at least twice a week to survey users on new features and policies.

Although eBay is known primarily for consumer-to-consumer actions, many small businesses have discovered they can sell older equipment and excess inventory through eBay. After a downturn in the aerospace industry, Reliable Tools Inc. sold a few items on eBay, including a $7,000, 2,300-pound milling machine. The California machine tool shop now sells about $1 million a month, accounting for 75 percent of its business. Increasingly, larger multinational firms are setting up shop on eBay as well. Sun Microsystems and IBM, for example, have their own webpages within eBay's computer category from which they market products, primarily to small and midsize business customers.

For many small businesses, eBay serves as their retail outlet. An estimated 724,000 individuals derive all or most of their income from selling products on the auction site; eBay has also spawned a number of "Trading Assistants," independent companies that act as intermediaries to help consumers and businesses sell goods on its site. AuctionDrop, for example, provides six sites in San Francisco where sellers can drop off goods for the small business to auction on eBay, after which it collects 40 percent of the sales price as a commission, on top of the transaction fee charged by eBay. The company, which handles up to 1,000 items per day, plans to expand to four more locations around the United States.

To maintain customer confidence in auction transactions, eBay has taken numerous steps to avoid fraud. Although fraud occurs in only 0.01 percent of all eBay transactions, even a few fraudulent activities generate negative publicity and ill will, and could jeopardize the firm's reputation for quality transactions. To battle the potential for fraud, the company modified its user agreement to permit the barring of any user from the auction site and established feedback forms that allow buyers and sellers to rate each other based on their experiences. The company also offers escrow, payment processing, and credit card protection services through PayPal, Billpoint, and other providers, which further reduce the potential for fraud. The firm also established the Trust & Safety Department to look for suspicious activities and assist law enforcement agents in battling fraud.

By providing an easy-to-use site for consumers and businesses to buy and sell goods and remaining proactive, eBay has essentially become the poster child for a successful Internet venture. With strong leadership from Meg Whitman, Internet insiders believe the company will continue to serve as a model for electronic commerce.[70]

### Questions for Discussion

1. Which of the basic characteristics of e-marketing is most important to eBay?
2. Describe eBay's marketing mix. How does this mix differ from that of a more traditional, "brick-and-mortar" discount store?
3. Online fraud has been a factor in some consumers' reluctance to use auction sites by eBay (and perhaps in the rise in intermediary companies). Has eBay done enough to prevent fraud on its site? What else could the company do to improve its services?

## CHAPTER 9

# Marketing Research and Information Systems

## Mystery Shoppers on the Case

Since the 1940s, many companies have used "mystery shoppers" to visit their retail establishments and report on whether the stores were adhering to the companies' standards of service. Today, companies that would like a candid assessment of an average customer's experience at their places of business can hire a mystery shopping company—a firm that hires mystery shoppers to evaluate goods and services for corporate clients, analyzes the feedback, and provides that analysis to its corporate clients. About 500 companies make up the $600 million "mystery shopper" industry.

Mystery shoppers enter establishments pretending to be regular customers. They evaluate the appearance of the store and assess how they are treated by employees. Some use digital cameras and computer equipment to document these observations. Many mystery shoppers work on a part-time basis and do so to earn free merchandise, meals, movies, and other goods. A few work full time.

These mystery shoppers provide valuable information that helps companies improve their organizations and refine their marketing strategies. Some

## OBJECTIVES

1. To describe the basic steps in conducting marketing research

2. To explore the fundamental methods of gathering data for marketing research

3. To describe the nature and role of information systems in marketing decision making

4. To understand how such tools as databases, decision support systems, and the Internet facilitate marketing research

5. To identify key ethical and international considerations in marketing research

companies take the input of mystery shoppers to heart and base company bonuses on employee performance during mystery inspections. Although a number of companies are now using online and phone customer surveys to judge performance—a practice that costs far less than employing mystery shoppers—many companies still rely on these mystery inspections and feel the results help them raise the bottom line—customer satisfaction.[1] ■

Mystery shoppers enable marketers to implement the marketing concept by helping them acquire information about whether and how their goods and services satisfy the desires of target market customers. When used effectively, such information facilitates relationship marketing by helping marketers focus their efforts on meeting and even anticipating the needs of their customers. Marketing research and information systems that can provide practical and objective information to help firms develop and implement marketing strategies therefore are essential to effective marketing.

In this chapter, we focus on how marketers gather information needed to make marketing decisions. First, we define marketing research and examine the individual steps of the marketing research process, including various methods of collecting data. Next, we look at how technology aids in collecting, organizing, and interpreting marketing research data. Finally, we consider ethical and international issues in marketing research.

# The Importance of Marketing Research

**marketing research** The systematic design, collection, interpretation, and reporting of information to help marketers solve specific marketing problems or take advantage of marketing opportunities

**Marketing research** is the systematic design, collection, interpretation, and reporting of information to help marketers solve specific marketing problems or take advantage of marketing opportunities. As the word *research* implies, it is a process for gathering information not currently available to decision makers. The purpose of marketing research is to inform an organization about customers' needs and desires, marketing opportunities for particular goods and services, and changing attitudes and purchase patterns of customers. Market information increases marketers' ability to respond to customer needs, which leads to improved organizational performance.[2] Detecting shifts in buyers' behaviors and attitudes helps companies stay in touch with the ever-changing marketplace. Fast-food marketers, for example, would be very interested to know that young men ages 18 to 24 average 20 trips a month to fast-food establishments, compared with about 15 trips a month for all fast-food diners. The billions that consumers spend dining out represent a tremendous opportunity for those companies willing to invest the resources to understand this market.[3] Strategic planning requires marketing research to facilitate the process of assessing such opportunities or threats.

Marketing research can help a firm better understand market opportunities, ascertain the potential for success for new products, and determine the feasibility of a particular marketing strategy. JCPenney, for example, conducted extensive research to learn more about a core segment of shoppers who weren't being adequately reached by department stores: middle-income mothers between the ages of 35 and 54. The research involved asking 900 women about their casual clothes preferences. Later the firm conducted in-depth interviews with 30 women about their clothing needs, feelings about fashion, and shopping experiences. The research helped the company recognize that this "missing middle" segment of shoppers was frustrated with the choices and quality of clothing available in their price range and stressed out by the experience of shopping for clothes for themselves. Armed with this information, Penney launched two new lines of moderately priced, quality casual women's clothing, including one by designer Nicole Miller.[4] A study by SPSS Inc. found that the most common reasons for conducting marketing research surveys included determining satisfaction (43 percent); product development (29 percent); branding (23

**Value of Marketing Research**
Mindfield provides services to help companies better understand their customers' behavior.

percent); segmentation (18 percent); awareness, trend tracking, and concept testing (18 percent); and business markets (11 percent).[5]

All sorts of organizations use marketing research to help them develop marketing mixes to match the needs of customers. Supermarkets, for example, have learned from marketing research that roughly half of all Americans prefer to have their dinners ready in 15 to 30 minutes. Such information highlights a tremendous opportunity for supermarkets to offer high-quality "heat and eat" meals to satisfy this growing segment of the food market. Political candidates also depend on marketing research to understand the scope of issues their constituents view as important. National political candidates may spend millions surveying voters to better understand issues and craft their images accordingly.

The real value of marketing research is measured by improvements in a marketer's ability to make decisions. Marketers should treat information in the same manner they use other resources, and they must weigh the costs of obtaining information against the benefits. Information should be judged worthwhile if it results in marketing activities that better satisfy the firm's target customers, lead to increased sales and profits, or help the firm achieve some other goal.

# The Marketing Research Process

To maintain the control needed to obtain accurate information, marketers approach marketing research as a process with logical steps: (1) locating and defining problems or issues, (2) designing the research project, (3) collecting data, (4) interpreting research findings, and (5) reporting research findings (see Figure 9.1). These steps should be viewed as an overall approach to conducting research rather than as a rigid set of rules to be followed in each project. In planning research projects, marketers must consider each step carefully and determine how they can best adapt the steps to resolve the particular issues at hand.

## Locating and Defining Problems or Research Issues
The first step in launching a research study is problem or issue definition, which focuses on uncovering the nature and boundaries of a situation or question related to marketing strategy or implementation. The first sign of a problem is typically a

**figure 9.1**

**THE FIVE STEPS OF THE MARKETING RESEARCH PROCESS**

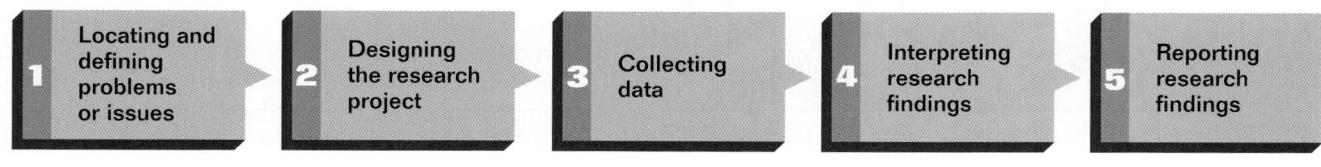

departure from some normal function, such as failure to attain objectives. If a corporation's objective is a 12 percent sales increase and the current marketing strategy resulted in a 6 percent increase, this discrepancy should be analyzed to help guide future marketing strategies. Declining sales, increasing expenses, and decreasing profits also signal problems. Customer relationship management (CRM) is frequently based on analysis of existing customers. However, research indicates that this information could be biased and therefore misleading when making decisions related to identifying and acquiring new customers.[6] Armed with this knowledge, a firm could define a problem as finding a way to adjust for biases stemming from existing customers when gathering data or to develop methods for gathering information to help find new customers. Conversely, when an organization experiences a dramatic rise in sales or some other positive event, it may conduct marketing research to discover the reasons and maximize the opportunities stemming from them.

Marketing research often focuses on identifying and defining market opportunities or changes in the environment. When a firm discovers a market opportunity, it may need to conduct research to understand the situation more precisely so it can craft an appropriate marketing strategy. For example, when General Motors saw that 42 percent of Hummer H3 buyers were women (compared to 26.3 percent of H2 buyers), it recognized an opportunity to position the smaller sport-utility vehicle to appeal to women buyers.[7]

To pin down the specific boundaries of a problem or an issue through research, marketers must define the nature and scope of the situation in a way that requires probing beneath the superficial symptoms. The interaction between the marketing manager and the marketing researcher should yield a clear definition of the research need. Researchers and decision makers should remain in the problem or issue definition stage until they have determined precisely what they want from marketing research and how they will use it. Deciding how to refine a broad, indefinite problem or issue into a precise, researchable statement is a prerequisite for the next step in the research process.

### Designing the Research Project

Once the problem or issue has been defined, the next step is creating a **research design**, an overall plan for obtaining the information needed to address it. This step requires formulating a hypothesis and determining what type of research is most appropriate for testing the hypothesis to ensure the results are reliable and valid.

**research design** An overall plan for obtaining the information needed to address a research problem or issue

**hypothesis** An informed guess or assumption about a certain problem or set of circumstances

**Developing a Hypothesis.** The objective statement of a marketing research project should include hypotheses based on both previous research and expected research findings. A **hypothesis** is an informed guess or assumption about a certain problem or set of circumstances. It is based on all the insight and knowledge available about the problem or circumstances from previous research studies and other sources. As information is gathered, the researcher can test the hypothesis. For example, a food marketer such as H. J. Heinz might propose the hypothesis that children today have considerable influence on their families' buying decisions regarding ketchup and other grocery products. A marketing researcher would then gather data, perhaps through surveys of children and their parents, and draw conclusions as to whether the hypothesis is correct. Movie theater, sports arena, and concert venue owners wondering why sales are down sharply have hypothesized that consumers are staying home more because of rising event prices, widespread availability of home theaters and broadband Internet access, as well as families' increasingly busy schedules.[8] Mar-

**snapshot**

# 300 million marketing opportunities

**How the population grows.**

One birth every
7 seconds

One death every
14 seconds

One international
migrant (net gain)
every 26 seconds

*Source:* Data from U.S. Census Bureau's POPClock Projection.

keters could test these hypotheses by manipulating prices or offering strong incentives for consumers to return. Sometimes several hypotheses are developed during an actual research project; the hypotheses that are accepted or rejected become the study's chief conclusions.

**Types of Research.** The nature and type of research varies based on the research design and the hypotheses under investigation. Marketers may elect to conduct either exploratory research or conclusive research. While each has distinct purposes, the major differences between them are formalization and flexibility rather than the specific research methods used. Table 9.1 summarizes the differences.

*Exploratory Research.* When marketers need more information about a problem or want to make a tentative hypothesis more specific, they may conduct **exploratory research.** The main purpose of exploratory research is to better understand a problem or situation and/or to help identify additional data needs or decision alternatives.[9] Consider that until recently, there was no research available to help marketers understand how consumers perceive the terms *clearance* versus *sale* in describing a discounted price event. An exploratory study asked one group of 80 consumers to write down their thoughts about a store window sign that said "sale" and another group of 80 consumers about a store window sign that read "clearance." The results revealed that consumers expected deeper discounts when the term *clearance* was used, and they expected the quality of the clearance products to be lower than that of products on sale.[10] This exploratory research helped marketers better understand how consumers view these terms and opened up the opportunity for additional research hypotheses about decision alternatives for retail pricing.

*Conclusive Research.* **Conclusive research** is designed to verify insights through an objective procedure to help marketers make decisions. It is used when the marketer has one or more alternatives in mind and needs assistance in the final stages of decision making.[11] For example, exploratory research revealed that clearance and sale terms send different signals to consumers, but in order to make a decision, a

**exploratory research** Research conducted to gather more information about a problem or to make a tentative hypothesis more specific

**conclusive research** Research designed to verify insights through objective procedures and to help marketers in making decisions

**table 9.1  DIFFERENCES BETWEEN EXPLORATORY AND CONCLUSIVE RESEARCH**

| Research Project Components | Exploratory Research | Conclusive Research |
|---|---|---|
| Research purpose | General: to generate insights about a situation | Specific: to verify insights and aid in selecting a course of action |
| Data needs | Vague | Clear |
| Data sources | Ill defined | Well defined |
| Data collection form | Open-ended, rough | Usually structured |
| Sample | Relatively small; subjectively selected to maximize generalization of insights | Relatively large; objectively selected to permit generalization of findings |
| Data collection | Flexible; no set procedure | Rigid; well-laid-out procedure |
| Data analysis | Informal; typically nonquantitative | Formal; typically quantitative |
| Inferences/recommendations | More tentative than final | More final than tentative |

**Source:** A. Parasuraman, Dhruv Grewal, and R. Krishnan, *Marketing Research,* p. 64. Copyright © 2004 by Houghton Mifflin Company. Used by permission.

well-defined and structured research project could be used to help marketers decide which approach is best for a specific set of products and target consumers. The study would be specific to selecting a course of action and typically quantitative using methods that can be verified. Two types of conclusive research are descriptive and experimental research.

**descriptive research** Research conducted to clarify the characteristics of certain phenomena to solve a particular problem

If marketers need to understand the characteristics of certain phenomena to solve a particular problem, **descriptive research** can aid them. Descriptive studies may range from general surveys of customers' education, occupation, or age to specifics on how often teenagers consume sports drinks or how often customers buy new pairs of athletic shoes. For example, if Nike and Reebok want to target more young women, they might ask 15- to 35-year-old females how often they work out, how frequently they wear athletic shoes for casual use, and how many pairs of athletic shoes they buy in a year. Such descriptive research can be used to develop specific marketing strategies for the athletic-shoe market. Descriptive studies generally demand much prior knowledge and assume the problem or issue is clearly defined. For example, a survey of automobile buyers found that those who use the Internet to search for vehicles are more likely to be younger and more educated and to spend more time searching in general.[12] Some descriptive studies require statistical analysis and predictive tools. The marketer's major task is to choose adequate methods for collecting and measuring data.

**experimental research** Research that allows marketers to make causal inferences about relationships

Descriptive research is limited in providing evidence necessary to make causal inferences (i.e., that variable $X$ causes a variable $Y$). **Experimental research** allows marketers to make causal deductions about relationships.[13] Such experimentation requires that an independent variable (one not influenced by or dependent on other variables) be manipulated and the resulting changes in a dependent variable (one contingent on, or restricted to, one value or set of values assumed by the independent variable) be measured. For example, when Coca-Cola introduced Dasani flavored waters, managers needed to estimate sales at various potential price points. In some markets, Dasani was introduced at $6.99/six pack. By holding variables such as advertising and shelf position constant, Coca-Cola could manipulate the price variable to study its effect on sales. If sales increased 40 percent when the price was reduced by $2, then managers could make an informed decision about the effect of price on sales. Coca-Cola could also use experimental research to manipulate other variables such as advertising or in-store shelf position to determine their effect on sales. Manipulation of the causal variable and control of other variables is what makes experimental research unique. As a result, it can provide much stronger evidence of cause and effect than data collected through descriptive research.

**reliability** A condition existing when a research technique produces almost identical results in repeated trials

**Research Reliability and Validity.** In designing research, marketing researchers must ensure that research techniques are both reliable and valid. A research technique has **reliability** if it produces almost identical results in repeated trials. However, a reliable technique is not necessarily valid. To have **validity**, the research method must measure what it is supposed to measure, not something else. For example, although a group of customers may express the same level of satisfaction based on a rating scale, as individuals they may not exhibit the same repurchase behavior because of different personal characteristics. This result may cause the researcher to question the validity of the satisfaction scale if the purpose of rating satisfaction was to estimate potential repurchase behavior.[14] A study to measure the effect of advertising on sales would be valid if advertising could be isolated from other factors or variables that affect sales. The study would be reliable if replications of it produced the same results.

**validity** A condition existing when a research method measures what it is supposed to measure

## Collecting Data

The next step in the marketing research process is collecting data to help prove (or disprove) the research hypothesis. The research design must specify what types of data to collect and how they will be collected.

**primary data** Data observed and recorded or collected directly from respondents

**secondary data** Data compiled both inside and outside the organization for some purpose other than the current investigation

**Types of Data.** Marketing researchers have two types of data at their disposal. **Primary data** are observed and recorded or collected directly from respondents. This type of data must be gathered by observing phenomena or surveying people of interest. **Secondary data** are compiled both inside and outside the organization for some purpose other than the current investigation. Secondary data include general reports supplied to an enterprise by various data services and internal and online databases. Such reports might concern market share, retail inventory levels, and customers' buying behavior. Commonly, secondary data are already available in private or public reports or have been collected and stored by the organization itself. Due to the opportunity to obtain data via the Internet, more than half of all marketing research now comes from secondary sources.

**Sources of Secondary Data.** Marketers often begin the data collection phase of the marketing research process by gathering secondary data. They may use available reports and other information from both internal and external sources to study a marketing problem.

Internal sources of secondary data can contribute tremendously to research. An organization's own database may contain information about past marketing activities, such as sales records and research reports, which can be used to test hypotheses and pinpoint problems. From sales reports, for example, a firm may be able to determine not only which product sold best at certain times of the year but also which colors and sizes customers preferred. Such information may have been gathered for management or financial purposes.[15]

Accounting records are also an excellent source of data but, surprisingly, are often overlooked. The large volume of data an accounting department collects does not automatically flow to other departments. As a result, detailed information about costs, sales, customer accounts, or profits by product category may not be easily accessible to the marketing area. This condition develops particularly in organizations that do not store marketing information on a systematic basis. A third source of internal secondary data is competitive information gathered by the sales force.

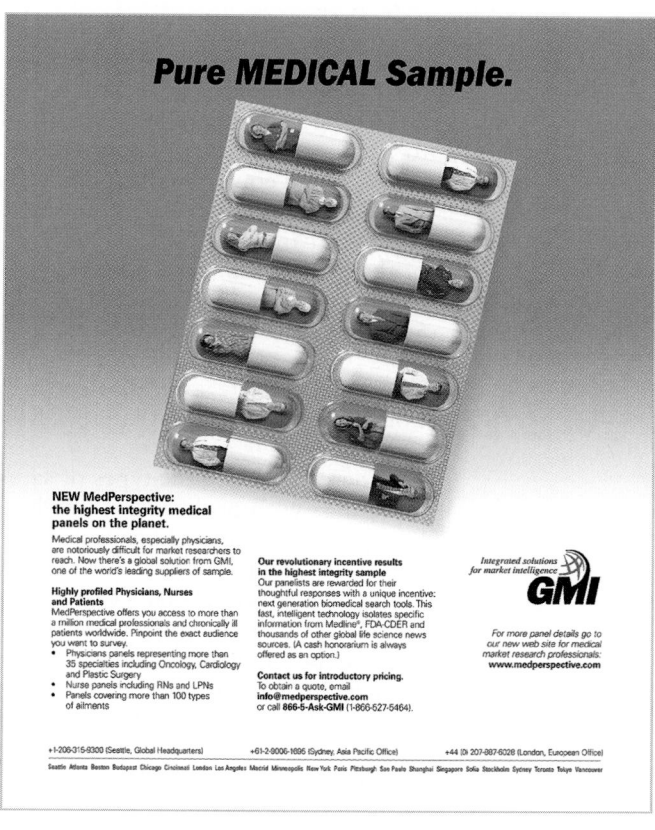

**Primary Data Collection**

GMI works with physicians, nurses, and patients to help pharmaceutical companies collect primary data on over 100 ailments.

External sources of secondary data include trade associations, periodicals, government publications, unpublished sources, and online databases. Trade associations such as the American Marketing Association offer guides and directories rife with information. Periodicals such as *Business Week,* the *Wall Street Journal, Sales & Marketing Management, Advertising Age, Marketing Research,* and *Industrial Marketing* publish general information that can help marketers define problems and develop hypotheses. *Survey of Buying Power,* an annual supplement to *Sales & Marketing Management,* contains sales data for major industries on a county-by-county basis. Many marketers also consult federal government publications such as the *Statistical Abstract of the United States,* the *Census of Business,* the *Census of Agriculture,* and the *Census of Population*; some of these government publications are available through online information services or the Internet. Although the government still conducts its primary census every ten years, it now surveys 250,000 households every month, providing marketers with a more up-to-date demographic picture of the nation's population every year. Target executives, for example, use such data to make merchandising and marketing decisions and to identify promising locations for new Target stores.[16]

In addition, companies may subscribe to services, such as ACNielsen or Information Resources, Inc. (IRI), that track retail sales and other information. For example, IRI tracks consumer purchases using in-store, scanner-based technology. Marketing firms can purchase information from IRI about a product category, such as frozen orange juice, as secondary data.[17] Small businesses may be unable to afford such services, but they can still find a wealth of information through industry publications and trade associations.[18]

**Methods of Collecting Primary Data.** Collection of primary data is a lengthier, more expensive, and more complex process than collection of secondary data. To gather primary data, researchers use sampling procedures, survey methods, and observation. These efforts can be handled in-house by the firm's own research department or contracted to a private research firm such as ACNielsen; Information Resources, Inc.; or IMS International.

*Sampling.* Because the time and resources available for research are limited, it is almost impossible to investigate all the members of a target market or other population. A **population,** or "universe," includes all the elements, units, or individuals of interest to researchers for a specific study. For example, for a Gallup poll designed to predict the results of a presidential election, all registered voters in the United States would constitute the population. By systematically choosing a limited number of units—a **sample**—to represent the characteristics of a total population, researchers can project the reactions of a total market or market segment. (In the case of the presidential poll, a representative national sample of several thousand registered voters would be selected and surveyed to project the probable voting outcome.) **Sampling** in marketing research, therefore, is the process of selecting representative units from a total population. Sampling techniques allow marketers to predict buying behavior fairly accurately on the basis of the responses from a representative portion of the population of interest. Most types of marketing research employ sampling techniques.

There are two basic types of sampling: probability sampling and nonprobability sampling. With **probability sampling**, every element in the population being studied has a known chance of being selected for study. Random sampling is a form of probability sampling. When marketers employ **random sampling**, all the units in a population have an equal chance of appearing in the sample. The various events that can occur have an equal or known chance of taking place. For example, a specific card in a regulation deck should have a 1/52 probability of being drawn at any one time. Sample units are ordinarily chosen by selecting from a table of random numbers statistically generated so that each digit, 0 through 9, will have an equal probability of occurring in each position in the sequence. The sequentially numbered elements of a population are sampled randomly by selecting the units whose numbers appear in the table of random numbers.

**population** All the elements, units, or individuals of interest to researchers for a specific study

**sample** A limited number of units chosen to represent the characteristics of a total population

**sampling** The process of selecting representative units from a total population

**probability sampling** A sampling technique in which every element in the population being studied has a known chance of being selected for study

**random sampling** A type of probability sampling in which all units in a population have an equal chance of appearing in the sample

**stratified sampling** A type of probability sampling in which the population of interest is divided into groups according to a common attribute and a random sample is then chosen within each group

**nonprobability sampling** A sampling technique in which there is no way to calculate the likelihood that a specific element of the population being studied will be chosen

**quota sampling** A nonprobability sampling technique in which researchers divide the population into groups and then arbitrarily choose participants from each group

Another type of probability sampling is **stratified sampling**, in which the population of interest is divided into groups according to a common attribute and a random sample is then chosen within each group. The stratified sample may reduce some of the error that could occur in a simple random sample. By ensuring that each major group or segment of the population receives its proportionate share of sample units, investigators avoid including too many or too few sample units from each group. Samples are usually stratified when researchers believe there may be variations among different types of respondents. For example, many political opinion surveys are stratified by gender, race, age, and/or geographic location.

The second type of sampling, **nonprobability sampling**, is more subjective than probability sampling because there is no way to calculate the likelihood that a specific element of the population being studied will be chosen. Quota sampling, for example, is highly judgmental because the final choice of participants is left to the researchers. In **quota sampling**, researchers divide the population into groups and then arbitrarily choose participants from each group. A study of people who wear eyeglasses, for example, may be conducted by interviewing equal numbers of men and women who wear eyeglasses. In quota sampling, there are some controls—usually limited to two or three variables, such as age, gender, or race—over the selection of participants. The controls attempt to ensure that representative categories of respondents are interviewed. Because quota samples are not probability samples, not everyone has an equal chance of being selected, and sampling error therefore cannot be measured statistically. Quota samples are used most often in exploratory studies, when hypotheses are being developed. Often a small quota sample will not be projected to the total population, although the findings may provide valuable insights into a problem. Quota samples are useful when people with some common characteristic are found and questioned about the topic of interest. A probability sample used to study people allergic to cats, for example, would be highly inefficient.

*Survey Methods.* Marketing researchers often employ sampling to collect primary data through mail, telephone, online, or personal interview surveys. The results of such surveys are used to describe and analyze buying behavior. Selection of a survey method depends on the nature of the problem or issue; the data needed to test the hypothesis; and the resources, such as funding and personnel, available to the researcher. Marketers may employ more than one survey method depending on the goals of the research. The SPSS Inc. survey of American Marketing Association members found that 43.8 percent use telephone surveys; 39.3 percent, web-based surveys; 36.8 percent, focus groups; 19 percent, mail surveys; 11.8 percent, e-mail surveys; and 9.6 percent, in-person interviews.[19] Table 9.2 (on p. 248) summarizes and compares the advantages of the various survey methods.

Gathering information through surveys is becoming increasingly difficult because fewer people are willing to participate. Many people believe responding to surveys takes up too much scarce personal time, especially as surveys become longer and more detailed. Others have concerns about how much information marketers are gathering and whether their

**Collecting Data Through Survey**
Greenfield Online creates and executes online surveys for clients who want to know more about their customers.

| table 9.2 | COMPARISON OF THE FOUR BASIC SURVEY METHODS | | | |
|---|---|---|---|---|
| | **Mail Surveys** | **Telephone Surveys** | **Online Surveys** | **Personal Interview Surveys** |
| **Economy** | Potentially lower in cost per interview than telephone or personal surveys if there is an adequate response rate. | Avoids interviewers' travel expenses; less expensive than in-home interviews. | The least expensive method if there is an adequate response rate. | The most expensive survey method; shopping mall and focus-group interviews have lower costs than in-home interviews. |
| **Flexibility** | Inflexible; questionnaire must be short and easy for respondents to complete. | Flexible because interviewers can ask probing questions, but observations are impossible. | Less flexible; survey must be easy for online users to receive and return; short, dichotomous, or multiple-choice questions work best. | Most flexible method; respondents can react to visual materials; demographic data are more accurate; in-depth probes are possible. |
| **Interviewer bias** | Interviewer bias is eliminated; questionnaires can be returned anonymously. | Some anonymity; may be hard to develop trust in respondents. | Interviewer bias is eliminated, but e-mail address on the return eliminates anonymity. | Interviewers' personal characteristics or inability to maintain objectivity may result in bias. |
| **Sampling and respondents' cooperation** | Obtaining a complete mailing list is difficult; nonresponse is a major disadvantage. | Sample limited to respondents with telephones; devices that screen calls, busy signals, and refusals are a problem. | Sample limited to respondents with computer access; the available e-mail address list may not be a representative sample for some purposes. | Not-at-homes are a problem, which may be overcome by focus-group and shopping mall interviewing. |

**mail survey** A research method in which respondents answer a questionnaire sent through the mail

**telephone survey** A research method in which respondents' answers to a questionnaire are recorded by an interviewer on the phone

privacy is being invaded. The unethical use of selling techniques disguised as marketing surveys has also led to decreased cooperation. These factors contribute to nonresponse rates for any type of survey.

In a **mail survey**, questionnaires are sent to respondents, who are encouraged to complete and return them. Mail surveys are used most often when the individuals in the sample are spread over a wide area and funds for the survey are limited. A mail survey is less expensive than a telephone or personal interview survey as long as the response rate is high enough to produce reliable results. The main disadvantages of this method are the possibility of a low response rate and of misleading results if respondents differ significantly from the population being sampled. One method of improving response rates involves attaching a brief note with a personal message on a Post-it note to the survey packet. Response rates to these surveys are not only higher, but the quality and the timeliness of the responses are also improved.[20]

Premiums or incentives that encourage respondents to return questionnaires have been effective in developing panels of respondents who are interviewed regularly by mail. Such mail panels, selected to represent a target market or market segment, are especially useful in evaluating new products and providing general information about customers, as well as records of their purchases (in the form of purchase diaries). Mail panels and purchase diaries are much more widely used than custom mail surveys, but both panels and purchase diaries have shortcomings. People who take the time to fill out a diary may differ from the general population based on income, education, or behavior, such as the time available for shopping activities.

In a **telephone survey**, an interviewer records respondents' answers to a questionnaire over a phone line. A telephone survey has some advantages over a mail survey. The rate of response is higher because it takes less effort to answer the telephone and talk than to fill out and return a questionnaire. If there are enough interviewers, a telephone survey can be conducted very quickly. Thus, political candidates or organizations seeking an immediate reaction to an event may choose this method. In addition, a telephone survey permits interviewers to gain rapport with respondents and ask probing questions.

However, only a small proportion of the population likes to participate in telephone surveys. Just one-third of Americans are willing to participate in telephone interviews, down from two-thirds 20 years ago.[21] This poor image can significantly limit participation and distort representation in a telephone survey. Moreover, telephone surveys are limited to oral communication; visual aids or observation cannot be included. Interpreters of results must make adjustments for individuals who are not at home or do not have telephones. Many households are excluded from telephone directories by choice (unlisted numbers) or because the residents moved after the directory was published. Potential respondents often use telephone answering machines, voice mail, or caller ID to screen or block calls. Moreover, an increasing number of younger Americans are giving up their fixed telephone lines in favor of cellular or wireless phones.[22] These issues have serious implications for the use of telephone samples in conducting surveys. Some adjustment must be made for groups of respondents that may be undersampled because of a smaller-than-average incidence of telephone listings. Nondirectory telephone samples can overcome such bias. Various methods are available, including random-digit dialing (adding random numbers to the telephone prefix) and plus-one telephone sampling (increasing the last digit of a directory number by 1). These methods make it feasible to dial any working number, whether or not it is listed in a directory. However, these methods do not address the fact that younger Americans are increasingly favoring their cellphones, which marketing researchers may not call.[23]

Online surveys are evolving as an alternative to telephone surveys. In an **online survey**, questionnaires can be transmitted to respondents who have agreed to be contacted and have provided their e-mail addresses. Because e-mail is semi-interactive, recipients can ask for clarification of specific questions or pose questions of their own. The potential advantages of e-mail surveys are quick response and lower cost than traditional mail, telephone, and personal interview surveys if the response rate is adequate. In addition, more firms are using their websites to conduct surveys. Online surveys can also make use of online communities—such as chat rooms, web-based forums, blogs, and newsgroups—to identify trends in interests and consumption patterns. Movies, consumer electronics, food, and computers are popular topics in many online communities.[24] Indeed, by "listening in" on these ongoing conversations, marketers may be able to identify new product opportunities and consumer needs. Moreover, this type of online data can be gathered at little incremental cost compared to alternative data sources.[25] Evolving technology and the interactive nature of the Internet allow for considerable flexibility in designing online questionnaires.

Given the growing number of households that have computers with Internet access, marketing research is likely to rely heavily on online surveys in the future. Furthermore, as negative attitudes toward telephone surveys render that technique less representative and more expensive, the integration of e-mail, fax, and voice mail functions into one computer-based system provides a promising alternative for survey research. E-mail surveys have especially strong potential within organizations whose employees are networked and for associations that publish members' e-mail addresses. However, there are some ethical issues to consider when using e-mail for marketing research, such as spam (unsolicited e-mail) and privacy.

In a **personal interview survey**, participants respond to questions face to face. Various audiovisual aids—pictures, products, diagrams, or prerecorded advertising copy—can be incorporated into a personal interview. Rapport gained through direct interaction usually permits more in-depth interviewing, including probes, follow-up questions, or psychological tests. In addition, because personal interviews can be longer, they may yield more information. Finally, respondents can be selected more carefully, and reasons for nonresponse can be explored.

One such research technique is the **in-home (door-to-door) interview**. The in-home interview offers a clear advantage when thoroughness of self-disclosure and

**online survey** A research method in which respondents answer a questionnaire via e-mail or on a website

**personal interview survey** A research method in which participants respond to survey questions face to face

**in-home (door-to-door) interview** A personal interview that takes place in the respondent's home

**focus-group interview** A research method involving observation of group interaction when members are exposed to an idea or a concept

elimination of group influence are important. In an in-depth interview of 45 to 90 minutes, respondents can be probed to reveal their real motivations, feelings, behaviors, and aspirations.

The object of a **focus-group interview** is to observe group interaction when members are exposed to an idea or a concept. General Motors, for example, used focus groups comprised of celebrity athletes, actors, and musicians, including XZibit, as part of its effort to redesign the Cadillac Escalade SUV and CTS sedan.[26] Focus-group interviews are often conducted informally, without a structured questionnaire, in small groups of 8 to 12 people. They allow customer attitudes, behaviors, lifestyles, needs, and desires to be explored in a flexible and creative manner. Questions are open-ended and stimulate respondents to answer in their own words. Researchers can ask probing questions to clarify something they do not fully understand or something unexpected and interesting that may help explain buying behavior. For example, Ford may use focus groups to determine whether to change its advertising to emphasize a vehicle's safety features rather than its style and performance. On the other hand, focus-group participants do not always tell the truth. Some participants may be less than honest in an effort to be sociable or to receive money and/or food in exchange for their participation. Research has found a poor correlation between stated intent and actual purchase behavior.[27] It may be necessary to use separate focus groups for each major market segment studied—men, women, and age groups—and experts recommend the use of at least two focus groups per segment in case one group is unusually idiosyncratic.[28]

**customer advisory boards** Small groups of actual customers who serve as sounding boards for new product ideas and offer insights into their feelings and attitudes toward a firm's products and other elements of marketing strategy

More organizations are starting **customer advisory boards**, which are small groups of actual customers who serve as sounding boards for new product ideas and offer insights into their feelings and attitudes toward a firm's products, promotion,

# A Look-Look at Trendsetters

Look-Look.com is an online, real-time service that provides accurate and reliable information, research, and news about trendsetting youths ages 14 to 30. With this age group spending an estimated $140 billion a year, many companies are willing to shell out an annual subscription fee of about $20,000 for access to this valuable data.

Look-Look pays more than 35,000 handpicked, prescreened young people from all over the world to e-mail the company information about their styles, trends, opinions, and ideas. This group of selected youth represents the trendsetters—forward-thinking innovators who influence their peers. (Although trendsetters account for only about 20 percent of the youth population, they influence the other 80 percent.) Look-Look also has 20 photographers who travel the globe capturing youth trends in photos.

Through the Internet and the company's intranet, Look-Look clients have access to results of surveys and polls. These clients can uncover information on the latest fashion and technology trends, entertain-

ment preferences, eating and drinking habits, and health and beauty issues of today's young people. They can also access the City Guide, which lists most preferred shops, hangouts, and restaurants in selected cities. Clients who may want to know the answer to a specific question can key that question into a search feature and reach a worldwide focus group 24 hours a day. Clients include an apparel company, video game manufacturers, a cosmetics company, beverage firms, and movie studios. Look-Look co-presidents DeeDee Gordon and Sharon Lee believe that full understanding of the youth culture requires a constant dialogue with young people—an understanding not achieved by a once- or twice-a-year focus group or by traditional market research.

## marketing ENTREPRENEURS

**Marc Ecko**

HIS BUSINESS: Ecko Unlimited

FOUNDED: 1993

SUCCESS: $400 million/year revenues

When he was 20 years old, graffiti artist Marc Milecofsky started a clothing line with just six hand-painted T-shirt designs. The line, Ecko Unlimited, took off when rapper Chuck D and director Spike Lee were seen in Ecko's shirts. Now, with annual revenue in the neighborhood of $400 million a year, Ecko Unlimited has become one of the hottest urban apparel firms on the market. Ecko stays up to date on what consumers want by hanging out and talking with people in social hot spots, and focuses on point-of-sale instead of mass-media advertising in order to connect with consumers. Ecko now offers a variety of lines and products that include gloves, hats, watches, outerwear, underwear, and shoes.

**telephone depth interview** An interview that combines the traditional focus group's ability to probe with the confidentiality provided by telephone surveys

**shopping mall intercept interviews** A research method that involves interviewing a percentage of individuals passing by "intercept" points in a mall

**on-site computer interview** A variation of the shopping mall intercept interview in which respondents complete a self-administered questionnaire displayed on a computer monitor

pricing, and other elements of marketing strategy. While these advisory boards help companies maintain strong relationships with valuable customers, they can also provide great insight into marketing research questions.[29] Northwest Airlines, for example, formed an 11-member Customer Advisory Board on Disabilities to obtain guidance and recommendations on how the airline can better serve air travelers with disabilities.[30]

Still another option is the **telephone depth interview**, which combines the traditional focus group's ability to probe with the confidentiality provided by a telephone survey. This type of interview is most appropriate for qualitative research projects among a small targeted group that is difficult to bring together for a traditional focus group because of members' professions, locations, or lifestyles. Respondents can choose the time and day for the interview. Although this method is difficult to implement, it can yield revealing information from respondents who otherwise would be unwilling to participate in marketing research.[31]

The nature of personal interviews has changed. In the past, most personal interviews, which were based on random sampling or prearranged appointments, were conducted in the respondent's home. Today most personal interviews are conducted in shopping malls. **Shopping mall intercept interviews** involve interviewing a percentage of individuals passing by certain "intercept" points in a mall. Like any face-to-face interviewing method, mall intercept interviewing has many advantages. The interviewer is in a position to recognize and react to respondents' nonverbal indications of confusion. Respondents can be shown product prototypes, videotapes of commercials, and the like, and asked for their reactions. The mall environment lets the researcher deal with complex situations. For example, in taste tests, researchers know that all the respondents are reacting to the same product, which can be prepared and monitored from the mall test kitchen. In addition to the ability to conduct tests requiring bulky equipment, lower cost and greater control make shopping mall intercept interviews popular.

An **on-site computer interview** is a variation of the shopping mall intercept interview in which respondents complete a self-administered questionnaire displayed on a computer monitor. A computer software package can be used to conduct such interviews in shopping malls. After a brief lesson on how to operate the software, respondents can proceed through the survey at their own pace. Questionnaires can be adapted so that respondents see only those items (usually a subset of an entire scale) that may provide useful information about their attitudes.[32]

*Questionnaire Construction.* A carefully constructed questionnaire is essential to the success of any survey. Questions must be clear, easy to understand, and directed toward a specific objective; that is, they must be designed to elicit information that meets the study's data requirements. Researchers need to define the objective before trying to develop a questionnaire because the objective determines the substance of the questions and the amount of detail. A common mistake in constructing questionnaires is to ask questions that interest the researchers but do not yield information useful in deciding whether to accept or reject a hypothesis. Finally, the most important rule in composing questions is to maintain impartiality.

The questions are usually of three kinds: open-ended, dichotomous, and multiple-choice.

**Open-Ended Question**

How do you feel about broadband Internet access for your computer?

_____

_____

_____

**Dichotomous Question**

Do you presently have broadband access at home, work, or school?

Yes _____ No _____

**Multiple-Choice Question**

What age group are you in?

Under 20 _____

20–29 _____

30–39 _____

40–49 _____

50–59 _____

60 and over _____

    Problems may develop in the analysis of dichotomous or multiple-choice questions when responses for one outcome outnumber others. For example, a dichotomous question asking respondents to choose between "buy" or "not buy" might require additional sampling from the disproportionately smaller group if there were not enough responses to analyze.[33]

    Researchers must also be very careful about questions that a respondent might consider too personal or that might require an admission of activities that other people are likely to condemn. Questions of this type should be worded to make them less offensive.

***Observation Methods.*** In using observation methods, researchers record individuals' overt behavior, taking note of physical conditions and events. Direct contact with them is avoided; instead, their actions are examined and noted systematically. For instance, researchers might use observation methods to answer the question "How long does the average McDonald's restaurant customer have to wait in line before being served?" Observation may include the use of ethnographic techniques, such as watching customers interact with a product in a real-world environment.

    Kimberly-Clark researchers employed ethnographic techniques when they asked a few consumers to wear a glasses-mounted camera so that they could observe how the consumers used Huggies baby wipes. The research revealed that parents were changing their babies on top of beds, floors, and even washing machines where they were struggling with wipe containers requiring two hands. Based on this research, the company redesigned the package so that the product can more easily be used with one hand.[34]

    Observation may also be combined with interviews. For example, during a personal interview, the condition of a respondent's home or other possessions may be observed and recorded. The interviewer can also directly observe and confirm such demographic information as race, approximate age, and gender.

    Data gathered through observation can sometimes be biased if the person is aware of the observation process. However, an observer can be placed in a natural market environment, such as a grocery store, without influencing shoppers' actions. If the presence of a human observer is likely to bias the outcome or if human sensory abilities are inadequate, mechanical means may be used to record behavior. Mechanical observation devices include cameras, recorders, counting machines, scanners, and equipment that records physiological changes. A special camera can be used to record the eye movements of people as they look at an advertisement; the camera detects the sequence of reading and the parts of the advertisement that receive greatest attention. The electronic scanners used in supermarkets are very useful in marketing research: they provide accurate data on sales and customers' purchase patterns, and marketing researchers may buy such data from the supermarkets.

Observation is straightforward and avoids a central problem of survey methods: motivating respondents to state their true feelings or opinions. However, observation tends to be descriptive. When it is the only method of data collection, it may not provide insights into causal relationships. Another drawback is that analyses based on observation are subject to the observer's biases or the limitations of the mechanical device.

## Interpreting Research Findings

After collecting data to test their hypotheses, marketers need to interpret the research findings. Interpretation of the data is easier if marketers carefully plan their data analysis methods early in the research process. They should also allow for continual evaluation of the data during the entire collection period. They can then gain valuable insights into areas that should be probed during the formal interpretation.

The first step in drawing conclusions from most research is to display the data in table format. If marketers intend to apply the results to individual categories of the things or people being studied, cross-tabulation may be useful, especially in tabulating joint occurrences. For example, using the two variables of gender and purchase rates of automobile tires, a cross-tabulation could show how men and women differ in purchasing automobile tires.

**statistical interpretation** Analysis of what is typical or what deviates from the average

After the data are tabulated, they must be analyzed. **Statistical interpretation** focuses on what is typical or what deviates from the average. It indicates how widely responses vary and how they are distributed in relation to the variable being measured. When marketers interpret statistics, they must take into account estimates of

**Interpreting Research**

Companies like Burke can help interpret the data collected from market research and offer insights into the areas to be investigated.

expected error or deviation from the true values of the population. The analysis of data may lead researchers to accept or reject the hypothesis being studied. Data require careful interpretation by the marketer. If the results of a study are valid, the decision maker should take action; if a question has been incorrectly or poorly worded, however, the results may produce poor decisions. Consider the research conducted for a food marketer that asked respondents to rate a product on criteria such as "hearty flavor," as well as how important each criterion was to the respondent. Although such results may have had utility for advertising purposes, they were less helpful in product development because it was not possible to discern respondents' meaning of "hearty flavor."[35] Managers must understand the research results and relate them to a context that permits effective decision making.

### Reporting Research Findings

The final step in the marketing research process is to report the research findings. Before preparing the report, the marketer must take a clear, objective look at the findings to see how well the gathered facts answer the research question or support or negate the initial hypotheses. In most cases, it is extremely doubtful that the study can provide everything needed to answer the research question. Thus, the researcher must point out the deficiencies, and the reasons for them, in the report.

The report of research results is usually a formal, written document. Researchers must allow time for the writing task when they plan and schedule the project. Because the report is a means of communicating with the decision makers who will use the research findings, researchers need to determine beforehand how much detail and supporting data to include. They should keep in mind that corporate executives prefer reports that are short, clear, and simply expressed. Researchers often give their summary and recommendations first, especially if decision makers do not have time to study how the results were obtained. A technical report allows its users to analyze data and interpret recommendations because it describes the research methods and procedures and the most important data gathered. Thus, researchers must recognize the needs and expectations of the report user and adapt to them.

Bias and distortion can be a major problem if the researcher is intent on obtaining favorable results. For example, research analyzing consumers' reports of their frequency of using long-distance telephone calls, letters, cards, and visits for personal communication found that some groups underreport their usage, whereas other groups overreport it. In particular, researchers found that consumers underestimate the duration of lengthy telephone calls but overestimate the length of short ones; in general, people tend to overestimate both the frequency and duration of their telephone calls. Without this information, companies relying on survey results may get a distorted view of the market for long-distance telephone services by mistakenly judging it to be larger and more homogeneous than it really is.[36]

Marketing researchers want to know about behavior and opinions, and they want accurate data to help them in making decisions. Careful wording of questions is very important because a biased or emotional word can dramatically change the results. Marketing research and marketing information systems can provide an organization with accurate and reliable customer feedback, which a marketer must have to understand the dynamics of the marketplace. As managers recognize the benefits of marketing research, they assign it a much larger role in decision making.

# Using Technology to Improve Marketing Information Gathering and Analysis

Technology is making information for marketing decisions increasingly accessible. The ability of marketers to track customer buying behavior and to better discern what buyers want is changing the nature of marketing. Customer relationship management is being enhanced by integrating data from all customer contacts and com-

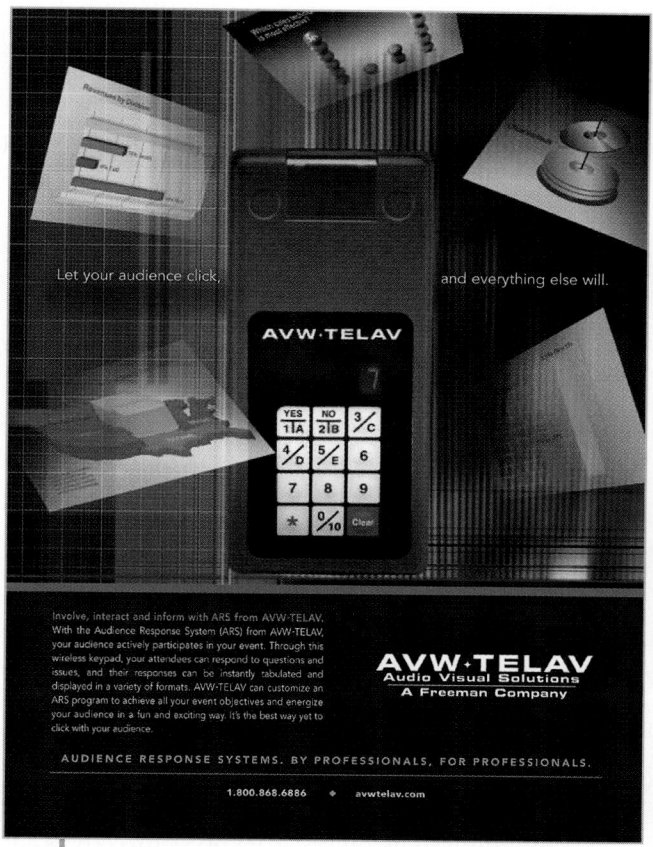

**Using Technology**
AVW-TELAV and Blackbaud provide high-tech audience response systems to assist in data collection.

**marketing information system (MIS)** A framework for managing and structuring information gathered regularly from sources inside and outside the organization

bining that information to improve customer retention. Information technology permits internal research and quick information gathering to help marketers better understand and satisfy customers. For example, company responses to e-mail complaints as well as to communications through mail, telephone, and personal contact can be used to improve customer satisfaction, retention, and value.[37] Armed with such information, marketers can fine-tune marketing mixes to satisfy their customers' needs.

The integration of telecommunications and computer technologies is allowing marketers to access a growing array of valuable information sources related to industry forecasts, business trends, and customer buying behavior. Electronic communication tools can be effectively used to gain accurate information with minimal customer interaction. Most marketing researchers have e-mail, voice mail, teleconferencing, and fax machines at their disposal. In fact, many firms use marketing information systems to network all these technologies and organize all the marketing data available to them. In this section, we look at marketing information systems and specific technologies that are helping marketing researchers obtain and manage marketing research data.

## Marketing Information Systems

A **marketing information system (MIS)** is a framework for the day-to-day management and structuring of information gathered regularly from sources both inside and outside the organization. As such, an MIS provides a continuous flow of information about prices, advertising expenditures, sales, competition, and distribution expenses. Anheuser-Busch, for example, uses a system called BudNet that compiles information about past sales at individual stores, inventory, competitors' displays and prices, and a host of other information collected by distributors' sales representatives on handheld computers. BudNet allows managers to respond quickly to changes in

**Interactive Marketing Research**
Workplace Print Media helps its customers to find customers.

competitors' strategies with an appropriate promotional message, package, display, or discount.[38]

The main focus of the MIS is on data storage and retrieval, as well as on computer capabilities and management's information requirements. Regular reports of sales by product or market categories, data on inventory levels, and records of salespeople's activities are examples of information that is useful in making decisions. In the MIS, the means of gathering data receive less attention than do the procedures for expediting the flow of information.

An effective MIS starts by determining the objective of the information, that is, by identifying decision needs that require certain information. The firm can then specify an information system for continuous monitoring to provide regular, pertinent information on both the external and internal environment. FedEx, for example, has developed interactive marketing systems to provide instantaneous communication between the company and its customers. Via either telephone or the Internet, customers can track their packages and receive immediate feedback concerning delivery. The company's website provides valuable information about customer usage and allows customers to express directly what they think about company services. The evolving telecommunications and computer technologies are allowing marketing information systems to cultivate one-to-one relationships with customers.

## Databases

Most marketing information systems include internal databases. As mentioned in Chapter 8, a database is a collection of information arranged for easy access and retrieval. Databases allow marketers to tap into an abundance of information useful in making marketing decisions: internal sales reports, newspaper articles, company news releases, government economic reports, bibliographies, and more, often accessed through a computer system. Information technology has made it possible to develop databases to guide strategic planning and help improve customer services. When Pulte Homes, the nation's top homebuilder, analyzed information in its database, it realized that 80 percent of its home buyers were selecting the same countertops, carpet, fixtures, lighting, and the like. The company used that information to streamline its 2,000 floor plans and reduce the number of fixtures and other home features to better match customer desires and to improve overall efficiency and decision making.[39] Many commercial websites require consumers to register and provide personal information to access the site or make a purchase. Frequent flier programs permit airlines to ask loyal customers to participate in surveys about their needs and desires, and to track their best customers' flight patterns by time of day, week, month, and year. Supermarkets gain a significant amount of data through checkout scanners tied to store discount cards. In fact, one of the best ways to predict market behavior is the use of database information gathered through loyalty programs or other transaction-based processes.[40]

Marketing researchers can also use commercial databases developed by information research firms, such as LexisNexis, to obtain useful information for marketing decisions. Many of these commercial databases are accessible online for a fee. They

# Data Mining at Wal-Mart

Wal-Mart is not only the world's largest retailer, it also operates the world's largest data warehouse, an organizationwide data collection and storage system that gathers data from all of the firm's critical operation systems as well as from selected external data sources. Wal-Mart's data warehouse contains more than 460 terabytes of data stored on mainframe computers; experts believe the Internet comprises less than half that amount of data.

Wal-Mart collects reams of data about products and customers primarily from checkout scanners at its Wal-Mart discount and Sam's Club membership stores. Clerks and managers may also use wireless handheld units to gather additional inventory data. The company stores the detailed data and classifies it into categories such as product, individual store, or region. The system also serves as a basis for the Retail Link decision-support system between Wal-Mart and its suppliers. Retail Link permits some vendors, like Kraft, to access data about how well their products are selling at Wal-Mart stores.

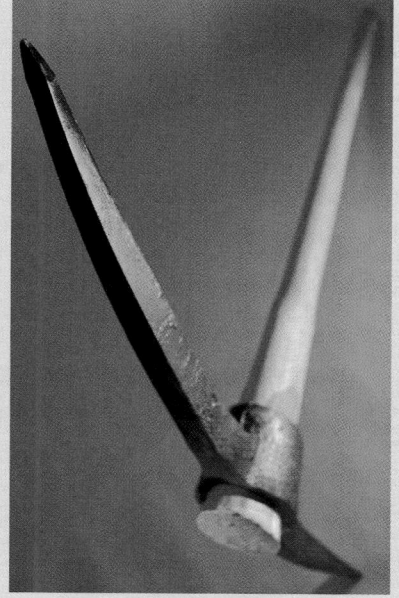

The mountain of data Wal-Mart collects helps boost efficiency dramatically by matching product supplies to demand. This information, for example, helped the firm determine to stock not only flashlights but also extra strawberry Pop-Tarts prior to a hurricane in Florida. It seems that Pop-Tart sales increase as much as seven times their normal rate ahead of a hurricane. The data may also help the company track supplier performance, set ideal prices, and even determine how many cashiers to schedule at a certain store on a certain day. Most important, it helps the retailer avoid carrying too much inventory or not having enough to satisfy demand.

can also be obtained in printed form or on computer compact discs (CD-ROMs). With most commercial databases, the user typically conducts a computer search by keyword, topic, or company, and the database service generates abstracts, articles, or reports that can then be printed out. Accessing multiple reports or a complete article may cost extra.

Information provided by a single firm on household demographics, purchases, television viewing behavior, and responses to promotions such as coupons and free samples is called **single-source data**.[41] For example, Behavior Scan, offered by Information Resources, Inc., screens about 60,000 households in 26 U.S. markets. This single-source information service monitors consumer household televisions and records the programs and commercials watched. When buyers from these households shop in stores equipped with scanning registers, they present Hotline cards (similar to credit cards) to cashiers. This enables each customer's identification to be electronically coded so the firm can track each product purchased and store the information in a database. It is important to gather longitudinal (long-term) information on customers to maximize the usefulness of single-source data.[42]

## Marketing Decision Support Systems

A **marketing decision support system (MDSS)** is customized computer software that aids marketing managers in decision making by helping them anticipate the effects of certain decisions. Some decision support systems have a broader range and offer greater computational and modeling capabilities than spreadsheets; they let managers explore a greater number of alternatives. For example, an MDSS can determine

**single-source data** Information provided by a single marketing research firm

**marketing decision support system (MDSS)** Customized computer software that aids marketing managers in decision making

how sales and profits might be affected by higher or lower interest rates or how sales forecasts, advertising expenditures, production levels, and the like, might affect overall profits. For this reason, MDSS software is often a major component of a company's marketing information system. Customized decision support systems can support a customer orientation and customer satisfaction in business marketing.[43] Some decision support systems incorporate artificial intelligence and other advanced computer technologies.

## The Internet and Online Information Services

The Internet has evolved as a most powerful communication medium, linking customers and companies around the world in computer networks via e-mail, forums, webpages, and more. Growth of the Internet, and especially the World Wide Web, has launched an entire industry that is working to make marketing information easily accessible to both marketing firms and customers.

Table 9.3 lists a number of websites that can be valuable resources for marketing research. The U.S. Census Bureau, for example, uses the World Wide Web to disseminate information that may be useful to marketing researchers, particularly through the *Statistical Abstract of the United States* and data from the most recent census. Among the companies that exploit census data for marketing decisions are Starbucks, which analyzes the data to assess potential coffee shop sites, and Blockbuster, which mines the data to help determine how many copies of a particular movie or video game to offer at each store.[44]

| table 9.3 | RESOURCES FOR MARKETING INFORMATION |
| --- | --- |
| **Government Sources** | |
| FedWorld | **www.fedworld.gov** |
| U.S. Census Bureau | **www.census.gov** |
| U.S. Department of State | **www.state.gov** |
| **Commercial Sources** | |
| ACNielsen | **www.acnielsen.com** |
| Arbitron | **www.arbitron.com** |
| Gallup | **www.gallup.com** |
| Information Resources, Inc. | **www.infores.com** |
| **Periodicals and Books** | |
| *Advertising Age* | **www.adage.com** |
| *Bloomberg Report* | **www.bloomberg.com** |
| *Business 2.0* | **www.business2.com** |
| *Business Week* | **www.businessweek.com** |
| *Fast Company* | **www.fastcompany.com** |
| *Fortune* | **www.fortune.com** |
| *Inc.* | **www.inc.com** |
| *Sales & Marketing Management* | **www.salesandmarketing.com** |

With two decades of data collection experience, Western Wats knows how to get the specific information you need quickly and accurately. **Opinion Outpost**, our online research panel, delivers reliable data under time-compressed project schedules with the highest quality available in the industry. We provide the research you have come to know and trust, at the price you've been searching for.

**Our panel members are waiting**
. . . and they've got opinions.

**Call**
**(877)254-1234**

Opinion Outpost.     Western Wats®

www.opinionoutpost.com

**Internet Research**

Opinion Outpost provides its customers with research delivered by a readily available online panel.

Companies can also mine their own websites for useful information. Amazon.com, for example, has built a relationship with its customers by tracking the types of books and music they purchase. Each time a customer logs on to the website, the company can offer recommendations based on the customer's previous purchases. Such a marketing system helps the company track the changing desires and buying habits of its most valued customers.

Marketing researchers can also subscribe to online services such as MSN, AOL, and LexisNexis. These services typically offer their subscribers such specialized services as databases, news services, and forums, as well as access to the Internet itself. Marketers can subscribe to "mailing lists" that periodically deliver electronic newsletters to their computer screens, and they can participate in on-screen discussions with thousands of network users. This enhanced communication with a firm's customers, suppliers, and employees provides a high-speed link that boosts the capabilities of the firm's marketing information system. Many marketers turn to search engines like Google for information for free.

While most webpages are open to anyone with Internet access, big companies like Cisco Systems also maintain internal webpages, called *intranets,* that allow employees to access such internal data as customer profiles and product inventory—information once hidden in databases only technicians could unlock. Such sensitive corporate information can be protected from outside users of the World Wide Web by special security software called *firewalls.* IBM uses its intranets to help its 300,000 employees around the world collaborate on projects. In addition to improving communications, the system has helped the company slash training and travel expenses by nearly $400 million.[45]

# Issues in Marketing Research

## The Importance of Ethical Marketing Research

Marketing managers and other professionals are relying more and more on marketing research, marketing information systems, and new technologies to make better decisions. It is therefore essential that professional standards be established by which to judge the reliability of marketing research. Such standards are necessary because of the ethical and legal issues that develop in gathering marketing research data. In addition, the relationships between research suppliers, such as marketing research agencies, and the marketing managers who make strategy decisions require ethical behavior. Organizations such as the Marketing Research Association have developed codes of conduct and guidelines to promote ethical marketing research. To be effective, such guidelines must instruct marketing researchers on how to avoid misconduct. Following are nine guidelines interviewers should follow when introducing a questionnaire.[46]

1. Allow interviewers to introduce themselves by name.

2. State the name of the research company.

3. Indicate this is a marketing research project.

4. Explain there will be no sales involved.

5. Note the general topic of discussion (if this is a problem in a "blind" study, a statement such as "consumer opinion" is acceptable).

6. State the likely duration of the interview.

7. Assure the anonymity of the respondent and confidentiality of all answers.

8. State the honorarium if applicable (for many business-to-business and medical studies, this is done up front for both qualitative and quantitative studies).

9. Reassure the respondent with a statement such as, "There are no right or wrong answers, so please give thoughtful and honest answers to each question" (recommended by many clients).

## International Issues in Marketing Research

As we saw in Chapter 7, sociocultural, economic, political, legal, and technological forces vary in different regions of the world. These variations create challenges for organizations attempting to understand foreign customers through marketing research. The marketing research process we describe in this chapter is used globally, but to ensure the research is valid and reliable, data-gathering methods may have to be modified to allow for regional differences. For example, experts have found that Latin Americans do not respond well to focus groups or in-depth interviews lasting more than 90 minutes. Researchers therefore need to adjust their tactics to generate information useful for marketing products in Latin America.[47] To ensure that global and regional differences are satisfactorily addressed, many companies retain a research firm with experience in the country of interest. Most of the largest marketing research firms derive a significant share of their revenues from research conducted outside the United States. As Table 9.4 indicates, VNU, Inc., the largest marketing research firm in the world, received 48 percent of its revenues from outside the United States.[48]

Experts recommend a two-pronged approach to international marketing research. The first phase involves a detailed search for and analysis of secondary data to gain greater understanding of a particular marketing environment and to pinpoint issues that must be taken into account in gathering primary research data. Secondary data can be particularly helpful in building a general understanding of the market, including economic, legal, cultural, and demographic issues, as well as in assessing the risks of doing business in that market and in forecasting demand.[49] Marketing researchers often begin by studying country trade reports from the U.S. Department of Commerce as well as country-specific information from local sources, such as a

| table 9.4 | TOP MARKETING RESEARCH FIRMS | |
|---|---|---|
| Company | Global Revenues (millions U.S. dollars) | % Revenues from Outside U.S. |
| 1. VNU, Inc. | 3,429 | 47.7 |
| 2. IMS Health, Inc. | 1,569 | 63.6 |
| 3. Westat, Inc. | 398 | – |
| 4. TNS U.S. | 1,732 | 77.2 |
| 5. Information Resources, Inc. | 573 | 33.6 |

**Source:** "Honomichl Top 50," *Marketing News*, June 15, 2005, pp. H1+.

country's website, and trade and general business publications such as the *Wall Street Journal*. These sources can offer insights into the marketing environment in a particular country and can even indicate untapped market opportunities abroad.

The second phase involves field research using many of the methods described earlier, including focus groups and telephone surveys, to refine a firm's understanding of specific customer needs and preferences. Specific differences among countries can have a profound influence on data gathering. For example, in-home (door-to-door) interviews are illegal in some countries. In China, few people have regular telephone lines, making telephone surveys both impractical and nonrepresentative of the total population. Primary data gathering may have a greater chance of success if the firm employs local researchers who better understand how to approach potential respondents and can do so in their own language.[50] Regardless of the specific methods used to gather primary data, whether in the United States or abroad, the goal is to better understand the needs of specific target markets to craft the best marketing strategy to satisfy the needs of customers in each market, as we will see in the next chapter.

## SUMMARY

Marketing research is the systematic design, collection, interpretation, and reporting of information to help marketers solve specific marketing problems or take advantage of marketing opportunities. It is a process for gathering information not currently available to decision makers. Marketing research can help a firm better understand market opportunities, ascertain the potential for success for new products, and determine the feasibility of a particular marketing strategy. The value of marketing research is measured by improvements in a marketer's ability to make decisions.

To maintain the control needed to obtain accurate information, marketers approach marketing research as a process with logical steps: (1) locating and defining problems or issues, (2) designing the research project, (3) collecting data, (4) interpreting research findings, and (5) reporting research findings.

The first step in launching a research study, problem or issue definition, focuses on uncovering the nature and boundaries of a situation or question related to marketing strategy or implementation. When a firm discovers a market opportunity, it may need to conduct research to understand the situation more precisely so it can craft an appropriate marketing strategy.

In the second step, marketing researchers design a research project to obtain the information needed to address it. This step requires formulating a hypothesis and determining what type of research to employ to test the hypothesis so the results are reliable and valid. A hypothesis is an informed guess or assumption about a problem or set of circumstances. Marketers conduct exploratory research when they need more information about a problem or want to make a tentative hypothesis more specific; they use conclusive research to verify insights through an objective procedure. Research is considered reliable if it produces almost identical results in repeated trials; it is valid if it measures what it is supposed to measure.

For the third step of the research process, collecting data, two types of data are available. Primary data are observed and recorded or collected directly from respondents; secondary data are compiled inside or outside the organization for some purpose other than the current investigation. Sources of secondary data include an organization's own database and other internal sources, periodicals, government publications, unpublished sources, and online databases. Methods of collecting primary data include sampling, surveys, observation, and experimentation. Sampling involves selecting representative units from a total population. In probability sampling, every element in the population being studied has a known chance of being selected for study. Nonprobability sampling is more subjective than probability sampling because there is no way to calculate the likelihood that a specific element of the population being studied will be chosen. Marketing researchers employ sampling to collect primary data through mail, telephone, online, or personal interview surveys. A carefully constructed questionnaire is essential to the success of any survey. In using observation methods, researchers record respondents' overt behavior and take note of physical conditions and events. In an experiment, marketing researchers attempt to maintain certain variables while measuring the effects of experimental variables.

To apply research data to decision making, marketers must interpret and report their findings properly—the final two steps in the marketing research process. Statistical interpretation focuses on what is typical or what deviates from the average. After interpreting the research findings, the researchers must prepare a report on the findings that the decision makers can understand and use. Researchers must also take care to avoid bias and distortion.

Many firms use computer technology to create a marketing information system (MIS), a framework for managing and structuring information gathered regularly from sources both inside and outside the organization. A database is a collection of information arranged for easy access and retrieval. A marketing decision support system (MDSS) is customized computer software that aids marketing managers in decision making by helping them anticipate the effects of certain decisions. Online information services and the Internet also enable marketers to communicate with customers and obtain information.

Eliminating unethical marketing research practices and establishing generally acceptable procedures for conducting research are important goals of marketing research. Both domestic and international marketing use the same marketing research process, but international marketing may require modifying data-gathering methods to address regional differences.

**ACE self-test**

Please visit the student website at **www.prideferrell.com** for ACE Self-Test questions that will help you prepare for exams.

## IMPORTANT TERMS

Marketing research
Research design
Hypothesis
Exploratory research
Conclusive research
Descriptive research
Experimental research
Reliability
Validity
Primary data

Secondary data
Population
Sample
Sampling
Probability sampling
Random sampling
Stratified sampling
Nonprobability sampling
Quota sampling
Mail survey

Telephone survey
Online survey
Personal interview survey
In-home (door-to-door) interview
Focus-group interview
Customer advisory boards
Telephone depth interview
Shopping mall intercept interview

On-site computer interview
Statistical interpretation
Marketing information system (MIS)
Single-source data
Marketing decision support system (MDSS)

## DISCUSSION & REVIEW QUESTIONS

1. What is marketing research? Why is it important?

2. Describe the five steps in the marketing research process.

3. What is the difference between defining a research problem and developing a hypothesis?

4. Describe the different types of approaches to marketing research and indicate when each should be used.

5. Where are data for marketing research obtained? Give examples of internal and external data.

6. What is the difference between probability sampling and nonprobability sampling? In what situation would random sampling be best? Stratified sampling? Quota sampling?

7. Suggest some ways to encourage respondents to cooperate in mail surveys.

8. If a survey of all homes with listed telephone numbers is to be conducted, what sampling design should be used?

9. Describe some marketing problems that could be solved through information gained from observation.

10. What is a marketing information system, and what should it provide?

11. Define a database. What is its purpose, and what does it include?

12. How can marketers use online services and the Internet to obtain information for decision making?

13. What role does ethics play in marketing research? Why is it important that marketing researchers be ethical?

14. How does marketing research in other countries differ from marketing research in the United States?

## APPLICATION QUESTIONS

1. After observing customers' traffic patterns, Bashas' Markets repositioned the greeting card section in its stores, and card sales increased substantially. To increase sales for the following types of companies, what information might marketing researchers want to gather from customers?

   a. Furniture stores

   b. Gasoline outlets/service stations

   c. Investment companies

   d. Medical clinics

2. When a company wants to conduct research, it must first identify a problem or possible opportunity to market its goods or services. Choose a company in your city that you think might benefit from a research project. Develop a research question and outline a method to approach this question. Explain why you think the research question is relevant to the organization and why the particular methodology is suited to the question and the company.

3. Input for marketing information systems can come from internal or external sources. ACNielsen Corporation is the largest provider of single-source marketing research in the world. Identify two firms in your city that might benefit from internal sources and two that might benefit from external sources. Explain why these sources would be useful to these companies. Suggest the type of information each company should gather.

4. Suppose you are opening a health insurance brokerage firm and want to market your services to small businesses with fewer than 50 employees. Determine which database for marketing information you will use in your marketing efforts, and explain why you will use it.

globalEDGE™

1. Your firm is considering entering the Japanese information technology market, and you have been asked to analyze the top 10 Japanese companies in this industry. One way to begin your research on this market segment is to access *BusinessWeek*'s Global 1,000 firms by using the search term "top global companies" at **http://globaledge.msu.edu/ibrd**. Once there, click on the Country-by-Country scoreboard to find the best document for analysis. Considering the criteria given, prepare a summary that includes the largest and smallest firms. In addition, describe which firms are the most and least healthy.

2. For a marketing research company, an important element in gathering data for a market is the level of information technology (IT) infrastructure that exists. NationMaster.com's website offers a subcategory of Personal Computers (PCs) that can provide insight on the level of personal computer (PC) usage in a country. Use the search term "compare various statistics" at **http://globaledge.msu.edu/ibrd** to reach NationMaster.com. Select the Media category and then the subcategory of Personal Computers (PCs). Give a summary of the top 15 countries as ranked by the number of PCs used. From this specified list of markets, include an assessment of the three countries with the most and least access to PCs. What conclusions can you make?

## INTERNET Exercise

Visit **www.prideferrell.com** for resources to help you master the material in this chapter, plus materials that will help you expand your marketing knowledge, including Internet exercise updates, ACE Self-Tests, hotlinks to companies featured in this chapter, and much more.

## World Association of Opinion and Marketing Research Professionals

The World Association of Opinion and Marketing Research Professionals (ESOMAR, founded as the European Society for Opinion and Marketing Research in 1948) is a nonprofit association for marketing research professionals. ESOMAR promotes the use of opinion and marketing research to improve marketing decisions in companies worldwide and works to protect personal privacy in the research process. Visit the association's website at **www.esomar.nl**.

1. How can ESOMAR help marketing professionals conduct research to guide marketing strategy?
2. How can ESOMAR help marketers protect the privacy of research subjects when conducting marketing research in other countries?
3. ESOMAR introduced the first professional code of conduct for marketing research professionals in 1948. The association continues to update the document to address new technology and other changes in the marketing environment. According to ESOMAR's code, what are the specific professional responsibilities of marketing researchers?

## Video Case 9.1

## Getting to the Heart of the Matter: Research Design at LSPMA

Lake, Snell, Perry, Mermin & Associates, Inc. (LSPMA) is a national public opinion and political strategy research firm. Its expertise lies in conducting objective opinion polls to assess the attitudes and behaviors of important target groups that concern its clients. The Washington, D.C.–based firm is nationally recognized for its knowledge of women's issues, children's and youth's concerns, and environmental political issues. Among the company's clients are the Democratic National Committee, the Democratic Governor's Association, Sierra Club, Planned Parenthood, Human Rights Campaign, Emily's List, and the Kaiser Foundation. LSPMA also conducts regular polls for *U.S. News & World Report,* and with the Terrance Group it conducts the Battleground Poll, which surveys the year's political landscape and draws attention to critical issues that Washington insiders can't afford to ignore. In 2005 LPSMA acquired the Washington- and San Diego–based polling firm Decision Research, giving it even greater capacity to conduct research for both business and political clients.

LSPMA's primary goal is to discover what the public thinks for people who want to know. Its staff serves as among the Democratic Party's leading strategists, acting as tacticians and senior advisers to dozens of political incumbents and challengers at all levels of the electoral process, as well as to a wide range of advocacy organizations, nonprofit organizations, and foundations. Its client base is split evenly among three groups: political candidates such as senators and governors; progressive issue organizations that want research on social issues such as poverty, education, health care, and teen pregnancy; and foundations or major institutions such as the American Cancer Society.

Through research techniques, including reconnaissance and espionage, LSPMA gathers and presents hard data regarding what specific segments of the public think about certain issues or candidates. LSPMA's work helps clients identify potential problems or opportunities and determine what strategies and messages would best help them achieve their goals and reach their target audiences. It is important to know what different segments of the population think, feel, and need so that advertising can then be targeted at the people that organizations want to reach. LSPMA uses a variety of methods, including telephone interviews, online polls, and focus groups, to create portraits of groups of people, such as "soccer moms," "waitress moms," or "NASCAR dads," so that its clients can understand these segments and recognize important trends.

Research allows LSPMA's clients to know what Americans are thinking and helps them determine how to target those segments of the population who are likely to think their firm has the right product or the right candidate. It allows clients to understand where they are most vulnerable and where they have the greatest opportunities to gain more support. By knowing which people feel strongly, which are sitting on the fence, and which are capable of changing their opinions, it is possible to segment people depending on what they think and how they act and behave. Once organizations know whom to target and which issues are most important to those they wish to target, they can narrow their approaches to accomplish their goals in the most cost-efficient way.

There are many reasons to segment the public. Since people are different, segmentation enables marketers and pollsters to cluster together like-minded people to better understand who they are. It is then possible to craft a message that precisely targets a particular audience. Markets can be segmented by age, gender, education, geographic region, income, or race to create new ways of looking at a group that tends to behave similarly.

There are pitfalls to segmentation, however. It can sometimes make people seem more diverse than they actually are. For example, women hold similar views on 80 percent of political issues. Segmentation can help an individual or organization only so much; the rest depends on the hottest new trends. Few groups are static or truly homogeneous, which means that continuous research is necessary to remain up to date with changes in attitudes and behaviors and to ensure that messages still reach their target audiences.

Like all marketing research firms, LSPMA plans its marketing research strategy well in advance, including such details as deciding what questions to ask, which audience to target, in what setting to target them, what time frame to use, and how to manage costs. It enables the firm to know what it has to do and how to do it. All research firms, regardless of their clients, create information for more informed understanding and decisions. [51]

### Questions for Discussion

1. Why do political organizations need marketing research conducted by LSPMA?
2. What is the relationship between marketing research conducted by LSPMA and identifying the needs and wants of specific market segments?
3. Why would a business rely on a marketing research firm that is heavily into political polling?

---

## Case 9.2     Best Buy Uncovers Angels in the Market

Best Buy Company, Inc. is a retailer of consumer electronics, home-office products, entertainment software, appliances, and related services. One of the company's goals is to make life easier and more fun for consumers. To meet that objective, the company's retail environment focuses on educating customers on the features and benefits of technology and entertainment products. The Minneapolis-based firm operates more than 930 retail stores across the United States and in Canada under the names Best Buy, Future Shop, GeekSquad, and Magnolia Audio Video, as well as an outlet store on eBay.

Best Buy operates in the highly competitive consumer electronics retail industry and must compete against other electronics retailers, specialty home-office retailers, mass merchants, home improvement superstores, and a growing number of direct-to-consumer alternatives. It also competes against independent dealers, regional chain discount stores, wholesale clubs, video rental stores, and other specialty retail stores. There is also increasing pressure from online sites, which offer entertainment as downloads, as well as pay-per-view cable television companies.

Best Buy collects data on nearly every transaction made, rain check issued, and call-center problem resolved for 75 million customers. To discover what its customers want and need, the company developed a database that incorporated information from 19 customer touch points including point of sale, and enhanced it with Experian's INSOURCESM consumer marketing data to develop a complete picture of its customers. It gained further insight by using purchase histories to study its customers' current as well as their future needs through segmentation analysis. This allowed Best Buy to develop and identify new customer segments, to better understand existing customers, to more precisely target promotions, and to identify key locations for expansion.

Best Buy collects data from its transactions and from mailing lists; it also has demographic information from local census numbers, surveys of customers, and targeted focus groups. In 2004 it launched a customer loyalty program called Reward Zone, which today has more than 6 million members from whom the company hopes to gain valuable insights. Best Buy retains Larry Selden, a professor at Columbia University's Graduate

Schools of Business, as a consultant. Selden argued that losses produced by what he calls "devil" customers can wipe out profits generated by "angels." Through its consultation with Selden and its data analysis with Experian, Best Buy identified its angel and devil customers. The angels were customers who bought high definition TVs, portable electronics, and newly released DVDs without waiting for markdowns or rebates. The devils bought products, applied for their rebates, and then returned the products and bought them back again at returned-merchandise discounts. Best Buy then categorized its angel customers into five segments:

- The Small Business customer ("BBfB"): These customers use Best Buy's products and services to enhance the profitability of their businesses.

- The Young Entertainment Enthusiast ("Buzz"): These are active younger men who want the latest technology and entertainment. They are early adopters who are interested in buying and showing off the latest gadgets.

- The Affluent Professional ("Barry"): These customers want the best technology and entertainment experience, and they do not mind spending to get the best, regardless of the cost. They are enthusiasts of action movies and cameras.

- The Busy Suburban Mom ("Jill"): These customers want to enrich their children's lives with technology and entertainment. They are busy but willing to talk about helping their families. They are smart and affluent but usually avoid electronics stores because the products intimidate them. "Jills" are typically the main shopper for the family and will make purchases based on staff recommendations.

- The Tech-Savvy Family Man ("Ray"): These are family men who want technology to improve their lives. They are practical adopters of technology and entertainment.

Best Buy's new "customer-centric" operating model focuses on these five key segments. The company launched the initiative with 67 stores, each of which would analyze the demographics of its local market and then choose one or two of these groups to be their focus. Each store would then stock merchandise for and include elements designed to appeal to the targeted segments. Executives believe that this model offers customers a richer in-store experience, including better shopping assistance, and also provides more of the goods and services that they want. It also empowers employees to recognize unique sets of customers and to build offerings and experiences to meet their needs. In fact, employees receive training in how to differentiate the customer types and how to help each.

To encourage its angel customers, Best Buy sends out associates with pink umbrellas to escort the Jills to and from their cars on rainy days. Personal Shopping Assistants have been provided to help Jills from the moment they enter the stores till they leave via the express checkout. For Barrys, there are comfortable couches for watching large TVs hooked up to high-end sound systems; even popcorn is included to add to the atmosphere. Magnolia Home Theatre specialists provide personalized expert advice. For Buzzes, Best Buy has set up video game areas with leather chairs and game players hooked to mammoth plasma-screen TVs, and TVs and games just a short walk from the area.

To discourage the undesirable devil customers, Best Buy is cutting back on promotions and sales tactics that tend to attract them, and it is also removing many of them from mailing lists. The company is also enforcing a 15 percent restocking fee on returned merchandise to discourage customers who return items with the intention of repurchasing them at "open-box" discounts. Best Buy is experimenting with reselling returned merchandise over the Internet, so the products do not reappear in the store where they were originally purchased.

Best Buy has already converted 85 stores to the new customer-centered model and plans to convert all of its U.S. Best Buy stores within three years. The 67 stores that underwent conversion in 2005 have reported a sales increase of 8.2 percent for the portion of the year in which they operated under the customer centricity model. Compared to an average store sales gain of 1.9 percent at other U.S. Best Buy stores, this is a considerable gain. However, due to one-time conversion costs and a higher expense structure, the selling, general, and administrative expenses for the converted stores were higher than for that of other U.S. Best Buy stores for the same period. Nonetheless, Best Buy believes that the profitability of stores operating under the customer-centered platform will improve over time, which is similar to its historical experience with new-store openings.[52]

### Questions for Discussion

1. From what internal and secondary sources did Best Buy acquire the data that helped it develop its customer centricity initiative?
2. How did Best Buy employ database marketing to better satisfy its customers?
3. How are the data gathered by Best Buy useful in customer relationship management?

# Target Markets: Segmentation, Evaluation, and Positioning

## Whole Foods and Baby Food

Whole Foods Markets is taking market segmentation to another level—it's targeting customers before they're born! Since 1980, the company has targeted customers with an interest in all-natural lifestyles. Today, it is the world's leading supermarket chain specializing in natural and organic foods. The company has sales in excess of $4 billion through more than 181 stores in the United States, Canada, and the United Kingdom.

Now Whole Foods, in partnership with *Mothering* magazine, has introduced a program called "Whole Baby" that targets expectant and new mothers. The Whole Baby program helps mothers prepare for their growing families by providing information on proper nutritional habits and on lifestyle topics ranging from prenatal care to baby's first foods.

In developing the program, Whole Foods commissioned a survey to evaluate the attitudes and interests of expectant and new mothers. When women were asked to identify their biggest concerns about having a baby, the issues most mentioned were money (56 percent), losing pregnancy weight (47 percent), and baby's health (44 percent). When asked about natural and organic foods, the survey found that 42 percent of the women thought that eating natural or organic foods was important, but that 38 percent didn't know the health advantages of these foods. Armed with this information, Whole Baby was developed to help new mothers learn about the benefits of healthier foods and lifestyles.

The program consists of free educational booklets available at Whole Foods Market stores. These guides contain money-saving coupons for the natural products that most appeal to mothers and information about parenting, as well as important nutritional information for pregnant women and new mothers. The program also includes free Whole Baby sample kits. These reusable tote bags contain product samples, information, and special offers from a variety of sponsors such as Burt's Bees, Earth's Best, Hylands, *Mothering* magazine, Seventh Generation, Stonyfield Farms, and Traditional Medicinals, which can be redeemed at Whole Foods Market stores.

## OBJECTIVES

1. To learn what a market is
2. To understand the differences among general targeting strategies
3. To become familiar with the major segmentation variables
4. To know what segment profiles are and how they are used
5. To understand how to evaluate market segments
6. To identify the factors that influence the selection of specific market segments for use as target markets
7. To understand positioning
8. To become familiar with sales forecasting methods

267

Whole Foods Market is also partnering with *Mothering* magazine to offer a Whole Baby lecture series in New York City, Philadelphia, Chicago, and Atlanta. These free talks provide new mothers with everything they need to know about natural foods, nourishment, raising healthy children, and breastfeeding.

Whole Foods Markets knows that the birth of a baby often gets new parents thinking about adopting healthier lifestyles. The Whole Baby program seems to be a natural for introducing this target market to Whole Foods.[1] ■

To compete effectively, Whole Foods Markets has singled out specific customer groups toward which it will direct its marketing efforts. Any organization that wants to succeed must identify its customers and develop and maintain marketing mixes that satisfy the needs of those customers.

In this chapter, we explore markets and market segmentation. Initially we define the term *market* and discuss the major requirements of a market. Then we examine the steps in the target market selection process, including identifying the appropriate targeting strategy, determining which variables to use for segmenting consumer and business markets, developing market segment profiles, evaluating relevant market segments, and selecting target markets. Then we examine the concept of positioning products in customers' minds. Finally, we discuss various methods for developing sales forecasts.

# What Are Markets?

The word *market* has a number of meanings. People sometimes use it to refer to a specific location where products are bought and sold—for example, a flea market. A large geographic area may also be called a market. Sometimes *market* refers to the relationship between supply and demand of a specific product, as in the question "How is the market for digital cameras?" *Market* may also be used as a verb, meaning "sell something."

We defined the term *market* in Chapter 2 as a group of people who, as individuals or as organizations, have needs for products in a product category and have the ability, willingness, and authority to purchase such products. In general use, the term *market* sometimes refers to the total population, or mass market, that buys products. However, our definition is more specific: it refers to groups of people seeking products in a specific product category. For example, students are part of the market for textbooks, as well as the markets for software, pens, paper, food, music, and other products. Obviously our complex economy has many different markets.

As stated in our definition, for a market to exist, the people in the aggregate must meet the following four requirements:

1. They must need or desire a particular product. If they do not, that aggregate is not a market.

2. They must have the ability to purchase the product. Ability to purchase is a function of buying power, which consists of resources such as money, goods, and services that can be traded in an exchange situation.

3. They must be willing to use their buying power.

4. They must have the authority to buy the specific products

Individuals can have the desire, the buying power, and the willingness to purchase certain products but may not be authorized to do so. For example, teenagers may have the desire, the money, and the willingness to buy liquor, but a liquor producer does not consider them a market because teenagers are prohibited by law from buying alcoholic beverages. An aggregate of people that lacks any one of the four requirements thus does not constitute a market.

# Target Market Selection Process

In Chapter 1, we pointed out that the first of two major components of developing a marketing strategy is to select a target market. Although marketers may employ several methods for target market selection, generally they use a five-step process. This process is shown in Figure 10.1, and we discuss it in the following sections.

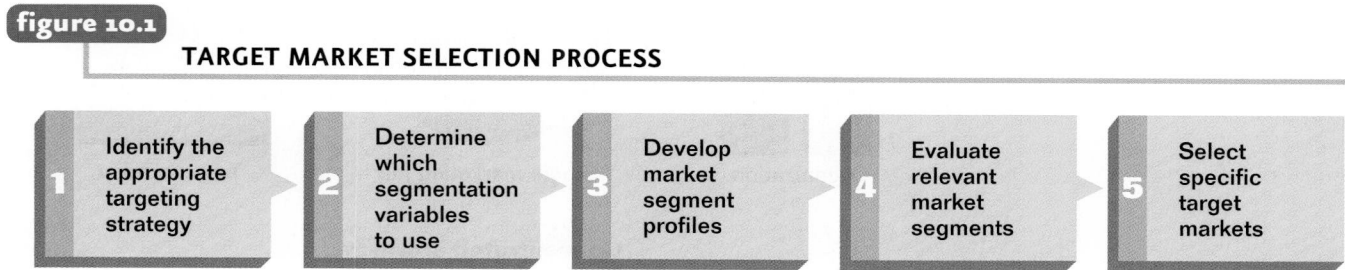

**figure 10.1**

**TARGET MARKET SELECTION PROCESS**

1 Identify the appropriate targeting strategy → 2 Determine which segmentation variables to use → 3 Develop market segment profiles → 4 Evaluate relevant market segments → 5 Select specific target markets

# Step 1: Identify the Appropriate Targeting Strategy

Recall from Chapter 1 that a target market is a group of people or organizations for which a business creates and maintains a marketing mix specifically designed to satisfy the needs of group members. The strategy used to select a target market is affected by target market characteristics, product attributes, and the organization's objectives and resources. Figure 10.2 (on p. 270) illustrates the three basic targeting strategies: undifferentiated, concentrated, and differentiated.

## Undifferentiated Targeting Strategy

An organization sometimes defines an entire market for a particular product as its target market. When a company designs a single marketing mix and directs it at the entire market for a particular product, it is using an **undifferentiated targeting strategy**. As Figure 10.2 shows, the strategy assumes that all customers in the target market for a specific kind of product have similar needs, and thus the organization can satisfy most customers with a single marketing mix. This mix consists of one type of product with little or no variation, one price, one promotional program aimed at everybody, and one distribution system to reach most customers in the total market. Products marketed successfully through the undifferentiated strategy include staple food items, such as sugar and salt, and certain kinds of farm produce.

The undifferentiated targeting strategy is effective under two conditions. First, a large proportion of customers in a total market must have similar needs for the product, a situation termed a **homogeneous market**. A marketer using a single marketing mix for a total market of customers with a variety of needs would find that the marketing mix satisfies very few people. A "universal car" meant to suit everyone would fulfill very few customers' needs for cars because it would not provide the specific attributes a particular person wants. Second, the organization must be able to develop and maintain a single marketing mix that satisfies customers' needs. The company must be able to identify a set of needs common to most customers in a total market and have the resources and managerial skills to reach a sizable portion of that market.

Although customers may have similar needs for a few products, for most products their needs decidedly differ. In such instances, a company should use a concentrated or a differentiated strategy.

**undifferentiated targeting strategy** A strategy in which an organization defines an entire market for a particular product as its target market, designs a single marketing mix, and directs it at that market

**homogeneous market** A market in which a large proportion of customers have similar needs for a product

## figure 10.2

### TARGETING STRATEGIES

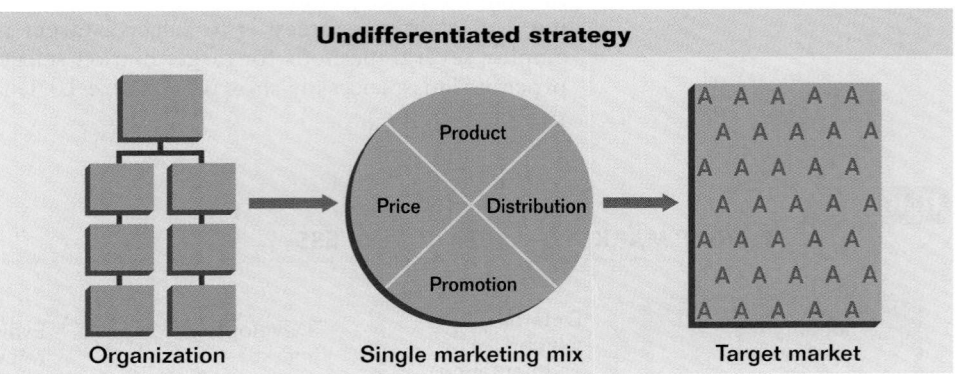

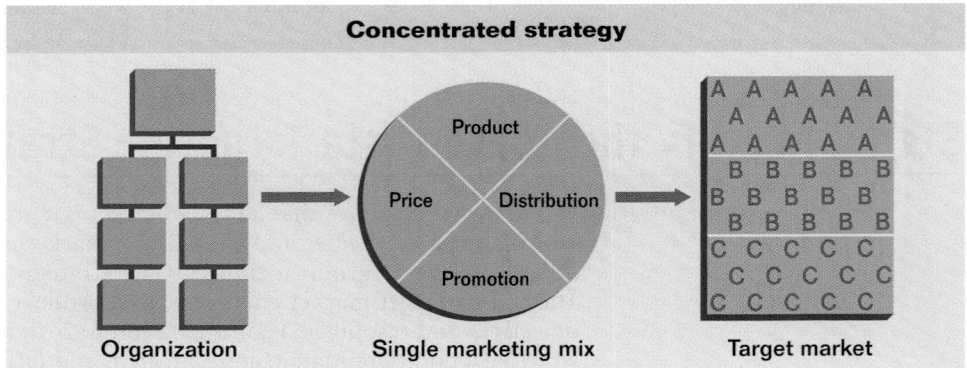

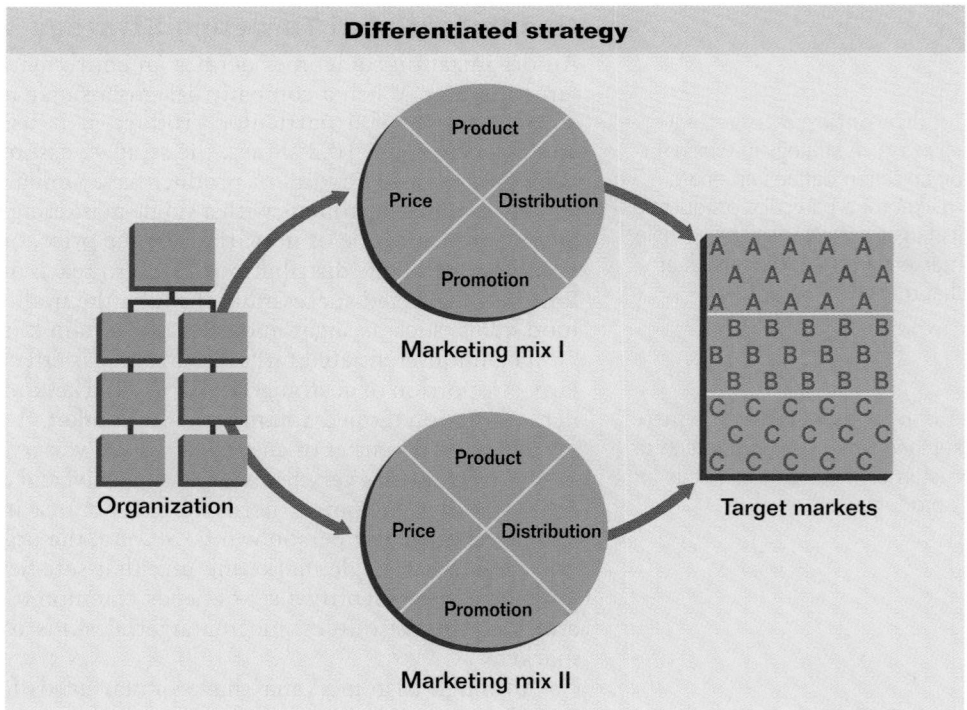

The letters in each target market represent potential customers. Customers with the same letters have similar characteristics and similar product needs.

**heterogeneous market** A market made up of individuals or organizations with diverse needs for products in a specific product class

**market segmentation** The process of dividing a total market into groups with relatively similar product needs to design a marketing mix that matches those needs

**market segment** Individuals, groups, or organizations sharing one or more similar characteristics that cause them to have similar product needs

**concentrated targeting strategy** A market segmentation strategy in which an organization targets a single market segment using one marketing mix

## Concentrated Targeting Strategy Through Market Segmentation

Not everyone wants the same type of car, furniture, or clothes. A market made up of individuals or organizations with diverse product needs is called a **heterogeneous market**. For example, some individuals want an economical car, while others desire a status symbol, and still others seek a roomy and comfortable vehicle. The automobile market thus is heterogeneous.

For such heterogeneous markets, market segmentation is appropriate. **Market segmentation** is the process of dividing a total market into groups, or segments, consisting of people or organizations with relatively similar product needs. The purpose is to enable a marketer to design a marketing mix that more precisely matches the needs of customers in the selected market segment. A **market segment** consists of individuals, groups, or organizations sharing one or more similar characteristics that cause them to have relatively similar product needs. The automobile market is divided into many different market segments. Hyundai, for example, aims its Sonata at the mid-size sedan market segment as opposed to aiming at all car buyers.[2] The main rationale for segmenting heterogeneous markets is that a company is better able to develop a satisfying marketing mix for a relatively small portion of a total market than to develop a mix that meets the needs of all people. Market segmentation is widely used. Fast-food chains, soft-drink companies, magazine publishers, hospitals, and banks are just a few types of organizations that employ market segmentation.

For market segmentation to succeed, five conditions must exist. First, customers' needs for the product must be heterogeneous; otherwise, there is little reason to segment the market. Second, segments must be identifiable and divisible. The company must find a characteristic or variable for effectively separating individuals in a total market into groups containing people with relatively uniform needs for the product. Third, the total market should be divided so that segments can be compared with respect to estimated sales potential, costs, and profits. Fourth, at least one segment must have enough profit potential to justify developing and maintaining a special marketing mix for that segment. Finally, the company must be able to reach the chosen segment with a particular marketing mix. Some market segments may be difficult or impossible to reach because of legal, social, or distribution constraints. For instance, marketers of Cuban rum and cigars cannot market to U.S. consumers because of political and trade restrictions.

When an organization directs its marketing efforts toward a single market segment using one marketing mix, it is employing a **concentrated targeting strategy**. Porsche focuses on the luxury sports car segment and directs all its marketing efforts toward high-income individuals who want to own high-performance sports cars. Mont Blanc, a German company famous for its high-quality writing pens, targets its products to individuals within the writing instrument market who value high-end, collectable writing instruments.[3] Notice in Figure 10.2 that the organization using the concentrated strategy is aiming its marketing mix only at "B" customers.

The chief advantage of the concentrated strategy is that it allows a firm to specialize. The firm analyzes characteristics and needs of a distinct customer group and then focuses all its energies on satisfying that group's needs. A firm may generate a large sales volume by reaching a single segment. Also, concentrating on a single segment permits a firm with limited resources to compete with larger organizations that may have overlooked smaller segments.

Specialization, however, means that a company puts all its eggs in one basket, which can be hazardous. If a company's sales depend on a single segment and the segment's demand for the product declines, the company's financial strength also deteriorates. Moreover, when a firm penetrates one segment and becomes well entrenched, its popularity may keep it from moving into other segments. For example, it is very unlikely that Mont Blanc could or would want to compete with Bic in the low-end, disposable-pen market segment.

## Differentiated Targeting Strategy Through Market Segmentation

**differentiated targeting strategy** A strategy in which an organization targets two or more segments by developing a marketing mix for each segment

With a **differentiated targeting strategy**, an organization directs its marketing efforts at two or more segments by developing a marketing mix for each segment (refer to Figure 10.2). After a firm uses a concentrated strategy successfully in one market segment, it sometimes expands its efforts to include additional segments. For example, Fruit of the Loom underwear has traditionally been aimed at one segment: men. However, the company now markets underwear for women and children as well. Marketing mixes for a differentiated strategy may vary as to product features, distribution methods, promotion methods, and prices.

A firm may increase sales in the aggregate market through a differentiated strategy because its marketing mixes are aimed at more people. For example, Gap, which established its retail apparel reputation by targeting people under 25, now targets several age groups, from infants to people over 60, with Gap, Banana Republic, and Old Navy stores. The company's newest stores, Forth & Towne, are aimed at women age 35 and up.[4] A company with excess production capacity may find a differentiated strategy advantageous because the sale of products to additional segments may absorb excess capacity. On the other hand, a differentiated strategy often demands more production processes, materials, and people. Thus, production costs may be higher than with a concentrated strategy.

# The Uploaded Photo at the End of the Bar

**M**any singles who are tired of the dating scene are going digital to search for a partner. And why not, when online dating boasts as high as a 94 percent success rate? Digital dating services use target marketing concepts to find singles the perfect mate. Today, online dating services are the biggest paid content on the Internet, with sales estimated at $1 billion. Approximately 20 to 30 million U.S. singles and millions more internationally visit an online dating site each month. Online dating is now the world's most popular means for meeting a romantic partner. There are hundreds of online dating websites in the United States. Some highly targeted sites are BlackSinglesConnection.com for African Americans; Terra.com, which targets the Hispanic market; JDate.com for Jewish daters; and TattooedSingles.com for ink enthusiasts. Other specialized singles sites exist for bikers, smokers, Democrats, Republicans, and NASCAR fans.

Using MatchMobile, daters can upload their profiles and search for dates on their cellphones. If users find a prospect, they can contact them by text messages. 3G Dating Agency takes it a step further by allowing video messaging between potential dates. Comcast Digital Cable is offering customers the opportunity to watch and upload video profiles on their TVs.

What if you fear that your online friend may be an in-person nightmare? Truedater.com gives singles from any online personal site the ability to rate their dates and give feedback on the truthfulness of their claims. Call it consumer love protection.

All digital dating services require demographic information from their members, which allows these companies to be more precise in determining matches. Among the most sophisticated researchers is eHarmony.com, which asks its members to answer a 436-question assessment that will help match marriage-minded couples based on 29 dimensions of compatibility. These dimensions are grouped into core traits and vital attributes.

With digital-assisted dating, your perfect mate may be just the press of a button away.

### Differentiated Targeting

Many companies use differentiated strategy by targeting more than one market segment. In the ads shown here, Visa hopes to attract young parents and Mont Blanc targets those who give business gifts. Both organizations aim multiple marketing mixes at multiple target markets.

# Step 2: Determine Which Segmentation Variables to Use

**segmentation variables**
Characteristics of individuals, groups, or organizations used to divide a market into segments

**Segmentation variables** are the characteristics of individuals, groups, or organizations used to divide a market into segments. For example, location, age, gender, or rate of product usage can all be bases for segmenting markets.

To select a segmentation variable, several factors are considered. The segmentation variable should relate to customers' needs for, uses of, or behavior toward the product. Stereo marketers might segment the stereo market based on income and age, but not on religion, because people's stereo needs do not differ due to religion. Furthermore, if individuals or organizations in a total market are to be classified accurately, the segmentation variable must be measurable. Age, location, and gender are measurable because such information can be obtained through observation or questioning. In contrast, segmenting a market on the basis of, say, intelligence is extremely difficult because this attribute is harder to measure accurately.

A company's resources and capabilities affect the number and size of segment variables used. The type of product and degree of variation in customers' needs also dictate the number and size of segments targeted. In short, there is no best way to segment markets.

Choosing a segmentation variable or variables is a critical step in targeting a market. Selecting an inappropriate variable limits the chances of developing a successful marketing strategy. To help you better understand potential segmentation variables, we next examine the major types of variables used to segment consumer markets and the types used to segment business markets.

## Variables for Segmenting Consumer Markets

A marketer using segmentation to reach a consumer market can choose one or several variables from an assortment of possibilities. As Figure 10.3 (on p. 274) shows, segmentation variables can be grouped into four categories: demographic, geographic, psychographic, and behavioristic.

## figure 10.3

### SEGMENTATION VARIABLES FOR CONSUMER MARKETS

**Demographic variables**
- Age
- Gender
- Race
- Ethnicity
- Income
- Education
- Occupation
- Family size
- Family life cycle
- Religion
- Social class

**Geographic variables**
- Region
- Urban, suburban, rural
- City size
- County size
- State size
- Market density
- Climate
- Terrain

**Psychographic variables**
- Personality attributes
- Motives
- Lifestyles

**Behavioristic variables**
- Volume usage
- End use
- Benefit expectations
- Brand loyalty
- Price sensitivity

**Gender-Based Segmentation**

Razor manufacturers target men with certain products and women with other products.

**Demographic Variables.** Demographers study aggregate population characteristics such as the distribution of age and gender, fertility rates, migration patterns, and mortality rates. Demographic characteristics that marketers commonly use in segmenting markets include age, gender, race, ethnicity, income, education, occupation, family size, family life cycle, religion, and social class. Marketers rely on these de-

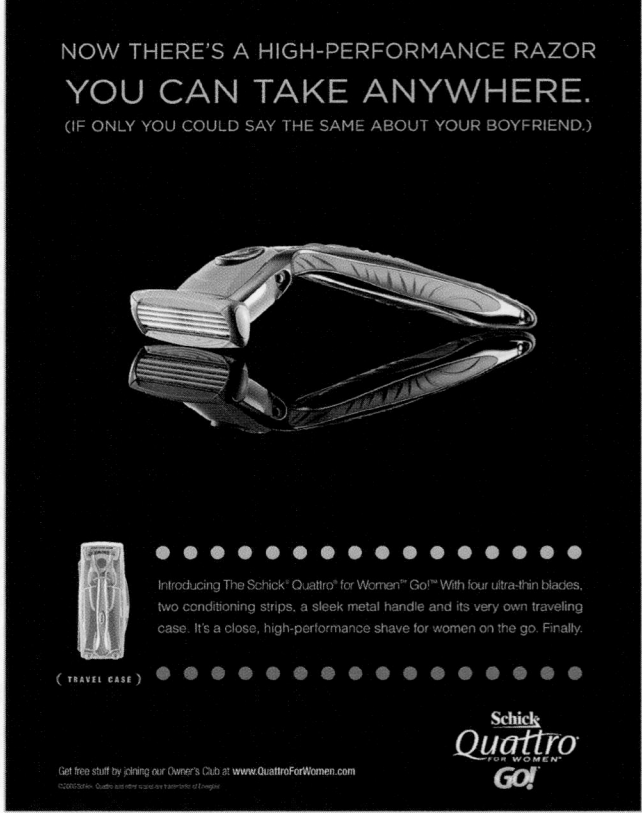

**figure 10.4**

## SPENDING LEVELS OF THREE AGE GROUPS FOR SELECTED PRODUCT CATEGORIES

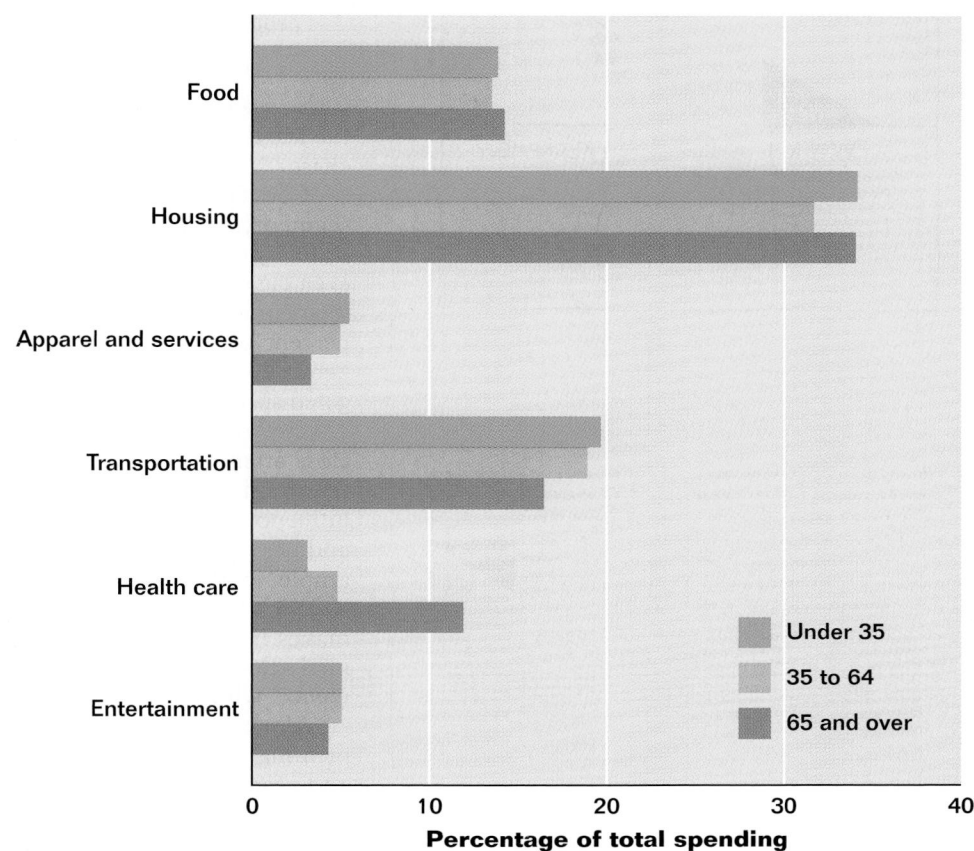

Legend:
- Under 35
- 35 to 64
- 65 and over

Categories (top to bottom): Food, Housing, Apparel and services, Transportation, Health care, Entertainment

X-axis: Percentage of total spending (0, 10, 20, 30, 40)

**Source:** "Consumer Expenditures in 2003," Report 986, U.S. Department of Labor, Bureau of Labor Statistics, September 2005.

mographic characteristics because they are often closely linked to customers' needs and purchasing behaviors and can be readily measured. Like demographers, a few marketers even use mortality rates. Service Corporation International (SCI), the largest U.S. funeral services company, attempts to locate its facilities in higher-income suburban areas with high mortality rates. SCI operates more than 2,800 funeral service locations, cemeteries, and crematoriums.[5]

Age is a commonly used variable for segmentation purposes. Marketers need to be aware of age distribution and how that distribution is changing. All age groups under 55 are expected to decrease by the year 2025, while all age categories 55 and older are expected to increase. In 1970, the average age of a U.S. citizen was 27.9; currently it is about 38.6.[6] As Figure 10.4 shows, Americans 65 and older spend as much or more on food, housing, and health care compared to Americans in the two younger age groups.

Many marketers recognize the purchase influence of children and are targeting more marketing efforts at them. Disney, for example, has created a free Internet game called Virtual Magic Kingdom aimed primarily at 7- to 12-year-olds. This game is targeted to those consumers who will appreciate the online multiplayer game, namely, vacation-influencing children.[7] As a group, parents of children ages 4 to 12 have annual incomes in excess of $40 billion. Numerous products are aimed specifically at children—toys, clothing, food and beverages, and entertainment such as movies and TV cable channels. In addition, children in this age group influence $500 billion of parental spending yearly.[8] In households with only one parent or those in which both parents work, children often take on additional responsibilities

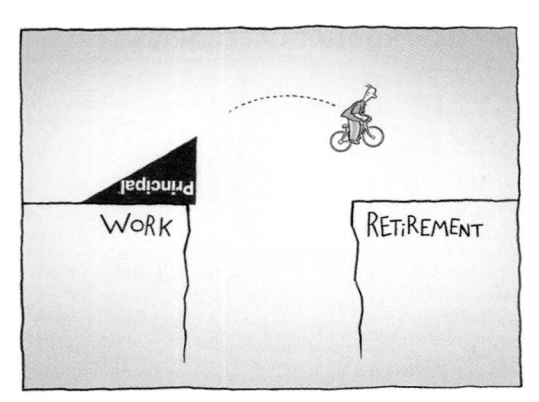

*Need a lift?*

GETTING TO RETIREMENT can seem like a pretty daunting task. What do you do? How much should you save? Where do you begin? Fortunately, this is where The Principal can help. We have everything you need to plan for retirement, from simple tools to help you get started to a wide range of financial products – including IRAs, annuities, investments, insurance and banking. And as the nation's 401(k) leader, we know how to make the whole process as simple as possible. So no matter how far away retirement might seem, The Principal can give you an edge in getting there.

Retirement
Investments
Insurance
Banking

**Principal®**
*Financial Group™*

WE'LL GIVE YOU AN EDGE™

*To learn more, contact your financial professional or visit principal.com*

©2005 Principal Financial Services, Inc. "The Principal," "Principal Financial Group" and the Edge Design are registered service marks and the illustrated character and "We'll Give You An Edge" are service marks of Principal Financial Services, Inc. Insurance issued by Principal Life Insurance Company. Securities offered through Princor Financial Services Corporation, (800) 247-4123, member SIPC. Bank products offered through Principal Bank,® member FDIC, Equal Housing Lender. Principal Life, Princor,® Principal Bank and Principal Financial Services, Inc., are members of the Principal Financial Group,® Des Moines, IA 50392. Insurance and annuities are not FDIC insured, not obligations or deposits of Principal Bank, not guaranteed by Principal Bank, and are subject to investment risks, including possible loss of the principal invested. #692592007

### Age-Based Segmentation

In this ad, Principle Financial Group touts its retirement plans and looks for potential customers among those people planning for retirement.

such as cooking, cleaning, and grocery shopping, and thus influence the types of products and brands these households purchase.

Gender is another demographic variable commonly used to segment markets, including the markets for clothing, soft drinks, nonprescription medications, toiletries, magazines, and even cigarettes. The U.S. Census Bureau reports that girls and women account for 50.8 percent and boys and men for 49.2 percent of the total U.S. population.[9] Some deodorant marketers use gender segmentation: Secret and Soft and Dri are targeted specifically at women, whereas Degree and Mitchum are directed toward men. Food and beverage companies are paying close attention to women and have determined that all important food marketing trends are partially the result of women's influence in the home. Foods offering convenience, portability, and easy preparation have a good chance of success. For example, cereal maker Kellogg Company spun off its Rice Krispies Treats from its Rice Krispies line, and its convenience makes it the most popular snack bar in the country, with annual sales topping $140 million. Its easy portability and convenience, which appeals to women consumers, is a factor.[10]

Marketers also use race and ethnicity as variables for segmenting markets for such products as food, music, clothing, and cosmetics and for services such as banking and insurance. The U.S. Hispanic population illustrates the importance of ethnicity as a segmentation variable. This ethnic group is growing five times faster than the general population. Consequently Campbell Soup, Procter & Gamble, and other companies are targeting Hispanic consumers, viewing this segment as attractive because of its size and growth potential. Asian Americans are another important subculture for many companies. Sears, for example, in an effort to better market to Asian Americans, African Americans, and Hispanics, has redesigned its apparel departments in stores located in cities with large multiethnic populations. These revisions include new in-store signage, updated merchandising displays, and new brands that appeal to an ethnically diverse audience.[11]

Because income strongly influences people's product needs, it often provides a way to divide markets. Income affects people's ability to buy and their desires for certain lifestyles. Product markets segmented by income include sporting goods, housing, furniture, cosmetics, clothing, jewelry, home appliances, automobiles, and electronics.

Among the factors influencing household income and product needs are marital status and the presence and age of children. These characteristics, often combined and called the *family life cycle*, affect needs for housing, appliances, food and beverages, automobiles, and recreational equipment. Using the information in Table 10.1, consider how life cycle stages affect the purchase of beverages.

Marketers also use many other demographic variables. For instance, dictionary publishing companies segment markets by education level. Some insurance companies segment markets using occupation, targeting health insurance at college students and at younger workers with small employers that do not provide health coverage. Family life cycles can be broken down in various ways. Figure 10.5 (on p. 278) shows a breakdown into nine categories. The composition of the U.S. household in relation to the family life cycle has changed considerably over the last several decades.

**table 10.1   LIFE CYCLE STAGES INFLUENCE BEVERAGE PURCHASES**

**Percentage of All Dollars Spent Annually in Each Beverage Category, by Life Stage**

| | Carbonated Beverages | Coffee | Juices, Refrigerated | Soft Drinks, Noncarb. | Bottled Water | All Remaining Carb. Bev. (Diet) | All Remaining Carb. Bev. (Reg.) | Coffee, Liquid |
|---|---|---|---|---|---|---|---|---|
| Young singles (ages 18–34) | 2% | 1% | 2% | 2% | 2% | 2% | 1% | 3% |
| Childless younger couples (two adults, 18–34) | 4% | 3% | 4% | 4% | 6% | 4% | 4% | 8% |
| New families (2 adults, 1 or more children <6) | 5% | 3% | 5% | 8% | 6% | 4% | 5% | 4% |
| Maturing families (2 adults, 1 or more children, not all <6 or +12) | 26% | 19% | 22% | 36% | 22% | 21% | 30% | 19% |
| Established families (1 or more children, all +12) | 12% | 9% | 10% | 10% | 10% | 9% | 14% | 12% |
| Middle-aged singles (35–54) | 7% | 5% | 7% | 4% | 9% | 9% | 7% | 7% |
| Middle-aged childless couples (2 adults, 35–54) | 18% | 17% | 16% | 14% | 18% | 19% | 16% | 18% |
| Empty-nesters (2 adults, +55, no children at home) | 20% | 32% | 24% | 17% | 20% | 24% | 17% | 21% |
| Older singles (55+) | 7% | 11% | 10% | 6% | 7% | 8% | 6% | 8% |
| Total | 100% | 100% | 100% | 100% | 100% | 100% | 100% | 100% |

**Source:** *American Demographics,* "Drink Me" by Matthew Grimm. Feb. 2000, pp. 62–63. Copyright © 2000. Reprinted with permission from *American Demographics.*

Single-parent families are on the rise, meaning that the "typical" family no longer consists of a married couple with children. Since 1970, the number of households headed by a single mother increased from 12 percent to 26 percent of total family households, and that number grew from 1 percent to 6 percent for families headed by a single father. Another factor influencing the family life cycle is that the increase in median marrying age for women has increased from 20.8 years to 25.3 years since 1970, while for men it increased from 23.2 years to 27.1 years. Additionally, the proportion of women ages 20 to 24 who have never been married has more than doubled over this time, and for women ages 30 to 34 this number has nearly tripled. Other important changes in the family life cycle include the rise in the number of people living alone and the number of unmarried couples living together.[12] Tracking these changes helps marketers satisfy the needs of particular target markets through new marketing mixes. For example, MicroMarketing, Inc. helps companies target customers through what it calls Lifestage Marketing. MicroMarketing can create a direct mail campaign aimed at groups such as people who recently moved, soon-to-be newlyweds, recent high school and college graduates, and expectant parents. By focusing on such narrow target markets, MicroMarketing boasts a return on investments of up to 2000 percent.[13]

**Geographic Variables.** Geographic variables—climate, terrain, city size, population density, and urban/rural areas—also influence consumer product needs. Markets may be divided into regions because one or more geographic variables can cause customers to differ from one region to another. A company selling products to a national market might divide the United States into the following regions: Pacific,

**figure 10.5**

## FAMILY LIFE CYCLE STAGES AS A PERCENTAGE OF ALL HOUSEHOLDS

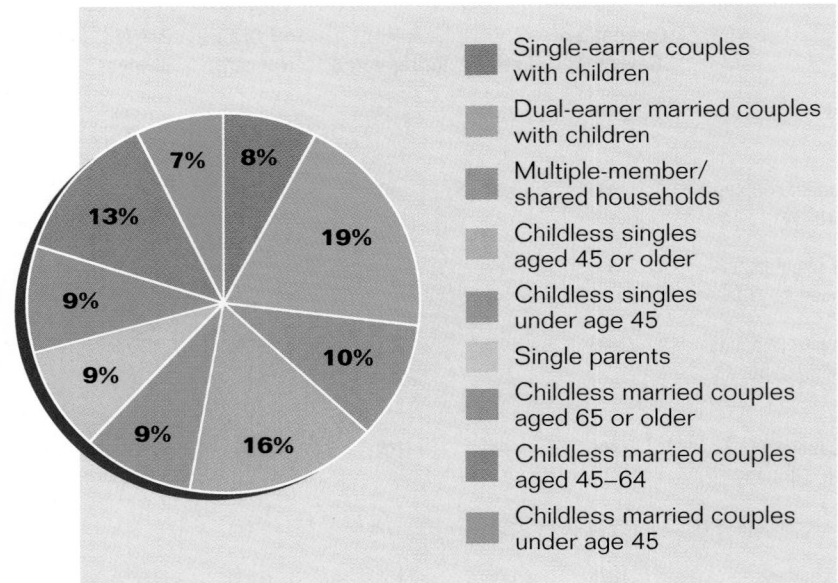

- Single-earner couples with children
- Dual-earner married couples with children
- Multiple-member/ shared households
- Childless singles aged 45 or older
- Childless singles under age 45
- Single parents
- Childless married couples aged 65 or older
- Childless married couples aged 45–64
- Childless married couples under age 45

**Source:** Jason Fields, "America's Families and Living Arrangements: 2003," *Current Population Reports,* U.S. Census Bureau, 2003.

Southwest, Central, Midwest, Southeast, Middle Atlantic, and New England. A firm operating in one or several states might regionalize its market by counties, cities, zip code areas, or other units.

City size can be an important segmentation variable. Some marketers focus efforts on cities of a certain size. For example, one franchised restaurant organization will not locate in cities of fewer than 200,000 people. It concluded that a smaller population base would result in inadequate profits. Other firms actively seek opportunities in smaller towns. A classic example is Wal-Mart, which initially located only in small towns.

Because cities often cut across political boundaries, the U.S. Census Bureau developed a system to classify metropolitan areas (any area with a city or urbanized area with a population of at least 50,000 and a total metropolitan population of at least 100,000). Metropolitan areas are categorized as one of the following: a metropolitan statistical area (MSA), a primary metropolitan statistical area (PMSA), or a consolidated metropolitan statistical area (CMSA). An MSA is an urbanized area encircled by nonmetropolitan counties and is neither socially nor economically dependent on any other metropolitan area. A metropolitan area within a complex of at least 1 million inhabitants can elect to be named a PMSA. A CMSA is a metropolitan area of at least 1 million consisting of two or more PMSAs. Of the 20 CMSAs, the five largest—New York, Los Angeles, Chicago, San Francisco, and Philadelphia—account for 20 percent of the U.S. population. The federal government provides a considerable amount of socioeconomic information about MSAs, PMSAs, and CMSAs that can aid in market analysis and segmentation.

**market density** The number of potential customers within a unit of land area

**geodemographic segmentation** A method of market segmentation that clusters people in zip code areas and smaller neighborhood units based on lifestyle and demographic information

**Market density** refers to the number of potential customers within a unit of land area, such as a square mile. Although market density relates generally to population density, the correlation is not exact. For example, in two different geographic markets of approximately equal size and population, market density for office supplies would be much higher in one area if it contained a much greater proportion of business customers than the other area. Market density may be a useful segmentation variable because low-density markets often require different sales, advertising, and distribution activities than do high-density markets.

A number of marketers are using geodemographic segmentation. **Geodemographic segmentation** clusters people in zip code areas and even smaller neighborhood units based on lifestyle information and especially demographic data such as income, education, occupation, type of housing, ethnicity, family life cycle, and level of urbanization. These small, precisely described population clusters help marketers isolate demographic units as small as neighborhoods where the demand for specific products is strongest. Information companies such as Donnelley Marketing Information Services, Claritas, and C.A.C.I., Inc. provide geodemographic data services called Prospect Zone, PRIZM, and Acorn, respectively. PRIZM is based on a classification of the more than 500,000 U.S. neighborhoods into one of 40 cluster types, such as "shotguns and pickups," "money and brains," and "gray power."

**micromarketing**  An approach to market segmentation in which organizations focus precise marketing efforts on very small geographic markets

Geodemographic segmentation allows marketers to engage in micromarketing. **Micromarketing** is the focusing of precise marketing efforts on very small geographic markets, such as community and even neighborhood markets. Providers of financial and health-care services, retailers, and consumer products companies use micromarketing. Special advertising campaigns, promotions, retail site location analyses, special pricing, and unique retail product offerings are a few examples of micromarketing facilitated through geodemographic segmentation.

Climate is commonly used as a geographic segmentation variable because of its broad impact on people's behavior and product needs. Product markets affected by climate include air-conditioning and heating equipment, clothing, gardening equipment, recreational products, and building materials.

**Psychographic Variables.** Marketers sometimes use psychographic variables, such as personality characteristics, motives, and lifestyles, to segment markets. A

# Se Habla Español: Banks Target Hispanics

It is estimated that more than 50 percent of the nation's 40 million Hispanics do not have checking or savings accounts. Until recently, these consumers could not cash a payroll check in a bank but had to turn instead to a check-cashing store, paying a fee of 2 to 3 percent of the check's value plus, in some cases, a transaction fee. Recognizing that the Hispanic population is growing rapidly, more financial firms are reaching out to these customers with new products.

To target Hispanics, financial companies are not just adding Spanish-speaking staff and running Spanish-language advertisements. They are increasingly offering unique products such as mortgages based on individual taxpayer ID numbers rather than social security numbers and intercountry fund-transfer services. Such remittance services are especially valuable for the 50 percent of Hispanic immigrants who regularly send money back to relatives in their former countries, with Mexico alone receiving nearly $20 billion annually.

Wells Fargo & Company, the nation's fourth largest bank, began targeting Hispanic customers in the nineteenth century. In addition to increasing its Spanish-speaking staff and redecorating a number of branches with Mexican themes, it also joined forces with pawn shop operator Cash America International to put check-cashing machines into grocery and convenience stores. Bank of America initiated a Spanish-language promotional campaign and introduced Safe-Send, a remittance service that allows Hispanics with new Bank of America checking accounts to send money to Mexico without transfer fees. Customers of bank-operated check-cashing stores generally report friendlier environments and lower transaction fees. By targeting an underserved market with technology and desirable products, many banks have been able to boost their profits and build relationships with more customers.

**Lifestyle Segmentation**

In these advertisements, the CESAR brand targets people who love their small dogs and Master-Card appeals to golfers.

psychographic dimension can be used by itself to segment a market or it can be combined with other types of segmentation variables.

Personality characteristics can be useful for segmentation when a product resembles many competing products and consumers' needs are not significantly related to other segmentation variables. However, segmenting a market according to personality traits can be risky. Although marketing practitioners have long believed consumer choice and product use vary with personality, until recently marketing research had indicated only weak relationships. It is hard to measure personality traits accurately, especially since most personality tests were developed for clinical use, not for segmentation purposes.

When appealing to a personality characteristic, a marketer almost always selects one that many people view positively. Individuals with this characteristic, as well as those who would like to have it, may be influenced to buy that marketer's brand. Marketers taking this approach do not worry about measuring how many people have the positively valued characteristic; they assume a sizable proportion of people in the target market either have it or want to have it.

When motives are used to segment a market, the market is divided according to consumers' reasons for making a purchase. Personal appearance, affiliation, status, safety, and health are examples of motives affecting the types of products purchased and the choice of stores in which they are bought. Marketing efforts based on health and fitness motives can be a point of competitive advantage. For example, Yum! Brands, Inc. (Taco Bell, Long John Silver's, Pizza Hut, KFC, and A&W Restaurants) teamed up with Bally Total Fitness to pair a free trial membership, valued at $50, with each restaurant's better-for-you menu items. This partnership will appeal to fitness motivated individuals and will create a link between fitness and the restaurants of Yum! Brands.[14]

Lifestyle segmentation groups individuals according to how they spend their time, the importance of things in their surroundings (homes or jobs, for example), beliefs about themselves and broad issues, and some demographic characteristics, such as income and education.[15] Lifestyle analysis provides a broad view of buyers because it encompasses numerous characteristics related to people's activities (work, hobbies, entertainment, sports), interests (family, home, fashion, food, technology), and opinions (politics, social issues, education, the future). For example, homeownership is valued by most income and age segments. Recent studies show, however, that 49 percent of Generation Xers (born between 1964 and 1973) own homes and account for 16.5 percent of the home furnishing market and 19.9 percent of furniture purchases. Unlike baby boomers (born 1946–1963), Generation X homeowners often research products for their homes on the Web and later buy those products in-store. In addition, their decisions on major home improvements are often decided based on how those improvements will affect the home's resale value.[16]

One of the most popular consumer lifestyle frameworks is a survey from SRI Consulting Business Intelligence. The company's VALS Program uses a survey to help classify consumers into eight basic groups. The segmentation is based on psychological characteristics that are correlated with purchase behavior and four key demographics. The eight groups are Innovators, Thinkers, Achievers, Experiencers, Believers, Strivers, Makers, and Survivors. This VALS questionnaire is then attached to larger surveys that focus on particular products, services, leisure activities, or media preferences to learn about the lifestyles of the eight groups. Figure 10.6 (on p. 282) is an example of VALS data showing the proportion of each VALS group that purchased a mountain bike, purchased golf clubs, owns a fishing rod, and goes hunting. VALS research is also used to create new products as well as to segment existing markets. VALS systems have been developed for the United States, Japan, and the United Kingdom.[17]

Many other lifestyle classification systems exist. Several companies, such as Experían's BehaviorBank, collect lifestyle data on millions of consumers.

**Behavioristic Variables.** Firms can divide a market according to some feature of consumer behavior toward a product, commonly involving some aspect of product use. For example, a market may be separated into users—classified as heavy, moderate, or light—and nonusers. To satisfy a specific group, such as heavy users, marketers may create a distinctive product, set special prices, or initiate special promotion and distribution activities. Per capita consumption data help identify different levels of usage. For example, the Beverage Market Index shows that per capita consumption of bottled water varies from 9.0 gallons in the East Central states (Illinois, Indiana, Kentucky, Michigan, Ohio, West Virginia, and Wisconsin) to 34.5 gallons in the Southwest (Arizona, New Mexico, Oklahoma, and Texas).[18]

How customers use or apply products may also determine the method of segmentation. To satisfy customers who use a product in a certain way, some feature—say, packaging, size, texture, or color—may be designed precisely to make the product easier to use, safer, or more convenient.

**benefit segmentation** The division of a market according to benefits that consumers want from the product

**Benefit segmentation** is the division of a market according to benefits that consumers want from the product. Although most types of market segmentation assume a relationship between the variable and customers' needs, benefit segmentation differs in that the benefits customers seek *are* their product needs. Consider that a customer who purchases over-the-counter cold relief medication may be specifically interested in two benefits: stopping a runny nose and relieving chest congestion. Thus, individuals are segmented directly according to their needs. By determining the desired benefits, marketers may be able to divide people into groups seeking certain sets of benefits. The effectiveness of such segmentation depends on three conditions: (1) the benefits sought must be identifiable; (2) using these benefits, marketers must be able to divide people into recognizable segments; and (3) one or more of the resulting segments must be accessible to the firm's marketing efforts. Both Timberland and Avia, for example, segment the foot apparel market based on benefits sought.

As this discussion shows, consumer markets can be divided according to numerous characteristics. Business markets are segmented using different variables, as we will see in the following section.

## figure 10.6

### VALS TYPES AND SPORTS PREFERENCES

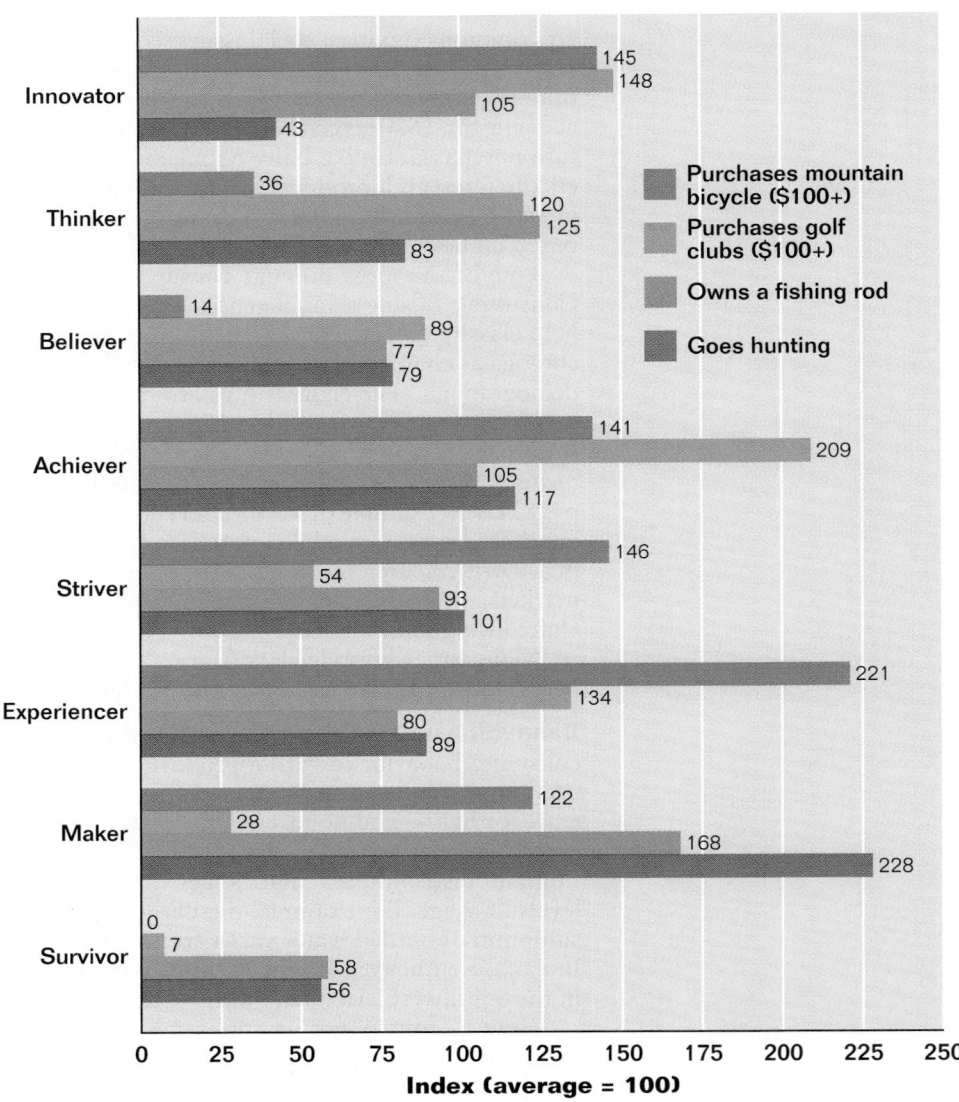

Legend:
- Purchases mountain bicycle ($100+)
- Purchases golf clubs ($100+)
- Owns a fishing rod
- Goes hunting

Innovator: 145, 148, 105, 43
Thinker: 36, 120, 125, 83
Believer: 14, 89, 77, 79
Achiever: 141, 209, 105, 117
Striver: 146, 54, 93, 101
Experiencer: 221, 134, 80, 89
Maker: 122, 28, 168, 228
Survivor: 0, 7, 58, 56

Index (average = 100)

**Source:** VALS™ Program. SRI Consulting Business Intelligence. Reprinted with permission.

## Variables for Segmenting Business Markets

Like consumer markets, business markets are frequently segmented. Marketers segment business markets according to geographic location, type of organization, customer size, and product use.

**Geographic Location.** Earlier we noted that the demand for some consumer products can vary considerably among geographic areas because of differences in climate, terrain, customer preferences, and similar factors. Demand for business products also varies according to geographic location. For example, producers of certain types of lumber divide their markets geographically because their customers' needs vary from region to region. Geographic segmentation may be especially appropriate for reaching industries concentrated in certain locations. Furniture and textile producers, for example, are concentrated in the Southeast.

**Type of Organization.** A company sometimes segments a market by types of organizations within that market. Different types of organizations often require different product features, distribution systems, price structures, and selling strategies.

Given these variations, a firm may either concentrate on a single segment with one marketing mix (a concentration targeting strategy) or focus on several groups with multiple mixes (a differentiated targeting strategy). A carpet producer, for example, could segment potential customers into several groups, such as automobile makers, commercial carpet contractors (firms that carpet large commercial buildings), apartment complex developers, carpet wholesalers, and large retail carpet outlets.

**Customer Size.** An organization's size may affect its purchasing procedures and the types and quantities of products it wants. Size can thus be an effective variable for segmenting a business market. To reach a segment of a particular size, marketers may have to adjust one or more marketing mix components. For example, customers that buy in extremely large quantities are sometimes offered discounts. In addition, marketers often must expand personal selling efforts to serve large organizational buyers properly. Because the needs of large and small buyers tend to be quite distinct, marketers frequently use different marketing practices to reach various customer groups.

**Product Use.** Certain products, especially basic raw materials like steel, petroleum, plastics, and lumber, are used in numerous ways. How a company uses products affects the types and amounts of products purchased, as well as the purchasing method. For example, computers are used for engineering purposes, basic scientific research, and business operations such as word processing, accounting, and telecommunications. A computer maker therefore may segment the computer market by types of use because organizations' needs for computer hardware and software depend on the purpose for which products are purchased.

# Step 3: Develop Market Segment Profiles

A market segment profile describes the similarities among potential customers within a segment and explains the differences among people and organizations in different segments. A profile may cover such aspects as demographic characteristics, geographic factors, product benefits sought, lifestyles, brand preferences, and usage rates. Individuals and organizations within segments should be relatively similar with respect to several characteristics and product needs, and differ considerably from those within other market segments. Marketers use market segment profiles to assess the degree to which their possible products can match or fit potential customers' product needs. Market segment profiles help marketers understand how a business can use its capabilities to serve potential customer groups.

The use of market segment profiles benefits marketers in several ways. Such profiles help a marketer determine which segment or segments are most attractive to the organization relative to the firm's strengths, weaknesses, objectives, and resources. While marketers may initially believe certain segments are quite attractive, development of market segment profiles may yield information that indicates the opposite. For the market segment or segments chosen by the organization, the information included in market segment profiles can be highly useful in making marketing decisions.

# Step 4: Evaluate Relevant Market Segments

After analyzing the market segment profiles, a marketer is likely to identify several relevant market segments that require further analysis and eliminate certain segments from consideration. To further assess relevant market segments, several important factors, including sales estimates, competition, and estimated costs associated with each segment, should be analyzed.

## Sales Estimates

Potential sales for a market segment can be measured along several dimensions, including product level, geographic area, time, and level of competition.[19] With respect to product level, potential sales can be estimated for a specific product item (for example, Diet Coke) or an entire product line (Coca-Cola Classic, Caffeine-Free Coke, Diet Coke, Caffeine-Free Diet Coke, Vanilla Coke, Diet Vanilla Coke, Cherry Coca-Cola, and Diet Cherry Coca-Cola comprise one product line). A manager must also determine the geographic area to include in the estimate. In relation to time, sales estimates can be short range (one year or less), medium range (one to five years), or long range (longer than five years). The competitive level specifies whether sales are being estimated for a single firm or for an entire industry.

**Market potential** is the total amount of a product that customers will purchase within a specified period at a specific level of industrywide marketing activity. Market potential can be stated in terms of dollars or units. For example, with the aging of the large baby boomer generation, the market potential for medical instruments and medications to treat congestive heart failure, hypertension, and other cardiovascular conditions is estimated to reach over $20 billion by 2013.[20] A segment's market potential is affected by economic, sociocultural, and other environmental forces. Marketers must assume a certain general level of marketing effort in the industry when they estimate market potential. The specific level of marketing effort varies from one firm to another, but the sum of all firms' marketing activities equals industrywide marketing efforts. A marketing manager must also consider whether and to what extent industry marketing efforts will change.

**Company sales potential** is the maximum percentage of market potential that an individual firm within an industry can expect to obtain for a specific product. Several factors influence company sales potential for a market segment. First, the market potential places absolute limits on the size of the company's sales potential. Second, the magnitude of industrywide marketing activities has an indirect but definite impact on the company's sales potential. Those activities have a direct bearing on the size of the market potential. When Domino's Pizza advertises home-delivered pizza, for example, it indirectly promotes pizza in general; its commercials may indirectly help sell Pizza Hut's and other competitors' home-delivered pizza. Third, the intensity and effectiveness of a company's marketing activities relative to competitors' affect the size of the company's sales potential. If a company spends twice as much as any of its competitors on marketing efforts and if each dollar spent is more effective in generating sales, the firm's sales potential will be quite high compared to competitors'.

There are two general approaches to measuring company sales potential: breakdown and buildup. In the **breakdown approach**, the marketing manager first develops a general economic forecast for a specific time period. Next, the manager estimates market potential based on this economic forecast. Then the manager derives the company's sales potential from the general economic forecast and estimate of market potential. In the **buildup approach**, the marketing manager begins by estimating how much of a product a potential buyer in a specific geographic area, such as a sales territory, will purchase in a given period. The manager then multiplies that amount by the total number of potential buyers in that area. The manager performs the same calculation for each geographic area in which the firm sells products and then adds the totals for each area to calculate market potential. To determine company sales potential, the manager must estimate, based on planned levels of company marketing activities, the proportion of the total market potential the company can obtain.

**market potential** The total amount of a product that customers will purchase within a specified period at a specific level of industrywide marketing activity

**company sales potential** The maximum percentage of market potential that an individual firm within an industry can expect to obtain for a specific product

**breakdown approach** Measuring company sales potential based on a general economic forecast for a specific period and the market potential derived from it

**buildup approach** Measuring company sales potential by estimating how much of a product a potential buyer in a specific geographic area will purchase in a given period, multiplying the estimate by the number of potential buyers, and adding the totals of all the geographic areas considered

snapshot

**How much do we spend on pets?** Approximately 63% of U.S. households own a pet. Since 1994, spending on pets has more than doubled.

2005 — $36
2002 — $30
1998 — $23
1994 — $17

Billions of dollars

*Source:* APPMA's 2005/2006 National Pet Owners Survey.

## Competitive Assessment

Besides obtaining sales estimates, it is crucial to assess competitors already operating in the segments being considered. Without competitive information, sales estimates may be misleading. A market segment that seems attractive based on sales estimates may prove much less so following a competitive assessment. Such an assessment should ask several questions about competitors: How many exist? What are their strengths and weaknesses? Do several competitors have major market shares and together dominate the segment? Can our company create a marketing mix to compete effectively against competitors' marketing mixes? Is it likely that new competitors will enter this segment? If so, how will they affect our firm's ability to compete successfully? Answers to such questions are important for proper assessment of the competition in potential market segments.

The actions of a national food company that considered entering the dog food market illustrate the importance of competitive assessment. Through a segmentation study, the company determined that dog owners could be divided into three segments according to how they viewed their dogs and dog foods. One group treated their dogs as companions and family members. These individuals were willing to pay relatively high prices for dog foods and wanted a variety of types and flavors so their dogs would not get bored. The second group saw their dogs as performing a definite utilitarian function, such as protecting family members, playing with children, guarding the property, or herding farm animals. These people wanted a low-priced, nutritious dog food and were not interested in a wide variety of flavors. Dog owners in the third segment were found to actually hate their dogs. These people wanted the cheapest dog food they could buy and were not concerned with nutrition, flavor, or variety. The food company examined the extent to which competitive brands were serving all these dog owners and found that each segment contained at least three well-entrenched competing brands, which together dominated the segment. The company's management decided not to enter the dog food market because of the strength of the competing brands.

### Cost Estimates

To fulfill the needs of a target segment, an organization must develop and maintain a marketing mix that precisely meets the wants and needs of individuals and organizations in that segment. Developing and maintaining such a mix can be expensive. Distinctive product features, attractive package design, generous product warranties, extensive advertising, attractive promotional offers, competitive prices, and high-quality personal service consume considerable organizational resources. Indeed, to reach certain segments, the costs may be so high that a marketer concludes the segment is inaccessible. Another cost consideration is whether the organization can effectively reach a segment at costs equal to or below competitors' costs. If the firm's costs are likely to be higher, it will be unable to compete in that segment in the long run.

# Step 5: Select Specific Target Markets

An important initial consideration in selecting a target market is whether customers' needs differ enough to warrant the use of market segmentation. If segmentation analysis shows customer needs to be fairly homogeneous, the firm's management may decide to use the undifferentiated approach, discussed earlier. However, if customer needs are heterogeneous, which is much more likely, one or more target markets must be selected. On the other hand, marketers may decide not to enter and compete in any of the segments.

Assuming one or more segments offer significant opportunities to achieve organizational objectives, marketers must decide in which segments to participate. Ordinarily information gathered in the previous step—about sales estimates, competitors, and cost estimates—requires careful consideration in this final step to determine long-term profit opportunities. Also, the firm's management must investigate whether the organization has the financial resources, managerial skills, employee expertise, and facilities to enter and compete effectively in selected segments. Furthermore, the requirements of some market segments may be at odds with the firm's overall objectives, and the possibility of legal problems, conflicts with interest groups, and technological advancements could make certain segments unattractive.

In addition, when prospects for long-term growth are taken into account, some segments may appear very attractive and others less desirable.

Selecting appropriate target markets is important to an organization's adoption and use of the marketing concept philosophy. Identifying the right target market is the key to implementing a successful marketing strategy, whereas failure to do so can lead to low sales, high costs, and severe financial losses. A careful target market analysis places an organization in a better position to both serve customers' needs and achieve its objectives.

# Product Positioning and Repositioning

**product positioning** Creating and maintaining a certain concept of a product in customers' minds

Once a target market is selected, a firm must consider how to position its product. **Product positioning** refers to the decisions and activities intended to create and maintain a certain concept of the firm's product (relative to competitive brands) in customers' minds. When marketers introduce a product, they try to position it so that it appears to have the characteristics that the target market most desires. This projected image is crucial. Crest is positioned as a fluoride toothpaste that fights cavities, and Close-Up is positioned as a whitening toothpaste that enhances the user's sex appeal, as shown in Figure 10.7.

## Perceptual Mapping

A product's position is the result of customers' perceptions of the product's attributes relative to those of competitive brands. Buyers make numerous purchase decisions

**figure 10.7**

**TOOTHPASTE PRODUCT POSITIONS**

| Brand | Product position |
|---|---|
| Colgate Total | Fights full range of oral health problems |
| Close-Up | Sexy, whitener, great breath for kissing |
| Crest | Powerful fluoride cavity fighter |
| Aim | Milder taste than other brands, kid-friendly |
| Arm & Hammer | Popular baking soda mixed with toothpaste |
| AquaFresh | Kills germs, for young adults |
| Biotene | Reduces bacteria and germs in mouth |
| Oral-B | High quality, dentist approved |
| Rembrandt | Higher quality whitening |
| Sensodyne | Especially for sensitive teeth |
| Mentadent | Baking soda and peroxide for fresh breath |
| Ultrabrite | Low priced whitener, removes stains |

**Product Positioning**

Colgate positions its Total toothpaste as the superior plaque fighter.

on a regular basis. To avoid a continuous reevaluation of numerous products, buyers tend to group, or "position," products in their minds to simplify buying decisions. Rather than allowing customers to position products independently, marketers often try to influence and shape consumers' concepts or perceptions of products through advertising. Marketers sometimes analyze product positions by developing perceptual maps, as shown in Figure 10.8 (on p. 288). Perceptual maps are created by questioning a sample of consumers about their perceptions of products, brands, and organizations with respect to two or more dimensions. To develop a perceptual map like the one in Figure 10.8, respondents would be asked how they perceive selected pain relievers in regard to price and type of pain for which the products are used. Also, respondents would be asked about their preferences for product features to establish "ideal points" or "ideal clusters," which represent a consensus about what a specific group of customers desires in terms of product features. Then marketers can compare how their brand is perceived compared with the ideal points.

## Bases for Positioning

Marketers can use several bases for product positioning. A common basis for positioning products is to use competitors. A firm can position a product to compete head-on with another brand, as PepsiCo has done against Coca-Cola, or to avoid competition, as 7Up has done relative to other soft-drink producers. Head-to-head competition may be a marketer's positioning objective if the product's performance characteristics are at least equal to those of competitive brands and if the product is priced lower. Head-to-head positioning may be appropriate even when the price is higher if the product's performance characteristics are superior. For example, the no-calorie sweetener Splenda is positioned as a healthier sugar substitute through its campaign slogan "Made from sugar so it tastes like sugar." Splenda also competes head-to-head through advertisements that indicate how it is unlike other no-calorie sweeteners because it is heat tolerant and can be used in baking as a cup-for-cup

**figure 10.8**

## HYPOTHETICAL PERCEPTUAL MAP FOR PAIN RELIEVERS

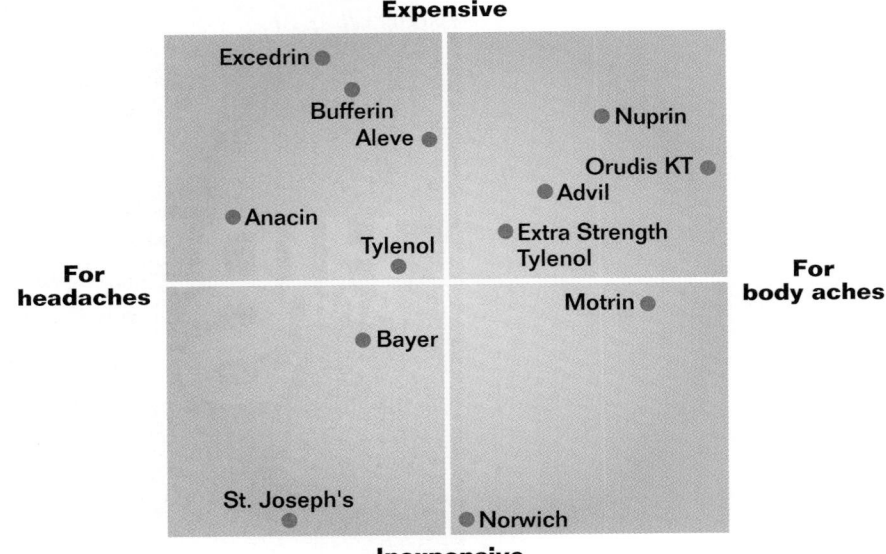

sugar substitute.[21] Conversely, positioning to avoid competition may be best when the product's performance characteristics do not differ significantly from competing brands. Moreover, positioning a brand to avoid competition may be appropriate when that brand has unique characteristics that are important to some buyers. Volvo, for example, has for years positioned itself away from competitors by focusing on the safety characteristics of its cars. Whereas some auto companies mention safety issues in their advertisements, many are more likely to focus on style, fuel efficiency, performance, or terms of sale. Avoiding competition is critical when a firm introduces a brand into a market in which the company already has one or more brands. Marketers usually want to avoid cannibalizing sales of their existing brands, unless the new brand generates substantially larger profits.

A product's position can be based on specific product attributes or features. For example, the Apple iPod is positioned based on product attributes such as its unique shape, its storage capacity (stores thousands of songs), and its access to iTunes music store. If a product has been planned properly, its features will give it the distinct appeal needed. Style, shape, construction, and color help create the image and the appeal. If buyers can easily identify the benefits, they are, of course, more likely to purchase the product. When the new product does not offer certain preferred attributes, there is room for another new product.

Other bases for product positioning include price, quality level, and benefits provided by the product. For example, Era detergent provides stain treatment and stain removal. Also, a positioning basis employed by some marketers is the target market. This type of positioning relies heavily on promoting the types of people who use the product.

### Repositioning

Positioning decisions are not just for new products. Evaluating the positions of existing products is important because a brand's market share and profitability may be strengthened by product repositioning. For example, several years ago Kraft was on the verge of discontinuing Cheez Whiz because its sales had declined considerably. After Kraft marketers repositioned Cheez Whiz as a fast, convenient, microwavable cheese sauce, its sales rebounded and achieved new heights. When introducing a new product into a product line, one or more existing brands may have to be repositioned to minimize cannibalization of established brands and ensure a favorable position for the new brand.

Repositioning can be accomplished by physically changing the product, its price, or its distribution. Rather than making any of these changes, marketers sometimes reposition a product by changing its image through promotional efforts. Finally, a marketer may reposition a product by aiming it at a different target market.

# Developing Sales Forecasts

**sales forecast** The amount of a product a company expects to sell during a specific period at a specified level of marketing activities

After a company targets its market and positions its product, it needs a **sales forecast**—the amount of a product the company expects to sell during a specific period at a specified level of marketing activities. The sales forecast differs from the company sales potential. It concentrates on what actual sales will be at a certain level of company marketing effort, whereas the company sales potential assesses what sales are possible at various levels of marketing activities, assuming certain environmental conditions will exist. Businesses use the sales forecast for planning, organizing, implementing, and controlling their activities. The success of numerous activities depends on this forecast's accuracy. Common problems in failing companies are improper planning and lack of realistic sales forecasts. Overly ambitious sales forecasts can lead to overbuying, overinvestment, and higher costs.

To forecast sales, a marketer can choose from a number of forecasting methods, some arbitrary and others more scientific, complex, and time consuming. A firm's choice of method or methods depends on the costs involved, type of product, market characteristics, time span of the forecast, purposes of the forecast, stability of the historical sales data, availability of required information, managerial preferences, and forecasters' expertise and experience.[22] Common forecasting techniques fall into five categories: executive judgment, surveys, time series analysis, regression analysis, and market tests.

## Executive Judgment

**executive judgment** A sales forecasting method based on the intuition of one or more executives

At times, a company forecasts sales chiefly on the basis of **executive judgment**, the intuition of one or more executives. This approach is unscientific but expedient and inexpensive. Executive judgment may work reasonably well when product demand is relatively stable and the forecaster has years of market-related experience. However, because intuition is swayed most heavily by recent experience, the forecast may be overly optimistic or overly pessimistic. Another drawback to intuition is that the forecaster has only past experience as a guide for deciding where to go in the future.

## Surveys

**customer forecasting survey** A survey of customers regarding the quantities of products they intend to buy during a specific period

Another way to forecast sales is to question customers, sales personnel, or experts regarding their expectations about future purchases. In a **customer forecasting survey**, marketers ask customers what types and quantities of products they intend to buy during a specific period. This approach may be useful to a business with relatively few customers. For example, Intel, which markets to a limited number of companies (primarily computer manufacturers), could conduct customer forecasting surveys effectively. PepsiCo, in contrast, has millions of customers and could not feasibly use a customer survey to forecast future sales.

Customer surveys have several drawbacks. Customers must be able and willing to make accurate estimates of future product requirements. Although some organizational buyers can estimate their anticipated purchases accurately from historical buying data and their own sales forecasts, many cannot make such estimates. In addition, customers may not want to take part in a survey. Occasionally a few respondents give answers they know are incorrect, making survey results inaccurate. Moreover, customer surveys reflect buying intentions rather than actual purchases. Customers' intentions may not be well formulated, and even when potential purchasers have definite buying intentions, they do not necessarily follow through on them. Finally, customer surveys consume much time and money.

**sales force forecasting survey** A survey of a firm's sales force regarding anticipated sales in their territories for a specified period

In a **sales force forecasting survey**, the firm's salespeople estimate anticipated sales in their territories for a specified period. The forecaster combines these territorial estimates to arrive at a tentative forecast. A marketer may survey the sales staff for several reasons. The most important is that the sales staff is closer to customers on a daily basis than other company personnel and therefore should know more about customers' future product needs. Moreover, when sales representatives assist in developing the forecast, they are more likely to work toward its achievement. In addition, forecasts can be prepared for single territories, divisions consisting of several territories, regions made up of multiple divisions, and the total geographic market. Thus, the method provides sales forecasts from the smallest geographic sales unit to the largest.

A sales force survey also has limitations. Salespeople may be too optimistic or pessimistic due to recent experiences. In addition, salespeople tend to underestimate sales potential in their territories when they believe their sales goals will be determined by their forecasts. They also dislike paperwork because it takes up time that could be spent selling. If preparation of a territorial sales forecast is time consuming, the sales staff may not do the job adequately.

Nonetheless, sales force surveys can be effective under certain conditions. The salespeople as a group must be accurate, or at least consistent, estimators. If the aggregate forecast is consistently over or under actual sales, the individual who develops the final forecast can make the necessary adjustments. Assuming the survey is well administered, the sales force can have the satisfaction of helping to establish reasonable sales goals and the assurance that its forecasts are not being used to set sales quotas.

**expert forecasting survey** Sales forecasts prepared by experts outside the firm, such as economists, management consultants, advertising executives, or college professors

When a company wants an **expert forecasting survey**, it hires professionals to help prepare the sales forecast. These experts are usually economists, management consultants, advertising executives, college professors, or other individuals outside the firm with solid experience in a specific market. Drawing on this experience and their analyses of available information about the company and the market, experts prepare and present forecasts or answer questions regarding a forecast. Using experts is expedient and relatively inexpensive. However, because they work outside the firm, these forecasters may be less motivated than company personnel to do an effective job.

**Delphi technique** A procedure in which experts create initial forecasts, submit them to the company for averaging, and then refine the forecasts

A more complex form of the expert forecasting survey incorporates the Delphi technique. In the **Delphi technique**, experts create initial forecasts, submit them to the company for averaging, and have the results returned to them so they can make individual refined forecasts. The premise is that the experts will use the averaged results when making refined forecasts and these forecasts will be in a narrower range. The procedure may be repeated several times until the experts, each working separately, reach a consensus on the forecasts. The ultimate goal in using the Delphi technique is to develop a highly accurate sales forecast.

**time series analysis** A forecasting method that uses historical sales data to discover patterns in the firm's sales over time and generally involves trend, cycle, seasonal, and random factor analyses

## Time Series Analysis

With **time series analysis**, the forecaster uses the firm's historical sales data to discover a pattern or patterns in the firm's sales over time. If a pattern is found, it can be used to forecast sales. This forecasting method assumes that past sales patterns will continue in the future. The accuracy, and thus usefulness, of time series analysis hinges on the validity of this assumption.

In a time series analysis, a forecaster usually performs four types of analysis: trend, cycle, seasonal, and random fac-

**marketing ENTREPRENEURS**

**Tim Keck and Chris Johnson**
THEIR BUSINESS: The *Onion*
FOUNDED: As juniors in college
SUCCESS: Revenues of $7 million a year

Tim Keck and Chris Johnson, students at the University of Wisconsin, took out an $8,000 loan to start the *Onion*, a free paper they distributed from their dorm that spoofed university events. The paper immediately began to profit and after the first year, the pair decided to sell the *Onion* to a couple of their collaborators. Since then, printed versions of the weekly have been launched in five cities, which together with the online version (**www.theonion.com**) reach more than 3 million readers weekly. The bulk of the paper's revenues stem from newspaper and web advertisers.

**trend analysis** An analysis that focuses on aggregate sales data over a period of many years to determine general trends in annual sales

**cycle analysis** An analysis of sales figures for a period of three to five years to ascertain whether sales fluctuate in a consistent, periodic manner

**seasonal analysis** An analysis of daily, weekly, or monthly sales figures to evaluate the degree to which seasonal factors influence sales

**random factor analysis** An analysis attempting to attribute erratic sales variations to random, nonrecurrent events

**regression analysis** A method of predicting sales based on finding a relationship between past sales and one or more independent variables, such as population or income

**market test** Making a product available to buyers in one or more test areas and measuring purchases and consumer responses to marketing efforts

tor. **Trend analysis** focuses on aggregate sales data, such as the company's annual sales figures, covering a period of many years to determine whether annual sales are generally rising, falling, or staying about the same. Through **cycle analysis**, a forecaster analyzes sales figures (often monthly sales data) from a period of three to five years to ascertain whether sales fluctuate in a consistent, periodic manner. When performing a **seasonal analysis**, the analyst studies daily, weekly, or monthly sales figures to evaluate the degree to which seasonal factors, such as climate and holiday activities, influence sales. In a **random factor analysis**, the forecaster attempts to attribute erratic sales variations to random, nonrecurrent events, such as a regional power failure, a natural disaster, or political unrest in a foreign market. After performing each of these analyses, the forecaster combines the results to develop the sales forecast. Time series analysis is an effective forecasting method for products with reasonably stable demand, but not for products with highly erratic demand.

## Regression Analysis

Like time series analysis, regression analysis requires the use of historical sales data. In **regression analysis**, the forecaster seeks to find a relationship between past sales (the dependent variable) and one or more independent variables, such as population, per capita income, or gross domestic product. Simple regression analysis uses one independent variable, whereas multiple regression analysis includes two or more independent variables. The objective of regression analysis is to develop a mathematical formula that accurately describes a relationship between the firm's sales and one or more variables; however, the formula indicates only an association, not a causal relationship. Once an accurate formula is established, the analyst plugs the necessary information into the formula to derive the sales forecast.

Regression analysis is useful when a precise association can be established. However, a forecaster seldom finds a perfect correlation. Furthermore, this method can be used only when available historical sales data are extensive. Thus, regression analysis is futile for forecasting sales of new products.

## Market Tests

A **market test** involves making a product available to buyers in one or more test areas and measuring purchases and consumer responses to distribution, promotion, and price. Test areas are often cities with populations of 200,000 to 500,000, but can be larger metropolitan areas or towns with populations of 50,000 to 200,000. For example, ACNielsen Market Decisions, a marketing research firm, conducts market tests for client firms in Boise, Tucson, Colorado Springs, Peoria, Evansville, Charleston, and Portland, in addition to custom test markets in cities chosen by clients.[23] A market test provides information about consumers' actual rather than intended purchases. In addition, purchase volume can be evaluated in relation to the intensity of other marketing activities such as advertising, in-store promotions, pricing, packaging, and distribution. Forecasters base their sales estimates for larger geographic units on customer response in test areas.

Because it does not require historical sales data, a market test is effective for forecasting sales of new products or sales of existing products in new geographic areas. A market test also gives a marketer an opportunity to test various elements of the marketing mix. However, these tests are often time consuming and expensive. In addition, a marketer cannot be certain that consumer response during a market test represents the total market response or that such a response will continue in the future.

## Using Multiple Forecasting Methods

Although some businesses depend on a single sales forecasting method, most firms use several techniques. Sometimes a company is forced to use multiple methods when marketing diverse product lines, but even a single product line may require several forecasts, especially when the product is sold to different market segments. Thus, a producer of automobile tires may rely on one technique to forecast tire sales for new cars and on another to forecast sales of replacement tires. Variation in the length of needed forecasts may call for several forecasting methods. A firm that employs one method for a short-range forecast may find it inappropriate for long-range forecasting. Sometimes a marketer verifies results of one method by using one or more other methods and comparing outcomes.

## SUMMARY

A market is an aggregate of people who, as individuals or as organizations, have needs for products in a product class and have the ability, willingness, and authority to purchase such products.

In general, marketers employ a five-step process when selecting a target market. Step 1 is to identify the appropriate targeting strategy. When a company designs a single marketing mix and directs it at the entire market for a particular product, it is using an undifferentiated targeting strategy. The undifferentiated strategy is effective in a homogeneous market, whereas a heterogeneous market needs to be segmented through a concentrated targeting strategy or a differentiated targeting strategy. Both these strategies divide markets into segments consisting of individuals, groups, or organizations that have one or more similar characteristics and thus can be linked to similar product needs. When using a concentrated strategy, an organization directs marketing efforts toward a single market segment through one marketing mix. With a differentiated targeting strategy, an organization directs customized marketing efforts at two or more segments.

Certain conditions must exist for effective market segmentation. First, customers' needs for the product should be heterogeneous. Second, the segments of the market should be identifiable and divisible. Third, the total market should be divided so that segments can be compared with respect to estimated sales, costs, and profits. Fourth, at least one segment must have enough profit potential to justify developing and maintaining a special marketing mix for that segment. Fifth, the firm must be able to reach the chosen segment with a particular marketing mix.

Step 2 is determining which segmentation variables to use. Segmentation variables are the characteristics of individuals, groups, or organizations used to divide a total market into segments. The segmentation variable should relate to customers' needs for, uses of, or behavior toward the product. Segmentation variables for consumer markets can be grouped into four categories: demographic (e.g., age, gender, income, ethnicity, family life cycle), geographic (population, market density, climate), psychographic (personality traits, motives, lifestyles), and behavioristic (volume usage, end use, expected benefits, brand loyalty, price sensitivity). Variables for segmenting business markets include geographic location, type of organization, customer size, and product use.

Step 3 in the target market selection process is to develop market segment profiles. Such profiles describe the similarities among potential customers within a segment and explain the differences among people and organizations in different market segments. Step 4 is evaluating relevant market segments, which requires that several important factors—including sales estimates, competition, and estimated costs associated with each segment—be determined and analyzed. Step 5 involves the actual selection of specific target markets. In this final step, the company considers whether customers' needs differ enough to warrant segmentation and which segments to target.

Product positioning relates to the decisions and activities that create and maintain a certain concept of the firm's product in customers' minds. It plays a role in market segmentation. Organizations can position a product to compete head to head with another brand or to avoid competition. Repositioning by making physical changes in the product, changing its price or distribution, or changing its image can boost a brand's market share and profitability.

A sales forecast is the amount of a product the company actually expects to sell during a specific period at a specified level of marketing activities. To forecast sales, marketers can choose from a number of methods. The choice depends on various factors, including the costs involved, type of product, market characteristics, and time span and purposes of the forecast. There are five categories of forecasting techniques: executive judgment, surveys, time series analysis, regression analysis, and market tests. Executive judgment is based on the intuition of one or more executives. Surveys include customer, sales force, and expert forecasting surveys. Time series analysis uses the firm's historical sales data to discover patterns in the firm's sales over time and employs four major types of analyses: trend, cycle, seasonal, and random factor. With regression analysis, forecasters attempt to find a relationship between past sales and one or more independent variables. Market testing involves making a product available to buyers in one or more test areas and measuring purchases and consumer responses to distribution, promotion, and price. Many companies employ multiple forecasting methods.

**ACE self-test**   Please visit the student website at **www.prideferrell.com** for ACE Self-Test questions that will help you prepare for exams.

## IMPORTANT TERMS

Undifferentiated targeting strategy
Homogeneous market
Heterogeneous market
Market segmentation
Market segment
Concentrated targeting strategy
Differentiated targeting strategy

Segmentation variables
Market density
Geodemographic segmentation
Micromarketing
Benefit segmentation
Market potential
Company sales potential
Breakdown approach
Buildup approach

Product positioning
Sales forecast
Executive judgment
Customer forecasting survey
Sales force forecasting survey
Expert forecasting survey
Delphi technique
Time series analysis

Trend analysis
Cycle analysis
Seasonal analysis
Random factor analysis
Regression analysis
Market test

## DISCUSSION & REVIEW QUESTIONS

1.  What is a market? What are the requirements for a market?

2.  In your local area, identify a group of people with unsatisfied product needs who represent a market. Could this market be reached by a business organization? Why or why not?

3.  Outline the five major steps in the target market selection process.

4.  What is an undifferentiated strategy? Under what conditions is it most useful? Describe a present market situation in which a company is using an undifferentiated strategy. Is the business successful? Why or why not?

5.  What is market segmentation? Describe the basic conditions required for effective segmentation. Identify several firms that use market segmentation.

6.  List the differences between concentrated and differentiated strategies, and describe the advantages and disadvantages of each.

7.  Identify and describe four major categories of variables that can be used to segment consumer markets. Give examples of product markets that are segmented by variables in each category.

8.  What dimensions are used to segment business markets?

9.  Define *geodemographic segmentation*. Identify several types of firms that might employ this type of market segmentation, and explain why.

10. What is a market segment profile? Why is it an important step in the target market selection process?

11. Describe the important factors that marketers should analyze to evaluate market segments.

12. Why is a marketer concerned about sales potential when trying to select a target market?

13. Why is selecting appropriate target markets important for an organization that wants to adopt the marketing concept philosophy?

14. What is product positioning? Under what conditions would head-to-head product positioning be appropriate? When should head-to-head positioning be avoided?

15. What is a sales forecast? Why is it important?

16. What are the two primary types of surveys a company might use to forecast sales? Why would a company use an outside expert forecasting survey?

17. Under what conditions are market tests useful for sales forecasting? What are the advantages and disadvantages of market tests?

18. Under what conditions might a firm use multiple forecasting methods?

## APPLICATION QUESTIONS

1.  MTV Latino targets the growing Hispanic market in the United States. Identify another product marketed to a distinct target market. Describe the target market, and explain how the marketing mix appeals specifically to that group.

2.  Generally marketers use one of three basic targeting strategies to focus on a target market: (1) undifferentiated, (2) concentrated, or (3) differentiated. Locate an article that describes the targeting strategy of a particular organization. Describe the target market, and explain the strategy being used to reach that market.

3. The stereo market may be segmented according to income and age. Discuss two ways the market for each of the following products might be segmented.
   a. Candy bars
   b. Travel agency services
   c. Bicycles
   d. Hair spray

4. Product positioning aims to create a certain concept of a product in consumers' minds relative to its competition. For example, Pepsi is positioned in direct competition with Coca-Cola, whereas Volvo has traditionally positioned itself away from competitors by emphasizing its cars' safety features. Following are several distinct positions in which an organization may place its product. Identify a product that would fit into each position.
   a. High price/high quality
   b. Low price
   c. Convenience
   d. Uniqueness

5. If you were using a time series analysis to forecast sales for your company for the next year, how would you use the following sets of sales figures?

   a. 1998 $145,000    2003 $149,000
      1999 $144,000    2004 $148,000
      2000 $147,000    2005 $180,000
      2001 $145,000    2006 $191,000
      2002 $148,000    2007 $227,000

b.

| | 2005 | 2006 | 2007 |
|---|---|---|---|
| Jan. | $12,000 | $14,000 | $16,000 |
| Feb. | $13,000 | $14,000 | $15,500 |
| Mar. | $12,000 | $14,000 | $17,000 |
| Apr. | $13,000 | $15,000 | $17,000 |
| May | $15,000 | $17,000 | $20,000 |
| June | $18,000 | $18,000 | $21,000 |
| July | $18,500 | $18,000 | $21,500 |
| Aug. | $18,500 | $19,000 | $22,000 |
| Sep. | $17,000 | $18,000 | $21,000 |
| Oct. | $16,000 | $15,000 | $19,000 |
| Nov. | $13,000 | $14,000 | $19,000 |
| Dec. | $14,000 | $15,000 | $18,000 |

   c. 2005 sales increased 21.2 percent (opened an additional store in 2005)

      2006 sales increased 18.8 percent (opened another store in 2006)

globalEDGE™

1. One approach for marketers to evaluate the level of expectations among consumers is to analyze a city's standard of living. A comparison of the overall quality of life across a variety of cities can be accomplished by analyzing Mercer's "Top 50 Rankings for Quality of Living." This ranking can be accessed by using the search term "overall quality of life" at **http://globaledge.msu.edu/ibrd**. In addition to the likelihood that market offerings may be more expensive in certain cities, marketers may determine which cities have higher expectations of product and service quality. What are the top five cities in the United States? What cities rank in the top five worldwide? Can the locations of these cities complicate or simplify a differentiated marketing strategy campaign?

2. The level of a country's urbanization can have profound implications for marketers. While a variety of resources may provide insight on this topic, data from the Population Reference Bureau's website may be useful. This data can be found by using the search term "data query tool" at **http://globaledge.msu.edu/ibrd**. Once you get to the Population Reference Bureau website, the level of urban population statistic can be found under the All Variables category. What is the level of urbanization of the United States? Choose four additional countries and compare your results with the United States. What particular challenges might you need to consider in markets with higher or lower levels of urbanization?

## INTERNET Exercise

Visit www.prideferrell.com for resources to help you master the material in this chapter, plus materials that will help you expand your marketing knowledge, including Internet exercise updates, ACE Self-Tests, hotlinks to companies featured in this chapter, and much more.

### iExplore

iExplore is an Internet company that offers a variety of travel and adventure products. Learn more about its goods, services, and travel advice through its website at www.iexplore.com.

1. Based on the information provided at the website, what are some of iExplore's basic products?
2. What market segments does iExplore appear to be targeting with its website? What segmentation variables is the company using to segment these markets?
3. How does iExplore appeal to comparison shoppers?

## Video Case 10.1   Jordan's Furniture: Shoppertaining Its Target Market

Samuel Tatelman began selling furniture out of the back of his truck in Waltham, Massachusetts, in 1918. Today his grandsons, Eliot and Barry, sell more furniture per square foot at Jordan's Furniture than at any other furniture retailer in the country and attract record numbers of guests each week. With just four stores, Jordan's Furniture has grown from 15 employees 25 years ago to over 1,000 today. Jordan's Furniture is also in the process of a massive expansion and plans to double its number of both stores and employees in the next few years.

The company has broken just about all industry standards. Inventory turns over at a rate of 13 times a year, compared to an average of 1 to 2 times a year in most furniture stores. Advertising expenditures are 2 percent, while the industry average is 7 percent. Sales per square foot are $950, whereas most furniture stores average $150 in sales per square foot.

When the brothers took over the business in 1973, they decided to focus their efforts on the 18- to 34-year-old market segment. While most furniture stores do not target specific customers, the Tatelmans felt that people with first homes or new families would need furniture more. To bring customers, even those not currently shopping for furniture, into the stores (particularly young families), the brothers invented what they call "shoppertainment" and created stores that were imaginative, fun, and a little Disney-like. Their "shoppertainment" concept paid off because the stores now host more than 4,000 visitors on an average weekend.

When customers walk into a Jordan's Furniture store, they might be greeted with a welcome map, be offered freshly baked chocolate chip cookies, or receive a hearty greeting from an animatronic Elvis. "We've taken furniture shopping and given it new life by making it more of a fun experience rather than this 'God, I have to go furniture shopping' [experience]," says Eliot. "Beantown," a re-creation of Boston made of 25 million jelly beans stands next to an ice cream stand. Indoor fireworks and jazz music enliven a re-creation of New Orleans's famous Bourbon Street, complete with amusement rides for kids, animated characters, and snack stands. Jordan's Furniture also offers a flight simulator and trapeze lessons to adventurous customers. A 300-seat IMAX theater brings customers in for a movie, but they leave the store by walking through showrooms of furniture.

The stores are strategically laid out to make the shopping experience not only fun, but also easy. Instead of arranging furniture by manufacturer, Jordan's Furniture puts all of its categories together so customers can see all of their offerings at the same time. "If you came in looking for a bedroom set, we'll make it easy to see every bedroom set we carry," says Eliot. The stores are also equipped with Dell workstations so that employees can quickly look up product details and pricing. Their Sleep Lab (complete with white-coated "Sleep Technicians") offers a questionnaire that helps customers find a mattress suited for maximum personal comfort. The showrooms are also equipped with low-level lighting that dim when customers lay down on a mattress.

With so many families making Jordan's Furniture a weekend outing and school groups visiting the IMAX on field trips, Jordan's Furniture has expanded its product mix to include nursery and children's furniture. The playful displays of hanging basketballs and soccer balls are designed especially to appeal to young tastes. The youth department uses painted murals to create a fun atmosphere. A safari-themed room showcases bunk beds and lofts.

Jordan's Furniture has also added an infants' section with soft white track lights. Since each department at Jordan's Furniture has its own theme music to set the tone, soft lullabies can be heard in the nursery section. Because of the high volume of families visiting the stores, Jordan's Furniture nursery products have been successful based on word of mouth alone.

By taking the focus off furniture and putting it on people, Jordan's Furniture has pulled ahead of its com-

petitors. "A lot of people look at their business strictly from the cash register's point of view. I can stand outside and watch people leaving and coming in and see smiles on their faces. When they're walking out smiling, happy, and having a good time," says Tatelman, "I know the cash register is going to be ringing."[24,25]

### Questions for Discussion

1. What type of targeting strategy is Jordan's Furniture using?
2. Describe and evaluate the company's target market.
3. Discuss the positioning of Jordan's Furniture's bedding products.

## Case 10.2   IKEA's Leksvik and Klippan Sofas: Coming to a Living Room Near You

For more than 60 years, the Swedish firm IKEA has marketed simple but stylish home furnishings for cost-conscious customers who don't mind assembling their purchases to save money. In addition to welcoming shoppers in its stores, IKEA invites customers to shop online and through catalogs. Traditional furniture stores display beautiful home furnishings for high-end customers with deep pockets and little inclination to attach legs to a table or bolt together a bed frame. In contrast, IKEA's strategy is "to offer a wide range of home furnishings with good design and function at prices so low that as many people as possible will be able to afford them." Its products are of wide range—from frying pans and lamps to kitchen cabinets and living room suites—and come in styles that can be easily coordinated.

To keep prices low for its thrifty customers, IKEA is relentless in looking for ways to cut costs in manufacturing, marketing, warehousing, raw materials, and sales and then pass the savings along. For example, it buys raw materials in bulk and searches the world for efficient suppliers to keep per-unit costs low. It uses a special software package to collect price quotes from suppliers and streamline the purchasing process. For a company that buys from 1,300 suppliers in 53 countries, even small efficiencies quickly add up to significant savings. More cost savings come from shipping furniture unassembled in flat boxes and having customers assemble their purchases at home. Low cost is not the only consideration, however. IKEA also requires its suppliers to abide by a code of conduct that forbids child labor, sets minimum standards for working conditions, and protects the environment.

Although IKEA's customers are frugal, they want to buy fashionable furniture that fits their personalities and lifestyles. In fact, the store's appeal cuts across demographic lines. Some customers who can well afford to shop at the poshest emporiums come to IKEA because they like the combination of chic design, down-to-earth functionality, and speedy assembly. Not every item must be assembled, but those that do are accompanied by simple, step-by-step instructions, which reassure even the most inexperienced do-it-yourselfer.

If customers get hungry as they walk through one of IKEA's cavernous stores, they can drop into the informal store restaurant for a quick snack or a light meal of delicacies from IKEA's home country. The most popular dish is Swedish meatballs: customers devour 150 million of these tiny meatballs every year.

Customers in many countries have responded enthusiastically to IKEA's formula of fashionable, affordable, and functional furniture. After expanding beyond Sweden to Norway and Denmark, the company opened stores in Europe, Australia, Canada, and, in 1985, the United States. More recently, IKEA has opened stores in Russia, Japan, and China, with additional U.S. outlets on the way.

Product names such as Leksvik bookcases and Klippan sofas are known throughout the world and reflect IKEA's Swedish origins. However, the company translates its catalogs into 36 languages and distributes 160 million copies every year. Here again, IKEA looks for ways to minimize expenses. It has all products photographed at one of Europe's largest studios and transmits the images electronically to printing facilities in the different regions where the catalogs will be distributed, saving on shipping and mailing costs. Every detail, from paper quality to type size, is scrutinized to identify new cost efficiencies.

IKEA's targeting strategy has helped it become a cult global brand. Every year, 410 million people go shopping in IKEA stores. The combined annual sales of home furnishings (and restaurant meals) in all of its 226 stores is nearly $18 billion. North America is one of IKEA's most important markets because it accounts for 16 percent of sales, and there are plans to have 50 stores open by 2010. No matter how large and fast IKEA grows, its focus will remain on keeping costs low

to continue satisfying its target market's need for reasonably priced, well-designed, assemble-it-yourself home furnishings.[26]

## Questions for Discussion

1. Is IKEA's targeting strategy concentrated or undifferentiated? Explain your answer.
2. Which of the variables for segmenting consumer markets is IKEA using, and why are these variables appropriate?
3. What combination of techniques might IKEA apply when preparing sales forecasts for North America?

## Strategic Case 4    Reebok Races into the Urban Market

Reebok wants to give front-runner Nike a run for its money in the race for market share in athletic footwear, apparel, and equipment. Reebok, based in Canton, Massachusetts, gained speed from the 1980s into the early 1990s by marketing special aerobics shoes for women. Then Nike pulled way ahead with new clothing and equipment endorsed by high-profile athletes such as Michael Jordan and Tiger Woods. Nike has remained the market leader, completely outdistancing all competitors to dominate the industry with $10.7 billion in annual sales and a 35 percent share of the U.S. sportswear market. In contrast, Reebok's U.S. market share is about one-half that of Nike, and its $3.5 billion in annual sales is about one-third of Nike's. Now Reebok is seeking to close the distance by changing its selection of target markets. In the process, it is aiming to change consumers' perceptions of and attitudes toward its brand and its products with the objective of boosting both sales and profits.

### Breaking Tradition with Hip-Hop

Traditionally sneaker manufacturers have captured market attention by signing successful or fast-rising sports stars to promote their shoes. Reebok still likes to link its brand to popular sports. Its multimillion-dollar contract with basketball's Yao Ming is one of the industry's most expensive deals, and it has many other sports figures under contract, including tennis star Venus Williams. The fierce rivalry with Nike continues on the playing field. Reebok has lucrative contracts to make branded hats for the National Basketball Association and to supply the National Football League with uniforms and equipment. Nike has an exclusive contract to provide performance apparel to all 30 major league baseball teams.

Looking beyond sports, Reebok's marketers investigated the urban market, where fashion rather than performance is the deciding factor in buying decisions. Urban teens tend to be extremely style conscious, buying as many as 10 pairs of athletic-style shoes a year so they can be seen in the very latest thing. Many are also fans of hip-hop music and buy clothing designed by hip-hop celebrities such as Jay-Z, Sean "P. Diddy" Combs, and Russell Simmons.

Reebok's marketing research confirmed this market's considerable buying power and the influence of hip-hop artists. To effectively reach this market, Reebok needed a new brand, new products, and new promotional efforts. First, the company took the focus off its mainstream Reebok brand by creating Rbk as a new brand specifically for the urban market. Next, it partnered with hip-hop artists such as Jay-Z and 50 Cent to develop special footwear collections, backed by targeted promotional efforts emphasizing style with attitude.

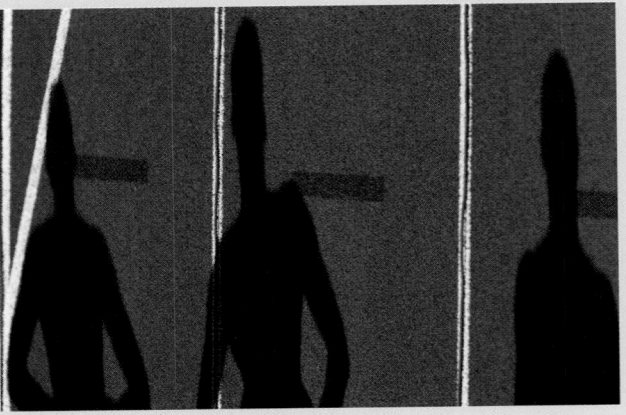

### New Street Credibility

Reebok found it was tapping into a significant market opportunity. Right after Reebok introduced soft-leather, flat-soled S. Carter shoes (after Jay-Z's original name, Shawn Carter), the line sold out. Demand for the $100 shoes quickly spiked so high that eager buyers bid up to $250 for one pair on the eBay auction site. Within eight months, the company had shipped 500,000 pairs to retailers around the country and was preparing to launch a second S. Carter shoe.

On the heels of this success, Reebok introduced G-Unit footwear, named after a hit song by the rapper 50 Cent, who says, "Reebok's Rbk Collection is the real thing when it comes to connecting with the street and hip-hop culture." Hip-hop's Eve was also asked to design a shoe. "She is one of the first artists in the campaign who has male and female appeal, urban and suburban," observes Reebok's director of global advertising. "She is as much a fashion icon as a music icon."

Moreover, the company found a way to bring sports and hip-hop together by launching the 13 Collection line of shoes by basketball star Allen Iverson. Iverson promoted the line by appearing in a series of fast-paced commercials filmed in rap-video style. Although he was shown playing basketball for a second or two, the commercials focused more on his off-court style than his on-court technique.

Despite the added credibility that such celebrities bring to the Rbk brand, the strategy entails some risks. Fads in street fashion and music can come and go at a dizzying pace, which means a shoe that is red-hot one day may be ice-cold the next. Moreover, Reebok might feel the repercussions if one of its celebrities gets into trouble. Still, the company's chief marketing officer is committed to the strategy. "With athletes, they wear the shoes for the length of a basketball season," he comments. "With hip-hop, the publicity is intense but short, just like movies." The advantage, he says, is that "you'll know very quickly whether you hit or miss."

## Targeting Urban Markets in China

In pursuit of growth, Reebok is also targeting promising global markets. China is high on its list of priorities. Interest in sports is skyrocketing there, thanks in part to Chinese basketball star Yao Ming's move to the NBA. According to company research, 93 percent of Chinese males ages 13 to 25—a prime market for athletic shoes—watch NBA broadcasts on a regular basis. Reebok's Asia Pacific general manager cites one projection showing 50 percent annual growth in footwear sales. His prediction: "It's hard to say what the [actual sales] numbers are going to be, but they are going to be huge."

To make the most of this opportunity, Reebok has set up "Yao's House" basketball courts around central Shanghai. Each features the Reebok trademark and a giant *Sports Illustrated* cover showing the basketball star. By giving teens and young adults a place to hone their slam dunks, Reebok hopes to shape their attitudes toward its products. "The trends are made in the urban areas and on street basketball courts, just like in the United States," says one Reebok executive.

Reebok is not the only athletic-shoe manufacturer entering this market. Nike sponsors a basketball court in Beijing, New Balance is building awareness of its shoes, and Pony is selling sneakers in Beijing, Shanghai, and Guandong. With the Summer Olympics coming to Beijing in 2008, sports fever is likely to spread throughout the major cities.

## Reebok's New Vector

Nike has its Swoosh, one of the most recognized trademarks in the world. Now Reebok has its Vector, a streamlined trademark designed to communicate the brand's attributes in a fast, fun way. The idea is to make the Vector synonymous with Reebok, just as the Swoosh is synonymous with Nike. "Our research suggests that consumers react better to logos than words, and it's a very effective marketing tool," stresses Reebok's head of marketing.

In addition, the company is giving its brand a touch of glamour with showcase stores in major U.S. cities. In New York City, for example, Reebok opened a new men's store right next to its women's store. Both feature footwear, apparel, and accessories, and both share the building with the Reebok Sport Club/NY. The displays are as stylish as the products, showing a mix of cashmere sweaters, varsity jackets, wristwatches, and sunglasses, along with shoes. "We want people to say, 'I didn't know Reebok made that,'" notes Reebok's vice president of retail. CEO Paul Fireman sums things up as follows: "The ultimate thing we are striving for is not brand recognition, but how people perceive us."[27]

## Questions for Discussion

1. What segmentation variables is Reebok using for its products? Why are these variables appropriate?
2. Which of the three targeting strategies is Reebok applying? Explain.
3. What influences on the consumer buying decision process appear to have the most impact on Reebok's customers' purchase decisions?
4. In terms of segmentation and buying behavior, explain the meaning of this statement by a Reebok executive: "The trends are made in the urban areas and on street basketball courts, just like in the United States."

# part 5

# Product Decisions

We are now prepared to analyze the decisions and activities associated with developing and maintaining effective marketing mixes. In Parts 5 through 8, we focus on the major components of the marketing mix: product, distribution, promotion, and price. **Part 5** explores the product component of the marketing mix. **Chapter 11** introduces basic concepts and relationships that must be understood to make effective product decisions. **Chapter 12** analyzes a variety of dimensions regarding product management, including line extensions and product modification, new-product development, and product deletions. **Chapter 13** discusses branding, packaging, and labeling. **Chapter 14** explores the nature, importance, and characteristics of service.

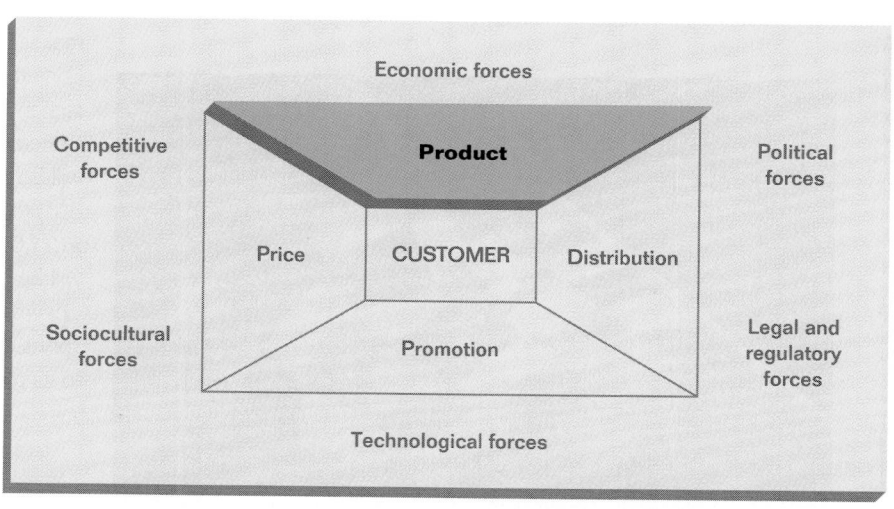

# CHAPTER 11

# Product Concepts

1. To understand the concept of a product

2. To explain how to classify products

3. To examine the concepts of product item, product line, and product mix and understand how they are connected

4. To understand the product life cycle and its impact on marketing strategies

5. To describe the product adoption process

6. To understand why some products fail and some succeed

## Corvette C6 Bests the Big Boys

The Chevy Corvette has been an American icon for more than 50 years. Although it is Chevrolet's most expensive car, with a starting price of $44,000, it is a relative bargain given its Porsche-like performance. The latest 'Vette, the C6 (for sixth-generation Corvette), has been completely redesigned to draw the attention of two-seat sports performance car lovers. The C6's standard 6-liter V8 engine rates at 400 horsepower, and the car's modest 3,200-pound weight allows it to go from 0 to 60 in 4.1 seconds—and ultimately to achieve 186 miles per hour. A special-edition Z06 model rates at 500 horsepower. To hop into the C6 you just push a button, and for a bit extra you can add even more high-tech features such as a navigation system and XM satellite radio.

*Road and Track* magazine compared a $54,000 Corvette C6 with an $89,000 Porsche 911, and concluded that the two cars gave a "remarkably similar racetrack performance." In speed, ability to maintain agility, and grip on the road, the cars are quite similar; the big difference is in terms of styling and design. The magazine named the Corvette C6 the best all-round sports car even over tough competitors from Porsche, Dodge, BMW, Honda, Mercedes, and Nissan.

To promote the launch of the new car Mattel released a large-scale (1:18) Hot Wheels model of the muscle car. GM also inked a deal with premium guitar maker Paul Reed Smith Guitars to put the Corvette logo on some custom-designed guitars and the PRS name on a C6 race car. General Motors predicts that most C6 buyers will be males between the ages of 35 and 50, probably college graduates with a $121,000 median household income. There will be only about 31,000 sold per year, and Chevrolet will use the Corvette as its flagship sports car to gain visibility and attract attention to its complete product line.[1] ■

**T**he product is an important variable in the marketing mix. Products such as the Corvette can be a firm's most important asset. If a company's products do not meet customers' desires and needs, the firm will fail unless it makes adjustments. Developing successful products such as the Corvette requires knowledge of fundamental marketing and product concepts.

In this chapter, we first define *product* and discuss how buyers view products. Next, we examine the concepts of product line and product mix. We then explore the stages of the product life cycle and the effect of each life cycle stage on marketing strategies. Then, we outline the product adoption process. Finally, we discuss the factors that contribute to a product's failure or success.

# What Is a Product?

**good**  A tangible physical entity

**service**  An intangible result of the application of human and mechanical efforts to people or objects

**idea**  A concept, philosophy, image, or issue

As defined in Chapter 1, a *product* is a good, a service, or an idea received in an exchange. It can be either tangible or intangible and includes functional, social, and psychological utilities or benefits. It also includes supporting services, such as installation, guarantees, product information, and promises of repair or maintenance. Thus, the 4-year/50,000-mile warranty that covers most new automobiles is part of the product itself. A **good** is a tangible physical entity, such as an iPod Nano music player or a Subway sandwich. A **service**, in contrast, is intangible; it is the result of the application of human and mechanical efforts to people or objects. Examples of services include a performance by Nelly, online travel agency bookings, medical examinations, child day care, real estate services, and martial arts lessons. (Chapter 14 provides a detailed discussion of services.) An **idea** is a concept, philosophy, image, or issue. Ideas provide the psychological stimulation that aids in solving problems or adjusting to the environment. For example, MADD (Mothers Against Drunk Driving) promotes safe consumption of alcohol and stricter enforcement of laws against drunk driving. It is helpful to think of a total product offering as having a combination of three interdependent elements: the core product itself, its supplemental features, and its symbolic or experiential value. See Figure 11.1 for an illustration. Consider that some people buy new tires for their basic utility (e.g., Sears' Guardsman III), while some look for safety (e.g., Michelin), and others buy on the basis of brand name or exemplary performance (e.g., Pirelli).

The core product consists of a product's fundamental utility or main benefit. Broadband Internet services, for instance, offer speedy Internet access, but some buyers want additional features such as wireless connectivity anywhere they go. The core product usually addresses a fundamental need of the consumer. When you buy bottled water, you can buy a store brand, name brand such as Dasani and Aquafina brands, or more exclusive brands such as Voss of Norway. Regardless of price, each alternative will quench your thirst. Retailers such as Target and Wal-Mart specialize in offering core products of a generally acceptable quality level at competitive prices. Hotels such as Clarion and the Hampton Inn specialize in providing quality services at affordable prices.

A product's supplemental features provide added value or attributes in addition to its core utility or benefit. Supplemental products can also provide installation, delivery, training, and financing. These supplemental attributes are not required to make the core product function effectively, but they help differentiate one product brand from another. The Starwood Hotel chain, for example, introduced a new concept called

**figure 11.1**

**THE TOTAL PRODUCT**

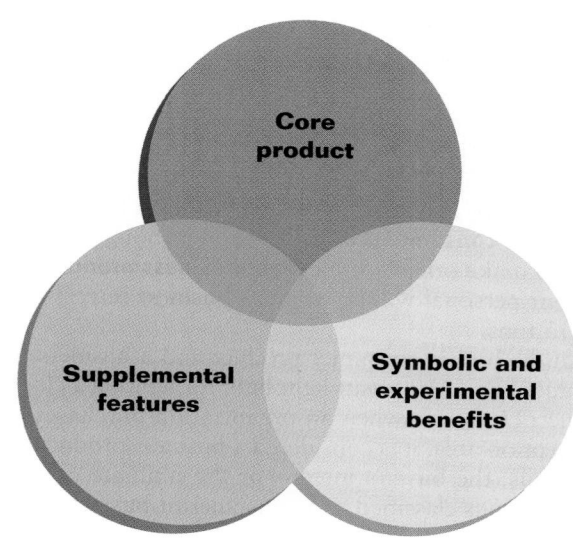

Core product

Supplemental features

Symbolic and experimental benefits

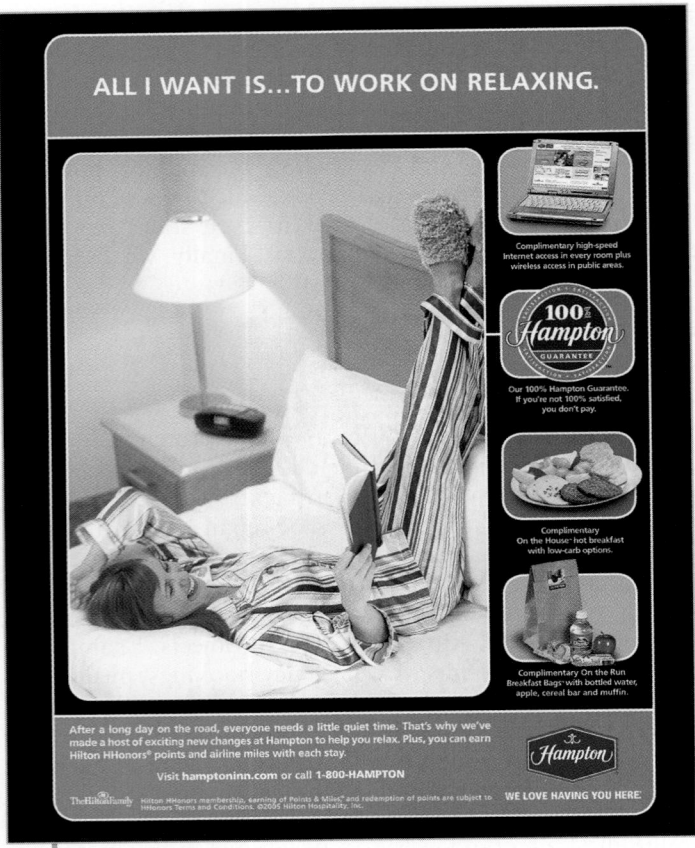

ALL I WANT IS...TO WORK ON RELAXING.

Complimentary high-speed Internet access in every room plus wireless access in public areas.

100% Hampton GUARANTEE

Our 100% Hampton Guarantee. If you're not 100% satisfied, you don't pay.

Complimentary On the House® hot breakfast with low-carb options.

Complimentary On the Run Breakfast Bags® with bottled water, apple, cereal bar and muffin.

After a long day on the road, everyone needs a little quiet time. That's why we've made a host of exciting new changes at Hampton to help you relax. Plus, you can earn Hilton HHonors® points and airline miles with each stay.

Visit hamptoninn.com or call 1-800-HAMPTON

*Hampton*    WE LOVE HAVING YOU HERE!

**What Is a Product?**

Hampton Inn provides a service based on consumers' expectations of a relaxing hotel environment.

Aloft that offers well-appointed "loft-like" guest rooms that appeal to business travelers at a mid-level price range. Hyatt offers a hotel concept that features larger rooms and work areas, free high-speed Internet, large flat-screen TVs, CD and DVD players, and cordless phones.[2] These supplemental features add real value to the core product of overnight hotel stays.

Finally, customers also receive benefits based on their experiences with the product. In addition, many products have symbolic meaning for buyers. For some consumers, the simple act of shopping gives symbolic value and improves their attitudes. Some stores capitalize on this value by striving to create a special experience for customers. For example, you can buy stuffed toys at many retailers, but at Build-A-Bear, you can choose the type of animal, stuff it yourself, give it a heart, create a name complete with a birth certificate, as well as give the toy a bath and clothe and accessorize it. The atmosphere and décor of a retail store, the variety and depth of product choices, the customer support, even the sounds and smells all contribute to the experiential element. When you check into a Hotel Monaco, not only do you get a great room with down comforters, bed toppers, and pillows, but you can also "check out" a fish as your companion during your stay. Customers credit the Hotel Monaco with providing a differentiated, enjoyable stay and become loyal customers. These symbolic and experiential features are all part of the Hotel Monaco total product.

Thus, when buyers purchase a product, they are really buying the benefits and satisfaction they think the product will provide. A Rolex watch, for example, is purchased to make a statement of success, not just for telling time. Services in particular are purchased on the basis of expectations. Expectations, suggested by images, promises, and symbols, as well as processes and delivery, help consumers make judgments about tangible and intangible products. Products are formed by the activities and processes that help satisfy expectations. Starbucks, for example, did not invent the coffee shop, but it did make high-quality coffee beverages readily available around the world with standardized service and in stylish, comfortable stores. Often symbols and cues are used to make intangible products more tangible, or real, to the consumer. Allstate Insurance Company, for example, uses giant hands to symbolize security, strength, and friendliness.

# Classifying Products

**consumer products** Products purchased to satisfy personal and family needs

**business products** Products bought to use in an organization's operations, to resell, or to make other products

Products fall into one of two general categories. Products purchased to satisfy personal and family needs are **consumer products**. Products bought to use in a firm's operations, to resell, or to make other products are **business products**. Consumers buy products to satisfy their personal wants, whereas business buyers seek to satisfy the goals of their organizations.

The same item can be both a consumer product and a business product. For example, when a consumer buys a 100-watt light bulb for lighting a closet, it is classified as a consumer product. However, when an organization purchases a 100-watt light bulb for lighting a reception area, it is considered a business product because it is used in daily operations. Thus, the buyer's intent—or the ultimate use of the product—determines whether an item is classified as a consumer or business product.

## marketing ENTREPRENEURS

**Arielle Eckstut, Jonah Shaw, and Jason Dorf**

**THEIR BUSINESS:** LittleMissMatched

**FOUNDED:** 2003

**SUCCESS:** 600,000 socks now in 600 stores

While pondering the great mystery of socks disappearing in the laundry, Arielle Eckstut, Jonah Shaw, and Jason Dorf recognized an opportunity to market socks that don't match. They targeted young girls ages 8 to 12 with their LittleMissMatched brand socks. A package of just one sock goes for $2, a package with three unmatched socks for $5, and a package with seven mixed socks for $10. Customers then use their imaginations to pair the socks (into 19,900 possible combinations) according to color, design, or their own sense of style. Today LittleMiss-Matched has expanded its concept to flip-flops, pajamas, and other garments that can be mismatched for fun and fashion for adults and toddlers as well as for preteens.

Product classifications are important because classes of products are aimed at particular target markets, which affects distribution, promotion, and pricing decisions. Furthermore, appropriate marketing strategies vary among the classes of consumer and business products. In short, how a product is classified can affect the entire marketing mix. In this section, we examine the characteristics of consumer and business products and explore the marketing activities associated with some of these products.

### Consumer Products

The most widely accepted approach to classifying consumer products is based on characteristics of consumer buying behavior. It divides products into four categories: convenience, shopping, specialty, and unsought products. However, not all buyers behave in the same way when purchasing a specific type of product. Thus, a single product can fit into several categories. To minimize this problem, marketers think in terms of how buyers *generally* behave when purchasing a specific item. In addition, they recognize that the "correct" classification can be determined only by considering a particular firm's intended target market. Examining the four traditional categories of consumer products can provide further insight.

**convenience products** Relatively inexpensive, frequently purchased items for which buyers exert minimal purchasing effort

**Convenience Products.** **Convenience products** are relatively inexpensive, frequently purchased items for which buyers exert only minimal purchasing effort. They range from bread, soft drinks, and chewing gum to gasoline and newspapers. The buyer spends little time planning the purchase or comparing available brands or sellers. Today time has become one of our most precious assets, and many consumers therefore buy products at the closest location to preserve time for other activities. Even a buyer who prefers a specific brand will readily choose a substitute if the preferred brand is not conveniently available.

Classifying a product as a convenience product has several implications for a firm's marketing strategy. A convenience product is normally marketed through many retail outlets. Examples of typical outlets include 7-Eleven, Exxon Mobil, and Starbucks. Starbucks, for example, has opened locations inside airports, hotels, and grocery stores, and half of its company-owned stores now have drive-through lanes to ensure that customers can get coffee whenever or wherever the desire strikes.[3] Because sellers experience high inventory turnover, per-unit gross margins can be relatively low. Producers of convenience products, such as Altoid mints, expect little promotional effort at the retail level and thus must provide it themselves with advertising and sales promotion. Packaging is also an important element of the marketing mix for convenience products. The package may have to sell the product because many convenience items are available only on a self-service basis at the retail level.

**shopping products** Items for which buyers are willing to expend considerable effort in planning and making purchases

**Shopping Products.** **Shopping products** are items for which buyers are willing to expend considerable effort in planning and making the purchase. Buyers spend much time comparing stores and brands with respect to prices, product features, qualities, services, and perhaps warranties. Shoppers may compare products at a number of outlets such as Best Buy, Circuit City, Sears, or Home Depot. Appliances, bicycles, furniture, stereos, cameras, and shoes exemplify shopping products. These products are expected to last a fairly long time and thus are purchased less frequently than convenience items. Although shopping products are more expensive than

**Convenience Products**

White bread is a typical convenience product. Sara Lee adds whole grain to increase the health benefit.

convenience products, few buyers of shopping products are particularly brand loyal. Most consumers, for example, are not brand loyal for computers and clothing. If they were, they would be unwilling to shop and compare among brands. Even when they are brand loyal, they may still spend considerable time comparing the features of different models of a brand. A consumer looking for a new Maytag washing machine, for example, may explore the company's website to compare the features of different washers before talking to a salesperson. Regardless of the number of brands of interest, buyers may also consult buying guides such as *Consumer Reports* or visit consumer information websites such as **www.epinions.com** to view others' opinions or ratings of brands and models before making an actual purchase.

To market a shopping product effectively, a marketer considers several key issues. Shopping products require fewer retail outlets than convenience products. Because shopping products are purchased less frequently, inventory turnover is lower, and marketing channel members expect to receive higher gross margins. Although large sums of money may be required to advertise shopping products, an even larger percentage of resources is likely to be used for personal selling. Usually the producer and the marketing channel members expect some cooperation from one another with respect to providing parts and repair services and performing promotional activities. In certain situations, both shopping products and convenience products may be marketed in the same location. HEB, a privately held Texas grocery chain, recently implemented a new store concept called HEB Plus. These stores carry everything from toys and home entertainment products to area rugs and high-end televisions as well as the traditional groceries and ethnic foods in which HEB excels.[4]

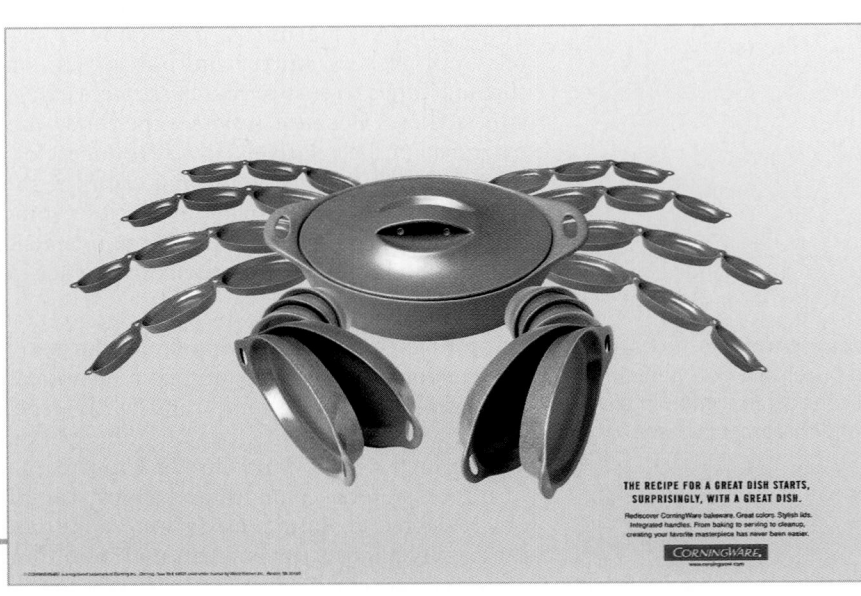

**Shopping Brands**

Corning Ware produces reliable cookware that are shopping products for most consumers.

**Specialty Products**

Seven Cycles makes custom bikes—a specialty product.

The average cyclist doesn't need a custom bike...

Then again, who's average?

There are those who say that the average cyclist doesn't need a custom bike. Well we say that's the type of thinking that produces average bikes. Because when it comes right down to it, **average is just another word for compromise.** So while other companies build bikes for the "the average cyclist", we build yours.

www.sevencycles.com   telephone 617.923.7774   email info@sevencycles.com

**seven** cycles

One Bike. Yours.

**specialty products** Items with unique characteristics that buyers are willing to expend considerable effort to obtain

**Specialty Products.** **Specialty products** possess one or more unique characteristics, and generally buyers are willing to expend considerable effort to obtain them. Buyers actually plan the purchase of a specialty product; they know exactly what they want and will not accept a substitute. Examples of specialty products include a Mont Blanc pen and a one-of-a-kind piece of baseball memorabilia, such as a ball signed by Babe Ruth. When searching for specialty products, buyers do not compare alternatives; they are concerned primarily with finding an outlet that has the preselected product available. Tag Heuer, for example, issued a special Indy 500 watch designed especially for racing fans.

The fact that an item is a specialty product can affect a firm's marketing efforts in several ways. Specialty products are often distributed through a limited number of retail outlets. Like shopping products, they are purchased infrequently, causing lower inventory turnover and thus requiring relatively high gross margins.

**unsought products** Products purchased to solve a sudden problem, products of which customers are unaware, and products that people do not necessarily think of buying

**Unsought Products.** **Unsought products** are products purchased when a sudden problem must be solved, products of which customers are unaware, and products that people do not necessarily think of purchasing. Emergency medical services and automobile repairs are examples of products needed quickly to solve a problem. A consumer who is sick or injured has little time to plan to go to an emergency medical center or a hospital. Likewise, in the event of a broken fan belt on the highway, a consumer will likely seek out the nearest auto repair facility to get back on the road as quickly as possible. Computer users must purchase antivirus and spyware detection software to protect their computers even though they may not want to make such purchases. In such cases, speed and problem resolution are far more important than price and other features buyers might consider if they had more time for decision making. Companies such as ServiceMaster (Rescue Rooter and Furniture Medic) and First Service (Colliers International and CMN International) are making the purchases of these unsought products more bearable by building trust with consumers through recognizable brands and superior functional performance.[5]

## Business Products

Business products are usually purchased on the basis of an organization's goals and objectives. Generally the functional aspects of the product are more important than the psychological rewards sometimes associated with consumer products. Business products can be classified into seven categories according to their characteristics and intended uses: installations, accessory equipment, raw materials, component parts, process materials, MRO supplies, and business services.

## Business Products

Sato Barcode label printers are a business product, as are Caterpillar lift trucks.

**installations** Facilities and non-portable major equipment

**accessory equipment** Equipment used in production or office activities that does not become a part of the final physical product but is used in production or office activities

**raw materials** Basic natural materials that become part of a physical product

**Installations.** **Installations** include facilities, such as office buildings, factories, and warehouses, and major equipment that are nonportable, such as production lines and very large machines. Major equipment usually is used for production purposes. Some major equipment is custom-made to perform specific functions for a particular organization; other items are standardized and perform similar tasks for many types of firms. Normally installations are expensive and intended to be used for a considerable length of time. Because they are so expensive and typically involve a long-term investment of capital, purchase decisions are often made by high-level management. Marketers of installations frequently must provide a variety of services, including training, repairs, maintenance assistance, and even financial assistance.

**Accessory Equipment.** **Accessory equipment** does not become a part of the final physical product but is used in production or office activities. Examples include file cabinets, fractional-horsepower motors, calculators, and tools. Compared with major equipment, accessory items are usually much cheaper, purchased routinely with less negotiation, and treated as expense items rather than capital items because they are not expected to last as long. Accessory products are standardized items that can be used in several aspects of a firm's operations. More outlets are required for distributing accessory equipment than for installations, but sellers do not have to provide the numerous services expected of installations marketers.

**Raw Materials.** **Raw materials** are the basic natural materials that actually become part of a physical product. They include minerals, chemicals, agricultural products, and materials from forests and oceans. They are usually bought and sold according to grades and specifications, and in relatively large quantities. Rose oil and jasmine are examples of raw materials in making perfume. The Kashi Company buys organic raw materials including whole grain wheat, oats, barley, and other grains for its Go Lean Crunch and Heart to Heart cereals.

**component parts** Items that become part of the physical product and are either finished items ready for assembly or items that need little processing before assembly

**Component Parts.** **Component parts** become part of the physical product and are either finished items ready for assembly or products that need little processing before assembly. Although they become part of a larger product, component parts often can be easily identified and distinguished. Spark plugs, tires, clocks, brakes, and switches are all component parts of an automobile. German-based Robert Bosch GmbH, the world's largest auto parts maker, supplies 30 percent of the 46 million antilock brakes installed in vehicles worldwide.[6] Buyers purchase such items according to their own specifications or industry standards. They expect the parts to be of specified quality and delivered on time so that production is not slowed or stopped. Producers that are primarily assemblers, such as most lawn mower and computer manufacturers, depend heavily on suppliers of component parts.

**process materials** Materials that are used directly in the production of other products but are not readily identifiable

**Process Materials.** **Process materials** are used directly in the production of other products. Unlike component parts, however, process materials are not readily identifiable. For example, a salad dressing manufacturer includes vinegar in its salad dressing. The vinegar is a process material because it is included in the salad dressing but is not identifiable. As with component parts, process materials are purchased according to industry standards or the purchaser's specifications.

**MRO supplies** Maintenance, repair, and operating items that facilitate production and operations but do not become part of the finished product

**MRO Supplies.** **MRO supplies** are maintenance, repair, and operating items that facilitate production and operations but do not become part of the finished product. Paper, pencils, oils, cleaning agents, and paints are in this category. MRO supplies are commonly sold through numerous outlets and are purchased routinely. To ensure supplies are available when needed, buyers often deal with more than one seller.

**business services** Intangible products that many organizations use in their operations

**Business Services.** **Business services** are the intangible products that many organizations use in their operations. They include financial, legal, marketing research, information technology, and janitorial services. Firms must decide whether to provide their own services internally or obtain them from outside the organization. This decision depends on the costs associated with each alternative and how frequently the services are needed. For example, few firms have the resources to provide global overnight delivery services efficiently, so most companies rely on FedEx, UPS, DHL, and other service providers.

# Product Line and Product Mix

Marketers must understand the relationships among all the products of their organization to coordinate the marketing of the total group of products. The following concepts help describe the relationships among an organization's products.

**product item** A specific version of a product

A **product item** is a specific version of a product that can be designated as a distinct offering among an organization's products. An L. L. Bean flannel shirt represents a product item. A **product line** is a group of closely related product items that are considered to be a unit because of marketing, technical, or end-use considerations. For example, Procter & Gamble, with the acquisition of Gillette, has hundreds of brands that fall into one of 22 product lines ranging from deodorants to paper products.[7] The exact boundaries of a product line (although sometimes blurred) are usually indicated by using descriptive terms such as "frozen dessert" product line or "shampoo" product line. To develop the optimal product line, marketers must understand buyers' goals. In the personal computer industry, for example, companies are likely to expand their product lines when industry barriers are low or perceived market opportunities exist. Firms with high market share are likely to expand their product lines aggressively, as are marketers with relatively high prices or limited product lines.[8] Specific product items in a product line usually reflect the desires of different target markets or the different needs of consumers.

**product line** A group of closely related product items viewed as a unit because of marketing, technical, or end-use considerations

**product mix** The composite, or total, group of products that an organization makes available to customers

A **product mix** is the composite, or total, group of products that an organization makes available to customers. For example, all the health-care, beauty-care, laundry and cleaning, food and beverage, paper, cosmetic, and fragrance products that Procter & Gamble manufactures constitute its product mix. The **width of product mix** is

**width of product mix** The number of product lines a company offers

## figure 11.2   THE CONCEPTS OF PRODUCT MIX WIDTH AND DEPTH APPLIED TO U.S. PROCTER & GAMBLE PRODUCTS

| | Laundry detergents | Toothpastes | Bar soaps | Deodorants | Shampoos | Tissue/Towel |
|---|---|---|---|---|---|---|
| **Depth** | Ivory Snow 1930 | Gleem 1952 | Ivory 1879 | Old Spice 1948 | Pantene 1947 | Charmin 1928 |
| | Dreft 1933 | Crest 1955 | Camay 1926 | Secret 1956 | Head & Shoulders 1961 | Puffs 1960 |
| | Tide 1946 | | Zest 1952 | Sure 1972 | Vidal Sassoon 1974 | Bounty 1965 |
| | Cheer 1950 | | Safeguard 1963 | | Pert Plus 1979 | |
| | Bold 1965 | | Oil of Olay 1993 | | Ivory 1983 | |
| | Gain 1966 | | | | Infusium 23 1986 | |
| | Era 1972 | | | | Physique 2000 | |
| | Febreze Clean Wash 2000 | | | | Herbal Essence 2001 | |

**Width**

Source: Reprinted by permission of the Proctor and Gamble Company.

---

**depth of product mix** The average number of different products offered in each product line

### Product Line and Product Mix

All-natural salad dressings is one of Newman's Own product lines. Horizon provides a complete line of dairy products.

measured by the number of product lines a company offers. Robert Bosch GmbH, for example, offers multiple product lines including automotive technology components such as brakes and stability control systems, consumer products such as household appliances, and business products such as packaging machines.[9] The **depth of product mix** is the average number of different products offered in each product line. Figure 11.2 shows the width and depth of a part of Procter & Gamble's product mix. Procter & Gamble is known for using distinctive branding, packaging, and consumer advertising to promote individual items in its detergent product line. Tide, Bold, Gain, Cheer, and Era—all Procter & Gamble detergents—share the same distribution channels and similar manufacturing facilities, but each is promoted as a distinctive product, adding depth to the product line.

# Product Life Cycles and Marketing Strategies

**product life cycle** The progression of a product through four stages: introduction, growth, maturity, and decline

Just as biological cycles progress from birth through growth and decline, so do product life cycles. As Figure 11.3 (on p. 312) shows, a **product life cycle** has four major stages: introduction, growth, maturity, and decline. As a product moves through its life cycle, the strategies relating to competition, promotion, distribution, pricing, and market information must be periodically evaluated and possibly changed. Astute marketing managers use the life cycle concept to make sure the introduction, alteration, and termination of a product are timed and executed properly. By understanding the typical life cycle pattern, marketers are better able to maintain profitable products and drop unprofitable ones.

## Introduction

**introduction stage** The initial stage of a product's life cycle; its first appearance in the marketplace when sales start at zero and profits are negative

The **introduction stage** of the product life cycle begins at a product's first appearance in the marketplace, when sales start at zero and profits are negative. Profits are below zero because initial revenues are low, and the company generally must cover large expenses for promotion and distribution. Notice in Figure 11.3 how sales should move upward from zero, and profits should also move upward from a position in which they are negative because of high expenses.

Developing and introducing a new product can mean an outlay of $100 million or more. Cadbury Schweppes, for example, spent two years and millions of dollars to develop Trident Splash, a sugar-free gum with a candy shell and a liquid center, which it markets to adults for 99 cents a package.[10] And while the importance of new products is significant, the risk of new-product failure is quite high, depending on the industry. Although LeapFrog introduced the LeapPad educational reading toy with

# Kellogg Lures the Global Breakfast Bunch

Thanks to the vision of its founder, W. K. Kellogg, the Kellogg Company has been investing in international markets for almost 100 years. Many international consumers actually consider Kellogg brands to be "of local origin." And many of them are right: today, Kellogg products are produced in 17 countries and marketed in more than 180.

The United Kingdom is Kellogg's largest European area of business; popular products are Special K Lite Bites, Frosties Light, and yogurt-coated versions of Special K and All-Bran. The company uses a number of themed promotions and health challenges associated with various Kellogg products as successful marketing tools in Europe because of the region's focus on health and wellness.

Growth in Italy, Spain, and Latin America is strong, particularly in Mexico, where the company is building a manufacturing facility for producing cereals and snack foods. Anemia is a common problem in Latin America, so Kellogg initiated its Defensa K campaign to promote the nutritional value of its products, especially iron content. Popular brands in Latin America are Nutri-Grain and All-Bran cereals, Choco Krispies bars, and Pop-Tarts. Marketing campaigns with sports themes are popular.

The Asian Pacific is another growth front for Kellogg, where competition is strong. Kellogg offers new varieties of cereals and bars in Australia and a new version of Frosties with less sugar in South Korea. The initial response to these introductions is positive. Kellogg's campaigns in Australia, India, and Japan focus primarily on health.

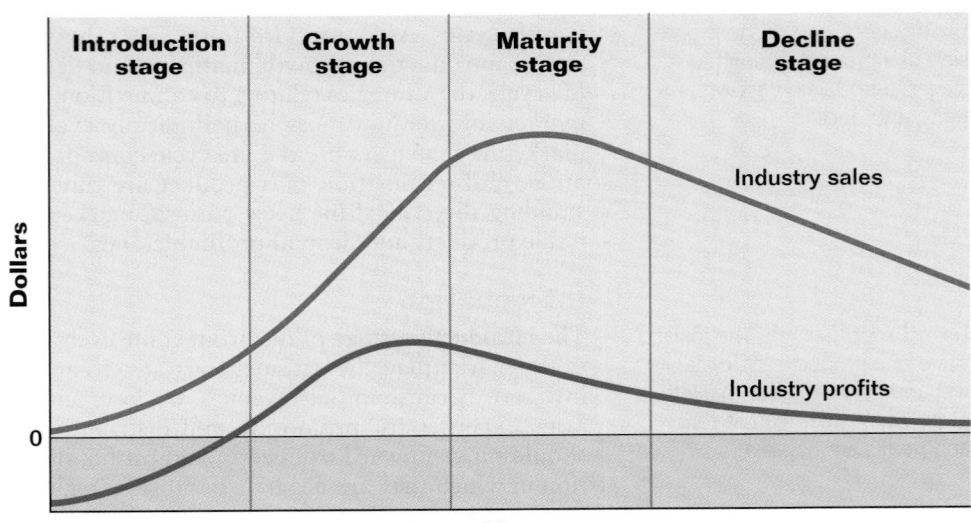

**figure 11.3**

# THE FOUR STAGES OF THE PRODUCT LIFE CYCLE

tremendous success, the company has since struggled to find a successful follow-up. Parents today want their kids to learn while playing, but children just want to have fun. To thrive, LeapFrog must adapt to changing expectations from both children and their parents.[11] Because of high risks and costs, few product introductions represent revolutionary inventions. More typically, product introductions involve a new packaged convenience food, a new model of automobile, or a new fashion in clothing rather than a major product innovation. The more marketing-oriented the firm, the more likely it will be to launch innovative, new-to-the-market products.[12]

Potential buyers must be made aware of the new product's features, uses, and advantages. Two difficulties may arise at this point. First, sellers may lack the resources, technological knowledge, and marketing know-how to launch the product successfully. Firms without large budgets can still attract attention by giving away free samples, as Essence of Vali did with its aromatherapy products. Another small-budget tactic is to gain visibility through media appearances. Dave Dettman, a.k.a. Dr. Gadget, specializes in promoting new products on television news and talk programs. Companies such as Sony, Disney, Warner Brothers, and others have hired Dr. Gadget to help with the introduction of new products.[13] Second, the initial product price may have to be high to recoup expensive marketing research or development costs. Given these difficulties, it is not surprising that many products never get beyond the introduction stage.

Most new products start off slowly and seldom generate enough sales to bring immediate profits. As

**New Products**

Miracle-Gro Liquafeed promotes new product adoption.

buyers learn about the new product, marketers should be alert for product weaknesses and make corrections quickly to prevent the product's early demise. Marketing strategy should be designed to attract the segment that is most interested in the product and has the fewest objections. As the sales curve moves upward and the break-even point is reached, the growth stage begins.

## Growth

**growth stage** The product life cycle stage when sales rise rapidly and profits reach a peak, then start to decline

During the **growth stage**, sales rise rapidly and profits reach a peak, then start to decline (see Figure 11.3). The growth stage is critical to a product's survival because competitive reactions to the product's success during this period will affect the product's life expectancy. When Splenda, a sugar substitute, was introduced, sales rose quickly as consumers switched from other low-calorie sweetners. Sales rose even more quickly when restaurants such as McDonald's and Starbucks began offering Splenda in single-serving packets.[14]

Profits begin to decline late in the growth stage as more competitors enter the market, driving prices down and creating the need for heavy promotional expenses. At this point, a typical marketing strategy encourages strong brand loyalty and competes with aggressive emulators of the product. During the growth stage, the organization tries to strengthen its market share and develop a competitive niche by emphasizing the product's benefits. Aggressive pricing, including price cuts, is also typical during this stage.

As sales increase, management must support the momentum by adjusting the marketing strategy. The goal is to establish and fortify the product's market position by encouraging brand loyalty. To achieve greater market penetration, segmentation may have to be used more intensely. That would require developing product variations to satisfy the needs of people in several different market segments. Apple, for example, introduced two variations on its wildly popular iPod MP3 player. The iPod Mini, a slimmer, more colorful device, and the iPod Shuffle, a more affordable iPod, have helped expand Apple's market penetration in the competitive MP3 player industry.[15] Marketers should also analyze competing brands' product positions relative to their own brands and take corrective actions.

Gaps in geographic market coverage should be filled during the growth period. As a product gains market acceptance, new distribution outlets usually become easier to obtain. Marketers sometimes move from an exclusive or a selective exposure to a more intensive network of dealers to achieve greater market penetration. Marketers must also make sure the physical distribution system is running efficiently so that customers' orders are processed accurately and delivered on time.

Promotion expenditures may be slightly lower than during the introductory stage but are still quite substantial. As sales increase, promotion costs should drop as a percentage of total sales. A falling ratio between promotion expenditures and sales should contribute significantly to increased profits. The advertising messages should stress brand benefits. Coupons and samples may be used to increase market share.

After recovering development costs, a business may be able to lower prices. As sales volume increases, efficiencies in production can result in lower costs. These savings may be passed on to buyers. For example, when satellite navigation systems for cars were initially introduced, the price was $5,000 or more. As demand soared, manufacturers were able to take advantage of economies of scale to reduce production costs and lower prices to less than $2,000 within several years.[16] If demand remains strong and there are few competitive threats, prices tend to remain stable. If price cuts are feasible, they can help a brand gain market share and discourage new competitors from entering the market.

# Crossover SUV sales soar

**Crossover SUV sales grow as sales of traditional SUVs wane.**

In millions

3 — Traditional SUVs

2

1 — **1.8 million** — Crossover SUVs

0

1995     2000     2006

**2.4 million**

**2.3 million**

*Source:* Ford Motor.

## Maturity

During the **maturity stage**, the sales curve peaks and starts to decline and profits continue to fall (see Figure 11.3). This stage is characterized by intense competition because many brands are now in the market. Competitors emphasize improvements and differences in their versions of the product. As a result, during the maturity stage, weaker competitors are squeezed out or lose interest in the product.

During the maturity phase, the producers who remain in the market are likely to change their promotional and distribution efforts. Advertising and dealer-oriented promotions are typical during this stage of the product life cycle. Marketers must also take into account that as the product reaches maturity, buyers' knowledge of it attains a high level. Consumers of the product are no longer inexperienced generalists; instead they are experienced specialists. Marketers of mature products sometimes expand distribution into global markets. Often the products have to be adapted to more precisely fit differing needs of global customers.

Because many products are in the maturity stage of their life cycles, marketers must know how to deal with these products and be prepared to adjust their marketing strategies. As Table 11.1 shows, there are many approaches to altering marketing strategies during the maturity stage. As noted in the table, to increase the sales of mature products, marketers may suggest new uses for them. Arm & Hammer has boosted demand for its baking soda with this method. As customers become more experienced and knowledgeable about products during the maturity stage (particularly about business products), the benefits they seek may change as well, necessitating product modifications. Consider that traditional truck-based sport-utility vehicles, such as the Ford Explorer and GMC Tahoe, have reached maturity and their sales are beginning to decline. Facing rising gasoline costs, consumers became interested in "crossovers," car-based utility vehicles like the Honda Pilot, BMW X3, Porsche Cayenne, and Saturn Vue. Automakers responded to this interest with more models and features. With their improved ride, handling,

| table 11.1 | SELECTED APPROACHES FOR MANAGING PRODUCTS IN THE MATURITY STAGE |
|---|---|
| **Approach** | **Examples** |
| Develop new product uses | Knox gelatin used as a plant food<br>Arm & Hammer baking soda marketed as a refrigerator deodorant<br>Cheez Whiz promoted as a microwavable cheese sauce |
| Increase product usage among current users | Multiple packaging used for products in which a larger supply at the point of consumption actually increases consumption (such as for soft drinks or beer) |
| Increase number of users | Global markets or small niches in domestic markets pursued |
| Add product features | Traditional SUVs slowly replaced by crossover vehicles<br>Satellite radio systems in automobiles |
| Change package sizes | Single-serving sizes introduced<br>Travel-size packages of personal-care products introduced |
| Increase product quality | Life of light bulbs increased<br>Reliability and durability of U.S.-made automobiles increased |
| Change nonproduct marketing mix variables—promotion, price, distribution | Focus of Dr Pepper advertisements shifted from teenagers to people ages 18 to 54<br>A package of dishwasher detergent containing one-third more product offered for the same price<br>Computer hardware marketed through mail-order outlets |

and fuel economy, crossovers are in a rapid sales growth stage at the expense of traditional SUVs.[17]

Three general objectives can be pursued during the maturity stage:

1. *Generate cash flow.* This is essential for recouping the initial investment and generating excess cash to support new products.

2. *Maintain share of market.* Companies with marginal market share must decide whether they have a reasonable chance to improve their position or whether they should drop out.

3. *Increase share of customer.* Whereas *market share* refers to the percentage of total customers a firm holds, *share of customer* relates to the percentage of each customer's needs that the firm is meeting. For example, many banks have added new services (brokerage, financial planning, auto leasing, etc.) to gain more of each customer's financial services business. Likewise, many supermarkets are seeking to increase share of customer by adding services such as restaurants, movie rentals, and dry cleaning to provide one-stop shopping for their customers' household needs.[18]

During the maturity stage, marketers actively encourage dealers to support the product. Dealers may be offered promotional assistance in lowering their inventory costs. In general, marketers go to great lengths to serve dealers and provide incentives for selling their brands.

Maintaining market share during the maturity stage requires moderate, and sometimes large, promotion expenditures. Advertising messages focus on differentiating a brand from the field of competitors, and sales promotion efforts are aimed at both consumers and resellers.

# Fifty Years of Pain Relief

In 2005, Tylenol celebrated 50 years of pain relief. Originally created to alleviate pain in children, McNeil Laboratories introduced Tylenol in 1955 as Children's Tylenol Elixir, available only with a prescription. After Johnson & Johnson bought McNeil Lab, it introduced Tylenol for adults in 1961. Since then, the acetaminophen-based pain reliever has become the most popular of its kind on the market for both children and adults.

Europeans began using acetaminophen in 1893, but it remained unfamiliar in the United States until the Tylenol brand was launched. Today Tylenol is more popular than ever because it is less likely to interfere with other medications and has fewer complications than

Vioxx, Bextra, ibuprofen, and naproxen. Although studies indicate that aspirin is still the safest pain medication to use in most cases, many doctors and patients alike are confident in and prefer Tylenol for pain relief.

In 1982, seven people died from cyanide-laced Tylenol found in several bottles of Tylenol in Chicago. Johnson & Johnson worked swiftly to deal with the crisis, ultimately recalling 264,000 Tylenol bottles from Chicago stores and advising customers to exchange any bottles they had on hand for new, sealed ones. Although the recall cost the company about $100 million, it was a worthwhile investment. Given the company's straightforward response, consumer confidence in the brand rebounded after just a few months. As a result of the incident, the company introduced containers with multiple seals. Today consumers have tamperproof packaging on many items found at the pharmacy or grocery store due to Johnson & Johnson's response to the Tylenol-tampering crisis.

A greater mixture of pricing strategies is used during the maturity stage. Strong price competition is likely and may ignite price wars. Firms also compete in ways other than price, such as through product quality or service. In addition, marketers develop price flexibility to differentiate offerings in product lines. Markdowns and price incentives are common. Prices may have to be increased, however, if distribution and production costs rise.

### Decline

During the **decline stage**, sales fall rapidly (refer to Figure 11.3). When this happens, the marketer considers pruning items from the product line to eliminate those not earning a profit. The marketer may also cut promotion efforts, eliminate marginal distributors, and, finally, plan to phase out the product. Consider the Thermador Car Cooler, a cone-shaped evaporative device that hung on a car's passenger-side window, which was widely used before air conditioning to lower a car's internal temperature by as much as 20 degrees in dry climates. The Thermador Car Cooler is long gone, but you may recognize the Thermador name as a high-end appliance maker.[19]

An organization can justify maintaining a product only as long as the product contributes to profits or enhances the overall effectiveness of a product mix. Kodak, after spending $1 billion over eight years to develop its Advantix photography system, pulled the plug after sales declined by 75 percent.[20]

In this stage, marketers must determine whether to eliminate the product or try to reposition it to extend its life. Usually a declining product has lost its distinctiveness because similar competing products have been introduced. Competition engenders increased substitution and brand switching as buyers become insensitive to minor product differences. For these reasons, marketers do little to change a product's style, design, or other attributes during its decline. New technology or social trends, product substitutes, or environmental considerations may also indicate that the time has come to delete the product.

During a product's decline, outlets with strong sales volumes are maintained and unprofitable outlets are weeded out. An entire marketing channel may be eliminated if it does not contribute adequately to profits. An outlet not previously used, such as a factory outlet, is sometimes used to liquidate remaining inventory of an obsolete product. As sales decline, the product becomes more inaccessible, but loyal buyers seek out dealers who still carry it.

Spending on promotion efforts is usually reduced considerably. Advertising of special offers may slow the rate of decline. Sales promotions, such as coupons and premiums, may temporarily recapture buyers' attention. As the product continues to decline, the sales staff shifts its emphasis to more profitable products.

The marketing manager has two options during the decline stage: attempt to postpone the decline or accept its inevitability. Many firms lack the resources to renew a product's demand and are forced to consider harvesting or divesting the product or the strategic business unit (SBU). The *harvesting* approach employs a gradual reduction in marketing expenditures and a less resource-intensive marketing mix. A company adopting the *divesting* approach withdraws all marketing support from the declining product or SBU. It may continue to sell the product until losses are sustained or arrange for another firm to acquire the product. The Home Depot, for example, made the tough decision to divest its Crossroads stores for farm dwellers and move human and financial resources to Home Depot Expo, a chain for upscale consumers engaged in major renovations or remodeling projects.[21]

Because most businesses have a product mix consisting of multiple products, a firm's destiny is rarely tied to one product. A composite of life cycle patterns forms when various products in the mix are at different cycle stages: as one product is declining, other products are in the introduction, growth, or maturity stage. Marketers must deal with the dual problem of prolonging the lives of existing products and introducing new products to meet organizational sales goals.

# Product Adoption Process

**product adoption process**
The five-stage process of buyer acceptance of a product: awareness, interest, evaluation, trial, and adoption

Acceptance of new products—especially new-to-the-world products—usually doesn't happen overnight. In fact, it can take a very long time. People are sometimes cautious or even skeptical about adopting new products, as indicated by some of the remarks quoted in Table 11.2. Customers who eventually accept a new product do so through an adoption process. The stages of the **product adoption process** are as follows:

1. *Awareness.* The buyer becomes aware of the product.

2. *Interest.* The buyer seeks information and is receptive to learning about the product.

3. *Evaluation.* The buyer considers the product's benefits and decides whether to try it.

4. *Trial.* The buyer examines, tests, or tries the product to determine if it meets his or her needs.

5. *Adoption.* The buyer purchases the product and can be expected to use it again whenever the need for this general type of product arises.[22]

In the first stage, when individuals become aware that the product exists, they have little information about it and are not concerned about obtaining more. Consumers enter the interest stage when they are motivated to get information about the product's features, uses, advantages, disadvantages, price, or location. During the

**table 11.2   MOST NEW IDEAS HAVE THEIR SKEPTICS**

"I think there is a world market for maybe five computers."

—Thomas Watson, chairman of IBM, 1943

"This 'telephone' has too many shortcomings to be seriously considered as a means of communication. The device is inherently of no value to us."

—Western Union internal memo, 1876

"The wireless music box has no imaginable commercial value. Who would pay for a message sent to nobody in particular?"

—David Sarnoff's associates in response to his urgings for investment in the radio in the 1920s

"The concept is interesting and well-formed, but in order to earn better than a 'C,' the idea must be feasible."

—A Yale University management professor in response to Fred Smith's paper proposing reliable overnight delivery service (Smith went on to found Federal Express Corporation)

"Who the hell wants to hear actors talk?"

—H. M. Warner, Warner Brothers, 1927

"A cookie store is a bad idea. Besides, the market research reports say America likes crispy cookies, not soft and chewy cookies like you make."

—Banker's response to Debbie Fields's idea of starting Mrs. Fields' Cookies

"We don't like their sound, and guitar music is on the way out."

—Decca Recording Company rejecting the Beatles, 1962

evaluation stage, individuals consider whether the product will satisfy certain criteria that are crucial to meeting their specific needs. In the trial stage, they use or experience the product for the first time, possibly by purchasing a small quantity, taking advantage of free samples, or borrowing the product from someone. Supermarkets, for instance, frequently offer special promotions to encourage consumers to taste products. During this stage, potential adopters determine the usefulness of the product under the specific conditions for which they need it.

Individuals move into the adoption stage by choosing a specific product when they need a product of that general type. However, entering the adoption process does not mean the person will eventually adopt the new product. Rejection may occur at any stage, including the adoption stage. Both product adoption and product rejection can be temporary or permanent. This adoption model has several implications when launching a new product. First, the company must promote the product to create widespread awareness of its existence and its benefits. Samples or simulated trials should be arranged to help buyers make initial purchase decisions. At the same time, marketers should emphasize quality control and provide solid guarantees to reinforce buyer opinion during the evaluation stage. Finally, production and physical distribution must be linked to patterns of adoption and repeat purchases.

When an organization introduces a new product, people do not begin the adoption process at the same time, nor do they move through the process at the same speed. Of those who eventually adopt the product, some enter the adoption process rather quickly, whereas others start considerably later. For most products, there is also a group of nonadopters who never begin the process. For business marketers, success in managing production innovation, diffusion, and adoption requires great adaptability and significant effort in understanding customers.[23]

Depending on the length of time it takes them to adopt a new product, consumers fall into one of five major adopter categories: innovators, early adopters, early majority, late majority, and laggards.[24] Figure 11.4 illustrates each adopter category and the percentage of total adopters it typically represents. **Innovators** are the first to adopt a new product; they enjoy trying new products and tend to be venturesome. **Early adopters** choose new products carefully and are viewed as "the people to check with" by those in the remaining adopter categories. People in the **early majority** adopt a new product just prior to the average person; they are deliberate and cautious in trying new products. Individuals in the **late majority** are quite skeptical of new products but eventually adopt them because of economic necessity or social pressure. **Laggards**, the last to adopt a new product, are oriented toward the past. They are suspicious of new products, and when they finally adopt the innovation, it may already have been replaced by a new product.

**innovators** First adopters of new products

**early adopters** Careful choosers of new products

**early majority** Individuals who adopt a new product just prior to the average person

**late majority** Skeptics who adopt new products when they feel it is necessary

**laggards** The last adopters, who distrust new products

## figure 11.4

### DISTRIBUTION OF PRODUCT ADOPTER CATEGORIES

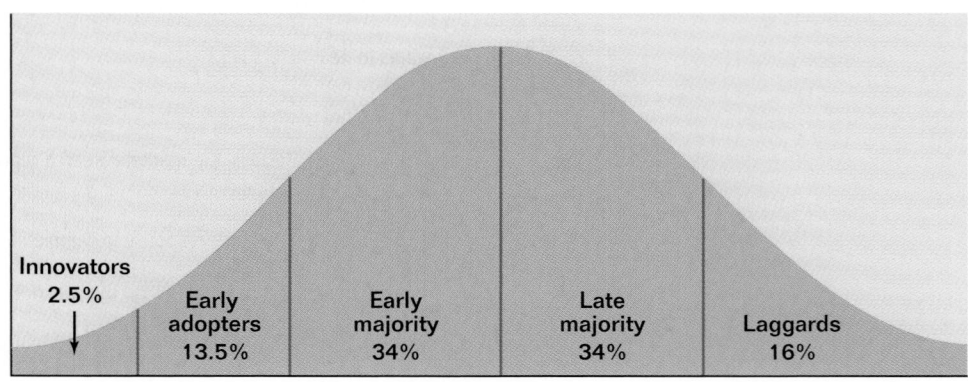

**Source:** Adapted with permission of The Free Press, a division of Simon & Schuster Adult Publishing Group, from *Diffusion of Innovations,* Fourth Edition, by Everett M. Rogers. Copyright © 1995 by Everett M. Rogers. Copyright © 1962, 1971, 1983 by The Free Press. All rights reserved.

## Why Some Products Fail and Others Succeed

Thousands of new products are introduced annually, and many fail. Statistical bureaus, consulting firms, and trade publications estimate that one in three new products fails each year; others report an annual new-product failure rate as high as 80 to 90 percent. The annual cost of product failures to U.S. firms can reach $100 billion. Failure and success rates vary from organization to organization, but in general consumer products fail more often than business products. Being one of the first brands launched in a product category is no guarantee of success. Table 11.3 shows examples of recent product successes and failures.

Products fail for many reasons. One of the most common reasons is the company's failure to match product offerings to customer needs. When products do not offer value and lack the features customers want, they fail in the marketplace. For example, Coca-Cola's C2 and PepsiCo's Pepsi Edge, both targeted at low-carbohydrate dieters with their mid-range calorie count, ultimately garnered just 1 percent share of the market together because low-carb dieters generally avoid products with any refined sugar.[25] Ineffective or inconsistent branding has also been blamed for product failures. Examples of products that failed due to failure to convey the right message or image include Gerber Singles (gourmet food for adults packaged in baby food jars), Microsoft's Bob (a "social interface" cartoon character that many users perceived as juvenile), and Gillette's For Oily Hair Only shampoo.[26] Other reasons cited for new-product failure include technical or design problems, poor timing, overestimation of market size, ineffective promotion, and insufficient distribution.

When examining the problem of product failure, it is important to distinguish the degree of failure. Absolute failure occurs when an organization loses money on a new product because it is unable to recover development, production, and marketing costs. This product usually is deleted from the product mix. Relative product failure occurs when a product returns a profit but does not meet a company's profit or market share objectives. If a company repositions or improves a relative product failure, that product may become a successful member of the product line. Some products experience relative product failure after years of success. Campbell Soup, for example, has been growing slowly for many years. The company continues to focus on its condensed-soup product line but has done little to improve packaging, promotion, or distribution. This leaves Campbell Soup with a core product whose market share has fallen 21 percent during a recent four-year period.[27]

| table 11.3   PRODUCT SUCCESSES AND FAILURES | |
|---|---|
| **Successes** | **Failures** |
| Smith Kline Beecham Nicoderm CQ | R. J. Reynolds Premier smokeless cigarettes |
| Canon Elph digital camera | Cadillac Allante luxury cars |
| Palm PDAs | Apple Lisa personal computer |
| Coca-Cola Dasani water | Heinz Ketch Salsa |
| Starbucks coffee shops | Nestlé Panache coffee |
| Procter & Gamble Pantene shampoos | Gillette For Oily Hair shampoo |
| Tide High Efficiency laundry detergent | Drel Home Dry Cleaning Kits |
| Procter & Gamble Swiffer mop and dusting cloths | S. C. Johnson Allercare aerosol spray, carpet powder, and dust mite powder |
| Bacardi Breezers | Bud and Michelob Dry Beer |

In contrast to this gloomy picture of new-product failure, some new products are very successful. Perhaps the most important ingredient for success is the product's ability to provide a significant and perceivable benefit to a sizable number of customers. New products with an observable advantage over similar available products, such as more features, ease of operation, or improved technology, have a greater chance to succeed. Sometimes a product is simply in touch with consumers' feelings and taste. Consider the Whoopie Pie, a Maine product similar to the Moon Pie sold in the South. Critical to launching a product that will achieve market success is effective planning and management. Companies that follow a systematic, customer-focused plan for new-product development, such as Procter & Gamble, and 3M, are well positioned to launch successful products.

## SUMMARY

A product is a good, a service, or an idea received in an exchange. It can be either tangible or intangible and includes functional, social, and psychological utilities or benefits. When consumers purchase a product, they are buying the benefits and satisfaction they think the product will provide.

Products can be classified on the basis of the buyer's intentions. Consumer products are those purchased to satisfy personal and family needs. Business products are purchased for use in a firm's operations, to resell, or to make other products. Consumer products can be subdivided into convenience, shopping, specialty, and unsought products. Business products can be classified as installations, accessory equipment, raw materials, component parts, process materials, MRO supplies, or business services.

A product item is a specific version of a product that can be designated as a distinct offering among an organization's products. A product line is a group of closely related product items that are viewed as a unit because of marketing, technical, or end-use considerations. The product mix is the composite, or total, group of products that an organization makes available to customers. The width of the product mix is measured by the number of product lines the company offers. The depth of the product mix is the average number of different products offered in each product line.

The product life cycle describes how product items in an industry move through four stages: introduction, growth, maturity, and decline. The life cycle concept is used to ensure that the introduction, alteration, and termination of a product are timed and executed properly. The sales curve is at zero at introduction, rises at an increasing rate during growth, peaks at maturity, and then declines. Profits peak toward the end of the growth stage of the product life cycle. The life expectancy of a product is based on buyers' wants, the availability of competing products, and other environmental conditions. Most businesses have a composite of life cycle patterns for various products. It is important to manage existing products and develop new ones to keep the overall sales performance at a desired level.

When customers accept a new product, they usually do so through a five-stage adoption process. The first stage is awareness, when buyers become aware that a product exists. Interest, the second stage, occurs when buyers seek information about the product. In the third stage, evaluation, buyers consider the product's benefits and decide whether to try it. The fourth stage is trial, when buyers examine, test, or try the product to determine if it meets their needs. The last stage is adoption, when buyers actually purchase the product and use it whenever a need for this general type of product arises.

Of the thousands of new products introduced every year, many fail. Absolute failure occurs when an organization loses money on a new product. Absolute failures are usually removed from the product mix. Relative failure occurs when a product returns a profit but fails to meet a company's objectives. Reasons for product failure include failure to match product offerings to customer needs, poor timing, and ineffective or inconsistent branding. New products that succeed provide significant and observable benefits to customers. Products that have perceivable advantages over similar products also have a better chance to succeed. Effective marketing planning and product management are important factors in a new product's chances of success.

**ACE self-test**

Please visit the student website at **www.prideferrell.com** for ACE Self-Test questions that will help you prepare for exams.

## IMPORTANT TERMS

| | | | |
|---|---|---|---|
| Good | Unsought products | Product item | Maturity stage |
| Service | Installations | Product line | Decline stage |
| Idea | Accessory equipment | Product mix | Product adoption process |
| Consumer products | Raw materials | Width of product mix | Innovators |
| Business products | Component parts | Depth of product mix | Early adopters |
| Convenience products | Process materials | Product life cycle | Early majority |
| Shopping products | MRO supplies | Introduction stage | Late majority |
| Specialty products | Business services | Growth stage | Laggards |

## DISCUSSION & REVIEW QUESTIONS

1. List the tangible and intangible attributes of a pair of Nike athletic shoes. Compare its benefits with those of an intangible product such as a hairstyling in a salon.

2. A product has been referred to as a "psychological bundle of satisfaction." Is this a good definition of a product? Why or why not?

3. Is a personal computer sold at a retail store a consumer product or a business product? Defend your answer.

4. How do convenience products and shopping products differ? What are the distinguishing characteristics of each type of product?

5. In the category of business products, how do component parts differ from process materials?

6. How does an organization's product mix relate to its development of a product line? When should an enterprise add depth to its product lines rather than width to its product mix?

7. How do industry profits change as a product moves through the four stages of its life cycle?

8. What is the relationship between the concepts of product mix and product life cycle?

9. What are the stages in the product adoption process, and how do they affect the commercialization phase?

10. What are the five major adopter categories describing the length of time required for a consumer to adopt a new product, and what are the characteristics of each?

11. In what ways does the marketing strategy for a mature product differ from the marketing strategy for a growth product?

12. What are the major reasons for new-product failure?

## APPLICATION QUESTIONS

1. Choose a familiar clothing store. Describe its product mix, including its depth and width. Evaluate the mix and make suggestions to the owner.

2. Tabasco pepper sauce is a product that has entered the maturity stage of the product life cycle. Name products that would fit into each of the four stages: introduction, growth, maturity, and decline. Describe each product and explain why it fits in that stage.

3. Generally buyers go through a product adoption process before becoming loyal customers. Describe your experience in adopting a product you now use consistently. Did you go through all the stages of the process?

4. Identify and describe a friend or family member who fits into each of the following adopter categories. How would you use this information if you were product manager for a fashion-oriented, medium-priced clothing retailer such as J. Crew or JCPenney?

   a. Innovator

   b. Early adopter

   c. Early majority

   d. Late majority

   e. Laggard

1. A firm's ability to innovate and develop new-product concepts is usually determined by the level of inventiveness and adeptness to adjust to market demands. As a result, successful firms generally benefit from an increase in revenue and publicity in magazines devoted to business innovation. *Business 2.0* annually ranks the fastest-growing companies, which often have the greatest rates of innovation. The ranking can be accessed by using the search term "business innovation" at **http://globaledge. msu.edu/ibrd**. Once you reach the *Business 2.0* website, click on Lists, and then choose the Fastest-Growing Companies option. Based on the *Business 2.0* List of Fastest-Growing Companies, what are the top ten fastest-growing companies? Which industry appears currently to have the most successful commercial innovativeness? Why do you think this industry is thriving?

2. The development of concepts for new products requires a firm to devote resources to research and development (R&D). While insight on different firms' R&D strategies and expenditures may be readily available in annual reports, *Technology Review,* a magazine of innovation, can consolidate this data in its Corporate R&D Scorecard to yield a more comprehensive analysis. The report can be accessed by using the search term "magazine of innovation" at **http://globaledge.msu.edu/ibrd**. Which three industries in a recent report devote the most resources to R&D? Which three industries allocate the least? What does this allow you to conclude about the characteristics of each industry?

## INTERNET Exercise

### Goodyear Tire & Rubber Company

In addition to providing information about the company's products, Goodyear's website helps consumers find the exact products they want and will even direct them to the nearest Goodyear retailer. Visit the Goodyear site at **www.goodyear.com**.

1. How does Goodyear use its website to communicate information about the quality of its tires?
2. How does Goodyear's website demonstrate product design and features?
3. Based on what you learned at the website, describe what Goodyear has done to position its tires.

## Video Case 11.1  There's No Place Like . . . Starbucks

Starbucks was founded in 1971 by three partners in Seattle's renowned open-air Pike Place Market. In 1982, after returning from a trip to coffee bar haven Milan, Italy (with its 1,500 coffee bars), Howard Schultz recognized an opportunity to develop a similar retail coffee-bar culture in Seattle and joined the company as director of retail operations and marketing. Three years later, the company tested the first downtown Seattle coffeehouse, served the first Starbucks Café latte, and introduced its Christmas blend. Since then Starbucks has been expanding across the United States and around the globe and now operates 10,801 locations in 37 countries. It opens about three new stores a day and serves more than 30 million customers a week.

Starbucks purchases and roasts high-quality whole coffee beans and resells them, along with fresh brewed coffees, Italian-style espresso beverages, cold blended beverages, bottled water, complementary food items, coffee-related accessories and equipment, premium teas, and a line of compact discs, primarily through company-operated retail stores. Starbucks also sells coffee and tea products and licenses its trademark through other channels, and, through some of its partners, Starbucks produces and sells bottled Frappuccino coffee drinks, DoubleShot espresso drinks, and a line of super-premium ice cream.

Starbucks locates its walk-in stores in high-traffic, high-visibility locations. While Starbucks can be found in a few shopping malls, the company generally focuses on locations that provide convenient access for pedestrians and drivers. The stores are designed to provide an inviting coffee-bar environment that is an important part of the Starbucks experience. Because the company is flexible with regard to size and format, it can locate stores in or near a variety of settings, including downtown and suburban retail centers, office buildings, and university campuses. It can also situate retail stores in select rural and off-highway locations to serve a broader array of customers outside major metropolitan markets and further expand brand awareness. To provide a greater degree of access and convenience for nonpedestrian customers, the company has increased development of stores with drive-through lanes.

Starbucks constantly strives to update its products and introduces new drinks with each season. At Christmastime 2005, drinks such as peppermint mochas and gingerbread lattes helped push earnings up 20 percent for the quarter. An eggnog latte introduced in 2004 proved so popular that the company introduced a new chai tea version of the drink the next year. Starbucks also tries hard to keep up with consumer desires and needs, for example, by introducing a low-calorie version of its popular frappuccino, which has about 30 to 40 percent fewer calories than the original. While the low-cal frappuccino has been very successful, not all new products are. In 2006 Starbucks pulled Chantico, its "drinkable dessert," from the menu. Chantico was marketed to resemble the thick, sweet hot chocolate drinks found in European cafés, but it was available without any variations in a 6-ounce size. The limitations proved fatal: at Starbucks, customers are used to dictating not only the size of their coffee drinks but also the host of other specifics, such as whether they want them regular or decaf; with nonfat, whole, or soy milk; with sugar-free or regular flavor shots; and with extras like whipped cream and caramel.

Starbucks's executives believe that the experience customers have in its stores should be the same in any country. The company tries to foster brand loyalty by increasing repeat business. One of the ways it has done so is through the Starbucks Card, a reloadable stored-value card that was introduced in 2001. It hit the $1 billion mark in October 2004 for total activations and reloads, and more than 58 million cards have been activated to date. The typical Starbucks customer visits Starbucks about 18 times a month.

Starbucks has been ranked on *Fortune*'s "100 Best Companies to Work For" list for eight years and in 2005 ranked 29th. The company offers both full- and part-time employees a comprehensive benefits package that includes stock-option grants through *Bean Stock*, as well as health, medical, dental, and vision benefits. It also embraces diversity as an essential component of doing business. The company has 91,056 employees; 11,444 are outside the United States. Of these, 28 percent are minorities and 64 percent are women. However, being a great employer does take its toll. In 2005, Starbucks spent more on health insurance for its employees than on raw materials required to brew its coffee. The company has faced double-digit increases in insurance costs each of the last four years. Nonetheless, the Starbucks's benefits policy is a key reason that it has notably low employee turnover and high productivity.

In the process of trying to establish Starbucks as the most recognized and respected brand of coffee in the world, the company has also built an excellent reputation for social responsibility and business ethics. Starbucks pays coffee farmers premium prices to help them make profits and support their families. It is also involved in social development programs that invest in programs to build schools, health clinics, and other projects that benefit coffee-growing communities. It collaborates with farmers through the Farmer Support Center, located in Costa Rica, to provide technical support and training that promotes high-quality coffee for the future. It strives to buy conservation and certified coffees, including Fair Trade Certified, shade grown, and certified organic coffee, to promote responsible environmental and economic efforts. In 2005 Starbucks ranked 42nd on *Business Ethics*'s "100 Best Corporate Citizens" list, up from its 2004 position of 45th. Starbucks's sense of social responsibility, fair trade, and support for the environment are a part of the total product it markets for consumers who are concerned about these social issues.[28]

### Questions for Discussion

1. What is the total product that Starbucks markets?
2. What is the role of the development of new products in Starbucks's success?
3. Why do you think some new Starbucks products succeed and others, like Chantico, fail?

## Case 11.2    Dell Mixes It Up

From MP3 music players and an online music store to flat-screen televisions to home theater projectors, Dell is filling out its product mix with goods and services for the entire household. The company, formerly known as Dell Computer, wants to build on its dominance of the personal computer market by making inroads into the lucrative $100 billion world of consumer electronics. Based in Round Rock, Texas, Dell made its name selling computers directly to customers through its website. In the future, the company expects to derive an ever-larger portion of revenues and profits from a wider mix of products for use beyond the home office.

This drive for diversification started with the introduction of the Dell Axim handheld computer—in direct competition with Palm and other established rivals—followed one year later by a second Axim model. Because the Axims are priced lower than most comparable products, Dell's entry forced Hewlett-Packard and other competitors to lower prices to protect their market share. The company used the same approach when it began selling printers and ink cartridges on its website, again competing directly with Hewlett-Packard. Even some Dell insiders were surprised when printer sales in the first six months were two times higher than forecasted sales.

Now the stage was set for a more comprehensive move into electronics designed for the digital home. Founder Michael Dell and his team envisioned consumers using a personal computer (from Dell, of course) to control televisions, music players, and other products all around the house. They began the planning process by carefully examining electronics products made by nearly 90 manufacturers. They also analyzed consumers' needs, buying patterns, and complaints about incompatibility problems between new and older products. Based on all of this research, they developed an ultra-bright, flat-screen LCD television, a Dell Digital Jukebox (DJ) to store and play music files, and a home theater projector for viewing DVDs and other entertainment. These new products were introduced in time for the holiday buying season, along with the Dell Music Store (selling downloadable music files) and software preloaded on Dell computers to help consumers manage digital entertainment files.

These new products, like the printers and handheld computers before them, put Dell squarely in the middle of a competitive battle with well-established rivals. The Dell DJ competes with Apple's iPod digital music player. The Dell Music Store sells downloadable music files in competition with Apple's iTunes store and other online retailers of digital music. The LCD television not only challenges Sony's television business but sets up a different kind of confrontation about which appliance will serve as the control center of home entertainment. Dell is putting its brand and money behind the computer as the controlling appliance, whereas Sony is putting its resources behind the television as the controlling appliance. "Now is the time for TVs to be reborn," comments a Sony spokesperson.

Although Dell started with only a product or two in each new line, it is gradually adding depth and expanding the width of its product mix. The company is not looking to pioneer new lines; it specializes in applying new technology, adding new features, and making production more efficient. As Dell gains experience with consumer electronics products, it finds ways to lower costs while enhancing each new model. Meanwhile Hewlett-Packard is focusing more on consumer products with the introduction of more than 150 new products, including digital cameras designed for compatibility with its color printers. Samsung and Sony are aggressively targeting segments of the home entertainment market with plasma televisions, home theater projectors, and other products.

Can Dell triumph in such a dynamic and competitive environment? The company certainly knows how to keep prices low by wringing the most productivity out of its direct distribution method. It also knows how to stay close to customers and find out what they want. Finally, with a 20-year history of marketing technology-based products, Dell is among the best-known brands in the country. "We've come out of nowhere to be the number-three consumer brand in the U.S. in less than five years, while Coca-Cola has been doing it for 100 years," says Dell's general manager of consumer business for the United States. "We're not in this to be number three. Number one is the only target around here."[29]

### Questions for Discussion

1. As a product, how can the Dell DJ music player be classified? Why?
2. While Dell has successfully marketed computers directly to customers, are customers likely to be willing to purchase consumer electronics such as home theater systems direct from Dell?
3. How far can Dell widen its product mix without hurting the company's credibility? For example, what might be the impact of new products such as Dell motorcycles or Dell frozen pastries?

# Developing and Managing Products

## One Sweet Brand

By replacing three hydrogen-oxygen groups with three chlorine atoms in a sugar molecule, scientists at Tate & Lyle PLC and researchers at Queen Elizabeth College in London created sucralose—which we know as Splenda—in 1976. Six hundred times sweeter than sugar, Splenda is not absorbed by the body as a carbohydrate. To market the sweetener, Tate & Lyle partnered with McNeil Nutritional (part of Johnson & Johnson). It reached North America when it was approved for consumption in Canada in 1991; the U.S. Food and Drug Administration approved its use in food in 1998. Initially, Splenda was available in only limited quantities via the Internet, but it became available in grocery and other retail stores and restaurants in 2000. In just five short years, Splenda became a household word.

Analysts attribute the sweetener's success to an intelligent, gradual introduction strategy. McNeil Nutritional first targeted diabetics via the Internet to help build interest and demand. Only later did the company begin marketing to grocery stores and restaurants as well as to niche food and beverage companies such as Atkins Nutritional. Although you might think Splenda's marketers would take aim at its direct competition Sweet'N Low, Equal, and other artificial sweeteners, McNeil chose to go head to head against the sugar market. The company promoted Splenda as "made from sugar, so it tastes like sugar" with the implication that Splenda is more natural than other imitation sweeteners. The strategy worked: by 2005 Splenda had revenues greater than sugar brands Domino and C&H; it surpassed sales of Equal and Sweet'N Low in 2004.

There are those that are critical of Splenda. In 2005 the Sugar Association and several other groups sued, not over the sweetner's safety, but over its "made from sugar, so it tastes like sugar" marketing claim. The association also launched a website (**www.truthaboutsplenda.com**) to inform consumers that Splenda is in fact a chemical. (A 2004 survey had revealed that 47 percent of Splenda users believe it is a "natural" product.)

OBJECTIVES

1. To understand how companies manage existing products through line extensions and product modifications

2. To describe how businesses develop a product idea into a commercial product

3. To understand the importance of product differentiation and the elements that differentiate one product from another

4. To examine how product deletion is used to improve product mixes

5. To describe organizational structures used for managing products

Despite the lawsuits, Splenda continues to gain popularity. McDonald's is replacing Sweet'N Low packets with Splenda at 13,700 U.S. stores. Workers at Starbucks had to hide Splenda packets to keep customers from taking handfuls of them. Dunkin' Donuts and Peet's Coffee & Tea have also begun stocking it in response to high demand. Splenda is now used in more than 3,000 foods and beverages, including Diet Coke, Diet Pepsi, and 7-Up, many displaying the Splenda logo on their own labels.

Building the Splenda brand is important not only for increasing revenue, but also in putting it at the forefront of the sucralose market. The patents on the process of making sucralose expired in 2006, opening the door for other companies to make products containing sucralose on their own. However, McNeil is not concerned. The company has plans to expand into Europe and to continue to innovate to keep the Splenda brand in the number 1 spot.[1] ■

To compete effectively and achieve their goals, organizations like the marketer of Splenda must be able to adjust their product mixes in response to changes in customers' needs. To provide products that satisfy target markets and achieve the firm's objectives, a marketer must develop, alter, and maintain an effective product mix. An organization's product mix may require adjustment for a variety of reasons. Because customers' attitudes and product preferences change over time, their desire for certain products may wane. Coca-Cola, for example, has seen sales of carbonated drinks decline as consumers seek alternatives such as bottled water. The decline is particularly worrisome given that the cola giant gets 82 percent of its sales from soft drinks. Thus, the company introduced more than 1,000 new products in 2005, including Diet Coke with Splenda, flavored Dasani water, and the low-calorie Powerade sports drink. Coke also plans to introduce new juice, water, coffee, and iced-tea products over the next few years.[2] In some cases, a company needs to alter its product mix for competitive reasons. A marketer may have to delete a product from the mix because a competitor dominates the market for that product. Similarly, a firm may have to introduce a new product or modify an existing one to compete more effectively. A marketer may expand the firm's product mix to take advantage of excess marketing and production capacity.

In this chapter, we examine several ways to improve an organization's product mix, including management of existing products, development of new products, product differentiation, and elimination of weak products from the product mix. First, we discuss managing existing products through effective line extension and product modification. Next, we examine the stages of new-product development. Then we look at the ways companies differentiate their products in the marketplace and discuss product positioning and repositioning. Next, we examine the importance of deleting weak products and the methods companies use to eliminate them. Finally, we look at the organizational structures used to manage products.

# Managing Existing Products

An organization can benefit by capitalizing on its existing products. By assessing the composition of the current product mix, a marketer can identify weaknesses and gaps. This analysis can then lead to improvement of the product mix through line extension and product modification.

## Line Extensions

**line extension** Development of a product that is closely related to existing products in the line but is designed specifically to meet different customer needs

A **line extension** is the development of a product closely related to one or more products in the existing product line but designed specifically to meet somewhat different customer needs. For example, Speedo, long known for its bathing suits, introduced high-performance winter-sport suits at the 2006 Winter Olympics.[3]

Many of the so-called new products introduced each year are in fact line extensions. Line extensions are more common than new products because they are a less

Four wholesome grains.
One great-tasting snack.

New TOSTITOS® Multigrain Tortilla Chips are made with the wholesome goodness of four grains. They're a fun, great-tasting snack that your family will love and a perfect companion to 100% all-natural TOSTITOS® Salsa.

**Line Extensions**

Tostitos grew through line extensions.

expensive, lower-risk alternative for increasing sales. A line extension may focus on a different market segment or be an attempt to increase sales within the same market segment by more precisely satisfying the needs of people in that segment. Clorox, for example, introduced the Clorox Toilet Wand, which incorporates Clorox bleach.[4] Line extensions are also used to take market share from competitors. Nestlé, the category leader in bottled waters, introduced a four-flavor line of water called Pure Life Splash in direct response to Coca-Cola and Pepsi's latest line extensions.[5] However, one side effect of employing a line extension is that it may result in a more negative evaluation of the core product.[6]

## Product Modifications

**product modification** Changes in one or more characteristics of a product

**Product modification** means changing one or more characteristics of a product. A product modification differs from a line extension in that the original product does not remain in the line. For example, U.S. automakers use product modifications annually when they create new models of the same brand. Once the new models are introduced, the manufacturers stop producing last year's model. Like line extensions, product modifications entail less risk than developing new products.

Product modification can indeed improve a firm's product mix, but only under certain conditions. First, the product must be modifiable. Second, customers must be able to perceive that a modification has been made. Third, the modification should make the product more consistent with customers' desires so it provides greater satisfaction. One drawback to modifying a successful product is that the consumer who had experience with the original version of the product may view a modified version as a riskier purchase.[7] There are three major ways to modify products: quality, functional, and aesthetic modifications.

THE NEW ENVOY DENALI WITH AVAILABLE TOUCH-SCREEN NAVIGATION SYSTEM. OUR MOST LUXURIOUS APPOINTMENTS. OUR MOST ADVANCED IDEAS. AND OUR HIGHEST LEVEL OF ENGINEERING. ALL LIE BEHIND THIS GRILLE. VISIT GMC.COM/DENALI. WE ARE PROFESSIONAL GRADE.™  **ENVOY DENALI**

**Product Modification**

Automakers often use product modification to grow. GM provides a touch-screen navigation system in its Denali; the Ford Five Hundred offers a raised cabin for better road visibility.

**quality modifications** Changes relating to a product's dependability and durability

**Quality Modifications.** **Quality modifications** are changes relating to a product's dependability and durability. The changes usually are executed by altering the materials or the production process. For example, Energizer increased its product's durability by using better materials—a larger cathode and anode interface—that make batteries last longer. For a service, such as a sporting event or air travel, quality modifications may involve enhancing the emotional experience that makes the consumer passionate and loyal to the brand.

Reducing a product's quality may allow an organization to lower its price and direct the item at a different target market. In contrast, increasing the quality of a product may give a firm an advantage over competing brands. Higher quality may enable a company to charge a higher price by creating customer loyalty and lowering customer sensitivity to price. However, higher quality may require the use of more expensive components and processes, thus forcing the organization to cut costs in other areas. Some firms, such as Caterpillar, are finding ways to increase quality while reducing costs.

**functional modifications** Changes affecting a product's versatility, effectiveness, convenience, or safety

**Functional Modifications.** Changes that affect a product's versatility, effectiveness, convenience, or safety are called **functional modifications**; they usually require redesign of the product. Product categories that have undergone considerable functional modification include office and farm equipment, appliances, cleaning products, and telecommunications services. For example, Gillette, which has achieved great success with its three-blade Mach3 shaving system, introduced the five-blade Fusion in both manual and battery-powered versions and priced at a 30 percent premium. The new system's blades are 30 percent closer together than before.[8]

Functional modifications can make a product useful to more people and thus enlarge its market. They can place a product in a favorable competitive position by providing benefits that competing brands do not offer. They can also help an organization achieve and maintain a progressive image. Finally, functional modifications are sometimes made to reduce the possibility of product liability lawsuits.

**aesthetic modifications** Changes relating to the sensory appeal of a product

**Aesthetic Modifications.** **Aesthetic modifications** change the sensory appeal of a product by altering its taste, texture, sound, smell, or appearance. A buyer making a purchase decision is swayed by how a product looks, smells, tastes, feels, or sounds. Thus, an aesthetic modification may strongly affect purchases. For years, automobile

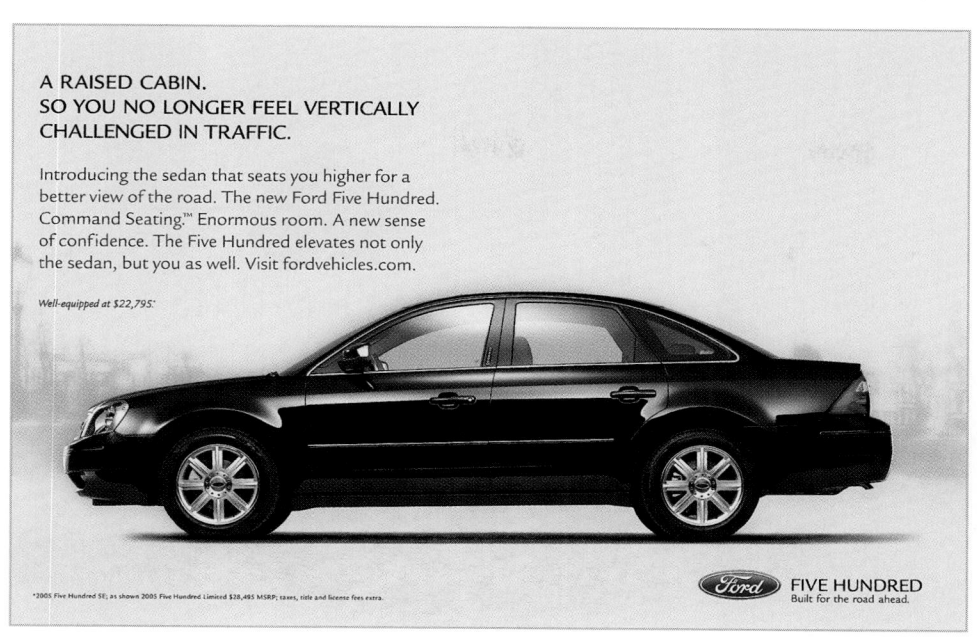

A RAISED CABIN.
SO YOU NO LONGER FEEL VERTICALLY
CHALLENGED IN TRAFFIC.

Introducing the sedan that seats you higher for a better view of the road. The new Ford Five Hundred. Command Seating.™ Enormous room. A new sense of confidence. The Five Hundred elevates not only the sedan, but you as well. Visit fordvehicles.com.

*Well-equipped at $22,795*

*2005 Five Hundred SE; as shown 2005 Five Hundred Limited $28,495 MSRP; taxes, title and license fees extra.*

Ford   FIVE HUNDRED
Built for the road ahead.

makers have relied on quality and aesthetic modifications. For example, the Ford Mustang has been around in one form or another since 1964. The latest modification has a retro look that dates back to the Mustang's muscle car heritage but also includes new safety features.[9]

Aesthetic modifications can help a firm differentiate its product from competing brands and thus gain a sizable market share. Eastern Spice & Flavors, for example, localizes its spice blends to match the tastes of various regional markets around the world.[10] The major drawback in using aesthetic modifications is that their value is determined subjectively. Although a firm may strive to improve the product's sensory appeal, customers may actually find the modified product less attractive.

## Developing New Products

A firm develops new products as a means of enhancing its product mix and adding depth to a product line. However, developing and introducing new products is frequently expensive and risky. For example, Kellogg decided to discontinue Kellogg's Cereal Mates after just two years in the marketplace. Cereal Mates consisted of two components: Corn Flakes, Fruit Loops, Mini Wheats, or Frosted Flakes cereal and aseptically packaged milk. The product failed because Americans do not care for warm milk on cereal and found the aseptically packaged milk unappealing; some customers viewed the product as slightly overpriced.[11] As we discussed in the previous chapter, new-product failures occur frequently and can create major financial problems for organizations, sometimes even causing them to go out of business.

Failure to introduce new products is also risky. Both Ford Motor and General Motors have lost market share to Japanese and Korean automakers in recent years as sales of some of their most profitable models have declined. Chrysler, however, has maintained market share with successful new products.[12]

The term *new product* can have more than one meaning. A genuinely new product offers innovative benefits. However, products that are different and distinctly better are often viewed as new. The following items are product innovations of the last 30 years: Post-it Notes, cellphones, personal computers, PDAs, digital music players, satellite radio, and digital video recorders. Thus, a new product can be an innovative product that has never been sold by any organization, such as the digital camera was when introduced for the first time. A radically new product involves a complex developmental process, including an extensive business analysis to determine the potential for success.[13] It can also be a product that a given firm has not marketed previously, although similar products have been available from other companies, such as Crayola School Glue. Eddie Bauer, best known for its rugged outdoor wear, extended this image with the introduction of a new line of men's cologne. It was considered a new product because Eddie Bauer had not previously marketed cologne or cosmetics. Finally, a product can be viewed as new when it is brought to one or more markets from another market. For example, making the Saturn VUE SUV available in Japan was viewed as a new-product introduction in Japan.

**Example of a New Product**
M&M's introduces two new products—Mega M&M's and M&M's Minis—to satisfy consumers' candy needs.

**new-product development process** A seven-phase process for introducing products: idea generation, screening, concept testing, business analysis, product development, test marketing, and commercialization

**idea generation** Seeking product ideas to achieve organizational objectives

Before a product is introduced, it goes through the seven phases of the **new-product development process** shown in Figure 12.1: (1) idea generation, (2) screening, (3) concept testing, (4) business analysis, (5) product development, (6) test marketing, and (7) commercialization. A product may be dropped (and many are) at any stage of development. In this section, we look at the process through which products are developed, from idea inception to fully commercialized product.

## Idea Generation

Businesses and other organizations seek product ideas that will help them achieve their objectives. This activity is **idea generation**. The fact that only a few ideas are good enough to be commercially successful underscores the challenge of the task.

Although some organizations get their ideas almost by chance, firms that try to manage their product mixes effectively usually develop systematic approaches for generating new-product ideas. Indeed, in organizations there is a relationship between the amount of market information gathered and the number of ideas generated by work groups.[14] At the heart of innovation is a purposeful, focused effort to identify new ways to serve a market.

New-product ideas can come from several sources. They may stem from internal sources: marketing managers, researchers, sales personnel, engineers, or other organizational personnel. Brainstorming and incentives or rewards for good ideas are typical intrafirm devices for stimulating development of ideas. For example, the idea for 3M Post-it adhesive-backed notes came from an employee. As a church choir member, he used slips of paper to mark songs in his hymnal. Because the pieces of paper kept falling out, he suggested developing an adhesive-backed note. New-product ideas may also arise from sources outside the firm, such as customers, competitors, advertising agencies, management consultants, and private

## figure 12.1

### PHASES OF NEW-PRODUCT DEVELOPMENT

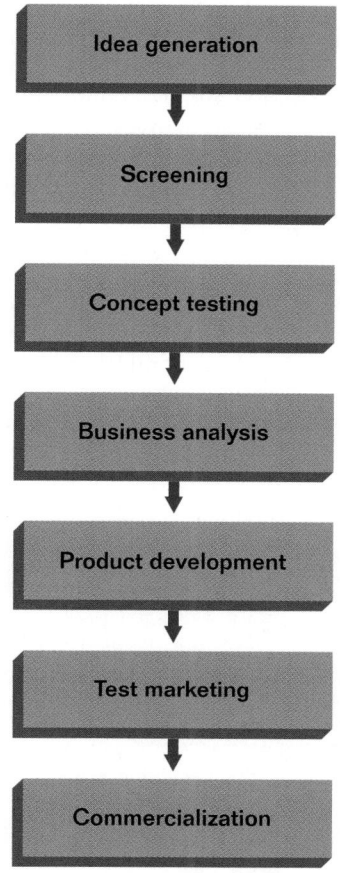

Idea generation

Screening

Concept testing

Business analysis

Product development

Test marketing

Commercialization

**screening** Selecting the ideas with the greatest potential for further review

research organizations. Procter & Gamble gets 35 percent of its ideas from inventors and outside consultants.[15] Consultants are often used as sources for stimulating new-product ideas. IDEO, based in Palo Alto, California, is a design firm that helps corporate clients develop innovative products and service environments. Developing new-product alliances with other firms has also been found to enhance the acquisition and use of information useful for creating new-product ideas.[16] Asking customers what they want from products and organizations has helped many firms become successful and remain competitive.

### Screening

In the process of **screening**, the ideas with the greatest potential are selected for further review. During screening, product ideas are analyzed to determine whether they match the organization's objectives and resources. If a product idea results in a product similar to the firm's existing offerings, marketers must assess the degree to which the new product could cannibalize the sales of current products. The company's overall abilities to produce and market the product are also analyzed. Keeping the product idea in focus and on track by understanding consumer needs and wants is the key to success.[17] Other aspects of an idea to be weighed are the nature and wants of buyers and possible environmental changes. At times a checklist of new-product requirements is used when making screening decisions. This practice encourages evaluators to be systematic and thus reduces the chances of overlooking some pertinent fact. Most new-product ideas are rejected during the screening phase.

---

**marketing ENTREPRENEURS**

**Alex Fisher and Stew Maloney**

THEIR BUSINESS: Planet Dog

FOUNDED: 1997

SUCCESS: Nearly 850 products sold through 2,000 stores around the world

Add Alex Fisher and Stew Maloney to the ranks of business founders who sketched their business plan on a napkin. Their plan for Planet Dog has grown into a successful dog-centric retailer based in Portland, Maine. It markets dog-tested toys, bones, leashes, beds, and other products through a website, catalog, and national retailers such as PetSmart and PETCO. From the beginning Fisher and Maloney focused on designing products to please dogs and infused their small business with a fun, free-thinking philosophy, where "there's no such thing as a bad idea." The fast-growing company sets aside 10 percent of profits for its charitable foundation. There's also a Planet Cat and a company store in Portland.

## Concept Testing

**concept testing** Seeking a sample of potential buyers' responses to a product idea

To evaluate ideas properly, it may be necessary to test product concepts. In **concept testing**, a small sample of potential buyers is presented with a product idea through a written or oral description (and perhaps a few drawings) to determine their attitudes and initial buying intentions regarding the product. For a single product idea, an organization can test one or several concepts of the same product. Concept testing is a low-cost procedure that allows a company to determine customers' initial reactions to a product idea before it invests considerable resources in research and development. Input from online communities may also be beneficial in the product development process.[18] The results of concept testing can help product development personnel better understand which product attributes and benefits are most important to potential customers.

Figure 12.2 shows a concept test for a proposed tick and flea control product. Notice that the concept is briefly described and then a series of questions is presented. The questions vary considerably depending on the type of product being tested. Typical questions are: In general, do you find this proposed product attractive? Which benefits are especially attractive to you? Which features are of little or no interest to you? Do you feel this proposed product would work better for you than the product you currently use? Compared with your current product, what are

# Demeter Makes Scents of New Products

Marketers at Demeter Fragrance Library are always sniffing out ideas for new products. In an industry where well-known brands are supported by millions of dollars worth of packaging, sampling, and advertising, Demeter has made its name by concentrating on the development of offbeat scents such as Dirt, Snow, Birthday Cake, and Sugar Cane. It now sells more than $10 million worth of fragrances yearly through Sephora, Anthropologie, and other retailers in the United States and Europe.

Many of Demeter's ideas for new colognes, body lotions, and bath gels are inspired by aromas in the natural world, the smell of places such as New Zealand, or by favorite foods such as apple pie. "Our Wet Garden scent started out as a version of what became

Greenhouse," explains fragrance maker and Demeter co-founder Christopher Gable. "It had the aroma of fresh green wetness, but not the humidity, so it became something else equally beautiful."

Customers sometimes provide inspiration for new scents, as well. Gable once asked a customer, "What aroma do you really want that you can't get?" When the customer responded, "It's the scent that comes when I first turn on my air conditioner in May," Gable recognized the aroma as mildew. The company proceeded to develop Mildew, which Gable says "is lovely and has quite a following."

Among Demeter's newest fragrances are scents that evoke a particular mood or experience. Its Attitude Adjustment Cologne Sprays include Always Calm, Always Energetic, and Always Happy. According to Chris Gable, founder, its Kahala fragrances, which include Guava Nectar and Hawaiian Surf, are intended to "deliver the Hawaiian context and concept in an authentic, original, and sophisticated way."

**figure 12.2**

## CONCEPT TEST FOR A TICK AND FLEA CONTROL PRODUCT

**Product description**

An insecticide company is considering the development and introduction of a new tick and flea control product for pets. This product would consist of insecticide and a liquid dispensing brush for applying the insecticide to dogs and cats. The insecticide is in a cartridge that is installed in the handle of the brush. The insecticide is dispensed through the tips of the bristles when they touch the pet's skin (which is where most ticks and fleas are found). The actual dispensing works very much like a felt-tip pen. Only a small amount of insecticide actually is dispensed on the pet because of this unique dispensing feature. Thus, the amount of insecticide that is placed on your pet is minimal compared to conventional methods of applying a tick and flea control product. One application of insecticide will keep your pet free from ticks and fleas for fourteen days.

**Please answer the following questions:**

1. In general, how do you feel about using this type of product on your pet?

2. What are the major advantages of this product compared with the existing product that you are currently using to control ticks and fleas on your pet?

3. What characteristics of this product do you especially like?

4. What suggestions do you have for improving this product?

5. If it is available at an appropriate price, how likely are you to buy this product?

      Very likely    Semi-likely    Not likely

6. Assuming that a single purchase would provide 30 applications for an average-size dog or 48 applications for an average-size cat, approximately how much would you pay for this product?

the primary advantages of the proposed product? If this product were available at an appropriate price, would you buy it? How often would you buy this product? How could this proposed product be improved?

## Business Analysis

**business analysis** Evaluating the potential impact of a product idea on the firm's sales, costs, and profits

During the **business analysis** stage, the product idea is evaluated to determine its potential contribution to the firm's sales, costs, and profits. In the course of a business analysis, evaluators ask a variety of questions: Does the product fit in with the organization's existing product mix? Is demand strong enough to justify entering the market, and will the demand endure? What types of environmental and competitive changes can be expected, and how will these changes affect the product's future sales, costs, and profits? Are the organization's research, development, engineering, and production capabilities adequate to develop the product? If new facilities must be constructed, how quickly can they be built and how much will they cost? Is the necessary financing for development and commercialization on hand or obtainable at terms consistent with a favorable return on investment?

In the business analysis stage, firms seek market information. The results of customer surveys, along with secondary data, supply the specifics needed to estimate potential sales, costs, and profits.

For many products in this stage (when they are still just product ideas), forecasting sales accurately is difficult. This is especially true for innovative and completely new products. Organizations sometimes employ break-even analysis to determine how many units they would have to sell to begin making a profit. At times an organization also uses payback analysis, in which marketers compute the time period required to recover the funds that would be invested in developing the new product. Because break-even and payback analyses are based on estimates, they are usually viewed as useful but not particularly precise during this stage.

## Product Development

**product development** Determining if producing a product is feasible and cost effective

**test marketing** A limited introduction of a product in geographic areas chosen to represent the intended market

**Product development** is the phase in which the organization determines if it is technically feasible to produce the product and if it can be produced at costs low enough to make the final price reasonable. To test its acceptability, the idea or concept is converted into a prototype, or working model. The prototype should reveal tangible and intangible attributes associated with the product in consumers' minds. The product's design, mechanical features, and intangible aspects must be linked to wants in the marketplace. Through marketing research and concept testing, product attributes important to buyers are identified. These characteristics must be communicated to customers through the design of the product. Honda Motor, for example, developed a prototype minivan that targets Japan's growing population of pet owners with pet-friendly features such as paneled floors and seats that convert to a holding pen. Displayed at the Tokyo Auto Show, the prototype helped Honda assess interest in the concept.[19]

After a prototype is developed, its overall functioning must be tested. Its performance, safety, convenience, and other functional qualities are tested both in a laboratory and in the field. Functional testing should be rigorous and lengthy enough to test the product thoroughly. Manufacturing issues that come to light at this stage may require adjustments. When Cadbury Schweppes was developing its new Trident Splash gum, production problems necessitated changes in the ingredients. One combination resulted in a too-soft gum that jammed machines; another combination resulted in the gum's liquid center leaking during trial deliveries. Finding just the right recipe required months.[20]

A crucial question that arises during product development is how much quality to build into the product. For example, a major dimension of quality is durability. Higher quality often calls for better materials and more expensive processing, which increase production costs and, ultimately, the product's price. In determining the specific level of quality, a marketer must ascertain approximately what price the target market views as acceptable. In addition, a marketer usually tries to set a quality level consistent with that of the firm's other products. Obviously the quality of competing brands is also a consideration.

The development phase of a new product is frequently lengthy and expensive; thus, a relatively small number of product ideas are put into development. If the product appears sufficiently successful during this stage to merit test marketing, then, during the latter part of the development stage, marketers begin to make decisions regarding branding, packaging, labeling, pricing, and promotion for use in the test marketing stage.

## Test Marketing

**Test marketing** is a limited introduction of a product in geographic areas chosen to represent the intended market. Heineken test marketed Heineken Premium Light in Providence, Tampa, Phoenix, and Dallas for several months before rolling out the product.[21] Its aim is to determine the extent to which potential customers will buy the product. Test marketing is not an extension of the development

**Product Development**

In the product development stage, Lays tested consumer acceptance of its Cheddar & Sour Cream flavored potato chips.

NOW CHEESE LOVERS REALLY HAVE SOMETHING TO SMILE ABOUT.

Baked!

Lay's

CHEDDAR & SOUR CREAM

NATURALLY BAKED FLAVORED POTATO CRISPS

The irresistible taste of real cheddar cheese on a baked potato crisp. They're delicious, yet sensible. This is snacking without the compromise.

Lay's

get your smile on.

stage; it is a sample launching of the entire marketing mix. Test marketing should be conducted only after the product has gone through development and initial plans have been made regarding the other marketing mix variables. Companies use test marketing to lessen the risk of product failure. The dangers of introducing an untested product include undercutting already profitable products and, should the new product fail, loss of credibility with distributors and customers.

Test marketing provides several benefits. It lets marketers expose a product in a natural marketing environment to measure its sales performance. While the product is being marketed in a limited area, the company can strive to identify weaknesses in the product or in other parts of the marketing mix. A product weakness discovered after a nationwide introduction can be expensive to correct. Moreover, if consumers' early reactions are negative, marketers may be unable to persuade consumers to try the product again. Thus, making adjustments after test marketing can be crucial to the success of a new product. On the other hand, test marketing results may be positive enough to warrant accelerating the product's introduction. Test marketing also allows marketers to experiment with variations in advertising, pricing, and packaging in different test areas and to measure the extent of brand awareness, brand switching, and repeat purchases resulting from these alterations in the marketing mix.

Selection of appropriate test areas is very important because the validity of test marketing results depends heavily on selecting test sites that provide accurate

# Concept Development: Seasons 52 Hits the Target

Seasons 52 is the latest concept restaurant developed by Darden Restaurants, Inc., the world's largest casual dining company. Seasons 52 boasts a seasonally inspired menu with the freshest goods available served in a casual atmosphere. With four Florida locations and one in Atlanta, Seasons 52 targets those who are striving to live fit, active lives and are concerned about the quality and nutrition of their food. The restaurants are warm and contemporary with soft lighting, rich earth tones, and live trees, and feature nightly live entertainment.

All menu items at Seasons 52 have fewer than 475 calories, significantly lower than competing restaurants; are nutritionally balanced; and are not fried. In the summer, the menu's focus is on fresh fruits and vegetables such as stone fruits,

melons, peppers, sweet corn, and tomatoes. More rustic flavors are featured in the fall, including squash, pumpkin, mushrooms, and cranberries. In the winter, the restaurant may offer Maui onions, Comice pears from Oregon, and California-grown Delta asparagus. Desserts include low-calorie, smaller portion versions of key lime pie, butterscotch pudding, or Rocky Road ice cream. Menu items are competitively priced. Appetizers sell for less than $10, entrees range in the mid-teens, and desserts are priced at less than $5.

Restaurants have one of the highest failure rates of any business, but Darden has experience; its other chains include Red Lobster, Olive Garden, Smokey Bones, and Bahama Breeze. When its Olive Garden concept was developed, the company studied consumer likes and dislikes about local Italian restaurants. Based on this research, Olive Garden featured larger tables, chairs with wheels for easy access, and larger portions. The Olive Garden was an immediate success. Darden's experience and Seasons 52's seasonally inspired, healthy menu appear poised to score another hit.

| table 12.1 | POPULAR TEST MARKETS IN THE UNITED STATES |
|---|---|

| Rank | City |
|---|---|
| 1 | Albany, NY |
| 2 | Rochester, NY |
| 3 | Greensboro, NC |
| 4 | Birmingham, AL |
| 5 | Syracuse, NY |
| 6 | Charlotte, NC |
| 7 | Nashville, TN |
| 8 | Eugene, OR |
| 9 | Wichita, KS |
| 10 | Richmond, VA |

**Source:** "Which American City Provides the Best Consumer Test Market?" *Business Wire,* May 24, 2004.

representation of the intended target market. Table 12.1 lists some of the most popular test market cities. The criteria used for choosing test market cities depend on the product's attributes, the target market's characteristics, and the firm's objectives and resources.

Test marketing is not without risks. It is expensive, and competitors may try to interfere. A competitor may attempt to "jam" the test program by increasing its own advertising or promotions, lowering prices, and offering special incentives, all to combat recognition and purchase of the new brand. Any such tactics can invalidate test results. Sometimes, too, competitors copy the product in the testing stage and rush to introduce a similar product. It is therefore desirable to move to the commercialization phase as soon as possible after successful testing. On the other hand, some firms have been known to heavily promote new products long before they are ready for the market to discourage competitors from developing similar new products.

Because of these risks, many companies use alternative methods to measure customer preferences. One such method is simulated test marketing. Typically consumers at shopping centers are asked to view an advertisement for a new product and are given a free sample to take home. These consumers are subsequently interviewed over the phone and asked to rate the product. The major advantages of simulated test marketing are greater speed, lower costs, and tighter security, which reduce the flow of information to competitors and reduce jamming. Gillette's Personal Care Division, for example, spends less than $200,000 for a simulated test that lasts three to five months. A live test market costs Gillette $2 million, counting promotion and distribution, and takes one to two years to complete. Several marketing research firms, such as ACNielsen Company, offer test marketing services to provide independent assessment of proposed products.

Clearly not all products that are test marketed are launched. At times, problems discovered during test marketing cannot be resolved. Procter & Gamble, for example, test marketed a new plastic wrap product called Impress in Grand Junction, Colorado, but decided not to launch the brand nationally based on the results of test marketing.[22]

## Commercialization

**commercialization** Refining and finalizing plans and budgets for full-scale manufacturing and marketing of a product

During the **commercialization** phase, plans for full-scale manufacturing and marketing must be refined and finalized and budgets for the project prepared. Early in the commercialization phase, marketing management analyzes the results of test marketing to find out what changes in the marketing mix are needed before introducing the product. The results of test marketing may tell marketers to change one or more of the product's physical attributes, modify the distribution plans to include more retail outlets, alter promotional efforts, or change the product's price. However, as more and more changes are made based on test marketing findings, the test marketing projections may become less valid.

During the early part of this stage, marketers must not only gear up for larger-scale production but also make decisions about warranties, repairs, and replacement parts. The type of warranty a firm provides can be a critical issue for buyers, especially when expensive, technically complex goods such as appliances are involved. Maytag, for example, provides a money-back guarantee on its refrigerators. Establishing an effective system for providing repair services and replacement parts is necessary to maintain favorable customer relationships. Although the producer may furnish these services directly to buyers, it is more common for the producer to provide such services through regional service centers. Regardless of how services are provided, it is important to customers that they be performed quickly and correctly.

The product enters the market during the commercialization phase. When introducing a product, a firm may spend enormous sums for advertising, personal selling,

**Commercialization**

Stanley successfully develops innovative products and rolls them out nationally.

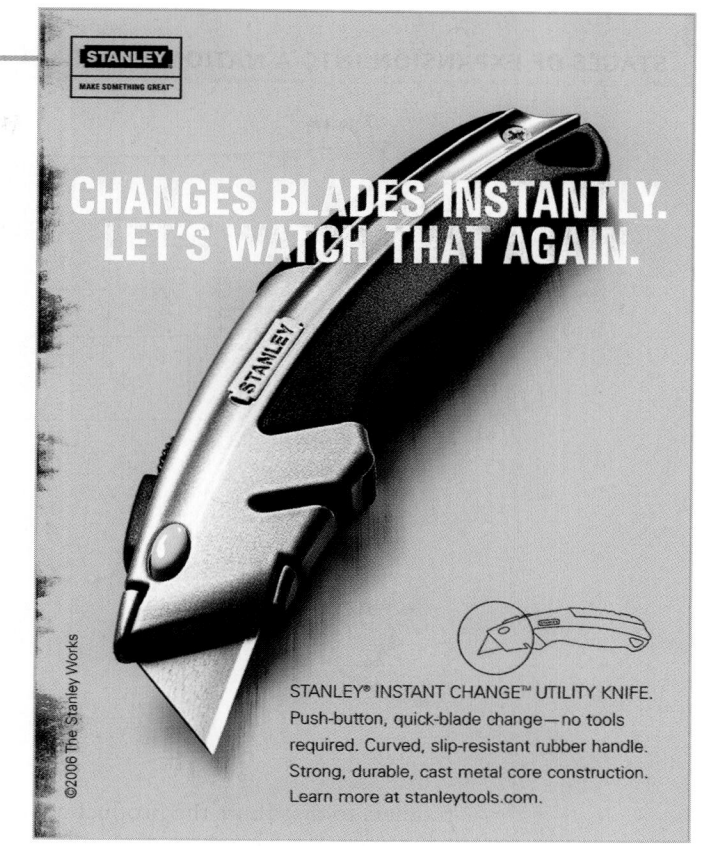

STANLEY® INSTANT CHANGE™ UTILITY KNIFE.
Push-button, quick-blade change—no tools required. Curved, slip-resistant rubber handle. Strong, durable, cast metal core construction. Learn more at stanleytools.com.

and other types of promotion, as well as for plant and equipment. Such expenditures may not be recovered for several years. Smaller firms may find this process difficult, but even so they may use press releases, blogs, podcasts, and other tools to capture quick feedback as well as promote the new product. Another low-cost promotional tool is product reviews in newspapers and magazines, which can be especially helpful when they are positive and target the same customers.

Usually products are not launched nationwide overnight but are introduced through a process called a *roll-out*. With a roll-out, a product is introduced in stages, starting in one set of geographic areas and gradually expanding into adjacent areas. It may take several years to market the product nationally. Sometimes the test cities are used as initial marketing areas, and the introduction of the product becomes a natural extension of test marketing. A product test marketed in Sacramento, Fort Collins, Abilene, Springfield, and Jacksonville, as the map in Figure 12.3 (on p. 338) shows, could be introduced first in those cities. After the stage 1 introduction is complete, stage 2 could include market coverage of the states where the test cities are located. In stage 3, marketing efforts might be extended into adjacent states. All remaining states would then be covered in stage 4.

Gradual product introductions do not always occur state by state; other geographic combinations, such as groups of counties that overlap across state borders, are sometimes used. Products destined for multinational markets may also be rolled out one country or region at a time. After Heineken test marketed its Heineken Premium Light beer in several cities in the United States, it gradually rolled out the product's distribution nationally.[23] Gradual product introduction is desirable for several reasons. First, it reduces the risks of introducing a new product. If the product fails, the firm will experience smaller losses if it introduced the item in only a few geographic areas than if it marketed the product nationally. Second, a company cannot introduce a product nationwide overnight because a system of wholesalers and

## figure 12.3

### STAGES OF EXPANSION INTO A NATIONAL MARKET DURING COMMERCIALIZATION

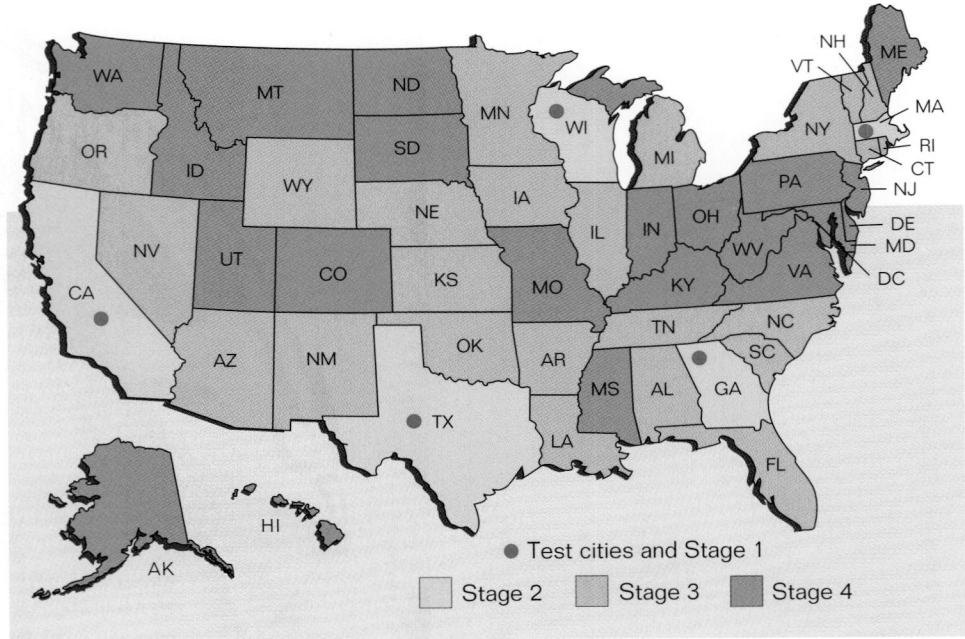

● Test cities and Stage 1

☐ Stage 2    ☐ Stage 3    ☐ Stage 4

retailers to distribute the product cannot be established so quickly; developing a distribution network may take considerable time. Third, if the product is successful, the number of units needed to satisfy nationwide demand for it may be too large for the firm to produce in a short time. Finally, it allows for fine tuning of the marketing mix to better satisfy target customers. Procter & Gamble, for example, originally conceived of Febreze deodorizer as a fabric-care product, but over time, the company's view of the highly successful brand evolved into an air freshening line because that's how consumers indicated they were using it.[24]

Despite the good reasons for introducing a product gradually, marketers realize this approach creates some competitive problems. A gradual introduction allows competitors to observe what the firm is doing and to monitor results just as the firm's own marketers are doing. If competitors see that the newly introduced product is successful, they may quickly enter the same target market with similar products. In addition, as a product is introduced region by region, competitors may expand their marketing efforts to offset promotion of the new product.

# Product Differentiation Through Quality, Design, and Support Services

**product differentiation** Creating and designing products so that customers perceive them as different from competing products

Some of the most important characteristics of products are the elements that distinguish them from one another. **Product differentiation** is the process of creating and designing products so that customers perceive them as different from competing products. Customer perception is critical in differentiating products. Perceived differences might include quality, features, styling, price, or image. A crucial element used to differentiate one product from another is the brand, discussed in the next chapter. In this section, we examine three aspects of product differentiation that companies must consider when creating and offering products for sale: product quality, product design and features, and product support services. These aspects involve the company's attempt to create real differences among products.

## Product Quality

**quality** The overall characteristics of a product that allow it to perform as expected in satisfying customer needs

**Quality** refers to the overall characteristics of a product that allow it to perform as expected in satisfying customer needs. The words *as expected* are very important to this definition because quality usually means different things to different customers. For some, durability signifies quality. Among the most durable products on the market today is the Craftsman line of tools at Sears; indeed, Sears provides a lifetime guarantee on the durability of its tools. For other consumers, a product's ease of use may indicate quality.

The concept of quality also varies between consumer and business markets. Consumers consider high-quality products to be reliable, durable, and easy to maintain. For business markets, technical suitability, ease of repair, and company reputation are important characteristics. Unlike consumers, most organizations place far less emphasis on price than on product quality.

**level of quality** The amount of quality a product possesses

One important dimension of quality is **level of quality**, the amount of quality a product possesses. The concept is a relative one; that is, the quality level of one product is difficult to describe unless it is compared with that of other products. For example, Burger King had suffered years of declining quality perceptions relative to other hamburger chains. After a new CEO instituted a number of changes, Burger King's customer satisfaction is at an all-time high according to the University of Michigan's American Customer Satisfaction Index, while rival McDonald's has seen its customer satisfaction decline.[25] How high should the level of quality be? It depends on the product and the costs and consequences of a product failure.

**consistency of quality** The degree to which a product has the same level of quality over time

A second important dimension is consistency. **Consistency of quality** refers to the degree to which a product has the same level of quality over time. Consistency means giving consumers the quality they expect every time they purchase the product. Like level of quality, consistency is a relative concept; however, it implies a quality comparison within the same brand over time. The quality level of McDonald's french fries is generally consistent from one location to another. If FedEx delivers more than 99 percent of overnight packages on time, its service has consistent quality.

**Product Quality**

Fair trade supports market premiums for small farmers to ensure the highest quality.

The consistency of product quality can also be compared across competing products. It is at this stage that consistency becomes critical to a company's success. Companies that can provide quality on a consistent basis have a major competitive advantage over rivals. FedEx, for example, is viewed as more consistent in delivery schedules than the U.S. Postal Service. In simple terms, no company has ever succeeded by creating and marketing low-quality products. Many companies have taken major steps, such as implementing total quality management (TQM), to improve the quality of their products.

By and large, higher product quality means marketers will charge a higher price for the product. This fact forces marketers to consider quality carefully in their product-planning efforts. Not all customers want or can afford the highest-quality products available. Thus, some companies offer products with moderate quality.

### Product Design and Features

**product design** How a product is conceived, planned, and produced

**Product design** refers to how a product is conceived, planned, and produced. Design is a very complex topic because it involves the total sum of all the product's physical characteristics. Many companies are known for the outstanding designs of their products: Sony for personal electronics, Hewlett-Packard for printers, Apple for computers and music players, and JanSport for backpacks. Good design is one of the best competitive advantages any brand can possess.

**styling** The physical appearance of a product

One component of design is **styling**, or the physical appearance of the product. The style of a product is one design feature that can allow certain products to sell very rapidly. Good design, however, means more than just appearance; it also involves a product's functioning and usefulness. For example, a pair of jeans may look great, but if they fall apart after three washes, clearly the design was poor. Most consumers seek out products that both look good and function well.

**product features** Specific design characteristics that allow a product to perform certain tasks

**Product features** are specific design characteristics that allow a product to perform certain tasks. By adding or subtracting features, a company can differentiate its products from those of the competition. Chrysler promotes its line of minivans as having more features related to passenger safety—dual air bags, steel-reinforced doors, and integrated child safety seats—than any other auto company. Product features can also be used to differentiate products within the same company. For example, Nike offers both a walking shoe and a run-walk shoe for specific consumer needs. In these cases, the company's products are sold with a wide range of features,

**customer services** Human or mechanical efforts or activities that add value to a product

from low-priced "base" or "stripped-down" versions to high-priced, prestigious "feature-packed" ones. The automotive industry regularly sells products with a wide range of features. In general, the more features a product has, the higher its price and, often, the higher its perceived quality.

For a brand to have a sustainable competitive advantage, marketers must determine the product designs and features that customers desire. Information from marketing research efforts and from databases can help in assessing customers' product design and feature preferences. Being able to meet customers' desires for product design and features at prices they can afford is crucial to a product's long-term success. Marketers must be careful not to misrepresent or overpromise regarding product features or product performance.

### Product Support Services

Many companies differentiate their product offerings by providing support services. Usually referred to as **customer services**, these services include any human or mechanical efforts or activities a company provides that

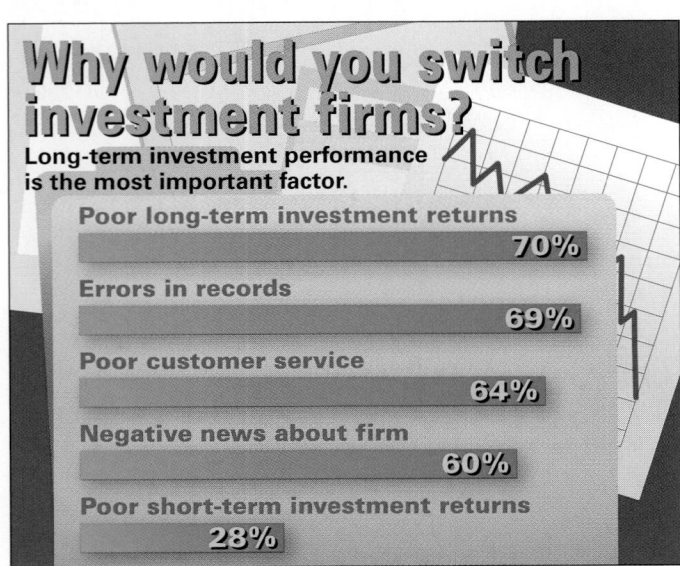

**snapshot**

**Why would you switch investment firms?**
**Long-term investment performance is the most important factor.**

Poor long-term investment returns — **70%**
Errors in records — **69%**
Poor customer service — **64%**
Negative news about firm — **60%**
Poor short-term investment returns — **28%**

*Source:* Data from TIAA-CREF Trust in America survey. Margin of error is ±3 percentage points.

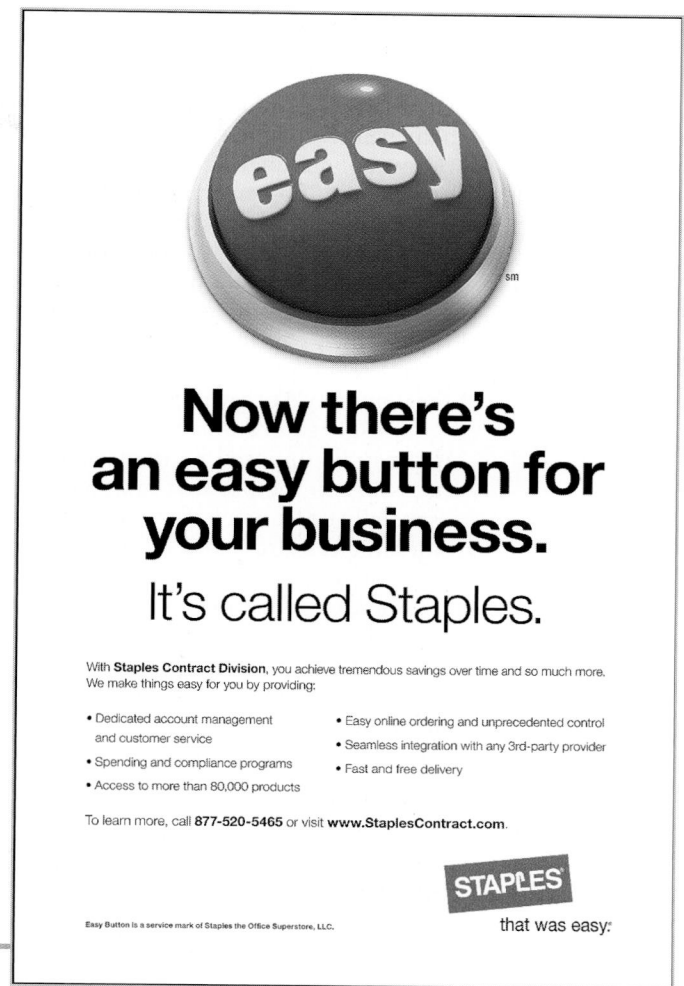

**Product Support Services**

Staples promotes support services to save businesses time and money.

add value to a product.[26] Examples of customer services include delivery and installation, financing arrangements, customer training, warranties and guarantees, repairs, layaway plans, convenient hours of operation, adequate parking, and information through toll-free numbers. For example, many hotel chains, including Holiday Inn, Marriott International, and Hilton Hotels, offer web-based reservation services for their customers' convenience. Their websites also provide information about the hotels' prices, amenities, and frequent-guest programs.

Whether as a major or minor part of the total product offering, all marketers of goods sell customer services. Providing good customer service may be the only way a company can differentiate its products when all products in a market have essentially the same quality, design, and features. This is especially true in the computer industry. When buying a laptop computer, for example, consumers shop more for fast delivery, technical support, warranties, and price than for product quality and design. Through research, a company can discover the types of services customers want and need. For example, some customers are more interested in financing, whereas others are more concerned with installation and training. The level of customer service a company provides can profoundly affect customer satisfaction. The American Customer Satisfaction Index, compiled by the National Quality Research Center at the University of Michigan, ranks customer satisfaction among a wide variety of businesses. Dissatisfied customers may curtail their overall spending, which could stifle economic growth.[27]

# Product Deletion

**product deletion** Eliminating a product from the product mix when it no longer satisfies a sufficient number of customers

Generally a product cannot satisfy target market customers and contribute to the achievement of the organization's overall goals indefinitely. **Product deletion** is the process of eliminating a product from the product mix, usually because it no longer satisfies a sufficient number of customers. Nikon, for example, discontinued seven film camera models, leaving the Japanese firm with just two film camera models on the market, in order to focus on digital cameras.[28] A declining product reduces an organization's profitability and drains resources that could be used to modify other products or develop new ones. A marginal product may require shorter production runs, which can increase per-unit production costs. Finally, when a dying product completely loses favor with customers, the negative feelings may transfer to some of the company's other products.

Most organizations find it difficult to delete a product. A decision to drop a product may be opposed by managers and other employees who believe the product is necessary to the product mix. Salespeople who still have some loyal customers are especially upset when a product is dropped. In such cases, companies may spend considerable resources and effort to change a slipping product's marketing mix to improve its sales and thus avoid having to eliminate it.

Some organizations delete products only after the products have become heavy financial burdens. Delta Airlines, for example, eliminated its Song discount airline subsidiary after entering bankruptcy proceedings.[29] A better approach is some form of systematic review in which each product is evaluated periodically to determine its impact on the overall effectiveness of the firm's product mix. Such a review should analyze the product's contribution to the firm's sales for a given period, as well as estimate future sales, costs, and profits associated with the product. It should also gauge the value of making changes in the marketing strategy to improve the product's performance. A systematic review allows an organization to improve product performance and ascertain when to delete products. Procter & Gamble, for example, discontinued its White Cloud brand of toilet tissue in the early 1990s after determining the product did not match customer needs. However, after Wal-Mart acquired the rights to the name, White Cloud was repositioned as a premium private-label brand and expanded to include laundry detergent, fabric softener, and dryer sheets. Ironically, these products now compete head to head with Procter & Gamble's Tide laundry detergent and Downy fabric softener in Wal-Mart stores.[30]

Basically there are three ways to delete a product: phase it out, run it out, or drop it immediately (see Figure 12.4). A *phase-out* allows the product to decline without a

**figure 12.4**

## PRODUCT DELETION PROCESS

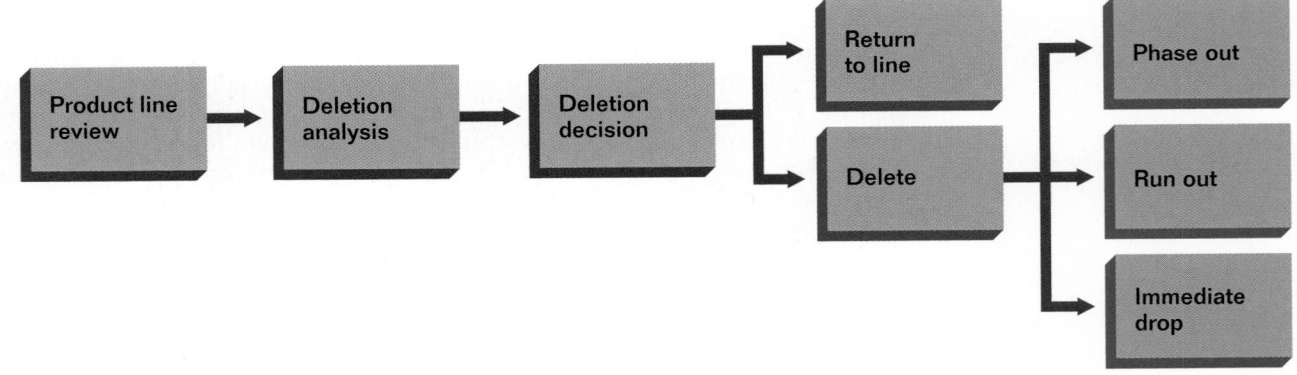

**Source:** Martin L. Bell, *Marketing: Concepts and Strategy,* 3rd ed., p. 267; Copyright © 1979, Houghton Mifflin Company. Reprinted by permission of Mrs. Martin L. Bell.

change in the marketing strategy; no attempt is made to give the product new life. Nikon, for example, simply allowed sales of its discontinued film cameras to continue until their supplies ran out.[31] A *run-out* exploits any strengths left in the product. Intensifying marketing efforts in core markets or eliminating some marketing expenditures, such as advertising, may cause a sudden jump in profits. This approach is commonly taken for technologically obsolete products, such as older models of computers and calculators. Often the price is reduced to generate a sales spurt. The third alternative, an *immediate drop* of an unprofitable product, is the best strategy when losses are too great to prolong the product's life.

# Organizing to Develop and Manage Products

After reviewing the concepts of product line and mix and life cycles, it should be obvious that managing products is a complex task. Often the traditional functional form of organization, in which managers specialize in such business functions as advertising, sales, and distribution, does not fit a company's needs. In this case, management must find an organizational approach that accomplishes the tasks necessary to develop and manage products. Alternatives to functional organization include the product or brand manager approach, the market manager approach, and the venture team approach.

**product manager** The person within an organization responsible for a product, a product line, or several distinct products that make up a group

**brand manager** The person responsible for a single brand

A **product manager** is responsible for a product, a product line, or several distinct products that make up an interrelated group within a multi-product organization. A **brand manager** is responsible for a single brand. General Foods, for example, has one brand manager for Maxim coffee and one for Maxwell House coffee. A product or brand manager operates cross-functionally to coordinate the activities, information, and strategies involved in marketing an assigned product. Product managers and brand managers plan marketing activities to achieve objectives by coordinating a mix of distribution, promotion (especially sales promotion and advertising), and price. They must consider packaging and branding decisions, and work closely with personnel in research and development, engineering, and production. Marketing research helps product managers understand consumers and find target markets. The product or brand manager approach to organization is used by many large, multiple-product companies. General Motors, for example, supports new-vehicle introductions by assigning brand managers who previously worked on successful launches.[32]

**market manager** The person responsible for managing the marketing activities that serve a particular group of customers

A **market manager** is responsible for managing the marketing activities that serve a particular group of customers. This organizational approach is particularly effective when a firm engages in different types of marketing activities to provide products to diverse customer groups. A company might have one market manager for business markets and another for consumer markets. These broad market categories might be broken down into more limited market responsibilities.

**venture team** A cross-functional group that creates entirely new products that may be aimed at new markets

A **venture team** creates entirely new products that may be aimed at new markets. Unlike a product or market manager, a venture team is responsible for all aspects of developing a product: research and development, production and engineering, finance and accounting, and marketing. Venture team members are brought together from different functional areas of the organization. In working outside established divisions, venture teams have greater flexibility to apply inventive approaches to develop new products that can take advantage of opportunities in highly segmented markets. Companies are increasingly using such cross-functional teams for product development in an effort to boost product quality. Quality may be positively related to information integration within the team, customers' influence on the product development process, and a quality orientation within the firm.[33] When a new product has demonstrated commercial potential, team members may return to their functional areas, or they may join a new or existing division to manage the product.

## SUMMARY

Organizations must be able to adjust their product mixes to compete effectively and achieve their goals. A product mix can be improved through line extension and product modification. A line extension is the development of a product closely related to one or more products in the existing line but designed specifically to meet different customer needs. Product modification is the changing of one or more characteristics of a product. This approach can be effective when the product is modifiable, when customers can perceive the change, and when customers want the modification. Quality modifications relate to a product's dependability and durability. Functional modifications affect a product's versatility, effectiveness, convenience, or safety. Aesthetic modifications change the sensory appeal of a product.

Developing new products can enhance a firm's product mix and add depth to the product line. A new product may be an innovation that has never been sold by any organization; a product that a given firm has not marketed previously, although similar products have been available from other organizations; or a product brought from one market to another.

Before a product is introduced, it goes through a seven-phase new-product development process. In the idea generation phase, new-product ideas may come from internal or external sources. In the process of screening, ideas are evaluated to determine whether they are consistent with the firm's overall objectives and resources. Concept testing, the third phase, involves having a small sample of potential customers review a brief description of the product idea to determine their initial perceptions of the proposed product and their early buying intentions. During the business analysis stage, the product idea is evaluated to determine its potential contribution to the firm's sales, costs, and profits. In the product development stage, the organization determines if it is technically feasible to produce the product and if it can be produced at a cost low enough to make the final price reasonable. Test marketing is a limited introduction of a product in areas chosen to represent the intended market. Finally, in the commercialization phase, full-scale production of the product begins and a complete marketing strategy is developed.

Product differentiation is the process of creating and designing products so that customers perceive them as different from competing products. Product quality, product design and features, and product support services are three aspects of product differentiation that companies consider when creating and marketing products. Product quality includes the overall characteristics of a product that allow it to perform as expected in satisfying customer needs. The level of quality is the amount of quality a product possesses. Consistency of quality is the degree to which a product has the same level of quality over time. Product design refers to how a product is conceived, planned, and produced. Components of product design include styling (the physical appearance of the product) and product features (the specific design characteristics that allow a product to perform certain tasks). Companies often differentiate their products by providing support services, usually called customer services. Customer services are human or mechanical efforts or activities that add value to a product.

Product deletion is the process of eliminating a product that no longer satisfies a sufficient number of customers. Although a firm's personnel may oppose product deletion, weak products are unprofitable, consume too much time and effort, may require shorter production runs, and can create an unfavorable impression of the firm's other products. A product mix should be systematically reviewed to determine when to delete products. Products to be deleted can be phased out, run out, or dropped immediately.

Often the traditional functional form of organization does not lend itself to the complex task of developing and managing products. Alternative organizational forms include the product or brand manager approach, the market manager approach, and the venture team approach. A product manager is responsible for a product, a product line, or several distinct products that make up an interrelated group within a multi-product organization. A brand manager is responsible for a single brand. A market manager is responsible for managing the marketing activities that serve a particular group or class of customers. A venture team is sometimes used to create entirely new products that may be aimed at new markets.

ACE
self-test

Please visit the student website at **www.prideferrell.com** for ACE Self-Test questions that will help you prepare for exams.

## IMPORTANT TERMS

Line extension
Product modifications
Quality modifications
Functional modifications
Aesthetic modifications
New-product development
  process

Idea generation
Screening
Concept testing
Business analysis
Product development
Test marketing
Commercialization

Product differentiation
Quality
Level of quality
Consistency of quality
Product design
Styling
Product features

Customer services
Product deletion
Product manager
Brand manager
Market manager
Venture team

## DISCUSSION & REVIEW QUESTIONS

1. What is a line extension, and how does it differ from a product modification?

2. Compare and contrast the three major approaches to modifying a product.

3. Identify and briefly explain the seven major phases of the new-product development process.

4. Do small companies that manufacture just a few products need to be concerned about developing and managing products? Why or why not?

5. Why is product development a cross-functional activity—involving finance, engineering, manufacturing, and other functional areas—within an organization?

6. What is the major purpose of concept testing, and how is it accomplished?

7. What are the benefits and disadvantages of test marketing?

8. Why can the process of commercialization take a considerable amount of time?

9. What is product differentiation, and how can it be achieved?

10. Explain how the term *quality* has been used to differentiate products in the automobile industry in recent years. What are some makes and models of automobiles that come to mind when you hear the terms *high quality* and *poor quality*?

11. What types of problems does a weak product cause in a product mix? Describe the most effective approach for avoiding such problems.

12. What type of organization might use a venture team to develop new products? What are the advantages and disadvantages of such a team?

## APPLICATION QUESTIONS

1. When developing a new product, a company often test markets the proposed product in a specific area or location. Suppose you wish to test market your new, revolutionary SuperWax car wax, which requires only one application for a lifetime finish. Where and how would you test market your new product?

2. A product manager may make quality, functional, or aesthetic modifications when modifying a product. Identify a familiar product that recently was modified, categorize the modification (quality, func-

tional, or aesthetic), and describe how you would have modified it differently.

3. Phasing out a product from the product mix often is difficult for an organization. Visit a retail store in your area, and ask the manager what products he or she has had to discontinue in the recent past. Find out what factors influenced the decision to delete the product and who was involved in the decision. Ask the manager to identify any products that should be but have not been deleted, and try to ascertain the reason.

1. A part of developing and managing new or existing products is to understand more about the competitive environment in which your firm's innovations may be commercialized. You are attempting to define the type of competitive structure of the future industry of the new product currently under development. The Industry Research Desk's website has developed 18 steps to assist in this process. The information can be accessed by using the search term "18 steps" at **http://globaledge. msu.edu/ibrd**. Once you reach the Industry Research Desk website, scroll down to Step 11 for the website's definitions of each of the following four types of competitive structure (note that this site uses the term *types of competition*): monopoly, oligopoly, monopolistic competition, and pure competition. How many different types of competition does your resource list? What are the differences between these different types of competition? Can you give examples of each type?

2. Before your firm decides to develop a new product for a specific industry, you have been asked to survey the level and quality of innovation in the biotechnology, computer software, and semiconductor industries. *Technology Review,* a magazine of innovation, can help you identify the firms with the highest and lowest levels of innovation in each industry. Access this journal by using the search term "magazine of innovation" at **http://globaledge.msu.edu/ibrd** and then click on the pdf link in the first sentence of the welcome page to download the report. What are considered the top companies' core competencies? Given this information, what do you think may be important in the coming years in each industry?

## INTERNET Exercise

Visit **www.prideferrell.com** for resources to help you master the material in this chapter, plus materials that will help you expand your marketing knowledge, including Internet exercise updates, ACE Self-Tests, hotlinks to companies featured in this chapter, and much more.

### Merck & Company

Merck, a leading global pharmaceutical company, develops, manufactures, and markets a broad range of health-care products. In addition, the firm's Merck-Medco Managed Care Division manages pharmacy benefits for more than 40 million Americans. The company has established a website to serve as an educational and informational resource for Internet users around the world. To learn more about the company and its research, visit its award-winning site at **www.merck.com**.

1. What products has Merck developed and introduced recently?
2. What role does research play in Merck's success? How does research facilitate new-product development at Merck?
3. Find Merck's mission statement. Is Merck's focus on research consistent with the firm's mission and values?

## Video Case 12.1    Newbury Comics Uncovers the Cool Stuff

Newbury Comics is an independently owned retailer that specializes in music, movies, and pop-culture goods. Over its 25 years through 24 New England stores, it has gained a devoted following. Founders Mike Dreese and John Brusger continue to own and operate Newbury Comics, and provide a consistent guiding force that advocates new ideas, encourages experimentation, and offers an alternative to large corporations.

MIT college roommates Dreese and Brusger started Newbury Comics in 1978. Brusger was an avid comic collector, and Dreese often accompanied him to comic conventions. Before long, they decided to open a comic books store in a small studio apartment in the middle of a bohemian Boston neighborhood. At first they sold only comics, but they gradually added other products to their mix. In 1979, Mike Dreese went to England and brought back records from U2, the Sex Pistols, and the Ramones. Newbury Comics was the first store in the United States to sell these albums, sometimes up to nine months before they were produced for the U.S. market. As importers of punk music, the store soon had a strong niche. Many bands that have been spotlighted by Newbury Comics, like Coldplay, Nirvana, the Strokes, and the Beastie Boys, have gone on to major careers. Some even credit their success to Newbury Comics. Now the company sells mainly digitized home entertainment products and pop-culture products that range from leather jackets and belts to hats, DVDs and Pokemon cards.

Products and inventory are extremely important to Newbury Comics. It combs the world looking for interesting and provocative merchandise and constantly adds new products in order to give its customers more of what they want in a one-stop-shopping experience. In a world increasingly dominated by "big box" mass merchant retailers, Newbury Comics stands out by supporting independent artists and cultural visionaries and recognizing the importance of offering products that entertain or challenge its customers' perceptions of the world. It also strives to offer exceptional customer service.

Newbury Comics stays ahead of the curve in marketing techniques, too. It had real-time systems in place four or five years ahead of its competition, enabling the company to update buyers on how products were selling every three minutes. This allows Newbury to place orders quickly if demand escalates for a particular product. The company gives its buyers great flexibility in the products they can buy. Buyers are constantly looking for interesting new products while trying to avoid flops, which could sink the company. Stocking the wrong product or the wrong assortment of products could result in excess inventory that will have to be sold at discounted prices and potential losses for the company. Finding the right products, such as Pokemon cards, can result in huge gains. The Pokemon cards were a gamble, because they did not appeal to Newbury's regular target customer, yet the company wound up making $4 million a year on the small packs of fantasy cards sold to eight-year-old boys.

Newbury Comics continually evaluates every product sold in its stores. It analyzes every square foot of the stores based on product groups to determine what the gross profit is for each inch of the store. It has such a wide variety of products that its stores are full. It is therefore essential to identify opportunities and maximize every inch of space. These analyses are used to make dramatic changes in product displays, product mixes, and even the number of products available in each store.

Although Newbury Comics stores have a wide range of products, there are some products that some segments of the community find difficult to deal with or even offensive. Consequently, the firm maintains an external legal team to ensure that it is in compliance with the law and to help address unpredictable legal events

that occur in the normal course of doing business. Some complaints from special interest groups have made it all the way to court.

Newbury Comics is also well respected by its suppliers. It would rather pay 5 percent more and get all the supply it needs of a hot item than bicker with a supplier over price. Its excellent relationship with suppliers has enabled the small business to scoop the market regularly—a big advantage in an industry where more than half the products are made in China and can require at least three months' lead-time for reorder. The company pays its bills promptly. This sometimes puts the company ahead of buyers who don't pay their bills so quickly when a particularly hot item is in limited supply. Failing to have the right item in stock can be extremely critical.

Newbury Comics believes that the best form of customer service is not having personnel walking around with phony smiles saying, "How can I help you?" but rather simply having what the customer wants on the shelf. It believes it can better serve its customers by focusing on products. Although anticipating which new products will become the next big things and avoiding buying the products that don't sell are challenges, Newbury's success proves that experimentation with new ideas and products can be a risk worth taking.[34]

## Questions for Discussion

1. How does Newbury Comics find new products to serve its target market?
2. What are the product differentiation characteristics or elements that distinguish Newbury Comics?
3. What is the customer service that helps Newbury Comics be successful?

## Case 12.2     Using the 3Rs and 3M

3M, the $20 billion company formerly known as Minnesota Mining and Manufacturing, markets diverse products in nearly 200 countries. The century-old company has a long-held reputation for innovative new products ranging from waterproof sandpaper and masking tape to Scotchguard fabric protector and Post-it Notes. It drives new-product development by carefully managing the 3Rs: risk, reward, and responsibility. 3M has more than a century of experience in successfully developing and managing a diverse mix of consumer and business products. Post-it Notes and Scotch-Brite scouring pads are just two of 3M's well-known brand names. The company also creates products for very specific uses, such as light-reflective coatings for street signs and medicinal creams for fighting skin-based viruses.

Day in and day out, 6,500 employees follow the 3R system as they search for new technologies and applications that could conceivably become 3M's next blockbuster product. The first R, risk, is a vital element in decisions about whether a product idea is promising enough to be developed into a prototype, test marketed, and ultimately brought to market through commercialization. Rather than take the safer path of incrementally improving existing products, 3M is taking calculated risks in its search for major breakthroughs. Its ambitious goals are to introduce twice the number of new products and triple the number of successful products that it has in the past.

Risks are evaluated relative to the second R, reward. Through the 3M Acceleration system, managers filter out ideas with lower profit potential and concentrate company resources on the few hundred ideas with higher profit potential. The point is to more productively support corporate growth by bringing high-potential products to market faster. Executives monitor all the ideas that make it into the Acceleration program to ensure speedy progress toward commercialization and measure the rewards in terms of revenue and profits.

With respect to the third R, responsibility, Lead User Teams—cross-functional groups of up to six employees—are responsible for new-product development. Along with technical and marketing staff, a team may have members from manufacturing, finance, procurement, or other departments, depending on its focus. Each team investigates product ideas to satisfy the unspoken or unrecognized needs of its customer segment. "They are taught to set their sights on exploring the areas where the possibilities for discovery are greatest because the pre-existing knowledge is most slim," says one 3M manager. This entails systematically examining trends that barely register today to consider products so advanced that "even the 'early adopters' have not yet arrived."

In addition to team responsibility, 3M has a long-standing tradition of nurturing independent research into potential new products. This encourages innovation from within and has led to new products and processes that benefited the company as well as its customers. Staff scientists are allowed to spend up to 15 percent of their time on self-directed projects that they think will blossom into commercially feasible products. They can request funding from their own business units or any other 3M unit to pursue the best ideas. If they are unable to obtain funding from a business unit, they can apply for a company-sponsored independent research grant of up to $100,000. Employees are also eligible for awards that honor outstanding achievement in new-product development, technology, and quality.

Along with the 3Rs, 3M is relying on DFSS—Design for Six Sigma—to boost product quality and development efficiency. The Six Sigma program takes quality far beyond simple error measurement and reduction: it teaches employees to incorporate the customer perspective early in the development process. More than 36,000 managers and scientists around the world have already received training in Six Sigma. These techniques "allow us to be more closely connected to the market and give us a much higher probability of success in our new-product designs," says 3M's vice president of research and development. The program has been so successful that the company is teaching its customers to apply Six Sigma techniques to improve their processes and products.

Finally, 3M is expediting new-product development by transferring 400 scientists from the corporate research and development department to specific business units. "By bringing more of our technical people into 3M businesses, we are strengthening our ability to commercialize new products now and well into the future," explains the CEO. "Now technical people can play more of a role in transforming pipeline projects into marketplace realities."[35]

### Questions for Discussion

1. Why would 3M apply quality improvement techniques to the design of new products?
2. What effect is the 3M Acceleration program likely to have on each stage of the new-product development process?
3. Evaluate 3M's goals of launching twice the number of new products and triple the number of successful products compared with previous years. Are these goals practical and attainable? How might these goals affect the efforts of 3M's Lead User Teams?

# Branding and Packaging

## Depend on Del Monte

At San Francisco–based Del Monte Foods, the motto is simply this: "Nourishing Families, Enriching Lives." Del Monte stands by this mission and sells more than $3 billion of a variety of nutritious brands for people and their pets. You can find conveniently packaged Del Monte products on grocery store shelves everywhere and in eight out of ten U.S. homes.

Del Monte's most recognized brands include Del Monte, S&W, Contadina, and StarKist. In addition to appreciating consumers' concerns about health—many of Del Monte's products are preservative-free and with low or no salt—Del Monte acknowledges that many people today simply don't have time to cook nourishing meals from scratch. So it markets healthy products that can be easily and quickly prepared. Some are even intended to be eaten on the run. Del Monte knows too that 55 percent of today's families have dogs or cats. Del Monte's pet brands include Kibbles 'n Bits, 9Lives, Pounce, and Pup-Peroni. All of these brands are known for their quality and are formulated with all of pets' nutritional needs in mind, from weight control to dental hygiene.

Del Monte has offered premium, high-quality foods for more than 100 years, and the company continues to move forward in offering products geared toward health and quality of life.[1] ■

**B**rands, components of brands, packages, and labels are part of a product's tangible features, the verbal and physical cues that help customers identify the products they want and influence their choices when they are unsure. As such, branding and packaging play an important role in marketing strategy. A successful brand like Del Monte is distinct and memorable; without one, a firm could not differentiate its products, and shoppers' choices would essentially be arbitrary. A good package design is cost effective, safe, environmentally responsible, and valuable as a promotional tool.

In this chapter, we first discuss branding, its value to customers and marketers, brand loyalty, and brand equity. Next, we examine the various types of brands. We then consider how companies choose and protect brands, the various branding policies employed, co-branding, and brand licensing. We look at packaging's critical role as part of the product. Next, we explore the functions of packaging, issues to consider in packaging design, how the package can be a major element in marketing strategy, and packaging criticisms. Finally, we discuss the functions of labeling and relevant legal issues.

# Branding

**brand** A name, term, design, symbol, or other feature that identifies a seller's products and differentiates them from competitors' products

**brand name** The part of a brand that can be spoken, including letters, words, and numbers

**brand mark** The part of a brand not made up of words, such as a symbol or design

**trademark** A legal designation of exclusive use of a brand

Marketers must make many decisions about products, including choices about brands, brand names, brand marks, trademarks, and trade names. A **brand** is a name, term, design, symbol, or any other feature that identifies one seller's good or service as distinct from those of other sellers. A brand may identify one item, a family of items, or all items of that seller.[2] A **brand name** is the part of a brand that can be spoken—including letters, words, and numbers—such as 7Up. A brand name is often a product's only distinguishing characteristic. Without the brand name, a firm could not differentiate its products. To consumers, a brand name is as fundamental as the product itself. Indeed, many brand names have become synonymous with the product, such as Scotch Tape and Xerox copiers. Through promotional activities, the owners of these brand names try to protect them from being used as generic names for tape and photocopiers, respectively.

The element of a brand that is not made up of words—often a symbol or design—is a **brand mark**. Examples of brand marks include McDonald's Golden Arches, Nike's "swoosh," and the stylized silhouette of Apple's iPod. A **trademark** is a legal designation indicating that the owner has exclusive use of a brand or a part of a

**Brand Mark**

Morton Salt's "girl with an umbrella" is an example of a brand mark.

THE SECRET'S OUT.

Holly's CATERING

It's the secret ingredient chefs have always used to make their dishes gourmet. Morton® Coarse Kosher Salt. Now you know.
*For recipes, visit www.mortonsalt.com*

brand and others are prohibited by law from using it. To protect a brand name or brand mark in the United States, an organization must register it as a trademark with the U.S. Patent and Trademark Office. In 2003, the Patent and Trademark Office registered more than 146,000 new trademarks.[3] Finally, a **trade name** is the full legal name of an organization, such as Ford Motor Company, rather than the name of a specific product.

**trade name** The full legal name of an organization

### Value of Branding

Both buyers and sellers benefit from branding. Brands help customers identify specific products that they do and do not like, which in turn facilitates the purchase of items that satisfy their needs and reduces the time required to purchase the product. Without brands, product selection would be quite random because buyers would have no assurance they were purchasing what they preferred. The purchase of certain brands can be a form of self-expression. For example, clothing brand names are important to many teenage boys; names such as Tommy Hilfiger, Polo, Champion, Guess, and Nike give manufacturers an advantage in the marketplace. A brand also helps buyers evaluate the quality of products, especially when they are unable to judge a product's characteristics; that is, a brand may symbolize a certain quality level to a customer, and in turn the person lets that perception of quality represent the quality of the item. A brand helps reduce a buyer's perceived risk of purchase. In addition, a psychological reward may come from owning a brand that symbolizes status. The Mercedes-Benz brand in the United States is an example.

Sellers benefit from branding because each company's brands identify its products, which makes repeat purchasing easier for customers. Branding helps a firm introduce a new product that carries the name of one or more of its existing products because buyers are already familiar with those brands. Branding also facilitates promotional efforts because the promotion of each branded product indirectly promotes all other similarly branded products. Branding also fosters brand loyalty. To the extent that buyers become loyal to a specific brand, the company's market share for that product achieves a certain level of stability, allowing the firm to use its resources more efficiently. Once a firm develops some degree of customer loyalty for a brand, it can maintain a fairly consistent price rather than continually cutting the price to attract customers. A brand is as much of an asset as the company's building or machinery. When marketers increase their brand's value, they also raise the total asset value of the organization. (We discuss brand value in more detail later in this chapter.) At times, marketers must decide whether to change a brand name. This is a difficult decision because the value in the existing brand name must be given up to gain the potential to build a higher value in a new brand name.

There is a cultural dimension to branding. Most brand experiences are individual, and each consumer confers his or her own social meaning onto brands. For some brands, such as Harley-Davidson, Google, and Apple, this can result in an almost cultlike following. These brands often develop a community of loyal customers that communicate through online forums, blogs, podcasts, and other means. These brands may even help consumers develop their identities and self-concepts and serve as forms of self-expression. In fact, the term *cultural branding* has been used to explain how a brand conveys a powerful myth that consumers find useful in cementing their identities.[4]

It is important to recognize that because a brand exists independently in the consumer's mind, it is not directly controlled by the marketer. Every aspect of a brand is subject to a consumer's emotional involvement,

**snapshot**

**Rising copyright registrations**

Number of copyright registrations received.

515,612    661,469

2000    2004

*Source:* Data from United States Copyright Office.

interpretation, and memory. By understanding how branding influences purchases, marketers can foster customer loyalty.[5]

### Brand Loyalty

**brand loyalty** A customer's favorable attitude toward a specific brand

As we just noted, creating and maintaining customer loyalty toward a brand is a major benefit of branding. **Brand loyalty** is a customer's favorable attitude toward a specific brand. If brand loyalty is strong enough, customers may consistently purchase this brand when they need a product in that product category. Customer satisfaction with a brand is the most common reason for loyalty to that brand.[6] Although brand loyalty may not result in a customer's purchasing a specific brand all the time, the

# Bingham Hill: A Great Brand Name Is Not Enough

Inspired by the fact that many artisan cheeses widely available in Europe were not available in the United States, Tom and Kristi Johnson started the Bingham Hill Cheese Company in 1999 in Fort Collins, CO. Seeing the success of local microbreweries such as New Belgium (creator of Fat Tire ale) and O'Dell's (creator of 90 Schilling), the Johnsons began talking with the microbrewery owners, who provided advice on all the aspects of starting a specialty business, including guidance on acquiring equipment and supplies. They ultimately chose to model Bingham Hill after the microbreweries, even calling it a "microcheesery." Bingham Hill's first batch of Rustic Blue was an instant hit, winning first place in the blue cheese class of the American Cheese Society's annual competition. The Johnsons sent samples of Rustic Blue to a number of stores, and the orders flooded in.

One thing that made the Bingham Hill brand stand out is the hand-made artisan cheese. Hand-made cheese is stirred, cut, ladled, turned, and inspected daily. Even in the midst of growth, the Johnsons continued hand-making cheese. The Johnsons continued to experiment and learn about the craft of cheese making. They were known also for their spreadable cheeses, which are not aged, cutting down on costs for space and time. The Johnsons also created new products made from goat's and sheep's milk.

In 2005, Bingham Hill cheeses won 10 medals at the annual World Cheese Awards in London. The company became one of just three national specialty cheese makers, and its products were regularly requested by top restaurants and chefs.

One important early customer of Bingham Hill was the California specialty foods retailer Trader Joe's. However, the cheese proved to be so popular that Bingham Hill simply could not supply its 200 stores with enough cheese. Although the Johnsons made significant investments to expand to accommodate Trader Joe's and other hoped-for large accounts, the small firm could not keep up with demand. Trader Joe's eventually eliminated the brand. Facing a huge bill for the expansion, rising costs, and the loss of a major customer, the company closed its doors in 2006. The state of Wisconsin offered the Johnsons financial incentives to move the firm to Wisconsin, but the owners were unwilling to move so far from family and friends.

*Always in season.* Enjoying the fresh taste of real fruit has never been easier. Now all the sweet goodness of DOLE comes in an unbreakable, resealable plastic jar. So the only thing that's going to get spoiled is you. Choose Mandarin Orange, Peach, Pineapple or Tropical Fruit. Each one is ripe and ready to be picked in the packaged fruit aisle. **Life is Sweet.**

**Brand Insistence**
Many consumers insist on a particular brand of packaged fruit.

brand is at least viewed as a potentially viable choice in the set of brands being considered for purchase. Development of brand loyalty in a customer reduces his or her risks and shortens the time spent buying the product. However, the degree of brand loyalty for products varies from one product category to another. For example, it is challenging to develop brand loyalty for most products because customers can usually judge a product's quality and do not need to refer to a brand as an indicator of quality. Brand loyalty also varies by country. Customers in France, Germany, and the United Kingdom tend to be less brand-loyal than U.S. customers.

Three degrees of brand loyalty exist: recognition, preference, and insistence. **Brand recognition** occurs when a customer is aware that the brand exists and views it as an alternative purchase if the preferred brand is unavailable or if the other available brands are unfamiliar. This is the mildest form of brand loyalty. The term *loyalty* clearly is used very loosely here. One of the initial objectives when introducing a new brand is to create widespread awareness of the brand to generate brand recognition.

**brand recognition** The degree of brand loyalty in which the customer is aware the brand exists and views the brand as an alternative purchase if their preferred brand is unavailable.

**brand preference** The degree of brand loyalty in which a customer prefers one brand over competitive offerings

**brand insistence** The degree of brand loyalty in which a customer strongly prefers a specific brand and will accept no substitute

**brand equity** The marketing and financial value associated with a brand's strength in a market

**Brand preference** is a stronger degree of brand loyalty: a customer definitely prefers one brand over competitive offerings and will purchase this brand if available. However, if the brand is not available, the customer will accept a substitute brand rather than expending additional effort finding and purchasing the preferred brand. A marketer is likely to be able to compete effectively in a market when a number of customers have developed brand preference for its specific brand.

When **brand insistence** occurs, a customer strongly prefers a specific brand, will accept no substitute, and is willing to spend a great deal of time and effort to acquire that brand. If a brand-insistent customer goes to a store and finds the brand unavailable, he or she will seek the brand elsewhere rather than purchase a substitute brand. Brand insistence is the strongest degree of brand loyalty; it is a brander's dream. However, it is the least common type of brand loyalty. Customers vary considerably regarding the product categories for which they may be brand insistent. Can you think of products for which you are brand insistent? Perhaps it's a brand of deodorant, soft drink, jeans, or even pet food (if your pet is brand insistent).

Brand loyalty in general seems to be declining, partly because of marketers' increased reliance on sales, coupons, and other short-term promotions and partly because of the sometimes overwhelming array of similar new products from which customers can choose. Several recent studies indicate that brand loyalty is declining for all age groups and especially among consumers age 50 and older.[7]

Building brand loyalty is a major challenge for many marketers. It is an extremely important issue. The creation of brand loyalty significantly contributes to an organization's ability to achieve a sustainable competitive advantage.

## Brand Equity

A well-managed brand is an asset to an organization. The value of this asset is often referred to as brand equity. **Brand equity** is the marketing and financial value associated with a brand's strength in a market. Besides the actual proprietary brand assets, such as patents and trademarks, four major elements underlie brand equity: brand

## Figure 13.1

### MAJOR ELEMENTS OF BRAND EQUITY

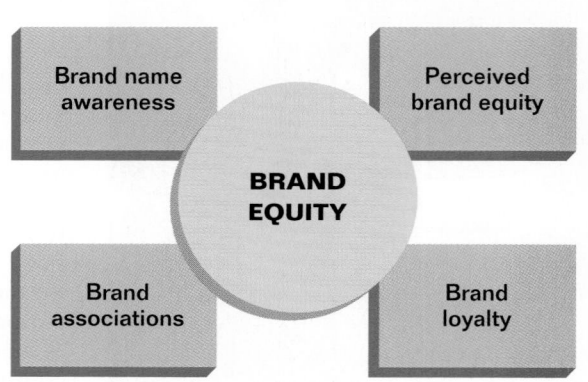

name awareness, brand loyalty, perceived brand quality, and brand associations (see Figure 13.1).[8]

Awareness of a brand leads to brand familiarity, which in turn results in a level of comfort with the brand. A familiar brand is more likely to be selected than an unfamiliar brand because the familiar brand is often viewed as more reliable and of more acceptable quality. The familiar brand is likely to be in a customer's consideration set, whereas the unfamiliar brand is not.

Brand loyalty is an important component of brand equity because it reduces a brand's vulnerability to competitors' actions. Brand loyalty allows an organization to keep its existing customers and avoid spending an enormous amount of resources gaining new ones. Loyal customers provide brand visibility and reassurance to potential new customers. Because customers expect their brands to be available when and where they shop, retailers strive to carry the brands known for their strong customer following.

Customers associate a particular brand with a certain level of overall quality. A brand name may be used as a substitute for judgment of quality. In many cases, customers can't actually judge the quality of the product for themselves and instead must rely on the brand as a quality indicator. Perceived high brand quality helps support a premium price, allowing a marketer to avoid severe price competition. Also, favorable perceived brand quality can ease the introduction of brand extensions, since the high regard for the brand will likely translate into high regard for the related products.

The set of associations linked to a brand is another key component of brand equity. At times a marketer works to connect a particular lifestyle or, in some instances, a certain personality type with a specific brand. For example, customers associate Michelin tires with protecting family members; a De Beers diamond with a loving, long-lasting relationship ("A Diamond Is Forever"); and Dr Pepper with a unique taste. These types of brand associations contribute significantly to the brand's equity. Brand associations are sometimes facilitated by using trade characters, such as the Jolly Green Giant, the Pillsbury Dough Boy, and Charlie the Tuna. Placing these trade characters in advertisements and on packages helps consumers link the ads and packages to the brands.

Although difficult to measure, brand equity represents the value of a brand to an organization. An organization

**Stimulating Brand Associations**

Kellogg's uses Tony the Tiger, a trademarked character, to stimulate favorable brand associations.

may buy a brand from another company at a premium price because outright brand purchase may be less expensive and less risky than creating and developing a brand from scratch. For example, The J. M. Smucker Company purchased International Multifoods Corporation primarily to acquire the Pillsbury, Hungry Jack, Pet, and other brands.[9] Brand equity helps give a brand the power to capture and maintain a consistent market share, which provides stability to the organization's sales volume.

Table 13.1 lists the 10 global brands with the greatest economic value, as compiled by *Business Week* magazine. *Business Week*'s top 100 brands account for nearly 30 percent of the market value of the firms that own them. The Coca-Cola brand, for example, represents two-thirds of the Coca-Cola Company's market capitalization.[10] Any company that owns a brand listed in Table 13.1 would agree that the economic value of that brand is likely to be the greatest single asset the organization possesses. A brand's overall economic value rises and falls with the brand's profitability, brand awareness, brand loyalty, and perceived brand quality and with the strength of positive brand associations.

## Types of Brands

**manufacturer brands** A brand initiated by its producer

**private distributor brands** A brand initiated and owned by a reseller

There are three categories of brands: manufacturer, private distributor, and generic. **Manufacturer brands** are initiated by producers and ensure that producers are identified with their products at the point of purchase—for example, Green Giant, Compaq Computer, and Levi's jeans. A manufacturer brand usually requires a producer to become involved in distribution, promotion, and, to some extent, pricing decisions. Brand loyalty is encouraged by promotion, quality control, and guarantees; it is a valuable asset to a manufacturer. The producer tries to stimulate demand for the product, which tends to encourage sellers and resellers to make the product available.

**Private distributor brands** (also called *private brands, store brands,* or *dealer brands*) are initiated and owned by resellers, that is, wholesalers or retailers. The major characteristic of private brands is that the manufacturers are not identified on the products. Retailers and wholesalers use private distributor brands to develop more efficient promotion, generate higher gross margins, and change store image. Safeway stores, for example, use private brands to compete against deep discounters and have a magazine to promote their brands. There are private-label products at every price point and in every category from trash bags to ice cream.[11] Private distributor brands give retailers or wholesalers freedom to purchase products of a specified quality at the lowest cost without disclosing the identities of the manufacturers. Wholesaler brands include IGA (Independent Grocers' Alliance) and Topmost (General Grocer). Familiar retailer brand names include Sears' Kenmore and JCPenney's Arizona. Many successful private brands are distributed nationally. Kenmore appliances are as well known as most manufacturer brands. Sometimes retailers with successful private distributor brands start manufacturing their own products to gain more control over product costs, quality, and design in the hope of increasing profits. Sales of private labels are now growing at more than twice the rate of brand names and account for 15 percent of packaged goods revenues in supermarkets. Some private brands have even gone upscale, such as Whole Food's 365 line of organic goods and Safeway's Rancher's Reserve premium beef.[12] Supermarket private brands are popular globally, too.

Competition between manufacturer brands and private distributor brands (sometimes called "the

### table 13.1   THE WORLD'S MOST VALUABLE BRANDS

| Brand | Brand Value (In Billion $) |
|-------|----------------------------|
| Coca-Cola | 67.5 |
| Microsoft | 59.9 |
| IBM | 53.4 |
| GE | 47.0 |
| Intel | 35.6 |
| Nokia | 26.5 |
| Disney | 26.4 |
| McDonald's | 26.0 |
| Toyota | 24.8 |
| Marlboro | 21.2 |

**Source:** From "The Top 100 Global Brands Scoreboard," *Business Week,* http://bwnt.businessweek.com/brand/2005/ (accessed May 1, 2006). Reprinted by permission of *Business Week*. The brand valuations draw on publicly available information, which has not been independently investigated by Interbrand. Data: Interbrand Corp., J. P. Morgan Chase & Co., Citigroup, Morgan Stanley, *Business Week.*

## Selecting a Brand Name

Marketers consider a number of factors in selecting a brand name. First, the name should be easy for customers (including foreign buyers, if the firm intends to market its products in other countries) to say, spell, and recall. Short, one-syllable names, such as Cheer, often satisfy this requirement. Second, the brand name should indicate the product's major benefits and, if possible, suggest in a positive way the product's uses and special characteristics; negative or offensive references should be avoided. For example, the brand names of such household cleaning products as Ajax dishwashing liquid, Vanish toilet bowl cleaner, Formula 409 multipurpose cleaner, Cascade dishwasher detergent, and Wisk laundry detergent connote strength and effectiveness. Research suggests that consumers are more likely to recall and to evaluate favorably names that convey positive attributes or benefits.[14] Third, to set it apart from competing brands, the brand should be distinctive. If a marketer intends to use a brand for a product line, that brand must be compatible with all products in the line. Finally, a brand should be designed so that it can be used and recognized in all types of media. Finding the right brand name has become a challenging task because many obvious product names have already been used. After acquiring the AmeriSuites hotel chain, Hyatt changed the brand name to Hyatt Place not only to emphasize the new chain's revamped interiors and exteriors, but also to capitalize on its own more recognizable name.[15]

How are brand names devised? Brand names can be created from single or multiple words—for example, Bic or Dodge Grand Caravan. Letters and numbers are used to create such brands as IBM PC or Z71. Words, numbers, and letters are combined to yield brand names such as Mazda MX-5 Miata or BMW Z4 Roadster. To avoid terms that have negative connotations, marketers sometimes use fabricated words that have absolutely no meaning when created—for example, Kodak and Exxon. Occasionally a brand is simply brought out of storage and used as is or modified. Firms often maintain banks of registered brands, some of which may have been used in the past. Cadillac, for example, has a bank of approximately 360 registered trademarks. The LaSalle brand, used in the 1920s and 1930s, could be called up for a new Cadillac model in the future. Possible brand names sometimes are tested in focus groups or other settings to assess customers' reactions.

Who actually creates brand names? Brand names can be created internally by the organization. Sometimes a name is suggested by individuals who are close to the product's development. Some organizations have committees that participate in brand name creation and approval. Large companies that introduce numerous new products annually are likely to have a department that develops brand names. At times, outside consultants and companies that specialize in brand name development are used. For example, Philip Morris hired Landor Associates to develop its new name, Altria Group.[16]

Although most of the important branding considerations apply to both goods and services, branding a service has some additional dimensions. The service brand is usually the same as the company name. Financial companies, such as Fidelity Investments and Charles Schwab Discount Brokerage, have established strong brand recognition. These companies have used their names to create an image of value and friendly, timely, responsible, accurate, and knowledgeable customer assistance. Service providers (such as United Airlines) are perceived by customers as having one brand name, even though they offer multiple products (first class, business class, and coach). Because the service brand name and company name are so closely interrelated, a service brand name must be flexible enough to encompass a variety of current services, as well as new ones the company may offer in the future. Geographical references such as *western* and descriptive terms such as *trucking* limit the scope of possible associations with the brand name. Because Southwest Airlines now flies to many parts of the country, its name has become too limited in its scope of associations. *Humana*, with its connotations of kindness and compassion, is flexible enough to encompass all services that a hospital, insurance plan, or health-care facility offers. Frequently a service marketer employs a symbol along with its brand name to make the brand distinctive and communicate a certain image.

## Protecting a Brand

A marketer should also design a brand so that it can be protected easily through registration. A series of court decisions has created a broad hierarchy of protection based on brand type. From most protectable to least protectable, these brand types are fanciful (Exxon), arbitrary (Dr Pepper), suggestive (Spray 'n Wash), descriptive (Minute Rice), and generic (aluminum foil). Generic brands are not protectable. Surnames and descriptive, geographic, or functional names are difficult to protect.[17] Because of their designs, some brands can be legally infringed on more easily than others. Although registration protects trademarks domestically for ten years and trademarks can be renewed indefinitely, a firm should develop a system for ensuring that its trademarks are renewed as needed.

To protect its exclusive rights to a brand, a company must ensure that the brand is not likely to be considered an infringement on any brand already registered with the U.S. Patent and Trademark Office. This task may be complex because infringement is determined by the courts, which base their decisions on whether a brand causes consumers to be confused, mistaken, or deceived about the source of the product. McDonald's is one company that aggressively protects its trademarks against infringement; it has brought charges against a number of companies with *Mc* names because it fears the use of that prefix will give consumers the impression that these companies are associated with or owned by McDonald's. Auto Shack changed its name to AutoZone when faced with legal action from Tandy Corporation, owner of Radio Shack. Tandy maintained that it owned the name *Shack*. After research showed that virtually every auto supply store in the country used *auto* in its name, *zone* was deemed the best word to pair with *auto*.

A marketer should guard against allowing a brand name to become a generic term used to refer to a general product category. Generic terms cannot be protected as exclusive brand names. For example, *aspirin, escalator,* and *shredded wheat*—all brand names at one time—eventually were declared generic terms that refer to product classes. Thus, they could no longer be protected. To keep a brand name from becoming a generic term, the firm should spell the name with a capital letter and use it as an adjective to modify the name of the general product class, as in Kool-Aid Brand Soft Drink Mix.[18] Including the word *brand* just after the brand name is also helpful. An organization can deal with this problem directly by advertising that its brand is a trademark and should not be used generically. The firm can also indicate that the brand is a registered trademark by using the symbol ®.

**Protecting a Brand**

Xerox works hard to protect its brand name so that people do not use "Xerox" to mean generic photocopying.

## marketing ENTREPRENEURS

**Elise and Evan MacMillan**

THEIR BUSINESS: The Chocolate Farm

FOUNDED AT AGES: 10 and 13

SUCCESS: Revenues of $1 million a year

After her first chocolate-making session with her grandmother at age 3, Elise MacMillan was hooked on the candy business. Over the next seven years, she experimented with chocolate until she perfected her signature product—chocolates in the shape of animals. Her brother Evan joined the venture when he drafted a financial plan. Shortly thereafter the two secured a bank loan and launched the business online (**www.chocolatefarm.com**). Elise continues to develop new chocolate products for the brand, while her brother handles the Denver-based company's finances and website.

In the interest of strengthening trademark protection, Congress enacted the Trademark Law Revision Act in 1988, the only major federal trademark legislation since the Lanham Act of 1946. The purpose of this more recent legislation is to increase the value of the federal registration system for U.S. firms relative to foreign competitors and to better protect the public from counterfeiting, confusion, and deception.

A U.S. firm that tries to protect a brand in a foreign country frequently encounters problems. In many countries, brand registration is not possible; the first firm to use a brand in such a country automatically has the rights to it. In some instances, U.S. companies actually have had to buy their own brand rights from a firm in a foreign country because the foreign firm was the first user in that country.

Marketers trying to protect their brands must also contend with brand counterfeiting. In the United States, for instance, one can purchase counterfeit General Motors parts, Cartier watches, Louis Vuitton handbags, Walt Disney character dolls, Warner Brothers clothing, Mont Blanc pens, and a host of other products illegally marketed by manufacturers that do not own the brands. Annual losses caused by counterfeit products are estimated at between $250 billion and $350 billion. Many counterfeit products are manufactured overseas—in Turkey, China, Thailand, Italy, and Colombia, for example—but some are counterfeited in the United States. Counterfeit products are often hard to distinguish from the real brands. Products most likely to be counterfeited are well-known brands that appeal to a mass market and products whose physical materials are inexpensive relative to the products' prices. Microsoft estimates that its revenues would double if counterfeiting of its brand name products were eliminated. Some $40 billion a year are lost in the computer software business because of counterfeit and pirated products. Brand fraud results not only in lost revenue for the brand's owner; it also results in a low-quality product for customers, distorts competition, affects investment levels, reduces tax revenues and legitimate employment, creates safety risks, and affects international relations. It also likely affects customers' perceptions of the brand due to the counterfeit product's inferior quality.

## Branding Policies

Before establishing branding policies, a firm must decide whether to brand its products at all. If a company's product is homogeneous and similar to competitors' products, it may be difficult to brand. Raw materials such as coal, sand, and farm produce are hard to brand because of the homogeneity and physical characteristics of such products.

If a firm chooses to brand its products, it may opt for one or more of the following branding policies: individual, family, or brand extension branding. **Individual branding** is a policy of giving each product a different name. Sara Lee uses individual branding among its many divisions, which include Hanes underwear, L'eggs pantyhose, Champion sportswear, Jimmy Dean, Bali, Ball Park, and other vastly diverse brands. A major advantage of individual branding is that if an organization introduces a poor product, the negative images associated with it do not contaminate the company's other products. An individual branding policy may also facilitate market segmentation when a firm wishes to enter many segments of the same market. Separate, unrelated names can be used and each brand aimed at a specific segment.

**individual branding** A branding policy in which each product is given a different name

**family branding** Branding all of a firm's products with the same name or part of the name

In **family branding**, all of a firm's products are branded with the same name or part of the name, such as Kellogg's Frosted Flakes, Kellogg's Rice Krispies, and Kellogg's Corn Flakes. In some cases, a company's name is combined with other words to brand items. Arm & Hammer uses its name on all its products, along with a generic description of the item, such as Arm & Hammer Heavy Duty Detergent, Arm & Hammer Pure Baking Soda, and Arm & Hammer Carpet Deodorizer. Unlike individual branding, family branding means the promotion of one item with the family brand promotes the firm's other products. Other major companies that use family branding include Mitsubishi, Kodak, and Fisher-Price.

**brand extension** An organization uses one of its existing brands to brand a new product in a different product category

A **brand extension** occurs when a firm uses one of its existing brands to brand a new product in a different product category. For example, Procter & Gamble employed a brand extension when it named a new product Ivory Shampoo. Another example is when Bic, the maker of disposable pens, introduced Bic disposable razors and Bic lighters. A brand extension should not be confused with a line extension, which involves using an existing brand on a new product in the same product category, such as new flavors or sizes. For example, when the maker of Tylenol, McNeil Consumer Products, introduced Extra Strength Tylenol P.M., the new product was a line extension because it was in the same category. Researchers have found that there may be an opportunity to charge a premium price relative to comparable products when extending a strong brand into a new product category because of consumers' perceptions of lower risk associated with a known brand name.[19]

Marketers share a common concern that if a brand is extended too many times or extended too far outside its original product category, the brand can be significantly weakened. For example, Miller Brewing Company has extended its brand to Miller Lite, Genuine Draft, Draft Lite, Ice, Ice Lite, Milwaukee's Best, Ice House, and Red Dog, but so many extensions may confuse customers and encourage them to en-

**Family Branding**

Walden Farms uses Family Branding.

gage in considerable brand switching. The Nabisco Snackwell brand initially appeared only on crackers, cookies, and snack bars, all of which fall into the baked-snack category. However, extending the brand to yogurts and gelatin mixes goes further afield. Although some experts might caution Nabisco against extending the Snackwell brand to this degree, some evidence suggests that brands can be successfully extended to less closely related product categories through the use of advertisements that extend customers' perceptions of the original product category. For example, Waterford, an upscale Irish brand of crystal, extended its name to writing instruments when seeking sales growth beyond closely related product categories such as china, cutlery, and table linens.[20]

An organization is not limited to a single branding policy. A company that uses primarily individual branding for many of its products may also use brand extensions. Branding policy is influenced by the number of products and product lines the company produces, the characteristics of its target markets, the number and types of competing products available, and the size of the firm's resources.

## Co-Branding

**co-branding** Using two or more brands on one product

**Co-branding** is the use of two or more brands on one product. Marketers employ co-branding to capitalize on the brand equity of multiple brands. It is popular in a number of processed food categories and in the credit card industry. The brands used for co-branding can be owned by the same company. For example, Kraft's Lunchables product teams the Kraft cheese brand with Oscar Mayer lunchmeats, another Kraft-owned brand. The brands may also be owned by different companies. Credit card companies such as American Express, Visa, and MasterCard, for instance, team up with other brands such as General Motors, AT&T, and many airlines.

Effective co-branding capitalizes on the trust and confidence customers have in the brands involved. The brands should not lose their identities, and it should be clear to customers which brand is the main brand. For example, it is fairly obvious that Kellogg owns the brand and is the main brander of Kellogg's Healthy Choice Cereal. (The Choice brand is owned by ConAgra.) It is important for marketers to understand that when a co-branded product is unsuccessful, both brands are

# Iams Aims at Pet Lovers

To many people today, pets are part of their families, and they want their pets to have the best. Iams, which markets the Iams and Eukanuba pet food brands, recognized this trend and shifted its focus. Today, it markets high-quality pet food, fancy pet treats, sauces, and other items that allow pet lovers to spoil their pets. For example, the company created Multi-Cat cat food for customers concerned about feeding cats in multi-cat households in which one cat might be overweight while another was not.

Now owned by Procter & Gamble, Iams has begun marketing pet products that mirror those intended for humans. For example, the company now applies a technology borrowed from P&G's Crest toothpaste to put a tarter-control coating on all adult pet food. The coating was added to pet treats in 2006. Iams also plans to produce a line of pet shampoo.

Iams faces stiff competition from Nestlé's Purina and Wal-Mart's Ol'Roy, but it is currently the number 1 national pet food brand based on dollar sales. And it continues to research new possibilities in pet supplies. For example, it is currently looking into creating pet products connected to P&G's Swiffer and Febreze brands. The company is also branching out through its Iams Pet Imaging Centers and by offering pet health insurance.

Now accepted on Jupiter

[ Mount Jupiter, British Columbia ]

**And the millions of other places on Earth you do business.**
The Diners Club® Card. Now accepted at nearly 24 million MasterCard® merchant locations worldwide.

The Diners Club Card with global MasterCard acceptance provides your business with a powerhouse end-to-end expense management tool that delivers the functionality and information needed to drive bottom-line savings. It's also a powerful tool in the hands of those who rely on those decisions. When you or your employees have a question, our best-in-class customer service connects you with a real person to speak with any time, day or night. Add our award-winning Club Rewards® Program, and choosing the Diners Club Card is a smart business decision and an easy one to make.

For more information, go to dinersclubus.com/btn or call 1 800 999-9093

© 2006 Citicorp Diners Club Inc. All rights reserved.

**Co-Branding**
Citi Corp offers a co-brand credit card with Diners Club International and MasterCard.

implicated in the product failure. To gain customer acceptance, the brands involved must represent a complementary fit in the minds of buyers. Trying to link a brand like Harley-Davidson with a brand like Healthy Choice will not achieve co-branding objectives because customers are not likely to perceive these brands as compatible.

Co-branding can help an organization differentiate its products from those of competitors. By using the product development skills of a co-branding partner, an organization can create a distinctive product. For example, fashion designer Giorgio Armani and carmaker Mercedes-Benz have teamed up to produce a Mercedes cabriolet with leather seats, dashboard, and a leather steering wheel designed by Armani. The two are considering joint marketing events and advertising.[21] Co-branding can also allow the partners to take advantage of each other's distribution capabilities.

While co-branding has been used for a number of years, it began to grow in popularity in the 1980s when Monsanto aggressively promoted its NutraSweet product as an ingredient in such well-known brands as Diet Coke. Later a rival sweetner, Splenda, was co-branded with Diet Coke, Starbucks, and many other brands. Intel, too, has capitalized on ingredient co-branding through its "Intel Inside" program. The effectiveness of ingredient co-branding relies heavily on continued promotional efforts by the ingredient's producer.

### Brand Licensing

**brand licensing** An agreement whereby a company permits another organization to use its brand on other products for a licensing fee

A popular branding strategy involves **brand licensing**, an agreement in which a company permits another organization to use its brand on other products for a licensing fee. Royalties may be as low as 2 percent of wholesale revenues or higher than 10 percent. Mattel, for example, licensed Warner Brothers' Harry Potter brand for use on board games and toys to tie in with the first movie based on the wildly popular book series. Warner was guaranteed royalties of $20 million from Mattel's licensing fee of 15 percent of gross revenues earned on these branded products.[22] The licensee is responsible for all manufacturing, selling, and advertising functions, and bears the costs if the licensed product fails. Not long ago only a few firms licensed their corporate trademarks, but today licensing is a multibillion-dollar business. The top U.S. licensing company is Walt Disney Company. The NFL, the NCAA, NASCAR, and Major League Baseball are all in the top ten in retail sales of licensed products.

The advantages of licensing range from extra revenues and low-cost or free publicity to new images and trademark protection. For example, Coca-Cola has licensed its trademark for use on glassware, radios, trucks, and clothing in the hope of protecting its trademark. However, brand licensing has drawbacks. The major disadvantages are a lack of manufacturing control, which could hurt the company's name, and bombarding consumers with too many unrelated products bearing the same name. Licensing arrangements can also fail because of poor timing, inappropriate distribution channels, or mismatching of product and name.

# Packaging

Packaging involves the development of a container and a graphic design for a product. A package can be a vital part of a product, making it more versatile, safer, and easier to use. Like a brand name, a package can influence customers' attitudes toward a product and thus affect their purchase decisions. For example, several producers of jellies, sauces, and ketchups have packaged their products in squeezable containers to make use and storage more convenient. Package characteristics help shape buyers' impressions of a product at the time of purchase or during use. In this section, we examine the main functions of packaging and consider several major packaging decisions.

## Packaging Functions

Effective packaging involves more than simply putting products in containers and covering them with wrappers. First, packaging materials serve the basic purpose of protecting the product and maintaining its functional form. Fluids such as milk, orange juice, and hair spray need packages that preserve and protect them. The packaging should prevent damage that could affect the product's usefulness and thus lead to higher costs. Because product tampering has become a problem, several packaging techniques have been developed to counter this danger. Some packages are also designed to deter shoplifting.

**Convenience**

Crystal Light on-the-go packets are convenient.

Another function of packaging is to offer convenience to consumers. For example, small aseptic packages—individual-size boxes or plastic bags that contain liquids and do not require refrigeration—strongly appeal to children and young adults with active lifestyles. The size or shape of a package may relate to the product's storage, convenience of use, or replacement rate. Small, single-serving cans of vegetables, for instance, may prevent waste and make storage easier.

A third function of packaging is to promote a product by communicating its features, uses, benefits, and image. Sometimes a reusable package is developed to make the product more desirable. For example, the Cool Whip package doubles as a food storage container.

Finally, packaging can be used to communicate symbolically the quality or premium nature of a product. It can also evoke an emotional response. Packaging has been a major force in bath and body products, especially those associated with the spa industry. The goal is to communicate what the product stands for and trigger an expected experience.[23]

## Major Packaging Considerations

In developing packages, marketers must take many factors into account. Obviously one major consideration is cost. Although a variety of packaging materials, processes, and designs are available, costs vary greatly. In recent years, buyers have shown a willingness to pay more for improved packaging, but there are limits. Marketers should conduct research to determine exactly how much customers are willing to pay for effective and efficient package designs.

As already mentioned, developing tamper-resistant packaging is very important for certain products. Although no package is tamperproof, marketers can develop packages that are difficult to contaminate. At a minimum, all packaging must comply with the Food and Drug Administration's packaging regulations. However, packaging should also make any product tampering evident to resellers and consumers. Although effective tamper-resistant packaging may be expensive to develop, when balanced against the costs of lost sales, loss of consumer confidence and company reputation, and potentially expensive product liability lawsuits, the costs of ensuring consumer safety are minimal.

Marketers should also consider how much consistency is desirable among an organization's package designs. No consistency may be the best policy, especially if a firm's products are unrelated or aimed at vastly different target markets. To promote an overall company image, a firm may decide that all packages should be similar or include one major element of the design. This approach is called **family packaging**. Sometimes it is used only for lines of products, such as Campbell's soups, Weight Watchers' foods, and Planter's nuts.

A package's promotional role is an important consideration. Through verbal and nonverbal symbols, the package can inform potential buyers about the product's content, features, uses, advantages, and hazards. A firm can create desirable images and associations by its choice of color, design, shape, and texture. Many cosmetics manufacturers, for example, design their packages to create impressions of richness, luxury, and exclusivity. A package performs a promotional function when it is designed to be safer or more convenient to use if such characteristics help stimulate demand.

To develop a package that has a definite promotional value, a designer must consider size, shape, texture, color, and graphics. Beyond the obvious limitation that the package must be large enough to hold the product, a package can be designed to appear taller or shorter. Light-colored packaging may make a package appear larger, whereas darker colors may minimize the perceived size.

Colors on packages are often chosen to attract attention, and color can positively influence customers' emotions. People associate specific colors with certain feelings and experiences. For example,

- Blue is soothing; it is also associated with wealth, trust, and security.
- Gray is associated with strength, exclusivity, and success.
- Orange often signifies low cost.
- Red connotes excitement and stimulation.
- Purple is associated with dignity and stateliness.
- Yellow connotes cheerfulness and joy.
- Black is associated with being strong and masterful.[24]

When opting for color on packaging, marketers must judge whether a particular color will evoke positive or negative feelings when linked to a specific product. Rarely, for example, do processors package meat or bread in green materials because customers may associate green with mold. Marketers must also determine whether a specific target market will respond favorably or unfavorably to a particular color. Cosmetics for women are more likely to be sold in pastel packaging than are personal care products for men. Packages designed to appeal to children often use primary colors and bold designs. A relatively recent trend in packaging is colorless packages. Clear products and packaging connote a pure, natural product.

Packaging must also meet the needs of resellers. Wholesalers and retailers consider whether a package facilitates transportation, storage, and handling. Concentrated versions of laundry detergents and fabric softeners, for example, enable retailers to offer more product diversity within the existing shelf space. Resellers may refuse to carry certain products if their packages are cumbersome.

A final consideration is whether to develop packages that are environmentally responsible. Nearly one-half of all garbage consists of discarded plastic packaging, such as polystyrene containers, plastic soft-drink bottles, and carryout bags. Plastic packaging material does not biodegrade, and paper requires the destruction of valuable forests. Consequently a number of companies have changed to environmentally sensitive packaging; they are also recycling more materials. Procter & Gamble markets several cleaning products in a concentrated form, which requires less packaging than the ready-to-use version. H. J. Heinz is looking for alternatives to its plastic ketchup squeeze bottles. Other companies are also searching for alternatives to environmentally harmful packaging. In some instances, however, customers have objected to such switches because the newer environmentally responsible packaging may be less effective or more inconvenient. Therefore, marketers must carefully balance society's desire to preserve the environment against customers' desire for convenience.

## Packaging and Marketing Strategies

Packaging can be a major component of a marketing strategy. A new cap or closure, a better box or wrapper, or a more convenient container may give a product a competitive advantage. The right type of package for a new product can help it gain market recognition very quickly. The developers of the SpinBrush, a $5 electric toothbrush, has this in mind when they created packaging that allowed shoppers to turn the brush on in the store to see how it worked. This bold strategy helped sell more than 10 million units of SpinBrush in its first year on the shelves.[25] In the case of existing brands, marketers should reevaluate packages periodically. Marketers should view packaging as a major strategic tool, especially for consumer convenience products. For instance, in the food industry, jumbo and large package sizes for such products as hot dogs, pizzas, English muffins, frozen dinners, and biscuits have been very successful. When considering the strategic uses of packaging, marketers must also analyze the cost of packaging and package changes. Table 13.2 lists the biggest packaging spenders. In this section, we examine several ways to use packaging strategically.

**Altering the Package.**  At times, a marketer changes a package because the existing design is no longer in style, especially when compared with the packaging of competitive products. Arm & Hammer now markets a refillable plastic shaker for its baking soda. Quaker Oats hired a package design company to redesign its Rice-A-Roni package to give the product the appearance of having evolved with the times while retaining its traditional taste appeal. Rice-A-Roni had been experiencing a lag in sales because of increased competition. An overhaul of the product packaging to a refreshing and more up-to-date look was credited with a 20 percent increase in sales over the previous year. Similarly, Del Monte introduced a contemporary look for its tomato products and experienced a double-digit gain in the first year.

A package may be redesigned because new product features need to be highlighted or because new packaging materials have become available. An organization may decide to change a product's packaging to reposition the product or to make the product safer or more convenient to use. The J. M. Smucker Company introduced Crisco vegetable oil in its new Simple Measures container that includes a cap that doubles as a measuring cup. After measuring out the desired amount of oil and replacing the cap, any unused oil falls back into the bottle.[26]

**Secondary-Use Packaging.**  A secondary-use package can be reused for purposes other than its initial function. For example, a margarine container can be reused to store leftovers, and a jelly container can serve as a drinking glass. Customers often view secondary-use packaging as adding value to products, in which case its use should stimulate unit sales.

**Category-Consistent Packaging.**  With category-consistent packaging, the product is packaged in line with the packaging practices associated with a particular product category. Some product categories—for example, mayonnaise, mustard, ketchup, and peanut butter—have traditional package shapes. Other product categories are characterized by recognizable color combinations, such as red and white for soup and red, white, and blue for Ritz-like crackers. When an organization introduces a brand in one of these product categories, marketers will often use traditional package shapes and color combinations to ensure customers will recognize the new product as being in that specific product category.

**Innovative Packaging.**  Sometimes a marketer employs a unique cap, design, applicator, or other feature to make a product distinctive. Such packaging can be effective when the innovation makes the product safer or easier to use, or provides better protection for the product. Nestlé, for example, introduced its new Country Creamery ice cream in an innovative package

| table 13.2 | COMPANIES THAT SPEND THE MOST ON PACKAGING | |
|---|---|---|
| Anheuser-Busch | | Kraft General Foods |
| Campbell Soup | | Kraft USA |
| Coca-Cola | | Miller Brewing |
| Coca-Cola Foods | | PepsiCo |
| General Mills | | Procter & Gamble |

that included a plastic lid that's easy to remove, even when the product is frozen, and ribbed carton corners that make it easier to grip while scooping.[27] In some instances, marketers use innovative or unique packages that are inconsistent with traditional packaging practices to make the brand stand out from competitors. To distinguish their products, marketers in the beverage industry have long used innovative shapes and packaging materials. Unusual packaging sometimes requires expending considerable resources, not only on package design but also on making customers aware of the unique package and its benefit. Research suggests that uniquely shaped packages that attract attention are more likely to be perceived as containing a higher volume of product.[28]

**Multiple Packaging.** Rather than packaging a single unit of a product, marketers sometimes use twin packs, tri-packs, six-packs, or other forms of multiple packaging. For certain types of products, multiple packaging may increase demand because it increases the amount of the product available at the point of consumption (in one's house, for example). It may also increase consumer acceptance of the product by encouraging the buyer to try the product several times. Multiple packaging can make products easier to handle and store, as in the case of six-packs for soft drinks; it can also facilitate special price offers, such as two-for-one sales. However, multiple packaging does not work for all types of products. One would not use additional table salt, for example, simply because an extra box is in the pantry.

**Handling-Improved Packaging.** A product's packaging may be changed to make it easier to handle in the distribution channel—for example, by changing the outer carton or using special bundling, shrink-wrapping, or pallets. In some cases, the shape of the package is changed. An ice cream producer, for instance, may change from a cylindrical package to a rectangular one to facilitate handling. In addition, at the retail level, the ice cream producer may be able to get more shelf facings with a rectangular package than with a round one. Outer containers for products are sometimes changed so they will proceed more easily through automated warehousing systems.

## Criticisms of Packaging

The last several decades have brought a number of improvements in packaging. However, some packaging problems still need to be resolved. Some packages suffer from functional problems in that they simply do not work well. The packaging for flour and sugar is, at best, poor. Both grocers and consumers are very much aware that these packages leak and tear easily. Can anyone open and close a bag of flour without spilling at least a little bit? Certain packages, such as refrigerated biscuit cans, milk cartons with fold-out spouts, and potato chip bags, are frequently difficult to open. Research by Nestlé reveals that hard-to-open packages are among consumers' top complaints.[29] The traditional shapes of packages for products such as ketchup and salad dressing make the product inconvenient to use. Have you ever wondered when tapping on a ketchup bottle why the producer didn't put the ketchup in a mayonnaise jar?

Although many steps have been taken to make packaging safer, critics still focus on the safety issues. Containers with sharp edges and breakable glass bottles are sometimes viewed as a threat to safety. Certain types of plastic packaging and aerosol containers represent possible health hazards.

At times, packaging is viewed as deceptive. Package shape, graphic design, and certain colors may be used to make a product appear larger than it actually is. The inconsistent use of certain size designations, such as giant, economy, family, king, and super, can lead to customer confusion.

Finally, although customers in the United States traditionally prefer attractive, effective, convenient packaging, the cost of such packaging is high.

# Labeling

**labeling** Providing identifying, promotional, or other information on package labels

**universal product code (UPC)** A series of electronically readable lines identifying a product and containing inventory and pricing information

**Labeling** is very closely interrelated with packaging and is used for identification, promotional, informational, and legal purposes. Labels can be small or large relative to the size of the product and carry varying amounts of information. The sticker on a Chiquita banana, for example, is quite small and displays only the brand name of the fruit. A label can be part of the package itself or a separate feature attached to the package. The label on a can of Coke is actually part of the can, whereas the label on a two-liter bottle of Coke is separate and can be removed. Information presented on a label may include the brand name and mark, the registered trademark symbol, package size and content, product features, nutritional information, potential presence of allergens, type and style of the product, number of servings, care instructions, directions for use and safety precautions, the name and address of the manufacturer, expiration dates, seals of approval, and other facts.

For many products, the label includes a **universal product code (UPC)**, a series of electronically readable lines identifying the product and providing inventory and pricing information for producers and resellers. The UPC is electronically read at the retail checkout counter.

Labels can facilitate the identification of a product by displaying the brand name in combination with a unique graphic design. For example, Heinz ketchup is easy to identify on a supermarket shelf because the brand name is easy to read and the label has a distinctive crownlike shape. By drawing attention to products and their benefits, labels can strengthen an organization's promotional efforts. Labels may contain such promotional messages as the offer of a discount or a larger package size at the same price, or information about a new or improved product feature.

A number of federal laws and regulations specify information that must be included on the labels of certain products. Garments must be labeled with the name of the manufacturer, country of manufacture, fabric content, and cleaning instructions. Labels on nonedible items such as shampoos and detergents must include both safety precautions and directions for use. In 1966, Congress passed the Fair Packaging and Labeling Act, one of the most comprehensive pieces of labeling and packaging legislation. This law focuses on mandatory labeling requirements, voluntary adoption of packaging standards by firms within industries, and the provision of power to the Federal Trade Commission and the Food and Drug Administration to establish and enforce packaging regulations.

The Nutrition Labeling Act of 1990 requires the FDA to review food labeling and packaging, focusing on nutrition content, label format, ingredient labeling, food descriptions, and health messages. This act regulates much of the labeling on more than 250,000 products made by some 17,000 U.S. companies. Any food product for which a nutritional claim is made must have nutrition labeling that follows a standard format. Food product labels must state the number of servings per container, serving size, number of calories per serving, number of calories derived from fat, number of carbohydrates, and amounts of specific nutrients such as vitamins. In addition, new nutritional labeling requirements focus on the amounts of trans-fatty acids in food products. Although consumers have responded favorably to this type of information on labels, evidence as to whether they actually use it has been mixed.

The use of new technology in the production and processing of food has led to additional food labeling issues. The FDA now requires that a specific irradiation logo be used when labeling irradiated food products. In addition, the FDA has issued voluntary guidelines for food companies to follow if they choose to label foods as biotech-free or to promote biotech ingredients.[30]

Despite legislation to make labels as accurate and informative as possible, questionable labeling practices persist. The Center for Science in the Public Interest questions the practice of naming a product "Strawberry Frozen Yogurt Bars" when it contains strawberry flavoring but no strawberries, or of calling a breakfast cereal "lightly sweetened" when sugar makes up 22 percent of its ingredients. Many labels on vegetable oils say "no cholesterol," but many of these oils contain

| table 13.3 | PERCEIVED QUALITY AND VALUE OF PRODUCTS BASED ON COUNTRY OF ORIGIN* | | | | | | | |
|---|---|---|---|---|---|---|---|---|
| | "Made in U.S.A." | | "Made in Japan" | | "Made in Korea" | | "Made in China" | |
| | Value | Quality | Value | Quality | Value | Quality | Value | Quality |
| U.S. adults | 4.0 | 4.2 | 3.2 | 3.2 | 2.6 | 2.4 | 2.8 | 2.4 |
| Western Europeans | 3.3 | 3.4 | 3.5 | 3.5 | 2.8 | 2.4 | 2.9 | 2.4 |

* On a scale of 1 (low) to 5 (high).
**Source:** "American Demographics 2006 Consumer Perception Survey," *Advertising Age,* Jan. 2, 2006, p. 9. Data by Synovate.

saturated fats that can raise cholesterol levels. The Food and Drug Administration amended its regulations to forbid producers of vegetable oil from making "no cholesterol" claims on their labels.

Another area of concern is "green labeling." Consumers who are committed to making environmentally responsible or natural purchasing decisions are sometimes fooled by labels that claim a product is environmentally friendly or organic. The U.S. Public Interest Research Group accused several manufacturers of "greenwashing" customers, using misleading claims to sell products by playing on customers' concern for the environment. For example, some manufacturers put a recycling symbol on labels for products made of polyvinyl chloride plastic, which cannot be recycled in the vast majority of U.S. communities.

Of concern to many manufacturers are the Federal Trade Commission's guidelines regarding "Made in U.S.A." labels, a growing problem due to the increasingly global nature of manufacturing. The FTC requires that "all or virtually all" of a product's components be made in the United States if the label says "Made in U.S.A." Although the FTC recently considered changing its guidelines to read "substantially all," it rejected this idea and maintains the "all or virtually all" standard. In light of this decision, the FTC ordered New Balance to stop using the "Made in U.S.A." claim on its athletic-shoe labels because some components (rubber soles) are made in China. The "Made in U.S.A." labeling issue has not been totally resolved. The FTC criteria for using "Made in U.S.A." are likely to be challenged and subsequently changed.[31] Table 13.3 provides insight into just how important the "Made in USA" label can be for both Americans and western Europeans. It includes assessments of both quality and value for USA-, Japan-, Korea-, and Chinese-origin labels.

## SUMMARY

A brand is a name, term, design, symbol, or any other feature that identifies one seller's good or service and distinguishes it from those of other sellers. A brand name is the part of a brand that can be spoken. A brand mark is the element not made up of words. A trademark is a legal designation indicating that the owner has exclusive use of the brand or part of the brand and others are prohibited by law from using it. A trade name is the legal name of an organization. Branding helps buyers identify and evaluate products, helps sellers facilitate product introduction and repeat purchasing, and fosters brand loyalty.

Brand loyalty is a customer's favorable attitude toward a specific brand. If brand loyalty is strong enough, customers may consistently purchase a particular brand when they need a product in this product category. The three degrees of brand loyalty are brand recognition, brand preference, and brand insistence. Brand recognition occurs when a customer is aware that the brand exists and views it as an alternative purchase if the preferred brand is unavailable. With brand preference, a customer prefers one brand over competing brands and will purchase it if available. Brand insistence occurs when a customer will accept no substitute.

Brand equity is the marketing and financial value associated with a brand's strength. It represents the value of a brand to an organization. The four major elements underlying brand equity include brand name awareness, brand loyalty, perceived brand quality, and brand associations.

A manufacturer brand, initiated by the producer, ensures that the firm is associated with its products at the point of purchase. A private distributor brand is initiated and owned by a reseller, sometimes taking on the name of the store or distributor. Manufacturers combat growing competition from private distributor brands by developing multiple brands. A generic brand indicates only the product category and does not include the company name or other identifying terms.

When selecting a brand name, a marketer should choose one that is easy to say, spell, and recall and that alludes to the product's uses, benefits, or special characteristics. Brand names can be devised from words, letters, numbers, nonsense words, or a combination of these. Brand names are created inside an organization by individuals, committees, or branding departments and by outside consultants. Services as well as products are branded, often with the company name and an accompanying symbol that makes the brand distinctive or conveys a desired image.

Producers protect ownership of their brands through registration with the U.S. Patent and Trademark Office. A company must make certain the brand name it selects does not infringe on an already registered brand by confusing or deceiving consumers about the source of the product. In most foreign countries, brand registration is on a first-come, first-serve basis, making protection more difficult. Brand counterfeiting is becoming increasingly common and can undermine consumers' confidence in a brand.

Companies brand their products in several ways. Individual branding designates a unique name for each of a company's products, family branding identifies all of a firm's products with a single name, and brand extension branding applies an existing name to a new product in a different product category. Co-branding is the use of two or more brands on one product. Effective co-branding profits from the trust and confidence customers have in the brands involved. Finally, through a licensing agreement and for a licensing fee, a

firm may permit another organization to use its brand on other products. Brand licensing enables producers to earn extra revenue, receive low-cost or free publicity, and protect their trademarks.

Packaging involves development of a container and a graphic design for a product. Effective packaging offers protection, economy, safety, and convenience. It can influence a customer's purchase decision by promoting features, uses, benefits, and image. When developing a package, marketers must consider the value to the customer of efficient and effective packaging, offset by the price the customer is willing to pay. Other considerations include making the package tamper resistant, whether to use multiple packaging and family packaging, how to design the package as an effective promotional tool, how best to accommodate resellers, and whether to develop environmentally responsible packaging. Firms choose particular colors, designs, shapes, and textures to create desirable images and associations. Packaging can be an important part of an overall marketing strategy and can be used to target certain market segments. Modifications in packaging can revive a mature product and extend its product life cycle. Producers alter packages to convey new features or to make them safer or more convenient. If a package has a secondary use, the product's value to the consumer may increase. Category-consistent packaging makes products more easily recognizable to consumers. Innovative packaging enhances a product's distinctiveness. Consumers may criticize packaging that does not work well, poses health or safety problems, is deceptive in some way, or is not biodegradable or recyclable.

Labeling is closely interrelated with packaging and is used for identification, promotional, informational, and legal purposes. The labels of many products include a universal product code, a series of electronically readable lines identifying a product and containing inventory and pricing information. Various federal laws and regulations require that certain products be labeled or marked with warnings, instructions, nutritional information, manufacturer's identification, and the like. Despite legislation, questionable labeling practices persist, including misleading information about fat content and cholesterol, freshness, and recyclability of packaging.

ACE self-test

Please visit the student website at **www.prideferrell.com** for ACE Self-Test questions that will help you prepare for exams.

## IMPORTANT TERMS

Brand
Brand name
Brand mark
Trademark
Trade name
Brand loyalty

Brand recognition
Brand preference
Brand insistence
Brand equity
Manufacturer brands
Private distributor brands

Generic brands
Individual branding
Family branding
Brand extension
Co-branding
Brand licensing

Family packaging
Labeling
Universal product code
(UPC)

## DISCUSSION & REVIEW QUESTIONS

1. What is the difference between a brand and a brand name? Compare and contrast a brand mark and a trademark.

2. How does branding benefit consumers and marketers?

3. What are the three major degrees of brand loyalty?

4. What is brand equity? Identify and explain the major elements of brand equity.

5. Compare and contrast manufacturer brands, private distributor brands, and generic brands.

6. Identify the factors a marketer should consider in selecting a brand name.

7. The brand name Xerox is sometimes used generically to refer to photocopiers, and Kleenex is used to refer to facial tissues. How can the manufacturers protect their brand names, and why would they want to do so?

8. What is co-branding? What major issues should be considered when using co-branding?

9. What are the major advantages and disadvantages of brand licensing?

10. Describe the functions a package can perform. Which function is most important? Why?

11. What are the main factors a marketer should consider when developing a package?

12. In what ways can packaging be used as a strategic tool?

13. What are the major criticisms of packaging?

14. What are the major functions of labeling?

15. In what ways do regulations and legislation affect labeling?

## APPLICATION QUESTIONS

1. Identify two brands for which you are brand insistent. How did you begin using these brands? Why do you no longer use other brands?

2. General Motors introduced the subcompact Geo with a name that appeals to a world market. Invent a brand name for a line of luxury sports cars that also would appeal to an international market. Suggest a name that implies quality, luxury, and value.

3. When a firm decides to brand its products, it may choose one of several strategies. Name one company that uses each of the following strategies. How does each strategy help the company?

   a. Individual branding

   b. Family branding

   c. Brand extension

4. For each of the following product categories, choose an existing brand. Then, for each selected brand, suggest a co-brand and explain why the co-brand would be effective.

   a. Cookies

   b. Pizza

   c. Long-distance telephone service

   d. A sports drink

5. Packaging provides product protection; customer convenience; and promotion of image, key features, and benefits. Identify a product that uses packaging in each of these ways, and evaluate the effectiveness of the package for that function.

6. Identify a package that you believe is inferior. Explain why you think the package is inferior, and discuss your recommendations for improving it.

1. Brands are no longer a domestic phenomenon. In fact, many consumers now associate global brands with higher degrees of quality or prestige than more localized or even regionalized brands. Find data on this topic at *Business Week*'s Global Brands section by using the search term "global brands" at **http://globaledge.msu.edu/ibrd**. Once there, click on the Top 100 Brands Scorecard to the right. What are the top ten brands worldwide? Which countries are represented? Which brands from the overall study are from Germany? Summarize three German brands and compare each with a competing brand.

2. To understand which brands are currently in the market your firm is hoping to enter, you have been asked to collect market data on specific brands and models. Given that you are aware of the Industry Research Desk's resources on 18 steps to assist in understanding the development and management of products, you can address this issue effectively. Use the search term "18 steps" at **http://globaledge.msu.edu/ibrd** to reach the Industry Research Desk's 18 steps, and then scroll down to Step 9 for information concerning collectors of market data on specific brands and models. What are the two main information providers that may assist in your assessment of the marketplace?

## INTERNET Exercise

Visit **www.prideferrell.com** for resources to help you master the material in this chapter, plus materials that will help you expand your marketing knowledge, including Internet exercise updates, ACE Self-Tests, hotlinks to companies featured in this chapter, and much more.

### Pillsbury

Like other marketers of consumer products, Pillsbury has set up a website to inform and entertain consumers. Catering to the appeal of its most popular product spokesperson, Pillsbury has given its Dough Boy his own site. Visit him at **www.doughboy.com**.

1. What branding policy does Pillsbury seem to be using with regard to the products it presents on this site?
2. How does this Pillsbury website promote brand loyalty?
3. What degree of consistency exists in Pillsbury's packaging of its products displayed on the website?

## Video Case 13.1   New Belgium Brewing Company

The idea for New Belgium Brewing Company (NBB) began with a bicycling trip through Belgium, where some of the world's finest ales have been brewed for centuries. As Jeff Lebesch, a U.S. electrical engineer, cruised around the country on a fat-tired mountain bike, he wondered if he could produce such high-quality ales in his home state of Colorado. After returning home, Lebesch began to experiment in his Fort Collins basement. When his home-brewed experiments earned rave reviews from friends, Lebesch and his wife, Kim Jordan, decided to open the New Belgium Brewing Company in 1991. They named their first brew Fat Tire Amber Ale in honor of Lebesch's Belgian biking adventure.

Today New Belgium markets a variety of permanent and seasonal ales and pilsners. The standard line includes Sunshine Wheat, Blue Paddle Pilsner, Abbey Ale, Trippel Ale, and 1554 Black Ale, as well as the firm's number 1 seller, the original Fat Tire Amber Ale. NBB also markets seasonal beers, such as Frambozen and Abbey Grand Cru, released at Thanksgiving and Christmas, and Farmhouse Ale, sold during the early fall months. The firm also occasionally offers one-time-only brews—such as LaFolie, a wood-aged beer—that are sold only until the batch runs out. Bottle label designs employ "good ol' days" nostalgia. The Fat Tire label, for example, features an old-style cruiser bike with wide tires, a padded seat, and a basket hanging from the handlebars. All the label and packaging designs were created by the same watercolor artist, Jeff Lebesch's next-door neighbor.

New Belgium beers are priced to reflect their quality at about $7 per six-pack. This pricing strategy conveys the message that the products are special and of consistently higher quality than macrobrews, such as Budweiser and Coors, but also keeps them competitive with other microbrews, such as Pete's Wicked Ale, Pyramid Pale Ale, and Sierra Nevada. To demonstrate its appreciation for its retailers and business partners, New Belgium does not sell beer to consumers on-site at the brewhouse for less than the retailers charge.

Although Fat Tire was initially sold only in Fort Collins, distribution quickly expanded throughout the rest of Colorado. Customers can now find Fat Tire and other New Belgium offerings in 15 western states, including Washington, Montana, Texas, New Mexico, and Arizona. The brewery regularly receives e-mails and telephone inquiries as to when New Belgium beers will be available elsewhere.

Since its founding, NBB's most effective promotion has been via word-of-mouth advertising by customers devoted to the brand. The company initially avoided mass advertising, relying instead on small-scale, local promotions, such as print advertisements in alternative magazines, participation in local festivals, and sponsorship of alternative sports events. Through event sponsorships, such as the Tour de Fat and Ride the Rockies, NBB has raised thousands of dollars for various environmental, social, and cycling nonprofit organizations.

With expanding distribution, however, the brewery recognized a need to increase its opportunities for reaching its far-flung customers. It consulted with Dr. David Holt, an Oxford professor and branding expert. After studying the young company, Holt, together with marketing director Greg Owsley, drafted a 70-page "manifesto" describing the brand's attributes, character, cultural relevancy, and promise. In particular, Holt identified in New Belgium an ethos of pursuing creative activities simply for the joy of doing them well and in harmony with the natural environment. With the brand thus defined, New Belgium went in search of an advertising agency to help communicate that brand identity; it soon found Amalgamated, an equally young, independent New York advertising agency. Amalgamated created a $10 million advertising campaign for New Belgium that targets high-end beer drinkers, men ages 25 to 44, and highlights the brewery's image as being down to earth. The grainy ads focus on a man rebuilding a cruiser bike out of used parts and then riding it along pastoral country roads. The product appears in just five seconds of each ad between the tag lines, "Follow Your Folly . . . Ours Is Beer." The ads helped position the growing brand as whimsical, thoughtful,

and reflective. In addition to the ad campaign, the company maintained its strategy of promotion through event sponsorships.

NBB's marketing strategy has always involved pairing the brand with a concern for how the company's activities affect the natural environment. The brewery looks for cost-efficient, energy-saving alternatives to conducting business and reducing its impact on the environment. Thus, the company's employee-owners unanimously agreed to invest in a wind turbine, making NBB the first fully wind-powered brewery in the United States. The company further reduces its energy use with a steam condenser that captures and reuses the hot water from boiling the barley and hops in the production process to start the next brew; the steam is redirected to heat the floor tiles and de-ice the loading docks in cold weather. NBB also strives to recycle as many supplies as possible, including cardboard boxes, keg caps, office materials, and the amber glass used in bottling. The brewery stores spent barley and hop grains in an on-premise silo and invites local farmers to pick up the grains, free of charge, to feed their pigs. Another way NBB conserves energy is through the use of "sun tubes," which provide natural daytime lighting throughout the brewhouse all year long. NBB also encourages employees to reduce air pollution through alternative transportation. As an incentive, NBB gives each employee a "cruiser bike"—just like the one on the Fat Tire Amber Ale label and in the television ads—

after one year of employment to encourage biking to work.

Beyond its use of environment-friendly technologies and innovations, New Belgium Brewing Company strives to improve communities and enhance lives through corporate giving, event sponsorship, and philanthropic involvement. The company donates $1 per barrel of beer sold to various cultural, social, environmental, and drug and alcohol awareness programs across the 15 western states in which it distributes beer. Typical grants range from $2,500 to $5,000. Involvement is spread equally among the 15 states, unless a special need requires greater participation or funding. The brewhouse also maintains a community board where organizations can post community involvement activities and proposals. This board allows tourists and employees to see opportunities to help out the community and provides nonprofit organizations with a forum for making their needs known. Organizations can also apply for grants through the New Belgium Brewing Company website, which has a link designated for this purpose.

New Belgium's commitment to quality, the environment, and its employees and customers is clearly expressed in its stated purpose: "To operate a profitable brewery which makes our love and talent manifest." This dedication has been well rewarded with loyal customers and industry awards. From cutting-edge environmental programs and high-tech industry advancements to employee-ownership programs and a strong belief in giving back to the community, New Belgium demonstrates its desire to create a living, learning community. According to David Edgar, director of the Institute for Brewing Studies, "They've created a very positive image for their company in the beer-consuming public with smart decision making." Although some members of society do not believe a brewery can be socially responsible, New Belgium has set out to prove that for those who make the choice to drink responsibly, the company can do everything possible to contribute to society.[32]

### Questions for Discussion

1. How does New Belgium Brewing Company's social responsibility initiatives help build its brand?
2. Describe New Belgium's branding policy. How does it use packaging to further its brand image?
3. Assess New Belgium's brand equity.

## Case 13.2        The Harley-Davidson Brand Roars into Its Second Century

Harley-Davidson has roared up and down the fast track in its time. Named for the two founders, the company was started with one motorcycle built in a shed in 1903. Now Harley-Davidson annually sells more than 317,000 motorcycles across the United States, Japan, Europe, and soon China. During the 1970s, however, product quality suffered as Harley-Davidson expanded too quickly. The company was nearly out of business by the mid-1980s when management decided to reduce manufacturing output, focus on improving quality, and redesign its basic motorcycle engine. Customers noticed the difference, and sales began to accelerate.

Soon Harley-Davidson was well on the road to reclaiming the brand's market dominance in the United States and beating back competition from Yamaha, Honda, Suzuki, and Kawasaki. Despite higher demand, management was careful to increase production only slightly from year to year. This allowed closer control over quality, but it also meant dealers never had enough inventory on hand. As a result, eager customers sometimes waited one or two years for the more popular models and paid thousands of dollars over the regular price when a particularly desirable bike became available. Demand soared higher still when Harley-Davidson sold special limited-edition models to celebrate its centennial in 2003.

The motorcycle experience is central to Harley-Davidson's culture and marketing. Nearly half of the company's 8,200 employees own one of the firm's motorcycles—purchased from local dealers—so they know a great deal about how their products are used.

In addition, hundreds of employees attend cycling rallies around the country to mingle with customers, applying what they learn when developing new products and new marketing programs. After observing how riders personalized their bikes with unusual handlebars and unique paint jobs, Harley-Davidson launched a line of custom bikes complete with special accessories. These motorcycles sell for around $25,000 and are more profitable than regular sport and touring models, which fetch $8,000 to $17,000.

To its customers, the Harley-Davidson brand represents more than just two-wheeled transportation. When they line up to buy Harley-Davidson bikes, wear branded apparel, and participate in cross-country tours benefiting charities, customers are making a lifestyle choice. Nonmotorcycle products with the Harley-Davidson brand are so popular that they bring in revenues exceeding $10 million monthly. Customers snap up T-shirts in sizes from newborn to XXXL. They also buy leather jackets, teddy bears, blankets, drinking glasses, collectible pins, and hundreds of other branded items. In fact, some customers start out wearing Harley-Davidson clothing and then progress to buying Harley-Davidson motorcycles.

Owning a Harley-Davidson makes customers part of a brand-oriented motorcycle community. The Harley Owners Group (H.O.G.)—900,000 members strong—allows enthusiasts to connect with one another and with the brand. Annual rallies such as those held at Sturgis, South Dakota, and Daytona Beach, Florida, routinely draw 100,000 or more Harley-Davidson owners. When the company threw a week-long 100th birthday bash in Milwaukee, 250,000 bikers showed up to celebrate and shop for all manner of Harley-Davidson merchandise.

Nevertheless, the company may face a bumpy ride as it searches for ways to appeal to younger customers and fend off rivals. Fifteen years ago, the average age of a Harley-Davidson buyer was 35; today the average age is 46. Moreover, market share is beginning to slip as customers buy high-performance models from competitors. In response, Harley-Davidson is introducing sleek new models with liquid-cooled engines. Some of these new models can reach speeds up to 140 miles per hour. It has also opened a new factory to keep up with demand. Through the Rider's Edge program, the company is teaching a new generation of customers how to ride and care for their motorcycles.

Harley-Davidson remains on top of the North American market and has reported record sales for more than 19 consecutive years. One of the co-founder's grandsons, Willie G. Davidson, serves as senior vice president and rides his Harley to customer gatherings. What he calls "the rebel thing" is an integral part of the brand image. Harley owners may enjoy this image when they ride, and a large number change their leathers for business suits during the workweek. To stay on the road to higher sales and profits, Harley-Davidson will have to stay attuned to its customers' perceptions of this century-old brand.[33]

## Questions for Discussion

1. What might Harley-Davidson's employees do to measure brand equity as they mingle with customers at motorcycle rallies?
2. Should the company continue family branding or move to individual branding for new models of motorcycles? Explain.
3. What questions should Harley-Davidson ask of an apparel company that wants to license the Harley-Davidson brand to place on its clothing?

# Services Marketing

## Wicked: Casting a Spell on Broadway

Nearly 80 percent of Broadway shows close without breaking even. But *Wicked,* a musical "prequel" to Frank Baum's *Wizard of Oz* tales, was in the black just 14 months after it opened. Today it grosses about $1.3 million a week.

The $14 million production was one of the first Broadway shows to charge more than $100 per ticket. After the show garnered mixed reviews after opening, its producers discounted tickets by as much as 30 percent through mail offerings. The strategy to draw people in worked: within months, strong word of mouth began resulting in sold-out performances. The play debuted at the Gershwin Theater, but clones of the show have since opened in Chicago and London, and the Broadway version's 30-city tour was expected to draw 960,000 people in 2006.

In addition to traditional advertising, the show is promoted through websites and chat rooms, licensing deals, and karaoke contests. Related products include a 192-page coffee-table book, *Wicked* T-shirts, and themed necklaces targeted at teenage girls, one of the biggest market segments of the show's audience. But the show found its real following by the buzz its marketers created. Nancy Coyne, who runs Serino Coyne, Broadway's largest advertising and marketing agency, says the show spent many dollars on billboard advertising because the play's title and the image it uses—a black silhouette of a witch—is so powerful.

Due to a successful and flexible marketing strategy, *Wicked* is the number 1 show on Broadway. In 2004 it won three Tony Awards—for Best Scenic Design, Best Actress in a Musical, and Best Costume Design—as well as seven 2004 Drama Desk Awards. Now, that's *Wicked.*[1] ∎

## OBJECTIVES

1. To understand the nature and importance of services

2. To identify the characteristics of services that differentiate them from goods

3. To describe how the characteristics of services influence the development of marketing mixes for services

4. To understand the importance of service quality and explain how to deliver exceptional service quality

5. To explore the nature of nonprofit marketing

The products offered on Broadway—namely, entertainment—are services rather than tangible goods. This chapter presents concepts that apply specifically to products that are services. The organizations that market service products include for-profit firms, such as those offering financial, personal, and professional services, and nonprofit organizations, such as educational institutions, churches, charities, and governments.

We begin this chapter with a focus on the growing importance of service industries in our economy. We then address the unique characteristics of services. Next, we deal with the challenges these characteristics pose in developing and managing marketing mixes for services. We then discuss customers' judgment of service quality and the importance of delivering high-quality services. Finally, we define nonprofit marketing and examine the development of nonprofit marketing strategies.

# The Nature and Importance of Services

All products, whether goods, services, or ideas, are intangible to some extent. We previously defined a service as an intangible product involving a deed, a performance, or an effort that cannot be physically possessed.[2] Services are usually provided through the application of human and/or mechanical efforts directed at people or objects. For example, a service such as education involves the efforts of service providers (teachers) directed at people (students), whereas janitorial and interior decorating services direct their efforts at objects. Services can also involve the use of mechanical efforts directed at people (air transportation) or objects (freight transportation). A wide variety of services, such as health care and landscaping, involve both human and mechanical efforts. Although many services entail the use of tangibles such as tools and machinery, the primary difference between a service and a good is that a service is dominated by the intangible portion of the total product.

Services as products should not be confused with the related topic of customer services. Customer service involves any human or mechanical activity that adds value to the product.[3] While the core product may be a good, complementary services help create the total product. While customer service is a part of the marketing of goods, service marketers also provide customer services. For example, many service companies offer guarantees to their customers in an effort to increase value. Hampton Inns, a national chain of mid-price hotels, gives its guests a free night if they are not 100 percent satisfied with their stay (fewer than one-half of 1 percent of Hampton customers ask for a refund). In some cases, a 100 percent satisfaction guarantee or similar service commitment may motivate employees to provide high-quality service, not because failure to do so leads to personal penalties but because they are proud to be part of an organization that is so committed to good service.

The increasing importance of services in the U.S. economy has led many people to call the United States the world's first service economy. In most developed countries, including Germany, Japan, Australia, and Canada, services account for about 70 percent of the gross domestic product (GDP). More than one-half of new businesses are service businesses, and service employment is expected to continue to grow. These industries have absorbed much of the influx of women and minorities into the workforce. In the United States, some customer-contact jobs, especially call centers, have been outsourced—into the homes of U.S. workers, especially women. JetBlue, for example, has 1,400 reservation agents who work from their homes.[4]

One major catalyst in the growth of consumer services has been long-term economic growth (slowed only by a few recessions) in the United States, which has led to increased interest in financial services, travel, entertainment, and personal care. Lifestyle changes have similarly encouraged expansion of the service sector. The need for child care, domestic services, and other time-saving services has increased, and many consumers want to avoid such tasks as meal preparation, house cleaning, yard maintenance, and tax preparation. Consequently, franchise service operations such as Subway, Merry Maids, ChemLawn, and H&R Block have experienced rapid growth. Also, because Americans have become more health-, fitness-, and recreation-oriented, the demand for exercise and recreational facilities has escalated. In terms of demographics, the U.S. population is growing older, a fact that has promoted tremendous expansion of health-care services. Finally, the increasing number and complexity of high-tech goods have spurred demand for support services. Indeed, the services sector has been enhanced by dramatic changes in information technology. Entrepreneurs have emerged taking advantage of inexpensive computer hardware, free software, and broadband Internet access to launch new service-oriented businesses or to transform existing businesses to focus on services.[5] Consider service companies such as Google, eBay, and Amazon.com, which use technology to provide services to challenge and change traditional ways of conducting business.

Business services have prospered as well. Business services include support and maintenance, consulting, installation, equipment leasing, marketing research, advertising, temporary office personnel, and janitorial services. Expenditures for business services have risen even faster than expenditures for consumer services. The growth in business services has been attributed to the increasingly complex, specialized, and competitive business environment. IBM, for example, has shifted from a focus on computer hardware to consulting services and software applications.

One way to view services is from a theater framework with production elements such as actors, audience, a setting, and a performance. The actors (service workers) create a service (performance) for the audience (customers) in a setting (service environment) where the performance unfolds. Costumes (uniforms), props (devices, music, machines), and the setting (face-to-face or indirect through telephone or Internet) help complete the theatrical metaphor.[6] At Disney World, for example, all employees wear costumes, there is an entertainment setting, and most service contact with employees involves playing roles and engaging in planned skits. But the theatrical components are also visible in a Subway fast-food restaurant or on an airline flight. In addition, a performance involves a "script," a chronologically ordered representation of the steps that comprise the service performance from the customer's perspective.[7] Even sports events such as football, basketball, and hockey have sequences of events and rules that standardize the performance, even if the outcome depends on the performance itself.

# Characteristics of Services

The issues associated with marketing service products differ somewhat from those associated with marketing goods. To understand these differences, we need to look at the distinguishing characteristics of services. Services have six basic characteristics: intangibility, inseparability of production and consumption, perishability, heterogeneity, client-based relationships, and customer contact.[8]

### Intangibility

As already noted, the major characteristic that distinguishes a service from a good is intangibility. **Intangibility** means a service is not physical and therefore cannot be perceived by the senses. For example, it is impossible to touch the education that students derive from attending classes; the intangible benefit is becoming more knowledgeable. In addition, services cannot be physically possessed. Students obviously cannot physically possess knowledge as they can an iPod or a car. There is a direct relationship between the level of intangibility and consumers' use of brands as a cue to the nature and quality of the service. This means that brand name is more important for financial services than for a cellphone.[9]

Figure 14.1 (on p. 378) depicts a tangibility continuum from pure goods (tangible) to pure services (intangible). Pure goods, if they exist at all, are rare because practically all marketers of goods also provide customer services. Even a tangible product such as sugar must be delivered to the store, priced, and placed on a shelf before a customer can purchase it. Intangible, service-dominant products such as

**intangibility** The quality of being produced and consumed at the same time

## figure 14.1

### THE TANGIBILITY CONTINUUM

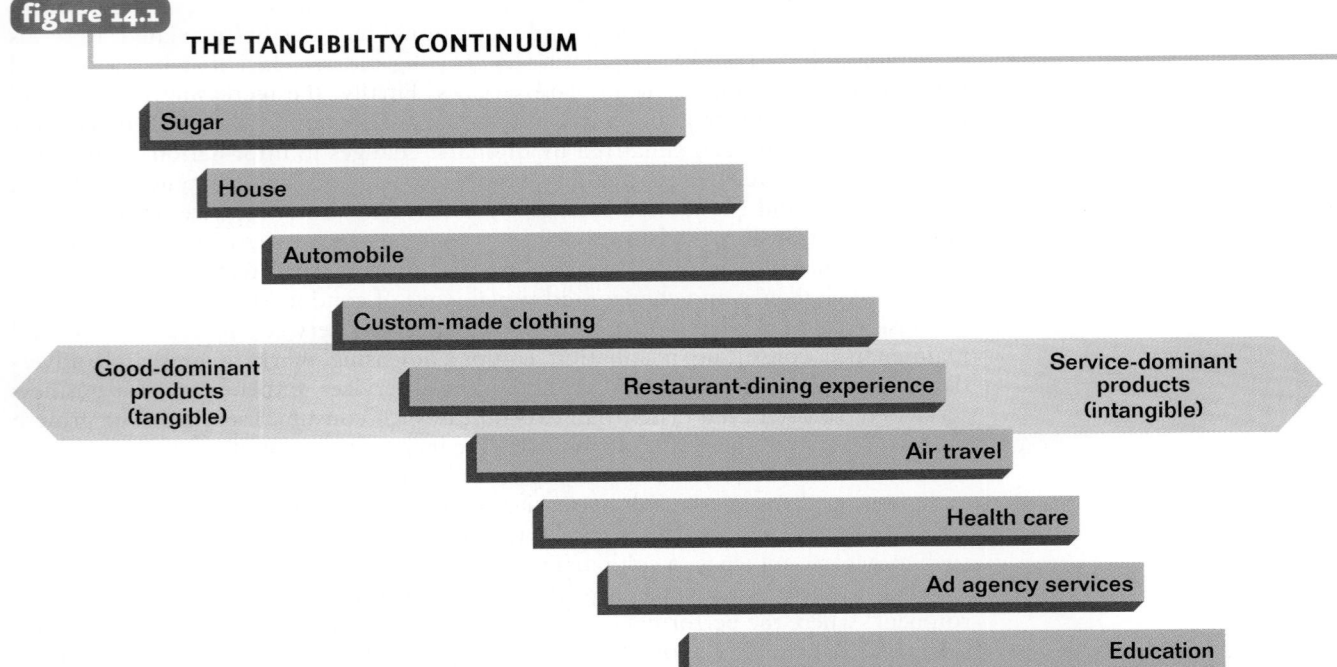

education or health care are clearly service products. But what about products near the center of the continuum? Is a restaurant such as Chili's a goods marketer or a service marketer? Services like airline flights have something tangible to offer, such as drinks and meals. An Internet search engine such as Google or a news site such as CNN or MSNBC is service-dominant. Knowing where the product lies on the continuum is important in creating marketing strategies for service-dominant products.

### Inseparability of Production and Consumption

**inseparability** The quality of being produced and consumed at the same time

Another important characteristic of services that creates challenges for marketers is **inseparability,** which refers to the fact that the production of a service cannot be separated from its consumption by customers. For example, air passenger service is produced and consumed simultaneously. In other words, services are often produced, sold, and consumed at the same time. In goods marketing, a customer can purchase a good, take it home, and store it until ready to use it. The manufacturer of the good may never see an actual customer. Customers, however, often must be present at the production of a service (such as investment consulting or surgery) and cannot take the service home. Because of inseparability, customers not only want a specific type of service but expect it to be provided in a specific way by a specific individual. For example, the production and consumption of a medical exam occur simultaneously, and the patient knows in advance who the physician is and generally understands how the exam will be conducted. Inseparability implies a shared responsibility between the customer and service provider. As a result, training programs for employees should stress the customer's role in the service experience to elevate their perceptions of shared responsibility and positive feelings.[10]

### Perishability

**perishability** The inability of unused service capacity to be stored for future use

Services are characterized by **perishability** in that the unused service capacity of one time period cannot be stored for future use. For example, empty seats on an airline flight today cannot be stored and sold to passengers at a later date. Other examples of service perishability include unsold basketball tickets, unscheduled dentists' appointment times, and empty hotel rooms. Although some goods, such as meat, milk, and produce, are perishable, goods generally are less perishable than services. If a

We'll save you money. What you do with it is up to you.

**The Hertz #1 Club®** gives you all sorts of discounts and savings. **Sign up free at hertz.com.** Far be it from us to tell you how to shop. But we can tell you how to save. For starters, The Hertz #1 Club gives you discounts on every vacation rental. Save on child and infant seat rentals. And we'll also keep you posted with special email offers for discounts on rentals, upgrades and more. Membership is free too. It's just one of the many ways Hertz #1 Club can get your vacation off to a great start. Just go to hertz.com/join to sign up. Rent the car. Keep the shoes. That's renting wisely.

*Hertz*
Rent Wisely.®

Hertz rents Fords and other fine cars. ® Reg. U.S. Pat. Off. © 2008 Hertz System, Inc.
**FOR YOUR INFORMATION:** Advance reservations are required. Standard rental conditions and return restrictions must be met. Restrictions apply. Minimum rental age is 25 (exceptions apply).

**Inseparability**

Hertz promotes both its service and its ability to save the customer money.

pair of jeans has been sitting on a department store shelf for a week, someone can still buy them the next day. Goods marketers can handle the supply-demand problem through production scheduling and inventory techniques. Service marketers do not have the same advantage and face several hurdles in trying to balance supply and demand. They can, however, plan for demand that fluctuates according to day of the week, time of day, or season.

## Heterogeneity

**heterogeneity** Variation in quality

Services delivered by people are susceptible to **heterogeneity,** or variation in quality. Quality of manufactured goods is easier to control with standardized procedures, and mistakes are easier to isolate and correct. Because of the nature of human behavior, however, it is very difficult for service providers to maintain a consistent quality of service delivery. This variation in quality can occur from one organization to another, from one service person to another within the same service facility, and from one service facility to another within the same organization. For example, one bank may provide more convenient hours and charge fewer fees than the one next door, or the retail clerks in one bookstore may be more knowledgeable and therefore more helpful than those in another bookstore owned by the same chain. In addition, the service a single employee provides can vary from customer to customer, day to day, or even hour to hour. Although many service problems are one-time events that cannot be predicted or controlled ahead of time, training and establishment of standard procedures can help increase consistency and reliability. Because research suggests that service employees with greater sensitivity toward people of different countries and cultures are more attentive and have better interpersonal skills, job satisfaction, and social satisfaction, training that improves cultural sensitivity should improve consistency of service quality in cross-cultural environments.[11]

Heterogeneity usually increases as the degree of labor intensiveness increases. Many services, such as auto repair, education, and hairstyling, rely heavily on

# Mississippi Power: Heroes in the Aftermath of Disaster

**A**fter Hurricane Katrina hit the Gulf Coast in 2005, Mississippi Power quickly and efficiently came to the rescue of its 195,000 customers—all of whom were left without power after the devastating storm. In only 12 days, the small utility managed to restore power to all customers for whom it was safe to do so, despite the loss of 65 percent of its transmission and distribution facilities.

Mississippi Power's values, as written on employees' ID badges, are "Unquestionable Trust, Superior Performance, Total Commitment." Facing the crisis, company executives had no choice but to take immediate action and trust that they could find solutions. Their resolve was strengthened by a "can-do" culture, years of hurricane experience, and a strong crisis-management plan. They appointed 20 storm directors and gave each complete authority to do whatever was necessary to get the job done. Each individual—from storm directors on down—was empowered to make decisions and solve problems on the spot. The results were phenomenal: people worked harder, found unconventional solutions, and restored power before the projected four-week deadline.

Those at Mississippi Power learned six valuable lessons in the wake of Katrina: (1) A good forecast pays off. (2) Back up your backup plans. (3) Know how to get help when you need it. (4) Seek breakthrough solutions. (5) Hard work and pride pay off. (6) Measure results. Although the Gulf Coast area is still recovering from Katrina, the people at Mississippi Power exceeded their own expectations by simply doing what needed to be done, and they saved money and restored service to their customers earlier than expected.

---

human labor. Other services, such as telecommunications, health clubs, and public transportation, are more equipment intensive. People-based services are often prone to fluctuations in quality from one time period to the next. For example, the fact that a hairstylist gives a customer a good haircut today does not guarantee that customer a haircut of equal quality from the same hairstylist at a later date or even a later hour. A morning customer may receive a better haircut than an end-of-the-day customer from the same stylist. Equipment-based services suffer from this problem to a lesser degree than people-based services. For instance, automated teller machines have reduced inconsistency in the quality of teller services at banks, and bar-code scanning has improved the accuracy of service at checkout counters in grocery stores.

### Client-Based Relationships

**client-based relationships**
Interactions that result in satisfied customers who use a service repeatedly over time

The success of many services depends on creating and maintaining **client-based relationships,** interactions that result in satisfied customers who use a service repeatedly over time.[12] In fact, some service providers, such as lawyers, accountants, and financial advisers, call their customers *clients* and often develop and maintain close, long-term relationships with them. For such service providers, it is not enough to attract customers. They are successful only to the degree to which they can maintain a group of clients who use their services on an ongoing basis. For example, an accountant may serve a family in his or her area for decades. If the members of this family like the quality of the accountant's services, they are likely to recommend the accountant to other families. If several families repeat this positive word-of-mouth communication, the accountant will likely acquire a long list of satisfied clients before long. This process is the key to creating and maintaining client-based relation-

**Characteristics of Services**
Hair stylists develop close client-based relationships.

ships. To ensure that it actually occurs, the service provider must take steps to build trust, demonstrate customer commitment, and satisfy customers so well that they become very loyal to the provider and unlikely to switch to competitors.

## Customer Contact

**customer contact** The level of interaction between provider and customer needed to deliver the service

Not all services require a high degree of customer contact, but many do. **Customer contact** refers to the level of interaction between the service provider and the customer necessary to deliver the service. High-contact services include health care, real estate, and legal and spa services. Examples of low-contact services are tax preparation, auto repair, and dry cleaning. Note that high-contact services generally involve actions directed toward people, who must be present during production. A hairstylist's customer, for example, must be present during the styling process. Because the customer must be present, the process of production may be just as important as its final outcome. Although it is sometimes possible for the service provider to go to the customer, high-contact services typically require that the customer go to the production facility. Thus, the physical appearance of the facility may be a major component of the customer's overall evaluation of the service. For example, when the physical setting fosters customer-to-customer interactions, it can lead to greater loyalty to an establishment and positive word-of-mouth communications.[13] While low-contact services do not require the customer's physical presence during delivery, the customer will likely need to be present to initiate and terminate the service. For example, customers of auto-repair services must bring in the vehicle and describe its symptoms, but often do not remain during the preparation process.

Employees of high-contact service providers are a very important ingredient in creating satisfied customers. A fundamental precept of customer contact is that satisfied employees lead to satisfied customers. In fact, employee satisfaction is the single most important factor in providing high-service quality. Thus, to minimize the problems customer contact can create, service organizations must

**Level of Customer Contact**
Online universities, such as Capella, maintain the level of contact through technology.

take steps to understand and meet the needs of employees by adequately training them, empowering them to make more decisions, and rewarding them for customer-oriented behavior.[14] To provide the quality of customer service that has made it the fastest-growing coffee retailer in the world, Starbucks provides extensive employee training. Employees receive about 25 hours of initial training, which includes memorizing recipes and learning the differences among a variety of coffees, proper coffee-making techniques, and many other skills that stress Starbucks's dedication to customer service. Starbucks has approximately 8,500 coffee shops and about 96,700 employees worldwide.[15]

# Developing and Managing Marketing Mixes for Services

The characteristics of services discussed in the previous section create a number of challenges for service marketers (see Table 14.1). These challenges are especially evident in the development and management of marketing mixes for services. Although such mixes contain the four major marketing mix variables—product, distribution, promotion, and price—the characteristics of services require that marketers consider additional issues.

**table 14.1  SERVICE CHARACTERISTICS AND MARKETING CHALLENGES**

| Service Characteristics | Resulting Marketing Challenges |
|---|---|
| Intangibility | Difficult for customer to evaluate.<br>Customer does not take physical possession.<br>Difficult to advertise and display.<br>Difficult to set and justify prices.<br>Service process is usually not protectable by patents. |
| Inseparability of production and consumption | Service provider cannot mass produce services.<br>Customer must participate in production.<br>Other consumers affect service outcomes.<br>Services are difficult to distribute. |
| Perishability | Services cannot be stored.<br>Balancing supply and demand is very difficult.<br>Unused capacity is lost forever.<br>Demand may be very time sensitive. |
| Heterogeneity | Service quality is difficult to control.<br>Service delivery is difficult to standardize. |
| Client-based relationships | Success depends on satisfying and keeping customers over the long term.<br>Generating repeat business is challenging.<br>Relationship marketing becomes critical. |
| Customer contact | Service providers are critical to delivery.<br>Requires high levels of service employee training and motivation.<br>Changing a high-contact service into a low-contact service to achieve lower costs is difficult to achieve without reducing customer satisfaction. |

**Sources:** K. Douglas Hoffman and John E. G. Bateson, *Services Marketing: Concepts, Strategies, and Cases,* 3rd ed. (Cincinnati: Thomson/South-Western, 2006); Valarie A. Zeithaml, A. Parasuraman, and Leonard L. Berry, *Delivering Quality Service: Balancing Customer Perceptions and Expectations* (New York: Free Press, 1990); Leonard L. Berry and A. Parasuraman, *Marketing Services: Competing through Quality* (New York: Free Press, 1991), p. 5.

## Development of Services

A service offered by an organization generally is a package, or bundle, of services consisting of a core service and one or more supplementary services. A core service is the basic service experience or commodity that a customer expects to receive. A supplementary service is a supportive one related to the core service and is used to differentiate the service bundle from competitors'. For example, Hampton Inns provides a room as a core service. Bundled with the room are such supplementary services as free local phone calls, cable television, and a complimentary continental breakfast.

As discussed earlier, heterogeneity results in variability in service quality and makes it difficult to standardize service delivery. However, heterogeneity provides one advantage to service marketers: it allows them to customize their services to match the specific needs of individual customers. Customization plays a key role in providing competitive advantage for the service provider. Being able to personalize the service to fit the exact needs of the customer accommodates individual needs, wants, or desires.[16] Subway, for example, tries to let each customer participate in developing his or her own customized sandwich. IBM determines a business's needs and then develops information technology services to provide a customized application. Health care is an example of an extremely customized service; the services provided differ from one patient to the next.

Such customized services can be expensive for both provider and customer, and some service marketers therefore face a dilemma: how to provide service at an acceptable level of quality in an efficient and economic manner and still satisfy individual customer needs. To cope with this problem, some service marketers offer standardized packages. For example, a spa may provide a number of treatments such as hair styling, facials, and massages for one price. When service bundles are standardized, the specific actions and activities of the service provider usually are highly specified. Automobile quick-lube providers frequently offer a service bundle for a single price; the specific work to be done on a customer's car is spelled out in detail. Various other equipment-based services are also often standardized into packages. For instance, cable television providers frequently offer several packages, such as "Basic," "Standard," and "Premier."

The characteristic of intangibility makes it difficult for customers to evaluate a service prior to purchase. A customer who is shopping for a pair of jeans can try them on before buying them, but how does she or he evaluate legal advice before receiving the service? Intangibility requires service marketers such as attorneys to market promises to customers. The customer is forced to place some degree of trust in the service provider to perform the service in a manner that meets or exceeds those promises. Service marketers must guard against making promises that raise customer expectations beyond what they can provide.

To cope with the problem of intangibility, marketers employ tangible cues, such as well-groomed, professional-appearing contact personnel and clean, attractive physical facilities, to help assure customers about the quality of the service. Most service providers uniform at least some of their high-contact employees. Uniforms help make the service experience more tangible and serve as physical

**Development of Services**
FTD provides many tangible cues to convey its delivery service.

evidence to signal quality, create consistency, and send cues to suggest a desired image.[17] Consider the professionalism, experience, and competence conveyed by an airline pilot's uniform. Life insurance companies sometimes try to make the quality of their policies more tangible by printing them on premium-quality paper and enclosing them in leather sheaths. Because customers often rely on brand names as an indicator of product quality, service marketers at organizations whose names are the same as their service brand names should strive to build a strong national image for their companies. For example, American Express, McDonald's, eBay, American Life, and America Online try to maintain strong, positive national company images because these names are the brand names of the services they provide.

The inseparability of production and consumption and the level of customer contact also influence the development and management of services. The fact that customers take part in the production of a service means other customers can affect the outcome of the service. For instance, if a nonsmoker dines in a restaurant without a no-smoking section, the overall quality of service experienced by the nonsmoking customer declines. For this reason, many restaurants have no-smoking sections and some prohibit smoking anywhere on their premises. Service marketers can reduce these problems by encouraging customers to share the responsibility of maintaining an environment that allows all participants to receive the intended benefits of the service.

## Distribution of Services

Marketers deliver services in a variety of ways. In some instances, customers go to a service provider's facility. For example, most health-care, dry-cleaning, and spa services are delivered at the provider's facilities. Some services are provided at the customer's home or business. Lawn care, air conditioning and heating repair, and carpet cleaning are examples. Other services are delivered primarily at "arm's length," meaning no face-to-face contact occurs between the customer and the service provider. A number of equipment-based services are delivered at arm's length, including electric, online, cable television, and telephone services. Providing high-quality customer service at arm's length can be costly but essential in keeping customers satisfied and maintaining market share. For example, many airlines, although trying to cut costs, are also increasing spending on refurbishing their websites to better serve customers. Companies such as United Airlines and American Airlines are working on user-friendly websites to draw customers to their online services as an alternative to going through an online travel agent like Orbitz or Travelocity.[18]

Marketing channels for services are usually short and direct, meaning the producer delivers the service directly to the end user. Some services, however, use intermediaries. For example, travel agents facilitate the delivery of airline services, independent insurance agents participate in the marketing of a variety of insurance policies, and financial planners market investment services.

Service marketers are less concerned with warehousing and transportation than are goods marketers. They are, however, very concerned about inventory management, especially balancing supply and demand for services. The service characteristics of inseparability and level of customer contact contribute to the challenges of demand management. In some instances, service marketers use appointments and reservations as approaches for scheduling delivery of services. Health-care providers, attorneys, accountants, auto mechanics, and restaurants often use appointments or reservations to plan and pace delivery of their services. To increase the supply of a service, marketers use multiple service sites and also increase the number of contact service providers at each site. National and regional eye-care and hair-care services are examples.

To make delivery more accessible to customers and increase the supply of a service, as well as reduce labor costs, some service providers have replaced some contact personnel with equipment. In other words, they have changed a high-contact service into a low-contact one. The banking industry is an example. By installing ATMs, banks have increased production capacity and reduced customer contact. In addition, a number of automated banking services are now available by telephone 24 hours a day. Such services have helped lower costs by reducing the need for customer service representatives. Changing the delivery of services from human to equipment has created some problems, however. Some customers complain that automated services are less personal. When designing service delivery, marketers must pay attention to the degree of personalization customers desire.

## Promotion of Services

The intangibility of services results in several promotion-related challenges to service marketers. Since it may not be possible to depict the actual performance of a service in an advertisement or display it in a store, explaining a service to customers can be a difficult task. Promotion of services typically includes tangible cues that symbolize the service. For example, Trans America uses its pyramid-shaped building to symbolize strength, security, and reliability, important features associated with insurance and other financial services. Similarly, the cupped hands Allstate uses in its ads symbolize personalized service and trustworthy, caring representatives. Although these symbols have nothing to do with the actual services, they make it much easier for customers to understand the intangible attributes associated with insurance services. To make a service more tangible, advertisements for services often show pictures of facilities, equipment, and service personnel. Marketers may also promote their services as a tangible expression of consumers' lifestyles.

Compared with goods marketers, service providers are more likely to promote price, guarantees, performance documentation, availability, and training and certification of contact personnel. The International Smart Tan Network, a trade association for indoor tanning salons, offers a certification course in professional standards for tanning facility operators. The association encourages salons to promote their "Smart Tan Certification" in advertising and throughout the salon as a measure of quality training.[19] When preparing advertisements, service marketers are careful to use concrete, specific language to help make services more tangible in customers' minds. Bear Stearns, for example, advertises that it was voted "America's most admired securities company." They are also careful not to promise too much regarding their services so that customer expectations do not rise to unattainable levels.

**Promotion of Services**

Costa cruise lines promotes the price of its European cruises.

Through their actions, service contact personnel can be directly or indirectly involved in the personal selling of services. Personal selling is often important because personal influence can help the customer visualize the benefits of a given service. Because service contact personnel may engage in personal selling, some companies invest heavily in training. Best Buy, for example, spends 5 percent of its payroll on employee training. On a salesperson's first day on the job, he or she gets a four-hour classroom session focused on how to fit into the company's sales force and the basics for providing customer satisfaction.[20]

As noted earlier, intangibility makes experiencing a service prior to purchase difficult, if not impossible in some cases. A car can be test driven, a snack food can be sampled in a supermarket, and a new brand of bar soap can be mailed to customers as a free sample. Some services also can be offered on a trial basis at little or no risk to the customer, but a number of services cannot be sampled before purchase. Promotional programs that encourage trial use of insurance, health care, or auto repair are difficult to design because even after purchase of such services, assessing their quality may require a considerable length of time. For example, an individual may purchase auto insurance from the same provider for ten years before filing a claim, but the quality of the coverage is based primarily on how the customer is treated and protected when a claim is made.

Because of the heterogeneity and intangibility of services, word-of-mouth communication is important in service promotion. What other people say about a service provider can have a tremendous impact on whether an individual decides to use that provider. Some service marketers attempt to stimulate positive word-of-mouth communication by asking satisfied customers to tell their friends and associates about the service and may even provide incentives for doing so.

## Pricing of Services

Prices for services can be established on several different bases. The prices of pest control services, dry cleaning, carpet cleaning, and health consultations are usually based on the performance of specific tasks. Other service prices are based on time. For example, attorneys, consultants, counselors, piano teachers, and plumbers often charge by the hour or day.

Some services use demand-based pricing. When demand for a service is high, the price also is high; when demand for a service is low, so is the price. The perishability of services means that when demand is low, the unused capacity cannot be stored and therefore is lost forever. Every empty seat on an airline flight or in a movie theater represents lost revenue. Some services are very time sensitive in that a significant number of customers desire the service at a particular time. This point in time is called *peak demand*. A provider of time-sensitive services brings in most of its revenue during peak demand. For an airline, peak demand is usually early and late in the day; for cruise lines, peak demand occurs in the winter for Caribbean cruises and in the summer for Alaskan cruises. Providers of time-sensitive services often use demand-based pricing to manage the problem of balancing supply and demand. They charge top prices during peak demand and lower prices during off-peak demand to encourage more customers to use the service. This is why the price of a matinee movie is often half the price of the same movie shown at night. Major airlines maintain sophisticated databases to help them adjust ticket prices to fill as many seats as possible on every flight. On a single day, each airline makes thousands of fare changes to maximize the use of its seating capacity and thus maximize its revenues. To accomplish this objective, many airlines have to overbook flights and discount fares.

When services are offered to customers in a bundle, marketers must decide whether to offer the services at one price, price them separately, or use a combination of the two methods. For example, some hotels offer a package of services at one price, while others charge separately for the room, phone service, breakfast, and even in-room safes. Some service providers offer a one-price option for a specific bundle of services and make add-on bundles available at additional charges. For example, a number of cable television companies offer a standard package of channels for one price and offer add-on channel packages for additional charges. Telephone services, such as call waiting and caller ID, are frequently bundled and sold as a package for one price.

Because of the intangible nature of services, customers sometimes rely heavily on price as an indicator of quality. If customers perceive the available services in a service category as being similar in quality, and if the quality of such services is difficult to judge even after these services are purchased, customers may seek out the lowest-priced provider. For example, many customers seek auto insurance providers with the lowest rates. If the quality of different service providers is likely to vary, customers may rely heavily on the price-quality association. For example, if you have to have an appendectomy, will you choose the surgeon who charges an average price of $1,500 or the surgeon who will take your appendix out for $399?

For certain types of services, market conditions may limit how much can be charged for a specific service, especially if the services in this category are perceived as generic in nature. For example, the prices charged by a self-serve laundromat are likely to be limited by the going price for laundromat services in a given community. Also, state and local government regulations may reduce price flexibility. Such regulations may substantially control the prices charged for auto insurance, utilities, cable television service, and even housing rentals.

# Service Quality

**service quality** Customers' perception of how well a service meets or exceeds their expectations

**search qualities** Tangible attributes that can be judged before the purchase of a product

**experience qualities** Attributes that can be assessed only during purchase and consumption of a service

Delivery of high-quality services is one of the most important and most difficult tasks any service organization faces. Because of their characteristics, services are very difficult to evaluate. Hence customers must look closely at service quality when comparing services. **Service quality** is defined as customers' perceptions of how well a service meets or exceeds their expectations.[21] A survey by Customer Care Alliance and Arizona State University found that 70 percent of consumers responding experienced "customer rage," indicating they were "extremely" or "very" upset about a negative service experience. More than 33 percent indicated they had raised their voices, while 13 percent admitted to using profanity when interacting with customer service representatives. While 75 percent of respondents wanted an explanation of why the problem occurred, only 18 percent got an explanation, and only 25 percent heard "I'm sorry" from a customer service representative.[22] Note that customers, not the organization, evaluate service quality. This distinction is critical because it forces service marketers to examine quality from the customer's viewpoint. Thus, it is important for service organizations to determine what customers expect and then develop service products that meet or exceed those expectations.

## snapshot

**Is customer service improving?**

Do you think the quality of customer service is better than 5 years ago?

Don't know 4%

About the same 40%

Yes 29%

No 27%

Source: Data from DHL Roper Public Affairs and Media Survey. Margin of error ± 3 percentage points.

### Customer Evaluation of Service Quality

The biggest obstacle for customers in evaluating service quality is the intangible nature of the service. How can customers evaluate something they cannot see, feel, taste, smell, or hear? Evaluation of a good is much easier because all goods possess **search qualities,** tangible attributes such as color, style, size, feel, or fit that can be evaluated prior to purchase. Trying on a new coat and taking a car for a test drive are examples of how customers evaluate search qualities. Services, on the other hand, have very few search qualities; instead, they abound in experience and credence qualities. **Experience qualities** are attributes, such as taste, satisfaction, or pleasure, which can be assessed only during the purchase and consumption of a service.[23] Restaurants and vacations are examples of services high in experi-

LONGER GOODBYES

SHORTER LINES

CHECK-IN KIOSKS

▲Delta
good goes around

*Earn 1,000 bonus SkyMiles® for each flown round-trip ticket purchased on*
delta.com

**Quality of Service**

Delta promises shorter lines, allowing longer goodbyes.

**credence qualities** Attributes that customers may be unable to evaluate even after purchasing and consuming a service

ence qualities. **Credence qualities** are attributes that customers may be unable to evaluate even after the purchase and consumption of the service. Examples of services high in credence qualities are surgical operations, automobile repairs, and legal representation. Most consumers lack the knowledge or skills to evaluate the quality of these types of services. Consequently they must place a great deal of faith in the integrity and competence of the service provider.

Despite the difficulties in evaluating quality, service quality may be the only way customers can choose one service over another. For this reason, service marketers live or die by understanding how consumers judge service quality. Table 14.2 defines five dimensions consumers use when evaluating service quality: tangibles, reliability, responsiveness, assurance, and empathy. Note that all of these dimensions have links to employee performance. Of the five, reliability is the most important in determining customer evaluations of service quality.[24]

Service marketers pay a great deal of attention to the tangibles of service quality. Tangible elements, such as the appearance of facilities and employees, are often the only aspects of a service that can be viewed before purchase and consumption. Indeed, research has found that a service provider's physical facilities have a very strong influence on customers' perceptions of quality.[25] Therefore, service marketers must ensure that these tangible elements are consistent with the overall image of the service.

Except for the tangibles dimension, the criteria customers use to judge service quality are intangible. For instance, how does a customer judge reliability? Since dimensions such as reliability cannot be examined with the senses, customers must rely on other ways of judging service. One of the most important factors in customer judgments of service quality is service expectations. Service expectations are influenced by past experiences with the service, word-of-mouth communication from other customers, and the service company's own advertising. For example, customers are usually eager to try a new restaurant, especially when friends recommend

## table 14.2   DIMENSIONS OF SERVICE QUALITY

| Dimension | Evaluation Criteria | Examples |
|---|---|---|
| Tangibles: Physical evidence of the service | Appearance of physical facilities Appearance of service personnel Tools or equipment used to provide the service | A clean and professional-looking doctor's office A clean and neatly attired repairperson The freshness of food in a restaurant The equipment used in a medical exam |
| Reliability: Consistency and dependability in performing the service | Accuracy of billing or recordkeeping Performing services when promised | An accurate bank statement A confirmed hotel reservation An airline flight departing and arriving on time |
| Responsiveness: Willingness or readiness of employees to provide the service | Returning customer phone calls Providing prompt service Handling urgent requests | A server refilling a customer's cup of tea without being asked An ambulance arriving within three minutes |
| Assurance: Knowledge/competence of employees and ability to convey trust and confidence | Knowledge and skills of employees Company name and reputation Personal characteristics of employees | A highly trained financial adviser A known and respected service provider A doctor's bedside manner |
| Empathy: Caring and individual attention provided by employees | Listening to customer needs Caring about customers' interests Providing personalized attention | A store employee listening to and trying to understand a customer's complaint A nurse counseling a heart patient |

**Sources:** Adapted from Leonard L. Berry and A. Parasuraman, *Marketing Services: Competing through Quality* (New York: Free Press, 1991 ); Valarie A. Zeithaml, A. Parasuraman, and Leonard L. Berry, *Delivering Quality Service: Balancing Customer Perceptions and Expectations* (New York: Free Press, 1990); A. Parasuraman, Leonard L. Berry, and Valarie A. Zeithaml, "An Empirical Examination of Relationships in an Extended Service Quality Model," *Marketing Science Institute Working Paper Series,* Report no. 90–112 (Cambridge, MA: Marketing Science Institute, 1990), p. 29.

it. These same customers may have also seen advertisements placed by the restaurant. As a result, they have an idea of what to expect when they visit the restaurant for the first time. When they finally dine there, the quality they experience will change the expectations they have for their next visit. That is why providing consistently high service quality is important. If the quality of a restaurant, or of any service, begins to deteriorate, customers will alter their own expectations and change their word-of-mouth communication to others accordingly.

### Delivering Exceptional Service Quality

Providing high-quality service on a consistent basis is very difficult. All consumers have experienced examples of poor service: late flight departures and arrivals, inattentive restaurant servers, rude bank employees, long lines. Obviously it is impossible for a service organization to ensure exceptional service quality 100 percent of the time. However, an organization can take many steps to increase the likelihood of providing high-quality service. First, though, the service company must consider the four factors that affect service quality: (1) analysis of customer expectations, (2) service quality specifications, (3) employee performance, and (4) management of service expectations (see Figure 14.2 on p. 390).[26]

**Analysis of Customer Expectations.** Providers need to understand customer expectations when designing a service to meet or exceed those expectations. Only then can they deliver good service. Customers usually have two levels of expectations: desired and acceptable. The desired level of expectations is what the customer really wants. If this level of expectations is provided, the customer will be very satisfied. The acceptable level of expectations is what the customer views as adequate. The difference between these two levels of expectations is called the customer's *zone of tolerance.*[27]

**figure 14.2**

## SERVICE QUALITY MODEL

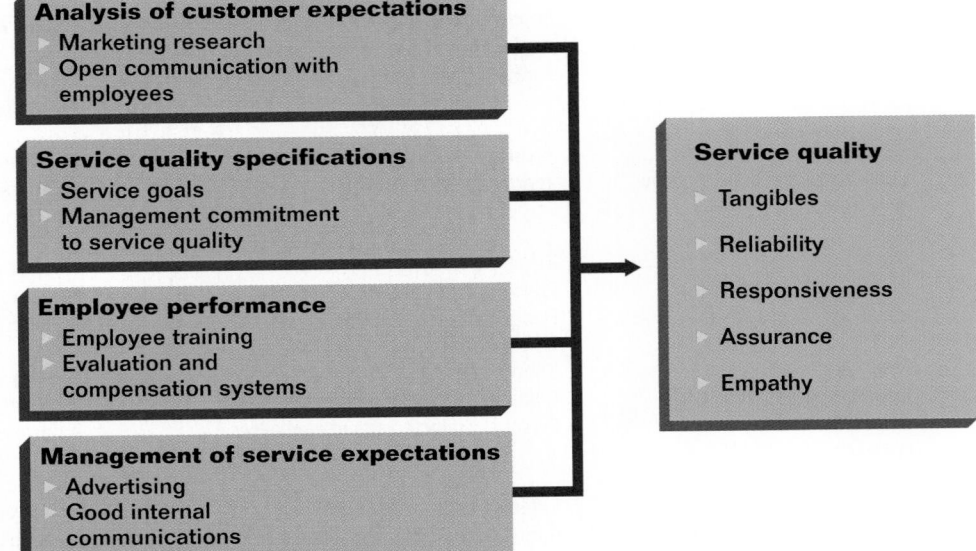

**Source:** Adapted from A. Parasuraman, Leonard L. Berry, and Valarie A. Zeithaml, "An Empirical Examination of Relationships in an Extended Service Quality Model," *Marketing Science Institute Working Paper Series,* Report no. 90–112, 1990. Reprinted by permission of Marketing Science Institute, and the authors.

Service companies sometimes use marketing research, such as surveys and focus groups, to discover customer needs and expectations. For instance, Ritz-Carlton Hotels conducted focus-group research to find out the level of service expected by high-tech executives and entrepreneurs, the target audience for its Silicon Valley resort hotel. Based on this analysis, the resort began offering guests around-the-clock tech support as well as high-speed web access, in-room video game consoles, safes to store laptop computers, and cellphone rentals.[28] Other service marketers, especially restaurants, use comment cards on which customers can complain or provide suggestions. Still another approach is to ask employees. Because customer contact employees interact daily with customers, they are in good positions to know what customers want from the company. Service managers should regularly interact with their employees by asking their opinions on the best way to serve customers.

**Service Quality Specifications.** Once an organization understands its customers' needs, it must establish goals to help ensure good service delivery. These goals, or service specifications, are typically set in terms of employee or machine performance. For example, a bank may require its employees to conform to a dress code. Likewise, the bank may require that all incoming phone calls be answered by the third ring. Specifications such as these can be very important in providing quality service as long as they are tied to the needs expressed by customers.

Perhaps the most critical aspect of service quality specifications is managers' commitment to service quality. Service managers who are committed to quality become role models for all employees in the organization. Such commitment motivates customer contact employees to comply with service specifications. It is crucial that all managers within the organization embrace this commitment, especially frontline managers, who are much closer to customers than higher-level managers.

**Employee Performance.** Once an organization sets service quality standards and managers are committed to them, the organization must find ways to ensure that customer contact employees perform their jobs well. Contact employees in most service industries (bank tellers, flight attendants, servers, sales clerks, etc.) are often the least trained and lowest-paid members of the organization. Service organizations must realize that contact employees are the most important link to the customer, and thus their performance is critical to customer perceptions of service quality. The way to ensure that employees perform well is to train them well so they understand how to do their jobs. Providing information about customers, service specifications, and the organization itself during the training promotes this understanding. The year-old company When Pigs Fly helps managers equip frontline workers at amusement parks, fairs, carnivals, and other amusement-related facilities with the training, tools, encouragement, and motivation they need to do their jobs well. Much of their training is targeted at the Generation Xers who staff these facilities. "Hospitality, customer service, safety—these things don't come naturally to kids," says company co-owner Patty Beazley.[29]

The evaluation and compensation system the organization uses also plays a part in employee performance. Many service employees are evaluated and rewarded on the basis of output measures, such as sales volume (automobile salespeople) or a low error rate (bank tellers). But systems using output measures overlook other major aspects of job performance, including friendliness, teamwork, effort, and customer satisfaction. These customer-oriented measures of performance may be a better basis for evaluation and reward. In fact, a number of service marketers use customer satisfaction ratings to determine a portion of service employee compensation.

**Management of Service Expectations.** Because expectations are so significant in customer evaluations of service quality, service companies recognize they must set realistic expectations about the service they can provide. They can set these expectations through advertising and good internal communication. In their advertisements, service companies make promises about the kind of service they will deliver. As already noted, a service company is forced to make promises because the intangibility of services prevents the organization from showing the benefits in the advertisement.

# Stay Tuned: Nick Has the Right Mix

Cable television network Nickelodeon—Nick for short—has to satisfy a number of tough audiences. Toddlers want fun programs such as *Blue's Clues* and the bilingual *Dora the Explorer*. School-age viewers enjoy wacky cartoons such as *Jimmie Neutron*. Younger teens tune in for programs like *All That*, while older teens watch the celebrity specials. And parents want to be sure that Nick's programs entertain and educate without violence or sex. Nick delivers for all these audiences, with ratings that top the list of basic cable networks.

Nick is known for its in-depth marketing research and its careful control of animation and production. Of course, no one can predict which shows will resonate with viewers, and the network has had both successes and disappointments. One surprise was the popularity of *SpongeBob SquarePants*, which first aired as a weekend series but has now become a Nick staple.

Nick has been able to profit not only from selling advertising time but also from licensing its brand for an ever-widening mix of goods and services. One of Nick's newest licensing ventures is a theme resort in Florida, the Nickelodeon Family Suites by Holiday Inn. In addition to waterslides, pools, and game rooms, the hotel offers breakfast with Nick characters and stages live shows starring Nick characters. Nick believes that viewers who enjoy its characters will look forward to staying at a Nick-themed hotel and is working with Holiday Inn to open several more resorts soon. Can the resort deliver the kind of service that is consistent with the Nick brand? Stay tuned.

## Where do you want to be?

Find your perfect place. It's easy with RE/MAX.

Whether you're dreaming of a second home in a faraway land – or your very first house right around the corner – just tell RE/MAX what you want.

RE/MAX agents average more experience than other agents. They know their markets and they care enough to get to know you, too.

Equal opportunity employers.     051790
©2006 RE/MAX International, Inc. All rights reserved.
Each RE/MAX® real estate office is independently owned and operated.

Nobody sells more real estate than RE/MAX. So wherever you are or want to be, we'll be there for you.

Visit remax.com for more online home listings than ever.

**RE/MAX**

Outstanding Agents. Outstanding Results.®
**remax.com®**

**Service Expectations**
Remax sets service expectations by asking customers to imagine the ideal living space.

However, the advertiser should not promise more than it can deliver. Doing so will likely mean disappointed customers.

To deliver on promises made, a company needs to have thorough internal communication among its departments, especially management, advertising, and store operations. Assume, for example, that a restaurant's radio advertisements guarantee service within five minutes or the meal is free. If top management or the advertising department fails to inform store operations about the five-minute guarantee, the restaurant will very likely fail to meet its customers' service expectations. Even though customers might appreciate a free meal, the restaurant will lose some credibility as well as revenue.

As mentioned earlier, word-of-mouth communication from other customers also shapes customer expectations. However, service companies cannot manage this "advertising" directly. The best way to ensure positive word-of-mouth communication is to provide exceptional service quality. It has been estimated that customers tell four times as many people about bad service as they do about good service.

# Nonprofit Marketing

**nonprofit marketing** Marketing activities conducted to achieve some goal other than ordinary business goals such as profit, market share, or return on investment

**Nonprofit marketing** includes marketing activities conducted by individuals and organizations to achieve some goal other than ordinary business goals such as profit, market share, or return on investment. Nonprofit marketing is divided into two categories: nonprofit-organization marketing and social marketing. Nonprofit-organization marketing is the use of marketing concepts and techniques by organizations whose goals do not include making profits. Social marketing promotes social causes, such as AIDS research and recycling.

Most of the previously discussed concepts and approaches to service products also apply to nonprofit organizations. Indeed, many nonprofit organizations provide mainly service products. In this section, we examine the concept of nonprofit marketing to determine how it differs from marketing activities in for-profit business organizations. We also explore the marketing objectives of nonprofit organizations and the development of their product strategies.

## How Is Nonprofit Marketing Different?

Many nonprofit organizations strive for effective marketing activities. Charitable organizations and supporters of social causes are major nonprofit marketers in this country. Political parties, unions, religious sects, and fraternal organizations also perform marketing activities, but they are not considered businesses. Whereas the chief beneficiary of a business enterprise is whoever owns or holds stock in it, in theory the only beneficiaries of a nonprofit organization are its clients, its members, or the public at large. The American Museum of Natural History, for example, is a non-profit service organization.

Nonprofit organizations have greater opportunities for creativity than most for-profit business organizations, but trustees or board members of nonprofit organiza-

**SHARE WHAT YOU KNOW. BECOME A MENTOR.**

It doesn't take special skills to mentor a young person—just a willingness
to listen, offer encouragement, and share what you've learned about life.
Mentoring programs in your community need more volunteers.

Visit **MENTORING.org**

Harvard School of Public Health  •  MENTOR  •  MetLife Foundation

**Nonprofit**

Nonprofit organizations promote
volunteer programs such as mentoring.

tions are likely to have difficulty judging the performance of the trained professionals they oversee. It is harder for administrators to evaluate the performance of professors or social workers than it is for sales managers to evaluate the performance of salespeople in a for-profit organization.

Another way nonprofit marketing differs from for-profit marketing is that nonprofit marketing is sometimes quite controversial. Nonprofit organizations such as Greenpeace, the National Rifle Association, and the National Organization for Women spend lavishly on lobbying efforts to persuade Congress, the White House, and even the courts to support their interests, in part because not all of society agrees with their aims. However, marketing as a field of study does not attempt to state what an organization's goals should be or to debate the issue of nonprofit versus for-profit business goals. Marketing tries only to provide a body of knowledge and concepts to help further an organization's goals. Individuals must decide whether they approve or disapprove of a particular organization's goal orientation. Most marketers would agree that profit and consumer satisfaction are appropriate goals for business enterprises, but would probably disagree considerably about the goals of a controversial nonprofit organization.

## Nonprofit Marketing Objectives

The basic aim of nonprofit organizations is to obtain a desired response from a target market. The response could be a change in values, a financial contribution, the donation of services, or some other type of exchange. Nonprofit marketing objectives are shaped by the nature of the exchange and the goals of the organization. These objectives should state the rationale for the organization's existence. An organization that defines its marketing objective as providing a product can be left without a purpose if the product becomes obsolete. However, servicing and adapting to the perceived needs and wants of a target public, or market, enhances an organization's chance to survive and achieve its goals.

## Developing Nonprofit Marketing Strategies

Nonprofit organizations develop marketing strategies by defining and analyzing a target market and creating and maintaining a total marketing mix that appeals to that market.

**Target Markets.** We must revise the concept of target markets slightly to apply it to nonprofit organizations. Whereas a business seeks out target groups that are potential purchasers of its product, a nonprofit organization may attempt to serve many diverse groups. For our purposes, a **target public** is a collective of individuals who have an interest in or a concern about an organization, a product, or a social cause. The terms *target market* and *target public* are difficult to distinguish for many nonprofit organizations. The target public of the Partnership for a Drug Free America consists of parents, adults, and concerned teenagers. However, the target market for the organization's advertisements consists of potential and current drug users. When an organization is concerned about changing values or obtaining a response from the public, it views the public as a market.[30]

In nonprofit marketing, direct consumers of the product are called **client publics** and indirect consumers are called **general publics**.[31] For example, the client public for a university is its student body, and its general public includes parents, alumni, and trustees. The client public usually receives most of the attention when an organization develops a marketing strategy.

**Developing a Marketing Mix.** A marketing mix strategy limits alternatives and directs marketing activities toward achieving organizational goals. The strategy should include a blueprint for making decisions about product, distribution, promotion, and price. These decision variables should be blended to serve the target market.

In developing the product, nonprofit organizations usually deal with ideas and services. Problems may evolve when an organization fails to define what it is providing. What product, for example, does the Peace Corps provide? Its services include vocational training, health services, nutritional assistance, and community development. It also markets the ideas of international cooperation and the implementation of U.S. foreign policy. The product of the Peace Corps is more difficult to define than the average business product. As indicated in the first part of this chapter, services are intangible and therefore need special marketing efforts. The marketing of ideas and concepts is likewise more abstract than the marketing of tangibles, and much effort is required to present benefits.

Distribution decisions in nonprofit organizations relate to how ideas and services will be made available to clients. If the product is an idea, selecting the right media to communicate the idea will facilitate distribution. By nature, services consist of assistance, convenience, and availability. Availability is thus part of the total service. Making a product such as health services available calls for knowledge of such retailing concepts as site location analysis.

Developing a channel of distribution to coordinate and facilitate the flow of nonprofit products to clients is a necessary task, but in a nonprofit setting the traditional concept of the marketing channel may need to be revised. The independent wholesalers available to a business enterprise do not exist in most nonprofit situations. Instead, a very short channel—nonprofit organization to client—is the norm because production and consumption of ideas and services are often simultaneous.

Making promotional decisions may be the first sign that a nonprofit organization is performing marketing activities. Non-

**target public** A collective of individuals who have an interest in or concern about an organization, product, or social cause

**client publics** Direct consumers of a product of a nonbusiness organization

**general publics** Indirect consumers of a product of a nonbusiness organization

---

## marketing ENTREPRENEURS

**Ercan Tutal**

HIS BUSINESS: The Alternative Camp for Disabled Individuals

SUCCESS: Organization has served more than 200,000 people

Located in Turkey, the Alternative Camp is a nonprofit organization that provides disabled persons with opportunities to participate in underwater sports such as diving. Tutal's organization has served more than 200,000 people and is funded entirely from the donations of generous businesses. So successful is his organization that the World Young Business Association granted him the Social Responsibility Award, and he recently was chosen to take part in the Olympic ceremonies as a torch bearer.

profit organizations use advertising and publicity to communicate with clients and the public. Direct mail remains the primary means of fundraising for social services, such as those provided by the Red Cross and Special Olympics. Some nonprofits use the immediacy of the Internet to reach fundraising and promotional goals. Nonprofits use the Internet as a form of e-commerce to accept online gifts and conduct online auctions, and many use application service providers to maintain software and save money.[32] Many nonprofit organizations also use personal selling, although they may call it by another name. Churches and charities rely on personal selling when they send volunteers to recruit new members or request donations. The U.S. Army uses personal selling when its recruiting officers attempt to persuade men and women to enlist. Special events to obtain funds, communicate ideas, or provide services are also effective promotional activities. Amnesty International, for example, has held worldwide concert tours featuring well-known musical artists to raise funds and increase public awareness of political prisoners around the world.

Although product and promotional techniques may require only slight modification when applied to nonprofit organizations, pricing is generally quite different and decision making is more complex. The different pricing concepts the nonprofit organization faces include pricing in user and donor markets. Two types of monetary pricing exist: *fixed* and *variable*. There may be a fixed fee for users, or the price may vary depending on the user's ability to pay. When a donation-seeking organization will accept a contribution of any size, it is using variable pricing.

**opportunity cost** The value of the benefit given up by choosing one alternative over another

The broadest definition of price (valuation) must be used to develop nonprofit marketing strategies. Financial price, an exact dollar value, may or may not be charged for a nonprofit product. Economists recognize the giving up of alternatives as a cost. **Opportunity cost** is the value of the benefit given up by selecting one alternative over another. According to this traditional economic view of price, if a nonprofit organization persuades someone to donate time to a cause or to change his or her behavior, the alternatives given up are a cost to (or a price paid by) the individual. Volunteers who answer phones for a university counseling service or a suicide hotline, for example, give up the time they could spend studying or doing other things and the income they might earn from working at a for-profit business organization.

For other nonprofit organizations, financial price is an important part of the marketing mix. Nonprofit organizations today are raising money by increasing the prices of their services or are starting to charge for services if they have not done so before. They are using marketing research to determine what kinds of products people will pay for. Pricing strategies of nonprofit organizations often stress public and client welfare over equalization of costs and revenues. If additional funds are needed to cover costs, the organization may solicit donations, contributions, or grants.

## SUMMARY

Services are intangible products involving deeds, performances, or efforts that cannot be physically possessed. They are the result of applying human or mechanical efforts to people or objects. Services are a growing part of the U.S. economy. They have six fundamental characteristics: intangibility, inseparability of production and consumption, perishability, heterogeneity, client-based relationships, and customer contact. Intangibility means that a service cannot be seen, touched, tasted, or smelled. Inseparability refers to the fact that the production of a service cannot be separated from its consumption by customers. Perishability means unused service capacity of one time period cannot be stored for future use. Heterogeneity is variation in service quality. Client-based rela-

tionships are interactions with customers that lead to the repeated use of a service over time. Customer contact is the interaction between providers and customers needed to deliver a service.

Core services are the basic service experiences customers expect; supplementary services are those that relate to and support core services. Because of the characteristics of services, service marketers face several challenges in developing and managing marketing mixes. To address the problem of intangibility, marketers use cues that help assure customers about the quality of their services. The development and management of service products are also influenced by the service characteristics of inseparability and level of customer contact. Some services require that customers come to the service provider's facility; others are delivered with no face-to-face contact. Marketing channels for services are usually short and direct, but some services employ intermediaries. Service marketers are less concerned with warehousing and transportation than are goods marketers, but inventory management and balancing supply and demand for services are important issues. The intangibility of services poses several promotion-related challenges. Advertisements with tangible cues that symbolize the service and depict facilities, equipment, and personnel help address these challenges. Service providers are likely to promote price, guarantees, performance documentation, availability, and training and certification of contact personnel. Through their actions, service personnel can be involved directly or indirectly in the personal selling of services.

Intangibility makes it difficult to experience a service before purchasing it. Heterogeneity and intangibility make word-of-mouth communication an important means of promotion. The prices of services are based on task performance, time required, or demand. Perishability creates difficulties in balancing supply and demand because unused capacity cannot be stored. The point in time when a significant number of customers desire a service is called peak demand; demand-based pricing results in higher prices charged for services during peak demand. When services are offered in a bundle, marketers must decide whether to offer them at one price, price them separately, or use a combination of the two methods. Because services are intangible, customers may rely on price as a sign of quality. For some services, market conditions may dictate the price; for others, state and local government regulations may limit price flexibility.

Service quality is customers' perception of how well a service meets or exceeds their expectations. Although one of the most important aspects of service marketing, service quality is very difficult for customers to evaluate because the nature of services renders benefits impossible to assess before actual purchase and consumption. These benefits include experience qualities, such as taste, satisfaction, or pleasure, and credence qualities, which customers may be unable to evaluate even after consumption. When com-

peting services are very similar, service quality may be the only way for customers to distinguish among them. Service marketers can increase the quality of their services by following the four-step process of understanding customer expectations, setting service specifications, ensuring good employee performance, and managing customers' service expectations.

Nonprofit marketing is marketing aimed at nonbusiness goals, including social causes. It uses most of the same concepts and approaches that apply to business situations. Whereas the chief beneficiary of a business enterprise is whoever owns or holds stock in it, the beneficiary of a nonprofit enterprise should be its clients, its members, or its public at large. The goals of a nonprofit organization reflect its unique philosophy or mission. Some nonprofit organizations have very controversial goals, but many organizations exist to further generally accepted social causes.

The marketing objective of nonprofit organizations is to obtain a desired response from a target market. Developing a nonprofit marketing strategy consists of defining and analyzing a target market and creating and maintaining a marketing mix. In nonprofit marketing, the product is usually an idea or a service. Distribution is aimed at the communication of ideas and the delivery of services. The result is a very short marketing channel. Promotion is very important to nonprofit marketing. Nonprofit organizations use advertising, publicity, and personal selling to communicate with clients and the public. Direct mail remains the primary means of fundraising for social services, but some nonprofits use the Internet for fundraising and promotional activities. Price is more difficult to define in nonprofit marketing because of opportunity costs and the difficulty of quantifying the values exchanged.

**ACE self-test**

Please visit the student website at **www.prideferrell.com** for ACE Self-Test questions that will help you prepare for exams.

## IMPORTANT TERMS

| | | | |
|---|---|---|---|
| Intangibility | Client-based relationships | Experience qualities | Client publics |
| Inseparability | Customer contact | Credence qualities | General publics |
| Perishability | Service quality | Nonprofit marketing | Opportunity cost |
| Heterogeneity | Search qualities | Target public | |

## DISCUSSION & REVIEW QUESTIONS

1. How important are services in the U.S. economy?

2. Identify and discuss the major characteristics of services.

3. For each marketing mix element, which service characteristics are most likely to have an impact? Explain.

4. What is service quality? Why do customers find it difficult to judge service quality?

5. Identify and discuss the five components of service quality. How do customers evaluate these components?

6. What is the significance of tangibles in service marketing?

7. How do search, experience, and credence qualities affect the way customers view and evaluate services?

8. What steps should a service company take to provide exceptional service quality?

9. How does nonprofit marketing differ from marketing in for-profit organizations?

10. What are the differences among clients, publics, and customers? What is the difference between a target public and a target market?

11. Discuss the development of a marketing strategy for a university. What marketing decisions must be made as the strategy is developed?

## APPLICATION QUESTIONS

1. Imagine you are the owner of a new service business. What is your service? Be creative. What are some of the most important considerations in developing the service, training salespeople, and communicating about your service to potential customers?

2. As discussed in this chapter, the characteristics of services affect the development of marketing mixes for services. Choose a specific service and explain how each marketing mix element could be affected by these service characteristics.

3. In advertising services, a company must often use symbols to represent the offered product. Identify three service organizations you have seen in outdoor, television, or magazine advertising. What symbols do these organizations use to represent their services? What message do the symbols convey to potential customers?

4. Delivering consistently high-quality service is difficult for service marketers. Describe an instance when you received high-quality service and an instance when you experienced low-quality service. What contributed to your perception of high quality? Of low quality?

1. Service marketing is sometimes associated with franchise chains that deliver products to fulfill a global need in the marketplace. Though there are magazines that rank the leading franchisers, an examination of the top 50 gives the analyst information for understanding the nature of franchising. Prepare a brief report based on information from the *Entrepreneur* Top Global Franchises. This ranking can be accessed by using the search term "top 200 franchisers" at **http://globaledge.msu.edu/ibrd**. In particular, which company has the highest startup costs? Given what you know, do you think the startup costs required for this company are justifiable?

2. To be a better "social enterprise" and deliver quality services, firms must better understand, communicate, and respond to customers. However, sometimes companies fail to interact with and help improve the communities they service. According to a report titled "The Three Ds of Customer Experience" by the Harvard Business School (HBS), as firms grow larger, they sometimes fall into a dominance trap. This research can be accessed by using the search term "social enterprise" at **http://globaledge.msu.edu/ibrd**. Once you reach the HBS website, use the search term "dominance trap." The relevant research is entitled "The Three Ds of Customer Experience." Based on this paper, define the concept of a dominance trap. Also, define and present three imperatives that may prevent this from occurring in a firm.

## INTERNET Exercise

### Matchmaker.com

The Internet abounds with dating sites, but few offer as much information about their members as Matchmaker.com. Matchmaker profiles are gleaned from a survey of some 60 question and essay responses. Check out the site at **www.matchmaker.com**.

1. Classify Matchmaker.com's product in terms of its position on the service continuum.
2. How does Matchmaker.com enhance customer service and foster better client-based relationships through its Internet marketing efforts?
3. Discuss the degree to which experience and credence qualities exist in the services offered by Matchmaker.com and other dating websites.

## Video Case 14.1    The New Wave of Marketing at New England Aquarium

From sea turtles and seals to penguins and porpoises, the nonprofit New England Aquarium houses an incredibly diverse array of creatures. Its 200,000-gallon tank, situated on a busy Boston wharf, serves as an underwater microcosm of the world's sea life. The aquarium wants to appeal to the broadest possible client and general publics. Its mission is "to present, promote, and protect the world of water." In line with this mission, the organization's products are both ideas (education and research) and services (conservation efforts and museum exhibits).

More than 1 million visitors annually stream through the aquarium's doors to see the sharks, watch divers feed the fish, listen to a lecture about penguins, or enjoy a special feature at the IMAX theater. Some visit the Aquarium Medical Center, an onsite hospital where specialists care for the facility's marine animals and treat sick or stranded animals from nearby beaches. Others opt for one of the Science at Sea boat rides or the half-day whale-watching cruises. The organization also maintains an aquatic exploration center in Rhode Island and a porpoise rehabilitation facility south of Boston.

Marketing brings in the money needed to support all these activities. In addition to admission fees and sales of branded merchandise, the aquarium operates a café, rents its premises for private parties, and solicits donations from individuals and businesses. Corporate sponsorships help pay for a wide range of educational activities. For example, EMC Corporation sponsors the Penguin Outreach Program, paying for Roast Beef the penguin to travel to local institutions in a special temperature-controlled van. It is also the sponsor of the Blue Lobster Bowl, a fast-paced quiz show in which high school students compete to show their knowledge of ocean-related subjects.

The Internet is an important and cost-effective marketing tool for the aquarium. Members of the public

can browse its website (**www.neaq.org**) to find out about current exhibits, scan the calendar of upcoming programs, donate money, become a member, or check the hours of operation and ticket prices. The website also explains the organization's many volunteer opportunities. Its staff of 1,000 volunteers, one of the nonprofit world's largest, contributes 100,000 hours of service yearly working with animals, exhibits, and programs. Many high school and college students volunteer so they can try out possible career choices. Hundreds of adults volunteer part-time as well.

The aquarium markets itself to volunteers because it needs assistance in nearly every department and has a very limited payroll budget. Therefore, Maureen C. Hentz, director of volunteer programs, is always looking for volunteers to supplement the paid staff in education, administration, animal rescue, and other areas. Hentz and her staff maintain an active schedule, going out into the community to build awareness of the aquarium's services and encouraging people to volunteer their time.

Admission fees help offset the cost of expanding the marine life collection, rehabilitating injured whales, and other expenses. However, the aquarium faces a delicate balancing act when pricing tickets. If admission fees seem too high, people may not visit or may visit less often. On the other hand, if admission fees are too low, the organization may not generate the revenue needed to cover ongoing operating costs and repay its considerable debt. The aquarium recently decided to raise its adult admission fees after attendance fell below expected levels because of a sluggish local economy and a drop in tourism. Financial concerns also caused the organization to cancel a $125 million expansion project that would have added 100,000 square feet of exhibit space to the Boston location.

Although the aquarium welcomes publicity about its services, it sometimes asks for special cooperation from media representatives. When the organization planned to release rescued seals into the ocean after rehabilitation, for example, it invited media representatives to cover the event. However, it requested that reporters not reveal the exact location in advance because of concerns that crowds would gather, jeopardizing a successful release.

Thanks to its new wave of marketing, the aquarium is fulfilling its mission. It is now Boston's top-drawing attraction. The IMAX theater remains one of its most popular features, and the whale-watching cruises usually depart with a full passenger load. Weekends are the busiest time, when neighborhood families and out-of-town visitors alike enjoy the world of water brought to life. The aquarium continues its leadership position in protecting marine life and conserving the aquatic environment.[33]

### Questions for Discussion

1. Who can be considered the aquarium's client public?
2. In addition to using the Web and attending community meetings, what other marketing efforts would help Maureen Hentz attract new aquarium volunteers?
3. How could the aquarium use pricing to manage its attendance?

## Case 14.2     Allstate: We're All in Good Hands

Customers value high-quality service and the service companies that provide it. The Allstate Corporation, the largest public personal insurance company in the United States, is one such service provider. The company offers 13 lines of insurance including auto, property, life, and business. It also offers retirement, investment, and banking services. Allstate serves about 17 million households and has offices in 49 U.S. states and in Canada. Allstate believes in bringing its customers value and prides itself on doing more than is expected of it in all areas. In the areas of customer relationships and social responsibility, Allstate stands out.

Allstate works hard to bring value to customers and all other stakeholders. The company has a strong commitment to high ethical standards. In today's climate of corporate scandal, this is a valuable asset for the company and builds strong long-term relationships with shareholders. The company has also managed and invested its capital in an ethical manner, thereby providing shareholders with long-term financial stability. Allstate is also focusing on building long-term customers.

In 2004, more than 1 million customers switched their auto insurance coverage to Allstate, and now the company is working to keep them. One way the company is retaining happy customers is by offering excellent claim management services. These services both strengthen the connection between the company and its customers (customers know they're in good hands) and

keep costs low. Allstate also focuses on streamlining its relationships with all individuals working with the company—employees and independent agents alike—so that they can then better provide clear, effective help to customers. They believe strongly in being good corporate citizens.

In addition, the company is committed to giving back to individuals and communities. For example, contributions from its subsidiaries fund an independent charity—the Allstate Foundation—which donates millions of dollars each year to causes that focus on three specific areas: economic empowerment; tolerance, inclusion, and diversity; and safe and vital communities. Each year the foundation also donates $1 million to nonprofit organizations through Agency Hands in the Community grants.

In 2005 both the Allstate Corporation and the Allstate Foundation came to the aid of those affected by hurricanes Katrina and Rita and the tsunami in South Asia, India, and Indonesia. In the wake of these devastating disasters, the Allstate Foundation established a $1 million Allstate Foundation Hurricane Recovery Fund designed to help hurricane victims begin to rebuild. The Allstate Corporation contributed $25,000 to the National Council of LaRaza Katrina Relief Fund and $50,000 to the Bush-Clinton Katrina Fund. It also agreed to match donations to the Black-AmericaWeb.com Relief Fund up to $250,000, and to donate $1,000 to the American Red Cross Hurricane

Katrina Relief Fund for each field goal completed by Allstate participating schools for the 2005 college football season. These contributions provided food, shelter, and schooling to those affected, as well as support to those who have offered to help hurricane victims. These significant donations came just months after the company raised $1.5 million for the Tsunami Disaster Recovery Fund through employee and agency donations and company-matched contributions.

Allstate also invests in municipal bonds and low-interest loans to support and grow urban neighborhoods. In addition, it is committed to helping the environment. At the company headquarters, lighting has been replaced both in and outside the buildings to cut down on energy consumption. The company is part of the Climate Resolve initiative—aimed to reduce greenhouse gas intensity. Employees who make use of public transportation are rewarded with subsidized tickets and complimentary shuttles to train stations. Allstate also works primarily with suppliers using recycled materials.

Seventy-five-year-old Allstate comes to the aid of not only its customers but also the global community at large. Edward M. Liddy, chairman and chief executive officer, explains, "One of the most rewarding aspects of working at Allstate is to see the way our employees and agencies help others in a time of crisis. I know it is what we do as a business, but it's more than a business for Allstaters." This commitment rings true not only in times of disaster but in the day-to-day workings of the company and its relationships with its customers and shareholders.[34]

## Questions for Discussion

1. Classify Allstate's product in terms of its position on the service continuum.
2. Describe Allstate's primary products using the six basic characteristics of services.
3. Discuss the degree to which experience and credence qualities exist in Allstate's services.

## Strategic Case 5   Radio Goes Sky-High at XM Satellite Radio

XM Satellite Radio is changing the world of radio. Until the company started on the road to static-free radio in 1997, when it paid more than $80 million for a federal license to broadcast digital radio, AM and FM radio stations had been free to all listeners, mainly because of commercial sponsorship. However, XM believed that commuters—and anyone else traveling by car for long periods—would be willing to pay for perfect 24-hour radio reception and dozens of channel choices anywhere in the United States. (After all, millions of viewers were paying for cable television service, even though they could watch broadcast television for free.) And it seems they were right. Today, XM has two satellites and offers 160 channels.

### Getting Ready for the Launch

Turning the concept of digital radio into reality cost XM more than $1 billion. First, the company had to design and launch two satellites into orbit over the United States. It set up satellite dishes to beam radio signals to the satellites and erected antennas on 800 buildings in major cities to reach local listeners across the country. In addition, XM created a vast library of digital recordings and built two performance studios to broadcast and record live musical performances.

Another big challenge was developing the radio equipment for customers' cars. XM planned to encode its satellite signals to prevent noncustomers from listening to its channels. The radio had to be capable of receiving and decoding the satellite signals yet compact enough to fit in a car. After building and testing prototypes, XM began manufacturing a radio about the size of a suitcase, to be connected to an antenna on the car's roof for proper reception. Initially customers had to retrofit their cars with XM radios. In time, the company arranged for General Motors, Honda, Audi, Nissan, and several other big automakers to offer factory-installed XM radios as options in their new cars.

### What to Broadcast, What to Charge?

At the same time the company was getting its technology in order, XM was conducting marketing research to determine the target market's listening tastes. Based on this research, the company decided to devote most of its radio stations to specific types of music, such as country, rap, jazz, blues, rock and roll, classic rock, international pop, instrumental classical music, and movie soundtracks. Some stations feature shows hosted by celebrities such as Bob Dylan, Snoop Dogg, and Wynton Marsalis. For more variety, it offers news-only, sports-only, talk-only, comedy-only, and children's stations, among other special-interest stations. For example, its talk-radio offerings include Air America Radio and Fox News Talk.

For sports fans, XM broadcasts Major League baseball and National Hockey League games, as well as NASCAR races.

Pricing involved a delicate balancing act. On the one hand, XM wanted to build a sizable base of subscribers, so its pricing had to be within customers' reach. On the other hand, the company was planning for long-term profitability and wanted to recoup some of its high startup costs. In the end, XM set a monthly subscription fee of $9.95 (later raised to $12.95) and priced its first radios at $300 or less. Within a year, the company launched smaller, less expensive radios for the home and for listening on the go. "We are an entertainment company, but we also recognized that if we were going to be successful, we had to rapidly drive down the cost of the equipment people needed to get our service," recalls an XM marketing analyst.

### Serious Competition from Sirius Satellite Radio

XM's new-product introduction has been successful. More than 5 million customers signed up in the first four years, and the company is preparing for even greater expansion, with profitability expected in the near future. In contrast, its only competitor, New York–based Sirius Satellite Radio, began operating a year after XM and has a smaller customer base, with 3 million customers. Like

XM, Sirius paid millions for a digital radio broadcast license, launched sophisticated satellites, and created specialized programming for 120 stations. And like XM, Sirius is looking to sports and celebrities to draw in new subscribers: In addition to National Football League, National Basketball Association, and National Hockey League games, Sirius has signed shock-jock Howard Stern, Martha Stewart, Eminem, and Pat Robertson to host shows.

Sirius charges a monthly subscription fee of $12.95 with discounts for multiyear contracts, but its channels are entirely commercial free. Sirius also sees drivers as the highest opportunity customer segment, so it has arranged for its radios to be preinstalled as options in cars manufactured by DaimlerChrysler, Ford, BMW, and several other automakers not covered by XM's deals. Sirius has also targeted the "aftermarket," retailers such as Best Buy and Circuit City, where consumers buy receivers for vehicles not already equipped with them.

### Tuning into Satellite Radio's Future

Satellite radio is gaining popularity at a much faster rate than cable television, VCRs, and CDs did after their introductions. As early majority adopters start tuning in to satellite radio, the industry could be serving an estimated 25 million customers by 2010. A Sirius official sees even bigger numbers ahead once the late majority group and the laggards get interested in the product: "We believe there are 350 million potential subscribers in the United States alone." Responding to critics who doubt that pay radio will become big business, Sirius's CEO observes, "People said no one would ever pay for satellite television, and now it has

21 million subscribers. The same thing is going to be true here."

One of XM's recent innovations is a $50 radio that can be connected to a personal computer, complete with software for switching between channels. It also began broadcasting weather and traffic reports for the 21 largest U.S. cities to draw listeners who otherwise would have tuned into local AM or FM stations for this information. Today XM customers must have the company's radio equipment to receive XM channels, just as Sirius customers must have its equipment to receive Sirius channels. That will change in a few months, when new radios capable of receiving either company's channels become available. Still, XM's CEO expects to maintain his company's market dominance by putting the emphasis on program content. "The technology is only the facilitator," he says. "Music connects so personally to people. We're putting the passion back into radio."[35]

### Questions for Discussion

1. How is XM Satellite Radio differentiating its product from that of Sirius?
2. What role has quality played in XM's product development and management?
3. At what stage of the product life cycle is satellite radio? How is the rate of adoption affecting the product's progression through the life cycle?
4. Evaluate the brand names of XM Satellite Radio and Sirius Satellite Radio. What are the strengths and weaknesses of each brand name? Which is the better brand name? Why?

**part**

# 6

## Distribution Decisions

Developing products that satisfy customers is important, but it is not enough to guarantee successful marketing strategies. Products must also be available in adequate quantities in accessible locations at the times when customers desire them. **Part 6** deals with the distribution of products and the marketing channels and institutions that help make products available. **Chapter 15** discusses the structure and functions of marketing channels and presents an overview of institutions that make up these channels. **Chapter 16** analyzes the types of wholesalers and their functions, as well as the decisions and activities associated with the physical distribution of products, such as order processing, materials handling, warehousing, inventory management, and transportation. **Chapter 17** focuses on retailing and direct marketing, including types of retailers, nonstore retailing, franchising, and strategic retailing issues.

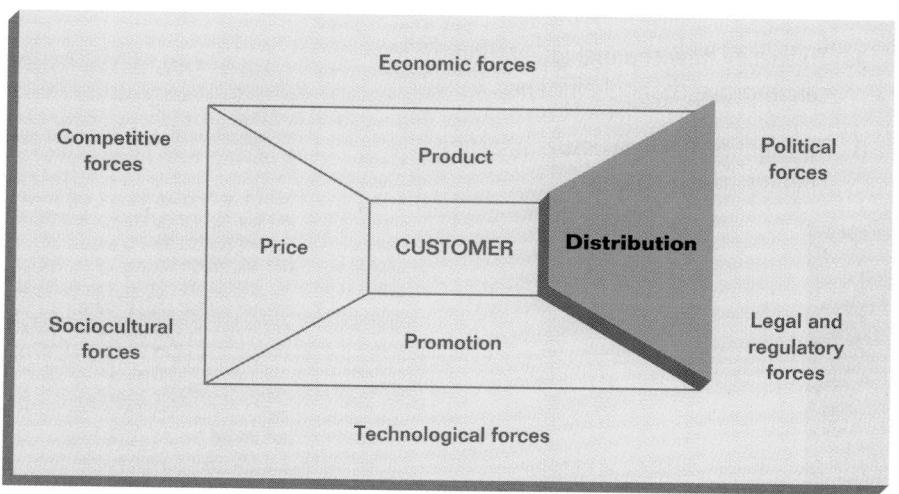

CHAPTER

# 15

# Marketing Channels and Supply Chain Management

## OBJECTIVES

1. To describe the nature and functions of marketing channels

2. Explain how supply chain management can facilitate distribution for the benefit of all channel members, especially customers

3. To identify the types of marketing channels

4. To understand the major factors that may affect the decisions associated with selecting marketing channels

5. To examine the major levels of marketing coverage

6. To explore the concepts of leadership, cooperation, and conflict in channel relationships

7. To specify how channel integration can improve channel efficiency

8. To examine the legal issues affecting channel management

### Radio Shack's Channel Challenge

Radio Shack believes in channel integration and cooperation. The electronics specialty retailer operates 5,046 company-owned stores, 1,788 dealer and franchisee outlets, regional distribution centers, and a shopping website. Its retail stores sell everything from high-end electronic products such as HDTVs, digital cameras, cellphones, and satellite navigational devices to low-end items like batteries, plugs, and connectors. And Radio Shack is the largest U.S. seller of mobile phones and accessories, which account for about a third of its sales.

The company faces competition from discounters such as Wal-Mart and Target as well as a growing range of stores owned by wireless service providers such as Verizon, Cingular, and T-Mobile. To maintain its position in wireless, where it has about 10 percent of the U.S. market, Radio Shack has agreements to operate more than 542 wireless kiosks in Sam's Warehouse Club locations and a growing network of more than 100 Sprint and Cingular branded kiosks in shopping malls.

Under the agreements, the Radio Shack name will not be used at these kiosk locations, and there will be no brand tie-in with the retail stores. Nonetheless, Radio Shack sees benefits in the arrangements. For one, Radio Shack's marketers believe the company will make incremental sales and profits through these partnerships that it would not have otherwise made since these customers were not shopping at Radio Shack stores.

In general then, Radio Shack's company-owned stores, dealerships, and franchisee stores compete amongst each other as well as with Sam's Club and the Sprint and Cingular kiosks that Radio Shack manages. When you consider that the company's website is in competition with all of these retail outlets, it is easy to see why maintaining marketing channel harmony may be challenging to Radio Shack.[1] ■

**distribution** The activities that make products available to customers when and where they want to purchase them

Radio Shack is expanding its operations to serve a greater number of customers through cost effective and efficient distribution practices. Decisions being made by Radio Shack marketers relate to the **distribution** component of the marketing mix, which focuses on the decisions and actions involved in making products available to customers when and where they want to purchase them. Choosing which channels of distribution to use is a major decision in the development of marketing strategies.

In this chapter, we focus on marketing channels. First, we discuss the nature of marketing channels and the need for intermediaries and then analyze the primary functions they perform. Next, we outline the types of marketing channels, discuss how they are selected, and explore how marketers determine the appropriate intensity of market coverage for a product. We then consider supply chain management, including behavioral patterns within marketing channels and forms of channel integration. Finally, we look at several legal issues affecting channel management.

# The Nature of Marketing Channels

**marketing channel** A group of individuals and organizations that direct the flow of products from producers to customers

A **marketing channel** (also called a *channel of distribution* or *distribution channel*) is a group of individuals and organizations that direct the flow of products from producers to customers. The major role of marketing channels is to make products available at the right time at the right place in the right quantities. Providing customer satisfaction should be the driving force behind marketing channel decisions. Buyers' needs and behavior are therefore important concerns of channel members.

Some marketing channels are direct, meaning that the product goes directly from the producer to the customer. For example, when a customer orders a computer from Dell, this product is sent from the manufacturer to the customer. Most channels, however, have marketing intermediaries. A **marketing intermediary** (or *middleman*) links producers to other intermediaries or to ultimate consumers through contractual arrangements or through the purchase and reselling of products. Marketing intermediaries perform the activities described in Table 15.1 (on p. 406). They also play key roles in customer relationship management, not only through their distribution activities but also by maintaining databases and information systems to help all members of the marketing channel maintain effective customer relationships. For example, eBay serves as a marketing intermediary between Internet sellers and buyers. eBay not only provides a forum for these exchanges, but it also keeps an extensive database of members' rankings to facilitate relationships among eBay channel members.[2]

**marketing intermediary** A middleman linking producers to other middlemen or ultimate consumers through contractual arrangements or through the purchase and resale of products

Wholesalers and retailers are examples of intermediaries. Wholesalers buy and resell products to other wholesalers, to retailers, and to industrial customers. Retailers purchase products and resell them to ultimate consumers. For example, your local supermarket probably purchased the Tylenol or Advil on its shelves from a wholesaler, which purchased that product, along with other over-the-counter and prescription drugs, from manufacturers such as McNeil Consumer Labs and Whitehall-Robins. Chapters 16 and 17 discuss the functions of wholesalers and retailers in marketing channels in greater detail.

Marketing channel members share certain significant characteristics. Each member has different responsibilities within the overall structure of the channel. Mutual profit and success for channel members are attained most readily when channel members cooperate to deliver satisfying products to customers.

**Table 15.1**   MARKETING CHANNEL ACTIVITIES PERFORMED BY INTERMEDIARIES

| Category of Marketing Activities | Possible Activities Required |
|---|---|
| Marketing information | Analyze sales data and other information in databases and information systems<br>Perform or commission marketing research |
| Marketing management | Establish strategic plans for developing customer relationships and organizational productivity |
| Facilitating exchanges | Choose product assortments that match the needs of customers<br>Cooperate with channel members to develop partnerships |
| Promotion | Set promotional objectives<br>Coordinate advertising, personal selling, sales promotion, publicity, and packaging |
| Price | Establish pricing policies and terms of sales |
| Physical distribution | Manage transportation, warehousing, materials handling, inventory control, and communication |

Although distribution decisions need not precede other marketing decisions, they are a powerful influence on the rest of the marketing mix. Channel decisions are critical because they determine a product's market presence and the product's accessibility to buyers. For example, because small businesses are more likely to purchase computers from office supply stores such as Office Depot or warehouse clubs such as Sam's, computer companies may be at a disadvantage without distribution through these outlets. Channel decisions have additional strategic significance because they entail long-term commitments. Thus, it is usually easier to change prices or promotional strategies than to change marketing channels.

Marketing channels serve many functions, including creating utility and facilitating exchange efficiencies. Although some of these functions may be performed by a

**Facilitating the Creation of Utility**

Organizations like Capgemini, which delivers outsourcing services, help businesses create utility.

single channel member, most functions are accomplished through both independent and joint efforts of channel members. When managed effectively, the relationships among channel members can also form supply chains that benefit all members of the channel, including the ultimate consumer.

## Marketing Channels Create Utility

Marketing channels create three types of utility: time, place, and possession. *Time utility* is having products available when customers want them. *Place utility* is created by making products available in locations where customers wish to purchase them. *Possession utility* means customers have access to the product to use or store for future use. Possession utility can occur through ownership or through arrangements that give the customer the right to use the product, such as a lease or rental agreement. Channel members sometimes create utility by assembling, preparing, or otherwise refining the product to suit individual customer needs.

## Marketing Channels Facilitate Exchange Efficiencies

Marketing intermediaries can reduce the costs of exchanges by efficiently performing certain services or functions. Even if producers and buyers are located in the same city, exchanges have associated costs. As Figure 15.1 shows, when 4 buyers seek products from 4 producers, 16 transactions are possible. If one intermediary serves both producers and buyers, the number of transactions can be reduced to 8. Intermediaries are specialists in facilitating exchanges. They provide valuable assistance because of their access to and control over important resources used in the proper functioning of marketing channels.

**figure 15.1**

### EFFICIENCY IN EXCHANGES PROVIDED BY AN INTERMEDIARY

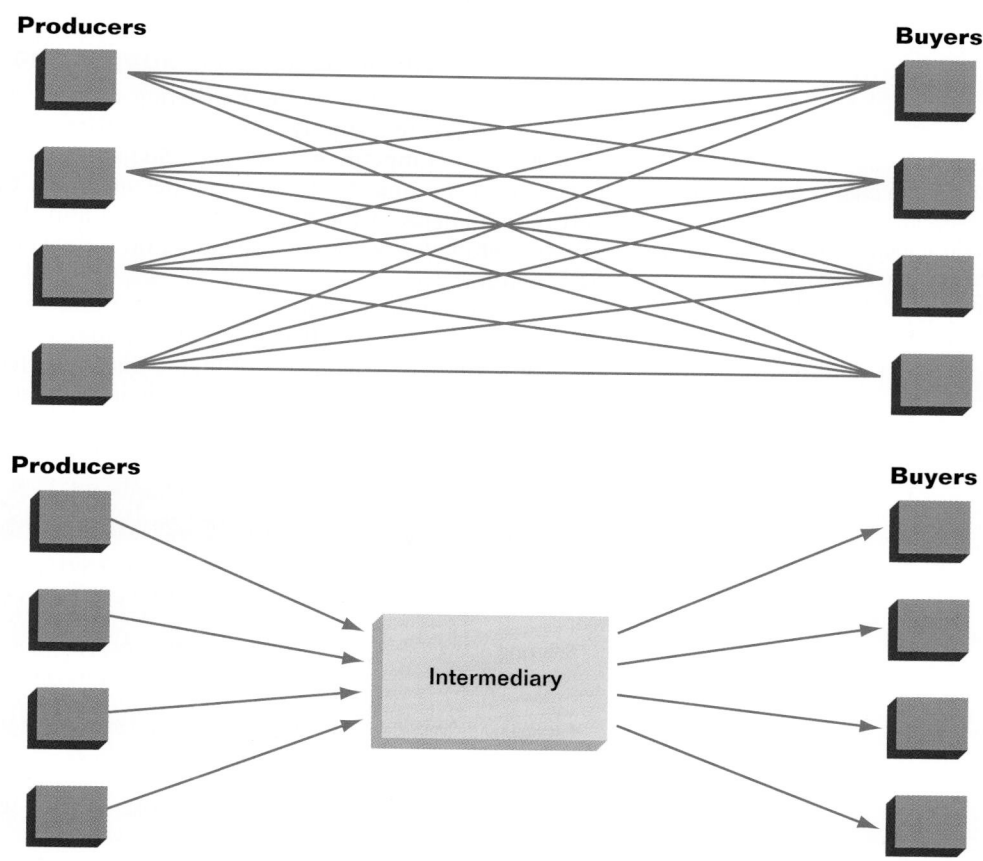

Nevertheless, the media, consumers, public officials, and other marketers freely criticize intermediaries, especially wholesalers. Critics accuse wholesalers of being inefficient and parasitic. Buyers often wish to make the distribution channel as short as possible, assuming the fewer the intermediaries, the lower the price will be. Because suggestions to eliminate them come from both ends of the marketing channel, wholesalers must be careful to perform only those marketing activities that are truly desired. To survive, they must be more efficient and more customer-focused than other marketing institutions.

Critics who suggest that eliminating wholesalers would lower customer prices do not recognize that this would not eliminate the need for services wholesalers provide. Although wholesalers can be eliminated, the functions they perform cannot. Other channel members would have to perform those functions, and customers would still have to pay for them. In addition, all producers would have to deal directly with retailers or customers, meaning every producer would have to keep voluminous records and hire enough personnel to deal with a multitude of customers. Customers might end up paying a great deal more for products because prices would reflect the costs of less efficient channel members.

To illustrate the efficiency of wholesalers' services, assume all wholesalers have been eliminated. Because there are approximately 1.1 million retailers, a widely purchased consumer product—say, candy—would require an extraordinary number of sales contacts, possibly more than a million, to maintain the current level of product exposure. For example, Mars, Inc., would have to deliver candy, purchase and service thousands of vending machines, establish warehouses all over the country, and maintain fleets of trucks. Selling and distribution costs for candy would skyrocket. Instead of a few contacts with food brokers, large retail organizations, and merchant wholesalers, candy manufacturers would have to make thousands of expensive contacts with and shipments to smaller retailers. Such an operation would be highly inefficient, and costs would be passed on to consumers. Candy bars would cost more and be harder to find. Clearly wholesalers are often more efficient and less expensive.

## Marketing Channels Form a Supply Chain

An important function of the marketing channel is the joint effort of all channel members to create a supply chain, a total distribution system that serves customers and creates a competitive advantage. **Supply chain management** refers to long-term partnerships among marketing channel members that reduce inefficiencies, costs, and redundancies in the marketing channel and develop innovative approaches to satisfy customers. Worldwide spending on supply chain management systems is over $19 billion.[3]

Supply chain management involves manufacturing, research, sales, advertising, shipping, and—most of all—cooperation and understanding of tradeoffs throughout the whole channel to achieve optimal levels of efficiency and service. Table 15.2 outlines the key tasks involved in supply chain management. Whereas traditional marketing channels tend to focus on producers, wholesalers, retailers, and customers, the

**supply chain management**
Long-term partnerships among marketing channel members that reduce inefficiencies, costs, and redundancies and develop innovative approaches to satisfy customers

| Table 15.2 | KEY TASKS IN SUPPLY CHAIN MANAGEMENT |
|---|---|
| Planning | Organizational and systemwide coordination of marketing channel partnerships to meet customers' product needs |
| Sourcing | Purchasing of necessary resources, goods, and services from suppliers to support all supply chain members |
| Facilitating delivery | All activities designed to move the product through the marketing channel to the end user |
| Relationship building | All marketing activities related to selling, service, and the development of long-term customer relationships |

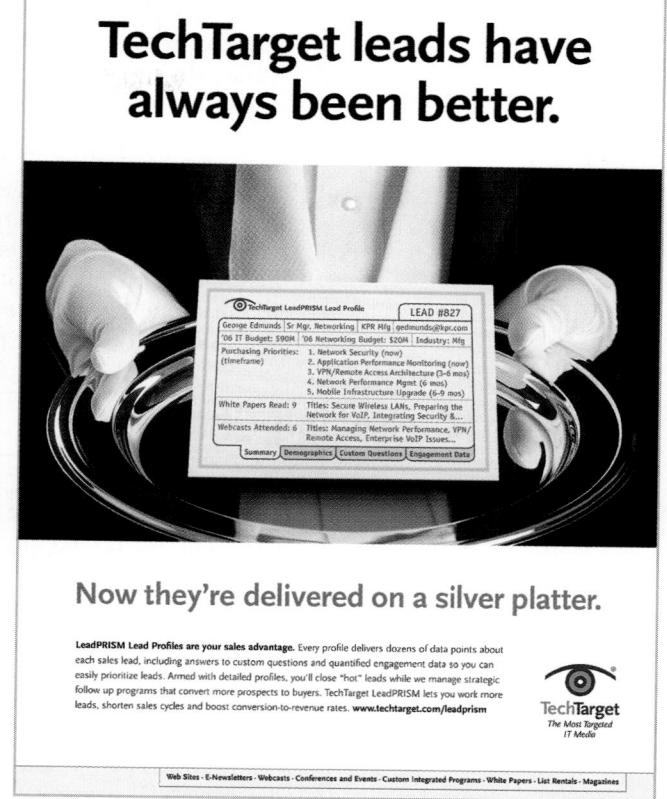

## Technology Facilitates Supply Chain Management

Technology-based tools help supply chain managers improve efficiency and coordination.

supply chain is a broader concept that includes facilitating agencies such as shipping companies, communication companies, and other organizations that indirectly take part in marketing exchanges. Thus, the supply chain includes all entities that facilitate product distribution and benefit from cooperative efforts. Supply chain management is helping more firms realize that optimizing supply chain costs through partnerships will improve all members' profits. All parties should focus on cooperating to reduce the costs of all affected channel members. Supply chains start with the customer and require the cooperation of channel members to satisfy customer requirements. When the buyer, the seller, marketing intermediaries, and facilitating agencies work together, the cooperative relationship results in compromise and adjustments that meet customers' needs regarding delivery, scheduling, packaging, or other requirements.

Most companies do not set out to develop a supply chain. Typically they see a need to rework the way they serve their customers. Often they need to increase the quality of a good or service, which results in such goals as reducing the time from production to customer purchase, decreasing transportation costs, or lowering information management or administrative costs. Achieving these goals to attain a more competitive position often requires that channel members cooperate and share information as well as accommodate one another's needs.

Technology has dramatically improved the capability of supply chain management on a global basis. With integrated information sharing among channel members, costs can be reduced, service improved, and value provided to the customer enhanced. Tools such as electronic billing, purchase order verification, bar-code technology, and image processing integrate needed data into the supply chain and improve overall performance. Intensely competitive industries operate the most sophisticated systems of supply chain management. Customer relationship management (CRM) systems exploit the information from supply chain partners' database and information systems to help all channel members make marketing strategy decisions that develop and sustain desirable customer relationships. Thus, managing relationships with supply chain partners is crucial to satisfying customers. CRM is gaining popularity with big companies like Hewlett-Packard and Amazon.com, which spend large sums of money on implementation and support for data mining and CRM analytical applications. By 2008, companies that supply CRM technology, such as Siebel, SAS, and NetIQ, are expected to bring in over $11 billion in revenues.[4]

Supply chain management is not just a buzzword. Reducing inventory and transportation costs, speeding order cycle times, cutting administrative and handling costs, and improving customer service are all improvements that provide rewards for *all* channel members. The rewards will come as companies determine their positions in the supply chain, identify their partners and their roles, and establish partnerships that focus on customer relationships.

# Types of Marketing Channels

Because marketing channels appropriate for one product may be less suitable for others, many different distribution paths have been developed. The various marketing channels can be classified generally as channels for consumer products and channels for business products.

### Channels for Consumer Products

Figure 15.2 illustrates several channels used in the distribution of consumer products. Channel A depicts the direct movement of goods from producer to consumers. Producers that sell goods directly from their factories to end users use direct marketing channels, as do companies that sell their own products via the Internet, such as Dell Computer. In fact, because Internet purchases have increased significantly, direct marketing via the Internet has become an important part of some companies' distribution strategies. Although direct marketing channels are the simplest, they are not necessarily the most effective distribution method. Faced with the strategic choice of going directly to the customer or using intermediaries, a firm must eval-

**figure 15.2**

**TYPICAL MARKETING CHANNELS FOR CONSUMER PRODUCTS**

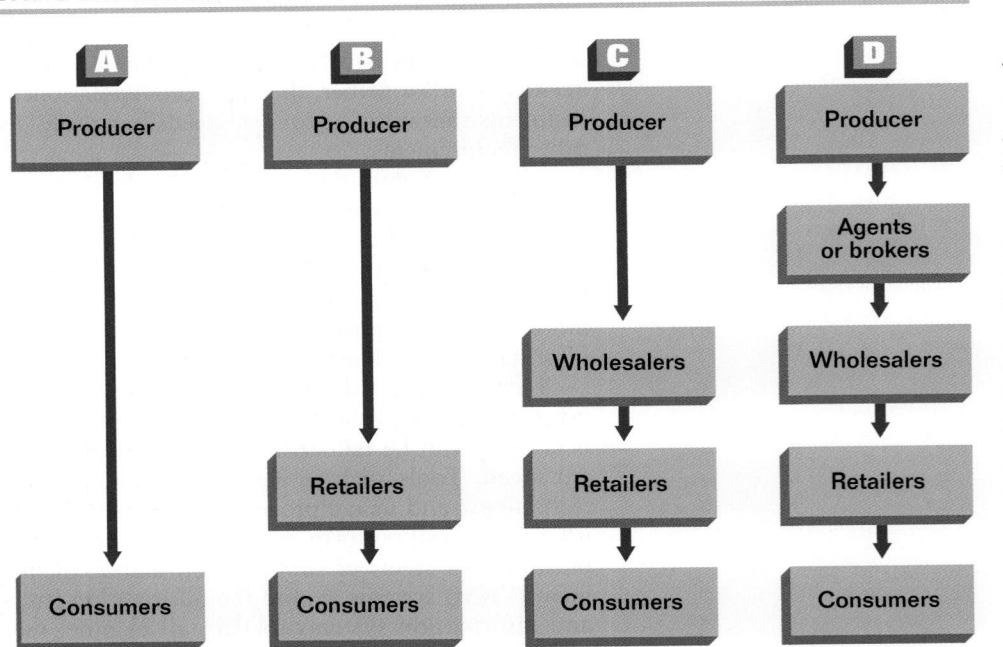

## marketing ENTREPRENEURS

**David Ansel**

THE BUSINESS: The Soup Peddler

FOUNDED: 2002

SUCCESS: Has grown from 17 Soupies to 2,000

David Ansel, a software developer, followed his girlfriend to Austin, Texas; there, neither the relationship nor his job prospects panned out. To make ends meet, Ansel began making soup and selling it to his neighbors, delivering it in a cooler he pulled behind his yellow bicycle. After he outgrew his own kitchen, he leased space in a local Thai restaurant after hours. His delicious, home-made soups quickly gained a following well beyond his South Austin neighborhood. Today, the Soup Peddler has its own production facility, employs a crew of eight, and delivers soup all over Austin in two orange refrigerated trucks (although Ansel still uses his bike to deliver soup to his own neighborhood).

uate the benefits to customers of going direct versus the transaction costs involved in using intermediaries. Several companies provide supply chain management software to assist customers in managing sales orders, procurement, warehousing, transportation, and customer service. For example, Manhattan Associates is a U.S. company specializing in supply chain management software. Jeff Baum, senior vice president of international operations, said the newest tool to increase supply chain efficiency is the radio frequency identification tag. The RFID emits a signal containing detailed information about a product, which is expected to eclipse the bar code and cut labor-intensive intervention in retail logistics.

Channel B, which moves goods from the producer to a retailer and then to customers, is a frequent choice of large retailers since it allows them to buy in quantity from manufacturers. Retailers such as Kmart and Wal-Mart sell clothing, stereos, and many other items purchased directly from producers. New automobiles and new college textbooks are also sold through this type of marketing channel. Primarily nonstore retailers, such as L.L. Bean and J. Crew, also use this type of channel.

A long-standing distribution channel, especially for consumer products, channel C takes goods from the producer to a wholesaler, then to a retailer, and finally to consumers. It is a practical option for producers that sell to hundreds of thousands of customers through thousands of retailers. A single producer finds it hard to do business directly with thousands of retailers. Consider the number of retailers marketing Wrigley's chewing gum. It would be extremely difficult, if not impossible, for Wrigley to deal directly with each retailer that sells its brand of gum. Manufacturers of tobacco products, some home appliances, hardware, and many convenience goods sell their products to wholesalers, which then sell to retailers, which in turn do business with individual consumers.

Channel D, through which goods pass from producer to agents to wholesalers to retailers and then to consumers, is frequently used for products intended for mass distribution, such as processed foods. For example, to place its cracker line in specific retail outlets, a food processor may hire an agent (or a food broker) to sell the crackers to wholesalers. Wholesalers then sell the crackers to supermarkets, vending machine operators, and other retail outlets.

Contrary to popular opinion, a long channel may be the most efficient distribution channel for some consumer goods. When several channel intermediaries perform specialized functions, costs may be lower than when one channel member tries to perform them all.

### Channels for Business Products

Figure 15.3 (on p. 412) shows four of the most common channels for business products. As with consumer products, manufacturers of business products sometimes work with more than one level of wholesalers.

Channel E illustrates the direct channel for business products. In contrast to consumer goods, more than half of all business products, especially expensive equipment, are sold through direct channels. Business customers prefer to communicate directly with producers, especially when expensive or technically complex products are involved. For this reason, business buyers prefer to purchase expensive and highly complex mainframe computers directly from IBM and other mainframe producers. Intel has established direct marketing channels for selling its microprocessor

figure 15.3

**figure 15.3**   TYPICAL MARKETING CHANNELS FOR BUSINESS PRODUCTS

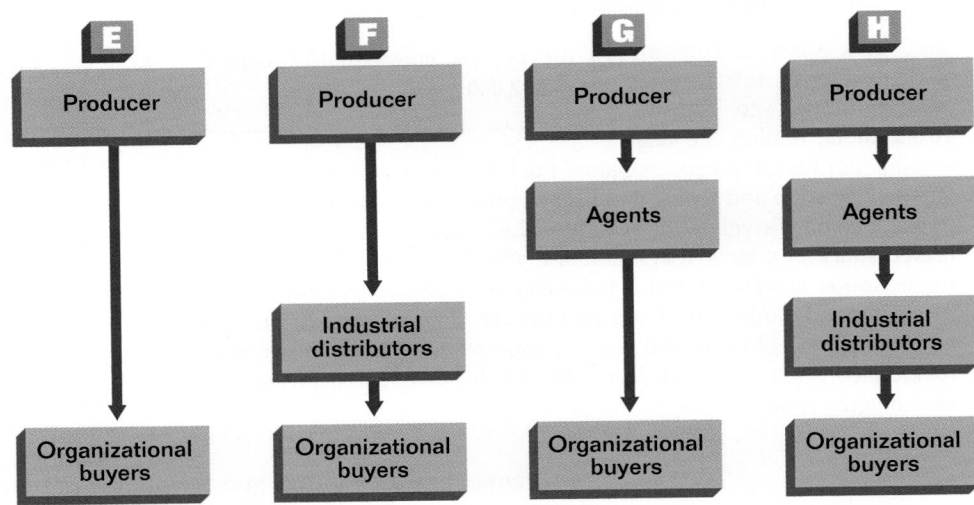

chips to computer manufacturers. In these circumstances, a customer wants the technical assistance and personal assurances that only a producer can provide.

In the second business products channel, channel F, an industrial distributor facilitates exchanges between producer and customer. An **industrial distributor** is an independent business that takes title to products and carries inventories. Industrial distributors usually sell standardized items such as maintenance supplies, production tools, and small operating equipment. Some industrial distributors carry a wide variety of product lines. Others specialize in one or a small number of lines. Industrial distributors are carrying an increasing percentage of business products. Industrial distributors can be most effectively used when a product has broad market appeal, is easily stocked and serviced, is sold in small quantities, and is needed on demand to avoid high losses.

Industrial distributors offer sellers several advantages. They can perform the needed selling activities in local markets at a relatively low cost to a manufacturer and reduce a producer's financial burden by providing customers with credit services. Also, because industrial distributors usually maintain close relationships with their customers, they are aware of local needs and can pass on market information to producers. By holding adequate inventories in their local markets, industrial distributors reduce producers' capital requirements.

Using industrial distributors has several disadvantages, however. Industrial distributors may be difficult to control since they are independent firms. Because they often stock competing brands, a producer cannot depend on them to sell its brand aggressively. Furthermore, since industrial distributors maintain inventories, they incur numerous expenses; consequently they are less likely to handle bulky or slow-selling items or items that need specialized facilities or extraordinary selling efforts. In some cases, industrial distributors lack the technical knowledge necessary to sell and service certain products.

The third channel for business products, channel G, employs a *manufacturers' agent,* an independent businessperson who sells complementary products of several producers in assigned territories and is compensated through commissions. Unlike an industrial distributor, a manufacturers' agent does not acquire title to the products and usually does not take possession. Acting as a salesperson on behalf of the producers, a manufacturers' agent has little or no latitude in negotiating prices or sales terms.

Using manufacturers' agents can benefit an organizational marketer. These agents usually possess considerable technical and market information and have an

**industrial distributor** An independent business organization that takes title to industrial products and carries inventories

established set of customers. For an organizational seller with highly seasonal demand, a manufacturers' agent can be an asset because the seller does not have to support a year-round sales force. The fact that manufacturers' agents are paid on a commission basis may also be an economical alternative for a firm that has highly limited resources and cannot afford a full-time sales force.

Certainly the use of manufacturers' agents is not problem-free. Even though straight commissions may be cheaper, the seller may have little control over manufacturers' agents. Because of the compensation method, manufacturers' agents generally prefer to concentrate on their larger accounts. They are often reluctant to spend time following up sales, putting forth special selling efforts, or providing sellers with market information when such activities reduce the amount of productive selling time. Because they rarely maintain inventories, manufacturers' agents have a limited ability to provide customers with parts or repair services quickly.

Finally, channel H includes both a manufacturers' agent and an industrial distributor. This channel may be appropriate when the producer wishes to cover a large geographic area but maintains no sales force due to highly seasonal demand or because it cannot afford a sales force. This type of channel can also be useful for a business marketer that wants to enter a new geographic market without expanding its existing sales force.

## Multiple Marketing Channels and Channel Alliances

**dual distribution** The use of two or more marketing channels to distribute the same product to the same target market

**strategic channel alliance** An agreement whereby the products of one organization are distributed through the marketing channels of another

To reach diverse target markets, manufacturers may use several marketing channels simultaneously, with each channel involving a different group of intermediaries. For example, a manufacturer uses multiple channels when the same product is directed to both consumers and business customers. When Del Monte markets ketchup for household use, the product is sold to supermarkets through grocery wholesalers or, in some cases, directly to retailers, whereas ketchup going to restaurants or institutions follows a different distribution channel. In some instances, a producer may prefer **dual distribution,** the use of two or more marketing channels to distribute the same products to the same target market. For example, Kellogg sells its cereals directly to large retail grocery chains (Channel B) and to food wholesalers that, in turn, sell them to retailers (Channel C). Another example of dual distribution is a firm that sells products through retail outlets and its own mail-order catalog or website. Dual distribution, however, can cause dissatisfaction among wholesalers and smaller retailers when they must compete with large retail grocery chains that make direct purchases from manufacturers such as Kellogg. The practice of dual distribution has been challenged as being anticompetitive. We discuss the legal dimensions of dual distribution later in this chapter.

A **strategic channel alliance** exists when the products of one organization are distributed through the marketing channels of another. The products of the two firms are often similar with respect to target markets or uses, but they are not direct competitors. For example, a brand of bottled

**OVER 40 BLENDS TO CHOOSE FROM.**

**PACE YOURSELF.**

Find out what flavor you are at Millstone.com

### Using Multiple Marketing Channels
Many products—including Millstone Coffee—are marketed through multiple distribution channels.

water might be distributed through a marketing channel for soft drinks, or a domestic cereal producer might form a strategic channel alliance with a European food processor. Alliances can provide benefits for both the organization that owns the marketing channel and the company whose brand is being distributed through the channel.

# Selecting Marketing Channels

Selecting appropriate marketing channels is important. While the process varies across organizations, channel selection decisions usually are significantly affected by one or more of the following factors: customer characteristics, product attributes, type of organization, competition, marketing environmental forces, and characteristics of intermediaries (see Figure 15.4).

### Customer Characteristics

Marketing managers must consider the characteristics of target market members in channel selection. As we have discussed, the channels appropriate for consumers are different than those for business customers. A different marketing channel will be required for business customers purchasing carpet for commercial buildings compared to consumers purchasing carpet for their homes. As already mentioned, business customers often prefer to deal directly with producers (or very knowledgeable channel intermediaries such as industrial distributors), especially for highly technical or expensive products such as mainframe computers, jet airplanes, and large mining machines. Moreover, business customers are more likely to buy complex products requiring strict specifications and technical assistance and/or to buy in considerable quantities.

**figure 15.4**

**SELECTING MARKETING CHANNELS**

Consumers, on the other hand, generally buy limited quantities of a product, purchase from retailers, and often don't mind limited customer service. Additionally, when customers are concentrated in a small geographic area, a more direct channel may be ideal, but when many customers are spread across an entire state or nation, distribution through multiple intermediaries is likely to be more efficient.

## Product Attributes

The attributes of the product can have a strong influence on the choice of marketing channels. Marketers of complex and expensive products such as automobiles will likely employ short channels, as will marketers of perishable products such as dairy and produce. Less expensive, more standardized products such as soft drinks and canned goods can employ longer channels with many intermediaries. In addition, channel decisions may be affected by a product's sturdiness: fragile products that require special handling are more likely to be distributed through shorter channels to minimize the risk of damage. Firms that desire to convey an exclusive image for their products may wish to limit the number of outlets available.

## Type of Organization

Clearly, the characteristics of the organization will have a great impact on the distribution channels chosen. Due to their sheer size, larger firms may be better able to negotiate better deals with vendors or other channel members. Compared to small firms, they may be in better positions to have more distribution centers, which may reduce delivery times to customers. A smaller regional company using regional or local channel members may be in a position to better serve customers in that region compared to a larger, less flexible organization. Compared to smaller organizations, large companies can use an extensive product mix as a competitive tool. Smaller firms may not have the resources to develop their own sales force, to ship their products long distances, to store or own products, or to extend credit. In such cases, they may have to include other channel members that have the resources to provide these services to customers efficiently and cost effectively.

## Competition

Competition is also an important factor for supply chain managers to consider. The success or failure of a competitor's marketing channel may encourage or dissuade an organization from considering a similar approach. A firm may also be forced to adopt a similar strategy to remain competitive. In a highly competitive market, it is important for a company to keep its costs low so that it can underprice its competitors if necessary.

## Marketing Environmental Forces

Environmental forces can also play a role in channel selection. Adverse economic conditions might force an organization to use a low-cost channel, even though customer satisfaction is reduced. In contrast, a booming economy might allow a company to choose a channel that previously had been too costly to consider. The introduction of new technology might cause an organization to add or modify its channel strategy. For instance, as the Internet became a powerful marketing communication tool, many companies were forced to go online to remain competitive. Government regulations can also affect channel selection. As new labor and environmental regulations are passed, an organization may be forced to modify its existing distribution channel structure. Firms may choose to make the changes before regulations are passed in order to appear compliant or to avoid legal issues. Governmental regulations can also include trade agreements with other countries that complicate the supply chain.

## Characteristics of Intermediaries

When an organization believes that a current intermediary is not adequately promoting the organization's products, it may reconsider its channel choices. In these instances, the company may choose another channel member to handle its products. Alternatively, it may choose to eliminate intermediaries, and to perform the functions itself. Alternatively, an existing intermediary may not offer an appropriate mix of services, forcing an organization to change to another intermediary.

# Intensity of Market Coverage

In addition to deciding which marketing channels to use to distribute a product, marketers must determine the intensity of coverage that a product should get, that is, the number and kinds of outlets in which it will be sold. This decision depends on the characteristics of the product and the target market. To achieve the desired intensity of market coverage, distribution must correspond to behavior patterns of buyers. In Chapter 11, we divided consumer products into four categories—convenience products, shopping products, specialty products, and unsought products—according to how consumers make purchases. In considering products for purchase, consumers take into account replacement rate, product adjustment (services), duration of consumption, time required to find the product, and similar factors.[5] These variables directly affect the intensity of market coverage. As shown in Figure 15.5, the three major levels of market coverage are intensive, selective, and exclusive distribution.

## Intensive Distribution

**intensive distribution** Using all available outlets to distribute a product

**Intensive distribution** uses all available outlets for distributing a product. Intensive distribution is appropriate for convenience products such as bread, chewing gum, soft drinks, and newspapers. Convenience products have a high replacement rate and require almost no service. To meet these demands, intensive distribution is necessary, and multiple channels may be used to sell through all possible outlets. For example, soft drinks, snacks, laundry detergent, and aspirin are available at convenience stores, service stations, supermarkets, discount stores, and other types of retailers. To consumers, availability means a store is located nearby and minimum time is necessary to search for the product at the store. Sales may have a direct relationship to product availability. The successful sale of such products as bread and milk at service stations or of gasoline at convenience grocery stores illustrates that the availability of these products is more important than the nature of the outlet. Companies such as Procter & Gamble that produce consumer packaged items rely on intensive distribution for many of their products (for example, soaps, detergents, food and juice products, and personal-care products) because consumers want ready availability.

**selective distribution** Using only some available outlets to distribute a product

**figure 15.5**

**INTENSITY OF MARKET COVERAGE**

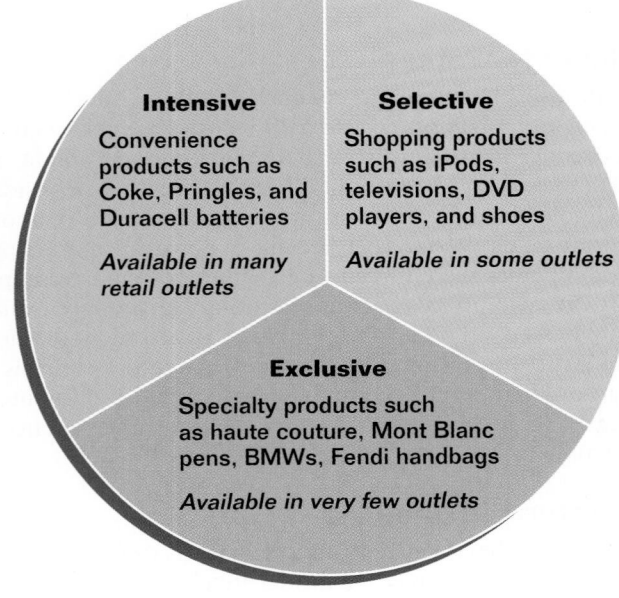

**Intensive**

Convenience products such as Coke, Pringles, and Duracell batteries

*Available in many retail outlets*

**Selective**

Shopping products such as iPods, televisions, DVD players, and shoes

*Available in some outlets*

**Exclusive**

Specialty products such as haute couture, Mont Blanc pens, BMWs, Fendi handbags

*Available in very few outlets*

## Selective Distribution

**Selective distribution** uses only some available outlets in an area to distribute a product. Selective distribution is appropriate for shopping products; durable goods such as televisions, stereos, and home computers usually fall into this category. These products are more expensive than convenience goods, and consumers are willing to spend more time visiting several retail outlets to compare prices, designs, styles, and other features. For example, Hermes Parfums launched Eau des Merveilles, an exclusive new scent and related products, only in selected high-end retailers. It expected to generate more than $25 million in retail volume its first year.[6]

**NEW MOUTHWATERINGLY COOL WATERMELON REMARKABLY LONG LASTING**

**Intensive Distribution**

Chewing gum, like Extra, is distributed through intensive distribution.

**exclusive distribution** Using a single outlet in a fairly large geographic area to distribute a product

*snapshot*

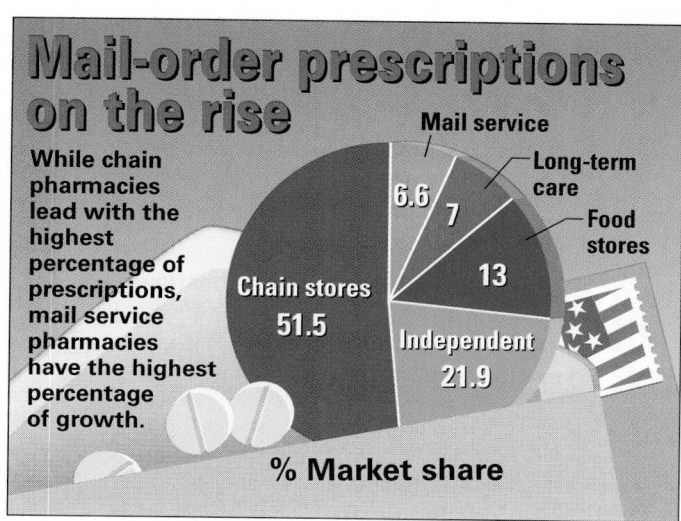

**Mail-order prescriptions on the rise**

While chain pharmacies lead with the highest percentage of prescriptions, mail service pharmacies have the highest percentage of growth.

Mail service — 6.6
Long-term care — 7
Food stores — 13
Chain stores 51.5
Independent 21.9

**% Market share**

*Source:* IMS Health October 2005.

Selective distribution is desirable when a special effort, such as customer service from a channel member, is important to customers. Shopping products require differentiation at the point of purchase. To motivate retailers to provide adequate presale service, selective distribution and company-owned stores are often used. Many business products are sold on a selective basis to maintain some control over the distribution process. For example, agricultural herbicides are distributed on a selective basis because dealers must offer services to buyers such as instructions about how to apply herbicides safely or the option to have the dealer apply the herbicide. Evinrude outboard motors are also sold by dealers on a selective basis.

## Exclusive Distribution

**Exclusive distribution** uses only one outlet in a relatively large geographic area. Exclusive distribution is suitable for products purchased infrequently, consumed over a long period of time, or requiring service or information to fit them to buyers' needs. It is also used for expensive, high-quality products, such as Porsche automobiles. It is not appropriate for convenience products and many shopping products.

Exclusive distribution is often used as an incentive to sellers when only a limited market is available for products. For example, automobiles such as the Bentley, made by Rolls-Royce, are sold on an exclusive basis, and Patek Philippe watches, which may sell for $10,000 or more, are available in only a few select locations. A producer using exclusive distribution generally expects dealers to carry a complete inventory, send personnel for sales and service training, participate in promotional programs, and provide excellent customer service. Some products are appropriate for exclusive distribution when first introduced, but as competitors enter the market and the product moves through its life cycle, other types of market coverage and distribution channels often become necessary. A problem that can arise with exclusive distribution (and selective distribution) is that unauthorized resellers acquire and sell products, violating the agreement between a manufacturer and its exclusive authorized dealers. This has been a problem for Rolex, another manufacturer of prestige watches.

# Supply Chain Management

To fulfill the potential of effective supply chain management and ensure customer satisfaction, marketing channels require leadership, cooperation, and management of channel conflict. They may also require consolidation of marketing channels through channel integration.

## Channel Leadership, Cooperation, and Conflict

Each channel member performs a different role in the distribution system and agrees (implicitly or explicitly) to accept certain rights, responsibilities, rewards, and sanctions for nonconformity. Moreover, each channel member holds certain expectations of other channel members. Retailers, for instance, expect wholesalers to maintain adequate inventories and deliver goods on time. Wholesalers expect retailers to honor payment agreements and keep them informed of inventory needs.

Channel partnerships facilitate effective supply chain management when partners agree on objectives, policies, and procedures for physical distribution efforts associated with the supplier's products. Such partnerships eliminate redundancies and reassign tasks for maximum systemwide efficiency. One of the best-known partnerships is that between Wal-Mart and Procter & Gamble. Procter & Gamble locates some of its staff near Wal-Mart's purchasing department in Bentonville, Arkansas, to establish and maintain the supply chain. Sharing information through a cooperative computer system, Procter & Gamble monitors Wal-Mart's inventory and additional data to determine production and distribution plans for its products. The results are increased efficiency, decreased inventory costs, and greater satisfaction for the customers of both companies. At this time, some suppliers have been unwilling or unable to make this level of commitment. In this section we discuss channel member behavior, including leadership, cooperation, and conflict, that marketers must understand to make effective channel decisions.

**Channel Leadership.** Many marketing channel decisions are determined by consensus. Producers and intermediaries coordinate efforts for mutual benefit. Some marketing channels, however, are

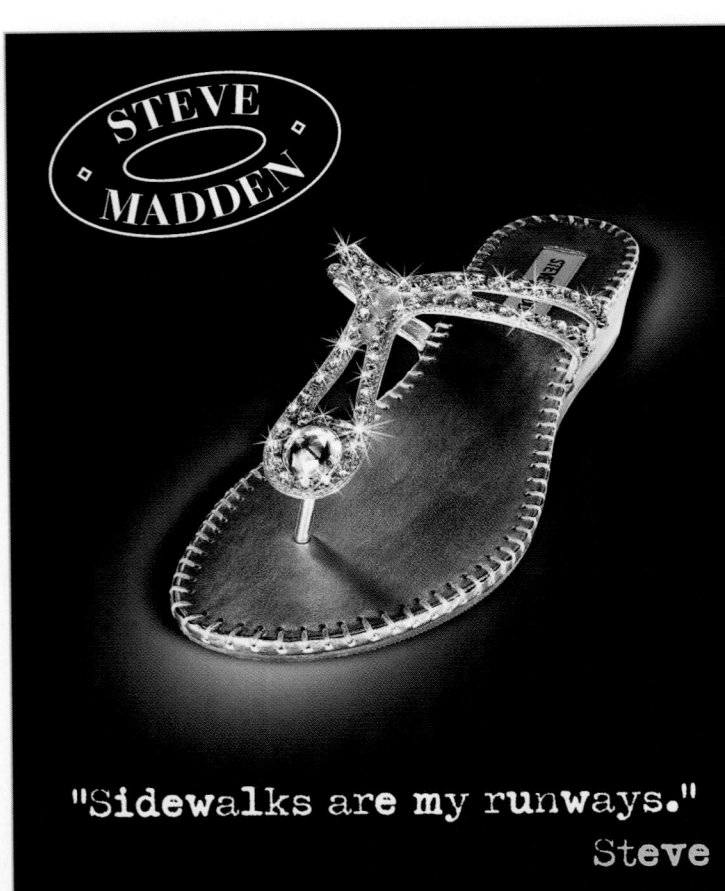

**Channel Leadership**
The manufacturer of Steve Madden shoes provides channel leadership in the distribution channels for its products.

**channel captain** The dominant member of a marketing channel or supply chain

**channel power** The ability of one channel member to influence another member's goal achievement

organized and controlled by a single leader, or **channel captain** (also called *channel leader*). The channel captain may be a producer, wholesaler, or retailer. Channel captains may establish channel policies and coordinate development of the marketing mix. Wal-Mart, for example, dominates the supply chain for its retail stores by virtue of the magnitude of its resources (especially information management) and strong, nationwide customer base. To become a captain, a channel member must want to influence overall channel performance. To attain desired objectives, the captain must possess **channel power,** the ability to influence another channel member's goal achievement. The member that becomes the channel captain will accept the responsibilities and exercise the power associated with this role.

When a manufacturer's large-scale production efficiency demands that it increase sales volume, the manufacturer may exercise power by giving channel members financing, business advice, ordering assistance, advertising services, sales and service training, and support materials. For example, U.S. automakers provide these services to retail automobile dealerships. However, these manufacturers also place numerous requirements on their retail dealerships with respect to sales volume, sales and service training, and customer satisfaction.

As already noted, retailers may also function as channel captains. With the rise in power of national chain stores and private-brand merchandise, many large retailers such as Wal-Mart are doing so. Small retailers too may assume leadership roles when they gain strong customer loyalty in local or regional markets. These retailers control many brands and sometimes replace uncooperative producers. Increasingly, leading retailers are concentrating their buying power with fewer suppliers and, in the process, improving their marketing effectiveness and efficiency. Single-source supply relationships are often successful, whereas multiple-source supply relationships based on price competition are decreasing. Long-term commitments enable retailers to place smaller and more frequent orders as needed rather than waiting for large volume discounts or placing huge orders early in the season and assuming the risks associated with carrying a larger inventory.

Wholesalers assume channel leadership roles as well, although they were more powerful decades ago, when many manufacturers and retailers were smaller, underfinanced, and widely scattered. Today wholesaler leaders may form voluntary chains with several retailers, which they supply with bulk buying or management services; these chains may also market their own brands. In return, the retailers shift most of their purchasing to the wholesaler leader. The Independent Grocers' Alliance (IGA) is one of the best-known wholesaler leaders in the United States. IGA's power is based on its expertise in advertising, pricing, and purchasing knowledge that it makes available to independent business owners. Other wholesaler leaders help retailers with store layouts, accounting, and inventory control.

**Channel Cooperation.** Channel cooperation is vital if each member is to gain something from other members. Cooperation enables retailers, wholesalers, and suppliers to speed up inventory replenishment, improve customer service, and cut the costs of bringing products to the consumer.[7] Without cooperation, neither overall channel goals nor member goals can be realized. All channel members must recognize that the success of one firm in the channel depends in part on other member firms. Thus, marketing channel members should make a coordinated effort to satisfy market requirements. Channel cooperation leads to greater trust among channel members and improves the overall functioning of the channel. It also leads to more satisfying relationships among channel members.

There are several ways to improve channel cooperation. If a marketing channel is viewed as a unified supply chain competing with other systems, individual members will be less likely to take actions that create disadvantages for other members. Similarly, channel members should agree to direct efforts toward common objectives so channel roles can be structured for maximum marketing effectiveness, which in turn can help members achieve individual objectives. A critical component in cooperation is a precise definition of each channel member's tasks. This provides a basis for reviewing the intermediaries' performance and helps reduce conflicts because each channel member knows exactly what is expected of it.

**Channel Conflict.** Although all channel members work toward the same general goal—distributing products profitably and efficiently—members may sometimes disagree about the best methods for attaining this objective. However, if self-interest creates misunderstanding about role expectations, the end result is frustration and conflict for the whole channel. For individual organizations to function together, each channel member must clearly communicate and understand role expectations. Communication difficulties are a potential form of channel conflict because ineffective communication leads to frustration, misunderstandings, and ill-coordinated strategies, jeopardizing further coordination.

The increased use of multiple channels of distribution, driven partly by new technology, has increased the potential for conflict between manufacturers and intermediaries. For example, Hewlett-Packard makes products available directly to consumers through its website (**www.hewlett-packard.com**), thereby competing directly with existing distributors and retailers.[8] Channel conflicts also arise when intermediaries overemphasize competing products or diversify into product lines traditionally handled by other intermediaries. Sometimes conflict develops because producers strive to increase efficiency by circumventing intermediaries. Such conflict is occurring in marketing channels for computer software. A number of software-only stores are establishing direct relationships with software producers, bypassing wholesale distributors altogether.

# IBM: Outsupplying the Competition

Thirty years ago, it took 24 hours to rack up $10 billion in foreign exchange transactions. Today, the same amount of trade occurs in a single second. Globalization has raised the competitive stakes, forcing companies to compete on more than just product features and price. Companies can now achieve competitive differentiation based on how well they deliver the right product to the right place at the right time. For example, a Japanese manufacturer uses a logistics partner to configure its digital camera packaging to fit the requirements of individual retail chains. Free memory cards or carrying cases are packaged with the cameras, enabling retailers to differentiate themselves. By providing more value to its customers, this manufacturer has developed a competitive advantage over competing camera suppliers.

Bob Moffat, a senior vice president of IBM's integrated supply chain group, puts it this way, "When people work on a supply chain, they work on cost, but it's really how they take that cost and cash advantage and use it as a competitive advantage or weapon in the marketplace." Members of Moffat's organization have been working to reduce the number of days that sales revenue goes uncollected. That doesn't happen by changing terms and conditions, says Moffat. It comes from making sure the right data is in the billing system, that bills are accurate, and the necessary backup documentation is attached, all of which minimize the number of billing disputes initiated by customers.

For a corporation with more than $89 billion in annual sales, speeding collections by one day frees up almost $250 million in cash that can be used for new-product development, increased advertising, or other programs to give IBM an advantage over its competition. IBM's supply chain management has been so successful that it is now offering Business Transformation Outsourcing, a service that provides its own supply chain management solutions and technology to other companies.

The supply chain has clearly evolved to more than a distribution system.

When a producer that has traditionally used franchised dealers broadens its retailer base to include other types of retail outlets, considerable conflict can arise. When Goodyear intensified its market coverage by allowing Sears and Discount Tire to market Goodyear tires, its action antagonized 2,500 independent Goodyear dealers.

Although there is no single method for resolving conflict, partnerships can be reestablished if two conditions are met. First, the role of each channel member must be specified. To minimize misunderstanding, all members must be able to expect unambiguous, agreed-on performance levels from one another. Second, members of channel partnerships must institute certain measures of channel coordination, which requires leadership and benevolent exercise of control. To prevent channel conflict from arising, producers or other channel members may provide competing resellers with different brands, allocate markets among resellers, define policies for direct sales to avoid potential conflict over large accounts, negotiate territorial issues among regional distributors, and provide recognition to certain resellers for their importance in distributing to others.

## Channel Integration

Channel members can either combine and control most activities or pass them on to another channel member. Channel functions may be transferred between intermediaries and to producers and even to customers. However, a channel member cannot eliminate functions; unless buyers themselves perform the functions, they must pay for the labor and resources needed to perform them.

Various channel stages may be combined under the management of a channel captain either horizontally or vertically. Such integration may stabilize supply, reduce costs, and increase coordination of channel members.

**vertical channel integration**
Combining two or more stages of the marketing channel under one management

**Vertical Channel Integration.** **Vertical channel integration** combines two or more stages of the channel under one management. This may occur when one member of a marketing channel purchases the operations of another member or simply performs the functions of another member, eliminating the need for that intermediary.

Whereas members of conventional channel systems work independently, participants in vertical channel integration coordinate efforts to reach a desired target market. In this more progressive approach to distribution, channel members regard other members as extensions of their own operations. Vertically integrated channels are often more effective against competition because of increased bargaining power and sharing of information and responsibilities. At one end of a vertically integrated channel, a manufacturer might provide advertising and training assistance, and the retailer at the other end might buy the manufacturer's products in large quantities and actively promote them.

**vertical marketing systems (VMSs)** A marketing channel managed by a single channel member to achieve efficient, low-cost distribution aimed at satisfying target market customers

Integration has been successfully institutionalized in marketing channels called **vertical marketing systems (VMSs),** in which a single channel member coordinates or manages channel activities to achieve efficient, low-cost distribution aimed at satisfying target market customers. Vertical integration brings most or all stages of the marketing channel under common control or ownership. The Limited, a retail clothing chain, uses a wholly owned subsidiary, Mast Industries, as its primary supply source. Radio Shack operates as a vertical marketing system, encompassing both wholesale and retail functions. Because efforts of individual channel members are combined in a VMS, marketing activities can be coordinated for maximum effectiveness and economy, without duplication of services. Vertical marketing systems are competitive, accounting for a significant share of retail sales in consumer goods.

Most vertical marketing systems take one of three forms: corporate, administered, or contractual. A *corporate VMS* combines all stages of the marketing channel, from producers to consumers, under a single owner. For example, the Limited established a corporate VMS that operates corporate-owned production facilities and retail stores. Supermarket chains that own food-processing plants and large retailers that purchase wholesaling and production facilities are other examples of corporate VMSs.

In an *administered VMS*, channel members are independent, but a high level of interorganizational management is achieved through informal coordination. Members of an administered VMS, for example, may adopt uniform accounting and ordering procedures and cooperate in promotional activities for the benefit of all partners. Although individual channel members maintain autonomy, as in conventional marketing channels, one channel member (such as a producer or large retailer) dominates the administered VMS so that distribution decisions take the whole system into account. Because of its size and power, Intel exercises a strong influence over distributors and manufacturers in its marketing channels, as do Kellogg (cereal) and Magnavox (televisions and other electronic products).

Under a *contractual VMS*, the most popular type of vertical marketing system, channel members are linked by legal agreements spelling out each member's rights and obligations. Franchise organizations, such as McDonald's and KFC, are contractual VMSs. Other contractual VMSs include wholesaler-sponsored groups, such as IGA (Independent Grocers' Alliance) stores, in which independent retailers band together under the contractual leadership of a wholesaler. Retailer-sponsored cooperatives, which own and operate their own wholesalers, are a third type of contractual VMS.

**horizontal channel integration** Combining organizations at the same level of operation under one management

**Horizontal Channel Integration.** Combining organizations at the same level of operation under one management constitutes **horizontal channel integration.** An organi-

# Partnering Helps Drive Toyota to the Top

To do a better job of reaching and satisfying customers through improved channel efficiencies, companies and channel members must choose their partners carefully, communicate clearly, and agree on the expectations and obligations of both sides.

Excelling at channel partnerships is one of the many reasons that Toyota is one of the world's leading automakers. Toyota has long been praised for its production system, which focuses on standardized processes and tooling. But the company believes in continual improvement, both for Toyota and its suppliers. Toyota's channel partnerships are based on the principle that product knowledge is intellectual property, but process knowledge is shared. Toyota offers process improvement lessons to its suppliers, disseminating information across Toyota's channel. The company even developed the Bluegrass Automotive Manufacturers Association in the United States, which provides information on the best practices in the industry to all members.

Toyota also works with suppliers to help them develop more efficient practices, which brings the benefit of standardization beyond production and into supply chain management. Toyota believes that unless every partner is working together to lower costs and raise efficiency, the goal will never be met. Despite evidence of the importance of working with channel partners, however, only 6 percent of businesses that responded to a recent survey said that they standardize with supply channel partners.

Companies that do business globally face the challenge of partnering with hundreds or thousands of channel members, sometimes across vast distances. Toyota famously tackled this challenge by creating multiple short channels. Toyota has built 47 plants in 26 markets outside Japan to reduce costs by shortening the supply channel. Avoiding the high cost of importing has improved Toyota's profits. In fact, as U.S. car companies move overseas, Toyota is building more factories in the United States, including a strategically located truck factory in Texas.

Through partnering with suppliers, Toyota hopes to increase efficiencies to ensure its ability to remain highly competitive in the global automotive business.

zation may integrate horizontally by merging with other organizations at the same level in the marketing channel. The owner of a dry-cleaning firm, for example, might buy and combine several other dry-cleaning establishments. Horizontal integration may enable a firm to generate sufficient sales revenue to integrate vertically as well.

Although horizontal integration permits efficiencies and economies of scale in purchasing, marketing research, advertising, and specialized personnel, it is not always the most effective method of improving distribution. Problems of size often follow, resulting in decreased flexibility, difficulties in coordination, and the need for additional marketing research and large-scale planning. Unless distribution functions for the various units can be performed more efficiently under unified management than under the previously separate managements, horizontal integration will neither reduce costs nor improve the competitive position of the integrating firm.

# Legal Issues in Channel Management

The numerous federal, state, and local laws governing channel management are based on the general principle that the public is best served by protecting competition and free trade. Under the authority of such federal legislation as the Sherman Antitrust Act and the Federal Trade Commission Act, courts and regulatory agencies determine under what circumstances channel management practices violate this underlying principle and must be restricted. Although channel managers are not expected to be legal experts, they should be aware that attempts to control distribution functions may have legal repercussions. The following practices are among those frequently subject to legal restraint.

## Dual Distribution

Earlier we noted that some companies may use dual distribution by using two or more marketing channels to distribute the same products to the same target market. Hewlett-Packard, for example, sells computers directly to consumers through a toll-free telephone line and a website, as well as through electronics retailers such as Best Buy. Courts do not consider this practice illegal when it promotes competition. A manufacturer can also legally open its own retail outlets. But the courts view as a threat to competition a manufacturer that uses company-owned outlets to dominate or drive out of business independent retailers or distributors that handle its products. In such cases, dual distribution violates the law. To avoid this interpretation, producers should use outlet prices that do not severely undercut independent retailers' prices.

## Restricted Sales Territories

To tighten control over distribution of its products, a manufacturer may try to prohibit intermediaries from selling its products outside designated sales territories. Intermediaries themselves often favor this practice because it gives them exclusive territories, allowing them to avoid competition for the producer's brands within these territories. In recent years, the courts have adopted conflicting positions in regard to restricted sales territories. Although the courts have deemed restricted sales territories a restraint of trade among intermediaries handling the same brands (except for small or newly established companies), they have also held that exclusive territories can actually promote competition among dealers handling different brands. At present, the producer's intent in establishing restricted territories and the overall effect of doing so on the market must be evaluated for each individual case.

**tying agreement** An agreement in which a supplier furnishes a product to a channel member with the stipulation that the channel member must purchase other products as well

## Tying Agreements

When a supplier (usually a manufacturer or franchiser) furnishes a product to a channel member with the stipulation that the channel member must purchase other products as well, a **tying agreement** exists. Suppliers may institute tying agreements to move weaker products along with more popular items, or a franchiser may tie purchase of equipment and supplies to the sale of franchises, justifying the policy as necessary for quality control and protection of the franchiser's reputation.

A related practice is *full-line forcing,* in which a supplier requires that channel members purchase the supplier's entire line to obtain any of the supplier's products. Manufacturers sometimes use full-line forcing to ensure that intermediaries accept new products and that a suitable range of products is available to customers.

The courts accept tying agreements when the supplier alone can provide products of a certain quality, when the intermediary is free to carry competing products as well, and when a company has just entered the market. Most other tying agreements are considered illegal.

### Exclusive Dealing

**exclusive dealing** A situation in which a manufacturer forbids an intermediary to carry products of competing manufacturers

When a manufacturer forbids an intermediary to carry products of competing manufacturers, the arrangement is called **exclusive dealing.** Manufacturers receive considerable market protection in an exclusive-dealing arrangement and may cut off shipments to intermediaries that violate the agreement.

The legality of an exclusive-dealing contract is generally determined by applying three tests. If the exclusive dealing blocks competitors from as much as 10 percent of the market, if the sales revenue involved is sizable, and if the manufacturer is much larger (and thus more intimidating) than the dealer, the arrangement is considered anticompetitive.[9] If dealers and customers in a given market have access to similar products or if the exclusive-dealing contract strengthens an otherwise weak competitor, the arrangement is allowed.

### Refusal to Deal

For more than 75 years, the courts have held that producers have the right to choose channel members with which they will do business (and the right to reject others). Within existing distribution channels, however, suppliers may not legally refuse to deal with wholesalers or dealers merely because these wholesalers or dealers resist policies that are anticompetitive or in restraint of trade. Suppliers are further prohibited from organizing some channel members in refusal-to-deal actions against other members that choose not to comply with illegal policies.

## SUMMARY

A marketing channel, or channel of distribution, is a group of individuals and organizations that direct the flow of products from producers to customers. The major role of marketing channels is to make products available at the right time at the right place and in the right amounts. In most channels of distribution, producers and consumers are linked by marketing intermediaries, or middlemen. The two major types of intermediaries are retailers, which purchase products and resell them to ultimate consumers, and wholesalers, which buy and resell products to other wholesalers, retailers, and business customers.

Marketing channels serve many functions. They create time, place, and possession utility by making products available when and where customers want them and providing customers with access to product use through sale or rental. Marketing intermediaries facilitate exchange efficiencies, often reducing the costs of exchanges by performing certain services and functions. Although critics suggest eliminating wholesalers, someone must perform their functions in the marketing channel. Because intermediaries serve both producers and buyers, they reduce the total number of transactions that otherwise would be needed to move products from producer to ultimate users.

Marketing channels also form a supply chain, a total distribution system that serves customers and creates a competitive advantage. Supply chain management refers to long-term partnerships among channel members working together to reduce inefficiencies, costs, and redundancies and to develop innovative approaches to satisfy customers. The supply chain includes all entities—shippers and other firms that facilitate distribution, as well as producers, wholesalers, and retailers—that distribute products and benefit from cooperative efforts. Supply chains start with the customer and require the cooperation of channel members to satisfy customer requirements.

Channels of distribution are broadly classified as channels for consumer products and channels for business products. Within these two broad categories, different marketing channels are used for different products. Although consumer goods can move directly from producer to consumers, consumer product channels that include wholesalers and retailers are usually more economical and efficient. Distribution of business products differs from that of consumer products in the types of channels used. A direct distribution channel is common in business marketing. Also used are channels containing industrial distributors, manufacturers' agents, and a combination of agents and distributors. Most producers have multiple or dual channels so the distribution system can be adjusted for various target markets.

Selecting an appropriate marketing channel is a crucial decision for supply chain managers. To determine which channel is most appropriate, managers must think about customer characteristics, the type of organization, product attributes, competition, environmental forces, and the availability and characteristics of intermediaries. Careful consideration of these factors will assist a supply chain manager in selecting the correct channel.

A marketing channel is managed such that products receive appropriate market coverage. In choosing intensive distribution, producers strive to make a product available to all possible dealers. In selective distribution, only some outlets in an area are chosen to distribute a product. Exclusive distribution usually gives a single dealer rights to sell a product in a large geographic area.

Each channel member performs a different role in the system and agrees to accept certain rights, responsibilities, rewards, and sanctions for nonconformance. Although many marketing channels are determined by consensus, some are organized and controlled by a single leader, or channel captain. A channel captain may be a producer, wholesaler, or retailer. Channels function most effectively when members cooperate; when they deviate from their roles, channel conflict can arise.

Integration of marketing channels brings various activities under one channel member's management. Vertical integration combines two or more stages of the channel under one management. The vertical marketing system (VMS) is managed centrally for the mutual benefit of all channel members. Vertical marketing systems may be corporate, administered, or contractual. Horizontal integration combines institutions at the same level of channel operation under a single management.

Federal, state, and local laws regulate channel management to protect competition and free trade. Courts may prohibit or permit a practice depending on whether it violates this underlying principle. Various procompetitive legislation applies to distribution practices. Channel management practices frequently subject to legal restraint include dual distribution, restricted sales territories, tying agreements, exclusive dealing, and refusal to deal. When these practices strengthen weak competitors or increase competition among dealers, they may be permitted; in most other cases, when competition may be weakened considerably, they are deemed illegal.

**ACE self-test**

Please visit the student website at **www.prideferrell.com** for ACE Self-Test questions that will help you prepare for exams.

## IMPORTANT TERMS

Distribution
Marketing channel
Marketing intermediary
Supply chain management
Industrial distributor
Dual distribution

Strategic channel alliance
Intensive distribution
Selective distribution
Exclusive distribution
Channel captain
Channel power

Vertical channel
 integration
Vertical marketing systems
 (VMSs)
Horizontal channel
 integration

Tying agreement
Exclusive dealing

## DISCUSSION & REVIEW QUESTIONS

1. Describe the major functions of marketing channels. Why are these functions better accomplished through combined efforts of channel members?

2. Can one channel member perform all the channel functions? Explain your answer.

3. "Shorter channels are usually a more direct means of distribution and therefore are more efficient." Comment on this statement.

4. List several reasons consumers often blame intermediaries for distribution inefficiencies.

5. Compare and contrast the four major types of marketing channels for consumer products. Through which type of channel is each of the following products most likely to be distributed?
   a. New automobiles
   b. Saltine crackers
   c. Cut-your-own Christmas trees
   d. New textbooks
   e. Sofas
   f. Soft drinks

6. Outline the four most common channels for business products. Describe the products or situations that lead marketers to choose each channel.

7. Describe an industrial distributor. What types of products are marketed through an industrial distributor?

8. Under what conditions is a producer most likely to use more than one marketing channel?

9. Identify and describe the factors that may influence marketing channel selection decisions.

10. Explain the differences among intensive, selective, and exclusive methods of distribution.

11. "Channel cooperation requires that members support the overall channel goals to achieve individual goals." Comment on this statement.

12. Name and describe firms that use (a) vertical integration and (b) horizontal integration in their marketing channels.

13. Explain the major characteristics of each of the three types of vertical marketing systems (VMSs): corporate, administered, and contractual.

14. Under what conditions are tying agreements, exclusive dealing, and dual distribution judged illegal?

## APPLICATION QUESTIONS

1. *Supply chain management* refers to long-term partnerships among channel members working together to reduce inefficiencies, costs, and redundancies and to develop innovative approaches to satisfy customers. Select one of the following companies and explain how supply chain management could increase marketing productivity.
   a. Dell Computer
   b. FedEx
   c. Nike
   d. Taco Bell

2. Organizations often form strategic channel alliances when they find it more profitable or convenient to distribute their products through the marketing channel of another organization. Find an article in a newspaper or on the Internet that describes such a strategic channel alliance. Briefly summarize the article and indicate the benefits each organization expects to gain.

3. Marketers can select from three major levels of market coverage when determining the number and

kinds of outlets in which to sell a product: intensive, selective, or exclusive distribution. Characteristics of the product and its target market determine the intensity of coverage a product should receive. Indicate the intensity level best suited for the following products, and explain why it is appropriate.
   a. Personal computer
   b. Deodorant
   c. Canon digital cameras
   d. Nike athletic shoes

4. Describe the decision process you might go through if you were attempting to determine the most appropriate distribution channel for one of the following:
   a. Shotguns for hunters
   b. Women's lingerie
   c. Telephone systems for small businesses
   d. Toy trucks for two-year-olds

1. Your firm is looking for competitive alternatives in its supply chain management strategy. One method is to reduce costs by relocating the U.S.-based manufacturing of your food processing division. The Competitive Alternatives website can assist with your analysis. Access this site by using the search term "competitive alternatives" at **http://globaledge.msu.edu/ibrd.** Once you reach the Competitive Alternatives website, click on the Download tab and then download the International Report (Volume 1). Based on the results of relative costs in an analysis by industry and operation, to which country should you relocate your firm's operations based on information from the Competitive Alternatives website? Compare this with the results focused on particular cities in the same report.

What are the five most promising cities listed? Does this change your decision on the relocation of your food processing division?

2. As conduct in international marketing channels typically involves the shipment of cargo around the world, managers must understand the different terms involved in the handling and delivery of "world cargo." Define the following terms: CFR, CIF, and CIP based on information from the World Cargo Alliance website. The information required can be accessed by using the search term "world cargo" at **http://globaledge.msu.edu/ibrd.** In each of these three shipment conditions, which party is required to clear the goods under consideration for export?

## INTERNET Exercise

Visit **www.prideferrell.com** for resources to help you master the material in this chapter, plus materials that will help you expand your marketing knowledge, including Internet exercise updates, ACE Self-Tests, hotlinks to companies featured in this chapter, and much more.

## iSuppli

Distribution bottlenecks can be an expensive problem for any business. Trying to prevent such problems is iSuppli, an Internet supply chain management tool that links all members of a supply chain, from the supplier's system to the retailer's storefront system. Learn more about this innovative tool at **www.isuppli.com**.

1. Does iSuppli represent a new type of marketing channel? Why or why not?
2. Why would firms be cautious when deciding whether to use iSuppli?
3. Do you think iSuppli represents the future of supply chain management? Why or why not?

## Video Case 15.1   SmarterKids, SmarterCompany

Marketing through online retailing, mail-order catalogs, and direct sales to institutional customers can be a difficult juggling act for any company, but Excelligence Learning Corporation is up to the challenge of channel management. One of the stars of its Early Childhood division is SmarterKids, a website targeting parents who want to buy quality educational toys. Other Excelligence divisions develop new educational toys, market supplies and furniture to schools through printed catalogs, and offer products for schools to buy for resale during fundraising drives. Together, they help Excelligence ring up $121 million in annual sales.

Excelligence maintains a sales force of 51 representatives who visit schools and child-care facilities to sell the full array of company products. In addition, it publishes a magazine and maintains a website for educators who work with preschool and elementary school students. Because Excelligence has so many businesses focused on children and education, it is in a unique position to effectively manage the flow of products to each of its target markets.

Consider the SmarterKids site (**www.smarterkids.com**), which serves as a consumer marketing channel for products made by the parent company as well as by outside manufacturers. Many toy retailers try to compete with industry giants such as Toys 'R' Us by stocking a huge number of products. SmarterKids takes a different approach. Rather than compete on the basis of an extensive product mix, SmarterKids narrows the choices by having a team of teachers individually test each product. The teachers even watch every video and play every computer game being considered for the website. Then they rate the products using hundreds of criteria, including ease of use, creativity, educational approach, and durability. The result is a smaller but much more focused selection of approximately 4,000 products that meet SmarterKids's extremely demanding criteria for advancing children's development and education.

SmarterKids's marketers know that parents have limited time and do not want to wander endlessly through cavernous stores looking at a dizzying array of toys that may or may not be right for their children. Ideally parents want to buy products that their children—newborns to teenagers—will enjoy for more than a few days. And they want to buy products that will help children develop their skills and build their knowledge. Customers may well be impressed by the number of toys a retailer stocks. However, many will find more value in buying from SmarterKids because it helps narrow the choices to a manageable subset of

toys, games, movies, and books that make sense for a particular child.

When customers log onto the colorful SmarterKids website, they can search for toys in four ways. First, they can search according to age categories (such as birth to one year old or preschool age). Second, they can choose a particular toy category (such as puzzles, music, or books). Third, they can search by developmental area (such as language, creative expression, or sensory development). Fourth, they can enter a keyword (such as a brand name or type of toy). In addition, the homepage highlights toys that are sold exclusively by SmarterKids, toys that are best sellers in their category, and discounted toys featured in the site's clearance section. Then, instead of pushing a shopping cart through endless miles of cramped aisles, customers simply point and click to browse and buy. Thus, SmarterKids makes the online shopping experience more efficient and more productive for its time-pressured customers.

Parents can also access special sections of the SmarterKids site to learn more about six child developmental areas. The site explains why each area of development is important and posts a number of fun, easy activities for home use. No SmarterKids toys are needed. Instead, the activities are designed to bring parents and children together for a few minutes of educational playtime involving simple household items such as pots and pans or sponges. These sections represent an evolution from the detailed, personalized assessments that SmarterKids once offered on the site.

SmarterKids has found through research that customers who take full advantage of the site's information and activities wind up purchasing twice as much as those who don't. More data means the retailer can do a better job of buying the most appropriate toys and planning e-mail newsletters and other targeted promotions. The idea is to establish and strengthen connections with customers by showing that SmarterKids is dedicated to satisfying their needs and the needs of their children. Big stores may have bigger inventories, but SmarterKids believes its retailing strategy is smarter for long-term customer loyalty. "If you are able to develop a trusting relationship with consumers, they're going to come back time and time again," says the CEO.[10]

### Questions for Discussion

1. What is Excelligence's approach to channel integration?
2. Some toys are sold to parents through the direct selling "party plan." Should SmarterKids use this channel in addition to online retailing? Explain.
3. Under what conditions would a toy manufacturer be as interested in marketing its products through SmarterKids as it would through Toys 'R' Us?

## Case 15.2    Grainger Wires the Channel for Business Products

Need an electric motor or a hard hat? W. W. Grainger has dozens for sale—among the many thousands of products showcased in its voluminous catalogs and on its website. Grainger is an industrial distributor offering virtually one-stop shopping for producer, government, and institutional markets seeking a wide range of maintenance, repair, and operating (MRO) supplies. With 600 distribution facilities spread across North America, the company can time shipments to arrive quickly when business customers place orders.

William W. Grainger founded the Illinois-based company in the 1920s as a wholesaler of electric motors. To build sales, Grainger mailed out postcards about his offerings and compiled a catalog titled *MotorBook*. In less than a decade, he was operating 15 U.S. sales branches to serve business customers from coast to coast. By 1949, he had expanded his branch network to 30 states.

Son David Grainger, now senior chairperson, continued the founder's expansion strategy. In the 1980s and 1990s, the company opened high-tech regional distribution centers in Kansas, Georgia, and Texas to supplement its Chicago-area facilities and slash fulfillment time for orders placed by customers around the country. Grainger also expanded its geographic reach by buying Acklands Ltd., a Canadian distributor of automotive and industrial safety products.

By the mid-1990s, Grainger was getting wired. Recognizing that the Internet could bring in many more business customers at a lower cost, management created Grainger.com as a comprehensive online catalog site. Over the years, the company continued to refine its web presence by posting informative resources, adding live-chat customer assistance, a virtual tour of the site for new customers, special international services, and web-only price promotions to bring customers back to the site again and again. Within the first three years of operation, annual web sales grew from $3 million to $267 million as customers flocked to the online catalog, which features many more items than the 80,000 products shown in a typical printed Grainger catalog.

Not all of Grainger's Internet initiatives have been as successful, however. The company had high hopes for its Material Logic division covering three web-based distribution sites. TotalMRO.com was designed as an industrywide portal with catalogs from Grainger and competing distributors. MROverstocks.com was created as an auction site for discontinued or excess industrial products. FindMRO.com was designed as a search site for specialized and hard-to-find industrial products. After launching the three sites, Grainger tried to interest competing distributors and outside investors in buying a stake in Material Logic. The company had spent more than $100 million on its web operations and sought outside funding to support its aggressive movement into electronic procurement. But when no one stepped forward to invest, Grainger quickly shut down the unprofitable division. At the same time, FindMRO.com was becoming popular, so it was merged into the existing Grainger.com operation.

Today Grainger sells $5 billion worth of industrial products every year. Approximately 10 percent of total sales revenues come from the profitable Grainger.com site, and the percentage continues to rise as more customers switch from paper-based to electronic purchasing. Despite its Internet success, Grainger is not abandoning its branch system. In line with the changing demographics of its customer base, the company is reassessing the intensity of its market coverage in major metropolitan areas. It has closed two older branches, opened three new branches, expanded or relocated seven branches, and hired more sales staff. The company has also opened convenient on-site branches for two big customers, Florida State University and Langley Air Force Base. "Grainger's multi-channel model is what distinguishes us from our competition," the CEO emphasizes. "No other company has as broad a product line with tens of thousands of items immediately available all across the country."

Grainger is showing major customers such as the U.S. Postal Service how to better manage their supply chains and cut costs throughout the procurement process. It is also helping customers plan and budget for unexpected and infrequent MRO purchases. Customers often need parts right away to repair machines that break down without warning, but they want to minimize equipment downtime and the expense of storing all replacement parts on hand at all times. Grainger uses sophisticated software to analyze how often customers of similar sizes buy spare parts and related products and then suggests how individual businesses can find an appropriate balance of inventory and planned purchasing for these products.

To handle future volume more productively, Grainger is opening an additional nine automated distribution centers and implementing a new logistics network. The added efficiency will allow the company to lower its inventory investment by $100 million while profitably serving more customers. More efficiencies are ahead as the company, already the largest industrial distributor in North America, aggressively pursues higher market share and higher profits.[11]

### Questions for Discussion

1. Why would a competing industrial distributor even consider investing in a portal designed by Grainger?
2. Is Grainger in a position to be a channel captain? Explain.
3. Why would a hospital buy from Grainger instead of buying directly from producers?

# Wholesaling and Physical Distribution

## McKesson: A Wholesale Powerhouse

McKesson Corporation is a pharmaceutical wholesaler health-care giant that touches the lives of millions of people every day. With annual revenues of more than $80 billion, McKesson ranks as the sixteenth largest industrial company and leads pharmaceutical distribution and supply chain management in the United States. Over 40,000 neighborhood drugstores, retail chains, and health-care facilities count on McKesson to help them operate their pharmacies with the highest possible quality, safety, and efficiency. McKesson delivers more than half of wholesale pharmaceutical products and is the largest supplier of generic pharmaceuticals in the United States.

McKesson services its customers through a network of 30 highly automated distribution centers in the United States. It provides a number of services for retailers, including bulk repackaging, inventory forecasting, and automated replenishment, as well as claims adjudication, claims reconciliation, managed-care networking, patient outcomes management, and profitability analysis. Obviously, patient safety is paramount to McKesson's business. It has invested heavily over the last several years to achieve operational excellence by upgrading systems to achieve the highest quality products. According to company records, this has resulted in a 99.9 percent accuracy rate in customer fulfillment.

## OBJECTIVES

1. To understand the nature of wholesaling in the marketing channel

2. To explain wholesalers' functions

3. To understand how wholesalers are classified

4. To recognize how physical distribution activities are integrated into marketing channels and overall marketing strategies

5. To discuss the major objectives of physical distribution

6. To examine the major physical distribution functions of order processing, inventory management, materials handling, warehousing, and transportation

7. To discuss the strategic implications of physical distribution systems

The mix of services that McKesson offers to its customer is important in maintaining a competitive advantage. For example, McKesson recently launched Auto-Rx-Net, a monthly pricing service that automatically updates pharmaceutical prices based on competitive rates in retailers' respective market areas. Prescription prices are automatically adjusted to competitive conditions on branded and generic drugs to optimize a pharmacy's profit margins. McKesson also provides its retailers with accounts receivable management to help them improve cash flow and better manage inventory.

McKesson and other intermediaries are changing how wholesalers are compensated. Pharmaceutical wholesalers used to stock up on inventory from manufacturers, control the market, and earn profits based on whatever up-charge they could get from retailers. Today, the distribution process is so efficient that wholesalers charge manufacturers a specific fee for the service of distributing their products to the point of sale or redistribution—and manufacturers pay it.[1] ∎

Wholesalers like McKesson help make products available to customers when and where they want them. Wholesalers often play a key role in supply chain management and physical distribution. Companies rely heavily on physical distribution, a crucial set of functions in supply chain management, because it includes those activities associated with handling and moving products through the marketing channel.

In this chapter, we explore the role of wholesaling and physical distribution in supply chain management. First, we examine the importance of wholesalers in marketing channels, including their functions and classifications. Next, we consider critical physical distribution concepts, including order processing, inventory management, materials handling, warehousing, and transportation. We conclude this chapter by examining some strategic implications of physical distribution systems.

# The Nature of Wholesaling

**wholesaling** Transactions in which products are bought for resale, for making other products, or for general business operations

**wholesaler** An individual or organization that sells products that are bought for resale, for making other products, or for general business operations

**Wholesaling** refers to all transactions in which products are bought for resale, for making other products, or for general business operations. A **wholesaler** is an individual or organization that sells products that are bought for these purposes. In other words, wholesalers buy products and resell them to reseller, government, and institutional users. Wholesaling does not include exchanges with ultimate consumers. For example, SYSCO, the nation's number one food-service distributor, supplies restaurants, hotels, schools, industrial caterers, and hospitals with everything from frozen and fresh food and paper products to medical and cleaning supplies. There are approximately 438,000 wholesaling establishments in the United States,[2] and more than half of all products sold in this country pass through these firms.

Table 16.1 lists the major activities wholesalers perform, but individual wholesalers may perform more or fewer functions than the table shows. Distribution of all goods requires wholesaling activities whether or not a wholesaling firm is involved. Wholesaling activities are not limited to goods; service companies, such as financial institutions, also use active wholesale networks. For example, some banks buy loans in bulk from other financial institutions as well as making loans to their own retail customers.

Wholesalers perform services for other organizations in the marketing channel. They bear primary responsibility for the physical distribution of products from manufacturers to retailers. In addition, they may establish information systems that help producers and retailers better manage the supply chain from producer to customer. Many wholesalers are using information technology and the Internet to allow their employees, customers, and suppliers to share information between intermediaries and facilitating agencies such as trucking companies and warehouse firms. For example, FedEx, which serves as a facilitating agency in providing overnight or even same-day delivery of packages, provides online tracking of packages for the benefit

| table 16.1 | MAJOR WHOLESALING FUNCTIONS |
| --- | --- |
| Supply chain management | Creating long-term partnerships among channel members |
| Promotion | Providing a sales force, advertising, sales promotion, and publicity |
| Warehousing, shipping, and product handling | Receiving, storing, and stock keeping<br>Packaging<br>Shipping outgoing orders<br>Materials handling<br>Arranging and making local and long-distance shipments |
| Inventory control and data processing | Processing orders<br>Controlling physical inventory<br>Recording transactions<br>Tracking sales data for financial analysis |
| Risk taking | Assuming responsibility for theft, product obsolescence, and excess inventories |
| Financing and budgeting | Extending credit<br>Borrowing<br>Making capital investments<br>Forecasting cash flow |
| Marketing research and information systems | Providing information about markets<br>Conducting research studies<br>Managing computer networks to facilitate exchanges and relationships |

of its customers. Other firms are making their databases and marketing information systems available to their supply chain partners to facilitate order processing, shipping, reward product development, and to share information about changing market conditions and customer desires. As a result, some wholesalers play a key role in supply chain management decisions.

## Services Provided by Wholesalers

Wholesalers provide essential services to both producers and retailers. By initiating sales contacts with a producer and selling diverse products to retailers, wholesalers serve as an extension of the producer's sales force. Wholesalers also provide financial assistance. They often pay for transporting goods; they reduce a producer's warehousing expenses and inventory investment by holding goods in inventory; they extend credit and assume losses from buyers who turn out to be poor credit risks; and when they buy a producer's entire output and pay promptly or in cash, they are a source of working capital. Wholesalers also serve as conduits for information within the marketing channel, keeping producers up to date on market developments and passing along the manufacturers' promotional plans to other intermediaries. Using wholesalers therefore gives producers a distinct advantage because the specialized services wholesalers perform allow producers to concentrate on developing and manufacturing products that match customers' needs and wants.

Many producers would prefer more direct interaction with retailers. Wholesalers, however, are more likely to have closer contact with retailers because of their strategic position in the marketing channel. Although a producer's own sales force is probably more effective at selling, the costs of maintaining a sales force and performing functions normally done by wholesalers are sometimes higher than the benefits received from an independent sales staff. Wholesalers can spread sales costs over many more products than can most producers, resulting in lower costs per product unit.

For these reasons, many producers shift informational, financing, and physical distribution activities, such as transportation and warehousing, to wholesalers. Thus, the wholesaler often becomes a major link in the supply chain, creating an optimal level of efficiency and customer service.

Wholesalers support retailers by assisting with marketing strategy, especially the distribution component. Wholesalers also help retailers select inventory. They are often specialists on market conditions and experts at negotiating final purchases. In industries in which obtaining supplies is important, skilled buying is indispensable. For example, Atlanta-based Genuine Parts Company (GPC), the nation's top automotive parts wholesaler, has more than 70 years of experience in the auto parts business, which helps the company serve its customers effectively. GPC supplies more than 300,000 replacement parts (from 150 different suppliers) to 6,000 NAPA Auto Parts stores.[3] Effective wholesalers make an effort to understand the businesses of their customers. They can reduce a retailer's burden of looking for and coordinating supply sources. If the wholesaler purchases for several buyers, all customers can share

# Wholesale Marketer: The Internet Intermediary

The Internet is providing new opportunities not only for one-on-one buying and selling, but also for intermediaries. Wholesale Marketer is a high-volume wholesaler that supplies products to retailers such as Best Buy and Circuit City, as well as to online selling channels like eBay and EZ2 Auction. Thanks to online customers, it has been the number 1 wholesaler in the United States for the last two years.

Wholesale Marketer sells top name brands like JVC, Canon, Black and Decker, Sony, and Polo in 12 different categories such as electronics, clothing, outdoor, health and fitness, books, and household appliances. The company offers more than 150,000 products from 13 warehouses around the country.

Wholesale Marketer provides many services to customers. Most importantly, products are shipped directly to customers from the manufacturer or producer in the quantity ordered (from one to hundreds of units). Consequently, Wholesale Marketer's customers do not have their money tied up in inventory. This means its customers do not need to own or rent a warehouse, worry about logistics or meeting minimum quantity commitments, pay for packaging materials, deal with a myriad of wholesalers, handle returns, or manage back-orders.

Pricing is another major selling point for Wholesale Marketer. All prices are wholesale, which range from 33 to 75 percent off manufacturer suggested retail price. Its prices are low because the company does not make a profit from the goods it sells. Wholesale Marketer passes along the prices and fees that suppliers, wholesalers, and manufacturers charge it without taking an upcharge. Both operations and profits are funded entirely from membership fees, which range from $300 to $400 per member per year.

Wholesale Marketer is a new type of wholesaler that has found a way to provide value to customers through the Internet.

expenses. Furthermore, whereas a manufacturer's salesperson offers retailers only a few products at a time, independent wholesalers always have a wide range of products available. Thus, through partnerships, wholesalers and retailers can forge successful relationships for the benefit of customers.

Buying in large quantities and delivering to customers in smaller lots enable wholesalers to perform physical distribution activities efficiently. These activities (discussed later in this chapter) include order processing, inventory planning, materials handling, warehousing, and transportation. Wholesalers furnish greater service than might be feasible for a producer's or retailer's own physical distribution system. Furthermore, wholesalers offer quick and frequent delivery, even when demand fluctuates. They can do so at low cost, which lets the producer and the wholesalers' customers avoid risks associated with holding large inventories.

The distinction between services performed by wholesalers and those provided by other businesses has blurred in recent years. Changes in the competitive nature of business, especially the growth of strong retail chains such as Wal-Mart, Home Depot, and Best Buy, are changing supply chain relationships. In many product categories, such as electronics, furniture, and even food products, retailers have discovered they can deal directly with producers, performing wholesaling activities themselves at a lower cost. An increasing number of retailers are relying on computer technology to expedite ordering, delivery, and handling of goods. Technology is thus allowing retailers to take over many wholesaling functions. When a wholesaler is eliminated from a marketing channel, the functions, listed in Table 16.1, still have to be performed by a member of the marketing channel, whether a producer, retailer, or facilitating agency. These wholesaling activities are critical components of supply chain management.

## Types of Wholesalers

Wholesalers are classified according to several criteria. Whether a wholesaler is independently owned or owned by a producer influences how it is classified. Wholesalers can also be grouped according to whether they take title to (own) the products they handle. The range of services provided is another criterion used for classification. Finally, wholesalers are classified according to the breadth and depth of their product lines. Using these criteria, we discuss three general types of wholesaling establishments: merchant wholesalers, agents and brokers, and manufacturers' sales branches and offices.

**Merchant Wholesalers.** **Merchant wholesalers** are independently owned businesses that take title to goods, assume risks associated with ownership, and generally buy and resell products to other wholesalers, business customers, or retailers. A producer is likely to rely on merchant wholesalers when selling directly to customers would be economically unfeasible. Merchant wholesalers are also useful for providing market coverage, making sales contacts, storing inventory, handling orders, collecting market information, and furnishing customer support. Some merchant wholesalers are even involved in packaging and developing private brands to help retail customers be competitive. Merchant wholesalers go by various names, including *wholesaler, jobber, distributor, assembler, exporter,* and *importer.* They fall into one of two broad categories: full-service and limited-service (see Figure 16.1 on p. 436).

*Full-Service Wholesalers.* **Full-service wholesalers** perform the widest possible range of wholesaling functions. Customers rely on them for product availability, suitable assortments, breaking large quantities into smaller lots, financial assistance, and technical advice and service. Universal Corporation, the world's largest buyer and processor of leaf tobacco, is an example of a full-service wholesaler. Based in Richmond, Virginia, the firm buys, resells, packs, and ships tobacco, and provides financing for its customers, which include cigarette manufacturers such as Philip Morris (which accounts for a significant portion of Universal's sales). Universal is also involved in sales of lumber, rubber, tea, nuts, dried fruit, and other products, and has operations in 40 countries.[4] Full-service wholesalers handle either consumer or business products and provide numerous marketing services to their customers. Many

**merchant wholesaler** An independently owned business that takes title to goods, assumes ownership risks, and buys and resells products to other wholesalers, business customers, or retailers

**full-service wholesaler** A merchant wholesaler that performs the widest range of wholesaling functions

## figure 16.1

### TYPES OF MERCHANT WHOLESALERS

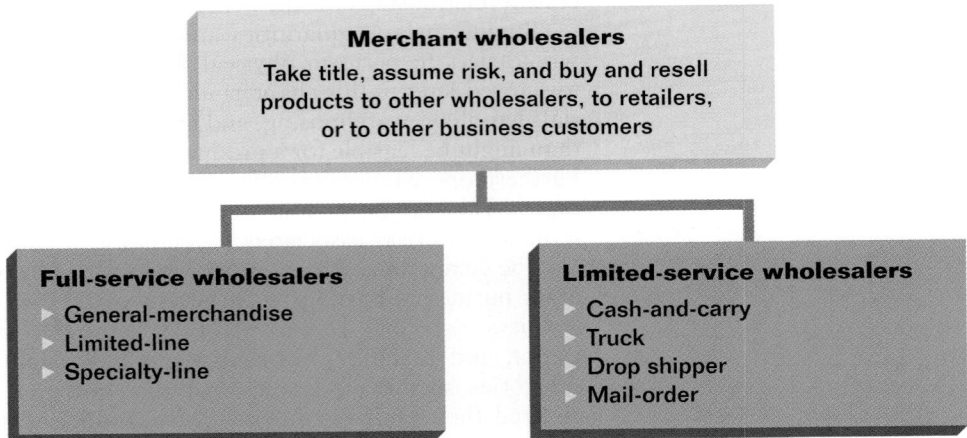

large grocery wholesalers help retailers with store design, site selection, personnel training, financing, merchandising, advertising, coupon redemption, and scanning. Although full-service wholesalers often earn higher gross margins than other wholesalers, their operating expenses are also higher because they perform a wider range of functions. Full-service wholesalers are categorized as general-merchandise, general-line, and specialty-line wholesalers.

**General-merchandise wholesalers** carry a wide product mix but offer limited depth within product lines. They deal in such products as drugs, nonperishable foods, cosmetics, detergents, and tobacco. **General-line wholesalers** carry only a few product lines, such as groceries, lighting fixtures, or oil-well drilling equipment, but offer an extensive assortment of products within those lines. Bergen Brunswig Corporation, for example, is a general-line wholesaler of pharmaceuticals and health and beauty aids. General-line wholesalers provide a range of services similar to those of general-merchandise wholesalers. **Specialty-line wholesalers** offer the narrowest range of products, usually a single product line or a few items within a product line. Wholesalers that specialize in shellfish, fruit, or other food delicacies are specialty-line wholesalers. Red River Commodities, for example, is the leading importer (specialty-line wholesaler) of nuts, seeds, and dried fruits in the United States.[5] **Rack jobbers** are a type of specialty-line wholesalers that own and maintain display racks in supermarkets, drugstores, and discount and variety stores. They set up displays, mark merchandise, stock shelves, and keep billing and inventory records; retailers need to furnish only space. Rack jobbers specialize in nonfood items with high profit margins, such as health and beauty aids, books, magazines, hosiery, and greeting cards.

*Limited-Service Wholesalers.* **Limited-service wholesalers** provide fewer marketing services than full-service wholesalers and specialize in just a few functions. Producers perform the remaining functions or pass them on to customers or to other intermediaries. Limited-service wholesalers take title to merchandise but often do not deliver merchandise, grant credit, provide marketing information, store inventory, or plan ahead for customers' future needs. Because they offer restricted services, limited-service wholesalers are compensated with lower rates and have smaller profit margins than full-service wholesalers. The decision about whether to use a limited-service or a full-service wholesaler depends on the structure of the marketing channel and the need to manage the supply chain to provide competitive advantage. Although certain types of limited-service wholesalers are few in number, they are important in the distribution of such products as specialty foods, perishable items, construction materials, and coal. Table 16.2 summarizes the services provided by four typical limited-service wholesalers: cash-and-carry wholesalers, truck wholesalers, drop shippers, and mail-order wholesalers.

**general-merchandise wholesaler** A full-service wholesaler with a wide product mix but limited depth within product lines

**general-line wholesaler** A full-service wholesaler that carries only a few product lines but many products within those lines

**specialty-line wholesaler** A full-service wholesaler that carries only a single product line or a few items within a product line

**rack jobber** A type of specialty-line wholesaler that owns and maintains display racks in stores

**limited-service wholesaler** A merchant wholesaler that provides some services and specializes in a few functions

| table 16.2 | SERVICES THAT LIMITED-SERVICE WHOLESALERS PROVIDE | | | |
|---|---|---|---|---|
| | Cash-and-Carry | Truck | Drop Shipper | Mail-Order |
| Physical possession of merchandise | Yes | Yes | No | Yes |
| Personal sales calls on customers | No | Yes | No | No |
| Information about market conditions | No | Some | Yes | Yes |
| Advice to customers | No | Some | Yes | No |
| Stocking and maintenance of merchandise in customers' stores | No | No | No | No |
| Credit to customers | No | No | Yes | Some |
| Delivery of merchandise to customers | No | Yes | No | No |

**cash-and-carry wholesaler** A limited-service wholesaler whose customers pay cash and furnish transportation

**truck wholesaler** A limited-service wholesaler that transports products directly to customers for inspection and selection

**drop shipper** A limited-service wholesaler that takes title to goods and negotiates sales but never actually takes possession of products

**mail-order wholesaler** A wholesaler who uses catalogs instead of a sales force to sell products to retail and business buyers

**agent** An intermediary that represents either buyers or sellers on a permanent basis

**broker** An intermediary that brings buyers and sellers together temporarily

**Cash-and-carry wholesalers** are intermediaries whose customers—usually small businesses—pay cash and furnish transportation. Cash-and-carry wholesalers typically handle a limited line of products with a high turnover rate, such as groceries, building materials, and electrical or office supplies. Many small retailers whose accounts are refused by other wholesalers survive because of cash-and-carry wholesalers. **Truck wholesalers**, sometimes called *truck jobbers*, transport a limited line of products directly to customers for on-the-spot inspection and selection. They are often small operators who own and drive their own trucks. They usually have regular routes, calling on retailers and other institutions to determine their needs. **Drop shippers**, also known as *desk jobbers*, take title to goods and negotiate sales but never actually take possession of products. They forward orders from retailers, business buyers, or other wholesalers to manufacturers and arrange for carload shipments of items to be delivered directly from producers to these customers. They assume responsibility for products during the entire transaction, including the costs of any unsold goods. **Mail-order wholesalers** use catalogs instead of sales forces to sell products to retail and business buyers. Wholesale mail-order houses generally feature cosmetics, specialty foods, sporting goods, office supplies, and automotive parts. Mail-order wholesaling enables buyers to choose and order particular catalog items for delivery through United Parcel Service, the U.S. Postal Service, or other carriers. This is a convenient and effective method of selling small items to customers in remote areas that other wholesalers might find unprofitable to serve. The Internet has enabled mail-order wholesalers to sell products via their own websites and have the products shipped by the manufacturers.

**Agents and Brokers.** Agents and brokers negotiate purchases and expedite sales but do not take title to products (see Figure 16.2 on p. 438). Sometimes called *functional middlemen*, they perform a limited number of services in exchange for a commission, which is generally based on the product's selling price. **Agents** represent either buyers or sellers on a permanent basis, whereas **brokers** are intermediaries that buyers or sellers employ temporarily.

Although agents and brokers perform even fewer functions than limited-service wholesalers, they are usually specialists in particular products or types of

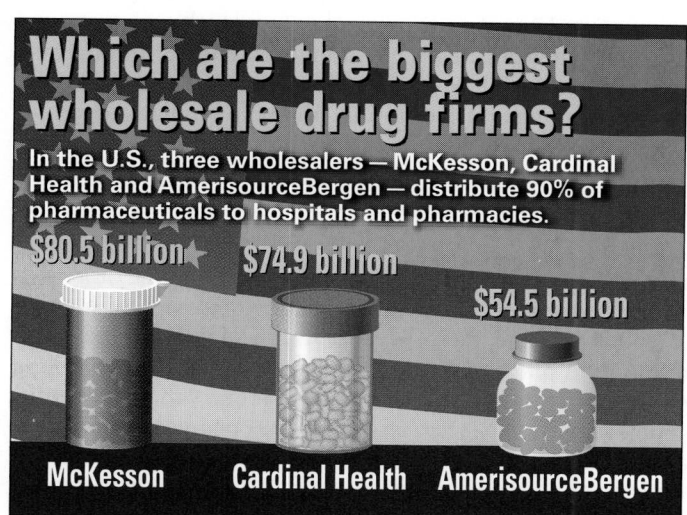

Source: Data from Bloomberg 2005.

## figure 16.2

### TYPES OF AGENTS AND BROKERS

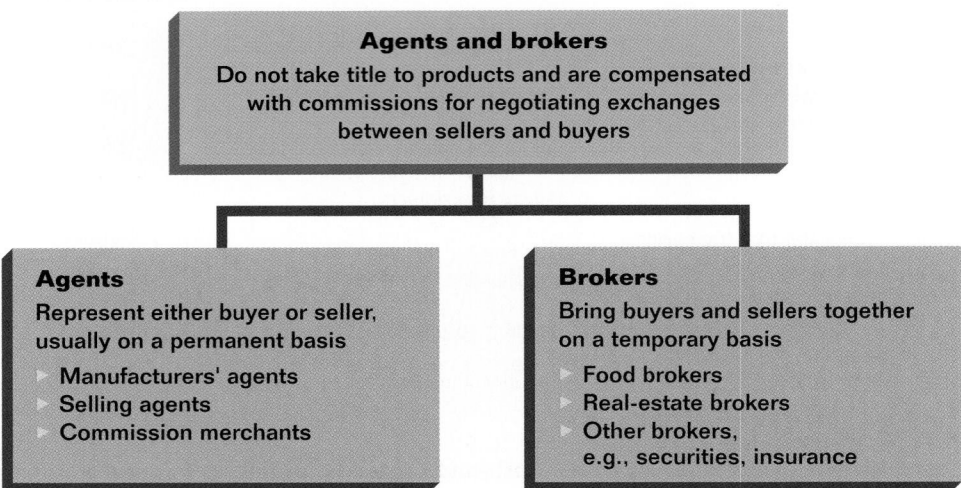

customers and can provide valuable sales expertise. They know their markets well and often form long-lasting associations with customers. Agents and brokers enable manufacturers to expand sales when resources are limited, to benefit from the services of a trained sales force, and to hold down personal selling costs. Despite the advantages they offer, agents and brokers face increased competition from merchant wholesalers, manufacturers' sales branches and offices, and direct-sales efforts through manufacturer-owned websites. We look here at three types of agents—manufacturers' agents, selling agents, and commission merchants—and at the broker's role in bringing about exchanges between buyers and sellers. Table 16.3 summarizes the services agents and brokers provide.

**manufacturers' agent** An independent intermediary that represents two or more sellers and usually offers customers complete product lines

*Manufacturers' Agents.* **Manufacturers' agents**, which account for more than half of all agent wholesalers, are independent intermediaries that represent two or more sellers and usually offer customers complete product lines. They sell and take orders year-round, much as a manufacturer's sales force does. Restricted to a particular territory, a manufacturers' agent handles noncompeting and complementary products. The relationship between the agent and the manufacturer is governed by written contracts that outline territories, selling price, order handling, and terms of sale related to delivery, service, and warranties. Manufacturers' agents have little or no control over producers' pricing and marketing policies. They do not extend credit and may be unable to provide technical advice. They do occasionally store and transport products, assist producers with planning and promotion, and help retailers advertise. Some maintain a service organization; the more services offered, the higher the agent's commission. Manufacturers' agents are commonly used in sales of apparel, machinery and equipment, steel, furniture, automotive products, electrical goods, and certain food items.

**selling agent** An intermediary that markets a whole product line or a manufacturer's entire output

*Selling Agents.* **Selling agents** market either all of a specified product line or a manufacturer's entire output. They perform every wholesaling activity except taking title to products. Selling agents usually assume the sales function for several producers simultaneously and are often used in place of marketing departments. In fact, selling agents are used most often by small producers or by manufacturers that have difficulty maintaining a marketing department because of seasonal production or other factors. In contrast to manufacturers' agents, selling agents generally have no territorial limits and have complete authority over prices, promotion, and distribution. To avoid conflicts of interest, selling agents represent noncompeting product lines. They play a key role in advertising, marketing research, and credit policies of the sellers they represent, at times even advising on product development and packaging.

| table 16.3 | SERVICES THAT AGENTS AND BROKERS PROVIDE | | | |
|---|---|---|---|---|
| | Manufacturers' Agents | Selling Agents | Commission Merchants | Brokers |
| Physical possession of merchandise | Some | Some | Yes | No |
| Long-term relationship with buyers or sellers | Yes | Yes | Yes | No |
| Representation of competing product lines | No | No | Yes | Yes |
| Limited geographic territory | Yes | No | No | No |
| Credit to customers | No | Yes | Some | No |

**commission merchant** An agent that receives goods on consignment from local sellers and negotiates sales in large, central markets

*Commission Merchants.* **Commission merchants** receive goods on consignment from local sellers and negotiate sales in large, central markets. Sometimes called *factor merchants*, these agents have broad powers regarding prices and terms of sale. They specialize in obtaining the best price possible under market conditions. Most often found in agricultural marketing, commission merchants take possession of truckloads of commodities, arrange for necessary grading or storage, and transport the commodities to auctions or markets where they are sold. When sales are completed, the agents deduct commissions and sales expenses, and then turn over the remaining revenue to the producer. Commission merchants also offer planning assistance and sometimes extend credit, but usually do not provide promotional support.

A broker's primary purpose is to bring buyers and sellers together. Thus, brokers perform fewer functions than other intermediaries. They are not involved in financing or physical possession, have no authority to set prices, and assume almost no risks. Instead they offer customers specialized knowledge of a particular commodity and a network of established contacts. Brokers are especially useful to sellers of certain types of products, such as supermarket products and real estate. Food brokers, for example, sell food and general merchandise to retailer-owned and merchant wholesalers, grocery chains, food processors, and business buyers.

**Manufacturers' Sales Branches and Offices.** Sometimes called *manufacturers' wholesalers*, manufacturers' sales branches and offices resemble merchant wholesalers' operations. **Sales branches** are manufacturer-owned intermediaries that sell products and provide support services to the manufacturer's sales force. Situated away from the manufacturing plant, they are usually located where large customers are concentrated and demand is high. They offer credit, deliver goods, give promotional assistance, and furnish other services. In many cases, they carry inventory (although this practice often duplicates functions of other channel members and is now declining). Customers include retailers, business buyers, and other wholesalers. Manufacturers of electrical supplies, such as Westinghouse Electric, and of plumbing supplies, such as American Standard, often have branch operations. Sales branches are also common in the lumber and automotive parts industries.

**sales branches** A manufacturer-owned intermediary that sells products and provides support services to the manufacturer's sales force

**sales office** A manufacturer-owned operation that provides services normally associated with agents

**Sales offices** are manufacturer-owned operations that provide services normally associated with agents. Like sales branches, they are located away from manufacturing plants; unlike branches, they carry no inventory. A manufacturer's sales office (or branch) may sell products that enhance the manufacturer's own product line. Companies such as Campbell Soup provide diverse services to their wholesale and retail customers. Hiram Walker, a liquor producer, imports wine from Spain to increase the number of products its sales offices can offer wholesalers.

Manufacturers may set up these branches or offices to reach their customers more effectively by performing wholesaling functions themselves. A manufacturer may also set up such a facility when specialized wholesaling services are not available through existing intermediaries. A manufacturer's performance of wholesaling and physical distribution activities through its sales branch or office may strengthen supply chain efficiency. In some situations, though, a manufacturer may bypass its sales office or branches entirely—for example, if the producer decides to serve large retailer customers directly.

# The Nature of Physical Distribution

**physical distribution** Activities used to move products from producers to consumers and other end users

**Physical distribution,** also known as *logistics,* refers to the activities used to move products from producers to consumers and other end users. These activities include order processing, inventory management, materials handling, warehousing, and transportation. Planning an efficient physical distribution system is crucial to developing an effective marketing strategy because it can decrease costs and increase customer satisfaction. Speed of delivery, service, and dependability are often as important to customers as costs. Companies that have the right goods in the right place, at the right time, in the right quantity, and with the right support services are able to sell more than competitors that do not. For example, a construction equipment dealer with a low inventory of replacement parts requires fast, dependable service from component suppliers when it needs parts not in stock. Even when the demand for products is unpredictable, suppliers must be able to respond quickly to inventory needs. In such cases, physical distribution costs may be a minor consideration when compared with service, dependability, and timeliness.

Physical distribution deals with the physical movement and storage of products and supplies both within and among marketing channel members. Physical distribution systems must meet the needs of both the supply chain and customers. Distribution activities are thus an important part of supply chain planning and require the cooperation of all partners. Often one channel member manages physical distribution for all channel members.

**outsourcing** Contracting physical distribution tasks to third parties that do not have managerial authority within the marketing channel

Within the marketing channel, physical distribution activities may be performed by a producer, a wholesaler, or a retailer, or they may be outsourced. In the context of distribution, **outsourcing** is the contracting of physical distribution tasks to third parties that do not have managerial authority within the marketing channel. Most physical distribution activities can be outsourced to third-party firms that have special expertise in such areas as warehousing, transportation, inventory management, and information technology. Some manufacturing firms, for example, outsource delivery services to Penske Truck Leasing, a joint venture between GE and Penske Corporation. Penske Truck has in turn outsourced some of its own activities, including some scheduling, billing, and invoicing services to employees and contractors in Mexico and India. Outsourcing has saved Penske $15 million and helped the company improve efficiency and customer service.[6] Cooperative relationships with third-party organizations, such as trucking companies, warehouses, and data-service providers, can help reduce marketing channel costs and boost service and customer satisfaction for all supply chain partners. For example, a number of e-businesses, as well as some traditional brick-and-mortar ones, have outsourced physical distribution activities, including shipping and warehousing, to build a supply chain of strategic partners to maximize customer service. Such relationships are increasingly being integrated in the supply chain to achieve physical distribution objectives. When choosing companies through which to outsource, marketers take care to use efficient firms that will help the outsourcing company provide excellent customer service.

## Physical Distribution Objectives

For most companies, the main objectives of physical distribution are to decrease costs and transit time while increasing customer service. However, few distribution systems achieve these goals in equal measure. The large inventories and rapid transportation necessary for good customer service drive up costs. Supply chain managers therefore strive for a reasonable balance among service, costs, and resources. They determine what level of customer service is acceptable and realistic, and then develop a "system" outlook to minimize total distribution costs and cycle time.

**Meeting Customer Service Standards.** In physical distribution, availability, timeliness, and accuracy are important dimensions of customer service. Companies set customer service standards based on one or a combination of these three dimensions. *Availability* refers to the percentage of orders that can be filled directly from a company's existing inventory. *Timeliness* refers to how quickly the product is shipped out to the customer. For example, some organizations set a service standard of shipping the product within 24 hours. *Accuracy* refers to whether the product the customer ordered is the product that is shipped to the customer. Some organizations have achieved better than a 99 percent order accuracy rate.

Customers seeking a high level of customer service may also want sizable inventories, efficient order processing, availability of emergency shipments, progress reports, postsale services, prompt replacement of defective items, and warranties. Customers' inventory requirements influence the expected level of physical distribution service. Business customers seeking to reduce their inventory storage and shipping costs may expect wholesalers or third-party firms to take responsibility for maintaining inventory in the marketing channel or to assume the cost of premium transportation. Because service needs vary from customer to customer, companies must analyze, and adapt to, customer preferences. Attention to customer needs and preferences is crucial to increasing sales and obtaining repeat orders. Failure to provide the desired level of service may mean loss of customers.

Companies must also examine the service levels competitors offer and match or exceed those standards when the costs of providing the services are justified by the sales generated. Many companies guarantee service performance to win customers. Services are provided most effectively when service standards are developed and stated in measurable terms, for example, "98 percent of all orders filled within 48 hours." Standards should be communicated clearly to both customers and employees, and diligently enforced. Many service standards outline delivery times and specify provisions for back-ordering, returning goods, and obtaining emergency shipments.

**Reducing Total Distribution Costs.** Although physical distribution managers try to minimize the costs associated with order processing, inventory management, materials handling, warehousing, and transportation, decreasing costs in one area often raises costs in another. Figure 16.3 shows the percentage of total costs that physical distribution functions represent. A total-cost approach to physical distribution enables managers to view physical distribution as a system rather than a collection of

**Source:** From Davis Database, 2005. Reprinted by permission of Establish Inc./Herbert W. Davis and Company.

**figure 16.3**  **PROPORTIONAL COST OF EACH PHYSICAL DISTRIBUTION FUNCTION AS A PERCENTAGE OF TOTAL DISTRIBUTION COSTS**

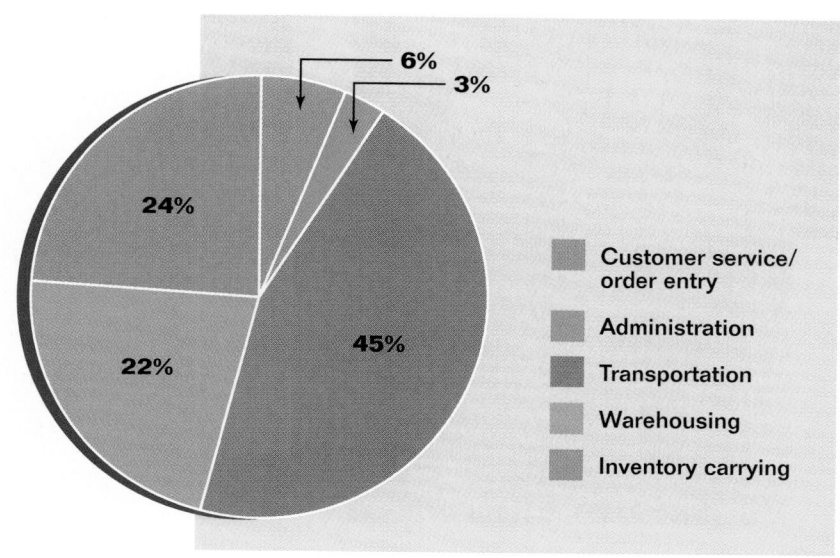

unrelated activities. This approach shifts the emphasis from lowering the separate costs of individual activities to minimizing overall distribution costs.

The total-cost approach involves analyzing the costs of all distribution alternatives, even those considered too impractical or expensive. Total-cost analyses weigh inventory levels against warehousing expenses, materials costs against various modes of transportation, and all distribution costs against customer service standards. Costs of potential sales losses from lower performance levels must also be considered. In many cases, accounting procedures and statistical methods are used to figure total costs. When hundreds of combinations of distribution variables are possible, computer simulations are helpful. A distribution system's lowest total cost is never the result of using a combination of the cheapest functions. Instead, it is the lowest overall cost compatible with the company's stated service objectives. For example, the Amerex Group buys materials and finished products from all over the world; consolidates them at various factories, where they are turned into men's, women's, and children's outerwear; and then packs and ships either to customers or to warehouses. The firm's supply chain management system was inflexible, expensive to maintain, and not particularly helpful in tracking so many elements. The fast-growing company asked Computer Generated Solutions to craft and implement an automated system called Blue Cherry. The system ultimately helped Amerex save $650,000 a year and eliminate 22 positions.[7]

Physical distribution managers must be sensitive to the issue of cost tradeoffs. Higher costs in one functional area of a distribution system may be necessary to achieve lower costs in another. Tradeoffs are strategic decisions to combine (and recombine) resources for greatest cost effectiveness. When distribution managers regard the system as a network of integrated functions, tradeoffs become useful tools in implementing a unified, cost-effective distribution strategy.

**Reducing Distribution Costs**

Distribution-related organizations, such as New Breed and Data2Logistics, help companies improve efficiencies and reduce costs.

THERE'S MONEY TO BE FOUND IN YOUR BUSINESS. YOU JUST HAVE TO KNOW WHERE TO LOOK.

We suggest you look in your supply chain. Most likely, it harbors vast unrealized possibilities. New Breed will help you harness the potential in your supply chain to increase efficiencies and realize greater profits. We're so confident that we can uncover opportunities in your supply chain that we base our fees on how effectively we execute the solutions we identify. And because we have our own existing infrastructure of facilities and technology, you'll make no capital investment. Our redesign of one national client's supply chain resulted in hundreds of millions of dollars that went straight to the company's bottom line. If you'd like to know what we can do for you, give us a call at 1-866-4-NEW-BREED or visit our website at www.new-breed.com.

NB
NEW BREED

DISTRIBUTION SERVICES
CRITICAL LOGISTICS
SUPPLY CHAIN CONSULTING

Let us enlighten you

data logistics

Does your freight bill process leave you in the dark? Shed light on the subject with Data2Logistics. We provide the business intelligence you need to reduce costs and improve your bottom line.

You can rely on us to audit your freight bills, allocate charges to the appropriate cost center and process invoices for payment. But even more important, Data2Logistics brings actionable information, not just access to data. Our total solution helps you to:

- Benchmark transportation costs
- Analyze rate changes and bid proposals
- Control accessorial charges
- Track routing guide compliance
- Identify your least cost carrier

Data2Logistics, the nation's largest freight bill processor, has the people, experience and industry knowledge to meet your needs. Call us to brighten the outlook on your transportation costs today.

609-683-3934    www.data2logistics.com    Ship Smarter and $ave

**cycle time** The time needed to complete a process

**Reducing Cycle Time.** Another important goal of physical distribution involves reducing **cycle time**, the time needed to complete a process. Doing so can reduce costs and/or increase customer service. Many companies, particularly manufacturers, overnight delivery firms, major news media, and publishers of books of current interest, are using cycle time reduction to gain a competitive advantage. FedEx believes so strongly in this concept that, in the interest of being the fastest provider of overnight delivery, it conducts research on reducing cycle time and identifying new management techniques and procedures for its employees. Seattle's Boeing Company is considering the construction of a plant to be run by two major suppliers and built next to Boeing's proposed 7E7 assembly plant. The plant would assemble about 75 percent of the 7E7's fuselage and deliver it to Boeing's final assembly plant next door. This arrangement not only would reduce cycle time but would save transportation costs on large pieces.[8]

## Physical Distribution Functions

As we saw earlier, physical distribution includes the activities necessary to get products from producers to customers. In this section we take a closer look at these activities, which include order processing, inventory management, materials handling, warehousing, and transportation.

**order processing** The receipt and transmission of sales order information

**Order Processing.** **Order processing** is the receipt and transmission of sales order information. Although management sometimes overlooks the importance of these activities, efficient order processing facilitates product flow. Computerized order processing provides a database for all supply chain members to increase their productivity. When carried out quickly and accurately, order processing contributes to customer satisfaction, decreased costs and cycle time, and increased profits.

Order processing entails three main tasks: order entry, order handling, and order delivery. Order entry begins when customers or salespeople place purchase orders via telephone, mail, e-mail, or website. Electronic ordering is less time consuming than a manual, paper-based ordering system and reduces costs. In some companies, sales representatives receive and enter orders personally, handle complaints, prepare progress reports, and forward sales order information.

Order handling involves several tasks. Once an order is entered, it is transmitted to a warehouse, where product availability is verified, and to the credit department, where prices, terms, and the customer's credit ratings are checked. If the credit department approves the purchase, warehouse personnel (sometimes assisted by automated equipment) pick and assemble the order. If the requested product is not in stock, a production order is sent to the factory or the customer is offered a substitute.

When the order has been assembled and packed for shipment, the warehouse schedules delivery with an appropriate carrier. If the customer pays for rush service, overnight delivery by FedEx, UPS, or another overnight carrier is used. The customer is sent an invoice, inventory records are adjusted, and the order is delivered.

Whether to use a manual or an electronic order-processing system depends on which method provides the greater speed and accuracy within cost limits. Manual processing suffices for small-volume orders and is more

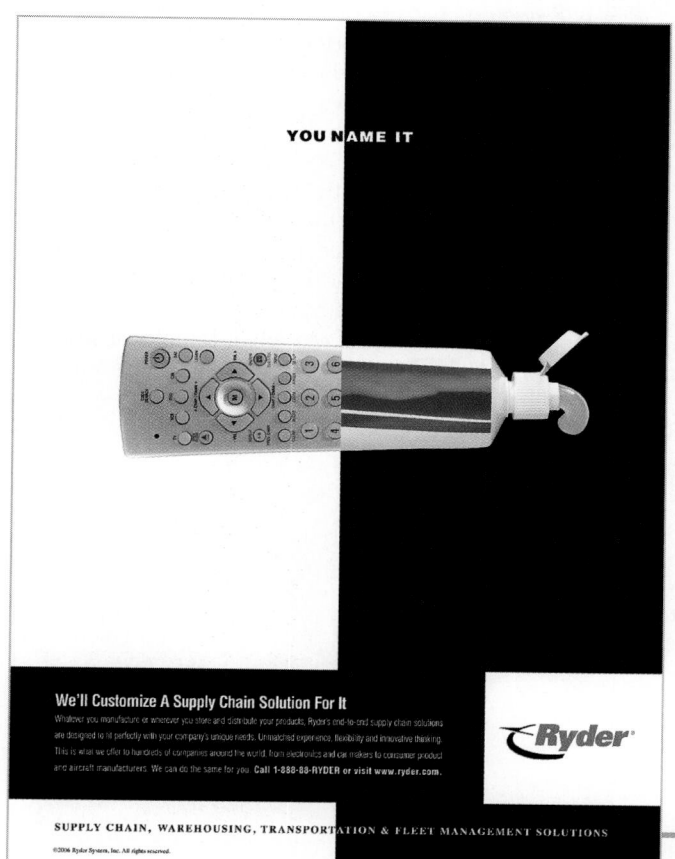

YOU NAME IT

**We'll Customize A Supply Chain Solution For It**
*Ryder*
SUPPLY CHAIN, WAREHOUSING, TRANSPORTATION & FLEET MANAGEMENT SOLUTIONS

**Improving Physical Distribution Functions**
Many companies provide both hardware and software to improve physical distribution efficiency.

**electronic data interchange (EDI)** A computerized means of integrating order processing with production, inventory, accounting, and transportation

flexible in certain situations. Most companies, however, use **electronic data interchange (EDI)**, which uses computer technology to integrate order processing with production, inventory, accounting, and transportation. Within the supply chain, EDI functions as an information system that links marketing channel members and outsourcing firms together. It reduces paperwork for all members of the supply chain and allows them to share information on invoices, orders, payments, inquiries, and scheduling. Consequently many companies have pushed their suppliers toward EDI to reduce distribution costs and cycle times. For example, Dobbs, an airline food-service company, requires all of its vendors to be EDI-equipped.

**inventory management** Developing and maintaining adequate assortments of products to meet customers' needs

**Inventory Management.** **Inventory management** involves developing and maintaining adequate assortments of products to meet customers' needs. Because a firm's investment in inventory usually represents a significant portion of its total assets, inventory decisions have a major impact on physical distribution costs and the level of customer service provided. When too few products are carried in inventory, the result is *stockouts*, or shortages of products, which in turn result in brand switching, lower sales, and loss of customers. When too many products (or too many slow-moving products) are carried, costs increase, as do risks of product obsolescence, pilferage, and damage. The objective of inventory management is to minimize inventory costs while maintaining an adequate supply of goods to satisfy customers. To achieve this objective, marketers focus on two major issues: when to order and how much to order.

# Skechers Sprints Ahead with Wireless Inventory Management

How can a fashion footwear firm manage the flow of 60,000 individual products to thousands of retail stores around the world? In its early years, Skechers, a California company known for making stylish men's, women's, and children's shoes, relied on a network of wholesalers to service retail accounts outside the United States. Then it opened a huge distribution center in Belgium to supplement its distribution center in California. Because the popularity of specific fashion footwear can be unpredictable, the company must have inventory ready to ship at a moment's notice. Skechers holds extra inventory in outside warehouses and shifts products between facilities as needed to fill orders in each distribution center. Searching the 1.5 million square feet of warehouse space to find a pair of shoes in a particular style, color, and size would be a major headache if not for the company's state-of-the-art inventory management system.

When a case of shoes arrives from a Skechers factory, the wireless system picks up information about the contents and records where all items are transported and stored. As stores submit orders,

the wireless system identifies each item's location, notes which products are being shipped to which store, deducts the products from current inventory levels, prepares shipping documents, and arranges for invoicing.

Thanks to this wireless system, Skechers can count all of its inventory in less than two days instead of the five days required before the company went wireless. The system automatically issues a warning if it detects any errors or discrepancies. This puts Skechers in a better position to fill store orders completely and correctly. Moreover, employees no longer have the tedious task of manually entering every shipment that enters or leaves the warehouse.

To determine when to order, a marketer calculates the *reorder point*, the inventory level that signals the need to place a new order. To calculate the reorder point, the marketer must know the order lead time, the usage rate, and the amount of safety stock required. The *order lead time* refers to the average time lapse between placing the order and receiving it. The *usage rate* is the rate at which a product's inventory is used or sold during a specific time period. *Safety stock* is the amount of extra inventory a firm keeps to guard against stockouts resulting from above-average usage rates and/or longer-than-expected lead times. The reorder point can be calculated using the following formula:

$$\text{Reorder Point} = (\text{Order Lead Time} \times \text{Usage Rate}) + \text{Safety Stock}$$

Thus, if order lead time is 10 days, usage rate is 3 units per day, and safety stock is 20 units, the reorder point is 50 units.

**just-in-time (JIT)** An inventory management approach in which supplies arrive just when needed for production or resale

Efficient inventory management with accurate reorder points is crucial for firms that use a **just-in-time (JIT)** approach, in which supplies arrive just as they are needed for use in production or for resale. When using JIT, companies maintain low inventory levels and purchase products and materials in small quantities whenever they need them. Usually there is no safety stock, and suppliers are expected to provide consistently high-quality products. Just-in-time inventory management requires a high level of coordination between producers and suppliers, but it eliminates waste and reduces inventory costs significantly. This approach has been used successfully by many well-known firms, including DaimlerChrysler, Harley-Davidson, and Dell Computer, to reduce costs and boost customer satisfaction. When a JIT approach is used in a supply chain, suppliers often move close to their customers.

**materials handling** Physical handling of tangible goods, supplies, and resources

**Materials Handling.** **Materials handling**, the physical handling of tangible goods, supplies, and resources, is an important factor in warehouse operations, as well as in transportation from points of production to points of consumption. Efficient procedures and techniques for materials handling minimize inventory management costs, reduce the number of times a good is handled, improve customer service, and increase customer satisfaction. Systems for packaging, labeling, loading, and movement must be coordinated to maximize cost reduction and customer satisfaction. A growing number of firms are turning to radio waves to track materials tagged with radio frequency ID (RFID) through every phase of handling.

Product characteristics often determine handling. For example, the characteristics of bulk liquids and gases determine how they can be moved and stored. Internal packaging is also an important consideration in materials handling; goods must be packaged correctly to prevent damage or breakage during handling and transportation. Most companies employ packaging consultants to help them decide which packaging materials and methods will result in the most efficient handling.

Unit loading and containerization are two common methods used in materials handling. With *unit loading*, one or more boxes are placed on a pallet or skid; these units can then be efficiently loaded by mechanical means such as forklifts, trucks, or conveyor systems. *Containerization* is the consolidation of many items into a single large container, which is sealed at its point of origin and opened at its destination. Containers are usually 8 feet wide, 8 feet high, and 10 to 40 feet long. They can be conveniently stacked and shipped via train, barge, or ship. Once containers reach their destinations, wheel assemblies can be added to make them suitable for ground transportation. Because individual items are not handled in transit, containerization greatly increases efficiency and security in shipping.

**warehousing** The design and operation of facilities for storing and moving goods

**Warehousing.** **Warehousing**, the design and operation of facilities for storing and moving goods, is another important physical distribution function. Warehousing provides time utility by enabling firms to compensate for dissimilar production and consumption rates. When mass production creates a greater stock of goods than can be sold immediately, companies may warehouse the surplus until customers are ready to buy. Warehousing also helps stabilize prices and availability of seasonal items.

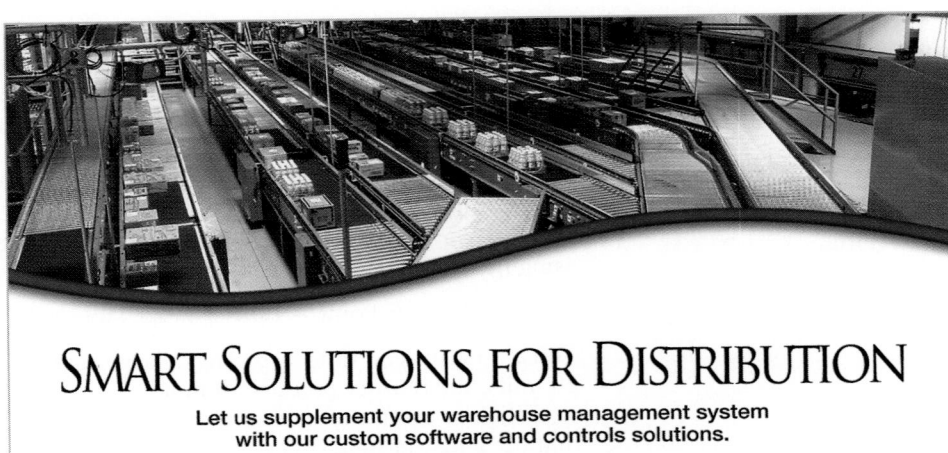

**Warehousing**
Specialized information technology is helping managers to operate warehouses more efficiently.

**private warehouse** A company-operated facility for storing and shipping products

**public warehouse** A business that leases storage space and related physical distribution facilities to other firms

Warehousing is not simply the storage of products. The basic distribution functions warehouses perform include receiving, identifying, sorting, and dispatching goods to storage; holding goods in storage until needed; recalling and assembling stored goods for shipment; and dispatching shipments. When warehouses receive goods by carloads or truckloads, they break down the shipments into smaller quantities for individual customers.

The choice of warehouse facilities is an important strategic consideration. The right type of warehouse allows a company to reduce transportation and inventory costs or improve service to customers. The wrong type of warehouse may drain company resources. Beyond deciding how many facilities to operate and where to locate them, a company must determine which type of warehouse is most appropriate. Warehouses fall into two general categories: private and public. In many cases, a combination of private and public facilities provides the most flexible warehousing approach.

Companies operate **private warehouses** for storing and shipping their own products. A firm usually leases or purchases a private warehouse when its warehousing needs in a given geographic market are substantial and stable enough to warrant a long-term commitment to a fixed facility. Private warehouses are also appropriate for firms that require special handling and storage and that want control of warehouse design and operation. Retailers such as Sears, Radio Shack, and Kmart find it economical to integrate private warehousing with purchasing and distribution for their retail outlets. When sales volumes are fairly stable, ownership and control of a private warehouse may provide benefits such as property appreciation. Private warehouses, however, face fixed costs such as insurance, taxes, maintenance, and debt expense. They also limit flexibility when firms wish to move inventories to more strategic locations. Before tying up capital in a private warehouse or entering into a long-term lease, a company should consider its resources, level of expertise in warehouse management, and the role of the warehouse in its overall marketing strategy. Many private warehouses are being eliminated by direct links between producers and customers, reduced cycle times, and outsourcing to public warehouses.

**Public warehouses** lease storage space and related physical distribution facilities to other firms. They sometimes provide such distribution services as receiving, unloading, inspecting, and reshipping products; filling orders; providing financing; displaying products; and coordinating shipments. Public warehouses are especially

## marketing ENTREPRENEURS

**Dineh Mohajer**

HER BUSINESS: Hard Candy Cosmetics

FOUNDED AT AGE: 22

SUCCESS: More than 60 colors of nail polish available nationwide

Unable to find nail polish to match her baby blue sandals, Dineh Mohajer mixed some old nail polish colors together and created a new color she called "Sky." She received so many compliments on the unusual color that she decided to market her creation. Fred Segal, a prestigious boutique in Los Angeles, was the first to introduce her Hard Candy Cosmetics samples. An instant success, many boutiques began placing large orders. Eventually, Dineh rented a warehouse and hired a full-time staff to help her meet the demand. Hard Candy Cosmetics now operates out of three offices (California, Maryland, and Florida), offers more than 60 shades of nail polish, makes a full line of other cosmetics, and is available at boutiques throughout the country.

Source: http://www.hardcandy.com/cs/aboutUs.cfm

useful to firms that have seasonal production or low-volume storage needs, have inventories that must be maintained in many locations, are testing or entering new markets, or own private warehouses but occasionally require additional storage space. Public warehouses also serve as collection points during product recall programs. Whereas private warehouses have fixed costs, public warehouses offer variable (and often lower) costs because users rent space and purchase warehousing services only as needed.

Many public warehouses furnish security for products being used as collateral for loans, a service provided at either the warehouse or the site of the owner's inventory. *Field public warehouses* are established by public warehouses at the owner's inventory location. The warehouser becomes custodian of the products and issues a receipt that can be used as collateral for a loan. Public warehouses also provide *bonded storage*, a warehousing arrangement in which imported or taxable products are not released until the products' owners pay U.S. customs duties, taxes, or other fees. Bonded warehouses enable firms to defer tax payments on such items until they are delivered to customers.

**distribution center** A large, centralized warehouse that focuses on moving rather than storing goods

**Distribution centers** are large, centralized warehouses that receive goods from factories and suppliers, regroup them into orders, and ship them to customers quickly; their focus is on movement of goods rather than storage.[9] Distribution centers are specially designed for the rapid flow of products. They are usually one-story buildings (to eliminate elevators) with access to transportation networks such as major highways or railway lines. Many distribution centers are highly automated, with computer-directed robots, forklifts, and hoists that collect and move products to loading docks. Although some public warehouses offer such specialized services, most distribution centers are privately owned. They serve customers in regional markets and, in some cases, function as consolidation points for a company's branch warehouses. Distribution centers are typically located within 500 miles of half of a company's market.

Distribution centers offer several benefits, the most important being improved customer service. They ensure product availability by maintaining full product lines, while the speed of their operations cuts delivery time to a minimum. Distribution centers also reduce costs. Instead of making many smaller shipments to scattered warehouses and customers, factories ship large quantities of goods directly to distribution centers at bulk rates, thus lowering transportation costs. Furthermore, rapid inventory turnover lessens the need for warehouses and cuts storage costs. Overstock.com, for example, operates a 350,000-square-foot distribution center in Salt Lake City to process all the name-brand housewares, electronics, toys, sporting goods, and gifts it markets through a website. Efficiency in distribution operations helps the firm offer deep discounts and stay on top of busy holiday seasons.[10] Some distribution centers facilitate production by receiving and consolidating raw materials and providing final assembly for certain products.

**transportation** The movement of products from where they are made to where they are used

**Transportation.** **Transportation**, the movement of products from where they are made to where they are used, is the most expensive physical distribution function. Because product availability and timely deliveries depend on transportation functions, transportation decisions directly affect customer service. A firm may even build its distribution and marketing strategy around a unique transportation system if that system can ensure on-time deliveries and thereby give the firm a competitive edge. Companies may build their own transportation fleets (private carriers) or out-source the transportation function to a common or contract carrier.

**Transportation Modes.** There are five basic transportation modes for moving physical goods: railroads, trucks, waterways, airways, and pipelines. Each mode offers distinct advantages. Many companies adopt physical handling procedures that facilitate the use of two or more modes in combination. Figure 16.4 indicates the percentage of intercity freight carried by each transportation mode; Table 16.4 shows typical transportation modes for various products.

Railroads such as Union Pacific and Canadian National carry heavy, bulky freight that must be shipped long distances over land. Railroads commonly haul minerals, sand, lumber, chemicals, and farm products, as well as low-value manufactured goods and an increasing number of automobiles. They are especially efficient for transporting full carloads, which can be shipped at lower rates than smaller quantities because they require less handling. Many companies locate factories or warehouses near major rail lines or on spur lines for convenient loading and unloading.

Trucks provide the most flexible schedules and routes of all major transportation modes because they can go almost anywhere. Because trucks have a unique ability to move goods directly from factory or warehouse to customer, they are often used in conjunction with other forms of transport that cannot provide door-to-door deliveries. Although trucks usually travel much faster than trains, they are more expensive and somewhat more vulnerable to bad weather. They are also subject to size and weight restrictions on the products they carry. Trucks are sometimes criticized for high levels of loss and damage to freight and for delays caused by rehandling small shipments. In response, the trucking industry has turned to computerized tracking of shipments and the development of new equipment to speed loading and unloading. Marten Transport Ltd. in Wisconsin charges its customers for the time drivers have to wait and rewards clients that help keep things moving. Using a satellite-tracking system, the company can track when a driver arrives at a site and how long it takes to load and unload freight. The data are shared with customers, and Marten and its customers work together to eliminate wasteful practices. Marten has lost customers, but has also reduced rates to others who have expedited loading and unloading.[11]

Waterways are the cheapest method of shipping heavy, low-value, nonperishable goods such as ore, coal, grain, and petroleum products. Water carriers offer considerable capacity. Powered by tugboats and towboats, barges that travel along inter-

**figure 16.4**

## PROPORTION OF INTERCITY FREIGHT CARRIED BY VARIOUS TRANSPORTATION MODES

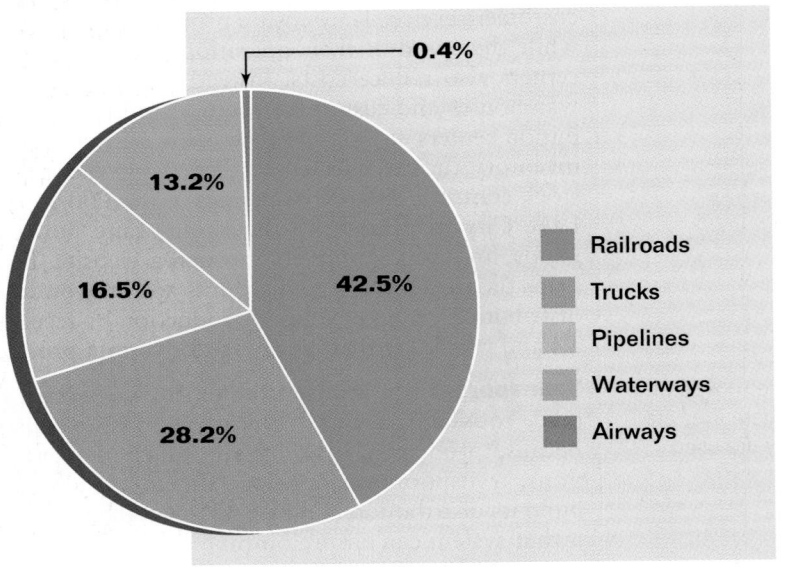

**Source:** U.S. Bureau of the Census, *Statistical Abstract of the United States,* 2006 (Washington, DC: Government Printing Office, 2006), p. 694.

| table 16.4 | **TYPICAL TRANSPORTATION MODES FOR VARIOUS PRODUCTS** | | | |
| --- | --- | --- | --- | --- |
| **Railroads** | **Trucks** | **Waterways** | **Airways** | **Pipelines** |
| Coal | Clothing | Petroleum | Flowers | Oil |
| Grain | Paper goods | Chemicals | Perishable food | Processed coal |
| Chemicals | Computers | Iron ore | Instruments | Natural gas |
| Lumber | Books | Bauxite | Emergency parts | Water |
| Automobiles | Livestock | Grain | Overnight mail | Chemicals |
| Steel | | | | |

coastal canals, inland rivers, and navigation systems can haul at least ten times the weight of one rail car, and oceangoing vessels can haul thousands of containers. However, many markets are inaccessible by water transportation unless supplemented by rail or truck. Furthermore, water transport is extremely slow and sometimes comes to a standstill during freezing weather. Companies depending on waterways may ship their entire inventory during the summer and then store it for winter use. Droughts and floods also create difficulties for users of inland waterway transportation. Nevertheless, the extreme fuel efficiency of water transportation and the continuing globalization of marketing will likely increase its use in the future.

Air transportation is the fastest but most expensive form of shipping. It is used most often for perishable goods; for high-value, low-bulk items; and for products requiring quick delivery over long distances, such as emergency shipments. Some air carriers transport combinations of passengers, freight, and mail. Despite its expense, air transit can reduce warehousing and packaging costs and losses from theft and damage, thus helping to lower total costs (but truck transportation needed for

**Trucking**

A number of transportation services are provided through trucks.

pickup and final delivery adds to cost and transit time). Although air transport accounts for less than 1 percent of total ton-miles carried, its importance as a mode of transportation is growing. In fact, the success of many businesses is now based on the availability of overnight air delivery service provided by such organizations as UPS, DHL, FedEx, RPS Air, and the U.S. Postal Service. Amazon.com, for example, ships via UPS many products ordered online within a day of order.

Pipelines, the most highly automated transportation mode, usually belong to the shipper and carry the shipper's products. Most pipelines carry petroleum products or chemicals. The Trans-Alaska Pipeline, owned and operated by a consortium of oil companies that includes Exxon, Mobil, and BP-Amoco, transports crude oil from remote oil-drilling sites in central Alaska to shipping terminals on the coast. Slurry pipelines carry pulverized coal, grain, or wood chips suspended in water. Pipelines move products slowly but continuously and at relatively low cost. They are dependable and minimize the problems of product damage and theft. However, contents are subject to as much as 1 percent shrinkage, usually from evaporation. Pipelines have also been a concern to environmentalists, who fear installation and leaks could harm plants and animals.

*Choosing Transportation Modes.* Distribution managers select a transportation mode based on the combination of cost, speed, dependability, load flexibility, accessibility, and frequency that is most appropriate for their products and generates the desired level of customer service. Table 16.5 shows relative ratings of each transportation mode by these selection criteria.

Marketers compare alternative transportation modes to determine whether benefits from a more expensive mode are worth higher costs. Air freight carriers such as FedEx promise many benefits, such as speed and dependability, but at much higher costs than other transportation modes. When such benefits are less important, marketers prefer lower costs. Bicycles, for instance, are often shipped by rail because an unassembled bicycle can be shipped more than 1,000 miles on a train for as little as $3.60. Bicycle wholesalers plan purchases far enough in advance to capitalize on this cost advantage. Companies such as Accuship can assist marketers in analyzing a variety of transportation options. This Internet firm's software gives corporate users, such as Coca-Cola and the Home Shopping Network, information about the speed and cost of different transportation modes. It allows them to select shippers and then track shipments online. Accuship processes nearly 1 million shipments every day.[12]

*Speed* is measured by the total time a carrier has possession of goods, including the time required for pickup and delivery, handling, and movement between points of origin and destination. Speed obviously affects a marketer's ability to provide service, but other, less obvious implications are important as well. Marketers take advantage of transit time to process orders for goods en route, a capability especially important to agricultural and raw materials shippers. Some railroads also let carloads in transit be redirected for maximum flexibility in selecting markets. A carload of peaches, for instance, may be shipped to a closer destination if the fruit is in danger of ripening too quickly.

**table 16.5  RELATIVE RATINGS OF TRANSPORTATION MODES BY SELECTION CRITERIA**

| Mode | Cost | Speed | Dependability | Load Flexibility | Accessibility | Frequency |
|---|---|---|---|---|---|---|
| Railroads | Moderate | Average | Average | High | High | Low |
| Trucks | High | Fast | High | Average | Very high | High |
| Waterways | Very low | Very slow | Average | Very high | Limited | Very low |
| Airways | Very high | Very fast | High | Low | Average | Average |
| Pipelines | Low | Slow | High | Very low | Very limited | Very high |

*Dependability* of a transportation mode is determined by the consistency of service provided. Marketers must be able to count on carriers to deliver goods on time and in an acceptable condition. Along with speed, dependability affects a marketer's inventory costs, including sales lost when merchandise is not available. Undependable transportation necessitates higher inventory levels to avoid stockouts, whereas reliable delivery service enables customers to carry smaller inventories at lower cost. Security problems vary considerably among transportation modes and are a major consideration in carrier selection. A firm does not incur costs directly when goods are lost or damaged because the carrier is usually held liable. Nevertheless, poor service and lack of security indirectly lead to increased costs and lower profits because damaged or lost goods are unavailable for immediate sale or use.

*Load flexibility* is the degree to which a transportation mode can provide appropriate equipment and conditions for moving specific kinds of goods and can be adapted for moving other products. Many products must be shipped under controlled temperature and humidity. Other products, such as liquids or gases, require special equipment or facilities for shipment. A marketer with unusual transport needs can consult the *Official Railway Equipment Register*, which lists the various types of cars and equipment each railroad owns. As Table 16.5 shows, waterways and railroads have the highest load flexibility, whereas pipelines have the lowest.

*Accessibility* refers to a carrier's ability to move goods over a specific route or network. For example, marketers evaluating transportation modes for reaching Great Falls, Montana, would consider rail lines, truck routes, and scheduled airline service but would eliminate water-borne carriers because Great Falls is inaccessible by water. Some carriers differentiate themselves by serving areas their competitors do not. After deregulation, many large railroad companies sold off or abandoned unprofitable routes, making rail service inaccessible to facilities located on spur lines. Some marketers were forced to buy or lease their own truck fleets to get their products to market. In recent years, small, short-line railroad companies have started buying up track and creating networks of low-cost feeder lines to reach underserved markets.

*Frequency* refers to how often a company can send shipments by a specific transportation mode. When using pipelines, shipments can be continuous. A marketer shipping by railroad or waterway is limited by the carriers' schedules.

**Coordinating Transportation.** To take advantage of the benefits offered by various transportation modes and compensate for deficiencies, marketers often combine and coordinate two or more modes. In recent years, **intermodal transportation**, as this integrated approach is sometimes called, has been facilitated by new developments within the transportation industry.

Several kinds of intermodal shipping are available. All combine the flexibility of trucking with the low cost or speed of other forms of transport. Containerization facilitates intermodal transportation by consolidating shipments into sealed containers for transport by *piggyback* (shipping that uses both truck trailers and railway flatcars), *fishyback* (truck trailers and water carriers), and *birdyback* (truck trailers and air carriers). As transportation costs have increased, intermodal shipping has gained popularity.

Specialized outsource agencies provide other forms of transport coordination. Known as **freight forwarders**, these firms combine shipments from several organizations into efficient lot sizes. Small loads (less than 500 pounds) are much more expensive to ship than full carloads or truckloads, which frequently requires consolidation. Freight forwarders take small loads from various marketers, buy transport space from carriers, and arrange for goods to be delivered to buyers. Freight forwarders' profits come from the margin between the higher, less-than-carload rates they charge each marketer and the lower carload rates they themselves pay. Because large shipments require less handling, use of freight forwarders can speed delivery. Freight forwarders can also determine the most efficient carriers and routes. They are useful for shipping goods to foreign markets because freight forwarders know how

**intermodal transportation** Two or more transportation modes used in combination

**freight forwarder** An organization that consolidates shipments from several firms into efficient lot sizes

## ONE PROVIDER.
## ALL MODES.
## GLOBALLY.

*For the Chemical and Process Industries*

www.odysseylogistics.com

**ODYSSEY** LOGISTICS & TECHNOLOGY

39 Old Ridgebury Road   Danbury, CT  06810
203-448-3900

© Odyssey Logistics & Technology Corp. All rights reserved.

**Intermodal Transportation**

Odyssey offers intermodal transportation capabilities.

**megacarrier** A freight transportation firm that provides several modes of shipment

to clear customs, pay duties, and handle the necessary paperwork. Some companies prefer to outsource their shipping to freight forwarders because the latter provide door-to-door services.

Another transportation innovation is the development of **megacarriers**, freight transportation firms that offer several shipment methods, including rail, truck, and air service. CSX, for example, has trains, barges, container ships, trucks, and pipelines, thus offering a multitude of transportation services. In addition, air carriers have increased their ground transportation services. As they expand the range of transportation alternatives, carriers too put greater stress on customer service.

## Strategic Issues in Physical Distribution

The physical distribution functions discussed in this chapter—order processing, inventory management, materials handling, warehousing, and transportation—account for about half of all marketing costs. Whether performed by a producer, wholesaler, or retailer, or outsourced to some other firm, these functions have a significant impact on customer service and satisfaction, which are of primary importance to all members of the supply chain.

The strategic importance of physical distribution is evident in all elements of the marketing mix. Product design and packaging must allow for efficient stacking, storage, transport, and tracking. Differentiating products by size, color, and style must take into account additional demands placed on warehousing and shipping facilities. Competitive pricing may depend on a firm's ability to provide reliable delivery or emergency shipments of replacement parts. Firms trying to lower inventory costs may offer quantity discounts to encourage large purchases. Promotional campaigns must be coordinated with distribution functions so that advertised products are available to buyers and order-processing departments can handle additional sales orders efficiently. Channel members must consider warehousing and transportation

**Strategic Physical Distribution**
Most organizations incorporate physical distribution functions into their marketing strategies.

costs, which may influence a firm's policy on stockouts or its decision to centralize (or decentralize) inventory.

Improving physical distribution starts by closing the gap with customers. The entire supply chain must understand and meet customers' requirements. An effective way to improve physical distribution is to integrate processes across the boundaries of all members of the supply chain. The full scope of the physical distribution process includes suppliers, manufacturers, wholesalers, retailers, transportation firms, and warehouses. To work well, the process requires a formal, integrated plan to balance supply and demand within a defined time period. Physical distribution can also be improved by developing cooperative relationships with suppliers of component parts and services. These relationships should emphasize joint improvement. Cooperation can be enhanced through information technology that allows channel partners to work together to plan production and physical distribution activities; improve the efficiency and safety of product handling and movement; and reduce waste and costs for the benefit of all channel members, including the customer.

No single distribution system is ideal for all situations, and any system must be evaluated continually and adapted as necessary. Pressures to adjust service levels or to reduce costs may lead to a total restructuring of supply chain relationships. The ensuing changes in transportation, warehousing, materials handling, and inventory may affect speed of delivery, reliability, and economy of service. Recognizing that changes in any major distribution function may affect all other functions, marketing strategists consider customers' changing needs and preferences. Customer-oriented marketers analyze the characteristics of their target markets and plan distribution systems to provide products in the right place, at the right time, and at acceptable costs.

## SUMMARY

Wholesaling consists of all transactions in which products are bought for resale, for making other products, or for general business operations. Wholesalers are individuals or organizations that facilitate and expedite exchanges that are primarily wholesale transactions. For producers, wholesalers are a source of financial assistance and information; by performing specialized accumulation and allocation functions, they allow producers to concentrate on manufacturing products. Wholesalers provide retailers with buying expertise, wide product lines, efficient distribution, and warehousing and storage.

Merchant wholesalers are independently owned businesses that take title to goods and assume ownership risks. They are either full-service wholesalers, offering the widest possible range of wholesaling functions, or lim-

ited-service wholesalers, providing only some marketing services and specializing in a few functions. Full-service merchant wholesalers include general-merchandise wholesalers, which offer a wide but relatively shallow product mix; general-line wholesalers, which offer extensive assortments within a few product lines; specialty-line wholesalers, which carry only a single product line or a few items within a line; and rack jobbers, which own and service display racks in supermarkets and other stores. Limited-service merchant wholesalers include cash-and-carry wholesalers, which sell to small businesses, require payment in cash, and do not deliver; truck wholesalers, which sell a limited line of products from their own trucks directly to customers; drop shippers, which own goods and negotiate sales but never take possession of products; and mail-order wholesalers, which sell to retail and business buyers through direct-mail catalogs.

Agents and brokers, sometimes called functional middlemen, negotiate purchases and expedite sales in exchange for a commission, but they do not take title to products. Usually specializing in certain products, they can provide valuable sales expertise. Whereas agents represent buyers or sellers on a permanent basis, brokers are intermediaries that buyers and sellers employ on a temporary basis to negotiate exchanges. Manufacturers' agents offer customers the complete product lines of two or more sellers. Selling agents market a complete product line or a producer's entire output and perform every wholesaling function except taking title to products. Commission merchants are agents that receive goods on consignment from local sellers and negotiate sales in large, central markets.

Manufacturers' sales branches and offices are owned by manufacturers. Sales branches sell products and provide support services for the manufacturer's sales force in a given location. Sales offices carry no inventory and function much as agents do.

Physical distribution, or logistics, refers to the activities used to move products from producers to customers and other end users. These activities include order processing, inventory management, materials handling, warehousing, and transportation. An efficient physical distribution system is an important component of an overall marketing strategy because it can decrease costs and increase customer satisfaction. Within the marketing channel, physical distribution activities are often performed by a wholesaler, but they may be performed by a producer or retailer, or outsourced to a third party.

The main objectives of physical distribution are to decrease costs and transit time while increasing customer service. Physical distribution managers strive to balance service, distribution costs, and resources. Because customers' service needs vary, companies must adapt to them. They must also offer service comparable to or better than competitors' and develop and communicate desirable customer service policies. Costs of providing service are minimized most effectively through the total-cost approach, which evaluates costs of the distribution system as a whole rather than as a collection of separate activities. Reducing cycle time, the time required to complete a process, is also important.

Order processing is the receipt and transmission of sales order information. It consists of three main tasks. Order entry begins when customers or salespeople place purchase orders by mail, e-mail, telephone, or computer. Order handling involves verifying product availability, checking customer credit, and preparing products for shipping. Order delivery is provided by the carrier most suitable for a desired level of customer service. Order processing can be done manually, but it is usually accomplished through electronic data interchange (EDI), a computerized system that integrates order processing with production, inventory, accounting, and transportation.

The objective of inventory management is to minimize inventory costs while maintaining a supply of goods adequate for customers' needs. To avoid stockouts without tying up too much capital in inventory, firms must have systematic methods for determining a reorder point, the inventory level that signals the need to place a new order. When firms use the just-in-time approach, products arrive just as they are needed for use in production or resale.

Materials handling, the physical handling of products, is an important factor in warehouse operations, as well as in transportation from points of production to points of consumption. Systems for packaging, labeling, loading, and movement must be coordinated to maximize cost reduction and customer satisfaction. Basic handling systems include unit loading, which entails placing boxes on pallets or skids and using mechanical devices to move them, and containerization.

Warehousing involves the design and operation of facilities for storing and moving goods. Private warehouses are operated by companies for the purpose of distributing their own products. Public warehouses are businesses that lease storage space and related physical distribution facilities to other firms. Distribution centers are large, centralized warehouses specially designed for rapid movement of goods to customers. In many cases, a combination of private and public facilities is the most flexible warehousing approach.

Transportation adds time and place utility to a product by moving it from where it is made to where it is purchased and used. The basic modes of transporting goods are railroads, trucks, waterways, airways, and pipelines. The criteria marketers use when selecting a transportation mode are cost, speed, dependability, load flexibility, accessibility, and frequency. Intermodal transportation allows marketers to combine advantages of two or more modes of transport. Freight forwarders coordinate transport by combining small shipments from several organizations into efficient lot sizes, while megacarriers offer several shipment methods.

Physical distribution functions account for about half of all marketing costs and have a significant impact on customer satisfaction. Effective marketers are therefore actively involved in the design and control of physical distribution systems. Physical distribution affects every element of the marketing mix: product, price, promotion, and distribution. To satisfy customers, marketers consider customers' changing needs and shifts within major distribution functions. They then adapt existing physical distribution systems for greater effectiveness.

Please visit the student website at **www.prideferrell.com** for ACE Self-Test questions that will help you prepare for exams.

ACE self-test

## IMPORTANT TERMS

Wholesaling
Wholesaler
Merchant wholesaler
Full-service wholesaler
General-merchandise
  wholesaler
General-line wholesaler
Specialty-line wholesaler
Rack jobber
Limited-service wholesaler

Cash-and-carry wholesaler
Truck wholesaler
Drop shipper
Mail-order wholesaler
Agent
Broker
Manufacturers' agent
Selling agent
Commission merchant
Sales branch

Sales office
Physical distribution
Outsourcing
Cycle time
Order processing
Electronic data
  interchange (EDI)
Inventory management
Just-in-time (JIT)
Materials handling

Warehousing
Private warehouse
Public warehouse
Distribution center
Transportation
Intermodal transportation
Freight forwarder
Megacarrier

## DISCUSSION & REVIEW QUESTIONS

1. What is wholesaling?
2. What services do wholesalers provide to producers and retailers?
3. What is the difference between a full-service merchant wholesaler and a limited-service merchant wholesaler?
4. Drop shippers take title to products but do not accept physical possession of them, whereas commission merchants take physical possession of products but do not accept title. Defend the logic of classifying drop shippers as wholesale merchants and commission merchants as agents.
5. Why are manufacturers' sales offices and branches classified as wholesalers? Which independent wholesalers are replaced by manufacturers' sales branches? Which independent wholesalers are replaced by manufacturers' sales offices?
6. Discuss the cost and service tradeoffs involved in developing a physical distribution system.
7. What factors must physical distribution managers consider when developing a customer service mix?
8. What are the main tasks involved in order processing?

9. Discuss the advantages of using an electronic order-processing system. Which types of organizations are most likely to use electronic order processing?
10. Explain the tradeoffs inventory managers face when reordering products or supplies. How is the reorder point computed?
11. How does a product's package affect materials handling procedures and techniques?
12. What is containerization? Discuss its major benefits.
13. Explain the major differences between private and public warehouses. What is a field public warehouse?
14. Distribution centers focus on the movement of goods. Describe how distribution centers are designed for the rapid flow of products.
15. Compare and contrast the five major transportation modes in terms of cost, speed, dependability, load flexibility, accessibility, and frequency.
16. Discuss ways marketers can combine or coordinate two or more modes of transportation. What is the advantage of doing so?

## APPLICATION QUESTIONS

1. Contact a local retailer with which you do business, and ask the manager to describe the store's relationship with one of its wholesalers. Using Table 16.1 as a guide, identify the activities the wholesaler performs. Are any of the functions shared by both the retailer and the wholesaler?

2. Assume you are responsible for the physical distribution of computers at a mail-order company. What would you do to ensure product availability, timely delivery, and quality service for your customers?

3. The type of warehouse facilities used has important strategic implications for a firm. What type of warehouse would be most appropriate for the following situations, and why?

   a. A propane gas company recently entered the market in the state of Washington. The company's customers need varied quantities of propane on a timely basis and, at times, on short notice.

   b. A suntan lotion manufacturer has little expertise in managing warehouses and needs storage space in several locations in the Southeast.

   c. A book publisher must have short cycle time to get its products to customers quickly and needs to send the products to many different retailers.

4. Marketers select a transportation mode based on cost, speed, dependability, load flexibility, accessibility, and frequency (see Table 16.5). Identify a product and then select a mode of transportation based on these criteria. Explain your choice.

---

**globalEDGE™**

1. Like many firms in your industry, your firm sources materials from abroad. The shipment of materials vital to the manufacturing process of a new line of high-quality, water-resistant winter sweaters is currently missing. You had expected the shipment four weeks ago, but the tracking information you have is outdated. To determine whether your shipment entered the United States, you must consult with the Global Statistics website, which can be accessed by using the search term "global statistics" at **http://globaledge.msu.edu/ibrd**. Once you reach the Global Statistics website, click on the Charts link at the top right. Using this information, find the largest domestic container ports and seaports. This will direct your search and help you resolve the im-

pending manufacturing emergency. Where will you be traveling to begin your investigation?

2. Your firm is planning to construct a network of distribution centers throughout the country to complement your current factories. To ensure the locations chosen are the best, use the search term "competitive alternatives" at **http://globaledge.msu.edu/ibrd** to access the Competitive Alternatives website. Once you reach the Competitive Alternatives website, click on the Download tab and then download the International Report (Volume 1). Identify the five most important quality-of-life factors that currently drive site selection for manufacturing firms. Has this changed from previous reports?

---

**INTERNET Exercise**

Visit **www.prideferrell.com** for resources to help you master the material in this chapter, plus materials that will help you expand your marketing knowledge, including Internet exercise updates, ACE Self-Tests, hotlinks to companies featured in this chapter, and much more.

### FedEx

FedEx has become a critical link in the distribution network of both small and large firms. With its efficient and strategically located superhub in Memphis, FedEx has truly revolutionized the shipping industry. View the company's website at **www.fedex.com**.

1. Comment on how the website's overall design reflects the services the site promotes.
2. Why does FedEx so prominently display a "News" area on its website?
3. Does FedEx differentiate between small and large customers on its website? Why or why not?

Video Case 16.1   **Stuffing It at Coca-Cola**

The Coca-Cola Company, founded in the late 1800s, is the largest beverage company in the world with customers in more than 200 countries. The company's brands are many of the most recognized; they include Coca-Cola, Diet Coke, Fanta, Sprite, Powerade, Minute Maid, and Dasani bottled water. Although Coca-Cola focused primarily on customers in the United States in its early years, it has since recognized and relentlessly pursued international opportunities. By the late 1990s, Coca-Cola dominated its market with more than 50 percent of international soft-drink sales. The company has always maintained a strong focus on bringing in, satisfying, and keeping loyal customers. Strategic, recognizable designs on bottles and cans and well-liked global advertising have contributed to the strong reputation the company holds. Coca-Cola consistently is rated the most valuable brand in the world.

Over the last ten years, Coca-Cola focused on traditional soft drinks while archrival PepsiCo gained a strong foothold on new-age drinks, formed a partnership with Starbucks, and expanded rapidly into the snack business. PepsiCo's Frito-Lay division has 60 percent of the U.S. snack-food market. Ten years ago Coca-Cola's market value was more than three times greater than PepsiCo. By 2006, PepsiCo had a market capitalization greater than Coca-Cola.

Coca-Cola has long focused on social responsibility issues. It makes donations to several foundations that focus on education and community improvement. Coca-Cola is also involved in issuing grants and scholarships both in the United States and internationally. It is also concerned with preserving the environment and helping stem the AIDS/HIV crisis in Africa. All of these contributions help Coca-Cola develop an emotional, trusting relationship with its customers. In 2005, Coca-Cola issued a 50-page report on corporate responsibility in Great Britain. Key accomplishments include supplier compliance and audits, recycling, open work environment, community investment, and an environmental advisory board. Coca-Cola has always prided itself on its strong reputation. The Harris Interactive and the Reputation Institute (creating reputation quotients for companies by measuring 20 perceived attributes) ranked Coca-Cola second in overall reputation in 1999. The company had long been featured on *Fortune* magazine's "America's Most Admired Companies" list. However, the company failed to make the 2000 *Fortune* list due to problems with performance and leadership in 1999. It was also eliminated from *Business Ethics* magazine's "100 Best Corporate Citizens" list in 2001. The 2005 *Business Ethics* 100 Best Corporate Citizens also did not include Coca-Cola.

Coca-Cola's problems in 1999 began with a contamination scare that had a negative effect on its European reputation. That year also brought a racial discrimination lawsuit by about 2,000 current and former African American employees against the company. The company settled the suit by paying $193 million. And then-CEO Doug Invester raised concentrate prices—a strategy that did not go over well with the company's bottlers. Overall, it was thought that the company did not handle these crises well. In addition to reflecting poorly on Coca-Cola's reputation, these crises had a negative impact on the firm's bottlers, distributors, suppliers, and other related third parties.

A major problem that Coca-Cola faced during this period was accusations of channel stuffing. Channel stuffing is the practice of shipping extra inventory to wholesalers and retailers at an excessive rate, typically before the end of a quarter. Essentially, a company counts the shipments as sales although the products often remain in warehouses or are later returned to the manufacturer. Channel stuffing tends to create the appearance of strong demand (or conceals declining demand) for a product, which may result in inflated financial statement earnings, misleading investors. Accusations of channel stuffing have been made recently against companies such as Krispy Kreme Donuts, Harley-Davidson, Clear One Communications, Symbol Technologies, Network Associates, Bristol-Myers, Taser International, and Intel.

In Coca-Cola's case, the company was accused of sending extra concentrate to Japanese bottlers from 1997 through 1999 in an effort to inflate its profit. The company was already under investigation after a former employee filed a lawsuit in 2000 accusing the company of fraud and improper business practices. In 2004, former finance officials for Coca-Cola reported finding statements of inflated earnings due to the company's shipping extra concentrate to Japan. Although the company settled the allegations, the Securities and Exchange Commission (SEC) did find that channel stuffing had occurred. However, what Coca-Cola had done was to pressure bottlers into buying additional concentrate in exchange for extended credit. Therefore, the sales were technically considered legitimate.

To settle with the SEC, Coke agreed to avoid engaging in channel stuffing in the future. The company also created an ethics and compliance office and is required to verify each financial quarter that it has not altered the terms of payment or extended special credit. The company further agreed to work to reduce the amount of concentrate held by international bottlers. Although the company settled with the SEC and the

Justice Department, it still faces a shareholder lawsuit regarding channel stuffing in Japan, North America, Europe, and South Africa.

Despite a solid focus on building and maintaining a strong, positive reputation and a firm dedication to social responsibility, Coca-Cola has had its major problems in competing with its major rival PepsiCo. The use of channel stuffing and other questionable practices has not been the answer to making the numbers.[13]

**Questions for Discussion**

1. How could channel stuffing at Coca-Cola affect its relationships with channel members such as bottlers?

2. In what ways could channel stuffing impact its own customer service standards?

3. Why would Coca-Cola risk its reputation by engaging in channel stuffing?

---

**Case 16.2**

# Distribution Technology: Wal-Mart's Power Tool

How does the world's largest retailer keep the shelves stocked at 6,000 stores while keeping prices low enough to attract 138 million shoppers worldwide every week? Physical distribution is the key. Since the first Wal-Mart opened in Rogers, Arkansas, in 1962, management has carefully balanced its inventory levels, delivery schedules, and transportation costs to ensure products arrive at the right stores at the right time and at the right price. Today the company uses information technology to coordinate the movement of products from suppliers to the loading docks of its 62 distribution centers and on to the company's Wal-Mart discount stores, Super-Center combination food/general merchandise outlets, Sam's Club warehouse stores, and Neighborhood Market grocery stores. Every day, Wal-Mart tracks 718 million items.

Through its Retail Link network, Wal-Mart collaborates with suppliers to forecast sales, plan future orders, and replenish stock automatically. Here is how the system works. The point-of-sale scanning equipment in each store captures item-by-item, brand-by-brand sales data. Using sophisticated database technology, Wal-Mart analyzes the sales patterns and historical results for the previous 65 weeks with all of its suppliers. Next, Wal-Mart and its suppliers agree on forecasts for future sales. Then they jointly decide on an order and delivery schedule to ensure inventory levels at each distribution center are appropriate for the forecasted store sales. Wal-Mart makes the system available to suppliers free of charge. In exchange, suppliers share detailed analyses of results and forecasts with Wal-Mart officials.

Retail Link works. During a pilot test with the maker of Listerine, Wal-Mart was able to boost its in-stock position from 87 percent to 98 percent while cutting the order fulfillment cycle time from 21 to 11 days. The supplier also benefited because it sold Wal-Mart an additional $8.5 million of Listerine and was able to better manage its production and delivery activities. Customers benefited because they were able to pick up

bottles of Listerine from store shelves when they wanted, and they saved money because low costs allow Wal-Mart to set everyday low prices.

Another technology that helps Wal-Mart streamline its physical distribution system is radio frequency identification (RFID). Wal-Mart requires its 100 largest suppliers to attach an RFID tag (bearing a computer chip, radio antenna, and identification number) to each case or pallet of merchandise. Using readers in its distribution centers, Wal-Mart picks up radio signals indicating which products are being received and in what quantities. Now the company can track inbound inventory on conveyer belts traveling 540 feet per minute without individually counting each container—and with complete accuracy. The technology has already yielded a 16 percent reduction of stockouts for certain products. Next-generation RFID technology will enable Wal-Mart to track shipments on much faster-moving conveyer belts.

Despite a global roster of 20,000 suppliers, Wal-Mart is always looking for ways to improve its supply chain management and gain flexibility, slash costs, and identify new supply sources around the world. For example, the company imports $12 billion worth of merchandise from China every year. It also maintains a private procurement website to request and receive supplier bids on contracts, centrally negotiate purchasing, and arrange shipping.

As the most powerful channel captain on the planet, Wal-Mart can command ever-higher efficiencies from its suppliers, squeeze additional costs from physical distribution due to economies of scale, and pass the savings on to consumers in the form of lower retail prices. Consider its private-brand George jeans, which were originally priced at $26.67. Wal-Mart reduced costs by purchasing in high volume directly from suppliers in Asia rather than working through wholesalers. It cut costs even further by refining materials handling and transportation. Now George jeans sell for $7.85—less than one-third of the old price.

As Wal-Mart spreads farther from its Arkansas base, management continues opening distribution centers and arranging transportation to ship merchandise to clusters of stores in the area. The company operates a huge truck fleet to transfer products from distribution centers to stores, but it also contracts with independent trucking firms to transport food and other specialized products. In the Northeast, for example, Wal-Mart receives and stores grocery products at an 868,000-square-foot food distribution center in Johnstown, New York. From there, trucks operated by Clarksville Refrigerated Lines bring orders to Wal-Mart stores across New England, New York, and Pennsylvania.

Similarly, a fleet of refrigerated trucks operated by M. S. Carriers transports perishable food products from Wal-Mart's food distribution center in Monroe, Georgia, to Sam's Club warehouse stores in five surrounding states.

Rather than reinvent the wheel for every distribution center and store in North America, Argentina, Brazil, Germany, the United Kingdom, Japan, China, and Korea, the company encourages each region to share its best distribution practices. As a result, Wal-Mart's German stores are benefiting from the U.S. stores' experience in reducing inventory levels and restocking more rapidly. Its Korean stores are replicating the Mexican operation's popular and profitable web-based grocery delivery program. The world's largest retailer is not finished expanding. As it opens hundreds of new stores in the coming years, it will keep honing its distribution skills to keep shelves stocked at the lowest possible cost.[14]

## Questions for Discussion

1. Why is physical distribution so important to Wal-Mart's marketing strategy?
2. Why does Wal-Mart prefer to deal directly with suppliers rather than buying from wholesalers?
3. How does Retail Link help Wal-Mart better control order processing and inventory management?

## CHAPTER 17

# Retailing and Direct Marketing

## The Container Store: Organizing Its Employees to Help You Organize Your Life

In 1978 the first The Container Store opened with a unique retailing concept—offer a mix of products to help people simplify their lives through storage and organization. Today the retailer has 34 locations across the United States and sells more than 10,000 innovative products to help customers save them space and, ultimately, time.

The Container Store has been consistently selected by *Fortune* magazine as one of the "100 Best Companies to Work For," and was ranked among the top three companies each year for the past five years. A key to the chain's success is its blue-aproned sales personnel. Trained to help customers put together home storage systems to fit their individual needs, salespeople provide unparalleled service, fresh organization ideas, and an interactive shopping experience. Customer service is so important to its operation that The Container Store names it its core competency. The company understands that to have outstanding customer service, it must have outstanding employees. All 2,500 employees—from salespeople to buyers to distribution center workers—are recognized as the firm's greatest asset.

## OBJECTIVES

1. To understand the purpose and function of retailers in the marketing channel

2. To identify the major types of retailers

3. To understand direct marketing and two other forms of nonstore retailing

4. To examine the major types of franchising and the benefits and weaknesses of franchising

5. To explore strategic issues in retailing

One of the company's business philosophies is that one "great" person equals three "good" people, so it aims to hire only "great" personnel—self-motivated and team-oriented people with strong basic values and a passion for customer service. Though they have varied backgrounds, most employees are college educated, and all share an enthusiasm for The Container Store. In an industry where turnover rates can run above 50 percent, barely 12 percent of the chain's employees leave each year. As The Container Store's CEO recently said, "The company's greatest challenge as it expands isn't capital expenditure or finding sites, but getting and keeping great people who can make the operational model work effectively."[1] ■

Retailers such as The Container Store, JCPenney, Home Depot, and Victoria's Secret are highly visible and accessible channel members to consumers. They are important links in the marketing channel because they are both marketers for and customers of producers and wholesalers. They perform many marketing functions, such as buying, selling, grading, risk taking, and developing and maintaining information databases about customers. Retailers are in strategic positions to develop relationships with consumers and partnerships with producers and intermediaries in the marketing channel.

In this chapter, we examine the nature of retailing and its importance in supplying consumers with goods and services. We discuss the major types of retail stores. Then we describe direct marketing and two other types of nonstore retailing. Next we look at franchising, a retailing form that continues to grow in popularity. Finally, we explore several strategic issues in retailing, including location, retail positioning, store image, scrambled merchandising, and the wheel of retailing.

# The Nature of Retailing

**retailing** All transactions in which the buyer intends to consume the product through personal, family, or household use

**retailer** An organization that purchases products for the purpose of reselling them to ultimate consumers

**Retailing** includes all transactions in which the buyer intends to consume the product through personal, family, or household use. Buyers in retail transactions are therefore the ultimate consumers. A **retailer** is an organization that purchases products for the purpose of reselling them to ultimate consumers. Although most retailers' sales are made directly to the consumer, nonretail transactions occasionally occur when retailers sell products to other businesses. Retailing often takes place in stores or service establishments, but it also occurs through direct selling, direct marketing, and vending machines outside stores.

Retailing is important to the national economy. Approximately 1.1 million retailers operate in the United States.[2] This number has remained relatively constant for the past 25 years, but sales volume has increased more than fourfold. Most personal income is spent in retail stores, and nearly one out of eight people employed in the United States works in a retail operation (Figure 17.1).

**figure 17.1**

## THE IMPORTANCE OF RETAILING IN THE U.S. ECONOMY

**In the U.S., retailing accounts for:**

| | |
|---|---|
| **15.6%** | of all businesses |
| **7.1%** | of the GDP* |
| **11.5%** | of employment |

*Gross Domestic Product

**Source:** U.S. Bureau of the Census, *Statistical Abstract of the United States,* 2006 (Washington, DC: Government Printing Office, 2006), pp. 407, 444, 513, 671.

Retailers add value, provide services, and assist in making product selections. They can enhance the value of the product by making the shopping experience more convenient, as in home shopping. Through its location, a retailer can facilitate comparison shopping; for example, car dealerships often cluster in the same general vicinity. Product value is also enhanced when retailers offer services, such as technical advice, delivery, credit, and repair services. Finally, retail sales personnel can demonstrate to customers how a product can help address their needs or solve a problem.

The value added by retailers is significant for both producers and ultimate consumers. Retailers are the critical link between producers and ultimate consumers because they provide the environment in which exchanges with ultimate consumers occur. Ultimate consumers benefit through retailers' performance of marketing functions that result in availability of broader arrays of products. Retailers play a major role in creating time, place, and possession utility and, in some cases, form utility.

Leading retailers such as Wal-Mart, Home Depot, Taco Bell, Macy's, and Toys 'R' Us offer consumers a place to browse and compare merchandise to find exactly what they need. However, such traditional retailing is being challenged by direct marketing channels that provide home shopping through catalogs, television, and the Internet. Traditional retailers are responding to this change in the retail environment in various ways. Wal-Mart, for example, is offering more upscale merchandise such as plasma TVs and more fashionable apparel as well as more extended warranties on merchandise.[3] It has also joined forces with fast-food giants McDonald's and KFC to attract consumers and offer them the added convenience of eating where they shop. In response to competition from Amazon.com, Barnes & Noble developed a website to sell books via the Internet.

New store formats and advances in information technology are making the retail environment highly dynamic and competitive. Instant-messaging technology is enabling online retailers to converse with customers so they don't click away to another site. For example, shoppers on the Lands' End website can chat, via keyboard, directly with a customer service representative about sizes, colors, or other product details. The key to success in retailing is to have a strong customer focus with a retail strategy that provides the level of service, product quality, and innovation that consumers desire. Partnerships among noncompeting retailers and other marketing channel members are providing new opportunities for retailers. For example, airports are leasing space to retailers such as The Sharper Image, McDonald's, Sunglass Hut, and The Body Shop. Kroger and Nordstrom have developed co-branded credit cards that offer rebates to customers at participating stores.

Retailers are also finding global opportunities. For example, both McDonald's and The Gap are now opening more international stores than domestic ones, a trend that is likely to continue for the foreseeable future. Wal-Mart and Home Depot are opening stores in Canada, Mexico, and South America. Increasingly, retailers from abroad, such as IKEA, Zara, and BP, are opening stores in the United States.

# Major Types of Retail Stores

Many types of retail stores exist. One way to classify them is by the breadth of products offered. Two general categories include general-merchandise retailers and specialty retailers.

## General-Merchandise Retailers

**general-merchandise retailer**
A retail establishment that offers a variety of product lines that are stocked in considerable depth

A retail establishment that offers a variety of product lines stocked in considerable depth is referred to as a **general-merchandise retailer**. The types of product offerings, mixes of customer services, and operating styles of retailers in this category vary considerably. The primary types of general-merchandise retailers are department stores, discount stores, supermarkets, superstores, hypermarkets, warehouse clubs, and warehouse and catalog showrooms (see Table 17.1 on p. 464).

| table 17.1 | GENERAL-MERCHANDISE RETAILERS | |
|---|---|---|
| **Type of Retailer** | **Description** | **Examples** |
| Department store | Large organization offering a wide product mix and organized into separate departments | Macy's, JCPenney, Sears |
| Discount store | Self-service, general-merchandise store offering brand name and private-brand products at low prices | Wal-Mart, Target, Kmart |
| Convenience store | Small self-service store offering a narrow product assortment in convenient locations | 7-Eleven, Circle K |
| Supermarket | Self-service store offering a complete line of food products and some nonfood products | Kroger, Albertson's, Winn-Dixie |
| Superstore | Giant outlet offering all food and nonfood products found in supermarkets, as well as most routinely purchased products | Wal-Mart Supercenters |
| Warehouse club | Large-scale, members-only establishment combining cash-and-carry wholesaling and discount retailing | Sam's Club, Costco |
| Warehouse showroom | Facility in a large, low-cost building with large on-premises inventories and minimal service | IKEA |
| Catalog showroom | Warehouse showroom in which consumers use catalogs to place orders for products, which are then filled directly in the warehouse area and picked up by buyers in the showroom | Service Merchandise |

**department store** A large retail organization characterized by a wide product mix and organized into separate departments to facilitate marketing efforts and internal management

**Department Stores. Department stores** are large retail organizations characterized by wide product mixes and staffs of at least 25 people. To facilitate marketing efforts and internal management in these stores, related product lines are organized into separate departments, such as cosmetics, housewares, apparel, home furnishings, and appliances. Often each department functions as a self-contained business, and buyers for individual departments are fairly autonomous.

Department stores are distinctly service oriented. Their total product may include credit, delivery, personal assistance, merchandise returns, and a pleasant atmosphere. Although some so-called department stores are actually large, departmentalized specialty stores, most department stores are shopping stores. Consumers can compare price, quality, and service at one store with those at competing stores. Along with large discount stores, department stores are often considered retailing leaders in a community and are found in most places with populations of more than 50,000.

Typical department stores, such as Macy's, Sears, Marshall Field's, Dillard's, and Neiman Marcus, obtain a large proportion of sales from apparel, accessories, and cosmetics. Other products these stores carry include gift items, luggage, electronics, home accessories, and sports equipment. Some department stores offer such services as automobile insurance, hair care, income tax preparation, and travel and optical services. In some cases, space for these specialized services is leased out, with proprietors managing their own operations and paying rent to the store.

**discount store** A self-service, general-merchandise store offering brand name and private-brand products at low prices

**Discount Stores. Discount stores** are self-service, general-merchandise outlets that regularly offer brand name and private-brand products at low prices. Discounters accept lower margins than conventional retailers in exchange for high sales volume. To keep inventory turnover high, they carry a wide but carefully selected assortment of products, from appliances to housewares and clothing. Major discount establishments also offer food products, toys, automotive services, garden supplies, and

**Department Stores**

Department stores like JC Penney offer a host of product lines and a number of customer services.

sports equipment. Wal-Mart, Target, and Kmart are the three largest discount stores. When Kmart Holding Corporation agreed to buy Sears, it introduced a smaller version of the Sears department store, called Sears Essentials, to compete with Target and Wal-Mart.[4] Many discounters are regional organizations, such as Venture, Bradlees, and Meijer. Most operate in large (50,000 to 80,000 square feet), no-frills facilities. Discount stores usually offer everyday low prices rather than relying on sales events.

Discount retailing developed on a large scale in the early 1950s, when postwar production began catching up with consumer demand for appliances, home furnishings, and other hard goods. Discount stores were often cash-only operations in warehouse districts, offering goods at savings of 20 to 30 percent over conventional retailers. Facing increased competition from department stores and other discount stores, some discounters have improved store services, atmosphere, and location, raising prices and sometimes blurring the distinction between discount store and department store. Other discounters continue to focus on price alone.

**Convenience Stores.** **Convenience stores** are small self-service stores that are open long hours and carry a narrow assortment of convenience items such as soft drinks and other beverages, snacks, newspapers, tobacco, and gasoline, and provide services such as automatic teller machines. The primary product offered by these stores is convenience. 7-Eleven's director of processed foods says, "When consumers visit a 7-Eleven, they seek something that will solve their immediate need. They are in the mood for a consumable product and want it right now, and expect the convenience store to deliver it."[5]

According to the National Association of Convenience Stores, there are 138,200 convenience stores in the United States with 1.5 million employees. They are typically less than 5,000 square feet; open 24 hours a day, 7 days a week; and stock about 500 items. In addition to many national chains, there are many family-owned independent convenience stores in operation.[6] The convenience store concept was developed in 1927 when Southland Ice in Dallas began stocking milk, eggs, and other products for customers replenishing their "ice" boxes. Southland eventually evolved into 7-Eleven, which now has 5,300 stores in the United States. Gasoline sales account for just one-third of the chain's total sales, which increasingly include upscale merchandise such as wine and high-end sandwiches and snacks.[7]

**convenience store** A small self-service store that is open long hours and carries a narrow assortment of products, usually convenience items

**supermarket** A large, self-service store that carries a complete line of food products, along with some nonfood products

**Supermarkets.** **Supermarkets** are large, self-service stores that carry a complete line of food products, as well as some nonfood products such as cosmetics and nonprescription drugs. Supermarkets are arranged in departments for maximum efficiency in stocking and handling products, but have central checkout facilities. They offer lower prices than smaller neighborhood grocery stores, usually provide free parking, and may also cash checks. Supermarkets must operate efficiently because net profits after taxes are usually less than 1 percent of sales. Supermarkets may be independently owned but are often part of a chain operation. Top U.S. supermarket chains include Kroger, Albertson's, Safeway, and A&P.

Today consumers make more than three-quarters of all grocery purchases in supermarkets. Even so, supermarkets' total share of the food market is declining because consumers now have widely varying food preferences and buying habits. Furthermore, in many communities shoppers can choose from a number of convenience stores, discount stores, and specialty food stores, as well as a wide variety of restaurants. Wal-Mart, for example, expects to generate more revenues in its "supermarket-type" stores than the top three U.S. supermarket chains—Kroger, Albertson's, and Safeway—combined. To continue to compete, Albertson's plans to make grocery shopping quick and easy with new technology that will eliminate checkout lines.[8]

**superstore** A giant retail outlet that carries food and nonfood products found in supermarkets, as well as most routinely purchased consumer products

**Superstores.** **Superstores**, which originated in Europe, are giant retail outlets that carry not only food and nonfood products ordinarily found in supermarkets but also routinely purchased consumer products. Besides a complete food line, superstores sell housewares, hardware, small appliances, clothing, personal-care products, garden products, and tires—about four times as many items as supermarkets. Services available at superstores include dry cleaning, automotive repair, check cashing, bill paying, and snack bars.

Superstores combine features of discount stores and supermarkets. Examples include Wal-Mart Supercenters, some Kroger stores, and Super Kmart Centers. To cut handling and inventory costs, superstores use sophisticated operating techniques and often have tall shelving that displays entire assortments of products. Superstores can have an area of as much as 200,000 square feet (compared with 20,000 square feet in traditional supermarkets). Sales volume is two to three times that of supermarkets, partly because locations near good transportation networks help generate the in-store traffic needed for profitability.

**hypermarket** A store that combines supermarket and discount store shopping in one location

**Hypermarkets.** **Hypermarkets** combine supermarket and discount store shopping in one location. Larger than superstores, they range from 225,000 to 325,000 square feet and offer 45,000 to 60,000 different types of low-priced products. They commonly allocate 40 to 50 percent of their space to grocery products and the remainder to general merchandise, including athletic shoes, designer jeans, and other apparel; refrigerators, televisions, and other appliances; housewares; cameras; toys; jewelry; hardware; and automotive supplies. Many lease space to noncompeting businesses such as banks, optical shops, and fast-food restaurants. All hypermarkets focus on low prices and vast selections. Although Kmart, Wal-Mart, and Carrefour (a French retailer) have operated hypermarkets in the United States, most of these stores were unsuccessful and closed. Such stores are too big for time-constrained U.S. shoppers. However, hypermarkets are successful in Europe, South America, and Mexico. For example, the hypermarket has become such a success in Mexico that the leading chains are currently waging a retail war. Wal-Mart de Mexico is leading the battle with annual sales of $11.7 billion, but competitors such as Soriana, with annual sales of $3.2 billion, are taking risks and fighting back.[9]

**warehouse club** A large-scale, members-only establishment that combines features of cash-and-carry wholesaling with discount retailing

**Warehouse Clubs.** **Warehouse clubs**, a rapidly growing form of mass merchandising, are large-scale, members-only selling operations combining cash-and-carry wholesaling with discount retailing. For a nominal annual fee (usually about $35), small retailers purchase products at wholesale prices for business use or for resale. Warehouse clubs also sell to ultimate consumers affiliated with government agencies, credit unions, schools, hospitals, and banks, but instead of paying a membership fee, individual consumers may pay about 5 percent more on each item than do business customers.

Sometimes called *buying clubs,* warehouse clubs offer the same types of products as discount stores, but in a limited range of sizes and styles. Whereas most discount stores carry around 40,000 items, a warehouse club handles only 3,500 to 5,000 products, usually acknowledged brand leaders. Sam's Club stores, for example, stock a little more than 4,000 items, with 1,400 available most of the time and the rest being one-time buys. Costco leads the warehouse club industry with sales of $52.9 billion. Sam's Club is second with $34.5 billion in store sales. A third company, BJ's Wholesale Club, which operates in the Northeast and Florida, has a much smaller market.[10] All these establishments offer a broad product mix, including food, beverages, books, appliances, housewares, automotive parts, hardware, and furniture. Warehouse clubs appeal to many price-conscious consumers and small retailers unable to obtain wholesaling services from large distributors. The average warehouse club shopper has more education, a higher income, and a larger household than the average supermarket shopper.

To keep prices lower than those of supermarkets and discount stores, warehouse clubs provide few services. They generally do not advertise, except through direct mail. Their facilities, often located in industrial areas, have concrete floors and aisles wide enough for forklifts. Merchandise is stacked on pallets or displayed on pipe racks. Customers must transport purchases themselves.

**warehouse showroom** A retail facility in a large, low-cost building with large on-premise inventories and minimal services

**Warehouse and Catalog Showrooms.** **Warehouse showrooms** are retail facilities with five basic characteristics: large, low-cost buildings; warehouse materials handling technology; vertical merchandise displays; large on-premises inventories; and minimal services. IKEA, a Swedish company, sells furniture, household goods, and kitchen accessories in warehouse showrooms and through catalogs around the world. Wickes Furniture and Levitz Furniture also operate warehouse showrooms. These high-volume, low-overhead operations stress fewer personnel and services. Lower costs are possible because some marketing functions have been shifted to consumers, who must transport, finance, and perhaps store merchandise. Most consumers carry away purchases in the manufacturers' cartons, although stores will deliver for a fee.

**Warehouse Showroom**

IKEA, is a warehouse showroom that markets furnishings and home accessories.

**catalog showroom** A warehouse showroom in which consumers use catalogs to place orders for products, which are then filled directly in the warehouse area and picked up by buyers in the showroom

In **catalog showrooms**, one item of each product is displayed, often in a locked case, with remaining inventory stored out of the buyer's reach. Using catalogs that have been mailed to their homes or are on store counters, customers order products by phone or in person. Clerks fill orders from the warehouse area, and products are presented in the manufacturers' cartons. In contrast to traditional catalog retailers, which offer no discounts and require that customers wait for delivery, catalog showrooms regularly sell below list price and often provide goods immediately.

Catalog showrooms usually sell jewelry, luggage, photographic equipment, toys, small appliances and housewares, sporting goods, and power tools. They advertise extensively and carry established brands and models that are not likely to be discontinued. Because catalog showrooms have higher product turnover, fewer losses through shoplifting, and lower labor costs than department stores, they are able to feature lower prices. However, they offer minimal services and customers often have to stand in line to examine items or place orders. The rapid growth of discounters and warehouse clubs is also putting pressure on catalog showrooms. Neiman Marcus Group Inc. is testing the concept of a catalog showroom inside two stores (one in Plano, Texas, and the other in suburban Chicago) as part of an effort to expand its retail formats.[11]

## Specialty Retailers

In contrast to general-merchandise retailers with their broad product mixes, specialty retailers emphasize narrow and deep assortments. Despite their name, specialty retailers do not sell specialty items (except when specialty goods complement the overall product mix). Instead, they offer substantial assortments in a few product lines. We examine three types of specialty retailers: traditional specialty retailers, off-price retailers, and category killers.

**traditional specialty retailer** A store that carries a narrow product mix with deep product lines

### Traditional Specialty Retailers

The Container Store is a specialty store that offers organizational products.

**Traditional Specialty Retailers. Traditional specialty retailers** are stores that carry a narrow product mix with deep product lines. Sometimes called *limited-line retailers*, they may be referred to as *single-line retailers* if they carry unusual depth in one main product category. Specialty retailers commonly sell such shopping products as apparel, jewelry, sporting goods, fabrics, computers, and pet supplies. The Limited, Radio Shack, Hickory Farms, The Gap, and Foot Locker are examples of retailers offering limited product lines but great depth within those lines.

Although the number of chain specialty stores is increasing, many specialty stores are independently owned. Florists, bakery shops, and bookstores are among the small, independent specialty retailers that appeal to local target markets, although these stores can be owned and managed by large corporations. Even if this kind of retailer adds a few supporting product lines, the store may still be classified as a specialty store.

Because they are usually small, specialty stores may have high costs in proportion to sales, and satisfying customers may require carrying some products with low turnover rates. However, these stores sometimes obtain lower prices from suppliers by purchasing limited lines of merchandise in large quantities. Successful specialty stores understand their customer types and know what products to carry, thus reducing the risk of unsold merchandise. Specialty stores usually offer better selections and more sales expertise than department stores, their main competitors. By capitalizing on fashion, service, personnel, atmosphere, and location, specialty retailers position themselves strategically to attract customers in specific market segments. Specialty stores may even become exclusive dealers in their markets for certain products.

**The Container Store®**
The Original Storage and Organization Store®

Chestnut Hill, MA 27 Boylston, Route 9 (just east of The Mall at Chestnut Hill) (617) 566-7480
Natick, MA Route 9 (just west of Natick Mall) (508) 655-8500
Store Hours: Monday - Saturday 9 am - 9 pm; Sunday 11 am - 6 pm
www.containerstore.com 1-800-733-3532

Through specialty stores, small-business owners provide unique services to match consumers' varied desires. For consumers dissatisfied with the impersonal nature of large retailers, the close, personal contact offered by a small specialty store can be a welcome change.

**Off-Price Retailers.** **Off-price retailers** buy manufacturers' seconds, overruns, returns, and off-season production runs at below-wholesale prices for resale to consumers at deep discounts. Unlike true discount stores, which pay regular wholesale prices for goods and usually carry second-line brand names, off-price retailers offer limited lines of national-brand and designer merchandise, usually clothing, shoes, and/or housewares. The number of off-price retailers has grown since the mid-1980s. Ross is an off-price clothing retailer that appeals to customers who want to "dress for less." Frequently found near other off-price retailers such as T.J. Maxx, Marshalls, Stein Mart, and Burlington Coat Factory, Ross targets customers with an annual household income of $50,000 to $60,000. To appeal to lower-income customers, Ross recently opened DD's Discounts in a number of small neighborhood shopping centers in California.[12]

Off-price stores charge 20 to 50 percent less than department stores for comparable merchandise but offer few customer services. They often feature community dressing rooms and central checkout counters. Some of these stores do not take returns or allow exchanges. Off-price stores may or may not sell goods with original labels intact. They turn over their inventory nine to 12 times a year, three times as often as traditional specialty stores. They compete with department stores for the same customers: price-conscious customers who are knowledgeable about brand names.

Another form of off-price retailer is the manufacturer's outlet mall, which makes available manufacturer overstocks and unsold merchandise from other retail outlets at discounted prices. Diverse manufacturers are represented in these malls.

To ensure a regular flow of merchandise into their stores, off-price retailers establish long-term relationships with suppliers that can provide large quantities of goods at reduced prices. Manufacturers may approach retailers with samples, discontinued products, or items that have not sold well. Also, retailers may seek out manufacturers, offering to pay cash for goods produced during the manufacturers' off season. Although manufacturers benefit from such arrangements, they also risk alienating their specialty and department store customers. Department stores tolerate off-price stores as long as they do not advertise brand names, limit merchandise to lower-quality items, and are located away from the department stores. When off-price retailers obtain large stocks of in-season, top-quality merchandise, tension builds between department stores and manufacturers.

**Category Killers.** Over the last two decades, a new breed of specialty retailer, the category killer, has evolved. A **category killer** is a very large specialty store that concentrates on a major product category and competes on the basis of low prices and enormous product availability. These stores are referred to as category killers because they expand rapidly and gain sizable market shares, taking business away from smaller, high-cost retail outlets. Examples of category killers include Home Depot and Lowe's (home-improvement chains); Staples, Office Depot, and Office-Max (office-supply chains); Borders and Barnes & Noble (booksellers); PETCO and PetSmart (pet-supply chains); and Best Buy and Circuit City (consumer electronics).

---

**off-price retailer** A store that buys manufacturers' seconds, overruns, returns, and off-season merchandise for resale to consumers at deep discounts

**category killer** A very large specialty store that concentrates on a major product category and competes on the basis of low prices and enormous product availability

### Category Killers

Some stores, like Lowe's, are referred to as category killers because of their enormous product mixes and low prices.

Fashion meets flora.

Visit Lowe's Garden Center today for our abundant selection of planters and accessories in styles ranging from classic to contemporary.

Items shown are metal with a copper finish: 16.5" Vase (227361), 8" Urn (273364), 11" Planter (273365).

© 2006 by Lowe's. All rights reserved. Lowe's and the gable design are registered trademarks of LF, LLC.

**LOWE'S**
Let's Build Something Together™

# Direct Marketing

**direct marketing** The use of the telephone, Internet, and nonpersonal media to introduce products to customers, who can then purchase them via mail, telephone, or the Internet

**nonstore retailing** The selling of products outside the confines of a retail facility

**catalog marketing** A type of marketing in which an organization provides a catalog from which customers make selections and place orders by mail, telephone, or the Internet

**Direct marketing** is the use of the telephone, Internet, and nonpersonal media to communicate product and organizational information to customers, who can then purchase products via mail, telephone, or the Internet. Direct marketing is one type of nonstore retailing. **Nonstore retailing** is the selling of products outside the confines of a retail facility. This form of retailing accounts for an increasing percentage of total sales. Direct marketing can occur through catalog marketing, direct-response marketing, telemarketing, television home shopping, and online retailing.

## Catalog Marketing

In **catalog marketing**, an organization provides a catalog from which customers make selections and place orders by mail, telephone, or the Internet. Catalog marketing began in 1872, when Montgomery Ward issued its first catalog to rural families. Today there are more than 7,000 catalog marketing companies in the United States, as well as a number of retail stores, such as JCPenney, that engage in catalog marketing. Some organizations, including Spiegel and JCPenney, offer a broad array of products spread over multiple product lines. Catalog companies such as Lands' End, Pottery Barn, and J. Crew offer considerable depth in one major line of products.

# Beyond the Maine Woods: L.L. Bean Branches Out

L.L. Bean, the well-known seller of outdoor clothing and equipment, is facing another hurdle in its successful history—how to change its way of doing business without changing its image.

Leon Leonwood Bean founded his company in Freeport, Maine, in 1912, the year after he made the first rubber-bottomed hunting boots. He sold his boots through a four-page mailer that he sent to hunters in Maine and to out-of-staters who held Maine hunting licenses. The business prospered as the company expanded its product line to outdoor clothing and hunting and fishing gear. Today the company is a global organization with annual sales in excess of $1.4 billion.

About 40 percent of its merchandise is sold through catalogs, 40 percent over the Internet, and 20 percent through five retail stores and 14 factory stores in or near Maine.

L.L. Bean's success has been primarily due to its high-quality, dependable products and a carefully constructed image of a Maine-based company that embraces the region's old-fashioned values of integrity, frugality, and quality.

In recent years, the marketplace has changed due to the emergence of savvy and aggressive competitors, three of which are each approaching annual sales of $1 billion. Eddie Bauer has over 400 locations across the United States; Eastern Mountain Sports (EMS) has 100 stores; and Gander Mountain has 98. For the most part, these competitors have built their businesses through retail sales outlets.

L.L. Bean plans to open more retail stores across the country to compete more effectively and grow long term. The challenge is to expand to new areas while maintaining its rustic Maine image. According to the current CEO, the important goal for the future is to convince people that the company still stands for the same things it did 40 years ago: outdoors, service, and quality products.

Still other catalog companies specialize in only a few products within a single line. Some catalog retailers—for instance, Crate and Barrel and The Sharper Image—have stores in major metropolitan areas. When Sears, Roebuck and Company acquired Lands' End, it continued to operate both entities separately, but found ways to incorporate Lands' End into Sears by opening mini Lands' End stores within Sears stores.[13]

The advantages of catalog retailing include efficiency and convenience for customers. The retailer benefits by being able to locate in remote, low-cost areas; save on expensive store fixtures; and reduce both personal selling and store operating expenses. On the other hand, catalog retailing is inflexible, provides limited service, and is most effective only for a selected set of products.

Catalog sales are about $132 billion annually and are expected to grow to $177 billion by 2008.[14] Even though the cost of mailing catalogs continues to rise, catalog sales are growing at double the rate of in-store retailing. Williams-Sonoma, for example, sells kitchenware and home and garden products through five catalogs, including Pottery Barn and Gardeners' Eden. Catalog sales have been increasing due to the convenience of catalog shopping. Product quality is often high, and because consumers can order by phone or Internet 24 hours a day, charge purchases to a credit card, and have the merchandise delivered to their door in one to two days, such shopping is much easier than going to a store.

## Direct-Response Marketing

**direct-response marketing** A type of marketing in which a retailer advertises a product and makes it available through mail or telephone orders

**Direct-response marketing** occurs when a retailer advertises a product and makes it available through mail or telephone orders. Generally a purchaser may use a credit card, but other forms of payment are acceptable. Examples of direct-response marketing include a television commercial offering a recording artist's musical collection available through a toll-free number, a newspaper or magazine advertisement for a series of children's books available by filling out the form in the ad or calling a toll-free number, and even a billboard promoting floral services available by calling 1-800-Flowers. Direct-response marketing is also conducted by sending letters, samples, brochures, or booklets to prospects on a mailing list and asking that they order the advertised products by mail or telephone. In general, products must be priced above $20 to justify the advertising and distribution costs associated with direct-response marketing.

## Telemarketing

**telemarketing** The performance of marketing-related activities by telephone

A number of organizations use the telephone to strengthen the effectiveness of traditional marketing methods. **Telemarketing** is the performance of marketing-related activities by telephone. Some organizations use a prescreened list of prospective clients. Telemarketing can help generate sales leads, improve customer service, speed up payments on past-due accounts, raise funds for nonprofit organizations, and gather marketing data.

Currently the laws and regulations regarding telemarketing, while in a state of flux, are becoming more restrictive. Many states have established do-not-call lists of customers who do not want to receive telemarketing calls from companies operating in their state. In 2003 the U.S. Congress implemented a national do-not-call registry for consumers who do not wish to receive telemarketing calls. By the end of that year, nearly one-third of the 166 million residential phone numbers in the United States had been listed on the registry. Companies are subject to a fine of up to $12,000 for each call made to a consumer listed on the national do-not-call registry.[15] The national registry is enforced by the Federal Trade Commission and the Federal Communications Commission.[16] Certain exceptions apply to no-call lists. A company can still use telemarketing to communicate with existing customers. In addition, charitable, political, and telephone survey organizations are not restricted by the national registry.

## Benefits of online marketing

Researchers report that the four major advantages of online marketing are increased revenue, greater visibility, cost savings, and reaching new customers.

| | |
|---|---|
| Increased revenue | 73% |
| Greater visibility | 58% |
| Cost savings | 56% |
| Reaching new customers | 54% |

Search [____] GO    Clothing   Footwear   Accessories   Home

*Source:* Multichannel Marketing 2005 Report, DMA.

**television home shopping** A form of selling in which products are presented to television viewers, who can buy them by calling a toll-free number and paying with a credit card

**online retailing** Retailing that makes products available to buyers through computer connections

## Television Home Shopping

**Television home shopping** presents products to television viewers, encouraging them to order through toll-free numbers and pay with credit cards. Home Shopping Network in Florida originated and popularized this format. There are several home shopping cable channels. A few of these channels specialize in certain product categories. The most popular products sold through television home shopping are jewelry (40 percent of total sales), clothing, housewares, and electronics.

Home shopping channels have grown so rapidly in recent years that more than 60 percent of U.S. households have access to home shopping programs. Home Shopping Network and QVC are two of the largest home shopping networks. Approximately 60 percent of home shopping sales revenues come from repeat purchasers.

The television home shopping format offers several benefits. Products can be easily demonstrated, and an adequate amount of time can be spent showing the product so to make viewers well informed. The length of time a product is shown depends not only on the time required for doing demonstrations but also on whether the product is selling. Once the calls peak and begin to decline, a new product is shown. Another benefit is that customers can shop at their convenience from the comfort of their homes.

## Online Retailing

**Online retailing** makes products available to buyers through computer connections. The phenomenal growth of Internet use has created new retailing opportunities. Many retailers have set up websites to disseminate information about their companies and products. Although most retailers with websites use them primarily to promote products, a number of companies, including Barnes & Noble, REI, Lands' End, and OfficeMax, sell goods online. Consumers can purchase hard-to-find items, such as Pez candy dispensers and Elvis memorabilia, on eBay. Banks and brokerage firms have established websites to give customers direct access to manage their accounts and enable them to trade online. With advances in computer technology continuing and consumers ever more pressed for time, online retailing will continue to escalate.

Excited. Can't sleep. Mind racing. Is it love, or vacation?

Expedia.com
enjoy your trip.

**Online Retailing**

Expedia is an online retailer of travel-related services.

## marketing ENTREPRENEURS

**Joseph Tantillo**

HIS BUSINESS: Greekgear.com

FOUNDED: 1999

SUCCESS: Revenues of $1.9 million a year

After his daughter was born, Joseph Tantillo wanted a job that would enable him to work from home. His membership in a fraternity during his college years inspired him to launch Greekgear.com, a website that sells personalized merchandise such as T-shirts, hats, jewelry, and license plates to Greek organizations across the country. In its second month, the site served just three customers; today it is the largest online source of "Greek" merchandise. Tantillo's company, Express Design Group, has since launched more online retail sites—Coedgear.com, Guidogear.com, and MyChristianGear.com—that together with GreekGear.com pull in 3 million customers annually.

Although online retailing represents a major retailing venue, security remains an issue. In a recent survey conducted by the Business Software Alliance, about 75 percent of Internet users expressed concerns about shopping online. The major issues are identity theft and credit card theft.

# Other Types of Nonstore Retailing

Besides direct marketing, there are two other major types of nonstore retailing: direct selling and automatic vending.

## Direct Selling

**direct selling** Marketing products to ultimate consumers through face-to-face sales presentations at home or in the workplace

**Direct selling** is the marketing of products to ultimate consumers through face-to-face sales presentations at home or in the workplace. Traditionally called *door-to-door selling*, direct selling in the United States began with peddlers more than a century ago and has since grown into a sizable industry of several hundred firms. Although direct sellers historically used a cold-canvass, door-to-door approach to finding prospects, many companies today, such as World Book, Kirby, Amway, Mary Kay, and Avon, use other approaches. They initially identify customers through the mail, the telephone, the Internet, or shopping mall intercepts and set up appointments.

Direct selling sometimes uses the "party plan," which can occur in the customer's home or workplace. With a party plan, the customer acts as a host and invites a number of friends and associates to view merchandise in a group setting, where a salesperson demonstrates products. The congenial party atmosphere helps to overcome customers' reluctance and encourages them to buy. Direct selling through the party plan requires effective salespeople who can identify potential hosts and provide encouragement and incentives for them to organize a gathering of friends and associates. Tupperware and Mary Kay were the pioneers of this selling technique, paving the way for companies like the Pampered Chef to grow from a basement business into a corporation that brings in over $700 million in revenues annually.[17]

Direct selling has both benefits and limitations. It gives the marketer an opportunity to demonstrate the product in an environment—usually customers' homes—where it would most likely be used. The door-to-door seller can give the customer personal attention, and the product can be presented to the customer at a convenient time and location. Personal attention to the customer is the foundation on which some direct sellers, such as Mary Kay, have built their businesses. Because commissions for salespeople are so high, ranging from 30 to 50 percent of the sales price, and great effort is required to isolate promising prospects, overall costs of direct selling make it the most expensive form of retailing. Furthermore, some customers view direct selling negatively, owing to unscrupulous and fraudulent practices used by some direct sellers in the past. Some communities even have local ordinances that control or, in some cases, prohibit direct selling. Despite these negative views held by some individuals, direct selling is still alive and well, bringing in revenues of over $29 billion a year.[18]

### Automatic Vending

**automatic vending** The use of machines to dispense products

**Automatic vending** is the use of machines to dispense products. It accounts for less than 2 percent of all retail sales. Video game machines provide an entertainment service, and many banks offer automatic teller machines (ATMs), which dispense cash and perform other services.

Automatic vending is one of the most impersonal forms of retailing. Small, standardized, routinely purchased products (e.g., chewing gum, candy, newspapers, cigarettes, soft drinks, coffee) can be sold in machines because consumers usually buy them at the nearest available location. Machines in areas of heavy traffic provide efficient and continuous service to consumers. Such high-volume areas may have more diverse product availability—for example, hot and cold sandwiches, and even hot pizza. WonderPizzaUSA, for example, markets an on-site pizzeria vending machine to workplaces. The machines—about the size of two soft-drink vending machines—cook the pizzas in about two minutes using infrared rays. They can hold up to 100 pizzas, which sell for about $6 each.[19]

Since vending machines need only a small amount of space and no sales personnel, this retailing method has some advantages over stores. The advantages are partly offset, however, by the high costs of equipment and frequent servicing and repairs.

# Franchising

**franchising** An arrangement in which a supplier (franchiser) grants a dealer (franchisee) the right to sell products in exchange for some type of consideration

**Franchising** is an arrangement in which a supplier, or franchiser, grants a dealer, or franchisee, the right to sell products in exchange for some type of consideration. The franchiser may receive some percentage of total sales in exchange for furnishing equipment, buildings, management know-how, and marketing assistance to the franchisee. The franchisee supplies labor and capital, operates the franchised business, and agrees to abide by the provisions of the franchise agreement. Table 17.2 lists the top 20 U.S. franchises, type of product, and startup costs.

Because of changes in the international marketplace, shifting employment options in the United States, the expanding U.S. service economy, and corporate interest in more joint venture activity, franchising is rapidly increasing. Franchising companies and their franchisees account for an estimated $1.5 trillion in annual U.S. retail sales from 767,483 franchised small businesses in 75 industries. Franchising accounts for more than 40 percent of all U.S. retail sales and employs nearly 10 million people.[20] In this section, we look at major types of retail franchises and the advantages and disadvantages of franchising.

### Major Types of Retail Franchises

Retail franchise arrangements fall into three general categories. In one arrangement, a manufacturer authorizes a number of retail stores to sell a certain brand name item. This franchise arrangement, one of the oldest forms, is common in sales of cars and trucks, farm equipment, shoes, paint, earth-moving equipment, and petroleum. In the second type of retail franchise, a producer licenses distributors to sell a given product to retailers. This arrangement is common in the soft-drink industry. Most national manufacturers of soft-drink syrups, including Coca-Cola, Dr Pepper, and PepsiCo, grant franchises to bottlers, which in turn serve retailers. In the third type of retail franchise, a franchiser supplies brand names, techniques, or other services instead of complete products. The franchiser may provide certain production and distribution services, but its primary role in the arrangement is careful development and control of marketing strategies. This approach to franchising is very common today and is used by such organizations as Holiday Inn, AAMCO, McDonald's, Dairy Queen, KFC, and H&R Block.

**table 17.2**  **TOP 20 U.S. FRANCHISES AND THEIR STARTUP COSTS**

| Rank* | Franchise | Description | Number of Franchise Outlets Worldwide | Startup Costs |
|---|---|---|---|---|
| 1 | Subway | Sandwiches, salads | 24,815 | $70,000–$220,000 |
| 2 | Quizno's | Sandwiches, soups, salads | 4,306 | $71,700–$251,100 |
| 3 | Curves | Women's fitness and weight loss | 9,468 | $38,400–$53,500 |
| 4 | UPS Store | Postal, business, communications services | 5,465 | $138,700–$245,500 |
| 5 | Jackson-Hewitt | Tax preparation services | 4,871 | $49,800–$94,000 |
| 6 | Dunkin' Donuts | Doughnuts, baked goods | 6,127 | $179,000–$1.6 million |
| 7 | Jani-King | Commercial cleaning | 11,728 | $11,300–$34,100 |
| 8 | RE/MAX Int'l | Real estate | 6,019 | $20,000–$200,000 |
| 9 | 7-Eleven | Convenience stores | 25,139 | Varies |
| 10 | Liberty Tax Service | Income tax preparation services | 1,723 | $42,300–$52,400 |
| 11 | Domino's Pizza | Pizza, breadsticks, buffalo wings | 7,231 | $141,400–$415,100 |
| 12 | Pizza Hut | Pizza | 9,722 | $1.1 million–$1.7 million |
| 13 | Sonic Drive-In Restaurants | Drive-in restaurants | 2,426 | $710,000–$2.3 million |
| 14 | Century 21 Real Estate | Real estate | 7,560 | $11,700–$522,500 |
| 15 | Jan-Pro Franchising | Commercial cleaning | 4,106 | $3,300–$49,900 |
| 16 | McDonald's | Hamburgers, chicken, salads | 22,435 | $506,000–$1.6 million |
| 17 | ServiceMaster Clean | Commercial/residential cleaning and disaster restoration | 4,555 | $26,000–$102,300 |
| 18 | Kumon Math & Reading Centers | Supplemental education | 25,843 | $10,000–$30,000 |
| 19 | Coldwell Banker Real Estate | Real estate | 2,891 | $23,500–$490,500 |
| 20 | Jiffy Lube | Fast oil change | 1,916 | $214,000–$273,000 |

*Ranking is based primarily on financial strength and stability, growth rate, size of the system, number of years in business, startup costs, litigation, percentage of terminations, and whether the company provides financing.

**Source:** "Franchise 500® 2006 Rankings," www.entrepreneur.com/franzone/rank/0,6584,12-12-F5-2006-0,00.html (accessed May 1, 2006).

## Advantages and Disadvantages of Franchising

Franchising offers several advantages to both the franchisee and the franchiser. It enables a franchisee to start a business with limited capital and benefit from the business experience of others. Moreover, nationally advertised franchises, such as Service-Master and Burger King, are often assured of customers as soon as they open. If business problems arise, the franchisee can obtain guidance and advice from the franchiser at little or no cost. Franchised outlets are generally more successful than independently owned businesses. Fewer than 10 percent of franchised retail businesses fail during the first two years of operation, compared to approximately 50 percent of independent retail businesses. Also, the franchisee receives materials to use in local advertising and can benefit from national promotional campaigns sponsored by the franchiser.

Through franchise arrangements, the franchiser gains fast and selective product distribution without incurring the high cost of constructing and operating its own outlets. The franchiser therefore has more capital for expanding production and advertising. It can also ensure, through the franchise agreement, that outlets are maintained and operated according to its own standards. The franchiser benefits from the fact that the franchisee, being a sole proprietor in most cases, is likely to be very highly motivated to succeed. Success of the franchise means more sales, which translate into higher income for the franchiser.

Franchise arrangements also have several drawbacks. The franchiser can dictate many aspects of the business: decor, design of employees' uniforms, types of signs, and numerous details of business operations. In addition, franchisees must pay to use the franchiser's name, products, and assistance. Usually there is a one-time franchise fee and continuing royalty and advertising fees, often collected as a percentage of sales. For example, Subway requires franchisees to come up with $70,000 to $220,000 in startup costs. Franchisees often must work very hard, putting in 10- to 12-hour days six or seven days a week. In some cases, franchise agreements are not uniform; one franchisee may pay more than another for the same services. Finally, the franchiser gives up a certain amount of control when entering into a franchise agreement. Consequently individual establishments may not be operated exactly according to the franchiser's standards.

# Strategic Issues in Retailing

Consumers often have vague reasons for making retail purchases. Whereas most business purchases are based on economic planning and necessity, consumer purchases may result from social and psychological influences. Because consumers shop for a variety of reasons—to search for specific items, escape boredom, or learn about something new—retailers must do more than simply fill space with merchandise. They must make desired products available, create stimulating shopping environments, and develop marketing strategies that increase store patronage. In this section, we discuss how store location, retail positioning, store image, scrambled merchandising, and the wheel of retailing affect retailing objectives.

## Location of Retail Stores

Location, the least flexible of the strategic retailing issues, is one of the most important because location dictates the limited geographic trading area from which a store draws its customers. Retailers consider a variety of factors when evaluating potential locations, including location of the firm's target market within the trading area, kinds of products being sold, availability of public transportation, customer characteristics, and competitors' locations.

In choosing a location, a retailer evaluates the relative ease of movement to and from the site, including such factors as pedestrian and vehicular traffic, parking, and transportation. Some retailers prefer sites with high pedestrian traffic. Preliminary site investigations sometimes include a pedestrian count to determine how many passersby are prospective customers. The nature of the area's vehicular traffic is also analyzed.

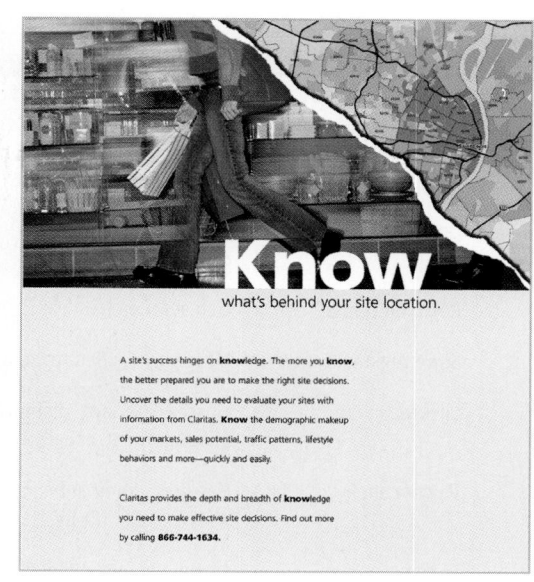

## Retail Location

The location of a retail store is crucial. There are a number of organizations that assist retailers to make retail site location decisions.

**neighborhood shopping center** A shopping center usually consisting of several small convenience and specialty stores

Because customers of certain retailers, such as service stations and many convenience stores, drive to these retail sites, overly congested locations should be avoided. Parking space must be adequate for projected demand, and transportation networks (major thoroughfares and public transit) must accommodate customers and delivery vehicles.

Retailers also evaluate the characteristics of the site itself: types of stores in the area; size, shape, and visibility of the lot or building under consideration; and rental, leasing, or ownership terms. Retailers look for compatibility with nearby retailers because stores that complement one another draw more customers for everyone. When making site location decisions, retailers select from among several general types of locations: freestanding structures, traditional business districts, traditional shopping centers, or nontraditional shopping centers.

**Freestanding Structures.** Freestanding structures are buildings unconnected to other buildings. Organizations may build such structures or lease or buy them. A retailer, for example, may find that its most successful stores are in freestanding structures close to a shopping mall but not in the mall. Use of freestanding structures allows retailers to physically position themselves away from or close to competitors. Quick-service oil change dealers and fast-food restaurants frequently use freestanding structures and locate close to each other. Toys 'R' Us and Home Depot also tend to locate in freestanding structures.

**Traditional Business Districts.** A traditional business district—the "downtown shopping district"—usually consists of structures attached to one another and located in a central part of a town or city. Often these structures are aging, and, in some cities, traditional business districts are decaying and are viewed as nonviable locations for retailers. However, many towns and cities are preserving or revitalizing their traditional business districts, thus making them attractive locations for certain types of retailers. Some cities have enclosed walkways, shut off streets from traffic, and provided free parking and transportation systems to help traditional business districts compete more effectively with shopping malls.

**Shopping Centers.** The major types of shopping centers are identified and described in Table 17.3 (on p. 478). **Neighborhood shopping centers** usually consist of several small convenience and specialty stores, such as small grocery stores, gas stations, and fast-food restaurants. Many of these retailers consider their target markets to be consumers who live within two to three miles of their stores, or ten minutes' driving time. Because most purchases are based on convenience or personal contact, there is usually little coordination of selling efforts within a neighborhood shopping center.

## table 17.3    TYPES AND CHARACTERISTICS OF SHOPPING CENTERS

| Type | Concept | Open or Enclosed? | Acreage | Number of Anchors | Radius of Primary Trade Area (Miles) |
|------|---------|-------------------|---------|-------------------|--------------------------------------|
| Neighborhood center | Convenience | Open | 3–15 | 1 or more | 3 |
| Community center | General merchandise, convenience | Open | 10–40 | 2 or more | 3–6 |
| Regional center | General merchandise, fashion | Enclosed | 40–100 | 2 or more | 5–15 |
| Superregional center | More variety than regional center | Enclosed | 60–120 | 3 or more | 5–25 |
| Lifestyle center | Upscale specialty, dining, and entertainment, usually national chains | Open | 10–40 | 0–2 | 8–12 |
| Power center | Category-dominant anchors, a few smaller businesses | Open | 25–80 | 3 or more | 5–10 |
| Outlet center | Manufacturers' outlet stores | Open | 10–50 | N/A | 25–75 |

**Source:** Adapted from "ICSC Shopping Center Definitions," International Council of Shopping Centers, p. 4, www.icsc.org/srch/lib/SCDEefinitions.pdf (accessed Feb. 3, 2006).

Generally product mixes consist of essential products, and depth of product lines is limited. Convenience stores are most successful when they are closer to consumers than, for example, supermarkets. A good strategy for neighborhood centers is to locate near hotels or interstate highways, or on the route to regional shopping centers.

**Community shopping centers** include one or two department stores and some specialty stores, as well as convenience stores. They draw consumers looking for shopping and specialty products not available in neighborhood shopping centers. Because these centers serve larger geographic areas, consumers must drive longer distances to community shopping centers than to neighborhood centers. Community shopping centers are planned and coordinated to attract shoppers. Special events, such as art exhibits, automobile shows, and sidewalk sales stimulate traffic. Overall management of a community shopping center looks for tenants that complement the center's total assortment of products. Such centers have wide product mixes and deep product lines.

**community shopping center**
A shopping center with one or two department stores, some specialty stores, and convenience stores

### Shopping Centers

Wrentham Village Premium Outlets in Massachusetts is one of the country's largest outlet centers and features many designer brands in an outdoor village setting.

**regional shopping center**
A type of shopping center with large department stores, the wide product mix, and the deep product lines of all shopping centers

**Regional shopping centers** usually have the largest department stores, the widest product mixes, and the deepest product lines of all shopping centers. Many shopping malls are regional shopping centers, although some are community shopping centers. Regional shopping centers carry most products found in a downtown shopping district. With 150,000 or more consumers in their target market, regional shopping centers must have well-coordinated management and marketing activities. Target markets may include consumers traveling from a distance to find products and prices not available in their hometowns.

Because of the expense of leasing space in regional shopping centers, tenants are more likely to be national chains than small, independent stores. Large centers usually advertise, have special events, furnish transportation to some consumer groups, maintain their own security forces, and carefully select the mix of stores. The largest of these centers, sometimes called **superregional shopping centers**, have the widest and deepest product mixes and attract customers from many miles away. These centers might host exclusive or high-end stores with fewer locations than most retail chains. Superregional centers often have special attractions such as skating rinks, amusement centers, or upscale restaurants. Mall of America, in the Minneapolis area, is the largest shopping mall in the United States with 520 stores, including Nordstrom and Bloomingdale's, and 100 restaurants and nightclubs. The shopping center also includes a theme park, Camp Snoopy, as well as a walk-through aquarium, 14-screen movie theater, hotels, miniature golf courses, and water slides.

**superregional shopping center**  A type of shopping center with the largest department stores, the widest product mix, and the deepest product lines of all shopping centers

Despite the success of Mall of America, some regional shopping centers are viewed as being out of touch with the needs of a changing population, struggling with massive debt accumulation, and in need of significant structural repair.[21] Indeed, fewer enclosed regional malls have been built in recent years; instead, developers have been opening shopping centers that often focus as much on entertainment as on shopping.[22]

**lifestyle shopping center**  A type of shopping center that is typically open-air and features upscale specialty, dining, and entertainment stores.

A **lifestyle shopping center** is typically an open-air shopping center that features upscale specialty, dining, and entertainment stores, usually owned by national chains, as well as fountains, benches, and other amenities that encourage "casual browsing." They are often located near affluent neighborhoods. Architectural design is an important aspect of these "mini-cities," which may include urban streets or parks, and is intended to encourage consumer loyalty by creating a sense of place. Some lifestyle centers are designed to resemble traditional "Main Street" shopping centers or have a central theme suggested by architecture.[23]

Some shopping centers may not include a traditional anchor department store. Most malls have one to three main anchor department stores to ensure a continuous stream of mall traffic. With traditional mall sales declining, this more recent type of shopping mall may be anchored by a store such as The Gap. Other likely stores for such malls include Toys 'R' Us, Circuit City, PetSmart, and Home Depot. Shopping center developers are combining off-price stores and small stores with category killers in **power shopping center** formats. The number of power shopping centers is growing, resulting in a variety of formats vying for the same retail dollar. To compete, existing region malls may have to adapt by changing their store mixes.

**power shopping center**  A type of shopping center that features off-price and small stores combined with category killers

**outlet shopping center**  A type of shopping center that features discount and factory outlet stores carrying manufacturer brands

**Outlet shopping centers** feature discount and factory outlet stores carrying traditional manufacturer brands, such as Van Heusen, Levi Strauss, HealthTex, and Wrangler. Some outlet centers feature upscale products. Manufacturers own these stores and make a special effort to avoid conflict with traditional retailers of their products. Manufacturers claim their stores are in noncompetitive locations; indeed, most factory outlet centers are located outside metropolitan areas. Not all factory outlets stock closeouts and irregulars, but most avoid comparison with discount houses. Factory outlet centers attract value-conscious customers seeking quality and major brand names. They operate in much the same way as regional shopping centers, but usually draw customers from a larger shopping radius; a portion of these stores' customers are sometimes tourists. Promotional activity is at the heart of these shopping centers. Craft and antique shows, contests, and special events attract a great deal of traffic.

**retail positioning** Identifying an unserved or underserved market segment and serving it through a strategy that distinguishes the retailer from others in the minds of consumers in that segment

**atmospherics** The physical elements in a store's design that appeal to consumers' emotions and encourage buying

**Store Image**

Pier 1 Imports stores utilize atmospherics, such as soft lighting, to attract customers.

## Retail Positioning

The large variety of shopping centers and expansion of product offerings by stores has intensified retailing competition. Retail positioning is therefore an important consideration. **Retail positioning** involves identifying an unserved or underserved market segment and serving it through a strategy that distinguishes the retailer from others in the minds of those customers. For example, Urban Outfitters, a specialty store chain, has carved out a unique retail position by stocking both new and recycled fashions, mixing apparel with housewares, and redecorating each of its 75 stores twice a month with original artwork to create an "intellectually stimulating" experience for its boutique-style stores.[24]

A retailer may position itself as a seller of high-quality, premium-priced products and provide many services. Neiman Marcus, for example, specializes in expensive, high-fashion clothing and jewelry, sophisticated electronics, and exclusive home furnishings, and provides wrapping and delivery, valet parking, and personal shopping consultants. Another type of retail organization may be positioned as a marketer of reasonable-quality products at everyday low prices. Pizza Hut, for example, has positioned itself as the value alternative by offering a variety of large pizzas at low prices. Its rival, Papa John's, has established a product quality position with the slogan "Better ingredients. Better pizza."

## Store Image

To attract customers, a retail store must project an image—a functional and psychological picture in the consumer's mind—that appeals to its target market. Store environment, category management, merchandise quality, and service quality are key determinants of store image.

**Atmospherics**, the physical elements in a store's design that appeal to consumers' emotions and encourage buying, help to create an image and position a retailer. Barnes and Noble, for example, uses murals of authors and framed classic book covers to convey a literary image.

Exterior atmospheric elements include the appearance of the storefront, display windows, store entrances, and degree of traffic congestion. Exterior atmospherics are particularly important to new customers, who tend to judge an unfamiliar store by its outside appearance and may not enter if they feel intimidated by the building or inconvenienced by the parking lot. Interior atmospheric elements include aesthetic considerations such as lighting, wall and floor coverings, dressing facilities, and store fixtures. Interior sensory elements contribute significantly to atmosphere. Color can attract shoppers to a retail display. Many fast-food restaurants use bright colors, such as red and yellow, because research suggests that these colors make customers feel hungrier and eat faster, which increases turnover. Sound is another important sensory component of atmosphere and may range from silence to subdued background sounds to music. One study indicated that retail customers shop for a longer period when exposed to unfamiliar music than they do when exposed to familiar music.[25] Many retailers believe shoppers who remain in their stores longer will, in fact, purchase more. A store's layout—arrangement of departments, width of aisles, grouping of products, and location of checkout areas—is another determinant of atmosphere. Department stores, restaurants, hotels, service stations, and specialty stores combine these elements in different ways to create specific atmospheres that may be perceived as warm, fresh, functional, or exciting. In one study, 90 percent of surveyed consumers ranked cleanliness—particularly in supermarkets—as the most important atmospheric element in choosing a shopping destination. Lighting, temperature, and

# PetSmart: Barking up the Right Tree

PetSmart, Inc., the world's largest retailer of pet-related products, operates more than 800 pet stores and offers more than 12,000 products in the United States and Canada. In addition to operating its retail outlets, the company runs a growing number of in-store PetsHotels, has a large pet-supply catalog business, and leads in online sales of pet products and information. PetSmart also offers pet training, grooming, day care, and adoption services.

PetSmart employs over 30,000 people in North America. In addition to its sales and store personnel, the retailer employs 1,500 accredited trainers who train more than 300,000 dogs annually. With its SmartPet Promise, customers are guaranteed 100 percent satisfaction, or their pets can take the training class again for free. PetSmart also has 6,600 certified pet stylists who groom and bathe more than 5 million dogs a year.

PetSmart is testing a Doggie Day Camp concept at its store in Pasadena, California, that provides daytime care and exercise for dogs. The Day Camp is an extension of its 26 PetsHotels that provide overnight and long-term boarding for pets. All PetsHotels feature caregivers who are hand-picked for their love of pets and are on the premises 24 hours a day. The company is not resting on its laurels. Pet-Smart has opened close to 200 new stores the last two years and a new distribution center in the Midwest. The company's CEO envisions the retailer eventually having 1,400 stores in North America. In 2005, the company changed its name from PetsMart to PetSmart because management felt the organization's primary goal was offering superior solutions rather than simply serving as a retailer of pet products.

aisle width were also ranked highly. Active elements such as in-store televisions were rated among the least influential.[26]

Retailers must assess the atmosphere the target market seeks and then adjust atmospheric variables to encourage desired consumer awareness and action. High-fashion boutiques generally strive for an atmosphere of luxury and novelty. Ralph Lauren's Polo Shops offer limited merchandise in large, open areas with props such as saddles or leather chairs adding to the exclusive look and image. On the other hand, discount department stores strive *not* to seem too exclusive and expensive. To appeal to multiple market segments, a retailer may create different atmospheres for different operations within the store; for example, the discount basement, the sports department, the housewares department, and the women's shoe department may each have a unique atmosphere.

Although heavily dependent on atmospherics, a store's image is also shaped by its reputation for integrity, number of services offered, location, merchandise assortments, pricing policies, promotional activities, and community involvement. Characteristics of the target market—social class, lifestyle, income level, and past buying behavior—help form store image as well. How consumers perceive the store can be a major determinant of store patronage. Consumers from lower socioeconomic groups tend to patronize small, high-margin, high-service food stores and prefer small, friendly loan companies over large, impersonal banks, even though the former charge higher interest. Affluent consumers tend to look for exclusive establishments offering high-quality products and prestigious labels. Retailers should be aware of the multiple factors contributing to store image and recognize that perceptions of image vary.

## Category Management

**Category management** is a retail strategy of managing groups of similar, often substitutable products produced by different manufacturers. An assortment of merchandise is customer and strategically driven to improve performance. Performance can be profit-per-square-foot of category space or average dollars purchased by customers in each category. Category management developed in the food industry because supermarkets were concerned about highly competitive behavior between manufacturers. Category management is a move toward a collaborative supply chain initiative to enhance consumer value. Wal-Mart, for example, has developed strong supplier relationships with firms such as Procter & Gamble. For category management to be successful, there should be the acquisition, analysis, and sharing of sales and consumer information between the retailer and manufacturer. The development of information about demand, consumer behavior, and optimal allocations of products should be available from one source. Firms such as SAS provide software to manage data associated with each step of the category management decision cycle. The key is cooperative interaction between the manufacturers of category products and the retailer to create maximum success for all parties in the supply chain. For example, supermarkets such as Safeway use category management to determine space for products such as cosmetics, cereals, and soups.

## Scrambled Merchandising

When retailers add unrelated products and product lines—particularly fast-moving items that can be sold in volume—to an existing product mix, they are practicing **scrambled merchandising**. Retailers adopting this strategy hope to accomplish one or more of the following: (1) convert stores into one-stop shopping centers, (2) generate more traffic, (3) realize higher profit margins, and (4) increase impulse purchases. In scrambled merchandising, retailers must deal with diverse marketing channels. Scrambled merchandising can also blur a store's image in consumers' minds, making it more difficult for a retailer to succeed in today's highly competitive, saturated markets. Finally, scrambled merchandising intensifies competition among traditionally distinct types of stores and forces suppliers to adjust distribution systems to accommodate new channel members.

## The Wheel of Retailing

As new types of retail businesses evolve, they strive to fill niches in a dynamic retailing environment. One hypothesis regarding the evolution and development of new types of retail stores is the **wheel of retailing**. According to this theory, new retailers enter the marketplace with low prices, margins, and status. Their low prices are usually the result of innovative cost-cutting procedures and soon attract imitators. Gradually, as these businesses attempt to broaden their customer base and increase sales, their operations and facilities become more elaborate and more expensive. They may move to more desirable locations, begin to carry higher-quality merchandise, or add services. Eventually they emerge at the high end of the price, cost, and service scales, competing with newer discount retailers following the same evolutionary process.[27]

Supermarkets, for example, have undergone many changes since their introduction in 1921. Initially they offered limited services and low food prices. Over time they developed a variety of new services, including free coffee, gourmet food sections, and children's play areas. Today supermarkets are being challenged by superstores, which offer more product choices and undercut supermarket prices.

Consider the evolution of department stores, discount stores, warehouse clubs, category killers, and online retailers. Department stores such as Sears started out as high-volume, low-cost merchants competing with general stores and other small retailers. Discount stores developed later in response to rising expenses of services in department stores. Many discount outlets now appear to be following the wheel of retailing by offering more services, better locations, quality inventories, and therefore higher prices. Some discount stores are almost indistinguishable from department stores. In response have emerged category killers, such as PetSmart and

Office Depot, which concentrate on a major product category and offer enormous product depth, in many cases at lower prices than discount stores. Even these retailers, however, seem to be following the wheel. Lowe's, a home improvement retailer, has added big-ticket items and more upscale brands, such as Laura Ashley.

The wheel of retailing, along with other changes in the marketing environment and in buying behavior itself, requires that retailers adjust to survive and compete. Consumers have less time than ever to shop. Shopping today centers on "needs fulfillment" and thus is more utilitarian and work oriented, a fact that many major retailing executives have noticed. As consumers have less time to shop and greater access to more sophisticated technology, retailing venues such as catalog retailing, television home shopping, and online retailing will take on greater importance. New retailers will evolve to capitalize on these opportunities, while those that cannot adapt will not survive.

## SUMMARY

Retailing includes all transactions in which buyers intend to consume products through personal, family, or household use. Retailers, organizations that sell products primarily to ultimate consumers, are important links in the marketing channel because they are both marketers for and customers of wholesalers and producers. Retailers add value, provide services, and assist in making product selections.

Retail stores can be classified according to the breadth of products offered. Two broad categories are general-merchandise retailers and specialty retailers. The primary types of general-merchandise retailers include department stores, discount stores, supermarkets, superstores, hypermarkets, warehouse clubs, and warehouse and catalog showrooms. Department stores are large retail organizations employing at least 25 people and characterized by wide product mixes of considerable depth for most product lines. Their products are organized into separate departments that function like self-contained businesses. Discount stores are self-service, low-price, general-merchandise outlets. A convenience store is a small self-service store that is open long hours and carries a narrow assortment of products, usually convenience items. Supermarkets are large, self-service food stores that also carry some nonfood products. Superstores are giant retail outlets that carry all the products found in supermarkets and most consumer products purchased on a routine basis. Hypermarkets offer supermarket and discount store shopping at one location. Warehouse clubs are large-scale, members-only discount operations. Warehouse and catalog showrooms are low-cost operations characterized by warehouse methods of materials handling and display, large inventories, and minimal services.

Specialty retailers offer substantial assortments in a few product lines. They include traditional specialty retailers, which carry narrow product mixes with deep product lines; off-price retailers, which sell brand name manufacturers' seconds and production overruns at deep discounts; and category killers, large specialty stores that concentrate on a major product category and

compete on the basis of low prices and enormous product availability.

Direct marketing is the use of the telephone, Internet, and nonpersonal media to communicate product and organizational information to customers, who can then purchase products via mail, telephone, or the Internet. Direct marketing is a type of nonstore retailing, the selling of goods or services outside the confines of a retail facility. Forms of direct marketing include catalog marketing, direct-response marketing, telemarketing, television home shopping, and online retailing. Two other types of nonstore retailing are direct selling and automatic vending. Direct selling is the marketing of products to ultimate consumers through face-to-face sales presentations at home or in the workplace. Automatic vending is the use of machines to dispense products.

Franchising is an arrangement in which a supplier grants a dealer the right to sell products in exchange for some type of consideration. Retail franchises are of three general types. A manufacturer may authorize a number of retail stores to sell a certain brand name item; a producer may license distributors to sell a given product to retailers; or a franchiser may supply brand names, techniques, or other services instead of a complete product. Franchise arrangements have a number of advantages and disadvantages over traditional business forms, and their use is increasing.

To increase sales and store patronage, retailers must consider strategic issues. Location determines the trading area from which a store draws its customers and should be evaluated carefully. When evaluating potential sites, retailers take into account a variety of factors, including the location of the firm's target market within the trading area, kinds of products sold, availability of public transportation, customer characteristics, and competitors' locations. Retailers can choose among several types of locations, including freestanding structures, traditional business districts, or shopping centers. The major types of shopping centers are neighborhood shopping centers, community shopping centers, regional shopping centers, superregional shopping centers, lifestyle shopping centers, power shopping centers, and outlet shopping centers.

Retail positioning involves identifying an unserved or underserved market segment and serving it through a strategy that distinguishes the retailer from others in those customers' minds. Store image, which various customers perceive differently, derives not only from atmosphere but also from location, products offered, customer services, prices, promotion, and the store's overall reputation. Atmospherics refers to the physical elements of a store's design that can be adjusted to appeal to consumers' emotions and thus induce them to buy. Category management is a retail strategy of managing groups of similar, often substitutable products produced by different manufacturers. Scrambled merchandising adds unrelated product lines to an existing product mix and is being used by a growing number of stores to generate sales.

The wheel of retailing hypothesis holds that new retail institutions start out as low-status, low-margin, and low-price operations. As they develop, they increase services and prices, and eventually become vulnerable to newer organizations, which enter the market and repeat the cycle.

**ACE self-test**

Please visit the student website at **www.prideferrell.com** for ACE Self-Test questions that will help you prepare for exams.

## IMPORTANT TERMS

Retailing
Retailer
General-merchandise retailer
Department store
Discount store
Convenience store
Supermarket
Superstore
Hypermarket
Warehouse club

Warehouse showroom
Catalog showroom
Traditional specialty retailer
Off-price retailer
Category killer
Direct marketing
Nonstore retailing
Catalog marketing
Direct-response marketing
Telemarketing

Television home shopping
Online retailing
Direct selling
Automatic vending
Franchising
Neighborhood shopping center
Community shopping center
Regional shopping center

Superregional shopping center
Lifestyle shopping center
Power shopping center
Outlet shopping center
Retail positioning
Atmospherics
Scrambled merchandising
Category management
Wheel of retailing

## DISCUSSION & REVIEW QUESTIONS

1. What value do retailers add to a product? What value do retailers add for producers and ultimate consumers?

2. Differentiate between the two general categories of retail stores based on breadth of product offering.

3. What are the major differences between discount stores and department stores?

4. How does a superstore differ from a supermarket?

5. In what ways are traditional specialty stores and off-price retailers similar? How do they differ?

6. Describe direct marketing and the other two major types of nonstore retailing. List some products you have purchased through these types of nonstore retailing in the last six months. Why did you choose this method for making your purchases instead of going to a retail outlet?

7. How is door-to-door selling a form of retailing? Some consumers believe direct-response orders bypass the retailer. Is this true? Explain.

8. Evaluate the following statement: "Telemarketing, television home shopping, and online retailing will eventually eliminate the need for traditional forms of retailing."

9. If you were opening a retail business, would you prefer to open an independent store or own a store under a franchise arrangement? Explain your preference.

10. What major issues should be considered when determining a retail site location?

11. Describe the major types of shopping centers. Give an example of each type in your area.

12. Discuss the major factors that help determine a retail store's image.

13. How does atmosphere add value to products sold in a store? How important is atmospherics for convenience stores?

14. Is it possible for a single retail store to have an overall image that appeals to sophisticated shoppers, extravagant buyers, and bargain hunters? Why or why not?

15. In what ways does the use of scrambled merchandising affect a store's image?

## APPLICATION QUESTIONS

1. Juanita wants to open a small retail store that specializes in high-quality, high-priced children's clothing. With what types of competitors should she be concerned in this competitive retail environment? Why?

2. Location of retail outlets is a primary issue in strategic planning. What initial steps would you recommend to Juanita (see question 1) when she considers a location for her store?

3. Different types of stores offer varying breadth and depth of assortments. Godiva Chocolate stores, for example, offer a very narrow assortment of products but provide great depth. Visit a discount store, a specialty store, or a department store, and report on the number of different product lines offered and the depth within each line.

4. Atmospherics is an important tool used by retailers in their efforts to position stores. Visit a retail store you shop in regularly. Identify the store and describe its atmospherics. Be specific about both exterior and interior elements, and indicate how the store is being positioned through its use of atmospherics.

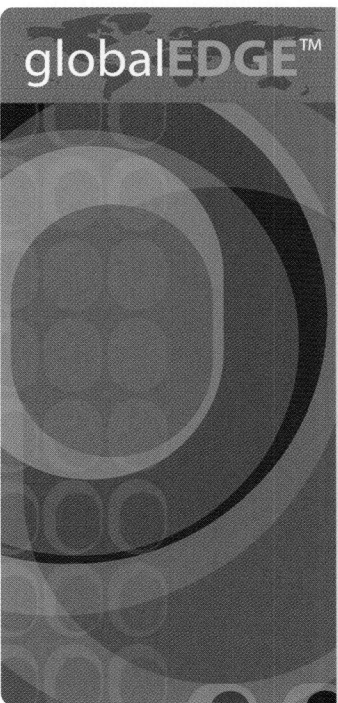

globalEDGE™

1. Some marketing analysts use the number of stores that a retailer has to indicate its level of marketing power. Seeking to emulate companies that have many retail stores, your firm has charged you with analyzing the National Retail Federation's *Stores* magazine. Access this site by using the search term "retail federation" at **http://globaledge.msu.edu/ibrd** and then follow the link to the Top 100 Specialty Retailers. Identify the top five specialty retailers rated in a definitive set of rankings for the most recent year. From which states do these firms originate? Given what you know about these retailers and their headquarters, which do you think might have less experience with retailers from countries other than the United States? Why might this be so?

2. You are an upper-level manager of a large retailing firm that currently is undertaking a primary initiative of international expansion. In your analysis on this topic, an important factor in choosing which markets to enter is the level of retail development in the countries targeted. Access the Global Retail Development Index website by using the search term "retail development" at **http://globaledge.msu.edu/ibrd**. What are four components that may assist in assessing the retail readiness of a country based on information provided by the Global Retail Development Index website? Can you name the top five emerging markets as ranked by an index on the topic? Are there any markets on your list that surprised you? Which three countries have the greatest market potential? Which market is the most stable?

## INTERNET Exercise

### Walmart.com

Wal-Mart provides a website where customers can shop for products, search for a nearby store, and even preorder new products. The website lets browsers see what's on sale and view company information. Access Wal-Mart's website at **www.walmart.com.**

1. How does Wal-Mart attempt to position itself on its website?
2. Compare the atmospherics of Wal-Mart's website to the atmospherics of a traditional Wal-Mart store. Are they consistent? If not, should they be?
3. Read the "Wal-Mart Story" on the website. Relate the firm's history to the wheel of retailing concept.

## Video Case 17.1    REI: The Great Outdoors—Inside

In 1938, 25 mountain climbers founded Recreational Equipment Inc. (REI) to pool their buying power for a better deal on ice axes and other climbing gear. From the start, REI was a consumer cooperative: a retail business that shares some of its profits with members. Today the Kent, Washington, retailer sells a vast array of outdoor sporting goods and apparel through 78 stores in 25 states, a printed catalog, and two websites. It also operates a travel service, REI Adventures, for those who want to paddle, climb, cycle, ski, hike, or enjoy a combination of outdoor activities while on vacation.

REI's store atmospherics are unique, making the shopping experience an adventure in itself. Every store contains a two-story climbing wall that customers are invited to scale when trying out gear before buying. For example, the store in Sandy, Utah, features a 22-foot-high climbing wall modeled after the granite walls of a local canyon. Like other stores in the chain, the Sandy store has demonstration areas devoted to camp stoves, water filter testing, and hiking boots. Surrounding these special areas are acres and acres of items that one employee calls "grown-up toys"—from kayaks and canteens to snow shoes and sleeping bags.

The store employees are enthusiastic about the merchandise they sell because they share their customers' love of the active life. "A passion for the outdoors comes first throughout REI and is a natural bond between employees and customers," observes REI's vice president of direct sales. "That passion and commitment to quality are reflected whether you're in an REI store, shopping online, or placing a catalog order on the phone." This may help explain REI's annual ranking in *Fortune* magazine's "100 Best Companies to Work For in America." Employees are trained to determine their customers' needs, demonstrate appropriate products, and help customers make informed buying decisions. The emphasis is on educating and satisfying customers rather than on trying to close as many sales as possible.

This emphasis is reflected in the attractive, easy-to-navigate design of REI.com. Customers can log on, select a product category, and scroll through thousands of pages filled with product details, product comparisons, and how-to articles about outdoor sports, recreation, and equipment. The company's discount website, REI-Outlet.com, also provides exten-

sive information about its marked-down products. Each REI store has several web kiosks where customers can browse the company's two websites and order any of the 50,000 products in stock for home delivery. If they prefer, customers can eliminate shipping fees by having online orders sent to a nearby store for pickup—an option chosen by more than 30 percent of REI-Outlet.com's customers.

Customers can become REI members by paying a one-time fee of $15. Because the retailer operates as a cooperative, members are eligible for refund vouchers of up to 10 percent on their total annual purchases from REI stores, catalogs, and websites. They also pay lower prices for equipment rented or repaired in REI stores and for travel packages arranged through REI Adventures.

One of REI's core values is its ongoing commitment to protecting the natural environment through contributions and volunteerism. The company donates thousands of dollars to support nature centers, open-space projects, youth recreation programs, land conservation, and related activities in each community where it does business. In all, REI's annual contributions total nearly $2 million. Moreover, as REI's president notes, store employees invest a great deal of "sweat equity" in the local community by volunteering their time to maintain hiking trails, clean up rivers, and preserve the environment in many other ways.

REI is not the only retailer pursuing the market for outdoor sporting goods and apparel. Bass Pro Shops, headquartered in Missouri, targets customers who like fishing, hunting, and boating with a huge catalog. Its 32 U.S. and Canadian stores offer demonstration areas for fishing and other sports, creating a focal point for customers. Cabela's operates 26 similar stores and an online catalog. Eastern Mountain Sports (EMS), headquartered in New Hampshire, operates 80 stores in eastern and midwestern states. REI must also compete with many independent stores and chain retailers that carry clothing and gear for the active lifestyle.

In this increasingly competitive climate, REI is relying on its innovative and appealing atmospherics as a key differentiating factor. It is also bringing customers back again and again through in-store demonstrations and an informative e-mail newsletter. Currently REI generates more than $840 million in revenue and serves 2 million customers a year. More growth is on the way with new store openings, new website features, and new "grown-up toys."[28]

## Questions for Discussion

1. Why would REI locate many of its stores in free-standing structures rather than in shopping centers?
2. What is the likely effect of REI's consumer cooperative structure on the retailer's ability to build customer relationships?
3. What is REI's retail positioning, and why is it appropriate for the target market?

---

## Case 17.2    Low Prices and Lots of Suprises at Costco

More than 20 years after Costco opened its first warehouse club store in Seattle, the company's philosophy can still be summed up as "pile 'em high, price 'em low." Costco stores are anything but fancy; in fact, the first store was located inside a warehouse. Yet nearly 46 million consumers and small-business owners pay $45 (fee may vary) annually so they can save on everything from mayonnaise, wine, and prescription medicines to handheld computers, truck-size snow tires, and fine art. In fact, customers never really know what products they will find each time they visit one of the 471 Costco warehouse stores around the world. Surprises are all part of the shopping experience at Costco.

"The art form of our business is intuition," says CEO James D. Sinegal. His buyers must choose carefully, because the typical Costco carries less than 10 percent of the number of products displayed in a Wal-Mart store. Moreover, Costco aims for a profit margin of no more than 14 percent, which means inventory must sell quickly. If products sell slowly, they will tie up precious cash that could be better spent on newer or more popular merchandise. Therefore, Costco's buyers watch for particularly hot products and product categories. When the chief electronics buyer noticed the cost of plasma-screen televisions dropping, for example, he took what he calls "an educated gamble" and placed a sizable order. The gamble paid off: the televisions, priced below $5,000, sold out quickly even before the year-end holiday shopping season.

Costco carries a broad and varied merchandise assortment, all priced low to move quickly. It sells 55,000 rotisserie chickens every day and $600 million worth of fine wines every year. It also sells 45 million hot dogs and 60,000 carats of diamonds annually. The hot dogs retail for $1.50 each, while a single piece of jewelry can retail for as much as $100,000. Well-known manufacturers' brands share shelf space with Kirkland Signature, Costco's private brand. Members may walk past stacks of best-selling books on the right and color printers on the left as they push their shopping carts down the aisle. This variety enhances the store's appeal, says the CEO: "Our customers don't drive 15 miles to save on a jar of peanut butter. They come for the treasure hunt." Among the treasures they might find: an $8,000 Suzuki grand piano, a $6,000 100-CD Wurlitzer jukebox, and a seven-carat diamond ring for $125,000. Such items now comprise 5 to 10 percent of Costco's sales.

Despite the low prices, Costco offers a generous return policy. Customers can return anything at any time. If dissatisfied with their membership, they can even get a full refund on that. The sole exception is computers, which cannot be brought back after six months. No receipt? No problem at Costco. Customers have ample opportunity to exchange or return items because they visit the stores frequently. Research shows that, on average, members visit Costco stores more than 11 times a year and spend $94 on each visit.

Costco's main competitor is Sam's Club, owned by Wal-Mart. Given Wal-Mart's buying power and channel leadership, Sam's Club can buy products at very low prices and get them to stores with unusual efficiency. Nonetheless, Costco tops Sam's Club in a number of ways. Each U.S. Costco store rings up, on average, $112 million worth of merchandise annually. By comparison, the average yearly sales of each U.S. Sam's Club store are $63 million. Whereas the average sales per square foot at Sam's Club is $497, Costco's equivalent figure is a whopping $797 per square foot. Although Sam's Club charges a lower membership fee, Costco's members are quite loyal, with a renewal rate of 86 percent. And they have a median income of $72,000 compared to Sam's customers, with a median income of $50,000.

In recent years, Costco has expanded by offering new services at low prices. For example, members can log onto the retailer's website (**www.costco.com**) and sign up for long-distance telephone service, apply for a mortgage, buy life insurance, or price a vacation trip. The company has also started a new chain of stores, Costco Home, which specializes in home furnishings. In warehouse retailing, however, Sam's Club remains the competitor to beat. Before Sam's Club opened stores in Canada, Costco prepared for the increased competition by remodeling some of its stores. And price wars sometimes break out when the two competitors battle for customers. The parent company of Sam's Club is by far the largest company in the world, but Costco is so adept at warehouse retailing that it continues to hold its own.[29]

## Questions for Discussion

1. How do Costco's atmospherics support its retail positioning?
2. Analyze the retail strategy represented by the new Costco Home chain.
3. How is Costco's retail positioning likely to be affected by its target profit margin of 14 percent?

## Strategic Case 6 — Direct Selling Mistine Cosmetics in Thailand

Better Way (Thailand) Company Limited was founded in 1988 by Thailand's "king of direct selling," Dr. Amornthep Deerojanawong, and Boonyakiat Chokwatana. Dr. Amornthep had worked as a medical doctor at Avon in Thailand, where he got the idea to start his own Thai-based cosmetics company. The company has become highly successful in Thailand using direct selling to launch its Mistine cosmetic brand. Although Thai people were not very familiar with the direct selling of cosmetics, within six years Mistine had become the leader in the consumer cosmetics market in Thailand, a market worth an estimated 25 billion baht (approximately US$635 million) and growing at a rate of 5–10 percent annually.

Better Way began with fewer than 100 products. Today, the company markets more than 4,000 makeup, skin-care, fragrance, and personal-care products. In addition, the company operates one retail store on the outskirts of Bangkok. Its warehouse is considered the largest cosmetics depot in Southeast Asia, with 1,170 regular employees.

The company primarily targets women who have a high school, occupational certificate level, or high occupational certificate level of education and have a monthly income of about US$125–200, as well as working women who have a monthly income of about US$200–300. Mistine's core target market, which accounts for 70–80 percent of its total revenues, are housewives with low to medium incomes. The company is expanding its customer base by targeting working people, men, and vocational school students, especially working people who have high purchasing power. There are now more than 420,000 customers nationwide.

Mistine positions itself as an Asian company marketing products developed and formulated specifically for the Asian woman. They are designed to blend well with the Asian skin tone and complexion. They are also made to better suit the warmer, more humid climate of the Asian region so that the product stays on longer and looks fresher.

### Mistine's Marketing Activities

Mistine products are manufactured by the best quality cosmetics manufacturers all over the world. Additional support is provided by Kolmar Laboratories, the largest and most experienced cosmetics manufacturer in the United States. An experienced production team develops hundreds of new and unique products each year, with at least two to three new products launched each month.

Every Mistine product is thoroughly inspected and tested before being delivered to the warehouse. Customers can be assured that they will receive the highest quality products, and, indeed, Mistine will replace or offer a full refund for any product for which a customers is not completely happy. "Our customer's satisfaction is what we care the most" is one of Mistine's slogans, which helps it to maintain its leadership in a competitive market.

Direct selling companies normally depend on word of mouth to develop brand awareness, recruit salespersons, and encourage product purchases. Better Way decided to do things differently by being the first direct selling company in Thailand to use mass media advertising. The company's continuous and award-winning advertising campaigns have been executed to build brand image and positioning in the customers' minds. Many products are promoted by popular celebrities.

### Sales Force Characteristics

Mistine's direct-sales system is a simple, single-level marketing (SLM) approach. The company recruits district managers who in turn recruit as many salespersons as they can manage. This approach meshes well with Thai culture and lifestyle. The benefit of this approach is that each salesperson earns full commission without having to share his or her earnings with others. Thus the more sales a salesperson makes, the more income he or she receives.

The company welcomes anyone—male or female—who has some free time on their hands and would like to earn money, make new friends, and develop their self-confidence to become a salesperson. Salespersons can plan their own schedules and routes in order to reach sales objectives and obtain rewards. If a salesperson achieves no sales within three selling periods, then he or she is automatically terminated. The annual turnover rate for the sales force is about 200 percent because, for most salespersons, selling Mistine products is a second job. Moreover, most of the salespersons do not have any sales experience. Although they receive up to 25–30 percent commission, if they are not determined and committed, they leave. Generally, about 70 percent are terminated within six selling periods.

Sales goals are set according to the sales promotion plans and advertising budget spent for a particular distribution period. The company offers major incentives, such as trips to Europe and gold jewelry, to all district managers who achieve sales goals.

With the belief that the salespersons can live without Mistine but Mistine cannot live without the salespersons, several programs have been launched to create employee loyalty to the company. Internal relationship programs such as the "Mistine Thank-You Concert" were organized in nine provinces around Thailand, aimed at gathering Mistine salespersons together as a family, as well as at showing that the company cares about and is responsible for its employees. The company also provides life insurance with coverage of US$50,000 for each salesperson, which is an unusual benefit in Thailand. Nonmonetary rewards and recognition incentives for salespersons include crystal trophies and photos in the hall of fame.

## Improving Sales Performance

In direct sales, the length of a selling period is crucial and shapes business operations. Normally, direct selling companies operate three-week selling periods, totaling 18 periods within a year. Mistine, however, found that most salespersons do not actually start selling products to customers until the last week of a selling period, meaning that the first two weeks are essentially wasted. Consequently, management decided to reduce the selling period to two weeks, resulting in 26 selling periods per year. This dramatic change was implemented despite objections. Ultimately, sales increased by 80 percent over the previous year, and salespersons became more active in selling the products.

These impressive sales increases occurred because of the reduced selling cycles and the positive attitude fostered throughout the company toward salespersons. One motto that employees of all levels still pledge to this day is "We will make Mistine No. 1."

## Growth and Expansion

Despite Mistine's great success with direct cosmetic sales, the company continues to strategize to maintain its market share amidst intense competition. To achieve its goals, the firm intends to continue recruiting new salespersons in order to increase sales and expand its marketing coverage area. It has increased its local promotion budget by 50 percent and developed 400 new product items to maintain its leading position. After observing that the sales of men's personal-care products have been increasing in department stores, Better Way launched nine men's products, including shampoo, deodorant, day and night cream, and sun protection lotion.

The company has formed a strategic alliance with DTAC, a leading telecommunications service provider, under the name "Mistine Corporate Solution," or MCS, which enables Mistine salespersons to call the 24-hour Mistine Call Center for free when using the DTAC cellular phone network system. This innovative direct-selling tool will help the salespersons in ordering products, requesting product information, and asking about promotions. This strategic alliance will help the company cut costs of about US$25,000 per month on phone charges.

To penetrate the teenage market segment, Mistine partnered with RS Promotions and employed D2B, an RS Promotions "boy band" popular among Thai teens, to present Mistine's Pink Magic lipstick. The campaign helped boost sales to teens by as much as 10 percent.

Recently Mistine has an aggressive strategy in its products and marketing communication in both domestic and international markets. The company opened manufacturing sites in the Philippines and Vietnam. Mistine has successfully offered products in Cambodia, Laos, and Myanmar. The success is due to its affordable price, which matches the income of the people in those countries. Moreover, its advertising campaigns that use popular actresses who are well known to people in those countries support its sales. Mistine will be exporting its cosmetic products to distributors in Taiwan and to China within two to three years. Hungary and Russia are potential markets in the future.[30]

## Questions for Discussion

1. Is it possible that having a retail outlet creates channel conflict? Explain.
2. From a customer's standpoint, what are the advantages or disadvantages of having a retail outlet? What about from the company's standpoint?
3. How would Mistine's use of mass media advertising influence the performance of its sales force?
4. Should Mistine's management expect to change marketing strategies when the company enters new international markets such as Hungary and Russia? Explain.
5. In what ways does the single-level direct-selling approach affects its turnover rates? Explain.

part

7

## Promotion Decisions

**P**art **7** focuses on communication with target market members and, at times, other groups. A specific marketing mix cannot satisfy people in a particular target market unless they are aware of the product and know where to find it. Some promotion decisions relate to a specific marketing mix; others are geared toward promoting the entire organization. **Chapter 18** discusses integrated marketing communications. It describes the communication process and the major promotional methods that can be included in promotion mixes. **Chapter 19** analyzes the major steps in developing an advertising campaign. It also explains what public relations is and how it can be used. **Chapter 20** deals with personal selling and the role it can play in a firm's promotional efforts. This chapter also explores the general characteristics of sales promotion and describes sales promotion techniques.

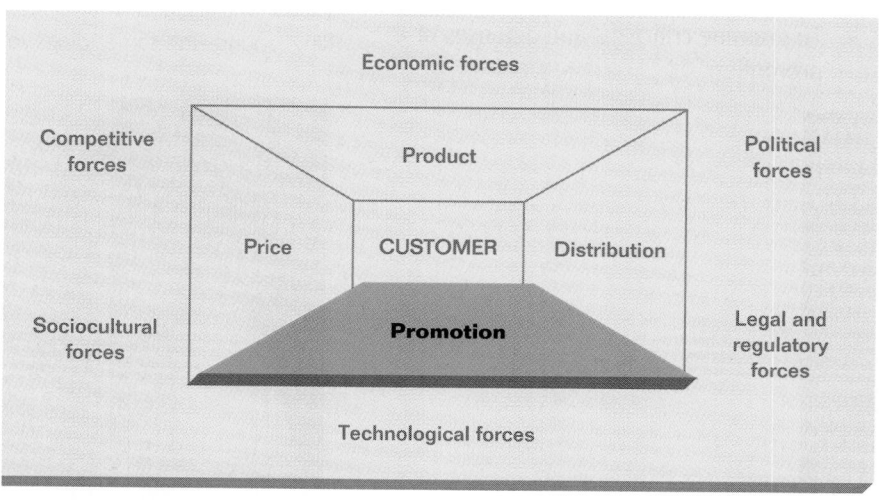

# Integrated Marketing Communications

## At Southwest Airlines, Fun Is in the Air

Although Southwest Airlines started small, today it is one of the largest airlines in the country, flying more than 70 million passengers a year to 62 cities on over 3,000 flights a day. The Texas-based company prides itself on its sense of humor and down-home attitude, which has been developed and advanced over the years through advertising, promotions, and public relations programs. Its national advertising campaigns ("You are now free to move about the country" and "Wanna get away?") are just the beginning. This is the airline that once paid an Elvis impersonator to serenade customers at the Manchester, New Hampshire, airport to celebrate its addition of flights to Las Vegas; the airline that's known for its line-dancing flight attendants who entertain passengers as they board.

The corporate culture owes a lot to the outgoing personality of the airline's co-founder, Herb Kelleher. But humor also serves as a way to make cheap travel more palatable. Handing out prizes at the gate to the passenger with the biggest hole in his sock or the traveler who has the most credit cards can be a sure way to make customers smile. These tactics also build worldwide customer allegiance. And the company strives to develop regional loyalty as well. After the Boston Red Sox won the 2004 World Series, Southwest put up billboards there that read, "You are now free to gloat around the country."

Southwest's recent "Ding" promotion is a terrific example of its use of integrated marketing communication. Customers can download software from the airline's website, and when Southwest offers a low fare it notifies them with a "ding" sound—the same "ding" you hear when airline captains turn off the seat-

belt sign; the same "ding" that precedes Southwest's well-known tagline, "You are now free to move about the country." The "Ding" TV commercial continues the company's humorous view: A young man in his office hears the "ding" from his computer and scrambles frantically over cubicle partitions to get to his desk to see the low fare. It's a creative campaign, but does it work? According to a survey, "Ding" promotion users are 45 percent more likely to book through Southwest. At current usage levels, that translates to more than $60 million per year.[1] ▣

O rganizations such as Southwest Airlines employ a variety of promotional methods to communicate with their target markets. Providing information to customers and other stakeholders is vital to initiating and developing long-term relationships with them.

This chapter looks at the general dimensions of promotion. First, we discuss the nature of integrated marketing communications. Next, we analyze the meaning and process of communication. We then define and examine the role of promotion and explore some of the reasons promotion is used. Then we consider major promotional methods and the factors that influence marketers' decisions to use particular methods. Next, we explain the positive and negative effects of personal and electronic word-of-mouth communication. Finally, we examine criticisms and defenses of promotion.

# The Nature of Integrated Marketing Communications

**integrated marketing communications** Coordination of promotion and other marketing efforts for maximum informational and persuasive impact

**Integrated marketing communications** refer to the coordination of promotion and other marketing efforts to ensure maximum informational and persuasive impact on customers. Coordinating multiple marketing tools to produce this synergistic effect requires a marketer to employ a broad perspective. A major goal of integrated marketing communications is to send a consistent message to customers. Masterfoods USA, for example, has attempted to integrate its well-known M&Ms brand with iconic consumer events such as the Academy Awards to help reinforce the fact that M&Ms are the number 1 snack food at the movies. In addition to humorous appearances by its "Red" and "Yellow" spokescharacters at pre-Oscar events, print ads for M&Ms featured a bingo game that consumers could play along with the awards ceremony, while television commercials offered tips for using M&Ms to host an Oscar party.[2] Indeed, research suggests that the use of such spokespersons results in more favorable brand images in integrated marketing communications.[3]

Because various units both inside and outside most companies have traditionally planned and implemented promotional efforts, customers have not always received consistent messages. Integrated marketing communications allow an organization to coordinate and manage its promotional efforts to transmit consistent messages. Integrated marketing communications also enable synchronization of promotion elements and can reduce overspending on elements that may produce a smaller return on investment.[4] Thus, this approach fosters not only long-term customer relationships but also the efficient use of promotional resources.

### Communication Channels

Numerous communications channels such as Yahoo are available for use in integrated marketing communication programs.

The concept of integrated marketing communications has been increasingly accepted for several reasons. Mass media advertising, a very popular promotional method in the past, is used less frequently today because of its high cost and lower effectiveness in reaching some target markets.[5] Marketers can now take advantage of more precisely targeted promotional tools, such as cable TV, direct mail, the Internet, special-interest magazines, CDs and DVDs, cellphones, and iPods. Database marketing is also allowing marketers to more precisely target individual customers. Until recently, suppliers of marketing communications were specialists. Advertising agencies provided advertising campaigns, sales promotion companies provided sales promotion activities and materials, and public relations organizations engaged in publicity efforts. Today a number of promotion-related companies provide one-stop shopping for the client seeking advertising, sales promotion, and public relations, thus reducing coordination problems for the sponsoring company. Because the overall cost of marketing communications has risen significantly, upper management demands systematic evaluations of communication efforts and a reasonable return on investment.

The specific communication vehicles employed and the precision with which they are used are changing as both information technology and customer interests become increasingly dynamic. For example, an increasing number of companies are running short advertisements during podcasts of TV shows and other videos that users download to their video iPods.[6] Earthlink sponsored podcasts from Washingtonpost.com for a month and ran 15-second ads in front of video clips.[7] Today marketers and customers have almost unlimited access to data about each other. Integrating and customizing marketing communications while protecting customer privacy has become a major challenge. However, research indicates that 75 percent of adult consumers want products customized to their personal needs, and 70 percent say they would be more loyal to companies that make an effort to discover their needs and tastes.[8] Through the Internet, companies can provide product information and services that are coordinated with traditional promotional activities. Communication relationships with customers can actually determine the nature of the product. For example, Reflect.com, an online cosmetics firm, mixes makeup for different skin types based on information exchanges with customers. Thus, consumers may be willing to exchange personal information for customized products.[9] The sharing of information and use of technology to facilitate communication between buyers and sellers are essential for successful customer relationship management.

# Promotion and the Communication Process

Communication is essentially the transmission of information. For communication to take place, both the sender and receiver of information must share some common ground. They must have a common understanding of the symbols, words, and pictures used to transmit information. An individual transmitting the following message may believe he or she is communicating with you:

在工廠吾人製造化粧品，在商店吾人銷售希望。

However, communication has not taken place if you don't understand the language in which the message is written.[10] Thus, we define **communication** as a sharing of meaning.[11] Implicit in this definition is the notion of transmission of information because sharing necessitates transmission.

As Figure 18.1 shows, communication begins with a source. A **source** is a person, group, or organization with a meaning it attempts to share with an audience. A source could be a salesperson wishing to communicate a sales message or an organization wanting to send a message to thousands of customers through an advertisement. De-

**communication** A sharing of meaning through the transmission of information

**source** A person, group, or organization with a meaning it tries to share with a receiver or an audience

## figure 18.1

### THE COMMUNICATION PROCESS

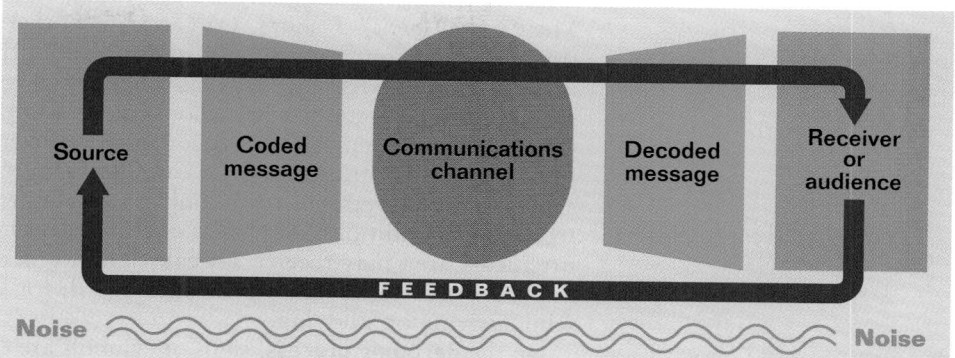

**receiver** The individual, group, or organization that decodes a coded message

**coding process** Converting meaning into a series of signs or symbols

**communications channel** The medium of transmission that carries the coded message from the source to the receiver

veloping a strategy can enhance the effectiveness of the source's communication. For example, a strategy in which a salesperson attempts to influence a customer's decision by eliminating competitive products from consideration has been found to be effective.[12] A **receiver** is the individual, group, or organization that decodes a coded message, and an *audience* is two or more receivers.

To transmit meaning, a source must convert the meaning into a series of signs or symbols representing ideas or concepts. This is called the **coding process**, or *encoding*. When coding meaning into a message, the source must consider certain characteristics of the receiver or audience. To share meaning, the source should use signs or symbols familiar to the receiver or audience. Research has shown that persuasive messages from a source are more effective when the appeal matches an individual's personality.[13] Marketers that understand this realize the importance of knowing their target market and ensuring that an advertisement, for example, uses language the target market understands. Thus, when General Mills advertises Cheerios, it does not mention all the ingredients used to make the cereal because some ingredients would have little meaning to consumers. Some notable problems have occurred in translating English advertisements into other languages to communicate with customers in global markets. For example, Coors's "Turn it loose" campaign was translated into Spanish as "Drink Coors and get diarrhea," while KFC's long-running slogan, "Finger lickin' good," was translated into Chinese as "Eat your fingers off." And Parker Pen was dismayed to learn that "Avoid embarrassment" (from a leaking pen) had been translated into "Avoid pregnancy" in Spanish.[14] Clearly it is important that people understand the language used in promotion.

When coding a meaning, a source needs to use signs or symbols that the receiver or audience uses to refer to the concepts the source intends to convey. Instead of technical jargon, explanatory language that helps consumers understand is more likely to result in positive attitudes and purchase intentions.[15] Marketers try to avoid signs or symbols that may have several meanings for an audience. For example, *soda* as a general term for soft drinks may not work well in national advertisements. Although in some parts of the United States the word means "soft drink," in other regions it may connote bicarbonate of soda, an ice cream drink, or something one mixes with Scotch whiskey.

To share a coded meaning with the receiver or audience, a source selects and uses a **communications channel**, the medium of transmission that carries the coded message from the source to the receiver or audience. Transmission media include ink on paper, air wave vibrations produced by vocal cords, chalk marks on a chalkboard, and electronically produced vibrations of air waves (in radio and television signals, for example).

When a source chooses an inappropriate communication channel, several problems may arise. The coded message may reach some receivers, but the wrong ones. For example, dieters embracing the Atkins low-carbohydrate diet are more likely to focus on communications relating to their food concerns, such as "Eat Meat Not Wheat" T-shirts, QVC's Low-Carb Hour, and fast-food chain advertisements that communicate information about the carbohydrate content of menu items.[16] An advertiser attempting to reach this group would need to take this information into account when choosing an appropriate communications channel. Coded messages may also reach intended receivers in incomplete form because the intensity of the transmission is weak. For example, radio and broadcast television signals are received effectively only over a limited range, which varies according to climatic conditions. Members of the target audience living on the fringe of the broadcast area may receive a weak signal; others well within the broadcast area may also receive an incomplete message if, for example, they listen to the radio while driving or studying.

In the **decoding process**, signs or symbols are converted into concepts and ideas. Seldom does a receiver decode exactly the same meaning the source coded. When the result of decoding differs from what was coded, noise exists. **Noise** is anything that reduces the clarity and accuracy of the communication; it has many sources and may affect any or all parts of the communication process. Noise sometimes arises within the communications channel itself. Radio static, poor or slow Internet connections, and laryngitis are sources of noise. Noise also occurs when a source uses signs or symbols that are unfamiliar to the receiver or have a meaning different from the one intended. Noise may also originate in the receiver; a receiver may be unaware of a coded message when perceptual processes block it out.

The receiver's response to a decoded message is **feedback** to the source. The source usually expects and normally receives feedback, although perhaps not immediately. During feedback, the receiver or audience is the source of a message directed toward the original source, which then becomes a receiver. Feedback is coded, sent through a communications channel, and decoded by the receiver, the source of the original communication. Thus, communication is a circular process, as indicated in Figure 18.1.

During face-to-face communication, such as occurs in personal selling and product sampling, verbal and nonverbal feedback can be immediate. Instant feedback lets communicators adjust messages quickly to improve the effectiveness of their communications. For example, when a salesperson realizes through feedback that a customer does not understand a sales presentation, the salesperson adapts the presentation to make it more meaningful to the customer. This may be why face-to-face sales presentations create higher behavioral intentions to purchase services than do telemarketing sales contacts.[17] In interpersonal communication, feedback occurs through talking, touching, smiling, nodding, eye movements, and other body movements and postures.

When mass communication such as advertising is used, feedback is often slow and difficult to recognize. Also, it may be several years before the effects of this promotion will be known. Feedback does exist for mass communication in the form of measures of changes in sales volume or in consumers' attitudes and awareness levels.

Each communication channel has a limit on the volume of information it can handle effectively. This limit, called **channel capacity**, is determined by the least efficient component of the communication process. Consider communications that depend on speech. An individual source can speak only so fast, and there is a limit to how much an individual receiver can take in aurally. Beyond that point, additional messages cannot be decoded; thus, meaning cannot be shared. Although a radio announcer can read several hundred words a minute, a one-minute advertising message should not exceed 150 words because most announcers cannot articulate words into understandable messages at a rate beyond 150 words per minute.

**decoding process** Converting signs or symbols into concepts and ideas

**noise** Anything that reduces a communication's clarity and accuracy

**feedback** The receiver's response to a decoded message

**channel capacity** The limit on the volume of information a communication channel can handle effectively

# The Role and Objectives of Promotion

**promotion** Communication to build and maintain relationships by informing and persuading one or more audiences

**Promotion** is communication that builds and maintains favorable relationships by informing and persuading one or more audiences to view an organization positively and to accept its products. Toward this end, many organizations spend considerable resources on promotion to build and enhance relationships with current and potential customers. For example, the lumber, pork, and milk industries promote the use of these products to stimulate demand with such catchphrases as "Be Constructive," "Pork: The Other White Meat," and "Got Milk?".[18] Marketers also indirectly facilitate favorable relationships by focusing information about company activities and products on interest groups (such as environmental and consumer groups), current and potential investors, regulatory agencies, and society in general. For example, some organizations promote responsible use of products criticized by society such as tobacco, alcohol, and violent movies. Companies sometimes promote programs that help selected groups. Yoplait, for instance, supports the Susan G. Komen Breast Cancer Research Foundation with its "Save Lids to Save Lives" campaign, which contributes 10 cents to the charity for every pink yogurt lid sent in by consumers.[19] Such cause-related marketing, as we discussed in Chapter 4, links the purchase of products to philanthropic efforts for one or more causes. By contributing to causes that its target markets support, cause-related marketing can help marketers boost sales and generate goodwill.

For maximum benefit from promotional efforts, marketers strive for proper planning, implementation, coordination, and control of communications. Effective management of integrated marketing communications is based on information about and feedback from customers and the marketing environment, often obtained from an organization's marketing information system (see Figure 18.2 on p. 498). How

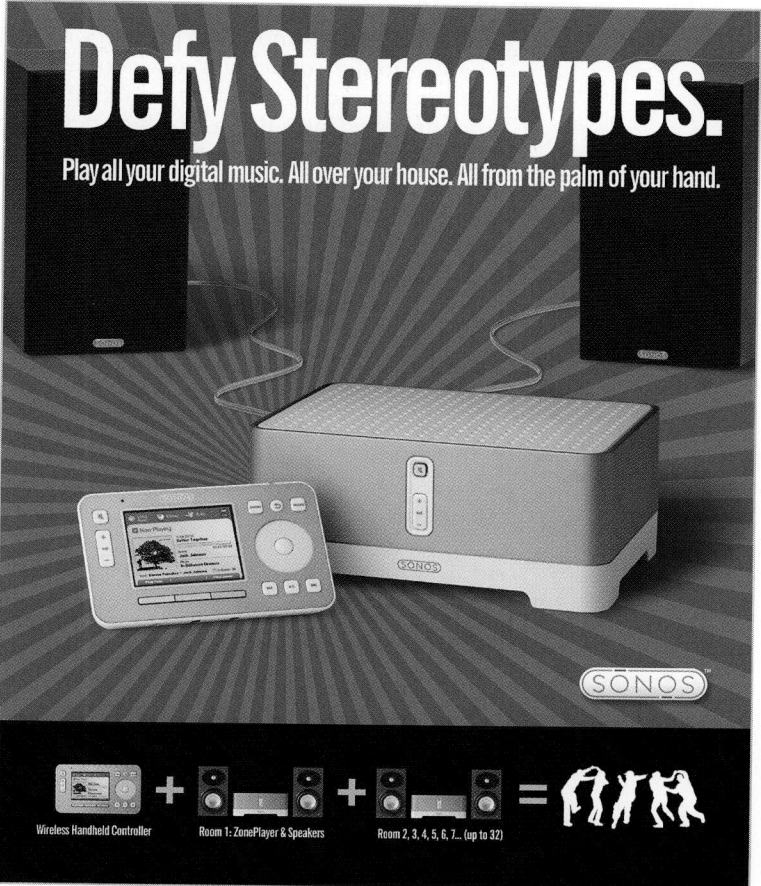

**Objectives of Promotion**

Marketers use promotional efforts to achieve a broad spectrum of objectives. What is the objective of this advertisement?

**figure 18.2**

## INFORMATION FLOWS ARE IMPORTANT IN INTEGRATED MARKETING COMMUNICATIONS

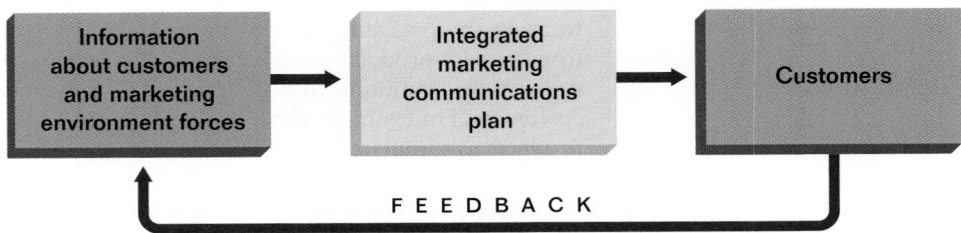

successfully marketers use promotion to maintain positive relationships depends to some extent on the quantity and quality of information the organization receives. Because customers derive information and opinions from many different sources, integrated marketing communications planning also takes into account informal methods of communication such as word of mouth and independent information sources on the Internet. Because promotion is communication that can be managed, we now analyze what communication is and how the communication process works.

Promotional objectives vary considerably from one organization to another and within organizations over time. Large firms with multiple promotional programs operating simultaneously may have quite varied promotional objectives. For the purpose of analysis, we focus on the eight promotional objectives shown in Table 18.1. Although the list is not exhaustive, one or more of these objectives underlie many promotional programs.

### Create Awareness

A considerable amount of promotion efforts focus on creating awareness. For an organization introducing a new product or a line extension, making customers aware of the product is crucial to initiating the product adoption process. A marketer that has invested heavily in product development strives to create product awareness quickly to generate revenues to offset the high costs of product development and introduction. To create awareness of its new Spicy Premium Chicken sandwich, for example, McDonald's passed out samples of the sandwich, coupons, T-shirts, and iPod covers in 14 cities.[20]

Creating awareness is important for existing products, too. Promotional efforts may aim to increase awareness of brands, product features, image-related issues (such as organizational size or socially responsive behavior), or operational characteristics (such as store hours, locations, and credit availability). Some promotional programs are unsuccessful because marketers fail to generate awareness of critical issues among a significant portion of target market members. For example, Chrysler Group effectively dropped an expensive campaign to launch its new Pacifica when sales failed to meet expectations. Chrysler wanted to target the new vehicle at younger, more affluent consumers. However, the company chose Celine Dion, the popular Canadian

| **table 18.1**  POSSIBLE OBJECTIVES OF PROMOTION | |
| --- | --- |
| Create awareness | Retain loyal customers |
| Stimulate demand | Facilitate reseller support |
| Encourage product trial | Combat competitive promotional efforts |
| Identify prospects | Reduce sales fluctuations |

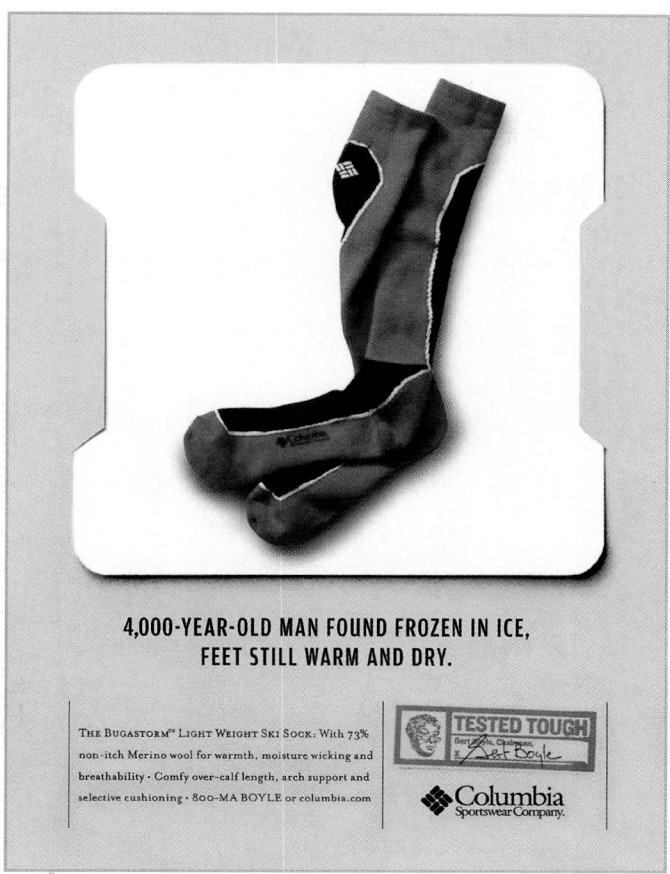

**4,000-YEAR-OLD MAN FOUND FROZEN IN ICE, FEET STILL WARM AND DRY.**

THE BUGASTORM™ LIGHT WEIGHT SKI SOCK: With 73% non-itch Merino wool for warmth, moisture wicking and breathability · Comfy over-calf length, arch support and selective cushioning · 800-MA BOYLE or columbia.com

TESTED TOUGH

Columbia
Sportswear Company.

**Selective Demand**

In this advertisement for ski socks, Columbia attempts to stimulate selective demand.

**primary demand** Demand for a product category rather than for a specific brand

**pioneer promotion** Promotion that informs consumers about a new product

**selective demand** Demand for a specific brand

singer, to appear in television commercials for the campaign and only later discovered that she appeals to a much older audience, with an average age of 52.[21]

## Stimulate Demand

When an organization is the first to introduce an innovative product, it tries to stimulate **primary demand**—demand for a product category rather than for a specific brand of product—through pioneer promotion. **Pioneer promotion** informs potential customers about the product: what it is, what it does, how it can be used, and where it can be purchased. Because pioneer promotion is used in the introductory stage of the product life cycle, meaning there are no competing brands, it neither emphasizes brand names nor compares brands. When Apple introduced the iPod, for instance, it initially attempted to stimulate primary demand by emphasizing the benefits of music players in general rather than the benefits of its specific brand. Primary-demand stimulation is not just for new products. At times an industry trade association rather than a single firm uses promotional efforts to stimulate primary demand.

To build **selective demand**, demand for a specific brand, a marketer employs promotional efforts that point out the strengths and benefits of a specific brand. Building selective demand also requires singling out attributes important to potential buyers. Selective demand can be stimulated by differentiating the product from competing brands in the minds of potential buyers. Selective demand can also be stimulated by increasing the number of product uses and promoting them through advertising campaigns, as well as through price discounts, free samples, coupons, consumer contests and games, and sweepstakes. Bennigan's, for example, launched an advertising campaign and held a thirtieth anniversary party to coincide with St. Patrick's Day to remind customers that the Irish-themed restaurant chain provides a fun environment where people can share good food.[22] Promotions for large package sizes or multiple-product packages are directed at increasing consumption, which in turn can stimulate demand. In addition, selective demand can be stimulated by encouraging existing customers to use more of the product.

## Encourage Product Trial

When attempting to move customers through the product adoption process, a marketer may successfully create awareness and interest, but customers may stall during the evaluation stage. In this case, certain types of promotion—such as free samples; coupons; test drives; or limited free-use offers, contests, and games—are employed to encourage product trial. Silk, for example, distributed coupons and samples to promote its new Silk Live! Smoothie product.[23] Whether a marketer's product is the first in a new product category, a new brand in an existing category, or simply an existing brand seeking customers, trial-inducing promotional efforts aim to make product trial convenient and low risk for potential customers.

## Identify Prospects

Certain types of promotional efforts aim to identify customers who are interested in the firm's product and are most likely to buy it. A marketer may use a magazine advertisement with a direct-response information form, requesting the reader to complete and mail the form to receive additional information. Some advertisements have toll-free numbers to facilitate direct customer response. Customers who fill out

**Encouraging Product Trial**

Sun Microsystems encourages product trial by offering free use for a selected time period.

information blanks or call the organization usually have higher interest in the product, which makes them likely sales prospects. The organization can respond with phone calls, follow-up letters, or personal contact by salespeople. Dun & Bradstreet, for example, offered a free article on customer relationship management to businesses that mailed in a card or called a toll-free number. This helped the consulting firm identify prospects to sell data used to develop and maintain customer relationships.

## Retain Loyal Customers

Clearly, maintaining long-term customer relationships is a major goal of most marketers. Such relationships are quite valuable. Promotional efforts directed at customer retention can help an organization control its costs because the costs of retaining customers are usually considerably lower than those of acquiring new ones. Frequent-user programs, such as those sponsored by airlines, car rental agencies, and hotels, aim to reward loyal customers and encourage them to remain loyal. Moët Hennessy, for example, introduced the Sparkling Circle, a membership club for 15,000 loyal customers.[24] Some organizations employ special offers that only their existing customers can use. To retain loyal customers, marketers not only advertise loyalty programs but also use reinforcement advertising, which assures current users they have made the right brand choice and tells them how to get the most satisfaction from the product.

## Facilitate Reseller Support

Reseller support is a two-way street: producers generally want to provide support to resellers to maintain sound working relationships, and in turn they expect resellers to support their products. When a manufacturer advertises a product to consumers, resellers should view this promotion as a form of strong manufacturer support. In some instances, a producer agrees to pay a certain proportion of retailers' advertising expenses for promoting its products. When a manufacturer is introducing a new consumer brand in a highly competitive product category, it may be difficult to persuade supermarket managers to carry this brand. However, if the manufacturer promotes the new brand with free sample and coupon distribution in the retailer's area, a supermarket manager views these actions as strong support and is much more likely to handle the product. To encourage wholesalers and retailers to increase their inventories of its products, a manufacturer may provide them with special offers and buying allowances. In certain industries, a producer's salesperson may provide support to a wholesaler by working with the wholesaler's customers (retailers) in the presentation and promotion of the products. Strong relationships with resellers are important to a firm's ability to maintain a sustainable competitive advantage. The use of various promotional methods can help an organization achieve this goal.

### Combat Competitive Promotional Efforts

At times a marketer's objective in using promotion is to offset or lessen the effect of a competitor's promotional program. This type of promotional activity does not necessarily increase the organization's sales or market share, but it may prevent a sales or market share loss. A combative promotional objective is used most often by firms in extremely competitive consumer markets, such as the fast-food and automobile industries. When some automakers began advertising their automobiles' ability to withstand collisions, as determined by crash tests conducted by various federal and private agencies, Volkswagen, BMW, Saturn, Mercedes-Benz, Toyota, and other firms quickly followed suit to combat their competitors' advertising. Although these ads were trying to promote safety records, the companies were also trying to prevent market share loss in a very competitive market.[25]

### Reduce Sales Fluctuations

Demand for many products varies from one month to another because of such factors as climate, holidays, and seasons. A business, however, cannot operate at peak efficiency when sales fluctuate rapidly. Changes in sales volume translate into changes in production, inventory levels, personnel needs, and financial resources. When promotional techniques reduce fluctuations by generating sales during slow periods, a firm can use its resources more efficiently.

Promotional techniques are often designed to stimulate sales during sales slumps. For example, advertisements promoting price reduction of lawn care equipment can increase sales during fall and winter months. During peak periods, a marketer may refrain from advertising to prevent stimulating sales to the point where the firm cannot handle all the demand. On occasion, an organization advertises that customers can be better served by coming in on certain days. A pizza outlet, for example, might distribute coupons that are valid only Monday through Thursday because on Friday through Sunday the restaurant is extremely busy.

To achieve the major objectives of promotion discussed here, companies must develop appropriate promotional programs. In the next section, we consider the basic components of such programs: the promotion mix elements.

# The Promotion Mix

**promotion mix** A combination of promotional methods used to promote a specific product

Several promotional methods can be used to communicate with individuals, groups, and organizations. When an organization combines specific methods to manage the integrated marketing communications for a particular product, that combination constitutes the promotion mix for that product. The four possible elements of a **promotion mix** are advertising, personal selling, public relations, and sales promotion (see Figure 18.3 on p. 502). For some products, firms use all four elements; for others, they use only two or three. In this section, we provide an overview of each promotion mix element; they are covered in greater detail in the next two chapters.

figure 18.3

**THE FOUR POSSIBLE ELEMENTS OF A PROMOTION MIX**

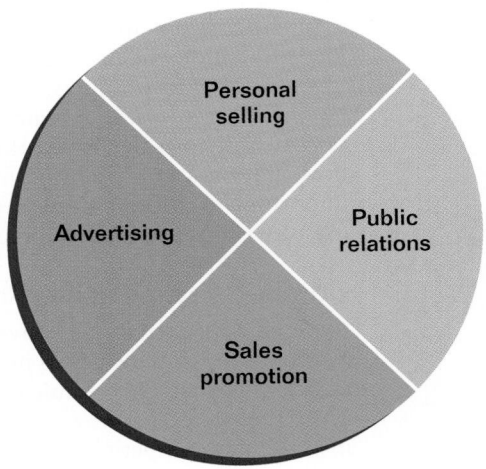

**Advertising as a Promotion Element**

The Garlic Company uses advertising and other elements in its promotion mix.

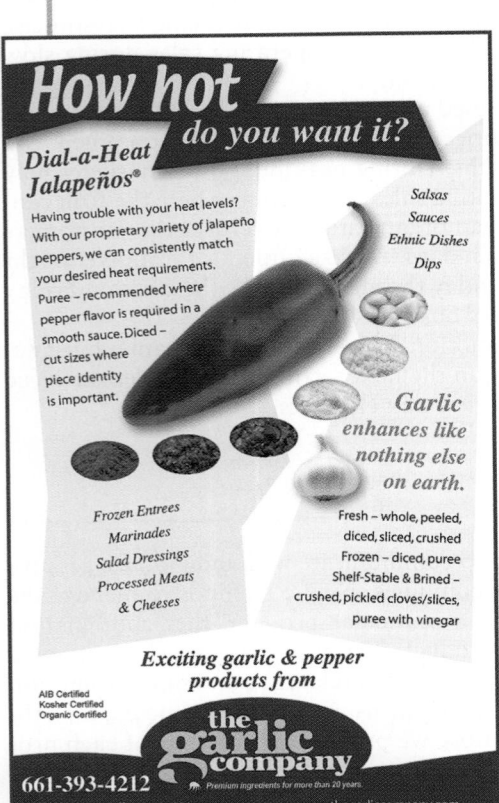

## Advertising

Advertising is a paid nonpersonal communication about an organization and its products transmitted to a target audience through mass media, including television, radio, the Internet, newspapers, magazines, direct mail, outdoor displays, and signs on mass transit vehicles. One company even placed advertisements—in the form of temporary tattoos of company logos—on the foreheads of college students.[26] Individuals and organizations use advertising to promote goods, services, ideas, issues, and people. Being highly flexible, advertising can reach an extremely large target audience or focus on a small, precisely defined segment. For instance, Burger King's advertising focuses on a large audience of potential fast-food customers, ranging from children to adults, whereas advertising for Gulfstream jets aims at a much smaller and more specialized target market.

Advertising offers several benefits. It is extremely cost efficient when it reaches a vast number of people at a low cost per person. For example, the cost of a four-color, full-page advertisement in *Time* magazine is $246,000. Because the magazine reaches more than 4 million subscribers, the cost of reaching 1,000 subscribers is about $62.[27] Advertising also lets the source repeat the message several times. Levi Strauss, for example, advertises on television, in magazines, and in outdoor displays. Advertising repetition has been found to be especially effective for brand name extensions beyond the original product category.[28] Furthermore, advertising a product a certain way can add to the product's value, and the visibility an organization gains from advertising can enhance its image. At times a firm tries to enhance its own or its product's image by including celebrity endorsers in advertisements. For example, the National Fluid Milk Processor Promotion Board's "milk moustache" campaign has featured Kelly Clarkson, Andy Roddick, Batman, Elvis impersonators, and the cast of "Scrubs."[29] Advertising has disadvantages as well. Even though the cost per person reached may be low, the absolute dollar outlay can be extremely high, especially for commercials during popular television shows. High costs can limit, and sometimes preclude, use of advertising in a promotion mix. Moreover, advertising rarely provides rapid feedback. Measuring its effect on sales

**Advertising Aimed at Prevention**

Merck & Co., Inc. uses the "Tell Someone" campaign to heighten awareness of cervical cancer and human papillomavirus (HPV).

is difficult, and it is ordinarily less persuasive than personal selling. In most instances, the time available to communicate a message to customers is limited to seconds, since people look at a print advertisement for only a few seconds and most broadcast commercials are 30 seconds or less. Of course, the use of infomercials can increase exposure time for viewers.

### Personal Selling

Personal selling is a paid personal communication that seeks to inform customers and persuade them to purchase products in an exchange situation. The phrase *purchase products* is interpreted broadly to encompass acceptance of ideas and issues. Telemarketing, described in Chapter 17 as direct selling over the telephone, relies heavily on personal selling. However, negative consumer attitudes and legislation restricting telemarketing have lessened its effectiveness as a personal selling technique.

Personal selling has both advantages and limitations when compared with advertising. Advertising is general communication aimed at a relatively large target audience, whereas personal selling involves more specific communication directed at one or several individuals. Reaching one person through personal selling costs considerably more than through advertising, but personal selling efforts often have greater impact on customers. Personal selling also provides immediate feedback, allowing marketers to adjust their messages to improve communication. It helps them determine and respond to customers' information needs.

When a salesperson and a customer meet face to face, they use several types of interpersonal communication. The predominant communication form is language, both spoken and written. A salesperson and

**Customer response rates to direct marketers**

| Media | Rate |
|---|---|
| Telephone | 8.55% |
| Coupon | 4.29% |
| Catalog | 3.67% |
| Banner/rich media ads | 3.52% |
| Direct mail | 2.77% |
| Email | 2.48% |
| Radio | 1.35% |
| Newspaper | 0.5% |
| Magazine | 0.17% |

Direct marketers' average rate by media type across twenty-one industries.

*Source:* The DMA 2005 Response Rate Report.

**kinesic communication** Communicating through the movement of head, eyes, arms, hands, legs, or torso

**proxemic communication** Communicating by varying the physical distance in face-to-face interactions

**tactile communication** Communicating through touching

customer frequently use **kinesic communication**, or communication through the movement of head, eyes, arms, hands, legs, or torso. Winking, head nodding, hand gestures, and arm motions are forms of kinesic communication. A good salesperson often can evaluate a prospect's interest in a product or presentation by noting eye contact and head nodding. **Proxemic communication**, a less obvious form of communication used in personal selling situations, occurs when either person varies the physical distance separating them. When a customer backs away from a salesperson, for example, he or she may be displaying a lack of interest in the product or expressing dislike for the salesperson. Touching, or **tactile communication**, is also a form of communication, although less popular in the United States than in many other countries. Handshaking is a common form of tactile communication both in the United States and elsewhere.

## Public Relations

While many promotional activities focus on a firm's customers, other stakeholders—suppliers, employees, stockholders, the media, educators, potential investors, government officials, and society in general—are important to an organization as well. To communicate with customers and stakeholders, a company employs public relations. Public relations is a broad set of communication efforts used to create and maintain favorable relationships between an organization and its stakeholders. Maintaining a positive relationship with one or more stakeholders can affect a firm's current sales and profits, as well as its long-term survival.

# Turkey Soda Garners Publicity with All the Trimmings

Despite its reputation for curious flavors, unique labels, and off-beat promotions, the management of Seattle-based Jones Soda Company was not prepared for the publicity generated by the release of their Thanksgiving-themed turkey- and gravy-flavored soft drink. Jones produced just a few thousand bottles of the seasonal flavor simply to draw attention to its other soft drinks, but Turkey & Gravy Soda sold out in a matter of hours. Although product developers at Jones characterized the product as a sipping soda rather than a thirst-satisfying one, the timing of its holiday release helped fuel its success.

In the weeks following the soft drink's introduction, the company's president, Peter Van Stolk, was contacted more than 500 times by the media, and gave nearly 100 radio interviews. Van Stolk further

maximized the public relations impact by mentioning in every interview that the company would donate all profits from Turkey & Gravy Soda to the Toys for Tots charity. And people loved talking about the soft drink that was purported to taste like "microwaved Thanksgiving leftovers." Paid advertising could never have generated as much interest in the oddly-flavored soda as this buzz marketing approach did.

Such publicity has been beneficial for this small firm that does very little advertising. Jones spends much of its promotion budget on sponsorships of "passionate young people" like skateboarder Tony Hawk, as well as on a website that allows nearly 500 unsigned bands to post their music for download. Such creativity in marketing certainly seems to have paid off for Jones Soda: its sales have doubled over the last four years, to more than $20 million.

Public relations uses a variety of tools, including annual reports, brochures, event sponsorship, and sponsorship of socially responsible programs aimed at protecting the environment or helping disadvantaged individuals. Nintendo, for example, is targeting older game players by hosting Super Bowl parties with men's magazines *Maxim* and *FHM,* as well as Spring Break parties and music tours, and it sponsored the Burton snowboarding championships.[30] Merrill Lynch sponsored a "Women of the World" art exhibit, which featured art by women artists from around the world, to help the financial services firm achieve its goal of targeting more affluent women.[31]

Other tools arise from the use of publicity, which is a component of public relations. Publicity is nonpersonal communication in news story form about an organization or its products, or both, transmitted through a mass medium at no charge. A few examples of publicity-based public relations tools are news releases, press conferences, and feature articles. When TiVo launched the personal video recorder, the company initially gave free devices to sports celebrities and select members of the entertainment industry to stimulate awareness and product trial. The company gained further publicity with news stories, product reviews, and strategic product placements in the mass media. TiVo may have chosen a public relations campaign over a more traditional advertising effort because its product enables consumers to bypass television commercials; use of personal video recorders is expected to reduce viewing of television advertisements by 19 percent by 2007.[32] Ordinarily public relations efforts are planned and implemented to be consistent with and support other elements of the promotion mix. Public relations efforts may be the responsibility of an individual or of a department within the organization, or the organization may hire an independent public relations agency.

Unpleasant situations and negative events, such as product tampering or an environmental disaster, may generate unfavorable public relations for an organization. For example, after Wal-Mart suffered negative publicity due to news stories and lawsuits related to its hiring practices, union management, and aggressive expansion policies, the company ran a full-page newspaper ad in more than 100 newspapers promoting its job creation, employee diversity, and employee-benefit packages.[33] To minimize the damaging effects of unfavorable coverage, effective marketers have policies and procedures in place to help manage any public relations problems.

Public relations should not be viewed as a set of tools to be used only during crises. To get the most from public relations, an organization should have someone responsible for public relations either internally or externally, and should have an ongoing public relations program.

## Sales Promotion

Sales promotion is an activity or material that acts as a direct inducement, offering added value or incentive for the product, to resellers, salespeople, or consumers. Examples include free samples, games, rebates, sweepstakes, contests, premiums, and coupons. For example, Trimspa sponsored a "Million Dollar Makeover Challenge," asking users of its weight-loss product to submit before and after photos of themselves to compete to win $1 million in prizes.[34] *Sales promotion* should not be confused with *promotion*; sales promotion is just one part of the comprehensive area of promotion. Marketers spend more on sales promotion than on advertising, and sales promotion appears to be a faster-growing area than advertising. Coupons are especially important; Table 18.2 (on p. 506) shows the product categories with the greatest distribution of coupons.

Generally, when companies employ advertising or personal selling, they depend on these activities continuously or cyclically. However, a marketer's use of sales promotion tends to be irregular. Many products are seasonal. A company such as Toro may offer more sales promotions in August than in the peak selling season of April or May, when more people buy tractors, lawn mowers, and other gardening equipment. Marketers frequently rely on sales promotion to improve the effectiveness of other promotion mix elements, especially advertising and personal selling. Decisions to cut sales promotion can have significant negative effects on a company. For example, Clorox decided to cut the promotion budget for Glad branded products two years in a row, in part to compensate for rising plastic resin prices. When competitors did not decrease their promotional budgets, Glad lost significant market share in trash bags (down 10.3 percent), food storage bags (down 10.6 percent), and lawn and leaf bags (down 23.2 percent).[35] In fact, research suggests that about one-third of a gain in sales from a sales promotion occurs at the expense of other brands in the same category.[36]

An effective promotion mix requires the right combination of components. To see how such a mix is created, we now examine the factors and conditions affecting the selection of promotional methods that an organization uses for a particular product.

# Selecting Promotion Mix Elements

Marketers vary the composition of promotion mixes for many reasons. Although a promotion mix can include all four elements, frequently a marketer selects fewer than four. Many firms that market multiple product lines use several promotion mixes simultaneously.

## Promotional Resources, Objectives, and Policies

The size of an organization's promotional budget affects the number and relative intensity of promotional methods included in a promotion mix. If a company's promotional budget is extremely limited, the firm is likely to rely on personal selling because it is easier to measure a salesperson's contribution to sales than to measure the sales effectiveness of advertising. Businesses must have sizable promotional budgets to use regional or national advertising. Procter & Gamble, for example, spends nearly $4 million a year on advertising its personal-care and cleaning products in the United States.[37] Organizations with extensive promotional resources generally include more elements in their promotion mixes, but having more promotional dollars to spend does not necessarily mean using more promotional methods.

An organization's promotional objectives and policies also influence the types of promotion selected. If a company's objective is to create mass awareness of a new convenience good, such as a breakfast cereal, its promotion mix probably leans heavily toward advertising, sales promotion, and possibly public relations. If a company hopes to educate consumers about the features of a durable good, such as a home ap-

| table 18.2 | PRODUCT CATEGORIES WITH THE GREATEST DISTRIBUTION OF COUPONS |
|---|---|
| 1. Household cleaners | 6. Condiments and gravies |
| 2. Prepared foods | 7. Personal soap and bath additives |
| 3. Detergents | 8. Frozen prepared foods |
| 4. Medications, remedies, health aids | 9. Cereal |
| 5. Paper products | 10. Skin care preparations |

**Source:** "September Is National Coupon Month," Promotion Marketing Association, press release, Sept. 2, 2003, www.couponmonth.com/pages/news.htm. © Copyright 2004 by Promotion Marketing Association, Inc./PMA Educational Foundation, Inc., 257 Park Ave. South, New York, NY 10010. All rights reserved, including the right to disseminate in any format or media. Reproduction of this work in any form is forbidden without written permission of the publisher. See also www.pmalink.org.

**Sales Promotion as a Promotion Mix Element**

SimDesk uses sales promotion (a free trial) and other elements in its promotion mix.

pliance, its promotion mix may combine a moderate amount of advertising, possibly some sales promotion designed to attract customers to retail stores, and a great deal of personal selling because this method is an efficient way to inform customers about such products. If a firm's objective is to produce immediate sales of nondurable services, the promotion mix will probably stress advertising and sales promotion. For example, dry cleaners and carpet-cleaning firms are more likely to use advertising with a coupon or discount rather than personal selling.

## Characteristics of the Target Market

Size, geographic distribution, and demographic characteristics of an organization's target market help dictate the methods to include in a product's promotion mix. To some degree, market size determines composition of the mix. If the size is limited, the promotion mix will probably emphasize personal selling, which can be very effective for reaching small numbers of people. Organizations selling to industrial markets and firms marketing products through only a few wholesalers frequently make personal selling the major component of their promotion mixes. When a product's market consists of millions of customers, organizations rely on advertising and sales promotion because these methods reach masses of people at a low cost per person.

Geographic distribution of a firm's customers also affects the choice of promotional methods. Personal selling is more feasible if a company's customers are concentrated in a small area than if they are dispersed across a vast region. When the company's customers are numerous and dispersed, advertising may be more practical.

Distribution of a target market's demographic characteristics, such as age, income, or education, may affect the types of promotional techniques a marketer selects, as well as the messages and images employed. The 2000 U.S. census found that so-called traditional families—those composed of married couples with children—account for fewer than one-quarter of all U.S. households, down from 30 percent in 1980 and 45 percent in 1960. To reach the three-quarters of households consisting of single parents,

ONE FRESH GROUND BEEF PATTY
SLICE OF AMERICAN
RED RIPE TOMATO
PICKLES AND MORE CRUNCHY PICKLES
WHOLE LEAF LETTUCE
ONIONS
KETCHUP
MUSTARD
NO MAYO, THANK YOU

IVETTE DOES THE IVETTE BURGER,
NOT JUST ANOTHER OFF-THE-RACK BURGER.

Don't compromise. Personalize. Wendy's® makes your hamburger right when you order it with the fresh toppings you say to put on. Do a hamburger made just for you.

Do what tastes right.™

Wendy's
OLD FASHIONED
HAMBURGERS

**Product Characteristics**

Inexpensive, frequently purchased convenience products, like those advertised here, require significant levels of advertising.

unmarried couples, singles, and "empty nesters" (whose children have left home), more companies are modifying the images used in their promotions. Charles Schwab, for example, featured celebrity single mother Sarah Ferguson, the Duchess of York, in commercials for its financial services.

## Characteristics of the Product

Generally promotion mixes for business products concentrate on personal selling, whereas advertising plays a major role in promoting consumer goods. This generalization should be treated cautiously, however. Marketers of business products use some advertising to promote products. Advertisements for computers, road-building equipment, and aircraft are fairly common, and some sales promotion is also used occasionally to promote business products. Personal selling is used extensively for consumer durables, such as home appliances, automobiles, and houses, whereas consumer convenience items are promoted mainly through advertising and sales promotion. Public relations appears in promotion mixes for both business and consumer products.

Marketers of highly seasonal products often emphasize advertising, and sometimes sales promotion as well, because off-season sales generally will not support an extensive year-round sales force. Although most toy producers have sales forces to sell to resellers, many of these companies depend chiefly on advertising to promote their products.

A product's price also influences the composition of the promotion mix. High-priced products call for personal selling because consumers associate greater risk with the purchase of such products and usually want information from a salesperson. Few people, for example, are willing to purchase a refrigerator from a self-service establishment. For low-priced convenience items, marketers use advertising rather than personal selling. Research suggests that consumers visiting a store specifically to purchase a product on sale are more likely to have read flyers and to have purchased other sale-priced products than consumers visiting the same store for other reasons.[38]

Another consideration in creating an effective promotion mix is the stage of the product life cycle. During the introduction stage, much advertising may be necessary for both business and consumer products to make potential users aware of them. For many products, personal selling and sales promotion are also helpful in this stage. In the growth and maturity stages, consumer services require heavy emphasis on advertising, whereas business products often call for a concentration of personal selling and some sales promotion. In the decline stage, marketers usually decrease all promotional activities, especially advertising.

Intensity of market coverage is still another factor affecting composition of the promotion mix. When products are marketed through intensive distribution, firms depend strongly on advertising and sales promotion. Many convenience products, such as lotions, cereals, and coffee, are promoted through samples, coupons, and money refunds. When marketers choose selective distribution, promotion mixes vary considerably. Items handled through exclusive distribution, such as expensive watches, furs, and high-quality furniture, typically require a significant amount of personal selling.

A product's use also affects the combination of promotional methods. Manufacturers of highly personal products, such as laxatives, nonprescription contraceptives, and feminine hygiene products, depend on advertising because many customers do not want to talk with salespeople about these products.

## Costs and Availability of Promotional Methods

Costs of promotional methods are major factors to analyze when developing a promotion mix. National advertising and sales promotion require large expenditures. However, if these efforts succeed in reaching extremely large audiences, the cost per individual reached may be quite small, possibly a few pennies. Some forms of advertising are relatively inexpensive. Many small, local businesses advertise products through local newspapers, magazines, radio and television stations, outdoor displays, and signs on mass transit vehicles.

Another consideration marketers explore when formulating a promotion mix is availability of promotional techniques. Despite the tremendous number of media vehicles in the United States, a firm may find that no available advertising medium effectively reaches a certain target market. The problem of media availability becomes more pronounced when marketers advertise in foreign countries. Some media, such as television, simply may not be available, or advertising on television may be illegal. In China, the State Administration for Radio, Film, and Television banned a Nike commercial that featured basketball star LeBron James besting a kung fu master and a pair of dragons in a video game. In recent years, the agency has cracked down on U.S. and Japanese advertisements that fail to "uphold national dignity and interest, and respect the motherland's culture."[39] Available media may not be open to certain types of advertisements. In some countries, advertisers are forbidden to make brand comparisons on television. Other promotional methods also have limitations. For instance, a firm may wish to increase its sales force but be unable to find qualified personnel.

## Push and Pull Channel Policies

**push policy** Promoting a product only to the next institution down the marketing channel

Another element marketers consider when planning a promotion mix is whether to use a push policy or a pull policy. With a **push policy**, the producer promotes the product only to the next institution down the marketing channel. In a marketing channel with wholesalers and retailers, the producer promotes to the wholesaler because in this case, the wholesaler is the channel member just below the producer (see Figure 18.4). Each channel member in turn promotes to the next channel member. A push policy normally stresses personal selling. Sometimes sales promotion and advertising are used in conjunction with personal selling to push the products down through the channel.

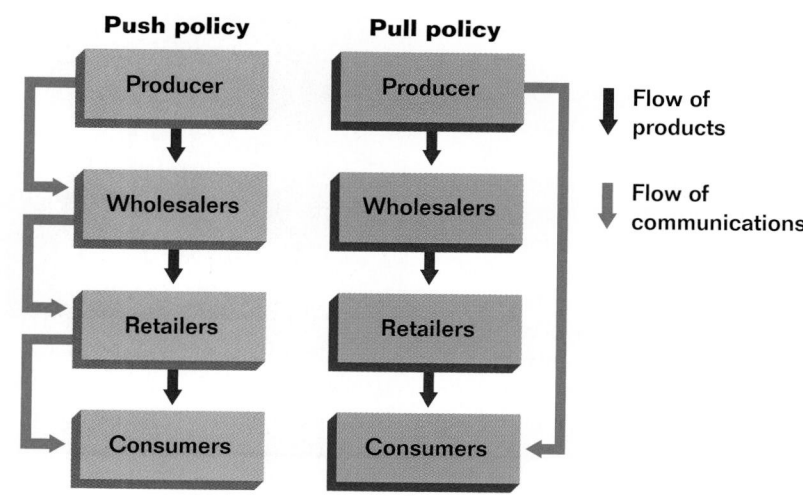

**figure 18.4**

**COMPARISON OF PUSH AND PULL PROMOTIONAL STRATEGIES**

**pull policy** Promoting a product directly to consumers to develop strong consumer demand that pulls products through the marketing channel

As Figure 18.4 shows, a firm using a **pull policy** promotes directly to consumers to develop strong consumer demand for its products. It does so primarily through advertising and sales promotion. Because consumers are persuaded to seek the products in retail stores, retailers in turn go to wholesalers or the producers to buy the products. This policy is intended to pull the goods down through the channel by creating demand at the consumer level. Consumers are told that if the stores don't have it, ask them to get it.

Push and pull policies are not mutually exclusive. At times an organization uses both simultaneously.

## Personal and Electronic Word-of-Mouth Communication

**word-of-mouth communication** Personal informal exchanges of communication that customers share with one another about products, brands, and companies

When making decisions about the composition of promotion mixes, marketers should recognize that commercial messages, whether from advertising, personal selling, sales promotion, or public relations, are limited in the extent to which they can inform and persuade customers and move them closer to making purchases. Depending on the type of customers and the products involved, buyers to some extent rely on word-of-mouth communication from personal sources such as family members and friends. **Word-of-mouth communication** is personal informal exchanges of communication that customers share with one another about products, brands, and companies.[40] Most customers are likely to be influenced by friends and family mem-

# P&G Buzzes Minors, Alarming Consumer Activists

Using a buzz marketing website called Tremor, Procter & Gamble (P&G) recruited 250,000 "connectors"—teens with lots of social connections—to talk up its products to other teenagers. P&G does not tell members of the "Tremor Crew" what to say and it does not pay them, but it does bestow coupons, samples, discounts, and free downloads. Members are not required to disclose their membership to anyone—not even their own parents.

Commercial Alert, a consumer-activist group, filed a complaint with the Federal Trade Commis-

sion, arguing that Tremor inappropriately targets minor children. The group also asked the federal agency to investigate whether such viral and buzz marketing efforts violate laws requiring the disclosure of commercial relationships. Commercial Alert argues that buzz marketing is deceptive and intrusive, takes advantage of the kindness of strangers, and involves turning people's friends and family against them for profit. P&G, however, contends that "we have been upfront with [our teens] to let them know that we are part of Procter & Gamble and a word-of-mouth marketing program."

Buzz marketing, now a $60 million business, has been controversial from the beginning. Consider the case of Sony Ericsson Mobile, which deployed fake tourists to ask bystanders in New York's Times Square to take their photos with a new camera phone and then chat with them about the phones. The "tourists," however, did not disclose their relationship to the company. The Word-of-Mouth Marketing Association has a code of ethics that encourages its members to be open and honest about their relationship with marketers in all communications. The Federal Trade Commission has not signaled its opinion on this growing form of promotion.

bers when making purchases. Word-of-mouth communication is very important when people are selecting restaurants and entertainment, and automotive, medical, legal, banking, and personal services such as hair care. Effective marketers who understand the importance of word-of-mouth communication attempt to identify opinion leaders and encourage them to try their products in the hope they will spread favorable word about them. Apple Computer, for example, relies on its devoted consumer following to spread by word of mouth their satisfaction with Apple products such as PowerBooks and iPods. Apple has built an "army of evangelists," ranging from teenagers to middle-aged adults, to make the product more visible and communicate the quality of the products to those around them.[41]

**buzz marketing** An attempt to gain acceptance of a product through word-of-mouth communications

**Buzz marketing** is an attempt to create a trend or acceptance of a product through word-of-mouth communications. The idea is that an accepted member of a social group will always be more credible than any other form of paid communication.[42] For example, Vespa Scooters paid models to ride and park its trendy motorbikes around the "in" cafés and fashionable retail establishments in Los Angeles in the hope of generating favorable word-of-mouth communication about the reissued European bikes. And Toyota parked its new Scions outside of raves and hip cafés, coffee shops, and clothing stores, where shoppers could take informal test drives to get the "buzz" going about the new marque.[43] Buzz marketing works best as a part of an integrated marketing communication program that also uses advertising, personal selling, sales promotion, and publicity. Marketers should not underestimate the importance of both word-of-mouth communication and personal influence, nor should they have unrealistic expectations about the performance of commercial messages.

In addition, customers are increasingly going online for information and opinions about goods and services as well as about the companies. Electronic word of mouth is communicating about products through websites, blogs, e-mail, or online forums. Users can go to a number of consumer-oriented websites, such as epinions.com and ConsumerReview.com. At these sites, they can learn about other consumers' feelings toward and experiences with specific products. Users can also search within product categories and compare consumers' viewpoints on various brands and models. Buyers can peruse Internet-based newsgroups, forums, and blogs to find word-of-mouth information. A consumer looking for a new cellphone service, for example, might inquire in forums about other participants' experiences and level of satisfaction to gain more information before making a purchase decision. A study by Forrester and Intelliseek found that more than 90 percent of consumers trust such recommendations they get from other consumers.[44] Electronic word of mouth is particularly important to consumers staying abreast of trends. For example, Facebook.com serves as an online dynamic yearbook for college and high school students. Facebook allows users to share interests as well as favorite movies, books, and television shows. The Pulse on Facebook tracks trends relating to each school. Students, for instance, can see which band is the most popular on their campus and how it compares to all schools. Consumers can also read or text-message their own reviews of movies or restaurants via their cellphones.

Word of mouth, no matter how it's transmitted, is not effective in all product categories. It seems to be most effective for new-to-market and more expensive products. Despite the obvious benefits of positive word of mouth, marketers must also recognize the potential dangers of negative word of mouth. This

**marketing ENTREPRENEURS**

**Mike Gellman**

THE BUSINESS: SpireMedia

FOUNDED: 1998

SUCCESS: More than $3 million in annual revenue

With just two computers, a fax machine, and one client (eBags), Mike Gellman founded Spire-Media, today Denver's biggest web-development firm. Twenty-five employees provide web strategy, information architecture, and business analysis services to 200 clients, to the tune of around $3.5 million annual revenue. The key to Gellman's success is that he produces quality work for his clients without a penny of outside financing, and word-of-mouth communication is his biggest promotion outlet. He maintains an open-book policy with his employees so that they are aware of how the business is doing and how they affect productivity. By growing slowly and acquiring clients from big competitors that went under in the 1990s, SpireMedia has become a successful company with clients such as Western Union, Qwest, Jeppessen, and even David Letterman.

is particularly important in dealing with online platforms that can reach more people and encourage consumers to "gang up" on a company or product. For example, music giant Sony BMG received negative press over a protest campaign that moved from online to the front of its office building. Sony had stopped production on the third album of its artist Fiona Apple after it decided the record was not radio-friendly. A copy of the album was mysteriously "leaked" on the Internet and soon became one of the most downloaded items online. Fans organized at websites and online forums to create petitions and mail apples to Sony's executives every day for several months. Sony agreed to release the album to stores after members of the online campaign picketed Sony's offices in New York and the story reached the mainstream media.[45]

**viral marketing** A strategy to get Internet users to share ads and promotions with their friends

**Viral marketing** is a strategy to get Internet users to share ads and promotions among friends. The concept is based on viral activitiesare spread among users through e-mail and website links. Burger King, for example, created the "Subservient Chicken" website, where visitors seem to be able to control a person in a chicken suit by typing in commands. Viral communications resulted in nearly 14 million visitors to the website in less than a year.[46]

# Criticisms and Defenses of Promotion

Even though promotional activities can help customers make informed purchasing decisions, social scientists, consumer groups, government agencies, and members of society in general have long criticized promotion. There are two main reasons for such criticism: promotion does have flaws, and it is a highly visible business activity that pervades our daily lives. Although complaints about too much promotional activity are almost universal, a number of more specific criticisms have been lodged. In this section, we discuss some of the criticisms and defenses of promotion.

### Is Promotion Deceptive?

One common criticism of promotion is that it is deceptive and unethical. During the nineteenth and early twentieth centuries, much promotion was blatantly deceptive. Although no longer widespread, some deceptive promotion still occurs. For example, T-Mobile paid $135,000 to the city of New York to settle a lawsuit accusing the company of misleading and confusing consumers with deceptive cellphone advertisements.[47] Questionable weight loss claims are made about various exercise devices and diet programs. Some promotions are unintentionally deceiving; for instance, when advertising to children, it is easy to mislead them because they are more naive than adults and less able to separate fantasy from reality. For this reason, the Federal Trade Commission monitors the ratings systems of the film, music, and electronic games industries as well as their advertising to children.[48] A promotion may also mislead some receivers because words can have diverse meanings for different people. However, not all promotion should be condemned because a small portion is flawed. Laws, government regulation, and industry self-regulation have helped decrease deceptive promotion.

### Does Promotion Increase Prices?

Promotion is also criticized for raising prices, but in fact it often tends to lower them. The ultimate purpose of promotion is to stimulate demand. If it does, the business should be able to produce and market products in larger quantities and thus reduce per-unit production and marketing costs, which can result in lower prices. For example, as demand for flat-screen TVs and MP3 players has increased, their prices have dropped. When promotion fails to stimulate demand, the price of the promoted product increases because promotion costs must be added to other costs. Promotion also helps keep prices lower by facilitating price competition. When firms advertise prices, their prices tend to remain lower than when they are not promoting prices. Gasoline pricing illustrates how promotion fosters price competition. Service stations with the highest prices seldom have highly visible price signs.

## Does Promotion Create Needs?

Some critics of promotion claim that it manipulates consumers by persuading them to buy products they do not need, hence creating "artificial" needs. In his theory of motivation, Abraham Maslow (discussed in Chapter 5) indicates that an individual tries to satisfy five levels of needs: physiological needs, such as hunger, thirst, and sex; safety needs; needs for love and affection; needs for self-esteem and respect from others; and self-actualization needs, that is, the need to realize one's potential. When needs are viewed in this context, it is difficult to demonstrate that promotion creates them. If there were no promotional activities, people would still have needs for food, water, sex, safety, love, affection, self-esteem, respect from others, and self-actualization.

Although promotion may not create needs, it does capitalize on them (which may be why some critics believe promotion creates needs). Many marketers base their appeals on these needs. For example, several mouthwash, toothpaste, and perfume advertisements associate these products with needs for love, affection, and respect. These advertisers rely on human needs in their messages, but they do not create the needs.

## Does Promotion Encourage Materialism?

Another frequent criticism of promotion is that it leads to materialism. The purpose of promoting goods is to persuade people to buy them; thus, if promotion works, consumers will want to buy more and more things. Marketers assert that values are instilled in the home and that promotion does not change people into materialistic consumers. However, the behavior of today's children and teenagers contradicts this view; many insist on high-priced, brand name apparel such as Gucci, Coach, Ralph Lauren, and Hummer.

## Does Promotion Help Customers Without Costing Too Much?

Every year firms spend billions of dollars for promotion. The question is whether promotion helps customers enough to be worth the cost. Consumers do benefit because promotion informs them about product uses, features, advantages, prices, and locations where they can buy the products. Consumers thus gain more knowledge about available products and can make more intelligent buying decisions. Promotion also informs consumers about services—for instance, health care, educational programs, and day care—as well as about important social, political, and health-related issues. For example, several organizations, such as the California Department of Health Services, inform people about the health hazards associated with tobacco use.

## Should Potentially Harmful Products Be Promoted?

Finally, some critics of promotion, including consumer groups and government officials, suggest that certain products should not be promoted at all. Primary targets are products associated with violence and other possibly unhealthy activities, such as handguns, alcohol, and tobacco. Cigarette advertisements, for example, promote smoking, a behavior proven to be harmful and even deadly. Tobacco companies, which spend billions on promotion, have countered criticism of their advertising by pointing out that advertisements for red meat and coffee are not censured even though these products may also cause health problems. Those who defend such promotion assert that as long as it is legal to sell a product, promoting that product should be allowed.

## SUMMARY

Integrated marketing communications is the coordination of promotion and other marketing efforts to ensure maximum informational and persuasive impact on customers.

Communication is a sharing of meaning. The communication process involves several steps. First, the source translates meaning into code, a process known as coding or encoding. The source should employ signs or symbols familiar to the receiver or audience. The coded message is sent through a communications channel to the receiver or audience. The receiver or audience then decodes the message and usually supplies feedback to the source. When the decoded message differs from the encoded one, a condition called noise exists.

Promotion is communication to build and maintain relationships by informing and persuading one or more audiences. Although promotional objectives vary from one organization to another and within organizations over time, eight primary objectives underlie many promotional programs. Promotion aims to create awareness of a new product, a new brand, or an existing product; to stimulate primary and selective demand; to encourage product trial through the use of free samples, coupons, limited free-use offers, contests, and games; to identify prospects; to retain loyal customers; to facilitate reseller support; to combat competitive promotional efforts; and to reduce sales fluctuations.

The promotion mix for a product may include four major promotional methods: advertising, personal selling, public relations, and sales promotion. Advertising is paid nonpersonal communication about an organization and its products transmitted to a target audience through a mass medium. Personal selling is paid personal communication that attempts to inform customers and persuade them to purchase products in an exchange situation. Public relations is a broad set of communication efforts used to create and maintain favorable relationships between an organization and its stakeholders. Sales promotion is an activity or material that acts as a direct inducement, offering added value or incentive for the product, to resellers, salespeople, or consumers.

The promotional methods used in a product's promotion mix are determined by the organization's promotional resources, objectives, and policies; characteristics of the target market; characteristics of the product; and cost and availability of promotional methods. Marketers also consider whether to use a push policy or a pull policy. With a push policy, the producer promotes the product only to the next institution down the marketing channel. Normally, a push policy stresses personal selling. Firms that use a pull policy promote directly to consumers, with the intention of developing strong consumer demand for the products. Once consumers are persuaded to seek the products in retail stores, retailers go to wholesalers or the producer to buy the products.

Most customers are likely to be influenced by friends and family members when making purchases. Word-of-mouth communication is personal, informal exchanges of communication that customers share with one another about products, brands, and companies. Customers may also choose to go online to find electronic word of mouth about products or companies. Buzz marketing is an attempt to gain acceptance of a product through word-of-mouth communications. Viral marketing is a strategy to get Internet users to share ads and promotions with their friends.

Promotional activities can help consumers make informed purchasing decisions, but they have also evoked many criticisms. Promotion has been accused of deception. Although some deceiving or misleading promotions do exist, laws, government regulation, and industry self-regulation minimize deceptive promotion. Promotion has been blamed for increasing prices, but it usually tends to lower them. When demand is high, production and marketing costs decrease, which can result in lower prices. Moreover, promotion helps keep prices lower by facilitating price competition. Other criticisms of promotional activity are that it manipulates consumers into buying products they do not need, that it leads to a more materialistic society, and that consumers do not benefit sufficiently from promotional activity to justify its high cost. Finally, some critics of promotion suggest that potentially harmful products, especially those associated with violence, sex, and unhealthy activities, should not be promoted at all.

**ACE self-test**

Please visit the student website at **www.prideferrell.com** for ACE Self-Test questions that will help you prepare for exams.

## IMPORTANT TERMS

| | | | |
|---|---|---|---|
| Integrated marketing communications | Decoding process | Selective demand | Word-of-mouth communication |
| Communication | Noise | Promotion mix | Buzz marketing |
| Source | Feedback | Kinesic communication | Viral marketing |
| Receiver | Channel capacity | Proxemic communication | |
| Coding process | Promotion | Tactile communication | |
| Communications channel | Primary demand | Push policy | |
| | Pioneer promotion | Pull policy | |

## DISCUSSION & REVIEW QUESTIONS

1. What does the term *integrated marketing communications* mean?

2. Define *communication* and describe the communication process. Is it possible to communicate without using all the elements in the communication process? If so, which elements can be omitted?

3. Identify several causes of noise. How can a source reduce noise?

4. What is the major task of promotion? Do firms ever use promotion to accomplish this task and fail? If so, give several examples.

5. Describe the possible objectives of promotion and discuss the circumstances under which each objective might be used.

6. Identify and briefly describe the four promotional methods an organization can use in its promotion mix.

7. What forms of interpersonal communication besides language can be used in personal selling?

8. How do target market characteristics determine which promotional methods to include in a promotion mix? Assume a company is planning to promote a cereal to both adults and children. Along what major dimensions would these two promotional efforts have to differ from each other?

9. How can a product's characteristics affect the composition of its promotion mix?

10. Evaluate the following statement: "Appropriate advertising media are always available if a company can afford them."

11. Explain the difference between a pull policy and a push policy. Under what conditions should each policy be used?

12. In which ways can word-of-mouth communication impact the effectiveness of a promotion mix for a product?

13. Which criticisms of promotion do you believe are the most valid? Why?

14. Should organizations be allowed to promote offensive, violent, sexual, or unhealthy products that can be legally sold and purchased? Support your answer.

## APPLICATION QUESTIONS

1. The overall objective of promotion is to stimulate demand for a product. Through television advertising, the American Dairy Association promotes the benefits of drinking milk, a campaign that aims to stimulate primary demand. Advertisements for a specific brand of milk focus on stimulating selective demand. Identify two television commercials, one aimed at stimulating primary demand and one aimed at stimulating selective demand. Describe each commercial and discuss how each attempts to achieve its objective.

2. Developing a promotion mix is contingent on many factors, including the type of product and the product's attributes. Which of the four promotional methods—advertising, personal selling, public relations, or sales promotion—would you emphasize if you were developing the promotion mix for the following products? Explain your answers.

   a. Washing machine
   b. Cereal
   c. Halloween candy
   d. Compact disc

3. Suppose marketers at Falcon International Corporation have come to you for recommendations on how to promote their products. They want to develop a comprehensive promotional campaign and have a generous budget with which to implement their plans. What questions would you ask them, and what would you suggest they consider before developing a promotional program?

4. Marketers must consider whether to use a push or a pull policy when deciding on a promotion mix (see Figure 18.4). Identify a product for which marketers should use each policy and a third product that might best be promoted using a mix of the two policies. Explain your answers.

**globalEDGE™**

1. Personalized marketing messages are important to appeal to the particular needs of individual customers. Due to the rapid globalization of your firm, you must determine which markets are more accepting of personalized messages to maximize the effect of your marketing campaign. Use the search term "Hofstede scores" at **http://globaledge.msu.edu/ibrd** to reach the Geert Hofstede Resource Center. Go to the link for Hofstede Scores, and then you can highlight all the scores and download them into a spreadsheet for analysis. Using Hofstede's scores, what are the top ten countries on this scale? Does this simplify or complicate the development of your firm's personalized marketing strategy?

2. The readiness of a global market's infrastructure is important for any integrated marketing campaign to communicate a similar message across different media (e.g., newspaper, magazine, radio, television, Internet) in an effective manner. One report that may be useful here is the Global Information Technology Report, which can be accessed by using the search term "global information technology" at **http://globaledge.msu.edu/ibrd**. Once there, find the most recent report. What are the ten markets with the most equipped infrastructures? Are there any surprises among the markets listed? What regions are represented in your report?

## INTERNET Exercise

Visit **www.prideferrell.com** for resources to help you master the material in this chapter, plus materials that will help you expand your marketing knowledge, including Internet exercise updates, ACE Self-Tests, hotlinks to companies featured in this chapter, and much more.

### MySpace Is the Music Place

MySpace isn't just for friends. It's also a unique promotional platform for musical artists, especially unsigned and independent artists. By creating a MySpace page, musicians can share their songs, post important dates, or even blog. MySpace music pages are different from record company websites because they feel more personal. Artists also take advantage of MySpace's viral nature by allowing other MySpace members to post their pictures, songs, and music videos on their own MySpace profile pages. Visit the website at **http://music.myspace.com** and look for your favorite artist or explore a new one.

1. Who is the target market for members?
2. What is being promoted to these individuals?
3. What are the promotional objectives of this website?
4. Is word-of-mouth communication occurring at this website? Explain.

## Video Case 18.1    Promoting "The Ultimate Driving Machine"

Careful targeting, consistent positioning, and a good match between message and media have all helped Bayerische Motoren Werke (better known as BMW) accelerate sales revenue on a relatively small advertising budget. The company, based in Munich, Germany, markets such well-known global brands as BMW, Mini, and Rolls-Royce, as well as BMW Motorcycles. Although other multibrand automobile manufacturers offer a range of vehicles for mass-market and upscale segments, BMW has followed a different route to profitability. The automaker focuses exclusively on high-end vehicles, targeting drivers who are affluent, successful, demanding of themselves and their cars, and interested in the time-saving convenience of automotive technology.

BMW uses television and magazine advertising to reinforce its brand image and to give the target audience a feeling for what the company calls "The Ultimate Driving Machine." Because its advertising budget is not as large as its competitors', BMW looks for ways to stand out in the crowd. For example, it likes to air television commercials supported by bursts of newspaper advertising; more than once it has signed on as the lone sponsor of television programs favored by its tar-

get audience. "TV advertising plays a vital role for us in building brand awareness, image, and desirability among members of the general public," notes a BMW marketing executive. "Without that type of broad appeal, a brand such as BMW would have less desirability within its target consumer groups."

The aim of every commercial is to help viewers picture themselves on the open road behind the wheel of a BMW; the car, not the driver or the scenery, is the star of the advertisement. The camera lingers on the vehicle's sleek lines, comfortable interior, high-tech features, and the familiar blue-and-white brand symbol. While the vehicle and the scenery may change from commercial to commercial, the ultimate objective is to motivate consumers to test-drive a BMW.

Movies have played a key role in BMW's promotions. The company has garnered huge waves of publicity from having the Mini featured in *The Italian Job* and arranging for James Bond to drive new BMWs. To reach Internet-savvy car buyers, BMW also hired top directors to make short films especially for Web view-

ing. Although the films ran online for only four years, they were viewed more than 100 million times, won numerous awards, and were later issued on DVD for free distribution to prospective buyers.

BMW's sales promotion efforts also include samples—in the form of extended test drives—as well as participation in major automotive trade shows. Eye-catching point-of-purchase displays in dealer showrooms support the overall integrated marketing communications effort by echoing selected images from the company's advertising. Price promotions are rare, although the company held its first end-of-year clearance sale on select U.S. models not long ago. The company has also offered special leasing deals to spark sales of its X3 model.

After a long stretch as head of marketing for BMW of North America, Jim McDowell switched jobs with Jack Pitney, who directed marketing for the company's Mini brand. Pitney has begun infusing BMW's marketing with some of the Mini's most successful promotional ideas. He plans to retain "The Ultimate Driving Machine" slogan for BMW's marketing communications because it resonates with the target audience and differentiates the brand from other premium competitors. BMW's worldwide positioning will not change, but with the launch of new models every year, the company will continue refining the promotion mix to attract new buyers, maintain brand image, and keep profits high.[49]

### Questions for Discussion

1. Evaluate BMW's use of movies in its integrated marketing communications program.
2. What types of objectives is BMW attempting to achieve through its television commercials?
3. How do BMW's extended test drives facilitate the personal selling efforts when customers visit a BMW dealership?

---

## Case 18.2    One Tough Mother at Columbia Sportswear

Eighty-one-year-old Gert Boyle is "one tough mother." Not only is she the chair of the board for Columbia Sportswear, she's also their spokeswoman. Gert assumed control of Columbia Sportswear 35 years ago after her husband Neil passed away from a sudden heart attack. Gert reported for duty a mere four days after Neil's death to take the reins of the growing company—a company that has flourished under her tough leadership.

Founded by Neil Boyle in 1938, Columbia Sportswear Company is a global leader in the design, sourcing, marketing, and distribution of active outdoor apparel and footwear. The $1.1 billion company employs more than 1,800 people and distributes and sells products in more than 70 countries to more than 12,000 retailers internationally. As one of the largest outerwear brands in the world and the leading seller of skiwear in the United States, the company has developed an international reputation for quality, performance, functionality, and value.

Columbia Sportswear has worked hard over the years to develop its image of offering high-quality products. It promotes itself and its products through event sponsorships, print and television advertising, and a strong public relations program. It is actively involved in event marketing. For example, the company signed up to be the official apparel sponsor of Jeep's "King of the Mountain" series, proclaimed as the richest and most prestigious professional snow racing series in the world. Columbia Sportswear will outfit the event staff and volunteers, as well as VIPs attending the event. Other sponsorships include events such as the Mt. Baker Banked Slalom snowboarding competition, which draws world-class snow boarders; the annual World Superpipe Championships; and the Ski Mountaineering Competition in Korea.

The company has used many approaches to promote the quality of its products. Their greatest success however, is a campaign featuring Gert and her son, Tim Boyle. This positioning is an outgrowth of the relationship that has existed between Gert and Tim since they began running the company together. According to people who know them, Tim and his mother have argued from the beginning about how to run Columbia Sportswear. A director of the company says, "Tim and Gert are a lot like the Jack Lemmon and Walter Matthau characters in *The Odd Couple*. They complain all the time, and yet they cherish each other."

Over 20 years ago, Borders, Perrin & Norrander, the company's advertising agency, came up with an idea to use the well-known relationship between Gert and her son to develop an identity for the company—an identity beyond technical claims about product quality. They developed an ad campaign that portrays Gert as "one tough mother" who uses her son to demonstrate that Columbia Sportswear clothes will protect whoever wears them under any weather conditions. In the many spots, Gert appears as a hard-driving mother who refuses to accept anything but the highest quality of products, both for her son and her company. The ads were so successful at positioning and promoting Columbia Sportswear's products, that Gert and Tim are now the company's ad staples.

Showing Gert put her son through a series of catastrophic tests to demonstrate the durability of the company's products doesn't just communicate product quality; it also establishes an identity in the customers' minds. In one commercial, Gert drives an SUV with Tim strapped on top through a series of severe weather situations to show that his clothing is protecting him. The ending scene is a close-up of the jacket he is wearing with the tagline "Tested Tough." This theme is continued throughout a series of commercials that depict Tim in a number of cold weather survival situations, such as being dropped on the top of a snow covered mountain by a helicopter piloted by Gert, being under the ice in a hockey arena (staying alive with a breathing tube), and being covered by snow with Gert driving the snow plow. In all cases, Tim is unharmed and Gert is unconcerned—all because he is wearing Columbia outerwear.

Columbia Sportswear's signature spot shows Gert in a biker bar. The audio track says: "In a world of rugged individuals only one is the toughest mother of them all. Mother Gert Boyle—maker of tough mother jeans." There is a close-up of Gert with a tattoo on her bicep that reads "Born to Nag" and the spot ends with a product shot of Columbia jeans. These irreverent and memorable ads appear to be working. Since their inception, Columbia Sportswear has carved out a 50 percent market share in its category. Now that's one tough mother![50]

## Questions for Discussion

1. Identify the key objectives of Columbia Sportswear's promotion program. Are the objectives the same or different for its advertising and for its event sponsorships?
2. Does Columbia Sportswear use integrated marketing communications? What suggestions, if any, would you make to strengthen the coordination of Columbia's promotion activities?
3. Describe the characteristics of Columbia's target market. Are they the same for advertising and event sponsorships? Explain.

## CHAPTER 19

# Advertising and Public Relations

## Aflac Hatches a (Q)Wacky Campaign

Before a duck touted its products, only 12 percent of the people in the United States had ever heard of Aflac—the American Family Life Assurance Company. Today, 90 percent of U.S. consumers know the 49-year-old Fortune 500 multi-billion-dollar insurance company. Since the Aflac duck made its first TV appearance four years ago, Aflac's sales have increased by 20 percent. Today, the company insures more than 40 million people worldwide, and the Aflac duck's "Aflac" quack has become part of the American vernacular.

Creating a brand icon often takes years and can require a massive ad budget. Aflac spends $45 million on commercial time annually. While not an insignificant sum, it is substantially lower than what McDonald's spends promoting Ronald McDonald, who has a lower Q score than the Aflac duck. A Q score is a survey measurement that marketers use to rate a character's familiarity and appeal. Energizer Batteries has spent approximately $1 billion on its veteran Energizer Bunny over the past 15 years. The Bunny also has a lower Q score than the Aflac duck.

The overwhelming success of Aflac's advertising campaign is surprising. It is not often that a humorous brand icon is used to represent a serious business like life and health insurance. Beyond the sheer creativity of the icon, the duck's success can be attributed to the company's guerrilla public relations campaign. Aflac's PR department is always on the lookout for opportunities to get free publicity for their web-footed friend. The Aflac duck has been featured on CNBC, *The Tonight Show with Jay Leno*, *Saturday Night Live*, and *Live with Regis and Kelly*. Aflac's publicity team has conducted two "Quack Attacks" on NBC's *Today Show*: Groups of 15 Aflac executives carry large plush duck toys on the show's outdoor set.

Recently, the Aflac duck was enshrined on Madison Avenue's Walk of Fame, an honor that identifies the beloved corporate mascot as one of America's favorite advertising icons. What did the duck say when he heard about this tribute? What else? *"Aflac!"*[1] ■

## OBJECTIVES

1. To describe the nature and types of advertising

2. To explore the major steps in developing an advertising campaign

3. To identify who is responsible for developing advertising campaigns

4. To examine the tools used in public relations

5. To analyze how public relations is used and evaluated

L arge organizations such as Aflac, as well as smaller companies, use conventional and online promotional efforts such as advertising to change their corporate images, launch new products, or promote current brands. In this chapter, we explore several dimensions of advertising and public relations. First, we focus on the nature and types of advertising. Next, we examine the major steps in developing an advertising campaign and describe who is responsible for developing such campaigns. We then discuss the nature of public relations and how it is used. We examine various public relations tools and ways to evaluate the effectiveness of public relations. Finally, we focus on how companies deal with unfavorable public relations.

# The Nature and Types of Advertising

Advertising permeates our daily lives. At times, we view it positively; at other times, we avoid it. Some advertising informs, persuades, or entertains us; some bores, annoys, or even offends us.

**advertising** Paid nonpersonal communication about an organization and its products transmitted to a target audience through mass media

As mentioned in Chapter 18, **advertising** is a paid form of nonpersonal communication transmitted through mass media, such as television, radio, the Internet, newspapers, magazines, direct mail, outdoor displays, and signs on mass transit vehicles. In Boston, for example, some taxicabs sport a cup of Starbucks coffee magnetically attached to their roofs.[2] Organizations use advertising to reach a variety of audiences ranging from small, specific groups, such as stamp collectors in Idaho, to extremely large groups, such as all athletic-shoe purchasers in the United States.

When asked to name major advertisers, most people immediately mention business organizations. However, many nonbusiness types of organizations, including governments, churches, universities, and charitable organizations, employ advertising to communicate with stakeholders. For example, the United Kingdom's government spends more than $350 million a year on advertising to advise, influence, or gently chastise its citizens.[3] In 2004, the U.S. government was the twenty-fifth largest advertiser in the country, spending approximately $1.2 billion on advertising.[4] Although we analyze advertising in the context of business organizations here, much of the material applies to all types of organizations. For example, the Mexican Tourism Board developed an advertising campaign tagged "Closer Than Ever" to encourage Americans and Canadians to continue spending their leisure time and money in Mexico. Tourism is Mexico's third-largest source of foreign currency, and visitors from the United States account for 90 percent of international tourists to Mexico.[5]

**institutional advertising** Advertising that promotes organizational images, ideas, and political issues

**advocacy advertising** Advertising that promotes a company's position on a public issue

**product advertising** Advertising that promotes the uses, features, and benefits of products

**pioneer advertising** Advertising that tries to stimulate demand for a product category rather than a specific brand by informing potential buyers about the product

Advertising is used to promote goods, services, ideas, images, issues, people, and anything else advertisers want to publicize or foster. Depending on what is being promoted, advertising can be classified as institutional or product advertising. **Institutional advertising** promotes organizational images, ideas, and political issues. It can be used to create or maintain an organizational image. Institutional advertisements may deal with broad image issues, such as organizational strength or the friendliness of employees. They may also aim to create a more favorable view of the organization in the eyes of noncustomer groups such as shareholders, consumer advocacy groups, potential stockholders, or the general public. When a company promotes its position on a public issue—for instance, a tax increase, abortion, gun control, or international trade coalitions—institutional advertising is referred to as **advocacy advertising**. Institutional advertising may be used to promote socially approved behavior such as recycling and moderation in consuming alcoholic beverages. Philip Morris, for example, has run television advertisements encouraging parents to talk to their children about not smoking. Research has identified a number of themes that advertisers can use to increase the effectiveness of antismoking messages for adolescents.[6] This type of advertising not only has societal benefits but also helps build an organization's image.

**Product advertising** promotes the uses, features, and benefits of products. There are two types of product advertising: pioneer and competitive. **Pioneer advertising** focuses on stimulating demand for a product category (rather than a specific brand)

**competitive advertising** Advertising that points out a brand's special features, uses, and advantages relative to competing brands

**comparative advertising** Advertising that compares two or more brands on the basis of one or more product characteristics

**reminder advertising** Advertising used to remind consumers about an established brand's uses, characteristics, and benefits

**reinforcement advertising** Advertising that assures users they chose the right brand and tells them how to get the most satisfaction from it

by informing potential customers about the product's features, uses, and benefits. This type of advertising is employed when the product is in the introductory stage of the product life cycle. **Competitive advertising** attempts to stimulate demand for a specific brand by promoting the brand's features, uses, and advantages, sometimes through indirect or direct comparisons with competing brands. Advertising effects on sales must reflect competitors' advertising activities. The type of competitive environment will determine the most effective industry approach.

To make direct product comparisons, marketers use a form of competitive advertising called **comparative advertising**, which compares the sponsored brand with one or more identified competing brands on the basis of one or more product characteristics. Miller Brewing, for example, ran advertisements comparing Miller Lite's 96 calories and 3.2 grams of carbohydrates to the 110 calories and 6.6 grams of carbohydrates in Bud Light, owned by Anheuser-Busch.[7] Often the brands promoted through comparative advertisements have low market shares and are compared with competitors that have the highest market shares in the product category. Product categories that commonly use comparative advertising include soft drinks, toothpaste, pain relievers, foods, tires, automobiles, and detergents. Under the provisions of the 1988 Trademark Law Revision Act, marketers using comparative advertisements in the United States must not misrepresent the qualities or characteristics of competing products. Other countries may have laws that are stricter or less strict with regard to comparative advertising.

Other forms of competitive advertising include reminder and reinforcement advertising. **Reminder advertising** tells customers that an established brand is still around and still offers certain characteristics, uses, and advantages. **Reinforcement advertising** assures current users they have made the right brand choice and tells them how to get the most satisfaction from that brand.

# Developing an Advertising Campaign

**advertising campaign** The creation and execution of a series of advertisements to communicate with a particular target audience

An **advertising campaign** involves designing a series of advertisements and placing them in various advertising media to reach a particular target audience. As Figure 19.1 indicates, the major steps in creating an advertising campaign are (1) identifying and

**figure 19.1**

## GENERAL STEPS IN DEVELOPING AND IMPLEMENTING AN ADVERTISING CAMPAIGN

8 Evaluate advertising effectiveness
7 Execute campaign
6 Create advertising message
5 Develop media plan
4 Determine advertising appropriation
3 Create advertising platform
2 Define advertising objectives
1 Identify and analyze target audience

STUDYING ROCKET SCIENCE IS MORE FUN WHEN YOU ACTUALLY HAVE ROCKETS.

There's only one place you can get hands-on training with the most advanced technology in the world and that's the U.S. Navy. If you're up to the challenge, log on the Life Accelerator at navy.com or call 1.800.USA.NAVY.

© 2004. Paid for by the U.S. Navy. All rights reserved.

NAVY
accelerateyourlife

**Target Audience**
This advertisement for the Navy is aimed at individuals who are in the 18 to 24 age category.

analyzing the target audience, (2) defining the advertising objectives, (3) creating the advertising platform, (4) determining the advertising appropriation, (5) developing the media plan, (6) creating the advertising message, (7) executing the campaign, and (8) evaluating advertising effectiveness. The number of steps and the exact order in which they are carried out may vary according to the organization's resources, the nature of its product, and the type of target audience to be reached. Nevertheless, these general guidelines for developing an advertising campaign are appropriate for all types of organizations.

### Identifying and Analyzing the Target Audience

The **target audience** is the group of people at whom advertisements are aimed. Advertisements for Barbie cereal are targeted toward young girls who play with Barbie dolls, whereas those for Special K cereal are directed at health-conscious adults. Identifying and analyzing the target audience are critical processes; the information yielded helps determine other steps in developing the campaign. The target audience may include everyone

**target audience** The group of people at whom advertisements are aimed

in the firm's target market. Marketers may, however, direct a campaign at only a portion of the target market. For example, Nissan, after recognizing that 10 to 12 percent of its buyers are Hispanic, expanded its advertising program to Spanish-language TV. The Japanese automaker ran its first Spanish ad for the Quest minivan after learning that one in two southwestern buyers of the van is Latino.[8]

Advertisers research and analyze advertising targets to establish an information base for a campaign. Information commonly needed includes location and geographic distribution of the target group; the distribution of demographic factors, such as age, income, race, gender, and education; lifestyle information; and consumer attitudes regarding purchase and use of both the advertiser's products and competing products. The exact kinds of information an organization finds useful depend on the type of product being advertised, the characteristics of the target audience, and the type and amount of competition. Generally, the more an advertiser knows about the target audience, the more likely the firm is to develop an effective advertising campaign. When the advertising target is not precisely identified and properly analyzed, the campaign may fail, as illustrated in the boxed feature.

### Defining the Advertising Objectives

The advertiser's next step is to determine what the firm hopes to accomplish with the campaign. Because advertising objectives guide campaign development, advertisers should define objectives carefully. Advertising objectives should be stated clearly, precisely, and in measurable terms. Precision and measurability allow advertisers to evaluate advertising success at the end of the campaign in terms of whether objectives have been met. To provide precision and measurability, advertising objectives should contain benchmarks and indicate how far the advertiser wishes to move from these standards. If the goal is to increase sales, the advertiser should state the current sales level (the benchmark) and the amount of sales increase sought through advertising. An advertising objective should also specify a time frame so that advertisers know exactly how long they have to accomplish the objective. An advertiser with average monthly sales of $450,000 (the benchmark) might set the following objective: "Our primary advertising objective is to increase average monthly sales from $450,000 to $540,000 within 12 months."

If an advertiser defines objectives on the basis of sales, the objectives focus on increasing absolute dollar sales or unit sales, increasing sales by a certain percentage, or increasing the firm's market share. Even though an advertiser's long-run goal is to increase sales, not all campaigns are designed to produce immediate sales. Some campaigns aim to increase product or brand awareness, make consumers' attitudes more favorable, or heighten consumers' knowledge of product features. If the goal is to increase product awareness, the objectives are stated in terms of communication. A specific communication objective might be to increase product feature awareness from 0 to 40 percent in the target audience by the end of six months. For example, Curves, a women-only fitness center chain, set an objective of 120,000 phone calls to its toll-free line after it launched its first national advertising campaign. The response was actually twice the stated goal in the campaign's first nine months.[9]

# Risky Business: Using Celebrity Endorsers

Using celebrities to endorse products is not without potential pitfalls. First, managers overawed by star power may be all too willing to sign deals, even when research suggests that a celebrity is not a good match for a particular product or target market. Celebrities are their own brands, and marketers must remain aware of the preexisting image the celebrity represents. (Estée Lauder kept this is mind when hiring Gwyneth Paltrow to attract a younger market for its Pleasures perfume.) A megastar celebrity can easily overshadow the brand, and ads that feature him or her can end up serving as more of an advertisement for the celebrity than for the product.

The company's products could even become discredited. Consider, for example, that Nike signed Tiger Woods to a five-year $100 million deal to use its Nike Tour Accuracy golf ball. But when his tournament performance lagged, Tiger ditched Nike for a competitor's ball.

Another danger is the possibility that a spokesperson will engage in scandalous behavior, as in the case of supermodel Kate Moss, who publicly admitted to using cocaine after a London paper published incriminating pictures of her that were taken by a camera phone. The scandal cost Moss over $9 million in endorsements, as she was dropped as the spokesmodel for Chanel's Coco Mademoiselle perfume, British clothing giant Hennes & Mauritz (H&M), designer clothier Burberry, and New York jeweler H. Stern. H&M released a statement announcing the cancellation of a planned advertising campaign by arguing that Moss's confessed behavior was inconsistent with the retailer's position against the use of illegal drugs. The scandal also cost Gloria Vanderbilt, which had just spent a large portion of its advertising budget photographing Moss for a new campaign that was cancelled.

Other problems may arise if celebrities are linked with too many products and become overexposed; marketers may want to be cautious when considering a celebrity who is already endorsing another product. Celebrity endorsements can also be significantly more expensive, often with lackluster results. The Gap spent $38 million to have fashion icon and *Sex and the City* star Sarah Jessica Parker appear in commercial, print, and outdoor ads. When sales plummeted, the campaign was deemed a failure, and The Gap dropped Parker. Despite all these risks, however, ad campaigns featuring celebrities are still common, and often boost a company's sales.

## Creating the Advertising Platform

Before launching a political campaign, party leaders develop a political platform stating major issues that are the basis of the campaign. Like a political platform, an **advertising platform** consists of the basic issues or selling points that an advertiser wishes to include in the advertising campaign. New Balance, for example, launched a campaign that mocks professional athletes while reminding its 25- to 49-year-old target market about the joys of competing for fun and the love of sports.[10] A single advertisement in an advertising campaign may contain one or several issues from the platform. Although the platform sets forth the basic issues, it does not indicate how to present them.

An advertising platform should consist of issues important to customers. One of the best ways to determine those issues is to survey customers about what they consider most important in the selection and use of the product involved. Selling features must not only be important to customers, they should also be strongly competitive features of the advertised brand. For example, New Balance's "Love or Money" campaign stemmed in part from Internet research that found that many people have become disturbed by the behavior of well-known professional athletes, some of whom receive millions of dollars a year in endorsements from New Balance's competitors.[11]

Although research is the most effective method for determining what issues to include in an advertising platform, it is expensive. Therefore, an advertising platform is most commonly based on opinions of personnel within the firm and of individuals in the advertising agency, if an agency is used. This trial-and-error approach generally leads to some successes and some failures.

**advertising platform** Basic issues or selling points to be included in an advertising campaign

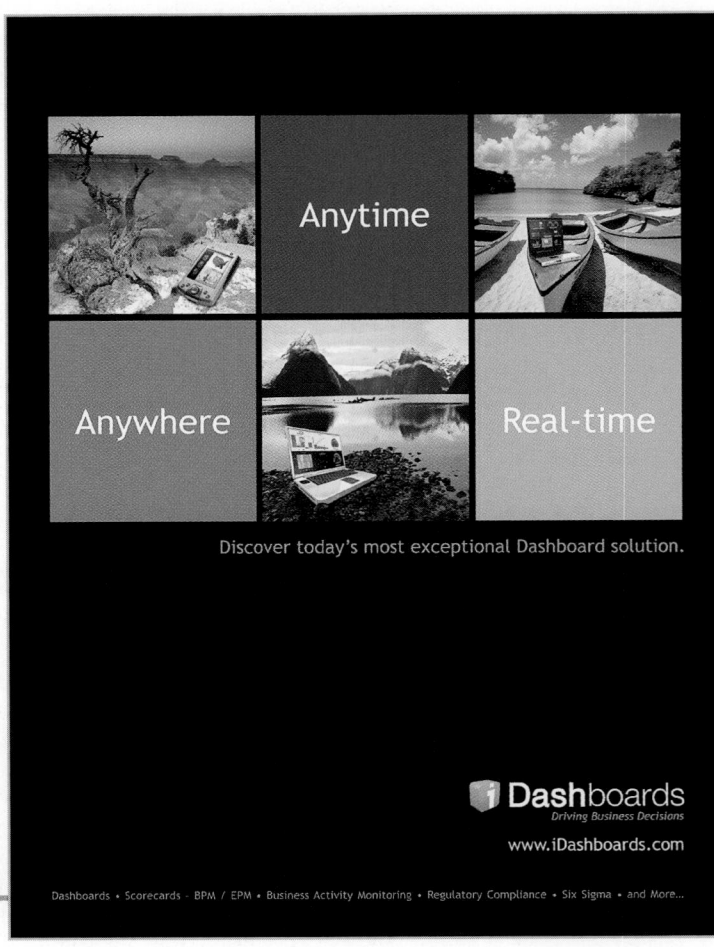

**Advertising Platform**

An advertising platform normally contains multiple issues. An ad can focus on one platform issue or on multiple issues, as shown in this iDashboards advertisement.

Because the advertising platform is a base on which to build the advertising message, marketers should analyze this stage carefully. A campaign can be perfect in terms of selection and analysis of its target audience, statement of its objectives, media strategy, and the form of its message. But the campaign will ultimately fail if the advertisements communicate information that consumers do not deem important when selecting and using the product.

### Determining the Advertising Appropriation

**advertising appropriation** The advertising budget for a specific time period

The **advertising appropriation** is the total amount of money a marketer allocates for advertising for a specific time period. New Balance, for example, planned to spend $21 million on its "Love or Money" campaign.[12] It is difficult to determine how much to spend on advertising for a specific period because the potential effects of advertising are so difficult to measure precisely.

**objective-and-task approach** Budgeting for an advertising campaign by first determining its objectives and then calculating the cost of all the tasks needed to attain them

Many factors affect a firm's decision about how much to appropriate for advertising. Geographic size of the market and the distribution of buyers within the market have a great bearing on this decision. As Table 19.1 (on p. 526) shows, both the type of product advertised and the firm's sales volume relative to competitors' sales volumes also play parts in determining what proportion of revenue to spend on advertising. Advertising appropriations for business products are usually quite small relative to product sales, whereas consumer convenience items, such as soft drinks, soaps, and cosmetics, generally have large advertising expenditures relative to sales.

**percent-of-sales approach** Budgeting for an advertising campaign by multiplying the firm's past and expected sales by a standard percentage

Of the many techniques used to determine the advertising appropriation, one of the most logical is the **objective-and-task approach**. Using this approach, marketers determine the objectives a campaign is to achieve and then attempt to list the tasks required to accomplish them. The costs of the tasks are calculated and added to arrive at the total appropriation. This approach has one main problem: marketers sometimes have trouble accurately estimating the level of effort needed to attain certain objectives. A coffee marketer, for example, may find it extremely difficult to determine how much of an increase in national television advertising is needed to raise a brand's market share from 8 to 10 percent.

**competition-matching approach** Determining an advertising budget by trying to match competitors' advertising outlays

In the more widely used **percent-of-sales approach**, marketers simply multiply the firm's past sales, plus a factor for planned sales growth or decline, by a standard percentage based on both what the firm traditionally spends on advertising and the industry average. This approach, too, has a major flaw: it is based on the incorrect assumption that sales create advertising rather than the reverse. A marketer using this approach during declining sales will reduce the amount spent on advertising, but such a reduction may further diminish sales. Though illogical, this technique has been favored because it is easy to use.

Another way to determine advertising appropriation is the **competition-matching approach**. Marketers following this approach try to match their major competitors' appropriations in absolute dollars or to allocate the same percentage of sales for advertising that their competitors do. Although a marketer should be aware of what competitors spend on advertising, this technique should not be used alone because the firm's competitors probably have different advertising objectives and different resources available for advertising. Many companies and advertising agencies review competitive spending on a quarterly basis, comparing competitors' dollar expenditures on print, radio, and television with their own spending levels. Competitive tracking of this nature occurs at both the national and regional levels.

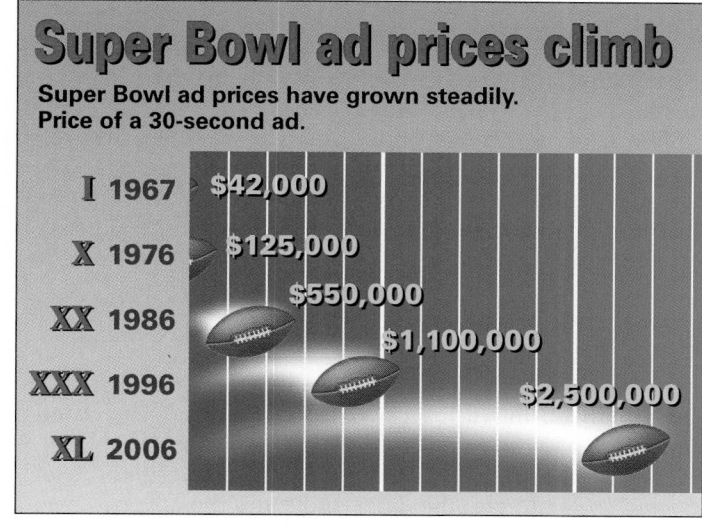

## Super Bowl ad prices climb

**Super Bowl ad prices have grown steadily.
Price of a 30-second ad.**

I 1967   $42,000
X 1976   $125,000
XX 1986   $550,000
XXX 1996   $1,100,000
XL 2006   $2,500,000

*Source:* Brooks Barnes, "Super Bowl Draws 6% More Viewers Than Last Year," *The Wall Street Journal*, Feb. 7, 2006, p. B10; "Super Bowl Statistics," *Advertising Age*, www.adage.com/page.cms?pageId=684 (accessed Feb. 7, 2006); CBS News, Feb. 7, 2005, www.cbsnews.com/stories2005/02/07/earlyshow/main672016.shtml.

| table 19.1 | TWENTY LEADING NATIONAL ADVERTISERS | | |
|---|---|---|---|
| Organization | Advertising Expenditures ($ millions) | U.S. Sales ($ millions) | Advertising Expenditures as % of Sales |
| 1. General Motors | 3,997 | 134,380 | 3.0 |
| 2. Procter & Gamble | 3,920 | 23,688 | 16.5 |
| 3. Time Warner | 3,283 | 33,572 | 9.8 |
| 4. Pfizer | 2,957 | 29,539 | 10.0 |
| 5. SBC Communications | 2,687 | 40,787 | 6.6 |
| 6. DaimlerChrysler | 2,462 | 80,224 | 3.1 |
| 7. Ford Motor | 2,458 | 100,208 | 2.5 |
| 8. Walt Disney | 2,242 | 24,012 | 9.3 |
| 9. Verizon | 2,197 | 69,269 | 3.2 |
| 10. Johnson & Johnson | 2,176 | 27,770 | 7.8 |
| 11. GlaxoSmithKline | 1,828 | 17,513 | 10.4 |
| 12. Sears Holding | 1,823 | 31,230 | 5.8 |
| 13. Toyota Motor | 1,821 | 55,007 | 3.3 |
| 14. General Electric | 1,819 | 90,954 | 2.0 |
| 15. Sony | 1,665 | 19,741 | 8.4 |
| 16. Nissan Motor | 1,540 | 34,709 | 4.4 |
| 17. Altria Group | 1,399 | 39,966 | 3.5 |
| 18. McDonald's | 1,389 | 24,390 | 5.7 |
| 19. L'Oreal | 1,341 | 4,711 | 28.5 |
| 20. Unilever | 1,319 | 11,231 | 11.7 |

**Source:** *Advertising Age,* June 27, 2005, pp. S-2, S-3, S-18.

**arbitrary approach** Budgeting for an advertising campaign as specified by a high-level executive in the firm

At times marketers use the **arbitrary approach**, which usually means a high-level executive in the firm states how much to spend on advertising for a certain period. The arbitrary approach often leads to underspending or overspending. Although hardly a scientific budgeting technique, it is expedient.

Deciding how large the advertising appropriation should be is critical. If the appropriation is set too low, the campaign cannot achieve its full potential. When too much money is appropriated, overspending results and financial resources are wasted.

### Developing the Media Plan

**media plan** A plan that specifies the media vehicles to be used and the schedule for running advertisements

As Figure 19.2 shows, advertisers spend tremendous amounts on advertising media. These amounts have grown rapidly during the past two decades. To derive maximum results from media expenditures, marketers must develop effective media plans. A **media plan** sets forth the exact media vehicles to be used (specific magazines, television stations, newspapers, and so forth) and the dates and times the advertisements will appear. The plan determines how many people in the target audience will be exposed to the message. It also determines, to some degree, the effects of the message on those individuals. Media planning is a complex task requiring thorough analysis of the target audience. Sophisticated computer models have been developed to attempt to maximize the effectiveness of media plans.

**figure 19.2**

## PERCENTAGE OF ADVERTISING SPENDING BY MEDIA CATEGORY: 1985 VS. 2005

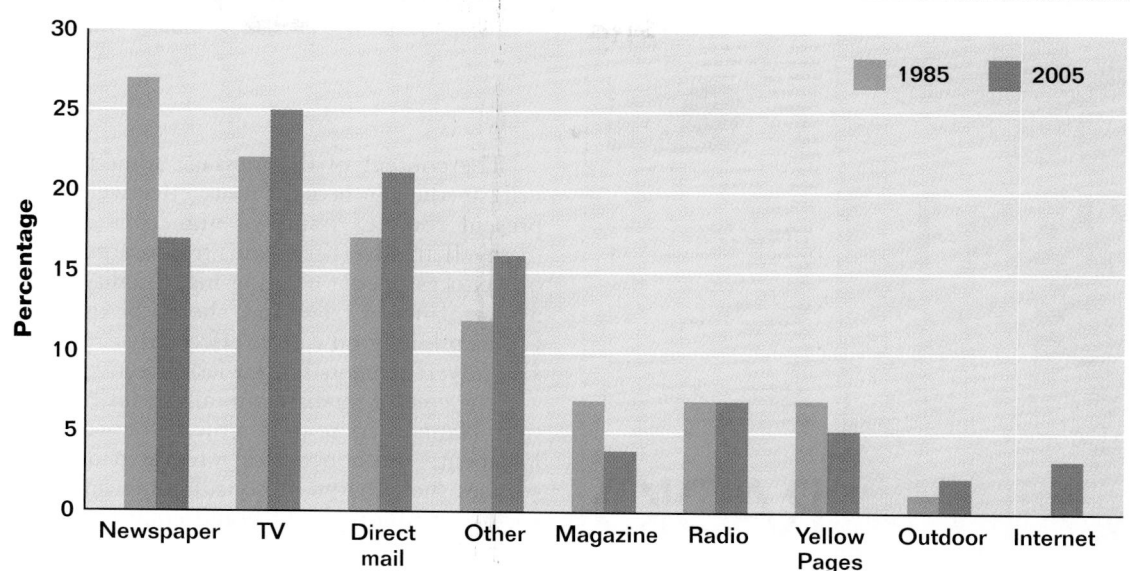

**Sources:** "Ad Spending Totals by Media," *Advertising Age,* June 27, 2005, p. S-21; Robert J. Coen, "Coen: Little Ad Growth," *Advertising Age,* May 6, 1991, pp. 1, 16.

To formulate a media plan, the planners select the media for the campaign and prepare a time schedule for each medium. The media planner's primary goal is to reach the largest number of people in the advertising target that the budget will allow. A secondary goal is to achieve the appropriate message reach and frequency for the target audience while staying within budget. *Reach* refers to the percentage of consumers in the target audience actually exposed to a particular advertisement in a stated period. *Frequency* is the number of times these targeted consumers are exposed to the advertisement.

Media planners begin with broad decisions but eventually make very specific ones. They first decide which kinds of media to use: radio, television, the Internet, newspapers, magazines, direct mail, outdoor displays, or signs on mass transit vehicles. Internet advertising in particular is growing, with companies spending $4 billion in 2004 to run ads alongside Internet searches in sites like Yahoo! and Google.[13] They assess different formats and approaches to determine which are most effective. Some media plans are highly focused and use just one medium. The media plans of manufacturers of consumer packaged goods can be quite complex and dynamic.

Media planners take many factors into account when devising a media plan. They analyze location and demographic characteristics of consumers in the target audience because people's tastes in media differ according to demographic groups and locations. There are radio stations especially for teenagers, magazines for men ages 18 to 34, and television cable channels aimed at women in various age groups. Media planners also consider the sizes and types of audiences that specific media reach. Anheuser-Busch, for example, cut back on network television advertising in favor of more cable television and Internet advertising in response to changing consumer media habits. In particular, men and women ages 21 to 34, a key segment for Anheuser-Busch, are spending more of their viewing time on cable networks.[14] Declining broadcast television ratings have led many companies to explore alternative media, including not only cable television and Internet advertising but also ads on cellphones and product placements in video games. Several data services collect and periodically provide information about circulations and audiences of various media.

### Media Selection

Media planners have many types of media options from which to choose. Qualitative factors are considered when making media choices, and databases provide quantitative profiles on specific media alternatives.

The content of the message sometimes affects media choice. Print media can be used more effectively than broadcast media to present complex issues or numerous details in single advertisements. If an advertiser wants to promote beautiful colors, patterns, or textures, media offering high-quality color reproduction, such as magazines or television, should be used instead of newspapers. For example, food can be effectively promoted in full-color magazine advertisements but far less effectively in black and white.

The cost of media is an important but troublesome consideration. Planners try to obtain the best coverage possible for each dollar spent. The concept of integrated marketing communications stresses the benefits of coordinating and building synergy across various media to build brand equity. Overspending is less likely with an integrated approach to multimedia advertising.[15] However, there is no accurate way to compare the cost and impact of a television commercial with the cost and impact of a newspaper advertisement. A **cost comparison indicator** lets an advertiser compare the costs of several vehicles within a specific medium (such as two mag-

**cost comparison indicator** A means of comparing the costs of advertising vehicles in a specific medium in relation to the number of people reached

azines) in relation to the number of people each vehicle reaches. The *cost per thousand (CPM)* is the cost comparison indicator for magazines; it shows the cost of exposing 1,000 people to a one-page advertisement.

Figure 19.2 shows the extent to which each medium is used and how it has changed since 1980. For example, the proportion of total advertising dollars spent on television has risen since 1980 and surpassed that spent on newspapers. The major media classes are shown in Table 19.2.

Like media selection decisions, media scheduling decisions are affected by numerous factors, such as target audience characteristics, product attributes, product seasonality, customer media behavior, and size of the advertising budget. There are three general types of media schedules: continuous, flighting, and pulsing. When a *continuous* schedule is used, advertising runs at a constant level with little variation throughout the campaign period. With a *flighting* schedule, advertisements run for set periods of time, alternating with periods in which no ads run. For example, an advertising campaign might have an ad run for two weeks, then suspend it for two weeks, and then run it again for two weeks. A *pulsing* schedule combines continuous and flighting schedules: during the entire campaign, a certain portion of advertising runs continuously, and during specific time periods of the campaign, additional advertising is used to intensify the level of communication with the target audience.

So the next time you buy a shampoo or a refrigerator, you may want to think about how that brand came to your mind and whether you associate it with a television show or a movie.

### Creating the Advertising Message

The basic content and form of an advertising message are a function of several factors. A product's features, uses, and benefits affect the content of the message. Characteristics of the people in the target audience—gender, age, education, race, income, occupation, lifestyle, and other attributes—influence both content and form. When Procter & Gamble promotes Crest toothpaste to children, the company emphasizes daily brushing and cavity control. When marketing Crest to adults, P&G stresses tartar and plaque control. To communicate effectively, advertisers use words, symbols,

| table 19.2 | ADVANTAGES AND DISADVANTAGES OF MAJOR MEDIA CLASSES |

| Medium | Advantages | Disadvantages |
|---|---|---|
| Newspapers | Reaches large audience; purchased to be read; geographic flexibility; short lead time; frequent publication; favorable for cooperative advertising; merchandising services | Not selective for socioeconomic groups or target market; short life; limited reproduction capabilities; large advertising volume limits exposure to any one advertisement |
| Magazines | Demographic selectivity; good reproduction; long life; prestige; geographic selectivity when regional issues are available; read in leisurely manner | High costs; 30–90 day average lead time; high level of competition; limited reach; communicates less frequently |
| Direct mail | Little wasted circulation; highly selective; circulation controlled by advertiser; few distractions; personal; stimulates actions; use of novelty; relatively easy to measure performance; hidden from competitors | Very expensive; lacks editorial content to attract readers; often thrown away unread as junk mail; criticized as invasion of privacy; consumers must choose to read the ad |
| Radio | Reaches 95 percent of consumers; highly mobile and flexible; very low relative costs; ad can be changed quickly; high level of geographic and demographic selectivity; encourages use of imagination | Lacks visual imagery; short life of message; listeners' attention limited because of other activities; market fragmentation; difficult buying procedures; limited media and audience research |
| Television | Reaches large audiences; high frequency available; dual impact of audio and video; highly visible; high prestige; geographic and demographic selectivity; difficult to ignore | Very expensive; highly perishable message; size of audience not guaranteed; amount of prime time limited; lack of selectivity in target market |
| Internet | Immediate response; potential to reach a precisely targeted audience; ability to track customers and build databases; highly interactive medium | Costs of precise targeting are high; inappropriate ad placement; effects difficult to measure; concerns about security and privacy |
| Yellow Pages | Wide availability; action and product category oriented; low relative costs; ad frequency and longevity; nonintrusive | Market fragmentation; extremely localized; slow updating; lack of creativity; long lead times; requires large space to be noticed |
| Outdoor | Allows for frequent repetition; low cost; message can be placed close to point of sale; geographic selectivity; operable 24 hours a day; high creativity and effectiveness | Message must be short and simple; no demographic selectivity; seldom attracts readers' full attention; criticized as traffic hazard and blight on countryside; much wasted coverage; limited capabilities |

**Sources:** William F. Arens, *Contemporary Advertising* (Burr Ridge, IL: Irwin/McGraw-Hill, 2004); George E. Belch and Michael Belch, *Advertising and Promotion* (Burr Ridge, IL: Irwin/McGraw-Hill, 2004).

and illustrations that are meaningful, familiar, and appealing to people in the target audience.

An advertising campaign's objectives and platform also affect the content and form of its messages. If a firm's advertising objectives involve large sales increases, the message may include hard-hitting, high-impact language and symbols. When campaign objectives aim to increase brand awareness, the message may use much repetition of the brand name and words and illustrations associated with it. Thus, the advertising platform is the foundation on which campaign messages are built.

Choice of media obviously influences the content and form of the message. Effective outdoor displays and short broadcast spot announcements require concise, simple messages. Magazine and newspaper advertisements can include considerable detail and long explanations. Because several kinds of media offer geographic selectivity, a precise message can be tailored to a particular geographic section of the target audience. Some magazine publishers produce **regional issues**, in which advertisements and editorial content of copies appearing in one geographic area differ

**regional issues** Versions of a magazine that differ across geographic regions from those appearing in other areas. As Figure 19.3 shows, *Time* magazine publishes eight regional issues. A company advertising in *Time* might decide to use one message in the New England region and another in the rest of the nation. A company may also choose to advertise in only one region. Such geographic selectivity lets a firm use the same message in different regions at different times.

**copy** The verbal portion of advertisements

**Copy.** **Copy** is the verbal portion of an advertisement and may include headlines, subheadlines, body copy, and signature. Not all advertising contains all of these copy elements. Even handwritten notes on direct-mail advertising that say, "Try this. It works!" seem to increase requests for free samples.[16] The headline is critical because often it is the only part of the copy that people read. It should attract readers' attention and create enough interest to make them want to read the body copy. The subheadline, if there is one, links the headline to the body copy and sometimes serves to explain the headline.

Body copy for most advertisements consists of an introductory statement or paragraph, several explanatory paragraphs, and a closing paragraph. Some copywriters have adopted guidelines for developing body copy systematically: (1) identify a specific desire or problem, (2) recommend the product as the best way to satisfy that desire or solve that problem, (3) state product benefits and indicate why the product is best for the buyer's particular situation, (4) substantiate advertising claims, and (5) ask the buyer to take action. When substantiating claims, it is important to present the substantiation in a credible manner. The proof of claims should help strengthen both the image of the product and company integrity. Typeface selection can help advertisers create a desired impression using fonts that are engaging, reassuring, or very prominent.[17]

The signature identifies the advertisement's sponsor. It may contain several elements, including the firm's trademark, logo, name, and address. The signature should be attractive, legible, distinctive, and easy to identify in a variety of sizes.

**figure 19.3**

**GEOGRAPHIC DIVISIONS FOR *TIME* REGIONAL ISSUES**

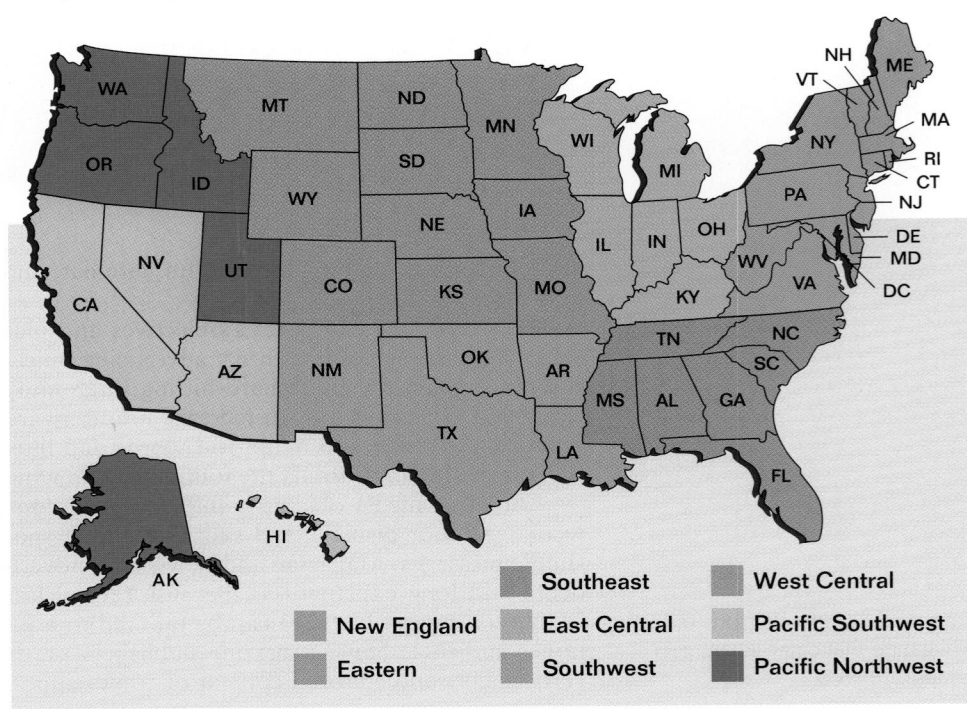

Legend:
- Southeast
- West Central
- New England
- East Central
- Pacific Southwest
- Eastern
- Southwest
- Pacific Northwest

**Source:** *Time* Magazine.
© 2006 Time Inc. Reprinted by permission.

**Components of a Print Ad**
This Xerox ad contains all the major components of a print advertisement.

Headline

Illustration

Subheadline

Body Copy

Signature

**storyboard**  A blueprint combining copy and visual material to show the sequence of major scenes in a commercial

**artwork**  An advertisement's illustrations and layout

**illustrations**  Photos, drawings, graphs, charts, and tables used to spark audience interest in an advertisement

**layout**  The physical arrangement of an advertisement's illustration and copy

Because radio listeners often are not fully "tuned in" mentally to what they're hearing on the radio, radio copy should be informal and conversational to attract listeners' attention. Radio messages are highly perishable and should consist of short, familiar terms, which increase their impact. The length should not require a rate of speech exceeding approximately two and one-half words per second.

In television copy, the audio material must not overpower the visual material, and vice versa. However, a television message should make optimal use of its visual portion, which can be very effective for product demonstrations. Copy for a television commercial is sometimes initially written in parallel script form. Video is described in the left column and audio in the right. When the parallel script is approved, the copywriter and artist combine copy with visual material by using a **storyboard**, which depicts a series of miniature television screens showing the sequence of major scenes in the commercial. Beneath each screen is a description of the audio portion to be used with that video segment. Technical personnel use the storyboard as a blueprint when producing the commercial.

**Artwork.** **Artwork** consists of an advertisement's illustrations and layout. **Illustrations** are often photographs but can also be drawings, graphs, charts, and tables. Illustrations are used to draw attention, encourage audiences to read or listen to the copy, communicate an idea quickly, or communicate ideas that are difficult to express. Illustrations can be more important in capturing attention than text or brand elements, independent of size.[18] They are especially important because consumers tend to recall the visual portions of advertisements better than the verbal portions. Advertisers use a variety of illustration techniques. They may show the product alone, in a setting, or in use, or show the results of the product's use. Illustrations can also take the form of comparisons, contrasts, diagrams, and testimonials.

The **layout** of an advertisement is the physical arrangement of the illustration and the copy (headline, subheadline, body copy, and signature). These elements can be arranged in many ways. The final layout is the result of several stages of layout preparation. As it moves through these stages, the layout promotes an exchange of ideas among people developing the advertising campaign and provides instructions for production personnel.

**Black and White Versus Color**

This example highlights the importance of using color when advertising certain products.

**pretest** Evaluation of advertisements performed before a campaign begins

**consumer jury** A panel of a product's existing or potential buyers who pretest ads

## Executing the Campaign

Execution of an advertising campaign requires extensive planning and coordination because many tasks must be completed on time and several people and firms are involved. Production companies, research organizations, media firms, printers, photoengravers, and commercial artists are just a few of the people and firms contributing to a campaign.

Implementation requires detailed schedules to ensure that various phases of the work are done on time. Advertising management personnel must evaluate the quality of the work and take corrective action when necessary. In some instances, changes are made during the campaign so it meets objectives more effectively. Sometimes one firm develops a campaign and another executes it.

## Evaluating Advertising Effectiveness

A variety of ways exist to test the effectiveness of advertising. They include measuring achievement of advertising objectives; assessing effectiveness of copy, illustrations, or layouts; and evaluating certain media.

Advertising can be evaluated before, during, and after the campaign. An evaluation performed before the campaign begins is called a **pretest**. A pretest usually attempts to evaluate the effectiveness of one or more elements of the message. To pretest advertisements, marketers sometimes use a **consumer jury**, a panel of existing or potential buyers of the advertised product. Jurors judge one or several dimensions of two or more advertisements. Such tests are based on the belief that consumers are more likely than advertising experts to know what influences them. Companies can also solicit the assistance of marketing research firms to help assess ads. PepsiCo, for example, relies on Information Resources Inc.'s (IRI) BehaviorScan to pretest new commercials in Eau Claire, Wisconsin, and Cedar Rapids, Iowa. IRI sends different Pepsi product ads to participating households and then analyzes their purchasing activity to test the ads' effectiveness.[19]

To measure advertising effectiveness during a campaign, marketers usually rely on "inquiries." In a campaign's initial stages, an advertiser may use several adver-

# The U.S. Army: A Tough Sell

**A**rmy recruiters have it tough. For the first time in its history, the U.S. Army is attempting to recruit an all-volunteer military amidst a protracted war. Complicating efforts are the dropping approval rates of the war in Iraq and daily reports of continuing violence. Just as detrimental is the fact that potential recruits are often being raised by parents who never served in the armed forces and would prefer that their children attend college. Due to

these issues, the Army is falling dangerously short on its recruiting quotas (the amounts needed to keep a war-time army staffed and functioning), and relying heavily on advertising and promotions to fix the problem.

This year, the Army will spend more than $200 million, the government's largest advertising expenditure, in an attempt to bring more than 165,000 new soldiers into its active duty, reserve, and National Guard ranks. It plans to do this with a multi-pronged approach. The "Army of One" television campaign focuses on providing information to both prospects and influencers (such as parents, teachers, and peers), by encouraging them to visit the Army's website, which outlines the benefits and variety of careers in the Army. The Army is also posting a large number of ads on Internet career sites such as Monster and CareerBuilder, on Google and Yahoo!, and on military-themed blogs and websites.

The Army targets high-potential segments with commercials on Spanish-language television and radio and Spanish-language websites. It also uses nontraditional media. For example, it has used a Humvee to tool around urban neighborhoods and pump out hip-hop music. The Army also sponsors a NASCAR race car, a National Hotrod Racing Association car, and professional bull riders and cowboys.

tisements simultaneously, each containing a coupon, form, or toll-free phone number through which potential customers can request information. The advertiser records the number of inquiries returned from each type of advertisement. If an advertiser receives 78,528 inquiries from advertisement A, 37,072 from advertisement B, and 47,932 from advertisement C, advertisement A is judged superior to advertisements B and C. Internet advertisers can also assess how many people "clicked" on an ad to obtain more product information. Before the launch of the Nissan 350Z, Nissan asked advertising agency TBWA/Chiat/Day to create an interactive Internet banner ad for the new sports car. In just 30 days, 50,000 clicked the ads, and Nissan ultimately saw 75,000 preorders for the car even before it went on sale.[20]

**posttest** Evaluation of advertising effectiveness after the campaign

Evaluation of advertising effectiveness after the campaign is called a **posttest**. Advertising objectives often determine what kind of posttest is appropriate. If the objectives focus on communication—to increase awareness of product features or brands or to create more favorable customer attitudes—the posttest should measure changes in these dimensions. Advertisers sometimes use consumer surveys or experiments to evaluate a campaign based on communication objectives. These methods are costly, however.

For campaign objectives stated in terms of sales, advertisers should determine the change in sales or market share attributable to the campaign. However, changes in sales or market share brought about by advertising cannot be measured precisely; many factors independent of advertisements affect a firm's sales and market share. Competitors' actions, regulatory actions, and changes in economic conditions, consumer preferences, and weather are only a few factors that might enhance or diminish a company's sales or market share. By using data about past and current sales and advertising expenditures, advertisers can make gross estimates of the effects of a campaign on sales or market share.

**recognition test**  A posttest in which respondents are shown the actual ad and asked if they recognize it

**unaided recall test**  A posttest in which respondents are asked to identify ads they have recently seen but are given no recall clues

**aided recall test**  A posttest that asks respondents to identify recent ads and provides clues to jog their memories

Because it is difficult to determine the direct effects of advertising on sales, many advertisers evaluate print advertisements according to how well consumers can remember them. Posttest methods based on memory include recognition and recall tests. Such tests are usually performed by research organizations through surveys. In a **recognition test**, respondents are shown the actual advertisement and asked whether they recognize it. If they do, the interviewer asks additional questions to determine how much of the advertisement each respondent read. When recall is evaluated, respondents are not shown the actual advertisement but instead are asked about what they have seen or heard recently. For Internet advertising, research suggests that the longer a person is exposed to a website containing a banner advertisement, the more likely he or she is to recall the ad.[21]

Recall can be measured through either unaided or aided recall methods. In an **unaided recall test**, respondents identify advertisements they have seen recently but are not shown any clues to help them remember. A similar procedure is used with an **aided recall test**, but respondents are shown a list of products, brands, company names, or trademarks to jog their memories. For example, the long-running national youth anti-drug media campaign by the Office of National Drug Control Policy has nearly 70 percent recognition and recall among youth and 55 percent among parents.[22] Several research organizations, such as Daniel Starch, provide research services that test recognition and recall of advertisements.

The major justification for using recognition and recall methods is that people are more likely to buy a product if they can remember an advertisement about it than if they cannot. However, recalling an advertisement does not necessarily lead to buying the product or brand advertised. Researchers also use a sophisticated technique called *single-source data* to help evaluate advertisements. With this technique, individuals' behaviors are tracked from television sets to checkout counters. Monitors are placed in preselected homes, and microcomputers record when the television set is on and which station is being viewed. At the supermarket checkout, the individual in the sample household presents an identification card. Checkers then record the purchases by scanner, and data are sent to the research facility. Some single-source data companies provide sample households with scanning equipment for use at home to record purchases after returning from shopping trips. Single-source data provide information that links exposure to advertisements with purchase behavior.

# Who Develops the Advertising Campaign?

An advertising campaign may be handled by an individual or by a few people within the firm, by the firm's own advertising department, or by an advertising agency.

In very small firms, one or two individuals are responsible for advertising (and for many other activities as well). Usually these individuals depend heavily on personnel at local newspapers and broadcast stations for copywriting, artwork, and advice about scheduling media.

In certain large businesses, especially large retail organizations, advertising departments create and implement advertising campaigns. Depending on the size of the advertising program, an advertising department may consist of a few multiskilled individuals or a sizable number of specialists such as copywriters, artists, media buyers, and technical production coordinators. Advertising departments sometimes obtain the services of independent research organizations and hire freelance specialists when a particular project requires it.

Many firms employ an advertising agency to develop advertising campaigns. New Belgium Brewing, for example, contracted with Amalgamated, a New York agency, to create its first $10 million advertising campaign.[23] When an organization uses an advertising agency, the firm and the agency usually develop the advertising campaign jointly. How much each participates in the campaign's total development depends on the working relationship between the firm and the agency. Ordinarily a firm relies on the agency for copywriting, artwork, technical production, and formulation of the media plan.

**marketing**
ENTREPRENEURS

**Cathey Finlon**

THE BUSINESS: McClain Finlon Advertising

FOUNDED: 1982

SUCCESS: $125 million in billings

In 1982 Cathey Finlon started her first ad agency with only $250 cash, a typewriter, and some art pads. Now, McClain Finlon Advertising is the highest earning, independently owned ad agency in Denver. The secret of Finlon's success comes from cutting-edge tactics that use a different language to market to a new generation of consumers. One example is a controversial Breckenridge Ski Resort ad campaign that employed words such as *bitch* to target young men. Although the ads were heavily criticized and caused an uproar among Denver locals, they earned several advertising awards for creativity from the Denver Advertising Federation and went on to compete nationally. Some McClain Finlon clients include Vespa, Xcel Energy, Sun Microsystems, and the Denver Zoo.

Advertising agencies assist businesses in several ways. An agency, especially a large one, can supply the services of highly skilled specialists—not only copywriters, artists, and production coordinators but also media experts, researchers, and legal advisers. Agency personnel often have broad advertising experience and are usually more objective than a firm's employees about the organization's products.

Because an agency traditionally receives most of its compensation from a 15 percent commission paid by the media from which it makes purchases, firms can obtain some agency services at low or moderate costs. If an agency contracts for $400,000 of television time for a firm, it receives a commission of $60,000 from the television station. Although the traditional compensation method for agencies is changing and now includes other factors, media commissions still offset some costs of using an agency.

Like advertising, public relations can be a vital element in a promotion mix. We turn to this topic next.

# Public Relations

**public relations** Communication efforts used to create and maintain favorable relations between an organization and its stakeholders

**Public relations** is a broad set of communication efforts used to create and maintain favorable relationships between an organization and its stakeholders. An organization communicates with various stakeholders, both internal and external, and public relations efforts can be directed toward any and all of them. A firm's stakeholders can include customers, suppliers, employees, stockholders, the media, educators, potential investors, government officials, and society in general.

Public relations can be used to promote people, places, ideas, activities, and even countries. It is often used by nonprofit organizations to achieve their goals. Public relations focuses on enhancing the image of the total organization. Assessing public attitudes and creating a favorable image are no less important than direct promotion of the organization's products. Because the public's attitudes toward a firm are likely to affect the sales of its products, it is very important for firms to maintain positive public perceptions. In addition, employee morale is strengthened if the public perceives the firm positively.[24] Although public relations can make people aware of a company's products, brands, or activities, it can also create specific company images, such as innovativeness or dependability. Companies such as Green Mountain Coffee Roasters, Patagonia, Sustainable Harvest, and Honest Tea have reputations for being socially responsible not only because they engage in socially responsible behavior but because their actions are reported through news stories and other public relations efforts. By getting the media to report on a firm's accomplishments, public relations helps the company maintain positive public visibility. Some firms use public relations for a single purpose; others use it for several purposes.

## Public Relations Tools

Companies use a variety of public relations tools to convey messages and create images. Public relations professionals prepare written materials, such as brochures, newsletters, company magazines, news releases, and annual reports that reach and influence their various stakeholders.

**Annual Report**

Annual reports, when appropriately designed, can generate favorable public relations.

**publicity** A news story type of communication about an organization and/or its products transmitted through a mass medium at no charge

**news release** A short piece of copy publicizing an event or a product

**feature article** A manuscript of up to 3,000 words prepared for a specific publication

**captioned photograph** A photograph with a brief description of its contents

**press conference** A meeting used to announce major news events

Public relations personnel also create corporate identity materials, such as logos, business cards, stationery, and signs that make firms immediately recognizable. Speeches are another public relations tool. Because what a company executive says publicly at meetings or to the media can affect the organization's image, the speech must convey the desired message clearly.

Event sponsorship, in which a company pays for part or all of a special event, such as a benefit concert or a tennis tournament, is another public relations tool. Examples are Home Depot's sponsorship of NASCAR and the U.S. Olympic team. Sponsoring special events can be an effective means of increasing company or brand recognition with relatively minimal investment. Event sponsorship can gain companies considerable amounts of free media coverage. An organization tries to ensure that its product and the sponsored event target a similar audience and that the two are easily associated in customers' minds. For example, corporate sponsors of professional beach volleyball, such as McDonald's, Nissan, and Budweiser, benefited from more than 1 billion media impressions during the 2004 season.[25] Public relations personnel also organize unique events to "create news" about the company. These may include grand openings with celebrities, prizes, hot-air balloon rides, and other attractions that appeal to a firm's publics.

Publicity is a part of public relations. **Publicity** is communication in news story form about the organization, its products, or both, transmitted through a mass medium at no charge. Although public relations has a larger, more comprehensive communication function than publicity, publicity is a very important aspect of public relations. Publicity can be used to provide information about goods or services; to announce expansions, acquisitions, research, or new-product launches; or to enhance a company's image.

The most common publicity-based public relations tool is the **news release**, sometimes called a *press release*, which is usually a single page of typewritten copy containing fewer than 300 words and describing a company event or product. A news release gives the firm's or agency's name, address, phone number, and contact person. Automakers and other manufacturers sometimes use news releases when introducing new products or making significant announcements. When Whole Foods Market purchased wind credits equal to 100 percent of all the energy used in its stores, facilities, distribution centers, and offices, making it the first Fortune 500 company to do so, it sent out news releases to newspapers, magazines, television contacts, and suppliers, resulting in public relations in the form of magazine and newspaper articles and television coverage.[26] As Table 19.3 shows, news releases tackle a multitude of specific issues. A **feature article** is a manuscript of up to 3,000 words prepared for a specific publication. A **captioned photograph** is a photograph with a brief description explaining its contents. Captioned photographs are effective for illustrating new or improved products with highly visible features.

There are several other kinds of publicity-based public relations tools. A **press conference** is a meeting called to announce major news events. Media personnel are invited to a press conference and are usually supplied with written materials and photographs. Letters to the editor and editorials are sometimes prepared and sent to newspapers and magazines. Videos and audiotapes may be distributed to broadcast stations in the hope they will be aired.

Publicity-based public relations tools offer several advantages, including credibility, news value, significant word-of-mouth communications, and a perception of media endorsement. The public may consider news coverage more truthful and credible than an advertisement because the media are not paid to provide the information. In addi-

| table 19.3 | POSSIBLE ISSUES FOR PUBLICITY RELEASES | |
|---|---|---|
| Changes in marketing personnel | Packaging changes | |
| Support of a social cause | New products | |
| Improved warranties | New slogan | |
| Reports on industry conditions | Research developments | |
| New uses for established products | Company's history and development | |
| Product endorsements | Employment, production, and sales records | |
| Quality awards | Award of contracts | |
| Company name changes | Opening of new markets | |
| Interviews with company officials | Improvements in financial position | |
| Improved distribution policies | Opening of an exhibit | |
| International business efforts | History of a brand | |
| Athletic event sponsorship | Winners of company contests | |
| Visits by celebrities | Logo changes | |
| Reports on new discoveries | Speeches of top management | |
| Innovative marketing activities | Merit awards | |
| Economic forecasts | Anniversary of inventions | |

tion, stories regarding a new-product introduction or a new environmentally responsible company policy, for example, are handled as news items and are likely to receive notice. Finally, the cost of publicity is low compared with the cost of advertising.[27]

Publicity-based public relations tools have some limitations. Media personnel must judge company messages to be newsworthy if the messages are to be published or broadcast at all. Consequently messages must be timely, interesting, accurate, and in the public interest. It may take a great deal of time and effort to convince media personnel of the news value of publicity releases, and many communications fail to qualify. Although public relations personnel usually encourage the media to air publicity releases at certain times, they control neither the content nor the timing of the communication. Media personnel alter length and content of publicity releases to fit publishers' or broadcasters' requirements and may even delete the parts of messages that company personnel view as most important. Furthermore, media personnel use publicity releases in time slots or positions most convenient for them. Thus, messages sometimes appear in locations or at times that may not reach the firm's target audiences. Although these limitations can be frustrating, properly managed publicity-based public relations tools offer an organization substantial benefits.

## Evaluating Public Relations Effectiveness

Because of the potential benefits of good public relations, it is essential that organizations evaluate the effectiveness of their public relations campaigns. Research can be conducted to determine how well a firm is communicating its messages or image to its target audiences. *Environmental monitoring* identifies changes in public opinion affecting an organization. A *public relations audit* is used to assess an organization's image among the public or to evaluate the effect of a specific public relations program. A *communications audit* may include a content analysis of messages, a readability

**Contact:**    Sean Greenwood
                Ben & Jerry's PR Poobah
                802-846-1500, ext. 7701
                sean.greenwood@benjerry.com

                                        **FOR IMMEDIATE RELEASE**

### BEN & JERRY'S TAKES STALK IN ITS PACKAGING
#### New Environmentally Friendly Corn Based Cup To Be Used at Scoop Shops Nationwide

Sept 5, 2006 - It's the one combination the Vermont company never tried: ice cream and corn. However, for the environment it could be a field of dreams.

Ben & Jerry's is switching to a new line of 100% corn based cold drink cups for use in their Scoop Shops starting this fall. The ecologically friendly cups are made from American grown corn, are environmentally sustainable and are fully compostable in commercial or industrial facilities. Specialty printed with Ben & Jerry's unmistakable colorful cow and pasture scene, the two sizes of new cups replace traditional petroleum based packaging for smoothies and frozen drinks.

"The cob does the job!" remarked Graham Rigby, Brand Manager at the company's headquarters. "We still have many improvements to make, but this is one switch we can be proud of."

Founded on a sustainable corporate culture, Ben & Jerry's strives to minimize the negative impact of its business practices on the environment. The ice cream maker has undertaken campaigns from helping family farms to offsetting its manufacturing plants emissions. It was the first frozen food business to introduce an unbleached paperboard container in 1998 and the mission continues with the use of Fabri-Kal's Greenware line of cold drink cups.

Headquartered in Kalamazoo, Michigan and in continuous operation since 1950, Fabri-Kal is one of the largest converters of the corn-based material used in the creation of the cups. More information about the Greenware line of products may be found at the company's website at www.f-k.com.

Ben & Jerry's, a wholly-owned autonomous subsidiary of Unilever, operates its business on a three-part mission statement emphasizing product quality, economic reward and a commitment to the community. The company produces a wide variety of super-premium ice cream and ice cream novelties which they distribute through many channels including 580 franchised Scoop Shops and PartnerShops worldwide.

\* Greenware is a registered trademark of Fabri-Kal Corporation

**Press Release**

Press releases are often used as a way to spread news about a company.

study, or a readership survey. If an organization wants to measure the extent to which stakeholders view it as being socially responsible, it can conduct a *social audit*.

One approach to measuring the effectiveness of publicity-based public relations is to count the number of exposures in the media. To determine which releases are published in print media and how often, an organization can hire a clipping service, a firm that clips and sends news releases to client companies. To measure the effectiveness of television coverage, a firm can enclose a card with its publicity releases requesting that the television station record its name and the dates when the news item is broadcast (although station personnel do not always comply). Some television and radio tracking services exist, but they are extremely costly.

Counting the number of media exposures does not reveal how many people have actually read or heard the company's message or what they thought about the message afterward. However, measuring changes in product awareness, knowledge, and attitudes resulting from the publicity campaign helps yield this information. To assess these changes, companies must measure these levels before and after public relations campaigns. Although precise measures are difficult to obtain, a firm's marketers should attempt to assess the impact of public relations efforts on the organization's sales. For example, critics' reviews of films can affect the films' box office performance. Interestingly, negative reviews (publicity) harm revenue more than positive reviews help revenue in the early weeks of a film's release.[28]

## Dealing with Unfavorable Public Relations

Thus far, we have discussed public relations as a planned element of the promotion mix. However, companies may have to deal with unexpected and unfavorable public relations resulting from an unsafe product, an accident resulting from product use, controversial actions of employees, or some other negative event or situation. For example, an airline that experiences a plane crash faces a very tragic and distressing situation. Charges of anticompetitive behavior against Microsoft have raised public concern and generated unfavorable public relations for that organization. The public's image of the Body Shop as a socially responsible company diminished considerably when it was reported that the company's actions were less socially responsible than its promotion promised. Unfavorable coverage can have quick and dramatic effects. After Martha Stewart was convicted on securities fraud charges, the stock of her firm, Martha Stewart Living Omnimedia, plummeted, advertisers abandoned her self-titled magazine, and her show was dumped.[29] A single negative event that generates public relations can wipe out a company's favorable image and destroy positive customer attitudes established through years of expensive advertising campaigns and other promotional efforts. Moreover, today's mass media, including online services and the Internet, disseminate information faster than ever before, and bad news generally receives considerable media attention.

To protect its image, an organization needs to prevent unfavorable public relations or at least lessen its effect if it occurs. First and foremost, the organization should try to prevent negative incidents and events through safety programs, inspections, and effective quality control procedures. However, because negative events can befall even the most cautious firms, an organization should have plans in place to handle them when they do occur. Firms need to establish policies and procedures for reducing the adverse impact of news coverage of a crisis or controversy. In most cases, organizations should expedite news coverage of negative events rather than try to discourage or block them. If news coverage is suppressed, rumors and other misinformation may replace facts.

An unfavorable event can easily balloon into serious problems or public issues and become very damaging. By being forthright with the press and public and taking prompt action, a firm may be able to convince the public of its honest attempts to deal with the situation, and news personnel may be more willing to help explain complex issues to the public. Dealing effectively with a negative event allows an organization to lessen, if not eliminate, the unfavorable impact on its image. Consider that after Martha Stewart went to prison even while appealing her conviction, public sympathy for her situation helped quadruple her firm's stock, and she had two new television shows waiting for her when she left prison in 2005.[30]

## SUMMARY

Advertising is a paid form of nonpersonal communication transmitted to consumers through mass media such as television, radio, the Internet, newspapers, magazines, direct mail, outdoor displays, and signs on mass transit vehicles. Both business and nonbusiness organizations use advertising. Institutional advertising promotes organizational images, ideas, and political issues. When a company promotes its position on a public issue such as taxation, institutional advertising is referred to as advocacy advertising. Product advertising promotes uses, features, and benefits of products. The two types of product advertising are pioneer advertising, which focuses on stimulating demand for a product category rather than a specific brand, and competitive advertising, which attempts to stimulate demand for a specific brand by indicating the brand's features, uses, and advantages. To make direct product comparisons, marketers use comparative advertising, which compares two or more brands. Two other forms of competitive advertising are reminder advertising, which reminds customers about an established brand's uses, characteristics, and benefits, and reinforcement advertis-

ing, which assures current users they have made the right brand choice.

Although marketers may vary in how they develop advertising campaigns, they should follow a general pattern. First, they must identify and analyze the target audience, the group of people at whom advertisements are aimed. Second, they should establish what they want the campaign to accomplish by defining advertising objectives. Objectives should be clear, precise, and presented in measurable terms. Third, marketers must create the advertising platform, which contains basic issues to be presented in the campaign. Advertising platforms should consist of issues important to consumers. Fourth, advertisers must decide how much money to spend on the campaign; they arrive at this decision through the objective-and-task approach, percent-of-sales approach, competition-matching approach, or arbitrary approach.

Advertisers must then develop a media plan by selecting and scheduling media to use in the campaign. Some factors affecting the media plan are location and demographic characteristics of the target audience, content of the message, and cost of the various media. The basic content and form of the advertising message are affected by product features, uses, and benefits; characteristics of the people in the target audience; the campaign's objectives and platform; and the choice of media. Advertisers use copy and artwork to create the message. The execution of an advertising campaign requires extensive planning and coordination.

Finally, advertisers must devise one or more methods for evaluating advertisement effectiveness. Pretests are evaluations performed before the campaign begins; posttests are conducted after the campaign. Two types of posttests are a recognition test, in which respondents are shown the actual advertisement and asked whether they recognize it, and a recall test. In aided recall tests, respondents are shown a list of products, brands, company names, or trademarks to jog their memories. In unaided tests, no clues are given.

Advertising campaigns can be developed by personnel within the firm or in conjunction with advertising agencies. A campaign created by the firm's personnel may be developed by one or more individuals or by an advertising department within the firm. Use of an advertising agency may be advantageous because an agency provides highly skilled, objective specialists with broad experience in advertising at low to moderate costs to the firm.

Public relations is a broad set of communication efforts used to create and maintain favorable relationships between an organization and its stakeholders. Public relations can be used to promote people, places, ideas, activities, and countries, and to create and maintain a posi-

tive company image. Some firms use public relations for a single purpose; others use it for several purposes. Public relations tools include written materials, such as brochures, newsletters, and annual reports; corporate identity materials, such as business cards and signs; speeches; event sponsorships; and special events. Publicity is communication in news story form about an organization, its products, or both, transmitted through a mass medium at no charge. Publicity-based public relations tools include news releases, feature articles, captioned photographs, and press conferences. Problems that organizations confront in using publicity-based public relations include reluctance of media personnel to print or air releases and lack of control over timing and content of messages.

To evaluate the effectiveness of their public relations programs, companies conduct research to determine how well their messages are reaching their audiences. Environmental monitoring, public relations audits, and counting the number of media exposures are all means of evaluating public relations effectiveness. Organizations should avoid negative public relations by taking steps to prevent negative events that result in unfavorable publicity. To diminish the impact of unfavorable public relations, organizations should institute policies and procedures for dealing with news personnel and the public when negative events occur.

**ACE self-test**

Please visit the student website at **www.prideferrell.com** for ACE Self-Test questions that will help you prepare for exams.

## IMPORTANT TERMS

| | | | |
|---|---|---|---|
| Advertising | Target audience | Cost comparison indicator | Recognition test |
| Institutional advertising | Advertising platform | Regional issues | Unaided recall test |
| Advocacy advertising | Advertising appropriation | Copy | Aided recall test |
| Product advertising | Objective-and-task approach | Storyboard | Public relations |
| Pioneer advertising | Percent-of-sales approach | Artwork | Publicity |
| Competitive advertising | Competition-matching approach | Illustrations | News release |
| Comparative advertising | | Layout | Feature article |
| Reminder advertising | Arbitrary approach | Pretest | Captioned photograph |
| Reinforcement advertising | Media plan | Consumer jury | Press conference |
| Advertising campaign | | Posttest | |

## DISCUSSION & REVIEW QUESTIONS

1. What is the difference between institutional and product advertising?

2. What is the difference between competitive advertising and comparative advertising?

3. What are the major steps in creating an advertising campaign?

4. What is a target audience? How does a marketer analyze the target audience after identifying it?

5. Why is it necessary to define advertising objectives?

6. What is an advertising platform, and how is it used?

7. What factors affect the size of an advertising budget? What techniques are used to determine an advertising budget?

8. Describe the steps in developing a media plan.

9. What is the function of copy in an advertising message?

10. Discuss several ways to posttest the effectiveness of advertising.

11. What role does an advertising agency play in developing an advertising campaign?

12. What is public relations? Whom can an organization reach through public relations?

13. How do organizations use public relations tools? Give several examples you have observed recently.

14. Explain the problems and limitations associated with publicity-based public relations.

15. In what ways is the effectiveness of public relations evaluated?

16. What are some sources of negative public relations? How should an organization deal with unfavorable public relations?

## APPLICATION QUESTIONS

1. An organization must define its objectives carefully when developing an advertising campaign. Which of the following advertising objectives would be most useful for a company, and why?

   a. The organization will spend $1 million to move from second in market share to market leader.

   b. The organization wants to increase sales from $1.2 million to $1.5 million this year to gain the lead in market share.

   c. The advertising objective is to gain as much market share as possible within the next 12 months.

   d. The advertising objective is to increase sales by 15 percent.

2. Copy, the verbal portion of advertising, is used to move readers through a persuasive sequence called AIDA: attention, interest, desire, and action. To achieve this, some copywriters have adopted guidelines for developing advertising copy. Select a print ad and identify how it (1) identifies a specific problem, (2) recommends the product as the best solution to the problem, (3) states the product's advantages and benefits, (4) substantiates the ad's claims, and (5) asks the reader to take action.

3. Advertisers use several types of publicity mechanisms. Look through some recent newspapers and magazines, and identify a news release, a feature article, and a captioned photograph used to publicize a product. Describe the type of product.

4. Negative public relations can harm an organization's marketing efforts if not dealt with properly. Identify a company that was recently the target of negative public relations. Describe the situation and discuss the company's response. What did marketers at this company do well? What, if anything, would you recommend that they change about their response?

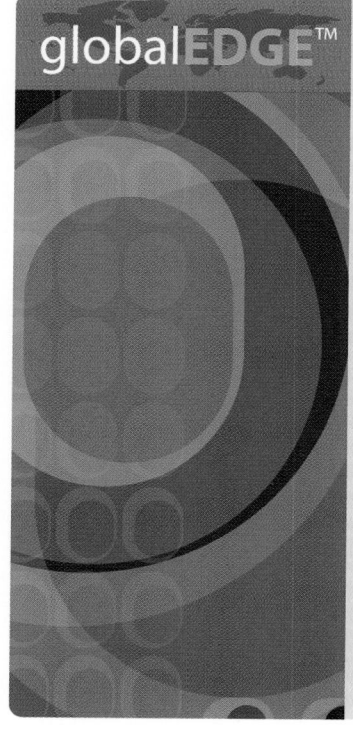

globalEDGE™

1. An essential component of advertising and public relations in marketing is a firm's ability to impart information to the most advanced consumers in a fast and efficient manner. To better focus your firm's communications worldwide in technologically savvy regions, you have been asked to survey the state of mobile technology by examining a report found on the GSM World website. Access this report by using either the search term "mobile" or "GSM" at **http://globaledge.msu.edu/ibrd.** and then go to the Media Centre option at the top and click on GSM Statistics. Find the most recent quarterly report. What are the three most technologically savvy regions in the world? What does GSM represent?

2. Your firm is planning to begin advertising a new line of products exclusively to women. However, before doing so, you must determine which markets to use to guide the design as well as where to implement the testing of the product and advertising concepts. Access the NationMaster.com's Gender Development Index using the search term "compare various statistics" at **http://globaledge.msu.edu/ibrd.** Once there, under the Facts & Statistics heading, select the People category in the drop-down box to the right and the subcategory of Gender Development Index to download this data into a spreadsheet for analysis. Based on information in the Gender Development Index, establish the five countries you will target for the advertising and public relations campaign. What types of complications might you encounter in the transition from testing to mass marketing your product? Is there a country you may want to enter first once design and testing is completed?

## LEGO Company

LEGO Company has been making toys since 1932 and has become one of the most recognized brand names in the toy industry. With the company motto "Only the best is good enough," it is no surprise that LEGO Company has developed an exciting and interactive website. See how the company promotes LEGO products and encourages consumer involvement with the brand by visiting **www.lego.com**.

1. Which type of advertising is LEGO Company using on its website?
2. What target audience is LEGO attempting to reach through its website?
3. Identify the advertising objectives LEGO is attempting to achieve through its website.

## Video Case 19.1  Vail Resorts Uses Public Relations to Put out a Fire

Vail Resorts, Inc. is one of the leading resort operators in North America. The company operates four ski resorts in Colorado, including Vail, Keystone, Beaver Creek, and Breckenridge, as well as one in Lake Tahoe, which borders northern California and Nevada. Vail Mountain has become the most popular ski destination in the United States, with 1.6 million skier visits in the 2004–2005 season. *SKI* magazine has ranked Vail as one of the best ski resorts in North America since 1988.

Despite its success, the company experienced a very challenging year in 1998. In October of that year, just two weeks before the beginning of the ski season, the Vail Mountain resort suffered the largest "ecoterrorist" event in U.S. history. Several structures, including Patrol Headquarters, the Two Elk restaurant, and Camp One, were burned to the ground, and four chair lift operator buildings were damaged. Total damages exceeded $12 million. The deliberately and strategically set fires disabled three central lifts and the biggest restaurant and guest service center on the mountain.

Shortly after the fires, the Earth Liberation Front (ELF), a radical environmental organization, claimed responsibility. In an e-mail, ELF, which splintered off the better-known Earth First! organization, claimed to have set the fires to protest a planned expansion of the resort, which, the group argued, would threaten habitat needed to reintroduce the Canada lynx, an endangered wild cat. In the e-mail, ELF said, "Putting profits ahead of Colorado's wildlife will not be tolerated." ELF's communiqué also warned skiers to stay away from the resort "for your safety and convenience." However, Earth First! and many other environmental groups, which had protested Vail's controversial plans to expand into lynx habitat, were quick to condemn ELF's firebombing at Vail. More than seven years later,

one suspect was arrested on charges related to six ecoterrorism attacks but has not gone to trial.

As with most disasters, the mass media quickly swarmed the scene at Vail Mountain, and the resulting stories published around the country were not always beneficial to Vail Mountain and nearby Vail, Colorado—or accurate. Some newspapers reported that all ski lifts had been destroyed and that the resort would be unable to open for the season. A few reported that the nearby town of Vail was on fire, including hotels.

Vail Resorts responded to the misinformation by launching a direct-mail campaign to communicate with everyone who had made reservations for ski vacations through Vail Central Reservations, as well as to travel agents and individual hotels in town. The company reassured skiers that the resort would indeed open and would be a safe place for their families to vacation. Vail Resorts managed to salvage the season and make it successful, despite the havoc wreaked by the fires.

Vail Resorts, like many firms, had a generic crisis plan in place at the time of the incident. However, some analysts contend that the degree to which the company followed that plan was questionable. In hindsight, Vail management has stated that things might have gone more smoothly in the first 48 hours after the crisis if they had adhered more closely to that plan. For example, managers now recognize that they did not use their staff as effectively as possible. Instead of clearly defining responsibilities up front, staff members were called up somewhat randomly, adding to the confusion surrounding the event. The plan also failed to address communication with employees. Resort management quickly decided that keeping employees fully informed was a top priority because they were the best ambassadors to the public.

Crisis management has been defined as preparation for low-probability or unexpected events that could threaten an organization's viability, reputation, or profitability. It has traditionally been viewed as "damage control," with little preplanning taking place. However, with the changing global political climate, events such as terrorist attacks and workplace violence have become more common, increasing the need for crisis management and disaster recovery planning for businesses. Even small companies are beginning to recognize the need to plan for the unexpected.

Crisis management and disaster recovery are critical for most organizations that deal with large numbers of customers, especially in the recreation and entertainment industries. The negative publicity resulting from a crisis can be potentially more devastating than a natural disaster such as an earthquake or a technological disruption such as a major power failure. The disruption of routine operations and paralysis of employees and customers in the face of crisis can reduce productivity, destroy long-established reputations, and erode public confidence in a company. Crisis planning can arm a company with tools and procedures to manage a crisis, protect a company's image, and reduce unfavorable publicity. By being forthright with the press and

the public and taking prompt action, companies may be able to convince the public of their honest attempts to resolve the situation, and news media may be more willing to help explain complex issues to the public. Effectively dealing with a negative event allows an organization to reduce the unfavorable impact on its image.

In the case of Vail Resorts, managers believe they could have followed their previously established crisis management plan more closely. During the two days immediately following the fires, management was disorganized and employees and Vail residents were confused about the future of the resort. Ultimately Vail chose to be honest and open with the media and its employees, which helped the resort weather the crisis with its image intact. The company's direct-mail campaign to vacationers also helped preserve public trust in the company.

To prepare for unexpected events, all firms should develop a crisis management program, which includes four basic steps: conducting a crisis audit, making contingency plans, assigning a crisis management team, and practicing the plan. Conducting a crisis audit involves assessing the potential impacts of different events, such as the death of an executive or a natural disaster. *Contingency planning* refers to the development of backup plans for emergencies that specify actions to be taken and their expected consequences. Crisis management teams should also be designated so that key areas, such as media relations and legal affairs, are covered in case of emergency. Finally, companies should practice the crisis management plan and regularly update it as necessary so that all employees are familiar with the plan.[31]

## Questions for Discussion

1. What tools did Vail Resorts use to respond to the crisis?
2. Evaluate Vail Resorts' response to the crisis. What did the firm do right? What else could it have done to relieve public concerns about the safety of the resort as well as its controversial expansion into the habitat of an endangered species?
3. How can creating a crisis management and disaster recovery plan help a company protect its reputation, customer relationships, and profits?

## Case 19.2      Harry Potter and the Power of PR

Public relations magic has catapulted every Harry Potter book to the top of the best-seller lists and transformed every Harry Potter movie into a box-office hit. Worldwide, nearly 300 million copies of J. K. Rowling's Harry Potter books and more than $1 billion in tickets to Harry Potter movies have been sold to date. In the words of one children's literature expert, the enormous popularity of the series has made reading "an event with the glitz of a movie premiere." It has also made the author an instant celebrity—and now a billionaire.

The magic started with the U.K. release of *Harry Potter and the Philosopher's Stone* (published by Scholastic in the United States as *Harry Potter and the Sorcerer's Stone*). Sales of this first book picked up quickly, fueled by publicity about Hogwarts and wizardry, the author's background, and even the heft of the book. As the buzz carried across the Atlantic, Scholastic printed 50,000 copies for the U.S. market. However, the publisher was unprepared for the unprecedented demand and had to reprint this debut book again and again. Readers remained enchanted with the young wizard's adventures, boosting sales of each successive book in the series. In all, Scholastic has sold 26 million of the first book, 24 million of the second, 19 million of the third, 18 million of the fourth, and 16 million of the fifth.

To build anticipation and excitement for the sixth book, *Harry Potter and the Half-Blood Prince,* none of the 11 million copies printed for the U.S. market were sold before midnight on the official launch date. Advertising and sales promotion not only boosted sales, they provoked considerable media coverage as well. Bookstores invited readers to preorder the new book and show up at 12:01 A.M.—dressed up as Harry, Hermione, or another character from the series—to pick up their purchases. Barnes & Noble, the country's largest book retailer, offered the book at a 40 percent discount and sold 1.3 million copies in the first 48 hours. Amazon.com discounted the book by 43 percent and delivered 1.5 million copies to customers on the launch date. Borders sold 850,000 copies in the 24

hours following the launch, with a few stores staying open around the clock. Libraries and schools kept enthusiasm high with Harry Potter parties, parades, and trivia contests.

In addition, all kinds of people connected with the book made public appearances, including author Rowling and Jim Dale, the Shakespearean actor who narrated the audiobook. Reporters sought out children and parents, educators, librarians, literacy professionals, and child psychologists to discuss the Harry Potter phenomenon. Media coverage continued for weeks as a prelude to the holiday-season release of the *Harry Potter and the Goblet of Fire* movie, just a few months away.

As the premiere date approached, Warner Brothers briefed reporters on every detail of the production. The studio also posted movie previews, games, newsletters, and more on its Harry Potter website (**www.harry potter.com**). The film's teenage stars made news everywhere as they met fans, reporters, and television personalities. The public-relations barrage paid off: *Harry Potter and the Goblet of Fire* smashed box-office records, with $400 million worth of movie tickets sold worldwide in the first 10 days.

Warner Brothers kept its PR activities going to bring fans back to movie houses a second and third time. For example, it sent Katie Leung, who plays Cho Chang, to visit China. "China is not a market that is used to frequent talent visits, so having Katie Leung there during our second week of release will contribute to maintaining the momentum on the movie," said a studio executive. Clearly, Harry Potter knows the power of PR.[32]

### Questions for Discussion

1. What would you suggest that Scholastic do to increase sales of earlier Harry Potter books through public relations?
2. How might Warner Brothers use event sponsorship to promote sales of Harry Potter movies on DVD?
3. How can online marketing communications be used to drive the sales of future Harry Potter books

# Personal Selling and Sales Promotion

## Holy Cow! Promotion at Chick-fil-A

Like most restaurant chains, Chick-fil-A uses sales promotions to bring customers into its restaurants. But unlike other fast-food chains, it doesn't imitate its competitors.

McDonald's, Burger King, and Denny's invest millions of dollars into marketing kids' meals with toys that are popularized through movies, television, and storybook characters. Chick-fil-A puts its money into teaching kids through books and CDs. One of its most successful promotions was a series of children's books that teaches basic money skills. This five-book series covers topics like work, spending, saving, giving, and contentment. The booklets were free with a kid's meal and an additional 99-cent purchase. Another kid's meal promotion was built around Veggie Tales CDs that teach children life-lessons, including the importance of family and forgiveness.

The Atlanta-based Chick-fil-A, Inc. is the nation's second-largest quick-service chicken restaurant chain, with more than 1,240 restaurants in 38 states. The chain, which adds around 60 locations annually, has a tradition of giving away a free year's supply of Chick-fil-A food to the first 100 customers on the opening day of each new restaurant. This event has attracted fans from across the country who camp out in all types of weather to be among the first in line. Almost $3 million in free Chick-fil-A meals have been given away since this promotion began.

While serious about its children's premiums, the company is not against having fun with its promotions. For the past decade, Chick-fil-A has run its "Eat Mor Chikin" campaign, which features cows that encourage beefeaters to switch to chicken out of self-preservation. The chain has even designated July 15 as Cow Appreciation Day, when customers receive a free combo meal if they arrive at a restaurant dressed as a cow. The cows have become the restaurant's mascots, appearing on clothing and other merchandise that can be purchased at Chick-fil-A locations or from its website.

The chain also uses the bovine theme in its annual calendars, dubbed "Cows in Shining Armor," which depict

## OBJECTIVES

1. To understand the major purposes of personal selling

2. To describe the basic steps in the personal selling process

3. To identify the types of sales force personnel

4. To recognize new types of personal selling

5. To understand sales management decisions and activities

6. To explain what sales promotion activities are and how they are used

7. To explore specific consumer and trade sales promotion methods

**545**

cows in various heroic situations. Now in its ninth year, the Chick-fil-A cow calendar has become the largest-selling calendar in the United States—more than doubling the sales of even *Sports Illustrated*'s wildly popular swimsuit calendar.

Like its competition, Chick-fil-A will no doubt continue to use sales promotion to drive its business, but don't expect this company to be cowed into following the crowd.[1] ∎

For many organizations, such as Chick-fil-A, targeting customers with appropriate sales promotions can play a major role in maintaining long-term, satisfying customer relationships, which in turn contribute to the company's success. As we saw in Chapter 18, personal selling and sales promotion are two possible elements in a promotion mix. Sales promotion is sometimes a company's sole promotional tool, although it is generally used in conjunction with other promotion mix elements. It is playing an increasingly important role in marketing strategies. Personal selling is becoming more professional and sophisticated, with sales personnel acting more as consultants and advisers.

In this chapter, we focus on personal selling and sales promotion. We first consider the purposes of personal selling and then examine its basic steps. Next, we look at types of salespeople and how they are selected. After taking a look at several new types of personal selling, we discuss major sales force management decisions, including setting objectives for the sales force and determining its size; recruiting, selecting, training, compensating, and motivating salespeople; managing sales territories; and controlling and evaluating sales force performance. Then we examine several characteristics of sales promotion, reasons for using sales promotion, and sales promotion methods available for use in a promotion mix.

# The Nature of Personal Selling

**personal selling** Paid personal communication that attempts to inform customers and persuade them to buy products in an exchange situation

**Personal selling** is paid personal communication that attempts to inform customers and persuade them to purchase products in an exchange situation. For example, a Hewlett-Packard (HP) salesperson describing the benefits of the company's servers, PCs, and printers to a small-business customer is engaging in personal selling. In fact, HP has a Small Business Initiative to reach more than 550,000 small businesses in the United States.[2] Personal selling gives marketers the greatest freedom to adjust a message to satisfy customers' information needs. It is the most precise of all promotion methods, enabling marketers to focus on the most promising sales prospects. Other promotion mix elements are aimed at groups of people, some of whom may not be prospective customers. However, personal selling is generally the most expensive element in the promotion mix. The average cost of a sales call is more than $400.[3]

Millions of people, including increasing numbers of women, earn their living through personal selling. Sales careers can offer high income, a great deal of freedom, a high level of training, and a high degree of job satisfaction. Although the public may harbor negative perceptions of personal selling, unfavorable stereotypes of salespeople are changing thanks to the efforts of major corporations, professional sales associations, and academic institutions. Research indicates that personal selling will continue to gain respect as professional sales associations develop and enforce ethical codes of conduct.[4]

Personal selling goals vary from one firm to another. However, they usually involve finding prospects, persuading prospects to buy, and keeping customers satisfied. Identifying potential buyers interested in the organization's products is critical. Because most potential buyers seek information before making purchases, salespeople can ascertain prospects' informational needs and then provide relevant information. To do so, sales personnel must be well trained regarding both their products and the selling process in general.

Salespeople must be aware of their competitors. They must monitor the development of new products and keep abreast of competitors' sales efforts in their sales

## marketing ENTREPRENEURS

**Lara Merriken**

**THE BUSINESS:** LäraBars

**FOUNDED:** 2000

**SUCCESS:** 11 employees and a reputation for quality

Lara Merriken, an avid hiker and founder of Humm Foods, wanted an alternative to the sugar- and junk-filled energy bars that were available on the market, so she started experimenting with recipes using a simple food processor. The result was the LäraBar, a snack bar made only with all-natural quality ingredients, without preservatives or refined sugar. She finished her first order of 500 bars by hand in her home kitchen. As demand increased, so did the size of her operation. Lara initially got her product into stores by presenting them to her former employer, Whole Foods. Her ability to personally sell the product made the difference. She now has 11 employees (two of which are her dogs) and distributes LäraBars to local natural foods stores throughout Colorado, as well as to some grocers in California and in Canada. LäraBars now retail at around $1.99 each or $29.99 for a case of 16. For Lara Merriken, a super-high-quality product and good marketing equals success.

territories, how often and when the competition calls on their accounts, and what the competition is saying about their product in relation to its own. Salespeople must emphasize the benefits their products provide, especially when competitors' products do not offer those specific benefits.

Few businesses survive solely on profits from one-time customers. For long-run survival, most marketers depend on repeat sales, and thus need to keep their customers satisfied. In addition, satisfied customers provide favorable word-of-mouth communications, thus attracting new customers. Although the whole organization is responsible for achieving customer satisfaction, much of the burden falls on salespeople because they are almost always closer to customers than anyone else in the company and often provide buyers with information and service after the sale. Indeed, research shows that a firm's marketing orientation has a positive influence on salespeople's attitudes, commitment, and influence on customer purchasing intentions.[5] Such contact gives salespeople an opportunity to generate additional sales and offers them a good vantage point for evaluating the strengths and weaknesses of the company's products and other marketing mix components. Their observations help develop and maintain a marketing mix that better satisfies both the firm and its customers.

**prospecting** Developing a list of potential customers

# Elements of the Personal Selling Process

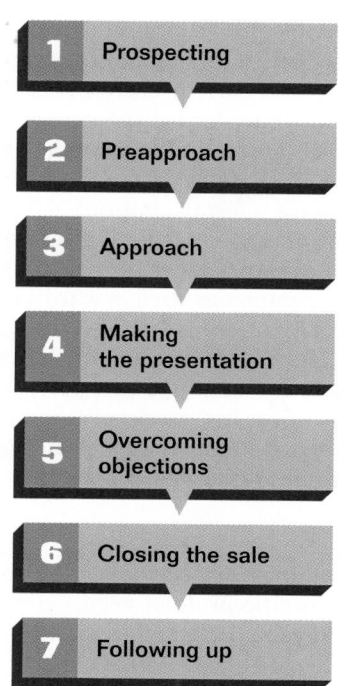

**figure 20.1**

**GENERAL STEPS IN THE PERSONAL SELLING PROCESS**

1 Prospecting

2 Preapproach

3 Approach

4 Making the presentation

5 Overcoming objections

6 Closing the sale

7 Following up

The specific activities involved in the selling process vary among salespeople and selling situations. No two salespeople use exactly the same selling methods. Nonetheless, many salespeople move through a general selling process. This process consists of seven steps, outlined in Figure 20.1: prospecting, preapproach, approach, making the presentation, overcoming objections, closing the sale, and following up.

## Prospecting

Developing a list of potential customers is called **prospecting**. Salespeople seek names of prospects from company sales records, trade shows, commercial databases, newspaper announcements (of marriages, births, deaths, and so on), public records, telephone directories, trade association directories, and many other sources. Sales personnel also use responses to advertisements that encourage interested persons to send in information request forms. Seminars and

**Prospecting**

Salesgenie.com helps companies connect with the right potential business customers.

meetings targeted at particular types of clients, such as attorneys or accountants, may also produce leads.

A number of salespeople prefer to use referrals—recommendations from current customers—to find prospects. Obtaining referrals requires that the salesperson have a good relationship with the current customer and therefore must have performed well before asking the customer for help. As might be expected, a customer's trust in and satisfaction with a salesperson influences his or her willingness to provide referrals.[6] Research shows that 1 referral is as valuable as 12 cold calls. Also, 80 percent of clients are willing to give referrals, but only 20 percent are ever asked. According to sales experts, the advantages of using referrals are that the resulting sales leads are highly qualified, sales rates are higher, initial transactions are larger, and the sales cycle is shorter.[7] Some companies even reward customers for referring their salespeople to new prospects by offering discounts off future purchases.[8]

Consistent activity is critical to successful prospecting. Salespeople must actively search the customer base for qualified prospects who fit the target market profile. After developing the prospect list, a salesperson evaluates whether each prospect is able, willing, and authorized to buy the product. Based on this evaluation, prospects are ranked according to desirability or potential.

## Preapproach

Before contacting acceptable prospects, a salesperson finds and analyzes information about each prospect's specific product needs, current use of brands, feelings about available brands, and personal characteristics. In short, salespeople need to know what potential buyers and decisionmakers consider most important and why they need a specific product.[9] The most successful salespeople are thorough in their preapproach, which involves identifying key decisionmakers, reviewing account histories and problems, contacting other clients for information, assessing credit histories and problems, preparing sales presentations, identifying product needs, and obtaining relevant literature. Many companies employ information technology and customer relationship management systems to scour their databases and thus identify the most profitable products and customers. These systems can also help sales departments manage leads, track customers, develop sales forecasts, and measure performance.[10] A salesperson with a lot of information about a prospect is better equipped to develop a presentation that precisely communicates with that prospect.

## Approach

**approach** The manner in which a salesperson contacts a potential customer

The **approach**, the manner in which a salesperson contacts a potential customer, is a critical step in the sales process. In more than 80 percent of initial sales calls, the purpose is to gather information about the buyer's needs and objectives. Creating a favorable impression and building rapport with prospective clients are important tasks in the approach because the prospect's first impressions of the salesperson are usually lasting ones. During the initial visit, the salesperson strives to develop a relationship rather than just push a product. Indeed, coming across as a "salesperson" may not be the best approach because some people are put off by strong selling tactics. Experts recommend using a neutral tone and normal conversational speech to improve the odds of making a sale.[11] The salesperson may have to call on a prospect several times before the product is considered. The approach must be designed to deliver value to targeted customers. If the sales approach is inappropriate, the salesperson's efforts are likely to have poor results.

One type of approach is based on referrals: the salesperson approaches the prospect and explains that an acquaintance, an associate, or a relative suggested the call. The salesperson who uses the "cold canvass" approach calls on potential customers without prior consent. Repeat contact is another common approach: when making the contact, the salesperson mentions a previous meeting. The exact type of approach depends on the salesperson's preferences, the product being sold, the firm's resources, and the prospect's characteristics.

## Making the Presentation

During the sales presentation, the salesperson must attract and hold the prospect's attention, stimulate interest, and spark a desire for the product. The salesperson should have the prospect touch, hold, or use the product. If possible, the salesperson should demonstrate the product or invite the prospect to use it. Automobile salespeople, for example, typically invite potential buyers to test drive the vehicle that interests them. Audiovisual equipment and software may also enhance the presentation.

During the presentation, the salesperson must not only talk, but also listen. The sales presentation gives the salesperson the greatest opportunity to determine the prospect's specific needs by listening to questions and comments and observing responses. Even though the salesperson plans the presentation in advance, she or he must be able to adjust the message to meet the prospect's informational needs. Research demonstrates that adapting the message in response to the customer's needs generally enhances performance, particularly in new-task or modified rebuy purchase situations.[12]

## Overcoming Objections

An effective salesperson usually seeks out a prospect's objections in order to address them. If they are not apparent, the salesperson cannot deal with them, and the prospect may not buy. One of the best ways to overcome objections is to anticipate and counter them before the prospect raises them. However, this approach can be risky because the salesperson may mention objections that the prospect would not have raised. If possible, the salesperson should handle objections as they arise. They can also be addressed at the end of the presentation.

**Closing the Sale**

Hoover's Online provides detailed information that can help close sales.

**closing** The stage in the personal selling process when the salesperson asks the prospect to buy the product

## Closing the Sale

**Closing** is the stage in the personal selling process when the salesperson asks the prospect to buy the product. During the presentation, the salesperson may use a *trial close* by asking questions that assume the prospect will buy. The salesperson might ask the potential customer about financial terms, desired colors or sizes, or delivery arrangements. Reactions to such questions usually indicate how close the prospect is to buying. Properly asked questions may allow prospects to uncover their own problems and identify solutions themselves. One questioning approach uses broad questions (*what, how, why*) to probe or gather information and focused questions (*who, when, where*) to clarify and close the sale. A trial close allows prospects to indicate indirectly that they will buy the product without having to say those sometimes difficult words, "I'll take it."

A salesperson should try to close at several points during the presentation because the prospect may be ready to buy. An attempt to close the sale may result in objections. Thus, closing can uncover hidden objections, which the salesperson can then address. One closing strategy involves asking the potential customer to place a low-risk tryout order.

### Following Up

After a successful closing, the salesperson must follow up the sale. In the follow-up stage, the salesperson determines whether the order was delivered on time and installed properly, if installation was required. He or she should contact the customer to learn if any problems or questions regarding the product have arisen. The follow-up stage is also used to determine customers' future product needs.

# Types of Salespeople

To develop a sales force, a marketing manager decides what kind of salesperson will sell the firm's products most effectively. Most business organizations use several different kinds of sales personnel. Based on the functions performed, salespeople can be classified into three groups: order getters, order takers, and support personnel. One salesperson can, and often does, perform all three functions.

### Order Getters

**order getter** A salesperson who sells to new customers and increases sales to current customers

To obtain orders, a salesperson informs prospects and persuades them to buy the product. The **order getter's** job is to increase sales by selling to new customers and increasing sales to present customers. This task is sometimes called *creative selling*. It requires that salespeople recognize potential buyers' needs and give them necessary information. Order getting is frequently divided into two categories: current-customer sales and new-business sales.

**Current-Customer Sales.** Sales personnel who concentrate on current customers call on people and organizations that have purchased products from the firm before. These salespeople seek more sales from existing customers by following up previous sales. Current customers can also be sources of leads for new prospects.

**New-Business Sales.** Business organizations depend to some degree on sales to new customers. New-business sales personnel locate prospects and convert them into buyers. In many organizations, salespeople help generate new business, but organizations that sell real estate, insurance, appliances, heavy industrial machinery, and automobiles depend in large part on new-customer sales.

## Order Takers

Taking orders is a repetitive task salespeople perform to perpetuate long-lasting, satisfying customer relationships. **Order takers** primarily seek repeat sales, generating the bulk of many firms' total sales. One of their major objectives is to be certain that customers have sufficient product quantities where and when needed. Most order takers handle orders for standardized products that are purchased routinely and do not require extensive sales efforts. The role of order takers is changing, however, as the position moves more toward one that identifies and solves problems to better meet the needs of customers. There are two groups of order takers: inside order takers and field order takers.

**order takers** A salesperson who primarily seeks repeat sales

**Inside Order Takers.** In many businesses, inside order takers, who work in sales offices, receive orders by mail, telephone, and the Internet. Certain producers, wholesalers, and retailers have sales personnel who sell from within the firm rather than in the field. Some inside order takers communicate with customers face to face; retail salespeople, for example, are classified as inside order takers. As more orders are placed through the Internet, the role of the inside order taker continues to change.

**Field Order Takers.** Salespeople who travel to customers are outside, or field, order takers. Often customers and field order takers develop interdependent relationships. The buyer relies on the salesperson to take orders periodically (and sometimes to deliver them), and the salesperson counts on the buyer to purchase a certain quantity of products periodically. Use of small computers has improved the field order taker's inventory and order-tracking capabilities.

## Support Personnel

**support personnel** Sales staff members who facilitate selling but usually are not involved solely with making sales

**Support personnel** facilitate selling but usually are not involved solely with making sales. They engage primarily in marketing industrial products, locating prospects, educating customers, building goodwill, and providing service after the sale. There are many kinds of sales support personnel; the three most common are missionary, trade, and technical salespeople.

**missionary salespeople** Support salespeople, usually employed by a manufacturer, who assist the producer's customers in selling to their own customers

**Missionary Salespeople.** **Missionary salespeople**, usually employed by manufacturers, assist the producer's customers in selling to their own customers. Missionary salespeople may call on retailers to inform and persuade them to buy the manufacturer's products. When they succeed, retailers purchase products from wholesalers, which are the producer's customers. Manufacturers of medical supplies and pharmaceuticals often use missionary salespeople, called *detail reps*, to promote their products to physicians, hospitals, and retail druggists.

**trade salespeople** Salespeople involved mainly in helping a producer's customers promote a product

**Trade Salespeople.** **Trade salespeople** are not strictly support personnel because they usually take orders as well. However, they direct much effort toward helping customers, especially retail stores, promote the product. They are likely to restock shelves, obtain more shelf space, set up displays, provide in-store demonstrations, and distribute samples to store customers. Food producers and processors commonly employ trade salespeople.

**technical salespeople** Support salespeople who give technical assistance to a firm's current customers

**Technical Salespeople.** **Technical salespeople** give technical assistance to the organization's current customers, advising them on product characteristics and applications, system designs, and installation procedures. Because this job is often highly technical, the salesperson usually has formal training in one of the physical sciences or in engineering. Technical sales personnel often sell technical industrial products such as computers, heavy equipment, and steel.

When hiring sales personnel, marketers seldom restrict themselves to a single category because most firms require different types of salespeople. Several factors dictate how many of each type a particular company should have. Product use, characteristics, complexity, and price influence the kind of sales personnel used, as do the number and characteristics of customers. The types of marketing channels and the intensity and type of advertising also affect the composition of a sales force.

# Selected Types of Selling

Personal selling has become an increasingly complex process due in large part to rapid technological innovation. Most importantly, the focus of personal selling is shifting from selling a specific product to building long-term relationships with customers by finding solutions to their needs, problems, and challenges. As a result, the roles of salespeople are changing. Among the new philosophies for personal selling are team selling and relationship selling.

## Team Selling

**team selling** The use of a team of experts from all functional areas of a firm, led by a salesperson, to conduct the personal selling process

Many products, particularly expensive high-tech business products, have become so complex that a single salesperson can no longer be expert in every aspect of the product and purchase process. **Team selling**, which involves the salesperson joining with people from the firm's financial, engineering, and other functional areas, is appropriate for such products. The salesperson takes the lead in the personal selling process, but other members of the team bring their unique skills, knowledge, and resources to the process to help customers find solutions to their own business challenges. Selling teams may be created to address a particular short-term situation or they may be formal, ongoing teams. Team selling is advantageous in situations calling for detailed knowledge of new, complex, and dynamic technologies such as jet aircraft and medical equipment. It can be difficult, however, for highly competitive salespersons to adapt to a team-selling environment.

## Relationship Selling

**relationship selling** The building of mutually beneficial long-term associations with a customer through regular communications over prolonged periods of time

**Relationship selling**, also known as consultative selling, involves building mutually beneficial long-term associations with a customer through regular communications over prolonged periods of time. Like team selling, it is especially used in business-to-business marketing. Relationship selling involves finding solutions to customers' needs by listening to them, gaining a detailed understanding of their organizations, understanding and caring about their needs and challenges, and providing support after the sale. At Computer Discount Warehouse (CDW), relationship selling is based on helping customers succeed. Before hurricanes struck Florida, for example, some CDW account managers contacted clients in the paths of the storms and suggested computer back-up storage and battery solutions that could help their businesses weather the storms with greater confidence.[13]

# Managing the Sales Force

The sales force is directly responsible for generating one of an organization's primary inputs: sales revenue. Without adequate sales revenue, businesses cannot survive. In addition, a firm's reputation is often determined by the ethical conduct of its sales force. The morale and ultimately the success of a firm's sales force depend in large part on adequate compensation, room for advancement, sufficient training, and management support—all key areas of sales management. Salespeople who are not satisfied with these elements may leave. Evaluating the input of salespeople is an important part of sales force management because of its strong bearing on a firm's success.

We explore eight general areas of sales management: establishing sales force objectives, determining sales force size, recruiting and selecting salespeople, training sales personnel, compensating salespeople, motivating salespeople, managing sales territories, and controlling and evaluating sales force performance.

## Establishing Sales Force Objectives

To manage a sales force effectively, sales managers must develop sales objectives. Sales objectives tell salespeople what they are expected to accomplish during a specified time period. They give the sales force direction and purpose, and serve as standards for evaluating and controlling the performance of sales personnel. Sales objectives should be stated in precise, measurable terms and should specify the time period and geographic areas involved.

Sales objectives are usually developed for both the total sales force and individual salespeople. Objectives for the entire force are normally stated in terms of sales volume, market share, or profit. Volume objectives refer to dollar or unit sales. For example, the objective for an electric drill producer's sales force might be to sell $18 million worth of drills, or 600,000 drills annually. When sales goals are stated in terms of market share, they usually call for an increase in the proportion of the firm's sales relative to the total number of products sold by all businesses in that industry. When sales objectives are based on profit, they are generally stated in terms of dollar amounts or return on investment.

Sales objectives, or quotas, for individual salespeople are commonly stated in terms of dollar or unit sales volume. Other bases used for individual sales objectives include average order size, average number of calls per time period, and ratio of orders to calls.

## Determining Sales Force Size

Sales force size is important because it influences the company's ability to generate sales and profits. Moreover, size of the sales force affects the compensation methods used, salespeople's morale, and overall sales force management. Sales force size must be adjusted periodically because a firm's marketing plans change along with markets and forces in the marketing environment. One danger in cutting back the size of the sales force to increase profits is that the sales organization may lose strength and resiliency, preventing it from rebounding when growth occurs or better market conditions prevail.

Several analytical methods can help determine optimal sales force size. One method involves determining how many sales calls per year are necessary for the organization to serve customers effectively and then dividing this total by the average number of sales calls a salesperson makes annually. A second method is based on marginal analysis, in which additional salespeople are added to the sales force until the cost of an additional salesperson equals the additional sales generated by that person. Although marketing managers may use one or several analytical methods, they normally temper decisions with subjective judgments.

## Recruiting and Selecting Salespeople

To create and maintain an effective sales force, sales managers must recruit the right type of salespeople. In **recruiting**, the sales manager develops a list of qualified applicants for sales positions. Effective recruiting efforts are a vital part of implementing the strategic sales force plan and can help assure successful organizational performance.[14] Costs of hiring and training a salesperson are soaring, reaching more than $60,000 in some industries. Thus, recruiting errors are expensive.

To ensure the recruiting process results in a pool of qualified applicants, a sales manager establishes a set of qualifications before beginning to recruit. Although

**recruiting** Developing a list of qualified applicants for sales positions

marketers have tried for years to identify a set of traits characterizing effective sales-people, no set of generally accepted characteristics yet exists. Experts agree that good salespeople exhibit optimism, flexibility, self-motivation, empathy, and the ability to network and maintain long-term customer relationships. One trait that may be use-ful in sensing customer reactions and generally being flexible is emotional intelligence: being in touch with one's own feelings and those of others.[15] Today companies are increasingly seeking applicants capable of employing relationship-building and con-sultative approaches.[16]

Sales managers must determine what set of traits best fits their companies' par-ticular sales tasks. Two activities help establish this set of required attributes. First, the sales manager should prepare a job description listing specific tasks salespeo-ple are to perform. Second, the manager should analyze characteristics of the firm's successful salespeople, as well as those of ineffective sales personnel. From the job description and analysis of traits, the sales manager should be able to develop a set of specific requirements and be aware of potential weaknesses that could lead to failure.

A sales manager generally recruits applicants from several sources: departments within the firm, other firms, employment agencies, educational institutions, respon-dents to advertisements, and individuals recommended by current employees. The specific sources depend on the type of salesperson required and the manager's expe-riences with particular sources.

The process of recruiting and selecting salespeople varies considerably from one company to another. Companies intent on reducing sales force turnover are likely to have strict recruiting and selection procedures. State Farm Life Insurance, for exam-ple, strives to retain customers by having low sales force turnover. Applicants for the job of State Farm insurance agent must go through a year-long series of interviews, tests, and visits with agents before finding out if they have been hired. Approximately 80 percent of State Farm agents are still employed four years after being hired, com-pared with an industry average of only 30 percent.

Sales management should design a selection procedure that satisfies the company's specific needs. Some organizations use the specialized services of other companies to hire sales personnel. The process should include steps that yield the information re-quired to make accurate selection decisions. However, because each step incurs a cer-tain amount of expense, there should be no more steps than necessary. Stages of the selection process should be sequenced so that the more expensive steps, such as a physical examination, occur near the end. Fewer people will then move through higher-cost stages.

Recruitment should not be sporadic; it should be a continuous activity aimed at reaching the best applicants. The selection process should systematically and effec-tively match applicants' characteristics and needs with the requirements of specific selling tasks. Finally, the selection process should ensure that new sales personnel are available where and when needed.

## Training Sales Personnel

Many organizations have formal training programs; others depend on informal, on-the-job training. Some systematic training programs are quite extensive, whereas oth-ers are rather short and rudimentary. Whether the training program is complex or sim-ple, developers must consider what to teach, whom to train, and how to train them.

A sales training program can concentrate on the company, its products, or sell-ing methods. Training programs often cover all three. Such programs can be aimed at newly hired salespeople, experienced salespeople, or both. Training for experi-enced company salespeople usually emphasizes product information, although sales-people must also be informed about new selling techniques and changes in company plans, policies, and procedures. Ordinarily, new sales personnel require comprehen-sive training, whereas experienced personnel need both refresher courses on estab-lished products and training regarding new-product information.

Sales training may be done in the field, at educational institutions, in company fa-cilities, and/or online using web-based technology. For many companies, online train-

**Sales Training**

Companies like Richardson offer specialized programs to assist the training process either at a physical location or online.

ing saves time and money, and helps salespeople learn about new products quickly. Some firms train new employees before assigning them to a specific sales position. Others put them into the field immediately, providing formal training only after they have gained some experience. Training programs for new personnel can be as short as several days or as long as three years; some are even longer. Sales training for experienced personnel is often scheduled when sales activities are not too demanding. Because experienced salespeople usually need periodic retraining, a firm's sales management must determine the frequency, sequencing, and duration of these efforts.

Sales managers, as well as other salespeople, often engage in sales training, whether daily on the job or periodically during sales meetings. Salespeople sometimes receive training from technical specialists within their own organizations. In addition, a number of outside companies specialize in providing sales training programs. Materials for sales training programs range from videos, texts, online materials, manuals, and cases to programmed learning devices and audio- and videocassettes. Lectures, demonstrations, simulation exercises, and on-the-job training can all be effective teaching methods. The choice of methods and materials for a particular sales training program depends on type and number of trainees, program content and complexity, length and location, size of the training budget, number of teachers, and teacher preferences.

## Compensating Salespeople

To develop and maintain a highly productive sales force, a business must formulate and administer a compensation plan that attracts, motivates, and retains the

# Pampered Chef

Doris Christopher's experience as a home economics teacher and homemaker helped her recognize a need for kitchen tools and techniques to minimize the time busy moms spend cooking. Inspired to help others preserve the tradition of family mealtimes, she founded the Pampered Chef out of the basement of her Chicago home in 1980.

Christopher modeled her business around home demonstration parties, which are sales presentations in which she showed people how to use the proper kitchen tools with real food. These parties offered the kind of show-and-tell that gave customers a "try-before-you-buy" experience. Christopher sold $175 worth of kitchenware at her first in-home

show. She expanded her direct-selling organization by following the personal selling process with in-home presentation as the heart of the sales process.

At first, Christopher handled all of the demonstrations herself, but in 1981 she took on her first outside "kitchen consultant" salesperson. By the end of that year, she had a dozen sales consultants and had established a commission incentive for selling the products. She also began holding sales meetings in her home, training sales consultants in effective techniques for making presentations, demonstrating recipes, and introducing new products.

Today more than 70,000 Pampered Chef Kitchen consultants sell more than 200 products with annual sales of $700 million. Doris Christopher's approach to personal selling, inspired by her dedication to family and home, helped to create a successful privately held company.

most effective individuals. The plan should give sales management the desired level of control and provide sales personnel with acceptable levels of income, freedom, and incentive. It should be flexible, equitable, easy to administer, and easy to understand. Good compensation programs facilitate and encourage proper treatment of customers. Obviously it is quite difficult to incorporate all of these requirements into a single program.

Developers of compensation programs must determine the general level of compensation required and the most desirable method of calculating it. In analyzing the required compensation level, sales management must ascertain a salesperson's value to the company on the basis of the tasks and responsibilities associated with the sales position. Sales managers may consider a number of factors, including salaries of other types of personnel in the firm, competitors' compensation plans, costs of sales force turnover, and nonsalary selling expenses. The average low-level salesperson earns about $65,000 annually (including commissions and bonuses), whereas a high-level, high-performing salesperson can make as much as $155,000 a year, as shown in Figure 20.2.[17]

Sales compensation programs usually reimburse salespeople for selling expenses, provide some fringe benefits, and deliver the required compensation level. To achieve this, a firm may use one or more of three basic compensation methods: straight salary, straight commission, or a combination of the two. Table 20.1 (on p. 558) lists the major characteristics, advantages, and disadvantages of each method. In a **straight salary compensation plan**, salespeople are paid a specified amount per time period, regardless of selling effort. This sum remains the same until they receive a pay increase or decrease. Although this method is easy to administer and affords salespeople financial security, it provides little incentive for them to boost selling efforts. In a **straight commission compensation plan**, salespeople's compensation is determined solely by sales for a given period. A commission may be based on a single percentage of sales or on a sliding scale involving several sales levels and percentage rates. While this method motivates sales personnel to escalate their selling efforts, it

**straight salary compensation plan** Paying salespeople a specific amount per time period, regardless of selling effort

**straight commission compensation plan** Paying salespeople according to the amount of their sales in a given time period

**figure 20.2**

## AVERAGE SALARIES FOR SALES REPRESENTATIVES

**Source:** Christine Galea, "3rd annual Compensation Survey," *Sales and Marketing Management,* May 2003, pp. 32–36. © VNU Business Media, Inc. Reprinted with permission from *Sales and Marketing Management.*

**combination compensation plan** Paying salespeople a fixed salary plus a commission based on sales volume

offers them little financial security, and it can be difficult for sales managers to maintain control over the sales force. For these reasons, many firms offer a **combination compensation plan** in which salespeople receive a fixed salary plus a commission based on sales volume. Some combination programs require that a salesperson exceed a certain sales level before earning a commission; others offer commissions for any level of sales. This method is the most popular, as indicated in Table 20.1.

When selecting a compensation method, sales management weighs the advantages and disadvantages listed in the table. Research suggests that sales managers may be moving away from individual performance-based commissions and toward salary- and team-based compensation methods.[18] For example, the Container Store, which markets do-it-yourself organizing and storage products, prefers to pay its sales staff salaries that are 50 to 100 percent higher than those offered by rivals instead of basing pay on commission plans.[19]

## Motivating Salespeople

Although financial compensation is an important incentive, additional programs are necessary for motivating sales personnel. A sales manager should develop a systematic approach for motivating salespeople to be productive. Effective sales force motivation is achieved through an organized set of activities performed continuously by the company's sales management.

Sales personnel, like other people, join organizations to satisfy personal needs and achieve personal goals. Sales managers must identify those needs and goals and strive to create an organizational climate that allows each salesperson to fulfill them. Enjoyable working conditions, power and authority, job security, and opportunity to excel are effective motivators, as are company efforts to make sales jobs more productive and efficient. At the Container Store, for example, sales personnel receive hundreds of hours of training about the company's products every year so they can help customers solve organization and storage problems.[20] Sales contests and other incentive programs can also be effective motivators. These can motivate salespeople to increase sales or add new accounts, promote special items, achieve greater volume per sales call, and cover territories more thoroughly. However, companies need to understand salespersons' preferences when designing contests in order to make them effective in increasing sales.[21] Some companies find such contests powerful tools for motivating sales personnel to achieve company goals. In smaller firms lacking the resources for a formal incentive program, a simple but public "thank-you" from management at a sales meeting, along with a small-denomination gift card, can be rewarding.[22]

| table 20.1 | CHARACTERISTICS OF SALES FORCE COMPENSATION METHODS | | | |
|---|---|---|---|---|
| **Compensation Method** | **Use (%)*** | **When Especially Useful** | **Advantages** | **Disadvantages** |
| Straight salary | 17.5 | Compensating new salespersons; firm moves into new sales territories that require developmental work; sales requiring lengthy presale and postsale services | Gives salespeople security; gives sales managers control over salespeople; easy to administer; yields more predictable selling expenses | Provides no incentive; necessitates closer supervision of salespeople; during sales declines, selling expenses remain constant |
| Straight commission | 14.0 | Highly aggressive selling is required; nonselling tasks are minimized; company uses contractors and part-timers | Provides maximum amount of incentive; by increasing commission rate, sales managers can encourage salespeople to sell certain items; selling expenses relate directly to sales resources | Salespeople have little financial security; sales managers have minimum control over sales force; may cause salespeople to give inadequate service to smaller accounts; selling costs less predictable |
| Combination | 68.5 | Sales territories have relatively similar sales potential; firm wishes to provide incentive but still control sales force activities | Provides certain level of financial security; provides some incentive; can move sales force efforts in profitable direction | Selling expenses less predictable; may be difficult to administer |

*Figures computed from *Dartnell's 30th Sales Force Compensation Survey*, Dartnell Corporation, Chicago, 1999.
**Source:** Charles Futrell, *Sales Management* (Ft. Worth: Dryden Press), 2001, pp. 307–316.

Properly designed incentive programs pay for themselves many times over, and sales managers are relying on incentives more than ever. Recognition programs that acknowledge outstanding performance with symbolic awards, such as plaques, can be very effective when carried out in a peer setting. The most common incentive offered by companies is cash, followed by gift cards and travel.[23] Travel reward programs can confer a high-profile honor, provide a unique experience that makes recipients feel special, and build camaraderie among award-winning salespeople. However, some recipients of travel awards may feel they already travel too much on the job. Cash rewards are easy to administer, are always appreciated by recipients, and appeal to all demographic groups. However, cash has no visible "trophy" value and provides few "bragging rights." The benefits of awarding merchandise are that the items have visible trophy value. In addition, recipients who are allowed to select the merchandise experience a sense of control, and merchandise awards can help build momentum for the sales force. The disadvantages of using merchandise are that employees may have lower perceived value of the merchandise and that the company may experience greater administrative problems. Some companies outsource their incentive programs to companies that specialize in the creation and management of such programs.

## Managing Sales Territories

The effectiveness of a sales force that must travel to customers is somewhat influenced by management's decisions regarding sales territories. When deciding on territories, sales managers must consider size, shape, routing, and scheduling.

**Creating Sales Territories.** Several factors enter into the design of a sales territory's size and shape. First, sales managers must construct territories that allow sales potential to be measured. Sales territories often consist of several geographic

**Motivating Salespeople**

Synygy provides sales compensation management solutions. Properly managed incentive programs motivate appropriate sales force behaviors, and thus drive sales performance.

units, such as census tracts, cities, counties, or states, for which market data are obtainable. Sales managers usually try to create territories with similar sales potential or requiring about the same amount of work. If territories have equal sales potential, they will almost always be unequal in geographic size. Salespeople with larger territories have to work longer and harder to generate a certain sales volume. Conversely, if sales territories requiring equal amounts of work are created, sales potential for those territories will often vary. If sales personnel are partially or fully compensated through commissions, they will have unequal income potential. Many sales managers try to balance territorial workloads and earning potential by using differential commission rates. At times, sales managers use commercial programs to help them balance sales territories. Although a sales manager seeks equity when developing and maintaining sales territories, some inequities always prevail.

A territory's size and shape should also help the sales force provide the best possible customer coverage and should minimize selling costs. Customer density and distribution are important factors.

**Routing and Scheduling Salespeople.** The geographic size and shape of a sales territory are the most important factors affecting the routing and scheduling of sales calls. Next in importance is the number and distribution of customers within the territory, followed by sales call frequency and duration. Those in charge of routing and scheduling must consider the sequence in which customers are called on, specific roads or transportation schedules to be used, number of calls to be made in a given period, and time of day the calls will occur. In some firms, salespeople plan their own routes and schedules with little or no assistance from the sales manager. In others, the sales manager is responsible. No matter who plans the routing and scheduling, the major goals should be to minimize salespeople's nonselling time (time spent traveling and waiting) and maximize their selling time. Planners should try to achieve these goals so that a salesperson's travel and lodging costs are held to a minimum.

## Controlling and Evaluating Sales Force Performance

To control and evaluate sales force performance properly, sales management needs information. A sales manager cannot observe the field sales force daily and thus relies on salespeople's call reports, customer feedback, and invoices. Call reports identify the customers called on and present detailed information about interactions with those clients. Sales personnel often must file work schedules indicating where they plan to be during specific time periods. Data about a salesperson's interactions with customers and prospects can be included in the company's customer relationship management system. This information provides insights about the salesperson's performance.

Dimensions used to measure a salesperson's performance are determined largely by sales objectives, normally set by the sales manager. If an individual's sales objective is stated in terms of sales volume, that person should be evaluated on the basis of sales volume generated. Even if a salesperson is assigned a major objective, he or she is ordinarily expected to achieve several related objectives as well. Thus, salespeople are often judged along several dimensions. Sales managers evaluate many performance indicators, including average number of calls per day, average sales per customer, actual sales relative to sales potential, number of new-customer orders, average cost per call, and average gross profit per customer.

To evaluate a salesperson, a sales manager may compare one or more of these dimensions with predetermined performance standards. However, sales managers commonly compare a salesperson's performance with that of other employees operating under similar selling conditions, or the salesperson's current performance with past performance. Sometimes management judges factors that have less direct bearing on sales performance, such as personal appearance, product knowledge, and ethical standards. One concern is the tendency to reprimand top sellers less severely than poor performers for engaging in unethical selling practices.[24]

After evaluating salespeople, sales managers take any needed corrective action to improve sales force performance. They may adjust performance standards, provide additional training, or try other motivational methods. Corrective action may demand comprehensive changes in the sales force.

# The Nature of Sales Promotion

**sales promotion** An activity and/or material intended to induce resellers or salespeople to sell a product or consumers to buy it

**Sales promotion** is an activity or material, or both, that acts as a direct inducement, offering added value or incentive for the product, to resellers, salespeople, or consumers. It encompasses all promotional activities and materials other than personal selling, advertising, and public relations. In competitive markets, where products are very similar, sales promotion provides additional inducements that encourage product trial and purchase.

Marketers often use sales promotion to facilitate personal selling, advertising, or both. Companies also employ advertising and personal selling to support sales promotion activities. For example, marketers frequently use advertising to promote contests, free samples, and premiums. The most effective sales promotion efforts are highly interrelated with other promotional activities. Decisions regarding sales promotion often affect advertising and personal selling decisions, and vice versa.

Sales promotion can increase sales by providing extra purchasing incentives. Many opportunities exist to motivate consumers, resellers, and salespeople to take desired actions. Some kinds of sales promotion are designed specifically to stimulate resellers' demand and effectiveness, some are directed at increasing consumer demand, and some focus on both consumers and resellers. Regardless of the purpose, marketers must ensure that sales promotion objectives are consistent with the organization's overall objectives, as well as with its marketing and promotion objectives.

When deciding which sales promotion methods to use, marketers must consider several factors, particularly product characteristics (size, weight, costs, durability, uses, fea-

## 10% off
### INSTALLED CARPET
Offer valid 10/6 – 11/20.

Offer applies to all in-stock and Special Order carpet purchased and installed through Lowe's. Discount applies to carpet, pad and installation charges.

Cannot be combined with any other offers or applied to prior purchases. In-home estimate fee must be received by 11/20. See store for details.

Improving Home Improvement

**Coupon Retailer**
A retailer coupon is a sales promotion method used to attract customers away from other retailers.

tures, and hazards) and target market characteristics (age, gender, income, location, density, usage rate, and shopping patterns). How products are distributed and the number and types of resellers may determine the type of method used. The competitive and legal environment may also influence the choice.

The use of sales promotion has increased dramatically over the last 20 years, primarily at the expense of advertising. This shift in how promotional dollars are used has occurred for several reasons. Heightened concerns about value have made customers more responsive to promotional offers, especially price discounts and point-of-purchase displays. Thanks to their size and access to checkout scanner data, retailers have gained considerable power in the supply chain and are demanding greater promotional efforts from manufacturers to boost retail profits. Declines in brand loyalty have produced an environment in which sales promotions aimed at persuading customers to switch brands are more effective. Finally, the stronger emphasis placed on improving short-term performance results calls for greater use of sales promotion methods that yield quick (although perhaps short-lived) sales increases.[25]

In the remainder of this chapter, we examine several consumer and trade sales promotion methods, including what they entail and what goals they can help marketers achieve.

## Consumer Sales Promotion Methods

**consumer sales promotion methods** Sales promotion techniques that encourage consumers to patronize specific stores or try particular products

**Consumer sales promotion methods** encourage or stimulate consumers to patronize specific retail stores or try particular products. Consumer sales promotion methods initiated by retailers often aim to attract customers to specific locations, whereas those used by manufacturers generally introduce new products or promote established brands. In this section we discuss coupons, cents-off offers, money refunds and rebates, frequent-user incentives, point-of-purchase displays, demonstrations, free samples, premiums, consumer contests and games, and consumer sweepstakes.

**coupon** A written price reduction used to encourage consumers to buy a specific product

**Coupons.** **Coupons** reduce a product's price and aim to prompt customers to try new or established products, increase sales volume quickly, attract repeat purchasers, or introduce new package sizes or features. Savings are deducted from the purchase price. Coupons are the most widely used consumer sales promotion technique. Although billions of coupons are distributed annually, less than 2 percent are redeemed.[26] Even so, about 76 percent of all consumers use coupons, yielding $3 billion in annual savings.[27] Figures 20.3 and 20.4 (fig. 20.4 on p. 562) show that consumers' incomes and ages have surprisingly little effect on coupon usage. Although some firms have tried to scale back their use of coupons and other sales promotion methods in favor of an everyday low price strategy, some groups of consumers have resisted these efforts, perhaps preferring the sense of achievement they experience from buying products on sale and/or with a coupon.[28]

**figure 20.3**

### EFFECT OF INCOME ON COUPON USAGE

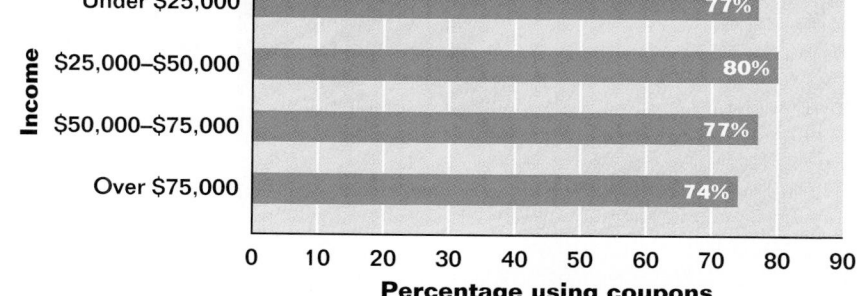

**Source:** "All About Coupons," Promotion Marketing Association, www.couponmonth.com/pages/allabout.htm (accessed May 5, 2006).

## figure 20.4

### EFFECT OF AGE ON COUPON USAGE

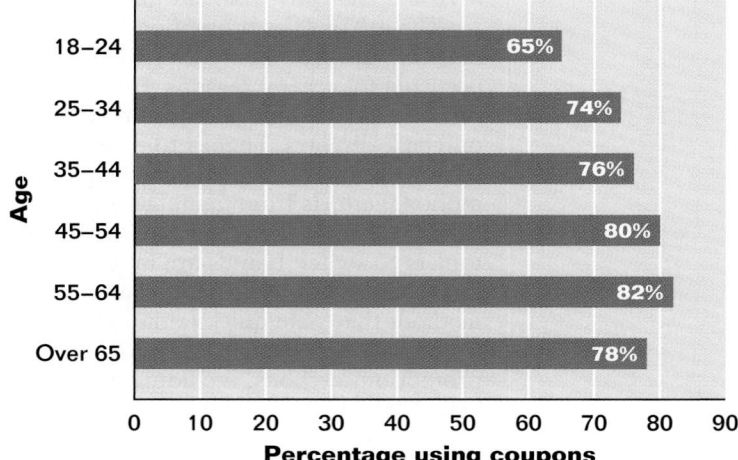

**Source:** "All About Coupons," Promotion Marketing Association, www.couponmonth.com/pages/allabout.htm (accessed May 5, 2006).

For best results, the coupons should be easily recognized and state the offer clearly. The nature of the product (seasonal demand for it, life cycle stage, frequency of purchase) is the prime consideration in setting up a coupon promotion. Paper coupons are distributed on and inside packages, through freestanding inserts, in print advertising, and through direct mail. Electronic coupons are distributed online, via in-store kiosks, through shelf dispensers in stores, and at checkout counters.[29] When deciding on the distribution method for coupons, marketers should consider strategies and objectives, redemption rates, availability, circulation, and exclusivity. The largest number of coupons distributed are for household cleaners, condiments, frozen foods, medications and health aids, and paper products. The coupon distribution and redemption arena has become very competitive. To avoid losing customers, many grocery stores will redeem any coupons offered by competitors. Also, to draw customers to their stores, grocers double and sometimes even triple the value of customers' coupons.

Coupons offer several advantages. Print advertisements with coupons are often more effective at generating brand awareness than are print ads without coupons. Generally, the larger the coupon's cash offer, the better the recognition generated. Coupons reward present product users, win back former users, and encourage purchases in larger quantities. Because they are returned, coupons also let a manufacturer determine whether it reached the intended target market. The advantages of using electronic coupons over paper coupons include lower cost per redemption, greater targeting ability, improved data-gathering capabilities, and greater experimentation capabilities to determine optimal face values and expiration cycles.[30]

Drawbacks of coupon use include fraud and misredemption, which can be expensive for manufacturers. The Coupon Information Council estimates that coupon fraud—including counterfeit Internet coupons as well as coupons cashed in under false retailer names—amounts to $500 million a year in the United States.[31] Another disadvantage, according to some experts, is that coupons are losing their value; because so many manufacturers offer them, consumers have

*Source:* Maritz Loyalty Marketing.

learned not to buy without some incentive, whether a coupon, a rebate, or a refund. Furthermore, brand loyalty among heavy coupon users has diminished, and many consumers redeem coupons only for products they normally buy. It is believed that about three-fourths of coupons are redeemed by people already using the brand on the coupon. Thus, coupons have questionable success as an incentive for consumers to try a new brand or product. An additional problem with coupons is that stores often do not have enough of the coupon item in stock. This situation generates ill will toward both the store and the product.

**cents-off offer** A promotion that allows buyers to pay less than the regular price to encourage purchase

**Cents-off offers.** With **cents-off offers**, buyers pay a certain amount less than the regular price shown on the label or package. Similar to coupons, this method can serve as a strong incentive for trying new or unfamiliar products and is commonly used in product introductions. It can stimulate product sales, multiple purchases, yield short-lived sales increases, and promote products during off seasons. It is an easy method to control and is often used for specific purposes. If used on an ongoing basis, however, cents-off offers reduce the price for customers who would buy at the regular price and may also cheapen a product's image. In addition, the method often requires special handling by retailers who are responsible for giving the discount at the point of sale.

**money refund** A sales promotion technique offering consumers a specified amount of money when they mail in a proof of purchase, usually for multiple product purchases

**Money refunds.** With **money refunds**, consumers submit proof of purchase and are mailed a specific amount of money. Usually manufacturers demand multiple product purchases before consumers qualify for money refunds. Marketers employ money refunds as an alternative to coupons to stimulate sales. Money refunds, used primarily to promote trial use of a product, are relatively low in cost. However, they sometimes generate a low response rate, and thus have limited impact on sales.

**rebate** A sales promotion technique in which a consumer receives a specified amount of money for making a single product purchase

**Rebates.** With **rebates**, the consumer is sent a specified amount of money for making a single product purchase. Rebates are generally given on more expensive products than money refunds and are used to encourage customers. Marketers also use rebates to reinforce brand loyalty, provide promotion buzz for salespeople, and advertise the product. On larger items, such as cars, rebates are often given at the point of sale. Most rebates, however, especially on smaller items, are given after the sale, usually through a mail-in process.

One problem with money refunds and rebates is that many people perceive the redemption process as too complicated. Only about 40 percent of individuals who purchase rebated products actually apply for the rebates.[32] Because of this, many marketers allow customers to apply for a rebate online, which eliminates the need for forms that may confuse customers and frustrate retailers. Consumers may also have negative perceptions of manufacturers' reasons for offering rebates. They may believe the products are untested or have not sold well. If these perceptions are not changed, rebate offers may actually degrade product image and desirability. On the other hand, rebates and low interest rates have been found to have a positive effect on car and truck sales.[33]

**Frequent-User Incentives.** Greeting cards aren't the only ones offered by Hallmark. To reward loyal customers, the company offers the Hallmark Gold Crown Card that allows frequent card buyers to accrue points which are redeemable for merchandise. Many firms develop incentive programs to reward customers who engage in repeat (frequent) purchases.[34] For

**GET A BONUS CREDIT FOR EVERY ROUNDTRIP BOOKED ON southwest.com.**

**Frequent-User Incentives**

To encourage customer loyalty, Southwest Airlines offers frequent-user incentive programs.

# Creative Promotion Tops Pizza Hut's Menu

Pizza Hut has gobbled up more than 40 percent of the U.S. pizza market with nearly 7,500 locations and $5.2 billion in annual revenue. Competition in the pizza business is heating up, however, with lots of special products, promotions, and pricing by challengers Domino's and Papa John's. So to maintain its dominance and keep customers coming back for more, Pizza Hut is cooking up an ever-expanding menu of creative promotions.

Every time the chain launches a new type of pizza, it blankets the nation with advertising supplemented by direct mail and signage in each Pizza Hut restaurant. When introducing the 16-inch Big New Yorker pizza, for example, Pizza Hut aired splashy television commercials geared to the "family dinner" market. The direct-mail campaign created excitement about the pizza by offering prizes such as a family holiday in Europe.

Competition is so intense that, despite higher costs for cheese and other ingredients, Pizza Hut and its rivals frequently offer money-saving coupons. In fact, visitors to Pizza Hut's website can click to print coupons. Moreover, to reward repeat purchasing, Pizza Hut now invites customers to join the Very into Pizza (VIP) program. For a $14.99 annual fee, members receive one free large pizza when they enroll and free breadsticks once a month for a year. When they place two or more $10 orders in a month, VIP members are eligible for a free large pizza.

Pizza Hut—owned by Yum Brands, which also owns KFC and Taco Bell—appeals to racing fans by sponsoring a NASCAR team and airing television commercials featuring Jeff Gordon and other well-known drivers. It continues the NASCAR theme with the Family Race Pack meal, a complete package of pizza, breadsticks, cinnamon sticks, soda, napkins, cups, and plates. Watch for more promotions ahead as Pizza Hut pushes for even more market share—and higher profits.

example, most major airlines offer frequent flier programs that reward customers who have flown a specified number of miles with free tickets for additional travel. Frequent-user incentives foster customer loyalty to a specific company or group of cooperating companies. They are favored by service businesses such as airlines, auto rental agencies, hotels, and local coffee shops. The U.K.'s Tesco supermarket chain, for example, uses its Clubcard program to reward shoppers' loyalty with a 1 percent rebate on their grocery purchases. Club members also receive a customized quarterly magazine. The long-running loyalty program has helped elevate Tesco to become the U.K.'s number 1 supermarket.[35]

**point-of-purchase (P-O-P) materials** Signs, window displays, display racks, and similar devices used to attract customers

**Point-of-Purchase Materials and Demonstrations. Point-of-purchase (P-O-P) materials** include outdoor signs, window displays, counter pieces, display racks, and self-service cartons. Innovations in P-O-P displays include sniff-teasers, which give off a product's aroma in the store as consumers walk within a radius of 4 feet, and computerized interactive displays. These items, often supplied by producers, attract attention, inform customers, and encourage retailers to carry particular products. A retailer is likely to use point-of-purchase materials if they are attractive, informative, well-constructed, and in harmony with the store's image.

**demonstration** A sales promotion method a manufacturer uses temporarily to encourage trial use and purchase of a product or to show how a product works

**Demonstrations** are excellent attention getters. Manufacturers offer them temporarily to encourage trial use and purchase of a product or to show how a product works. Because labor costs can be extremely high, demonstrations are not used widely. They can be highly effective for promoting certain types of products, such as appliances, cosmetics, and cleaning supplies. Even automobiles can be demonstrated, not only by a salesperson but also by the prospective buyer during a test drive. General

Motors, for example, launched an advertising campaign to encourage more prospective buyers to test drive new vehicles. The "Sleep on It" campaign resulted in more than 350,000 consumers taking GM vehicles home overnight and ultimately more than 100,000 sales.[36] Cosmetics marketers, such as Merle Norman and Clinique, sometimes offer potential customers "makeovers" to demonstrate product benefits and proper application.

**free sample** A sample of a product given out to encourage trial and purchase

**Free Samples.** Marketers use **free samples** to stimulate trial of a product, increase sales volume in the early stages of a product's life cycle, and obtain desirable distribution. Sampling is the most expensive sales promotion method because production and distribution—at local events, by mail or door-to-door delivery, online, in stores, and on packages—entail high costs. Schick, for example, gave away 200,000 Quattro for Women razors outside of office buildings in Chicago, New York, Philadelphia, and San Francisco.[37] Many consumers prefer to get their samples by mail. In designing a free sample, marketers should consider factors such as seasonal demand for the product, market characteristics, and prior advertising. Free samples usually are inappropriate for slow-turnover products. Despite high costs, use of sampling is increasing. In a given year, almost three-fourths of consumer product companies may use sampling. Distribution of free samples through websites such as StartSampling.com and FreeSamples.com is growing.

**premium** An item offered free or at a minimal cost as a bonus for purchasing a product

**Premiums.** **Premiums** are items offered free or at minimal cost as a bonus for purchasing a product. Like the prize in the Cracker Jack box, premiums are used to attract competitors' customers, introduce different sizes of established products, add variety to other promotional efforts, and stimulate consumer loyalty. Creativity is essential when using premiums; to stand out and achieve a significant number of redemptions, the premium must match both the target audience and the brand's image. Premiums must also be easily recognizable and desirable. Premiums are placed on or inside packages and can also be distributed by retailers or through the mail. Examples include a service station giving a free carwash with a fill-up, a free toothbrush available with a tube of toothpaste, and a free plastic storage box given with the purchase of Kraft Cheese Singles.

**consumer contest** Sales promotion methods in which individuals compete for prizes based on their analytical or creative skills

**Consumer Contests.** In **consumer contests**, individuals compete for prizes based on their analytical or creative skills. This method can be used to generate retail traffic and frequency of exposure to promotional messages, and may be used in conjunction with other sales promotional methods, such as coupons. Although total participation may be lower in consumer contests than in games or sweepstakes, contestants are typically more highly involved. For example, Cingular invited customers to submit pictures taken on their camera phones resembling the image in its "Raising the Bar" ad campaign. The winner, a graduate student at Texas A&M University, received $50,000 for his picture.

**consumer game** Sales promotion method in which individuals compete for prizes based primarily on chance

**Consumer Games.** In **consumer games**, individuals compete for prizes based primarily on chance. Games are typically conducted over a longer period of time than contests since the goal of a game is to stimulate repeat business. Games are commonly used by fast-food chains, soft-drink companies, and hotels and often require that customers collect game pieces such as bottle caps or stickers. Because collecting multiple pieces may be necessary to win, the game stimulates repeated business. Games are often developed and handled by an independent public relations firm. This outsourcing is especially common for large companies as an independent firm is especially useful in assisting companies to navigate federal and state laws applying to games. Although games may increase sales temporarily, it is unproven whether games impact a company's long-term sales.

Marketers considering games should exercise care. Problems or errors may anger customers and could result in a lawsuit. McDonald's' wildly popular Monopoly game promotion, in which customers collect Monopoly real estate pieces on drink and french fry packages, has been tarnished by both fraud and lawsuits. After six successful years, McDonald's was forced to end the annual promotion when a crime ring, including employees of the promotional firm running the game, were convicted of stealing millions of dollars in winning game pieces. McDonald's reintroduced the Monopoly game in 2003, featuring heightened security. However, the Monopoly promotion is once again under scrutiny as it is the focus of a class action lawsuit filed by Burger King franchisees, who claim their customers were lured away by the false promises of McDonald's game.[38]

**consumer sweepstakes** A sales promotion in which entrants submit their names for inclusion in a drawing for prizes

**Sweepstakes.** Entrants in a **consumer sweepstakes** submit their names for inclusion in a drawing for prizes. Hostess, for example, sponsored a "Treats and Tracks" online game with trips to see Danica Patrick, Leilani Munter, and Melanie Troxel in auto races in Daytona, Indianapolis, or Las Vegas as prizes.[39] Sweepstakes are employed more often than consumer contests and tend to attract a greater number of participants. However, contestants are usually more involved in consumer contests and games than in sweepstakes, even though total participation may be lower. Contests, games, and sweepstakes may be used in conjunction with other sales promotion methods, such as coupons.

## Trade Sales Promotion Methods

**trade sales promotion methods** Methods intended to persuade wholesalers and retailers to carry a producer's products and market them aggressively

To encourage resellers, especially retailers, to carry their products and promote them effectively, producers use trade sales promotion methods. **Trade sales promotion methods** attempt to persuade wholesalers and retailers to carry a producer's products and market them more aggressively. These methods include buying allowances, buy-back allowances, scan-back allowances, merchandise allowances, cooperative advertising, dealer listings, free merchandise, dealer loaders, premium or push money, and sales contests.

**buying allowance** A temporary price reduction to resellers for purchasing specified quantities of a product

**Trade Allowances.** Many manufacturers offer trade allowances to encourage resellers to carry a product or stock more of it. One such trade allowance is a **buying allowance**, a temporary price reduction offered to resellers for purchasing specified quantities of a product. A soap producer, for example, might give retailers $1 for each case of soap purchased. Such offers provide an incentive for resellers to handle new products, achieve temporary price reductions, or stimulate purchase of items in larger-than-normal quantities. The buying allowance, which takes the form of money, yields profits to resellers and is simple and straightforward. There are no restrictions on how resellers use the money, which increases the method's effectiveness. One drawback of buying allowances is that customers may buy "forward," that is, buy large amounts that keep them supplied for many months. Another problem is that competitors may match (or beat) the reduced price, which can lower profits for all sellers.

**buy-back allowance** A sum of money given to a reseller for each unit bought after an initial promotion deal is over

A **buy-back allowance** is a sum of money that a producer gives to a reseller for each unit the reseller buys after an initial promotional deal is over. This method is a secondary incentive in which the total amount of money resellers receive is proportional to their purchases during an initial consumer promotion, such as a coupon offer. Buy-back allowances foster cooperation during an initial sales promotion effort and stimulate repurchase afterward. The main disadvantage of this method is expense.

**scan-back allowance** A manufacturer's reward to retailers based on the number of pieces scanned

A **scan-back allowance** is a manufacturer's reward to retailers based on the number of pieces moved through the retailers' scanners during a specific time period. To participate in scan-back programs, retailers are usually expected to pass along savings to consumers through special pricing. Scan-backs are becoming widely used by manufacturers because they link trade spending directly to product movement at the retail level.

**merchandise allowance** A manufacturer's agreement to pay resellers certain amounts of money for providing special promotional efforts, such as setting up and maintaining a display

A **merchandise allowance** is a manufacturer's agreement to pay resellers certain amounts of money for providing promotional efforts such as advertising or point-of-purchase displays. This method is best suited to high-volume, high-profit, easily handled products. A drawback is that some retailers perform activities at a minimally acceptable level simply to obtain allowances. Before paying retailers, manufacturers usually verify their performance. Manufacturers hope that retailers' additional promotional efforts will yield substantial sales increases.

**cooperative advertising** An arrangement in which a manufacturer agrees to pay a certain amount of a retailer's media costs for advertising the manufacturer's products

**dealer listings** An advertisement that promotes a product and identifies the names of participating retailers that sell the product

**free merchandise** A manufacturer's reward given to resellers that purchase a stated quantity of products

**dealer loader** A gift, often part of a display, given to a retailer that purchases a specified quantity of merchandise

**premium (push) money** Extra compensation to salespeople for pushing a line of goods

**sales contest** A sales promotion method used to motivate distributors, retailers, and sales personnel through recognition of outstanding achievements

**Cooperative Advertising and Dealer Listings. Cooperative advertising** is an arrangement in which a manufacturer agrees to pay a certain amount of a retailer's media costs for advertising the manufacturer's products. The amount allowed is usually based on the quantities purchased. As with merchandise allowances, a retailer must show proof that advertisements did appear before the manufacturer pays the agreed-on portion of the advertising costs. These payments give retailers additional funds for advertising. Some retailers exploit cooperative-advertising agreements by crowding too many products into one advertisement. Not all available cooperative advertising dollars are used. Some retailers cannot afford to advertise, while others can afford it but do not want to advertise. A large proportion of all cooperative advertising dollars is spent on newspaper advertisements.

**Dealer listings** are advertisements promoting a product and identifying participating retailers that sell the product. Dealer listings can influence retailers to carry the product, build traffic at the retail level, and encourage consumers to buy the product at participating dealers.

**Free Merchandise and Gifts.** Manufacturers sometimes offer **free merchandise** to resellers that purchase a stated quantity of products. Occasionally free merchandise is used as payment for allowances provided through other sales promotion methods. To avoid handling and bookkeeping problems, the "free" merchandise usually takes the form of a reduced invoice.

A **dealer loader** is a gift to a retailer that purchases a specified quantity of merchandise. Dealer loaders are often used to obtain special display efforts from retailers by offering essential display parts as premiums. For example, a manufacturer might design a display that includes a sterling silver tray as a major component and give the tray to the retailer. Marketers use dealer loaders to obtain new distributors and to push larger quantities of goods.

**Premium Money. Premium money** (or **push money**) is additional compensation offered by the manufacturer to salespeople as an incentive to push a line of goods. This method is appropriate when personal selling is an important part of the marketing effort; it is not effective for promoting products sold through self-service. Premium money often helps a manufacturer obtain a commitment from the sales force, but it can be very expensive.

**Sales Contests.** A **sales contest** is designed to motivate distributors, retailers, and sales personnel by recognizing outstanding achievements. To be effective, this method must be equitable for all individuals involved. One advantage is that it can achieve participation at all distribution levels. Positive effects may be temporary, however, and prizes are usually expensive.

## SUMMARY

Personal selling is the process of informing customers and persuading them to purchase products through paid personal communication in an exchange situation. The three general purposes of personal selling are finding prospects, persuading them to buy, and keeping customers satisfied.

Many salespeople, either consciously or unconsciously, move through a general selling process as they sell products. In prospecting, the salesperson develops a list of potential customers. Before contacting prospects, the salesperson conducts a preapproach that involves finding and analyzing information about prospects and their needs. The approach is the manner in which the salesperson contacts potential customers. During the

sales presentation, the salesperson must attract and hold the prospect's attention to stimulate interest in and desire for the product. If possible, the salesperson should handle objections as they arise. During the closing, the salesperson asks the prospect to buy the product or products. After a successful closing, the salesperson must follow up the sale.

In developing a sales force, marketing managers consider which types of salespeople will sell the firm's products most effectively. The three classifications of salespeople are order getters, order takers, and support personnel. Order getters inform both current customers and new prospects and persuade them to buy. Order takers seek repeat sales and fall into two categories:

inside order takers and field order takers. Sales support personnel facilitate selling, but their duties usually extend beyond making sales. The three types of support personnel are missionary, trade, and technical salespeople. The roles of salespeople are changing. Team selling involves the salesperson joining with people from the firm's financial, engineering, and other functional areas. Relationship selling involves building mutually beneficial long-term associations with a customer through regular communications over prolonged periods of time.

Sales force management is an important determinant of a firm's success because the sales force is directly responsible for generating the organization's sales revenue. Major decision areas and activities are establishing sales force objectives; determining sales force size; recruiting, selecting, training, compensating, and motivating salespeople; managing sales territories; and controlling and evaluating sales force performance.

Sales objectives should be stated in precise, measurable terms and specify the time period and geographic areas involved. The size of the sales force must be adjusted occasionally because a firm's marketing plans change along with markets and forces in the marketing environment.

Recruiting and selecting salespeople involves attracting and choosing the right type of salesperson to maintain an effective sales force. When developing a training program, managers must consider a variety of dimensions, such as who should be trained, what should be taught, and how training should occur. Compensation of salespeople involves formulating and administering a compensation plan that attracts, motivates, and retains the right types of salespeople. Motivated salespeople

should translate into high productivity. Managing sales territories focuses on such factors as size, shape, routing, and scheduling. To control and evaluate sales force performance, sales managers use information obtained through salespeople's call reports, customer feedback, and invoices.

Sales promotion is an activity or a material (or both) that acts as a direct inducement, offering added value or incentive for the product to resellers, salespeople, or consumers. Marketers use sales promotion to identify and attract new customers, introduce new products, and increase reseller inventories. Sales promotion techniques fall into two general categories: consumer and trade. Consumer sales promotion methods encourage consumers to patronize specific stores or try a particular product. These sales promotion methods include coupons; cents-off offers; money refunds and rebates; frequent-user incentives; point-of-purchase displays; demonstrations; free samples and premiums; and consumer contests, games, and sweepstakes. Trade sales promotion techniques can motivate resellers to handle a manufacturer's products and market them aggressively. These sales promotion techniques include buying allowances, buy-back allowances, scan-back allowances, merchandise allowances, cooperative advertising, dealer listings, free merchandise, dealer loaders, premium (or push) money, and sales contests.

**ACE self-test**

Please visit the student website at **www.prideferrell.com** for ACE Self-Test questions that will help you prepare for exams.

---

## IMPORTANT TERMS

| | | | |
|---|---|---|---|
| Personal selling | Recruiting | Money refund | Buying allowance |
| Prospecting | Straight salary compensation plan | Rebate | Buy-back allowance |
| Approach | | Point-of-purchase (P-O-P) materials | Scan-back allowance |
| Closing | Straight commission compensation plan | Demonstration | Merchandise allowance |
| Order getter | | Free sample | Cooperative advertising |
| Order taker | Combination compensation plan | Premium | Dealer listing |
| Support personnel | | Consumer contest | Free merchandise |
| Missionary salespeople | Sales promotion | Consumer game | Dealer loader |
| Trade salespeople | Consumer sales promotion methods | Consumer sweepstakes | Premium money (or push money) |
| Technical salespeople | | Trade sales promotion methods | Sales contest |
| Team selling | Coupon | | |
| Relationship selling | Cents-off offer | | |

## DISCUSSION & REVIEW QUESTIONS

1. What is personal selling? How does personal selling differ from other types of promotional activities?

2. What are the primary purposes of personal selling?

3. Identify the elements of the personal selling process. Must a salesperson include all these elements when selling a product to a customer? Why or why not?

4. How does a salesperson find and evaluate prospects? Do you consider any of these methods to be ethically questionable? Explain.

5. Are order getters more aggressive or creative than order takers? Why or why not?

6. Why are team selling and relationship selling becoming more prevalent?

7. Identify several characteristics of effective sales objectives.

8. How should a sales manager establish criteria for selecting sales personnel? What do you think are the general characteristics of a good salesperson?

9. What major issues or questions should management consider when developing a training program for the sales force?

10. Explain the major advantages and disadvantages of the three basic methods of compensating salespeople. In general, which method would you prefer? Why?

11. What major factors should be taken into account when designing the size and shape of a sales territory?

12. How does a sales manager, who cannot be with each salesperson in the field on a daily basis, control the performance of sales personnel?

13. What is sales promotion? Why is it used?

14. For each of the following, identify and describe three techniques and give several examples: (a) consumer sales promotion methods and (b) trade sales promotion methods.

15. What types of sales promotion methods have you observed recently? Comment on their effectiveness.

## APPLICATION QUESTIONS

1. Briefly describe an experience you have had with a salesperson at a clothing store or an automobile dealership. Describe the steps the salesperson used. Did the salesperson skip any steps? What did the salesperson do well? Not so well? Would you describe the salesperson as an order getter, an order taker, or a support salesperson? Why? Did the salesperson perform more than one of these functions?

2. Leap Athletic Shoe, Inc., a newly formed company, is in the process of developing a sales strategy. Market research indicates sales management should segment the market into five regional territories. The sales potential for the North region is $1.2 million; for the West region, $1 million; for the Central region, $1.3 million; for the South Central region, $1.1 million; and for the Southeast region, $1 million. The firm wishes to maintain some control over the training and sales processes because of the unique features of its new product line, but Leap marketers realize the salespeople need to be fairly aggressive in their efforts to break into these markets. They would like to provide the incentive needed for the extra selling effort. What type of sales force compensation method would you recommend to Leap? Why?

3. Consumer sales promotions aim to increase sales of a particular retail store or product. Identify a familiar type of retail store or product. Recommend at least three sales promotion methods that could effectively promote the store or product. Explain why you would use these methods.

4. Producers use trade sales promotions to encourage resellers to promote their products more effectively. Identify which method or methods of sales promotion a producer might use in the following situations, and explain why the method would be appropriate.

   a. A golf ball manufacturer wants to encourage retailers to add a new type of golf ball to current product offerings.

   b. A life insurance company wants to increase sales of its universal life products, which have been lagging recently (the company has little control over sales activities).

   c. A light bulb manufacturer with an overproduction of 100-watt bulbs wants to encourage its grocery store chain resellers to increase their bulb inventories.

**globalEDGE™**

1. Your firm has recently developed a revolutionary new chemical that is widely applicable, nearly costless, and does not harm the environment. However, before widespread production, you must identify the largest manufacturing companies worldwide that may be interested in your new product. The *IndustryWeek*'s IW 1000 ranking should prove useful for this task. This can be found using the search term "largest manufacturing companies" at **http://globaledge.msu.edu/ibrd.** From there, follow the link to the IW 1000 Database and then choose the Chemicals industry as a choice criterion. What are the ten largest chemical companies as ranked by sales? Because your firm is based in the United States and focused on the domestic market, which companies are feasible to target for a comprehensive sales strategy? If you were planning to enter a new market, which would it be?

2. Your Seattle-based maritime business is currently enjoying profitable conditions. Because your firm and national competitors have been catching an overabundance of fresh shrimp in recent weeks, you have noticed that the domestic market is currently saturated. You are unsure of the options that may exist internationally, so you decide to export through a local agent to assist in selling your products overseas. Find potential agents by using the search term "products overseas" at **http://globaledge.msu.edu/ibrd.** to reach the FASonline website. Enter appropriate criteria. How many agents do you find that are near your offices when you search FASonline's website? Which will you choose?

---

**INTERNET Exercise**

Visit **www.prideferrell.com** for resources to help you master the material in this chapter, plus materials that will help you expand your marketing knowledge, including Internet exercise updates, ACE Self-Tests, hotlinks to companies featured in this chapter, and much more.

### TerrAlign

TerrAlign offers consulting services and software products designed to help a firm maximize control and deployment of its field sales representatives. Review its website at **www.terralign.com**.

1. Identify three features of TerrAlign software that are likely to benefit salespeople.
2. Identify three features of TerrAlign software that are likely to benefit sales managers.
3. Why might field sales professionals object to the use of software from TerrAlign?

---

**Video Case 20.1**    ## IBM Sales Force Sells Solutions

In recent years, IBM has worked hard to reposition itself from a supplier of information technology hardware and software to a company that provides business solution services. In their own words, "We measure ourselves today by how well we help clients solve their biggest and most pressing problems." Obviously, successful problem solving leads to an increase in customers and an increase in goods and services sold.

Although IBM is still the world's largest provider of IT hardware and software, it regards this as the means to an end. The company relies heavily on its global sales force to make the transition from a goods to a solution services provider. The enormous task of changing the company's focus cannot be overstated.

Personal selling has always been a fundamental aspect of IBM's business philosophy and is one of the foundations of the company's success: IBM has customers in 174 countries who speak 165 languages. The company's sales force makes 18 billion client contacts a year and addresses 350,000 sales opportunities per day.

As in all organizations, IBM's change comes from the top. Last year Samuel J. Palmisano, IBM's chair, president, and chief executive officer, led a process of examining and redefining the company's core values. One of the first core values identified was "dedication to every client's success." From a sales perspective, this is achieved through consultative or solution selling, which brings all of IBM's resources and expertise together to solve customer problems. This requires that the sales force thoroughly understand their customers' business environments and deliver the correct answers to their questions. As Palmisano points out, the company's business model has changed. It used to be "invent, build, and sell." Today it is "craft, solve, and deliver the solution."

Not surprisingly, solution selling has brought new challenges to the sales force. IBM believes that salespeople are not born, but trained. The company puts its salespeople through an extensive five-month training program that encompasses three major areas of focus: IBM's commitment to its customers, techniques of collaborative selling, and techniques for gaining understanding of a company's resources and infrastructure. For large projects, salespeople often work in teams comprised of one sales leader and four to five sales specialists who have expertise relevant to the project.

For the most part, IBM salespeople use the Socratic method of selling. This involves asking open-ended questions to better understand their customers' problems, desires, and needs. As might be expected, solution (or pull) selling is more complex than product (or push) selling. The salesperson's role in solution selling is to gather information concerning the customer's business problem, provide a point of view, solve the problem (with the help of other team members), and determine the potential impact on the customer's business once the recommended solution is implemented.

The most accurate and important indicator of the success of the solutions service is customer reaction. An example of IBM achieving its sales objective of "insuring our clients are successful," is their Sales Connections Program. Actuate, an Independent Software Vendor (ISV) and IBM customer, used the Sales Connection website to express concerns about a customer dragging its feet on an applications deal. IBM discovered that the person Actuate was working with lacked the authority to close the deal. IBM provided Actuate with the correct contact person and the sale was quickly closed.

Another example is IBM's Software-as-a-Service program. Software-as-a-Service delivers software via the Internet. This eliminates the need for companies to buy, build, manage, and maintain applications that address areas such as accounting, human resources, customer relationship management, and enterprise resource planning. Companies benefit from this concept because they can reduce their operational costs and maintenance expenses, therefore increasing profits. In an effort to sell this service more broadly, an IBM sales team designed a sales incentive that awards a 10 percent referral fee and additional marketing incentives to IBM customers that submit leads resulting in business for IBM. The marketing incentives include direct mail, telemarketing, advertising, and technical resources to help businesses generate leads. This program enabled one of IBM's customers to generate 800 sales leads in one year.

With this kind of dedication, there is little doubt that IBM's solutions service will continue its success.[40]

### Questions for Discussion

1. What are the advantages for IBM in selling solutions rather than goods?
2. Why is solution selling more complex than hardware and software selling? Identify the sales skills needed for each approach.
3. What are some ways that IBM can measure the effectiveness of its solutions or consultative selling?

## Case 20.2    Fraud Forces Sub Club Closing

With 21,000 outlets, Subway Restaurants is the fastest growing fast-food chain. It is so successful that the number of sandwiches sold annually would wrap around the earth at least six times. Subway's success is based on high-quality food and loyal customers drawn by Subway's offerings of healthy sandwiches made to order and Sub Club stamps. Subway's Sub Club has been a staple of the chain for over 25 years and is one of the most popular frequent-user incentive programs ever. Under the Sub Club system, customers would be rewarded with a stamp when purchasing a 6-inch sandwich (two stamps for a foot-long sandwich). After collecting eight stamps, the customer received a free 6-inch sandwich. The stamps were dutifully collected by many loyal customers and helped increase Subway's repeat business. If the club was so popular with customers, why did Subway abruptly shut it down?

Aside from posting signs in its restaurants, Subway made no official announcements of its decision to end its 25-year program. The posted signs indicated only that the program was closing, without providing the reason for Subway's decision. Many loyal customers vented on blogs and online message boards over the sudden and mysterious demise of the club. Media soon began pointing to fraud as the culprit. It turns out that, armed with laser printers and photo editing software, it was relatively easy for counterfeiters to reproduce the Sub Club card and stamps, and franchisees were redeeming these fake stamps and losing money. The imitation stamps were being distributed online, especially through eBay. (At one point, eBay had over 50 separate auctions of Sub Club stamps and cards.) The counterfeiters were selling the stamps in large quantities for thousands of dollars. Two Virginia Tech students were arrested for forging stamps when reported by the owner of a local Subway franchise.

Counterfeiting wasn't the only method of fraud. A portion of the Sub Club stamp auctions on eBay featured authentic stamps, some in quantities as large as an entire roll. These authentic stamps were being stolen by Subway employees. The stolen stamps hurt franchisees because they were redeemed without accompanying sales. Although Subway insists that the amount of money lost via stamp fraud was not significant, it is apparent that the problem was significant enough to end the Sub Club.

The Sub Club is not the only customer loyalty program to be targeted by counterfeiters. Cold Stone Creamery also had to discontinue its customer loyalty program due to counterfeiting. Its punch-card program rewarded customers with a free scoop of ice cream when their cards were completely punched.

Franchisees have been evaluating Sub Club alternatives, and some have been tested in certain markets. One is the plastic Subway Cash Card, which can be loaded with up to $100 for purchases at any Subway. In initial tests, customers bought more and completed purchases faster with the cards than with cash, and the program allows Subway to print targeted promotional offers on each cardholder's receipt. Subway has even established a website to make card management easier (**www.mysubwaycard.com**). Card holders can add money, check point totals, or order cards to be sent as gifts.

Another alternative that is being tested in 15 states is the Subway Rewards Card. In this program, customers receive one point for every dollar spent with the card. They can later redeem points for menu items such as a 6-inch sub (50 points), soft drinks (20 points), a cookie (10 points), or a foot-long sandwich (75 points).

Subway continues to float ideas to replace its submerged Sub Club; surely a successful customer loyalty program will surface.[41]

### Questions for Discussion

1. What is the major reason for Subway to have the Sub Club?
2. Given that Subway is a large, well-established organization with over 21,000 stores, does Subway need a customer loyalty program like the Sub Club?
3. If Subway wanted to restart the Sub Club, what recommendations would you make to avoid the problems that led to the Club being closed?

## Strategic Case 7        T-Mobile Promotes with Celebrity Sidekicks

Look out America, here comes Big Pink! With the purchase of U.S. wireless carrier VoiceStream Wireless, Germany's Deutsche Telekom became the first European company to cross the Atlantic and join the highly competitive U.S. wireless phone market. Deutsche Telekom envisioned becoming the world's first single-branded international cellular phone service. Operating as T-Mobil in Germany, it added an 'e' for a more English-friendly calling card. T-Mobile, in six different countries—including the United States—was born.

Promoting a product in any market can be difficult, but T-Mobile was faced with the unique challenge of promoting its single brand in six different markets and across continents. Nikesh Arora, who heads up global marketing for T-Mobile, was up for the challenge: "... on the marketing side you need a one-brand approach, which means you have common products and common ways of representing the business. We have to make sure we have exciting offers for our customers in every market," says Arora. "I have to build a solid, sustainable, and differentiated brand." When developing the promotion strategy, Arora and his team decided to look at the positive: "We had to sit down and decide what is common across all of the markets and what the key strength of T-Mobile today is." To reach its goal of promoting a consistent brand image, T-Mobile uses a single advertising agency that handles all of its advertising in all six countries.

T-Mobile started out as a genuine underdog in the United States's already established wireless phone market; pitting itself against strong competitors such as Cingular, Verizon, Sprint, and NexTel. The company has more than met the challenge. T-Mobile is the fastest growing wireless carrier in the United States, boasting as many as 1.4 million new subscribers per quarter and totaling over 21 million customers in the United States alone. How has T-Mobile become a major competitor in the U.S. wireless phone market? Effective promotion efforts have helped.

### T-Mobile's Star-Studded Promotion Efforts

As an unknown European brand, T-Mobile had to seek ways to create a definitive brand image in the United States among brands that were already well established. To create a recognizable brand, T-Mobile hired Academy Award—winning actress Catherine Zeta-Jones. The highly recognizable Welsh-born actress has been instrumental in building the brand image in the United States by appearing in television, print, and radio ads. Because Zeta-Jones is so well known, customers not only noticed the company's ads but also remembered them. Although Zeta-Jones is the official spokesperson,

she isn't the only star behind T-Mobile's promotion. The company rolled out the red carpet when introducing its high-end multimedia device, the Sidekick. T-Mobile used a long lineup of celebrities in television ads and promotional events. The television commercials featured rapper Snoop Dogg using his T-Mobile Sidekick to message a long series of celebrities—such as Paris Hilton, Wee Man from MTV's *Jackass*, Wayne Newton, and Burt Reynolds—for help in doing his laundry. The goal of the advertisement wasn't just to sell a lot of Sidekicks but to establish T-Mobile as a hip, young, and cool brand.

The company reinforces this message by sponsoring events such as ESPN's X Games and parties featuring hot musical acts such as the Black Eyed Peas and the Pussycat Dolls. T-Mobile has made sure that its Sidekick is photographed in the hands of Hollywood's hottest trend-setting stars, such as Beyoncé, Lindsay Lohan, Jessica Simpson, and Nicky and Paris Hilton. T-Mobile also offers special editions of the Sidekick, partnered by hip L.A. clothing line Juicy Couture and urban artist Mister Cartoon. The Juicy Couture Sidekick is baby pink with the designer brand's signature Scottie dogs emblazoned on the back. Juicy Couture also offers jewelry charms, velour wristlets, and trendy carrying cases customized for the T-Mobile Sidekick.

The Mister Cartoon Sidekick is decorated with the artist's drawings. T-Mobile also partners with NYC Peach, the company that decorated Paris Hilton's infamously hijacked Sidekick. NYC Peach will completely customize a Swarovski crystal design for T-Mobile Sidekicks.

T-Mobile doesn't rely on celebrities just for its Sidekick. It sponsors the T-Mobile All Access Concert Series featuring intimate venues with hot musical acts such as Kelly Clarkson, Gavin DeGraw, Simple Plan, and Good Charlotte. To cross-promote the tour, subscribers could download free ring tones of performances or wallpapers of the touring musicians.

T-Mobile also has a multiyear marketing partnership as Official Wireless Services Partner with the NBA and WNBA. This agreement allows T-Mobile to reach a wide market of basketball fans. T-Mobile is integrated into all NBA and WNBA broadcasts and events. It also offers special basketball-related content on its phones, such as participation in NBA All-Star balloting, MVP voting for the NBA All-Star Game and the championship finals, as well as the latest NBA-related news, statistics, and other fun features. T-Mobile is confident that this partnership will broaden its exposure and enhance its youth-targeted image.

Some of T-Mobile's ads poke fun at competitors. One commercial featured two grocery store employees locked in a walk-in freezer. Although suffering from hypothermia, they refuse to call for help because they are outside of their network and don't want to be charged roaming fees. Another ad features a series of parents angry at their children because of high cellphone overages. To promote its flat-rate text messaging plan, a T-Mobile ad shows a suspicious dad roaming the house hoping to catch his children sending text messages. These ads poke fun at common consumer complaints within the wireless phone industry and provide T-Mobile as the provider with a solution. These ads set T-Mobile apart as the company that understands the frustration of wireless bills and overage charges.

### T-Mobile's Customers "Get More" Customer Service

T-Mobile lacks some of the multimedia services offered by competitors such as iTunes and live TV. T-Mobile attributes their growth without multimedia to exceptional customer service. It ranked number 1 on J. D. Power & Associates' industry survey in "Overall Customer Satisfaction," "Customer Care," and "Call Quality." Its mission is not only to remain at the top of its industry in customer service but also to eventually become the most highly respected service company across industries. To maintain this goal, T-Mobile's CEO Robert Dotson and Chief Marketing Officer

Mike Butler visit a large number of T-Mobile stores every quarter. Butler says that the purpose of the visits is not to lecture employees but to learn from them: "We come away with a list of items we're going to address to help deliver better customer service in the future." Many of the ideas expressed by T-Mobile store employees have been incorporated by the company. One suggested change was to provide more detailed information to potential customers about service coverage. T-Mobile developed color-coded maps that allow potential customers to view the coverage in their area as specifically as at street level. "[W]e would rather they went down the street to someone else than sign up with us and be unhappy," says Butler. T-Mobile even christened its headquarters as "T-Mobile Field Service," because it feels that the purpose of its headquarters is to assist field employees with the necessary tools to deliver outstanding customer service. Many of T-Mobile's ads focus on this dedication to customer service. It believes that "Get More" is not just a tagline but a promise that every customer will get more service, more savings, and more features.

### What's Ahead for T-Mobile?

Some industry analysts speculate that T-Mobile might be the next target of a buyout or that it will be unable to compete against the multimedia features being offered by other service providers. But T-Mobile remains optimistic and fully expects to continue growing by focusing on excellent customer service and more traditional cellphone features. T-Mobile is betting on the idea that cellphone users find chatting with friends and family more important than other features. Only time will tell if this strategy will pay off; but T-Mobile's track record indicates they might be right.[42]

### Questions for Discussion

1. What kind of brand image does T-Mobile want to build through its celebrity-packed promotion efforts?
2. What celebrities should T-Mobile use in its advertisements? Why?
3. How would T-Mobile's choice of promotional partners, such as Juicy Couture and the NBA, attract or discourage customers from selecting T-Mobile's phone services?
4. In what ways is T-Mobile supporting its personal selling activities at the retail level?
5. T-Mobile promotes its highly rated customer service as a selling point. Do you think it is effective against competitors that promote high-tech multimedia features? Explain.

part

8

## Pricing Decisions

To provide a satisfying marketing mix, an organization must set a price acceptable to target market members. Pricing decisions can have numerous effects on other parts of the marketing mix. For example, price can influence how customers perceive the product, what types of marketing institutions are used to distribute the product, and how the product is promoted. **Chapter 21** discusses the importance of price and looks at some characteristics of price and nonprice competition. It explores fundamental concepts such as demand, elasticity, marginal analysis, and break-even analysis. Then the chapter examines the major factors that affect marketers' pricing decisions. **Chapter 22** discusses six major stages in the process marketers use to establish prices.

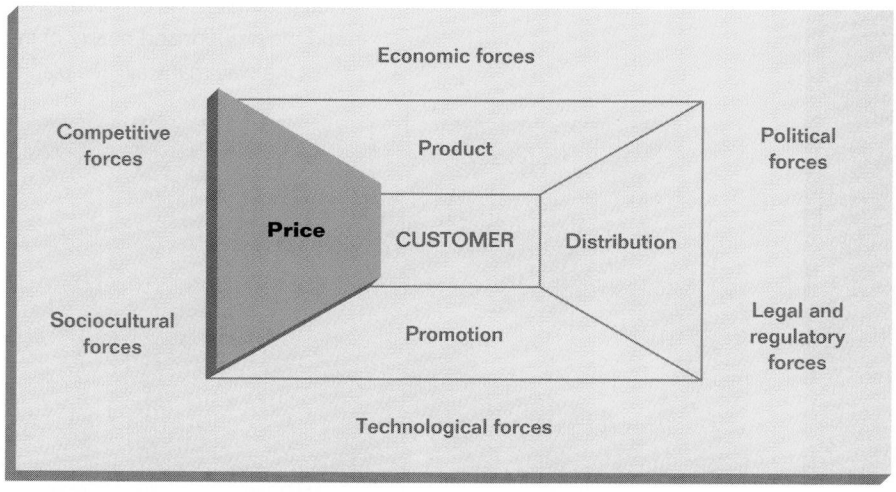

# Pricing Concepts

## Striking a Balance: Airlines Weigh Demand, Costs to Survive

By the fall of 2005, more than half of the major U.S. airline companies were operating under Chapter 11 bankruptcy protection. Two, United and US Airways, had been directly affected by the 9/11 terrorist attacks. United had two planes hijacked, and US Airways was not able to fly out of Washington Reagan National Airport, one of its main hubs, for a considerable time. Delta and Northwest, which both filed for Chapter 11 in September 2005, were not directly affected by 9/11. Analysts pinpoint Delta and Northwest's problems as failures to keep up with low-cost airlines, lower fares, and rising fuel prices caused by several hurricanes that devastated the Gulf Coast.

Delta and Northwest, along with many of the other long-standing airlines, have made little effort to compete with the new low-fare carriers that have popped up in recent years, such as Southwest Airlines. Some experts believe the major carriers didn't initially think the discounters would last, but in fact, most appear to be doing quite well.

To continue flying while dealing with bankruptcy and strong competition, both United Airlines and US Airways had to reduce their "flying capacity" by around 15 percent. United also slashed employee pay, benefits, and pensions. Delta and Northwest will likely have to make similar changes, such as fare increases, limitations on cities to which the airlines will fly, use of aircraft types, and the amount and quality of in-flight service.

One way many airlines plan to boost revenues is by adding more international flights. Delta, for example, intends to increase its flights to Europe and Latin America. There is great demand for flights to Asia. Currently, only Continental and United Airlines are flying "ultralong haul"—nonstop international flights—although these flights represent a small portion of their overall flights. Although U.S. airlines are looking to international travel as a way out of financial woes, few can

afford to get into the ultralong haul market. However, all the companies currently operating under Chapter 11 plan to continue with flights for the foreseeable future and hope to come through the process intact. One—United—emerged from bankruptcy protection in 2006 after 38 months.[1] ■

**M**any airlines use pricing as a tool to compete against major rivals and help boost sales industrywide. However, new low-cost competitors have emerged that also employ pricing as a major competitive tool, but their cost structure enables them to be more profitable. In other industries, many successful firms do not necessarily have the lowest prices; rather, they use various other pricing strategies.

In this chapter, we focus first on the nature of price and its importance to marketers. We then consider some characteristics of price and nonprice competition. Next, we discuss several pricing-related concepts such as demand, elasticity, and break-even analysis. Then we examine in some detail the numerous factors that can influence pricing decisions. Finally, we discuss selected issues related to pricing products for business markets.

# The Nature of Price

**price** The value exchanged for products in a marketing exchange

**barter** The trading of products

The purpose of marketing is to facilitate satisfying exchange relationships between buyer and seller. **Price** is the value exchanged for products in a marketing exchange. Many factors may influence the assessment of value, including time constraints, price levels, perceived quality, and motivations to use available information about prices.[2] In most marketing situations, the price is apparent to both buyer and seller. However, price does not always take the form of money paid. In fact, trading of products, or **barter**, is the oldest form of exchange. Money may or may not be involved.

Buyers' interest in price stems from their expectations about the usefulness of a product or the satisfaction they may derive from it. Because buyers have limited resources, they must allocate those resources to obtain the products they most desire. Buyers must decide whether the utility gained in an exchange is worth the buying power sacrificed. Almost anything of value—ideas, services, rights, and goods—can be assessed by a price. In our society, financial price is the measurement of value commonly used in exchanges.

## Terms Used to Describe Price

Value can be expressed in different terms for different marketing situations. For instance, students pay *tuition* for a college education. Automobile insurance companies charge a *premium* for protection from the cost of injuries or repairs stemming from an automobile accident. An officer who stops you for speeding writes a ticket that requires you to pay a *fine,* while a lawyer you hire to defend you in traffic court charges a *fee.* Airlines and taxi cabs charge a *fare.* A *toll* is charged for the use of bridges or toll roads. *Rent* is paid for the use of equipment or an apartment. A *commission* is remitted to a broker for the sale of real estate. *Dues* are paid for membership in a club or group. A *deposit* is made to hold or lay away merchandise. *Tips* help pay food servers for their services. *Interest* is charged for a loan, and *taxes* are paid for government services. Although price may be expressed in a variety of ways, its purpose is to quantify and express the value of the items in a marketing exchange.

## The Importance of Price to Marketers

As pointed out in Chapter 12, developing a product may be a lengthy process. It takes time to plan promotion and to communicate benefits. Distribution usually requires a long-term commitment to dealers that will handle the product. Often price is the only thing a marketer can change quickly to respond to changes in demand or to actions of competitors. Under certain circumstances, however, the price variable may be relatively inflexible.

Price is a key element in the marketing mix because it relates directly to the generation of total revenue. The following equation is an important one for the entire organization:

$$\text{Profit} = \text{Total Revenue} - \text{Total Costs}$$

$$\text{Profits} = (\text{Price} \times \text{Quantity Sold}) - \text{Total Costs}$$

Prices affect an organization's profits in several ways because it is a key component of the profit equation and can be a major determinant of quantities sold. For example, price is a top priority for Hewlett-Packard in gaining market share and improving financial performance.[3] Furthermore, total costs are influenced by quantities sold.

Because price has a psychological impact on customers, marketers can use it symbolically. By pricing high, they can emphasize the quality of a product and try to increase the prestige associated with its ownership. By lowering a price, marketers can emphasize a bargain and attract customers who go out of their way to save a small amount of money. Thus, as this chapter details, price can have strong effects on a firm's sales and profitability.

# Price and Nonprice Competition

**price competition** Emphasizing price as an issue and matching or beating competitors' prices

The competitive environment strongly influences the marketing mix decisions associated with a product. Pricing decisions are often made according to the price or nonprice competitive situation in a particular market. Price competition exists when consumers have difficulty distinguishing competitive offerings and marketers emphasize low prices. Nonprice competition involves a focus on marketing mix elements other than price.

## Price Competition

When engaging in **price competition**, a marketer emphasizes price as an issue and matches or beats competitors' prices. To compete effectively on a price basis, a firm should be the low-cost seller of the product. If all firms producing the same product charge the same price for it, the firm with the lowest costs is the most profitable. Firms that stress low price as a key marketing mix element tend to market standardized products. A seller competing on price may change prices frequently, or at least must be willing and able to do so. Consider that when Southwest Airlines moved into the Denver market, where Frontier Airlines is headquartered, Frontier's stock price fell 28 percent. Frontier had to cut fares 20 percent to compete with Southwest's introductory $59 and up one-way fare. However, Frontier's non-fuel costs are lower than Southwest's, and it offers passengers Direct TV and roomier seats. So far, Frontier's flights remain near capacity.[4] Whenever competitors change their prices, the company usually responds quickly and aggressively.

**Price Competition**
Snapfish competes on price.

# Netflix: Still Outpricing the Competition

**N**etflix, founded in 1997, is currently the top online DVD subscription service in the United States. Its most popular service charges customers $17.99 a month for an unlimited number of DVD rentals, although only three DVDs can be rented at any particular time. Once finished with a DVD, the customer sends it back through the mail, and a new DVD from his or her stored list is shipped to replace it. Netflix charges no late fees, and there are no time limits on how long a person takes to watch a DVD.

When Wal-Mart and Blockbuster entered the online DVD rental business, each offered the service at lower prices than Netflix. After a time, Wal-Mart developed a joint venture with Netflix, and now the companies promote each other's services. Blockbuster, which originally offered its online rental service for $14.99 a month, is expected to raise its price by $3 a month. Nonetheless, Netflix added a $9.99 per month subscription tier for customers willing to rent just one DVD at a time. While a recent ForeSee Results' survey ranked Netflix number 1 in customer satisfaction, the key seems to be inventory. Netflix currently offers more than 45,000 DVD titles—far exceeding any video rental store and most online sites.

In addition to remaining responsive to price, Netflix continues to delve into new areas of the online rental business. The company's new Friends Network, for example, allows a customer's friends to view the movies on the customer's stored list and to read his or her movie reviews. The company is also experimenting with allowing customers to download movies directly to their computers. Netflix's highly personalized website enables the firm to cut down on employee costs. In 2005 the company had more than 3 million customers but just 43 customer service representatives.

Price competition gives marketers flexibility. They can alter prices to account for changes in their costs or respond to changes in demand for the product. If competitors try to gain market share by cutting prices, a company competing on a price basis can react quickly to such efforts. However, a major drawback of price competition is that competitors too have the flexibility to adjust prices. If they quickly match or beat a company's price cuts, a price war may ensue. For example, a price war has developed in the market for high-speed Internet access, with prices for cable-modem service dropping below $20 a month in some areas.[5] Chronic price wars such as this one can substantially weaken organizations.

## Nonprice Competition

**nonprice competition** Emphasizing factors other than price to distinguish a product from competing brands

**Nonprice competition** occurs when a seller decides not to focus on price and instead emphasizes distinctive product features, service, product quality, promotion, packaging, or other factors to distinguish its product from competing brands. Thus, nonprice competition allows a company to increase its brand's unit sales through means other than changing the brand's price. Mars, for example, markets not only Snickers and M&Ms, but also has an upscale candy line called ethel's chocolates. With the tagline, "no mystery middles," Ethel's chocolates competes on the basis of taste, attractive appearance, and hip packaging and thus has little need to engage in price competition.[6] A major advantage of nonprice competition is that a firm can build customer loyalty toward its brand. If customers prefer a brand because of nonprice factors, they may not be easily lured away by competing firms and brands. In contrast, when price is the primary reason customers buy a particular brand, a competitor is often able to attract those customers through price cuts. However, some surveys show that the proportion of customers who base their purchase decisions solely on price is fairly small.[7]

Nonprice competition is effective only under certain conditions. A company must be able to distinguish its brand through unique product features, higher product quality, effective promotion, distinctive packaging, or excellent customer service. For example, Vermont Pure, a New England bottled-water producer, used superior service and customer-oriented delivery to compete against the bottled water offerings of Coca-Cola, PepsiCo, and Nestlé. The firm's focus on the service aspects of bottled water helped boost its sales by 15 percent.[8] Buyers not only must be able to perceive these distinguishing characteristics but must also view them as important. The distinguishing features that set a particular brand apart from competitors should be difficult, if not impossible, for competitors to imitate. Finally, the firm must extensively promote the brand's distinguishing characteristics to establish its superiority and set it apart from competitors in the minds of buyers.

Even a marketer that is competing on a nonprice basis cannot ignore competitors' prices. It must be aware of them and sometimes be prepared to price its brand near or slightly above competing brands. Therefore, price remains a crucial marketing mix component even in environments that call for nonprice competition.

# Analysis of Demand

Determining the demand for a product is the responsibility of marketing managers, who are aided in this task by marketing researchers and forecasters. Marketing research and forecasting techniques yield estimates of sales potential, or the quantity of a product that could be sold during a specific period. These estimates are helpful in establishing the relationship between a product's price and the quantity demanded.

## The Demand Curve

**demand curve**  A graph of the quantity of products expected to be sold at various prices if other factors remain constant

For most products, the quantity demanded goes up as the price goes down, and the quantity demanded goes down as the price goes up. Intel, for example, knows that lowering prices boosts demand for its Pentium PC processors. Thus, an inverse relationship exists between price and quantity demanded. As long as the marketing environment and buyers' needs, ability (purchasing power), willingness, and authority to buy remain stable, this fundamental inverse relationship holds.

Figure 21.1 illustrates the effect of one variable, price, on the quantity demanded. The classic **demand curve** ($D_1$) is a graph of the quantity of products expected to be sold at various prices if other factors remain constant.[9] It illustrates that as price falls, quantity demanded usually rises. Demand depends on other factors in the marketing mix, including product quality, promotion, and distribution. An improvement in any of these factors may cause a shift to, say, demand curve $D_2$. In such a case, an increased quantity ($Q_2$) will be sold at the same price ($P$).

Many types of demand exist, and not all conform to the classic demand curve shown in Figure 21.1. Prestige products, such as selected perfumes and jewelry, tend to sell better at high prices than at low ones. These products are desirable partly because their expense makes buyers feel elite. If the price fell drastically and many people owned these products, they would lose some of their appeal.

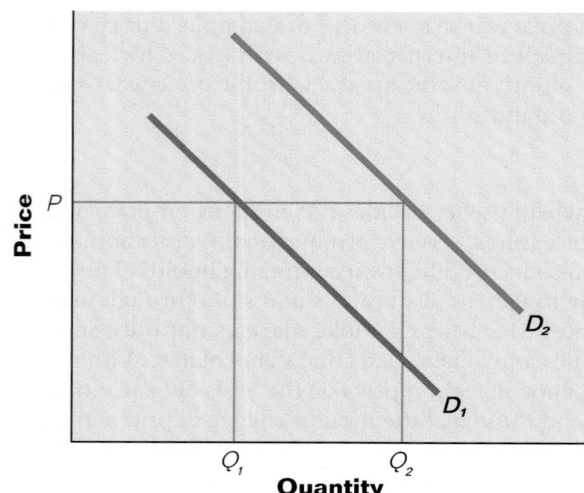

**figure 21.1**  DEMAND CURVE ILLUSTRATING THE PRICE–QUANTITY RELATIONSHIP AND INCREASE IN DEMAND

## figure 21.2   DEMAND CURVE ILLUSTRATING THE RELATIONSHIP BETWEEN PRICE AND QUANTITY FOR PRESTIGE PRODUCTS

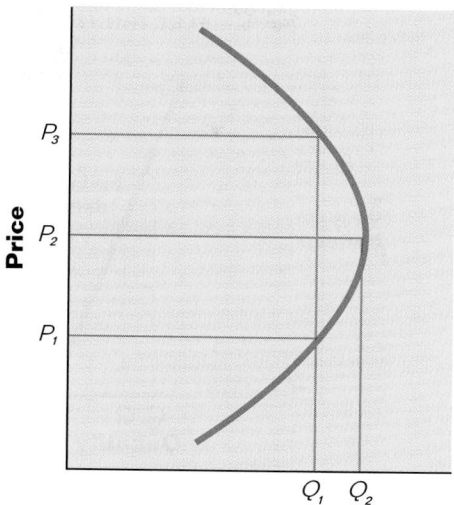

The demand curve in Figure 21.2 shows the relationship between price and quantity demanded for prestige products. Quantity demanded is greater, not less, at higher prices. For a certain price range—from $P_1$ to $P_2$—the quantity demanded ($Q_1$) goes up to $Q_2$. After a certain point, however, raising the price backfires: if the price goes too high, the quantity demanded goes down. The figure shows that if price is raised from $P_2$ to $P_3$, quantity demanded goes back down from $Q_2$ to $Q_1$.

### Demand Fluctuations

Changes in buyers' needs, variations in the effectiveness of other marketing mix variables, the presence of substitutes, and dynamic environmental factors can influence demand. Restaurants and utility companies experience large fluctuations in demand daily. Toy manufacturers, fireworks suppliers, and air-conditioning and heating contractors also face demand fluctuations because of the seasonal nature of their products. The demand for online services, beef, and flat-screen TVs has changed over the last few years. In the case of flat-screen plasma and LCD TVs, demand accelerated as prices dropped by as much as 50 percent.[10] In some cases, demand fluctuations are predictable. It is no surprise to restaurants and utility company managers that demand fluctuates. However, changes in demand for other products may be less predictable, leading to problems for some companies. Other organizations anticipate demand fluctuations and develop new products and prices to meet consumers' changing needs.

### Assessing Price Elasticity of Demand

Up to this point, we have seen how marketers identify the target market's evaluation of price and its ability to purchase and how they examine demand to learn whether price is related inversely or directly to quantity. The next step is to assess price elasticity of demand. **Price elasticity of demand** provides a measure of the sensitivity of demand to changes in price. It is formally defined as the percentage change in quantity demanded relative to a given percentage change in price (see Figure 21.3 on p. 582).[11] The percentage change in quantity demanded caused by a percentage change in price is much greater for elastic demand than for inelastic demand. For a product such as electricity, demand is relatively inelastic: when its price increases, say, from $P_1$ to $P_2$, quantity demanded goes down only a little, from $Q_1$ to $Q_2$. For products such as recreational vehicles, demand is relatively elastic: when price rises sharply, from $P_1$ to $P_2$, quantity demanded goes down a great deal, from $Q_1$ to $Q_2$.

**price elasticity of demand** A measure of the sensitivity of demand to changes in price

## figure 21.3

### ELASTICITY OF DEMAND

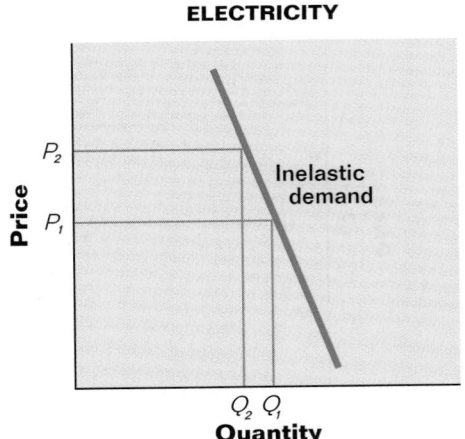
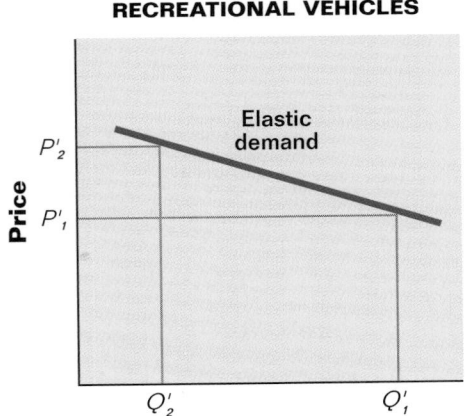

If marketers can determine the price elasticity of demand, setting a price is much easier. By analyzing total revenues as prices change, marketers can determine whether a product is price elastic. Total revenue is price times quantity; thus, 10,000 rolls of wallpaper sold in one year at a price of $10 per roll equals $100,000 of total revenue. If demand is *elastic*, a change in price causes an opposite change in total revenue: an increase in price will decrease total revenue, and a decrease in price will increase total revenue. *Inelastic* demand results in a change in the same direction as total revenue: an increase in price will increase total revenue, and a decrease in price will decrease total revenue. In the hotel industry, for example, research has found that demand for hotel rooms is inelastic regardless of whether they are in budget motels or luxury hotels.[12] The following formula determines the price elasticity of demand:

$$\text{Price Elasticity of Demand} = \frac{(\% \text{ Change in Quantity Demanded})}{(\% \text{ Change in Price})}$$

For example, if demand falls by 8 percent when a seller raises the price by 2 percent, the price elasticity of demand is $-4$ (the negative sign indicating the inverse relationship between price and demand). If demand falls by 2 percent when price is increased by 4 percent, elasticity is $-\frac{1}{2}$. The less elastic the demand, the more beneficial it is for the seller to raise the price. Products without readily available substitutes and for which consumers have strong needs (for example, electricity or appendectomies) usually have inelastic demand.

Marketers cannot base prices solely on elasticity considerations. They must also examine the costs associated with different sales volumes and evaluate what happens to profits.

# Demand, Cost, and Profit Relationships

The analysis of demand, cost, and profit is important because customers are becoming less tolerant of price increases, forcing manufacturers to find new ways to control costs. In the past, many customers desired premium brands and were willing to pay extra for those products. Today customers pass up certain brand names if they can pay less without sacrificing quality. To stay in business, a company must set

## marketing ENTREPRENEURS

**Pankaj Arora**

**HIS BUSINESS:** paWare and Pankaj Arora Software

**FOUNDED AT AGE:** 14

**SUCCESS:** Offered a salary of $100,000/year

Though a seemingly typical 16-year-old high school student, Pankaj Arora's extracurricular activities include heading up two technology-based businesses. Arora runs both paWare, a web design and custom-computer company, and Pankaj Arora Software, which develops and distributes software with ZDNet. Already a business savvy entrepreneur, Arora is not seduced by the idea of making millions. In fact, he turned down a $100,000/year offer from a Minneapolis consulting firm so he could continue to improve his shareware and freeware technologies. Clearly, Arora has proven himself to be a hot commodity within the high-tech industry, but for now he says he is just doing what he likes to do.

**fixed costs** Costs that do not vary with changes in the number of units produced or sold

**average fixed cost** The fixed cost per unit produced

**variable costs** Costs that vary directly with changes in the number of units produced or sold

**average variable cost** The variable cost per unit produced

**total cost** The sum of average fixed and average variable costs times the quantity produced

**average total cost** The sum of the average fixed cost and the average variable cost

**marginal cost (MC)** The extra cost incurred by producing one more unit of a product

**marginal revenue (MR)** The change in total revenue resulting from the sale of an additional unit of a product

prices that not only cover its costs but also meet customers' expectations. In this section, we explore two approaches to understanding demand, cost, and profit relationships: marginal analysis and break-even analysis.

## Marginal Analysis

Marginal analysis examines what happens to a firm's costs and revenues when production (or sales volume) changes by one unit. Both production costs and revenues must be evaluated. To determine the costs of production, it is necessary to distinguish among several types of costs. **Fixed costs** do not vary with changes in the number of units produced or sold. For example, a wallpaper manufacturer's cost of renting a factory does not change because production increases from one to two shifts a day or because twice as much wallpaper is sold. Rent may go up, but not because the factory has doubled production or revenue. **Average fixed cost** is the fixed cost per unit produced and is calculated by dividing fixed costs by the number of units produced.

**Variable costs** vary directly with changes in the number of units produced or sold. The wages for a second shift and the cost of twice as much wallpaper are extra costs incurred when production is doubled. Variable costs are usually constant per unit; that is, twice as many workers and twice as much material produce twice as many rolls of wallpaper. **Average variable cost**, the variable cost per unit produced, is calculated by dividing the variable costs by the number of units produced.

**Total cost** is the sum of average fixed costs and average variable costs times the quantity produced. The **average total cost** is the sum of the average fixed cost and the average variable cost. **Marginal cost (MC)** is the extra cost a firm incurs when it produces one more unit of a product.

Table 21.1 (on p. 584) illustrates various costs and their relationships. Notice that average fixed cost declines as output increases. Average variable cost follows a U shape, as does average total cost. Because average total cost continues to fall after average variable cost begins to rise, its lowest point is at a higher level of output than that of average variable cost. Average total cost is lowest at 5 units at a cost of $22.00, whereas average variable cost is lowest at 3 units at a cost of $11.67. As Figure 21.4 (on p. 584) shows, marginal cost equals average total cost at the latter's lowest level. In Table 21.1, this occurs between 5 and 6 units of production. Average total cost decreases as long as marginal cost is less than average total cost and increases when marginal cost rises above average total cost.

**Marginal revenue (MR)** is the change in total revenue that occurs when a firm sells an additional unit of a product. Figure 21.5 (on p. 585) depicts marginal revenue and a demand curve. Most firms in the United States face downward-sloping demand curves for their products; in other words, they must lower their prices to sell additional units. This situation means that each additional unit of product sold provides the firm with less revenue than the previous unit sold. MR then becomes less than average revenue, as Figure 21.5 (on p. 585) shows. Eventually MR reaches zero, and the sale of additional units actually hurts the firm.

However, before the firm can determine whether a unit makes a profit, it must know its cost, as well as its revenue, because profit equals revenue minus cost. If MR is a unit's addition to revenue and MC is a unit's addition to cost, MR minus MC tells us whether the unit is profitable. Table 21.2 (on p. 585) illustrates the relationships among price, quantity sold, total revenue, marginal revenue, marginal cost, and total cost. It indicates where maximum profits are possible at various combinations

## table 21.1    COSTS AND THEIR RELATIONSHIPS

| 1 Quantity | 2 Fixed Cost | 3 Average Fixed Cost (2) ÷ (1) | 4 Average Variable Cost | 5 Average Total Cost (3) + (4) | 6 Total Cost (5) × (1) | Marginal Cost |
|---|---|---|---|---|---|---|
| 1 | $40 | $40.00 | $20.00 | $60.00 | $60 | |
| | | | | | | $10 |
| 2 | 40 | 20.00 | 15.00 | 35.00 | 70 | |
| | | | | | | 2 |
| 3 | 40 | 13.33 | 10.67 | 24.00 | 72 | |
| | | | | | | 18 |
| 4 | 40 | 10.00 | 12.50 | 22.50 | 90 | |
| | | | | | | 20 |
| 5 | 40 | 8.00 | 14.00 | 22.00 | 110 | |
| | | | | | | 30 |
| 6 | 40 | 6.67 | 16.67 | 23.33 | 140 | |
| | | | | | | 40 |
| 7 | 40 | 5.71 | 20.00 | 25.71 | 180 | |

of price and cost. Notice that the total cost and the marginal cost figures in Table 21.2 are calculated and appear in Table 21.1.

Profit is the highest where MC = MR (see Table 21.2). In this table, note that at a quantity of 4 units, profit is the highest and MR − MC = 0. The best price is $33, and the profit is $42. Up to this point, the additional revenue generated from an extra unit sold exceeds the additional cost of producing it. Beyond this point, the additional cost of producing another unit exceeds the additional revenue generated, and profits decrease. If the price were based on minimum average total cost—$22 (Table 21.1)—it would result in a lower profit of $40 (Table 21.2) for 5 units priced at $30 versus a profit of $42 for 4 units priced at $33.

### figure 21.4

**TYPICAL MARGINAL COST AND AVERAGE TOTAL COST RELATIONSHIP**

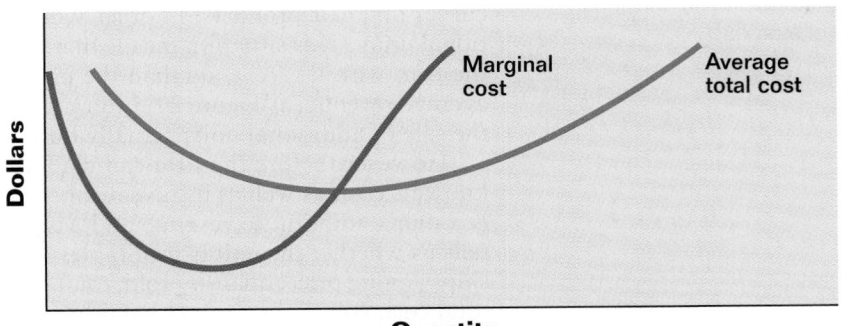

### figure 21.5   TYPICAL MARGINAL REVENUE AND AVERAGE REVENUE RELATIONSHIP

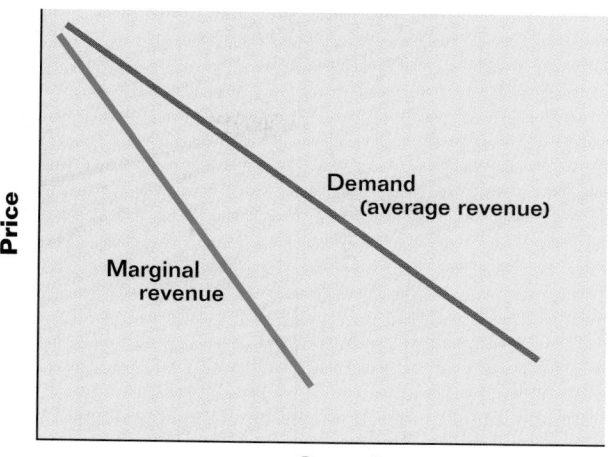

Graphically combining Figures 21.4 and 21.5 into Figure 21.6 (on p. 586) shows that any unit for which MR exceeds MC adds to a firm's profits, and any unit for which MC exceeds MR subtracts from profits. The firm should produce at the point where MR equals MC because this is the most profitable level of production.

This discussion of marginal analysis may give the false impression that pricing can be highly precise. If revenue (demand) and cost (supply) remained constant, prices could be set for maximum profits. In practice, however, cost and revenue change frequently. The competitive tactics of other firms or government action can quickly undermine a company's expectations of revenue. Thus, marginal analysis is only a model from which to work. It offers little help in pricing new products before costs and revenues are established. On the other hand, in setting prices of existing products, especially in competitive situations, most marketers can benefit by understanding the relationship between marginal cost and marginal revenue.

### table 21.2   MARGINAL ANALYSIS METHOD FOR DETERMINING THE MOST PROFITABLE PRICE

| 1 Price | 2 Quantity Sold | 3 Total Revenue (1) × (2) | 4 Marginal Revenue | 5 Marginal Cost | 6 Total Cost | 7 Profit (3) − (6) |
|---|---|---|---|---|---|---|
| $57 | 1 | $ 57 | $ 57 | $ 60 | $ 60 | − $ 3 |
| 50 | 2 | 100 | 43 | 10 | 70 | 30 |
| 38 | 3 | 114 | 14 | 2 | 72 | 42 |
| **33*** | **4** | **132** | **18** | **18** | **90** | **42** |
| 30 | 5 | 150 | 18 | 20 | 110 | 40 |
| 27 | 6 | 162 | 12 | 30 | 140 | 22 |
| 25 | 7 | 175 | 13 | 40 | 180 | −5 |

*Boldface indicates the best price-profit combination.

**figure 21.6** COMBINING THE MARGINAL COST AND MARGINAL REVENUE CONCEPTS FOR OPTIMAL PROFIT

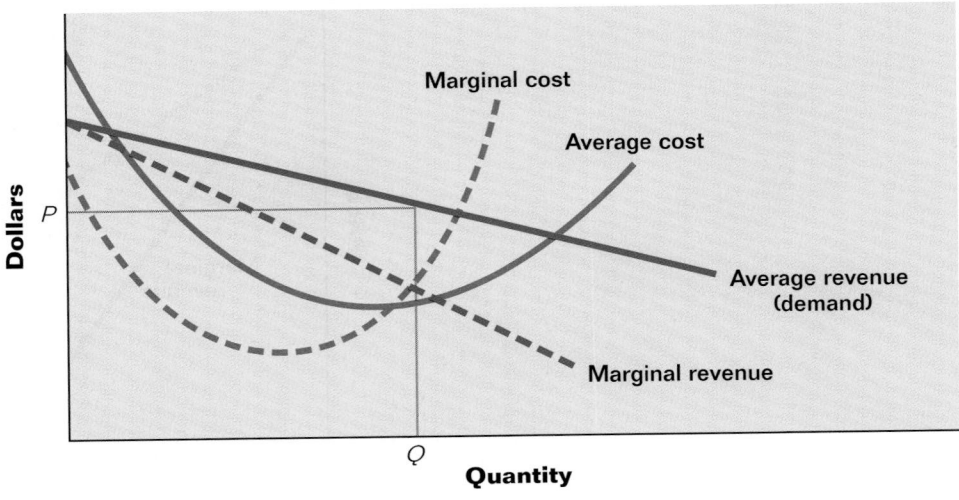

### Break-Even Analysis

**break-even point** The point at which the costs of producing a product equal the revenue made from selling the product

The point at which the costs of producing a product equal the revenue made from selling the product is the **break-even point**. If the wallpaper manufacturer has total annual costs of $100,000 and sells $100,000 worth of wallpaper in the same year, the company has broken even.

Figure 21.7 illustrates the relationships among costs, revenue, profits, and losses involved in determining the break-even point. Knowing the number of units necessary to break even is important in setting the price. If a product priced at $100 per unit has an average variable cost of $60 per unit, the contribution to fixed costs is $40. If total fixed costs are $120,000, the break-even point in units is determined as follows:

$$\text{Breakeven Point} = \frac{\text{Fixed Costs}}{\text{Per-Unit Contribution to Fixed Costs}}$$

$$= \frac{\text{Fixed Costs}}{\text{Price} - \text{Variable Costs}}$$

$$= \frac{\$120,000}{\$40}$$

$$= 3,000 \text{ Units}$$

To calculate the break-even point in terms of dollar sales volume, the seller multiplies the break-even point in units by the price per unit. In the preceding example, the break-even point in terms of dollar sales volume is 3,000 (units) times $100, or $300,000.

To use break-even analysis effectively, a marketer should determine the break-even point for each of several alternative prices. This determination allows the marketer to compare the effects on total revenue, total costs, and the break-even point for each price under consideration. Although this comparative analysis may not tell the marketer exactly what price to charge, it will identify highly undesirable price alternatives that should definitely be avoided.

Break-even analysis is simple and straightforward. It does assume, however, that the quantity demanded is basically fixed (inelastic) and that the major task in setting prices is to recover costs. It focuses more on how to break even than on how to achieve a pricing objective, such as percentage of market share or return on invest-

## figure 21.7

### DETERMINING THE BREAK-EVEN POINT

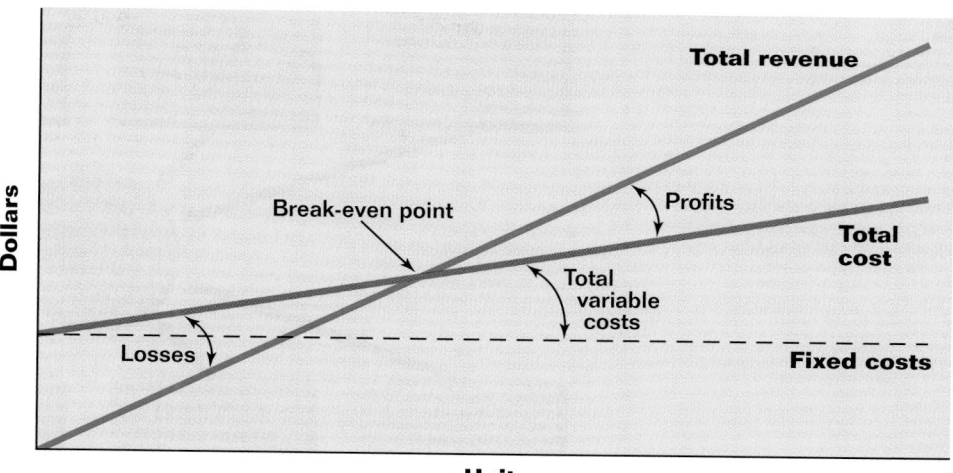

ment. Nonetheless, marketing managers can use this concept to determine whether a product will achieve at least a break-even volume.

# Factors Affecting Pricing Decisions

Pricing decisions can be complex because of the number of factors to consider. Frequently there is considerable uncertainty about the reactions to price among buyers, channel members, and competitors. Price is also an important consideration in marketing planning, market analysis, and sales forecasting. It is a major issue when assessing a brand's position relative to competing brands. Most factors that affect pricing decisions can be grouped into one of the eight categories shown in Figure 21.8 (on p. 588). In this section, we explore how each of these groups of factors enters into price decision making.

## Organizational and Marketing Objectives

Marketers should set prices that are consistent with the organization's goals and mission. For example, a retailer trying to position itself as value oriented may wish to set prices that are quite reasonable relative to product quality. In this case, a marketer would not want to set premium prices on products but would strive to price products in line with this overall organizational goal.

Pricing decisions should also be compatible with the firm's marketing objectives. For instance, suppose one of a producer's marketing objectives is a 12 percent increase in unit sales by the end of the following year. Assuming buyers are price sensitive, increasing the price or setting a price above the average market price would not be in line with this objective.

## Types of Pricing Objectives

The types of pricing objectives a marketer uses obviously have considerable bearing on the determination of prices. For example, an organization that uses pricing to increase its market share would likely set the brand's price below those of competing brands of similar quality to attract competitors' customers. A marketer sometimes uses temporary price reductions in the hope of gaining market share. If a business needs to raise cash quickly, it will likely use temporary price reductions such as sales, rebates, and special discounts. We examine pricing objectives in more detail in the next chapter.

**figure 21.8**

**FACTORS THAT AFFECT PRICING DECISIONS**

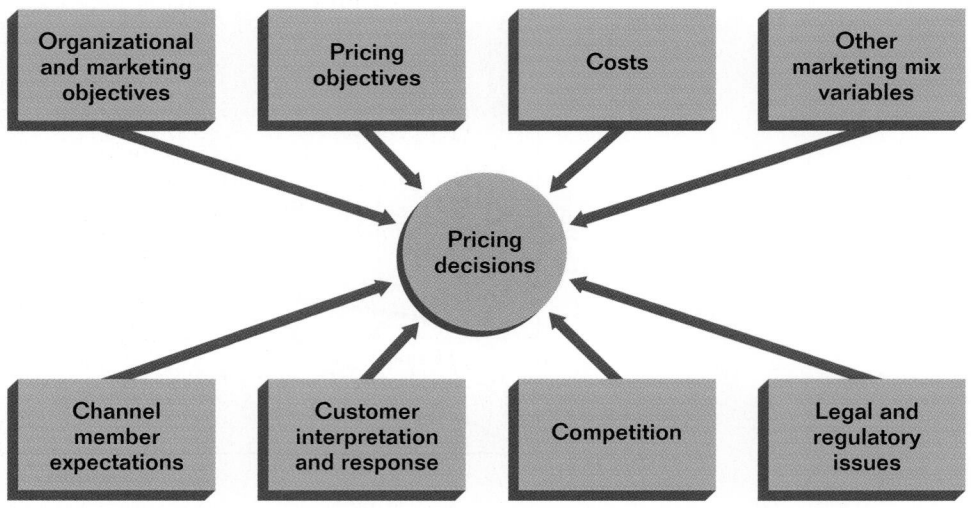

## Costs

Clearly costs must be an issue when establishing price. A firm may temporarily sell products below cost to match competition, generate cash flow, or even increase market share, but in the long run it cannot survive by selling its products below cost. Even a firm that has a high-volume business cannot survive if each item is sold slightly below its cost. A marketer should be careful to analyze all costs so they can be included in the total cost associated with a product.

To maintain market share and revenue in an increasingly price-sensitive market, many marketers have concentrated on reducing costs. In the highly competitive computer industry, for example, IBM constantly looks for ways to lower the cost of developing, producing, and marketing computers and related products. As a cost-cutting move, the company recently relocated 4,750 managerial and engineering jobs to India, where labor costs are significantly lower.[13]

Labor-saving technologies, a focus on quality, and efficient manufacturing processes have brought productivity gains that translate into reduced costs and lower prices for customers. In an industry ravaged by labor concerns and monetary losses, Southwest Airlines has managed to stay one step ahead of its larger rivals. Southwest is the low-fare leader on more of the top 100 routes in the United States than the three largest airlines—American, Delta, and United. One reason for the Texas-based airline's success is its ability to control costs. Southwest's per-seat mile costs are somewhat lower than those of its "big three" rivals. However, Southwest now faces competition from other low-cost airlines such as JetBlue and Frontier.

Besides considering the costs associated with a particular product, marketers must take into account the costs the product shares with others in the product line. Products often share some costs, particularly the costs of research and development, production, and distribution. Most marketers view a product's cost as a minimum, or floor, below which the product cannot be priced.

## Other Marketing Mix Variables

All marketing mix variables are highly interrelated. Pricing decisions can influence evaluations and activities associated with product, distribution, and promotion variables. A product's price frequently affects the demand for that item. A high price, for instance, may result in low unit sales, which in turn may lead to higher production costs per unit. Conversely, lower per-unit production costs may result from a low price. For many products, buyers associate better product quality with a high price and poorer product quality with a low price. This perceived price–quality relationship influences customers' overall image of products or brands. Sony, for example, prices its television sets higher than average to help communicate that Sony televisions are high-quality electronic products. Consumers recognize the Sony brand name, its reputation for quality, and the prestige associated with buying Sony products. Individuals who associate quality with a high price are likely to purchase products with well-established and recognizable brand names.[14]

The price of a product is linked to several dimensions of its distribution. Premium-priced products are often marketed through selective or exclusive distribution; lower-priced products in the same product category may be sold through intensive distribution. For example, Cross pens are distributed through selective distribution and Bic pens through intensive distribution. Moreover, an increase in physical distribution costs, such as shipping, may have to be passed on to customers. Soaring ocean-shipping rates, for example, increased the price of imported commodities and goods in the United States when the supply of ships trailed the demand for ocean-shipping services.[15] When setting a price, the profit margins of marketing channel members, such as wholesalers and retailers, must also be considered. Channel members must be adequately compensated for the functions they perform.

Price may determine how a product is promoted. Bargain prices are often included in advertisements. Premium prices are less likely to be advertised, though they are sometimes included in advertisements for upscale items such as luxury cars or fine jewelry. Higher-priced products are more likely than lower-priced ones to require personal selling. Furthermore, the price structure can affect a salesperson's relationship with customers. A complex pricing structure takes longer to explain to customers, is more likely to confuse potential buyers, and may cause misunderstandings that result in long-term customer dissatisfaction. For example, the pricing structures of many airlines are complex and frequently confuse ticket sales agents and travelers alike.

## Channel Member Expectations

When making price decisions, a producer must consider what members of the distribution channel expect. A channel member certainly expects to receive a profit for the functions it performs. The amount of profit expected depends on what the intermediary could make if it were handling a competing product instead. Also, the amount of time and the resources required to carry the product influence intermediaries' expectations.

Channel members often expect producers to give discounts for large orders and prompt payment. At times, resellers expect producers to provide several support activities such as sales training, service training, repair advisory service, cooperative advertising, sales promotions, and perhaps a program for returning unsold merchandise to the producer. These support activities clearly have associated costs that a producer must consider when determining prices.

## Customers' Interpretation and Response

When making pricing decisions, marketers should address a vital question: How will our customers interpret our prices and respond to them? *Interpretation* in this context refers to what the price means or what it communicates to customers. Does the price mean "high quality" or "low quality," or "great deal," "fair price," or "rip-off"? Customer *response* refers to whether the price will move customers closer to purchase of the product and the degree to which the price enhances their satisfaction with the purchase experience and with the product after purchase.

**snapshot**

**What is a fair price?**

What people in industrial nations said would be a "fair price" for a gallon of gas.

UK $5.16
Germany $4.87
South Korea $4.11
France $4.08
Spain $3.32
Australia $2.94
Canada $2.72
United States $1.99

*Source:* Data from Ipsos-Public Affairs. Margin of error ±3.1–3.2 percentage points.

Customers' interpretation of and response to a price are to some degree determined by their assessment of value, or what they receive compared with what they give up to make the purchase. In evaluating what they receive, customers consider product attributes, benefits, advantages, disadvantages, the probability of using the product, and possibly the status associated with the product. In assessing the cost of the product, customers likely will consider its price, the amount of time and effort required to obtain it, and perhaps the resources required to maintain it after purchase. Consider that research shows that an increasing number of investors with at least $500,000 of assets to invest are using full-service brokers, which suggests that these customers view the costs of full-service brokerage services as more acceptable, given the return on their investments.[16]

At times, customers interpret a higher price as higher product quality. They are especially likely to make this price–quality association when they cannot judge the quality of the product themselves. This is not always the case, however; whether price is equated with quality depends on the types of customers and products involved. Obviously marketers that rely on customers making a price–quality association and that provide moderate- or low-quality products at high prices will be unable to build long-term customer relationships.

When interpreting and responding to prices, how do customers determine if the price is too high, too low, or about right? In general, they compare prices with internal or external reference prices. An **internal reference price** is a price developed in the buyer's mind through experience with the product. It reflects a belief that a product should cost approximately a certain amount. To arrive at an internal reference price, consumers may consider one or more values, including what they think the product "ought" to cost, the price usually charged for it, the last price paid they paid, the highest and lowest amounts they would be willing to pay, the price of the brand they usually buy, the average price of similar products, the expected future price, and the typical discounted price.[17] As consumers, our experiences have given each of us internal reference prices for a number of products. For example, most of us have a reasonable idea of how much to pay for a six-pack of soft drinks, a loaf of bread, or a gallon of milk. For the product categories with which we have less experience, we rely more heavily on external reference prices. An **external reference price** is a comparison price provided by others, such as retailers or manufacturers. For example, a retailer in an advertisement might state, "While this product is sold for $100 elsewhere, our price is only $39.95." When attempting to establish a reference price in customers' minds by advertising a higher price against which to compare the company's real price, a marketer must make sure the higher price is realistic because if it is not, customers will not use this price when establishing or altering their reference prices.[18] Customers' perceptions of prices are also influenced by their expectations about future price increases, by what they paid for the product recently, and by what they would like to pay for the product. Other factors affecting customers' perceptions of whether the price is right include time or financial constraints, the costs associated with searching for lower-priced products, and expectations that products will go on sale.

Buyers' perceptions of a product relative to competing products may allow the firm to set a price that differs significantly from rivals' prices. If the product is deemed superior to

**internal reference price** A price developed in the buyer's mind through experience with the product

**external reference price** A comparison price provided by others

## Why do you think they're so cheap?

You know the saying: You get what you pay for.
In this case, what you're getting
are zinc batteries that rely on
different, less powerful technology.
That's why Duracell® will last up to
4 times longer than one of these
so-called "Heavy Duty" batteries.

TRUS±ED EVERYWHERE™

**External Reference and Price**

Duracell compares its quality to its direct competitors and justifies its price.

# Clearance? On Sale? Where's the Better Deal?

**W**hen you're out shopping, how do you respond to discounts labeled *sale* versus *clearance*? Although several states have taken legal action against retailers for their use of the term *sale*, especially when used as a reference price ("Was $89.95. Now only $59.95"), there has been almost no research or regulatory guidance on the use of the term *clearance*. Researchers believe consumers associate *clearance* with the end of a season, excess inventories, or even products that may be discontinued. In reality, the term is used widely and in many different contexts that depend only on the seller's interpretation. Most retailers are aware that consumers want to buy at discount, but attitude toward and perception of price cues influence consumers' reaction to a discount. Almost 80 percent of automobiles, furniture, and kitchenware were purchased at a discount.

An experiment was conducted to provide greater insight into consumers' perception of the term *clearance*. One group of respondents was asked to write down their thoughts after driving past a store and seeing a large sign in the window saying *clearance*. Another was given the same task using the word *sale*. The experiment revealed that a *clearance* sign leads people to expect or maintain larger discounts, more favorable attitude toward promotion, a greater retailer obligation to reduce price, a greater sense that the retailer would be going out of business, and concerns about product quality. This research suggests that *clearance* is a more powerful term to use in influencing consumer perceptions about price discounts. Although states have been active in prosecuting deceptive advertising claims involving sale prices when the reference price cannot be substantiated, the use of clearance prices has yet to be regulated unless it is coupled with the word *sale*.

---

most of the competition, a premium price may be feasible. However, even products with superior quality can be overpriced. Strong brand loyalty sometimes provides the opportunity to charge a premium price. On the other hand, if buyers view a product less than favorably (though not extremely negatively), a lower price may generate sales.

In the context of price, buyers can be characterized according to their degree of value consciousness, price consciousness, and prestige sensitivity. Marketers that understand these characteristics are better able to set pricing objectives and policies. **Value-conscious** consumers are concerned about both price and quality of a product.[19] These consumers may perceive value as quality per unit of price or as not only economic savings but also the additional gains expected from one product over a competitor's brand. The first view is appropriate for commodities such as bottled water, bananas, and gasoline. If a value-conscious consumer perceives that quality of gasoline to be the same for Exxon and Shell, he or she will go to the station with the lower price. For consumers looking not just for economic value but additional gains they expect from one brand over another, a product differentiation value could be associated with benefits and features that are believed to be unique.[20] For example, a BMW may be considered to be better than a Cadillac. To appeal to the value-conscious consumer, Apple Computer recently introduced the Mac Mini and iPod Shuffle, more compact versions of their respective counterparts offered at discount prices.[21] **Price-conscious** individuals strive to pay low prices.[22] They want the lowest prices and would respond to Wal-Mart's claim that "we sell for less." A price-conscious pet food buyer, for example, would probably purchase Wal-Mart's Ol' Roy

**value conscious** Concerned about price and quality of a product

**price conscious** Striving to pay low prices

**Prestige Products**

Embraer offers high-quality prestige products like the Phenom 100.

**prestige sensitive** Drawn to products that signify prominence and status

brand because it is the lowest priced dog food and satisfies a basic need. **Prestige-sensitive** buyers focus on purchasing products that signify prominence and status.[23] For example, the Porsche Cayenne, one of the highest-priced sport-utility vehicles ever marketed, created record sales and profits for Porsche. Only 18 percent of Cayenne buyers had previously owned a Porsche; many of the rest were attracted to a vehicle with the prestige associated with the Porsche name.[24]

On the other hand, some consumers vary in their degree of value, price, and prestige consciousness. In some segments, consumers are increasingly "trading up" to higher-status products in categories such as automobiles, home appliances, restaurants, and even pet food, yet remain price conscious regarding cleaning and grocery products. This trend has benefited marketers such as Starbucks, Sub-Zero, BMW, Whole Foods, and PETCO, which can charge premium prices for high-quality, prestige products, as well as Sam's Club and Costco, which offer basic household products at everyday low prices.[25] Indeed, it appears that a new "mass class" market is emerging in part due to technology and communication advances, the prevalence of designer goods, and the proliferation of counterfeit goods. As a result, more designers like Karl Lagerfeld are creating exclusive designer originals for upscale markets and less expensive mass market goods for a much broader target audience.[26]

## Competition

A marketer needs to know competitors' prices so it can adjust its own prices accordingly. This does not mean a company will necessarily match competitors' prices; it may set its price above or below theirs. However, for some organizations (such as airlines), matching competitors' prices is an important strategy for survival.

When adjusting prices, a marketer must assess how competitors will respond. Will competitors change their prices and, if so, will they raise or lower them? In

**Competitive Industry and Price**

Gold's Gym is part of a competitive industry and uses price to win customers.

Who knows.
You could be the next governor.

Straight on Foothill. Left on Altadena.    goldsgym.com

Chapter 3, we described several types of competitive market structures. The structure that characterizes the industry to which a firm belongs affects the flexibility of price setting. For example, because of reduced pricing regulation, firms in the telecommunications industry have moved from a monopolistic market structure to an oligopolistic one, which has resulted in significant price competition.

When an organization operates as a monopoly and is unregulated, it can set whatever prices the market will bear. However, the company may not price the product at the highest possible level to avoid government regulation or to penetrate a market by using a lower price. If the monopoly is regulated, it normally has less pricing flexibility; the regulatory body lets it set prices that generate a reasonable but not excessive return. A government-owned monopoly may price products below cost to make them accessible to people who otherwise could not afford them. Transit systems, for example, sometimes operate this way. However, government-owned monopolies sometimes charge higher prices to control demand. In some states with state-owned liquor stores, the price of liquor is higher than in states where liquor stores are not owned by a government body.

The automotive and aircraft industries exemplify oligopolies, in which only a few sellers operate and barriers to competitive entry are high. Companies in such industries can raise their prices in the hope competitors will do the same. When an organization cuts its price to gain a competitive edge, other companies are likely to follow suit. Thus, very little advantage is gained through price cuts in an oligopolistic market structure.

A market structure characterized by monopolistic competition has numerous sellers with product offerings that are differentiated by physical characteristics, features, quality, and brand images. The distinguishing characteristics of its product may allow a company to set a different price than its competitors. However, firms in a monopolistic competitive market structure are likely to practice nonprice competition, discussed earlier in this chapter.

Under conditions of perfect competition, many sellers exist. Buyers view all sellers' products as the same. All firms sell their products at the going market price, and buyers will not pay more than that. This type of market structure, then, gives a marketer no flexibility in setting prices. Farming, as an industry, has some characteristics of perfect competition. Farmers sell their products at the going market price. At times, for example, corn, soybean, and wheat growers have had bumper crops and been forced to sell them at depressed market prices.

## Legal and Regulatory Issues

As discussed in Chapter 3, legal and regulatory issues influence pricing decisions. To curb inflation, the federal government can invoke price controls, freeze prices at certain levels, or determine the rates at which firms may increase prices. In some states and many other countries, regulatory agencies set prices on such products as insurance, dairy products, and liquor.

Many regulations and laws affect pricing decisions and activities in the United States. The Sherman Antitrust Act prohibits conspiracies to control prices, and in interpreting the act, courts have ruled that price fixing among firms in an industry is illegal. Marketers must refrain from fixing prices by developing independent pricing policies and setting prices in ways that do not even hint at collusion. Both the Federal Trade Commission Act and the Wheeler-Lea Act prohibit deceptive pricing. In establishing prices, marketers must guard against deceiving customers.

The Robinson-Patman Act has had a strong impact on pricing decisions. For various reasons, marketers may wish to sell the same type of product at different prices. Provisions in the Robinson-Patman Act, as well as those in the Clayton Act, limit the use of such price differentials. **Price discrimination**, the practice of employing price differentials that tend to injure competition by giving one or more buyers a competitive advantage over other buyers, is prohibited by law. However, not all price differentials are discriminatory. A marketer can use price differentials if they do not hinder competition, if they result from differences in the costs of selling or transportation to various customers, or if they arise because the firm has had to cut its price to a particular buyer to meet competitors' prices.

**price discrimination** Employing price differentials that injure competition by giving one or more buyers a competitive advantage

## Pricing for Business Markets

Business markets consist of individuals and organizations that purchase products for resale, for use in their own operations, or for producing other products. Establishing prices for this category of buyers sometimes differs from setting prices for consumers. Differences in the size of purchases, geographic factors, and transportation considerations require sellers to adjust prices. In this section, we discuss several issues unique to the pricing of business products, including discounts, geographic pricing, and transfer pricing.

### Price Discounting

Producers commonly provide intermediaries with discounts, or reductions, from list prices. Although many types of discounts exist, they usually fall into one of five categories: trade, quantity, cash, seasonal, and allowance. Table 21.3 summarizes some reasons to use each type of discount and provides examples.

**trade (functional) discount** A reduction off the list price a producer gives to an intermediary for performing certain functions

**quantity discount** A deduction from list price for purchasing in large quantities

**Trade Discounts.** A reduction off the list price given by a producer to an intermediary for performing certain functions is called a **trade**, or **functional**, **discount**. A trade discount is usually stated in terms of a percentage or series of percentages off the list price. Intermediaries are given trade discounts as compensation for performing various functions, such as selling, transporting, storing, final processing, and perhaps providing credit services. Although certain trade discounts are often a standard practice within an industry, discounts vary considerably among industries. It is important that a manufacturer provide a trade discount large enough to offset the intermediary's costs, plus a reasonable profit, to entice the reseller to carry the product.

**Quantity Discounts.** Deductions from list price that reflect the economies of purchasing in large quantities are called **quantity discounts**. Quantity discounts are used in many industries and pass on to the buyer cost savings gained through economies of scale.

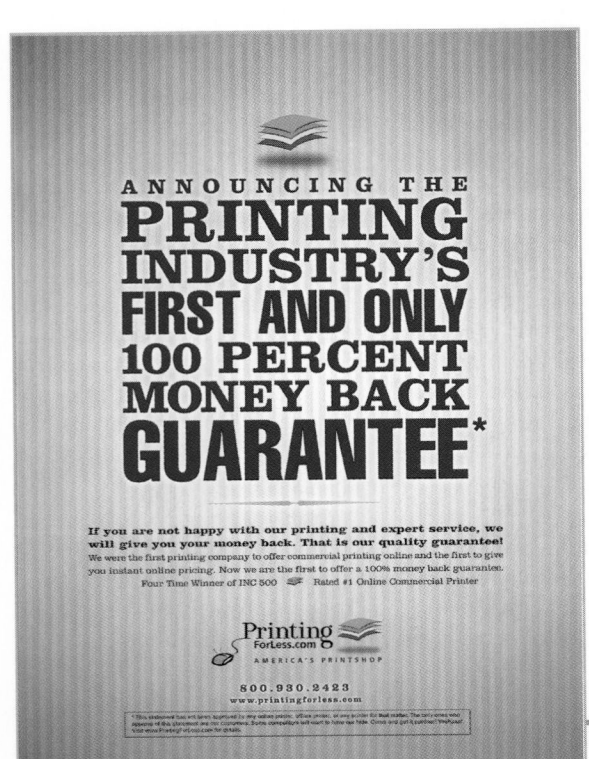

**Pricing for Business Markets**

Printingforless.com offers a 100% money back guarantee to assure its business customer of quality printing services.

## table 21.3   DISCOUNTS USED FOR BUSINESS MARKETS

| Type | Reasons for Use | Examples |
|---|---|---|
| Trade (functional) | To attract and keep effective resellers by compensating them for performing certain functions, such as transportation, warehousing, selling, and providing credit | A college bookstore pays about one-third less for a new textbook than the retail price a student pays |
| Quantity | To encourage customers to buy large quantities when making purchases and, in the case of cumulative discounts, to encourage customer loyalty | Large department store chains purchase some women's apparel at lower prices than do individually owned specialty stores |
| Cash | To reduce expenses associated with accounts receivable and collection by encouraging prompt payment of accounts | Numerous companies serving business markets allow a 2 percent discount if an account is paid within 10 days |
| Seasonal | To allow a marketer to use resources more efficiently by stimulating sales during off-peak periods | Florida hotels provide companies holding national and regional sales meetings with deeply discounted accommodations during the summer months |
| Allowance | In the case of a trade-in allowance, to assist the buyer in making the purchase and potentially earn a profit on the resale of used equipment; in the case of a promotional allowance, to ensure that dealers participate in advertising and sales support programs | A farm equipment dealer takes a farmer's used tractor as a trade-in on a new one

Nabisco pays a promotional allowance to a supermarket for setting up and maintaining a large, end-of-aisle display for a two-week period |

**cumulative discount** A quantity discount aggregated over a stated period

**noncumulative discount** A one-time price reduction based on the number of units purchased, the size of the order, or the product combination purchased

**cash discount** A price reduction given to buyers for prompt payment or cash payment

**seasonal discount** A price reduction given to buyers for purchasing goods or services out of season

**allowance** A concession in price to achieve a desired goal

Quantity discounts can be either cumulative or noncumulative. **Cumulative discounts** are quantity discounts aggregated over a stated time period. Purchases totaling $10,000 in a three-month period, for example, might entitle the buyer to a 5 percent, or $500, rebate. Such discounts are intended to reflect economies in selling and to encourage the buyer to purchase from one seller. **Noncumulative discounts** are one-time reductions in prices based on the number of units purchased, the dollar value of the order, or the product mix purchased. Like cumulative discounts, these discounts should reflect some economies in selling or trade functions.

**Cash Discounts.**  A **cash discount**, or price reduction, is given to a buyer for prompt payment or cash payment. Accounts receivable are an expense and a collection problem for many organizations. A policy to encourage prompt payment is a popular practice and sometimes a major concern in setting prices.

Discounts are based on cash payments or cash paid within a stated time. For example, "2/10 net 30" means that a 2 percent discount will be allowed if the account is paid within 10 days. If the buyer does not make payment within the 10-day period, the entire balance is due within 30 days without a discount. If the account is not paid within 30 days, interest may be charged.

**Seasonal Discounts.**  A price reduction to buyers that purchase goods or services out of season is a **seasonal discount**. These discounts let the seller maintain steadier production during the year. For example, automobile rental agencies offer seasonal discounts in winter and early spring to encourage firms to use automobiles during the slow months of the automobile rental business.

**Allowances.**  Another type of reduction from the list price is an **allowance**, a concession in price to achieve a desired goal. Trade-in allowances, for example, are price reductions granted for turning in a used item when purchasing a new one. Allowances help make the buyer better able to make the new purchase. This type of discount is popular in the aircraft industry. Another example is a promotional allowance, a price reduction granted to dealers for participating in advertising and sales support programs intended to increase sales of a particular item.

## Geographic Pricing

**geographic pricing** Reductions for transportation and other costs related to the physical distance between buyer and seller

**geographic pricing** involves reductions for transportation costs or other costs associated with the physical distance between buyer and seller. Prices may be quoted as F.O.B. (free-on-board) factory or destination. An **F.O.B. factory** price indicates the price of the merchandise at the factory, before it is loaded onto the carrier, and thus excludes transportation costs. The buyer must pay for shipping. An **F.O.B. destination** price means the producer absorbs the costs of shipping the merchandise to the customer. This policy may be used to attract distant customers. Although F.O.B. pricing is an easy way to price products, it is sometimes difficult to administer, especially when a firm has a wide product mix or when customers are widely dispersed. Because customers will want to know about the most economical method of shipping, the seller must be informed about shipping rates.

**F.O.B. factory** The price of merchandise at the factory, before shipment

**F.O.B. destination** A price indicating the producer is absorbing shipping costs

To avoid the problems involved in charging different prices to each customer, **uniform geographic pricing**, sometimes called *postage-stamp pricing*, may be used. The same price is charged to all customers regardless of geographic location, and the price is based on average shipping costs for all customers. Gasoline, paper products, and office equipment are often priced on a uniform basis.

**uniform geographic pricing** Charging all customers the same price, regardless of geographic location

**Zone pricing** sets uniform prices for each of several major geographic zones; as the transportation costs across zones increase, so do the prices. For example, a Florida manufacturer's prices may be higher for buyers on the Pacific Coast and in Canada than for buyers in Georgia.

**zone pricing** Pricing based on transportation costs within major geographic zones

**Base-point pricing** is a geographic pricing policy that includes the price at the factory, plus freight charges from the base point nearest the buyer. This approach to pricing has virtually been abandoned because of its questionable legal status. The policy resulted in all buyers paying freight charges from one location, such as Detroit or Pittsburgh, regardless of where the product was manufactured.

**base-point pricing** Geographic pricing that combines factory price and freight charges from the base point nearest the buyer

When the seller absorbs all or part of the actual freight costs, **freight absorption pricing** is being used. The seller might choose this method because it wishes to do business with a particular customer or to get more business; more business will cause the average cost to fall and counterbalance the extra freight cost. This strategy is used to improve market penetration and to retain a hold in an increasingly competitive market.

**freight absorption pricing** Absorption of all or part of actual freight costs by the seller

## Transfer Pricing

**transfer pricing** Prices charged in sales between an organization's units

**Transfer pricing** occurs when one unit in an organization sells a product to another unit. The price is determined by one of the following methods:

- *Actual full cost:* calculated by dividing all fixed and variable expenses for a period into the number of units produced

- *Standard full cost:* calculated based on what it would cost to produce the goods at full plant capacity

- *Cost plus investment:* calculated as full cost plus the cost of a portion of the selling unit's assets used for internal needs

- *Market-based cost:* calculated at the market price less a small discount to reflect the lack of sales effort and other expenses

The choice of transfer pricing method depends on the company's management strategy and the nature of the units' interaction. An organization must also ensure that transfer pricing is fair to all units involved in the transactions.

## SUMMARY

Price is the value exchanged for products in marketing transactions. Price is not always money paid; barter, the trading of products, is the oldest form of exchange. Price is a key element in the marketing mix because it relates directly to generation of total revenue. The profit factor can be determined mathematically by multiplying price by quantity sold to get total revenue and then subtracting total costs. Price is the only variable in the marketing mix that can be adjusted quickly and easily to respond to changes in the external environment.

A product offering can compete on either a price or a nonprice basis. Price competition emphasizes price as the product differential. Prices fluctuate frequently, and price competition among sellers is aggressive. Nonprice competition emphasizes product differentiation through distinctive features, service, product quality, or other factors. Establishing brand loyalty by using nonprice competition works best when the product can be physically differentiated and the customer can recognize these differences.

An organization must determine the demand for its product. The classic demand curve is a graph of the quantity of products expected to be sold at various prices if other factors hold constant. It illustrates that as price falls, the quantity demanded usually increases. However, for prestige products, there is a direct positive relationship between price and quantity demanded: demand increases as price increases. Next, price elasticity of demand, the percentage change in quantity demanded relative to a given percentage change in price, must be determined. If demand is elastic, a change in price causes an opposite change in total revenue. Inelastic demand results in a parallel change in total revenue when a product's price is changed.

Analysis of demand, cost, and profit relationships can be accomplished through marginal analysis or break-even analysis. Marginal analysis examines what happens to a firm's costs and revenues when production (or sales volume) is changed by one unit. Marginal analysis combines the demand curve with the firm's costs to develop a price that yields maximum profit. Fixed costs do not vary with changes in the number of units produced or sold; average fixed cost is the fixed cost per unit produced. Variable costs vary directly with changes in the number of units produced or sold. Average variable cost is the variable cost per unit produced. Total cost is the sum of average fixed cost and average variable cost times the quantity produced. The optimal price is the point at which marginal cost (the cost associated with producing one more unit of the product) equals marginal revenue (the change in total revenue that occurs when one additional unit of the product is sold). Marginal analysis is only a model; it offers little help in pricing new products before costs and revenues are established.

Break-even analysis, determining the number of units that must be sold to break even, is important in setting price. The point at which the costs of production equal the revenue from selling the product is the break-even point. To use break-even analysis effectively, a marketer should determine the break-even point for each of several alternative prices. This makes it possible to compare the effects on total revenue, total costs, and the break-even point for each price under consideration. However, this approach assumes the quantity demanded is basically fixed and the major task is to set prices to recover costs.

Eight factors enter into price decision making: organizational and marketing objectives, pricing objectives, costs, other marketing mix variables, channel member expectations, customer interpretation and response, competition, and legal and regulatory issues. When setting prices, marketers should make decisions consistent with the organization's goals and mission. Pricing objectives heavily influence price-setting decisions. Most marketers view a product's cost as the floor below which a product cannot be priced. Because of the interrelationship among the marketing mix variables, price can affect product, promotion, and distribution decisions. The revenue channel members expect for their functions must also be considered when making price decisions.

Buyers' perceptions of price vary. Some consumer segments are sensitive to price, but others may not be. Thus, before determining price, a marketer needs to be aware of its importance to the target market. Knowledge of the prices charged for competing brands is essential to allow the firm to adjust its prices relative to competitors'. Government regulations and legislation also influence pricing decisions. Several laws aim to enhance competition in the marketplace by outlawing price fixing and deceptive pricing. Legislation also restricts price differentials that can injure competition. Moreover, the government can invoke price controls to curb inflation.

Unlike consumers, business buyers purchase products for resale, for use in their own operations, or for producing other products. When adjusting prices, business sellers consider the size of the purchase, geographic factors, and transportation requirements. Producers commonly provide discounts off list prices to intermediaries. The categories of discounts include trade, quantity, cash, seasonal, and allowance. A trade discount is a price reduction for performing such functions as storing, transporting, final processing, or providing credit services. If an intermediary purchases in large enough quantities, the producer gives a quantity discount, which can be either cumulative or noncumulative. A cash discount is a price reduction for prompt payment or payment in cash. Buyers who purchase goods or services out of season may be granted a seasonal discount. An allowance, such as a trade-in allowance, is a concession in price to achieve a desired goal.

Geographic pricing involves reductions for transportation costs or other costs associated with the physical distance between buyer and seller. With an F.O.B. factory price, the buyer pays for shipping from the factory. An F.O.B. destination price means the producer pays for shipping; this is the easiest way to price products, but it is difficult to administer. When the seller charges a fixed average cost for transportation, it is using uniform geographic pricing. Zone prices are uniform within major geographic zones; they increase by zone as transportation costs increase. With base-point pricing, prices are adjusted for shipping expenses incurred by the seller from the base point nearest the buyer. Freight absorption pricing occurs when a seller absorbs all or part of the freight costs.

ACE self-test

Please visit the student website at **www.prideferrell.com** for ACE Self-Test questions that will help you prepare for exams.

## IMPORTANT TERMS

Price
Barter
Price competition
Nonprice competition
Demand curve
Price elasticity of demand
Fixed costs
Average fixed cost
Variable costs
Average variable cost

Total cost
Average total cost
Marginal cost (MC)
Marginal revenue (MR)
Break-even point
Internal reference price
External reference price
Value conscious
Price conscious
Prestige sensitive

Price discrimination
Trade (functional) discount
Quantity discount
Cumulative discount
Noncumulative discount
Cash discount
Seasonal discount
Allowance
Geographic pricing

F.O.B. factory
F.O.B. destination
Uniform geographic pricing
Zone pricing
Base-point pricing
Freight absorption pricing
Transfer pricing

## DISCUSSION & REVIEW QUESTIONS

1. Why are pricing decisions important to an organization?

2. Compare and contrast price and nonprice competition. Describe the conditions under which each form works best.

3. Why do most demand curves demonstrate an inverse relationship between price and quantity?

4. List the characteristics of products that have inelastic demand, and give several examples of such products.

5. Explain why optimal profits should occur when marginal cost equals marginal revenue.

6. Chambers Company has just gathered estimates for conducting a break-even analysis for a new product. Variable costs are $7 a unit. The additional plant will cost $48,000. The new product will be charged $18,000 a year for its share of general overhead.

Advertising expenditures will be $80,000, and $55,000 will be spent on distribution. If the product sells for $12, what is the break-even point in units? What is the break-even point in dollar sales volume?

7. In what ways do other marketing mix variables affect pricing decisions?

8. What types of expectations may channel members have about producers' prices? How might these expectations affect pricing decisions?

9. How do legal and regulatory forces influence pricing decisions?

10. Compare and contrast a trade discount and a quantity discount.

11. What is the reason for using the term *F.O.B.*?

12. What are the major methods used for transfer pricing?

## APPLICATION QUESTIONS

1. Price competition is intense in the fast-food, air travel, and personal computer industries. Discuss a recent situation in which companies had to meet or beat a rival's price in a price-competitive industry. Did you benefit from this situation? Did it change your perception of the companies and/or their products?

2. Customers' interpretations and responses regarding a product and its price are an important influence on marketers' pricing decisions. Perceptions of price are affected by the degree to which a customer is value conscious, price conscious, or prestige sensitive. Discuss how value consciousness, price consciousness, and prestige sensitivity influence the buying decision process for the following products:
   a. A new house
   b. Weekly groceries for a family of five
   c. An airline ticket
   d. A soft drink from a vending machine

globalEDGE™

1. A fundamental component of the price of newsprint in the world market is its supply and demand. At the national level, information can typically be gathered based on a country's imports and exports. Using the Food and Agriculture Organization (FAO) of the United Nations website as a resource devoted to food and agriculture, find Canadian, Mexican, and U.S. trade statistics concerning the newsprint industry. Use the search term "food and agriculture" at **http://globaledge.msu.edu/ibrd** to reach the FAOSTAT website, then click on the All Data link at the top. From the next page, choose Production and then ForeSTAT. Click on "newsprint" in the Commodity drop-down box and then choose the most recent year available in the Year drop-down box. Then, holding the CTRL key down for multiple choices in the country information drop-down boxes, Select Canada, Mexico, and the U.S. Finally, in the Subject drop-down box, first choose "Import quantity (tonnes/m3)" and then "Export quantity (tonnes)" to conduct separate searches to access the data. From the three countries surveyed, which could be said to increase the price of newsprint in the world market? Which might decrease its price?

2. Business strategists and economists sometimes use a consumer price index (CPI) in their decision models. In fact, some organizations perform a comparison across countries to inform the public of consumer pricing trends. A report titled "Consumer Price Indices (CPI) for OECD Countries" should prove helpful in answering this question. Access this report by using the search term "comparison across countries" at **http://globaledge.msu.edu/ibrd.** Once you reach the OECD webpage, click on "View Long Abstract" for the link for Consumer Price Indices (CPI) for OECD Countries. What is a CPI generally used to measure?

## INTERNET Exercise

### Autosite

Autosite offers car buyers a free, comprehensive website to find the invoice prices for almost all car models. The browser can also access a listing of all the latest new-car rebates and incentives. Visit this site at **www.autosite.com**.

1. Find the lowest-priced Lexus available today, and examine its features. Which Lexus dealer is closest to you?
2. If you wanted to purchase this Lexus, what are the lowest monthly payments you could make over the longest time period?
3. Is this free site more credible than a "pay" site? Why or why not?

## Video Case 21.1 | JetBlue's Flight Plan for Profitability

When David Neeleman sold his Utah-based airline to Southwest Airlines in 1994, he signed a contract agreeing not to compete in the air travel industry for five years. By the time the five years ended, the entrepreneur had created a new flight plan—and found $160 million in financial backing—for his full-throttle return to the skies with a customer-friendly, low-fare airline called JetBlue. Today that airline serves 35 cities in the United States, Puerto Rico, the Bahamas, and the Dominican Republic, and it has become the number 4 airline flying out of New York City.

Neeleman and his management team decided to base the startup airline in New York City after they thoroughly analyzed the area's air travel patterns. "Essentially, New Yorkers were prisoners," explains John Owen, JetBlue's chief financial officer. "They had only low-quality, high-fare airlines to choose from. Their expectations were at [the] bottom." New York travelers also had to contend with crowds and delays at nearby La Guardia Airport unless they were willing to venture eight miles farther to fly from John F. Kennedy International Airport. Unlike some metropolitan airports, JFK is not a regional hub for major airlines or for low-fare carriers such as Southwest. Seizing an opportunity to trade off a slightly less convenient location for less competition and better on-time performance, Neeleman secured more than 70 takeoff and landing slots at JFK Airport, enough to accommodate JetBlue's projected growth through its first five years.

Neeleman understands price is a top consideration for travelers. He therefore has sharpened his pencil to keep JetBlue's ticket prices highly competitive to attract vacationers as well as business travelers. Major carriers such as Delta typically quote dozens of fares between two locations, depending on time of day and other factors. JetBlue's everyday pricing structure is far simpler and avoids complicated requirements such as Saturday-night stayovers. Neeleman says the fares are based on demand and that JetBlue uses pricing to equalize the loads

on the flights so no jet takes off empty while another is completely full. Thus, fares for Sunday-night flights tend to be higher because of higher demand, whereas Tuesday-night flights may be priced lower due to lower demand. Still, the CEO observes that JetBlue's highest fare generally undercuts the lowest fare of its competitors.

JetBlue's promotional fares are even lower. When inaugurating service between New York and California, the airline offered a one-way fare of $99, an extraordinarily low price for a nonstop, cross-country flight. Neeleman points out that low fares stimulate traffic, which helps JetBlue weather the turbulence of tough economic times and challenges such as the falloff in air travel that occurred after the September 11 terrorist attacks. JetBlue's flights have an average passenger load of 85 percent of full capacity, compared with an industry average load of 68.4 percent.

Neeleman and his team have made other decisions to set their startup apart from other new airline ventures. Whereas many new carriers buy used jets, JetBlue flies new, state-of-the-art, environmentally friendly Airbus A320 jets with seat-back personal video screens. Rather than squeeze in the maximum 180 seats that A320s can hold, JetBlue flies with only 162, which allows passengers more leg room. In addition, the jets are outfitted with roomier leather seats, which cost twice as much as regular seat fabric but last twice as long. More important, passengers feel pampered when they sink into the leather seats and enjoy free DirectTV programming, which also differentiates JetBlue from other low-fare airlines.

Another advantage of flying new jets is higher fuel efficiency. Because of their dual engines and weight, A320s can operate on 60 percent of the amount of fuel burned by an equivalent jet built decades earlier. As a result, JetBlue has not had to raise ticket prices to compensate for rising fuel costs even as the airline expands beyond the East Coast to western destinations such as

Long Beach, California, and Seattle. In addition, because JetBlue's technicians work on only one type of jet, they become highly proficient at their maintenance tasks, which saves time and money. New jets come with a five-year warranty, so JetBlue has to budget only for routine maintenance service.

From its first day of operation, JetBlue has relied on Internet bookings to minimize sales costs. Travelers who buy tickets directly through the company's website (**www.jetblue.com**) get a special discount and are also eligible for online specials, such as "Get It Together" fares designed for two people traveling together. By the airline's second year, it was selling 50 percent of its tickets via the Internet. JetBlue also set up a special web-based service to encourage travel agents to buy tickets for their customers online.

JetBlue's total costs equal about 6.5 cents per mile, well below the per-mile costs of most major competitors. In turn, its low cost structure allows the airline to keep ticket prices low while delivering a comfortable flying experience. Neeleman's decision to fly from JFK Airport also means JetBlue's on-time record is generally better than those of the big airlines, another important consideration for business travelers and vacationers alike. Not surprisingly, JetBlue flew into profitability just months after its launch, and Neeleman aims to keep the airline's revenues and profits soaring in the future.[27]

## Questions for Discussion

1. In an industry where pricing has driven many firms out of business or into bankruptcy protection, why does JetBlue compete so successfully on the basis of price?
2. How does JetBlue use pricing to deal with demand fluctuations?
3. Is a businessperson's demand for air travel likely to be relatively elastic or inelastic? Is a vacationer's demand for air travel likely to be relatively elastic or inelastic?
4. What other factors related to pricing are most important to JetBlue's management when making pricing decisions?

---

## Case 21.2 — Priceline.com: Name Your Price

Priceline.com, the original name-your-price website, has had a challenging few years. The site invites customers to name the price they are willing to pay for an airline ticket, a hotel room, a rental car, tours and attractions, a mortgage, or a cruise. In its first four months of operation, the company sold 40,000 airline tickets and continues to attract more than 1 million visitors a week. At peak times, it sells a ticket every 70 seconds to one of its 11 million registered customers.

However, Priceline only recently recorded its first profit since the company burst onto the Internet with much fanfare in 1998. Like other e-businesses, Priceline has employed a substantial promotional budget to build awareness and attract customers. The company has also been saddled with costs incurred by its withdrawal from ill-fated attempts to expand its product mix to include name-your-price groceries, gasoline, and insurance. On top of these challenges, Priceline is learning to deal with competition now that it is no longer the only name-your-price site on the Web.

Travel services remain Priceline's most popular offering. Unsold airline seats and hotel rooms are wasted; they cannot be stored in warehouses for later sale. Priceline.com, which provides an anonymous link between buyers and sellers, gives buyers an opportunity to pay a price they can afford and sellers the chance to reduce waste by accepting a buyer's offer. Because planes fly with more than 500,000 empty seats a day, waste and lost revenues are a major problem for airlines, and many therefore cooperate with Priceline.com.

How does Priceline.com's airline ticket service work? Using the lowest available advance purchase fares as a guideline, customers go to the Priceline site, enter their destinations and travel dates, offer a price for a ticket, and type in their credit card numbers. Travel must begin in the United States, and customers must be flexible regarding the time of day they are willing to travel. However, destinations can be worldwide, and there are no blackout dates or advance purchase requirements. After receiving an offer, Priceline searches ticket availability on participating airlines. Within an hour or less (one day for international flights), Priceline lets the customer know whether his or her offer has been accepted, charges the credit card, and processes the tickets. Customers whose offers are rejected can try again. This web-based pricing system is so original that the U.S. Patent and Trademark Office granted Priceline a patent on the method.

Shopping at Priceline.com sounds easy and economical, and most of its customers agree. Critics, however, point out some drawbacks in Priceline's airline ticket service. In addition to committing themselves to fly at hours that will not be specified until after their offers are accepted, customers must be willing to take flights that may include one or more stops or connections and possibly a long layover. Tickets are nonrefundable, cannot be changed, and earn no frequent flier miles. Some reporters who have tested Priceline's system complain the airfares are not always the lowest available and conclude that the site works best for people who must fly on short notice and can't meet advance purchase requirements for lower fares.

Customers can also use Priceline to name their price for hotel rooms in major U.S. cities. First, they enter their destination, dates, number of rooms, desired quality level of the hotel (two, three, four, or five stars), and how much they are willing to pay per night. As with the airline ticket system, they have to provide a credit card number so Priceline can lock in the reservation if it finds accommodations that meet their criteria. Priceline searches its database of participating hotels for one with a rate at or below the customer's request, books the room, buys it from the hotel, and charges the customer $5 more than the price it paid. Priceline guarantees its hotel prices and promises that if customers can find a better price for a similar room online, the company will refund the difference. This Priceline service has become so popular that it now represents more than half of all booked offers on Priceline. Customers are also reserving more rental cars, helping to boost Priceline's overall revenues and contributing to its profitability.

Although Priceline had no name-your-price competition in its early years, other travel sites now offer variations on this pricing approach. Expedia, backed by Microsoft, offers Flight Price Matcher, a service very similar to Priceline's—so similar, in fact, that Priceline sued for patent infringement (a settlement calls for Expedia to pay royalties to Priceline). Expedia customers don't find out which airline they are using or when their flights leave until their bids have been accepted, which takes up to 15 minutes. Hotwire.com, started by several major airlines, invites customers to bid on airline tickets, rental cars, and hotel rooms. Unlike Expedia and Priceline, Hotwire allows customers one hour to make a decision once they find out whether their price has been accepted, but they still don't learn all the details until they have agreed to the purchase.

Because travelers have become savvier about searching out special Internet deals, online travel is experiencing tremendous growth. However, the rise in discount airlines and simplified fare structures and online deals from traditional airlines has dented Priceline's blind bidding airfare business by as much as 40 percent. In 2005, the company added a service booking airlines with published airfares, and growth in that area has grown sharply despite competition from sites such as Orbitz and Expedia. Priceline.com hopes its value-conscious strategy will prove irresistible to a large number of travelers, bringing them again and again to Priceline's site rather than to competing sites.[28]

## Questions for Discussion

1. What effect do name-your-price sites seem to be having on demand for travel services? What are the implications for price elasticity of demand?
2. Does the pricing facilitated by Priceline.com result in price or nonprice competition?
3. What are the advantages and disadvantages of Priceline.com's pricing approach for buyers? For sellers?

# Setting Prices

## Levis: High-End Low Riders

Levi Strauss & Company, known for its 501s and affordable prices, is breaking into the premium jeans market. The company, which has been making jeans since the 1800s, wants a part of the fast-growing $1 billion market for upscale denim. The premium jean market is dominated by brands such as Earl Jeans, Seven for All Mankind, Citizens for Humanity, and True Religion. Levi's is entering the market with its Capital E collection, selling for between $110 and $180 a pair.

People in the fashion industry fear that Levi's reputation as a long-standing, reliable, inexpensive department store brand may harm its chances in the upscale market. To compete, Levi's must prove that its premium line has the quality and style comparable to other high-end brands.

Levi's joined with the Warhol Foundation to create the 2006 Andy Warhol Factory X collection, based on the art of Andy Warhol, a lover of Levi's jeans. (The "Lux" jeans from this line sell for nearly $300!) The company also threw an "underground" party to promote its Ultimate boot-cut jeans with the help of cast members from the hit TV show, *Desperate Housewives*. In addition, the company opened new Levi's stores in Beverly Hills, California, and Georgetown, Washington, D.C., to market both the company's popular Red Tab jeans collection as well as the high-end collection.

Levi's Premium collection may contribute a small portion of the company's revenue, but right now it is driving the company's innovation. After seeing losses for several years, the company is seeing positive sales results in the premium markets in Europe and Asia. Overall premium sales saw more than a 100 percent increase in 2004.[1] ■

## OBJECTIVES

**1.** To describe the six major stages of the process used to establish prices

**2.** To explore issues related to developing pricing objectives

**3.** To understand the importance of identifying the target market's evaluation of price

**4.** To examine how marketers analyze competitors' prices

**5.** To describe the bases used for setting prices

**6.** To explain the different types of pricing strategies

L evi Strauss became a leading marketer of blue jeans by offering a quality product at a competitive price, which helped the firm gain market share and a strong reputation for more than 100 years. Because price has such a profound impact on a firm's success, finding the right pricing strategy is crucial. Indeed, some firms have developed products, especially software, to help client companies find the best price for their own products. One such firm is Zilliant, which assists airlines and hotels in finding optimum prices.[2] Selecting a pricing strategy is one of the fundamental components of the process of setting prices.

In this chapter, we examine six stages of a process marketers can use when setting prices. Figure 22.1 illustrates these stages. Stage 1 is the development of a pricing objective that is compatible with the organization's overall and marketing objectives. Stage 2 entails assessing the target market's evaluation of price. Stage 3 involves evaluating competitors' prices, which helps determine the role of price in the marketing strategy. Stage 4 requires choosing a basis for setting prices. Stage 5 is the selection of a pricing strategy, or the guidelines for using price in the marketing mix. Stage 6, determining the final price, depends on environmental forces and marketers' understanding and use of a systematic approach to establishing prices. These stages are not rigid steps that all marketers must follow; rather, they are guidelines that provide a logical sequence for establishing prices.

# Development of Pricing Objectives

**pricing objectives** Goals that describe what a firm wants to achieve through pricing

**Pricing objectives** are goals that describe what a firm wants to achieve through pricing. Developing pricing objectives is an important task because pricing objectives form the basis for decisions about other stages of pricing. Thus, pricing objectives must be stated explicitly, and the statement should include the time frame for accomplishing them.

Marketers must ensure that pricing objectives are consistent with the organization's marketing objectives and with its overall objectives because pricing objectives influence decisions in many functional areas, including finance, accounting, and production. A marketer can use both short- and long-term pricing objectives and can employ one or multiple pricing objectives. For instance, a firm may wish to increase market share by 18 percent over the next three years, achieve a 15 percent return on investment, and promote an image of quality in the marketplace.

In this section, we examine some of the pricing objectives companies might set for themselves. Table 22.1 shows the major pricing objectives and typical actions associated with them.

**figure 22.1**

**STAGES FOR ESTABLISHING PRICES**

1 Development of pricing objectives

2 Assessment of target market's evaluation of price

3 Evaluation of competitors' prices

4 Selection of a basis for pricing

5 Selection of a pricing strategy

6 Determination of a specific price

| table 22.1 | PRICING OBJECTIVES AND TYPICAL ACTIONS TAKEN TO ACHIEVE THEM |
|---|---|
| **Objective** | **Possible Action** |
| Survival | Adjust price levels so the firm can increase sales volume to match organizational expenses |
| Profit | Identify price and cost levels that allow the firm to maximize profit |
| Return on investment | Identify price levels that enable the firm to yield targeted ROI |
| Market share | Adjust price levels so the firm can maintain or increase sales relative to competitors' sales |
| Cash flow | Set price levels to encourage rapid sales |
| Status quo | Identify price levels that help stabilize demand and sales |
| Product quality | Set prices to recover research and development expenditures and establish a high-quality image |

## Survival

A fundamental pricing objective is survival. Most organizations will tolerate set-backs such as short-run losses and internal upheaval if necessary for survival. Because price is a flexible variable, it is sometimes used to keep a company afloat by increasing sales volume to levels that match expenses. For example, a women's apparel retailer may run a three-day, 60-percent-off sale to generate enough cash to pay creditors, employees, and rent.

## Profit

Although a business may claim that its objective is to maximize profits for its own-ers, the objective of profit maximization is rarely operational because its achieve-ment is difficult to measure. Because of this difficulty, profit objectives tend to be set at levels that the owners and top-level decision makers view as satisfactory. Specific profit objectives may be stated in terms of either actual dollar amounts or a percent-age of sales revenues. For example, when Procter & Gamble introduced the Gillette Fusion five-blade razor, it set a price 30 percent higher than its Mach 3 three-blade products. With an overall 72 percent market share, P&G hopes the Fusion family of shaving products will help boost profits.[3]

## Return on Investment

Pricing to attain a specified rate of return on the company's investment is a profit-related pricing objective. Most pricing objectives based on return on investment (ROI) are achieved by trial and error because not all cost and revenue data needed to project the return on investment are available when setting prices. General Motors, for example, uses ROI pricing objectives. Many pharmaceutical companies also use ROI pricing objectives because of their great investment in research and development.

## Market Share

Many firms establish pricing objectives to maintain or increase market share, a prod-uct's sales in relation to total industry sales. Toyota, for example, priced its Prius hybrid at a reasonable price that helped consumers afford the car and, in turn, built a strong market share in the hybrid category.[4] Many firms recognize that high rela-tive market shares often translate into higher profits. The Profit Impact of Market

Strategies (PIMS) studies, conducted over the last 30 years, have shown that both market share and product quality heavily influence profitability. Thus, marketers often use an increase in market share as a primary pricing objective.

Maintaining or increasing market share need not depend on growth in industry sales. Remember that an organization can increase its market share even if sales for the total industry are flat or decreasing. On the other hand, an organization's sales volume may increase while its market share decreases if the overall market is growing.

### Cash Flow

Some organizations set prices so they can recover cash as quickly as possible. Financial managers understandably seek to quickly recover capital spent to develop products. This objective may have the support of a marketing manager who anticipates a short product life cycle. Although it may be acceptable in some situations, the use of cash flow and recovery as an objective oversimplifies the contribution of price to profits. If this pricing objective results in high prices, competitors with lower prices may gain a large share of the market.

### Status Quo

In some cases, an organization is in a favorable position and, desiring nothing more, may set an objective of status quo. Status quo objectives can focus on several dimensions, such as maintaining a certain market share, meeting (but not beating) competitors' prices, achieving price stability, and maintaining a favorable public image. A status quo pricing objective can reduce a firm's risks by helping to stabilize demand for its products. The use of status quo pricing objectives sometimes minimizes pricing as a competitive tool, leading to a climate of nonprice competition in an industry. Professionals such as accountants and attorneys often operate in such an environment.

### Product Quality

A company may have the objective of leading its industry in product quality. This goal normally dictates a high price to cover the costs of achieving high product quality and, in some instances, the costs of research and development. For example, Bentley Motors uses premium prices to help signal the quality of its hand-made cars, which can cost from $190,000 to well over $300,000 depending on accessories and options.[5] As previously mentioned, the PIMS studies have shown that both product quality and market share are good indicators of profitability. The products and brands that customers perceive to be of high quality are more likely to survive in a competitive marketplace. High quality usually enables a marketer to charge higher prices for the product.

**Product Quality**
American Ironhorse produces quality motorcycles.

# At Whole Foods Market, Pricing Signals Quality

Supermarket chain Whole Foods Market caters to customers who are generally concerned with health and wellness. Many of the stores' regular customers are vegetarians, and people committed to eating organic foods and free range poultry. Many Whole Foods stores feature local produce, meats, and cheeses, and have dining areas that resemble contemporary coffee houses. Whole Foods Market has also adopted a premium pricing strategy that seems to be generating healthy profits.

Whole Foods Market is able to charge a premium for its products by appealing to consumers' increasing desire to be healthy and because of their willingness to pay a little more for quality products that are organic, natural, and environmentally friendly. The company's executives say that their goal is to offer first-rate products that provide great value to their customers, and they define *high value* as "a product of high quality at a competitive price." From their perspective, the high quality of Whole Foods' products justifies their premium prices. Product presentation, variety, and the Whole Foods Market shopping experience also tempt customers to linger in the stores and buy more than they might in a typical grocery store.

In an age when customers are going to great lengths to look younger and feel better, Whole Foods Market is well positioned. It is currently growing at twice the rate of its closest competition and has had a 20 percent increase in annual sales over the past few years. Moreover, it has virtually no debt, which is almost unheard of in the grocery industry. While no one can predict whether the success of high-end grocery stores with their premium pricing will continue, things certainly look positive.

## Assessment of the Target Market's Evaluation of Price

Despite the general assumption that price is a major issue for buyers, the importance of price depends on the type of product, the type of target market, and the purchase situation. For example, buyers are probably more sensitive to gasoline prices than to luggage prices. With respect to the type of target market, adults may have to pay more than children for certain products. The purchase situation also affects the buyer's view of price. Most moviegoers would never pay in other situations the prices charged for soft drinks, popcorn, and candy at movie concession stands. By assessing the target market's evaluation of price, a marketer is in a better position to know how much emphasis to put on price. Information about the target market's price evaluation may also help a marketer determine how far above the competition the firm can set its prices.

Because some consumers today are seeking less expensive products and shopping more selectively, some manufacturers and retailers are focusing on the value of their products. Value combines a product's price and quality attributes, which customers use to differentiate among competing brands. Consumers are looking for good deals on products that provide better value for their money. They may also view products that have highly desirable attributes, such as organic content or time-saving features, as having great value. Consumers are increasingly willing to pay a higher price for food that is convenient and time saving, as illustrated in Table 22.2 (on p. 608). Companies that offer both low prices and high quality, such as Target and Best Buy, have altered consumers' expectations about how much quality they must sacrifice for low prices.[6] Even retail atmospherics can influence consumers' perceptions of price:

| table 22.2 | EXAMPLES OF PERCEPTIONS OF PRODUCT VALUE |
| --- | --- |
| **Basic, Cost-Effective Product** | **Expensive, Time-Saving Product** |
| 1 head romaine lettuce, $1.99 | 1 bag EarthGreens organic romaine hearts, $3.99 |
| 1 sandwich with Welch's jelly, Jif peanut butter, white bread, 46¢ | 1 Smucker's Uncrustables ready-made peanut butter and jelly sandwich, 82¢ |
| 24 oz. Clorox Liquid Bleach, roll of Viva paper towels, $2.69 | 1 package Clorox Disinfecting Wipes, $3.49 |

**Source:** "Stop Getting Eaten Alive by Grocery Bills," *Money*, Jan. 2006, p. 34.

the use of soft lights and colors has been found to have a positive influence on perception of price fairness.[7] Understanding the importance of a product to customers, as well as their expectations about quality and value, helps marketers correctly assess the target market's evaluation of price.

# Evaluation of Competitors' Prices

In most cases, marketers are in a better position to establish prices when they know the prices charged for competing brands. Learning competitors' prices may be a regular function of marketing research. Some grocery and department stores, for example, have full-time comparative shoppers who systematically collect data on prices. Companies may also purchase price lists, sometimes weekly, from syndicated marketing research services.

Finding out what prices competitors are charging is not always easy, especially in producer and reseller markets. Competitors' price lists are often closely guarded. Even if a marketer has access to competitors' price lists, those lists may not reflect the actual prices at which competitive products are sold because those prices may be established through negotiation.

Knowing the prices of competing brands can be very important for a marketer. Competitors' prices and the marketing mix variables they emphasize partly determine how important price will be to customers. A marketer in an industry in which price competition prevails needs competitive price information to ensure its prices are the same as, or lower than, competitors' prices. In some instances, an organization's prices are designed to be slightly above competitors' prices to give its products an exclusive image. In contrast, another company may use price as a competitive tool and price its products below those of competitors. Category killers like Staples and Home Depot have acquired large market shares through highly competitive pricing.[8]

# Selection of a Basis for Pricing

The three major dimensions on which prices can be based are cost, demand, and competition. The selection of the basis to use is affected by the type of product, the market structure of the industry, the brand's market share position relative to competing brands, and customer characteristics. In this section, we discuss each basis separately. However, when setting prices, an organization generally considers two or all three of these dimensions, even if one is the primary basis on which it determines prices. For example, if an organization is using cost as a basis for setting prices, marketers in that organization are also aware of and concerned about competitors' prices. If a company is using demand as a basis for pricing, those making pricing decisions still must consider costs and competitors' prices. Fairchild Semiconductor uses software to assess

*Source:* Data from Bureau of Transportation Statistics.

**cost-based pricing** Adding a dollar amount or percentage to the cost of the product

**cost-plus pricing** Adding a specified dollar amount or percentage to the seller's cost

**markup pricing** Adding to the cost of the product a predetermined percentage of that cost

all three dimensions, as well as buying behavior, manufacturing capacity, inventories, and product life cycles, in setting prices for its 44,000 products.[9]

## Cost-Based Pricing

With **cost-based pricing**, a dollar amount or percentage is added to the cost of the product. This approach thus involves calculations of desired profit margins. Cost-based pricing does not necessarily take into account the economic aspects of supply and demand, nor must it relate to just one pricing strategy or pricing objective. Cost-based pricing is straightforward and easy to implement. Two common forms of cost-based pricing are cost-plus and markup pricing.

**Cost-Plus Pricing.** With **cost-plus pricing**, the seller's costs are determined (usually during a project or after a project is completed), and then a specified dollar amount or percentage of the cost is added to the seller's cost to establish the price. Cost-plus pricing and competition-based pricing are in fact the most common bases for pricing services.[10] When production costs are difficult to predict, cost-plus pricing is appropriate. Projects involving custom-made equipment and commercial construction are often priced using this technique. The government frequently uses such cost-based pricing in granting defense contracts. One pitfall for the buyer is that the seller may increase costs to establish a larger profit base. Furthermore, some costs, such as overhead, may be difficult to determine. In periods of rapid inflation, cost-plus pricing is popular, especially when the producer must use raw materials that are fluctuating in price. In industries in which cost-plus pricing is common and sellers have similar costs, price competition may not be especially intense.

**Markup Pricing.** With **markup pricing**, commonly used by retailers, a product's price is derived by adding a predetermined percentage of the cost, called *markup*, to the cost of the product. Although the percentage markup in a retail store varies from one category of goods to another—35 percent of cost for hardware items and 100 percent of cost for greeting cards, for example—the same percentage is often used to determine the prices on items within a single product category, and the percentage markup may be largely standardized across an industry at the retail level. Using a rigid percentage markup for a specific product category reduces pricing to a routine task that can be performed quickly.

Markup can be stated as a percentage of the cost or as a percentage of the selling price. The following example illustrates how percentage markups are determined and points out the differences in the two methods. Assume a retailer purchases a can of tuna at 45 cents, adds 15 cents to the cost, and then prices the tuna at 60 cents. Here are the figures:

$$\text{Markup as a Percentage of Cost} = \frac{\text{Markup}}{\text{Cost}}$$
$$= \frac{15}{45}$$
$$= 33.3\%$$

$$\text{Markup as a Percentage of Selling Price} = \frac{\text{Markup}}{\text{Selling Price}}$$
$$= \frac{15}{60}$$
$$= 25.0\%$$

Obviously, when discussing a percentage markup, it is important to know whether the markup is based on cost or selling price.

Markups normally reflect expectations about operating costs, risks, and stock turnovers. Wholesalers and manufacturers often suggest standard retail markups that are considered profitable. To the extent that retailers use similar markups for the same product category, price competition is reduced. In addition, using rigid markups is convenient and is the major reason retailers, which face numerous pricing decisions, favor this method.

## Demand-Based Pricing

**demand-based pricing** Pricing based on the level of demand for the product

Marketers sometimes base prices on the level of demand for the product. When **demand-based pricing** is used, customers pay a higher price when demand for the product is strong and a lower price when demand is weak. For example, hotels that otherwise attract numerous travelers often offer reduced rates during lower-demand periods. Some long-distance telephone companies, such as Sprint and AT&T, also use demand-based pricing by charging peak and off-peak rates. To use this pricing basis, a marketer must be able to estimate the amounts of a product consumers will demand at different prices. The marketer then chooses the price that generates the highest total revenue. Obviously the effectiveness of demand-based pricing depends on the marketer's ability to estimate demand accurately.

Compared with cost-based pricing, demand-based pricing places a firm in a better position to reach higher profit levels, assuming buyers value the product at levels sufficiently above the product's cost.

## Competition-Based Pricing

**competition-based pricing** Pricing influenced primarily by competitors' prices

With **competition-based pricing**, an organization considers costs to be secondary to competitors' prices. The importance of this method increases when competing products are relatively homogeneous and the organization is serving markets in which price is a key purchase consideration. A firm that uses competition-based pricing may choose to price below competitors' prices, above competitors' prices, or at the same level. Airlines use competition-based pricing, often charging identical fares on the same routes. Online travel services such as Orbitz, Expedia, and Priceline.com have also employed competition-based pricing. If you want to sell your home without the aid of a realtor, how do you determine the value of your home and thus a competitive asking price? One website, **www.zillow.com**, provides a free estimate of your home's value based on its size and the sale of comparable homes in the area.[11] While you may think your home is worth as much as a castle, if you set the asking

**Demand-Based Pricing**

Woodstock Inn & Resort uses demand-based pricing to reflect seasonal needs for its resort property.

price too high above comparable homes for sale, buyers will likely choose one with a lower price.

Although not all introductory marketing texts have exactly the same price, they do have similar prices. The price the bookstore paid to the publishing company for this textbook was determined on the basis of competitors' prices. Competition-based pricing can help a firm achieve the pricing objective of increasing sales or market share. Competition-based pricing may necessitate frequent price adjustments. For example, for many competitive airline routes, fares are adjusted often.

# Selection of a Pricing Strategy

A pricing strategy is an approach or a course of action designed to achieve pricing and marketing objectives. Generally pricing strategies help marketers solve the practical problems of establishing prices. Table 22.3 lists the most common pricing strategies, which we discuss in this section.

## Differential Pricing

An important issue in pricing decisions is whether to use a single price or different prices for the same product. Using a single price has several benefits. A primary advantage is simplicity. A single price is easily understood by both employees and customers, and since many salespeople and customers dislike having to negotiate a price, it reduces the chance of an adversarial relationship developing between marketer and customer. The use of a single price does create some challenges, however. If the single price is too high, a number of potential customers may be unable to afford the product. If it is too low, the organization loses revenue from those customers who would have paid more had the price been higher.

**differential pricing** Charging different prices to different buyers for the same quality and quantity of product

**Differential pricing** means charging different prices to different buyers for the same quality and quantity of product. For differential pricing to be effective, the market must consist of multiple segments with different price sensitivities, and the method should be used in a way that avoids confusing or antagonizing customers. Customers paying the lower prices should not be able to resell the product to the individuals and organizations paying higher prices, unless that is the seller's intention. Differential pricing can occur in several ways, including negotiated pricing, secondary-market discounting, periodic discounting, and random discounting.

**table 22.3   COMMON PRICING STRATEGIES**

| | |
|---|---|
| **Differential Pricing** | **Psychological Pricing** |
| Negotiated pricing | Reference pricing |
| Secondary-market pricing | Bundle pricing |
| Periodic discounting | Multiple-unit pricing |
| Random discounting | Everyday low prices |
| **New-Product Pricing** | **Odd-Even Pricing** |
| Price skimming | Customary pricing |
| Penetration pricing | Prestige pricing |
| **Product-Line Pricing** | **Promotional Pricing** |
| Captive pricing | Price leaders |
| Premium pricing | Special-event pricing |
| Bait pricing | Comparison discounting |
| Price lining | |
| | **Professional Pricing** |

**negotiated pricing** Establishing a final price through bargaining between seller and customer

**secondary-market pricing** Setting one price for the primary target market and a different price for another market

**periodic discounting** Temporary reduction of prices on a patterned or systematic basis

**random discounting** Temporary reduction of prices on an unsystematic basis

**Negotiated Pricing.** **Negotiated pricing** occurs when the final price is established through bargaining between seller and customer. Negotiated pricing occurs in a number of industries and at all levels of distribution. Cutler-Hammer/Eaton streamlined its contract-negotiations process for more than 90,000 products by reducing quote response times and implementing automatic acceptance of offers.[12] Even when there is a predetermined stated price or a price list, manufacturers, wholesalers, and retailers may negotiate to establish the final sales price. Consumers commonly negotiate prices for houses, cars, and used equipment.

**Secondary-Market Pricing.** **Secondary-market pricing** means setting one price for the primary target market and a different price for another market. Often the price charged in the secondary market is lower. However, when the costs of serving a secondary market are higher than normal, secondary-market customers may have to pay a higher price. Examples of secondary markets include a geographically isolated domestic market, a market in a foreign country, and a segment willing to purchase a product during off-peak times. For example, some restaurants offer special "early-bird" prices during the early evening hours, movie theaters offer senior citizen and afternoon matinee discounts, and some textbooks and pharmaceutical products are sold for considerably less in certain foreign countries than in the United States. Secondary markets give an organization an opportunity to use excess capacity and stabilize the allocation of resources.

**Periodic Discounting.** **Periodic discounting** is the temporary reduction of prices on a patterned or systematic basis. Many retailers, for example, have annual holiday sales. Some women's apparel stores have two seasonal sales each year: a winter sale in the last two weeks of January and a summer sale in the first two weeks of July. Automobile dealers regularly discount prices on current models in the fall, when the next year's models are introduced. From the marketer's point of view, a major problem with periodic discounting is that because the discounts follow a pattern, customers can predict when the reductions will occur and may delay their purchases until they can take advantage of the lower prices.

**Random Discounting.** To alleviate the problem of customers knowing when discounting will occur, some organizations employ **random discounting**; that is, they temporarily reduce their prices on an unsystematic basis. When price reductions of a product occur randomly, current users of that brand are likely unable to predict when the reductions will occur and thus will not delay their purchases. In the automobile industry, with the increasing reliance on sales, rebates, and incentives such as 0 percent financing, random discounting has become nearly continuous discounting, and some analysts have expressed concern that automakers will find it difficult to "wean" consumers off the generous incentives as the economy improves.[13] Marketers also use random discounting to attract new customers. For example, Lever Brothers may temporarily reduce the price of one of its bar soaps in the hope of attracting new customers.

Whether they use periodic discounting or random discounting, retailers often employ tensile pricing when putting products on sale. *Tensile pricing* refers to a broad statement about price reductions as opposed to detailing specific price discounts. Examples of tensile pricing would be statements such as

**Secondary-Market Pricing**

Because of the product type, purchasers of Jeldwen windows may be one-time customers.

"20 to 50 percent off," "up to 75 percent off," and "save 10 percent or more." Generally, using and advertising the tensile price that mentions only the maximum reduction (such as "up to 50 percent off") generates the highest customer response.[14]

### New-Product Pricing

Setting the base price for a new product is a necessary part of formulating a marketing strategy. The base price is easily adjusted (in the absence of government price controls), and its establishment is one of the most fundamental decisions in the marketing mix. The base price can be set high to recover development costs quickly or provide a reference point for developing discount prices for different market segments. When a marketer sets base prices, it also considers how quickly competitors will enter the market, whether they will mount a strong campaign on entry, and what effect their entry will have on the development of primary demand. Two strategies used in new-product pricing are price skimming and penetration pricing.

**price skimming** Charging the highest possible price that buyers who most desire the product will pay

**penetration pricing** Setting prices below those of competing brands to penetrate a market and gain a significant market share quickly

**Price Skimming.** **Price skimming** means charging the highest possible price that buyers who most desire the product will pay. The Porsche Cayenne, for example, has a starting price of $56,000, considerably higher than those for other sport-utility vehicles.[15] This approach provides the most flexible introductory base price. Demand tends to be inelastic in the introductory stage of the product life cycle.

Price skimming can provide several benefits, especially when a product is in the introductory stage of its life cycle. A skimming policy can generate much-needed initial cash flows to help offset sizable development costs. Price skimming protects the marketer from problems that arise when the price is set too low to cover costs. When a firm introduces a product, its production capacity may be limited. A skimming price can help keep demand consistent with the firm's production capabilities. The use of a skimming price may attract competition into an industry because the high price makes that type of business appear quite lucrative. In reality, companies price new products for less than they could or should. In such cases, companies risk not only failing to maximize potential profits but also establishing a lower market value in buyers' minds.[16] New-product prices should be based on both the value to the customer and competitive products.

**Penetration Pricing.** With **penetration pricing**, prices are set below those of competing brands to penetrate a market and gain a large market share quickly. Perhaps the ultimate penetration pricing strategy was implemented by the Arctic Monkeys. The U.K. rock band handed out free CDs of its music at early performances, and fans e-mailed the music to friends. The resulting viral effort led to a recording contract for the band, which has the fastest selling debut album in British music history.[17] This approach is less flexible for a marketer than price skimming because it is more difficult to raise a penetration price than to lower or discount a skimming price. It is not unusual for a firm to use a penetration price after having skimmed the market with a higher price.

Penetration pricing can be especially beneficial when a marketer suspects that competitors could enter the market easily. If penetration pricing allows the

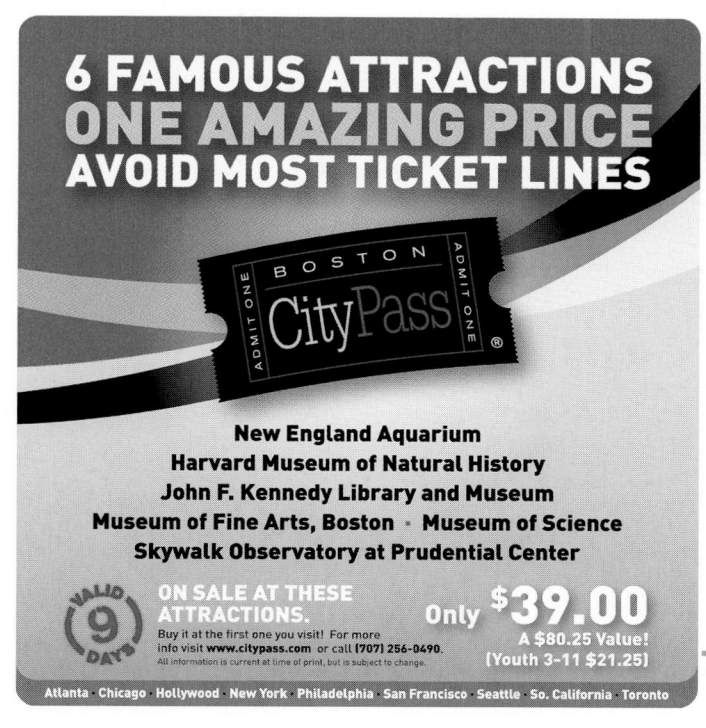

**Penetration Pricing**
CityPass uses penetration pricing to sell its discounts to city visitors.

marketer to gain a large market share quickly, competitors may be discouraged from entering the market. In addition, because the lower per-unit penetration price results in lower per-unit profit, the market may not appear to be especially lucrative to potential new entrants. Apple prices its iPod digital music players at penetration prices. Although retailers such as Best Buy and Circuit City earn very little profit on iPods, they benefit from selling iPod accessories. Many iPod buyers purchase at least two accessories, and the market for accessories such as speakers and covers is expected to double. Moreover, 40 percent of vehicles sold in the United States will offer some sort of iPod integration this year.[18]

### Product-Line Pricing

**product-line pricing** Establishing and adjusting prices of multiple products within a product line

Rather than considering products on an item-by-item basis when determining pricing strategies, some marketers employ product-line pricing. **Product-line pricing** means establishing and adjusting the prices of multiple products within a product line. When marketers use product-line pricing, their goal is to maximize profits for an entire product line rather than focusing on the profitability of an individual product. Product-line pricing can lend marketers flexibility in price setting. For example, marketers can set prices so that one product is quite profitable while another increases market share due to having a lower price than competing products.

Before setting prices for a product line, marketers evaluate the relationship among the products in the line. When products in a line are complementary, sales increases in one item raise demand for other items. For instance, desktop printers and

# Counting on the Games, Microsoft Prices Xbox Below Cost

**M**icrosoft raised eyebrows when it used captive pricing for its Xbox 360 video game system. According to an iSuppli survey, the parts used to make the 360 cost the company $470 prior to factoring in assembly; however, the system retails for $399—a $71 loss. Factoring in additional items such as power supply, cables, and controllers boosts the loss for each Xbox to $126. Microsoft has said that it may break even on the unit by 2007 with the help of sales on games for the Xbox, but in 2005, Microsoft's home entertainment division lost $391 million on sales of $3.3 billion. So why is the company producing a product on which it loses money?

For one thing, the cost of each game for the Xbox 360 has increased by $10 over the previous version. Also, multiplayer game functions cost $70 a year. Xbox users who network receive lots of online offers to buy more Microsoft products such as games and game add-ons. It appears that Microsoft expects to profit not only from game software and networking access but also from additional software buys made by those who want to make their Xboxes part of their home entertainment systems. The new Xbox system connects to a television and allows users to view photographs, play music, and more, as well as playing games. Microsoft assumes that all the extra operating products will be purchased after the Xbox is purchased.

Bill Gates and the Microsoft team are confident that the Xbox will soon begin to turn a profit; time, of course, will tell. Let the games begin!

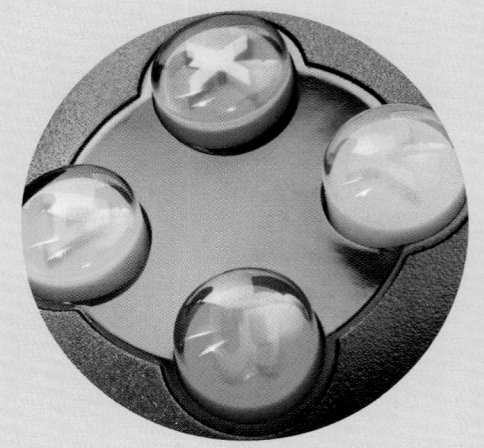

toner cartridges are complementary products. When products in a line function as substitutes for one another, buyers of one product in the line are unlikely to purchase one of the other products in the same line. In this case, marketers must be sensitive to how a price change for one of the brands may affect the demand not only for that brand but also for the substitute brands. For example, if decision makers at Procter & Gamble were considering a price change for Tide detergent, they would be concerned about how the price change might influence sales of Cheer, Bold, and Gain.

When marketers employ product-line pricing, they have several strategies from which to choose. These include captive pricing, premium pricing, bait pricing, and price lining.

**captive pricing** Pricing the basic product in a product line low while pricing related items higher

**Captive Pricing.**  With **captive pricing**, the basic product in a product line is priced low while items required to operate or enhance it are priced higher. For example, a manufacturer of cameras and film may set the price of the cameras at a level low enough to attract customers but set the film price relatively high because to use the cameras, customers must continue to purchase film. Printer companies have used this pricing strategy: providing relatively low-cost, low-margin printers and selling ink cartridges to generate significant profits. Gillette and other razor manufacturers know if you can sell a new razor handle to customers at little or no cost, you can generate revenues with blades. Likewise, Sirius and XM Satellite Radio cut the prices of receivers, which sell for as little as $30, to sell the annual radio service for about $150/year.[19]

**premium pricing** Pricing the highest-quality or most versatile products higher than other models in the product line

**Premium Pricing.**  **Premium pricing** is often used when a product line contains several versions of the same product; the highest-quality products or those with the most versatility are given the highest prices. Other products in the line are priced to appeal to price-sensitive shoppers or to buyers who seek product-specific features.

**bait pricing** Pricing an item in a product line low with the intention of selling a higher-priced item in the line

Marketers that use a premium strategy often realize a significant portion of their profits from premium-priced products. Examples of product categories that commonly use premium pricing are small kitchen appliances, beer, ice cream, and cable television service.

**Bait Pricing.**  To attract customers, marketers may put a low price on one item in the product line with the intention of selling a higher-priced item in the line; this strategy is known as **bait pricing**. For example, a computer retailer might advertise its lowest-priced computer model, hoping that when customers come to the store they will purchase a higher-priced one. This strategy can facilitate sales of a line's higher-priced products. As long as a retailer has sufficient quantities of the advertised low-priced model available for sale, this strategy is considered acceptable. In contrast, *bait and switch* is an activity in which retailers have no intention of selling the bait product; they use the low price merely to entice customers into the store to sell them higher-priced products. Bait and switch is considered unethical, and in some states it is illegal as well.

As I See It, #1 in a photographic series by Jean Claude Maillard.

The Serpentine Bronze Vessel—lavatory. May your bathroom have great drama.

1-800-4-KOHLER. ext. XXX
Kohler.com/serpentine

THE BOLD LOOK OF **KOHLER.**

**Premier Pricing**
Kohler uses unique ad to sell its high-end products.

**price lining** Setting a limited number of prices for selected groups or lines of merchandise

**Price Lining.** When an organization sets a limited number of prices for selected groups or lines of merchandise, it is using **price lining**. A retailer may have various styles and brands of similar-quality men's shirts that sell for $15 and another line of higher-quality shirts that sell for $22. Price lining simplifies customers' decision making by holding constant one key variable in the final selection of style and brand within a line.

The basic assumption in price lining is that the demand for various groups or sets of products is inelastic. If the prices are attractive, customers will concentrate their purchases without responding to slight changes in price. Thus, a women's dress shop that carries dresses priced at $85, $55, and $35 may not attract many more sales with a drop to, say, $83, $53, and $33. The "space" between the price of $85 and $55, however, can stir changes in consumer response. With price lining, the demand curve looks like a series of steps, as shown in Figure 22.2.

Another type of price lining is subscription services. Cable or satellite TV subscribers choose different packages or groupings of channels with different prices. Likewise, subscribers to subscription DVD rental services such as Netflix can choose a membership price based on the number of DVDs they want to receive at one time.

## Psychological Pricing

**psychological pricing** Pricing that attempts to influence a customer's perception of price to make a product's price more attractive

**reference pricing** Pricing a product at a moderate level and positioning it next to a more expensive model or brand

Learning the price of a product is not always a pleasant experience for customers. It is sometimes surprising (as at a movie concession stand) and sometimes downright horrifying; most of us have been afflicted with "sticker shock." **Psychological pricing** attempts to influence a customer's perception of price to make a product's price more attractive. In this section, we consider several forms of psychological pricing: reference pricing, bundle pricing, multiple-unit pricing, everyday low prices (EDLP), odd-even pricing, customary pricing, and prestige pricing.

**Reference Pricing.** **Reference pricing** means pricing a product at a moderate level and positioning it next to a more expensive model or brand in the hope that the customer will use the higher price as an external reference price (i.e., a comparison price). Because of the comparison, the customer is expected to view the moderate price favorably. Reference pricing is based on the "isolation effect," meaning an alternative is less attractive when viewed by itself than when compared with other alternatives. When you go to Best Buy or Circuit City to buy a DVD player, a moderately priced DVD player may appear especially attractive because it offers most of the important attributes of the more expensive alternatives on display and at a lower price. It is not unusual for an organization's moderately priced private brands to be

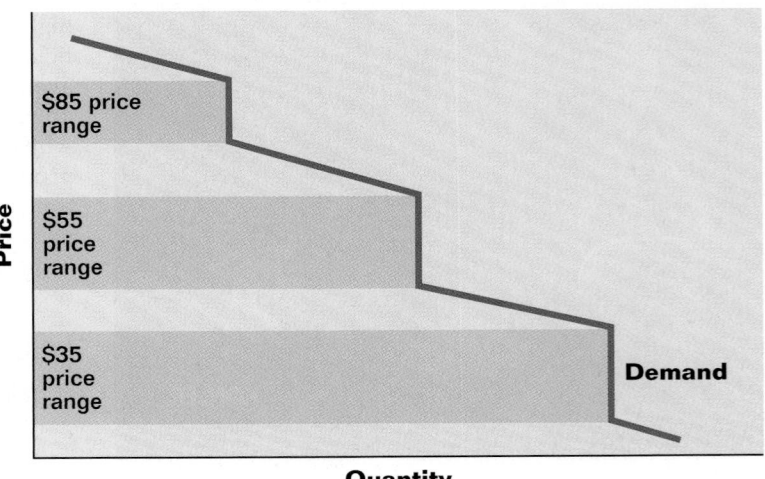

**figure 22.2**

**PRICE LINING**

*Price* (vertical axis)

$85 price range

$55 price range

$35 price range

**Demand**

**Quantity**

## marketing ENTREPRENEURS

**W**hile snorkeling on a family vacation in Hawaii, Rich Stachowski could hardly mask his elation when he spotted a giant sea turtle. Unfortunately, he was unable to share this experience with his family when he couldn't catch their attention underwater. Determined to remedy this problem, he designed a device using a soccer cone, a snorkel, and duct tape, which enabled him to project his voice in water. He called his invention the Water Talkie, and formed a company called Short Stack to market Water Talkies and develop swimming pool toys. The Water Talkie idea took off when Toys 'R' Us bought more than 50,000 units. Stachowski eventually sold his company to Wild Planet Toys for more than $1 million.

**Rich Stachowski**

HIS BUSINESS: Water Talkies

FOUNDED AT AGE: 10

SUCCESS: Sold his business for over $1 million

positioned alongside more expensive, better-known manufacturer brands. On the other hand, many private store brands are raising their prices in an effort to boost these products' image.[20]

**Bundle Pricing.** **Bundle pricing** is packaging together two or more products, usually complementary ones, to be sold at a single price. Many fast-food restaurants, for example, offer combination meals at a price that is lower than the combined prices of each item priced separately. Most telephone and cable television providers bundle local telephone service, high-speed Internet access, and digital cable television for one monthly fee. To attract customers, the single bundled price is usually considerably less than the sum of the prices of the individual products. The opportunity to buy the bundled combination of products in a single transaction may be of value to the customer as well. Marketing research models suggest that marketers can develop heterogeneous bundles of products with optimal prices for different market segments.[21] Bundle pricing not only helps increase customer satisfaction; by bundling slow-moving products with products with higher turnover, an organization can also stimulate sales and increase revenues. It may also help build customer loyalty and reduce "churn," that is, losing dissatisfied customers to rivals.[22] Selling products as a package rather than individually may also result in cost savings. Bundle pricing is commonly used for banking and travel services, computers, and automobiles with option packages.

Some companies, however, are unbundling packages in favor of a more itemized approach sometimes called *à la carte pricing*. This approach gives customers the opportunity to pick and choose only the products they want without having to purchase additional products in the bundle that may not be right for their purposes.[23] For example, some television viewers have expressed a preference to subscribe only to their favorite channels rather than a predetermined package of channels.[24] At online music services such as iTunes and Rhapsody, customers can pick and choose individual songs to download instead of buying a complete CD.[25] Furthermore, with the help of the Internet, comparison shopping has become more convenient than ever, allowing customers to price items and create their own mixes. Nevertheless, bundle pricing continues to appeal to customers who prefer the convenience of a package.[26]

**Multiple-Unit Pricing.** **Multiple-unit pricing** occurs when two or more identical products are packaged together and sold at a single price. This normally results in a lower per-unit price than the price regularly charged. Multiple-unit pricing is commonly used for twin-packs of potato chips, four-packs of light bulbs, and six- and twelve-packs of soft drinks. Customers benefit from the cost saving and convenience this pricing strategy affords. A company may use multiple-unit pricing to attract new customers to its brands and, in some instances, to increase consumption of them. When customers buy in larger quantities, their consumption of the product may increase. For example, multiple-unit pricing may encourage a customer to buy larger quantities of snacks, which are likely to be consumed in higher volume at the point of consumption simply because they are available. However, this is not true for all products. For instance, greater availability at the point of consumption of light bulbs, bar soap, and table salt is not likely to increase usage.

Discount stores and especially warehouse clubs, such as Sam's Club and Costco, are major users of multiple-unit pricing. For certain products in these stores, customers receive significant per-unit price reductions when they buy packages containing multiple units of the same product, such as an eight-pack of canned tuna fish.

**bundle pricing** Packaging together two or more complementary products and selling them at a single price

**multiple-unit pricing** Packaging together two or more identical products and selling them at a single price

**everyday low prices (EDLP)**
Pricing products low on a consistent basis

**odd-even pricing** Ending the price with certain numbers to influence buyers' perceptions of the price or product

**customary pricing** Pricing on the basis of tradition

**prestige pricing** Setting prices at an artificially high level to convey prestige or a quality image

**Prestige Pricing**

Dorfman Sterling Jewelry uses prestige pricing.

DORFMAN
STERLING

UNFORGETTABLE
GIFTS AND JEWELRY FOR ALL OCCASIONS.

**Everyday Low Prices (EDLP).** To reduce or eliminate the use of frequent short-term price reductions, some organizations use an approach referred to as **everyday low prices (EDLP)**. With EDLP, a marketer sets a low price for its products on a consistent basis rather than setting higher prices and frequently discounting them. Everyday low prices, though not deeply discounted, are set far enough below competitors' prices to make customers feel confident they are receiving a fair price. EDLP is employed by retailers such as Wal-Mart and manufacturers such as Procter & Gamble. A company that uses EDLP benefits from reduced losses from frequent markdowns, greater stability in sales, and decreased promotional costs. The furniture industry, where consumers' greatest concern seems to be price relative to quality, has taken a cue from Wal-Mart. Traditionally dominated by U.S. manufacturing, even long-standing U.S. companies such as Timberlake are now offering lower-priced furniture made overseas to compete more effectively.[27]

A major problem with EDLP is that customers have mixed responses to it. Over the last several years, many marketers have inadvertently "trained" customers to expect and seek out deeply discounted prices. In some product categories, such as apparel, finding the deepest discount has become almost a national consumer sport. Thus, failure to provide deep discounts can be a problem for certain marketers. In some instances, customers simply don't believe everyday low prices are what marketers claim they are but are instead a marketing gimmick.

**Odd-Even Pricing.** Through **odd-even pricing**—ending the price with certain numbers—marketers try to influence buyers' perceptions of the price or the product. Odd pricing assumes more of a product will be sold at $99.95 than at $100. Theoretically, customers will think, or at least tell friends, that the product is a bargain—not $100, but $99 and change. Also, customers will supposedly think the store could have charged $100 but instead cut the price to the last cent, to $99.95. Some claim, too, that certain types of customers are more attracted by odd prices than by even ones. Research has found a higher-than-expected demand associated with prices ending in 9 in print advertisements.[28] Odd prices are far more common today than even prices.

Even prices are often used to give a product an exclusive or upscale image. An even price supposedly will influence a customer to view the product as being a high-quality, premium brand. A shirt maker, for example, may print on a premium shirt package a suggested retail price of $42.00 instead of $41.95; the even price of the shirt is used to enhance its upscale image.

**Customary Pricing.** With **customary pricing**, certain goods are priced primarily on the basis of tradition. Recent economic uncertainties have made most prices fluctuate fairly widely, but the classic example of the customary, or traditional, price is the price of a candy bar. For years, a candy bar cost 5 cents. A new candy bar would have had to be something very special to sell for more than a nickel. This price was so sacred that rather than change it, manufacturers increased or decreased the size of the candy bar itself as chocolate prices fluctuated. Today, of course, the nickel candy bar has disappeared. However, most candy bars still sell at a consistent, but obviously higher, price. Thus, customary pricing remains the standard for this market.

**Prestige Pricing.** With **prestige pricing**, prices are set at an artificially high level to convey prestige or a quality image. Prestige pricing is used especially when buyers associate a higher price with higher quality. Pharmacists report that some consumers complain when a prescription does not cost enough; apparently some consumers associate a drug's price with its potency. Typical product categories in which selected products are prestige priced include perfumes, liquor, jewelry, and cars. Although traditionally appliances have not been prestige priced, upscale appliances have appeared in recent years to capitalize on the willingness of some consumer segments to "trade up" for high-quality products. These consumers do not mind paying extra for a Subzero refrigerator, a Viking commercial range, or a Whirlpool Duet washer and dryer because these products offer high quality as well as a level of prestige. The Whirlpool Duet washer and dryer, for example, are priced at $2,300 per pair—about $1,500 more than conventional washers and dryers—but offer high performance, large loads, gentle cleaning, and energy efficiency.[29] If these producers lowered their prices dramatically, the new prices would be inconsistent with the perceived high-quality images of their products. From gold clubs to handbags, prestige products are selling at record levels. Consider some of the prestige products shown in Table 22.4 that were selected as the best by *Smart Money* magazine. For example, spending on pets has escalated to $36 billion a year, rivaling what some families spend on their children. Some consumers are willing to pay as much as $1,000 for designer dogs like the "puggle," a beagle-pug mix, for their nice dispositions, intelligence, and smaller sizes.[30]

## Professional Pricing

**professional pricing** Fees set by people with great skill or experience in a particular field

**Professional pricing** is used by people who have great skill or experience in a particular field. Professionals often believe their fees (prices) should not relate directly to the time and effort spent in specific cases; rather, a standard fee is charged regardless of the problems involved in performing the job. Some doctors' and lawyers' fees are prime examples, such as $75 for a checkup, $2,000 for an appendectomy, and $995 for a divorce. Other professionals set prices in other ways. Like other marketers, professionals have costs associated with facilities, labor, insurance, equipment, and supplies. Certainly costs are considered when setting professional prices.

The concept of professional pricing carries the idea that professionals have an ethical responsibility not to overcharge customers. In some situations, a seller can charge customers a high price and continue to sell many units of the product. Medicine offers several examples. If a person with diabetes requires one insulin treatment per day to survive, she or he will probably buy that treatment whether its price is $1 or $10. In fact, the patient surely would purchase the treatment even if the price rose. In these situations, sellers could charge exorbitant fees. Drug companies claim that despite their positions of strength in this regard, they charge ethical prices rather than what the market will bear.

## Promotional Pricing

As an ingredient in the marketing mix, price is often coordinated with promotion. The two variables are sometimes so closely interrelated that the pricing policy is promotion oriented. Types of promotional pricing include price leaders, special-event pricing, and comparison discounting.

### table 22.4   SAMPLE PRESTIGE PRODUCT PRICES

| | | |
|---|---|---|
| Fine Pens | Mont Blanc's Meisterstuck Solitaire Classique | $710 |
| Digital cameras | Cannon EOS Digital Rebel XT | $1,000 |
| Handbags | Miu Miu's classic suede handbag | $750 |
| Golf drivers | TaylorMade r5 D Dual | $350 |
| Sports watches | TAG Heuer's Formula 1 Chronotimer | $995 |
| Men's jeans | John Varrantos jeans | $195 |

**Source:** Maggie Dunphy, "The Best of Everything," *Smart Money*, Dec. 2005, pp. 67–75.

**price leader** A product priced below the usual markup, near cost, or below cost

**Price Leaders.** Sometimes a firm prices a few products below the usual markup, near cost, or below cost, which results in prices known as **price leaders**. This type of pricing is used most often in supermarkets and restaurants to attract customers by giving them especially low prices on a few items. Management hopes that sales of regularly priced products will more than offset the reduced revenues from the price leaders.

**special-event pricing** Advertised sales or price cutting linked to a holiday, a season, or an event

**Special-Event Pricing.** To increase sales volume, many organizations coordinate price with advertising or sales promotions for seasonal or special situations. **Special-event pricing** involves advertised sales or price cutting linked to a holiday, a season, or an event. If the pricing objective is survival, special sales events may be designed to generate the necessary operating capital. Special-event pricing entails coordination of production, scheduling, storage, and physical distribution. Whenever a sales lag occurs, special-event pricing is an alternative that marketers should consider.

**comparison discounting** Setting a price at a specific level and comparing it with a higher price

**Comparison Discounting.** **Comparison discounting** sets the price of a product at a specific level and simultaneously compares it with a higher price. The higher price may be the product's previous price, the price of a competing brand, the product's price at another retail outlet, or a manufacturer's suggested retail price. Customers may find comparative discounting informative, and it can have a significant impact on their purchases. However, overuse of comparison pricing may reduce customers' internal reference prices, meaning they no longer believe the higher price is the regular or normal price.[31]

Because this pricing strategy has on occasion led to deceptive pricing practices, the Federal Trade Commission has established guidelines for comparison discounting. If the higher price against which the comparison is made is the price formerly charged for the product, the seller must have made the previous price available to customers for a reasonable period of time. If the seller presents the higher price as the one charged by other retailers in the same trade area, it must be able to demonstrate that this claim is true. When the seller presents the higher price as the manufacturer's suggested retail price, the higher price must be similar to the price at which a reasonable proportion of the product was sold. Some manufacturers' suggested retail prices are so high that very few products are actually sold at those prices. In such cases, comparison discounting would be deceptive. An example of deceptive comparison discounting occurred when a major retailer put 93 percent of its power tools on sale, with discounts ranging from 10 to 40 percent. The retailer's frequent price reductions meant the tools sold at sale prices most of the year. Thus, comparisons with regular prices were deemed to be deceptive.

# Determination of a Specific Price

A pricing strategy will yield a certain price. However, this price may need refinement to make it consistent with pricing practices in a particular market or industry. When Blockbuster eliminated late fees for movie rentals, it probably did not anticipate that revenue would fall by nearly 10 percent. Given increasing competition from online movie rental and pay-per-view services, the company will need to evaluate its overall pricing strategy in light of decreased profitability.[32]

Pricing strategies should help in setting a final price. If they are to do so, marketers must establish pricing objectives; have considerable knowledge about target market customers; and determine demand, price elasticity, costs, and competitive factors. Also, the way pricing is used in the marketing mix will affect the final price.

In the absence of government price controls, pricing remains a flexible and convenient way to adjust the marketing mix. The online brokerage arm of American Express, for example, sets prices on a sliding scale based on how much service support each customer uses. Customers who conduct all their securities trades without going through Amex employees pay lower prices than those who work with the firm's financial advisers to complete trades. As a result, American Express can provide the exact services each customer requires at an appropriate price.[33] In many situations, prices can be adjusted quickly—over a few days or even in minutes. Such flexibility is unique to this component of the marketing mix.

## SUMMARY

The six stages in the process of setting prices are (1) developing pricing objectives, (2) assessing the target market's evaluation of price, (3) evaluating competitors' prices, (4) choosing a basis for pricing, (5) selecting a pricing strategy, and (6) determining a specific price. Setting pricing objectives is critical because pricing objectives form a foundation on which the decisions of subsequent stages are based. Organizations may use numerous pricing objectives, including short-term and long-term ones, and different objectives for different products and market segments. Pricing objectives are overall goals that describe the role of price in a firm's long-range plans. There are several major types of pricing objectives. The most fundamental pricing objective is the organization's survival. Price usually can be easily adjusted to increase sales volume or combat competition to help the organization stay alive. Profit objectives, which are usually stated in terms of sales dollar volume or percentage change, are normally set at a satisfactory level rather than at a level designed to maximize profits. A sales growth objective focuses on increasing the profit base by raising sales volume. Pricing for return on investment (ROI) has a specified profit as its objective. A pricing objective to maintain or increase market share links market position to success. Other types of pricing objectives include cash flow, status quo, and product quality. Assessing the target market's evaluation of price tells the marketer how much emphasis to place on price and may help determine how far above the competition the firm can set its prices. Understanding how important a product is to customers relative to other products, as well as customers' expectations of quality, helps marketers correctly assess the target market's evaluation of price.

A marketer needs to be aware of the prices charged for competing brands. This allows the firm to keep its prices in line with competitors' prices when nonprice competition is used. If a company uses price as a competitive tool, it can price its brand below competing brands.

The three major dimensions on which prices can be based are cost, demand, and competition. When using cost-based pricing, the firm determines price by adding a dollar amount or percentage to the cost of the product. Two common cost-based pricing methods are cost-plus and markup pricing. Demand-based pricing is based on the level of demand for the product. To use this method, a marketer must be able to estimate the amounts of a product buyers will demand at different prices. Demand-based pricing results in a high price when demand for a product is strong and a low price when demand is weak. In the case of competition-based pricing, costs and revenues are secondary to competitors' prices.

A pricing strategy is an approach or a course of action designed to achieve pricing and marketing objectives. Pricing strategies help marketers solve the practical problems of establishing prices. The most common pricing strategies are differential pricing, new-product pricing, product-line pricing, psychological pricing, professional pricing, and promotional pricing.

When marketers employ differential pricing, they charge different buyers different prices for the same quality and quantity of products. Negotiated pricing, secondary-market discounting, periodic discounting, and random discounting are forms of differential pricing. With negotiated pricing, the final price is established through bargaining between seller and customer. Secondary-market pricing involves setting one price for the primary target market and a different price for another market; often the price charged in the secondary market is lower. Marketers employ periodic discounting when they temporarily lower their prices on a patterned or systematic basis; the reason for the reduction may be a seasonal change, a model-year change, or a holiday. Random discounting occurs on an unsystematic basis.

Two strategies used in new-product pricing are price skimming and penetration pricing. With price skimming, the organization charges the highest price that buyers who most desire the product will pay. A penetration price is a low price designed to penetrate a market and gain a significant market share quickly.

Product-line pricing establishes and adjusts the prices of multiple products within a product line. This strategy includes captive pricing, in which the marketer prices the basic product in a product line low and prices of related items higher; premium pricing, in which prices on higher-quality or more versatile products are set higher than those on other models in the product line; bait pricing, in which the marketer tries to attract customers by pricing an item in the product line low with the intention of selling a higher-priced item in the line; and price lining, in which the organization sets a limited number of prices for selected groups or lines of merchandise. Organizations that employ price lining assume the demand for various groups of products is inelastic.

Psychological pricing attempts to influence customers' perceptions of price to make a product's price more attractive. With reference pricing, marketers price a product at a moderate level and position it next to a more expensive model or brand. Bundle pricing is packaging together two or more complementary products and selling them at a single price. With multiple-unit pricing, two or more identical products are packaged together and sold at a single price. To reduce or eliminate use of frequent short-term price reductions, some organizations employ everyday low pricing (EDLP), setting a low price for products on a consistent basis. When employing odd-even pricing, marketers try to influence buyers' perceptions of the price or the product by ending the price with certain numbers. Customary pricing is based on traditional prices. With prestige pricing, prices are set at an artificially high level to convey prestige or a quality image.

Professional pricing is used by people who have great skill or experience in a particular field, therefore allowing them to set the price. This concept carries the idea that professionals have an ethical responsibility not to overcharge customers. As an ingredient in the marketing mix, price is often coordinated with promotion. The two variables are sometimes so closely interrelated that the pricing policy is promotion oriented. Promotional pricing includes price leaders, special-event pricing, and comparison discounting.

Price leaders are products priced below the usual markup, near cost, or below cost. Special-event pricing involves advertised sales or price cutting linked to a holi-

day, season, or event. Marketers that use a comparison discounting strategy price a product at a specific level and compare it with a higher price.

Once a price is determined by using one or more pricing strategies, it needs to be refined to a final price consistent with the pricing practices in a particular market or industry.

**ACE self-test**

Please visit the student website at **www.prideferrell.com** for ACE Self-Test questions that will help you prepare for exams.

## IMPORTANT TERMS

Pricing objectives
Cost-based pricing
Cost-plus pricing
Markup pricing
Demand-based pricing
Competition-based pricing
Differential pricing
Negotiated pricing

Secondary-market pricing
Periodic discounting
Random discounting
Price skimming
Penetration pricing
Product-line pricing
Captive pricing
Premium pricing

Bait pricing
Price lining
Psychological pricing
Reference pricing
Bundle pricing
Multiple-unit pricing
Everyday low prices
  (EDLP)

Odd-even pricing
Customary pricing
Prestige pricing
Professional pricing
Price leader
Special-event pricing
Comparison discounting

## DISCUSSION & REVIEW QUESTIONS

1. Identify the six stages in the process of establishing prices.

2. How does a return on investment pricing objective differ from an objective of increasing market share?

3. Why must marketing objectives and pricing objectives be considered when making pricing decisions?

4. Why should a marketer be aware of competitors' prices?

5. What are the benefits of cost-based pricing?

6. Under what conditions is cost-plus pricing most appropriate?

7. A retailer purchases a can of soup for 24 cents and sells it for 36 cents. Calculate the markup as a percentage of cost and as a percentage of selling price.

8. What is differential pricing? In what ways can it be achieved?

9. For what types of products would price skimming be most appropriate? For what types of products would penetration pricing be more effective?

10. Describe bundle pricing and give three examples using different industries.

11. What are the advantages and disadvantages of using everyday low prices?

12. Why do customers associate price with quality? When should prestige pricing be used?

13. Are price leaders a realistic approach to pricing? Explain your answer.

## APPLICATION QUESTIONS

1. Price skimming and penetration pricing are strategies commonly used to set the base price of a new product. Which strategy is more appropriate for the following products? Explain.

a. Short airline flights between cities in Florida

b. A DVD player

c. A backpack or book bag with a lifetime warranty

d. Season tickets for a newly franchised NBA basketball team

2. Price lining is used to set a limited number of prices for selected lines of merchandise. Visit a few local retail stores to find examples of price lining. For what types of products and stores is this practice most common? For what types of products and stores is price lining not typical or feasible?

3. Professional pricing is used by people who have great skill in a particular field, such as doctors, lawyers, and business consultants. Find examples (advertisements, personal contacts) that reflect a professional-pricing policy. How is the price established? Are there any restrictions on the services performed at that price?

4. Organizations often use multiple pricing objectives. Locate an organization that uses several pricing objectives, and discuss how this approach influences the company's marketing mix decisions. Are some objectives oriented toward the short term and others toward the long term? How does the marketing environment influence these objectives?

globalEDGE™

1. Your firm may purchase raw materials from the Czech Republic. Initial estimates put the cost of your first shipment at 1 billion Czech koruna. Find out how much this is in U.S. dollars by using the search term "foreign exchange markets" at **http://globaledge.msu.edu/ibrd**. Once you reach the FX Street webpage, click on the Currency Converter. Using your abilities to navigate foreign exchange markets, how much is this amount in U.S. dollars?

2. You have been asked to make a comparison across countries to determine which countries have had the highest inflation over the past 12 months. This knowledge may help in projecting which countries' markets may not perform as well as expected due to rising costs and decreased consumer spending. This information can be found in the Consumer Price Indices (CPI) for OECD countries by using the search term "comparison across countries" at **http://globaledge.msu.edu/ibrd**. Once you reach the OECD webpage, download the report titled "Consumer Price Indices (CPI) for OECD Countries" to find the three countries with the highest inflation for consumer prices.

## INTERNET Exercise

Visit **www.prideferrell.com** for resources to help you master the material in this chapter, plus materials that will help you expand your marketing knowledge, including Internet exercise updates, ACE Self-Tests, hotlinks to companies featured in this chapter, and much more.

### T-Mobile

T-Mobile has attempted to position itself as a low-cost cellular phone service provider. A person can purchase a calling plan, a cellular phone, and phone accessories at its website. Visit the T-Mobile website at **www.t-mobile.com**.

1. Determine the various nationwide calling rates available in your city.
2. How many different calling plans are available in your area?
3. What type of pricing strategy is T-Mobile using on its rate plans in your area?

# Video Case 22.1     The Price Is Right at New Balance

William Riley founded New Balance Arch Company in Boston during the early twentieth century. Riley, an English immigrant, made arch supports and prescription footwear for people with problem feet, and was committed to helping people. His daughter and son-in-law took over the business in the 1950s and spearheaded the development of the company's first performance running shoe in 1961. Since then, New Balance has developed a reputation for quality manufacturing, superior fit, and technological innovation in athletic shoes. These are values the current owners of the privately held company, Jim and Anne Davis, strive to maintain even in a highly competitive industry. Today, the firm sells $1.2 billion worth of athletic shoes and apparel.

In the United States, New Balance operates facilities in Boston; Lawrence, Massachusetts; and Maine, where the bulk of the manufacturing operations are located. The company employs about 2,000 people, three-quarters of whom are actually involved in manufacturing. New Balance also maintains wholly owned subsidiaries in Britain, Germany, France, Australia, New Zealand, Mexico, Canada, and South Africa. It has a variety of licensees and distributorships around the globe, including Latin America, the Asia-Pacific Basin, India, and the eastern European region, which has been merged into the European region. Like many of its competitors, New Balance has manufacturing facilities in China and Taiwan. Unlike its competitors, the company also manufactures shoes in Vietnam, but uses Vietnam solely to supply European and other marketplaces rather than the United States.

New Balance's goal is to create and market performance-oriented products that live up to their reputations and create satisfied customers. When customers buy New Balance shoes from a store, they will judge the company's products based on whether the shoes provide proper support and are appropriate for the intended activity. Indeed, at New Balance, developing a new product begins with customer needs in a particular category—for instance, running. Key decisions are made: For what type of runner will the shoe be designed? How many miles do they run? What is the runner's body

makeup? A product segment, such as running shoes, will contain a spectrum of products in a range of prices, from entry level to high performance.

Although costs and prices are not the key factors in marketing athletic shoes, they are very important. At New Balance, pricing starts at the very beginning of the product development process. In the first stage of development, a separate firm is hired to prepare a marketing brief, which gives the company some information about the target customer, what special features the shoe design should include, and the target price margin to yield adequate profits.

From the beginning, the design, development, and marketing teams consider costs a part of the marketing strategy. They look at material costs, labor costs, and overhead costs, as well as any special treatments the shoe design may include, such as specially molded pieces, labels, or embroidery. This information is used to create a rough cost estimate that will be a major factor in the retail price.

Material costs are a key factor. Upscale high-performance products may contain more expensive materials and technology, and thus sell for higher prices. Lower-end products may employ less technology and use different materials that perform at a different level. This variation in technology and materials permits New Balance to offer a variety of products at different prices to serve various market segments for athletic shoes.

Competitors' prices are also an important part of New Balance's pricing strategy. When New Balance develops an $80 cushioning shoe, it examines $80 cushioning shoes from competitors, comparing features as well as appearance and color. New Balance often purchases competing shoes to get an idea of what is on the market and how its product stacks up to the competition. The company constantly strives to improve its products and make them stand out against the competition.

At this point, New Balance contracts with the manufacturer to make a prototype, which gives a more realistic estimate of material costs, labor costs, and the costs of any extra work needed in actually making the product. Based on these actual costs, adjustments are made to materials, manufacturing, and shoe details to meet cost standards and requirements.

Jim Sciabarrasi, Corporate Manager of Sourcing, Purchasing, and Logistics, helped develop New Balance's costing and pricing system. When Sciabarrasi joined the company, no such process was in place. One team of people would set the projected cost and another team would take charge of negotiating with the manufacturer to get that particular price. This created frustrating situations for employees. Sciabarrasi's new integrated system of product costing and development ensures that real value is created for each product.

New Balance is a brand that focuses on fit and performance for both consumers and resellers. Integrity is a core value and creates a sense of honesty and genuineness in buyer-seller relationships. The company extends its view of integrity into all marketing and

advertising decisions. For example, because New Balance is "about" the value, performance, and sincerity of its products, it avoids celebrity endorsers. The company believes a customer will choose its products not because they have been endorsed by the athletic star of the week or represent a fashion statement but because they are the right shoe for that customer. However, the company has benefited from the celebrity status of some of its more famous customers, including musician Willie Nelson and former president Bill Clinton.[34]

### Questions for Discussion

1. What pricing objectives does New Balance seem to employ?
2. What type of pricing strategy is New Balance using?
3. What other pricing tools does New Balance employ?

---

**Case 22.2**              ## GM: Reducing Reliance on Rebates

Automakers have been using incentives to attract customers since 1912, when Henry Ford gave rebate checks to Model T buyers. The idea of incentives has remained popular throughout the years, although the offers themselves have varied, ranging from lease promotions and special financing offers to cash rebates. Incentives are a form of random discounting, temporary reductions of prices on an unsystematic basis; however, they have become almost ubiquitous in promoting sales of automobiles. Although incentives are credited with increasing sales and market share, automakers are now being criticized for abusing incentives, leading to decreased profits and poor brand image. The growing reliance on sales, rebates, and 0 percent financing has made it difficult to wean consumers off incentives.

When General Motors introduced aggressive cash rebates and 0 percent financing to boost sales after the attacks of September 11, 2001, the company never expected to keep riding on rebates for more than four years. GM executives credit the incentive program with providing many benefits for the company, including preserving market share and keeping GM's factories running. The latter is important because GM's labor costs are relatively fixed due to its contract with the United Auto Workers union, which requires the firm to pay unemployment benefits equal to 95 percent of normal pay to any laid-off workers. Thus, even if the company cuts production, its labor cost would remain the same. GM has therefore chosen to use incentives to

equalize sales and production rather than cutting production to meet demand. To understand General Motors' fear of reducing incentives, it is constructive to know that every percentage point of market share translates into millions of dollars in profit, according to Morgan Stanley.

Although GM has made several attempts to cut back on incentives (for example, launching the Chevrolet Cobalt with rebates no larger than $1,500, compared to the $4,000 rebate offered on the Chevrolet Cavalier that the Cobalt replaced), consumers have failed to cooperate. Between June and September 2005, GM extended its "employee discount" to every customer buying a new car or truck. However, the employee-discount promotion was quickly emulated by rivals Ford Motor and DaimlerChrysler (and soon after, even by marketers in other industries). But when the automakers ended the popular discount, vehicle sales hit the brakes. At GM, sales dove 26 percent in the month after the promotion ended. Thus, while the discounts gave all three automakers their third highest sales months in history, they did not help their bottom lines. The vice president of GM's North American marketing later admitted the promotion might have been a mistake.

The problem with incentives is that they erode profit. For example, in 2005 General Motors lost $5 billion on global auto sales, compared to 2002 when it netted $2.6 billion. Rebates may also give the impression of operating in a distressed atmosphere. There is little doubt that large rebates may suggest to consumers that a product's quality and reliability are not up to par. An important element of product quality is the amount of quality a product possesses. Because this concept is relative, a company that offers deep discounts may give consumers the impression of less quality. On the other hand, it would be desirable to use product design, styling, or other product features that would enhance and maintain a high-quality concept of the firm's product relative to competitive brands. Rebates and the cost of long-term loans can also undermine the resale value of an automaker's vehicles.

Alternatives to direct consumer incentives include discounting to dealers, who can then make decisions about how much of the discounts to pass along to consumers. Another approach is nonprice competition, using promotions that encourage consumers to visit a dealership. For example, General Motors gave away 1,000 new cars and trucks worth $25 million to prospective buyers who visited a GM dealership. General Motors expected the giveaway to attract 40 to 50 percent more showroom traffic during months that are historically slow. Another approach is to build more niche cars that generate greater profits. Some "must-have" models include the Chevy SSR Pickup, Pontiac GTO, and Cadillac XLR. Volkswagen is also applying this approach. Volkswagen CEO Bernd Pischetsrieder says he would rather let U.S. sales fall substantially, preserving brand image and resale value, than to use incentives.

An important question for all automobile companies is how to go about reducing incentives. Because incentive-driven sales persuaded many consumers to replace their cars during the economic downturn at the beginning of the century, little pent-up demand remains for new vehicles. Worse, consumers seem to have become addicted to incentives and unwilling to make a purchase without them. Volkswagen plans to "stick to its guns" and attempt to break consumers of the incentive habit. The company's new Touareg SUV is a good example of a unique, high-quality offering that can be sold at sticker price with few deals.

GM is now redesigning 90 percent of its passenger car lineup over the next three years in the hope of being able to compete on nonprice attributes. It is also introducing value pricing for many models, eliminating the practice of haggling with dealers. However, in the face of sluggish sales during a period of rising fuel prices, GM and its rivals were forced to slash prices on sport-utility vehicles and to offer incentives such as free gas or 0 percent financing to keep cars moving off showroom lots. The value of marketing in this industry is illustrated by the effectiveness of price incentives to manage demand. The challenge is to find other promotional methods that can effectively communicate the benefits and value of GM's products.[35]

## Questions for Discussion

1. What pricing objectives does General Motors seem to be using? How do these objectives help dictate the firm's use of periodic discounting and incentives?
2. What type of pricing strategy is GM using?
3. What risks does an automaker such as Volkswagen, Toyota, or BMW face in going against the industry by avoiding price incentives?

## Strategic Case 8   Napster 2.0: The Cat Is Back

Napster was the brainchild of Shawn Fanning, a 17-year-old freshman at Northeastern University who left college to develop a technology to trade music over the Internet. The technology was commercialized through Napster, which allowed computer users to share high-quality digital recordings (MP3s) of music via the Internet using its proprietary MusicShare software. Napster didn't actually store the recordings on its own computers; rather, it provided an index of all the songs available on the computers of members who were logged on to the service. In other words, Napster functioned as a sort of clearinghouse through which members could search by artist or song title, identify MP3s of interest, and download their choices from other members' hard drives. Napster quickly became one of the most popular sites on the Internet, claiming some 15 million users in little more than a year. Indeed, so many college students were downloading songs from Napster that many universities were forced to block the site from their systems to regain bandwidth.

From the beginning, Napster's service was as controversial as it was popular. Barely a year after its 1999 launch, Napster was sued by the Recording Industry Association of America (RIAA), which represents major recording companies such as Universal Music, BMG, Sony Music, Warner Music Group, and EMI. The RIAA claimed that Napster's service violated copyright laws by allowing users to swap music recordings for free. The RIAA also sought an injunction to stop the downloading of copyrighted songs and damages for lost revenue. The RIAA argued that song swapping via Napster and similar firms had cost the music industry more than $300 million in lost sales. Metallica, a heavy-metal band, and rap star Dr. Dre filed sep-

arate lawsuits accusing Napster of copyright infringement and racketeering. Lars Ulrich, Metallica's drummer, told a Senate committee that he believed Napster users were basically stealing from the band every time they downloaded one of its songs.

### The Fall of Napster

On July 26, 2000, U.S. District Judge Marilyn Patel granted the RIAA's request for an injunction and ordered Napster to stop making copyrighted recordings available for download. This order would have effectively destroyed the company by pulling the plug on its most popular feature. However, on July 28, just nine hours before Napster would have shut down, the Ninth Circuit Court of Appeals stayed that order, granting Napster a last-minute reprieve until the lawsuits could be tried in court. Despite the brief reprieve, Napster was ultimately found guilty of direct copyright infringement of RIAA members' musical recordings, and that ruling was upheld on appeal on February 12, 2001. The District Court of Appeals refuted all of Napster's defense tactics and ordered the company to stop allowing its millions of users to download and share copyrighted material without properly compensating the owners of that material. In late September 2001, Napster agreed to pay $26 million for past distribution of unauthorized music and made a proposal that would let songwriters and musicians distribute their music on Napster for a fee. This settlement would have covered as many as 700,000 songs, but Napster still needed an agreement before it could legally distribute the music. However, after several failed attempts to reach a suitable compromise with the recording industry, and with litigation expenses mounting, the company entered Chapter 11 bankruptcy proceedings in June 2002 as a last-gasp effort to reach a deal with Bertelsmann AG, Napster's strategic partner.

The final nail in the coffin for Napster came on September 3, 2002, when a Delaware bankruptcy judge blocked the sale of the company to Bertelsmann, ruling that negotiations with the German media company had not been made at arm's length and in good faith. Bertelsmann had agreed to pay creditors $8 million for Napster's assets. According to the bankruptcy petition, the company had assets of $7.9 million and debts of $101 million as of April 30, 2002. Shortly after the judge's ruling, Napster laid off nearly all of its 42-person staff and proceeded to convert its Chapter 11 reorganization into a Chapter 7 liquidation. At the time, Napster appeared to be doomed.

### The Digital Music Revolution

The United States is the largest music market in the world, accounting for 40 percent of all global sales and almost 33 percent of all unit sales. However, the future of traditional music sales—CDs and albums—appears bleak. CD sales declined by 31 percent over a three-year period; the sale of DVDs increased, but only by a slight 4 percent. One major reason for the decline in music sales is changing consumer preferences. Although consumers value CDs because they provide "long-term" entertainment, an RIAA survey found that many believe CDs cost too much. The RIAA's research indicates that a significant number of consumers do not fully understand the variables that play a role in the overall pricing of a CD. Consumers counter that they resent paying $13 to $18 for a CD to get only one or two popular songs. Thus many consumers find downloading music an appealing alternative to high CD prices.

With Napster out of the picture and the RIAA bringing lawsuits against individual downloaders of music online, other online music providers were rapidly getting their houses in order. One of the first was AOL, which launched MusicNet with 20 music streams and 20 downloads for $3.95 per month. Apple's iTunes was by far the heaviest hitter to join the foray into online music with 99-cent downloads. Other services were available as well:

- Rhapsody (**www.real.com/rhapsody/**), a division of RealNetworks, whose RealPlayer is ubiquitous on millions of PCs. Rhapsody offers 1.5 million songs for download.

- MusicMatch (**www.musicmatch.com**), a major partner with Dell, which preinstalls MusicMatch Jukebox on all new PCs. MusicMatch offers 900,000 songs for download.

- BuyMusic.com (**www.buymusic.com**), a subsidiary of Buy.com, that offers 885,000 songs for download.

- walmart.com, which entered the online music business. Naturally, the discount chain would undercut the competition with 88-cents-per-song downloads.

- Amazon.com has top CDs for as low as $12.99, breakthrough artists for less, and some free downloads.

Worldwide, there are now 335 legal downloading services, with more than 2 million songs available. The number of registered users of Napster and other music download services grew from 1.5 million to 2.8 million in 2005. Thus it has become clear to both sides of the music-downloading controversy that online music distribution is here to stay. It was only a matter of time until a compromise could be reached among the recording studios, the artists, and the various online music providers.

Some thorny issues remained to be resolved, however. First, because even pay-for-download services are not immune to piracy, the recording industry wanted to develop technology that would prevent downloaders from swapping files on their own even after making a legitimate purchase. To protect the artists, the industry also wanted to limit the number of times a song can be downloaded and copied. Suggestions included using the MD5 hash—a digital fingerprint—or using software that monitors sound patterns to detect illegal copies. A second issue was the development of a revenue model. Should MP3 files be available individually, as one file in a complete album, or both? Should pricing be based on a per-download basis or on an unlimited basis for a monthly subscription fee?

### The Rise of Napster 2.0

In late 2002, Napster's name and assets were purchased by Roxio, a company well known for its "CD-burning" software. After much fanfare and excitement, Roxio revived Napster as Napster 2.0 on October 29, 2003. The new fee-based service offers 1 million songs for download—giving it one of the largest online catalogs currently available in the industry—at 99 cents per track or $9.95 per album. Users can also pay $9.95 per month for unlimited music streaming to their desktops. Perhaps most important, Napster's relaunch came with the blessing of five major record labels. Napster has also developed a number of partnerships with Microsoft, Gateway, Yahoo!, and Samsung that gave it an advantage during its relaunch. Napster's partnership with Samsung led to the creation of the Samsung YP-910GS, a 20-gigabyte digital audio player that is fully integrated with Napster 2.0. The device allows users to transfer songs from Napster directly to the unit via a USB connection. The player also boasts an integrated FM transmitter that allows users to broadcast MP3 playback through their home or car stereo systems. In addition, Napster subscribers receive the industry's leading CD creation software package, developed by parent company Roxio, as a bonus.

Although the reborn Napster currently offers a large catalog of songs, it continues to face competition from a growing number of firms, particularly iTunes, Rhapsody, and MusicMatch. Apple's iTunes is likely to pose the biggest threat to Napster. iTunes currently offers more than 2 million songs and adds thousands more weekly. It also offers a wide selection of audio books, music videos, and television show episodes. Moreover, the popularity of Apple's iPod MP3 player confers on Apple a distinct advantage: the iPod provides customers with a perfect vehicle to get the music they desire. The iTunes software application works for both Macintosh and Windows operating systems. The service is easy to use and boasts fewer restrictions than MusicNet and other brand competitors. As a result, iTunes has developed a high customer satisfaction rating.

Other competitors include the thousands of offline and online music record stores that offer CDs and other merchandise, as well as satellite radio and, increasingly, music downloads via mobile phones. Moreover, there are still websites from which music can be downloaded free of charge, albeit illegally. Some potential customers would rather risk getting caught than pay for the music.

As with any technology-based service, new competition is often unseen and swift. With subscribers of peer-to-peer networks, such as Kazaa, being targeted by the Recording Industry Association of America, any or all of these services may move toward a pay-for-play service to avoid being hassled by the RIAA. In addition, competition exists from major retailers such as Wal-Mart and Amazon.com and from traditional music retailers such as Tower Records, Sam Goody, Best Buy, and Circuit City. In addition, some insiders have speculated that Microsoft will launch a service of its own. Given the existing and future competition, it is imperative that Napster make its brand the market leader in a short period of time.[36]

## Questions for Discussion

1. What factors seem to have the greatest influence on Napster 2.0's pricing decisions? Explain.
2. What appear to be Napster's primary pricing objectives?
3. Assess the level of price competition in the music industry as a whole and within the online music distribution business specifically.
4. Evaluate Napster's pricing strategy of charging 99 cents per song. Under what circumstances should the company consider changing that strategy?

# Careers in Marketing

## Changes in the Workplace

Between one-fourth and one-third of the civilian workforce in the United States is employed in marketing-related jobs. Although the field offers a multitude of diverse career opportunities, the number of positions in each area varies. For example, millions of workers are employed in many facets of sales, but relatively few people work in public relations and marketing research.

Many nonbusiness organizations now recognize that they perform marketing activities. For that reason, the number of marketing positions in government agencies, hospitals, charitable and religious groups, educational institutions, and similar organizations is increasing. Today's nonprofit organizations are competitive and better managed, with job growth rates often matching those of private-sector firms. Another area ripe with opportunities is the World Wide Web. The federal government makes more sales to consumers online than even Amazon.com. With so many businesses setting up websites, demand will rise for people who have the skills to develop and design marketing strategies for the Web.

Many workers outplaced from large corporations are choosing an entrepreneurial path, creating still more new opportunities for first-time job seekers. Even some individuals with secure managerial positions are leaving corporations and heading to smaller companies, toward greater responsibility and autonomy. The traditional career path used to be graduation from college, then a job with a large corporation, and a climb up the ladder to management. This pattern has changed, however. Today people are more likely to experience a career path of sideways "gigs" rather than sequential steps up a corporate ladder.

## Career Choices Are Major Life Choices

Many people think career planning begins with an up-to-date résumé and a job interview.[1] In reality, it begins long before you prepare your résumé. It starts with *you* and what you want to become. In some ways, you have been preparing for a career ever since you started school. Everything you have experienced during your lifetime you can use as a resource to help you define your career goals. Since you will likely spend more time at work than at any other single place during your lifetime, it makes sense to spend that time doing something you enjoy. Unfortunately, some people just work at a *job* because they need money to survive. Other people choose a *career* because of their interests and talents or a commitment to a particular profession. Whether you are looking for a job or a career, you should examine your priorities.

## Personal Factors Influencing Career Choices

Before choosing a career, you need to consider what motivates you and what skills you can offer an employer. The following questions may help you define what you consider important in life:

1. *What types of activities do you enjoy?* Although most people know what they enjoy in a general way, a number of interest inventories exist. By helping you determine specific interests and activities, these inventories can help you land a job that will lead to a satisfying career. In some cases, it may be sufficient just to list the activities you enjoy, along with those you dislike. Watch for patterns that may influence your career choices.

2. *What do you do best?* All jobs and all careers require employees to be able to "do something." It is extremely important to assess what you do best. Be honest with yourself about your ability to succeed in a specific job. It may help to make a list of your strongest job-related skills. Also, try looking at your skills from an employer's perspective: What can you do that an employer would be willing to pay for?

3. *What kind of education will you need?* The amount of education you need is determined by the type of career you choose. In some careers, it is impossible to get an entry-level position without at least a college degree. Other careers may also require technical or hands-on skills. Generally, additional education increases your potential earning power.

4. *Where do you want to live?* Initially, some college graduates will want to move to a different part of the country before entering the job market, whereas others may prefer to reside close to home, friends, and relatives. In reality, successful job applicants must be willing to go where the jobs are. The location of an entry-level job may be influenced by the type of marketing career selected. For example, some of the largest advertising agencies are in New York, Chicago, and Los Angeles. Likewise, large marketing research organizations are based in metropolitan areas. On the other hand, sales positions and retail management jobs are available in medium-size as well as large cities.

# Job Search Activities

When people begin to search for a job, they often first go online or turn to the classified ads in their local newspaper. Those ads are an important source of information about jobs in a particular area, but they are only one source. Many other sources can lead to employment and a satisfying career. Because there is a wealth of information about career planning, you should be selective in both the type and the amount of information you use to guide your job search.

In recent years the library, a traditional job-hunting tool, has been joined by the Internet. Both the library and the Internet are sources of everything from classified newspaper ads and government job listings, to detailed information on individual companies and industries. You can use either resource to research an area of employment or a particular company that interests you. In addition, the Internet allows you to check electronic bulletin boards for current job information, exchange ideas with other job seekers through online discussion groups or e-mail, and get career advice from professional counselors. You can also create your own webpage to inform prospective employers about your qualifications. You may even have a job interview online. Many companies use their websites to post job openings, accept applications, and interview candidates.

As you start your job search, you may find the following websites helpful. (Addresses of additional career-related websites can be accessed through the Student Career Center at **www.prideferrell.com.**)

America's Job Bank: **www.ajb.dni.us**

This massive site contains information on nearly 250,000 jobs. Listings come from 1,800 state employment offices around the country and represent every line of work, from professional and technical to blue-collar, and from entry level on up.

CareerBuilder.com: **www.careerbuilder.com**

This site is one of the largest on the Internet, with more than 900,000 jobs to view. The site allows a job seeker to find jobs, post résumés, get advice and career resources, and obtain information on career fairs.

Hoover's Online: **www.hoovers.com**

Hoover's offers a variety of job search tools, including information on potential employers and links to sites that post job openings.

The Monster Board: **www.monster.com**

The Monster Board carries hundreds of job listings and offers links to related sites, such as company homepages and sites with information about job fairs.

Federal jobs: **www.fedworld.gov/jobs/jobsearch.html**

If you are interested in working for a government agency, this site lists positions all across the country. You can limit your search to specific states or do a general cross-country search for job openings.

Other web addresses for job seekers include:

**www.careers-in-marketing.com**

**www.marketingjobs.com**

**www.starthere.com/jobs**

**www.careermag.com**

**www.salary.com**

In addition to the library and the Internet, the following sources can be of great help when trying to find the "perfect job":

1. *Campus placement offices.* Colleges and universities have placement offices staffed by trained personnel specialists. In most cases, these offices serve as clearinghouses for career information. The staff may also be able to guide you in creating a résumé and preparing for a job interview.

2. *Professional sources and networks.* A network is a group of people—friends, relatives, and professionals—who are in a position to exchange information, including information about job openings. According to many job applicants, networking is one of the best sources of career information and job leads. Start with as many people as you can think of to establish your network. (The Internet can be very useful in this regard.) Contact these people and ask specific questions about job opportunities they are aware of. Also, ask each individual to introduce or refer you to someone else who may be able to help you in your job search.

3. *Private employment agencies.* Private employment agencies charge a fee for helping people find jobs. Typical fees can be as high as 15 to 20 percent of an employee's first-year salary. The fee may be paid by the employer or the employee. Like campus placement offices, private employment agencies provide career counseling, help create résumés, and provide preparation for job interviews. Before you use a private employment agency, be sure you understand the terms of any contract or agreement you sign. Above all, make sure you know who is responsible for paying the agency's fee.

4. *State employment agencies.* The local office of your state employment agency is a valuable source of information about job openings in your immediate area. Some job applicants are reluctant to use state agencies because most jobs available through them are for semiskilled or unskilled workers. From a practical standpoint, though, it can't hurt to consult state employment agencies. They will have information about some professional and managerial positions available in your area, and you will not be charged a fee if you obtain a job through one of these agencies.

Many graduates want a job immediately and are discouraged at the thought that an occupational search can take months. But people seeking entry-level jobs should expect their job search to take considerable time. Of course, the state of the economy and whether employers generally are hiring can shorten or extend a job search.

During a job search, you should use the same work habits that effective employees use on the job. Resist the temptation to "take the day off" from job hunting. Instead, make a master list of the activities you want to accomplish each day. If necessary, force yourself to make contacts, do job research, or schedule interviews that might lead to job opportunities. (In fact, many job applicants look at the job hunt as their actual job and "work" full time at it until they find the job they want.) Above all, realize that an occupational search requires patience and perseverance. According to many successful applicants, perseverance may be the job hunter's most valuable trait.

# Planning and Preparation

The key to landing the job you want is planning and preparation—and planning begins with goals. In particular, it is important to determine your *personal* goals, decide on the role your career will play in reaching those goals, and then develop your *career* goals. Once you know where you are going, you can devise a feasible plan for getting there.

The time to begin planning is as early as possible. You must, of course, satisfy the educational requirements for the occupational area you desire. Early planning will give you the opportunity to do so. However, some of the people who will compete with you for the better jobs will also be fully prepared. Can you do more? Company recruiters say the following factors give job candidates a definite advantage.

■ *Work experience.* You can get valuable work experience in cooperative work/school programs, during summer vacations, or in part-time jobs during the school year. Experience in your chosen occupational area carries the most weight, but even unrelated work experience is useful.

■ *The ability to communicate well.* Verbal and written communication skills are increasingly important in all aspects of business. Yours will be tested in your letters to recruiters, in your résumé, and in interviews. You will use these same communication skills throughout your career.

■ *Clear and realistic job and career goals.* Recruiters feel most comfortable with candidates who know where they are headed and why they are applying for a specific job.

Again, starting early will allow you to establish well-defined goals, sharpen your communication skills (through elective courses, if necessary), and obtain solid work experience. To develop your own personal career plan, go to the **www.pride ferrell.com** student site and access the Student Career Center. There you will find personal career plan worksheets.

# The Résumé

An effective résumé is one of the keys to being considered for a good job. Because your résumé states your qualifications, experiences, education, and career goals, a potential employer can use it to assess your compatibility with the job requirements. The résumé should be accurate and current.

In preparing a résumé, it helps to think of it as an advertisement. Envision yourself as a product and the potential employers as your customer. To interest the customer in buying the product—hiring you—your résumé must communicate information about your qualities and indicate how you can satisfy the customer's needs—that is, how you can help the company achieve its objectives. The information in the résumé should persuade the organization to take a closer look at you by calling you in for an interview.

To be effective, the résumé should be targeted at a specific position, as Figure A.1 (on p. A-6) shows. This document is only one example of an acceptable résumé. The job target section is specific and leads directly to the applicant's qualifications for the job. The qualifications section details capabilities—what the applicant can do—and also shows that the applicant has an understanding of the job's requirements. Skills and strengths that relate to the specific job should be emphasized. The achievement section ("Experiences" in Figure A.1) indicates success at accomplishing tasks or goals on the job and at school. The work experience section in Figure A.1 includes an unusual listing, which might pique the interviewer's interest: "helped operate relative's blueberry farm in Michigan for three summers." It tends to inspire rather than satisfy curiosity, thus inviting further inquiry.

Another type of résumé is the chronological résumé, which lists work experience and educational history in order by date. This type of résumé is useful for those just entering the job market because it helps highlight education and work experience.

Common suggestions for improving résumés include deleting useless or outdated information, improving organization, using professional printing and typing, listing duties (not accomplishments), maintaining grammatical perfection, and avoiding an overly elaborate or fancy format.[2] Keep in mind that the person who will look at your résumé may have to sift through hundreds in the course of the day in addition to handling other duties. Consequently it is important to keep your résumé short (one page is best, never more than two), concise, and neat. Moreover, you want your résumé to be distinctive so it will stand out from all the others.

In addition to having the proper format and content, a résumé should be easy to read. It is best to use only one or two kinds of type and plain, white paper. When sending a résumé to a large company, several copies may be made and distributed. Textured, gray, or colored paper may make a good impression on the first person who sees the résumé, but it will not reproduce well for the others, who will see only a poor copy. You should also proofread your résumé with care. Typos and misspellings will grab attention—the wrong kind.

Along with the résumé itself, always submit a cover letter. In the letter, you can include somewhat more information than in your résumé and convey a message that expresses your interest and enthusiasm about the organization and the job.

## The Job Interview

In essence, your résumé and cover letter are an introduction. The deciding factor in the hiring process is the interview (or several interviews) with representatives of the firm. It is through the interview that the firm gets to know you and your qualifications. At the same time, the interview gives you a chance to learn about the firm.

Here again, preparation is the key to success. Research the firm before your first interview. Learn all you can about its products, its subsidiaries, the markets in which it operates, its history, the locations of its facilities, and so on. If possible, obtain and read the firm's most recent annual report. Be prepared to ask questions about the firm and the opportunities it offers. Interviewers welcome such questions. They

## A RÉSUMÉ TARGETED AT A SPECIFIC POSITION

**LORRAINE MILLER**
**2212 WEST WILLOW**
**PHOENIX, AZ 12345**
**(416) 862-9169**

EDUCATION: B.A. Arizona State University, 2004, Marketing, achieved a 3.4 on a 4.0 scale throughout college

POSITION DESIRED: Product manager with an international firm providing future career development at the executive level

QUALIFICATIONS:

- Communicates well with individuals to achieve a common goal
- Handles tasks efficiently and in a timely manner
- Understands advertising sales, management, marketing research, packaging, pricing, distribution, and warehousing
- Coordinates many activities at one time
- Receives and carries out assigned tasks or directives
- Writes complete status or research reports

EXPERIENCES:

- Assistant Editor of college paper
- Treasurer of the American Marketing Association (student chapter)
- Internship with 3-Cs Advertising, Berkeley, CA
- Student Assistantship with Dr. Steve Green, Professor of Marketing, Arizona State University
- Solo cross-Canada canoe trek, summer 2003

WORK RECORD:

| | | |
|---|---|---|
| 2003–Present | Blythe and Co., Inc. | |
| | —Junior Advertising Account Executive | |
| 2001–2002 | Student Assistant for Dr. Steve Green | |
| | —Research Assistant | |
| 2000–2001 | The Men | |
| | —Retail sales and consumer relations | |
| 1998–2000 | Farmer | |
| | —Helped operate relative's blueberry farm in Michigan for three summers | |

In some cases, education is more important than unrelated work experience because it indicates the career direction you desire despite the work experience you have acquired thus far.

expect you to be interested enough to spend some time thinking about your potential relationship with their organization.

Also, prepare to respond to questions the interviewer may ask. Table A.1 lists typical interview questions that job applicants often find difficult to answer. But don't expect interviewers to stick to the list given in the table or to the items appearing in your résumé. They will be interested in anything that helps them decide what kind of person and worker you are.

Make sure you are on time for your interview and are dressed and groomed in a businesslike manner. Interviewers take note of punctuality and appearance just as they do of other personal qualities. Bring a copy of your résumé, even if you already sent one to the firm. You may also want to bring a copy of your course transcript

## table A.1   INTERVIEW QUESTIONS JOB APPLICANTS OFTEN FIND DIFFICULT TO ANSWER

1. Tell me about yourself.

2. What do you know about our organization?

3. What can you do for us? Why should we hire you?

4. What qualifications do you have that make you feel you will be successful in your field?

5. What have you learned from the jobs you've held?

6. If you could write your own ticket, what would be your ideal job?

7. What are your special skills, and where did you acquire them?

8. Have you had any special accomplishments in your lifetime that you are particularly proud of?

9. Why did you leave your most recent job?

10. How do you spend your spare time? What are your hobbies?

11. What are your strengths and weaknesses?

12. Discuss five major accomplishments.

13. What kind of boss would you like? Why?

14. If you could spend a day with someone you've known or know of, who would it be?

15. What personality characteristics seem to rub you the wrong way?

16. How do you show your anger? What types of things make you angry?

17. With what type of person do you spend the majority of your time?

**Source:** Adapted from *The Ultimate Job Hunter's Guidebook,* 4th ed., by Susan D. Greene and Melanie C. L. Martel. Copyright © 2004 by Houghton Mifflin Company.

and letters of recommendation. If you plan to furnish interviewers with the names and addresses of references rather than with letters of recommendation, make sure you have your references' permission to do so.

Consider the interview itself as a two-way conversation rather than a question-and-answer session. Volunteer any information that is relevant to the interviewer's questions. If an important point is skipped in the discussion, don't hesitate to bring it up. Be yourself, but emphasize your strengths. Good eye contact and posture are also important; they should come naturally if you take an active part in the interview. At the conclusion of the interview, thank the recruiter for taking the time to see you.

In most cases, the first interview is used to *screen* applicants, that is, choose those who are best qualified. These applicants are then given a second interview and perhaps a third, usually with one or more department heads. If the job requires relocation to a different area, applicants may be invited there for these later interviews.

After the interviewing process is complete, applicants are told when to expect a hiring decision.

### After the Interview

Attention to common courtesy is important as a follow-up to your interview. You should send a brief note of thanks to the interviewer and give it as much care as you did your résumé and cover letter. A short, typewritten letter is preferred to a handwritten note or card, or an e-mail. Avoid not only typos, but also overconfident statements such as "I look forward to helping you make Universal Industries successful over the next decade." Even in the thank-you letter, it is important to show team spirit and professionalism, as well as to convey proper enthusiasm. Everything you say and do reflects on you as a candidate.

**snapshot**

## Job candidate mistakes

**In which job-application areas do candidates make the most mistakes?**

Interview **32%**

Resume **21%**

Cover letter **9%**

Reference checks **9%**

Interview follow-up **7%**

Screening call **6%**

*Source:* Data from Robert Half Finance & Accounting survey. Margin of error: ±2.

## After the Hire

Clearly, performing well in a job has always been a crucial factor in keeping a position. In a tight economy and job market, however, a person's attitude, as well as his or her performance, counts greatly. People in their first jobs can commit costly political blunders by being insensitive to their environments. Politics in the business world includes how you react to your boss, how you react to your coworkers, and your general demeanor. Here are a few rules to live by.

1. *Don't bypass your boss.* One major blunder an employee can make is to go over the boss's head to resolve a problem. This is especially hazardous in a bureaucratic organization. You should become aware of the generally accepted chain of command and, when problems occur, follow that protocol, beginning with your immediate superior. No boss likes to look incompetent, and making him or her appear so is sure to hamper or even crush your budding career. However, there may be exceptions to this rule in emergency situations. It is wise to discuss with your supervisor what to do in an emergency, before an emergency occurs.[3]

2. *Don't criticize your boss.* Adhering to the old adage "praise in public and criticize in private" will keep you out of the line of retaliatory fire. A more sensible and productive alternative is to present the critical commentary to your boss in a diplomatic way during a private session.

3. *Don't show disloyalty.* If dissatisfied with the position, a new employee may start a fresh job search, within or outside the organization. However, it is not advisable to begin a publicized search within the company for another position unless you have held your current job for some time. Careful attention to the political climate in the organization should help you determine how soon to start a new job campaign and how public to make it. In any case, it is not a good idea to publicize that you are looking outside the company for a new position.

4. *Don't be a naysayer.* Employees are expected to become part of the organizational team and to work together with others. Behaviors to avoid, especially if you are a new employee, include being critical of others; refusing to support others' projects; always playing devil's advocate; refusing to help others when a crisis occurs; and complaining all the time, even about such matters as the poor quality of the food in the cafeteria, the crowded parking lot, or the temperature in the office.

5. *Learn to correct mistakes appropriately.* No one likes to admit having made a mistake, but one of the most important political skills you can acquire is minimizing the impact of a blunder. It is usually advantageous to correct the damage as soon as possible to avoid further problems. Some suggestions: be the first to break the bad news to your boss, avoid being defensive, stay poised and don't panic, and have solutions ready for fixing the blunder.[4]

# Types of Marketing Careers

In considering marketing as a career, the first step is to evaluate broad categories of career opportunities in the areas of marketing research, sales, industrial buying, public relations, distribution management, product management, advertising, retail management, and direct marketing. Keep in mind that the categories described here are not all-inclusive and that each encompasses hundreds of marketing jobs.

## Marketing Research

Clearly, marketing research and information systems are vital aspects of marketing decision making. Marketing researchers survey customers to determine their habits, preferences, and aspirations. The information about buyers and environmental forces that research and information systems provide improves a marketer's ability to understand the dynamics of the marketplace and therefore make effective decisions.

Marketing research firms are usually employed by a client organization such as a provider of goods or services, a nonbusiness organization, a research consulting firm, or an advertising agency. The activities performed include concept testing, product testing, package testing, advertising testing, test market research, and new-product research.

Marketing researchers gather and analyze data relating to specific problems. A researcher may be involved in one or several stages of research depending on the size of the project, the organization of the research unit, and the researcher's experience. Marketing research trainees in large organizations usually perform a considerable amount of clerical work, such as compiling secondary data from the firm's accounting and sales records and from periodicals, government publications, syndicated data services, the Internet, and unpublished sources. A junior analyst may edit and code questionnaires or tabulate survey results. Trainees may also participate in gathering primary data through mail and telephone surveys, personal interviews, and observation. As a marketing researcher gains experience, he or she may become involved in defining problems and developing research questions; designing research procedures; and analyzing, interpreting, and reporting findings. Exceptional personnel may assume responsibility for entire research projects.

Although most employers consider a bachelor's degree sufficient qualification for a marketing research trainee, many specialized positions require a graduate degree in business administration, statistics, or other related fields. Today trainees are more likely to have a marketing or statistics degree than a liberal arts degree. Courses in statistics, information technology, psychology, sociology, communications, economics, and technical writing are valuable preparation for a career in marketing research.

The Bureau of Labor Statistics indicates that marketing research provides abundant employment opportunities, especially for applicants with graduate training in marketing research, statistics, economics, and the social sciences. Generally, the value of information gathered by marketing information and research systems rises as competition increases, thus expanding opportunities for prospective marketing research personnel.

The major career paths in marketing research are with independent marketing research agencies/data suppliers and marketing research departments in advertising agencies and other businesses. In a company in which marketing research plays a key role, the researcher is often a member of the marketing strategy team. Surveying or interviewing customers is the heart of the marketing research firm's activities. A statistician selects the sample to be surveyed, analysts design the questionnaire and synthesize the gathered data into a final report, data processors tabulate the data, and the research director controls and coordinates all these activities so each project is completed to the client's satisfaction.

Salaries in marketing research depend on the type, size, and location of the firm, as well as the nature of the position. Overall, salaries of marketing researchers have increased slightly during the last few years. However, the specific position within the marketing research field determines the degree of fluctuation.[5] Generally, starting salaries are somewhat higher and promotions somewhat slower than in other occupations requiring similar training. The typical salary for a market analyst is $24,000 to $50,000; a marketing research director can earn $75,000 to $200,000.[6]

## Sales

Millions of people earn a living through personal selling. Chapter 20 defines personal selling as paid personal communication that attempts to inform customers and persuade them to purchase products in an exchange situation. Although this definition describes the general nature of sales positions, individual selling jobs vary enormously with respect to the types of businesses and products involved, the educational background and skills required, and the specific activities sales personnel perform. Because the work is so varied, it offers numerous career opportunities for people with a wide range of qualifications, interests, and goals. The two types of career opportunities we discuss relate to business-to-business sales.

**Sales Positions in Wholesaling.** Wholesalers buy products intended for resale, for use in making other products, and for general business operations, and sell them directly to business markets. Wholesalers thus provide services to both retailers and producers. They can help match producers' products to retailers' needs and provide services that save producers time, money, and resources. Some activities a sales representative for a wholesaling firm is likely to perform include planning and negotiating transactions; assisting customers with sales, advertising, sales promotion, and publicity; facilitating transportation and storage; providing customers with inventory control and data processing assistance; establishing prices; and giving customers technical, managerial, and merchandising assistance.

The background needed by wholesale personnel depends on the nature of the product handled. A sales representative for a drug wholesaler, for example, needs extensive technical training and product knowledge, and may have a degree in chemistry, biology, or pharmacology. A wholesaler of standard office supplies, on the other hand, may find it more important that its sales staff be familiar with various brands, suppliers, and prices than have technical knowledge about the products. A person just entering the wholesaling field may begin as a sales trainee or hold a non-selling job that provides experience with inventory, prices, discounts, and the firm's customers. A college graduate usually enters a wholesaler's sales force directly. Competent salespeople also transfer from manufacturer and retail sales positions.

The number of sales positions in wholesaling is expected to grow about as rapidly as the average for all occupations. Earnings for wholesale personnel vary widely because commissions often make up a large proportion of their incomes.

**Sales Positions in Manufacturing.** A manufacturer's sales personnel sell the firm's products to wholesalers, retailers, and industrial buyers; they thus perform many of the same activities as a wholesaler's representatives. As in wholesaling, educational requirements for a sales position depend largely on the type and complexity of the products and markets. Manufacturers of nontechnical products usually hire college graduates who have a liberal arts or business degree and train them so they become knowledgeable about the firm's products, prices, and customers. Manufacturers of highly technical products generally prefer applicants who have degrees in fields associated with the particular industry and market.

Sales positions in manufacturing are expected to increase at an average rate. Manufacturers' sales personnel are well compensated and earn above-average salaries; most are paid a combination of salary and commission. Commissions vary according to the salesperson's efforts, abilities, and sales territory, as well as the type of products sold. Annual salary and/or commission for sales positions range from $63,511 to $78,348 for a sales manager and $30,000 to $52,000 for a field salesperson. A sales trainee would start at about $35,500 in business sales positions.[7]

## Industrial Buying

Industrial buyers, or purchasing agents, are responsible for maintaining an adequate supply of the goods and services an organization requires for its operations. In general, industrial buyers purchase all items needed for direct use in producing other products and for use in day-to-day operations. Industrial buyers in large firms often specialize in purchasing a single, specific class of products—for example, all petroleum-based lubricants. In smaller organizations, buyers may be responsible for many different categories of purchases, including raw materials, component parts, office supplies, and operating services.

An industrial buyer's main job is to select suppliers that offer the best quality, service, and price. When the products to be purchased are standardized, buyers may base their purchasing decisions on suppliers' descriptions of their offerings in catalogs and trade journals. Buyers who purchase highly homogeneous products often meet with salespeople to examine samples and observe demonstrations. Sometimes buyers must inspect the actual product before purchasing it; in other cases, they invite suppliers to bid on large orders. Buyers who purchase equipment made to specifications often deal directly with manufacturers. After choosing a supplier and placing an order, an industrial buyer usually must trace the shipment to ensure on-time delivery. Sometimes the buyer is also responsible for receiving and inspecting an order and authorizing payment to the shipper.

Training requirements for a career in industrial buying relate to the needs of the firm and the types of products purchased. A manufacturer of heavy machinery may prefer an applicant who has a background in engineering. A service company, on the other hand, may recruit liberal arts majors. Although not generally required, a college degree is becoming increasingly important for industrial buyers who wish to advance to management positions.

Employment prospects for industrial buyers are expected to increase faster than average. Opportunities will be excellent for individuals with master's degrees in business administration or bachelor's degrees in engineering, science, or business administration. Companies that manufacture heavy equipment, computer equipment, and communications equipment will need buyers with technical backgrounds.

## Public Relations

Public relations encompasses a broad set of communication activities designed to create and maintain favorable relationships between an organization and its stakeholders—customers, employees, stockholders, government officials, and society in general. Public relations specialists help clients create the image, issue, or message they wish to present and communicate it to the appropriate audience. According to the Public Relations Society of America, about 120,000 people work in public relations in the United States. Half the billings of the nation's 4,000 public relations agencies and firms come from Chicago and New York. The highest starting salaries are also found there. Communication is basic to all public relations programs. To communicate effectively, public relations practitioners must first gather data about the firm's stakeholders to assess their needs, identify problems, formulate recommendations, implement new plans, and evaluate current activities.

Public relations personnel disseminate large amounts of information to the organization's stakeholders. Written communication is the most versatile tool of public relations; thus, good writing skills are essential. Public relations practitioners must be adept at writing for a variety of media and audiences. It is not unusual for a person in public relations to prepare reports, news releases, speeches, broadcast scripts, technical manuals, employee publications, shareholder reports, and other communications aimed at both organizational personnel and external groups. In addition, a public relations practitioner needs a thorough knowledge of the production techniques used in preparing various communications. Public relations personnel also establish distribution channels for the organization's publicity. They must have a thorough understanding of the various media, their areas of specialization, the characteristics of their target audiences, and their policies regarding publicity. Anyone who hopes to succeed in public relations must develop close working relationships with numerous media personnel to enlist their interest in disseminating clients' communications.

A college education combined with writing or media-related experience is the best preparation for a career in public relations. Most beginners have a college degree in journalism, communications, or public relations, but some employers prefer a business background. Courses in journalism, business administration, marketing, creative writing, psychology, sociology, political science, economics, advertising, English, and public speaking are recommended. Some employers ask applicants to present a portfolio of published articles, scripts written for television or radio programs, slide presentations, and other work samples. Other agencies require written tests that include such tasks as writing sample press releases. Manufacturing firms, public utilities, transportation and insurance companies, and trade and professional associations are the largest employers of public relations personnel. In addition, sizable numbers of public relations personnel work for health-related organizations, government agencies, educational institutions, museums, and religious and service groups.

Although some larger companies provide extensive formal training for new personnel, most new public relations employees learn on the job. Beginners usually perform routine tasks such as maintaining files about company activities and searching secondary data sources for information to be used in publicity materials. More experienced employees write press releases, speeches, and articles, and help plan public relations campaigns.

Employment opportunities in public relations are expected to increase faster than the average for all occupations. One caveat is in order, however: competition for beginning jobs is keen. The prospects are best for applicants who have solid academic preparation and some media experience. Abilities that differentiate candidates, such as an understanding of information technology, are becoming increasingly important. Public relations account executives earn $30,000 to $45,000. Public relations agency managers earn in the $51,460 to $62,874 range.[8]

## Distribution Management

A distribution manager arranges for transportation of goods within firms and through marketing channels. Transportation is an essential distribution activity that permits a firm to create time and place utility for its products. It is the distribution manager's job to analyze various transportation modes and select the combination that minimizes cost and transit time while providing acceptable levels of reliability, capability, accessibility, and security.

To accomplish this task, a distribution manager performs many activities. First, the individual must choose one or a combination of transportation modes from the five major modes available: railroads, trucks, waterways, airways, and pipelines. The distribution manager must then select the specific routes the goods will travel and the particular carriers to be used, weighing such factors as freight classifications and regulations, freight charges, time schedules, shipment sizes, and loss and damage ratios. In addition, this person may be responsible for preparing shipping documents, tracing shipments, handling loss and damage claims, keeping records of freight rates, and monitoring changes in government regulations and transportation technology.

Distribution management employs relatively few people and is expected to grow about as fast as the average for all occupations in the near future. Manufacturing firms are the largest employers of distribution managers, although some distribution managers work for wholesalers, retail stores, and consulting firms. Salaries of experienced distribution managers vary but generally are much higher than the average for all nonsupervisory personnel. Entry-level positions are diverse, ranging from inventory control and traffic scheduling to operations or distribution management. Inventory management is an area of great opportunity because of increasing global competition. While salaries in the distribution field vary depending on the position and information technology skill requirements, entry salaries start at about $40,000.[9]

Most employers of distribution managers prefer to hire graduates of technical programs or people who have completed courses in transportation, logistics, distribution management, economics, statistics, computer science, management, marketing, and commercial law. A successful distribution manager is adept at handling technical data and is able to interpret and communicate highly technical information.

## Product Management

The product manager occupies a staff position and is responsible for the success or failure of a product line. Product managers coordinate most of the activities required to market a product. However, because they hold a staff position, they have relatively little actual authority over marketing personnel. Nevertheless, they take on a large amount of responsibility and typically are paid quite well relative to other marketing employees. Being a product manager can be rewarding both financially and psychologically, but it can also be frustrating because of the disparity between responsibility and authority.

A product manager should have a general knowledge of advertising, transportation modes, inventory control, selling and sales management, sales promotion, marketing research, packaging, pricing, and warehousing. The individual must be knowledgeable enough to communicate effectively with personnel in these functional areas and help assess alternatives when major decisions are being made.

Product managers usually need college training in an area of business administration. A master's degree is helpful, although a person usually does not become a product manager directly out of school. Frequently several years of selling and sales management experience are prerequisites for a product management position, which is often a major step in the career path of top-level marketing executives. Product managers can earn $60,000 to $120,000, while an assistant product manager starts at about $40,000.[10]

## Advertising

Advertising pervades our daily lives. Business and nonbusiness organizations use advertising in many ways and for many reasons. Advertising clearly needs individuals with diverse skills to fill a variety of jobs. Creativity, imagination, artistic talent, and expertise in expression and persuasion are important for copywriters, artists, and account executives. Sales and managerial abilities are vital to the success of advertising managers, media buyers, and production managers. Research directors must have a solid understanding of research techniques and human behavior. A related occupation is an advertising salesperson, who sells newspaper, television, radio, or magazine advertising to advertisers.

Advertising professionals disagree on the most beneficial educational background for a career in advertising. Most employers prefer college graduates. Some employers seek individuals with degrees in advertising, journalism, or business; others prefer graduates with broad liberal arts backgrounds. Still other employers rank relevant work experience above educational background.

"Advertisers look for generalists," says a staff executive of the American Association of Advertising Agencies. "Thus, there are just as many economics or general liberal arts majors as M.B.A.'s." Common entry-level positions in an advertising agency are found in the traffic department, account service (account coordinator), or the media department (media assistant). Starting salaries in these positions are often quite low, but to gain experience in the advertising industry, employees must work their way up in the system. Assistant account executives start at $25,000, while a typical account executive earns $30,000 to $50,000. Copywriters earn $30,000 to $50,000 a year.[11]

A variety of organizations employ advertising personnel. Although advertising agencies are perhaps the most visible and glamorous employers, many manufacturing firms, retail stores, banks, utility companies, and professional and trade associations maintain advertising departments. Advertising jobs are also available with television and radio stations, newspapers, and magazines. Other businesses that employ advertising personnel include printers, art studios, letter shops, and package design firms. Specific advertising jobs include advertising manager, account executive, research director, copywriter, media specialist, and production manager.

About 59 percent of advertising employees are between 25 and 44 years of age compared to 51 percent of all workers in the U.S. economy. Employment opportunities in advertising are expected to increase faster than the average for all occupations through 2008.[12]

## Retail Management

Although a career in retailing may begin in sales, there is more to retailing than simply selling. Many retail personnel occupy management positions. Besides managing the sales force, they focus on selecting and ordering merchandise, promotional activities, inventory control, customer credit operations, accounting, personnel, and store security.

Organization of retail stores varies. In many large department stores, retail management personnel rarely engage in actual selling to customers; these duties are performed by retail salespeople. Other types of retail organizations may require management personnel to perform selling activities from time to time.

Large retail stores offer a variety of management positions, including assistant buyers, buyers, department managers, section managers, store managers, division managers, regional managers, and vice president of merchandising. The following list describes the general duties of four of these positions; the precise nature of their duties may vary from one retail organization to another.

A section manager coordinates inventory and promotions and interacts with buyers, salespeople, and ultimate consumers. The manager performs merchandising, labor relations, and managerial activities, and usually works more than a 40-hour workweek.

The buyer's task is more focused. This fast-paced occupation involves much travel and pressure, and the need to be open-minded with respect to new, potentially successful items.

The regional manager coordinates the activities of several stores within a given area, usually monitoring and supporting sales, promotions, and general procedures.

The vice president of merchandising has a broad scope of managerial responsibility and reports to the organization's president.

Most retail organizations hire college graduates, put them through management training programs, and then place them directly in management positions. They frequently hire candidates with backgrounds in liberal arts or business administration. Sales positions and retail management positions offer the greatest employment opportunities for marketing students.

Retail management positions can be exciting and challenging. Competent, ambitious individuals often assume a great deal of responsibility very quickly and advance rapidly. However, a retail manager's job is physically demanding and sometimes entails long working hours. In addition, managers employed by large chain stores may be required to move frequently during their early years with the company. Nonetheless, positions in retail management often offer the chance to excel and gain promotion. Growth in retailing, which is expected to accompany the growth in population, is likely to create substantial opportunities during the next ten years. While a trainee may start in the $30,000 to $47,250 range, a store manager can earn from $50,000 to $200,000 depending on the size of the store.[13]

## Direct Marketing

One of the more dynamic areas in marketing is direct marketing, in which the seller uses one or more direct media (telephone, online, mail, print, or television) to solicit a response. The telephone is a major vehicle for selling many consumer products. Telemarketing is direct selling to customers using a variety of technological improvements in telecommunications. Direct-mail catalogs appeal to such market segments as working women and people who find going to retail stores difficult or inconvenient. Newspapers and magazines offer great opportunity, particularly in special market segments. *Golf Digest*, for example, is obviously a good medium for selling golfing equipment. Cable television provides many opportunities for selling directly to consumers. Home shopping channels, for instance, have been very successful. The Internet offers numerous direct marketing opportunities.

The most important asset in direct marketing is experience. Employers often look to other industries to locate experienced professionals. This preference means that if you can get an entry-level position in direct marketing, you will have an advantage in developing a career.

Jobs in direct marketing include buyers, such as department store buyers, who select goods for catalog, telephone, or direct-mail sales. Catalog managers develop marketing strategies for each new catalog that goes into the mail. Research/mail list management involves developing lists of products that will sell in direct marketing and lists of names of consumers who are likely to respond to a direct-mail effort. Order fulfillment managers direct the shipment of products once they are sold. The effectiveness of direct marketing is enhanced by periodic analysis of advertising and communications at all phases of contact with the consumer. Direct marketing involves all aspects of marketing decision making. Most positions in direct marketing involve planning and market analysis. Some direct marketing jobs involve the use of databases that include customer information, sales history, and other tracking data. A database manager might receive a salary of $53,750 to $88,750. A telemarketing director in business-to-business sales could receive a salary of about $35,000.[14]

## E-Marketing and Customer Relationship Management

Today only about 1.5 percent of all retail sales are conducted on the Internet.[15] Currently approximately one-half of all businesses order online. One characteristic of firms engaged in e-marketing is a renewed focus on relationship marketing by building customer loyalty and retaining customers—in other words, on customer relationship management (CRM). This focus on CRM is possible because of e-marketers' ability to target individual customers. This effort is enhanced over time as the customer invests more time and effort in "teaching" the firms what he or she wants.

Opportunities abound to combine information technology expertise with marketing knowledge. By providing an integrated communication system of websites, fax, telephone, and personal contacts, marketers can personalize customer relationships. Careers exist for individuals who can integrate the Internet as a touch point with customers as part of effective customer relationship management. Many Internet-only companies ("dot-coms") failed because they focused too heavily on brand awareness and did not understand the importance of an integrated marketing strategy.

The use of laptops, cellular phones, e-mail, voice mail, and other devices is necessary to maintain customer relationships and allow purchases on the Internet. A variety of jobs exist for marketers who have integrated technology into their work and job skills. Job titles include e-marketing manager, customer relationship manager, and e-services manager, as well as jobs in dot-coms.

Salaries in this rapidly growing area depend on technical expertise and experience. For example, a CRM customer service manager receives a salary in the $40,000 to $45,000 range. Database administrators earn salaries of approximately $70,500 to $90,000. With five years of experience in e-marketing, individuals responsible for online product offerings can earn from $50,000 to $85,000.

# Financial Analysis in Marketing*

Our discussion in this book focuses more on fundamental concepts and decisions in marketing than on financial details. However, marketers must understand the basic components of financial analyses to be able to explain and defend their decisions. In fact, they must be familiar with certain financial analyses to reach good decisions in the first place. To control and evaluate marketing activities, they must understand the income statement and what it says about their organization's operations. They also need to be familiar with performance ratios, which compare current operating results with past results and with results in the industry at large. We examine the income statement and some performance ratios in the first part of this appendix. In the second part, we discuss price calculations as the basis for price adjustments. Marketers are likely to use all these areas of financial analysis at various times to support their decisions and make necessary adjustments in their operations.

## The Income Statement

The income, or operating, statement presents the financial results of an organization's operations over a certain period. The statement summarizes revenues earned and expenses incurred by a profit center, whether a department, a brand, a product line, a division, or the entire firm. The income statement presents the firm's net profit or net loss for a month, quarter, or year.

Table B.1 (on p. A-18) is a simplified income statement for Stoneham Auto Supplies, a fictitious retail store. The owners, Rose Costa and Nick Schultz, see that net sales of $250,000 are decreased by the cost of goods sold and by other business expenses to yield a net income of $83,000. Of course, these figures are only highlights of the complete income statement, which appears in Table B.2 (on p. A-19).

The income statement can be used in several ways to improve the management of a business. First, it enables an owner or a manager to compare actual results with budgets for various parts of the statement. For example, Rose and Nick see that the total amount of merchandise sold (gross sales) is $260,000. Customers returned merchandise or received allowances (price reductions) totaling $10,000. Suppose the budgeted amount was only $9,000. By checking the tickets for sales returns and allowances, the owners can determine why these events occurred and whether the $10,000 figure could be lowered by adjusting the marketing mix.

After subtracting returns and allowances from gross sales, Rose and Nick can determine net sales, the amount the firm has available to pay its expenses. They are pleased with this figure because it is higher than their sales target of $240,000.

A major expense for most companies that sell goods (as opposed to services) is the cost of goods sold. For Stoneham Auto Supplies, it amounts to 18 percent of net sales. Other expenses are treated in various ways by different companies. In our example, they are broken down into standard categories of selling expenses, administrative expenses, and general expenses.

* We gratefully acknowledge the assistance of Jim L. Grimm, Professor Marketing, Illinois State University, in writing this appendix.

## table B.1    SIMPLIFIED INCOME STATEMENT FOR A RETAILER

**Stoneham Auto Supplies**
**Income Statement for the Year Ended**
**December 31, 2005**

| | |
|---|---|
| Net Sales | $250,000 |
| Cost of Goods Sold | 45,000 |
| Gross Margin | $205,000 |
| Expenses | 122,000 |
| Net Income | $ 83,000 |

The income statement shows that for Stoneham Auto Supplies, the cost of goods sold was $45,000. This figure was derived in the following way. First, the statement shows that merchandise in the amount of $51,000 was purchased during the year. In paying the invoices associated with these inventory additions, purchase (cash) discounts of $4,000 were earned, resulting in net purchases of $47,000. Special requests for selected merchandise throughout the year resulted in $2,000 in freight charges, which increased the net cost of delivered purchases to $49,000. When this amount is added to the beginning inventory of $48,000, the cost of goods available for sale during 2005 totals $97,000. However, the records indicate that the value of inventory at the end of the year was $52,000. Because this amount was not sold, the cost of goods that were sold during the year was $45,000.

Rose and Nick observe that the total value of their inventory increased by 8.3 percent during the year:

$$\frac{\$52,000 - \$48,000}{\$48,000} = \frac{\$4,000}{\$48,000} = \frac{1}{2} = 0825, \text{ or } 8.3\%$$

Further analysis is needed to determine whether this increase is desirable or undesirable. (Note that the income statement provides no details concerning the composition of the inventory held on December 31; other records supply this information.) If Nick and Rose determine that inventory on December 31 is excessive, they can implement appropriate marketing action.

Gross margin is the difference between net sales and cost of goods sold. Gross margin reflects the markup on products and is the amount available to pay all other expenses and provide a return to the owners. Stoneham Auto Supplies had a gross margin of $205,000:

| | |
|---|---|
| Net sales | $250,000 |
| Cost of goods sold | 45,000 |

Stoneham's expenses (other than cost of goods sold) during 2005 totaled $122,000. Observe that $53,000, or slightly more than 43 percent of the total, constituted direct selling expenses:

$$\frac{\$53,000 \; selling \; \text{expenses}}{\$122,000 \; total \; \text{expenses}} = .434, \text{ or } 43\%$$

The business employs three salespeople (one full time) and pays competitive wages. The selling expenses are similar to those in the previous year, but Nick and Rose wonder whether more advertising is necessary because the value of inventory increased by more than 8 percent during the year.

The administrative and general expenses are essential for operating the business. A comparison of these expenses with trade statistics for similar businesses indicates that the figures are in line with industry amounts.

Net income, or net profit, is the amount of gross margin remaining after deducting expenses. Stoneham Auto Supplies earned a net profit of $83,000 for the fiscal year ending December 31, 2005. Note that net income on this statement is figured before payment of state and federal income taxes.

Income statements for intermediaries and for businesses that provide services follow the same general format as that shown for Stoneham Auto Supplies in Table B.2. The income statement for a manufacturer, however, differs somewhat in

**table B.2   INCOME FOR A RETAILER**

**Stoneham Auto Supplies**
**Income Statement for the Year Ended December 31, 2005**

| | | | |
|---|---|---|---|
| **Gross Sales** | | | **$260,000** |
| Less: Sales returns and allowances | | | $ 10,000 |
| **Net Sales** | | | **$250,000** |
| **Cost of Goods Sold** | | | |
| Inventory, January 1, 2005 (at cost) | | $48,000 | |
| Purchases | $51,000 | | **$260,000** |
| Less: Purchase discounts | 4,000 | | |
| Net purchases | $47,000 | | |
| Plus: Freight-in | 2,000 | | |
| Net cost of delivered purchases | | $49,000 | |
| Cost of goods available for sale | | $97,000 | |
| Cost of goods sold | | | $ 45,000 |
| **Gross Margin** | | | **$205,000** |
| Expenses | | | |
| Selling expenses | | | |
| Sales salaries and commissions | $32,000 | | |
| Advertising | 16,000 | | |
| Sales promotions | 3,000 | | |
| Delivery | 2,000 | | |
| Total selling expenses | | $53,000 | |
| Administrative expenses | | | |
| Administrative salaries | $20,000 | | |
| Office salaries | 20,000 | | |
| Office supplies | 2,000 | | |
| Miscellaneous | 1,000 | | |
| Total administrative expenses | | $43,000 | |
| General expenses | | | |
| Rent | $14,000 | | |
| Utilities | 7,000 | | |
| Bad debts | 1,000 | | |
| Total general expenses | | $26,000 | |
| Total expenses | | | $ 122,000 |
| **Net Income** | | | **$ 83,000** |

## table B.3    COST OF GOODS SOLD FOR A MANUFACTURER

**ABC Manufacturing**
**Income Statement for the Year Ended December 31, 2005**

| | | | |
|---|---|---|---|
| **Cost of Goods Sold** | | | $ 50,000 |
| Finished goods inventory January 1, 2005 | | | |
| Cost of goods manufactured | | | |
| Work-in-process inventory, January 1, 2005 | | $ 20,000 | |
| Raw materials inventory, January 1, 2005 | $ 40,000 | | |
| Net cost of delivered purchases | $240,000 | | |
| Cost of goods available for use | $280,000 | | |
| Less: Raw materials inventory, December 31, 2005 | $ 42,000 | | |
| Cost of goods placed in production | | $238,000 | |
| Direct labor | | 32,000 | |
| Manufacturing overhead | | | |
| Indirect labor | $ 12,000 | | |
| Supervisory salaries | 10,000 | | |
| Operating supplies | 6,000 | | |
| Depreciation | 12,000 | | |
| Utilities | $ 10,000 | | |
| Total manufacturing overhead | | $ 50,000 | |
| Total manufacturing costs | | $320,000 | |
| Total work-in-process | | $340,000 | |
| Less: Work-in-process inventory, December 31, 2005 | | $ 22,000 | |
| **Cost of Goods Manufactured** | | | $ 318,000 |
| | | | $ 368,000 |
| **Cost of Goods Available for Sale** | | | 48,000 |
| Less: Finished goods inventory, December 31, 2005 | | | |
| **Cost of Goods Sold** | | | **$320,000** |

that "purchases" portion is replaced by "cost of goods manufactured." Table B.3 shows the entire Cost of Goods Sold section for a manufacturer, including cost of goods manufactured. In other respects, income statements for retailers and manufacturers are similar.

## Performance Ratios

Rose and Nick's assessment of how well their business did during fiscal year 2005 can be improved through use of analytical ratios. Such ratios enable a manager to compare the results for the current year with data from previous years and industry statistics. However, comparisons of the current income statement with income statements and industry statistics from other years are not very meaningful because factors such as inflation are not accounted for when comparing dollar amounts. More useful comparisons can be made by converting these figures to a percentage of net sales, as this section shows.

The first analytical ratios we discuss, the operating ratios, are based on the net sales figure from the income statement.

## Operating Ratios

Operating ratios express items on the income, or operating, statement as percentages of net sales. The first step is to convert the income statement into percentages of net sales, as illustrated in Table B.4 (on p. A-22). After making this conversion, the manager looks at several key operating ratios: two profitability ratios (the gross margin ratio and the net income ratio) and the operating expense ratio.

For Stoneham Auto Supplies, these ratios are determined as follows (see Tables B.2 and B.4 for supporting data):

$$\text{Gross Margin Ratio} = \frac{Gross\ Margin}{Net\ Sales} = \frac{\$205,000}{\$250,000} = 82\%$$

$$\text{Net Income Ratio} = 33.2\%$$

$$\text{Operating Expenses Ratio} = \frac{Total\ Expenses}{Net\ Sales} = \frac{\$122,000}{\$250,000} = 48.8\%$$

The gross margin ratio indicates the percentage of each sales dollar available to cover operating expenses and achieve profit objectives. The net income ratio indicates the percentage of each sales dollar that is classified as earnings (profit) before payment of income taxes. The operating expense ratio calculates the percentage of each dollar needed to cover operating expenses.

If Nick and Rose believe the operating expense ratio is higher than historical data and industry standards, they can analyze each operating expense ratio in Table B.4 to determine which expenses are too high and then take corrective action. After reviewing several key operating ratios, Nick and Rose, like many managers, will probably want to analyze all the items on the income statement. By doing so, they can determine whether the 8 percent increase in the value of their inventory was necessary.

## Inventory Turnover Rate

The inventory turnover rate, or stock-turn rate, is an analytical ratio that can be used to answer the question "Is the inventory level appropriate for this business?" The inventory turnover rate indicates the number of times an inventory is sold (turns over) during one year. To be useful, this figure must be compared with historical turnover rates and industry rates.

The inventory turnover rate is computed (based on cost) as follows:

$$\text{Inventory Turnover} = \frac{Cost\ of\ Goods\ Sold}{Average\ Inventory\ at\ Cost}$$

Rose and Nick would calculate the turnover rate from Table B.2 as follows:

$$\frac{Cost\ of\ Goods\ Sold}{Average\ Inventory\ at\ Cost} = \frac{\$45,000}{\$50,000} = 0.9\%$$

Their inventory turnover is less than once per year (0.9 times). Industry averages for competitive firms are 2.8 times. This figure convinces Rose and Nick that their investment in inventory is too large and they need to reduce their inventory.

## Return on Investment

Return on investment (ROI) is a ratio that indicates management's efficiency in generating sales and profits from the total amount invested in the firm. For Stoneham Auto Supplies, the ROI is 41.5 percent, which compares well with competing businesses.

We use figures from two different financial statements to arrive at ROI. The income statement, already discussed, gives us net income. The balance sheet, which states the firm's assets and liabilities at a given point in time, provides the figure for total assets (or investment) in the firm.

## table B.4  INCOME STATE COMPONENTS AS PERCENTAGE OF NET SALES

**Stoneham Auto Supplies**
**Income Statement as a Percentage of Net Sales for the Year Ended**
**December 31, 2005**

| | | | Percentage of Net Sales |
|---|---|---|---|
| **Gross Sales** | | | 103.8% |
| Less: Sales returns and allowances | | | 3.8 |
| **Net Sales** | | | 100.0% |
| **Cost of Goods Sold** | | | |
| Inventory, January 1, 2005 (at cost) | | 19.2% | |
| Purchases | 20.4% | | |
| Less: Purchase discounts | 1.6 | | |
| Net purchases | 18.8% | | |
| Plus: Freight-in | 0.8 | | |
| Net cost of delivered purchases | | 19.6 | |
| Cost of goods available for sale | | 38.8% | |
| Less: Inventory, December 31, 2005 (at cost) | | 20.8 | |
| Cost of goods sold | | | 18.0 |
| | | | |
| **Expenses** | | | |
| Selling expenses | | | |
| Sales salaries and commissions | 12.8% | | |
| Advertising | 6.4 | | |
| Delivery | 0.8 | | |
| Total selling expenses | | 21.2% | |
| Administrative expenses | | | |
| Administrative salaries | 8.0% | | |
| Office salaries | 8.0 | | |
| Office supplies | 0.8 | | |
| Miscellaneous | 0.4 | | |
| Total administrative expenses | | 17.2% | |
| General expenses | | | |
| Rent | 5.6% | | |
| Utilities | 2.8 | | |
| Bad debts | 0.4 | | |
| Miscellaneous | 1.6 | | |
| Total general expenses | | 10.4% | |
| Total expenses | | | 48.8 |
| Net Income | | | 33.2% |

The basic formula for ROI is

$$\text{ROI} = \frac{Net\ Income}{Total\ Investment}$$

For Stoneham Auto Supplies, net income is $83,000 (see Table B.2). If total investment (taken from the balance sheet for December 31, 2005) is $200,000, then

$$\text{ROI} = \frac{\$83,000}{\$200,000} = 0.415, \text{ or } 41.5\%$$

The ROI formula can be expanded to isolate the impact of capital turnover and the operating income ratio separately. Capital turnover is a measure of net sales per dollar of investment; the ratio is figured by dividing net sales by total investment. For Stoneham Auto Supplies,

$$\text{Capital Turnover} = \frac{Net\ Sales}{Total\ Investment} = \frac{\$250,000}{\$200,000} = 1.25$$

ROI is equal to capital turnover times the net income ratio. The expanded formula for Stoneham Auto Supplies is

$$\text{ROI} = \frac{Net\ Income}{Net\ Sales}$$

$$= \frac{\$250,000}{\$200,000} \times \frac{\$83,000}{\$250,000}$$

$$= (1.25)\,(33.2\%) = 41.5\%$$

# Price Calculations

An important step in setting prices is selecting a basis for pricing, as discussed in Chapter 22. The systematic use of markups, markdowns, and various conversion formulas helps in calculating the selling price and evaluating the effects of various prices.

## Markups

As discussed in the text, markup is the difference between the selling price and the cost of the item; that is, selling price equals cost plus markup. The markup must cover cost and contribute to profit; thus, markup is similar to gross margin on the income statement.

Markup can be calculated on either cost or selling price as follows:

$$\text{Markup as Percentage of Cost} = \frac{Amount\ Added\ to\ Cost}{Cost} = \frac{Dollar\ Markup}{Cost}$$

$$\text{Markup as Percentage of Selling Price} = \frac{Amount\ Added\ to\ Cost}{Selling\ Price} = \frac{Dollar\ Markup}{Selling\ Price}$$

Retailers tend to calculate the markup percentage on selling price.

To review the use of these markup formulas, assume an item costs $10 and the markup is $5:

$$\text{Selling Price} = \text{Cost} + \text{Markup}$$

$$\$15 = \$10 + \$5$$

Thus,

$$\text{Markup Percentage on Selling Price} = \frac{\$5}{\$10} = 50\%$$

$$\text{Markup Percentage on Selling Price} = \frac{\$5}{\$15} = 33\tfrac{1}{3}\%$$

It is necessary to know the base (cost or selling price) to use markup pricing effectively. Markup percentage on cost will always exceed markup percentage on price, given the same dollar markup, as long as selling price exceeds cost.

On occasion, we may need to convert markup on cost to markup on selling price, or vice versa. The conversion formulas are as follows:

$$\text{Markup Percentage on Selling Price} = \frac{Markup\ Percentage\ on\ Cost}{100\% + Markup\ Percentage\ on\ Cost}$$

$$\text{Markup Percentage on Cost} = \frac{Markup\ Percentage\ on\ Selling\ Price}{100\% - Markup\ Percentage\ on\ Selling\ Price}$$

For example, if the markup percentage on cost is $33\tfrac{1}{3}$ percent, the markup percentage on selling price is

$$\frac{33\tfrac{1}{3}\%}{100\% + 33\tfrac{1}{3}\%} = \frac{33\tfrac{1}{3}\%}{1.33\tfrac{1}{3}\%} = 25\%$$

If the markup percentage on selling price is 40 percent, the corresponding percentage on cost is as follows:

$$66\tfrac{2}{3}\%$$

Finally, we can show how to determine selling price if we know the cost of the item and the markup percentage on selling price. Assume an item costs $36 and the usual markup percentage on selling price is 40 percent. Remember that selling price equals markup plus cost. Thus, if

$$100\% = 40\% \text{ of Selling Price} + \text{Cost}$$

then,

$$60\% \text{ of Selling Price} = \text{Cost}$$

In our example, cost equals $36. Therefore,

$$0.6X = \$36$$

$$X = \frac{\$36}{0.6}$$

$$\text{Selling Price} = \$60$$

Alternatively, the markup percentage could be converted to a cost basis as follows:

$$66\tfrac{2}{3}\%$$

The selling price would then be computed as follows:

$$\text{Selling Price} = 66\tfrac{2}{3}\%(\text{Cost}) + \text{Cost}$$

$$= 66\tfrac{2}{3}\%(\$36) + \$36$$

$$= \$24 + \$36 = \$60$$

If you keep in mind the basic formula—selling price equals cost plus markup—you will find these calculations straightforward.

## Markdowns

Markdowns are price reductions a retailer makes on merchandise. Markdowns may be useful on items that are damaged, priced too high, or selected for a special sales event. The income statement does not express markdowns directly because the change in price is made before the sale takes place. Therefore, separate records of markdowns would be needed to evaluate the performance of various buyers and departments.

The markdown ratio (percentage) is calculated as follows:

$$\text{Markdown Percentage} = \frac{Dollar\ Markdowns}{Net\ Sales\ in\ Dollars}$$

In analyzing their inventory, Nick and Rose discover three special automobile jacks that have gone unsold for several months. They decide to reduce the price of each item from $25 to $20. Subsequently these items are sold. The markdown percentage for these three items is

$$\text{Markdown Percentage} = \frac{3(\$5)}{3(\$20)} = \frac{\$15}{\$60} = 25\%$$

Net sales, however, include all units of this product sold during the period, not just those marked down. If ten of these items were already sold at $25 each, in addition to the three items sold at $20, the overall markdown percentage would be

$$\text{Markdown Percentage} = \frac{3(\$5)}{10(\$25) + 3(\$20)}$$

$$= \frac{\$15}{\$250 + \$60} = \frac{\$15}{\$310} = 4.8\%$$

Sales allowances are also a reduction in price. Thus, the markdown percentage should include any sales allowances. It would be computed as follows:

$$\text{Markdown Percentage} = \frac{Dollar\ Markdowns + Dollar\ Allowances}{Net\ Sales\ in\ Dollars}$$

## Discussion and Review Questions

1. How does a manufacturer's income statement differ from a retailer's income statement?

2. Use the following information to answer questions a through c:

| TEA COMPANY | |
|---|---|
| **Fiscal year ended June 30, 2006** | |
| Net sales | $500,000 |
| Cost of goods sold | 300,000 |
| Net income | 50,000 |
| Average inventory at cost | 100,000 |
| Total assets (total investment) | 200,000 |

a. What is the inventory turnover rate for TEA Company? From what sources will the marketing manager determine the significance of the inventory turnover rate?

    **b.** What is the capital turnover ratio? What is the net income ratio? What is the return on investment (ROI)?

    **c.** How many dollars of sales did each dollar of investment produce for TEA Company?

**3.** Product A has a markup percentage on cost of 40 percent. What is the markup percentage on selling price?

**4.** Product B has a markup percentage on selling price of 30 percent. What is the markup percentage on cost?

**5.** Product C has a cost of $60 and a usual markup percentage of 25 percent on selling price. What price should be placed on this item?

**6.** Apex Appliance Company sells 20 units of product Q for $100 each and 10 units for $80 each. What is the markdown percentage for product Q?

# Sample Marketing Plan

This sample marketing plan for a hypothetical company illustrates how the marketing planning process described in Chapter 2 might be implemented. If you are asked to create a marketing plan, this model may be a helpful guide, along with the concepts in Chapter 2.

**❶ The Executive Summary,** one of the most frequently read components of a marketing plan, is a synopsis of the marketing plan. Although it does not provide detailed information, it does present an overview of the plan so readers can identify key issues pertaining to their roles in the planning and implementation processes. Although this is the first section in a marketing plan, it is usually written last.

**❷ The Environmental Analysis** presents information regarding the organization's current situation with respect to the marketing environment, the current target market(s), and the firm's current marketing objectives and performance.

**❸** This section of the environmental analysis considers relevant **external environmental forces** such as competitive, economic, political, legal and regulatory, technological, and sociocultural forces.

## Star Software, Inc., Marketing Plan

### ❶ I. EXECUTIVE SUMMARY

Star Software, Inc., is a small, family-owned corporation in the first year of a transition from first-generation to second-generation leadership. Star Software sells custom-made calendar programs and related items to about 400 businesses, which use the software mainly for promotion. As Star's business is highly seasonal, its 18 employees face scheduling challenges, with greatest demand during October, November, and December. In other months, the equipment and staff are sometimes idle. A major challenge facing Star Software is how to increase profits and make better use of its resources during the off-season.

An evaluation of the company's internal strengths and weaknesses and external opportunities and threats served as the foundation for this strategic analysis and marketing plan. The plan focuses on the company's growth strategy, suggesting ways it can build on existing customer relationships, and on the development of new products and/or services targeted to specific customer niches. Since Star Software markets a product used primarily as a promotional tool by its clients, it is currently considered a business-to-business marketer.

### ❷ II. ENVIRONMENTAL ANALYSIS

Founded as a commercial printing company, Star Software, Inc., has evolved into a marketer of high-quality, custom-made calendar software and related business-to-business specialty items. In the mid-1960s, Bob McLemore purchased the company and, through his full-time commitment, turned it into a very successful family-run operation. In the near future, McLemore's 37-year-old son, Jonathan, will take over as Star Software's president and allow the elder McLemore to scale back his involvement.

### ❸ A. The Marketing Environment

1. *Competitive forces.* The competition in the specialty advertising industry is very strong on a local and regional basis, but somewhat weak nationally. Sales figures for the industry as a whole are difficult to obtain since very little business is conducted on a national scale.

   The competition within the calendar industry is strong in the paper segment and weak in the software-based segment. Currently paper calendars hold a dominant market share of approximately 65 percent; however, the software-based segment is growing rapidly. The 35 percent market share held by software-based calendars is divided among many different firms. Star Software, which holds 30 percent of the software-based calendar market, is the only company that markets a software-based calendar on a national basis. As software-based calendars become more popular, additional competition is expected to enter the market.

2. *Economic forces.* Nationwide, many companies have reduced their overall promotion budgets as they face the need to cut expenses. However, most of these reductions have occurred in the budgets for mass media advertising (television, magazines, newspapers). While overall promotion budgets are shrinking, many companies are diverting a larger percentage of their budgets to sales promotion and specialty advertising. This trend is expected to continue as a weak, slow-growth economy forces most companies to focus more on the "value" they receive from their promotion dollars. Specialty advertising, such as can be done with a software-based calendar, provides this value.

3. *Political forces.* There are no expected political influences or events that could affect the operations of Star Software.

4. *Legal and regulatory forces.* In recent years, more attention has been paid to "junk mail." A large percentage of specialty advertising products are distributed by mail, and some of these products are considered "junk." Although this label is attached to the type of products Star Software makes, the problem of junk mail falls on Star's clients and not on the company itself. While legislation may be introduced to curb the tide of advertising delivered through the mail, the fact that more companies are diverting their promotion dollars to specialty advertising indicates that most do not fear the potential for increased legislation.

5. *Technological forces.* A major emerging technological trend involves personal digital assistants (PDAs). A PDA is a handheld device, similar in size to a large calculator, that can store a wide variety of information, including personal notes, addresses, and a calendar. Some PDAs, such as the BlackBerry, can be loaded with a cellphone and walkie-talkie. The user can e-mail and schedule on the electronic calendar. As this trend continues, current software-based calendar products may have to be adapted to match the new technology.

6. *Sociocultural forces.* In today's society, consumers have less time for work or leisure. The hallmarks of today's successful products are convenience and ease of use. In short, if the product does not save time and is not easy to use, consumers will simply ignore it. Software-based calendars fit this consumer need quite well. A software-based calendar also fits in with other societal trends: a move to a paperless society, the need to automate repetitive tasks, and the growing dependence on computers, for example.

**④** The analysis of current target markets assesses demographic, geographic, psychographic, and product usage characteristics of the target markets. It also assesses the current needs of each of the firm's target markets, anticipated changes in those needs, and how well the organization's current products are meeting those needs.

### ④ B. Target Market(s)

By focusing on commitment to service and quality, Star Software has effectively implemented a niche differentiation strategy in a somewhat diverse marketplace. Its ability to differentiate its product has contributed to superior annual returns. Its target market consists of manufacturers or manufacturing divisions of large corporations that move their products through dealers, distributors, or brokers. Its most profitable product is a software program for a PC-based calendar, which can be tailored to meet client needs by means of artwork, logos, and text. Clients use this calendar software as a promotional tool, providing a disk to their customers as an advertising premium. The calendar software is not produced for resale.

The calendar software began as an ancillary product to Star's commercial printing business. However, due to the proliferation of PCs and the growth in technology, the computer calendar soon became more profitable for Star than its wall and desktop paper calendars. This led to the sale of the commercial printing plant and equipment to employees. Star Software has maintained a long-term relationship with these former employees, who have added capabilities to reproduce computer disks and whose company serves as Star's primary supplier of finished goods. Star's staff focuses on further development and marketing of the software.

## C. Current Marketing Objectives and Performance

Star Software's sales representatives call on potential clients and, using a template demonstration disk, help them create a calendar concept. Once the sale has been finalized, Star completes the concept, including design, copywriting, and customization of the demonstration disk. Specifications are then sent to the supplier, located about 1,000 miles away, where the disks are produced. Perhaps what most differentiates Star from its competitors is its high level of service. Disks can be shipped to any location the buyer specifies. Since product development and customization of this type can require significant amounts of time and effort, particularly during the product's first year, Star deliberately pursues a strategy of steady, managed growth. Star Software markets its products on a company-specific basis. It has an annual reorder rate of approximately 90 percent and an average customer-reorder relationship of about eight years. The first year in dealing with a new customer is the most stressful and time consuming for Star's salespeople and product developers. Subsequent years are faster and significantly more profitable.

A company must set marketing objectives, measure performance against those objectives, and then take corrective action if needed.

The company is currently debt free except for the mortgage on its facility. However, about 80 percent of its accounts receivable are billed during the last three months of the calendar year. Seasonal account billings, along with the added travel of Star's sales staff during the peak season, pose a special challenge to the company. The need for cash to fund operations in the meantime requires the company to borrow significant amounts of money to cover the period until customer billing occurs. Star Software's marketing objectives include increases in both revenues and profits of approximately 10 percent over the previous year. Revenues should exceed $4 million, and profits are expected to reach $1.3 million.

### III. SWOT ANALYSIS

**5** A. Strengths

1. Star Software's product differentiation strategy is the result of a strong marketing orientation, commitment to high quality, and customization of products and support services.

2. There is little turnover among employees, who are well compensated and liked by customers. The relatively small staff size promotes camaraderie with coworkers and clients, and fosters communication and quick response to clients' needs.

3. A long-term relationship with the primary supplier has resulted in shared knowledge of the product's requirements, adherence to quality standards, and a common vision throughout the development and production process.

4. The high percentage of reorder business suggests a satisfied customer base, as well as positive word-of-mouth communication, which generates some 30 percent of new business each year.

**6** B. Weaknesses

1. The highly centralized management hierarchy (the McLemores) and lack of managerial backup may impede creativity and growth. Too few people hold too much knowledge.

2. Despite the successful, long-term relationship with the supplier, single-sourcing could make Star Software vulnerable in the event of a natural disaster, strike, or dissolution of the current supplier. Contingency plans for suppliers should be considered.

3. The seasonal nature of the product line creates bottlenecks in productivity and cash flow, places excessive stress on personnel, and strains the facilities.

4. Both the product line and the client base lack diversification. Dependence on current reorder rates could breed complacency, invite competition, or create a false sense of customer satisfaction. The development of a product that would make the software calendar obsolete would probably put Star out of business.

5. While the small size of the staff fosters camaraderie, it also impedes growth and new-business development.

6. Star Software is reactive rather than assertive in its marketing efforts because of its heavy reliance on positive word-of-mouth communication for obtaining new business.

7. Star's current facilities are crowded. There is little room for additional employees or new equipment.

**7** **Opportunities** are favorable conditions in the environment that could yield rewards for an organization if acted on properly.

**8** **Threats** are conditions or barriers that may prevent the organization from reaching its objectives.

**9** During the development of a marketing plan, marketers attempt to match internal strengths to external opportunities. In addition, they try to convert internal weaknesses into strengths and external threats into opportunities.

## C. Opportunities

1. Advertising expenditures in the United States exceed $132 billion annually. More than $25 billion of this is spent on direct-mail advertising and another $20 billion on specialty advertising. Star Software's potential for growth is significant in this market.

2. Technological advances have not only freed up time for Americans and brought greater efficiency but have also increased the amount of stress in their fast-paced lives. Personal computers have become commonplace, and personal information managers have gained popularity.

3. As U.S. companies look for ways to develop customer relationships rather than just close sales, reminders of this relationship could come in the form of acceptable premiums or gifts that are useful to the customer.

4. Computer-based calendars are easily distributed nationally and globally. The globalization of business creates an opportunity to establish new client relationships in foreign markets.

## D. Threats

1. Reengineering, right-sizing, and outsourcing trends in management may alter traditional channel relationships with brokers, dealers, and distributors or eliminate them altogether.

2. Calendars are basically a generic product. The technology, knowledge, and equipment required to produce such an item, even a computer-based one, is minimal. The possible entry of new competitors is a significant threat.

3. Theft of trade secrets and software piracy through unauthorized copying is difficult to control.

4. Specialty advertising through promotional items relies on gadgetry and ideas that are new and different. As a result, product life cycles may be quite short.

5. Single-sourcing can be detrimental or even fatal to a company if the buyer-supplier relationship is damaged or if the supplying company has financial difficulty.

6. Competition from traditional paper calendars and other promotional items is strong.

## E. Matching Strengths to Opportunities/Converting Weaknesses and Threats

1. The acceptance of technological advances and the desire to control time create a potential need for a computer-based calendar.

2. Star Software has more opportunity for business growth during its peak season than it can presently handle because of resource (human and capital) constraints.

3.  Star Software must modify its management hierarchy, empowering its employees through a more decentralized marketing organization.

4.  Star Software should discuss future growth strategies with its supplier and develop contingency plans to deal with unforeseen events. Possible satellite facilities in other geographic locations should be explored.

5.  Star Software should consider diversifying its product line to satisfy new market niches and develop nonseasonal products.

6.  Star Software should consider surveying its current customers and its customers' clients to gain a better understanding of their changing needs and desires.

**10** The development of marketing objectives is based on environmental analysis, SWOT analysis, the firm's overall corporate objectives, and the organization's resources. For each objective, this section should answer the question "What is the specific and measurable outcome and time frame for completing this objective?"

## **10** IV. MARKETING OBJECTIVES

Star Software, Inc., is in the business of helping other companies market their products and/or services. Besides formulating a marketing-oriented and customer-focused mission statement, Star Software should establish an objective to achieve cumulative growth in net profit of at least 50 percent over the next five years. At least half of this 50 percent growth should come from new, nonmanufacturing customers and from products that are nonseasonal or that are generally delivered in the off-peak period of the calendar cycle.

To accomplish its marketing objectives, Star Software should develop benchmarks to measure progress. Regular reviews of these objectives will provide feedback and possible corrective actions on a timely basis. The major marketing objective is to gain a better understanding of the needs and satisfaction of current customers. Since Star Software is benefiting from a 90 percent reorder rate, it must be satisfying its current customers. Star could use the knowledge of its successes with current clients to market to new customers. To capitalize on its success with current clients, the company should establish benchmarks to learn how it can improve the products it now offers through knowledge of clients' needs and specific opportunities for new product offerings. These benchmarks should be determined through marketing research and Star's marketing information system.

Another objective should be to analyze the billing cycle Star now uses to determine if there are ways to bill accounts receivable in a more evenly distributed manner throughout the year. Alternatively, repeat customers might be willing to place orders at off-peak cycles in return for discounts or added customer services.

Star Software should also create new products that can use its current equipment, technology, and knowledge base. It should conduct simple research and analyses of similar products or product lines with an eye toward developing specialty advertising products that are software based but not necessarily calendar related.

**11** The marketing plan clearly specifies and describes the target market(s) toward which the organization will aim its marketing efforts. The difference between this section and the earlier section covering target markets is that the earlier section deals with present target markets, whereas this section looks at future target markets.

**12** Though the marketing mix section in this plan is abbreviated, this component should provide considerable details regarding each element of the marketing mix: product, price, distribution, and promotion.

## 11  V. MARKETING STRATEGIES

### A. Target Market(s)

**Target market 1:** Large manufacturers or stand-alone manufacturing divisions of large corporations with extensive broker, dealer, or distributor networks

> Example: An agricultural chemical producer, such as Dow Chemical, distributes its products to numerous rural "feed and seed" dealers. Customizing calendars with Chicago Board of Trade futures or USDA agricultural report dates would be beneficial to these potential clients.

**Target market 2:** Nonmanufacturing, nonindustrial segments of the business-to-business market with extensive customer networks, such as banks, medical services, or financial planners

> Example: Various sporting goods manufacturers distribute to specialty shop dealers. Calendars could be customized to the particular sport, such as golf (with PGA, Virginia Slims, or other tour dates), running (with various national marathon dates), or bowling (with national tour dates).

**Target market 3:** Direct consumer markets for brands with successful licensing arrangements for consumer products, such as Coca-Cola

> Example: Products with major brand recognition and fan club membership, such as Harley-Davidson motorcycles or the Bloomington Gold Corvette Association, could provide additional markets for customized computer calendars. Environmental or political groups represent a nonprofit market. Brands with licensing agreements for consumer products could provide a market for consumer computer calendars in addition to the specialty advertising product, which would be marketed to manufacturers/dealers.

**Target market 4:** Industry associations that regularly hold or sponsor trade shows, meetings, conferences, or conventions

> Example: National associations, such as the National Dairy Association or the American Marketing Association, frequently host meetings or annual conventions. Customized calendars could be developed for any of these groups.

### 12  B. Marketing Mix

1. *Products.* Star Software markets not only calendar software but also the service of specialty advertising to its clients. Star's intangible attributes are its ability to meet or exceed customer expectations consistently, its speed in responding to customers' demands, and its anticipation of new customer needs. Intangible attributes are difficult for competitors to copy, thereby giving Star Software a competitive advantage.

2. *Price.* Star Software provides a high-quality specialty advertising product customized to its clients' needs. The value of this product and service is reflected in its premium price. Star should be sensitive to the price elasticity of its product and overall consumer demand.

3. *Distribution*. Star Software uses direct marketing. Since its product is compact, lightweight, and nonperishable, it can be shipped from a central location direct to the client via UPS, FedEx, or the U.S. Postal Service. The fact that Star can ship to multiple locations for each customer is an asset in selling its products.

4. *Promotion*. Since 90 percent of Star's customers reorder each year, the bulk of promotional expenditures should focus on new product offerings through direct-mail advertising and trade journals or specialty publications. Any remaining promotional dollars could be directed to personal selling (in the form of sales performance bonuses) of current and new products.

## VI. MARKETING IMPLEMENTATION

### A. Marketing Organization

**13** This section of the marketing plan details how the firm will be organized—by functions, products, regions, or types of customers—to implement its marketing strategies. It also indicates where decision making authority will rest within the marketing unit.

Because Star's current and future products require extensive customization to match clients' needs, it is necessary to organize the marketing function by customer groups. This will allow Star to focus its marketing efforts exclusively on the needs and specifications of each target customer segment. Star's marketing efforts will be organized around the following customer groups: (1) manufacturing group; (2) nonmanufacturing, business-to-business group; (3) consumer product licensing group; and (4) industry associations group. Each group will be headed by a sales manager who will report to the marketing director (these positions must be created). Each group will be responsible for marketing Star's products within that customer segment. In addition, each group will have full decision making authority. This represents a shift from the current, highly centralized management hierarchy. Frontline salespeople will be empowered to make decisions that will better satisfy Star's clients.

These changes in marketing organization will enable Star Software to be more creative and flexible in meeting customers' needs. Likewise, these changes will overcome the current lack of diversification in Star's product lines and client base. Finally, this new marketing organization will give Star a better opportunity to monitor the activities of competitors.

### B. Activities, Responsibility, and Timetables for Completion

**14** This component of the marketing plan outlines the specific activities required to implement the marketing plan, who is responsible for performing these activities, and when these activities should be accomplished based on a specified schedule.

All implementation activities are to begin at the start of the next fiscal year on April 1. Unless specified, all activities are the responsibility of Star Software's next president, Jonathan McLemore.

- On April 1, create four sales manager positions and the position of marketing director. The marketing director will serve as project leader of a new business analysis team, to be composed of nine employees from a variety of positions within the company.

- By April 15, assign three members of the analysis team to each of the following projects: (1) research potential new product offerings and clients, (2) analyze the current billing cycle and billing practices, and (3) design a customer survey project. The marketing director is responsible.

- By June 30, the three project groups will report the results of their analyses. The full business analysis team will review all recommendations.
- By July 31, develop a marketing information system to monitor client reorder patterns and customer satisfaction.
- By July 31, implement any changes in billing practices as recommended by the business analysis team.
- By July 31, make initial contact with new potential clients for the current product line. Each sales manager is responsible.
- By August 31, develop a plan for one new product offering, along with an analysis of its potential customers. The business analysis team is responsible.
- By August 31, finalize a customer satisfaction survey for current clients. In addition, the company will contact those customers who did not reorder for the 2005 product year to discuss their concerns. The marketing director is responsible.
- By January, implement the customer satisfaction survey with a random sample of 20 percent of current clients who reordered for the 2005 product year. The marketing director is responsible.
- By February, implement a new product offering, advertising to current customers and to a sample of potential clients. The business analysis team is responsible.
- By March, analyze and report the results of all customer satisfaction surveys and evaluate the new product offering. The marketing director is responsible.
- Reestablish the objectives of the business analysis team for the next fiscal year. The marketing director is responsible.

## VII. EVALUATION AND CONTROL

### A. Performance Standards and Financial Controls

A comparison of the financial expenditures with the plan goals will be included in the project report. The following performance standards and financial controls are suggested:

- The total budget for the billing analysis, new-product research, and the customer survey will be equal to 60 percent of the annual promotional budget for the coming year.
- The breakdown of the budget within the project will be a 20 percent allocation to the billing cycle study, a 30 percent allocation to the customer survey and marketing information system development, and a 50 percent allocation to new-business development and new-product implementation.

**15** This section details how the results of the marketing plan will be measured and evaluated. The control portion of this section includes the types of actions the firm can take to reduce the differences between the planned and the actual performance.

- Each project team is responsible for reporting all financial expenditures, including personnel salaries and direct expenses, for its segment of the project. A standardized reporting form will be developed and provided by the marketing director.

- The marketing director is responsible for adherence to the project budget and will report overages to the company president on a weekly basis. The marketing director is also responsible for any redirection of budget dollars as required for each project of the business analysis team.

- Any new product offering will be evaluated on a quarterly basis to determine its profitability. Product development expenses will be distributed over a two-year period, by calendar quarters, and will be compared with gross income generated during the same period.

## B. Monitoring Procedures

To analyze the effectiveness of Star Software's marketing plan, it is necessary to compare its actual performance with plan objectives. To facilitate this analysis, monitoring procedures should be developed for the various activities required to bring the marketing plan to fruition. These procedures include, but are not limited to, the following:

- A project management concept will be used to evaluate the implementation of the marketing plan by establishing time requirements, human resource needs, and financial or budgetary expenditures.

- A perpetual comparison of actual and planned activities will be conducted on a monthly basis for the first year and on a quarterly basis after the initial implementation phase. The business analysis team, including the marketing director, will report its comparison of actual and planned outcomes directly to the company president.

- Each project team is responsible for determining what changes must be made in procedures, product focus, or operations as a result of the studies conducted in its area.

**Accessibility**   The ability to obtain information available on the Internet. (8)

**Accessory equipment**   Equipment used in production or office activities that does not become a part of the final physical product but is used in production or office activities. (11)

**Addressability**   A marketer's ability to identify customers before they make a purchase. (8)

**Advertising**   Paid nonpersonal communication about an organization and its products transmitted to a target audience through mass media. (19)

**Advertising appropriation**   The advertising budget for a specific time period. (19)

**Advertising campaign**   The creation and execution of a series of advertisements to communicate with a particular target audience. (19)

**Advertising platform**   Basic issues or selling points to be included in an advertising campaign. (19)

**Advocacy advertising**   Advertising that promotes a company's position on a public issue. (19)

**Aesthetic modifications**   Changes relating to the sensory appeal of a product. (12)

**Agent**   An intermediary that represents either buyers or sellers on a permanent basis. (16)

**Aided recall test**   A posttest that asks respondents to identify recent ads and provides clues to jog their memories. (19)

**Allowance**   A concession in price to achieve a desired goal. (21)

**Approach**   The manner in which a salesperson contacts a potential customer. (20)

**Arbitrary approach**   Budgeting for an advertising campaign as specified by a high-level executive in the firm. (19)

**Artwork**   An advertisement's illustrations and layout. (19)

**Asia-Pacific Economic Cooperation (APEC)**   An alliance that promotes open trade and economic and technical cooperation among member nations throughout the world. (7)

**Atmospherics**   The physical elements in a store's design that appeal to consumers' emotions and encourage buying. (17)

**Attitude**   An individual's enduring evaluation of feelings about and behavioral tendencies toward an object or idea. (5)

**Attitude scale**   A means of measuring consumer attitudes by gauging the intensity of individuals' reactions to adjectives, phrases, or sentences about an object. (5)

**Automatic vending**   The use of machines to dispense products. (17)

**Average fixed cost**   The fixed cost per unit produced. (21)

**Average total cost**   The sum of the average fixed cost and the average variable cost. (21)

**Average variable cost**   The variable cost per unit produced. (21)

**Bait pricing**   Pricing an item in a product line low with the intention of selling a higher-priced item in the line. (22)

**Balance of trade**   The difference in value between a nation's exports and its imports. (7)

**Barter**   The trading of products. (21)

**Base-point pricing**   Geographic pricing that combines factory price and freight charges from the base point nearest the buyer. (21)

**Benchmarking**   Comparing the quality of the firm's goods, services, or processes with that of its best-performing competitors. (2)

**Benefit segmentation**   The division of a market according to benefits that consumers want from the product. (10)

**Better Business Bureau (BBB)**   A system of nongovernmental, independent, local regulatory agencies supported by local businesses that helps settle problems between customers and specific business firms. (3)

**Brand**   A name, term, design, symbol, or other feature that identifies a seller's products and differentiates them from competitors' products. (13)

**Brand competitors**   Firms that market products with similar features and benefits to the same customers at similar prices. (3)

**Brand equity**   The marketing and financial value associated with a brand's strength in a market. (13)

**Brand insistence**   The degree of brand loyalty in which a customer strongly prefers a specific brand and will accept no substitute. (13)

**Brand licensing**   An agreement whereby a company permits another organization to use its brand on other products for a licensing fee. (13)

**Brand loyalty**   A customer's favorable attitude toward a specific brand. (13)

**Brand manager**   The person responsible for a single brand. (12)

**Brand mark**   The part of a brand not made up of words, such as a symbol or design. (13)

**Brand name**   The part of a brand that can be spoken, including letters, words, and numbers. (13)

**Brand preference**   The degree of brand loyalty in which a customer prefers one brand over competitive offerings. (13)

**Breakdown approach**   Measuring company sales potential based on a general economic forecast for a specific period and the market potential derived from it. (10)

**Break-even point**   The point at which the costs of producing a product equal the revenue made from selling the product. (21)

**Broker**   An intermediary that brings buyers and sellers together temporarily. (16)

**Buildup approach**   Measuring company sales potential by estimating how much of a product a potential buyer in a specific geographic area will purchase in a given period, multiplying the estimate by the number of potential buyers, and adding the totals of all the geographic areas considered. (10)

**Bundle pricing** Packaging together two or more complementary products and selling them at a single price. (22)

**Business (organizational) buying behavior** The purchase behavior of producers, government units, institutions, and resellers. (6)

**Business analysis** Evaluating the potential impact of a product idea on the firm's sales, costs, and profits. (12)

**Business cycle** A pattern of economic fluctuations that has four stages: prosperity, recession, depression, and recovery. (3)

**Business market** Individuals or groups that purchase a specific kind of product for resale, direct use in producing other products, or use in general daily operations. (6)

**Business products** Products bought to use in an organization's operations, to resell, or to make other products. (11)

**Business services** Intangible products that many organizations use in their operations. (11)

**Buy-back allowance** A sum of money given to a reseller for each unit bought after an initial promotion deal is over. (20)

**Buying allowance** A temporary price reduction to resellers for purchasing specified quantities of a product. (20)

**Buying center** The people within an organization who make business purchase decisions. (6)

**Buying power** Resources, such as money, goods, and services that can be traded in an exchange. (3)

**Buzz marketing** An attempt to gain acceptance of a product through word-of-mouth communications. (18)

**Captioned photograph** A photograph with a brief description of its contents. (19)

**Captive pricing** Pricing the basic product in a product line low while pricing related items higher. (22)

**Cash-and-carry wholesaler** A limited-service wholesaler whose customers pay cash and furnish transportation. (16)

**Cash discount** A price reduction given to buyers for prompt payment or cash payment. (21)

**Catalog marketing** A type of marketing in which an organization provides a catalog from which customers make selections and place orders by mail, telephone, or the Internet. (17)

**Catalog showroom** A warehouse showroom in which consumers use catalogs to place orders for products, which are then filled directly in the warehouse area and picked up by buyers in the showroom. (17)

**Category killer** A very large specialty store that concentrates on a major product category and competes on the basis of low prices and enormous product availability. (17)

**Category management** A retail strategy of managing groups of similar, often substitutable products produced by different manufacturers. (17)

**Cause-related marketing** The practice of linking products to a particular social cause on an ongoing or short-term basis. (4)

**Centralized organization** A structure in which top-level managers delegate little authority to lower levels. (2)

**Cents-off offer** A gift, often part of a display, given to a retailer that purchases a specified quantity of merchandise (20)

**Channel capacity** The limit on the volume of information a communication channel can handle effectively. (18)

**Channel captain** The dominant member of a marketing channel or supply chain. (15)

**Channel power** The ability of one channel member to influence another member's goal achievement. (15)

**Client-based relationships** Interactions that result in satisfied customers who use a service repeatedly over time. (14)

**Client publics** Direct consumers of a product of a nonbusiness organization. (14)

**Closing** The stage in the personal selling process when the salesperson asks the prospect to buy the product. (20)

**Co-branding** Using two or more brands on one product. (13)

**Codes of conduct** Formalized rules and standards that describe what the company expects of its employees. (4)

**Coding process** Converting meaning into a series of signs or symbols. (18)

**Cognitive dissonance** A buyer's doubts shortly after a purchase about whether the decision was the right one. (5)

**Combination compensation plan** Paying salespeople a fixed salary plus a commission based on sales volume. (20)

**Commercialization** Refining and finalizing plans and budgets for full-scale manufacturing and marketing of a product. (12)

**Commission merchant** An agent that receives goods on consignment from local sellers and negotiates sales in large, central markets. (16)

**Common Market of the Southern Cone (MERCOSUR)** An alliance that promotes the free circulation of goods, services, and production factors, and has a common external tariff and commercial policy among member nations in South America. (7)

**Communications channel** The medium of transmission that carries the coded message from the source to the receiver. (18)

**Community** A sense of group membership or feeling of belonging by individual members. (8)

**Community shopping center** A shopping center with one or two department stores, some specialty stores, and convenience stores. (17)

**Company sales potential** The maximum percentage of market potential that an individual firm within an industry can expect to obtain for a specific product. (10)

**Comparative advertising** Advertising that compares two or more brands on the basis of one or more product characteristics. (19)

**Competition** Other organizations that market products that are similar to or can be substituted for a marketer's products in the same geographic area. (3)

**Competition-based pricing** Pricing influenced primarily by competitors' prices. (22)

**Competition-matching approach** Determining an advertising budget by trying to match competitors' advertising outlays. (19)

**Competitive advantage** The result of a company's matching a core competency to opportunities it has discovered in the marketplace. (2)

**Component parts** Items that become part of the physical product and are either finished items ready for assembly or items that need little processing before assembly. (11)

**Concentrated targeting strategy** A market segmentation strategy in which an organization targets a single market segment using one marketing mix. (10)

**Concept testing** Seeking a sample of potential buyers' responses to a product idea. (12)

**Conclusive research** Research designed to verify insights through objective procedures and to help marketers in making decisions. (9)

**Consideration set** A group of brands within a product category that a buyer views as alternatives for possible purchase. (5)

**Consistency of quality**    The degree to which a product has the same level of quality over time. (12)

**Consumer buying behavior**    The decision processes and purchasing activities of people who purchase products for personal or household use and not for business purposes. (5)

**Consumer buying decision process**    A five-stage purchase decision process that includes problem recognition, information search, evaluation of alternatives, purchase, and postpurchase evaluation. (5)

**Consumer contest**    Sales promotion methods in which individuals compete for prizes based on their analytical or creative skills. (20)

**Consumer game**    Sales promotion method in which individuals compete for prizes based primarily on chance. (20)

**Consumerism**    Organized efforts by individuals, groups, and organizations to protect consumers' rights. (3)

**Consumer jury**    A panel of a product's existing or potential buyers who pretest ads. (19)

**Consumer market**    Purchasers and household members who intend to consume or benefit from the purchased products and do not buy products to make profits. Buying behavior. (5)

**Consumer products**    Products purchased to satisfy personal and family needs (11)

**Consumer sales promotion methods**    Sales promotion techniques that encourage consumers to patronize specific stores or try particular products. (20)

**Consumer socialization**    The process through which a person acquires the knowledge and skills to function as a consumer. (5)

**Consumer sweepstakes**    A sales promotion in which entrants submit their names for inclusion in a drawing for prizes. (20)

**Contract manufacturing**    The practice of hiring a foreign firm to produce a designated volume of the domestic firm's product or a component of it to specification; the final product carries the domestic firm's name. (7)

**Control**    Customers' ability to regulate the information they view and the rate and sequence of their exposure to that information. (8)

**Convenience products**    Relatively inexpensive, frequently purchased items for which buyers exert minimal purchasing effort. (11)

**Convenience store**    A small self-service store that is open long hours and carries a narrow assortment of products, usually convenience items. (17)

**Cookie**    An identifying string of text stored on a website visitor's computer. (8)

**Cooperative advertising**    An arrangement in which a manufacturer agrees to pay a certain amount of a retailer's media costs for advertising the manufacturer's products. (20)

**Copy**    The verbal portion of advertisements. (19)

**Core competencies**    Things a firm does extremely well, which sometimes give it an advantage over its competition. (2)

**Corporate strategy**    A strategy that determines the means for utilizing resources in the various functional areas to reach the organization's goals. (2)

**Cost-based pricing**    Adding a dollar amount or percentage to the cost of the product. (22)

**Cost comparison indicator**    A means of comparing the costs of advertising vehicles in a specific medium in relation to the number of people reached. (19)

**Cost-plus pricing**    Adding a specified dollar amount or percentage to the seller's cost. (22)

**Coupon**    A written price reduction used to encourage consumers to buy a specific product. (20)

**Credence qualities**    Attributes that customers may be unable to evaluate even after purchasing and consuming a service. (14)

**Cultural relativism**    The concept that morality varies from one culture to another and that business practices are therefore differentially defined as right or wrong by particular cultures. (7)

**Cumulative discount**    A quantity discount aggregated over a stated period. (21)

**Customary pricing**    Pricing on the basis of tradition. (22)

**Customer advisory boards**    Small groups of actual customers who serve as sounding boards for new product ideas and offer insights into their feelings and attitudes toward a firm's products and other elements of marketing strategy. (9)

**Customer contact**    The level of interaction between provider and customer needed to deliver the service. (14)

**Customer forecasting survey**    A survey of customers regarding the quantities of products they intend to buy during a specific period. (10)

**Customer relationship management (CRM)**    Using information about customers to create marketing strategies that develop and sustain desirable customer relationships. (1)

**Customers**    The purchasers of organizations' products; the focal point of all marketing activities. (1)

**Customer services**    Human or mechanical efforts or activities that add value to a product. (12)

**Cycle analysis**    An analysis of sales figures for a period of three to five years to ascertain whether sales fluctuate in a consistent, periodic manner. (10)

**Cycle time**    The time needed to complete a process. (16)

**Database**    A collection of information arranged for easy access and retrieval. (8)

**Dealer listings**    An advertisement that promotes a product and identifies the names of participating retailers that sell the product. (20)

**Dealer loader**    A gift, often part of a display, given to a retailer that purchases a specified quantity of merchandise. (20)

**Decentralized organization**    A structure in which decision-making authority is delegated as far down the chain of command as possible. (2)

**Decline stage**    The stage of a product's life cycle when sales fall rapidly. (11)

**Decoding process**    Converting signs or symbols into concepts and ideas. (18)

**Delphi technique**    A procedure in which experts create initial forecasts, submit them to the company for averaging, and then refine the forecasts. (10)

**Demand-based pricing**    Pricing based on the level of demand for the product. (22)

**Demand curve**    A graph of the quantity of products expected to be sold at various prices if other factors remain constant. (21)

**Demonstration**    A sales promotion method a manufacturer uses temporarily to encourage trial use and purchase of a product or to show how a product works. (20)

**Department store**    A large retail organization characterized by a wide product mix and organized into separate departments to facilitate marketing efforts and internal management. (17)

**Depression**    A stage of the business cycle when unemployment is extremely high, wages are very low, total disposable income is at a minimum, and consumers lack confidence in the economy. (3)

**Depth of product mix**    The average number of different products offered in each product line. (11)

**Derived demand**    Demand for industrial products that stems from demand for consumer products. (6)

**Descriptive research**    Research conducted to clarify the characteristics of certain phenomena to solve a particular problem. (9)

**Differential pricing**    Charging different prices to different buyers for the same quality and quantity of product. (22)

**Differentiated targeting strategy**    A strategy in which an organization targets two or more segments by developing a marketing mix for each segment. (10)

**Digitalization**    The ability to represent a product, or at least some of its benefits, as digital bits of information. (8)

**Direct marketing**    The use of the telephone, Internet, and nonpersonal media to introduce products to customers, who can then purchase them via mail, telephone, or the Internet. (17)

**Direct ownership**    A situation in which a company owns subsidiaries or other facilities overseas. (7)

**Direct-response marketing**    A type of marketing in which a retailer advertises a product and makes it available through mail or telephone orders. (17)

**Direct selling**    Marketing products to ultimate consumers through face-to-face sales presentations at home or in the workplace. (17)

**Discount store**    A self-service, general-merchandise store offering brand name and private-brand products at low prices. (17)

**Discretionary income**    Disposable income available for spending and saving after an individual has purchased the basic necessities of food, clothing, and shelter. (3)

**Disposable income**    After-tax income. (3)

**Distribution**    The activities that make products available to customers when and where they want to purchase them. (15)

**Distribution center**    A large, centralized warehouse that focuses on moving rather than storing goods. (16)

**Drop shipper**    A limited-service wholesaler that takes title to goods and negotiates sales but never actually takes possession of products. (16)

**Dual distribution**    The use of two or more marketing channels to distribute the same product to the same target market. (15)

**Dumping**    The practice of charging high prices for products sold in domestic markets while selling the same products in foreign markets at low prices, often below the costs of exporting them. (7)

**Early adopters**    Careful choosers of new products. (11)

**Early majority**    Individuals who adopt a new product just prior to the average person. (11)

**Electronic commerce (e-commerce)**    Sharing business information, maintaining business relationships, and conducting business transactions by means of telecommunications networks. (8)

**Electronic data interchange (EDI)**    A computerized means of integrating order processing with production, inventory, accounting, and transportation. (16)

**Electronic marketing (e-marketing)**    The strategic process of creating, distributing, promoting, and pricing products for targeted customers in the virtual environment of the Internet. (8)

**Embargo**    A government's suspension of trade in a particular product or with a given country. (7)

**Empowerment**    Giving customer-contact employees authority and responsibility to make marketing decisions without seeking approval of their supervisors. (2)

**Environmental analysis**    The process of assessing and interpreting the information gathered through environmental scanning. (3)

**Environmental scanning**    The process of collecting information about forces in the marketing environment. (3)

**Ethical issue**    An identifiable problem, situation, or opportunity requiring a choice among several actions that must be evaluated as right or wrong, ethical or unethical. (4)

**European Union (EU)**    An alliance that promotes trade among its member countries in Europe. (7)

**Evaluative criteria**    Objective and subjective characteristics that are important to a buyer. (5)

**Everyday low prices (EDLP)**    Pricing products low on a consistent basis. (22)

**Exchange**    The provision or transfer of goods, services, or ideas in return for something of value. (1)

**Exchange controls**    Government restrictions on the amount of a particular currency that can be bought or sold. (7)

**Exclusive dealing**    A situation in which a manufacturer forbids an intermediary to carry products of competing manufacturers. (15)

**Exclusive distribution**    Using a single outlet in a fairly large geographic area to distribute a product. (15)

**Executive judgment**    A sales forecasting method based on the intuition of one or more executives. (10)

**Experience qualities**    Attributes that can be assessed only during purchase and consumption of a service. (14)

**Experimental research**    Research that allows marketers to make causal inferences about relationships. (9)

**Expert forecasting survey**    Sales forecasts prepared by experts outside the firm, such as economists, management consultants, advertising executives, or college professors. (10)

**Exploratory research**    Research conducted to gather more information about a problem or to make a tentative hypothesis more specific. (9)

**Exporting**    The sale of products to foreign markets. (7)

**Extended problem solving**    A consumer problem-solving process employed when purchasing unfamiliar, expensive, or infrequently bought products. (5)

**External customers**    Individuals who patronize a business. (2)

**External reference price**    A comparison price provided by others. (21)

**External search**    An information search in which buyers seek information from sources other than memory. (5)

**Family branding**    Branding all of a firm's products with the same name or part of the name. (13)

**Family packaging**    Using similar packaging for all of a firm's products or packaging that has one common design element. (13)

**Feature article**    A manuscript of up to 3,000 words prepared for a specific publication. (19)

**Feedback**    The receiver's response to a decoded message. (18)

**Fixed costs**    Costs that do not vary with changes in the number of units produced or sold. (21)

**F.O.B. destination**    A price indicating the producer is absorbing shipping costs. (21)

**F.O.B. factory**    The price of merchandise at the factory, before shipment. (21)

**Focus-group interview**   A research method involving observation of group interaction when members are exposed to an idea or a concept. (9)

**Franchising**   A form of licensing in which a franchiser, in exchange for a financial commitment, grants a franchisee the right to market its product in accordance with the franchiser's standards. (7)

**Franchising**   An arrangement in which a supplier (franchiser) grants a dealer (franchisee) the right to sell products in exchange for some type of consideration. (17)

**Free merchandise**   A manufacturer's reward given to resellers that purchase a stated quantity of products. (20)

**Free sample**   A sample of a product given out to encourage trial and purchase. (20)

**Freight absorption pricing**   Absorption of all or part of actual freight costs by the seller. (21)

**Freight forwarder**   An organization that consolidates shipments from several firms into efficient lot sizes. (16)

**Full-service wholesaler**   A merchant wholesaler that performs the widest range of wholesaling functions. (16)

**Functional modifications**   Changes affecting a product's versatility, effectiveness, convenience, or safety. (12)

**General Agreement on Tariffs and Trade (GATT)**   An agreement among nations to reduce worldwide tariffs and increase international trade. (7)

**General-line wholesaler**   A full-service wholesaler that carries only a few product lines but many products within those lines. (16)

**General-merchandise retailer**   A retail establishment that offers a variety of product lines that are stocked in considerable depth. (17)

**General-merchandise wholesaler**   A full-service wholesaler with a wide product mix but limited depth within product lines. (16)

**General publics**   Indirect consumers of a product of a nonbusiness organization. (14)

**Generic brands**   A brand indicating only the product category. (13)

**Generic competitors**   Firms that provide very different products that solve the same problem or satisfy the same basic customer need. (3)

**Geodemographic segmentation**   A method of market segmentation that clusters people in zip code areas and smaller neighborhood units based on lifestyle and demographic information. (10)

**Geographic pricing**   Reductions for transportation and other costs related to the physical distance between buyer and seller. (21)

**Globalization**   The development of marketing strategies that treat the entire world (or its major regions) as a single entity. (7)

**Good**   A tangible physical entity. (11)

**Government markets**   Federal, state, county, or local governments that buy goods and services to support their internal operations and provide products to their constituencies. (6)

**Gross domestic product (GDP)**   The market value of a nation's total output of goods and services for a given period; an overall measure of economic standing. (7)

**Growth stage**   The product life cycle stage when sales rise rapidly and profits reach a peak, then start to decline. (11)

**Heterogeneity**   Variation in quality. (14)

**Heterogeneous market**   A market made up of individuals or organizations with diverse needs for products in a specific product class. (10)

**Homogeneous market**   A market in which a large proportion of customers have similar needs for a product. (10)

**Horizontal channel integration**   Combining organizations at the same level of operation under one management. (15)

**Hypermarket**   A store that combines supermarket and discount store shopping in one location. (17)

**Hypothesis**   An informed guess or assumption about a certain problem or set of circumstances. (9)

**Idea**   A concept, philosophy, image, or issue. (11)

**Idea generation**   Seeking product ideas to achieve organizational objectives. (12)

**Illustrations**   Photos, drawings, graphs, charts, and tables used to spark audience interest in an advertisement. (19)

**Importing**   The purchase of products from a foreign source. (7)

**Import tariff**   A duty levied by a nation on goods bought outside its borders and brought in. (7)

**Impulse buying**   An unplanned buying behavior resulting from a powerful urge to buy something immediately. (5)

**Income**   For an individual, the amount of money received through wages, rents, investments, pensions, and subsidy payments for a given period. (3)

**Individual branding**   A branding policy in which each product is given a different name. (13)

**Industrial distributor**   An independent business organization that takes title to industrial products and carries inventories. (15)

**Inelastic demand**   Demand that is not significantly altered by a price increase or decrease. (6)

**Information inputs**   Sensations received through sight, taste, hearing, smell, and touch. (5)

**In-home (door-to-door) interview**   A personal interview that takes place in the respondent's home. (9)

**Innovators**   First adopters of new products. (11)

**Input-output data**   Information that identifies what types of industries purchase the products of a particular industry. (6)

**Installations**   Facilities and nonportable major equipment. (11)

**Institutional advertising**   Advertising that promotes organizational images, ideas, and political issues. (19)

**Institutional markets**   Organizations with charitable, educational, community, or other nonbusiness goals. (6)

**Intangibility**   The quality of being produced and consumed at the same time. (14)

**Integrated marketing communications**   Coordination of promotion and other marketing efforts for maximum informational and persuasive impact. (18)

**Intended strategy**   The strategy the company decided on during the planning phase and wants to use. (2)

**Intensive distribution**   Using all available outlets to distribute a product. (15)

**Interactivity**   The ability to allow customers to express their needs and wants directly to the firm in response to the firm's marketing communications. (8)

**Intermodal transportation**   Two or more transportation modes used in combination. (16)

**Internal customers**   A company's employees. (2)

**Internal marketing**   A management philosophy that coordinates internal exchanges between the organization and its employees to achieve successful external exchanges between the organization and its customers. (2)

**Internal reference price**   A price developed in the buyer's mind through experience with the product. (21)

**Internal search**   An information search in which buyers search their memories for information about products that might solve their problem. (5)

**International marketing**   Developing and performing marketing activities across national boundaries. (7)

**Introduction stage**   The initial stage of a product's life cycle; its first appearance in the marketplace when sales start at zero and profits are negative. (11)

**Inventory management**   Developing and maintaining adequate assortments of products to meet customers' needs. (16)

**Joint demand**   Demand involving the use of two or more items in combination to produce a product. (6)

**Joint venture**   A partnership between a domestic firm and a foreign firm or government. (7)

**Just-in-time (JIT)**   An inventory management approach in which supplies arrive just when needed for production or resale. (16)

**Kinesic communication**   Communicating through the movement of head, eyes, arms, hands, legs, or torso. (18)

**Labeling**   Providing identifying, promotional, or other information on package labels. (13)

**Laggards**   The last adopters, who distrust new products. (11)

**Late majority**   Skeptics who adopt new products when they feel it is necessary. (11)

**Layout**   The physical arrangement of an advertisement's illustration and copy. (19)

**Learning**   Changes in an individual's thought processes and behavior caused by information and experience. (5)

**Level of involvement**   An individual's intensity of interest in a product and the importance of the product for that person. (5)

**Level of quality**   The amount of quality a product possesses. (12)

**Licensing**   An alternative to direct investment requiring a licensee to pay commissions or royalties on sales or supplies used in manufacturing. (7)

**Lifestyle**   An individual's pattern of living expressed through activities, interests, and opinions. (5)

**Lifestyle shopping center**   A type of shopping center that is typically open-air and features upscale speciality, dining, and entertainment stores. (17)

**Limited problem solving**   A consumer problem-solving process used when purchasing products occasionally or needing information about an unfamiliar brand in a familiar product category. (5)

**Limited-service wholesaler**   A merchant wholesaler that provides some services and specializes in a few functions. (16)

**Line extension**   Development of a product that is closely related to existing products in the line but is designed specifically to meet different customer needs. (12)

**Mail-order wholesaler**   A wholesaler who uses catalogs instead a sales force to sell products to retail and business buyers. (16)

**Mail survey**   A research method in which respondents answer a questionnaire sent through the mail. (9)

**Manufacturer brands**   A brand initiated by its producer. (13)

**Manufacturers' agent**   An independent intermediary that represents two or more sellers and usually offers customers complete product lines. (16)

**Marginal cost (MC)**   The extra cost incurred by producing one more unit of a product. (21)

**Market**   A group of individuals and/or organizations that have needs for products in a product class and have the ability, willingness, and authority to purchase those products. (2)

**Market density**   The number of potential customers within a unit of land area. (10)

**Market growth/market share matrix**   A strategic planning tool based on the philosophy that a product's market growth rate and market share are important considerations in its determining marketing strategy. (2)

**Marketing**   The process of creating, distributing, promoting, and pricing goods, services, and ideas to facilitate satisfying exchanges relationships with customers and develop and maintain favorable relationships with stakeholders in a dynamic environment. (1)

**Marketing channel**   A group of individuals and organizations that direct the flow of products from producers to customers. (15)

**Marketing citizenship**   The adoption of a strategic focus for fulfilling the economic, legal, ethical, and philanthropic social responsibilities expected by stakeholders. (4)

**Marketing concept**   A philosophy that an organization should try to provide products that satisfy customers' needs through a coordinated set of activities that also allows the organization to achieve its goals. (1)

**Marketing control process**   Establishing performance standards, evaluating actual performance by comparing it with established standards and reducing the differences between desired and actual performance. (2)

**Marketing decision support system (MDSS)**   Customized computer software that aids marketing managers in decision making. (9)

**Marketing environment**   The competitive, economic, political, legal and regulatory, technological, and sociocultural forces that surround the customer and affect the marketing mix. (1)

**Marketing ethics**   Principles and standards that define acceptable marketing conduct as determined by various stakeholders. (4)

**Marketing implementation**   The process of putting marketing strategies into action. (2)

**Marketing information system (MIS)**   A framework for managing and structuring information gathered regularly from sources inside and outside the organization. (9)

**Marketing management**   The process of planning, organizing, implementing, and controlling marketing activities to facilitate exchanges effectively and efficiently. (1)

**Marketing mix**   Four marketing activities—product, distribution, promotion, and pricing—that a firm can control to meet the needs of customers within its target markets. (1)

**Marketing objective**   A statement of what is to be accomplished through marketing activities. (2)

**Marketing orientation**   An organizationwide commitment to researching and responding to customer needs. (1)

**Marketing plan**   A written document that specifies the activities to be performed to implement and control the organization's marketing activities. (2)

**Marketing planning**   The process of assessing marketing opportunities and resources, determining marketing objectives, defining marketing strategies, and establishing guidelines for implementation and control of the marketing program. (2)

**Marketing research**   The systematic design, collection, interpretation, and reporting of information to help marketers solve specific marketing problems or take advantage of marketing opportunities. (9)

**Marketing strategy** A plan of action for identifying and analyzing a target market and developing a marketing mix to meet the needs of that market. (2)

**Market manager** The person responsible for managing the marketing activities that serve a particular group of customers. (12)

**Market opportunity** A combination of circumstances and timing that permits an organization to take action to reach a particular target market. (2)

**Market potential** The total amount of a product that customers will purchase within a specified period at a specific level of industrywide marketing activity. (10)

**Market segment** Individuals, groups, or organizations sharing one or more similar characteristics that cause them to have similar product needs. (10)

**Market segmentation** The process of dividing a total market into groups with relatively similar product needs to design a marketing mix that matches those needs. (10)

**Market share** The percentage of a market that actually buys a specific product from a particular company. (2)

**Market test** Making a product available to buyers in one or more test areas and measuring purchases and consumer responses to marketing efforts. (10)

**Markup pricing** Adding to the cost of the product a predetermined percentage of that cost. (22)

**Maslow's hierarchy of needs** The five levels of needs that humans seek to satisfy, from most to least important. (5)

**Materials handling** Physical handling of tangible goods, supplies, and resources. (16)

**Maturity stage** The stage of a product's life cycle when the sales curve peaks and starts to decline, and profits continue to fall. (11)

**Media plan** A plan that specifies the media vehicles to be used and the schedule for running advertisements. (19)

**Megacarrier** A freight transportation firm that provides several modes of shipment. (16)

**Memory** The ability to access databases or data warehouses containing individual customer profiles and purchase histories and use these data in real time to customize a marketing offer. (8)

**Merchandise allowance** A manufacturer's agreement to pay resellers certain amounts of money for providing special promotional efforts, such as setting up and maintaining a display. (20)

**Merchant wholesaler** An independently owned business that takes title to goods, assumes ownership risks, and buys and resells products to other wholesalers, business customers, or retailers. (16)

**Micromarketing** An approach to market segmentation in which organizations focus precise marketing efforts on very small geographic markets. (10)

**Missionary salespeople** Support salespeople, usually employed by a manufacturer, who assist the producer's customers in selling to their own customers. (20)

**Mission statement** A long-term view, or vision, of what the organization wants to become. (2)

**Money refund** A sales promotion technique offering consumers a specified amount of money when they mail in a proof of purchase, usually for multiple product purchases. (20)

**Monopolistic competition** A competitive structure in which a firm has many potential competitors and tries to develop a marketing strategy to differentiate its product. (3)

**Monopoly** A competitive structure in which an organization offers a product that has no close substitutes, making that organization the sole source of supply. (3)

**Motive** An internal energizing force that directs a person's behavior toward satisfying needs or achieving goals. (5)

**MRO supplies** Maintenance, repair, and operating items that facilitate production and operations but do not become part of the finished product. (11)

**Multinational enterprise** A firm that has operations or subsidiaries in many countries. (7)

**Multiple sourcing** An organization's decision to use several suppliers. (6)

**Multiple-unit pricing** Packaging together two or more identical products and selling them at a single price (22)

**National Advertising Review Board (NARB)** A self-regulatory unit that considers challenges to issues raised by the National Advertising Division (an arm of the Council of Better Business Bureaus) about an advertisement. (3)

**Negotiated pricing** Establishing a final price through bargaining between seller and customer. (22)

**Neighborhood shopping center** A shopping center usually consisting of several small convenience and specialty stores. (17)

**New-product development process** A seven-phase process for introducing products: idea generation, screening, concept testing, business analysis, product development, test marketing, and commercialization. (12)

**New-task purchase** An initial purchase by an organization of an item to be used to perform a new job or solve a new problem. (6)

**Noise** Anything that reduces a communication's clarity and accuracy. (18)

**Noncumulative discount** A one-time price reduction based on the number of units purchased, the size of the order, or the product combination purchased. (21)

**Nonprice competition** Emphasizing factors other than price to distinguish a product from competing brands. (21)

**Nonprobability sampling** A sampling technique in which there is no way to calculate the likelihood that a specific element of the population being studied will be chosen. (9)

**Nonprofit marketing** Marketing activities conducted to achieve some goal other than ordinary business goals such as profit, market share, or return on investment. (14)

**Nonstore retailing** The selling of products outside the confines of a retail facility. (17)

**North American Free Trade Agreement (NAFTA)** An alliance that merges Canada, Mexico, and the United States into a single market. (7)

**North American Industry Classification System (NAICS)** An industry classification system that generates comparable statistics among the United States, Canada, and Mexico. (6)

**Objective-and-task approach** Budgeting for an advertising campaign by first determining its objectives and then calculating the cost of all the tasks needed to attain them. (19)

**Odd-even pricing** Ending the price with certain numbers to influence buyers' perceptions of the price or product. (22)

**Off-price retailer** A store that buys manufacturers' seconds, overruns, returns, and off-season merchandise for resale to consumers at deep discounts. (17)

**Offshoring** The practice of moving a business process that was done domestically at the local factory to a foreign country, regardless of whether the production accomplished in the foreign country is performed by the local company (e.g., in a wholly owned subsidiary) or a third party (e.g., subcontractor). (7)

**Oligopoly** A competitive structure in which a few sellers control the supply of a large proportion of a product. (3)

**Online retailing** Retailing that makes products available to buyers through computer connections. (17)

**Online survey** A research method in which respondents answer a questionnaire via e-mail or on a website. (9)

**On-site computer interview** A variation of the shopping mall intercept interview in which respondents complete a self-administered questionnaire displayed on a computer monitor.(9)

**Opinion leader** A member of an informal group who provides information about a specific topic to other group members. (5)

**Opportunity cost** The value of the benefit given up by choosing one alternative over another. (14)

**Order getter** A salesperson who sells to new customers and increases sales to current customers. (20)

**Order processing** The receipt and transmission of sales order information. (16)

**Order takers** A salesperson who primarily seeks repeat sales. (20)

**Organizational structure** The way in which a firm divides its operations into separate functions and/or value-adding units and coordinates its activities. (7)

**Outlet shopping center** A type of shopping center that features discount and factory outlet stores carrying manufacturer brands. (17)

**Outsourcing** The practice of contracting noncore operations with an organization that specializes in those operation. (7)

**Outsourcing** Contracting physical distribution tasks to third parties that do not have managerial authority within the marketing channel. (16)

**Patronage motives** Motives that influence where a person purchases products on a regular basis. (5)

**Penetration pricing** Setting prices below those of competing brands to penetrate a market and gain a significant market share quickly. (22)

**Percent-of-sales approach** Budgeting for an advertising campaign by multiplying the firm's past and expected sales by a standard percentage. (19)

**Perception** The process of selecting, organizing, and interpreting information inputs to produce meaning. (5)

**Performance standard** An expected level of performance against which actual performance can be compared. (2)

**Periodic discounting** Temporary reduction of prices on a patterned or systematic basis. (22)

**Perishability** The inability of unused service capacity to be stored for future use. (14)

**Personal interview survey** A research method in which participants respond to survey questions face to face. (9)

**Personality** A set of internal traits and distinct behavioral tendencies that result in consistent patterns of behavior in certain situations. (5)

**Personal selling** Paid personal communication that attempts to inform customers and persuade them to buy products in an exchange situation. (20)

**Physical distribution** Activities used to move products from producers to consumers and other end users. (16)

**Pioneer advertising** Advertising that tries to stimulate demand for a product category rather than a specific brand by informing potential buyers about the product. (19)

**Pioneer promotion** Promotion that informs consumers about a new product. (18)

**Point-of-purchase (P-O-P) materials** Signs, window displays, display racks, and similar devices used to attract customers. (20)

**Portal** A multiservice website that serves as a gateway to other websites. (8)

**Posttest** Evaluation of advertising effectiveness after the campaign. (19)

**Premium** An item offered free or at a minimal cost as a bonus for purchasing a product. (20)

**Premium (push) money** Extra compensation to salespeople for pushing a line of goods. (20)

**Premium pricing** Pricing the highest-quality or most versatile products higher than other models in the product line. (22)

**Press conference** A meeting used to announce major news events. (19)

**Prestige pricing** Setting prices at an artificially high level to convey prestige or a quality image. (22)

**Prestige sensitive** Drawn to products that signify prominence and status. (21)

**Pretest** Evaluation of advertisements performed before a campaign begins. (19)

**Price** The value exchanged for products in a marketing exchange. (21)

**Price competition** Emphasizing price as an issue and matching or beating competitors' prices. (21)

**Price conscious** Striving to pay low prices. (21)

**Price discrimination** Employing price differentials that injure competition by giving one or more buyers a competitive advantage. (21)

**Price elasticity of demand** A measure of the sensitivity of demand to changes in price. (21)

**Price leader** A product priced below the usual markup, near cost, or below cost. (22)

**Price lining** Setting a limited number of prices for selected groups or lines of merchandise. (22)

**Price skimming** Charging the highest possible price that buyers who most desire the product will pay. (22)

**Pricing objectives** Goals that describe what a firm wants to achieve through pricing. (22)

**Primary demand** Demand for a product category rather than for a specific brand. (18)

**Private distributor brands** A brand initiated and owned by a reseller. (13)

**Private warehouse** A company-operated facility for storing and shipping products. (16)

**Probability sampling** A sampling technique in which every element in the population being studied has a known chance of being selected for study. (9)

**Process materials** Materials that are used directly in the production of other products but are not readily identifiable. (11)

**Producer markets** Individuals and business organizations that purchase products to make profits by using them to produce other products or using them in their operations. (6)

**Product** A good, a service, or an idea. (1)

**Product adoption process** The five-stage process of buyer acceptance of a product: awareness, interest, evaluation, trial, and adoption. (11)

**Product advertising**   Advertising that promotes the uses, features, and benefits of products. (19)

**Product competitors**   Firms that compete in the same product class but market products with different features, benefits, and prices. (3)

**Product deletion**   Eliminating a product from the product mix when it no longer satisfies a sufficient number of customers. (12)

**Product design**   How a product is conceived, planned, and produced. (12)

**Product development**   Determining if producing a product is feasible and cost effective. (12)

**Product differentiation**   Creating and designing products so that customers perceive them as different from competing products. (12)

**Product features**   Specific design characteristics that allow a product to perform certain tasks. (12)

**Product item**   A specific version of a product. (11)

**Product life cycle**   The progression of a product through four stages: introduction, growth, maturity, and decline. (11)

**Product line**   A group of closely related product items viewed as a unit because of marketing, technical, or end-use considerations. (11)

**Product-line pricing**   Establishing and adjusting prices of multiple products within a product line. (22)

**Product manager**   The person within an organization responsible for a product, a product line, or several distinct products that make up a group. (12)

**Product modification**   Changes in one or more characteristics of a product. (12)

**Product positioning**   Creating and maintaining a certain concept of a product in customers' minds. (10)

**Professional pricing**   Fees set by people with great skill or experience in a particular field. (22)

**Promotion**   Communication to build and maintain relationships by informing and persuading one or more audiences. (18)

**Promotion mix**   A combination of promotional methods used to promote a specific product. (18)

**Prospecting**   Developing a list of potential customers. (20)

**Prosperity**   A stage of the business cycle characterized by low unemployment and relatively high total income, which together ensure high buying power (provided the inflation rate stays low). (3)

**Proxemic communication**   Communicating by varying the physical distance in face-to-face interactions. (18)

**Psychological influences**   Factors that in part determine people's general behavior, thus influencing their behavior as consumers. (5)

**Psychological pricing**   Pricing that attempts to influence a customer's perception of price to make a product's price more attractive. (22)

**Publicity**   A news story type of communication about an organization and/or its products transmitted through a mass medium at no charge. (19)

**Public relations**   Communication efforts used to create and maintain favorable relations between an organization and its stakeholders. (19)

**Public warehouse**   A business that leases storage space and related physical distribution facilities to other firms. (16)

**Pull policy**   Promoting a product directly to consumers to develop strong consumer demand that pulls products through the marketing channel. (18)

**Pure competition**   A market structure characterized by an extremely large number of sellers, none strong enough to significantly influence price or supply. (3)

**Push policy**   Promoting a product only to the next institution down the marketing channel. (18)

**Quality**   The overall characteristics of a product that allow it to perform as expected in satisfying customer needs. (12)

**Quality modifications**   Changes relating to a product's dependability and durability. (12)

**Quantity discount**   A deduction from list price for purchasing in large quantities. (21)

**Quota**   A limit on the amount of goods an importing country will accept for certain product categories in a specific period of time. (7)

**Quota sampling**   A nonprobability sampling technique in which researchers divide the population into groups and then arbitrarily choose participants from each group. (9)

**Rack jobber**   A type of specialty-line wholesaler that owns and maintains display racks in stores. (16)

**Random discounting**   Temporary reduction of prices on an unsystematic basis. (22)

**Random factor analysis**   An analysis attempting to attribute erratic sales variations to random, nonrecurrent events. (10)

**Random sampling**   A type of probability sampling in which all units in a population have an equal chance of appearing in the sample. (9)

**Raw materials**   Basic natural materials that become part of a physical product. (11)

**Realized strategy**   The strategy that actually takes place. (2)

**Rebate**   A sales promotion technique in which a consumer receives a specified amount of money for making a single product purchase. (20)

**Receiver**   The individual, group, or organization that decodes a coded message. (18)

**Recession**   A stage of the business cycle during which unemployment rises and total buying power declines, stifling both consumer and business spending. (3)

**Reciprocity**   An arrangement unique to business marketing in which two organizations agree to buy from each other. (6)

**Recognition test**   A posttest in which respondents are shown the actual ad and asked if they recognize it. (19)

**Recovery**   A stage of the business cycle in which the economy moves from recession or depression toward prosperity. (3)

**Recruiting**   Developing a list of qualified applicants for sales positions. (20)

**Reference group**   A group that a person identifies with so strongly that he or she adopts the values, attitudes, and behavior of group members. (5)

**Reference pricing**   Pricing a product at a moderate level and positioning it next to a more expensive model or brand. (22)

**Regional issues**   Versions of a magazine that differ across geographic regions. (19)

**Regional shopping center**   A type of shopping center with large department stores, the wide product mix, and the deep product lines of all shopping centers. (17)

**Regression analysis**   A method of predicting sales based on finding a relationship between past sales and one or more independent variables, such as population or income. (10)

**Reinforcement advertising**   Advertising that assures users they chose the right brand and tells them how to get the most satisfaction from it. (19)

**Relationship marketing**   Establishing long-term, mutually satisfying buyer-seller relationships. (1)

**Relationship selling**   The building of mutually beneficial long-term associations with a customer through regular communications over prolonged periods of time. (20)

**Reliability**   A condition existing when a research technique produces almost identical results in repeated trials. (9)

**Reminder advertising**   Advertising used to remind consumers about an established brand's uses, characteristics, and benefits. (19)

**Research design**   An overall plan for obtaining the information needed to address a research problem or issue. (9)

**Reseller markets**   Intermediaries that buy finished goods and resell them for profit. (6)

**Retailer**   An organization that purchases products for the purpose of reselling them to ultimate consumers. (17)

**Retailing**   All transactions in which the buyer intends to consume the product through personal, family, or household use. (17)

**Retail positioning**   Identifying an unserved or underserved market segment and serving it through a strategy that distinguishes the retailer from others in the minds of consumers in that segment. (17)

**Role**   Actions and activities that a person in a particular position is supposed to perform based on expectations of the individual and surrounding persons. (5)

**Routinized response behavior**   A consumer problem-solving process used when buying frequently purchased, low-cost items that require very little search-and-decision effort. (5)

**Sales force forecasting survey**   A survey of a firm's sales force regarding anticipated sales in their territories for a specified period. (10)

**Sales forecast**   The amount of a product a company expects to sell during a specific period at a specified level of marketing activities. (10)

**Sales office**   A manufacturer-owned operation that provides services normally associated with agents. (16)

**Sales promotion**   An activity and/or material intended to induce resellers or salespeople to sell a product or consumers to buy it. (20)

**Sample**   A limited number of units chosen to represent the characteristics of a total population. (9)

**Sampling**   The process of selecting representative units from a total population. (9)

**Scan-back allowance**   A manufacturer's reward to retailers based on the number of pieces scanned. (20)

**Scrambled merchandising**   The addition of unrelated products and product lines to an existing product mix, particularly fast-moving items that can be sold in volume. (17)

**Screening**   Selecting the ideas with the greatest potential for further review. (12)

**Search qualities**   Tangible attributes that can be judged before the purchase of a product. (14)

**Seasonal analysis**   An analysis of daily, weekly, or monthly sales figures to evaluate the degree to which seasonal factors influence sales. (10)

**Seasonal discount**   A price reduction given to buyers for purchasing goods or services out of season. (21)

**Secondary-market pricing**   Setting one price for the primary target market and a different price for another market. (22)

**Segmentation variables**   Characteristics of individuals, groups, or organizations used to divide a market into segments. (10)

**Selective demand**   Demand for a specific brand. (18)

**Selective distortion**   An individual's changing or twisting of information that is inconsistent with personal feelings or beliefs. (5)

**Selective distribution**   Using only some available outlets to distribute a product. (15)

**Selective exposure**   The process by which some inputs are selected to reach awareness and others are not. (5)

**Selective retention**   Remembering information inputs that support personal feelings and beliefs and forgetting inputs that do not. (5)

**Self-concept**   A perception or view of oneself. (5)

**Selling agent**   An intermediary that markets a whole product line or a manufacturer's entire output. (16)

**Service**   An intangible result of the application of human and mechanical efforts to people or objects. (11)

**Service quality**   Customers' perception of how well a service meets or exceeds their expectations. (14)

**Shopping mall intercept interviews**   A research method that involves interviewing a percentage of individuals passing by "intercept" points in a mall. (9)

**Shopping products**   Items for which buyers are willing to expend considerable effort in planning and making purchases. (11)

**Single-source data**   Information provided by a single marketing research firm. (9)

**Situational influences**   Influences resulting from circumstances, time, and location that affect the consumer buying decision process. (5)

**Social class**   An open group of individuals with similar social rank. (5)

**Social influences**   The forces other people exert on one's buying behavior. (5)

**Social responsibility**   An organization's obligation to maximize its positive impact and minimize its negative impact on society. (4)

**Sociocultural forces**   The influences in a society and its culture(s) that change people's attitudes, beliefs, norms, customs, and lifestyles. (3)

**Sole sourcing**   An organization's decision to use only one supplier. (6)

**Source**   A person, group, or organization with a meaning it tries to share with a receiver or an audience. (18)

**Special-event pricing**   Advertised sales or price cutting linked to a holiday, a season, or an event. (22)

**Specialty-line wholesaler**   A full-service wholesaler that carries only a single product line or a few items within a product line. (16)

**Specialty products**   Items with unique characteristics that buyers are willing to expend considerable effort to obtain. (11)

**Stakeholders**   Constituents who have a "stake" or claim in some aspect of a company's products, operations, markets, industry, and outcomes. (1)

**Statistical interpretation**   Analysis of what is typical or what deviates from the average. (9)

**Storyboard**   A blueprint combining copy and visual material to show the sequence of major scenes in a commercial. (19)

**Straight commission compensation plan**   Paying salespeople according to the amount of their sales in a given time period. (20)

**Straight rebuy purchase**   A routine purchase of the same products by a business buyer. (6)

**Straight salary compensation plan**   Paying salespeople a specific amount per time period, regardless of selling effort. (20)

**Strategic alliances** A partnership formed to create a competitive advantage on a worldwide basis. (7)

**Strategic business unit (SBU)** A division, product line, or other profit center within the parent company. (2)

**Strategic channel alliance** An agreement whereby the products of one organization are distributed through the marketing channels of another. (15)

**Strategic philanthropy** The synergistic use of organizational core competencies and resources to address key stakeholders' interests and achieve both organizational and social benefits. (4)

**Strategic windows** Temporary periods of optimal fit between the key requirements of a market and the particular capabilities of a firm competing in that market. (2)

**Styling** The physical appearance of a product. (12)

**Subcultures** A group of individuals whose characteristic values and behavior patterns are similar and different from those of the surrounding culture. (5)

**Supermarket** A large, self-service store that carries a complete line of food products, along with some nonfood products. (17)

**Superregional shopping center** A type of shopping center with the largest department stores, the widest product mix, and the deepest product lines of all shopping centers. (17)

**Superstore** A giant retail outlet that carries food and nonfood products found in supermarkets, as well as most routinely purchased consumer products. (17)

**Supply chain management** Long-term partnerships among marketing channel members that reduce inefficiencies, costs, and redundancies and develop innovative approaches to satisfy customers. (15)

**Support personnel** Sales staff members who facilitate selling but usually are not involved solely with making sales. (20)

**Sustainable competitive advantage** An advantage that the competition cannot copy. (2)

**SWOT analysis** Assessment of an organization's strengths, weaknesses, opportunities, and threats. (2)

**Tactile communication** Communicating through touching. (18)

**Target audience** The group of people at whom advertisements are aimed. (19)

**Target market** A specific group of customers on whom an organization focuses its marketing efforts. (1)

**Target public** A collective of individuals who have an interest in or concern about an organization, product, or social cause. (14)

**Team selling** The use of a team of experts from all functional areas of a firm, led by a salesperson, to conduct the personal selling process. (20)

**Technical salespeople** Support salespeople who give technical assistance to a firm's current customers. (20)

**Technology** The application of knowledge and tools to solve problems and perform tasks more efficiently. (3)

**Telemarketing** The performance of marketing-related activities by telephone. (17)

**Telephone depth interview** An interview that combines the traditional focus group's ability to probe with the confidentiality provided by telephone surveys. (9)

**Telephone survey** A research method in which respondents' answers to a questionnaire are recorded by an interviewer on the phone. (9)

**Television home shopping** A form of selling in which products are presented to television viewers, who can buy them by calling a toll-free number and paying with a credit card. (17)

**Test marketing** A limited introduction of a product in geographic areas chosen to represent the intended market. (12)

**Total budget competitors** Firms that compete for the limited financial resources of the same customers. (3)

**Total cost** The sum of average fixed and average variable costs times the quantity produced. (21)

**Total quality management (TQM)** A philosophy that uniform commitment to quality in all areas of the organization will promote a culture that meets customers' perceptions of quality. (2)

**Trade (functional) discount** A reduction off the list price a producer gives to an intermediary for performing certain functions. (21)

**Trademark** A legal designation of exclusive use of a brand. (13)

**Trade name** The full legal name of an organization. (13)

**Trade salespeople** Salespeople involved mainly in helping a producer's customers promote a product. (20)

**Trade sales promotion methods** Methods intended to persuade wholesalers and retailers to carry a producer's products and market them aggressively. (20)

**Trading company** A company that links buyers and sellers in different countries. (7)

**Traditional specialty retailer** A store that carries a narrow product mix with deep product lines. (17)

**Transfer pricing** Prices charged in sales between an organization's units. (21)

**Transportation** The movement of products from where they are made to where they are used. (16)

**Trend analysis** An analysis that focuses on aggregate sales data over a period of many years to determine general trends in annual sales. (10)

**Truck wholesaler** A limited-service wholesaler that transports products directly to customers for inspection and selection. (16)

**Tying agreement** An agreement in which a supplier furnishes a product to a channel member with the stipulation that the channel member must purchase other products as well. (15)

**Unaided recall test** A posttest in which respondents are asked to identify ads they have recently seen but are given no recall clues. (19)

**Undifferentiated targeting strategy** A strategy in which an organization defines an entire market for a particular product as its target market, designs a single marketing mix, and directs it at that market. (10)

**Uniform geographic pricing** Charging all customers the same price, regardless of geographic location. (21)

**Universal product code (UPC)** A series of electronically readable lines identifying a product and containing inventory and pricing information. (13)

**Unsought products** Products purchased to solve a sudden problem, products of which customers are unaware, and products that people do not necessarily think of buying. (11)

**Validity** A condition existing when a research method measures what it is supposed to measure. (9)

**Value** A customer's subjective assessment of benefits relative to costs in determining the worth of a product. (1)

**Value analysis** An evaluation of each component of a potential purchase. (6)

**Value conscious** Concerned about price and quality of a product. (21)

**Variable costs** Costs that vary directly with changes in the number of units produced or sold. (21)

**Vendor analysis** A formal, systematic evaluation of current and potential vendors. (6)

**Vertical channel integration** Combining two or more stages of the marketing channel under one management. (15)

**Vertical marketing systems (VMSs)** A marketing channel managed by a single channel member to achieve efficient, low-cost distribution aimed at satisfying target market customers. (15)

**Viral marketing** A strategy to get Internet users to share ads and promotions with their friends. (18)

**Warehouse club** A large-scale, members-only establishment that combines features of cash-and-carry wholesaling with discount retailing. (17)

**Warehouse showroom** A retail facility in a large, low-cost building with large on-premise inventories and minimal services. (17)

**Warehousing** The design and operation of facilities for storing and moving goods. (16)

**Wealth** The accumulation of past income, natural resources, and financial resources. (3)

**Wheel of retailing** A hypothesis holding that new retailers usually enter the market as low-status, low-margin, low-price operators but eventually evolve into high-cost, high-price merchants. (17)

**Wholesaler** An individual or organization that sells products that are bought for resale, for making other products, or for general business operations. (16)

**Wholesaling** Transactions in which products are bought for resale, for making other products, or for general business operations. (16)

**Width of product mix** The number of product lines a company offers. (11)

**Willingness to spend** An inclination to buy because of expected satisfaction from a product, influenced by the ability to buy and numerous psychological and social forces. (3)

**Word-of-mouth communication** Personal informal exchanges of communication that customers share with one another about products, brands, and companies. (18)

**World Trade Organization (WTO)** An entity that promotes free trade among member nations by eliminating trade barriers and educating individuals, companies, and governments about trade rules around the world. (7)

**Zone pricing** Pricing based on transportation costs within major geographic zones. (21)

## Chapter 1

1. Burt Helm, "The Sport of Extreme Marketing," *Business Week*, Mar. 14, 2005; Kerry A. Dolan, "The Soda with Buzz," *Forbes*, Mar. 28, 2005; Kathryn Masterson, "Crank Juice—As Energy Drinks Gain on Sodas in THR Market Selection Grows Too," *Chicago Tribune*, Dec. 5, 2005.
2. *Marketing News*, Sept. 15, 2004, p. 1.
3. Julie Schlosser, "DeWalt," in "Breakaway Brands," *Fortune*, Oct. 31, 2005, pp. 156–158.
4. Mark Jewell, "Dunkin' Donuts Eyes Turn Westward: Chain Evolves from No Frills," The [Fort Collins] *Coloradoan*, Jan. 17, 2005, p. E1.
5. Tom Lowry, "Wow! Yao!" *Business Week*, Oct. 25, 2004, pp. 86–90.
6. Kelly K. Spors, "Beyond Flowers: New Funeral Options Proliferate," *The Wall Street Journal*, Oct. 19, 2005, p. D2, http://online.wsj.com/public/us.
7. Jane Spencer, "Getting Your Health Care at Wal-Mart," *The Wall Street Journal*, Oct. 5, 2005, p. D1, http://online.wsj.com/public/us.
8. James Tenser, "Endorser Qualities Count More Than Ever," *Advertising Age*, Nov. 8, 2004, pp. S-2, S-4.
9. Eric Bontrager, "U.S. to Consumers: Turn Down Heat," *The Wall Street Journal*, Oct. 4, 2005, p. D2, http://online.wsj.com/public/us; Matthew L. Wald, "Shifting Message, Energy Officials Announce Conservation Plan," *The New York Times*, Oct. 4, 2005, http://www.nytimes.com/.
10. Lorrie Grant, "Scrimping to Splurge," *USA Today*, Jan. 28, 2005, p. 1B.
11. Chad Terhune, "Pepsi Outlines Ad Campaign for Healthy Food," *The Wall Street Journal*, Oct. 15, 2005, p. A4, http://online.wsj.com/public/us.
12. John Thaw, "Why Sharper Image Is Playing the Hits Again," *Business 2.0*, Nov. 2003, pp. 64–66.
13. Ajay K. Kohli and Bernard J. Jaworski, "Market Orientation: The Construct, Research Propositions, and Managerial Implications," *Journal of Marketing*, Apr. 1990, pp. 1–18; O. C. Ferrell, "Business Ethics and Customer Stakeholders," *Academy of Management Executive* 18 (May 2004): 126–129.
14. Eugene W. Anderson, Claes Fornell, and Sanal K. Mazvancheryl, "Customer Satisfaction and Shareholder Value," *Journal of Marketing* 68 (Oct. 2004): 172–185.
15. Kohli and Jaworski, "Market Orientation."
16. Kwaku Atuahene-Gima, "Resolving the Capability-Rigidity Paradox in New Product Innovation," *Journal of Marketing* 69 (Oct. 2005): 61–83.
17. Sunil Gupta, Donald R. Lehmann, and Jennifer Ames Stuart, "Valuing Customers," *Journal of Marketing Research 41* (Feb. 2004): 7–18.
18. Jean Halliday, "Nissan Delves into Truck Owner Psyche," *Advertising Age*, Dec. 1, 2003, p. 11.
19. Alan Grant and Leonard Schlesinger, "Realize Your Customers' Full Profit Potential," *Harvard Business Review*, Sept./Oct.

1995, p. 59; Peter C. Verhoef, "Understanding the Effect of Customer Relationship Management Efforts on Customer Retention and Customer Share Development," *Journal of Marketing*, Oct. 2003, p. 30.
20. Jagdish N. Sheth and Rajendras Sisodia, "More Than Ever Before, Marketing Is Under Fire to Account for What It Spends," *Marketing Management*, Fall 1995, pp. 13–14.
21. Lynette Ryals and Adrian Payne, "Customer Relationship Management in Financial Services: Towards Information-Enabled Relationship Marketing," *Journal of Strategic Marketing*, Mar. 2001, p. 3.
22. O. C. Ferrell and Michael Hartline, *Marketing Strategy* (Mason, OH: South-Western, 2005), p. 114.
23. Roland T. Rust, Katherine N. Lemon, and Valarie A. Zeithaml, "Return on Marketing: Using Customer Equity to Focus Marketing Strategy," *Journal of Marketing* 68 (Jan. 2004): 109–127.
24. Rajkumar Venkatesan and V. Kumar, "A Customer Lifetime Value Framework for Customer Selection and Resource Allocation Strategy," *Journal of Marketing* 68 (Oct. 2004): 106–125.
25. Ryals and Payne, "Customer Relationship Management in Financial Services," pp. 3–27.
26. Natalie Mizik and Robert Jacobson, "Trading Off Between Value Creation and Value Appropriation: The Financial Implications of Shifts in Strategic Emphasis," *Journal of Marketing*, Jan. 2003, pp. 63–76.
27. Ferrell and Hartline, *Marketing Strategy*, p. 104.
28. "Kids' Food Pyramid Launched," CNN, Sept. 28, 2005, http://www.cnn.com./
29. "Charitable Giving Rises Nearly 5 Percent to Nearly $250 Billion in 2004," Giving USA, American Association of Fundraising Counsel, press release, June 14, 2005, http://www.aafrc.org/press_releases/index.cfm?pg=trustreleases/tsunamigifts.html.
30. Steve Lohr, "Is IBM's Lenovo Proposal a Threat to National Security?" *The New York Times*, Jan. 31, 2005, www.nytimes.com.
31. Keith Regan, "Report: Online Sales Top $100 Billion," *E-Commerce Times*, June 1, 2004, www.ecommercetimes.com/story/34148.html.
32. "A Perfect Fit: Staples and Kids in Need," *Chain Store Age*, Oct. 2005, p. 78.
33. Sources: Thomas Caywood, "Bagel Company Finagles Hollow New Idea," *The Boston Herald*, Jan. 6, 2005, via LexisNexis; Donna Hood Crecca, "Higher Calling," Chain Leader, Dec. 2002, p. 14; Finagle a Bagel, www.finagleabagel.com (accessed Apr. 13, 2005); "Finagle Sees a Return to More Normal Business Mode," *Foodservice East*, Fall 2002, pp. 1, 17; "Sloan Grads Bet Their Money on Bagels," *Providence Business News*, Oct. 25, 1999, p. 14; "State Fare: Finagle A Bagel, Boston," *Restaurants and Institutions*, Oct. 1, 2002, www.rimag.com/1902/sr.htm; interview with Laura B. Trust and Alan Litchman, Feb. 25, 2003.

34. Sources: "A Brief History of CART and Champ Car Racing," *Fullspeed Database*, Feb. 17, 2003, www.fsdb.net/champcar/history/index.htm; "Champ Car Announces Management Changes," Motorsport.com, July 16, 2005, www.motorsport.com/news/article.asp?ID=197605&FS=BUSINESS; "Champ Car Team Owner and Legendary Actor Paul Newman Partners with Friend and Fellow Racer Eddie Wachs to Form Newman/Wachs Racing Atlantic Team," Champ Car World Series, Nov. 4, 2005, www.champcarworldseries.com/News/Article.asp?ID=9816; Mark Cipollini, "Branding CART and Their Race Cars," AutoRacing1.com, Nov. 9, 2000, www.autoracing1.com/MarkC/001109Branding.htm; Daniel Kaplan, "CART Tries Turnaround," *Sports Business Journal*, www.sportsbusinessjournal.com/article.cms?articleId=26881&s=1; Robin Miller, "New Owners Could Focus on Streets," RPM//espn.go.com/rpm/cart/2003/0810/159430.html; Robin Miller, "Pook Looking to Privatize Company," RPM//espn.go.com/rpm/cart/2003/0615/1568383.html; "Open Wheel Racing Series Pursues the Acquisition of Championship Auto Racing Teams," *Champ Car News*, Sept. 18, 2003, www.cart.com/News/Article.asp?ID=7058&print=true; Chapman Rackaway, "Eccelstone to the Rescue?" *Racing News Online*, Oct. 23, 2002, www.racingnewsonline.com/story.do?id=55630; "Sherman-Williams Brings Colorful New Outlook to Partnership with Champ Car World Series and Champ Car Atlantic Series," Champ Car World Series, press release, Nov. 2, 2005, www.champcarworldseries.com/News/Article.asp?ID=9814; "State of the Series: Steve Johnson," Champ Car World Series, Sept. 20, 2005, www.champcarworldseries.com/News/Article.asp?ID=9665; Bob Zeller, "CART vs. IRL: Who Won the War?" *Car and Driver Online*, Feb. 2004, www.caranddriver.com/article.asp?section_id=4&article_id=7719&page_numbers=1. Don Roy, Middle Tennessee State University, assisted in the preparation of this case.

## Chapter 2

1. "It's Saturday Morning All the Time," CNN, Nov. 4, 2005, www.cnn.com/2005/US/08/12/cereality/index.html; Joann Louiglio, "Totally Cereal-ous: All-Cereal Restaurant," *The [Fort Collins] Coloradoan*, Dec. 2004, pp. E1, E2; Cereality, www.cereality.com (accessed Apr. 13, 2006); "A Cereal Store for Cereal (Seriously)," *Business 2.0*, Oct. 2004, p. 42; "Carb Appeal," *Fortune Small Business*, Oct. 2004, p. 28.
2. O. C. Ferrell and Michael Hartline, *Marketing Strategy* (Mason, OH: South-Western, 2005), p. 10.
3. Christian Homburg, Karley Krohmer, and John P. Workman, Jr., "A Strategy Implementation Perspective of Market Orientation," *Journal of Business Research*, 57 (2004): 1331–1340.
4. Ferrell and Hartline, *Marketing Strategy*.
5. Abraham Lustgarten, "iPod," in "Breakaway Brands," *Fortune*, Oct. 31, 2005, pp. 154–156.
6. J. Chris White, P. Rajan Varadarajan, and Peter A. Dacin, "Market Situation Interpretation and Response: The Role of Cognitive Style, Organizational Culture, and Information Use," *Journal of Marketing*, July 2003, pp. 63–79.
7. Ferrell and Hartline, *Marketing Strategy*, p. 51.
8. Graham J. Hooley, Gordon E. Greenley, John W. Cadogan, and John Fahy, "The Performance Impact of Marketing Resources," *Journal of Business Research*, 58 (2005): 18–27.
9. Steven Gray, "Wendy's Stumbles with Baja Fresh," *The Wall Street Journal*, Jan. 4, 2005, p. B7, http://online.wsj.com/public/us.
10. Derek F. Abell, "Strategic Windows," *Journal of Marketing*, July 1978, p. 21.
11. Michael Krauss, "EBay 'Bids' on Small-Biz Firms to Sustain Growth," *Marketing News*, Dec. 8, 2003, p. 6.
12. Catherine Yang with Jay Green, "You've Got Mail—But Not Enough Ads," *Business Week*, Oct. 25, 2004, p. 48.
13. Ibid.
14. Michael McCarthy, "CD Prices Hit Sour Note with Retail Buyers," *USA Today*, Dec. 2003, pp. 1B, 2B.
15. Ibid.
16. Douglas Bowman and Hubert Gatignon, "Determinants of Competitor Response Time to a New Product Introduction," *Journal of Marketing Research*, Feb. 1995, pp. 42–53.
17. Chuck Salter, "Ford's Escape Route," *Fast Company*, Oct. 2004, www.fastcompany.com/magazine/87/ford.html.
18. "Our Mission," *Celestial Seasonings*, www.celestialseasonings.com/whoweare/corporatehistory/mission.php (accessed Apr. 13, 2006).
19. Cláudia Simões, Sally Dibb, and Raymond P. Fisk, "Managing Corporate Identity," *Journal of the Academy of Marketing Science*, 33 (Apr. 2005):154–168.
20. Peter Asmus, "17th Annual Business Ethics Awards," *Business Ethics*, Fall 2005, pp. 18–20.
21. Laurence G. Weinzimmer, Edward U. Bond III, Mark B. Houston, and Paul C.Nystrom, "Relating Marketing Expertise on the Top Management Team and Strategic Market Aggressiveness to Financial Performance and Shareholder Value," *Journal of Strategic Marketing*, June 2003, pp. 133–159.
22. "Sara Lee Sells Coffee Business," *The Wall Street Journal*, Oct. 26, 2005, http://online.wsj.com/public/us.
23. Thomas Ritter and Hans Georg Gemünden, "The Impact of a Company's Business Strategy on Its Technological Competence, Network Competence and Innovation Success," *Journal of Business Research*, 57 (2004): 548–556.
24. Jean L. Johnson, Ruby Pui-Wan Lee, Amit Saini, and Bianca Grohmann, "Market-Focused Flexibility: Conceptual Advances and an Integrative Model," *Journal of the Academy of Marketing Science*, 31, no. 1 (2003):74–89.
25. Information Resouces, Inc., reported in Stephanie Thompson, "Nestlé, Hershey Figure Sticks Will Be Big Sellers," *Advertising Age*, Oct. 3, 2005, p. 3.
26. Robert D. Buzzell, "The PIMS Program of Strategy Research: A Retrospective Appraisal," *Journal of Business Research*, 57 (2004): 478–483.
27. George S. Day, "Diagnosing the Product Portfolio," *Journal of Marketing*, Apr. 1977, pp. 30–31.
28. Isabelle Maignan, O. C. Ferrell, and Linda Ferrell, "A Stakeholder Model for Implementing Social Responsibility in Marketing," *European Journal of Marketing*, 39 (Sept./Oct. 2005): 956–977.
29. Coca-Cola 2004 Annual Report, www2.coca-cola.com/investors/annualandotherreports/2004/pdf/Coca-Cola_10-K_Item_01.pdf (accessed Apr. 13, 2006).
30. Kate MacCarthur, "Franchisees Turn on Crispin's King," *Advertising Age*, Oct. 24, 2005, pp. 1, 42.
31. M. Fry and Michael J. Polonsky, "Examining the Unintended Consequences of Marketing," *Journal of Business Research*, 57 (2005):1303–1306.
32. Maignan, Ferrell, and Ferrell, "A Stakeholder Model for Implementing Social Responsibility in Marketing."
33. G. Tomas, M. Hult, David W. Cravens, and Jagdish Sheth, "Competitive Advantage in the Global Marketplace: A Focus on Marketing Strategy," *Journal of Business Research*, Jan. 2001, pp. 1–3.
34. Kwaku Atuahene-Gima and Janet Y. Murray, "Antecedents and Outcomes of Marketing Strategy Comprehensiveness," *Journal of Marketing*, 68 (Oct. 2004): 33–46.

35. "The Echo Boomers," 60 Minutes, Oct. 3, 2004, CBSNews.com; Michael J. Weiss, "To Be About to Be," *American Demographics*, Sept. 2003, pp. 28–36.
36. Nancy Einhart, "How the New T-Bird Went Off Course," *Business 2.0*, Nov. 2003, pp. 74–76.
37. Christian Homburg, John P. Workman, and Ove Jensen, "Fundamental Changes in Marketing Organization: The Movement Toward a Customer-Focused Organizational Structure," *Journal of the Academy of Marketing Science*, Fall 2000, pp. 459–478.
38. Weiss, "To Be About to Be," pp. 28–36.
39. Rajdeep Grewal and Patriya Tansuhaj, "The Chain of Effects from Brand Trust and Brand Affect to Brand Performance: The Role of Brand Loyalty," *Journal of Marketing*, Apr. 2001, pp. 67–80.
40. Steve Watkins, "Marketing Basics: The Four P's Are as Relevant Today as Ever," *Investor's Business Daily*, Feb. 4, 2002, p. A1.
41. Bent Dreyer and Kjell Grønhaug, "Uncertainty, Flexibility, and Sustained Competitive Advantage," *Journal of Business Research 57* (2004): 484–494.
42. Hemant C. Sashittat and Avan R. Jassawalla, "Marketing Implementation in Smaller Organizations: Definition, Framework, and Propositional Inventory," *Journal of the Academy of Marketing Science*, Winter 2001, pp. 50–69.
43. Ferrell and Hartline, *Marketing Strategy*, p. 257.
44. Weiss, "To Be About to Be," pp. 28–36.
45. Adapted from Nigel F. Piercy, *Market-Led Change* (Newton, MA: Butterworth, Heinemann, 1992), pp. 374–385.
46. Ian N. Lings, "Internal Market Orientation: Construct and Consequences," *Journal of Business Research*, 57 (2004): 405–413.
47. Sybil F. Stershic, "Internal Marketing Campaign Reinforces Service Goals," *Marketing News*, July 31, 1998, p. 11.
48. Kee-hung Lee and T. C. Edwin Cheng, "Effects of Quality Management and Marketing on Organizational Performance," *Journal of Business Research*, 58 (2005):446–456; Wuthichai Sittimalakorn and Susan Hart, "Market Orientation Versus Quality Orientation: Sources of Superior Business Performance," *Journal of Strategic Marketing*, 12 (Dec. 2004): 243–253.
49. Philip B. Crosby, Quality Is Free: *The Art of Making Quality Certain* (New York: McGraw-Hill, 1979), pp. 9–10.
50. Piercy, *Market-Led Change*.
51. Douglas W. Vorhies and Neil A. Morgan, "Benchmarketing Marketing Capabilities for Sustainable Competitive Advantage," *Journal of Marketing*, 69 (Jan. 2005): 80–94.
52. Kenneth W. Thomas and Betty A. Velthouse, "Cognitive Elements of Empowerment: An 'Interpretive' Model of Intrinsic Task Motivation," *Academy of Management Review*, Oct. 1990, pp. 666–681.
53. Ferrell and Hartline, *Marketing Strategy*.
54. Rohit Deshpande and Frederick E. Webster, Jr., "Organizational Culture and Marketing: Defining the Research Agenda," *Journal of Marketing*, Jan. 1989, pp. 3–15.
55. Kathleen Cholewka, "CRM: Lose the Hype and Strategize," *Sales & Marketing Management*, June 2001, pp. 27–28.
56. Eric M. Olson, Stanley F. Slater, and G. Tomas Hult, "The Performance Implications of Fit Among Business Strategy, Marketing Organization Structure, and Strategic Behavior," *Journal of Marketing*, 69 (July 2005):49–65.
57. Bernard J. Jaworski, "Toward a Theory of Marketing Control: Environmental Context, Control Types, and Consequences," *Journal of Marketing*, July 1988, pp. 23–39.
58. James R. Healey, "Hot, Fun, and Even Functional," *USA Today*, Nov. 26, 2004, p. 10D.
59. "Lincoln Continues to Break Records for Customer Satisfaction with Dealer Service," J. D. Powers & Associates, press release, July 20, 2005, www.jdpa.com/news/releases/pressrelease.asp?ID=2005092.
60. Brian Steinberg and Ann Zimmerman, "Lesson Learned, Wal-Mart Touts Lower Prices," *The Wall Street Journal*, Dec. 3, 2004, http://online.wsj.com/public/us.
61. Sources: "100 Best Corporate Citizens 2005," *Business Ethics*, Spring 2005, pp. 22–23; "200 Best Small Companies in America," *Forbes*, Oct. 14, 2005, www.forbes.com/lists/2005/23/GMAE.html; Green Mountain Coffee, www.greenmountaincoffee.com (accessed Apr. 13, 2006); Green Mountain Coffee Annual Report 10-K; "Green Mountain Coffee Roasters," Hoover's Online, www.hoovers.com/green-mountain-coffee/—ID__45721—/free-co-factsheet.xhtml?cm_ven=PAID&cm_cat=BUS&cm_pla=CO1&cm_ite=Green_Mountain_Coffee_Roasters_Inc (accessed Apr. 13, 2006).
62. Sources: "Greg Brenneman, Chairman and Chief Executive Officer, Burger King Corporation," Burger King Corporation, www.bk.com/CompanyInfo/bk_corporation/executive_team/brenneman.aspx (accessed Jan. 31, 2006); "Global Fact Sheet," Burger King, www.bk.com/CompanyInfo/bk_corporation/fact_sheets/global_facts.aspx (accessed Apr. 13, 2006); Bruce Horovitz, "CEO Turns the Flame Up," *USA Today*, May 23, 2005, p. 3B; Kate MacArthur, "Franchisees Turn on Crispin's King," *Advertising Age*, Oct. 24, 2005, pp. 1, 42; Elaine Walker, "Whopper of a Recovery?" *The Kansas City Star*, Sept. 24, 2005, pp. C-1, C-2.
63. Sources: Kate MacArthur, "Visa, FedEx Pony Up For Future Fund," *Advertising Age*, Nov. 14, 2005, pp. 1, 37; Ellen Florian Kratz, "For FedEx, It was Time to Deliver," *Fortune*, Oct. 3, 2005, p. 65; "Pass the Parcel," *Economist*, Feb. 11, 2006, p. 61; Robert W. Mooman, "The IT Traffic Solution," *Air Transport World*, Sep. 2005, p. 58; Patricia Sellers, "Bigger and BIGGER," *Fortune*, Sep. 5, 2005, pp. 104–107; "BW50: Delivering the Goods at FedEx," *Business Week Online*, June 13, 2005, www.businessweek.com; "DHL/Airborne Deal Could Shake Up U.S. Express Market," Logistics Management, Apr. 1, 2003, www.manufacturing.net; FedEx Corporation, 2003 Annual Report; FedEx Corporation, www.fedex.com (accessed Jan. 24, 2006); "FedEx to Buy Kinko's for $2.4B," CNN/Money, Dec. 30, 2003, http://money.cnn.com; "FedEx to Create Shanghai Hub Office," *AirWise News*, Oct. 24, 2003, http://news.airwise.com; "FedEx Ground Opens 'Super Hub,'" *Transportation & Distribution*, Nov. 2000, pp. 12–13; Kristin S. Krause, "Handling the Holiday Crush," *Traffic World*, Dec. 4, 2000, p. 33; Betsy McKay and Rick Brooks, "FedEx Will Buy Kinko's for $2.4 Billion in Cash," *The Wall Street Journal*, Dec. 30, 2003, http://online.wsj.com; Theo Mullen, "Delivery Wars Go High-Tech—FedEx Ground Sends Message with $80M Investment to Improve Package Tracking," *Internetweek*, Oct. 23, 2000, p. 18; Jayne O'Donnell, "FedEx–Postal Service Alliance Delivers Goods," *USA Today Online*, Jan. 11, 2001, www.usatoday.com/; "Post Office, FedEx to Work Together," *USA Today Online*, Jan. 10, 2001, www.usatoday.com/; Monica Roman, "FedEx Hitches Up a New Trucker," *Business Week*, Nov. 27, 2000, p. 66; Marc L. Songini, "FedEx Expects CRM System to Deliver," *Computerworld*, Nov. 6, 2000, p. 10; "UPS Wants Fed Probe into DHL–Airborne Deal," *San Francisco Business Times*, Mar. 27, 2003, www.bizjournals.com.

## Chapter 3

1. Shoemart, www.shoemart.com (accessed Jan. 22, 2006); "The Timberland Company CEO and CFO to Present at the Companies for Social Responsibility Investor Conference,"

*Business Wire*, Apr. 28, 2005, www.businesswire.com; "Any Company Can Create a Great Workplace, Our Mission Is to Help Them Do It," Great Place to Work Institute, www.greatplacetowork.com (accessed Jan.19, 2006); The Timberland Company, www.timberland.com (accessed Jan. 19, 2006).

2. Gina Chon, "Sales of SUVs Fall Sharply," *The Wall Street Journal*, Oct. 4, 2005, p. D1, http://online.wsj.com/public/us.

3. "U.S. Soft Drink Sales Flat in 2003, "Beverage Marketing Corporation Reports," Beverage Marketing Corporation, press release, Mar. 4, 2004, www.beveragemarketing.com/news2oo.htm.

4. O. C. Ferrell and Michael Hartline, *Marketing Strategy* (Mason, OH: South-Western, 2005), p. 58.

5. Ibid.

6. Rodolfo Vazquez, Maria Leticia Santos, and Luis Ignacio Álvarez, "Market Orientation, Innovation and Competitive Strategies in Industrial Firms," *Journal of Strategic Marketing*, Mar. 2001, pp. 69–90.

7. Eberhard Stickel, "Uncertainty Reduction in a Competitive Environment," *Journal of Business Research,* 51, no. 3 (2001): 169–177.

8. EContent, Nov. 2003, p. 23.

9. "Income Stable, Poverty Rate Increases, Percentage of Americans without Health Insurance Unchanged," U.S. Census Bureau, press release, Aug. 30, 2005, www.census.gov/Press-Release/www/releases/archives/income_wealth/005647.html.

10. Lorrie Grant, "Scrimping to Splurge," *USA Today*, Jan. 28, 2005, p. 1B.

11. Hall Dickler Kent Goldstein & Wood LLC, "Controversy over Food Advertising to Children," *AdLaw*, Oct. 20, 2003.

12. "Samsung Agrees to Plead Guilty and to Pay a $300 Million Criminal Fine for Role in Price Fixing Conspiracy, U.S. Department of Justice, press release, Oct. 13, 2005, www.usdoj.gov/atr/public/press_releases/2005/212002.htm; www.usdoj.gov/atr/public/press_releases/2003/201284.htm.

13. "Marketers of 'Smoke Away' Pay $1.3 Million to Settle FTC Charges," Federal Trade Commission, press release, Aug. 23, 2005, www.ftc.gov/opa/2005/08/emerson.htm.

14. "FTC Slams Pop-Up Spammer," *eWeek*, Nov. 6, 2003.

15. Sarah Ellison, "Why Kraft Decided to Ban Some Food Ads to Children," *The Wall Street Journal*, Oct. 31, 2005, p. A1, http://online.wsj.com/public/us.

16. Jeffrey Greenbaum, "Advertising Prescription Drugs?" *Shoot*, Oct. 7, 2005, p. 9.

17. David Tyler, "BBB Hangs Up on Cingular," *Rochester Democrat & Chronicle*, Sept. 10, 2005, www.rochesterdandc.com/apps/pbcs.dll/article?AID =/20050910/BUSINESS/509100309&SearchID =73220665966305.

18. "NAD Refers Advertising Claims by Aventis to the Government," National Advertising Division, press release, Oct. 4, 2004, www.nadreview.org.

19. Kate MacArthur, "Government to Mediate Vodka Ad Dispute; Grey Goose, Belvedere Fight Could Drag On," *Advertising Age*, Sept. 8, 2003, p. 92.

20. Chris Woodward, "Some Offices Opt for Cellphones Only," *USA Today*, Jan. 25, 2005, p. B1.

21. "New Subscribers to Telecom Services Continues Growing in 2005," Cellular-News.com, Oct. 5, 2005, www.cellular-news.com/story/12792.php.

22. Joseph Carroll, "Americans Inventory Their Gadgets," Gallup Poll News Service, Dec. 23, 2005.

23. Marcia A. Reed-Woodward, "Take the Work Home," *Black Enterprise*, Dec. 2005, p. 72.

24. Debbie McAlister, Linda Ferrell, and O. C. Ferrell, *Business and Society* (Boston: Houghton Mifflin, 2005), p. 85.

25. Ibid.

26. Ibid.

27. Vladimir Zwass, "Electronic Commerce: Structures and Issues," *International Journal of Electronic Commerce*, Fall 2000, pp. 3–23.

28. "Peace Corp. Seeks to Launch First PEO Business-to-Business Online Marketplace," *Business Wire*, July 31, 2003, p. 2086.

29. U.S. Bureau of the Census, Statistical Abstract of the United States, 2004 (Washington DC: Government Printing Office, 2005), p. 13.

30. Ibid., pp. 48, 51.

31. Ibid., p. 12.

32. Ibid., p. 8.

33. U.S. Bureau of the Census, "U.S. Interim Projections by Age, Sex, Race, and Hispanic Origin," Mar. 18, 2004, www.census.gov/ipc/www/usinterimproj/natprojtab01a.pdf.

34. Jeffrey M. Humphreys, "The Multicultural Economy 2005," Georgia Business and Economic Conditions 65 (Third Quarter, 2005), www.nmsdcus.org/infocenter/Multi_Cultural_economy05.pdf.

35. "Good Translations: Targeting a Multicultural Audience Takes More Than a Dictionary: It Takes Tact, Understanding, and Relevance," *PR Week*, Aug. 18, 2003.

36. Laura Clark Geist, "Big 3 Boost Effort to Win Minority Buyers; Growing Ethnic Groups Can Help Raise Market Share," *Automotive News*, Oct. 13, 2003.

37. William H. Redmond, "Intrusive Promotion as Market Failure: How Should Society Impact Marketing?" *Journal of Macromarketing* 25 (June 2005): 12–21.

38. Sources: Jennifer Soong, "The Sunshine Boys," *Worthwhile*, Premiere Issue 2004, p. 43; Thomas J. Ryan, "Lust for Life," *SBG*, Jan. 2006, p. 30; Jill Rose, "The Right Thing," *American Executive*, Aug. 2005; Rachel Bowie, "Good Feelings," *Boston Common*, Winter 2006, p. 62; Melonee McKinney Hurt, "Life is good.," *American Profile*, Oct.–Nov. 2005; Life is good., www.lifeisgood.com (accessed Apr. 13, 2006); Susan Reimer, "Brothers Spread Positive T-shirt Vibes," *Mail Tribune*, Sept. 1, 2005, Local Section; Brooke Donald, "Life is (Very) Good for Brothers Selling T-Shirts One at a Time," *USA Today*, July 9, 2005; Christopher O'Carroll, "It's Hip to be Happy," *UMass Magazine*, Fall 2004, www.umassmag.com.

39. Sources: "Frito-Lay Introduces New Lineup of Low-Carb Chips," *Long Island Business News*, Jan. 16, 2004; Theresa Howard, "Frito-Lay's New Stax to Take a Stand," *USA Today*, Aug. 15, 2003, p. 12B; Debbie Howell, "Good-for-You Munchies Best News in Snacks," *DSN Retailing Today*, Jan. 24, 2005, p. F6; Sonia Reyes, "Strategy: R-R-R-Ruffles Hopes Its Past Gives Future a Blast," *Brandweek*, June 23, 2003; "Snacking Now Made Easier with Frito-Lay's New Smart Snack Ribbon Label," PR Newswire, Aug. 5, 2003, www.prnewswire.com; Chad Terhune, "Frito-Lay to Refocus Marketing," *The Wall Street Journal*, Feb. 25, 2005, p. B3; Chad Terhune, "Pepsi Outlines Ad Campaign for Healthy Food," *The Wall Street Journal*, Oct. 15, 2005, p. A4; Stephanie Thompson, "Frito-Lay Defends Its Snack Turf Against all Comers, Salty or Sweet," *Advertising Age*, May 16, 2005, p. 16; Suzanne Vranica, "PepsiCo Sets Health-Snack Effort," *The Wall Street Journal*, Sept. 23, 2003, p. B6; Andrea K. Walker, "Potato-Chip Maker Now Targets 'Bad Fat,'" *FSView and Florida Flambeau*, Oct. 2, 2003; Judith Weinraub, "Getting the Fat Out," *Washington Post*, Nov. 12, 2003, p. F1.

## Chapter 4

1. Sources: Sarah Ellison, "Why Kraft Decided to Ban Some Food Ads to Children," *The Wall Street Journal*, Oct. 31, 2005, p. A1, http://online.wsj.com/public/us; Sarah Ellison and Janet Adamy, "Panel Faults Food Packaging for Kid Obesity,"

*The Wall Street Journal*, Dec. 7, 2005, http://online.wsj.com/public/us; "Kaiser Family Foundation Releases New Report on Role of Media in Childhood Obesity," Kaiser Family Foundation, press release, Feb. 24, 2004, www.kff.org/entmedia/entmedia022404nr.cfm; "Supersizing Europeans," in William M. Pride and O. C. Ferrell, *Foundations of Marketing*, 2nd ed. (Boston: Houghton Mifflin, 2006), p. 122; Melanie Warner, "Under Pressure, Food Producers Shift to Healthier Products," *The New York Times*, Dec. 16, 2005, www.nytimes.com.

2. Isabelle Maignan and O. C. Ferrell, "Corporate Social Responsibility and Marketing: An Integrative Framework," *Journal of the Academy of Marketing Science* 32 (Jan. 2004): 3–19.

3. Alex Berenson, "Big Drug Makers See Sales Decline with Their Image," *The New York Times*, Nov. 14, 2005, www.nytimes.com; "Report: Merck Aware of Vioxx Problems," *The Austin American-Statesman*, Nov. 2, 2004, http://statesman.com.

4. "About Avon," Avon, www.avoncompany.com/about/ (accessed Apr. 13, 2006); "The Avon Breast Cancer Crusade," Avon, www.avoncompany.com/women/avoncrusade/index.html (accessed Apr. 13, 2006).

5. Isabelle Maignan and O. C. Ferrell, "Antecedents and Benefits of Corporate Citizenship: An Investigation of French Businesses," *Journal of Business Research* 51, no. 1 (2001): 37–51.

6. Debbie McAlister, Linda Ferrell, and O. C. Ferrell, *Business and Society: A Strategic Approach to Social Responsibility* (Boston: Houghton Mifflin, 2005), pp. 38–40.

7. O. C. Ferrell, "Business Ethics and Customer Stakeholders," *Academy of Management Executive* 18 (May 2004): 126–129.

8. "Corporate Citizenship Report 2003–2004," Ford Motor Company, www.ford.com/en/company/about/corporateCitizenship/report/ (accessed Apr. 13, 2006).

9. Archie Carroll, "The Pyramid of Corporate Social Responsibility: Toward the Moral Management of Organizational Stake-holders," *Business Horizons*, July/Aug. 1991, p. 42.

10. William T. Neese, Linda Ferrell, and O. C. Ferrell, "An Analysis of Federal Mail and Wire Fraud Cases Related to Marketing," *Journal of Business Research* 58 (2005): 910–918.

11. Suzanne Sataline, "Office Depot Sues Staples over Ads Placed on Google," *The Wall Street Journal*, Oct. 21, 2005, http://online.wsj.com/public/us.

12. "2004 Contributions: $248.52 Billion by Source of Contributions," Giving USA, American Association of Fundraising Counsel, chart, www.aafrc.org/gusa/chartbysource.html (accessed Apr. 13, 2006).

13. Jessica Stannard-Friel, "Corporate Giving Responds to Hurricane Katrina," onPhilanthropy, Aug. 30, 2005, www.onphilanthropy.com/onthescene/os2005-08-30.html.

14. "American Express Launches Nationwide Campaign to Help Raise Awareness and Funds for St. Jude Children's Research Hospital," American Express, press release, Nov. 17, 2004, www.findarticles.com/p/articles/mi_m0EIN/is_2004_Nov_17/ai_n6363419.

15. Barbara A. Lafferty, Ronald E. Goldsmith, and G. Tomas M. Hult, "The Impact of the Alliance on the Partners: A Look at Cause-Brand Alliances," *Psychology & Marketing* 21, no. 7 (July 2004): 509–531, via ABI/INFORM Global.

16. Marianne Wilson, "Doing Good Is More Than a Feel-Good Option," *Chain Store Age*, Oct. 2005, pp. 77+.

17. McAlister, Ferrell, and Ferrell, *Business and Society*, p. 335.

18. Ibid.

19. Steve Quinn, "Wal-Mart Green with Energy," *The* [Fort Collins] *Coloradoan*, July 24, 2005, p. E1.

20. Keith Naughton, with Patrick Crowley, "Green," *Newsweek*, Nov. 22, 2004, pp. 50–56.

21. Peter Asmus, "17th Annual Business Ethics Awards," *Business Ethics*, Fall 2005, pp. 18–20.

22. Isabelle Maignan and Debbie Thorne McAlister, "Socially Responsible Organizational Buying: How Can Stakeholders Dictate Purchasing Policies?" *Journal of Macromarketing* 23 (Dec. 2003): 78–89.

23. Stephanie Thompson, "Aveda Pressures Mags to Go Green," *Advertising Age*, Nov. 29, 2004, p. 19.

24. "Certification," Home Depot, www.homedepot.com/HDUS/EN_US/corporate/corp_respon/certification.shtml (accessed Jan. 31, 2006).

25. "Better Banana Project," Chiquita, www.chiquita.com/chiquita/discover/owbetter.asp (accessed Apr. 13, 2006).

26. Paul Hawken and William McDonough, "Seven Steps to Doing Good Business," *Inc.*, Nov. 1993, pp. 79–90.

27. Jill Gabrielle Klein, N. Craig Smith, and Andrew John, "Why We Boycott: Consumer Motivations for Boycott Participation," *Journal of Marketing* 68 (July 2004): 92–109.

28. Christian Homburg and Andreas Fürst, "How Organizational Complaint Handling Drives Customer Loyalty: An Analysis of the Mechanistic and the Organic Approach," *Journal of Marketing* 69 (July 2005): 95–114.

29. Roger Bougie, Rik Pieters, and Marcel Zeelenberg, "Angry Customers Don't Come Back, They Get Back: The Experience and Behavioral Implications of Anger and Dissatisfaction in Services," *Journal of the Academy of Marketing Science* 31, no. 4 (2003): 377–393.

30. Asmus, "17th Annual Business Ethics Awards," p. 20.

31. "Take Charge of Education," Target, http://target.com/target_group/community_giving/take_charge_of_education.jhtml (accessed Apr. 13, 2006).

32. "Philanthropy," New Belgium Brewing Company, www.newbelgium.com/philanthropy.php (accessed Apr. 13, 2006).

33. McAlister, Ferrell, and Ferrell, *Business and Society*.

34. Thomas L. Carson, "Self-Interest and Business Ethics: Some Lessons of the Recent Corporate Scandals," *Journal of Business Ethics*, April 2003, pp. 389–394.

35. "Multi-Year Study Finds 21% Increase in Americans Who Say Corporate Support of Social Issues Is Important in Building Trust," Cone, Inc., press release, Dec. 8, 2004, www.coneinc.com/Pages/pr_30.html.

36. Mark Lisheron, "Texas Sues Sony Over Hidden Software That Can Hurt PCs," *The Austin American-Statesman*, Nov. 22, 2005, www.statesman.com; Ethan Smith, "Sony BMG Pulls Millions of CDs Amid Antipiracy-Software Flap," *The Wall Street Journal*, Nov. 17, 2005, p. D5, http://online.wsj.com/public/us.

37. "Hasbro: Do Not Pass Go, Ghettopoly," *USA Today*, Oct. 23, 2003, www.usatoday.com.

38. Tim Barnett and Sean Valentine, "Issue Contingencies and Marketers' Recognition of Ethical Issues, Ethical Judgments and Behavioral Intentions," *Journal of Business Research* 57 (2004): 338–346.

39. Betsy Querna, "The Big Pill Pitch," *U.S. News & World Report*, June 6, 2005, pp. 52–53.

40. David E. Sprott, Kenneth C. Mannign, and Anthony D. Miyazaki, "Grocery Price Setting and Quantity Surcharges," *Journal of Marketing*, July 2003, pp. 34–46.

41. Stephen Taub, "SEC Probing Harley Statements," CFO.com, July 14, 2005, www.cfo.com/article.cfm/4173321/c_4173841?f=archives&origin=archive.

42. Michael Josephson, "2004 Report Card: The Ethics of American Youth," Josephson Institute of Ethics, press release, www.josephsoninstitute.org/Survey2004/2004reportcard_pressrelease.htm.

43. Peggy H. Cunningham and O. C. Ferrell, "The Influence of Role Stress on Unethical Behavior by Personnel Involved in the Marketing Research Process" (working paper, Queens University, Ontario, 2004), p. 35.

44. Joseph W. Weiss, *Business Ethics: A Managerial, Stakeholder Approach* (Belmont, CA: Wadsworth, 1994), p. 13.

45. O. C. Ferrell, Larry G. Gresham, and John Fraedrich, "A Synthesis of Ethical Decision Models for Marketing," *Journal of Macromarketing*, Fall 1989, pp. 58–59.

46. Ethics Resource Center, "The Ethics Resource Center's 2005 *National Business Ethics Survey: How Employees View Ethics in Their Organizations*, 1994–2005" (Washington, DC: Ethics Resource Center, 2005), p. 16.

47. Barry J. Babin, James S. Boles, and Donald P. Robin, "Representing the Perceived Ethical Work Climate Among Marketing Employees," *Journal of the Academy of Marketing Science* 28, no. 3 (2000): 345–358.

48. Ferrell, Gresham, and Fraedrich, "A Synthesis of Ethical Decision Models for Marketing."

49. Lawrence B. Chonko and Shelby D. Hunt, "Ethics and Marketing Management: A Retrospective and Prospective Commentary," *Journal of Business Research* 50, no. 3 (2000): 235–244.

50. Linda K. Trevino and Stuart Youngblood, "Bad Apples in Bad Barrels: A Causal Analysis of Ethical Decision Making Behavior," *Journal of Applied Psychology* 75, no. 4 (1990): 378–385.

51. "Survey Documents State of Ethics in the Workplace," Ethics Resource Center, press release, Oct. 12, 2005, www.ethics.org/nbes/nbes2005/release.html.

52. Ethics Resource Center, "The Ethics Resource Center's 2005 *National Business Ethics Survey*," p. 29.

53. Gene R. Laczniak and Patrick E. Murphy, *Ethical Marketing Decisions: The Higher Road* (Boston: Allyn & Bacon, 1993), p. 14.

54. Marjorie Kelly, "Tyco's Ethical Makeover," *Business Ethics*, Summer 2005, pp. 14–19.

55. "HCA Ethics and Compliance," HCA Healthcare, http://ec.hcahealthcare.com (accessed Apr. 13, 2005); O.C. Ferrell, John Fraedrich, and Linda Ferrell, *Business Ethics: Ethical Decision Making and Cases*, 6th ed. (Boston: Houghton Mifflin, 2005), pp. 407–424.

56. "Social Responsibility Statement," American Apparel & Footwear Association, http://apparelandfootwear.org/4col.cfm?PageID 228 (accessed Apr. 13, 2006); "About WRAP," Worldwide Responsible Apparel Production, www.wrapapparel.org/modules.php?name=Content&pa=showpage&pid=3 (accessed Apr. 13, 2006).

57. James C. Hyatt, "Birth of the Ethics Industry," *Business Ethics*, Summer 2005, pp. 20–26.

58. Kelly, "Tyco's Ethical Makeover."

59. Hyatt, "Birth of the Ethics Industry"; Del Jones, "Law Rings up Growth in Worker Hotline Industry," *USA Today*, May 26, 2003, www.usatoday.com.

60. Jeff Leeds, "2 Are Fired at Clear Channel After a Misconduct Inquiry," *The New York Times*, Oct. 12, 2005, www.nytimes.com.

61. Sir Adrian Cadbury, "Ethical Managers Make Their Own Rules," *Harvard Business Review*, Sept./Oct. 1987, p. 33.

62. Caren Epstein, "Food Companies Marketing Products to People Living with Chronic Disease," *The* [Fort Colllins] *Coloradoan*, Nov. 13, 2005, p. E4.

63. Don Tapscott and David Ticoll, "The Naked Corporation," *The Wall Street Journal*, Oct. 14, 2003, http://online.wsj.com/public/us.

64. Ferrell, Fraedrich, and Ferrell, *Business Ethics*, pp. 27–30.

65. Isabelle Maignan, O. C. Ferrell, and Linda Ferrell, "A Stakeholder Model for Implementing Social Responsibility in Marketing," *European Journal of Marketing* 39 (Sept./Oct. 2005): 956–977.

66. "Multi-Year Study Finds 21% Increase in Americans Who Say Corporate Support of Social Issues Is Important in Building Trust."

67. Maignan, Ferrell, and Ferrell, "A Stakeholder Model for Implementing Social Responsibility in Marketing."

68. Sources: Catherine Colbert, "PETCO Animal Supplies, Inc.," Hoovers, www.hoovers.com/petco-(holding)/—ID__17256—/free-co-factsheet.xhtml (accessed Apr. 13, 2006); Corporate Governance—Code of Ethics, PETCO, http://ir.petco.com/phoenix.zhtml?c=93935&p=irol-govConduct (accessed Apr. 13, 2006); "Fortune 500 2005," CNN Money.com, http://money.cnn.com/magazines/fortune/fortune500/snapshots/2154.html; Michelle Higgins, "When the Dog's Hotel Is Better than Yours," *The Wall Street Journal*, June 30, 2004, p. D1; "Just Say No! Petco—the Place Where Pets Die," Kind Planet, www.kindplanet.org/petno.html; Ilene Lelchuk, "San Francisco Alleges Cruelty at 2 PETCOs," *San Francisco Chronicle*, June 19, 2002, www.anapsid.org/pettrade/petcoit2.html; "Lifestyle Trends Affect Pet Markets," PET AGE, Jan. 2006, www.petage.com/News010607.asp; Robert McMillan, "PETCO Settles Charge It Left Customer Data Exposed," NetworkWorld, Nov. 17, 2004, www.networkworld.com/news/2004/1117petcosettl.html; Chris Penttila, "Magic Markets," *Entrepreneur*, Sept. 2004, www.entrepreneur.com/article/0,4621,316866-2,00.html; "PETA and PETCO Announce Agreement," PETA, press release, Apr. 12, 2005, www.peta.org/feat/PETCOAgreement/default.asp; PETCO, www.petco.com (accessed Apr. 13, 2006); PETCO 10-K Annual Report; PETCO Annual Report to Shareholders; "Petco Animal Supplies," *Yahoo Finance*, http://finance.yahoo.com/q?s=PETC (accessed Apr.13, 2006); "PETCO Pays Fine to Settle Lawsuit," PETA Annual Review, 2004, www.peta.org/feat/annual_review04/notToAbuse.asp; "PETCO Foundation to 'Round-up' Support for Spay/Neuter Programs," PETCO, press release, July 13, 2005, Forbes.com, www.forbes.com/prnewswire/feeds/prnewswire/2005/07/13/prnewswire200507131335PR_NEWS_B_WES_LA_LAW067.html; "PETCO Lawsuit—Mistreating Animals San Diego, CA," May 28, 2004, Pet-Abuse.com, www.pet-abuse.com/cases/2373/CA/US; "PETCO Looks to the Web to Enhance Multi-Channel Marketing" Internet Retailer, Jan. 16, 2006; "PETCO's Bad Business Is Bad for Animals," PETA Animal Times, Spring 2003, www.peta.org/living/at-spring2003/comp2.html; "PETCO Settles FTC Charges," Federal Trade Commission, Nov. 17, 2004, www.ftc.gov/opa/2004/11/petco.htm; "PETCO Settles Suit Alleging Abuse, Overcharging," May 27, 2004, CBS News.com, www.anapsid.org/pettrade/petcocit2.html; "PETCO 'Spring a Pet' Campaign Blossoms for Animals Nationwide," PETCO, press release, May 11, 2005, Corporate Social Responsibility Press Releases, Center for Corporate Citizenship, Boston College, www.csrwire.com/ccc/article.cgi/3910.html; "The Pet Market—Market Assessment 2005," Research and Markets, Apr. 2005, www.researchandmarkets.com/reports/c26485/; "Pet Portion Control," Prevention, Feb. 2006, p. 201; "Pet Store Scandal: PETA Uncovers Shocking Back-Room Secrets," PETA Animal Times, Summer 2000, www.peta.org/living/at-summer2000/petco.html; "Say No to PETCO," PETA Animal Times, Spring 2002, www.peta.org/living/at-spring2002/specialrep/; Julie Schmidt, "Pet Bird Buyers Asking Sellers about Avian Flu," *USA Today*, Nov. 28, 2005; Jessica Stannard-Freil, "Corporate Philanthropy: PR or legitimate News?" OnPhilanthropy, May 20, 2005, www.onphilanthropy.com/tren_comm/tc2005-05-20.html.

69. Sources: Ford Motor Company, www.ford.com (accessed Apr. 13, 2006); John S. McClenahen, "Ford's Formidable Challenge," *Industry Week*, Feb. 1, 2003, www.industryweek.com/

currentArticles/asp/articles.asp?ArticleID=1379; Joann Muller, "Lean Green Machine," *Forbes*, Feb. 3, 2003, www.forbes.com/global/2003/0203023_print.html; "Our Route to Sustainability: Ford Sustainability Report," 2004/2005, Ford Motor Company, www.ford.com (accessed Apr. 13, 2006); Chuck Salter, "Ford's Escape Route," *Fast Company*, Oct. 2004, pp. 106+; Jason Sapsford, Phred Dvorak, and Jeffrey McCracken, "Ford Plans to Speed Up Production of Hybrid Vehicles," *The Wall Street Journal*, Sept. 22, 2005, p. A1, http://online.wsj.com/public/us.

70. TI Values and Principles and The TI Ethics Quick Test: Reprinted Courtesy of Texas Instruments. Sources: www.ti.com (accessed February 2006),TexasInstruments Annual Report 10-K,Texas Instruments training materials available for employees in brochure format titled: "Designing for the Environment", "Working with Suppliers", "Workplace Safety", "TI, the Law and You. A Survival Guide for Changing Times." Texas Instruments Corporate Social Responsibility Homepage: http://www.ti.com/corp/docs/csr/index.shtml (accessed 2/8/06) Texas Instruments Ethics Homepage: http://www.ti.com/corp/docs/company/citizen/ethics/index.shtml (accessed 2/6/06), The TI Code of Ethics: http://www.ti.com/corp/docs/investor/corpgov/valuesethicsconduct.pdf. Headline News: "TI named to 'Fortune' magazine's 100 Best Companies to Work for List" *Fortune*, 12 Jan 2005. http://infolinknews.ti.com/tinews/storydetail.tsp?storyId=106225 (accessed 2/2/06), "100 Best Corporate Citizens 2005," *Business Ethics,* The Magazine of Corporate Responsibility, Spring 2005. Thomas L. Friedman, "A Green Dream in Texas." *The New York Times.* January 18, 2006. "Ethics is the Cornerstone of TI," www.ti.com/corp/docs/company/citizen/ethics/benchmark.shtml (accessed Feb. 25, 2003).

## Chapter 5

1. PR Newswire, Packaged Facts, http://biz.yahoo.com/prnews (accessed Feb. 20, 2006); "Broadband Biggest Factor in Online Sales Growth," *The Retail Bulletin*, www.theretailbulletin.com (accessed Feb. 21, 2006); Juan Carlos Perez, "Online Sales in US to Grow Briskly through 2010, Study Says," ComputerWorld.com, www.computerworld.com (accessed Feb. 16, 2006); Kate Maddox, "Outsell Predicts Strong Growth in Online Marketing," BtoB, www.Btobonline.com (accessed Feb. 16, 2006).

2. Wayne D. Hoyer and Deborah J. MacInnis, *Consumer Behavior*, 3rd ed. (Boston: Houghton Mifflin, 2004), pp. 57–59.

3. "First Source for Car Shoppers in Online Households," *USA Today* Snapshot, Nov. 16, 2001, www.usatoday.com/snapshot.

4. Russell W. Belk, "Situational Variables and Consumer Behavior," *Journal of Consumer Research*, Dec. 1975, pp. 157–164.

5. "Sorry Cupid, Santa's the One Handing Out Engagement Rings This Year—and He's Buying Them Online," *PR Newswire*, Dec. 6, 2004.

6. Kim Ann Zimmermann, "Safeway Enters Online Grocery Turnstile," *E-Commerce Times*, Jan. 16, 2002, http://www.ecommercetimes.com.

7. Margaret Sheridan, "Made to Measure: Patient Satisfaction Surveys Provide Hospitals with Paths to Improvement," *Restaurants & Institutions*, Nov. 1, 2003, p. 69.

8. Laura Q. Hughes and Alice Z. Cuneo, "Lowe's Retools Image in Push Toward Women," *Advertising Age*, Feb. 26, 2001, www.adage.com; Amy Tsao, "Retooling Home Improvement," *Business Week Online*, Feb. 14, 2005, www.businessweek.com/bwdaily/dnflash/feb2005/nf20050214_3207_db_082.htm.

9. "Heinz Unveils New Blue Ketchup," *USA Today*, Apr. 7, 2003, www.usatoday.com/money/industries/food/2003-04-07-blue-ketchup_x.htm; Casey Keller, "So Far, It's Easy Being Green," *The New York Times*, Oct. 22, 2000, sec. 3, p. 2.

10. Maria Mooshil, "More Retailers Take Steps to Capture Women's Consumer Allegiance," *Chicago Tribune*, Jun 15, 2005, http://web.lexis-nexis.com.

11. Eric Wilson, "Her Name Already in Lights, A Star Seeks Fashion Credibility," *New York Times*, Feb. 11, 2005, Fashion, p. 11.

12. U.S. Bureau of the Census, "2004 American Community Survey Data Profile Highlights," http://factfinder.census.gov.

13. Jeffrey M. Humphreys, "The Multicultural Economy 2005," *Georgia Business and Economic Conditions* 65 (Third Quarter 2005), www.selig.uga.edu/forecast/GBEC/GBEC053Q.pdf.

14. Stuart Elliott, "Campaigns for Black Consumers," *The New York Times*, June 13, 2003.

15. Daimler Chrysler Corp., press release, www.csrwire.com (accessed Feb. 24, 2006).

16. "Hawaiian Punch Announces 2003 Black History Contest," www.blackvoices.com (accessed Jan. 20, 2006).

17. U.S. Bureau of the Census, "2004 American Community Survey Data Profile Highlights."

18. Ethnic Analysis, www.databankusa.com (accessed Jan. 18, 2006).

19. "Minority Buying Power to Triple," *Dallas Morning News*, Aug. 15, 2003.

20. Laurel Wentz, "Reebok Launches Web Site for U.S. Hispanic Market," *Advertising Age*, Nov. 15, 2005, www.adage.com.

21. Stuart Elliott, "Campaigns for Black Consumers" *The New York Times*, June 13, 2003.

22. Noel C. Paul, "Advertisers Slip into Spanish" *The Christian Science Monitor*, June 2, 2003.

23. U.S. Bureau of the Census, "2004 American Community Survey Data Profile Highlights"; Christina Hoag, "Asian-Americans Are Fastest Growing Group," *Miami Herald*, Apr. 7, 2003.

24. Humphreys, "The Multicultural Economy 2005."

25. Phuong Ly, "Immigrants Find a Taste of Home; Foreign Food Shops Expand to U.S. to Serve Old Customers—and New," *Washington Post*, Jan. 22, 2002, p. B1.

26. Sources: Consumer Reports, www.consumerreports.com (accessed Jan. 26, 2006); "Winner: Consumer Reports Staff," *The Quill*, June/July 2005; Roger Parloff, "The Ionic Breeze Is No Match for Consumer Reports," *Fortune*, Dec. 13, 2004; "Holiday Shopping Made Easy: Consumer Reports ShopSmart Mobile Subscription Service Helps On-the-Go Holiday Shoppers Buy the Best Gifts at the Best Prices," *AScribe Newswire*, Dec. 12, 2005, www.highbeam.com.

27. Sources: AutoTrader.com, www.autotrader.com (accessed Apr. 13, 2006); "AutoTrader.com Continues Summer Marketing Blitz with Television Buy," *PR Newswire*, June 30, 2003, www.prnewswire.com; "AutoTrader.com Gears Up for One-of-a-Kind Interactive Online Gaming Experience," AutoTrader, news release, Aug. 2, 2001, www.autotrader.com; "AutoTrader.com Has Highest Overall Satisfaction Among Used Vehicle Independent Sites in J. D. Power and Associates Study," AutoTrader.com, press release, Sept. 21, 2005, www.autotrader.com/about/pressroom/media/pressrelease_detail.jsp?article_id=18299; "How to Translate a TV Ad into an Online Promotion," MarketingSherpa.com, Nov. 1, 2001, www.emarketingtoher.com; Steve Jarvis, "Pedal to the Cyber-Metal," *Marketing News*, Jan. 21, 2002, pp. 6–7; Gregory Jordan, "Online, Used Car Lots That Cover the Nation," *The New York Times*, Oct. 22, 2003, p. G13 ; Chaz Osburn, "AutoTrader Adds Online Auction Listings," *Automotive News*, Jan. 13, 2003, p. 28.

## Chapter 6

1. Sources: "About Naturally Potatoes," Naturally Potatoes, www.naturallypotatoes.com/about.html (accessed Apr. 13, 2006); "Potatoes: Finding the Perfect Potato," Michael Foods, www.michaelfoods.com/products/potatoes.cfm (accessed Apr. 13, 2006); "Products: Potato Express," Reser's Fine Foods, www.resers.com/products/potatoexpress (accessed Apr. 13, 2006); "Retail," Naturally Potatoes, www.naturallypotatoes.com/retail.html (accessed Apr. 13, 2006); David Sharp, "Spuds Go the Way of Salad: Right Out of the Package," *The* [Fort Collins] *Coloradoan*, Aug. 28, 2005, p. E2.
2. "STP: Segmentation, Targeting, Positioning," American Marketing Association, www.marketingpower.com/content1488C381S3.php (accessed Dec. 17, 2005).
3. Ibid.
4. Matt Kelly, "Consortium Finds a Happy Ending," *eWeek*, Sept. 19, 2005, pp. C1, C4.
5. Michael D. Hutt and Thomas W. Speh, *Business Marketing Management* (Mason, OH: Thomson/South-Western, 2004), p. 93.
6. U.S. Bureau of the Census, Statistical Abstract of the United States, 2006 (Washington DC: Government Printing Office, 2006), pp. 671–672.
7. Ibid., p. 671.
8. Ibid., pp. 317–319.
9. Ibid., p. 272.
10. "Identix Wins the U.S. Department of State Facial Recognition Solicitation," *Business Wire*, Sept. 29, 2004.
11. Adina Genn, "E-Deals Even Small-Biz Playing Field," *Long Island Business News*, July 9, 2004.
12. Hussey Seating, www.husseyseating.com (accessed Apr. 13, 2006).
13. Das Narayandas and V. Kasturi Rangan, "Building and Sustaining Buyer-Seller Relationships in Mature Industrial Markets," *Journal of Marketing*, July 2004, p. 63.
14. "Dell Expands Global Services Capabilities with European Command Center," *Business Wire*, Dec. 1, 2004.
15. Alex R. Zablah, Wesley J. Johnston, and Danny N. Bellenger, "Transforming Partner Relationships through Technological Innovation," *Journal of Business & Industrial Marketing* 20 (Aug. 2005): 355–363.
16. Moin Uddin, "Loyalty Programs: The Ultimate Gift," *DSN Retailing Today*, Mar. 5, 2001, p. 12.
17. Cindy Claycomb and Gary L. Frankwick, "Dynamics of Buyers' Perceived Costs during a Relationship Development Process: An Empirical Assessment," *Journal of Business Research* 58 (2005): 1662–1671.
18. Lisa Harrington, "Right Moves," *Inbound Logistics*, Nov. 2005, pp. 37–40.
19. Leonidas C. Leonidou, "Industrial Buyers' Influence Strategies: Buying Situation Differences," *Journal of Business & Industrial Marketing* 20 (Jan. 2005): 33–42.
20. Joseph O'Reilly, "A Ready-Mix Transport Solution," *Inbound Logistics*, Nov. 2005, pp. 70–71.
21. Jeffrey Burt, "Gateway Eyes Small Businesses," *eWeek*, Sept. 5, 2005, www.eweek.com.
22. Frederick E. Webster, Jr., and Yoram Wind, "A General Model for Understanding Organizational Buyer Behavior," *Marketing Management*, Winter/Spring 1996, pp. 52–57.
23. Laura Heller, *DSN Retailing Today*, Jan. 10, 2005, pp. 13–14.
24. George S. Day and Katrina J. Bens, "Capitalizing on the Internet Opportunity," *Journal of Business & Industrial Marketing* 20 (2005): 160–168.
25. Steve Hamm, "GM's Way or the Highway," *Business Week*, Dec. 19, 2005, pp. 48–49.
26. Niklas Myhr and Robert E. Spekman, "Collaborative Supply-Chain Partnerships Built upon Trust and Electronically Mediated Exchange," *Journal of Business & Industrial Marketing* 20 (2005): 179–186.
27. "Development of NAICS," U.S. Census Bureau, www.census.gov/epcd/www/naicsdev.htm (accessed Apr. 13, 2006).
28. Sources: Lextant, www.lextant.com (accessed Apr. 13, 2006); Jon Udell, "Art and Science of Usability Analysis," *InfoWorld*, June 4, 2004, www.infoworld.com/article/04/06/ 04/23 FEuser-sb_1.html?INTEGRATED%20DEVELOPMENT %20ENVIRONMENT%20-%20IDE.
29. Sources: Adam L. Freeman, "WebMD Wants to Process Claims, Too," *The Wall Street Journal*, Nov. 19, 2003, p. 1; Milt Freudenheim, "WebMD Is Somewhat Stronger After Therapy," *The New York Times*, Feb. 4, 2002, p. C5; Karen Southwick, "WebMD May Be Due for a Checkup," c|net News, Apr. 26, 2004, news.com.com/2100-1011_3-5198935.html; WebMD, www.webmd.com (accessed Apr. 13, 2006); "WebMD Responds to Physicians' Complaints," *Information Week*, Jan. 28, 2004; "WebMD to Pay $280 Million for Medifax-EDI," *The New York Times*, Oct. 23, 2003, p. C4.

## Chapter 7

1. Sources: Leander Kahney, "The Cult of iPod," *Playlist*, http://playlistmag.com (accessed Jan. 18, 2006); iPod, www.apple.com/ipod/ipod.html (accessed Apr. 13, 2006); Louise Lee, "Sewing Up the iPod Market," *BusinessWeek*, Jan. 12, 2006, http://www.businessweek.com/technology/content/jan2006/tc20060112_086932.htm (accessed June 2, 2006); Mary Bellis, "Inventors of the Modern Computer," *About*, http://inventors.about.com/library/weekly/aa121598.htm (accessed Apr. 13, 2006); Apple Computer Inc., www.apple.com (accessed Apr. 13, 2006); Carol Glatz, "Vatican Radio Employees Present Pope with Specially Loaded iPod Nano," *The Catholic News Service*, www.catholicnews.com/data/stories/cns/0601282.htm (accessed Apr. 13, 2006).
2. U.S. Bureau of the Census, World Population Clock, www.census.gov/cgi.bin/ipc./popclockw (accessed Jan. 19, 2006); "Trade Statistics 2005," World Trade Organization, http://www.wto.org/english/res_e/statis_e/its2005_e/its2005_e.pdf (accessed Apr. 13, 2006).
3. Anthony Bianco and Wendy Zellner, "Is Wal-Mart Too Powerful?" *Business Week*, Oct. 6, 2003, pp. 100–110; Cora Daniels, "Mr. Coffee," *Fortune*, Apr. 14, 2003, pp. 139–140; Latest Counts of Wal-Mart, www.wal-martchina.com/english/news/stat.htm (accessed Apr. 13, 2006); The Future of Starbucks, http://netscape.fool.com/news/commentary/2005/commentary05021104.htm (accessed Apr. 13, 2006).
4. The Progressive Policy Institute, www.ppionline.org (accessed Apr. 13, 2006).
5. Export.gov, www.export.gov/comm_svc/about_us/about_home.html (accessed Apr. 13, 2006).
6. CIBERweb, http://ciberweb.msu.edu (accessed Apr. 13, 2006).
7. Gary A. Knight and S. Tamer Cavusgil, "Innovation, Organizational Capabilities, and the Born-Global Firm," *Journal of International Business Studies*, Mar. 2004, pp. 124–141.
8. Investor Relations at Amazon.com, http://amazon.com (accessed Feb. 8, 2006); *People's Daily Online*, http://english.people.com.cn/200501/27/eng20050127_172143.html (accessed Feb. 9, 2006).
9. Brian Bremner and Chester Dawson, "Can Anything Stop Toyota?" *Business Week*, Nov. 17, 2003, pp. 114–122.
10. United States of America v. Microsoft Corporation, http://usvms.gpo.gov (accessed Mar. 30, 2006); BBC News, Microsoft Corporation v. America Online (AOL), http://news.bbc.co.uk/1/hi/business/2949778.stm (accessed Mar. 30, 2006).
11. This Is Systembolaget, www.systembolaget.se/Applikationer/Knappar/InEnglish/Swedish_alcohol_re.htm (accessed Apr. 13, 2006).

12. George S. Yip, *Total Global Strategy* II (Upper Saddle River, NJ: Prentice Hall, 2003), Alan M. Rugman, *The Regional Multinationals: MNEs and "Global" Strategic Management* (Cambridge: Cambridge University Press, 2005).

13. Global Customers, Kimberly-Clark, www.kimberly-clark.com/investorinfo/AnnualReport2001/kc_customers.pdf (accessed Apr. 13, 2006); Oracle—Global Customer Program, www.oracle.com/customers/gcp/index.html (accessed Apr. 13, 2006); Sony—Customer Satisfaction, www.sony.net/SonyInfo/Environment/people/customers/satisfaction/index.html (accessed Apr. 13, 2006).

14. U.S. Bureau of the Census, Foreign Trade Statistics, www.census.gov/foreign-trade/statistics/historical/gandsbal.pdf (accessed Apr. 13, 2006).

15. Bureau of Economic Analysis, U.S. Department of Commerce, www.bea.gov/bea/dn/home/gdp.htm (accessed Apr. 13, 2006).

16. Ibid., pp. 824–826, 834.

17. CIBERweb, http://ciberweb.msu.edu (accessed Apr. 13, 2006).

18. American Marketing Association, Code of Ethics, www.marketingpower.com/content435.php (accessed Apr. 13, 2006).

19. Charles R. Taylor, George R. Franke, and Michael L. Maynard, "Attitudes Toward Direct Marketing and Its Regulation: A Comparison of the United States and Japan," *Journal of Public Policy & Marketing*, Fall 2000, pp. 228–237.

20. "Product Pitfalls Proliferate in Global Cultural Maze," *The Wall Street Journal*, May 14, 2001, p. B11.

21. Ibid.

22. Ibid.

23. Greg Botelho, "2003 Global Influentials: Selling to the World," CNN, Dec. 9, 2003, www.cnn.com.

24. Jeffrey G. Blodgett, Long-Chuan Lu, Gregory M. Rose, and Scott J. Vitell, "Ethical Sensitivity to Stakeholder Interests: A Cross-Cultural Comparison," *Journal of the Academy of Marketing Science* 29, no. 2 (2001): 190–202.

25. Thomas G. Brashear, Elzbieta Lepkowska-White, and Cristian Chelariu, "An Empirical Test of Antecedents and Consequences of Salesperson Job Satisfaction Among Polish Retail Salespeople," *Journal of Business Research*, Dec. 2003, pp. 971–978.

26. Zeynep Gürhan-Canli and Durairaj Maheswaran, "Cultural Variations in Country of Origin Effects," *Journal of Marketing Research*, Aug. 2000, pp. 309–317.

27. Joseph Albright and Marcia Kunstel, "Schlotzsky's First China Opening Less Than Red-Hot," *Austin American-Statesman*, May 27, 1998, www.austin360.com.

28. Isabelle Maignan and O. C. Ferrell, "Nature of Corporate Responsibilities: Perspectives from American, French, and German Consumers," *Journal of Business Research*, Jan. 2003, pp. 55–67.

29. Dave Izraeli and Mark S. Schwartz, "What We Can Learn from the Federal Sentencing Guidelines for Organizational Ethics," *Journal of Business Ethics*, July 1998, pp. 9–10.

30. "European Consumers Getting Comfortable with Online Channel," CyberAtlas, July 6, 2001, http://cyberatlas.internet.com/big_picture/geographics/article/0,,5911_794321,00.html.

31. "Population Explosion!" CLickZ Stats, Nov. 3, 2005, www.clickz.com/stats/sectors/geographics/article.php/5911_151151.

32. Click Z Network, "Euro Teens Respond to Online Advertising," www.clickz.com/stats/sectors/demographics/article.php/3586966 (accessed Apr. 13, 2006).

33. Elisa Batista, "Telcos Duke It Out over Iraq," Wired News, June 27, 2003, www.wired.com/news/politics/0,1283,59410,00.html; Ben Charny, "Study: Cell Phone Use to Double," cnet, Aug. 2003, http://news.com.com/2100–1039_3–5060745.html.

34. Louisa Kasdon Sidell, "The Economics of Inclusion," *Continental*, Apr. 2001, pp. 64–67.

35. Jim Carlton, "Stymied in Alaska, Oil Producers Flock to a New Frontier," *The Wall Street Journal*, Sept. 4, 2002, pp. A1, A15.

36. "Ethics in the Global Market," Texas Instruments, www.ti.com/corp/docs/company/citizen/ethics/market.shtml (accessed Apr. 13, 2006).

37. Business for Social Responsibility, www.bsr.org (accessed Apr. 13, 2006).

38. Geri Smith and Cristina Lindblad, "Mexico: Was NAFTA Worth It?" *Business Week*, Dec. 22, 2003, pp. 66–72.

39. U.S. Bureau of the Census, Statistical Abstract of the United States, 2002 (Washington, DC: Government Printing Office, 2003), pp. 824–826, 834; U.S. Department of Commerce, "NAFTA: A Decade of Strengthening a Dynamic Relationship," pamphlet, 2003, available at www.ustr.gov.

40. globalEDGE, Country Insights, http://globaledge.msu.edu (accessed Feb. 26, 2006).

41. U.S. Bureau of the Census, "Canada-U.S. Trade Statistics," www.census.gov/foreign-trade/balance/c1220.html#2006 (accessed Apr. 13, 2006).

42. William C. Symonds, "Meanwhile, to the North, NAFTA Is a Smash," *Business Week*, Feb. 27, 1995, p. 66.

43. U.S. Bureau of the Census, *Statistical Abstract of the United States, 2006* (Washington, DC: Government Printing Office, 2006), www.census.gov/statab/www (accessed Apr. 13, 2006).

44. globalEDGE, Country Insights, http://globaledge.msu.edu (accessed Feb. 26, 2006).

45. "Antecedents of the FTAA Process," FTAA, www.ftaa-alca.org/View_e.asp (accessed Apr. 8, 2004); "FTAA Fact Sheet," Market Access and Compliance, U.S. Department of Commerce, www.mac.doc.gov/ftaa2005/ftaa_fact_sheet.html (accessed Apr. 8, 2004).

46. "Archer Daniels to File NAFTA Claim Against Mexico," Inbound Logistics, Oct. 2003, p. 30.

47. Smith and Lindblad, "Mexico."

48. "The European Union at a Glance," Europa (European Union online), http://europa.eu.int/abc/index_en.htm (accessed Mar. 28, 2006).

49. Gateway to the European Union, http://europa.eu.int/index_en.htm (accessed Mar. 28, 2006).

50. Stanley Reed, with Ariane Sains, David Fairlamb, and Carol Matlack, "The Euro: How Damaging a Hit?" *Business Week*, Sept. 29, 2003, p. 63; "The Single Currency," CNN, July 3, 2001, www.cnn.com/SPECIALS/2000/eurounion/story/currency/.

51. "Common Market of the South (MERCOSUR): Agri-Food Regional Profile Statistical Overview," Agriculture and Agrifood Canada, Oct. 2002, http://atn-riae.agr.ca/latin/e3431.htm.

52. "About APEC," Asia-Pacific Economic Cooperation, www.apecsec.org.sg/apec/about_apec.html (accessed Apr. 13, 2006).

53. Asian Pacific Economic Cooperation, www.apec.org/content/apec/about_apec/achievements_and_benefits.html (accessed Apr. 13, 2006).

54. Smith and Lindblad, "Mexico."

55. Clay Chandler, "How to Play the China Boom," *Fortune*, Dec. 22, 2003, pp. 141–142.

56. Dexter Roberts and Frederik Balfour, "Is This Boom in Danger?" *Business Week*, Nov. 3, 2003, pp. 48–50.

57. World Trade Organization, www.wto.org/index.htm (accessed Apr. 13, 2006).

58. "What Is the WTO?" World Trade Organization, www.wto.org/english/thewto_e/whatis_e/whatis_e.htm (accessed Apr. 13, 2006).

59. "WTO: U.S. Steel Duties Are Illegal," *USA Today*, Nov. 10, 2003, http://usatoday.com.

60. "Bush Ends Steel Tariffs," *CNN/Money*, Dec. 4, 2003, http://cnnmoney.com.

61. Jan Johanson and Finn Wiedersheim-Paul, "The Internationalization of the Firm," *Journal of Management Studies*, Oct. 1975, pp. 305–322; Jan Johanson and Jan-Erik Vahlne, "The

Internationalization Process of the Firm—A Model of Knowledge Development and Increasing Foreign Commitments," *Journal of International Business Studies*, Spring/Summer 1977, pp. 23–32; S. Tamer Cavusgil and John R. Nevin, "Internal Determinants of Export Marketing Behavior: An Empirical Investigation," *Journal of Marketing Research*, Feb. 1981, pp. 114–119.

62. Pradeep Tyagi, "Export Behavior of Small Business Firms in Developing Economies: Evidence from the Indian Market," *Marketing Management Journal*, Fall/Winter 2000, pp. 12–20.

63. Berrin Dosoglu-Guner, "How Do Exporters and Non-Exporters View Their 'Country of Origin' Image Abroad?" *Marketing Management Journal*, Fall/Winter 2000, pp. 21–27.

64. Farok J. Contractor and Sumit K. Kundu, "Franchising Versus Company-Run Operations: Model Choice in the Global Hotel Sector," *Journal of International Marketing*, Nov. 1997, pp. 28–53.

65. Margreet F. Boersma, Peter J. Buckley, and Pervez N. Ghauri, "Trust in International Joint Venture Relationships," *Journal of Business Research*, Dec. 2003, pp. 1031–1042.

66. "What We're About," NUMMI, http://www.nummi.com/co_info.html (accessed Apr. 13, 2006).

67. William Q. Judge and Joel A. Ryman, "The Shared Leadership Challenge in Strategic Alliances: Lessons from the U.S. Healthcare Industry," *Academy of Management Executive*, May 2001, pp. 71–79.

68. Ibid.

69. Leslie Gornstein, "Retailers Cater to Growing U.S. Hispanic Population," *Pensacola News Journal*, June 17, 2001, p. 4B.

70. Jan Johanson and Finn Wiedersheim-Paul, "The Internationalization of the Firm," *Journal of Management Studies*, Oct. 1975, pp. 305–322; Jan Johanson and Jan-Erik Vahlne, "The Internationalization Process of the Firm—A Model of Knowledge Development and Increasing Foreign Commitments," *Journal of International Business Studies*, Spring/Summer 1977, pp. 23–32; D. Naidler, M. Gerstein, and R. Shaw, *Organization Architecture* (San Francisco: Jossey-Bass, 1992).

71. Clipsal Export Department, www.clipsal.com.au/trade/about_us/Export (accessed Apr. 13, 2006).

72. Botelho, "Selling to the World."

73. Theodore Levitt, "The Globalization of Markets," *Harvard Business Review*, May/June 1983, p. 92.

74. Deborah Owens, Timothy Wilkinson, and Bruce Keillor, "A Comparison of Product Attributes in a Cross-Cultural/Cross-National Context," *Marketing Management Journal*, Fall/Winter 2000, pp. 1–11.

75. Anil K. Gupta and Vijay Govindarajan, "Converting Global Presence into Global Competitive Advantage," *Academy of Management Executive*, May 2001, pp. 45–58.

76. Sources: "About IDG," International Data Group, www.idg.com/www/home.nsf/AboutIDGForm?OpenForm&region=WW (accessed Apr. 13, 2006); Sam Perkins and Neal Thornberry, "Corporate Entrepreneurship for Dummies," *Harvard Business School Publishing* (Case BAB114).

77. Sources: Rekha Balu, "Hop Faster, Energizer Bunny: Rayovac Batteries Roll On," *The Wall Street Journal*, June 15, 1999, p. B4; "Battle of the Blades Draws Corporate Blood," "For Mighty Gillette, These Are the Faces of War," *The New York Times*, Oct. 12, 2003, sec. 3, p. 1; The Gillette Company, www.gillette.com (accessed Apr. 13, 2006); Gillette 1999–2005 Annual Reports, http://www.pg.com/investors/annualreports.jhtml (accessed June 2, 2006); "Gillette's Edge," *Business Week*, Jan. 19, 1998, pp. 70–77; "Gillette, Schick End Legal War, but Battle in Market Rages On," Boston.com, www.boston.com/business/healthcare/articles/2006/02/17/gillette_schick_end_legal_war_but_battle_in_market_rages_on (accessed Apr. 13, 2006); "Wal-Mart Selling Its Own Brand of Alkaline Batteries," *The Wall Street Journal*, Dec. 10, 1999, pp. C4–C5. Don Roy, Middle Tennessee State University; Michael D. Hartline, Florida State University; and G. Tomas M. Hult, Michigan State University, assisted in the development of these case materials.

78. Deborah Adamson, "Trouble in Toyland," CBS MarketWatch, Mar. 8, 2000, http://cbs.marketwatch.com/; American Girl, www.americangirl.com (accessed Apr. 3, 2006); Bandai, www.bandai.com (accessed May 27, 2003); "Barbie Is Banned from Russia, Without Love," *The Observer*, Nov. 24, 2002, www.observer.co.uk/; Lisa Bannon, "Mattel Sees Untapped Market for Blocks: Little Girls," *The Wall Street Journal*, June 6, 2002, p. B-1; Lisa Bannon, "New Playbook: Taking Cues from GE, Mattel's CEO Wants Toy Maker to Grow Up," *The Wall Street Journal*, Nov. 14, 2001, p. A-1; Barbie, www.barbie.com (accessed May 27, 2003); Sherri Day, "As It Remakes Itself, Mattel Does Same for Barbie," *New York Times*, Nov. 9, 2002, p. C-1; Hot Wheels, www.hotwheels.com/ (accessed Apr. 3, 2006); Debbie Howell, "Top Brands 2002: A Longing for Labels' Returns," *DSN Retailing Today*, Oct. 28, 2002, pp. 24–27; Interbrand, "The 100 Best Brands," Business Week Online, Aug. 5, 2002, www.businessweek.com; "Iran Enforces Barbie Ban," Associated Press, May 23, 2002; Kate MacArthur, "Plastic Surgery: Barbie Gets Real Makeover," *Advertising Age*, Nov. 4, 2002, pp. 4, 53; Mattel, www.mattel.com (accessed Apr. 3, 2006); "Mattel Combines Girls, Boys Divisions, Cuts Management," Associated Press, Feb. 28, 2003; "Mattel, Inc. Launches Global Code of Conduct Intended to Improve Workplace, Workers' Standard of Living," Canada NewsWire, Nov. 21, 1997 (for more information on Mattel's code, contact the company at 310–252–3524); "Mattel Lands WB Master Toy Licenses," *Home Textiles Today*, Sep. 2002, p. 14; "Mattel Swings to Better Than Expected Profit," Reuters News & Financial Intelligence, Apr. 13, 2003, http://www.reuters.com/; My Scene Barbie, www.myscene.com (accessed May 27, 2003); Christopher Palmeri, "Mattel's New Toy Story," *Business Week*, Nov. 18, 2002, pp. 72–74; J. Alex Tarquino, "Barbie & Co. Reviving Mattel," *New York Times*, March 9, 2003, Section 3, p. 7. This case was prepared by Debbie Thorne McAlister and Laura Leigh Saenz, Texas State University–San Marcos, for classroom discussion rather than to illustrate either effective or ineffective handling of an administration situation. The authors acknowledge the work of Kevin Sample on previous versions of this case.

## Chapter 8

1. "More Monkeyshines? Or the Real Deal?," Jac Chebatoris, *Newsweek*, Feb. 6, 2006, p. 10; "Arctic Monkeys Earn Fastest-Selling U.K. Debut," Paul Sexton, *Billboard.com*, Jan. 30, 2006, www.billboard.com/bbcom/news/article_display.jsp?vnu_content_id=1001920504; "Arctic Monkeys Make Chart History," BBC News, Jan. 29, 2006, http://news.bbc.co.uk/go/pr/fr/-/1/hi/entertainment/4660394.stm; "Arctic Monkeys," Wikipedia,

2. Vladimir Zwass, "Electronic Commerce: Structures and Issues," *International Journal of Electronic Commerce*, Fall 1996, pp. 3–23.

3. Stan Crock, "Lockheed Martin," *Business Week*, Nov. 24, 2003, p. 85.

4. Michael J. Mandel and Robert D. Hof, "Rethinking the Internet," *Business Week*, Mar. 26, 2001, pp. 116–122.

5. Catherine Yang, "Homeland Security Dept.," *Business Week*, Nov. 24, 2003, p. 85.

6. Fang Wu, Vijay Mahajan, and Sridhar Balasubramanian, "An Analysis of E-Business Adoption and Its Impact on Business Performance," *Journal of the Academy of Marketing Science*, Fall 2003, pp. 425–447.

7. Michael Totty, "The Researcher," *The Wall Street Journal*, July 16, 2001, p. R20.

8. "Shop Around the Clock," *American Demographics*, Sept. 2003, p. 18.

9. David W. Stewart and Qin Zhao, "Internet Marketing, Business Models, and Public Policy," *Journal of Public Policy & Marketing*, Fall 2000, pp. 287–296.

10. Totty, "The Researcher."

11. Christopher Hart and Pete Blackshaw, "Internet Inferno," *Marketing Management*, Jan./Feb. 2006, p. 19.

12. John Eaton, "e-Word-of-Mouth Marketing," custom module for William M. Pride and O. C. Ferrell, *Marketing*, 14th ed. (Boston: Houghton Mifflin, 2006), www.prideferrell.com.

13. Christopher Hart and Pete Blackshaw, "Internet Inferno," *Marketing Management*, Jan./Feb. 2006, p. 21.

14. Ben Elgin, "A Search Engine for Every Subject," *Business Week*, Feb. 20, 2006, pp. 66–67.

15. Ronald L. Hess, Shankar Ganesan, and Noreen M. Klein, "Service Failure and Recovery: The Impact of Relationship Factors on Customer Satisfaction," *Journal of the Academy of Marketing Science*, Spring 2003, pp. 127–145.

16. "Turning to Tech," *Business Week*, Dec. 22, 2003, p. 83.

17. Jon Mark Giese, "Place Without Space, Identity Without Body: The Role of Cooperative Narrative in Community and Identity Formation in a Text-Based Electronic Community" (unpublished dissertation, Pennsylvania State University, 1996).

18. David Kirkpatrick and Daniel Roth, "Why There's No Escaping the Blog," *Fortune*, Jan. 10, 2005, pp. 44–50.

19. "Krispy Kreme's Secret Ingredient," *Business 2.0*, Sept. 2003, p. 36.

20. "Fact Sheet," eFairness, www.e-fairness.org/factsheet/factsheet.htm (accessed Apr. 13, 2006).

21. Jason Straziuso, "Internet Grocery Quietly Grows to $2.4 Billion Industry," *USA Today*, May 17, 2004, www.usatoday.com/tech/news/2004-05-17-groceries_x.htm.

22. "About Us," FreshDirect, www.freshdirect.com/about/index.jsp (accessed Apr. 13, 2006).

23. "Southwest Airlines Fact Sheet," Southwest Airlines, www.iflyswa.com/about_swa/press/factsheet.html (accessed Apr. 13, 2006).

24. Stephanie Anderson Forest, "Kinko's," *Business Week*, Nov. 24, 2003, p. 101.

25. Michael Arndt, "Yellow," *Business Week*, Nov. 24, 2003, pp. 100, 101.

26. Andrew Park, "Imperial Sugar," *Business Week*, Nov. 24, 2003, p. 98.

27. "Jupiter Research Forecasts Online Retail Spending Will Reach $144 Billion in 2010, a CAGR of 12% from 2005," Jupiter Media, press release, Feb. 6, 2006, www.jupitermedia.com/corporate/ releases/06.02.06-newjupresearch.html.

28. "Amazon.com Announces Free Cash Flow Surpasses $500 Million for the First Time; Customers Joined Amazon Prime at an Accelerated Rate," Amazon.com, press release, Feb. 2, 2006, http://phx.corporate-ir.net/phoenix.zhtml?c=176060&p=irol-newsArticle&ID=812301&highlight=.

29. Enid Burns, "Online Ads Influence Collegiate Set," ClickZ, Feb. 10, 2006, www.clickz.com/stats/sectors/demographics/article.php/3584441.

30. Enid Burns, "Online Seizes More of the Advertising Mix," ClickZ, Feb. 13, 2006, www.clickz.com/stats/sectors/advertising/article.php/3584801.

31. Asim Ansari and Carl F. Mela, "E-Customization," *Journal of Marketing Research*, May 2003, pp. 131–145.

32. Stephanie Stahl and John Soat, "Feeding the Pipeline: Procter & Gamble Uses IT to Nurture New Product Ideas," *Information Week*, Feb. 24, 2003, www.informationweek.com.

33. V. Kumar, "Customer Relationship Management," custom module for William M. Pride and O. C. Ferrell, *Marketing*, 14th ed. (Boston: Houghton Mifflin, 2006), www.prideferrell.com.

34. Ilaria Dalla Pozza and Guiliano Noci, "The Impact of Customer Relationship Management on Performance," in Jean L. Johnson and John Hulland, eds., 2006: AMA Winter Educators' Conference; *Marketing Theory and Applications* 17 (Winter 2006): 144–145.

35. C. B. Bhattacharya and Sankar Sen, "Consumer-Company Identification: A Framework for Understanding Consumers' Relationships with Companies," *Journal of Marketing*, Apr. 2003, pp. 76–88.

36. Peter C. Verhoef, "Understanding the Effect of Customer Relationship Management Efforts on Customer Retention and Customer Share Development," *Journal of Marketing*, Oct. 2003, pp. 30–45.

37. D. Aaker, V. Kumar, and G. Day, *Marketing Research*, 8th ed. (New York: Wiley & Sons, 2004).

38. Marlus Wübben and Florian von Wangenheim, "Predicting Customer Lifetime Duration and Future Purchase Levels: Simple Heuristics vs. Complex Models," in Jean L. Johnson and John Hulland, eds., 2006: AMA Winter Educators' Conference; *Marketing Theory and Applications* 17 (Winter 2006): 83–84.

39. Kumar, "Customer Relationship Management."

40. Christine McManus, "'Micro-Cheesery' Closes," *The* [Fort Collins] *Coloradoan*, Feb. 10, 2006, www.coloradoan.com.

41. V. Kumar, J. Andrew Peterson, and Robert P. Leone, "The Power of Customer Advocacy," in Jean L. Johnson and John Hulland, eds., 2006: AMA Winter Educators' Conference; *Marketing Theory and Applications* 17 (Winter 2006): 81–82.

42. O. C. Ferrell and Michael D. Hartline, *Marketing Strategy*, 3rd ed. (Mason, OH: South-Western, 2005), p. 72.

43. Werner J. Reinartz and V. Kumar, "The Impact of Relationship Characteristics on Profitable Lifetime Duration," *Journal of Marketing*, Jan. 2003, pp. 77–99.

44. Kumar, "Customer Relationship Management."

45. V. Kumar, G. Ramani, and T. Bohling, "Customer Lifetime Value Approaches and Best Practices Applications," *Journal of Interactive Marketing* 18, no. 3 (2004): 60–72.

46. Kumar, "Customer Relationship Management."

47. J. Bonasia, "Eyeing Growth in Customer Relationship Management Software," *Investors Business Daily*, Jan. 8, 2002, p. 7.

48. "Better Relationships, Better Business," *Business Week*, Special Advertising Section, Apr. 29, 2002.

49. Edward Prewitt, "How to Build Customer Loyalty in an Internet World," CIO, Jan. 1, 2002, www.cio.com/archive/010102/loyalty_content.html.

50. G. S. Day, *Capabilities for Forging Customer Relationships* (Cambridge, MA: Marketing Science Institute, 2000).

51. Michael Krauss, "At Many Firms, Technology Obscures CRM," *Marketing News*, Mar. 18, 2002, p. 5.

52. Emin Babakus, Ugur Yavas, Osman M. Karatepe, and Turgay Avci, "The Effect of Management Commitment to Service Quality on Employees' Affective and Performance Outcomes," *Journal of the Academy of Marketing Science*, Summer 2003, pp. 272–286.

53. Prewitt, "How to Build Customer Loyalty in an Internet World."

54. Ibid.

55. Ibid.

56. Dennis B. Arnett, Steve D. German, and Shelby D. Hunt, "The Identity Salience Model of Relationship Marketing Success: The Case of Nonprofit Marketing," *Journal of Marketing*, Apr. 2003, pp. 89–105.

57. David Pottruck and Terry Peace, "Listening to Customers in the Electronic Age," *Fortune*, May 2000, www.business2.com/articles/mag/0,1640,7700,00.html.

58. Stephenie Steitzer, "Commercial Websites Cut Back on Collections of Personal Data," *The Wall Street Journal*, Mar. 28, 2002, http://online.wsj.com/public/us.

59. Peter Loftus, "Yahoo Modifies Its Privacy Policy to Allow More Sharing of User Data," *The Wall Street Journal*, Mar. 28, 2002, http://online.wsj.com/public/us.

60. Steitzer, "Commercial Websites Cut Back on Collections of Personal Data."

61. "BBBOnLine Privacy Seal," BBBOnLine, www.BBBOnLine.org/privacy/index.asp (accessed Apr. 13, 2006).

62. "European Union Directive on Privacy," E-Center for Business Ethics, www.e-businessethics.com (accessed Apr. 13, 2006).

63. "Study: Spam Costing Companies $22 Billion a Year," CNN, Feb. 4, 2005, www.cnn.com.

64. Tim Hanrahan and Jason Fry, "Spammers, Human Mind Do Battle over Spelling," *The Wall Street Journal*, Feb. 9, 2004, http://online.wsj.com/public/us; Tom Zeller, "Law Barring Junk E-Mail Allows a Flood Instead," *The New York Times*, Feb. 1, 2005, www.nytimes.com.

65. Stephen H. Wildstrom, "Can Microsoft Stamp Out Piracy?" *Business Week Online*, Oct. 2, 2000, www.businessweek.com.

66. Burt Helm, "A Hard Ride for eDonkey," *Business Week*, Oct. 24, 2005, pp. 90–92.

67. Richard Waters, "Google's Image Search Breaches Publisher's Rights," *Financial Times*, Feb. 23, 2006, p. 15.

68. William T. Neese and Charles R. McManis, "Summary Brief: Law, Ethics and the Internet: How Recent Federal Trademark Law Prohibits a Remedy Against Cyber-squatters," Proceedings from the Society of Marketing Advances, Nov. 4–7, 1998.

69. Sources: Marty Gast, "Travelocity.com: A Glimpse Through History," *Travel News*, Dec. 23 2003, www.breakingtravelnews.com/article.php?story=20031222221110443&mode=print; Josh Roberts, "Travelocity, Expedia Aim to Prove Their Differences," *USA Today*, May 11, 2005, www.usatoday.com/travel/deals/inside/2005-05-11-column_x.htm; Travelocity, www.travelocity.com (accessed Apr. 13, 2006); "Travelocity.com LP," Hoovers, www.hoovers.com/travelocity/—ID__100249—/free-co-factsheet.xhtml (accessed Apr. 13, 2006).

70. Sources: Karen Bannan, "Sole Survivor," *Sales & Marketing Management*, July 2001, pp. 36–41; "eBay Announces Fourth Quarter and Full Year 2005 Results," eBay, press release, Jan. 18, 2006, http://investor.ebay.com/news/; "eBay: The World's Online Marketplace," eBay, http://pages.ebay.com/aboutebay/thecompany/companyoverview.html (accessed Apr. 13, 2006); Robert Goff, "Ebay's Cop," *Forbes*, June 25, 2001, p. 42; "Fiorina Tops Fortune List of Most Powerful Women," *Mercury News*, Oct. 1, 2003, www.mercurynews.com/mld/mercurynews/business/6904474.htm; Robert D. Hof, "The eBay Economy," *Business Week Online*, Aug. 25, 2003, www.businessweek.com/magazine/content/03_34/b3846650.htm; Robert D. Hof, "Online Extra: Q&A with eBay's Meg Whitman," Business Week Online, May 14, 2001, www.businessweek.com; Julia King, "Websites Crack Down on Fraud," *ComputerWorld*, Sept. 13, 1999, p. 1113; Chuck Lenatti, "Auction Mania," *Upside*, July 11, 1999, pp. 84–92; Ellen Messmer, "Ebay Acts to Curtail Internet Fraud," *Network World*, July 24, 2000, pp. 31, 34; "New Study Reveals 724,000 Americans Rely on eBay Sales for Income," eBay, press release, July 21, 2005, http://investor.ebay.com/ReleaseDetail.cfm?ReleaseID=170073&FYear=; Paul Sloan, "Retail Without the Risk," *Business 2.0*, Mar. 1, 2006, http://money.cnn.com/magazines/business2/business2_archive/2006/03/01/8370575/; Jon Swartz, "'E' in eBay Might Stand for Expansion," *USA Today*, Mar. 28, 2001, www.usatoday.com; Lizette Wilson, "Businesses Build Profits Helping Others Use Ebay," *San Francisco Business Times*, May 26, 2003, http://sanfrancisco.bizjournals.com/sanfrancisco/stories/2003/05/26/story8.html; Eric Young, "Ebay Says Fixed-Price Bazaar Will Open Next Quarter," *The Standard*, May 25, 2001, www.thestandard.com.

## Chapter 9

1. Sources: "Company History," Pacific Research Group, http://65.119.21.227/company/history.asp (accessed Apr. 14, 2006); Robert Frank, "How One Entrepreneur Lives Large—For Free," from *The Wall Street Journal* Online, June 11, 2003, www.startupjournal.com/ideas/services/20030611-frank.html; Matthew Heimer, "Mystery Shopper," *Smart Money*, Dec. 2005, pp. 96–101; "Our Programs: Digital On-Site Mystery Shopping," Pacific Research Group, http://65.119.21.227/programs/digital_onsite_shopping.asp (accessed Apr. 14, 2006).

2. Anne L. Souchon, John W. Cadogan, David B. Procter, and Belinda Dewsnap, "Marketing Information Use and Organisational Performance: The Mediating Role of Responsiveness," *Journal of Strategic Marketing*, 12 (Dec. 2004): 231–242.

3. Suzanne Vranica, "McDonald's Tries for 'Viral' Buzz," *The Wall Street Journal*, Feb. 8, 2005, http://online.wsj.com/public/us.

4. Ellen Byron, "New Penney: Chain Goes for 'Missing Middle,'" *The Wall Street Journal*, Feb. 14, 2005, http://online.wsj.com/public/us.

5. Catherine Arnold, "Self-Examination: Researchers Reveal State of MR in Survey," *Marketing News*, Feb. 1, 2005, pp. 55, 56.

6. Jacquelyn S. Thomas, "A Methodology for Linking Customer Acquisition to Customer Retention," *Journal of Marketing Research*, May 2001, pp. 262–268.

7. Jamie Lareau, "Hummer's H3 Thrives in Slow SUV Market Despite Higher Gas Prices," *AutoWeek*, Oct. 11, 2005, www.autoweek.com/news.cms?newsId=103335.

8. "Trading the Bleachers for the Couch," *Business Week Online*, Aug. 22, 2005, www.businessweek.com.

9. A. Parasuraman, Dhruv Grewal, and R. Krishnan, *Marketing Research* (Boston: Houghton Mifflin, 2004), p. 63.

10. Ken Manning, O. C. Ferrell, and Linda Ferrell, "Consumer Expectations of Clearance vs. Sale Prices," University of Wyoming, working paper, 2006.

11. Parasuraman, Grewal, and Krishnan, *Marketing Research*, p. 64.

12. Brian T. Ratchford, Myung-Soo Lee, and Debabrata Talukdar, "The Impact of the Internet on Information Search for Automobiles," *Journal of Marketing Research*, May 2003, pp. 193–209.

13. Parasuraman, Grewal, and Krishnan, *Marketing Research*, p. 73.

14. Vikas Mittal and Wagner A. Kamakura, "Satisfaction, Repurchase Intent, and Repurchase Behavior: Investigating the Moderating Effects of Customer Characteristics," *Journal of Marketing Research*, Feb. 2001, pp. 131–142.

15. "Internal Secondary Market Research," CCH Business Owner's Toolkit, www.toolkit.cch.com/text/P03_3020.asp (accessed Apr. 14, 2006).

16. Haya El Nasser, "Census Bureau No Longer Waiting 10 Years for Data," *The* [Fort Collins] *Coloradoan*, Jan. 17, 2005, p. A2.

17. "Information Resources, Inc.," *Marketing News*, June 15, 2005, pp. H1–H57.

18. "External Secondary Market Research," CCH Business Owner's Toolkit, www.toolkit.cch.com/text/P03_3011.asp (accessed Apr. 14, 2006).

19. Arnold, "Self-Examination."

20. Randy Garner, "Post-It Note Persuasion: A Sticky Influence," *Journal of Consumer Psychology* 15 (2005): 230–237.

21. John Harwood and Shirley Leung, "Hang-Ups: Why Some Pollsters Got It So Wrong This Election Day," *The Wall Street Journal*, Nov. 8, 2003, pp. A1, A6.
22. Ibid.
23. Ibid.
24. Robert V. Kozinets, "The Field Behind the Screen: Using Netnography for Marketing Research in Online Communities," *Journal of Marketing Research* 39 (Feb. 2002): 61–72.
25. Glen L. Urban and John R. Hauser, "'Listening In' to Find and Explore New Combinations of Customer Needs," *Journal of Marketing* 68 (Apr. 2004): 72–87.
26. "Where the Stars Design the Cars," *Business 2.0*, July 2005, p. 32.
27. Daniel Gross, "Lies, Damn Lies, and Focus Groups," *Slate*, Oct. 10, 2003, http://slate.msn.com/id/2089677/.
28. Peter DePaulo, "Sample Size for Qualitative Research," *Quirk's Marketing Research Review*, Dec. 2000, www.quirks.com.
29. Sean Geehan and Stacy Sheldon, "Connecting to Customers," *Marketing Management*, Nov./Dec. 2005, pp. 37–42.
30. "Customer Advisory Board on Disabilities," Northwest Airlines, www.nwa.com/services/onboard/special/cab.shtml (accessed Apr. 14, 2006).
31. Barbara Allan, "The Benefits of Telephone Depth Sessions," *Quirk's Marketing Research Review*, Dec. 2000, www.quirks.com.
32. Jagdip Singh, Roy D. Howell, and Gary K. Rhoads, "Adaptive Designs for Likert-Type Data: An Approach for Implementing Marketing Surveys," *Journal of Marketing Research*, Aug. 1990, pp. 304–321.
33. Bas Donkers, Philip Hans Franses, and Peter C. Verhoef, "Selective Sampling for Binary Choice Models," *Journal of Marketing Research*, Nov. 2003, pp. 492–497.
34. David Kiley, "Shoot the Focus Group," *Business Week Online*, Nov. 14, 2005, www.businessweek.com.
35. Thomas T. Semon, "Determine Survey's Purpose for Best Results," *Marketing News*, Jan. 6, 2003, p. 7.
36. Eunkyu Lee, Michael Y. Hu, and Rex S. Toh, "Are Consumer Survey Results Distorted? Systematic Impact of Behavioral Frequency and Duration on Survey Response Errors," *Journal of Marketing Research*, Feb. 2000, pp. 125–133.
37. Judy Strauss and Donna J. Hill, "Consumer Complaints by E-mail: An Exploratory Investigation of Corporate Responses and Customer Reactions," *Journal of Interactive Marketing*, Winter 2001, pp. 63–73.
38. Kevin Kelleher, "66,207,986 Bottles of Beer on the Wall," *Business 2.0*, via CNN, Feb. 25, 2004, www.cnn.com.
39. Thomas Mucha, "The Builder of Boomtown," *Business 2.0*, Sept. 2005, www.business2.com.
40. Noah Rubin Brier, John McManus, David Myron, and Christopher Reynolds, "'Zero-In' Heroes," *American Demographics*, Oct. 2004, pp. 36–45.
41. Laurence N. Goal, "High Technology Data Collection for Measurement and Testing," *Marketing Research*, Mar. 1992, pp. 29–38.
42. Philip Hans Franses, "How Nobel-Worthy Economics Relates to Databases," *Marketing News*, Mar. 12, 2001, p. 14.
43. Behrooz Noori and Mohammad Hossein Salimi, "A Decision-Support System for Business-to-Business Marketing," *Journal of Business & Industrial Marketing* 20 (2005): 226–236.
44. Amy Merrick, "New Population Data Will Help Marketers Pitch Their Products," *The Wall Street Journal*, Feb. 14, 2001, http://online.wsj.com/public/us.
45. Spencer E. Ante, "IBM," *Business Week*, Nov. 24, 2003, p. 84.
46. Source: Reprinted with permission of The Marketing Research Association, P.O. Box 230, Rocky Hill, CT 06067–0230, 860–257–4008.

47. Carlos Denton, "Time Differentiates Latino Focus Groups," *Marketing News*, Mar. 15, 2004, p. 52.
48. "Honomichl Top 50," *Marketing News*, June 15, 2005, p. H1+.
49. Lambeth Hochwald, "Are You Smart Enough to Sell Globally?" *Sales & Marketing Management*, July 1998, pp. 52–56.
50. Ibid.
51. Sources: Steve Bassill, "How to Implement a Winning Segment Strategy," *Marketing Profs.com*, Feb. 21, 2006, www.marketingprofs.com/6/bassill1.asp; Lake Snell Perry Mermin & Associates, www.lakesnellperry.com (accessed Apr. 14, 2006); "Leading Democratic Polling Firm Celebrates 10th Anniversary with New Partner," Lake Snell Perry Mermin & Associates, press release, Mar. 11, 2005, www.lakesnellperry.com/new/Mermin0311.htm.
52. Sources: Best Buy, www.bestbuy.com (accessed Apr. 14, 2006); "Best Buy Case Study," Experian, www.Experian.com (accessed Apr. 14, 2006); Ariana Eunjung Chu, "In Retail Profiling for Profit; Best Buy Stores Cater to Specific Customer Types," *The Washington Post*, Aug. 17, 2005, p. A1; Stacey Collett, "Turning Data into Dollars," *Computer World*, Sept. 23, 2004, www.computerworld.com; *Fiscal 2005 Annual Report*, Best Buy; Gary McWilliams, "Minding the Store: Analyzing Customers, Best Buy Decides Not All Are Welcome," *The Wall Street Journal*, Nov. 8, 2004, http://online.wsj.com/public/us.

## Chapter 10

1. Sources: "Whole Baby Program Introduces New Moms to Advantages of Natural and Organic Lifestyle for Their Growing Families, Whole Foods Market and *Mothering* Magazine Partner to Launch Informational Lecture Tour About Benefits of Natural Parenting," *PR Newswire*, Aug. 11, 2005; "Whole Foods Market Survey Reveals Expectant Moms Are Hungry for Natural and Organic Nutrition Guidance, Whole Baby Lecture Series Kicks-Off in New York City Sept. 22, National Experts Promote Health to Growing Families," *PR Newswire*, Sept. 19, 2005; Whole Foods Market, www.wholefoodsmarket.com (accessed Apr. 17, 2006); Whole Baby Lecture Series, www.wholebabylecture.com (accessed Apr. 17, 2006).
2. Mark Rechtin, "Hyundai Targets Sedan Superstars," *Automotive News*, Jan. 17, 2005, pp. 14–15.
3. Dan Higgins, "Pens, A Fountain of Inspiration," *The Times Union*, Nov. 5, 2004, p. E1.
4. Andrew Blum, with Louise Lee, "It Sure Ain't Old Navy," *Business Week*, Oct. 17, 2005, pp. 62–64.
5. Service Corporation International, www.hoovers.com (accessed Jan. 26, 2005).
6. Brad Edomondson, "America, New & Improved," *Advertising Age*, Jan. 2, 2006, p. 34.
7. "Disney Hopes Virtual Park Delivers Real-World Results," *Advertising Age*, Jan. 3, 2005, p. 4.
8. "Kids and Commercialism," Center for New American Dream, http://newdream.org/kids/facts.php (accessed Apr. 17, 2006).
9. U.S. Bureau of the Census, *Statistical Abstract of the United States*, 2004 (Washington, DC: Government Printing Office, 2005), p. 12.
10. Marvin Maties, "The New Product Game: Why Targeting Women Is Key," *Prepared Foods*, June 2003, p. 35.
11. Laura Heller, "Sears Targets Ethnic Customers with New Lines, Bilingual Associates," *DSN Retailing Today*, Oct. 25, 2004, p. 69.
12. Jason Fields, "America's Families and Living Arrangements: 2003," *Current Population Reports*, U.S. Census Bureau (Washington, DC: Government Printing Office, 2003), pp. 20–553.
13. Clients and Case Studies, www.micromarketing.com/clients/index.html (accessed Apr. 17, 2006).

14. "Yum, Bally Fitness Team Up for Promo," *Advertising Age*, Jan. 3, 2005, p. 2.
15. Joseph T. Plummer, "The Concept and Application of Life Style Segmentation," *Journal of Marketing*, Jan. 1974, p. 33.
16. "Catching Up with the Next Generation: They're Not Slackers Anymore," *PR Newswire*, Oct. 26, 2004.
17. SRI Consulting Business Intelligence, www.sric-bi.com/VALS (accessed Apr. 17, 2006).
18. Beverage World, "Beverage Market Index 2003," *VNU Business Media*, June 15, 2003.
    Philip Kotler, *Marketing Management: Analysis, Planning, Implementation, and Control*, 11th ed. (Englewood Cliffs, NJ: Prentice-Hall, 2003), p. 144.
19. "Analysis: Huge Cardiovascular Market Potential in Aging Baby Boomers," *Heart Disease Weekly* via NewsRX.com and NewsRX.net, Apr. 11, 2004, p. 92.
20. Sara Schaefer Munoz, "Food Group Joins Sugar Producers Critical of Splenda," *The Wall Street Journal*, Feb. 15, 2005, p. D4; Marian Burros, "Splenda's 'Sugar' Claim Unites Odd Couple of Nutrition Wars," *The New York Times*, Feb. 15, 2005, p. A12.
21. Charles W. Chase, Jr., "Selecting the Appropriate Forecasting Method," *Journal of Business Forecasting*, Fall 1997, pp. 2, 23, 28–29.
22. "ACNielsen Market Decisions: Controlled Market Testing," ACNielsen, http://us.acnielsen.com/products/rms_amd_controlledmktest.shtml (accessed Apr. 17, 2006).
23. Sources: Jordan's Furniture, www.jordans.com (accessed Apr. 17, 2006); "Three Customer-Centric Retailers," *Chain Store Age*, Oct. 2005, pp. 26–29.
24. & 25. "Jordan's Makes Furniture Shopping a Fun Event," *Metro Report Boston*, July 2005, p. 30; Janet Groeber, "That's Entertainment," *Display & Design Ideas*, May 2005, p. 22.
26. Sources: Kerry Capell, "IKEA: How the Swedish Retailer Became a Global Brand," *Business Week*, Nov. 14, 2005, pp. 96–106; "Facts and Figures," IKEA, www.ikea.com/ms/en_US (accessed Apr. 17, 2006); "IKEA's Growth Limited by Style Issues, Says CEO," *Nordic Business Report*, Jan. 21, 2004, www.nordicbusinessreport.com; "IKEA Sets New Heights with Cat," *Printing World*, Aug. 21, 2003, p. 3; "Stylish, Swedish, 60-ish: IKEA's a Global Phenomenon," *Western Mail*, May 20, 2003, p. 1; "Verticalnet's Supply Chain Software Upgrade, Packaging Wins Customers," *InternetWeek*, Sept. 3, 2003, www.internetworld.com.
27. Sources: Jennifer Carofano, "The Turnaround Gunning for the No. 1 Spot in Athletic Footwear, Reebok Cranked Up the Heat in 2003," *Footwear News*, Dec. 8, 2003, p. 22; Polly Devaney, "Reebok Shoots from the Hip-Hop in Sneaker Wars," *Marketing Week*, July 31, 2003, p. 21; Rosemary Feitelberg, "Eve to Rap Up Reebok Classic," *Women's Wear Daily*, Mar. 20, 2003, p. 8; www.hoovers.com; Morag Cuddeford Jones, "Reebok Has Spring in Its Step," *Brand Strategy*, Oct. 2003, p. 9; David Lipke, "Reebok Targets Men with New NYC Store," *Daily News Record*, Oct. 27, 2003, p. 14; Wayne Niemi, "Chasing China: With Several Major Athletic Players Betting Big on China, the Sneaker Wars Are Heating Up," *Footwear News*, Dec. 15, 2003, p. 12; Elizabeth Olson, "Being Chased by the Big Boys," *New York Times*, Nov. 27, 2003, p. C4; Joseph Pereira and Stephanie Kang, "Phat News: Rappers Choose Reebok Shoes," *The Wall Street Journal*, Nov. 14, 2003, p. B1; Reebok, www.rbk.com (accessed Jan. 24, 2006); Scott Van Voorhis, "Reebok Pitching Licensing Deal to MLB," *Boston Herald*, Jan. 15, 2004, p. 40.

**Chapter 11**

1. Sources: "1st: Chevrolet Corvette Coupe," *Road and Track*, Mar. 2004, pp. 74–76; Csaba Csere, "Simply the Fastest-Ever Production Vette," *Car and Driver*, Feb. 2005, p. 74;

James R. Healey, "Hot, Fun, and Even Functional," *USA Today*, Nov. 26, 2004, p. 10D; "Mattel Joins with GM to Roll Out Hot Wheels Corvette C6," Mattel, press release, Jan. 13, 2004, via http://collectibles.about.com/cs/automobiliaracing/a/blPRmattel11404.htm; Thane Peterson, "Going Topless in the Best Vette Yet," *Business Week Online*, Jun. 24, 2005, www.businessweek.com/bwdaily/dnflash/jun2005/nf20050624_3422.htm; Ron Perry, "Chevrolet Corvette vs. Porsche 911 Carrera S: Classic Warfare," *Road and Track*, Dec. 2004, pp. 87–96; Rachel Sams, "PRS Guitars Signs Pact with Corvette," *Baltimore Business Journal*, Jan. 15, 2005, http://baltimore.bizjournals.com/baltimore/stories/2005/01/17/daily2.html.
2. Jay Boehmer, "Three Hotel Chains Introduce Select Service Prototypes," *Business Travel News*, Oct. 17, 2005, pp. 10–34.
3. Greg Moss, "Starbucks Sees Growing Demand for Drive-Thrus," 9News.com, Dec. 27, 2005, www.9news.com.
4. Debbie Howell, "HEB Plus! Is at It Again—Turning Heads with a NEW GM Line," *DSN Retailing Today*, Dec. 19, 2005, pp. 3+.
5. Karen Richardson, "First Service's Odd Mix Works," *The Wall Street Journal*, Dec. 22, 2004, p. C4.
6. Joann Muller, "Parts for the Sensitive Car," *Forbes*, Nov. 28, 2005, pp. 204–208.
7. Traci Pardum, "Procter & Gamble: Adding More Goods to Its Bag," *IndustryWeek*, Oct. 13, 2005, www.industryweek.com/ReadArticle.aspx?ArticleID=10862&SectionID=5.
8. William P. Putsis, Jr., and Barry L. Bayus, "An Empirical Analysis of Firms' Product Line Decisions," *Journal of Marketing Research*, Feb. 2001, pp. 110–118.
9. Muller, "Parts for the Sensitive Car."
10. Deborah Ball, "Snack Attack: As Chocolate Sags, Cadbury Gambles on a Piece of Gum," *The Wall Street Journal*, Jan. 12, 2006, p. A1, http://online.wsj.com/public/us.
11. Susanna Hamner, "Why the Kids Are Dissing LeapFrog," *Business 2.0*, Nov. 2005, www.business2.com.
12. Brian A. Lukas and O. C. Ferrell, "The Effect of Market Orientation on Product Innovation," *Journal of the Academy of Marketing Science*, Feb. 2000, pp. 239–247.
13. "Who Is Dr. Gadget?" The Dettman Group, 2005, www.doctorgadget.com/Who_Is_Dr._Gadget.html.
14. Elizabeth Esfahani, "Finding the Sweet Spot," *Business 2.0*, Nov. 2005, www.business2.com.
15. Peter Lewis, "Play That Funky Music, White Toy," *Fortune*, Feb. 7, 2005, pp. 38–39.
16. Lee G. Cooper, "Structure Marketing Planning for Radically New Products," *Journal of Marketing*, Jan. 2000, pp. 1–16.
17. James R. Healey and Jayne O'Donnell, "Popularity of Crossovers Leaves SUVs in Dust," *USA Today*, Dec. 8, 2005, pp. 1B, 3B.
18. O. C. Ferrell and Michael Hartline, *Marketing Strategy* (Mason, OH: South-Western, 2005), pp. 172–173.
19. "A Really Cool Studey," *Road & Track*, Dec. 2005, p. 130.
20. Adam Horowitz, Mark Athitakis, Mark Lasswell, and Owen Thomas, "101 Dumbest Moments in Business," *Business 2.0*, Jan/Feb. 2005, pp. 103–112.
21. Ferrell and Hartline, *Marketing Strategy*, p. 174.
22. Adapted from Everett M. Rogers, *Diffusion of Innovations* (New York: Macmillan, 1962), pp. 81–86.
23. Arch G. Woodside and Wim Biemans, "Managing Relationships, Networks, and Complexity in Innovation, Diffusion, and Adoption Processes," *Journal of Business & Industrial Marketing* 20 (July 2005): 335–338.
24. Ibid., pp. 247–250.
25. Horowitz, Athitakis, Lasswell, and Thomas, "101 Dumbest Moments in Business."

26. Susan Casey, "Object-Oriented: Everything I Ever Needed to Know About Business I Learned in the Frozen Food Aisle," *eCompany,* Oct. 2000, www.ecompany.com.

27. Louis Lavelle, "What Campbell's New Chief Needs to Know," *Business Week,* June 25, 2001, p. 60.

28. Sources: "100 Best Corporate Citizens 2005," *Business Ethics,* Spring 2005, pp. 22–23; "Brewing Up a Strong Starbucks Alternative," MSNBC, Feb. 5, 2006, www.msnbc.msn.com/id/4163701/; "Coca-Cola May Take on Starbucks," MSNBC, Jan. 30, 2006, www.msnbc.msn.com/id/11101825/; "Company Fact Sheet," Starbucks, Feb. 2006, www.starbucks.com/aboutus/Company_Fact_Sheet_Feb06.pdf; "'Fortune 100 Best Companies to Work for 2006," *Fortune,* Jan. 12, 2005, http://money.cnn.com/magazines/fortune/bestcompanies/snapshots/1267.html; "Health Care Takes Its Toll on Starbucks," MSNBC, Sep. 14, 2005, www.msnbc.msn.com/id/9344634/; Adam Horowitz, David Jacobson, Mark Lasswell, and Owen Thomas, "101 Dumbest Moments in Business," *Business 2.0,* Feb. 1, 2006, http://money.cnn.com/magazines/business2/101dumbest/full_list/page6.html; "In Rare Flop, Starbucks Scraps Chocolate Drink," MSNBC, Feb. 10, 2006, www.msnbc.msn.com/id/11274445/; Starbucks, www.starbucks.com (accessed Apr. 17, 2006); Starbucks Annual Report 10-K; Winter, "Starbucks Everywhere," www.starbuckseverywhere.net/ (accessed Apr. 17, 2006).

29. Sources: "Dell at a Glance," Dell, www1.us.dell.com/content/topics/global.aspx/corp/background/en/facts?c=us&l=en&s=corp&~section=000&~ck=mn (accessed Apr. 17, 2006); Heather Green, "Consumer Electronics: Free-Falling Prices and Rocketing Sales," *Business Week,* Jan. 12, 2004, pp. 99–101; Bolaji Ojo, "Equipped with Hard Drive," *EBN,* Oct. 27, 2003, p. 2; Cathy Booth Thomas, "Dell Wants Your Home," *Time,* Oct. 6, 2003, pp. 48–50; Cynthia L. Webb, "Battle of the Consumer Electronics Giants," Washingtonpost.com, Sept. 26, 2003, www.washingtonpost.com.

## Chapter 12

1. Sources: Elizabeth Esfahani, "Finding the Sweet Spot," *Business 2.0,* Nov. 2005, www.business2.com; Judith Blake, "Splenda under Fire over Claims," *The Seattle Times,* Mar. 2, 2005, http://seattletimes.nwsource.com/html/foodwine/2002193747_splenda02.html; "Splenda Brand Timeline," Splenda, www.splenda.com/page.jhtml?id=splenda/newspromotions/press/timelines.inc (accessed Mar. 2, 2006).

2. Mary Jane Credeur, "Coke Poured Out 1,000 New Products in 2005," *USA Today,* Dec. 8, 2005, p. B5.

3. Bruce Horovitz, "Speedo Speeds Suits to Winter Athletes," *USA Today,* Dec. 1, 2005, p. 3B.

4. Brian Hindo, "Clorox: The Dirt on Innovation," Business Week Online, Nov. 3, 2005, www.businessweek.com

5. Kate MacArthur, "Drink Your Fruits, Veggies: Water's the New Fitness Fad," *Advertising Age,* Jan. 3, 2005, p. 4.

6. Chung K. Kim, Anne M. Lavack, and Margo Smith, "Consumer Evaluation of Vertical Brand Extensions and Core Brands," *Journal of Business Research,* Mar. 2001, pp. 211–222.

7. Maria Sääksjärvi and Minttu Lampinen, "Consumer Perceived Risk in Successive Product Generations," *European Journal of Innovation Management* 8 (June 2005): 145–156.

8. William C. Symonds, "Gillette's Five-Blade Wonder," *Business Week,* Sept. 15, 2005, www.businessweek.com.

9. Warren Brown, "Add Sunshine, Be Stirred: 2005 Mustang Convertible," *The Washington Post,* Jan. 16, 2005, p. G1.

10. Frank Franzak and Dennis Pitta, "New Product Development at Eastern Spice & Flavorings," *Journal of Product & Brand Management* 14 (2005): 462–467.

11. Robert M. McMath, "Kellogg's Cereal Mates: 'It's Not for Breakfast Anymore,'" *Failure Magazine,* Dec. 2003.

12. Scott Sprinzen and Robert Schulz, "Running on Empty in Detroit," Business Week Online, Dec. 9, 2005, www.businessweek.com.

13. Lee G. Cooper, "Strategic Marketing Planning for Radically New Products," *Journal of Marketing,* Jan. 2000, pp. 1–16.

14. Lisa C. Troy, David M. Szymanski, and P. Rajan Varadarajan, "Generating New Product Ideas: An Initial Investigation of the Role of Market Information and Organizational Characteristics," *Journal of the Academy of Marketing Science,* Jan. 2001, pp. 89–101.

15. "A. G. Lafley: Procter & Gamble," *Business Week,* Dec. 19, 2005, p. 62.

16. Aric Rindfleisch and Christine Moorman, "The Acquisition and Utilization of Information in New Product Alliances: A Strength-of-Ties Perspective," *Journal of Marketing,* Apr. 2001, pp. 1–18.

17. Jack Gordon and Bill Vernick, "What All Brands, CEOs Must Know About Developing Great New Products," *Cost Engineering* 47 (Nov. 2005): 8–9.

18. Dennis A. Pitta and Danielle Fowler, "Online Consumer Communities and Their Value to New Product Developers," *Journal of Product & Brand Management* 14 (2005): 283–291.

19. Jathon Sapsford, "Honda Caters to Japan's Pet Population Boom," *The Wall Street Journal,* Oct. 5, 2005, p. B1, http://online.wsj.com/public/us.

20. Deborah Ball, "As Chocolate Sags, Cadbury Gambles on a Piece of Gum," *The Wall Street Journal,* Jan. 12, 2006, p. A1, http://online.wsj.com/public/us.

21. Lisa Sanders, "Berlin Cameron Wins Heineken Light Beer Ad Campaign," *Advertising Age,* Dec. 27, 2005, www.adage.com.

22. "P&G Ends Test of Impress Plastic Wrap," *Advertising Age,* July 18, 2001, www.adage.com.

23. Sanders, "Berlin Cameron Wins Heineken Light Beer Ad Campaign."

24. Jack Neff, "Swiffer by Another Name," *Advertising Age,* Apr. 11, 2005, p. 11.

25. Bruce Horovitz, "CEO Turns the Flame Up," *USA Today,* May 23, 2005, p. 3B; Kate MacArthur, "What's Eating Burger King," *Advertising Age,* Jan. 26, 2004, pp. 1, 30.

26. Adapted from Michael Levy and Barton A. Weitz, *Retailing Management* (Burr Ridge, IL: Irwin/McGraw-Hill, 2001), p. 585.

27. American Customer Satisfaction Index, National Quality Research Center at the University of Michigan, www.theacsi.org/overview.htm (accessed Apr. 17, 2006).

28. "Nikon Will Stop Making Most Film Cameras," CNN, Jan. 12, 2006, www.cnn.com.

29. "Delta to Eliminate Discount Carrier Song," *The New York Times,* Oct. 28, 2005, www.nytimes.com.

30. Jack Neff, "White Clouds Could Bring Rain on P&G," *Advertising Age,* July 2, 2001, p. 4.

31. "Nikon Will Stop Making Most Film Cameras."

32. Julie Cantwell, "GM Redefines Role of Brand Managers," *Automotive News,* Jan. 14, 2002, p. 3.

33. Rajesh Sethi, "New Product Quality and Product Development Teams," *Journal of Marketing,* Apr. 2000, pp. 1–14.

34. Sources: Newbury Comics, www.newburycomics.com (accessed Apr. 17, 2006); Steve Traiman, "Relationship of Mutual Respect Reaps Rewards," *Billboard,* Sept. 27, 2003; Anne Zaleski, "You Learn by the Bonehead Mistakes," *Billboard,* Sept. 27, 2003.

35. Sources: Jennifer Bjorhus, "3M Unveils Drastic Shakeup of Research and Development Division," *Saint Paul Pioneer Press,* Sept. 27, 2003, www.twincities.com/mld/pioneerpress; John S. McClenahen, "New World Leader: 3M Co.'s James McNerney, CEO of the Year," *Industry Week,* Jan. 2004, pp.

36+; Rita Shor, "Managed Innovation: 3M's Latest Model for New Products," *Manufacturing and Technology News* (n.d.), www.manufacturingnews.com/news/editorials/shor.html; Tim Studt, "3M—Where Innovation Rules," *R&D*, Apr. 2003, pp. 20+; Robert Westervelt, "3M Reorganizes R&D Effort," *Chemical Week*, Oct. 5, 2003, p. 11; "Who We Are," 3M, http://solutions.3m.com/wps/portal/!ut/p/kcxml/04_ Sj9SPykssy0xPLMnMz0vM0Q9KzYsPDdaP0I8yizeID3LUL8h wVAQAOeGPLw!! (accessed Apr. 17, 2006).

## Chapter 13

1. Sources: "Company Profile," Del Monte, www.delmonte.com/ company/AboutUs/Profile.asp (accessed May 1, 2006); "Del Monte," Enterprise IG, www.enterpriseig.com/display/ BrandsDetails.asp?BrandID=222 (accessed May 1, 2006); Del Monte Foods 2005 Annual Report, pp. 1–9; "Del Monte Foods Company Reports Fiscal 2005 Fourth Quarter and Full Year Results; Announces Brand-Driven Strategic Plan, Including a $125 Million Share Repurchase Program," Business Wire, June 23, 2005, www.findarticles.com/p/articles/mi_m0EIN/is_2005_ June_23/ai_n13828072.

2. "Dictionary of Marketing Terms," American Marketing Association, www.marketingpower.com/mg-dictionary.php (accessed Jan. 18, 2006).

3. U.S. Bureau of the Census, *Statistical Abstract of the United States*, 2006 (Washington DC: Government Printing Office, 2006), p. 521.

4. Douglas B. Holt, *How Brands Become Icons: The Principles of Cultural Branding* (Boston: Harvard Business School Press, 2004).

5. Nigel Hollis, "Branding Unmasked," *Marketing Research*, Fall 2005, pp. 24–29.

6. Don E. Schultz, "The Loyalty Paradox," *Marketing Management*, Sept./Oct. 2005, pp. 10–11.

7. David J. Lipke, "Pledge of Allegiance," *American Demographics*, Nov. 2000, pp. 40–42.

8. David A. Aaker, *Managing Brand Equity: Capitalizing on the Value of a Brand Name* (New York: Free Press, 1991), pp. 16–17.

9. Smucker's Annual Report, 2005, The J. M. Smucker Company.

10. Joel Rubinson, "Framework for Growth," *Marketing Research*, Summer 2005, pp. 15–16.

11. Kelly Pate, "Private Brands Help Grocers Compete, Offer Higher Profit Margins," *The Denver Post*, July 30, 2003.

12. Janet Adamy, "New Food, New Look," *The Wall Street Journal*, Nov. 21, 2005, p. R8, http://online.wsj.com/public/us.

13. Marcel Corstjens and Rajiv Lal, "Building Store Loyalty Through Store Brands," *Journal of Marketing Research*, Aug. 2000, pp. 281–291.

14. Chiranjeev S. Kohli, Katrin R. Harich, and Lance Leuthesser, "Creating Brand Identity: A Study of Evaluation of New Brand Names," *Journal of Business Research* 58 (2005): 1506–1515.

15. Jay Boehmer, "Three Hotel Chains Introduce Select-Service Prototypes," *Business Travel News*, Oct. 17, 2005, via Business Source Premier.

16. Mike Beirne, "Philip Morris to Put New Name, Altria, Aloft," *Brandweek*, Dec. 16, 2002, p. 4.

17. Dorothy Cohen, "Trademark Strategy," *Journal of Marketing*, Jan. 1986, p. 63.

18. U.S. Trademark Association, "Trademark Stylesheet," no. 1A.

19. Devon Del Vecchio and Daniel C. Smith, "Brand-Extension Price Premiums: The Effects of Perceived Fit and Extension Product Category Risk," *Journal of Marketing Science* 33 (Apr. 2005): 184–196.

20. Vicki R. Lane, "The Impact of Ad Repetition and Ad Content on Consumer Perceptions of Incongruent Extensions," *Journal of Marketing*, Apr. 2000, pp. 80–91.

21. Alessandra Galloni, "Armani, Mercedes to Form Marketing, Design Venture," *Wall Street Journal Online*, Sept. 30, 2003, http://online.wsj.com/article/0,,SB106487258836292400,00. html.

22. Christopher Palmeri, "Mattel: Up the Hill Minus Jill," *Business Week*, Apr. 9, 2001, pp. 53–54.

23. Jeff Falk, "Splish, Splash—Packaging Takes a Bath," *Global Cosmetic Industry*, Dec. 2005, pp. 44+.

24. Thomas J. Madden, Kelly Hewett, and Martin S. Roth, "Managing Images in Different Cultures: A Cross-National Study of Color Meanings and Preferences," *Journal of International Marketing*, Winter 2000, p. 90.

25. Gary Grossman, "Put Some Pizzazz in Your Packaging," *Brandweek*, Jan. 17, 2005, p. 17.

26. Smucker's Annual Report, 2005.

27. Deborah Ball, "The Perils of Packaging: Nestlé Aims for Easier Openings," *The Wall Street Journal*, Nov. 17, 2005, p. B1, http://online.wsj.com/public/us.

28. Valerie Folkes and Shashi Matta, "The Effect of Package Shape on Consumers' Judgment of Product Volume: Attention as a Mental Contaminant," *Journal of Consumer Research*, Sept. 2004, p. 390.

29. Ball, "The Perils of Packaging."

30. "FDA Proposed New Rules for GM Foods," *Chemical Market Reporter*, Jan. 29, 2001, p. 7.

31. Federal Trade Commission, www.ftc.gov (accessed May 1, 2006).

32. Sources: Peter Asmus, "Goodbye Coal, Hello Wind," *Business Ethics*, July/Aug. 1999, pp. 10–11; Robert Baun, "New Belgium Hits Top 5 Among U.S. Specialty Brewers," *The [Fort Collins] Coloradoan*, Feb. 21, 2002, p. 09; Robert Baun, "What's in a Name? Ask the Makers of Fat Tire," *The [Fort Collins] Coloradoan*, Oct. 8, 2000, pp. E1, E3; Rachel Brand, "Colorado Breweries Bring Home 12 Medals in Festival," *Rocky Mountain [Denver] News*, www.insidedenver.com/ news/1008beer6.shtml (accessed Nov. 6, 2000); Stevi Deter, "Fat Tire Amber Ale," The Net Net, www.thenetnet.com/ reviews/fat.html (accessed May 1, 2006); DirtWorld.com, www.dirtworld.com/races/Colorado_race745.htm (accessed Nov. 6, 2000); Robert F. Dwyer and John F. Tanner, Jr., *Business Marketing* (Burr Ridge, IL: Irwin/McGraw-Hill, 1999), p. 104; "Fat Tire Amber Ale," *Achwiegut (The Guide to Austrian Beer)*, www.austrianbeer.com/beer/b000688.shtml (accessed Mar. 5, 2001); "Four Businesses Honored with Prestigious International Award for Outstanding Marketplace Ethics," Better Business Bureau, press release, Sept. 23, 2002, www.bbb.org/alerts/2002torchwinners.asp; Julie Gordon, "Lebesch Balances Interests in Business, Community," *The [Fort Collins] Coloradoan*, Feb. 26, 2003; Del I. Hawkins, Roger J. Best, and Kenneth A. Coney, *Consumer Behavior: Building Marketing Strategy*, 8th ed. (Burr Ridge, IL: Irwin/McGraw-Hill, 2001); David Kemp, Tour Connoisseur, New Belgium Brewing Company, personal interview by Nikole Haiar, Nov. 21, 2000; New Belgium Brewing Company, Ft. Collins, CO, www.newbelgium.com (accessed May 1, 2006); New Belgium Brewing Company Tour by Nikole Haiar, Nov. 20, 2000; "New Belgium Brewing Wins Ethics Award," *Denver Business Journal*, Jan. 2, 2003, http:// denver.bizjournals.com/denver/stories/2002/12/30/daily21. html; Dan Rabin, "New Belgium Pours It on for Bike Riders," *Celebrator Beer News*, Aug./Sept. 1998, www.celebrator.com/ 9808/rabin.html; Lisa Sanders, "This Beer Will Reduce Your Anxiety," *Advertising Age*, Jan. 17, 2005, p. 25; Bryan Simpson, "New Belgium Brewing: Brand Building Through Advertising and Public Relations," http://college.hmco.com/ instructors/catalog/misc/new_belgium_brewing.pdf (accessed May 1, 2006).

33. Sources: Monica Davey, "Harley at 100," *The New York Times*, Sept. 1, 2003, p. A1; Jonathan Fahey, "Love into Money," *Forbes*, Jan. 7, 2002, pp. 60–65; Harley-Davidson Company, www.harley-davidson.com (accessed May 1, 2006); "Harley-Davidson Reports Record Second Quarter," Harley-Davidson news release, July 16, 2003, www.harley-davidson.com; Abraham Lustgarten, "The 100 Best Companies to Work For: Harley-Davidson," *Fortune*, Jan. 12, 2004, p. 76; Ryan Nakashima, "Harley-Davidson Plans China Dealership," Forbes.com, Jan. 18, 2006, www.forbes.com/business/energy/feeds/ap/2006/01/18/ap2458631.html; Joseph Weber, "Harley Investors May Get a Wobbly Ride," *Business Week*, Feb. 11, 2002, p. 65; Mark Yost, "Harley-Davidson Centenary Bash Brings Out Armchair 'Rebels,'" *The Wall Street Journal*, Sept. 3, 2003, p. D4.

**Chapter 14**

1. Sources: Brooks Barnes, "How 'Wicked' Cast Its Spell," *The Wall Street Journal*, Oct. 22, 2005, p. A1, http://online.wsj.com/public/us; Michael Kuchwara, "One Woman Stands Behind Broadway's Best," MSNBC.com, Aug. 21, 2005, http://msnbc.com/id/8974469/page/2/; "Wicked," Internet Broadway Database, www.ibdb.com/production.asp?id= 13485 (accessed May 1, 2006), *Wicked*, www.wickedthemusical.com (accessed May 1, 2006).
2. Leonard L. Berry and A. Parasuraman, *Marketing Services: Competing through Quality* (New York: Free Press, 1991), p. 5.
3. Michael Levy and Barton A. Weitz, *Retailing Management* (Burr Ridge, IL: Irwin/McGraw-Hill, 2001), p. 585.
4. Michelle Conlin, "Call Centers in the Rec Room," *Business Week*, Jan 23, 2006, www.businessweek.com.
5. Matthew Maier, "Building the Next Google," *Business 2.0*, Nov. 1, 2005, p. 117.
6. Raymond P. Fisk, Stephen J. Grove, and Joby John, *Interactive Services Marketing* (Boston: Houghton Mifflin, 2003), p. 25.
7. Fisk, Grove, and John, *Interactive Services Marketing*, p. 59.
8. The information in this section is based on K. Douglas Hoffman and John E. G. Bateson, *Services Marketing: Concepts, Strategies, and Cases*, 3rd ed. (Cincinnati: Thomson/South-Western, 2006); Valarie A. Zeithaml, A. Parasuraman, and Leonard L. Berry, *Delivering Quality Service: Balancing Customer Perceptions and Expectations* (New York: Free Press, 1990).
9. Michael K. Brady, Brian L. Bourdeau, and Julia Heskel, "The Importance of Brand Cues in Intangible Service Industries: An Application to Investment Services," *Journal of Services Marketing* 19 (Oct. 2005): 401–410.
10. Jeremy J. Sierra and Shaun McQuitty, "Service Providers and Customers: Social Exchange Theory and Service Loyalty," *Journal of Services Marketing* 19 (Oct. 2005): 392–400.
11. Steve Sizoo, Richard Plank, Wilifried Iskat, and Hendrick Serrie, "The Effect of Intercultural Sensitivity on Employee Performance in Cross-Cultural Service Encounters," *Journal of Services Marketing* 29 (June 2005): 245–255.
12. J. Paul Peter and James H. Donnelly, *A Preface to Marketing Management* (Burr Ridge, IL: Irwin/McGraw-Hill, 2003), p. 212.
13. Robert Moore, Melissa L. Moore, and Michael Capella, "The Impact of Customer-to-Customer Interactions in a High Personal Contact Service Setting," *Journal of Services Marketing* 19 (July 2005): 482–491.
14. Michael D. Hartline and O. C. Ferrell, "Service Quality Implementation: The Effects of Organizational Socialization and Managerial Actions of Customer Contact Employee Behavior," *Marketing Science Institute Report*, no. 93–122 (Cambridge, MA: Marketing Science Institute, 1993).
15. Starbucks Corporation Fact Sheet, *Hoover's Online*, www.hoovers.com/starbucks/—ID__15745—/free-co-factsheet.xhtml (accessed May1, 2006).
16. Fisk, Grove, and John, *Interactive Services Marketing*, p. 56.
17. Ibid., p. 91.
18. Sam Schechner, "Testing Out Airline Web Sites," *The Wall Street Journal*, Feb. 15, 2005, p. D5.
19. International Smart Tan Network, www.smarttan.com/beta/page.php?pid=4 (accessed May 1, 2006).
20. Lesley Kump, "Teaching the Teachers," *Forbes*, Dec. 12, 2005, p. 121.
21. Zeithaml, Parasuraman, and Berry, *Delivering Quality Service*.
22. Dayana Yochim, "'Customer Rage' Is on the Rise," *The Motley Fool*, Nov. 3, 2005, via AOL.
23. Valarie A. Zeithaml, "How Consumer Evaluation Processes Differ between Goods and Services," in *Marketing of Services*, ed. James H. Donnelly and William R. George (Chicago: American Marketing Association, 1981), pp. 186–190.
24. A. Parasuraman, Leonard L. Berry, and Valarie A. Zeithaml, "An Empirical Examination of Relationships in an Extended Service Quality Model," *Marketing Science Institute Working Paper Series*, no. 90–112 (Cambridge, MA: Marketing Science Institute, 1990), p. 29.
25. Anja Reimer and Richard Kuehn, "The Impact of Servicescape on Quality Perception," *European Journal of Marketing* 39 (Jan. 2005): 785–808.
26. Valarie A. Zeithaml, Leonard L. Berry, and A. Parasuraman, "Communication and Control Processes in the Delivery of Service Quality," *Journal of Marketing*, Apr. 1988, pp. 35–48.
27. Valarie A. Zeithaml, Leonard L. Berry, and A. Parasuraman, "The Nature and Determinants of Customer Expectations of Service," *Journal of the Academy of Marketing Science*, Winter 1993, pp. 1–12.
28. Linda Himelstein, "'Room Service, Send Up a Techie,'" *Business Week*, Apr. 9, 2001, p. 10.
29. James Zoltak, "'When Pigs Fly' Teaches GenXers the Meaning of Customer Service," *Amusement Business*, Sept. 1, 2003.
30. Philip Kotler, *Marketing for Nonprofit Organizations*, 2nd ed. (Englewood Cliffs, NJ: Prentice-Hall, 1982), p. 37.
31. Ibid.
32. "Non-Profits Discover the Benefits of Using Software Through the Internet," *Fund Raising Management*, Apr. 2001, p. 36.
33. Sources: Thomas Caywood, "Red Ink at Beleaguered Aquarium," *Boston Herald*, Aug. 15, 2003, p. 23; Geoff Edgers, "With Eye on Growth, Aquarium Names New Chief," *Boston Globe*, June 15, 2005, www.bostonglobe.com; Jeffrey Krasner, "New England Aquarium Plunges into Financial Turmoil," *Boston Globe*, Dec. 13, 2002, www.boston.com/globe; New England Aquarium, www.neaq.org (accessed May 1, 2006); "New England Aquarium," EMC website, www.emc.com (accessed May 1, 2006).
34. Sources: "About Allstate," "The Allstate Corporation at a Glance," Allstate Insurance Company, www.allstate.com/about/pagerender.asp?page=allstate_at_a_glance.htm (accessed May 1, 2006); "Allstate CEO: Firms Should Be Politically Active," *USA Today*, July 18, 2005, http://www.usatoday.com/money/companies/management/2005-07-18-allstate_x.htm; "Community Commitment," "The Allstate Foundation," Allstate Insurance Company, www.allstate.com/Community/PageRender.asp?Page=foundation.html (accessed May 1, 2006); "Years Like 2004 Bring Out the Best in Allstate," The Allstate Corporation Summary Annual Report 2004, pp. 5–9.
35. Sources: Dan Thanh Dang, "Satellite Radio Industry Continues to Grow, Enter Mainstream," *The Baltimore Sun*, Nov. 16, 2003, www.sunspot.net; Stephen Holden, "High-Tech Quirkiness Restores Radio's Magic," *The New York Times*, Dec. 26, 2003, pp. E1+; "In Brief, Radio: XM Radio Ends '03 with

1.36 Million Users," *The Los Angeles Times,* Jan. 8, 2004, p. C3; David Pogue, "Satellite Radio Extends Its Orbit," *The New York Times,* Dec. 18, 2003, p. G1; "Satellite Scramble," *The Wall Street Journal,* http://online.wsj.com/documents/info-satellite04.html?printVersion=true (accessed Jan. 24, 2006); "Sirius Satellite Radio Hits Three Million Subscribers," *The Wall Street Journal,* Dec. 27, 2005, http://online.wsj.com; Brad Stone, "Greetings, Earthlings: Satellite Radio for Cars Is Taking Off and Adding New Features—Now Broadcasters Are Starting to Fight Back," *Newsweek,* Jan. 26, 2003, p. 55; David Welch, "Satellite Radio: Two for the Road," *Business Week,* Nov. 24, 2003, p. 144+.

**Chapter 15**

1. Sources: Jonathan Birchall, "Radio Shack Seeks the Right Retail Wavelength," *Financial Times (US Edition),* May 31, 2005, Business Life Section, p. 9; Laura Heller, "Radio Shack Inks Two Wireless Deals," *DSN Retailing Today,* Oct. 25, 2004, p. 5; Radio Shack, www.radioshackcorporation.com (accessed May 1, 2006).
2. "eBay: The World's Online Marketplace," ebay.com, http://pages.ebay.com/aboutebay/thecompany/companyoverview.html (accessed May 1, 2006).
3. "When Complexity Pays Off," CFO, *The Magazine for Financial Executives,* Winter 2003, p. 14.
4. "Trendspotting," *Intelligent Enterprises,* Mar. 2005, p. 17; Doug Henschen, "Content and CRM: Completing the Picture Intelligent Enterprise," *Intelligent Enterprises,* Mar. 2005, pp. 34+.
5. Leo Aspinwall, "The Marketing Characteristics of Goods," in *Four Marketing Theories* (Boulder: University of Colorado Press, 1961), pp. 27–32.
6. Jennifer Weil and Brid Costello, "Hermes Planning to Launch a Wonder," *WWD,* Dec. 12, 2003, p. 10.
7. Wroe Alderson, *Dynamic Marketing Behavior* (Homewood, IL: Irwin, 1965), p. 239.
8. Jonathan D. Hibbard, Nirmalya Kumar, and Louis W. Stern, "Examining the Impact of Destructive Acts in Marketing Channel Relationships," *Journal of Marketing Research,* Feb. 2001, pp. 45–61.
9. Anne T. Coughlan, Erin Anderson, Louis W. Stern, and Adel I. El-Ansary, *Marketing Channels* (Upper Saddle River, NJ: Prentice-Hall, 2001), pp. 368–369.
10. Sources: Hanna Aronovich, "Learning Curve," *U.S. Business Review,* Aug. 2005, www.usbusiness-review.com/content_archives/Aug05/07.html; Nichole Cipriani, "Testing Your Child—Online," *Parenting,* May 2001, p. 21; Excelligence Learning, www.excelligencelearning.com (accessed May 1, 2006); "Excelligence Learning Releases Third Quarter 2003 Results," Business Wire, Nov. 5, 2003, www.businesswire.com; Susan Holly, "Get Smarter," *PC Magazine,* Oct. 17, 2000, p. 19 ; SmarterKids, www.smarterkids.com (accessed May 1, 2006).
11. Sources: Alan Earls, "Valuing Exchanges," *Industrial Distribution,* Sept. 2000, p. E15; Victoria Fraza, "Grainger Branches Out," *Industrial Distribution,* Nov. 2003, p. 18; "Grainger Retreats, Closes Material Logic," *Industrial Distribution,* June 2001, p. 19; "Grainger Sets Growth Course by Expanding Market Presence," PR Newswire, Oct. 9, 2003, www.prnewswire.com; "Grainger Spruces Up Branches; Now Has Retail Look and Feel," *Purchasing,* July 14, 2005, pp. 121–125; "Grainger Takes New Look at Unplanned MRO Purchases," *Purchasing,* Sept. 1, 2005, pp. 53–55; James P. Miller, "Firm to Close Its Troubled Chicago-Area 'E-Procurement' Business," *Chicago Tribune,* Apr. 24, 2001, www.chicago.tribune.com; "Top Distributor Talks Business," *Industrial Distribution,* June 1, 2003, p. 46; "W. W. Grainger,"

Hoover's Online, www.hoovers.com (accessed May 1, 2006); "W. W. Grainger," *Hoover's Handbook of American Business 2001* (Austin, TX: Hoover's Business Press, 2001), pp. 1550–1551.

**Chapter 16**

1. Sources: James Frederick, "Pharmaceuticals Powerhouse Drives Growth with Integrated, Innovative Approach," *Drug Store News,* July 19, 2004; James Frederick, "Deal-Changing, Fee-for-Service Revolution on Track," *Drug Store News,* Aug. 22, 2005; McKesson Corporation, www.mckesson.com (accessed May 1, 2006).
2. U.S. Bureau of the Census, *Statistical Abstract of the United States,* 2006 (Washington, DC: Government Printing Office, 2006), p. 671.
3. Genuine Parts Company Fact Sheet, Hoover's Online, www.hoovers.com/free (accessed May 1, 2006).
4. Universal Corporation Fact Sheet, Hoover's Online, www.hoovers.com/free (accessed May 1, 2006).
5. Red River Commodities Inc. Fact Sheet, Hoover's Online, www.hoovers.com/free (accessed May 1, 2006); Red River Commodities, www.redriv.com (accessed May 1, 2006).
6. Pete Engardio, with Michael Arndt and Dean Foust, "The Future of Outsourcing," *Business Week,* Jan. 30, 2006, pp. 50–58.
7. Amy Roach Partridge, "Apparel Logistics & Technology: A Perfect Fit," *Inbound Logistics,* Nov. 2005, www.inboundlogistics.com/articles/features/1105_feature04.shtml.
8. Dominic Gates, "Boeing 7E7 Site Winner Will Get Second-Plant Bonus," *Seattle Times,* Nov. 19, 2003.
9. Anne T. Coughlan, Erin Anderson, Louis W. Stern, and Adel I. El-Ansary, *Marketing Channels* (Upper Saddle River, NJ: Prentice-Hall, 2001), p. 510.
10. Leslie Hansen Harps, "Best Practics in Today's Distribution Center," *Inbound Logistics,* May 2005, www.inboundlogistics.com/articles/features/0505_feature01.shtml.
11. Daniel Machalaba, "Trucker Rewards Customers for Good Behavior," *The Wall Street Journal Online,* Sept. 9, 2003, http://online.wsj.com/public/us.
12. Anne Stuart, "Express Delivery," *Inc. Tech 2001,* Mar. 15, 2001, pp. 54–56.
13. Sources: Katrina Brooker, "The Pepsi Machine." *Fortune,* Feb. 6, 2006, pp. 68–72; "Coca-Cola Company: Crisis and Reputation Management," in Debbie Thorne McAlister, O. C. Ferrell, and Linda Ferrell, *Business and Society: A Strategic Approach to Social Responsibility,* 2nd ed. (Boston: Houghton Mifflin, 2005), pp. 394–401; T. C. Doyle, "Channel Stuffing Rears Its Ugly Head," *VARBusiness,* May 6, 2003, www.varbusiness.com/showArticle.jhtml;jsessionid=PCVHTC51ICHQ0QSNDBCSKHSCJUMEKJVN?articleID=18823602; "Grand Jury to Investigate Coke on Channel Stuffing Allegations," *Atlanta Business Chronicle,* May 3, 2004, http://atlanta.bizjournals.com/atlanta/stories/2004/05/03/daily2.html; Majorie Kelly, "100 Best Corporate Citizens," *Business Ethics,* Spring 2005, pp. 20–23; Betsy McKay and Chad Terhune, "Coca-Cola Settles Regulatory Probe; Deal Resolves Allegations by SEC That Firm Padded Profit by 'Channel Stuffing,'" *The Wall Street Journal,* via http://proquest.umi.com/pqdweb?did=823831501&sid=1&Fmt=3&clientld=2945&RQT=309&Vname=PQD (accessed Nov. 8, 2005); Stephen Taub, "SEC Probing Harley Statements," CFO.com, July 13, 2005, www.cfo.com/article.cfm/4173321/c_4172651?f=archives&origin=archive.
14. Sources: Larisa Brass, "Technology Keeps Wal-Mart Out Front," *Knight Ridder Tribune Business News,* Feb. 24, 2005, p. 1; Anthony Bianco and Wendy Zellner, "Is Wal-Mart Too Powerful?" *Business Week,* Oct. 6, 2003, pp. 100–110; Alorie Gilbert, "Retail's Super Supply Chains—

Wal-Mart Inks Deal to Roll Out Private Trading Hub; Kmart Readies an Overhaul of Its Planning Systems," *Information Week,* Oct. 16, 2000, p. 22; Kris Hudson, "Wal-Mart Aims to Recharge Growth in Operating Profit," *The Wall Street Journal,* Nov. 9, 2005, http://online.wsj.com/public/us; Jean Kinsey, "A Faster, Leaner Supply Chain: New Uses of Information Technology," *American Journal of Agricultural Economics,* Nov. 15, 2000, p. 1123; Jack Neff, "Wal-Marketing: How to Benefit in Bentonville," *Advertising Age,* Oct. 6, 2003, p. 1; Liz Parks, "Wal-Mart Gets Onboard Early with Collaborative Planning," *Drug Store News,* Feb. 19, 2001, p. 14; "Ready for RFID?" *Information Week,* Jan. 5, 2004; "Trucking Company to Expand to Accommodate Wal-Mart," *Capital District Business Review,* May 7, 2001, p. 8; Wal-Mart, www.walmart.com (accessed May 1, 2006); "Wal-Mart Fuels Expansion at M.S. Carriers," *Memphis Business Journal,* July 28, 2000, p. 3; "World-Class Merchandising Model Leverages Global Synergies," *DSN Retailing Today,* June 2001, p. 15.

## Chapter 17

1. Sources: Mike Duff, "Top-Shelf Employees Keep Container Store On Track," *DSN Retailing Today,* Mar. 8, 2004; Dee Gill, "Train and Pay Staff Well, Container Store Keeps Lid On Staff Turnover," *Crain's Chicago Business,* Aug. 9, 2004; "The Container Store Deploys Micro Strategy to Improve Merchandising Insight," *PR Newswire,* May 5, 2005; The Container Store, www.containerstore.com (accessed May 1, 2006).

2. U.S. Bureau of the Census, *Statistical Abstract of the United States,* 2006 (Washington, DC: Government Printing Office, 2006), p. 671.

3. Ann Zimmerman and Kris Hudson, "Looking Upscale, Wal-Mart Begins a Big Makeover," *The Wall Street Journal,* Sept. 17, 2005, p. A1, http://online.wsj.com/public/us; Robert Berner, "Watch Out, Best Buy and Circuit City," *Business Week,* Nov. 21, 2005, pp. 46–48.

4. "A Different Type of Sears Store," *The New York Times,* Feb. 9, 2005, p. C5.

5. "Testing Ground, Why the Convenience Channel Is the Ideal Environment to Spur Consumer Trial," *Stagnito's New Products Magazine,* May 2005, p. 38.

6. "Industry Resources: PR Toolkit," National Association of Convenience Stores, www.nacsonline.com (accessed May 1, 2006).

7. Elizabeth Esfahani, "7-Eleven Gets Sophisticated," *Business 2.0,* Jan./Feb. 2005, pp. 93–100.

8. Stanley Holmes, "The Jack Welch of the Meat Aisle; Former GE Exec Larry Johnston Brings High-Tech to Troubled Albertson's," *Business Week,* Jan. 24, 2005, p. 60.

9. Richard C. Morais, "One Hot Tamale," *Forbes,* Dec. 27, 2004, p. 137.

10. Sam's Club Fact Sheet and Costco Wholesale Corporation Fact Sheet, Hoover's Online, www.hoovers.com/free (accessed May 1, 2006).

11. Paul Miller, "Neiman Marcus Tests Catalog Showrooms," *Catalog Age,* May 14, 2004.

12. Jenny Strasburg, "High Hopes for Low Prices; Ross Appeals to Bargain Hunters with DD's Discounts," *San Francisco Chronicle,* Aug. 14, 2004, p. C1.

13. Patrick Seitz, "After a Failure, Reinvent Yourself," *Investor's Business Daily,* Dec. 8, 2003, p. A08.

14. Pete Barlas, "Rising Security Fears Will Result in Less Shopping Online: Survey," *Investor's Business Daily,* Nov. 21, 2003.

15. Scott Frey, "Complying with Do-Not-Call," *National Underwriter Life & Health—Financial Services Edition,* Dec. 8, 2003, p. 17.

16. National Do Not Call Registry, https://www.donotcall.gov/default.aspx (accessed May 1, 2006).

17. Lucinda Hahn, "Pampered Life," *Chicago Tribune,* Jan. 18, 2005, p. 1.

18. "Fact Sheet: U.S. Direct Selling 2004," *Direct Selling Association,* www.dsa.org/pubs/numbers/05gofactsheet.pdf (accessed May 1, 2006).

19. Nick Bunkley, "Livonia Startup Makes Hot Pizza Easy as Pie," *The Detroit News,* Oct. 10, 2005, www.detnews.com/2005/business/0510/06/C01-339409.htm; Andrew Dietderich, "Pushbutton Pizza: Livonia Company Markets Vending-Machine Pies," *Crain's Detroit Business,* Oct. 17, 2005, p. 3.

20. International Franchise Association, www.franchise.org (accessed May 1, 2006).

21. Nora Ganim Barnes, "As the Mall Falls: Is Mall Entertainment Too Little, Too Late?" *Marketing Advances in the New Millennium,* Proceedings of the Society for Marketing Advances, 2000, pp. 51–54.

22. David Bodamer, "The Mall Is Dead," *Retail Traffic,* Apr. 1, 2005, www.retailtrafficmag.com/mag/retail_mall_dead/index.html.

23. Kurt Blumenau, "Are Target, Best Buy Really Upscale? Owners of 'Lifestyle' Shopping Centers Still Signing Retail Tenants," *The [Allentown, Pennsylvania] Morning Call,* May 29, 2005, via LexisNexis; "ICSC Shopping Center Definitions," International Council of Shopping Centers, www.icsc.org/srch/l.ib/SCDefinitions.pdf (accessed Feb. 2, 2006); Debra Hazel, "Wide-Open Spaces," *Chain Store Age,* Nov. 2005, p. 120.

24. Susanna Hamner, "Lessons from a Retail Rebel," *Business 2.0,* June 2005, p. 62.

25. Richard F. Yalch and Eric R. Spangenberg, "The Effects of Music in a Retail Setting on Real and Perceived Shopping Times," *Journal of Business Research,* Aug. 2000, pp. 139–147.

26. "Store Atmospherics Provide Competitive Edge," *Chain Store Age,* Dec. 2005, p. 74.

27. Stephen Brown, "The Wheel of Retailing: Past and Future," *Journal of Retailing,* Summer 1990, pp. 143–149.

28. Sources: "About REI," REI, www.rei.com/aboutrei/about_rei.html (accessed May 1, 2006); Bass Pro Shops, www.basspro.com (accessed May 1, 2006); Cabela's, www.cabelas.com (accessed May 1, 2006); Stephane Fitch, "Uphill Battle," *Forbes,* Apr. 25, 2005, pp. 62+; Mike Gorrell, "New REI Store Opens in Salt Lake City Area," *Salt Lake Tribune,* Mar. 28, 2003, www.sltrib.com; "REI Climbs to New Heights Online," *Chain Store Age,* Oct. 2003, p. 72; "REI Facts," REI, www.rei.com/aboutrei/business.html (accessed May 1, 2006); "Retailer Eastern Mountain Sports Opens Hamburg, N.Y. Store," *Buffalo News,* Dec. 1, 2003, www.buffalonews.com.

29. Sources: "The Costco Way," *Business Week,* Apr. 12, 2004, www.businessweek.com/magazine/content/04_15/b3878084_mz021.htm; Doug Desjardins, "Costco Comps Up 7%, Despite 4Q Lag," *DSN Retailing Today,* Oct. 27, 2003, p. 8; Doug Desjardins, "Costco Home to Expand in '04," *DSN Retailing Today,* Dec. 15, 2003, p. 8; John Helyar, "The Only Company Wal-Mart Fears," *Fortune,* Nov. 24, 2003, p. 158; Kris Hudson, "Warehouses Go Luxe," *The Wall Street Journal,* Nov. 11, 2005, p. B1, http://online.wsj.com/public/us; "Investor Relations: Company Profile," Costco, http://phx.corporate-ir.net/phoenix.zhtml?c=83830&p=irol-homeprofile (accessed May 1, 2006).

30. Sources: Better Way (Thailand) Company, www.mistine.co.th; Grammy Entertainment Public Company, www.gmmgrammy.com; RS Promotion Public Company, www.rs-promotion.co.th; Total Access Communication Public Company, www.dtac.co.th; "Mistine," Superbrands International, Nov. 24, 2004, www.superbrandsinternational.com/thailand/

vol1/images/member/pdf/Mistine_TH20041229.pdf; Jaturong Kobkaew, King of Direct Sales (Bangkok: Thai Public Relations and Publishing, 2002); Anuwat Dharamadhaj, "How Direct Selling Is Regulated and Managed in Different Markets in Thailand," 2002, www.hkdsa.org.hk/symposium/anuwat_ppt.pdf; "U*Star and GMM Grammy Artists," Krungthep Turakij, Oct. 2, 2004, www.bangkokbiznews.com; "Branding for Direct Selling," Business Thai, Dec. 12, 2003, http://bcm.arip.co.th; "Direct Selling," Marketeer, September 2003, p. 62; "U*Star to the Market," GoToManager, Sep. 13, 2003, www.gotomanager.com; "Direct Selling War," Krungthep Turakij, March 24, 2003, www.bangkokbiznews.com; "Big Five Direct Sellers," Business Thai, Oct. 12, 2001, http://bcm.arip.co.th; MK621 Competitive Strategies in Marketing; Reports on Thailand Direct Selling from MIM Class 16, Thammasat University, 2004; MIM Class 17, Thammasat University, 2005, prepared this case under the direction of Dr. O. C. Ferrell, Colorado State University, and Dr. Linda Ferrell, University of Wyoming, as the basis for classroom discussion.

## Chapter 18

1. Sources: Teresa F. Lindeman, "Southwest Airlines—Wacky Like a Fox, Underlying the Company's 'Aw Shucks' Approach Is an Airline with Killer Instincts and a Happy Bottom Line," Pittsburgh Post-Gazette, Feb. 18, 2005; "Southwest Airlines Offers Fare Deals Through Desktop Icon," Airline Industry Information, Feb. 28, 2005; "Compete, Inc.'s Latest Spark! Advisory Finds Users of Southwest Airlines' DING! Program Are 45% More Likely to Book through Southwest," Business Wire, Dec. 5, 2005; Southwest Airlines, www.southwest.com (accessed May 5, 2006).
2. Stephanie Thompson, "Masterfoods Ties M&M's to Movies with Oscar Effort," Advertising Age, Jan. 24, 2005, pp. 4, 54.
3. Judith A. Garretson and Scot Burton, "The Role of Spokespersons as Advertisement and Package Cues in Integrated Marketing Communications," Journal of Marketing 69 (Oct. 2005): 118–135.
4. Prasad A. Naik and Kalyon Raman, "Understanding the Impact of Synergy in Multimedia Communications," Journal of Marketing Research, Nov. 2003, pp. 375–388.
5. Ibid.
6. Suzanne Vranica, "Marketers Aim New Ads at Video iPod Users," The Wall Street Journal, Jan. 31, 2006, p. B1, http://online.wsj.com/public/us.
7. Pamela Parker, "Earthlink Runs Ads on Video Podcasts," ClickZ, Dec. 13, 2005, www.clickz.com/news/article.php/3570421.
8. Rebecca Gardyn, "Swap Meet: Customers Are Willing to Exchange Personal Information for Personalized Products," American Demographics, July 2001, pp. 51–55.
9. Ibid.
10. In case you do not read Chinese, the message, prepared by Chih Kang Wang, says, "In the factory we make cosmetics, and in the store we sell hope."
11. Terence A. Shimp, Advertising, Promotion, and Supplemental Aspects of Integrated Marketing Communications (Cincinnati: South-western, 2003), p. 81.
12. Judy A. Wagner, Noreen M. Klein, and Janet E. Keith, "Selling Strategies: The Effects of Suggesting a Decision Structure to Novice and Expert Buyers," Journal of the Academy of Marketing Science 29, no. 3 (2001): 289–306.
13. Salvador Ruiz and María Sicilia, "The Impact of Cognitive and/or Affective Processing Styles on Consumer Response to Advertising Appeals," Journal of Business Research 57 (2004): 657–664.
14. Anton Piësch, "Speaking in Tongues" Inc., June 2003, p. 50.
15. Samuel D. Bradley III and Robert Meeds, "The Effects of Sentence-Level Context, Prior Word Knowledge, and Need for Cognition on Information Processing of Technical Language in Print Ads," Journal of Consumer Psychology 14, no. 3 (2004): 291–302.
16. Mathew Boyle, "Atkins World," Fortune, Jan. 12, 2004, pp. 94–96.
17. David M. Szymanski, "Modality and Offering Effects in Sales Presentations for a Good Versus a Service," Journal of the Academy of Marketing Science 29, no. 2 (2001): 179–189.
18. Chad Terhune, "Wood Folks Hope for 'Got Milk' Success," The Wall Street Journal, Feb. 9, 2001, p. B7.
19. "Yoplait Is Committed to Fighting Breast Cancer!" Yoplait, www.yoplait.com/breastcancer_commitment.aspx (accessed May 5, 2006).
20. Amy Johannes, "McDonald's Debuts Coupons, Sampling Effort for Chicken Sandwich," Promo, Feb. 8, 2006, http://promomagazine.com/othertactics/mcds_spicychicken_020806/.
21. "Inside Chrysler's Celine Dion Advertising Disaster," Advertising Age, Nov. 24, 2003, www.adage.com/news.cms?newsID□39262; Thomas Mucha, "Why the Caveman Loves the Pitchman," Business 2.0, Apr. 2005, p. 39.
22. "Bennigan's Celebrates 30th Anniversary with Irish Bash," Promo, Jan. 12, 2006, http://promomagazine.com/eventmarketing/bennigans_30anniversary_011206/.
23. Patricia Odell, "Silk Goes Guerilla to Sample New Smoothie," Promo, Aug. 18, 2004, http://promomagazine.com/sampling/silk_goes_guerrilla/.
24. Betsy Spethmann, "Moët Fine Tunes Loyalty Premiums," Promo, Feb. 8, 2006, http://promomagazine.com/interactivemarketing/moet_loyaltypremiums_020806/.
25. Karen Lundegaard, "Car Crash Ads May Lose Impact," The Detroit News, Apr. 15, 2001, p. C1.
26. "Ad Space," Business Week, Jan. 12, 2004, p. 14.
27. "2006 Rates and Editions," Time, www.time.com/time/mediakit/editions/national/index.html (accessed May 5, 2006).
28. Vicki R. Lane, "The Impact of Ad Repetition and Ad Content on Consumer Perceptions of Incongruent Extensions," Journal of Marketing, Apr. 2000, pp. 80–91.
29. "Got Milk," National Fluid Milk Processor Promotion Board, www.whymilk.com (accessed May 5, 2006).
30. Beth Snyder Bulik, "Nintendo 'Maximi'-izes to Lure Older Generation of Gamers," Advertising Age, Feb. 7, 2005, p. 8.
31. Colleen DeBaise, "To Draw Women Investors, Firms Appeal to Senses," Marketing News, Feb. 15, 2005, p. 14.
32. Michael Krauss, "Television Advertising in a Time of TiVo," Marketing News, Jan. 6, 2003, p. 4.
33. "Wal-Mart on PR Blitz," CNN, Jan. 13, 2005, www.cnn.com.
34. "Trimspa Sweep Boats $1 Million Prize Pool," Promo, Jan. 4, 2005, http://promomagazine.com/games/trimspa_million_sweeps_010405/.
35. Jack Neff, "Clorox Gives in on Glad, Hikes Trade Promotion," Advertising Age, July 19, 2001, www.adage.com.
36. Harald J. Van Heerde, Sachin Gupta, and Dick R. Wittink, "Is 75% of the Sales Promotion Bump Due to Brand Switching? No, Only 33% Is," Journal of Marketing Research, Nov. 2003, pp. 481–491.
37. "National Advertisers Ranked 1 to 50," Advertising Age, June 27, 2005, pp. S2–S3.
38. Rockney G. Walters and Maqbul Jamil, "Exploring the Relationships Between Shopping Trip Type, Purchases of Products on Promotion, and Shopping Basket Profit," Journal of Business Research 56 (2003): 17–29.
39. Geoffrey A. Fowler, "China Bans Nike's LeBron Ad as Offensive to Nation's Dignity," The Wall Street Journal, Dec. 7, 2004, http://online.wsj.com/public/us.
40. John Eaton, "e-Word-of-Mouth Marketing," Teaching Module, Houghton Mifflin Company, 2006.

41. Alice Z. Cuneo, "Apple Transcends as Lifestyle Brand," *Advertising Age*, Dec. 15, 2003, pp. S-2, S-6.
42. Gerry Khermouch and Jeff Green, "Buzz Marketing," *Business Week*, July 30, 2001, pp. 50–51.
43. *Business 2.0*, Jan./Feb. 2005, pp. 67–68; Michael J. Weiss, "To Be About to Be," *American Demographics*, Sept. 2003, pp. 28–36.
44. "The New Realities of a Low-Trust World," *Advertising Age*, Feb. 13, 2006, www.adage.com.
45. Scott D. Lewis, "Fiona Apple vs. Sony," *The Oregonian*, Apr. 15, 2005, p. D1.
46. Nat Ives, "Interactive Viral Campaigns Ask Consumers to Spread the Word," *The New York Times*, Feb. 18, 2005, www.nytimes.com.
47. "T-Mobile Pays $135,000 to Settle City's Lawsuit for Deceptive Ads," New York City Department of Consumer Affairs, press release, Dec. 14, 2005, www.nyc.gov/html/dca/html/pr2005/pr_121405.shtml.
48. Deborah L. Vence, "Marketing to Minors Still Under Careful Watch," *Marketing News*, Mar. 31, 2003, p. 5.
49. Sources: Based on information from Matthew Creamer and Lisa Sanders, "BMW Seeks a 'Holistic' Ad Approach," *Automotive News*, Nov. 21, 2005, p. 10; "50 Years of Fame," *Marketing*, Sept. 21, 2005, p. 25; Neal E. Boudette, "Navigating Curves," *The Wall Street Journal*, Jan. 10, 2005, pp. A1+; Neal E. Boudette, "BMW's CEO Just Says 'No' to Protect Brand," *The Wall Street Journal*, Nov. 26, 2003, pp. B1+; "The Psychology of Luxury," *USA Today*, Dec. 15, 2003, www.usatoday.com; BMW North America, www.bmwusa.com (accessed May 5, 2006).
50. Sources: "Columbia Sportswear Named Official Apparel Sponsor of Jeep Ski/Snowboard Series," The Auto Channel, Dec. 1, 2005, www.theautochannel.com/news/2005/12/01/153912.html (accessed May 5, 2006); Erica Iacono, "Corporate Case Study—Columbia Sportswear Speaks to Many with One Voice," *PR Week*, Jan. 16, 2006; George Anders, "Drama's Profitable at Sportswear Maker—Columbia Run by Mother and Son," *The Seattle Times*, Oct. 12, 2005; Columbia Sportswear, www.columbia.com (accessed May 5, 2006).

## Chapter 19

1. Sources: Suzanne Vranica, "Aflac Duck's Stardom: Creativity on the Cheap," *Ventura County Star*, Aug. 1, 2004; "Aflac Takes Next Step in Defining Brand—Brand Evolution of Aflac—The Duck to Do More Than Just Quack Company Name," *PR Newswire*, Dec. 2, 2004; "Aflac Duck Enshrined on Advertising Walk of Fame—The Aflac Duck Receives Honor as a Favorite Icon During New York City's Second Annual Celebration of the Advertising Industry," *PR Newswire*, Sept. 26, 2005; Aflac, www.aflac.com (accessed May 5, 2006).
2. "Starbucks Revs Up Advertising with Taxi Rooftop Campaign," *Marketing News*, Feb. 1, 2005, p. 12.
3. Aaron O. Patrick, "U.K. Spends Millions Nagging Its Citizens," *The Wall Street Journal*, Jan. 24, 2006, p. B1, http://online.wsj.com/public/us.
4. "100 Leading National Advertisers," *Advertising Age*, June 27, 2005, pp. S-2, S-3.
5. Arundhati Parmar, "New Ads and Marketing Up Tourism to Mexico," *Marketing News*, Apr. 14, 2003, pp. 6, 8.
6. Cornelia Pechmann, Guangzhi Zhao, Marvin E. Goldberg, and Ellen Thomas Reibling, "What to Convey in Antismoking Advertisements for Adolescents: The Use of Protection Motivation Theory to Identify Effective Message Themes," *Journal of Marketing*, Apr. 2003, pp. 1–18.
7. Desiree J. Hanford, "Miller Lite's Ads, Price Gives Brand Some Momentum," Dow Jones Newswires, Oct. 22, 2003, http://online.wsj.com/public/us.
8. Laurel Wentz, "Nissan Boosts Hispanic Efforts," *Advertising Age*, Dec. 1, 2003, p. 26.
9. Kate Fitzgerald, "Curves International: Diane Heavin," *Advertising Age*, Nov. 17, 2003, p. S-6.
10. Joe Pereira, "New Balance Sneaker Ads Jab at Pro Athletes' Pretentions," *The Wall Street Journal*, Mar. 10, 2005, p. B1.
11. Ibid.
12. Ibid.
13. Marcelo Prince, "Red Hot Online Ad Market Boosts Google, Yahoo," *The Wall Street Journal*, Feb. 2, 2005, http://online.wsj.com/public/us.
14. Sarah Ellison, "Anheuser Will Raise Spending on Cable, Internet," *The Wall Street Journal*, Nov. 30, 2005, p. B3, http://online.wsj.com/public/us.
15. "Notion of Ad Overspending Lessens with Integrated Communications," *Marketing News*, Nov. 24, 2003, pp. 28, 30.
16. Daniel J. Howard and Roger A. Kerin, "The Effects of Personalized Product Recommendations on Advertisement Response Rates: The 'Try This. It Works!' Technique," *Journal of Consumer Psychology* 14, no. 3 (2004): 271–279.
17. Pamela W. Henderson, Joan L. Giese, and Joseph A. Cote, "Impression Management Using Typeface Design," *Journal of Marketing* 68 (Oct. 2004): 60–72.
18. Rik Pieters and Michel Wedel, "Attention Capture and Transfer in Advertising: Brand, Pictorial, and Text-Size Effects," *Journal of Marketing* 68 (Apr. 2004): 36–50.
19. Gerry Khermouch, "The Top 5 Rules of the Ad Game," *Business Week*, Jan. 20, 2003, p. 73.
20. Jean Halliday, "Z Series: Steven Wilhite," *Advertising Age*, Nov. 17, 2003, p. S-2.
21. Peter J. Danaher and Guy W. Mullarkey, "Factors Affecting Online Advertising Recall: A Study of Students," *Journal of Advertising Research* 43 (2003): 252–267.
22. "Media Campaign Fact Sheets," Office of National Drug Control Policy, www.mediacampaign.org/newsroom/factsheets/accomplishments.html (accessed May 5, 2006).
23. Lisa Sanders, "This Beer Spot Will Reduce Your Anxiety," *Advertising Age*, Jan. 17, 2005, p. 25.
24. George E. Belch and Michael A. Belch, *Advertising and Promotion* (Burr Ridge, IL: Irwin/McGraw-Hill, 2004), p. 570.
25. Deborah L. Vence, "Serves Them Right," *Marketing News*, Feb. 1, 2005, pp. 13, 16.
26. "Whole Foods Market Makes Largest Ever Purchase of Wind Energy Credits in United States," Whole Foods Markets, press release, Jan. 10, 2006, www.wholefoodsmarket.com/company/pr_01-10-06.html.
27. Belch and Belch, *Advertising and Promotion*, pp. 580–581.
28. Suman Basuroy, Subimal Chatterjee, and S. Abraham Ravid, "How Critical Are Critical Reviews? The Box Office Effects of Film Critics, Star Power, and Budgets," *Journal of Marketing*, Oct. 2003, pp. 103–117.
29. Keith Naughton, "Martha Breaks Out," *Newsweek*, Mar. 7, 2005, pp. 36–44.
30. Ibid.
31. Sources: Jeff Benard, "'Prime Suspect' Named in Two Elk Fire," *Summit [Colorado] Daily News*, Dec. 13, 2005, www.summitdaily.com/article/20051213/NEWS/112130036; Robert S. Boynton, "Powder Burn," *Outside*, Jan. 1999, http://outside.away.com/magazine/0199/9901vail.html; "Destination Vail," Vail Resorts, www.vailresorts.com/ourresorts.cfm?mode□vail (accessed May 5, 2006); "Earth Liberation Front Sets Off Incendiary at Vail Colorado," FactNet, www.factnet.org/cults/earth_liberation_front/vail_fire.html (accessed May 5, 2006); Robert Kreitner, *Management*, 9th ed. (Boston: Houghton Mifflin, 2004), p. 572; Sarah Love, "Investigation into Vail Fires Continues," *Mountain Zone News*, Nov. 4, 1998, http://classic.mountainzone.com/news/vail10–21.html.

32. Sources: Vicky Hallett, "The Power of Potter," *U.S. News & World Report,* July 25, 2005, p. 44; Jonathan Landreth, "Harry's Flame Heats Up China," *The Washington Post,* Nov. 26, 2005, p. C3; "Latest 'Potter' Spells Magic at Holiday Weekend Box Office," *The Wall Street Journal,* Nov. 28, 2005, p. B4; Jeffrey A. Trachtenberg and Deborah Ball, "A Magical Moment for Publishing," *The Wall Street Journal,* Jul. 18, 2005, p. B3.

## Chapter 20

1. Sources: Kristina Buchthal, "The Ten-Minute Manager's Guide To . . . Being Child-Friendly," *Restaurants and Institutions,* Feb. 15, 2006; "Thanksgiving Comes Early as Chick-fil-A Celebrates Restaurant Grand Opening in Chandler on Nov. 17," Market Wire, Nov. 16, 2005, www.marketwire.com/mw/ release_html_b1?release_id=101132; "Chick-fil-A President to Camp Out at San Antonio's Third Chick-fil-A Opening This Year—Nov. 17 Opening to Include a Free One-Year Supply of Chick-fil-A to the First 100 People in Line," Market Wire, Nov. 15, 2005, www.marketwire.com/mw/release_html_b1?release_ id=101312; "Herds of Customers Expected to Stampede Chick-fil-A Restaurants Nationwide on Cow Appreciation Day July 15—Chain Awards Free Meals to Cow-Dressed Customers," *PR Newswire US,* July 12, 2005; Chick-fil-A, www. chickfila.com (accessed May 5, 2006).

2. Jennifer Gilbert, "Small but Mighty," *Sales & Marketing Management,* Jan. 2004, p. 32.

3. "Research and Markets: The Cost of the Average Sales Call Today is More Than 400 Dollars," *M2 Presswire,* Feb. 28, 2006.

4. Jon M. Hawes, Anne K. Rich, and Scott M. Widmier, "Assessing the Development of the Sales Profession," *Journal of Personal Selling & Sales Management* 24 (Winter 2004): 27–37.

5. Eli Jones, Paul Busch, and Peter Dacin, "Firm Market Orientation and Salesperson Customer Orientation: Interpersonal and Intrapersonal Influence on Customer Service and Retention in Business-to-Business Buyer–Seller Relationships," *Journal of Business Research* 56 (2003): 323–340.

6. Julie T. Johnson, Hiram C. Barksdale, Jr., and James S. Boles, "Factors Associated with Customer Willingness to Refer Leads to Salespeople," *Journal of Business Research* 56 (2003): 257–263.

7. Sarah Lorge, "The Best Way to Prospect," *Sales & Marketing Management,* Jan. 1998, p. 80.

8. Andy Cohen, "Success with Referrals," *Sales & Marketing Management,* Sept. 2003, p. 12.

9. Bob Donath, "Tap Sales 'Hot Buttons' to Stay Competitive," *Marketing News,* Mar. 1, 2005, p. 8.

10. J. Bonasia, "Keep Sales Up by Finding New Customers, Focusing on Strengths," *Investor's Business Daily,* Mar. 25, 2002, p. A4.

11. "Lose the Sales Act," *Sales & Marketing Management,* Jan. 2004, p. 22.

12. Stephen S. Porter, Joshua L. Wiener, and Gary L. Frankwick, "The Moderating Effect of Selling Situation on the Adaptive Selling Strategy—Selling Effectiveness Relationship," *Journal of Business Research* 56 (2003): 275–281.

13. Chuck Salter, "The Soft Sell," *Fast Company,* Jan. 2005, pp. 72+.

14. Michael A. Wiles and Rosann L. Spiro, "Research Notes: Attracting Graduates to Sales Positions and the Role of Recruiter Knowledge: A Reexamination," *Journal of Personal Selling & Sales Management* 24 (Winter 2004): 39–48.

15. Julia Chang, "Born to Sell?" *Sales & Marketing Management,* July 2003, p. 34.

16. Greg W. Marshall, Daniel J. Goebel, and William C. Moncrief, "Hiring for Success at the Buyer–Seller Interface," *Journal of Business Research* 56 (2003): 247–255.

17. Christine Galea, "The 2005 Compensation Survey," *Sales & Marketing Management,* May 2005, p. 25.

18. Susan Mudambi, "Salesforce Compensation and the Web: Managing Change in the Information Age," *American Marketing Association,* Winter 2002, p. 489.

19. Kirk Shinkle, "All of Your People Are Salesmen: Do They Know? Are They Ready?" *Investor's Business Daily,* Feb. 6, 2002, p. A1.

20. Ibid.

21. William H. Murphy, Peter A. Dacin, and Neil M. Ford, "Sales Contest Effectiveness: An Examination of Sales Contest Design Preferences of Field Sales Forces," *Journal of the Academy of Marketing Science* 32, no. 2 (2004): 127–143.

22. Eilene Zimmerman, "Motivation on Any Budget," *Sales & Marketing Management,* Jan. 2004, pp. 37, 38.

23. Patricia Odell, "Motivating the Masses," *Promo,* Sept. 1, 2005, http://promomagazine.com.

24. Joseph A. Bellizzi and Ronald W. Hasty, "Supervising Unethical Sales Force Behavior: How Strong Is the Tendency to Treat Top Sales Performers Leniently?" *Journal of Business Ethics,* Apr. 2003, pp. 337–351.

25. George E. Belch and Michael A. Belch, *Advertising and Promotion* (Burr Ridge, IL: Irwin/McGraw-Hill, 2004), pp. 514–522.

26. Natalie Schwartz, "Clipping Path," *Promo's 12th Annual SourceBook 2005,* p. 15.

27. "All About Coupons," Coupon Council, www.couponmonth. com/pages/allabout.htm (accessed May 5, 2006); Natalie Schwartz, "Clipping Path," *Promo,* Apr. 1, 2004, http:// promomagazine.com/mag/marketing_clipping_path/.

28. Judith A. Garretson and Scot Burton, "Highly Coupon and Sale Prone Consumers: Benefits Beyond Price Savings," *Journal of Advertising Research* 43 (2003): 162–172.

29. Arthur L. Porter, "Direct Mail's Lessons for Electronic Couponers," *Marketing Management Journal,* Spring/Summer 2000, pp. 107–115.

30. Ibid.

31. Karen Holt, "Coupon Crimes," *Promo,* Apr. 1, 2004, http:// promomagazine.com/mag/marketing_coupon_crimes/.

32. Brian Grow, "The Great Rebate Runaround," *Business Week,* Dec. 5, 2005, pp. 34–37.

33. Richard F. Beltramini and Patricia S. Chapman, "Do Customers Believe in Automobile Industry Rebate Incentives?" *Journal of Advertising Research* 43 (2003): 16–24.

34. "Getting to Know You," *Chain Store Age,* Nov. 2005, p. 51.

35. Betsy Spethmann "Loyalty's Royalty," *Promo,* Mar. 1, 2004, http://promomagazine.com/othertactics/marketing_loyaltys_ royalty/.

36. Jean Halliday, "GM's 'Sleep on It' Test Drives: Christopher 'C. J.' Fraleigh," *Advertising Age,* Nov. 17, 2003, p. S-8.

37. Betsy Spethmann, "Schick Revved Quattro with Sampling," *Promo,* Dec. 26, 2005, http://promomagazine.com/sampling/ schick_sampling_122705/.

38. Amy Garber, "BK Franchisees File Class Action Suit Against McD," *Nation's Restaurant News,* Aug. 29, 2005, p. 1.

39. "Hostess Rallies Around Racing Divas," *Promo,* Feb. 8, 2006, http://promomagazine.com/contests/hostess_racingdivas_ 020806/.

40. Sources: "IBM Steps Up Efforts to Drive the Adoption of Software as a Service—Offers Broadest Range of Resources Enabling Business Partners to Transition to Rapid Delivery Model," Market Wire, Feb. 23, 2006, www.marketwire.com/ mw/release_html_b1?release_id=110803; Dan Neel, IBM Connects the Partner Dots," *Computer Reseller News,* Nov. 7,

2005; IBM, www.ibm.com (accessed May 5, 2006); Video Interviews with IBM employees: Dan Pelino, Greg Pushalla, Karen Lowe, Monica Chambers (accessed Feb. 28, 2006).

41. Sources: "Sinking the Sub Club," *Snopes*, June 2, 2005, www.snopes.com (accessed May. 5, 2006); Amy Johannes, "Subway Phases Out Sandwich Promo," *Promo*, June 6, 2005; "Subway Slated to Roll Out Massive Gift Card Program," *Nation's Restaurant News*, July 11, 2005, p. 60; Cara Baruzzi, "Counterfeit 'Sub Club' Cards Force Subway to Cancel Promotion," *New Haven Register*, June 3, 2005, www.nhregister.com; My Subway Card, www.mysubwaycard.com (accessed May 5, 2006); Jacob Ogles, "Fraud Sinks Subway's Club," *Wired News*, Sept. 25, 2005, www.wired.com (accessed May 5, 2006); Scott Leamon, "Police Accuse Pair of College Students with Forging Subway Sub Club Stamps," WSLS News Channel 10, Oct. 22, 2004, www.wsls.com (accessed May 5, 2006).

42. Sources: Li Yuan, "Cellphone Accessories Enter Realm of Couture," *Wall Street Journal*, Mar. 1, 2006, p. D5; Brad Stone, "More Fun For Your Mobile; Forget Mere Ringtones. 'Mobile Media' Have Arrived," *Newsweek*, Nov. 14, 2005, p. 36; Bob Garfield, "T-Mobile Spots Succeed Because They Ring True," *Advertising Age*, Aug. 22, 2005, p. 57; Alice Z. Cuneo, "T-Mobile's Novel Sell: Great Cell Service," *Advertising Age*, Nov. 28, 2005, p. 12; Matt Richtel and Ken Belson, "Yes, T-Mobile Is Profitable, But What to Do With It?," *The New York Times*, July, 11, 2005, C5 p. 6; "T-Mobile Heats Up Hollywood's Elite With the Debut of the New Limited Edition Versions of the T-Mobile Sidekick II," *PR Newswire*, Oct. 19, 2005; "T-Mobile Inks Broad Marketing Partnership with NBA and WNBA," *Business Wire*, Oct. 3, 2005; "T-Mobile Brings Today's Hottest Artists Up Close and Personal," *PR Newswire US*, July 27, 2005, www.prnewswire.com; "The Ideas Behind The Big Pink T," *Global Telecom Business*, Jan.–Feb. 2004, p. 40; "Deutsche Telekom AG: T-Mobile USA Posts Gain of 1.4 Million New Subscribers," *Wall Street Journal*, Jan. 27, 2006, p. 1; Alice Z. Cuneo, "T-Mobile Sprinkles Stardust on Sidekick II," *Advertising Age*, Nov. 22, 2004, p. 6; Kelly Hill, "T-Mobile USA Tops J.D. Power Customer Care Survey," *RCR Wireless News*, Jan. 30, 2006, p. 3; Dan Meyer, "Can T-Mobile USA Make It Alone?," *RCR Wireless News*, Apr. 18, 2005, p. 1; T-Mobile USA, www.t-mobile.com (accessed Mar. 17, 2006).

## Chapter 21

1. Sources: Marilyn Adams and Dan Reed, "Delta, Northwest File Chapter 11," *USA Today*, Sept. 15, 2005, p. 1B; "As One Airline Emerges, 2 Still in Bankruptcy," WCCO, Jan. 31, 2006, http://wcco.com/business/local_story_031071357.html; Barbara De Lollis and Barbara Hansen, "Airlines Gear Up for Ultralong Haul," *USA Today*, June 27, 2005, p. 1B; Dan Reed and Marilyn Adams, "Northwest on Brink of Filing for Bankruptcy," *USA Today*, Sept. 14, 2005, p. 1B.

2. Rajneesh Suri and Kent B. Monroe, "The Effects of Time Constraints on Consumers' Judgments of Prices and Products," *Journal of Consumer Research*, June 2003, p. 92.

3. "Hewlett-Packard," case study, Professional Pricing Society, www.pricingsociety.com/case_studies_details4.asp (accessed May 5, 2006).

4. Michael Arndt, "Frontier: Not About to Pack Its Bags," *Business Week Online*, Feb. 20, 2006.

5. Jon Swartz, "Price War Looms for High-Speed Net Access," *USA Today*, Nov. 14, 2003, p. 1B.

6. Lauren Young, "Candy's Getting Dandy," *Business Week*, Feb. 13, 2006, pp. 88–89.

7. David Aaker and Erich Joachimsthaler, "An Alternative to Price Competition," *American Demographics*, Sept. 2000, p. 11.

8. Frank Byrt, "Vermont Pure Seeks to Deliver Higher Margins by Shifting Focus," *The Wall Street Journal*, Feb. 16, 2005, p. 1.

9. Dictionary of Marketing Terms, American Marketing Association, www.marketingpower.com/mg-dictionary.php (accessed May 5, 2006).

10. Gary McWilliams and Evan Ramstad, "Where the TV Bargains Are," *The Wall Street Journal*, Jan. 17, 2006, p. D1, http://online.wsj.com/public/us.

11. Dictionary of Marketing Terms.

12. "Study: Hotel Demand Is Price Inelastic—So What Now?" *Hotels*, July 1, 2003, p. 14.

13. Carleen Hawn, "The Global Razor's Edge," *Fast Company*, Feb. 2004, pp. 27, 28.

14. Donald Lichtenstein, Nancy M. Ridgway, and Richard G. Netemeyer, "Price Perceptions and Consumer Shopping Behavior: A Field Study," *Journal of Marketing Research*, May 1993, pp. 234–245.

15. Robert Guy Matthews, "A Surge in Ocean-Shipping Rates Could Increase Consumer Prices," *The Wall Street Journal*, Nov. 4, 2003, http://online.wsj.com/public/us.

16. "Investing," *Business Week*, Feb. 13, 2006, p. 90.

17. Russell S. Winer, *Pricing* (Cambridge, MA: Marketing Science Institute, 2005), p. 20.

18. Bruce L. Alford and Brian T. Engelland, "Advertised Reference Price Effects on Consumer Price Estimates, Value Perception, and Search Intention," *Journal of Business Research*, May 2000, pp. 93–100.

19. Lichtenstein, Ridgway, and Netemeyer, "Price Perceptions and Consumer Shopping Behavior."

20. Gerald E. Smith and Thomas T. Nagle, "A Question of Value," *Marketing Management*, July/Aug. 2005, pp. 39–40.

21. Peter Burrows, "Apple's Down Market Gamble; By Launching a Much Cheaper Mac and iPod, Steve Jobs Is Appealing to Hordes of Price-Conscious Consumers," *Business Week Online*, Jan. 12, 2005.

22. Lichtenstein, Ridgway, and Netemeyer, "Price Perceptions and Consumer Shopping Behavior."

23. Ibid.

24. Gail Edmondson, "This SUV Can Tow an Entire Carmaker," *Business Week*, Jan. 19, 2004, pp. 40, 41.

25. Lorrie Grant, "Scrimping to Splurge," *USA Today*, Jan. 28, 2005, p. 1B; Linda Tischler, "The Price Is Right," *Fast Company*, Nov. 2003, p. 83.

26. Diane Brady, "Best Ideas," *Business Week*, Dec. 19, 2005, p. 80.

27. Sources: "Blue Skies: Is JetBlue the Next Great Airline—or Just a Little Too Good to Be True?" *Time*, July 30, 2001, p. 241; J. K. Dineen, "JetBlue Offering $99 Nonstop Coast-to-Coast Flights," *New York Daily News*, Aug. 15, 2001, www.nydailynews.com; David Grossman, "Business Traveler: Why Business Travelers Will Always Pay More to Fly," *USA Today*, Feb. 6, 2006, www.usatoday.com/travel/columnist/grossman/2006-02-06-grossman_x.htm; JetBlue, www.jetblue.com (accessed May 5, 2006); Dan Reed, "JetBlue Gains on Its Competition," *USA Today*, Aug. 13, 2003, p. 3B; Darren Shannon, "Three of a Kind," *Travel Agent*, July 23, 2001, p. 601.

28. Sources: Beth Cox, "Priceline Finds Some Room in the Hotel Market," *Internet News*, Feb. 24, 2003, www.internetnews.com; Greg Dalton, "Priceline Is Finally on the Ascent," *Industry Standard*, July 31, 2001, www.thestandard.com/article/0,1902,28394,00.html; Maryann Keller, "Inside Priceline's Sausage Factory," *Fortune*, Sept. 3, 2001, p. 42; Priceline.com, www.priceline.com (accessed May 5, 2006); "Priceline Incorporated," CNN/Money, http://money.cnn.com (accessed May 5, 2006); "Priceline Says Air Ticket Bid Business Fading," *USA Today*, Feb. 14, 2006, www.usatoday.com/travel/flights/

2006-02-14-priceline_x.htm; Clare Saliba, "Priceline, Expedia End Patent Flap," *E-Commerce Times*, Jan. 10, 2001, http://ecommercetimes.com/perl/story/?id56605; Jay Walker, "What Price Brand Loyalty?" *Marketing Week*, June 29, 2000, p. 53.

**Chapter 22**

1. Sources: Sarah Duxbury, "Levi's Planning Pair of Snazzy Denim Spots," *San Francisco Business Times*, May 9, 2005, http://sanfrancisco.bixjournals.com/sanfrancisco/stories/2005/05/09/story6.html; Theresa Howard, "Levi's Charms Buyers Back," *USA Today*, Oct. 24, 2004, www.usatoday.com/money/advertising/adtrack/2004-10-21-levis_x.htm; Stephanie Thompson, "Levi's Struggles to Redefine Itself as a Premium-Denim Purveyor," *Advertising Age*, July 11, 2005, p. 12.

2. Lori Hawkins, "If Price Is Right," *The Austin American-Statesman*, Feb. 13, 2006, www.statesman.com.

3. William C. Symonds and Robert Bernes, "Gillette's New Edge," *Business Week Online*, Feb. 6, 2006, (accessed May 6, 2006).

4. Kevin Schweitzer, "Hybrid Potential Limited Only by Price," *Chicago Tribune*, Feb. 11, 2005, p. 10.

5. "New Bentley Pricing," Automotive.com, www.automotive.com/new-cars/pricing/01/bentley/index.html (accessed May 6, 2006).

6. Robert J. Frank, Jeffrey P. George, and Laxman Narasimhan, "When Your Competitor Delivers More for Less," *McKinsey Quarterly*, www.Mckinseyquarterly.com (accessed May 6, 2006).

7. Barry J. Babin, David M. Hardesty, and Tracy A. Suter, "Color and Shopping Intentions: The Intervening Effect of Price Fairness and Perceived Affect," *Journal of Business Research*, July 2003, pp. 541–551.

8. David Moin, "Category Killers' Concerns: Overgrowth and Extinction," *WWD*, Jan. 6, 2005, p. 17.

9. "Fairchild Dynamic Pricing Team," Professional Pricing Society, case study, www.pricingsociety.com/case_studies_details3.asp (accessed May 6, 2006).

10. George J. Avlonitis and Kostis A. Indounas, "Pricing Objectives and Pricing Methods in the Services Sector," *Journal of Services Marketing* 19 (Jan. 2005): 47–57.

11. Stephen Gandel, "What's Your Home Worth? Get a 'Zesti-mate'," CNN/Money, Feb. 8, 2006, www.cnnmoney.com.

12. "Cutler-Hammer/Eaton Corporation," case study, Professional Pricing Society, www.pricingsociety.com/case_studies_details2.asp (accessed May 6, 2006).

13. "Can Detroit Break the Rebate Habit?" *Business Week*, Jan. 12, 2004, p. 110; Joann Muller, "Outpsyching the Car Buyer," *Forbes*, Feb. 17, 2003, p. 52.

14. Marla Royne Stafford and Thomas F. Stafford, "The Effectiveness of Tensile Pricing Tactics in the Advertising of Services," *Journal of Advertising*, Summer 2000, pp. 45–56.

15. Gail Edmondson, "This SUV Can Tow an Entire Carmaker," *Business Week*, Jan. 19, 2004, pp. 40, 41.

16. Michael Marn, Eric V. Roegner, and Craig C. Zawada, "Pricing New Products," *Inc.*, July 2003, http://pf.inc.com/articles/2003/07/pricing.html.

17. "Arctic Monkeys Play on Web Hype," CNN/Money, Feb. 2, 2006, www.cnnmoney.com.

18. Amanda Cantrell, "iPod Add-Ons: Boombox Purses, and More," CNN/Money, Jan. 12, 2006, www.cnnmoney.com.

19. John W. Schoen, "Stern's Move to Sirius a Hard Act to Follow," MSNBC, Jan. 9, 2006, www.msnbc.msn.com.

20. Daniel A. Sheinin and Janet Wagner, "Pricing Store Brands across Categories and Retailers," *Journal of Product & Brand Management* 12, no. 4 (2003): 201–220.

21. Jaihak Chung and Vithala R. Rao, "A General Choice Model for Bundles with Multiple-Category Products: Application to Market Segmentation and Optimal Pricing for Bundles," *Journal of Marketing Research*, May 2003, pp. 115–130.

22. Keith Damsell, "Telecom Bundling Seen Luring Customers," *The Globe and Mail*, Sept. 29, 2003, p. B8, via www.globe technology.com.

23. George Mannes, "The Urge to Unbundle," *Fast Company*, Feb. 2005, pp. 23–25.

24. Doug Halonen, "Watchdog Sets Sights on a la Carte," *TelevisionWeek*, Jan. 10, 2005, p. 8.

25. Russell S. Winer, *Pricing* (Cambridge, MA: Marketing Science Institute, 2005), p. 31.

26. Mannes, "The Urge to Unbundle."

27. "'Made in USA' Means Little to Furniture Buyers," MSNBC, Feb. 10, 2006, www.msnbc.com.

28. Keith S. Coulter, "The Influence of Print Advertisement Organization on Odd-Ending Price Image Effects," *Journal of Product & Brand Management* 11, no. 4 (2002): 319.

29. Lorrie Grant, "Scrimping to Splurge," *USA Today*, Jan. 28, 2005, p. 1B; Linda Tischler, "The Price Is Right," *Fast Company*, Nov. 2003, p. 83.

30. "Best Ideas," *Business Week*, Dec. 19, 2005, pp. 76–77.

31. Bruce L. Alford and Brian T. Engelland, "Advertised Reference Price Effects on Consumer Price Estimates, Value Perception, and Search Intention," *Journal of Business Research*, May 2000, pp. 93–100.

32. "Blockbuster Plans to Eliminate 300 Jobs," *Business Week Online*, Feb. 8, 2006 (accessed May 6, 2006).

33. Nigel Cox, "Amex Charges Ahead," *Smart Business*, Apr. 2001, pp. 123–128.

34. Sources: "Fact Sheet: New Balance Athletic Shoes, Inc.," New Balance, www.newbalance.com/cms-service/stream/pdf/?pdf_id=3948696 (accessed May 6, 2006); Interviews with Jim Sciabarrasi, Christine Epplett, and Paul Heffernan of New Balance, video, Houghton Mifflin Company, 2003; "New Balance Athletic Shoe, Inc.," Hoover's Online, www.hoovers.com/new-balance/—ID__42602—/free-co-factsheet.xhtml (accessed May 6, 2006); "Our History," New Balance, www.newbalance.com/aboutus/misc/history.html (accessed May 6, 2006).

35. Sources: Gina Chon, "Car Makers Forced to Pile on More Discounts," *The Wall Street Journal*, Oct. 25, 2005, p. D1, http://online.wsj.com/public/us; General Motors, www.gm.com (accessed May 6, 2006); "GM Exec Said to Regret Employee Discount," CNN, Jan. 5, 2006, www.cnn.com; David Guilford, "Apologize for Incentives? GM Loves 'Em," *Automotive News*, Aug. 18, 2003, p. 1, via Lexis-Nexis Academic Database; Lee Hawkins, "GM Cuts Prices on Most Vehicles," *The Wall Street Journal*, Jan. 11, 2006, p. D1, http://online.wsj.com/public/us; Chris Isidore, "GM Execs: No Let-Up on Incentives," CNN/Money, Jan. 5, 2004, via Lexis-Nexis Academic Database; Kathleen Kerwin and David Welch, "Can Detroit Break the Rebate Habit?" *Business Week*, Jan. 12, 2004, pp. 110–111; David Kiley, "GM Tries to Cut Cord on Costly Rebates," *USA Today*, Jan. 23, 2004, pp. 1B–2B; David Kiley, "The Incentive Trap: Owing More Than Trade-in's Worth," *USA Today*, Jan. 23, 2004, p. 2B; Alisa Priddle and David E. Zoia, "Are Incentives a Carrot or Noose?" *Ward's Dealer Business*, Aug. 1, 2003, p. 8, via Lexis-Nexis Academic Database; Jennifer Saranow, "Employee Discounts Now Everywhere," *The [Fort Collins] Coloradoan*, Aug. 28, 2005, pp. E1, E2.

36. Sources: "The Digital Music Report—2006," IFPI, www.ifpi.org/site-content/press/20060119d.html (accessed Feb. 23, 2006); "GartnerG2 Says 'Big 5' Record Labels Must Standardize Digital Music Delivery to Profit from the Market Opportunity," The Gartner Group, press release, Aug. 29, 2001, http://gartner.com/5_about/press_releases/2001/pr20010829c.html; Stephen Hinkle, "RIAA, Surrender Now!" Dmusic.com, http://news.dmusic.com/print/5026 (accessed Nov. 20, 2003); Bob Keefe, "Music File-Sharers Hit by New Round of Lawsuits," *The Austin American-Statesman*, Jan. 22, 2004, www.

statesman.com; Michael McCarthy, "CD Prices Hit Sour Note with Retailers, Buyers," *USA Today,* Dec. 8, 2003, pp. 2B, 2B; "Napster, But in Name Only," *Wired News,* July 28, 2003, www.wired.com/news/digiwood/0,1412,59798,00.html; Napster, www.napster.com (accessed Feb. 23, 2006); Michael Pastore, "The Online Music Debate Rambles On," Cyberatlas, July 24, 2000, http://cyberatlas.internet.com/markets/retailing/article/0,,6061_420571,00.html; Plunkett Research, www.plunkettresearch.com/technology/infotech_trends.htm (accessed Nov. 20, 2003); "U.S. Electronic Media and Entertainment," theinfoshop.com, www.the-infoshop.com/study/fi13558_electronic_media.html (accessed Nov. 20, 2003); Andrew Wallmeyer, "Wal-Mart to Offer Songs at 88 Cents a Download," *Wall Street Journal,* Dec. 18, 2003, http://online.wsj.com. Michael D. Hartline and O. C. Ferrell prepared this case for classroom discussion rather than to illustrate effective or ineffective handling of an administrative, legal, or ethical situation.

### Appendix A

1. This section and the three that follow are adapted from William M. Pride, Robert J. Hughes, and Jack R. Kapoor, *Business* (Boston: Houghton Mifflin, 2002), pp. A1–A9.

2. Sal Divita, "Résumé Writing Requires Proper Strategy," *Marketing News,* July 3, 1995, p. 6.
3. Andrew J. DuBrin, "Deadly Political Sins," *Wall Street Journal's Managing Your Career,* Fall 1993, pp. 11–13.
4. Ibid.
5. Cyndee Miller, "Marketing Research Salaries Up a Bit, but Layoffs Take Toll," *Marketing News,* June 19, 1995, p. 1.
6. Careers in Marketing, "Market Research—Salaries," www.careers-in-marketing.com/mrsal.htm (accessed May 9, 2006).
7. PayScale, www.payscale.com (accessed May 9, 2006)
8. Ibid.
9. Ibid.
10. Careers in Marketing, "Product Management—Salaries," www.careers-in-marketing.com/pmsal.htm (accessed May 9, 2006).
11. Careers in Marketing, "Advertising and Public Relations—Salaries," www.careers-in-marketing.com/adsal.htm (accessed May 9, 2006).
12. Ibid.
13. PayScale, www.payscale.com (accessed May 9, 2006).
14. Ibid.
15. PCWorld.com, www.pcworld.com (accessed May 9, 2006).

# Sources

## Chapter 1

p. 10 Lambert's Café History, distributed by Lambert's Café, 2515 E. Malone, Sikeston, MO 63801, 2005, pp. 1–80; Lambert's Café, www.throwedrolls.com (accessed Apr. 13, 2006).

## Chapter 2

p. 31 Alldorm.com (accessed Apr. 13, 2006); "Case study: All-Dorm," ecommstats, www.ecommstats.com/case_alldorm.jsp (accessed Apr. 13, 2006); Rachel Metz, "Setting Up the Dorm Remotely," *Wired*, Aug. 18, 2004, www.wired.com/new/school/0%2c1383%2c64601%2c00.html; Erin Ryan, "Classmates Click as Business Partners," *Santa Clara Magazine*, Fall 2003, www.scu.edu/scm/fall2003/bp-alldorm.cfm.

p. 36 Cynthia Crossen and Kortney Stringer, "A Merchant's Evolution," *The Wall Street Journal*, Nov. 18, 2004, pp. B1–B2; David Lieberman, "Retailing Giants Team Up," *USA Today*, Nov. 18, 2004, p. 1A; Amy Merrick and Dennis Berman, "Kmart to Buy Sears for $11.5 Billion," *The Wall Street Journal*, Nov. 18, 2004, pp. A1, A8; David Runk, "The Mind Behind the Merger," *The [Fort Collins] Coloradoan*, Nov. 18, 2004, pp. D7, D8; Allan Sloan, "It's Not About Retailing," *Newsweek*, Nov. 29, 2004, p. 41.

p. 38 David Gaffen, "Gillette Sparkles on Merger," *The Wall Street Journal*, Jan. 28, 2005, http://online.wsj.com/public/us; Atifa Hargrave-Silk, "P&G Broadening China Sweet Spot," *Media Asia*, Jan. 16, 2004, p. 3, accessed via Business Source Premier; Cliff Peale, "P&G in Deal to Buy Gillette," *USA Today*, Jan. 28, 2005, p. 1B; Procter & Gamble Annual Report, 2004, Procter & Gamble, www.pg.com/company/who_we_are/index.jhtml (accessed Apr. 13, 2006).

## Chapter 3

p. 73 "Hottest New Pet Products Unleashed at Global Pet Expo," *Business Wire*, Mar. 29, 2005, www.businesswire.com; Laura Koss-Feder, "Critter Comforts: The Boom in Pet Businesses Has Entrepreneurs Vying for Their Spots as Top Dog," *Entrepreneur*, Nov. 2005, p. 124; Kathleen M. Mangan, "Perks for Pets: Nutritional Supplements for Fluffy and Fido," E: *The Enforcement Magazine*, Nov.–Dec., 2004, www.emagazine.com.

p. 74 "The Able Jo Waldron," WomenOf, www.womenof.com/Articles/cb_3_29_04.asp (accessed May 2, 2006); "Now Hear This," ColoradoBiz 30 (Aug. 2003): 14; Christine Turner, "Inventing Technology That Matters," *Colorado Company*, Jan./Feb. 2004, www.coloradocompany.biz/jan_feb/inventing_technology.shtml.

p. 76 Jerry Adler, "The Boomer Files," *Newsweek*, Nov. 14, 2005, p. 50; Amy Gillentine, "Baby Boomers Still Shape Market, Say Experts," *Colorado Springs Business Journal*, Nov. 18, 2005, NEWS section; Stephanie Thompson, "Ten Trends to Watch For," *Advertising Age*, Dec. 19, 2005, p. 11; "Report: Aging Population Poses New Retailing Challenges," *Financial Wire* (Forest Hills), Jan. 17, 2006, p. 1.

## Chapter 4

p. 89 "Nestlé Boss Starts an African Crusade," *The Sunday Times*, Mar. 13, 2005, www.timesonline.co.uk/article/0,,2095-1522290,00.html;"The Nestlé Coffee Report," Faces of Coffee, Mar. 2004, Nestlé S.A., Public Affairs, www.nestle.com/NR/rdonlyres/4F893E04-4129-4E4C-92F1-91AF4C8C4738/0/2003_Coffee_Report.pdf; "The Nestlé Commitment to Africa," Africa Report, Nestlé, www.nestle.com/Our_Responsibility/Africa+Report/Overview/Africa+Report.htm (accessed Apr. 13, 2006).

p. 90 Anthony Bianco and Wendy Zellner, "Is Wal-Mart Too Powerful?" *Business Week*, Oct. 6, 2003, pp. 102–110; Cora Daniels, "Women vs. Wal-Mart," *Fortune*, July 21, 2003, pp. 79–82; Charles Fishman, "The Wal-Mart You Don't Know: Why Low Prices Have a High Cost," *Fast Company*, Dec. 2003, pp. 70–80; Daren Fonda, "Will Wal-Mart Steal Christmas?" *Time*, Dec. 8, 2003, pp. 54–56; Wal-Mart, www.walmart.com (accessed Apr. 13, 2006).

p. 91 Amy's Ice Cream, www.amysicecream.com (accessed Apr. 13, 2006); Renuka Rayasam, "Amy's Grows Up," *Austin American-Statesman*, Sept. 29, 2005, www.statesman.com.

## Chapter 5

p. 132 Bob Mook, "Entrepreneur of the Year Finalists Revealed," *Denver Business Journal*, Apr. 28, 1997; Bryan Tutt, "Give Your Kids the Biz—Of Their Own That Is," YoungBiz.com, June 18, 2003, www.youngbiz.com/aspindex.asp?fileName=family_biz/give_your_kids_the_biz.htm.

p. 134 Jennifer Davies, "Oh, Baby!—More Parents Are Paying Top Dollar to Give Their Infants and Toddlers Luxury Items," *The San Diego Union-Tribune*, Oct. 17, 2004; "In Hot Pursuit of Yoga Mama," *Business Week*, Nov. 7, 2005; "Today's Yoga Mamas Replace Soccer Moms and Evolve to All-Natural Lifestyle and Products," *PR Newswire*, Jan. 23, 2006, www.prnewswire.com; "Marketing to Moms—The Power of Yoga Mamas," ABC News Transcripts, Nov. 10, 2005, www.abcnews.com.

p. 136 Kathleen Hays, Gerri Willis, Valerie Morris, "Teen Moguls & Spotting Teen Buying Trends," *The Flipside*, Mar. 18, 2004; "Teen Clout Shows No Sign of Diminishing, Everyone Takes Note," *Business and Industry*, July 18, 2005; Jan Eisner, "Putting Brakes on Materialism: Teen Buying Power," *Knight Ridder Newspapers*, Sept. 20, 2004; Becky Sisco, "Sweet Buy and By; Research Finds a Few Changes in Teens' Purchasing Habits," *Telegraph Herald*, Jan. 9, 2005; "Teen Market Profile," Mediamark Research Inc., www.magazine.org (accessed Jan. 28, 2006).

## Chapter 6

p. 153 Brighton, www.brighton.com (accessed Apr. 13, 2006); "Building the Brighton Business," *Brighton View*, 2003, pp. 1–22; Interview with a Bryan, Texas, Brighton retailer, Dec. 18, 2003; "When You Can't Beat Them, Ambush Them," *Industry*, Oct. 1, 2004, www.businesswire.com.

p. 158 "Press Room: Background," IBM, www03.ibm.com/press/us/en/background.wss (accessed Apr. 13, 2006); Steve Hamm, "GM's Way or the Highway," *Business Week*, Dec. 19, 2005, pp. 48–49; IBM Annual Report 2004, IBM, pp. 1–7; Understanding

Our Company, An IBM Prospectus, IBM, Mar. 2005.
p. 161 GlobalTek Solutions, www.globalteksolutions.com/index. html (accessed Apr. 13, 2006); "GlobalTek Solutions: Small, Successful, and Led by a 15-Year-Old CEO," *Web Services Journal,* 2004, www.sys-con.com/webservices/article.cfm?id=199; Afshan Khoja, "Executive Watch," NewsLine, Sept. 2004, www.newsline.com.pk/NewsSep2004/executivesep.htm; Nichole L. Torres, "Generation Next," *Entrepreneur.com,* July 2004, www.entrepreneur.com/article/0,4621,299288-2,00.html.

## Chapter 7

p. 193 TCBY, www.tcby.com (accessed Apr. 13, 2006); Merger Place, "TCBY to Be Acquired by Capricorn Investors," http://mergerplace.bison.com/press/pr2-10tcby.html (accessed Apr. 13, 2006); *Entrepreneur.com,* www.entrepreneur.com/franzone/rank/0,6584,12-12-F5-2003-30,00.html (accessed Jan. 19, 2006).
p. 200 George Wehrfritz and Joe Cochrane, "The Biggest Sleeper," *NewsWeek International,* Mar. 6, 2006, http://www.msnbc.msn. com/id/11569226/site/newsweek (accessed June 2, 2006); globalEDGE Country Insights: Indonesia, http://globaledge.msu. edu/ibrd (accessed Apr. 13, 2006).

## Chapter 8

p. 219 Matt Drudge, "Anyone with a Modem Can Report on the World," Liberty Round Table: Essays, www.libertyroundtable.org/library/essay.drudge.html (accessed Apr. 13, 2006); Rich Ord, "Drudge Report Is Third Most Searched for News Source," *WebProNews,* Dec. 2, 2004, www.webpronews.com/news/ebusinessnews/wpn-45-20041202DrudgeReportIsThirdMostSearchedForNewsSource.html; Camille Paglia, "Drudge Match," *Radar Magazine,* www.radarmagazine.com/features/issue_02/drudge.html (accessed Feb. 16, 2005); "The Secrets of Drudge Inc.," *Business 2.0,* Apr. 2003, p. 56.
p. 222 "About Us," ING Direct, http://home.ingdirect. com/about/about.asp (accessed Oct. 25, 2006); "ING Direct Bank Does One Thing Noticeably Well," ING Direct, news release, March 7, 2004, http://home.ingdirect.com/about/aboutus_news. html#03072004; Lisa Sanders, "ING Café: Coffee, Tea or Mortgage," *Advertising Age,* June 14, 2004, p. 8; Matthew Sibel, "Where Money Doesn't Talk," *Forbes,* May 24, 2004, p. 176.
p. 228 "About Us," Informative, www.informative.com/aboutUs.html (accessed Oct. 25, 2006); Allison Fass, "Collective Opinion, Forget the Up-Close Focus Group. Newfangled Software Lets Lego, Procter & Gamble and Others Mine Ideas from Tens of Thousands of Opinionated Customers," *Forbes,* Nov. 28, 2005, pp. 76–79;
"The Communispace Difference," Communispace, www.communispace.com/difference.htm (accessed Oct. 25, 2006); "Customer Communities," Communispace, www.communispace.com/customer_c.htm (accessed Oct. 25, 2006); "Solutions and Services," Informative, www.informative.com/solutionsServices.html (accessed Oct. 25, 2006); "Technology and Services," Communispace, www.communispace.com/technology.htm (accessed Oct. 25, 2006).

## Chapter 9

p. 250 Stephanie Kang, "Trying to Connect with a Hip Crowd," *The Wall Street Journal,* Oct. 13, 2005, p. B3, http://online.wsj. com/public/us; Sarah Moore, "On Your Markets," *Working Woman,* Feb. 2001, p. 26; "Quest for Cool," Time, Sept. 2003, via www.looklook.com/looklook/html/Test_Drive_Press_Time. html; "What We Do," Look-Look.com, www.look-look.com/dynamic/looklook/ jsp/What_We_Do.jsp (accessed Apr. 14,

2006); "Who We Are," Look-Look.com, www.look-look.com/looklook/html/Test_Drive_Who_We_Are.html (accessed Apr. 14, 2006).
p. 251 Samantha Critchell, "Designer Marc Eckos Building a Fashion Empire," *The [Massachusetts] Standard-Times,* May 12, 2004, p. B1, www.southcoasttoday.com/daily/05-04/05-12-04/b01li040.htm; Ecko Unlimited, www.eckounltd.com (accessed Apr. 14, 2006); "Marc Ecko Fashion Collections," *First View,* www.firstview.com/alldesigners/MarcEcko.html#Anchor3 (accessed Apr. 14, 2006); Jordan Robertson, "Toe the Line Between Corporate and Cool," *Business 2.0,* Nov. 2004.
p. 257 Constance L. Hays, "What Wal-Mart Knows About Customers' Habits," *The New York Times,* Nov. 14, 2004, www. nytimes.com; Skip Kaltenheuser, "Innovative Air Force Data Warehouse Integrates Millions of Parts into One-Stop Supply Chain Visibility," *World Trade Magazine,* Jan. 1, 2005, www.worldtrademag.com/CDA/ArticleInformation/features/BNP__Features__Item/0,3483,140201,00.html; "Wal-Mart Expands Its Teradata Warehouse to Optimize Decision Support Capabilities 10/13/04," *Teradata,* press release, Oct. 13, 2004, www.teradata.com/t/page/128640/index.html.

## Chapter 10

p. 272 Jeremy Caplan, "Date.com Is So 2004," *Time,* June 20, 2005, p. 19; Katherine Davidson, "Specialized Dating Soars," *The New Hampshire Union Leader,* Oct. 24, 2004; "Internet Dating Is Projected to Soon Top $1,000,000,000 in Yearly Sales," *USA Today (Society for the Advancement of Education),* Aug. 2005; Nikitta A. Foston, "Love at First Byte: The Virtual World of Dating Online," *Ebony,* Oct. 2005; "Hairmax Int. Expands Personal Services into the One Billion Dollar On-Line Dating Industry," *Business Wire,* Sept. 24, 2004, www.businesswire.com; eHarmony, www.eHarmony.com (accessed Apr. 17, 2006); Match.com, www.match.com (accessed Apr. 17, 2006); True Dater, www.truedater.com (accessed Apr. 17, 2006); "94% Success Rate for Cyber Dating" *Manchester Online,* www. manchesteronline.co.uk (accessed Feb. 14, 2006).
p. 279 Brian Grow, "Tapping a Market That Is Hot, Hot, Hot," *Business Week,* Jan. 17, 2005, p. 36; "Innovations in Personal Finance for the Unbanked: Emerging Practices from the Field; Case Study; Cash & Save—Union Bank of California," Fannie Mae Foundation, www.fanniemaefoundation.org (accessed Apr. 17, 2006); Shaheen Pasha, "Banks Woo Hispanic Market," *CNN/Money,* Nov. 22, 2005, http://money.cnn.com.
p. 290 Nick Summers, "Fast Chat: Bloomin' Onion," *Newsweek,* Sept. 12, 2005, p. 16; *The Onion,* www.theonion.com (accessed Apr. 17, 2006).

## Chapter 11

p. 305 Emily Holt, "A Pair of Odd Socks," *Women's Wear Daily,* Aug. 9, 2004; Brendan I. Koerner, "A Salute to the Stray Sock," *The New York Times,* Oct. 3, 2004, sec. 3, p. 2; LittleMissMatched, www.littlemissmatched.com (accessed Apr. 17, 2006); "A Successful Mismatch," *CNN,* May 9, 2005, www.cnn.com; "The Sock of the New," *Boston Globe,* Oct. 14, 2004.
p. 311 Janet Adamy, "Kellogg Posts 11% Rise in Profits But Warns of Fuel-Cost Impact," *The Wall Street Journal,* Nov. 1, 2005, p. B5, http://online.wsj.com/public/us; "Kellogg Around the World," Kellogg, www.kelloggcompany.com/kelloggco/kellogg_around_the_world/index.html (accessed Apr. 17, 2006); "Our Company," Kellogg, www.kelloggcompany.com/kellog-gco/our_company/index.html (accessed Apr. 17, 2006); Staying on Track, Annual Report 2004, Kellogg Company, pp. 14–17.
p. 315 "At 50, Tylenol Brand Still Gaining Steam," MSNBC.com, Oct. 31, 2005, http://msnbc.msn.com/id/9879888; Linda A. Johnson,

"Tylenol Turns 50, Best-Known Acetaminophen Brand Gaining Steam on Its Safety Image," *The [Fort Collins] Coloradoan*, Nov. 6, 2005, pp. E1, E3.

## Chapter 12

p. 331 Planet Dog, www.planetdog.com (accessed Apr. 17, 2006); "Raise the Woof," *CNN*, Nov. 4, 2005, www.cnn.com/2005/US/03/28/otr.planet.dog/index.html; Stephanie Volo, "Unleash Your Commitment," *Fast Company*, Mar. 2003, www.fastcompany.com/fast50_02/people/culture/volo.html.

p. 332 "Beauty Diary: Demeter Fragrances," Sephora, www.sephora.com (accessed Apr. 17, 2006); Cassandra Chiacchio, "Dirt Has Been Sold," *WWD*, July 5, 2002, p. 1; "Demeter Fragrances Recreate Memories," Demeter Fragrance Library, press release, Nov. 1, 2005, www.demeterfragrance.com/pearlsofw.aspx?r=28; Matthew W. Evans, "Demeter to Launch Two New Brands," *WWD*, Feb. 25, 2004, p. 35; "World: Since Acquiring Demeter Fragrances in 2002, the Freedom Marketing Group Has Been Working Overtime," Cosmetics International Cosmetic Products Report, June 2004, p. 3.

p. 335 Joanna Soto, Carabello "Seasons 52 Making Georgia Debut at Perimeter Mall," *Atlanta Business Chronicle*, Oct. 17, 2005, www.bizjournals.com/atlanta/stories/2005/10/17/focus7.html; "Darden to Test Casually Sophisticated Fresh Grill and Wine Bar," PRNewswire, www.foodservice.com/news/company_news_detail.cfm?id=5369&company_name=Red%20Lobster (accessed Apr. 17, 2006); Seasons 52, www.seasons52.com (accessed Apr. 17, 2006).

## Chapter 13

p. 352 Julie Gordon, "Churning Up Cheese," MouCo News, June 24, 2001, http://mouco.com/sitecms/content/view/50/2/; Christine McManus, "Bingham Hill Returns," *The [Fort Collins] Coloradoan*, Nov. 11, 2005, p. D8; Christine McManus, " 'Micro-Cheesery' Closes," *The [Fort Collins]Coloradoan*, Feb. 10, 2006, www.coloradoan.com; Kate Sander, "Rustic Blue Won Bingham Hill Its Fame; Now Company Delves into New Cheeses," Cheese Market News, Sept. 2, 2005, www.cheesemarketnews.com/articlesearch/retailwatch/2005/rw02sept05.html; Kate Sander, "Bingham Hill Builds on Microbreweries' Success with Colorado 'Microcheesery,' " Cheese Market News, June 15, 2001, www.cheesemarketnews.com/articlesearch/retailwatch/2001/rw13jul01.html; Anna Wolfe, "Bingham Hill Quadruples Production Capacity," *Gourmet News*, Aug. 2005, via www.looksmartitalianfood.com/p/articles/mi_qa4024/is_200508/ai_n14851846.

p. 359 The Chocolate Farm, www.chocolatefarm.com (accessed May 1, 2006); "Generation Next," Devlin Smith, Entrepreneur, July 2004, www.entrepreneur.com/article/0,4621,299288-11,00.html; "Teen of the Month," iParenting.com, Feb. 2004, http://teenagerstoday.com/tom/0204.htm; "Teen Titans," *People*, Nov. 8, 2004, p. 129.

p. 361 "1. Good Boy!" 2005 Fast 50, Fast Company, www.fastcompany.com/fast50_05/winners/1.html (accessed May 1, 2006); Diane Brady, "Pets Are People, Too, You Know," *Business Week*, Nov. 28, 2005, p. 114; "The Iams Company," Iams, www.iamsco.com/en_US/jhtmls/iamsco/home/sw_ih_Home_page.jhtml?pti=IH&li=en_US&bc=C (accessed May 1, 2006); "The Iams Company Hires Dean of The Ohio State University's College of Veterinary Medicine," Business Wire, Jan. 9, 2004, www.findarticles.com/p/articles/mi_m0EIN/is_2004_Jan_9/ai_112007046/print.

## Chapter 14

p. 380 Dennis Cauchon, "The Little Company That Could," *USA Today*, Oct. 10, 2005, www.usatoday.com/money/companies/management/2005-10-09-mississippi-power-usat_x.htm; "News and Information," Mississippi Power, http://newsinfo.southernco.com/printArticle.asp? mnuType=sub&mnuItem=ni&id=1868&mnuOpco=mpc&category=000&layout=print (accessed May 1, 2006).

p. 391 Diane Brady and Gerry Khermouch, "How to Tickle a Child," *Business Week*, July 7, 2003, pp. 48–50; Joe Flint, "Testing Limits of Licensing," *The Wall Street Journal*, Oct. 9, 2003, p. B1; "He Lives in a Pineapple Under the Sea," *Hotel & Motel Management*, Nov. 3, 2003, p. 126; "Nickelodeon Sits Atop the Basic Cable Heap," MSNBC, Dec. 30, 2005, http://msnbc.msn.com/id/10562945; Karyn Strauss, "Move Over, Disney," *Hotels*, Jan. 2004, p. 13.

p. 394 Alternative Camp," www.alternativecamp.org (accessed May 1, 2006); "Ashoka Fellows-Turkey," Ashoka, www.ashoka.org/global/aw_ce_turkey.cfm (accessed May 1, 2006); Ercan Baysal, "World Acclaim for Young Business Achiever," Zaman Daily Online, Dec. 3, 2004, www.zaman.com/?bl=national&alt=&trh=20041203&hn=14389.

## Chapter 15

p. 411 Kitty Crider, "Off the Bike, the Soup Peddler Expands," *The Austin American-Statesman*, Sept. 14, 2005, www.statesman.com; Julie Powell, "Tale of the Soup Peddler," *Food & Wine*, Nov. 2005, pp. 204–214; The Soup Peddler, www.souppeddler.com (accessed May 1, 2006).

p. 420 "IBM to Enhance Its Supply Chain BTO Offering," *Market Wire*, Feb. 8, 2006; Mike Eskew, "The Art of Delivery: Why More CEOs Are Becoming Supply Chain Experts," *Chief Executive*, Aug.–Sept. 2004, p. 16; David Drickhamer, "Supply-Chain Superstars," *Industry Week*, May 2004, p. 58; Mike McInerney, "Supply Chain Strategic Alliances Can Help Logistics Teams Provide Value," *Pulp & Paper*, Oct. 2003, p. 58.

p. 422 Philip Evans and Bob Wolf, "Collaboration Rules," *Harvard Business Review*, July–Aug. 2005, p. 96; Kate Vitasek, Karl B. Manrodt, and Jeff Abbott, "What Makes a Supply Chain Lean?" *Supply Chain Management*, Oct. 1, 2005, p. 39; Clay Chandler, "Full Speed Ahead," *Fortune*, Feb. 7, 2005, p. 78.

## Chapter 16

p. 434 Wholesale Marketer, www.wholesalemarketer.com (accessed May 1, 2006); "EZ2 Companies, Inc. Partners with Wholesale Marketer to Offer Auction Users 150,000 Items," Business Wire, June 20, 2005; "Wholesale Marketer Adds Two Warehouses," Desert News, Nov 17, 2004.

p. 444 Ann Bednarz, "Footwear Maker Treads Wirelessly," *Network World*, Nov. 17, 2003, p. 23; Rishawn Biddle, "Skechers' Executives Dispute Wrongdoing in Distribution Deals," *Los Angeles Business Journal*, Apr. 21, 2003, p. 3; Karen M. Kroll, "Better Selling Through Kiosks," *MultiChannel Merchant*, Dec. 1, 2005; "Psion Teklogix's Wireless Inventory Management System Implemented at Skechers," *Canadian Corporate News*, Sept. 16, 2003.

p. 447 "Candy Girl," YoungBiz.com, June 16, 2003, www.youngbiz.com/aspindex.asp?fileName=career_gears/Turning%20%20Pro/candy_girl.htm; "Company History," www.hardcandy.com/cs/aboutUs.cfm (accessed May 1, 2006); Jeffrey Zaslow, "Strait Talk," *USA Weekend Magazine*, June 26, 1998.

## Chapter 17

p. 470 Paul Grimaldi, "Out of the Woods—After 93 years in Freeport, Maine, L.L. Bean Says It Has to Open a String of Retail Stores to Fend Off Its Competitors," *The Providence Journal*, July 24, 2005; Tux Terkel, "L.L. Bean Considers Retail, Distribution Expansion in Freeport, Maine," *Portland Press Herald*, Sept. 22, 2005; Clarke Canfield, "L.L. Bean Reports 17 Percent Surge in Holiday Sales," *The Associated Press State & Local Wire*, Jan. 9,

2006; L.L. Bean, www.llbean.com (accessed May 1, 2006).

p. 473 Will Buss, "Magazine to Feature Freeburg, Illinois, Design Business," *Belleville News-Democrat,* Sept. 29, 2004; Greek Gear, www.greekgear.com (accessed May 1, 2006); Susan Kerth, "In Gear," *St. Louis Business Journal,* Jan. 23, 2004; "On A Shoestring," Entrepreneur, Nov. 2004.

p. 481 Doug Desjardins, "PetSmart Rolls Out New Store Format: All Stores to Be Converted to Eagle II by End of 2006," *DSN Retailing Today,* Nov. 8, 2004; "PetSmart Selects Unicru to Find People Passionate About Pets—Top Specialty Retailer of Pet Food and Supplies Looks to Unicru to Hire the Best," *Business Wire,* Jan. 17, 2006; "Multimedia News Release—Mart or Smart?—Nations Largest Pet Retailer Grooms Smart New Brand," *PR Newswire,* Aug. 25, 2005.

## Chapter 18

p. 504 "About Jones Soda," Jones Soda, www.jonessoda.com/files_new/about.html (accessed May 5, 2006); "Jones Soda Swamped with Requests for Turkey & Gravy Soda," Jones Soda, press release, Nov. 20, 2003, www.jonessoda.com/stockstuff/pdf_documents/2003/tandg.pdf; Dave Joseph, "Jones Soda Creates a Pop Culture," *South Florida Sun-Sentinel,* Oct. 27, 2004, via www.jonessoda.com/media_archives/2004/041027-jones_soda_creates_pop_culture.pdf; Edward Popper, "Talking Turkey about Pop Culture," *Business Week,* Nov. 25, 2003, www.businessweek.com.

p. 510 Claire Atkinson, "Commercial Alert Seeks FTC Buzz Marketing Investigation," *Advertising Age,* Oct. 18, 2005, www.adage.com; "Buzz Marketing," Commercial Alert, www.commercialalert.org/issues-landing.php?subcategory_id=90&category=1 (accessed May 5, 2006); Matthew Creamer, "Is Buzz Marketing Illegal?" *Advertising Age,* Oct. 4, 2005, www.adage.com; Jeff Gelles, "New Buzz Tactic: Manipulating Teens," *Philadelphia Enquirer,* Oct. 31, 2005, via www.commercialalert.org/issues-article.php?article_id=816&subcategory_id=90&category=1; Andy Sernovitz, " 'Is Buzz Marketing Illegal' Story Rebutted," letter to the editor, *Advertising Age,* Oct. 10, 2005, www.adage.com.

p. 511 Adam Cole, "Mike Gelman of Spire Media," TechDenver Online, May 24, 2004, www.techdenver.com/viewpoint-23864-313.html; "DBJ's Best Places to Work 2005, *The Denver Business Journal,* Nov. 11, 2005, www.spiremedia.com/spiremedia2k5/?cid=6,123,162; SpireMedia, www.spiremedia.com (accessed May 5, 2006); Mike Taylor, "Unfunded Spire Outlasts Tech's Early High Fliers," *ColoradoBiz,* 30.

## Chapter 19

p. 523 Jim Hanas, "Special Report: Culture of Celebrity," *Advertising Age,* Feb. 20, 2006, p. S1; Nicholas Wapshott, "What Katy Did: The Value of Celebrity Endorsement," *The London Sunday Telegraph,* Sept. 25, 2005, p. 5; "H&M Drops Moss Over Cocaine Use," CNN, Sept. 20, 2005, www.cnn.com; David Kiley and Thomas Mucha, "Why the Caveman Loves the Pitchman," *Business 2.0,* Apr. 2005, p. 39.

p. 533 Mark Mazzetti, "U.S. Army a Tough Brand to Sell," *The Toronto Star,* Aug. 28, 2005; "Army Recruiting Campaign Focuses on Prospects, Influencers," *Congressional Quarterly,* Aug. 30, 2005; "U.S. Military Awards 1.35 Billion Dollar Recruitment Contract," *Agence French Presse,* Dec. 7, 2005; Jon Steinman, "U.S. Army Uses Web Sites to Get Recruits," *Deseret News [Salt Lake City],* May 9, 2005.

p. 535 McClain Finlon, www.mcclainfinlon.com (accessed May 5, 2006); Jane Stebbins, " 'Bitch' Ads Advance to National Competition," *Summit [Colorado] Daily,* April 3, 2003, www.summitdaily.com/article/20030403/NEWS/304030101/0/ARCHIVE; Mike Taylor, "Image Maker," *Coloradobiz,* May 2003; "That Was Then, This Is Now: McClain Finlon Celebrates Twenty Years in Advertis-

ing," *Create Magazine,* Nov. 8, 2005, www.createmagazine.com/news.cfm?IssueName=denver&NewsID=3740.

## Chapter 20

p. 547 Mike Adams, "Larabars Are Unique Food Bars with No Preservatives, No Refined Sugars: Exclusive Interview with Lara Merriken," NewsTarget.com, Dec. 5, 2004, www.newstarget.com/002690.html; Mike Adams, "Larabars Expand in Distribution, Bringing Real Food Bars to Health-Conscious Consumers: Exclusive Interview with Lara Merriken," NewsTarget.com, www.newstarget.com/002696.html (accessed May 5, 2006); LaraBar, www.larabar.com (accessed May 5, 2006); Mike Taylor, "Startup Junkies Get Monthly Fix," *ColoradoBiz* 30, no. 10 (2003): 52.

p. 556 Gregory K. Ericksen, "A Woman Entrepreneur Tells Her Story: Doris Christopher," in *Women Entrepreneurs Only: 12 Women Entrepreneurs Tell Their Success* (New York: Wiley, 1999); The Pampered Chef, www.pamperedchef.com (accessed May 5, 2006); "The Pampered Chef, Ltd.," Hoover's, www.hoovers.com (accessed May 5, 2006).

p. 564 "Pizza Hut Unveils 50 percent Bigger Pizza," *Marketing Week,* Dec. 1, 2005, p. 7; Richard Williamson, "Pizza Hut Partakes in 'Three Wishes,' " *Adweek Southwest,* Nov. 11, 2005; Richard Williamson, "Pizza Hut Turns Up Heat on Stuffed Crust," *Adweek Southwest,* April 2005; Gregg Cebrzynski, "Top Pizza Segment Chains Fight It Out on Familiar Turf," *Nation's Restaurant News,* June 27, 2005, pp. 118+; "Pizza Hut Starts Its Engines for First NASCAR Sponsorship," *Nation's Restaurant News,* May 9, 2005, p. 20; Pizza Hut, www.pizzahut.com (accessed May 5, 2006).

## Chapter 21

p. 579 Robert D. Hof, "Netflix 1, Wal-Mart 0," Business Week Online, May 20, 2005, via EBSCO Host Research Database; Tara Lemmey, "Push the Positive for Customers," Business Week Online, Sept. 13, 2005, via EBSCO Host Research Database; Jena McGregor, "High-Tech Achiever: Netflix, At Netflix, the Secret Sauce Is Software," *Fast Company,* Oct. 2005, p. 48, http://pf.fastcompany.com/magazine/99/open_customer-netflix.html; "Movies to Go," *Economist,* July 9, 2005, p. 57, via EBSCO Host Research Database; Timothy J. Mullaney and Robert Hof, "Netflix: Starring in Merger Story?" Business Week Online, Nov. 10, 2005, via EBSCO Host Research Database; Julie Schlosser, "Netflix Makes it Big in Hollywood," *Fortune,* June 13, 2005, p. 34, via EBSCO Host Research Database.

p. 583 Amy Fennell Christian, "What Is Success?" *Entrepreneur,* Jan. 2004, www.entrepreneur.com/tsu/article/0,5788,312524,00.html; Andrea Faiad, "Teen Tech Wizard," *YoungBiz.com,* Dec. 1999, www.youngbiz.com; "Pankaj Arora Software's Tumi Cursor Powerpack," www.paware.com/pastcp.

p. 591 Mercedes M. Cardona, "Affluent Shoppers Like Their Luxe Goods Cheap," *Advertising Age,* Dec. 1, 2003; Donald R. Lichtenstein, Scot Burton, and Paul M. Herr, "An Examination of the Effects of Information Consistency and Distinctiveness in a Reference Price Advertisement Context," *Journal of Applied Social Psychology,* Dec. 1993; Donald R. Lichtenstein, Scot Burton, and Eric Karson, "The Effect of Semantic Cues on Consumer Perceptions of Reference Price Advertisements," *Journal of Consumer Research,* Dec. 1991; Ken Manning, O. C. Ferrell, and Linda Ferrell, "A Comparison of Clearance and Sale Prices: An Empirical Investigation," working paper, University of Wyoming, 2006.

## Chapter 22

p. 607 Kathy Smith, "Whole Foods' Belmar Store Breaks New Ground for Food Shoppers," *CO Vine,* Winter 2005, pp. 25–28; Robert Walberg, "Is Whole Foods the Next Starbucks?" MSN

Money, May 19, 2005, http://moneycentral.msn.com/content/P116548.asp?Printer; "Whole Foods Market: Company: Declaration of Interdependence," Whole Foods Market, www.wholefoodsmarket.com/company/declaration.html (accessed May 6, 2005).

p. 614 Arik Hesseldahl, "For Every Xbox, A Big Fat Loss," *UPFront,* Dec. 5, 2005, p. 13; Thomas Jackson, "War of the New Machines," *Forbes,* Dec. 13, 2005, pp. 81–83, via EBSCO Host Research Database; Stephen Manes, "Generation X," *Forbes,* Dec. 12, 2005, pp. 70–72, via EBSCO Host Research Database; Frank Michael Russell, "Xbox 360 Pricing Strategy: Less than the Sum of Its Parts?" *Mercury News,* Nov. 23, 2005 (accessed January 18, 2006); Stephen H. Wildstrom, "Xbox: A Winner Only at Games," *Business Week,* Dec. 12, 2005 (accessed January 18, 2006), via EBSCO Host Research Database.

p. 617 Jacky Johnson, "Young and Inventive," *St. Petersburg Times,* Mar. 3, 2003, www.sptimes.com/2003/03/03/Xpress/Young_and_inventive.shtml; "Kid Inventors," *Wild Planet Kid Inventor Challenge,* www.kidinventorchallenge.com/kid_inventors/rich_stachowski.php (accessed May 6, 2006); "Teen Titans," *People,* Nov. 8, 2004, p. 129.

**CHAPTER 1** p. 2: Simeon Schatz/alwaystock LLC/Alamy; p. 5 (left): Reprinted with permission of Neutrogena Corp.; p. 5 (right): Reprinted with permission of ESPN; p. 10 (left): Courtesy of Citigroup, Inc. Used by permission. Photo copyright Robin Lynne Gibson/Workbook Stock; p. 10 (right): Copyright State Farm Mutual Automobile Insurance Company 2005. Used by Permission; p. 14 (top): Reprinted with permission of Rapala; p. 14 (bottom): Reprinted with permission of Procter & Gamble Productions, Inc.; p. 15: Dann Tardif/LWA/Blend Images/Alamy; p. 17 (left): Reprinted with permission of National Hemophilia Organization and Carliss Scaife; p. 17 (right): Reprinted with permission of the Susan G. Komen Breast Cancer Foundation; p. 18: Royalty-Free Corbis; p. 19: © 2006 EBAY INC. ALL RIGHTS RESERVED; p. 23: MedioImages/Getty Images.

**CHAPTER 2** p. 27: Brand X Pictures/Jupiter Images; p. 29: Courtesy of Unilever US, Inc. Used by permission.; p. 30: Reprinted with permission of La-Z-Boy Incorporated.; p. 31 (left): Reprinted with permission of Veterinary Pet Insurance; p. 31 (right): Reprinted with permission of Splintek; p. 32: Reprinted with permission of Leupold & Stevens, Inc.; p. 35: Reprinted with permission of Citigroup. Photo by Matthias Clamer/Getty Images; p. 36: Chicken Fee Photo/Creatas/Jupiter Images; p. 38: Comstock/Jupiter Images; p. 39: Reprinted with permission of Dyson; p. 50: fotosearch.com.

**STRATEGIC CASE 1** p. 52: Dex Image/Jupiter Images

**CHAPTER 3** p. 56: Photodisc Green/Getty Images; p. 59: Courtesy of Toyota North America. Used by permission; p. 60: Reprinted with permission of AMI Brands, LLC; p. 72 (left): Copyright 2006 – Monster, Inc. All Rights Reserved; p. 72 (right): Reprinted with permission of American Honda Motor Co., Inc. and Natalie Boehm Photography.; p. 73: Image Source/fotosearch.com; p. 75 (left): Reprinted with permission of Westphal/Stonewear Designs; p. 75 (right): Reprinted with permission of Bayer Healthcare, LLC, Consumer Care Division; p. 76: Photodisc Green/Getty Images; p. 78: Reprinted with permission of Miele; p. 82: Michael Dwyer/AP Photo.

**CHAPTER 4** p. 85: Con Bishop/Photodisc Red/Getty Images; p. 86: Reprinted with permission of The Rechargeable Battery Recycling Corporation; p. 88: Copyrighted by Chevron Corporation and used with permission; p. 89: Royalty-Free Corbis; p. 90: Dennis Kitchen/Stone/Getty Images; p. 93 (left): Reprinted with permission of Earth Share; p. 93 (right): Reprinted with permission of European Eco-label; p. 94: © The Muppets Holding Company, LLC. All Rights Reserved. Reprinted by Permission of FORD.; p. 99: Reprinted with permission of The National Youth Anti-Drug Media Campaign; p. 101: Reprinted with permission of The Humane Society of the United States; p. 105: Reprinted with permission of Siemens. Photo copyright Getty Images.; p. 108: Reprinted with permission of Merck & Co, Inc.; p. 111: Royalty-Free Corbis.

**STRATEGIC CASE 2** p. 114 Mickael David/Alamy.

**CHAPTER 5** p. 120: Rubberball/Jupiter Images; p. 124: Reprinted with permission of The Rechargeable Battery Recycling Corporation; p. 125: Courtesy of the Gilette Company; p. 128: M. C. Escher's "Sky and Water I" © 2006 The M. C. Escher Company – Baarn – Holland. All Rights Reserved. Used by permission; p. 130 (left): Reprinted with permission of the ASPCA; p. 130 (right): © 2006 Kashi Company. used by permission; p. 131: Reprinted with permission of Mothers Against Drunk Driving © 2006; p. 133: Reprinted by permission of The Creative Circus; p. 134: Benno de Wilde/Imageshop/Alamy; p. 136: George Doyle/Stockbyte Platinum/Getty Images; p. 140: Reprinted with permission of Burton Snowboards; p. 146: Randy Faris/Corbis.

**CHAPTER 6** p. 149: Jonelle Weaver/Photodisc Green/Getty Images; p. 152 (left): Reprinted with permission of The Garlic Company; p. 152 (right): Reprinted with permission of Carolina Turkeys; p. 153: Royalty-Free Corbis; p. 156: Reprinted with permission of Cargill Corporation; p. 157: Courtesy of Acushnet; p. 158: 56347893; p. 159 (left): Reprinted with permission of AVW-TELAV Audio Visual Solutions; p. 159 (right): Reprinted with permission of Magma Design Automation; p. 160: Property, copyright and reprinted with permission of Ashland; p. 164: Reprinted with permission of American Airlines; p. 170: PNC/Photodisc Red/Getty Images; p. 171: Ilianski/Alamy.

**CHAPTER 7** p. 173: Comstock/Jupiter Images; p. 175: Image and the InterContinental Hotels & Resorts © names appear courtesy of InterContinental Hotels Group.; p. 176: Reprinted with permission of Robb Allen, Richard Dolan, Stephen Jablonsky, Pat. James Longo. Courtesy of DataPipe; p. 181: Reprinted with permission of the American Indian College Fund. Used by permission.; p. 185: Reprinted with permission of Cargill Incorporated; p. 187: Reprinted with permission of Continental Airlines; p. 192: Ad courtesy of Orchard Network Ltd. Used by permission.; p. 200: Goodshot/Jupiter Images; p. 205: Comstock/Jupiter Images.

**STRATEGIC CASE 3** p. 208: © Creatas Images/Jupiter Images.

**CHAPTER 8** p. 212: AP Photo/Sang Tan; p. 214: Reprinted from REAL SIMPLE ® © Time Inc. All rights reserved.; p. 217 (left): Reprinted with permission of DirectoryNet, LLC; p. 217 (right): Reprinted with permission of Textile World/Billian Publishing, Inc.; p. 220: Reprinted with permission of Napster, LLC; p. 221 (left): Reprinted with permission of CareerBuilder.com; p. 221 (right): Copyright 2006 – Monster, Inc. All Rights Reserved.; p. 222: Courtesy, ING DIRECT; p. 225: Reprinted with permission of Lansmont Corporation; p. 228: Mitch Diamond/Alamy; p. 231: Reprinted with permission of SurfControl. Created by Banujo, Donkers and Brothers. Photo by Tim Bradley/TimBradley.com; p. 237: Image Source/Getty Images.

**CHAPTER 9** p. 239: Royalty-Free Corbis; p. 241: Courtesy of McMillion Research/Mindfield Online Panels; p. 245: Reprinted with permission of GMI (Global Market Institute, Inc.); p. 247: Reprinted with permission of Greenfield Online, Inc.; p. 250: Brand X Pictures/fotosearch.com; p. 253: Reprinted with permission of

Burke, Inc.; p. 255 (left): Reprinted with permission of AVW-TELAV Audio Visual Solutions; p. 255 (right): Reprinted with permission of Blackbaud, Inc. Photo copyright Eureka/Alamy; p. 256: Reprinted with permission of Workplace Print Media; p. 257: Steve Allen/Brand X Pictures/Alamy; p. 259: Reprinted with permission of Western Wats, Inc.; p. 264: Image 100/Jupiter Images.

**CHAPTER 10** p. 267: Royalty-Free Corbis; p. 272: Image Source; p. 273 (left): Reprinted with permission of Visa U. S. A. Inc.; p. 273 (right): Reprinted with permission of Montblanc NA LLC; p. 274 (left): Reprinted with permission of The Gillette Company; p. 274 (right): © 2006 Eveready Battery Company, Inc. Reprinted with permission.; p. 276: Reprinted with permission of The Principal Financial Group; p. 279: Image Source; p. 280 (left): CESAR® is a registered trademark of Mars, Incorporated and its affiliates. This trademark is used with permission. Mars, Incorporated is not associated with Pride/Ferrell. Advertisement is printed with permission of Mars, Incorporated. ©Mars, Inc 2008.; p. 280 (right): © 2006 MasterCard. All rights reserved. No reproduction or use of this material may be made without prior written consent of MasterCard International Incorporated.; p. 287: Reprinted with permission of Colgate Palmolive Company; p. 295: Royalty-Free Corbis.

**STRATEGIC CASE 4** p. 298: Karl Weatherly/PhotoDisc Green.

**CHAPTER 11** p. 302: Brand X Pictures/Jupiter Images; p. 304: Sean Murphy Photo; p. 306 (top): Reprinted with permission of Sara-Lee Food & Beverage, St. Louis, MO, © Sara Lee Corporation 2005.; p. 306 (bottom): Reprinted with permission of World Kitchen, LLC; p. 307: Reprinted with permission of Seven Cycles and MIBA Design; p. 308 (left): Reprinted with permission of SATO America, Inc.; p. 308 (right): Reprinted Courtesy of Caterpillar, Inc.; p. 310 (left): Reprinted with permission of Newman's Own, Inc.; p. 310 (right): Reprinted with permission of Horizon Organic; p. 311: MedioImages/Jupiter Images; p. 312: Reprinted with permission of The Scotts Miracle-Gro Company; p. 315: Image Source/Jupiter Images; p. 323: Royalty-Free Corbis.

**CHAPTER 12** p. 325: Royalty-Free Corbis; p. 327: Reprinted with permission of Frito-Lay, Inc.; p. 328: General Motors Corp. Used with permission, GM Media Archives; p. 329: Photographer Ken Stidwill www.acmephoto.com; p. 330 (left): M&M'S®, M&M'S® MINIS®, Mega M&M'S®, M-AZING®, and M_AZING® MINIS® are trademarks owned by Mars, Incorporated and its affiliates. These trademarks are used with permission. Mars, Incorporated is not associated with Houghton Mifflin Company. Advertisements printed with permission of Mars, Incorporated. ©Mars, Inc. 2008.; p. 330 (right): M&M'S®, M&M'S® MINIS®, Mega M&M'S®, M-AZING®, and M_AZING® MINIS® are trademarks owned by Mars, Incorporated and its affiliates. These trademarks are used with permission. Mars, Incorporated is not associated with Houghton Mifflin Company. Advertisements printed with permission of Mars, Incorporated. ©Mars, Inc. 2008.; p. 332: Demeter Fragrance Library; p. 334: Reprinted with permission of Frito-Lay, Inc.; p. 335: Digital Vision/Getty Images; p. 337: Reprinted with permission of The Stanley Works; p. 339: Reprinted with permission of Equal Exchange; p. 341: Reprinted with permission of Staples, Inc.; p. 347: Photodisc Green/Getty Images.

**CHAPTER 13** p. 349: Chris Batson/Alamy; p. 350: MORTON and the Umbrella Girl are registered trademarks of Morton International, Inc. Used with permission. Photography by Shane Morgan. Used with permission.; p. 352: Ingram Publishing/Jupiter Images; p. 353: Reprinted with permission of Dole Food Company, Inc.; p. 354: © 2006 Kellogg North America Company; p. 358: Reprinted with permission of Xerox Corporation; p. 360:

Reprinted with permission of Mitchell Berko, President, Walden Farms, Inc.; p. 361: Photodisc Green/Getty Images; p. 362: Reprinted with permission of Citicorp Diners Club Inc. Ad published in 2005.; p. 363: Reprinted by permission of Kraft Foods. Photographer: Richard Pierce.; p. 372: Image Source/Getty Images.

**CHAPTER 14** p. 375: Darren Kirk/Alamy; p. 379: © 2006 Hertz Systems, Inc. Hertz is a registered service mark and trademark of Hertz System, Inc. Photo by Altrendo Images/Getty Images; p. 380: Photodisc Red/Getty Images; p. 381 (top): Reprinted with permission of Amy Schiappa, Fringe Salon NY.; p. 381 (bottom): Reprinted with permission of Capella University; p. 383: Reprinted with permission of FTD; p. 385: Reprinted with permission of Costa Cruise Lines, N. V.; p. 388: Reprinted with permission of Delta Airlines, Inc.; p. 391: Blend Images/Getty Images; p. 392: Reprinted with permission of RE/MAX International, Inc. Photo by Ed Dosien; p. 393: Reprinted with permission of Harvard School of Public Health; p. 398: #200120937-001.

**STRATEGIC CASE 5** p. 401: Digital Vision/Getty Images.

**CHAPTER 15** p. 404: Royalty-Free Corbis; p. 406: Reprinted with permission of Capgemini; p. 409 (left): Reprinted with permission of Luther Brow, nVision Global Technology Solutions, Inc.; p. 409 (right): Reprinted with permission of TechTarget, Inc.; p. 413: Reprinted with permission of Procter & Gamble; p. 417: Reprinted with permission of Wm. Wrigley Jr. Company; p. 418: Reprinted with permission of Steve Madden Ltd.; p. 420: Age Fotostock/Fotosearch; p. 422: Cut and Deal/Gambling Stock Photograph/Alamy; p. 428: Dex Photo/Getty Images.

**CHAPTER 16** p. 431: PhotoDisc/Fotosearch.com; p. 434: Michael Blann/Getty Images; p. 442 (left): Reprinted with permission of New Breed Logistics, Inc.; p. 442 (right): Reprinted with permission of Data2Logistics, LLC; p. 443: Reprinted with permission of Ryder System, Inc.; p. 444: Image Source/Getty Images; p. 446: Reprinted with permission of Seayco Integrators, Inc.; p. 449 (left): Reprinted with permission of Conway Inc.; p. 449 (right): Reprinted with permission of Horizon Lines Inc. & BSY Associates; p. 452: Reprinted with permission of Odyssey Logistics & Technology Corporation; p. 453: Reprinted with permission of Stonepath Group; p. 458: Joseph Sohm-Visions of America/Getty Images.

**CHAPTER 17** p. 461: Royalty-Free Corbis; p. 465: AP/Wide World Photos; p. 467: Michael Newman/Photo Edit, Inc. p. 468: Reprinted with permission of The Container Store; p. 469: Reprinted with permission of Lowe's Companies, Inc.; p. 470: Image Ideas/Jupiter Images; p. 472: Reprinted with permission of Expedia, Inc.; p. 477 (left): Reprinted with permission of the Corporate Marketing Department of MapInfo Corporation.; p. 477 (right): Reprinted with permission of Claritas Inc.; p. 478: Reprinted with permission of Wrentham Village Premium Outlets; p. 480: Reprinted with permission of Pier 1 Imports; p. 481: Digital Vision/Getty Images; p. 486: Kimball Andrew Schmidt/Stock Connection Blue/Alamy.

**STRATEGIC CASE 6** p. 489: Brand X Pictures/Jupiter Images.

**CHAPTER 18** p. 492: Royalty-Free Corbis; p. 493: © 2006 Yahoo! Inc. YAHOO! And the YAHOO! logo are trademarks of Yahoo! Inc.; p. 497: Reprinted with permission of Sonos; p. 499: Reprinted with permission of Columbia Sportswear Company; p. 500: Copyright 2006 Sun Microsystems Inc. All rights reserved. Reprinted with permission of Sun Microsystems Inc.; p. 502: Reprinted with permission of The Garlic Company; p. 503: Reprinted with permission of Merck & Co., Inc.; p. 504: Comstock Imagery/Alamy; p. 507: Reprinted with permission of

Simdesk Technologies; p. 508: Reprinted with permission of Wendy's International, Inc.; p. 510: Peter Lowe/Stock Image/Pixland/Alamy; p. 517: Frank Whitney/Brand X Pictures.

**CHAPTER 19**    p. 519: Brand X Pictures/Alamy; p. 522: Reprinted with permission of CNRC the U. S. Navy; p. 523: Bramwell-slocker/Alamy; p. 524: Reprinted with permission of iDashboards; p. 528: Reprinted with permission of Clear Channel Radio; p. 531: Reprinted with permission of Xerox Corporation; p. 532: Reprinted with permission of Carolina Turkeys; p. 533: Royalty-Free Corbis; p. 536: Reprinted with permission of Steinway Musical/The Wyant Simboli Group; p. 538: Reprinted with permission of Ben & Jerry's; p. 542: Royalty-Free Corbis.

**CHAPTER 20**    p. 545: Royalty-Free Corbis; p. 548: Reprinted with permission of infoUSA; p. 550: Reprinted with permission of Hoover's, Inc., a D&B Company; p. 555: Reprinted with permission of Richardson; p. 556: TRBfoto/Getty Images; p. 559: Reprinted with permission of Synygy, Inc. Photo by Coneyl Jay/Getty Images; p. 560: Reprinted with permission of Lowe's Companies; p. 563: Reprinted with permission of Southwest Airlines; p. 564: Victoria Snowber/Getty Images; p. 571: AP Photo/Fabian Bimmer.

**STRATEGIC CASE 7**    p. 573: Ryan McVay/Getty Images.

**CHAPTER 21**    p. 576: Royalty-Free Corbis; p. 578: Reprinted with permission of Snapfish; p. 579: Royalty-Free Corbis; p. 590: Reprinted with permission of The Gillette Company; p. 591: Arthur S. Aubry/Getty Images; p. 592: Reprinted with permission of Leliam de Castro Raña, Embraer; p. 593: Reprinted with permission of Gold's Gym International; p. 594: Reprinted with permission of PrintingForLess.com; p. 600: Image Source/Getty Images.

**CHAPTER 22**    p. 603: Corbis Royalty-Free/Jupiter Images; p. 606: Courtesy of American Ironhorse Motorcycle Company Inc.; p. 607: Image Source/Jupiter Images; p. 610: Reprinted with permission of The Woodstock Inn & Resort; p. 612: Reprinted with permission of JELD-WEN © Windows & Doors, www.jeld-wen.com; p. 613: Reprinted with permission of CITYPASS, Inc.; p. 614: Joan Joannides/Alamy; p. 615: Reprinted with permission of Kohler. Photo courtesy of Jean Claude Maillard.; p. 618: Reprinted with permission of Dorfman Sterling; p. 624: Dynamic Graphics/Jupiter Images.

**STRATEGIC CASE 8**    p. 627: Nader Cserny/Getty Images.

Greenbaum, Jeffrey, N4
Greenley, Gordon E., N2
Gresham, Larry G., N6
Grewal, Dhruv, 243(table), N12
Grewal, Rajdeep, N3
Grimm, Jim L., A17
Grimm, Matthew, 277(table)
Grohmann, Bianca, N2
Gronhaug, Kjell, N3
Gross, Daniel, N13
Grossman, David, N23
Grossman, Gary, N16
Grove, Stephen J., N17
Grow, Brian, N22
Guilford, David, N24
Gupta, Anil K., N10
Gupta, Sachin, N20
Gupta, Sunil, N1
Gürha-Canli, Zeynep, N9
Gurney, Dan, 24

Hahn, Lucinda, N19
Haiar, Nikole, N16
Hallett, Vicky, N22
Halliday, Jean, N1, N21, N22
Halonen, Doug, N24
Hamm, Steve, N8
Hamner, Susanna, N14, N19
Hanford, Desiree J., N21
Hanrahan, Tim, N12
Hansen, Barbara, N23
Hardesty, David M., N24
Harich, Katrin R., N16
Harps, Leslie Hanson, N18
Harrington, Lisa, N8
Hart, Christopher, N11
Hart, Susan, N3
Hartline, Michael, 28(illus.), N1, N2, N3, N4, N14
Hartline, Michael D., N10, N11, N17, N25
Harwood, John, N13
Hasty, Ronald W., N22
Hauser, John R., N13
Hawes, Jon M., N22
Hawk, Tony, 504
Hawken, Paul, N5
Hawkins, Del I., N16
Hawkins, Lee, N24
Hawkins, Lori, N24
Hawn, Carleen, N23
Hazel, Debra, N19
Healey, James R., N3, N14
Heffernan, Paul, N24
Heimer, Matthew, N12
Heller, Laura, N8, N13, N18
Helm, Burt, N1, N12
Helyar, John, N19
Henderson, Pamela W., N21
Henschen, Doug, N18
Hentz, Maureen C., 398
Hernandez, Mirna, 23
Heskel, Julia, N17
Hess, Ronald L., N11
Hewett, Kelly, N16
Hibbard, Jonathan D., N18
Hickingbotham, Frank, 193
Higgins, Dan, N13
Higgins, Michelle, N6
Hill, Donna J., N13
Hilton, Nicky, 573
Hilton, Paris, 573, 574
Himelstein, Linda, N17
Hindo, Brian, N15

Hinkle, Stephen, N24
Hoag, Christina, N7
Hochwald, Lambeth, N13
Hof, Robert D., N10, N12
Hoffman, K. Douglas, 382(table), N17
Holden, Stephen, N17
Hollis, Nigel, N16
Holly, Susan, N18
Holmes, Stanley, N19
Holt, David, 372
Holt, Douglas B., N16
Holt, Karen, N22
Homburg, Christian, N2, N3, N5
Hooley, Graham J., N2
Horovitz, Bruce, N3, N15
Horowitz, Adam, N14, N15
Houston, Mark B., N2
Howard, Daniel J., N21
Howard, Theresa, N4, N24
Howell, Debbie, N4, N10, N14
Howell, Roy D., N13
Hoyer, Wayne D., 139(table), N7
Hu, Michael Y., N13
Hudson, Chris, N19
Hughes, Laura Q., N7
Hulland, John, N11
Hult, G. Thomas, N3
Hult, G. Thomas M., N5, N10
Hult, M., N2
Humphreys, Jeffrey M., N4, N7
Hunt, Shelby D., N6, N11
Hurt, Melonee McKinney, N4
Hutt, Michael D., N8
Hyatt, James C., N6

Iacono, Erica, N21
Indounas, Kostis A., N24
Invester, Douglas, 457
Isidore, Chris, N24
Iskat, Wilifried, N17
Iverson, Allen, 298
Ives, Nat, N21
Izraeli, David, N9

Jacobs, Bert, 82–83
Jacobs, John, 82–83
Jacobson, David, N15
Jacobson, Robert, N1
Jamil, Maqbul, N20
Jarvis, Jeff, 216
Jarvis, Steve, N7
Jassawalla, Avan R., N3
Jaworski, Bernard J., N1, N3
Jay-Z, 33, 298
Jealouse, Victoria, 140(illus.)
Jensen, Ove, N3
Jewell, Mark, N1
Joachismthaler, Erich, N23
Johannes, Amy, N20, N23
Johanson, Jan, N9, N10
John, Andrew, N5
John, Joby, N17
Johnson, Chris, 290
Johnson, Jean L., N2, N11
Johnson, Julie T., N22
Johnson, Kristi, 352
Johnson, Steve, N2
Johnson, Tom, 352
Johnston, Larry, N19
Johnston, Wesley J., N8
Jones, Del, N6
Jones, Eli, N22
Jones, Morag Cuddeford, N14
Jordan, Gregory, N7

Jordan, Kim, 371
Jordan, Michael, 298
Josephson, Michael, N5
Judge, William Q., N10

Kahney, Leander, N8
Kamakura, Wagner A., N12
Kang, Stephanie, N14
Kaplan, Daniel, N2
Karatepe, Osman M., N11
Keck, Tim, 290
Keefe, Bob, N24
Keillor, Bruce, N10
Keith, Janet E., N20
Kelleher, Herb, 492
Kelleher, Kevin, N13
Keller, Casey, N7
Keller, Maryann, N23
Kellogg, W.K., 311
Kelly, Marjorie, 87(table), N6, N18
Kelly, Matt, N8
Kemp, David, N16
Kennedy, John F., 95
Kerin, Roger A., N21
Kerwin, Kathleen, N24
Khermouch, Gerry, N21
Kiley, David, N13, N24
Kim, Chung K., N15
King, Julia, N12
Kinsey, Jean, N19
Kirkpatrick, David, N11
Klein, Jill Gabrielle, N5
Klein, Noreen M., N11, N20
Knight, Gary A., N8
Kobkaew, Jaturong, N20
Kohl, Jerry, 153
Kohli, Ajay K., N1
Kohli, Chirajeev S., N16
Kotler, Philip, N14, N17
Kozinets, Robert V., N13
Krasner, Jeffrey, N17
Kratz, Ellen Florian, N3
Krause, Kristin S., N3
Krauss, Michael, N2, N11, N20
Kreitner, Robert, N21
Krishnan, R., 243(table), N12
Krohmer, Karley, N2
Kuchwara, Michael, N17
Kuehn, Richard, N17
Kumar, Nirmalya, N18
Kumar, V., N1, N11
Kump, Leslie, N17
Kundu, Sumit K., N10
Kunstel, Marcia, N9

Laczniak, Gene R., N6
Lafferty, Barbara A., N5
Lafley, A.G., N15
Lagerfeld, Karl, 173, 592
Lambert, Agnes, 10
Lambert, Earl, 10
Lambert, Norman Ray, 10
Lampinen, Minttu, N15
Landreth, Jonathan, N22
Lane, Vicki R., N16, N20
Lareau, Jamie, N12
Lasswell, Mark, N14, N15
Lavack, Anne M., N15
Lavelle, Louis, N15
Leamon, Scott, N23
Lebesch, Jeff, 371
Lee, Eunkyu, N13
Lee, Kee-hung, N3
Lee, Louise, N8, N13

Prewitt, Edward, N11
Priddle, Alisa, N24
Pride, William M., N5, N11
Prince, Marcelo, N21
Procter, David B., N12
Pushalla, Greg, N23
Putsis, William P., Jr., N14

Querna, Betsy, N5
Quinn, Steve, N5

Rabin, Dan, N16
Rackaway, Chapman, N2
Ramage, Douglas, 200
Raman, Kalyon, N20
Ramani, G., N11
Ramstad, Evan, N23
Rangan, V. Kasturi, N8
Rao, Vithala R., N24
Ratchford, Brian T., N12
Ravid, S. Abraham, N21
Rechtin, Mark, N13
Redmond, William H., N4
Reed, Dan, N23
Reed, Stanley, N9
Reed-Woodward, Marcia A., N4
Regan, Keith, N1
Reibling, Elen Thomas, N21
Reimer, Anja, N17
Reimer, Susan, N4
Reinartz, Werner J., N11
Reyes, Sonia, N4
Reynolds, Burt, 573
Reynolds, Christopher, N13
Rhoads, Gary K., N13
Rich, Anne K., N22
Richardson, Karen, N14
Richtel, Matt, N23
Ridgeway, Nancy M., N23
Riley, William, 624
Rindfleisch, Aric, N15
Ritter, Thomas, N2
Roberts, Dexter, N9
Roberts, Josh, N12
Robertson, Heather, 23, 24
Robertson, Pat, 402
Robin, Donald P., N6
Roddick, Andy, 502
Roegner, Eric V., N24
Rogers, Everett M., 318(illus.), N14
Roman, Monica, N3
Rose, Gregory M., N9
Rose, Jill, N4
Roth, Daniel, N11
Roth, David, 27
Roth, Martin S., N16
Rowling, J.K., 544
Roy, Don, N2, N10
Rubinson, Joel, N16
Rugman, Alan M., N9
Ruiz, Salvador, N20
Rust, Roland T., N1
Ruth, Babe, 307
Ryals, Lynette, N1
Ryan, Thomas J., N4
Ryman, Joel A., N10

Sääksjärvi, Maria, N15
Saenz, Laura Leigh, N10
Saini, Amit, N2
Sains, Ariane, N9
Saliba, Clare, N24
Salimi, Mohammad Hossein, N13
Salter, Chuck, N2, N7, N22

Sample, Kevin, N10
Sams, Rachel, N14
Sanders, Lisa, N15, N16, N21
Santos, Maria Leticia, N4
Sapsford, Jason, N7
Sapsford, Jathon, N15
Saranow, Jennifer, N24
Sarnoff, David, 317(table)
Sarraille, Edmund, 228
Sashittat, Hermant C., N3
Sataline, Suzanne, N5
Schechner, Sam, N17
Schlesinger, Leonard, N1
Schlosser, Julie, N1
Schmidt, Julie, N6
Schoen, John W., N24
Schultz, Don E., N16
Schultz, Howard, 322
Schulz, Robert, N15
Schwartz, Mark S., N9
Schwartz, Natalie, N22
Schweitzer, Kevin, N24
Sciabarrasi, Jim, 625, N24
Segal, Fred, 447
Seitz, Patrick, N19
Selden, Larry, 265–266
Sellers, Patricia, N3
Semon, Thomas T., N13
Sen, Sankar, N11
Serrie, Hendrick, N17
Sethi, Rajesh, N15
Sexton, Paul, N10
Shakira, 141
Shannon, Darren, N23
Sharp, David, N8
Shaw, Jonah, 305
Shaw, R., N10
Sheinin, Daniel A., N24
Sheldon, Stacy, N13
Sheridan, Margaret, N7
Sheth, Jagdish N., N1, N2
Shinkle, Kirk, N22
Shor, Rita, N16
Shrimp, Terrence A., N20
Sicilia, María, N20
Sidell, Louise Kasdon, N9
Sierra, Jeremy J., N17
Simmons, Amy, 91
Simmons, Russell, 298
Simoes, Cláudia, N2
Simple Plan, 574
Simpson, Bryan, N16
Simpson, Jessica, 573
Sinegal, James D., 487
Singh, Jagdip, N13
Sisodia, Rajendras, N1
Sittimalakorn, Wuthichai, N3
Sizoo, Steve, N17
Slater, Stanley F., N3
Sloan, Paul, N12
Smith, Daniel C., N16
Smith, Ethan, N5
Smith, Fred, 317(table)
Smith, Frederick W., 52, 54
Smith, Gerald E., N23
Smith, Geri, N9
Smith, Margo, N15
Smith, N. Craig, N5
Snoop Dog, 401, 573
Snow, Tony, 6
Songini, Marc L., N3
Soong, Jennifer, N4
Souchon, Anne L., N12
Southwick, Karen, N8

Spangenberg, Eric R., N19
Speh, Thomas W., N8
Spekman, Robert E., N8
Spencer, Jane, N1
Spethman, Betsy, N20
Spethmann, Betsy, N22
Spiro, Rosann L., N22
Spors, Kelly K., N1
Sprinzen, Scott, N15
Sprott, David E., N5
Stachowski, Rich, 617
Stafford, Marla Royne, N24
Stafford, Thomas F., N24
Stannard-Friel, Jessica, N5, N6
Steele, Willian H., 206
Steinberg, Brian, N3
Steitzer, Stephenie, N12
Stern, Howard, 402
Stern, Louis W., N18
Stershic, Sybil F., N3
Stewart, David W., N11
Stewart, Martha, 402, 539
Stickel, Eberhard, N4
Stiller, Bob, 50
Stone, Brad, N18, N23
Strasburg, Jenny, N19
Strauss, Judy, N13
Straziuso, Jason, N11
Stuart, Anne, N18
Stuart, Jennifer Ames, N1
Studt, Tim, N16
Suri, Rajneesh, N23
Suter, Tracy A., N24
Swartz, Jon, N12, N23
Symonds, William C., N9, N15, N24
Szymanski, David M., N15, N20

Talukadar, Debabrata, N12
Tanner, John F., Jr., N16
Tansuhaj, Patriya, N3
Tantillo, Joseph, 473
Tapscott, Don, N6
Tarquino, Alex, N10
Tatelman, Barry, 295
Tatelman, Eliot, 295, 296
Tatelman, Samuel, 295
Taub, Stephen, N5, N18
Taylor, Charles R., N9
Tenser, James, N1
Terhune, Chad, N1, N4, N18, N20
Thaw, John, N1
Thomas, Jacquelyn S., N12
Thomas, Kathy Booth, N15
Thomas, Kenneth W., N3
Thomas, Owen, N14, N15
Thompson, Stephanie, N2, N4, N5, N20, N24
Thornberry, Neal, N10
Ticoll, David, N6
Tischler, Linda, N23, N24
Toh, Rex S., N13
Tomas, G., N2
Totty, Michael, N11
Trachtenberg, Jeffrey A., N22
Traiman, Steve, N15
Trevino, Linda K., N6
Troxel, Melanie, 566
Troy, Lisa C., N15
Trust, Laura, 23, 24
Trust, Laura B., N1
Tsao, Amy, N7
Turakij, Krungthep, N20
Tutal, Ercan, 394
Twain, Shania, 33

Accessibility
　e-marketing and, 219
　of transportation modes, 450(table),
　　451
Accessory equipment, 308
Accuracy, physical distribution and, 441
Achievers, 281, 282(illus.)
Addressability, e-marketing and, 216–217
Administered VMSs, 422
Adoption, in product adoption process,
　318, 318(illus.)
Advertising, 502–503, 520–535
　advocacy, 520
　careers in, A13–14
　comparative, 521
　competitive, 521
　cooperative, 567
　definition of, 520
　institutional, 520
　objectives of, 522–523
　pioneer, 520–521
　product, 520–521
　reinforcement, 521
　reminder, 521
　repetition in, 125
Advertising appropriation, 525–526,
　526(table)
Advertising campaigns, 521(illus.),
　521–534
　advertising appropriation and,
　　525–526, 526(table)
　advertising message for, 528–532,
　　530(illus.)
　advertising platform and, 524–525
　evaluating effectiveness of, 532–534
　executing, 532
　media plan for, 526–528, 527(illus.),
　　529(table)
　objectives of, defining, 522–523
　responsibility for developing, 534–535
　target audience of, identifying and
　　analyzing, 522
Advertising message, 528–532, 530(illus.)
Advertising platform, 524–525
Advocacy advertising, 520
Aesthetic modifications, 328–329
African American subculture, 141
Age, as segmentation variable, 275(illus.),
　275–276
Agents, 437–439, 438(illus.), 439(table)
Aided recall tests, 534
Air transportation, 449–450
A la carte pricing, 617
Allowances, 595, 595(table)
American Customer Satisfaction Index,
　64, 64(illus.)
American Marketing Association, Code of
　Ethics for Marketing on the Internet
　of, 232, 233(table)
Approach, 549

Arbitrary approach, 526
Artwork, for advertising, 531
Asian American subculture, 142
Asia-Pacific Economic Cooperation
　(APEC), 189
Aspirational reference groups, 137
Assemblers, 435–437, 436(illus.)
Atmospherics, 480–481
Attitudes, consumer buying decision
　process and, 131–132
Attitude scales, 132
Audience, in communication process, 495,
　496
Audits
　communications, 537–538
　public relations, 537
　social, 538
Automatic vending, 474
Availability
　physical distribution and, 441
　of promotional methods, 509
Average fixed cost, 583, 584(table)
Average total cost, 583, 584(illus.),
　584(table)
Average variable cost, 583, 584(table)
Awareness, creation of, by promotion,
　498–499
Awareness stage, in product adoption
　process, 317

Bait pricing, 615
Balance of trade, 178
Barter, 577
Base-point pricing, 596
B2B markets, see Business markets
Behavioristic segmentation variables, 282
Believers, 281, 282(illus.)
Benchmarking, 43
Benefit segmentation, 282
Better Business Bureau (BBB), 70–71
Blogs, 215
Bonded storage, 447
Boston Consulting Group (BCG) approach,
　37, 37(illus.)
Brand competitors, 59–60
Brand equity, 353–355, 354(illus.),
　355(table)
Brand extension, 360–361
Brand insistence, 353
Brand licensing, 362
Brand loyalty, 352–353
Brand managers, 343
Brand marks, 350
Brand names, 350, 352
　selection of, 357
Brand preference, 353
Brand recognition, 353
Brands/branding, 350–363
　brand equity and, 353–355, 354(illus.),
　　355(table)

　brand extension and, 360–361
　brand licensing and, 362
　brand loyalty and, 352–353
　brand name selection and, 357
　brand protection and, 358–359
　co-branding and, 361–362
　cultural, 351
　family, 360
　generic, 356
　individual, 359
　manufacturer, 355–356, 356(illus.)
　policies for, 359–361
　private distributor (dealer; store),
　　355–356
　types of brands and, 355–356,
　　356(illus.)
　value of, 351–352
Breakdown approach, 284
Break-even analysis, 586–587, 587(illus.)
Break-even point, 586
Brokers, 437–438, 438(illus.)
Buildup approach, 284
Bundle pricing, 617
Business analysis, in new product
　development process, 333–334
Business buying
　methods of, 157–158
　types of purchases and, 158–159
Business buying decisions, 161–165
　buying centers and, 161–162
　influences on, 164–165
　stages of process, 162–164, 163(illus.)
Business customers
　attributes of, 155
　characteristics of transactions with,
　　154–155
　estimating purchase potential of, 167
　primary concerns of, 155–157
Business cycle, 62
Business districts, retail stores in, 477
Businesses, marketing's importance to,
　17–18
Business for Social responsibility
　(BSR), 186
Business markets, 150–154
　government, 153–154
　institutional, 154
　pricing for, 594–596
　producer, 151, 151(table)
　reseller, 151–152
　segmentation variables for, 282–283
Business products, 304, 307–309
　demand for, 159–161
　marketing channels for, 411–413,
　　412(illus.)
Business services, 309
Business-to-business markets, see Business
　markets
Business-unit strategy, 36–37, 37(illus.)
*Business Week*, 246